THE OXFORD HANDBOOK OF 6~094 2014

REFUGEE AND FORCED MIGRATION STUDIES

Refugee and Forced Migration Studies has grown from being a concern of a relatively small number of scholars and policy researchers in the 1980s to a global field of interest with thousands of students worldwide studying displacement either from traditional disciplinary perspectives or as a core component of newer programmes across the Humanities and Social and Political Sciences. Today the field encompasses both rigorous academic research which may or may not ultimately inform policy and practice, as well as action-research focused on advocating in favour of refugees' needs and rights.

This authoritative *Handbook* critically evaluates the birth and development of Refugee and Forced Migration Studies, and analyses the key contemporary and future challenges faced by academics and practitioners working with and for forcibly displaced populations around the world. The 53 state-of-the-art chapters, written by leading academics, practitioners, and policymakers working in universities, research centres, think tanks, NGOs, and international organizations, provide a comprehensive and cutting-edge overview of the key intellectual, political, social, and institutional challenges arising from mass displacement in the world today. The chapters vividly illustrate the vibrant and engaging debates that characterize this rapidly expanding field of research and practice.

THE OXFORD HANDBOOK OF

REFUGEE AND FORCED MIGRATION STUDIES

Edited by
ELENA FIDDIAN-QASMIYEH
GIL LOESCHER
KATY LONG
NANDO SIGONA

OXFORD
UNIVERSITY PRESS

OXFORD
UNIVERSITY PRESS

Great Clarendon Street, Oxford, ox2 6DP,
United Kingdom

Oxford University Press is a department of the University of Oxford.
It furthers the University's objective of excellence in research, scholarship,
and education by publishing worldwide. Oxford is a registered trade mark of
Oxford University Press in the UK and in certain other countries

© The several contributors 2014, © Except chapter 14: Nicholas Van Hear

The moral rights of the authors have been asserted

First published 2014
First published in paperback 2016

Published in the United States of America by Oxford University Press
198 Madison Avenue, New York, NY 10016, United States of America

British Library Cataloguing in Publication Data
Data available

Library of Congress Cataloging in Publication Data
Data available

ISBN 978-0-19-965243-3 (Hbk.)
ISBN 978-0-19-877850-9 (Pbk.)

This book is dedicated to Belinda Allan, Arthur Helton, Sergio Vieira de Mello, Aristide Zolberg, and to all other friends and colleagues who contributed in such significant ways to the development of refugee studies and action for refugees, and yet are sadly no longer with us today

Foreword by the United Nations High Commissioner for Refugees (UNHCR)

We live in an age where more and more people are on the move; where conflicts and persecution drive millions from their homes each year; and where forced displacement grows increasingly protracted. There is enormous human suffering hidden behind the statistical trends, but at the same time I am impressed, again and again, by the resilience we encounter among those who have lost nearly everything. Displacement is no doubt one of the great contemporary challenges the world is facing, and as the international community remains ill prepared to prevent and resolve its root causes, millions of people continue to be affected year after year.

I am therefore grateful for this publication, and for the bridges it helps build between academic study and our everyday fieldwork and advocacy in forced displacement. The chapters of this Handbook carefully examine all the key elements for the protection of refugees, displaced persons, migrants, and other people on the move, identifying both obstacles and opportunities that are relevant to our work in the field, and which should rightly be contemplated by students of forced migration.

The chapters on shifting spaces and new paradigms of forced migration examine questions relating to encampment, urban refugees, internally displaced persons, and protracted refugee situations, which we at UNHCR are grappling with every day. Issues such as internal displacement and statelessness need to be put higher on the international agenda, and I welcome developments in institutional frameworks and partnerships that support this.

The authors draw attention to specific concerns such as the protection of children, older persons, and those with disabilities, as well as the gendered dimension of displacement (including sexual and gender-based violence). The increasing risks and dangers faced by refugees, asylum seekers, and others travelling in mixed migratory flows require the establishment of complementary national and regional strategies in order to mitigate pressure on the institution of asylum, and ensure that frameworks and tools translate effectively into better protection and assistance to people on the ground.

Taking stock, as this Handbook does, of new trends and root causes of displacement such as human trafficking and smuggling or climate change provides opportunities to explore the broader impact of migration on communities across the world. In particular, the dramatic demographic, economic, and social consequences of forced displacement highlight the need for strategic and complementary partnerships across disciplines. UNHCR, for example, is working closely with partners, governments, and civil society to help increase self-reliance while enabling positive impacts on local economies. Such essential protection activities will be supported by the Handbook's valuable regional analyses.

Today we stand at a critical juncture in the history of forced displacement and migration —faced with multiple emergencies, a 20-year high in the number of forcibly uprooted people, and complex mixed-migratory flows that increasingly include perilous sea journeys. This Handbook aptly highlights the multiple challenges defining the contemporary field of forced migration. A welcome collection of research in this changing context, it examines essential concepts from a theoretical perspective, but also considers the practical implications which affect operational actors, such as UNHCR and the people we work for.

It is encouraging to see developments in this field attracting the attention and acknowledgement that is warranted, and in an in-depth and meaningful manner. I commend the Oxford Refugee Studies Centre for providing this comprehensive overview, which covers nearly every aspect of contemporary refugee and forced displacement studies. In addition to being an essential tool for academics and students of forced migration, the comprehensive nature of this Handbook opens up the field to a wide range of stakeholders.

In particular, I hope that the Handbook will be a valuable tool for practitioners in the field and assist them in working together to protect a fundamental human value—that of providing refuge to people fleeing violence and persecution.

Geneva, March 2014

António Guterres
United Nations High Commissioner for Refugees

PREFACE

THIS project first began in early 2011, when we were all working at the University of Oxford's Refugee Studies Centre and searching for ways to mark the 30th Anniversary of the Centre's establishment. A commemorative book to be published in 2012 was suggested, with the aim of drawing on the considerable talents of the many scholars who have passed through the Refugee Studies Centre as academic staff, visiting researchers, and students since the Centre's birth in 1982. It was then noted (thank you, Claire) that there existed no single, comprehensive work surveying the development of the multidisciplinary field of refugee and forced migration studies as it exists today. What initially began as a 12-chapter volume therefore expanded into a major 52-chapter Handbook. While the influence of the Refugee Studies Centre on the structure of the Handbook is clear—both through the editors' current and former affiliations, and also with many of the contributors having links, past or present, with the Centre—the final product draws on an ever-expanding global network of Refugee and Forced Migration scholars, practitioners, and policymakers from a wide range of academic institutions, international organizations such as the United Nations High Commissioner for Refugees, and national governmental organizations and think tanks. It is our hope that this Handbook, in tracing the achievements of the field to date, will inspire new students and researchers to join this community.

ACKNOWLEDGEMENTS

WE would like to thank the following people for their invaluable support and feedback throughout different phases of the development of this Handbook. At Oxford University Press, we are grateful to Dominic Byatt for his enthusiasm for this project from our first encounter in 2011 and for commissioning this volume as part of the Oxford Handbook series; and to Sarah Parker, Jenny Nugee, Jashnie Jabson, Edwin Pritchard, and Joy Mellor for all of their help over the past two years. Elena would like to thank Yousif M. Qasmiyeh and Bissan-Maria Fiddian-Qasmiyeh for their encouragement and patience, especially in the wonderful but chaotic months following Bissan-Maria's arrival. Gil would like to thank Elena for reviewing a couple of the chapters he was responsible for, and Elena and Nando for dealing with some of the technical aspects of the editing. He would also like to thank Ann Loescher for encouraging him to take part in yet another long book project. Katy would like to thank Tim Moreton for all his support (and for finding a way for me to finish the editing process in the Californian sun) as well as colleagues at the London School of Economics and University of Edinburgh. Nando would like to thank Julia for all her support and encouragement and Robin for the wonderful and much needed after-work play time, as well as colleagues at the University of Birmingham's Institute for Research into Superdiversity, and the Oxford Diasporas Programme and Centre on Migration, Policy and Society at the University of Oxford. The editorial team would also like to thank all of our colleagues at the Refugee Studies Centre for their support and contribution to this ambitious project. Finally, we would like to thank António Guterres, the UN High Commissioner for Refugees, for contributing the Foreword to this volume, in adddition to Micheline Saunders-Gallemand for her assistance in this regard.

Contents

PART II SHIFTING SPACES AND SCENARIOS OF DISPLACEMENT

PART III LEGAL AND INSTITUTIONAL RESPONSES TO FORCED MIGRATION

PART IV ROOT CAUSES OF DISPLACEMENT

PART V LIVED EXPERIENCES AND REPRESENTATIONS OF FORCED MIGRATION

PART VI RETHINKING DURABLE SOLUTIONS

PART VII REGIONAL STUDIES: CURRENT REALITIES AND FUTURE CHALLENGES

LIST OF ABBREVIATIONS

ADB	Asian Development Bank
ADFL	Alliance of Democratic Forces for the Liberation of Congo–Zaire
AICHR	ASEAN Intergovernmental Commission on Human Rights
ANC	African National Congress
APD	Asylum Procedures Directive
APPRN	Asia Pacific Refugee Rights Network
ARV	Afghan Refugee Village
ASEAN	Association of Southeast Asian Nations
AVRR	Assisted Voluntary Return and Reintegration
BIA	Board of Immigration Appeals
CAT	Convention against Torture
CBSA	Canadian Border Services Agency
CDC	Center for Disease Control and Prevention
CEAS	Common European Asylum System
CIC	Citizenship and Immigration Canada
CIREFCA	International Conference on Central American Refugees
CJEU	Court of Justice of the European Union
CoE	Council of Europe
COMISAF	Commander ISAF
CPA	Comprehensive Plan of Action
CRED	Centre for Research on the Epidemiology of Disasters
CRS	Catholic Relief Services
CRS	Congressional Research Service
CSR	corporate social responsibility
DCO	Designated Countries of Origin
DHS	Department of Homeland Security
DIDR	development induced displacement and resettlement
DRC	Democratic Republic of Congo

EBRD	European Bank for Reconstruction and Development
ECHR	European Convention on Human Rights
ECJ	European Court of Justice
ECOMOG	Economic Community of West African States Monitoring Group
ECOSOC	UN Economic and Social Council
ECOWAS	Economic Community of West African States
ECR	Emergency Relief Coordinator
ECtHR	European Court of Human Rights
EPRDF	Ethiopian Peoples' Revolutionary Democratic Front
ETS	European Treaty Series
EU	European Union
EXCOM	Executive Committee
FDLR	Forces Démocratiques pour de Libération du Rwanda
FRELIMO	Frente de Libertação de Moçambique
GAD	Gender And Development
GAFM	Gender And Forced Migration
GAO	Government Accountability Office
GBV	gender-based violence
GDP	gross domestic product
GDPU	Gulu Disabled Person's Union
GIS	Geographical Information Systems
GLR	Great Lakes region
GOI	Government of India
GPS	Geographical Positioning System
HEP	humanitarian evacuation programme
HoA	Horn of Africa
HRIT	Heightened Risk Identification Tool
IACHR	Inter-American Commission on Human Rights
IASC	Inter-Agency Standing Committee
ICCPR	International Covenant on Civil and Political Rights
ICESCR	International Covenant on Economic, Social and Cultural Rights
ICMC	International Catholic Migration Commission
ICRC	International Committee of the Red Cross
IDMC	Internal Displacement Monitoring Centre
IDP	internally displaced person

IFC	International Finance Corporation
IFH	Interim Federal Health
IFI	international financing institution
IFRC	International Federation of Red Cross and Red Crescent Societies
ILC	International Law Commission
ILO	International Labour Organization
ILPA	Immigration Lawyers Practitioner Association
IOM	International Organization for Migration
IR	international relations
IRO	International Refugee Organization
ISAC	Inter-Agency Standing Committee
ISAF	International Security Assistance Force
IT	information technology
IWGIA	International Work Group for Indigenous Affairs
JH	Johns Hopkins
JRS	Jesuit Refugee Service
KT	Kantarawaddy Times
LGBTI	lesbian, gay, bisexual, transgender, and intersex
LTTE	Liberation Tigers of Tamil Eelam
MENA	Middle East and North Africa
MFI	microfinance institution
MPA	Mexico Plan of Action
MPLA	Popular Movement for the Liberation of Angola
MSF	Médecins Sans Frontières
MTS	Medium Term Strategy
NATO	North Atlantic Treaty Organization
NEFA	North East Frontier Agency
NGO	non-governmental organization
OAS	Organization of African States
OAS	Organization of American States
OAU	Organization of African Unity
OCHA	Office for the Coordination of Humanitarian Affairs
OECD	Organization for Economic Cooperation and Development
OFDA	Office of Foreign Disaster Assistance
OHCHR	Office of the High Commissioner for Human Rights

OSCIC	US Citizenship and Immigration Services
PDR	People's Democratic Republic
PNG	Papua New Guinea
PRS	protracted refugee situation
QD	Qualification Directive
RAD	Refugee Appeals Division
RAO	Refugee Affairs Officers
RENAMO	Mozambican Resistance Movement
RHTAC	Refugee Health Technical Assistance Center
RSD	refugee status determination
RSP	Refugee Studies Programme
SAARC	South Asian Association for Regional Cooperation
SAMP	Southern African Migration Programme
SGBV	sexual and gender based violence
SHV	Special Humanitarian Visa
SOHS	State of the Humanitarian System
SRS	Self-Reliance Strategy
SSD	statelessness status determination
SWAPO	South-West Africa People's Organization
TCO	transnational criminal organization
TGP	Three Gorges Project
TIP	Trafficking in Persons
TPS	temporary protected status
TPV	temporary protection visa
TRP	Temporary Resident Permit
UAE	United Arab Emirates
UGC	User Generated Content
UN.GIFT	United Nations Global Initiative to Fight Human Trafficking
UNAIDS	Joint United Nations Programme on HIV/AIDS
UNAMA	United Nations Assistance Mission in Afghanistan
UNCCP	United Nations Conciliation Commission on Palestine
UNCRC	United Nations Convention on the Rights of the Child
UNDP	United Nations Development Programme
UNGA	United Nations General Assembly

UNHCR	United Nations High Commissioner for Refugees
UNICEF	United National International Children's Emergency Fund
UNITA	National Union for the Total Liberation of Angola
UNRWA	United Nations Relief and Works Agency
UNSC	United Nations Security Council
UNTS	United Nations Treaty Series
USRAP	US Refugee Admissions Program
VoT	victims of trafficking
WAD	Women And Development
WCD	World Commission on Dams
WFP	World Food Programme
WHO	World Health Organization
WID	Women In Development
WIFM	Women In Forced Migration
WRC	Women's Refugee Commission

List of Contributors

Alastair Ager is Professor of Clinical Population and Family Health at the Mailman School of Public Health, Columbia University.

Susan Akram is Clinical Professor of Law, Boston University Law School.

Bridget Anderson is Professor of Migration and Citizenship at the University of Oxford where she is Deputy Director of the Centre on Migration, Policy and Society (COMPAS).

Oliver Bakewell is Co-Director of the International Migration Institute at the University of Oxford.

Bayram Balci is Visiting Scholar on the Middle East Program at the Carnegie Endowment for International Peace, Washington, DC.

Paula Banerjee is Associate Professor, Department of South and Southeast Asian Studies, University of Calcutta, and former President of the International Association for Study of Forced Migration.

Roland Bank is the Head of Protection in UNHCR's Representation for Austria and Germany in Berlin. In 2012–13, he was Departmental Lecturer in International Refugee and Human Rights Law at the Refugee Studies Centre, University of Oxford.

Michael Barnett is University Professor of International Affairs and Political Science, George Washington University.

Alexander Betts is University Lecturer in Refugee Studies and Forced Migration Studies and Fellow of Green Templeton College, University of Oxford.

Claudio Bolzman is Professor at the Department of Social Work, University of Applied Sciences Western Switzerland (HES-SO), and Senior Lecturer at the Department of Sociology, University of Geneva.

Megan Bradley is Fellow in Foreign Policy at the Brookings Institution, where she works with the Brookings-LSE Project on Internal Displacement.

Dawn Chatty is Professor of Anthropology and Forced Migration and Fellow of St Cross College at the University of Oxford. She is the Director of the Refugee Studies Centre.

Abel Chikanda is Post Doctoral Fellow, Global Development Studies, Queen's University, Kingston, Canada.

Michael Collyer is Senior Lecturer in Geography at the University of Sussex.

Jonathan Crush is Professor of Global Development Studies and Director of the Southern African Research Centre, Queen's University, Kingston, Canada.

Rebecca Dowd, Division of International Protection, UNHCR.

Alice Edwards is Chief of the Protection Policy and Legal Advice Section at UNHCR in Geneva. She is also Research Associate at the Refugee Studies Centre and Research Fellow at St Anne's College, University of Oxford, as well as Fellow of the University of Nottingham's Human Rights Law Centre.

Jérôme Elie is an independent historian and consultant on international migration and refugee issues.

Elena Fiddian-Qasmiyeh is Reader in Human Geography and Co-Director of the Migration Research Unit at the Department of Geography, University College London.

José H. Fischel de Andrade is Professor at the University of Milan, Italy, Visiting Professor at the University of Paris II (Panthéon-Assas), France, and UNHCR-Designated Judge at the National Court of Asylum (Cour Nationale de Droit d'Asile, CNDA) in Paris. He is a UNHCR senior staff member.

Marion Fresia is Assistant Professor at the Institute of Anthropology, University of Neuchâtel.

Matthew J. Gibney is Reader in Politics and Forced Migration and Official Fellow of Linacre College, University of Oxford. He is the Deputy Director of the Refugee Studies Centre.

Guy S. Goodwin-Gill is Professor of International Refugee Law and Fellow at All Souls College, University of Oxford.

Martin Gottwald is Deputy Representative, UNHCR Colombia.

Anne Hammerstad is Lecturer in International Relations, University of Kent.

Laura Hammond is Senior Lecturer in Development Studies at the School of Oriental and African Studies (SOAS), University of London.

Sari Hanafi is Associate Professor of Sociology at the Department of Social and Behavioral Sciences, American University of Beirut.

Randall Hansen holds a research chair in Political Science, University of Toronto, Canada.

Jason Hart is Senior Lecturer at the Department of Social and Policy Studies, University of Bath and Research Associate at the Refugee Studies Centre, University of Oxford.

David Hollenbach, SJ, is University Chair in Human Rights and International Justice, Theology Department, Boston College.

Lucy Hovil is Senior Researcher at the International Refugee Rights Initiative, Kampala. She was formerly the Senior Research and Advocacy Officer at the Refugee Law Project, at the Faculty of Law, Makerere University, Uganda.

Karen Jacobsen is Associate Professor at the Feinstein International Center, Tufts University.

Walter Kälin is Professor of Constitutional and International Public Law, University Bern and Senior Fellow at the Brookings-LSE project on Internal Displacement. From 2004 to 2010, he was the Representative of the UN Secretary-General on the Human Rights of Internally Displaced Persons and from 2005 to 2010 Co-Director of the Brookings-Bern project on Internal Displacement.

Gaim Kibreab is Professor and Course Director in Refugee Studies, Department of Social and Policy Studies, London South Bank University.

Loren B. Landau is the Director of the African Center for Migration and Society (ACMS) (formerly Forced Migration Studies Programme, FMSP) at the University of Witwatersrand in Johannesburg, South Africa.

Sarah Kenyon Lischer is Associate Professor of Political Science at the Department of Politics and International Affairs, Wake Forest University.

Gil Loescher is Visiting Professor, Refugee Studies Centre, University of Oxford, and Emeritus Professor, University of Notre Dame.

Katy Long is Visiting Scholar at Stanford University and Honorary Fellow at the University of Edinburgh.

Susan F. Martin holds the Donald G. Herzberg Chair in International Migration and is the Director of the Institute for the Study of International Migration in the School of Foreign Service at Georgetown University.

Jane McAdam is Professor of Law at the University of New South Wales, Australia.

Kirsten McConnachie is the Joyce Pearce Junior Research Fellow at Lady Margaret Hall and the Refugee Studies Centre, both at the University of Oxford.

Christopher McDowell is Reader in International Politics at the Department of International Politics, City University London.

Anne McNevin is Lecturer in Politics and International Relations at Monash University, Melbourne.

James Milner is Associate Professor in Political Science at Carleton University, Ottawa.

Mansha Mirza is Assistant Professor at the University of Illinois at Chicago.

Alessandro Monsutti is Research Director at the Programme for the Study of Global Migration, Graduate Institute of International and Development Studies, Geneva. He is also Research Associate at the Refugee Studies Centre, University of Oxford.

James Morrissey is Research Officer at the Refugee Studies Centre, University of Oxford.

Simon Russell is Senior Protection Officer, UNHCR.

Stephan Scheel is a postgraduate researcher in the Department of Politics and International Studies at the Open University.

Nando Sigona is Senior Lecturer and Deputy Director of the Institute for Research into Superdiversity at the University of Birmingham. He is also Associate Editor of the journal *Migration Studies* and Research Associate at the University of Oxford's Refugee Studies Centre.

Ninna Nyberg Sørensen is Senior Researcher and the Head of the research unit on Migration, Danish Institute for International Studies.

Vicki Squire is Associate Professor of International Security at the University of Warwick.

Finn Stepputat is Senior Researcher, research unit on Migration, Danish Institute for International Studies.

Vicky Tennant is Senior Policy Officer, UNHCR.

Volker Türk is Director of International Protection, UNHCR.

Nicholas Van Hear is Senior Researcher and Deputy Director at the Centre on Migration, Policy and Society (COMPAS), University of Oxford.

Joanne van Selm is Independent Consultant on Migration and Refugee Issues, Associate Director of Research at Eurasylum and Adjunct Professor at Georegetown University.

Laura van Waas is Senior Researcher and Manager of the Statelessness Programme, at Tilburg Law School in the Netherlands

Terence Wright is Professor of Visual Arts at the University of Ulster.

Roger Zetter is Emeritus Professor of Refugee Studies, University of Oxford. He retired as the fourth Director of the Refugee Studies Centre in September 2011.

CHAPTER 1

INTRODUCTION: REFUGEE AND FORCED MIGRATION STUDIES IN TRANSITION

ELENA FIDDIAN-QASMIYEH, GIL LOESCHER,
KATY LONG, AND NANDO SIGONA

INTRODUCTION

WHO a refugee is and how we can define and understand forced migration are central questions to studies of displacement and the multidisciplinary field of refugee and forced migration studies. While research often begins with these questions, answers usually remain elusive. Academics and practitioners alike continue to debate the contours of the field. *Inter alia*, they ask whether studies should focus on those crossing international borders in flight from persecution and who are therefore entitled to claim legal status as refugees, or whether the field should stretch to encompass the internally displaced, the trafficked, irregular migrants, second- and third-generation diasporas, and those at risk of deportation. If the latter is favoured, how far can refugee and forced migration studies stretch before its focus becomes too diffuse to be meaningful, blurring into the broader fields of Migration Studies, Human Rights, Development Studies, or International Politics?

There is no definitive consensus among researchers about where the boundaries of refugee and forced migration studies should be drawn, and the 52 chapters in this volume clearly demonstrate this, offering 52 different perspectives on this field of studies. However, they also vividly illustrate the vibrant and engaging debates that characterize what is a rapidly expanding field.

A Brief History of Refugee and Forced Migration Studies

Although the field of refugee and forced migration studies itself emerged in the 1980s, there is a long and important history of research into refugees and forced displacement across the Humanities and Social and Political Sciences. During the interwar and post-Second World War eras, for instance, historians examined refugee movements and the role of international organizations established to protect and assist refugees during this period (see Elie's chapter in this volume). While these early assessments were insufficiently critical of either the states or intergovernmental agencies, during the 1970s and early 1980s researchers became increasingly frank in their analyses (e.g. Tolstoy 1977; de Zayas 1979).[1]

Legal scholars were also active during this time, principally focusing on the provisions of national and international refugee instruments pertaining to refugee definitions, asylum and protection (see Goodwin-Gill, this volume). In the early 1980s legal scholars adopted a broader policy-oriented approach examining the domestic and foreign policy influences on Western refugee determination procedures (Martin 1982; Avery 1984), providing important insights into the effectiveness of refugee decision-making procedures, the role of UNHCR, and the impact of domestic and foreign policy factors on the implementation of refugee legal instruments.

Although Malkki notes that researchers positioned within geography and anthropology started to conduct research on 'Refugee Studies' more recently than historians and legal scholars (1995: 507), throughout these and later decades, research from across the social and political sciences explored individual, familial, and collective experiences of persecution, internment, and mass displacement in diverse contexts (see Chatty, this volume).[2] Most notably, perhaps, this includes Elizabeth Colson's political-anthropological research in Japanese-American internment camps in the 1940s and her analysis of colonized populations' experiences of displacement and forced resettlement in the 1950s and 1960s (Colson 1971).

By the early 1980s refugee and forced migration issues had become a globally salient issue, in part as a result of major protracted refugee situations in South-East Asia, Pakistan and Iran, the Horn of Africa, Southern Africa, and Mexico and Central America, as well as a substantial increase in the numbers of asylum seekers in Europe and North America. In response to these developments, organizations such as the Ford Foundation funded a number of research organizations and individuals to undertake projects dealing with these issues. The result was a growing body of work documenting the causes of refugee flows; emergency assistance programmes for refugees; transnational networks to assist refugees; and policy responses of particular states to refugee movements.[3]

Arguably one of the key scholarly contributions from this period was Barbara Harrell-Bond's ground-breaking *Imposing Aid* (1986). This research was influential not least because it reflected Harrell-Bond's conviction that research *about* refugees should be used *for* refugees, to uphold refugees' rights and agency throughout processes of displacement. Indeed, what is now often referred to as researchers' 'dual imperative' to promote academic knowledge and undertake ethical action (Jacobsen and Landau 2003) is closely tied to the assertion that there can be no 'justification for conducting research into situations of extreme human suffering if one does not have the alleviation of suffering as an explicit objective of one's research' (Turton 1996: 96).

Consequently, one of the most important developments during the 1980s was the emergence of refugee and forced migration studies as a distinct field of study and policy analysis (also see Malkki 1995), and the establishment of new research and teaching centres and policy institutes. These included the Refugee Studies Programme at the University of Oxford, the refugee programme at York University in Toronto, and the Refugee Policy Group in Washington DC; in addition, existing policy centres such as the US Committee for Refugees, the Lawyers Committee for Human Rights, and the European Council on Refugees and Exiles considerably strengthened their coverage and advocacy efforts for refugees and asylum seekers. Finally, two new academic journals, the *Journal of Refugee Studies* and the *Journal of International Refugee Law* were established in 1988 and 1989 respectively, and The International Research and Advisory Panel on Refugees and Other Displaced Persons (IRAP), which was the precursor to the International Association for the Study of Forced Migration (IASFM), was formed in 1990.

Over the last thirty years refugee and forced migration studies has grown from being a concern of a relatively small number of scholars and policy researchers to a global field of interest with thousands of students worldwide studying displacement either from traditional disciplinary perspectives or as a core component of newer programmes across the Humanities and Social and Political Sciences. Today the field encompasses both rigorous academic research which may or may not ultimately inform policy and practice as well as action-research focused on advocating in favour of refugees' needs and rights. This Handbook draws on an ever-expanding global network of scholars in refugee and forced migration studies, bringing together contributions from leading academics, practitioners, and policymakers working in universities, research centres, think tanks, NGOs, and international organizations around the world.

DEFINING THE FIELD: KEY DEBATES

Since the 1980s, refugee and forced migration studies has evolved beyond its original close ties to advocacy and policymaking, developing a more distinct identity as an independent field worthy of scholarly research. Increasingly, many researchers elect to use forced migration as a lens through which to contribute to a range of philosophical, political, and interpretative theory. Yet there can be little doubt that the study of forced migration is as relevant to the 'real world' as ever, with 7.6 million people having been newly displaced due to conflict or persecution in 2012 alone: an average of 23,000 people a day (UNHCR 2013). New and ongoing humanitarian crises continue to erupt, most recently—and with terrible consequences—across the Middle East and North

Africa, with the conflict in Syria described in April 2013 by the United Nations High Commissioner for Refugees, Antonio Guterres, as 'the most dramatic humanitarian crisis that we [UNHCR] have ever faced' (Chulov 2013). Meanwhile, two-thirds of refugees and displaced persons continue to wait in exile for over five years, in some cases for generations, with no solutions in sight for millions of Palestinians, Somalis, Afghans, or Colombians among others.

One of the great contemporary debates in refugee and forced migration studies is the extent to which research should be framed by urgent policy questions to respond to these and other crises. Policymakers frequently decry what they perceive to be a shift towards more abstract, intellectual concerns, while academics argue that more theoretical approaches contribute to important disciplinary debates and that completing policy relevant research is no substitute for rigorous intellectual analysis. This Handbook not only documents these different approaches to research, but shows how they can be complementary when used in combination. Indeed, there is a real and continuing need to collect accurate, representative, and meaningful qualitative and quantitative data in order to carefully map and better understand the scope, scale, causes, and consequences of forced migration. In addition to informing policymaking, evaluation and development, new concepts, methodological and interpretative frameworks, and theoretical modelling are equally fundamental to the wider framing of forced migrations, be they crises of conflict, citizenship, or capitalism.

Integral to the debate regarding policy-relevant and 'policy-irrelevant' research (Bakewell 2008) is an interrogation of the methods of data collection and analysis which have characterized a significant proportion of studies undertaken by scholars in the field to date, and whether such research is in fact well situated to inform policy. With much, if not most, research in the field having been primarily qualitative in nature, and often framed around detailed analyses of single case-studies (as is the classical ethnographic approach underpinning anthropology), the challenges of completing research which is simultaneously meaningful for displaced persons and communities, academics, practitioners, and policymakers are complex (Jacobsen and Landau 2008). Many of the Handbook's contributions represent and critically reflect upon these diverse methodological and interpretative frameworks, ranging from archival research and institutional history;[4] micro-, meso-, and macro-levels of analysis;[5] large-N statistical data sets and top-down research;[6] and technological tools such as remote sensing and Geographical Information Systems.[7] In turn, interpretative frameworks represented in the Handbook include normative approaches[8] and critical perspectives grounded in feminist, gender, and post-colonial theories.[9]

Just as the contested relationship between research, policy, and practice in refugee and forced migration studies is in evidence in many of the Handbook's chapters,[10] so too is the connection between definitions and experiences of forced versus voluntary migration, and how *forced* migration studies relates to and complements the wider field of Migration Studies. Some contributors, such as Bakewell, Van Hear, and Long, argue that it is often more appropriate to focus on processes of migration in and from conflict, and that in defending refugee and forced migration studies as a separate field, there is a risk that scholars are legitimizing labels that are—as Zetter (1991) warns us—deliberately constructed to exclude and to disempower. In contrast, others, including Gibney, Milner, and Goodwin-Gill point out that because being a *refugee* is qualitatively different from being a migrant (as it reflects a breakdown of a basic relationship between state and citizen), it is essential that we recognize this. What few on either side would dispute, however, is that the two areas of study are closely connected. Particularly at the edges of what is conventionally recognized as forced migration—when dealing with topics like diasporas and transnationalism, irregular migration, or economic livelihoods[11]—attempting to draw clear boundaries is unhelpful, and the most exciting research in these areas reflects the best insights from both the migration studies and forced migration studies traditions.

Despite these contests and caveats, which have fuelled considerable debate in recent years (see e.g. Martin 2004; Hathaway 2007), in practice, most researchers can nonetheless readily identify work that belongs to the field of refugee and forced migration studies. Most clearly, such research can be broadly considered to cover the study of those who have been identified by the international community as asylum seekers, refugees, internally displaced persons (IDPs), development induced displaced persons, or trafficked persons,[12] as well as all those whose claim to such labels may have been denied, but who have been forced to *move* against their will as a result of persecution, conflict, or insecurity. Interest in studying governmental, institutional, and international responses to such forced migrations reflects the extent to which law has influenced the development of the field.[13] Concurrently, detailed ethnographic studies and concern with documenting lived experiences of forced migration reflect the crucial contributions of anthropologists and sociologists to the field.

In addition to direct lived experiences of being forced to *flee*, a related set of studies centralize direct and inherited experiences of forced *immobility* and forced *sedentarization*.[14] These studies include research with individuals and groups born into protracted displacement who may not have personally experienced migration (forced or otherwise) and those who are 'internally stuck' or otherwise prevented from safely returning to their own or their families' places of origin in spite of a desperate desire to do so, including stateless persons and communities. Indeed, with reference to the latter, the causes, experiences, and implications of borders moving over people—as in the cases of the partition of India and the dissolution of the former Yugoslavia and the former Soviet Union[15]—in addition to people moving over borders, have gained increasing attention over the past few years.

Uniting the diverse disciplinary perspectives, methodologies, and areas of analysis outlined above—as aptly illustrated in this Handbook—is that refugee and forced migration studies is a subject focused on understanding and addressing *human* experiences of displacement and dispossession. Most explicitly, perhaps, scholars working within the traditions of anthropology and sociology have highlighted the heterogeneity of these human experiences, according for instance to age, gender, sexual orientation, health and disability status, or religious identity. Understanding this diversity is highly significant for political and institutional analyses of the nature and implications of state and non-state responses to forced migration which can variously aim to alleviate human suffering and uphold the rights of displaced persons, or to control and protect borders and territories by limiting and/or forcing the removal of certain bodies from these spaces.[16]

Acknowledging this diversity is equally significant in order to ensure that studies and policies of, about, and for forced migrants recognize the agency of affected individuals and groups, even in contexts of extreme violence, oppression, and control. Indeed, beyond academics', policymakers', and practitioners' analyses, forced migrants themselves are, of course, active agents, who represent their own and others' experiences of displacement through diverse means, including through refugee- and IDP-produced media.[17]

Harrell-Bond's seminal work (1986) argued that refugees are not a priori dependent and passive, but rather that humanitarian institutions and political structures have created and even demanded the dependency of forced migrants upon donors and providers of assistance. This suggests that there is a continuing need for both humanitarian and political responses to displacement on the one hand, and academic research across all disciplines on the other, to ensure that policies, studies, and discourses do not deny the agency of displaced persons, but rather aim to enhance their rights and capabilities within contexts of accelerated social and political change. Such approaches must, we would argue, simultaneously interrogate structures and mechanisms which unduly criminalize and subject forced migrants to securitization paradigms, but also those structures which concomitantly lead to an unrealistic and potentially equally oppressive idealization of certain groups of displaced persons.

It is, we hope, this commitment to upholding the human rights of displaced persons within the framework of international legal commitments and ethical values, wherever they may be located—in camps or cities; 'here' or 'there'; in the global North or global South—which connects scholars working on refugee and forced migration studies across the Humanities and Social and Political Sciences.

PART OUTLINES

This Handbook offers a comprehensive, global survey of these and many other key debates, issues and themes in refugee and forced migration studies. By critically tracing and evaluating the development of this multidisciplinary field, it assesses where refugee and forced migration studies has *come from*: as such, the individual chapters provide ideal entry points for researchers, policymakers, and practitioners beginning to engage with the diverse complex issues—ethical, political, and practical—that are connected to processes of displacement and forced migrations. Concurrently, the Handbook's contributors analyse the key contemporary and future challenges faced by academics and practitioners working with and for forcibly displaced populations around the world, thereby exploring where the field is *going*: the chapters therefore not only offer thematic overviews of state-of-the-art research, but also detailed assessments of the direction of current cutting-edge analyses and suggestions for future research agendas.

Approaches: Old and New

The Handbook begins by setting out the different disciplinary approaches that have been followed in exploring refugee and forced migration studies and the particular insights they bring to the study of displacement.

Part I opens with Jérôme Elie's chapter on the history of refugee and forced migration studies, an essay that asks why this field is so often considered 'ahistorical' and subject to neglect by historians, and makes a powerful case for more historical research. Guy Goodwin-Gill's chapter on the international law of refugee protection then discusses the legal tools, treaties, and national laws which prescribe or implement the obligations of states to refugees as well as the core protection functions and responsibilities of the Office of the United Nations High Commissioner for Refugees (UNHCR). In turn, Matthew Gibney's chapter on the ethical and normative questions that studying refugees and forced migration raise for political theorists underlines why studying displacement can offer important lessons for those interested in trying to understand much broader political theories of citizenship, nationality, and power. Alexander Betts further explores the position of refugees and other groups of forced migrants in the international political system, outlining the most prominent body of academic work on the international politics of forced migration and arguing that the discipline of international relations has an important role to play in understanding the challenges that transnational population movements play in the world today.

Turning to lived experiences of forced migration, Dawn Chatty argues that anthropology's unique contributions to the field of refugee and forced migration studies include carefully documenting what happens to people, their culture, and society when they are forcibly displaced and wrenched from their territorial moorings, or, indeed, when they are dispossessed through processes of forced sedentarization and involuntary immobility. Finn Stepputat and Ninna Nyberg Sørensen then examine the role of sociological methods, concepts, and theories in advancing our understanding of the causes, experiences, and impacts of forced migration on micro-, meso-, and macro-levels, in addition to highlighting the extent to which studies of forced migration can push disciplines such as sociology to adapt and develop new lenses and explanatory models.

Subsequently, Karen Jacobsen's chapter examines the pursuit of livelihood opportunities by refugees and other forced migrants outside of camps. In addition to outlining how the livelihoods of the forcibly displaced are different from those of other migrants, she argues that traditionally conceived and targeted refugee programmes should be reconceptualized and restructured as programmes that support both refugees and their hosts. Drawing the disciplinary part to a close, Michael Collyer notes that although geographical research into forced migration is dominated by subdisciplines of *human* geography, a growing body of literature examines relationships between forced migration and the *physical* environment; furthermore, he notes that developments in the range of research tools such as remote sensing and Geographical Information Systems (GIS) applications have reached a level of sophistication that has led to their widespread use in emergency response planning.

Shifting Spaces and Scenarios of Displacement

Part II of the Handbook considers how displacement can be experienced in different ways over space and time, focusing in particular on deconstructing the labels that define and limit research agendas and international responses to displacement, and challenging the idea that refugee and forced migration studies should be primarily concerned with refugees in camps in the developing world. It begins with Oliver Bakewell's chapter exploring tensions between the international community's interest in fixing refugee populations in camps and refugees' own practices of (often irregular) self-settlement in towns and cities. Loren Landau then examines the new interest in researching urban displacement, arguing that what has changed in the past decade is not displacement itself, but who we—as academics, policymakers, and practitioners—choose to see as displaced. In turn, James Milner's chapter considers the changing time scale of displacement, outlining the growing numbers of refugees and other forced migrants who spend years—if not decades—in exile and the need for researchers to adjust their focus to incorporate these protracted displacements. Returning to the question of physical spaces of displacement, Walter Kälin then traces the development of an international protection regime for internally displaced populations who have not crossed a border to become refugees, as well as the protection gaps that remain. In contrast, Nicholas van Hear writes about the transnational and diasporic links that connect refugees, asylum seekers, and other migrants from conflict across countries and continents. The final chapter, by Stephan Scheel and Vicki Squire, explores how many of those refugees and asylum seekers making transnational journeys are labelled as 'irregular migrants' by states who are anxious to make such movements illegitimate.

Legal and Institutional Responses to Forced Migration

Part III of the Handbook explores many of the legal, political, and institutional responses to forced migration, considering how practice, policy, and research in this area variously connect. Jane McAdam's chapter traces the growing connections between human rights, human rights law, and forced migration. This chapter examines the ways in which human rights law can assist and protect forced migrants who cross an international border but do not satisfy the legal definition of 'refugee' under the 1951 Refugee Convention or its regional counterparts. The part then examines the development of the two UN organizations with specific mandates for refugee protection and relief—UNHCR and the United Nations Relief and Works Agency (UNRWA). Gil Loescher's chapter discusses UNHCR's normative agenda as well as the effectiveness of the Office's work for refugee protection within the context of a changing international political system, and expanding global mobility regime, and a growing and diverse group of displaced people in need of assistance and protection. Susan Akram's chapter on UNRWA considers, from a legal perspective, whether the situation of Palestinian refugees is different from other refugees in the world and whether these differences affect Palestinians' rights to a durable solution to their plight. Michael Barnett's chapter examines the intertwined history of the international refugee regime and the international humanitarian order. From its origins in the late eighteenth century, humanitarianism has expanded today to protect more kinds of people affected by forced migration including those displaced by natural disasters.

Other chapters examine state responses to forced migration and the connections made between refugee flight and post-Cold War securitization discourses. Randall Hansen's chapter discusses the relationship between the nation state, borders, refugees, and citizenship while Anne Hammerstad's chapter on the securitization of forced migration underlines how the relatively recent growth in interest of the security dimensions of forced migration has coincided with the widening of the security agenda during the post-Cold War era. Several UNHCR staff members and their academic colleagues conclude this part with chapters on gaps in existing protection regimes for refugees, the problem of statelessness, and the challenges of humanitarian reform within the international system. In their chapter, Volker Türk and Rebecca Dowd point to a number of critical gaps or shortcomings in the contemporary international refugee protection regime and propose a series of suggestions to states to fill these protection gaps.

Subsequently, Alice Edwards' and Laura van Waas's chapter explores the historical development of the international legal regime for the protection of stateless persons, its relationship with the international refugee regime, and contemporary challenges to the prevention and reduction of statelessness, and points toward a number of promising developments for progress in this field. In the final chapter of this part of the Handbook, Simon Russell and Vicky Tennant present the recent history of humanitarian reform within the international system. In particular, the chapter analyses the changes in the architecture for addressing internal displacement and ongoing debates on institutional mandates and responsibilities, and assesses the implementation and practice of these reforms.

Root Causes of Displacement

Part IV critically evaluates the ways in which the 'drivers' of forced migration are identified by academics, policymakers, and affected persons, whilst simultaneously problematizing notions of mono-causality in favour of more complex and dynamic understandings of the multiple reasons which may underpin individual, familial, and collective experiences of forced (im)mobility. Sarah Lischer's chapter traces the development of research into mass flight caused by conflict and political or economic crisis, questioning the validity of quantitative and qualitative methods used to trace causality in such complex contexts of mass flux, and arguing in favour of mixed-methods, multidisciplinary research. Drawing on historical and contemporary examples alike, Christopher McDowell then examines how and why states forcibly remove citizens from specific spaces and places in the name of national development, assessing the nature, scope, and scale of such movements, as well as the ways in which different actors, including civil society networks and the international community, have attempted to respond to processes of internal displacement and involuntary resettlement. Roger Zetter and James Morrissey, like Lischer, problematize mainstream understandings of apolitical mono-causal depictions of 'climate induced displacement' through detailed multi-sited primary research with and about communities whose livelihoods are differently affected by processes of environmental stress according to their position within diverse systems of power. The final chapter in this part, by Bridget Anderson, in turn explores the multiple connections which exist between trafficking, smuggling, and forced migration, and, by tracing a genealogy of current discourse and policies on trafficking, further problematizes the binary between voluntary and forced migration.

Lived Experiences and Representations of Forced Migration

Part V brings to the fore the agency of refugees and examines different approaches to studying the diversity of refugees' and forced migrants' own lived experiences in flight and exile. The part begins with Nando Sigona's discussion of scholarly debates on 'refugee voices' and an exploration of the complex relationship between emic and etic narratives and representations of refugees' and IDPs' experiences. The chapters that follow focus on particular groups and identities within refugee populations which have historically been overlooked by practitioners, policymakers, and researchers. The first chapter by Jason Hart examines the significance of age and generation by providing an overview of some of the key features characterizing the study of children and forced migration as this has been pursued over the last quarter of a century. Elena Fiddian-Qasmiyeh then explores gendered experiences of exile and displacement highlighting the transition from documenting the particularities of female experiences, to a re-evaluation of the multiple ways in which processes of and responses to forced migration influence gender identities, roles, and relations. Complementing Hart's and Fiddian-Qasmiyeh's chapters, Claudio Bolzman's contribution on older refugees in turn shows how the experiences of older male and female forced migrants remain relatively unexplored. In the fifth chapter, Mansha Mirza argues that while people with disabilities represent a substantial subgroup among displaced populations, disability issues have nonetheless mostly been neglected within displacement-focused humanitarian programmes.

The analysis of the relationship between health status and health systems, and of the complex nexus between religion and forced migration, are addressed in the following two chapters of this part, respectively by Alastair Ager and David Hollenbach. Alastair Ager argues that the lens of health, a comparatively neglected area of study within the field of forced migration, provides significant insight into multiple dimensions of the lived experience of refugee populations. David Hollenbach analyses the role of religion in addressing the causes and experiences of forced migration and the responses to it, both by the displaced themselves and by organizations seeking to help them. In this part's final chapter, Terence Wright makes a further contribution to debates pertaining to 'refugee voices' by examining the changing patterns in representations of forced migration in the media, including a discussion of the roles of citizen and refugee/IDP journalists.

Rethinking Durable Solutions

The penultimate part of the Handbook turns to consider how we might 'solve' displacement—and what assessing the limitations of existing approaches can teach us. Katy Long's chapter argues that, given the rising numbers trapped in protracted displacement, traditional solutions are not working, and that there is a need to rethink our approach, in particular to consider how facilitating refugees' mobility might open up new possibilities for refugees to build their own transformative solutions. The part then continues to look at each of those traditional durable solutions— local integration, repatriation, and resettlement—in turn. Lucy Hovil similarly underlines the importance of refugees' autonomy and of centring solutions around citizenship in her survey of local integration, in which she argues local integration is not so much the 'forgotten' solution but the official 'forbidden' solution—despite clear evidence that even where it is prohibited, local integration happens on the ground. Laura Hammond writes about repatriation, considering why refugee return has dominated international efforts to solve crises, the problems that have resulted from this push to repatriate, and the difficult challenges faced by refugees who do return 'home'. Joanne van Selm then offers a comprehensive explanation of resettlement, both in terms of the highly political calculations that have determined its successes and failures, and its impact on the ground. Finally, Martin Gottwald's chapter looks at the language of burden sharing that is so often used by the international community, arguing that the very structures of the refugee protection regime explain why there is such resistance to pursuing fluid, dynamic, and comprehensive solutions.

Regional Studies: Current Realities and Future Challenges

The final part of the Handbook places the preceding debates and challenges in regional context, exploring the nature and implications of different geopolitical areas' specific social, political, and legal dynamics.

The first three chapters respectively explore displacement and forced migration in Sub-Saharan Africa. Marion Fresia contextualizes contemporary and ongoing processes of forced migration in West Africa, examining, *inter alia*, the role of the Economic Community of West African States and the European Union alike on the development of immigration discourses and policies in West Africa. In turn, Jonathan Crush and Abel

Chikanda outline five phases of displacement in the 'fifty years war' of Southern Africa, highlighting the advantages and limitations of national refugee legislation, and regional initiatives such as the Organization of African Unity (OAU) Refugee Convention and the African Union Convention for the Protection and Assistance of Internally Displaced Persons in Africa. Gaim Kibreab then traces the interconnected causes and experiences of forced migration within the Great Lakes and the Horn of Africa, critiquing mainstream encampment and self-settlement policies alike as means of preventing the local integration of displaced populations.

Sari Hanafi's chapter on the Middle East and North Africa also highlights the challenges of protracted encampment through case-studies of Palestinians in Lebanon and Sahrawis in South-West Algeria, and of local integration in urban contexts in the case of Iraqis in Jordan. Alessandro Monsutti and Bayram Balci subsequently explore one of the most emblematic recent cases of forced migration—protracted displacement in and from Afghanistan—alongside complex cases of forced migration and statelessness prompted by conflict and environmental stress in the Central Asian republics. Paula Banerjee's chapter on South Asia addresses a wide range of mass displacement scenarios, including the impact of the Partition of India/Pakistan, the constitution of and discrimination against stateless populations, and the impacts of development projects across the region. Kirsten McConnachie subsequently discusses the role of the Association of Southeast Asian Nations (ASEAN) and other regional initiatives in responding to conflict induced and disaster induced displacement and trafficking, before exploring responses to Indochinese refugees and refugees from Myanmar in detail. The connections between political shifts and migratory movements between South-East Asia, Australasia, and the Pacific Islands are explored through McNevin's chapter, with specific reference to Australia and New Zealand as destinations for asylum seekers and refugees, and Pacific Island states as source countries for climate induced and other forms of forced migration.

Three chapters then address displacement dynamics across the Americas, starting with José Fischel de Andrade's analysis of the history, evolution, and impacts of Latin America's unique protection regime, including a particular focus on the distinction between refuge on the one hand and territorial and diplomatic asylum on the other. Against the backdrop of the regional protection framework underpinned by the Organization of American States and the 1984 Cartagena Declaration on Refugees, Megan Bradley's chapter on Central America and the Caribbean explores civil society, national, and regional responses to diverse displacement scenarios, critically evaluating the impacts of the International Conference on Central American Refugees (CIREFCA). Susan Martin's chapter then explores North American states' roles as resettlement and donor states, in addition to critiquing the increasing restrictionism of the United States of America's and Canada's asylum systems. Finally, Bank's chapter on Europe draws this part of the Handbook to a close by examining the asylum and immigration policies and legislative frameworks created by the Council of Europe and the European Union. As such, Bank considers the extent to which developments in Europe have the potential to influence the interpretation of international refugee law across other regions of the world.

The Future of Refugee and Forced Migration Studies

The contributors to this Handbook—leading scholars, practitioners and policymakers in this field—provide insights to the likely directions which research in refugee and forced migration studies will take in the future, and the challenges the field will need to address as it evolves over the next 30 years.

One thing is clear: the *places* where research with and about refugees and forced migration takes place are changing. These changes are taking place in at least two regards.

First, an exponential growth in research tracing urban displacement has taken place since 2007, reflecting the fact that the majority of refugees and IDPs choose to live in cities, and correcting an earlier tendency to concentrate on the experiences of those in refugee camps. Furthermore, such a focus on urban displacement involves both international and internal displacement contexts. Indeed, the number of IDPs far outnumbers refugees in most displacement crises, and yet refugee and forced migration scholars have often been slow to focus on these groups, despite the important legal, political, and sociological questions that internal displacement raises. This is beginning to change, and the pace of such change is only likely to accelerate. Refugee and forced migration studies will increasingly concern itself with urban hosting settings and IDPs rather than refugee camps.

Second, a major shift is taking place in terms of the (geographical and intellectual) location and origins of scholars conducting research into refugee and forced migration studies. While many academics, practitioners, and policymakers working in this field to date have been situated in institutions in the global North, significant contributions to the field have long been made by researchers from across all regions of the world, even if 'southern'[18] academics' voices and publications (in different languages, institutions, and journals) have often had less reach due to structural conditions (Landau 2012; cf. Chimni 1998). With bodies such as the International Association for the Study of Forced Migration and leading journals such as the *Journal of Refugee Studies* increasingly showcasing the contributions of scholars and universities, practitioners, and organizations from across the global South, the future of refugee and forced migration studies will be closely tied to ongoing debates regarding the visibility, audibility, authenticity, and acceptability of different perspectives from diverse locations around the world. With reference to the acceptability of such research, Banerjee argues that 'the northern gaze is often turned away from the research done in the south, especially when it is considered too political. Our research cannot but be political because we have to live with the reality of forced migration every day and so our research, if not emancipatory, can become meaningless' (2012: 572).

The diversification of regional perspectives in academic research will also be paralleled by the increasing number of regional initiatives designed to respond to, and attempt to prevent, displacement.[19] Regional policies, institutions, and conventions are, of course, far from new innovations, as demonstrated throughout the twelve contributions in the Regional Studies section of the Handbook, and critical evaluations of so-called regional success stories such as the International Conference on Central American Refugees (CIREFCA) or the Comprehensive Plan of Action for Indochinese Refugees (CPA), and the OAU Refugee Convention and Cartagena Declaration. Nonetheless, a multiplicity of regional mechanisms and frameworks have been developed (including the Bali process and the 2011 Regional Cooperation Framework in the Asia and Pacific region) and, in the case of Conventions, presented for ratification over the past decade, requiring detailed analysis of their implications over the coming years. In particular, such research will explore the potential impacts of the African Union Convention for the Protection and Assistance of Internally Displaced Persons in Africa (known as the Kampala Convention), which entered into force on 6 December 2012, and whether different regions around the world will mirror or reject the Kampala Convention and the European Union's evolving asylum policy framework.

Other trends are less absolute, but many of the most exciting developments in refugee and forced migration studies are likely to take place at the edges of traditional areas of study. In particular, the overlap between migration studies and forced migration research studies will in all likelihood continue to increase. This reflects the growing body of existing work that shows that, on the ground and in lived experience, such distinctions are often arbitrary when trying to map movements from conflict and crisis situations, as well as increasing hostility towards immigration and scepticism about the possibility of integration in the West. A question that refugee and forced migration scholars have long wrestled with—how to frame the movement of those who migrate not because they are persecuted, but because they are poor—is likely to become increasingly salient. Human rights-based research—another field that has seen rapid growth—may provide one means of reconciling the study of forced migration with the politics of migration, through the language of rights.

There are also important gaps in our understanding of forced migration that closer collaboration with researchers working to document other forms of migration could help to fill. In particular, research in forced migration has tended to be overwhelmingly qualitative. This in part reflects the roots of the field in the gathering of both ethnographic and legal testimony that can document and challenge human suffering at the micro-level, but it has left notable gaps. One area requiring further engagement is that of the economics of forced migration. Perhaps the most referenced study to date in this regard is Kuhlman's work on the economic integration of refugees in Eastern Sudan, and refugees' impact on the economic behaviour and outcomes of the host population (Kuhlman 1991). While quantitative econometric studies have been conducted and circulated by and among economists (for instance: Ibáñez and Moya 2009; Alix-García and Saah 2010) there has nonetheless been little engagement with the economics of forced migration *as part of the* multidisciplinary field of refugee and forced migration studies. A major exception is the valuable work which has been undertaken to successfully incorporate a livelihoods perspective into forced migration research and programming, as discussed by Jacobsen in this volume. There is therefore a real need both for more quantitative researchers to engage with the economics of forced migration, and for qualitative researchers to engage with this existing and emerging literature in order to maximize the benefits of mixed-methods approaches to research, despite the methodological challenges that the complexities and uncertainties of forced migration flows inevitably entail.

The increasing recognition that future research agendas in refugee and forced migration studies must incorporate an economic perspective also underlines the (recurrent) trend to connect refugee and forced migration studies with not only humanitarian but also development work. The question of how displacement interacts with development processes has long occupied both policymakers and researchers (see Betts 2004), but answers remain uncertain.

With protracted displacements of five years or more now being the norm rather than the exception, researchers are also increasingly documenting the experiences of those who have never personally moved anywhere, but who have inherited their status as displaced people, and who live alongside equally deprived local citizens. Further exploration of the multifaceted legacies of exile and displacement across generations both in the intimate space of the household and at societal level will continue to enrich debates on durable solutions. It will also facilitate the establishment of a rich terrain for cross-fertilization with diaspora studies and historical analysis more broadly, the latter a contact zone currently not fully appreciated partly as a result of a research agenda in refugee and forced migration studies which is more oriented towards the immediacy of the here and the now.

The search for not just durable but *transformative* solutions for those trapped in protracted displacement is also likely to lead to continued efforts to incorporate forced migrants into existing 'migration and development' discourses. Equally, given the close connection between protracted displacement and prolonged conflict, links between peace and conflict studies and forced migration studies also need to be strengthened. This may further encourage refugee and forced migration scholars to focus not only on the displaced, but also to examine the needs and rights of those who are left behind and who are often rendered 'involuntarily immobile' (Carling 2002)—both in countries of origin and, after return, in countries of asylum.

Refugee and forced migration studies will also shift to incorporate new understandings not only of the consequences but also of the causes of forced migration. In particular, much work remains to be done in evaluating how climate change and accelerated environmental degradation are affecting patterns of migration, especially in weak and conflict-prone states. Furthermore, as the processes of urbanization, development, and post-conflict state-building described here accelerate, there is also likely to be a need for renewed attention to be paid to development induced displacement processes that pit individual rights against collective gain and pose new questions about power and ethics.

As exciting as these and other innovations may be, it is important that these new research fields are not developed at the cost of abandoning more traditional concerns. It is very clear that there is still a need for perceptive, thoughtful research that speaks directly to the original core concerns that underpin refugee and forced migration studies: who deserves international protection, and what should that protection look like? These concerns are closely linked to a much broader challenge that refugee and forced migration studies continues to face as it matures: how to manage the field's close connections with policy and advocacy communities, while simultaneously continuing to build upon Harrell-Bond's legacy of critiquing the nature and implications, both intended and unintended, of humanitarianism and the humanitarian regime (1987; also Fassin 2011; Weiss 2013).

As this Handbook documents, the field has its roots in advocacy and policy-relevant research. For many of us who have chosen to work in this field, our motivation is not just intellectual curiosity, but a sense of moral responsibility to try and account for some of the injustices experienced by refugees and other forced migrants, and to record testimonies that would otherwise be largely confined to the margins of history. Yet after 30 years, it is obvious that in many areas, the causes of continuing suffering stem not from research gaps, but a lack of political will to recognize the implications of very clear research findings. Similarly, as Bakewell (2008) has argued, research that blindly follows policy agendas rather than critically assessing such policy frameworks and breaking new ground is likely to offer few innovative conclusions. Recent decades have seen the development of a more rigorous approach to methodology, and refugee and forced migration scholars need to be equally determined to set their own research agendas. Of course, the value of refugee and forced migration studies lies in its determination to confront very real world problems, and yet this must involve challenging policymakers' conventional approaches by providing new accounts, new insights, and new frameworks. In a world where academic funding and research work will be increasingly measured by 'impact', refugee and forced migration scholars are undoubtedly well placed to contribute to public debates. Nonetheless, the field needs to remember that when it comes to the question of how to best ameliorate conditions, the right conclusions are often those that the powerful least want to hear. This is why it is important that refugee and forced migration studies retains a critical, independent edge.

Growing academic interest in refugee and forced migration issues is to be welcomed. However it also brings with it at least two significant challenges that may not be easy to reconcile. On the one hand, some research into refugee and forced migration issues is conducted by scholars in the social sciences who analyse refugee crises primarily in order to contribute to theoretical debates within existing academic canons. This is important, as it increasingly places refugee issues in the context of broader debates and avoids forced migration being viewed as a marginal, peripheral subject rather than a complex topic that should interest the brightest and best minds. Yet on the other hand, there is a real risk that refugee and forced migration studies may lose its distinct identity and the strengths that come from its rich cross-disciplinary tradition and humanitarian roots.

We argue that engaging with refugee and forced migration studies should not be based on a purely intellectual pursuit, divorced from the human realities of displacement and dispossession. However, if refugee and forced migration scholars *can* grow in complex intellectual and theoretical directions while ensuring that the fundamental concerns with the 'right to have rights' (Arendt 1951) that saw the field emerge three decades ago remain at the centre of the field, the future for refugee and forced migration studies remains bright. Given how bleak a future so many refugees, asylum seekers, and migrants continue to face in cities and camps across the globe, a vibrant and engaged community of refugee and forced migration scholars is particularly crucial now and in the decades to come. It is for this reason that we hope that the *Oxford Handbook of Refugee and Forced Migration Studies* will both help to inspire new researchers to join our field, and help to build a sense of common purpose linking, but not limiting, the diverse interests of existing researchers working in this complex, fascinating, and important field.

Notes

1. Important research on the impact of the early Cold War on international refugee policy was also undertaken by a group of historians based at the University of Lund in the mid- to late 1980s.
2. Also see Cirtautas 1957; Gordenker 1983.
3. Key references include, respectively, Aga Khan (1981); Chambers (1979) and Mason and Brown (1983); Gorman (1984) and Ferris (1985); and Loescher and Scanlan (1986).
4. For example, Elie's and Loescher's chapters
5. For instance, see Betts, Barnett, Chatty, and Stepputat and Sørensen in this volume.
6. See Lischer's chapter in particular.
7. As discussed in Collyer's contribution.
8. For instance, see Gibney and Hollenbach in this volume.
9. Examples include Anderson, Fiddian-Qasmiyeh, and Sigona in this volume.
10. In particular, see Landau, Long, Van Selm, and Zetter and Morrissey in this volume.
11. Respectively, Van Hear, Scheel and Squire, and Jacobsen in this volume.
12. These last three are explored in detail by Kälin, McDowell, and Anderson respectively.
13. For instance, see contributions by Goodwin-Gill, Betts, McAdam, Edwards and Van Waas, Türk and Dowd, Akram, Barnett, and Russell and Tennant.
14. For example, see Collyer's, Fresia's, and Hanafi's chapters.
15. These case-studies are discussed by Banerjee and Monsutti and Balci in this volume.
16. Chapters addressing these aims include Hansen and Hammerstad.
17. As discussed by Sigona, Fiddian-Qasmiyeh, and Wright.
18. Precisely who is considered to 'be' of the south or north, is of course a contested issue in and of itself, as noted by Landau's self-positioning as a 'southern researcher' despite his academic training in North American institutions, etc. (2012).
19. This trend also partly reflects a changing geography of asylum and the emergence of new asylum hubs, such as Brazil and South Africa.

References

Aga Khan, S. (1981) *Study on Human Rights and Massive Exoduses*. United Nations: Economic and Social Council, Commission on Human Rights, E/CN.4/1503

Alix-García, J., and Saah, D. (2010) 'The Effect of Refugee Inflows on Host Communities: Evidence from Tanzania'. *The World Bank Economic Review* 24(1): 148–70.

Arendt, H. (1951) *The Origins of Totalitarianism*. New York: Harvest.

Avery, C. (1984) 'Refugee Status Decision-Making in Ten Countries'. *Stanford Journal of International Law* 17: 183–241.

Bakewell, O. (2008) 'Research beyond the Categories: The Importance of Policy Irrelevant Research into Forced Migration'. *Journal of Refugee Studies* 21(4): 432–53.

Betts, A. (2004) 'International Cooperation and Targeting Development Assistance for Refugee Solutions: Lessons From the 1980s'. Geneva: UNHCR. New Issues in Refugee Research Working Paper, 107.

Carling, J. (2002) 'Migration in the Age of Involuntary Immobility: Theoretical Reflections and Cape Verdean Experiences'. *Journal of Ethnic and Migration Studies* 28(1): 5–42.

Chambers, R. (1979) 'Rural Refugees in Africa: What the Eyes do not See'. *Disasters* 3(4): 381–92.

Chimni, B. S. (1998) 'The Geopolitics of Refugee Studies: A View from the South'. *Journal of Refugee Studies* 11(4): 350–74.

Chulov, M. (2013) 'Half of Syrian Population "Will Need Aid by End of Year"'. *The Guardian*, 19 April.

Cirtautas, C. K. (1957) *The Refugee: A Psychological Study*. Boston: Meadow.

Colson, E. (1971) *The Social Consequences of Resettlement: The Impact of the Kariba Resettlement upon the Gwembe Tonga*. Manchester: University of Manchester Press.

Fassin, D. (2011) *Humanitarian Reason: A Moral History of the Present*. London: University of California Press.

Ferris, E. (1985) *Refugees and World Politics*. New York: Praeger.

Gordenker, L. (1983) 'Refugees in Developing Countries and Transnational Organisation'. *The Annals of the American Academy of Political and Social Science* 467: 62–77.

Gorman, R. (1984) 'Refugee Repatriation in Africa'. *The World Today* 40: 436–43.

Harrell-Bond, B. (1986) *Imposing Aid: Emergency Assistance to Refugees*. Oxford: Oxford University Press.

Hathaway, J. C. (2007) 'Forced Migration Studies: Could we Agree just to "Date"?' *Journal of Refugee Studies* 20(3): 349–69.

Ibáñez, A., and Moya, A. (2009) 'Do Conflicts Create Poverty Traps? Asset Losses and Recovery for Displaced Households in Colombia'. MICROCON Research Working Paper 10.

Jacobsen, K., and Landau, L. (2008) 'The Dual Imperative in Refugee Research: Some Methodological and Ethical Considerations in Social Science Research on Forced Migration'. *Disasters* 27(3): 185–206.

Kuhlman, T. (1991) 'The Economic Integration of Refugees in Developing Countries: A Research Model'. *Journal of Refugee Studies* 4: 1–20.

Landau, L. (2012) 'Communities of Knowledge or Tyrannies of Partnership: Reflections on North–South Research Networks and the Dual Imperative'. *Journal of Refugee Studies* 25(4): 555–70.

Loescher, G., and Scanlan, J. (1986) *Calculated Kindness: Refugees and America's Half-Open Door*. New York: Simon and Schuster.

Malkki, L. (1995) 'Refugees and Exile: From "Refugee Studies" to the National Order of Things'. *Annual Review of Anthropology* 24: 495–523.

Martin, D. (1982) 'Large-Scale Migrations of Asylum-Seekers'. *American Journal of International Law* 76: 598–605.

Martin, S. (2004) 'Making the UN Work: Forced Migration and Institutional Reform'. *Journal of Refugee Studies* 17(3): 301–18.

Mason, L., and Brown, R. (1983) *Rice, Rivalry and Politics*. Notre Dame, IN: University of Notre Dame Press.

Tolstoy, N. (1977) *Victims of Yalta*. London: Hodder and Stoughton.

Turton, D. (1996) 'Migrants and Refugees'. Pp. 96–110 in T. Allen (ed.), *In Search of Cool Ground: War, Flight, and Homecoming in Northeast Africa*. Trenton: Africa World Press.

UNHCR (2013) Global Trends 2012: Displacement—The New 21st Century Challenge. <http://unhcr.org/globaltrendsjune2013/UNHCR%20GLOBAL%20TRENDS%202012_V08_web.pdf>.

Weiss, T. (2013) *Humanitarian Business*. Cambridge: Polity.

Zayas, A. de (1979) *Nemesis at Potsdam*. London: Routledge and Kegan Paul.

Zetter, R. (1991) 'Labelling Refugees: Forming and Transforming a Bureaucratic Identity'. *Journal of Refugee Studies* 4(1): 39–61.

PART I

APPROACHES: OLD AND NEW

....

CHAPTER 2

HISTORIES OF REFUGEE AND FORCED MIGRATION STUDIES

....

JÉRÔME ELIE

INTRODUCTION

....

REFUGEE and forced migration studies have always involved a multiplicity of academic disciplines. Yet many believe the role of historians has been weak and poorly defined, history being 'notable by its absence' (Marfleet 2007: 136). This is partially explained by the discipline's focus on practical and current issues as well as its intimate connections with policy developments, notwithstanding critical approaches. In contrast, history has largely remained estranged from or unappealing to policy circles which 'rarely show interest in migrations of the past' (Marfleet 2007: 137–8) and tend to reinvent the wheel continuously (Loescher 2001: 33–4).

Consequently, the field is often believed to be deeply 'ahistorical'. Most strikingly, historians such as Tony Kushner and Peter Gatrell seem to concur, considering refugee history as an 'emerging field' sometimes best represented by 'amateur' historians, which has yet to produce its own specialized journal. Non-historians have demonstrated an 'inability to see history and refugees as linked or relevant,' whereas historians have shown 'actual resistance rather than simple apathy' in their engagement with the theme (Kushner 2006: 40; Gatrell 2007: 43–5).

In this context, how can one write about the histories of an 'ahistorical' field? Is there really such a general lack of historical studies on refugees and forced migrants or should we understand that historians have failed to address important aspects rather than the whole field? To be sure, historians and history are not totally absent. More accurately, historians have addressed refugee and forced migration issues without necessarily identifying their work with the field. They often situate their work within other (related) historiographical debates, such as the history of the slave trade, the two world wars, genocide, the Cold War, humanitarian interventions, transnational history, and so on. Histories have been written and debates, trends, or even historiographical schools can therefore be identified and discussed. However, there are undoubtedly much less general reflections on the historiography of refugees and forced migration. The objective of this chapter is to briefly provide such an overview, while explaining and questioning the claim of 'ahistory'.

An Overview of the Histories of Refugee and Forced Migration

Academic inquiry, including historical research on refugees and forced migrants, started long before the 'birth' of the discipline in the 1980s (Skran and Daughtry 2007: 15). Over the 1920s and 1930s scholars discussed the mass refugee movements produced during the First World War, thus announcing publications of the immediate post-Second World War era (e.g. Holborn 1939). This period is characterized by a richness of works on refugees, including voluminous studies (not necessarily written by historians) of the refugee camps left after the two world wars (e.g. Kulischer 1948; Proudfoot 1956).

In the immediate post-war years historians also focused importantly on the international organizations created in the 1920s–1930s and the 1940s–1950s. These legal-institutional accounts continued to dominate the literature during the 1960s–1970s as attested by Louise Holborn's influential history of UNHCR (1975). Despite claims to universality, the main focus remained for a long time on Western European issues. The study of the history of forced migration in Europe peaked in the 1980s, with publications such as Michael Marrus's overview of Europe's *Unwanted* (1985) and national perspectives akin to Wolfgang Jacobmeyer's major study of 'Displaced Persons' in Germany (1985).

Michael Marrus focused his attention on the masses of refugees in Europe, with the objective of tracing the emergent consciousness on the refugee phenomenon in a critical manner (Caestecker 2011). Also notable was Gérard Noiriel's *La Tyrannie du national* (1991). During the late 1980s, a number of studies appeared looking at non-European issues, or from non-European perspectives, often linked to the opening of national archives. Thus, Gil Loescher and John Scanlan's *Calculated Kindness* (1986) presented the first comprehensive critical survey of the US government's post-war policies toward the admission of refugees. Benny Morris's work on the *Birth of the Palestinian Refugee Problem* (1989) also marked the historiography of this sensitive area.

The end of the Cold War, 'combined with the postmodernist challenge to grand narratives helped unleash a new round of historical research' (Gatrell 2010: 2). From the early 1990s, many books on refugees appeared, launching a massive interest in the history of immigration and refugee flows. Policies towards immigrants and refugees became part of national histories, with more focused and detailed case-studies highlighting the role and interests of different political actors (particularly in receiving states). A major theme of those publications related to European states' policies and popular attitudes towards refugees in the 1930s, especially Jewish refugees from Germany (Carron 1999). In line with Marrus and Noiriel these books tended to be critical of the historical record (Deschodt and Huguenin 2001; London 2003). Research now continues especially with comparative endeavours such as Frank Caestecker and Bob Moore's volume on *Refugees from Nazi Germany and the Liberal European States* (2010).

It was also through the study of the interwar years that the historiography came back on the role of international organizations and the refugee regime with studies by Tommie Sjöberg on the Intergovernmental Committee on Refugees (1991), Claudena Skran on the emergence of the regime in interwar Europe (1995), and Gil Loescher's work on the global refugee crisis and his excellent although relatively short history of UNHCR (2001). Loescher aptly described the organization's shortcomings and the successive High Commissioners' drives to expand their mandate despite important constraints. He thus developed a useful corrective to Holborn's 'more whiggish approach' which presented UNHCR history as an 'inevitable progression toward an ever-widening realm of humanitarian intervention' (Peterson 2012: 327). More studies on UNHCR followed in connection to improved access to the documentation after the creation of its global archives in 1996 and the celebration of the organization's 50th anniversary (UNHCR 2000; Hanhimäki 2008). Much work remains to be done however as many organizations, particularly NGOs, still do not provide satisfactory access to and preservation of their archives.

The focus on UNHCR has however been questioned by researchers considering that it looms 'disproportionately large' in historical accounts of the early post-war period, especially given its 'modest and uncertain beginnings'. New perspectives should certainly recognize that the refugee regime developing in Europe after the war 'was only one part of a larger picture' (Holian and Cohen 2012: 316). Historians thus recently started looking more closely at other organizations (e.g. Reinisch 2008; Salvatici 2012) and at the significance of interactions between UNHCR and other non-state actors (Elie 2010). An important trend relates to the study of displaced persons as part of the history of humanitarianism and post-war relief and reconstruction programmes (e.g. Cohen 2011).

The diversification of research also led to reassessing heretofore neglected avenues of inquiries such as the history of forced displacement in the Russian and Soviet area (Gatrell 1999; Gousseff 2008), the history of refugee repatriation (Zieck 1997; Long 2013a) and gender dimensions (Schrover et al. 2008). Transnational history also went beyond simple (inter-)national histories, towards accounts of connections and circulations of people, goods, ideas and skills. For example, Peter Gatrell's book (2011) on World Refugee Year (1959–60) focuses on a specific global social movement and the role of multiple actors such as the United Nations, NGOs, and individuals.

Historians not only began to 'redress the Eurocentric bias by writing about other parts of the globe' (Gatrell 2010: 2), but also questioned the distinction between 'classical' refugees who had their origins in Europe and 'new' refugees from other parts of the world. This dichotomy implied that forced movements outside Europe only began after the resolution of the old continent's refugee crisis and forgot the 'already global nature of the refugee question in the early post-war period' (Ballinger 2012: 367). Historians often ignored that there were massive forced movements outside Europe during the 1950s and 1960s and even before. The partition of the Indian subcontinent, 'one of the greatest mass migrations in history' was a case in point, at least until Gyanendra Pandey's book (2001: 41). As argued by Holian and Cohen (2012: 315), although the Eurocentric approach has been questioned, no 'significantly different account of the early post-war period' appeared, displacing Europe 'from the conceptual and practical centre'. Historians are now just starting working in this direction (Peterson 2012; Madokoro 2012). In the process they also underline the causal links between the end of empires, the rise of the modern nation state and the emergence of mass refugee flows (Gatrell 2010: 2).

This brief overview excludes many more studies because of language limitations. However, it demonstrates that a relatively important literature exists. The meaning of the 'ahistorical' reputation thus remains unexplained. An answer may be found by looking more closely at the ways historians have reflected on this field, particularly with reference to classical issues of continuity and change.

Continuity and Change in Refugee and Forced Migration History

In this field, historiography has made important progress in the last few years. In the process, historians have looked to highlight elements of continuity and change, aiming to date and map the birth of the contemporary refugee phenomenon and determine what is so distinctive about the current era. In essence, historians recognize that the forced movement of people has a long history, but many consider refugees as a distinctly modern phenomenon, which emerged with the world wars. For example, Richard Bessel and Claudia Haake (2009: 3) consider forced displacements as 'hardly something novel or invented' but as a phenomenon whose occurrence and magnitude across the world is 'peculiarly modern'. Similarly, Marrus (1985: 3–5) has argued that people fleeing war and persecution 'have tramped across the European continent since time immemorial,' but that they only became an 'important problem of international politics' in the twentieth century. During this period, modern refugees appeared in greater numbers than ever before with vague legal status and posing problems on a radically new scale. Arguably, early modern tolerance towards displaced persons was replaced by hostile attitudes and policies linked to the development of ethno-nationalism and its links with the modern state, which made outsiders suspicious and undesirable (Marrus 2010).

Indeed, as Marfleet (2007: 139) remarks, the 'focus upon nation-states and relations within and among them' largely explains the widespread view that 'refugees did not appear as a meaningful category' until the mid-twentieth century. In this era states felt threatened by foreigners and therefore introduced tools to protect themselves from intruders epitomized by increased administrative control such as alien registration and the passport systems (Torpey 2000). Many factors combined to give the refugee issue a 'quantitatively and qualitatively new character': new modern technology facilitating travel and communication, the new scale and destructiveness of warfare, the expansion of a world capitalist economy, the emergence of modern race thinking and the triumph of national sovereignty (Bessel and Haake 2009: 3). The world wars accelerated these processes exponentially and brought a 'veritable avalanche of refugees' extending later on to other continents (Marrus 2010).

However, for other historians, the phenomenon has a much longer history. Olivier Forcade and Philippe Nivet (2008: 7) agree that the 'refugee fleeing a conflict' became a typical character after the world wars but claim that populations displaced by war have been major figures of European history at least since the sixteenth century. The early modern period saw individual departures or displacements in groups but also large flows. Well-known examples include the departure of more than 170,000 Huguenots from France around the Revocation of the Edict of Nantes (1685), but also the expulsion of more than 100,000 Jews from Spain after 1492 or the eviction at least 240,000 Moors from Spain after 1609 (Poussou 2008: 43–6). Those early modern displacements were numerically smaller than twentieth-century refugee movements but nonetheless represented major episodes in the history of Europe, some countries being particularly marked by forced exiles. As Gatrell (2010: 7) argued in reference to First World War refugee movements, 'impressions and proportions' do matter, as does the context in which these occurred. Although 'smaller than in the late 1940s,' the displacements certainly shocked contemporaries, especially in areas where refugees represented a large proportion of the population.

In the early modern era, host states were not always eager to welcome refugees especially in case of massive emigration. A major objective was often to get rid of them. Hostile attitudes sometimes led to suspicion and xenophobic sentiments (Poussou 2008: 54–6), an issue well studied for Huguenot refugees in Switzerland (Sautier et al. 1985). In any case, there was no question of putting refugees on an equal footing with the inhabitants of the host country and their treatment was usually rudimentary. If only because setting-up camps was difficult at the time, the reception of refugees was certainly very different from what it became in the contemporary era. Nevertheless, as noted by Jean-Pierre Poussou (2008: 56), reception conditions have hardly improved in the contemporary era.

Historians however do agree on a few factors that make the post-war era distinctive. At least two themes stand out: the issue of relief linked to the actions of governmental, international, and intergovernmental organizations and the causes of departures.

From the late fifteenth century private charitable initiatives and religious congregations provided relief to displaced persons. Later on, during the nineteenth century, the Balkans and the Ottoman Empire became genuine laboratories of humanitarian experiences (Forcade 2008: 337–8; Rodogno 2011). Public action gradually replaced private initiatives and the First World War acted as a powerful accelerator of this evolution. From this perspective, the 'real break, which led to a changeover in the figure of the refugee, certainly happened in the nineteenth century, before the First World War' rather than after any of the world wars (Forcade 2008: 332).

For Peter Gatrell (2010: 11–12), the important new dimension of the post-Second World War era was the 'emphasis on "rehabilitation" as something other than the restoration of physical capability' and a 'flurry of professional expertise' which had 'little or no counterpart in the interwar period'. He also identified elements of continuity and change in the refugee regime: while the interwar order had 'operated with a gradually evolving concept of a collective loss of protection,' the post-Second World War system, embodied by the 1951 Refugee Convention, established the individual 'well-founded fear of being persecuted' as the main criterion for legal recognition of the refugee status. Nevertheless, the modus operandi of the main refugee relief agencies bore similarities, especially in 'the dearth of resources at the disposal of both UNHCR and the League of Nations'. Both had very limited budgets and 'relied heavily on a number of non-governmental organisations to operate refugee relief programmes' (Gatrell 2010: 8–9; Elie 2013).

The second significant element of change relates to the causes of refugee flights, although the turning point seems to have happened again in the nineteenth (or even the late eighteenth) century. Although between the fifteenth and the nineteenth century, many displacements were caused by war, the bulk of refugee movements were linked to religious clashes. The early modern era has been 'particularly marked by the religious dimension of the forced movements' even if it could be mixed with other factors. Starting with the French Revolution, political dimensions took precedence as revolutionary France 'launched the phenomenon of mass exile for political reasons'. Throughout the nineteenth century, political refugees have been numerous although never on a comparable scale. Arguably, the process of purification implemented under the French Revolution had similarities with past searches for imposed religious unity but those never had the same organized character and ideological element. Those factors were to be found again later on, during the Russian Revolution and in Nazi Germany's actions (Poussou 2008: 68–9).

Finally, the examination of the causes of departure reminds us that the early modern era also witnessed waves of people moving 'internally' or for 'environmental' and socio-economic reasons, such as droughts, famines, and epidemics. This has relevance for this chapter since it indicates that historians have considered categorization as well as the analytical consequences of labels.

HISTORIANS AND LABELLING

To a large extent, the evolution from refugee to forced migration studies has revolved around a debate over the appropriate labels and their methodological implications (Zetter 1988). From the outset, the field of refugee studies has been 'dogged by terminological difficulties' and the relatively 'uncritical use and recycling' of a policy-based definition of refugees (Harrell-Bond 1998: 3; Black 2001: 63). According to Chimni, the 'legal definitions of "refugee" have always been partial and designed to serve state policy' and academia has failed to address this issue (Chimni 2009: 16). Historians did not necessarily position themselves within this debate but they developed their own reflections and efforts at defining their object of study.

One important (although basic) risk of the uncritical use of legal categories by historians is that of producing teleological and anachronistic studies. In this perspective, the historian's role is rather to question the categories adopted at different periods by states and international organizations and highlight the evolutions and modes of transformation of those labels over time. It is indeed critical to produce 'detailed accounts of the complex debates over eligibility in a wide range of contexts' (Ballinger 2012: 379). One way historians have tackled this challenge has been to suggest new or alternative terminology (Gatrell 2007; Bessel and Haake 2009) and show that some of the 'new' terms were actually used in the past and have a history. Thus, Alf Lüdtke reminded us recently that the term 'forced migration' was included in the fifteenth edition of the *Encyclopaedia Britannica* in the 1970s (2009: 16–17). Others have questioned the novelty of categories such as internally and environmentally displaced persons, so popular since the 1990s, by reminding readers that those were used before, even administratively. For example, Forcade and Nivet note that when the 'French Ministry of Interior established a refugee service during World War I or when Robert Schuman was appointed as Deputy Secretary of State for Refugee in 1940, it was to deal with "national refugees"' (Forcade and Nivet 2008: 8–9). This approach also includes the study of the origins and development of those 'new' categories (e.g. Weiss and Korn 2006).

Historians have looked at the evolution of labels, especially in connection with the history of the international regime and the work of international organizations. Claudena Skran and Gil Loescher's works stand out but recently a number of articles have also looked at the genesis and growth of the refugee conventions and definitions used in the interwar and post-war years (e.g. Einarsen 2011). In this context, echoing some anthropologists' criticisms about the refugee label, historians have recently questioned the historical foundations of the artificial distinction between refugees and migrants (Karatani 2005; Elie 2010; Long 2013b). Particularly noteworthy is the September 2012 issue of the *Journal of Refugee Studies*, which examines 'how "the refugee" as a distinct category of person developed in different post-war settings' (Holian and Cohen 2012: 317). Pamela Ballinger's contribution to this journal is particularly relevant since she highlights another potential risk of using labels, that of systematically excluding certain experiences and categories from history. Indeed, the omission of certain categories from national and international legal instruments 'should not be mistaken for an empirical reality'. Moreover, historians 'of refugee flows must remain on continual guard not to mistake the object of their analysis...with their unit of analysis' (Ballinger 2012: 367, 379).

This reminds us that it is crucial for research to be grounded in the historical context and reality of the time. Administrative categories rarely correspond fully to the political and sociological reality of displacements. For example, after the Second World War, not all displaced persons were considered as refugees and some were forced to return to their country of origin. On this basis, Frank Caestecker considers that it is imperative to 'go beyond the administrative category of policymaking and use an independent category of "refugee" to understand what happened on the ground'. According to him, the legal category of 'refugee' should 'certainly not discipline our knowledge'. Yet, wondering whether historians can act as 'eligibility officers for the human past,' he identifies one danger linked to the usual lack of 'sources which give us clues on the forced nature of the migration,' especially when officials do not provide relevant information (Caestecker 2011).

REFUGEE AND FORCED MIGRATION HISTORY 'FROM BELOW'

Since the 1980s, another recurrent theme in critical analyses of the field of refugee and forced migration studies has pointed towards the tendency of depicting displaced persons simply as mute, helpless victims rather than specific persons (see Sigona, this volume; Malkki 1996). As a result, the figure of the refugee or the forced migrant is often forgotten and repeatedly excluded from scholarly research. The field of history is no exception and the absence of the refugee from most historical writing is sometimes considered to be 'so marked that it constitutes a systematic exclusion'. Indeed, asking for the refugees to 'be re/instated on the historical record,' Marfleet expressed the opinion that historians have 'ignored most refugee movements and "silenced" those involved' (2007: 136–8).

This is arguably the real meaning of the term 'ahistorical'. It is not necessarily that history has neglected themes linked to refugee and forced migration processes but that historians have refrained from studying 'those involved'. In other words, the refugee or the forced migrant is 'less an unknown of history than a missing, untraceable and unnameable character of the historiography' (Forcade 2008: 332). Refugee history is seen as biased towards the history of states and international organizations. According to Kushner the history of refugees has been 'actively forgotten' (2006: 47), while for Marfleet, an important factor is also that the refugee voice challenges established national narratives (Marfleet 2007: 144).

Some historians have argued in favour of 'putting refugees at the centre rather than the margins of historical enquiry' (Gatrell 2010; 12). One recent historiographical trend is certainly the 'desire to find explanations for the "doings" of historical actors' (Lüdtke 2009: 13) and to produce life histories, including of the refugees (e.g. BenEzer 2002). In their book, Knox and Kushner (2001: 1) thus aim at exploring 'refugees' experiences and responses to their plight'. In doing so, they 'attempt to restore the humanity of refugees' and claim to develop the 'first social history of refugees' movements during the twentieth century and the first comparative one'.

To develop this kind of history, scholars face familiar dilemmas, related to the relevant methods of investigation and interpretation as well as the (un)availability of sources. Collecting information on individual refugees or forced migrants on the basis of international organizations' archives is difficult precisely because of staff members' tendency of 'talking at rather than talking with—or listening to—refugees' (Gatrell 2007: 54). Even with the best intentions, the collection of personal testimony is only a secondary activity. Valuable information on groups and eligibility criteria can be found in the UNHCR archives. However, only a small fraction of the individual cases files on refugees and refugee registration forms—likely to represent major sources of relevant data—have been preserved and those files are anyway closed for a period of 75 years to protect personal information (while most other records are available for research after 20 years).

The challenge is familiar to social historians, who since the 1960s pioneered the use of 'unconventional' archives of trade unions or local groups, thus answering E. P. Thompson's call for a history 'from below' (Marfleet 2007: 145; Gatrell 2010; 12). Some historians have actually recently used original sources to write very interesting histories of displacements, such as individual police files on Jewish refugees (Rünitz 2000). There are, however, a number of obstacles and methodological issues associated with the use of this type of sources, such as those linked to memories and recollections. Moreover, written contemporary accounts primarily emanate from educated individuals and social elites, which often represent only a fraction of the population. Thus, rural populations and craftsmen constituted the bulk of Huguenot refugees in Geneva, but they did not leave any memoirs (Poussou 2008: 50, 58). Historians also have to deal with the fact that personal accounts 'sometimes reach the light of day in unusual circumstances' (Gatrell 2007: 52) and that we lack an overview of existing testimonies, which may have an impact on the weight and interpretations we attach to those sources (Poussou 2008: 50).

An obvious corrective method has been the use of oral history which may add different perspectives to the research. Urvashi Butalia's study of the impact of Partition in India (2000) is one of the best examples of how oral testimony can complement other sources and help consider the individual experiences of displaced persons. It is certainly one way of ensuring that their voice is, for once, being heard. However, this approach also presents difficulties beyond language skills and the relative exclusion of earlier periods of history. There are the classical issues linked to how that voice is registered. Moreover, without reproducing the 'suspicion' discussed here, it is important not to over-interpret these testimonies and avoid considering those voices as the absolute and ultimate truth. Finally, the difficulty of approaching the refugees has to be taken into account (Harrell-Bond and Voutira 2007). Many obstacles hinder research, especially when one tries to access archival material or individuals in the 'South'.

Despite all the difficulties, historians have developed valuable efforts at redressing the imbalance in scholarship towards a better consideration of the 'refugee voice'. Only with increased initiatives of the kind presented here and with enhanced mixing of sources will the field become less 'ahistorical'.

CONCLUSION

History can bring important inputs by shedding light on the 'manifold ways in which past societies thought about refugees' (Holian and Cohen 2012: 324). Although still an emerging area of research, the preceding pages demonstrate that a rich body of historical scholarship exists. As attested by a number of ongoing research projects and recent conferences, historians' contributions to the field seem to represent a flourishing field of study. To be sure, there are still many shortcomings, such as the lack of 'history from below'. Methodological and archival difficulties may explain part of the research gap but historians have to better address those aspects if they are to shed the 'ahistorical' stigma. In doing so, they can certainly count on the interest of and the contribution from other academic disciplines and collaborations with anthropologists is certainly a most promising avenue.

However, for the dialogue to be productive, it is also important for other academics to show more interest in historical studies on refugees and forced migrants as well as more generally. When Philip Marfleet laments that 'researchers in the field of forced migration rarely undertake historical analyses' and seem to be 'averse to history' (2007: 136), he not only points to the shortcomings in historical studies on refugees and forced migrants but also to a lack of interest in history *tout court*. Refugee and forced migration scholars should engage more with the general historical contexts in which displacements develop. For fruitful exchanges to emerge, it may also be important to realize that more often than not, historians will aim to produce history of forced displacements for its own sake and not just with a 'utilitarian' perspective, i.e. to 'help' other scholars, as Marfleet requests (2007: 136). Historians will (hopefully) not necessarily select a research topic or an approach solely for the benefit of other disciplines, a specific field of study, or to feed into policy. Despite the inherent difficulties, meaningful engagement with historians has to be based on genuine interdisciplinary projects and consideration for historians' own perspectives. In other words, as historians move to take refugee and forced migration studies seriously, the wider refugee and forced migration studies community must start taking history seriously too.

REFERENCES

Ballinger, P. (2012) 'Entangled or "Extruded" Histories? Displacement, National Refugees, and Repatriation after the Second World War'. *Journal of Refugee Studies* 25(3): 366–86.

BenEzer, G. (2002) *The Ethiopian Jewish Exodus: Narratives of the Migration Journey to Israel, 1977–1985*. London: Routledge.

Bessel, R., and Haake, C. B. eds. (2009) *Removing Peoples: Forced Removal in the Modern World*. Oxford: Oxford University Press.

Black, R. (2001) 'Fifty Years of Refugee Studies: From Theory to Policy'. *International Migration Review* 35(1): 57–78.

Butalia, U. (2000) *The Other Side of Silence: Voices from the Partition of India*. Durham, NC: Duke University Press Books.

Caestecker, F. (2011) 'Refugees in the European Historiography: Beyond the Administrative Category'. Paper presented at the conference: Historiographies sans frontières. Les migrations internationales saisies par les histoires nationales (XIXe–XXe siècles), Paris, 4 October 2011. Podcast. <http://www.histoire-immigration.fr/2011/9/historiographies-sans-frontieres-les-migrations-internationales-saisies-par-les-histoires-nationales-xixe-xxe-siecles> (accessed 27 July 2012).

Caestecker, F., and Moore, B. (2010) *Refugees from Nazi Germany and the Liberal European States*. New York: Berghahn Books.

Carron, V. (1999) *Uneasy Asylum: France and the Jewish Refugee Crisis, 1933–1942*. Stanford, CA: Stanford University Press.

Chimni, B. S. (2009) 'The Birth of a "Discipline": From Refugee to Forced Migration Studies'. *Journal of Refugee Studies* 22(1): 11–29.

Cohen, G. D. (2011) *In War's Wake: Europe's Displaced Persons in the Postwar Order*. Oxford: Oxford University Press.

Deschodt, P.-J., and Huguenin, F. (2001) *La République xénophobe. 1917–1939, de la machine d'état au 'crime de bureau'. Les révélations des archives*. Paris: J.-C. Lattès.

Einarsen, T. (2011) 'Drafting History of the 1951 Convention and the 1967 Protocol'. Pp. 3–36 in A. Zimmermann (ed.), *The 1951 Convention Relating to the Status of Refugees and its 1967 Protocol: A Commentary*. Oxford: Oxford University Press.

Elie, J. (2010) 'The Historical Roots of Cooperation between the UN High Commissioner for Refugees and the International Organization for Migration'. *Global Governance* 16(3): 345–60.

Elie, J. (2013) 'Interactions et filiations entre organisations internationales autour de la question des réfugiés dans la période d'après-guerre (1946–1956)'. *Relations internationales* 152: 39–50.

Forcade, O. (2008). Conclusion. Pp. 331–40 in O. Forcade and P. Nivet (eds.), *Les Réfugiés en Europe du XVIe au XXe siècle*. Paris: Éditions Nouveau Monde.

Forcade, O., and Nivet, P. (2008) 'Pour une histoire des réfugiés dans l'Europe moderne et contemporaine'. Pp. 7–10 in O. Forcade and P. Nivet (eds.), *Les Réfugiés en Europe du XVIe au XXe siècle*. Paris: Éditions Nouveau Monde.

Gatrell, P. (1999) *A Whole Empire Walking: Refugees in Russia during World War One*. Bloomington: Indiana University Press.

Gatrell, P. (2007) 'Population Displacement in the Baltic Region in the Twentieth Century: From "Refugee Studies" to Refugee History'. *Journal of Baltic Studies* 38(1): 43–60.

Gatrell, P. (2010) 'The Making of the Modern Refugee'. Keynote Address for the Conference on 'Refugees in the Postwar World', Arizona State University, 8–9 April. Unpublished paper.

Gatrell, P. (2011) *Free World? The Campaign to Save the World's Refugees, 1956–1963*. New York: Cambridge University Press.

Gousseff, C. (2008) *L'Exil russe 1920–1939. La fabrique du réfugié apatride*. Paris: CNRS Éditions.

Hanhimäki, J. ed. (2008) 'UNHCR and the Global Cold War, 1971–1984'. *Refugee Survey Quarterly* 27(1).

Harrell-Bond, B. (1998). 'Refugee Studies at Oxford: "Some" History'. Paper presented at the conference 'The Growth of Forced Migration: New Directions in Research, Policy and Practice', Oxford, 25–7 March 1998, p. 7. <http://www.rsc.ox.ac.uk/publications/rsc-reports/history-refugee-studies/view> (accessed 27 July 2012).

Harrell-Bond, B. and Voutira, E. (2007) 'In Search of "Invisible" Actors: Barriers to Access in Refugee Research'. *Journal of Refugee Studies* 20(2): 281–98.

Holborn, L. W. (1939) 'The League of Nations and the Refugee Problem'. *Annals of the American Academy of Political and Social Science* 203: 124–35.

Holborn, L. W. (1975) *Refugees: A Problem of our Time: The Work of the United Nations High Commissioner for Refugees, 1951–1972*. Metuchen, NJ: The Scarecrow Press.

Holian, A. and Cohen, G. D. (eds.) (2012) 'Special Issue: The Refugee in the Postwar World, 1945–1960'. *Journal of Refugee Studies* 25(3).

Jacobmeyer, W. (1985) *Vom Zwangsarbeiter zum Heimatlosen Ausländer. Die Displaced Persons in Westdeutschland 1945–1951*. Göttingen: Vandenhoeck und Ruprecht.

Karatani, R. (2005) 'How History Separated Refugee and Migrant Regimes: In Search of Their Institutional Origins'. *International Journal of Refugee Law* 17(3): 517–41.

Knox, K., and Kushner, T. (2001) *Refugees in an Age of Genocide: Global, National and Local Perspectives during the Twentieth Century*. London: Frank Kass.

Kulischer, E. M. (1948) *Europe on the Move: War and Population Changes, 1917–47*. New York: Columbia University Press.

Kushner, T. (2006) *Remembering Refugees: Then and Now*. Manchester: Manchester University Press.

Loescher, G. (2001) *The UNHCR and World Politics: A Perilous Path*. Oxford: Oxford University Press.

Loescher, G., and Scanlan, J. A. (1986) *Calculated Kindness: Refugees and America's Half-Open Door, 1945 to the Present*. New York: The Free Press.

London, L. (2003) *Whitehall and the Jews, 1933–1948: British Immigration Policy, Jewish Refugees and the Holocaust*. Cambridge: Cambridge University Press.

Long, K. (2013a) *The Point of No Return: Refugees, Rights and Repatriation*. Oxford: Oxford University Press.

Long, K. (2013b) 'When Refugees Stopped Being Migrants: Movement, Labour and Humanitarian Protection'. *Migration Studies* 1(1): 4–26.

Lüdtke, A. (2009) 'Explaining Forced Migration'. Pp. 13–32 in R. Bessel and C. B. Haake (eds.), *Removing Peoples: Forced Removal in the Modern World*. Oxford: Oxford University Press.

Madokoro, L. (2012) 'Borders Transformed: Sovereign Concerns, Population Movements and the Making of Territorial Frontiers in Hong Kong, 1949–1967'. *Journal of Refugee Studies* 25(3): 407–27.

Malkki, L. H. (1996) 'Speechless Emissaries: Refugees, Humanitarianism, and Dehistoricization'. *Cultural Anthropology* 11(3): 377–404.

Marfleet, P. (2007) 'Refugees and History: Why We Must Address the Past'. *Refugee Survey Quarterly* 26(3): 136–48.

Marrus, M. (1985) *The Unwanted: European Refugees from the First World War through the Cold War*. Oxford: Oxford University Press.

Marrus, M. (2010). 'Refugees in Europe: Explaining the Forty Years' Crisis', Opening Keynote Lecture. Conference on 'The Forty Years' Crisis: Refugees in Europe, 1919–1959', 14–16 September 2010, Birkbeck, University of London. <http://www.bbk.ac.uk/history/about-us/events/future-events/the-forty-years-crisis-refugees-in-europe-1919-1959> (accessed 25 July 2012).

Morris, B. (1989) *The Birth of the Palestinian Refugee Problem, 1947–1949*. Cambridge: Cambridge University Press.

Noiriel, G. (1991) *La Tyrannie du National, le droit d'asile en Europe (1793–1993)*. Paris: Calmann-Levy.

Pandey, G. (2001) *Remembering Partition: Violence, Nationalism and History in India*. Cambridge: Cambridge University Press.

Peterson, G. (2012) 'The Uneven Development of the International Refugee Regime in Postwar Asia: Evidence from China, Hong Kong and Indonesia'. *Journal of Refugee Studies* 25(3): 326–43.

Poussou, J.-P. (2008) Les Réfugiés dans l'histoire de l'Europe à l'époque moderne'. Pp. 31–71 in O. Forcade and P. Nivet (eds.), *Les Réfugiés en Europe du XVIe au XXe siècle*. Paris: Éditions Nouveau Monde.

Proudfoot, M. (1956) *European Refugees: 1939–52. A Study in Forced Population Movement*. London: Faber & Faber.

Reinisch, J. (2008) '"We Shall Rebuild Anew a Powerful Nation": UNRRA, Internationalism and National Reconstruction in Poland'. *Journal of Contemporary History* 43(3): 451–76.

Rodogno, D. (2011) *Against Massacre: Humanitarian Interventions in the Ottoman Empire (1815–1914). The Birth of a Concept and International Practice*. Princeton: Princeton University Press.

Rünitz, L. (2000) *Danmark Og de Jodiske Flygtninge 1933–1940. En Bog Om Flygtninge Og Menneskerettigheder*. Copenhagen: Museum Tusculanum Press, 2000.

Salvatici, S. (2012) '"Help the People to Help Themselves": UNRRA Relief Workers and European Displaced Persons'. *Journal of Refugee Studies* 25(3): 428–51.

Sautier, J., et al. (1985) *Genève au temps de la Révocation de l'Edit de Nantes, 1680–1705*. Geneva: Droz.

Schrover, M., et al. (2008) *Illegal Migration and Gender in a Global and Historical Perspective*. Amsterdam: Amsterdam University Press.

Skran, C. (1995) *Refugees in Inter-War Europe: The Emergence of a Regime*. Oxford: Clarendon Press.

Skran, C., and Daughtry, C. N. (2007) 'The Study of Refugees before "Refugee Studies"'. *Refugee Survey Quarterly* 26(3): 15–35.

Sjöberg, T. (1991) *The Powers and the Persecuted: The Refugee Problem and the Intergovernmental Committee on Refugees (IGCR), 1938–1947*. Lund: Lund University Press.

Torpey, J. (2000) *The Invention of the Passport: Surveillance, Citizenship and the State*. Cambridge: Cambridge University Press.

UNHCR (2000) *The State of the World's Refugees 2000: Fifty Years of Humanitarian Action*. Oxford: Oxford University Press.

Weiss, T. G., and Korn, D. A. (2006) *Internal Displacement: Conceptualization and its Consequences*. New York: Routledge.

Zetter, R. (1988) 'Refugees and Refugee Studies: A Label and an Agenda'. *Journal of Refugee Studies* 1(1): 1–6.

Zieck, M. (1997) *UNHCR and Voluntary Repatriation of Refugees: A Legal Analysis*. The Hague: M. Nijhoff.

CHAPTER 3

THE INTERNATIONAL LAW OF REFUGEE PROTECTION

GUY S. GOODWIN-GILL

INTRODUCTION

THE movement of people between states, whether refugees or 'migrants', takes place in a context in which *sovereignty* remains important, and specifically that aspect of sovereign competence which entitles the state to exercise prima facie exclusive jurisdiction over its territory, and to decide who among non-citizens shall be allowed to enter and remain, and who shall be refused admission and required or compelled to leave. Like every sovereign power, this competence must be exercised within and according to law, and the state's right to control the admission of non-citizens is subject to certain well-defined exceptions in favour of those in search of refuge, among others. Moreover, the state which seeks to exercise migration controls *outside* its territory, for example, through the physical interception, 'interdiction', and return of asylum seekers and forced migrants, may also be liable for actions which breach those of its international obligations which apply extra-territorially (Goodwin-Gill 2011; Moreno Lax 2011, 2012).[1]

The international law of refugee protection, which is the source of many such exceptions, comprises a range of universal and regional conventions (treaties), rules of customary international law, general principles of law, national laws, and the ever-developing standards in the practice of states and international organizations, notably the Office of the United Nations High Commissioner for Refugees.

While the provision of material assistance—food, shelter, and medical care—is a critically important function of the international refugee regime, the notion of *legal protection* has a very particular focus. Protection in this sense means using the legal tools, including treaties and national laws, which prescribe or implement the obligations of states and which are intended to ensure that no refugee in search of asylum is penalized, expelled, or refouled, that every refugee enjoys the full complement of rights and benefits to which he or she is entitled *as a refugee*; and that the human rights of every refugee are guaranteed. Protection is thus based in the law; it may be wider than rights, but it begins with rights and rights permeate the whole. Moreover, while solutions remain the ultimate objective of the international refugee regime, this does not mean that the one goal is automatically subsumed within the other. That is, protection *is* an end in itself, so far as it serves to ensure the fundamental human rights of the individual. Neither the objective of solutions nor the imperatives of assistance, therefore, can displace the autonomous protection responsibility which is borne, in its disparate dimensions, by both states and UNHCR.

The modern law can now be traced back nearly 100 years, to legal and institutional initiatives taken by the League of Nations, first, in the appointment of a High Commissioner for Refugees in 1921, and then in agreement the following year on the issue of identity certificates to 'any person of Russian origin who does not enjoy or no longer enjoys the protection of the Government of the Union of Soviet Socialist Republics and who has not acquired another nationality'. After the Second World War, the refugee question became highly politicized (Goodwin-Gill 2008), and the UN's first institutional response to the problem—the International Refugee Organization (IRO), a specialized agency—was opposed by the Soviet Union and its allies, remaining funded by only 18 of the 54 governments which were then members of the United Nations. Notwithstanding the politics of the day, tens of thousands of refugees and displaced persons were resettled under IRO auspices, through government selection schemes, individual migration, and employment placement (Holborn 1975; Loescher and Scanlan 1986).

In 1951, the IRO was replaced by a new agency, an initially non-operational subsidiary organ of the UN General Assembly charged with providing 'international protection' to refugees and seeking permanent solutions. The Statute of the United Nations High Commissioner for Refugees (UNHCR) was adopted on 14 December 1950, and the Office came into being on 1 January 1951.[2] Its mandate was general and universal, including refugees recognized under earlier arrangements, as well as those outside their country of origin who were unable or unwilling to return there owing to well-founded fear of persecution on grounds of race, religion, nationality, or political opinion. Once a temporary agency, UNHCR was put on a permanent basis in 2003, when the General Assembly renewed its mandate 'until the refugee problem is solved'.[3]

From the start, UNHCR's protection responsibilities were intended to be complemented by a new refugee treaty, and the 1951 Convention relating to the Status of Refugees was finalized by states at a conference in Geneva in July 1951; it entered into force in 1954 (Goodwin-Gill 2009).[4] Notwithstanding the intended complementarity, there were already major differences between UNHCR's mandate, which was universal and general, unconstrained by geographical or temporal limitations, and the refugee definition forwarded to the Conference by the General Assembly. This reflected the reluctance of states to sign a 'blank cheque' for unknown numbers of future refugees, and so was restricted to those who became refugees by reason of events occurring before 1 January 1951; the Conference was to add a further option, allowing states to limit their obligations to refugees resulting from events occurring *in Europe* before the critical date.

The difficulty of maintaining a refugee definition bounded by time and space was soon apparent, but it was not until 1967 that the Protocol relating to the Status of Refugees helped to bridge the gap between UNHCR's mandate and the 1951 Convention.[5] The Protocol is often referred to as 'amending' the 1951 Convention, but in fact it does no such thing. States parties to the Protocol, which can be ratified or acceded to without becoming a party to the Convention, simply agree to apply Articles 2 to 34 of the Convention to refugees defined in Article 1 thereof, as if the dateline were omitted (Article I of the Protocol). Cape Verde, the United States of America, and Venezuela have acceded only to the Protocol; Madagascar and St Kitts and Nevis remain party only to the Convention; and Madagascar and Turkey have retained the geographical limitation. The Protocol required just six ratifications and it entered into force on 4 October 1967.

The Convention Refugee Definition

Article 1A(1) of the 1951 Convention applies the term 'refugee', first, to any person considered a refugee under earlier international arrangements. Then, Article 1A(2), read now together with the 1967 Protocol and without time or geographical limits, offers a general definition of the refugee as including any person who is outside their country or origin and unable or unwilling to return there or to avail themselves of its protection, owing to well-founded fear of persecution for reasons of race, religion, nationality, membership of a particular social group (an additional ground not found in the UNHCR Statute), or political opinion. Stateless persons may also be refugees in this sense, where country of origin (citizenship) is understood as 'country of former habitual residence'.

The refugee must be 'outside' his or her country of origin, and having crossed an international frontier is an intrinsic part of the quality of refugee, understood in the international legal sense. However, it is not necessary to have fled by reason of fear of persecution, or even actually to have been persecuted. The fear of persecution looks to the future, and can emerge during an individual's absence from their home country, for example, as a result of intervening political change.

Persecution and the Reasons for Persecution

Although central to the refugee definition, 'persecution' itself is not defined in the 1951 Convention. Articles 31 and 33 refer to threats to life or freedom, so clearly it includes the threat of death, or the threat of torture, or cruel, inhuman, or degrading treatment or punishment. A comprehensive analysis requires the general notion to be related to developments within the broad field of human rights,[6] and the recognition that fear of persecution and lack of protection are themselves interrelated elements. The persecuted do not enjoy the protection of their country of origin, while evidence of the lack of protection on either the internal or external level may create a presumption as to the likelihood of persecution and to the well-foundedness of any fear. However, there is no necessary linkage between persecution and government authority. A Convention refugee, by definition, must be *unable* or *unwilling* to avail him- or herself of the protection of the state or government, and the notion of inability to secure the protection of the state is broad enough to include a situation where the authorities cannot or will not provide protection, for example, against persecution by non-state actors.

The Convention does require that the persecution feared be for reasons of 'race, religion, nationality, membership of a particular social group, or political opinion'. This language, which recalls the language of non-discrimination in the Universal Declaration of Human Rights and subsequent human rights instruments, gives an insight into the characteristics of individuals and groups which are considered relevant to refugee protection. These reasons in turn show that the groups or individuals are identified by reference to a classification which ought to be irrelevant to the enjoyment of fundamental human rights, while persecution implies a violation of human rights of particular gravity; it may be the result of cumulative events or systemic mistreatment, but equally it could comprise a single act of torture (Hathaway 2005; Goodwin-Gill and McAdam 2007).

The Convention does not just say who is a refugee, but also sets out when refugee status comes to an end (Article 1C; for example, in the case of voluntary return, acquisition of a new, effective nationality, or change of circumstances in the country of origin). For political reasons, the Convention also puts Palestinian refugees outside its scope (at least while they continue to receive protection or assistance from other UN agencies; Article 1D); and it excludes those who are treated as nationals in their state of refuge (Article 1E). Finally, the Convention definition categorically excludes from the benefits of refugee status anyone who there are serious reasons to believe has committed a war crime, a serious non-political offence prior to admission, or acts contrary to the purposes and principles of the United Nations (Article 1F). From the beginning, therefore, the 1951 Convention has contained clauses sufficient to ensure that the serious criminal and the terrorist do not benefit from international protection.

Non-refoulement

Besides identifying the essential characteristics of the refugee, states party to the Convention also accept specific obligations which are crucial to achieving the goal of protection, and thereafter an appropriate solution. Foremost among these is the principle of *non-refoulement*. As set out in the Convention, this prescribes broadly that no refugee shall be returned in any manner whatsoever to any country where he or she would be at risk of persecution.[7]

The word *refoulement* derives from the French *refouler*, which means to drive back or to repel. The idea that a state ought not to return persons to other states in certain circumstances was first referred to in Article 3 of the 1933 Convention relating to the International Status of Refugees. It was not widely ratified, but a new era began with the

General Assembly's 1946 endorsement of the principle that refugees with valid objections should not be compelled to return to their country of origin.[8] An initial proposal that the prohibition of *refoulement* be absolute and without exception was qualified by the 1951 Conference, which added a paragraph to deny the benefit of *non-refoulement* to the refugee whom there are 'reasonable grounds for regarding as a danger to the security of the country... or who, having been convicted by a final judgment of a particularly serious crime, constitutes a danger to the community of that country.' Apart from such limited exceptions, however, the drafters of the 1951 Convention made it clear that refugees should not be returned, either to their country of origin or to other countries in which they would be at risk; they also categorically rejected a proposal allowing for 'cancellation' of refugee status in cases of criminal or delinquent behaviour after recognition.

Today, the principle of *non-refoulement* is not only the essential foundation for international refugee law, but also an integral part of human rights protection, implicit in the subject matter of many such rights, and a rule of customary international law.

CONVENTION STANDARDS OF TREATMENT

Every state is obliged to implement its international obligations in good faith, which often means incorporating international treaties into domestic law, and setting up appropriate mechanisms so that those who should benefit are identified and treated accordingly. The 1951 Convention is not self-applying, and while recognition of refugee status may be declaratory of the facts, the enjoyment of most Convention rights is necessarily contingent on such a decision being made by a state party. A procedure for the determination of refugee status thus goes a long way towards ensuring the identification of those entitled to protection, and makes it easier for a state to fulfil its international obligations.[9]

In addition to the core protection of *non-refoulement*, the 1951 Convention prescribes freedom from penalties for illegal entry (Article 31), and freedom from expulsion, save on the most serious grounds (Article 32). Article 8 seeks to exempt refugees from the application of exceptional measures which might otherwise affect them by reason only of their nationality, while Article 9 preserves the right of states to take 'provisional measures' on the grounds of national security against a particular person, but only 'pending a determination by the Contracting State that that person is in fact a refugee and that the continuance of such measures is necessary... in the interests of national security'.

States have also agreed to provide certain facilities to refugees, including administrative assistance (Article 25); identity papers (Article 27), and travel documents (Article 28); the grant of permission to transfer assets (Article 30); and the facilitation of naturalization (Article 34).

Given the further objective of a *solution* (assimilation or integration), the Convention concept of refugee *status* thus offers a point of departure in considering the appropriate standard of treatment of refugees within the territory of contracting states. It is at this point, where the Convention focuses on matters such as social security, rationing, access to employment and the liberal professions, that it betrays its essentially European origin; it is here, in the articles dealing with social and economic rights, that the great-est number of reservations are to be found, particularly among developing states. Otherwise, however, the Convention proposes, as a minimum standard, that refugees should receive at least that treatment which is accorded to non-citizens generally. In some contexts, 'most-favoured-nation' treatment is called for (Articles 15, 17(1)), in oth-ers, 'national treatment', that is, treatment no different from that accorded to citizens (Articles 4, 14, 16, 20, 22(1), 23, 24(1), 29).

REFUGEE DEFINITION AND PROTECTION
BEYOND THE CONVENTION

In addition to measures adopted at the universal level, the international legal protection of refugees and forced migrants benefits from regional arrangements and instruments which, in turn, may be refugee specific or oriented more generally to the protection of human rights.

In 1969, the Organization of African Unity (now the African Union) adopted the Convention on the Specific Aspects of Refugee Problems in Africa (Sharpe 2012).[10] Article I(1) incorporates the 1951 Convention definition, but paragraph (2) adds an approach more immediately reflecting the social and political realities of contempo-rary refugee movements. Also to be accepted as refugees are those compelled to flee owing to external aggression, occupation, foreign domination, or events seriously dis-turbing public order. In 1984, 10 Central American States adopted a similar approach in the (non-binding) Cartagena Declaration,[11] recognizing in addition flight from general-ized violence, internal conflicts, and massive violation of human rights. Two years later, in the extradition case of *Soering v United Kingdom*,[12] the European Court of Human Rights laid the essential foundations for protection from removal under the European Convention. In this first judgment in what is now a long and consistent body of juris-prudence, the court ruled that it would be a breach of the Convention to remove an individual to another state in which there were substantial grounds to believe that he or she would face a real risk of treatment contrary to Article 3, which prohibits torture or inhuman or degrading treatment. Later judgments have confirmed the applicability of this principle without exception, for example, in 'security' or criminal cases,[13] and in the context also of extra-territorial interception operations.[14]

This human rights jurisprudence contributed substantially to 'legislative' develop-ments within the European Union. These include the adoption of the 2001 Directive on Temporary Protection,[15] applicable to 'displaced persons' unable or unwilling to return to their country of origin, for example, because of armed conflict, endemic violence, or systematic or generalized violence, and whether or not they are Convention refugees;

and the 2004 Qualification Directive, which besides providing for recognition of Convention refugees, now also calls for 'subsidiary protection' in the case of those who would face a real risk of serious harm if returned to their country of origin (McAdam 2007).[16]

ASYLUM

No international instrument defines 'asylum'. Article 14 of the 1948 Universal Declaration of Human Rights simply says that 'Everyone has the right to seek and to enjoy in other countries asylum from persecution.' Article 1 of the 1967 UN Declaration on Territorial Asylum notes that 'Asylum granted by a State, in the exercise of its sovereignty, to persons entitled to invoke Article 14 of the Universal Declaration of Human Rights…shall be respected by all other States.' But it is for 'the State granting asylum to evaluate the grounds for the grant of asylum' (Goodwin-Gill 2012).

Neither instrument creates any binding obligations for states. Indeed, both texts suggest a considerable margin of appreciation with respect to who is granted asylum and what exactly this means. In practice, however, states' freedom of action is significantly influenced by 'external' constraints, which follow from an internationally recognized refugee definition, the application of the principle of *non-refoulement*, and the overall impact of human rights law. Regional instruments and doctrine have also had an important impact on the 'asylum question'. Again, the 1969 OAU Convention was among the first to give a measure of normative content to the discretionary competence of states to grant asylum (Article II).[17] Within the EU, the 2000 Charter of Fundamental Rights declares expressly that 'the right to asylum shall be guaranteed…', and that no one may be removed to a state where he or she faces a serious risk of the death penalty, torture, or other inhuman or degrading treatment or punishment (Articles 18, 19). The Qualification Directive provides in turn that member states 'shall grant' refugee status to those who satisfy the relevant criteria (Article 13; see also Article 8 of the Temporary Protection Directive) (Gil-Bazo 2008).

PROTECTION AND SOLUTIONS

UNHCR's responsibility to seek permanent solutions for the problem of refugees[18] is commonly translated into a preferential hierarchy, with voluntary repatriation as a first priority, followed by local asylum and resettlement in a third state.

The ultimate purpose of protection is not to ensure that refugees remain refugees for ever, and *voluntary repatriation* reflects the right of the individual to return to his or her country of citizenship. No universal instrument deals with this, but the 'right to return' is widely accepted as an inalienable incident of nationality. The only formal reference appears in the 1969 OAU Convention, Article 5(1) of which emphasizes that the 'essentially voluntary character of repatriation shall be respected in all cases and no refugee shall be repatriated against his will'. On several occasions, the UNHCR Executive Committee has proposed standards and guidelines for voluntary repatriation operations.[19] The general rule is that refugees should return *voluntarily* and in conditions of *security*, and the international community has a legal interest in the follow-up to any repatriation movement; the security of those returning and the implementation of amnesties and other guarantees are rightly considered matters of international concern, and therefore subject to monitoring against relevant legal standards.

Local integration, that is, residence and acceptance into the local community where the refugee first arrives, is the practical realization of asylum. States may be bound to the refugee definition and bound to observe the principle of *non-refoulement*, but they retain discretion as to whether to allow a refugee to settle locally; this point was underlined by the UNHCR Executive Committee in its 2005 Conclusion on local integration,[20] although with little if any regard or reference to states' other obligations under international law which govern the treatment of non-nationals on state territory.

Resettlement aims to accommodate a variety of objectives, the first being to provide a durable solution for refugees and the displaced, unable to return home or to remain in their country of first refuge. A further goal is to relieve the strain on receiving countries, sometimes in a quantitative way, at others in a political way, by assisting them in relations with countries of origin. Resettlement thus contributes to international solidarity and continued fulfilment of the fundamental principles of protection, but given the continuing relevance of the sovereign competence referred to above and the challenges of translating the principle of international cooperation into effective action,[21] it is difficult to see what more international law can contribute to this solution.

REFUGEES AND HUMAN RIGHTS

The refugee problem cannot be considered apart from the field of human rights as a whole, which touches on both causes and solutions, so that knowledge and appreciation of the rights at issue helps to understand the refugee concept. The treatment of refugees and asylum seekers within a state is governed not only by the refugee treaties, but also by the broader human rights treaties (and even rules of customary international law), which set out general standards, whether of a procedural or substantive nature (for example, the requirement that a remedy be provided for every violation of human rights; or the duty of a state to protect everyone within its territory or jurisdiction from torture). Here, local law and practice play an important role in ensuring that international rules are applied.

The 1951 Convention is frequently described as a 'human rights treaty', to be approached as a living instrument, evolving to meet the needs and challenges of the day. Given the subject matter and the inescapable linkage between human rights violations and forced displacement, this descriptive language is understandable. The Convention, however, is not like most other human rights treaties, and it is styled a convention relating to the *status* of refugees, rather than one on the rights of refugees. Moreover, it does not frame 'refugee rights' in terms of what 'every refugee' shall enjoy and 'no refugee' shall be denied; in this sense its approach differs markedly from that later adopted in the 1966 Covenants, the 1989 Convention on the Rights of the Child, or the 2006 Convention on the Rights of Persons with Disabilities. Whereas later human rights treaties tend to identify the individual as the point of departure—whether simply by virtue of being human, or a child, a woman, a worker, or someone with a disability—the practice of states and international organizations has itself helped to bring the concept of refugee rights into the foreground of international legal protection doctrine.

The 1951 Convention remains quite 'state-centric', in the sense that it represents undertakings and obligations, accepted between the parties, to respect, protect, or accord certain rights and benefits.[22] Sometimes a right may be stated simply, unqualified other than by reference to the refugee's lawful presence (Article 32), but at others, it has to be implied ('the refugee shall be allowed...': Article 32(2)), or must be assumed as the reverse side of a qualification to the competence of the state, rather than a right strictly correlative to duty (contracting states 'shall not expel a refugee...save on grounds of national security or public order': Article 32(1); 'shall not impose penalties....': Article 31; 'shall issue identity papers...': Article 27; and 'No contracting State shall expel or return ("refouler") a refugee...': Article 33(1)).

In addition to the 'protection gap' between the principle of *non-refoulement* and asylum in the sense of solution, there are further doctrinal gaps between the Convention/Protocol refugee regime and the seemingly broader regime, or regimes, of human rights protection. The 1969 Vienna Convention on the Law of Treaties provides no answer, for example, to the question of how far the general prohibition of discrimination in Article 26 of the 1966 International Covenant on Civil and Political Rights is to be applied to refugees;[23] or how, if at all, their specific entitlements under the 1951 Convention are to be 'updated' or 'expanded' in the light of parallel systems of protection which seem to be simultaneously applicable.

The practice of states at present provides no clear answers, save that states themselves appear to want to maintain the specific, refugee-focused approach of the 1951 Convention. The fundamental principles of refugee protection, particularly refuge, non-return, or '*non-refoulement*', are necessarily common material to both fields, but reports of human rights undermining the refugee protection regime[24] are likely exaggerated or premature, or just plain academic speculation.

EVALUATION AND CONCLUSION

The 1951 Convention is sometimes portrayed today as a relic of the Cold War, inadequate in the face of 'new' refugees from ethnic violence and gender-based persecution, insensitive to security concerns, particularly terrorism and organized crime, and even redundant, given the protection now due in principle to everyone under international human rights law.

The 1951 Convention does not deal with the question of admission, and neither does it oblige a state of refuge to accord asylum as such, or provide for the sharing of responsibilities (for example, by prescribing which state should deal with a claim to refugee status). The Convention does not address the question of 'causes' of flight, or make provision for prevention; its scope does not include internally displaced persons, and it is not concerned with the better management of international migration. At the regional level, and notwithstanding the 1967 Protocol, refugee movements have necessitated more focused responses, such as the 1969 OAU Convention and the 1984 Cartagena Declaration; while in Europe, the development of protection doctrine under the 1950 European Convention on Human Rights has led to the adoption of provisions on 'subsidiary' or 'complementary' protection within the legal system of the European Union.

Nevertheless, within the context of the international refugee regime, which brings together states, UNHCR, and other international organizations, the UNHCR Executive Committee, and non-governmental organizations, among others, the 1951 Convention continues to play an important part in the protection of refugees, in the promotion and provision of solutions for refugees, in ensuring the security and related interests of states, sharing responsibility, and generally promoting human rights. Ministerial Meetings of States Parties, convened in Geneva by the government of Switzerland to mark the 50th and 60th anniversaries of the Convention in December 2001 and December 2011, expressly acknowledged, 'the continuing relevance and resilience of this international regime of rights and principles...' and reaffirmed that the 1951 Convention and the 1967 Protocol 'are the foundation of the international refugee protection regime and have enduring value and relevance in the twenty-first century'.[25]

In many states, judicial and administrative procedures for the determination of refugee status have established the necessary legal link between refugee status and protection, contributed to a broader and deeper understanding of key elements in the Convention refugee definition, and helped to consolidate the fundamental principle of *non-refoulement*. While initially concluded as an agreement between states on the treatment of refugees, the 1951 Convention has inspired both doctrine and practice in which the language of refugee rights is entirely appropriate.

The concept of the refugee as an individual with a well-founded fear of persecution continues to carry weight, and to symbolize one of the essential, if not exclusive, reasons for flight. The scope and extent of the refugee definition, however, have matured under the influence of human rights law and practice, to the point that, in certain well-defined circumstances, the necessity for protection against the risk of harm can trigger an obligation to protect.

NOTES

1. See, among others, *Hirsi v Italy* (Appl. no. 27765/09), 23 February 2012; *R (European Roma Rights Centre and others) v Immigration Officer at Prague Airport and another (United Nations High Commissioner for Refugees intervening)* [2005] 2 AC 1, [2004] UKHL 55.
2. UNGA Resolution 428(V), 14 December 1950, Annex.
3. UNGA Resolution 58/153, 22 December 2003, para. 9.
4. 1951 Convention relating to the Status of Refugees: 189 UNTS 137. Text in Brownlie 2010 and Goodwin-Gill and McAdam 2007.
5. UNGA Resolution 2198 (XXI), 16 December 1966; 1967 Protocol relating to the Status of Refugees: 606 UNTS 267; text in Goodwin-Gill and McAdam 2007.
6. Cf. Article 1, 1984 Convention against Torture: 1465 UNTS 85; Article 7, 1966 International Covenant on Civil and Political Rights: 999 UNTS 171; Article 3, 1950 European Convention on Human Rights: ETS No 5; Article 6, 1969 American Convention on Human Rights: OAS Treaty Series No. 36 (1969); Article 5, 1981 African Charter on Human and Peoples' Rights: 1530 UNTS No. 26,363.
7. Article 3 of the 1984 Convention against Torture extends the same protection where there are substantial grounds for believing that a person to be returned would be in danger of being tortured.
8. UNGA Resolution 8(I), 12 February 1946.
9. See UNHCR, *Handbook on Procedures and Criteria for the Determination of Refugee Status*, Geneva: UNHCR, 1979; UNHCR Executive Committee Conclusion No. 8 (XXVIII), 1977: UN doc. A/AC.96/549, para. 36.
10. 1969 Convention on the Specific Aspects of Refugee Problems in Africa: 1000 UNTS 46; text in Brownlie 2010, Goodwin-Gill and McAdam 2007.
11. 1984 Cartagena Declaration on Refugees: OAS/Ser.L/V/II.66, doc. 10, rev. 1, 190–3; text in Goodwin-Gill and McAdam 2007.
12. *Soering v United Kingdom* (1989) 11 EHRR 439.
13. See, for example, *Chahal v United Kingdom* (1996) 23 EHRR 413.
14. *Hirsi v Italy* (Appl. no. 27765/09), 23 February 2012.
15. European Council Directive on Temporary Protection 2001/55/EC; text in Goodwin-Gill and McAdam 2007.
16. European Council Directive on Qualification and Status as Refugees of Persons otherwise in need of International Protection 2004/83/EC, Articles 2, 15; text in Goodwin-Gill and McAdam 2007. See also now Council Directive 2011/95/EU of the European Parliament and of the Council of 13 December 2011 on Standards for the Qualification of Third-Country Nationals or Stateless Persons as Beneficiaries of International Protection, for a Uniform Status for Refugees or for Persons Eligible for Subsidiary Protection, and for the Content of the Protection Granted (Recast), OJ 2011 No. L337/9; McAdam, this volume.
17. See also Article 12(3), 1981 African Charter of Human and Peoples' Rights; Article 22(7), 1969 American Convention on Human Rights.
18. UNGA Resolution 428(v), 14 December 1950, Annex, para. 1.
19. Executive Committee Conclusion No. 18, 1980; Executive Committee Conclusion No. 40, 1985; Executive Committee Conclusion No. 101, 2004.
20. Executive Committee Conclusion No. 104, 2005.
21. Cf. Article 1(3) UN Charter; UNGA res. 428(V), para. 20.

22. The 1984 Convention against Torture is somewhat similar in this respect.
23. Article 30 of the Vienna Convention deals with the application of successive treaties 'relating to the same subject-matter,' but not with the situation created by 'overlapping' multilateral treaties, in particular, those concerned with human rights.
24. Cited in McAdam, this volume.
25. Ministerial Communiqué, Intergovernmental event at the ministerial level of member states of the United Nations on the occasion of the 60th anniversary of the 1951 Convention relating to the Status of Refugees and the 50th anniversary of the 1961 Convention on the Reduction of Statelessness (7–8 December 2011): UN doc. HCR/MINCOMMS/2011/6, 8 December 2011.

REFERENCES

Brownlie, I., and Goodwin-Gill, G. S. (eds.) (2010) *Brownlie's Documents on Human Rights* (6th edn.). Oxford: Oxford University Press.

Gil-Bazo, M.-T. (2008) 'The Charter of Fundamental Rights of the European Union and the Right to be Granted Asylum in the Union's Law'. *Refugee Survey Quarterly* 27(3): 33.

Goodwin-Gill, G. S. (2008) 'The Politics of Refugee Protection'. *Refugee Survey Quarterly* 27: 8–23.

Goodwin-Gill, G. S. (2009) 'Introduction to the 1951 Convention/1967 Protocol relating to the Status of Refugees'. UN Audio-Visual Library of International Law, Historic Archives. <http://www.un.org/law/avl/>.

Goodwin-Gill, G. S. (2011) 'The Right to Seek Asylum: Interception at Sea and the Principle of *Non-refoulement*'. *International Journal of Refugee Law* 23: 443–57.

Goodwin-Gill, G. S. (2012) 'Introduction to the 1967 United Nations Declaration on Territorial Asylum'. UN Audio-Visual Library of International Law, Historic Archives. <http://www.un.org/law/avl/>.

Goodwin-Gill, G. S., and McAdam, J. (2007) *The Refugee in International Law* (3rd edn.). Oxford: Oxford University Press.

Hathaway, J. (2005) *The Rights of Refugees*. Cambridge: Cambridge University Press.

Holborn, L. (1975) *Refugees: A Problem of our Time*. Metuchen, NJ: The Scarecrow Press.

Loescher, G., and Scanlan, J. (1986) *Calculated Kindness*. New York: The Free Press, Macmillan.

McAdam, J. (2007) *Complementary Protection in International Refugee Law*. Oxford: Oxford University Press.

Marrus, M. R. (1985) *The Unwanted: European Refugees in the Twentieth Century*. New York: Oxford University Press.

Moreno Lax, V. (2011) 'Seeking Asylum in the Mediterranean: Against a Fragmentary Reading of EU Member States' Obligations Accruing at Sea'. *International Journal of Refugee Law* 23: 174–220

Moreno Lax, V. (2012) 'Hirsi v Italy or the Strasbourg Court v Extraterritorial Migration Control?' *Human Rights Law Review* 12(3): 1–25.

Sharpe, M. (2012) 'The 1989 African Refugee Convention: Innovations, Misconceptions, and Omissions'. *McGill Law Journal* 58(1): 1–52.

CHAPTER 4

POLITICAL THEORY, ETHICS, AND FORCED MIGRATION

MATTHEW J. GIBNEY

Introduction

FORCED migration raises profound ethical issues. Even attempting to define forced migration demands careful consideration. Why, for instance, do forced migration scholars describe refugees—people who choose to flee persecution—as forced migrants, but not suspected felons extradited to face trial in another country or non-citizens deported for violating immigration laws (Gibney 2013b)? After all, in each case, people are being forced to move. One explanation lies in the fact that forced migration is not simply a descriptive term; it is also an evaluative one, one which involves moral judgements about the legitimacy of the movement in question. It is generally considered morally acceptable for a Western state to send someone to stand trial in another democratic country (at least when there is a case to answer) or to deport undesirable non-citizens, but it is never acceptable to persecute people on the basis of their race, religion, or political opinion. A central aim of normative theory is to make explicit the values embodied in common practices liked forced migration and to subject these evaluations to moral scrutiny.

Typically the domain of political theorists, philosophers, and theologians, this kind of normative theorizing has traditionally been undervalued in forced migration studies. Particularly in its early years, forced migration scholarship tended to be policy focused, concerned primarily with improving the plight of refugees more or less directly (Black 2001). Legal approaches able to bring states directly to account and anthropological scholarship aimed at unpicking the micro-dynamics of forced migration were privileged. Ethical theorists, on the other hand, tended to eschew the phenomenon of forced migration, largely because of its empirical complexity and their professional tendency to focus on more abstract moral concerns. However, things have changed in recent years. As the field of forced migration scholarship has expanded and the issue of migration has become more politically controversial, social scientists have increasingly turned to normative issues surrounding forced migration and more political theorists and philosophers have seen displacement as worthy of sustained analytical attention.

This chapter looks at some of the fruits of the increasing focus on the normative issues raised by forced migration. It first discusses the areas that have garnered the most discussion and attention: who is a refugee and what are the moral responsibilities of states to such people? The chapter then outlines a number of key moral issues that have been addressed by scholars in their analyses of statelessness, deportation, undocumented migration, and refugee repatriation. This survey illustrates not only the vibrancy and range of normative discussion in the field of forced migration; it shows clearly how forced migration's central questions connect with contemporary academic discussions on the character of morally decent political communities.

ASYLUM AND OBLIGATIONS TO REFUGEES

No subject related to forced migration has received more attention from a normative perspective than the question of whether some forced migrants should have a special right to cross borders in search of international protection, or asylum. In particular, scholars have been concerned with who should be able to claim asylum, and what responsibilities states have to admit and protect those they recognize as refugees.

Who is a Refugee?

The focus on asylum has largely emerged as a consequence of concern by political theorists with the more general question of whether immigration controls are morally justifiable. Some liberals—most notably Joseph Carens—have argued that a commitment to liberal principles of equality and freedom demands that states allow the free movement of individuals between states (Carens 1992; Cole 2000). These scholars have had little reason (except when thinking about the non-ideal present world) to concern themselves with the question of how to define a refugee, as, in a world with open borders, all individuals regardless of their status would be free to move as migrants. But scholars who argue that, even under ideal conditions, immigration controls *are* acceptable (e.g. because they preserve the way of life or public culture of a citizen community)—immediately need to consider what should happen to those people who are *forced* to move. Almost without exception, defenders of immigration controls argue that states have a duty to offer some form of asylum that constrains their right to determine whom to admit and whom to exclude (Walzer 1983; Miller 2007; Wellmann 2008). This has led them to debate the question of who exactly should be recognized as a refugee, and provided with special protection.

In general, most scholars have seen the 1951 UN Refugee Convention's definition as being too arbitrary or narrow to provide a plausible normative account of who is owed asylum. Andrew Shacknove, for example, argued in 1986 that a more appropriate definition would classify refugees as 'persons whose basic needs are unprotected by their country of origin, who have no remaining recourse other than to seek international restitution of their needs' (1985: 277). Shacknove's definition has been very influential in part because it highlights the way that refugeehood involves a breaking of the political 'bond'—or, in traditional liberal terms, the social contract—between the individual and the state that lies at the heart of legitimate rule (1985: 275). The collapse of this relationship creates a duty on behalf of international society to provide protection to the individual concerned.

Shacknove's definition highlights some of the moral reasoning implicit in the Convention definition. However, rather than emphasizing the *reasons* (persecution on specified grounds) why an individual rights were violated as the basis for refugeehood, Shacknove's account requires only that individual's 'basic needs' are not protected (1985: 277). The question of what constitutes 'basic needs' is left unanswered. Is life-threatening poverty indicative of a broken social contract (and therefore sufficient grounds for claiming asylum), or must persecution be direct? Moreover, whereas the Convention demands that a refugee be outside her country of origin, Shacknove's definition states merely that the individual must be in a position where 'restitution is possible' (1985: 277). Shacknove's approach therefore expands the category of those who should be considered refugees in a way that can include victims of generalized violence, famine, environmental catastrophe or poverty, and those who have not crossed a border. Similarly expansive positions have been outlined by other normative theorists (e.g. Gibney 2004; Miller 2007).

However, this expansive trend has led to a backlash from some legal scholars. James Hathaway has responded that the Refugee Convention's requirement of persecution on a range of specific grounds is not arbitrary at all but rather a way of picking out 'the most deserving among the deserving' of people on the move (1997: 86). Because refugees are people who have been both denied fundamental rights and are socially and politically marginalized, they are less likely than other forced migrants to find protection at home. In contrast, Matthew Price (2009) has argued that what makes the refugee morally distinctive is her need for an alternative political membership (citizenship) rather than simply temporary protection, and that providing asylum is one way of morally condemning a persecutory state.

However, the arguments of these refugee definition puritans are not completely convincing. The question of who is the 'most deserving of the deserving' seems otiose if non-persecuted but threatened individuals (such as those facing indiscriminate bombing) are in imminent mortal danger. Moreover, many of the world's Convention refugees do not necessarily need (or get) citizenship in another country (cf. Bradley 2013b). There is also no reason for believing that a state providing protection to victims of generalized violence, or even those covered by the exclusion clauses of the Refugee Convention, does not (or cannot) express a degree of moral condemnation in Price's sense. It is understandable why one might seek to constrain the concept of the refugee: the reality of contemporary politics means that states are concerned with limiting refugee numbers, rather than admitting all those who might be judged to be morally deserving of asylum. Nonetheless, the refugee puritans fail to establish good moral grounds for prioritizing Refugee Convention refugees in the rationing of asylum.

How Should Duties to Refugees be Allocated between States?

Definitions matter because normative theorists see states as having responsibilities to refugees, including duties to grant them entrance (or even membership) which may clash with (what they adjudge to be) the legitimate expectations or rights of citizens. If one defines a refugee narrowly, the global pool of refugees is likely to be limited, and the duties of states to admit these individuals will not greatly impair their right to control borders; if the definition is broad, however, the pool will be large, and states might have onerous responsibilities that could dramatically impact upon a community's 'way of life' (Walzer 1983; Gibney 2004). But just how does a state incur responsibilities to any particular refugee and what are the limits of these responsibilities?

As in the case of the refugee definition, International Law provides a starting point for considering how responsibilities to refugees are incurred and what these might involve (see Goodwin-Gill, this volume). The cornerstone of legal refugee protection is the principle of *non-refoulement*, the requirement not to send back refugees to territories where their lives or fundamental freedoms would be at risk. This duty is effectively distributed on the basis of *location* (a state has a duty to those refugees who arrive at or in its territory) (Gibney 2000). Michael Walzer (1983) follows this approach, arguing that states have a duty not to expel refugees who arrive in their territory, in part because such people have already made their escape and sending them back would involve using force against desperate and helpless people, which is morally unacceptable (Walzer 1983: 49–51). But most normative theorists have been more sceptical of the location principle for two reasons. First, it tends to privilege (in practice) those refugees with access to the resources and ability to move in search of asylum (like young men), leaving many people endangered in their country of origin (Gibney 2004). This has led Singer and Singer to argue that states should offer asylum to those refugees most in danger, regardless of where they are located (Singer and Singer 1988). Walzer's position, they reason, unjustifiably privileges location over need, and acts (using force to expel refugees) over omissions (failing to save refugees in other countries when this is possible) (1988: 119–20). Growing international focus on internal displacement in the past two decades might be seen to reflect this concern.

A second worry is that the location principle leads to unjust distributions in refugee 'burdens' between *states* (Gibney 2007; Miller 2007; Owen 2012). States located near displacement generating states, typically poorer countries in the global South, tend to find themselves with the highest proportion of refugee claimants because they are the easiest to access. The resulting inequalities between states mock the idea of refugee protection as a common responsibility of the 'international society of states' (Owen 2012). In response, a number of theorists have argued that a just distribution needs to be more sensitive to the integrative abilities of particular states (e.g. level of GDP, size, political stability, etc.) (Gibney 2007; Miller 2007; Carens 2013). The result would be an allocation of refugees across states quite different from the current one, which, as already noted, is skewed towards poorer states.

The problem with this conclusion is that it is unclear what to do with it. To shuffle refugees between states for the sake of international justice would probably require riding roughshod over the choices of refugees themselves. Redistributing refugees runs the risk of reducing these people to mere commodities, especially if states are allowed to trade their refugee quotas as is proposed in some market systems (Schuck 1997; Anker, Fitzpatrick, and Shacknove 1998; Gibney 2007; Sandel 2012). While states could redistribute resources instead of refugees (financially compensating poorer states with their higher burdens), this is also morally dubious because it smacks of richer countries buying themselves out of asylum (Anker, Fitzpatrick, and Shacknove 1998). There appears to be a profound tension between doing justice to refugees and achieving justice between states (Gibney 2007).

Another way of distributing responsibilities internationally is to take into account the special responsibilities that particular states have to specific groups of refugees. The idea that states have a duty to refugees generated by wars they have initiated or participated in (e.g. Vietnam or Kosovo or Iraq), for example, is not new. But only recently has the idea of harm as a basis for asylum been systematically developed through the conceptualization of asylum as a form of reparation for injustice inflicted on refugees by third countries as a result of military aggression, supplying arms that stoke civil wars, and even support for human rights violating regimes (Souter 2013). That said, important challenges still remain in terms of identifying the kinds of harms that ought to give rise to a duty to grant asylum and in determining how these duties should be weighed against the more general humanitarian responsibilities of states to provide asylum.

What are the Limits of State Responsibilities to Refugees?

Even if one can identify a just principle for allocating refugees between states, there remains the difficult question of specifying the limits of a state's responsibilities to refugees. Is there a point at which a state is morally justified in refusing to accept any more refugees? Most normative theorists accept that there is in principle such a point, even if states are a long way from reaching it in practice.

Using a utilitarian calculus, Singer and Singer (1988) argue that a state must keep accepting refugees up to the point that the costs to the residents of the state of one extra refugee entrant are greater than the benefits yielded by that particular entrant. This situation, they think, might be reached when, for example 'tolerance in a multicultural society is breaking down' or strain on environmental resources becomes severe (Singer and Singer 1988: 127–8). Michael Walzer's criterion also has a consequentialist flavour, though it is one that attempts to reconcile the claims of communities with minimal universalist principles (1983). He argues that states are morally required to accept refugees when the costs of doing so are low; once further intake jeopardizes the character of a political community, however, exclusion is justified (1983: 49–50). Gibney specifies a similar limit with his 'humanitarian principle', though he argues that states are obliged to undertake a range of actions—shaping public opinion, participating in burden sharing, reducing the causes of refugee flight—that create a more conducive political environment for the acceptance of refugees (2004: 244). Joseph Carens, considering refugee policy from the perspective of non-ideal theory, accepts that 'public order constraints', including a fundamental threat to liberal society, would justify exclusion. He states, however, that this kind of circumstance is unlikely to emerge in practice (2013).

Thus most theorists reach a similar conclusion on the question of limits: accepting refugees is of profound moral importance, but a state is not obliged to take in refugees though the heavens fall. However, does this conclusion justify states actually *deporting* refugees to egregious human right violations (or even their likely death), not allowing more refugees to enter (and therefore leaving them at risk of continued persecution), or simply refusing to accept refugees admitted elsewhere for resettlement? Michael Walzer is one of the few scholars that confronts this issue directly. Despite the limitations of the mutual aid principle and his partiality towards community independence, in a well-known passage in *Spheres of Justice* (2003) Walzer refuses to condone the expulsion of refugees. The duties of responding to refugees may have their limits, he argues, but 'at the extreme, the claim of asylum is virtually undeniable' (1983: 51). This uncomfortable conclusion expresses powerfully the way the provision of asylum both relies upon and reveals the limits of closed forms of political community.

OTHER NORMATIVE ISSUES IN FORCED MIGRATION

If work on asylum has been the primary focus of normative investigation into forced migration, it hardly exhausts discussion in the field. Forced migration scholars have also addressed an array of questions that have implications far beyond the confines of forced migration. In a brief and necessarily selective discussion of these issues, this chapter now highlights how scholars have used different kinds of displacement to shed light on the following questions: what is the value of citizenship?; who should enjoy the protections of state members?; when is displacement justified?; and what are the conditions of just repatriation for refugees and displaced people?

What is the Value of Citizenship?

Forced migration scholars have contributed to understanding of why citizenship matters largely through their examination of the phenomenon of statelessness: the situation of individuals who lack of nationality and citizenship in any state whatsoever. Legal scholars have rightly highlighted the way that statelessness involves a lack of state protection and its associated rights. But it has been normative theorists who have provided the richest account of the dangers of statelessness and its inevitable injustices. No one has been more influential in this regard than the émigré political philosopher Hannah Arendt who, writing in the aftermath of the Second World War, drew upon the experiences of 1930s and 1940s, to characterize the stateless as suffering a loss of the very 'right to have rights' (1986: 296). To be without citizenship, Arendt believed, was not to be liberated from state power but rather to become completely subject to it. The stateless, in the words of Krause, experience a kind of 'total domination' characteristic of totalitarian regimes yet evidently possible even in formally democratic societies (Krause 2011: 25).

Discussion of statelessness's normative underpinnings has served to open up the category to other marginalized groups. Arendt, for example, did not distinguish in her work between formally stateless people (those with citizenship nowhere) and refugees (those who possessed citizenship but who faced persecution by their own government) (Bradley 2013a). For her, the normative core of the two groups was the same: each was denied political agency through the effective loss of membership, and each faced a situation of 'rightlessness' (Arendt 1986: 296). Contemporary scholars have (not without controversy) extended the concept of statelessness even further. For example, Krause sees the 'undocumented' as in many ways the inheritors of Arendt's stateless (2008: 26). Others have seen appropriate analogies to statelessness in the experience of groups including irregular migrants, guest-workers, even victims of internally displacement (Walzer 1983; Somers 2008; Gibney 2011; Sawyer and Blitz 2011).

However, if recent work illustrates the importance of citizenship, for some it also attempts to put citizenship in its place. Increasingly, scholars have used statelessness to highlight the practical reality and moral need for forms of membership beyond national citizenship. Agamben signals something of this change with his comment that the refugee (or stateless person) is 'nothing less than a border concept that radically calls into question the principles of the nation State and, at the same time, helps clear the field for a no longer delayable renewal of categories' (1995). Other scholars, including McNevin (2011) have seen something transformative in the paradoxical situation of undocumented migrants demonstrating publicly in support of their rights in countries like the US; while others have proposed new ways of (re)conceptualizing citizenship to incorporate rightless residents (migrants) (Benhabib 2004; Bauböck 2005; Kostakopoulou 2008; Gibney 2011). The stateless have thus been used to underline not only citizenship's current importance but also its evident limitations. To be incorporated into the order of national citizenship is to take on a range of obligations (as well as rights) and to be a member of an international system that chains people to states in a way that mocks consent-based governance and consigns some of the world's denizens to appallingly low life chances (Carens 1992).

Who is a Member?

Scholars examining issues of forced migration have also contributed to discussions on the moral boundaries of citizenship in modern societies. They have done so primarily through discussion of legitimate deportation power. The norm that states may not expel or deport their own citizens is a key feature of contemporary international law and a widely shared norm across states, partly constitutive of the distinction between refugee creation and legitimate expulsion (Gibney 2013b).

Informed by growing efforts across Western states to expel undocumented migrants and deport non-citizens convicted of crimes, Joseph Carens (2005, 2009) has provided an influential account of state responsibilities to non-citizens. He argues that after a certain period of residence, an individual accumulates a moral right to membership in the state (including its protection from deportation) because of the personal, social, and economic connections they have formed over time (Carens 2009). Not to recognize such people as members, Carens argues, violates liberal and democratic principles.

Carens's articulation of long-term residents as members chimes with the work by other scholars including Walzer (1983), Baubock (2005, 2008), Shachar (2009), and Gibney (2011). These theorists have each proposed standards for seeing some residents as members (and thus free from deportation power) by drawing upon some combination of liberal, republican, and communitarian thinking. From liberal and republican viewpoints, in any just society there should be congruence between the run of a state's coercive power and the boundaries of its membership. As Walzer has put it, any state that allows non-citizens to live and work in the state over an extended period while denying them access to the protections of membership risks being a 'tyranny' where citizens unilaterally decide the fate of non-citizen residents (1983). From a communitarian perspective, on the other hand, the view that one's individual identity (and thus claims to membership) are constructed by the social and cultural community in which one lives provides a strong moral foundation for seeing long-term resident non-citizens as part of the community of those who belong, especially when they arrived as children (Gibney 2011).

This overlapping consensus amongst normative theorists on non-citizen incorporation should not be exaggerated. There is wide variation amongst scholars on the specifics of the question of when individuals become insulated from deportation power. Some scholars argue that any claim to membership through length of residence ought to be qualified by other indicators of integration (law-abidingness, signs of involvement in the community, paying taxes, etc.) (Elshtain 2009; Shachar 2009). Nonetheless, the common presumption that questions of membership are subject to considerations of justice provides a basis for critically assessing current state practices of expulsion and exclusion.

When is Forced Migration Justifiable?

Forced migration is typically conceived of as an 'evil' (Penz 1997: 37), as something that ought morally to be avoided, but are there circumstances when it might be justifiable? This is a question that is obviously relevant to scholars of deportation, as states often claim that expulsion (particularly of convicted non-citizen criminals) increases public security (Gibney 2013b). But the matter has received most attention by way of discussions of development induced displacement and resettlement (DIDR).

DIDR involves the coordinated and state-sanctioned displacement of communities to facilitate development projects and is typically (though not exclusively) associated with the countries of the global South. What makes this displacement of particular interest is that the (coerced) movement of people is typically justified in utilitarian terms on the grounds that the development project in question (e.g. the building of a dam) will have benefits to the community as a whole (e.g. the electrification of areas without power) that far outweigh the suffering of the relatively small number of people that will be displaced. The key issue has been stated by Peter Penz: 'Even if it is recognized that displacement is bad because it involves harm or coercion, it is possible that is a justifiable evil...In particular, the question arises of whether the good that development does can morally outweigh its bad consequences, including uprooting people' (1997: 38).

A number of scholars of DIDR have drawn upon ethical theory to reflect on the losses for individuals and communities caused by displacement. In illuminating work, Drydyk (1999), for example, uses John Rawls's theory to conceptualize the costs of displacement to include damage to a community's 'self respect' caused by the loss of their 'cultural space and identity' and 'networks and associations' (1999: 4–5). The sophisticated reckoning of the costs of displacement evident in work like Drydyk's has provided the foundation for more demanding accounts of the terms under which DIDR might be morally acceptable. Peter Penz has helped map the moral terrain of DIDR by outlining three moral claims in conflict in DIDR situations—conceptions of the public interest; considerations of freedom, property, and (collective) self-determination; and matters of equity and justice, with the latter involving how the costs and benefits of the project are shared across the affected population (Penz 1997: 37–41). For Penz, the most pertinent of these considerations is self-determination, which requires that legitimate displacement involves consultation with the community at risk of displacement. Legitimate displacement needs to involve 'negotiated resettlement' and costs need to be 'fully compensated' (Penz 1997: 41).

One implication of recent discussions of DIDR is that there are situations in which the coerced movement of communities to make way for development projects can be morally justifiable. As Penz notes, the 'self-determination' of the community being displaced 'cannot be asserted in such unqualified terms that development which serves both the public interest and distributive justice is blocked' (1997: 41). Nonetheless, the displacement of communities and individuals cannot be morally justified simply by appealing to some utilitarian calculus; legitimate displacement requires a just *process*, with all the complexities that recent scholarship has made clear this entails.

Under What Conditions Should Refugees Return?

Repatriation is often presented as the most desirable means of ending refugee crises. It is therefore not surprising that the question of repatriation has been a focus of normatively inclined scholars. The question of under what conditions return might be 'just' is of particular importance for two different reasons: first, because refugees have typically escaped a position of acute vulnerability and their rights risk being violated once again upon return; second, because the question of whether refugees might have a *duty* to return to their country (because by doing so they may be able to help rebuild their country of origin or show gratitude to the state of asylum) is often a politically salient one.

While normative discussion of the legitimacy of repatriation programmes is not new (Weiner 1998; Barnett 2001), return processes have only recently begun to receive systematic normative attention (Bradley 2008, 2013a; Long 2008, 2013). Megan Bradley, for instance, has argued that there is an intimate connection between enabling a 'dignified return' by refugees (a stated goal of most international organizations involved in repatriation) and appropriate redress for the injustices experienced by those who have been forced to flee. For redress (or reparation) plays an essential role in asserting the dignity of refugees by showing that the rights of such people cannot be breached with impunity (2008: 306). Long's approach is similarly indebted to the idea of the social contract, though she carefully reworks the concept to highlight the challenges of just repatriation. She labels this approach '*em*patriation' because it involves the beginning or creation of a new relationship not a return to things as they were.

It is clear from the normative literature on repatriation that the conditions for a 'just return' involve far more than simply a cessation of hostilities or the emergence of a government that respects basic rights. A morally defensible account of when return is appropriate (or even obligatory) must involve reckoning with the relationship between the refugees and their country of asylum, respect for the dignity and autonomy of refugees as agents, and attention to the terms on which refugees will be (re)integrated into the country they originally fled.

CONCLUSION

This chapter shows that the ethics of forced migration is a diverse, growing, and vibrant area of scholarship. From its primary concentration on the question of asylum and refugees, the normative study of forced migration has recently branched out to consider the claims of repatriated refugees, people facing deportation, undocumented migrants, and a range of other groups. The claims of these forced migrants have served as a prism through which academics concerned with forced migration have critically questioned the moral boundaries of citizenship, the balance between the social good and the individual and group interest, the ethics of reparation for historical injustice, and the integration of marginalized people. There remain significant gaps: in particular, normative scholars have tended to be disproportionately concerned with the ethics of forced migration as it relates to the concerns and value frameworks of developed, Western, liberal states. Yet as the field of forced migration becomes more crowded and nuanced in the years ahead, the amount and quality of normative reflection on its main concerns seems only likely to grow rapidly.

References

Agamben, G. (1995) 'We Refugees'. *Symposium* 49(2): 114–19.

Anker, D., Fitzpatrick, J., and Shacknove, A. (1998) 'Crisis and Cure: A Reply to Hathaway/Neve and Schuck'. *Harvard Human Rights Journal* 11: 295.

Arendt, H. (1986) *The Origins of Totalitarianism*. London: Andre Deutsch.

Barnett, M. (2001) 'UNHCR and the Ethics of Repatriation'. *Forced Migration Review* 10: 31–4.

Bauböck, R. (2005) 'Expansive Citizenship—Voting beyond Territory and Membership'. *PS: Political Science & Politics* 38(4): 683–7.

Bauböck, R. (2008) *Stakeholder Citizenship: An Idea Whose Time Has Come?* Washington, DC: Migration Policy Institute.

Benhabib, S. (2004) *The Rights of Others*. Cambridge: Cambridge University Press.

Black, R. (2001) 'Fifty Years of Refugee Studies: From Theory to Policy'. *International Migration Review* 35(1): 57–78.

Bradley, M. (2008) 'Back to Basics: The Conditions of Just Refugee Returns'. *Journal of Refugee Studies* 21(3): 285–304.

Bradley, M. (2013a) *Refugee Repatriation: Justice, Responsibility and Redress*. Cambridge: Cambridge University Press.

Bradley, M. (2013b) 'Rethinking Refugeehood: Statelessness, Repatriation, and Refugee Agency'. *Review of International Studies*, 1–23.

Carens, J. (1992) 'Migration and Morality: A Liberal Egalitarian Perspective'. Pp. 25–47 in B. Barry and R. Goodin (eds.), *Free Movement*. London: Harvester Wheatsheaf.

Carens, J. (2005) 'On Belonging'. *The Boston Review* (Summer). <http://www.bostonreview.net/BR30.3/carens.html>.

Carens, J. H. (2009) 'The Case for Amnesty', *The Boston Review* (May/June). <http://bostonreview.net/BR34.3/ndf_immigration.php>.

Carens, J. H. (2013) *The Ethics of Immigration*. New York: Oxford University Press.

Cole, P. (2000) *Philosophies of Exclusion: Liberal Political Theory and Immigration*. Edinburgh: Edinburgh University Press.

Drydyk, J. (1999) 'Development-Induced Displacement and John Rawl's "General Conception" of Justice'. Project Report. CIDA-SICI Partnership Project II. <http://www3.carleton.ca/cove/papers/Displacement.rtf>.

Elshtain, J. B. (2009) 'The Sheer Length of Stay is not by itself Decisive'. *The Boston Review* (May/June). <http://bostonreview.net/BR34.3/ndf_immigration.php>.

Gibney, M. J. (2000) 'Asylum and the Principle of Proximity'. *Ethics, Place & Environment*, 3(3): 313–17.

Gibney, M. J. (2004) *The Ethics and Politics of Asylum*. Cambridge: Cambridge University Press.

Gibney, M. J. (2007) 'Forced Migration, Engineered Regionalism, and Justice between States'. Pp. 57–77 in S. Kneebone and F. Rawlings Sanei (eds.), *New Regionalism and Asylum Seekers*. Oxford: Berghahn.

Gibney, M. J. (2011) 'The Rights of Non-citizens to Membership'. Pp. 41–68 in C. Sawyer and B. Blitz (eds.), *Statelessness in the European Union: Displaced, Undocumented, Unwanted*. Cambridge: Cambridge University Press.

Gibney, M. J. (2013a) 'Should Citizenship Be Conditional?' *Journal of Politics*. In press.

Gibney, M. J. (2013b) 'Is Deportation a Form of Forced Migration?' *Refugee Survey Quarterly*. In press.

Hathaway, J. C. (1997) 'Is Refugee Status Really Elitist? An Answer to the Ethical Challenge'. Pp. 79–88 in J. Y. Carlier and D. Vanheule (eds.), *Europe and Refugees: A Challenge?* The Hague: Kluwer Law International.

Kostakopoulou, D. (2008) *The Future Governance of Citizenship*. Cambridge: Cambridge University Press.

Krause, M. (2011) 'Undocumented Migrants: An Arendtian Perspective'. Pp. 22–40 in C. Sawyer and B. K. Blitz (eds.), *Statelessness in the European Union*. Cambridge: Cambridge University Press.

Long, K. (2008) 'State, Nation, Citizen: Rethinking Repatriation'. Refugee Studies Centre, University of Oxford, Working Paper No. 48. Oxford.

Long, K. (2013) *The Point of No Return: Refugees, Rights and Repatriation*. Oxford: Oxford University Press.

McNevin, A. (2011) *Contesting Citizenship: Irregular Migrants and New Frontiers of the Political*. New York: Columbia University Press.

Miller, D. (2007) *National Responsibility and Global Justice*. Oxford: Oxford University Press.

Owen, D. (2012) 'In Loco Civitatis: On the Normative Structure of the International Refugee Regime'. Paper presented the CRASSH Conference, Cambridge University.

Penz, P. (1997) 'The Ethics of Development-Induced Displacement'. *Refuge*, 16(3): 38–41.

Penz, P., Drydyk, J., and Bose, P. S. (2011) *Displacement by Development: Ethics, Rights and Responsibilities*. Cambridge: Cambridge University Press.

Price, M. (2009) *Rethinking Asylum*. Cambridge: Cambridge University Press.

Sandel, M. J. (2012) *What Money Can't Buy: The Moral Limits of Markets*. New York: Farrar, Straus and Giroux.

Sawyer, C., and Blitz, B. K. (eds.) (2011) *Statelessness in the European Union: Displaced, Undocumented, Unwanted*. Cambridge: Cambridge University Press.

Schuck, P. H. (1997) 'Refugee Burden-Sharing: A Modest Proposal'. *Yale Journal of International Law*, 22: 243.

Shachar, A. (2009) *The Birthright Lottery: Citizenship and Global Inequality*. Cambridge, MA: Harvard University Press.

Shacknove, A. E. (1985) 'Who is a Refugee?' *Ethics* 95(2): 274–84.

Shklar, J. N. (1998) *Political Thought and Political Thinkers*. Chicago: University of Chicago Press.

Singer, P., and Singer R. (1988) 'The Ethics of Refugee Policy'. Pp. 111–30 in M. Gibney (ed.), *Open Borders, Closed Societies*. Westport, CT: Greenwood.

Somers, M. R. (2008). *Genealogies of Citizenship: Markets, Statelessness, and the Right to Have Rights*. Cambridge: Cambridge University Press.

Souter, J. (2013) 'Towards a Theory of Asylum as Reparation for Past Injustice'. *Political Studies*. <http://onlinelibrary.wiley.com/journal/10.1111/(ISSN)1467-9248/earlyview>.

Staples, K. (2012) *Retheorising Statelessness: A Background Theory of Membership in World Politics*. Edinburgh: Edinburgh University Press.

Walzer, M. (1983) *Spheres of Justice*. New York: Basic Books.

Weiner, M. (1998) 'The Clash of Norms: Dilemmas in Refugee Policies'. *Journal of Refugee Studies*, 11(4): 433–53.

Wellman, C. H. (2008) '*Immigration* and Freedom of Association'. *Ethics* 119(1): 109–41.

CHAPTER 5

....

INTERNATIONAL RELATIONS AND FORCED MIGRATION

....

ALEXANDER BETTS

INTRODUCTION

....

REFUGEES are often referred to as human rights violations made visible. However, refugees are more than simply a human rights issue. They are an inherent part of international politics (Betts and Loescher 2010). The refugee and the state system are two sides of the same coin, and the former cannot be understood without reference to the latter. The 'figure of the refugee' is an integral part of the international system, symbolizing the failure of the breakdown of the state-citizen-territory relationship assumed by the state system (Haddad 2008).

Even other categories of forced migration—such as internal displacement, statelessness, and environmental displacement—are only rendered meaningful by their mutually constitutive relationship to the state system. The common conceptual feature that connects these areas is the unwillingness or inability of the country of origin to ensure the protection of its own citizens, and hence the need for international protection. Forced migration is, by definition, indicative of a breakdown of the nation-state system. All forms of forced migration go to the core of questions of state sovereignty, and invite a host of other questions relating to security and the international political economy.

The causes, consequences, and responses to refugees and other categories of forced migration are all closely intertwined with world politics. The causes of refugee movements are underpinned by conflict, state failure, and the inequalities of international political economy. The consequences of movements have been associated with security, the spread of conflict, terrorism, and trans-nationalism. Responding to refugees represents a challenge to the facilitation of international cooperation and the role of international institutions and law. Situating forced migration within this larger context of world politics, opens up a vast potential research agenda.

Yet despite the political and international nature of forced migration, there has traditionally been relatively little work within international relations (IR) on refugees. IR has expanded its empirical focus beyond analysing war and peace and international security to address a range of areas such as the global economy, environment, human rights, and international trade. However, it has paid comparatively little attention to the international politics of forced migration.

The work that has attempted to 'bridge the divide' between IR and forced migration suggests that studying forced migration has enormous relevance for IR, touching upon issues relating to international cooperation, globalization, human rights, international organizations, regime complexity, the role of non-state actors, regionalism, North–South relations, transnationalism, the national politics of international institutions, and security. Therefore, making the study of forced migration part of mainstream IR has a potentially wide-ranging theoretical contribution to make to the discipline (Betts and Loescher 2010).

Furthermore, forced migration studies has rarely drawn upon the tools offered by IR to inform its analysis. Rather, social scientific research on refugees and forced migration has predominantly drawn upon disciplines such as anthropology, sociology, and geography to analyse the causes and consequences of human displacement. It has generally offered a 'bottom-up' perspective, placing the experiences of displaced people at the centre of its analysis. There is also a need for a complementary 'top-down' level of analysis to understand the macro-level structures that influence states' and other international actors' responses to forced migration. This is crucial because it is often the choices made by states and other political actors that determine outcomes for the displaced.

Gradually, a growing body of scholarship has begun to consider how patterns of forced migration relate to world politics. This chapter offers an intellectual history of the relationship between IR and forced migration, arguing that 'international relations and forced migration' can be divided into three broad waves of scholarship. First, it suggests that much of the early IR work on forced migration beginning during the Cold War was mainly empirical and can be thought of as *international history*. Second, it argues that since the late 1990s there has been a gradual move towards theorizing the international politics of forced migration but with a primary focus on *theorizing refugees and international relations*. Third, it argues that a new wave is gradually beginning to emerge which represents a *transnational turn*, with the greatest potential to contribute not only to understanding the politics of forced displacement but also to export ideas back to political science and international relations.

INTERNATIONAL POLITICAL HISTORY

At virtually every juncture in the evolution and development of the international system, the refugee has been a central figure. In Arendt's terms, refugees have been a 'vanguard of history', not only witnessing, but also being an integral aspect of, the changing architecture of world politics (Owens 2010). From the creation of the state system at the Peace of Westphalia in 1648, to the consolidation of the European state through the revolutions and state unifications of the nineteenth century, to the changing balance of power between the late nineteenth century and the two world wars, to decolonization and the creation of the post-Second World War international society, to the bipolarity of the Cold War, to the post-Cold War era, to globalization, 9/11, and the emergence of new transnational threats linked to terrorism and the environment, refugees have been a central feature of world politics. Not only have refugees been an unintended consequence of developments in the international system but they have also often had an important independent causal influence on the trajectory of world politics.

The most prominent body of academic work on the international politics of forced migration is within the area of international political history. This research lays the empirical groundwork for work on IR and refugees. It offers insights into the emergence and development of the international refugee regime and interaction with the changing international political context. Most of this work has been archival and strongly empirical, and so has not generally applied the conceptual and theoretical developments of IR.

Two pioneering and related volumes emerged in quick succession in the late 1980s, which established the link between IR and refugees. Gordenker's (1987) *Refugees in International Politics* was the first to outline the international institutional framework underpinning international cooperation on refugee protection, explaining the emergence of the refugee regime in the twentieth century, the challenges emerging to the scope of that regime at the end of the Cold War, and making a range of policy recommendations. Loescher and Monahan's (1989) edited volume *Refugees and International Relations* offered an interdisciplinary approach to the international politics of the refugee regime, drawing on history, sociology, and political science. The chapters collectively highlight, in the words of one contributor, that 'the refugee problem is essentially political' rather than humanitarian (Coles 1989: 394).

Both volumes are predominantly empirical and policy oriented rather than theoretical. Yet, what is striking is how few of the core international policy debates they address evolved in the subsequent decades. They discuss the challenge for the international refugee regime to adapt to people fleeing socio-economic rights and basic rights deprivations, referred to as 'extra-convention refugees' or 'de facto refugees' (Gordenker 1987), the need to cooperate to find durable solutions to long-standing refugee crises (Cuny and Stein 1989), the need to promote refugee self-reliance beyond encampment (Cuenod 1989), and the challenges posed by so-called irregular migration (Gallagher 1989).

Loescher's work as an international historian has established him as the leading authority on IR and forced migration. In *Calculated Kindness*, Loescher and Scanlan (1987) examine the history of US refugee policy during the Cold War, showing how foreign policy considerations consistently defined the US response to refugees fleeing from East to West. In *Beyond Charity*, Loescher (1996) considers the global challenges faced by the international refugee regime in the post-Cold War era, situating them within a broader historical context. He shows that refugees are an inherently political issue and must be addressed in a comprehensive way that not only ensures asylum but also engages with the underlying root causes of displacement. In *UNHCR and World Politics*, he (2001) provides an in-depth institutional history of the main Office of the United Nations High Commissioner for Refugees showing how the organization has had to walk a 'perilous path' in its relationship with states, needing to uphold humanitarian principles while working in a context defined by power and interests.

This approach has been complemented by work from the so-called English School of International Relations, traditionally the most historically and empirically focused approach to exploring the evolution of international society. Hedley Bull (2010), the founder of the English School, even wrote a posthumously published paper looking at the challenges of refugee protection within international society. Most notably, Haddad's (2008) *The Refugee in International Society*, examines the *longue durée* of the mutually constitutive relationship between the figure of the refugee and modern state system. She argues that, first, refugees can be understood to be an inevitable consequence of the state system, resulting from the breakdown of the assumed state-citizen-territory nexus implied by the Westphalian system and, secondly, that refugees reinforce the nation-state system by upholding a clear distinction between citizens and non-citizens.

Although refuge and sanctuary have been provided by city states and religious groups throughout history, the basis of the refugee regime emerged alongside the creation and consolidation of the modern state system. For Haddad (2008), the origins of the modern refugee regime can be found within the Peace of Westphalia of 1648, with the flight of the Huguenots in the seventeenth century after their expulsion by Louis XIV representing Europe's first refugee crisis. During the eighteenth and nineteenth centuries, refugee creation and protection was an integral part of the state-building process within Europe, with émigrés fleeing revolutions in France between 1789 and 1815, and elsewhere in Europe such as in Italy and Poland in 1848. Refugees were also an integral part of the changing balance of power in the context of the formation, consolidation, and expansion of the modern state system in the early part of the twentieth century. As the First World War accelerated the dismantling of multi-ethnic empires such as the Habsburg, Ottoman, and Prussian empires, large numbers of people were excluded from citizenship in the new national states, making displacement to the subsequent nation-building process. Recognition of this longer historical *durée* of the refugee in world politics, within the English School tradition of International Relations, has thereby contributed to showing how the figure of the refugee only makes sense when considered as closely related to the evolution of the state system (Skran 1995; Haddad 2008; Hurrell 2010).

Theorizing Refugees and International Relations

While this work has largely been empirical and historical in nature theoretically informed scholarship has more recently emerged, attempting to ask explanatory questions about the contemporary challenges of refugees and forced displacement. Such attempts have most notably been developed in Betts's (2009a) textbook *Forced Migration and Global Politics* and the related Betts and Loescher (2010) volume *Refugees in International Relations*, which have examined what IR theory can offer empirical questions within refugee and forced migration studies and vice versa.

The concepts that have emerged from IR have great relevance for understanding the relationship between forced migration and world politics. The area has immense relevance for a whole range of debates in IR, not least because of the way in which forced migration conceptually sits between debates on security, international political economy, and human rights. Within work on IR and Forced Migration, the two main strands of work have focused on analysis of the causes and consequences, which engage mainly with IR literature in international security, and work on responses to displacement, which draw mainly on IR literature on international cooperation.

International Security

Existing IR work on the causes and consequences of forced migration draws heavily on literature within international security (Snyder 2010; Roberts 2010), highlighting in particular that refugees are not only a consequence of insecurity and conflict but may also contribute to insecurity and conflict. In particular, since the end of the Cold War a growing body of work from IR scholars examines the empirical relationship between refugee movements and conflict and tries to identify the conditions under which refugees exacerbate conflict (Loescher 1992, 1993; Weiner 1993, 1995; Stedman and Tanner 2003; Lischer 2005; Salehyan and Gleditsch 2006).

In *Refugee Manipulation*, Stedman and Tanner (2003) identify the way in which refugees, and the refugee regime, have been manipulated, as resources of war, by both states and non-state actors. They show how refugees have been instrumentally used in conflicts by great powers and by groups in exile in ways that have had significant implications for international security. Building on this argument, Lischer (2005) explores, in *Dangerous Sanctuaries*, the conditions under which refugee crises represent a catalyst for the diffusion of conflict—both internal and inter-state. She claims that variation in the relationship between refugee crises and the exacerbation of conflict can be found in political explanations, based on the origin of the refugee crisis, the policy of the receiving state, and the influence of external state and non-state actors.

This recognition that refugees can, under certain conditions, be a catalyst for conflict has contributed to the development of the concept of 'spoilers'. In other words, in post-conflict situations, in particular, refugees and IDPs may, if they are not provided with adequate protection and durable solutions, become a barrier to the development of peace-building initiatives (Morris and Stedman 2008; Milner 2009). They may disrupt post-conflict reconstruction and peace building as returnees with property and rights-based claims, through remaining militarized groups in exile, by remaining outside of peace negotiations, postponing possibilities for repatriation, or refusing to renounce violence, for example. This recognition has been used to highlight the need to include a focus on refugees both in analysis of conflict and within policy initiatives relating to peace building.

Greenhill (2010)'s *Weapons of Mass Migration* shows how forced migration has frequently been an instrument of state foreign policy. She examines how illiberal regimes have often used 'strategically engineered migration' to impose costs and target state and thereby influence inter-state relations. Looking at a large-n data set from 1951 to 2006, and in-depth cases of Cuba, Kosovo, Haiti, and North Korea, she shows how strategic forced migration has shaped bilateral state relations by overwhelming host capacities and by violating norms that the target state cares about.

Reflecting a broader turn in security studies, the concept of human security, which shifts the referent object of security from the nation state to the individual, has also been increasingly applied to forced migration. This idea had significant resonance in the forced migration literature, allowing the refugee to be made the referent object of security and to critically examine how state-centric notions of security undermine the security of individual refugees and other forced migrants. Through a series of case studies, Newman's and Van Selm's (2003) *Refugees and Forced Displacement: International Security, Human Vulnerability, and the State* and Edwards and Ferstman's (2010) *Human Security and Non-Citizens* drew upon the human security literature to offer insights into the relationship between displacement and human security. Relatedly, a body of constructivist and critical scholarship has considered the conditions under which refugees and displaced populations are 'securitized', being perceived or identified as threats, in ways that legitimate certain forms of otherwise action against them (Hammerstadt 2010).

International Cooperation

A significant amount of the existing IR literature on responses to forced migration has examined the conditions under which international cooperation has taken place in the refugee regime (Betts 2009b; Cronin 2003; Suhrke 1998; Thielemann 2003) or has examined the role of UNHCR as the main international organization working on refugee protection (Loescher 2001; Barnett and Finnemore 2004; Betts, Bloom, and Omata 2012). In doing so, it has drawn upon, and contributed to, literature on international institutions within IR. One of the main intellectual challenges has been to understand the cooperation problem within the refugee regime, and the conditions under which it has historically been overcome. This has involved attempting to explain states' behaviour towards refugees; why and how they contribute to refugee protection; and the conditions under which international institutions like UNHCR are able to influence that behaviour.

States' contributions to refugee protection fall into two broad areas: asylum (contributing to the protection of refugees on their territory) and burden sharing (contributing to the protection of refugees on the territory of another state). Existing literature has explained the conditions under which cooperation takes place in both of these areas, identifying a different logic governing each. States' obligations to provide asylum to refugees who reach their territory are highly institutionalized in international law, whereas states have only weakly institutionalized obligations vis-à-vis burden-sharing. As such, while the former is partly subject to norm-driven behaviour, the latter is predominantly defined by interest-driven behaviour given its discretionary nature.

There is surprisingly little qualitative or quantitative work examining the complex question of why states contribute to asylum. Much scholarship on the politics of asylum in the North has been normative rather than explanatory (see, for example, Gibney 2004). In the South, one notable attempt to explain the politics of asylum from an IR perspective is Milner's (2009) *The Politics of Asylum in Africa*, which draws upon wider work on the African state in world politics. He looks at the cases of Tanzania, Kenya, and Guinea, explaining variation in the quality and quantity of asylum by variation in international burden sharing and the security consequences of hosting, as well as arguing that the contingency of history and state identity have mattered.

Most of the theoretical literature on cooperation in the refugee regime focuses on explaining Northern burden sharing—in the form of financial contributions or resettlement—to support protection in the South. There has been a significant academic debate on both the cooperation problem involved and the conditions under which it is likely to be overcome. In her pioneering article in the *Journal of Refugee Studies*, Suhrke (1998) argues that because refugee protection is a global public good, burden sharing is characterized by the game theoretical analogy of Prisoner's Dilemma, whereby, in the absence of highly institutionalized burden-sharing norms, states have strong incentives to free-ride on the provision of other states, and hence the prospects for international burden sharing are limited.

In contrast, Betts (2009b) argues in *Protection by Persuasion* that a better game theoretical analogy for the cooperation problem in the refugee regime is that of a Suasion Game, in which the regime is characterized by a fundamental North–South power asymmetry given the overwhelming majority of the world's refugees bring in the South. Northern donor states have little incentive to cooperate (provide burden sharing), while Southern host states have little choice but to cooperate (provide asylum). The outcome is a North–South impasse with serious consequences for protection and durable solutions. The historical challenge for UNHCR has been to overcome this cooperation problem. Exploring UNHCR's attempts to overcome the impasse, Betts find that issue-linkage—connecting refugee protection to states' wider interests in security, migration, and development—has been a crucial determinant of North–South cooperation.

Existing accounts of state contributions to refugee protection have therefore been mainly interest driven, and there has been relatively little in-depth exploration of the role of norms and values in determining asylum or burden sharing. One of the few notable constructivist contributions to the debate is by Barnett and Finnemore (2004), who use UNHCR as one of their primary case-studies in developing their understanding of international organizations. In *Rules for the World*, they examine the shift in UNHCR's mandate towards working on repatriation in the 1990s, arguing that rather than being passive, automotive actors that respond in predictable ways to states, international organizations such as UNHCR have their own organizational sociologies and pathologies that define their behaviour and change in their mandates over time.

Recently, Betts and Orchard's (2014) edited collection has explored how norms translate from the global to the national level in different areas of forced migration. In *Implementation and World Politics*, different chapter contributors explore how norms relating to the rights of refugees, IDPs, and returnees vary in how they translate into practice in different contexts. Yet, despite this there remain notable gaps in the existing literature on understanding the political role of norms within the forced migration context, and, with a few notable exceptions, a lack of theoretically informed work on the international politics of other areas of forced migration beyond refugees, such as IDPs, environmental displacement, and statelessness.

Towards a Transnational Turn

Reflecting the emphasis of much of IR theory, most of the existing theoretical work on the international politics of causes, consequences, and responses to forced migration has focused on inter-state relations. Furthermore, in most of these debates refugee and forced migration studies has been a net importer of concepts that have helped to elucidate the politics of forced migration without necessarily exporting outwards to IR. Yet, what, if anything, might the study of forced migration offer IR?

In many ways, IR itself is at a crossroads. Many of its dominant theories were conceived to understand and explain the inter-state relations of another era. Today, IR is struggling to develop concepts and theories to make sense of an increasingly transnational world, within which authority is diffusely located across a range of actors, processes, and levels of governance.

One of the most salient academic features of refugee studies and forced migration is that it is transnational. Within Migration Studies as a whole, there has been a 'transnational turn' (Vertovec 2004), which has partly shunned statist approaches to thinking about migration, while political science and international relations have struggled to move beyond statism. The study of the international politics of forced migration offers a unique space within which to bring transnationalism and the state together and ask how they interact.

IR, as a subdiscipline of political science, is attempting to wrestle with a number of core challenges relating to transnationalism, to which refugee and forced migration studies arguably has its greatest contribution to make, in particular regarding three emerging debates: the changing nature of global governance, the rise of non-state actors, and transnational political mobilization.

Global Governance

Global governance can be understood as either a process (all actions aimed at creating collective action among states or transnational actors) or as substance (the norms, rules, principles, and decision-making procedures that regulate the behaviour of states and transnational actors). The post-Second World War era created a United Nations-based framework of multilateral institutions, within which particular international organizations were given a clearly delineated de facto monopoly over particular issue areas. Since then, the nature of global governance has changed rapidly, and there has been significant institutional proliferation and fragmentation, with new parallel, overlapping, and nested institutions being created at the bilateral, regional, international, and even network levels of governance (Alter and Meunier 2009).

This broader trend has been replicated in forced migration. While the core of the refugee regime—based on UNHCR and the 1951 Convention—remains similar to at their inception, the wider structures of global forced migration governance have altered beyond recognition. Rather than speaking of a 'refugee regime', there is today arguably a 'refugee regime complex' (Betts 2010), within which a range of different institutions, at different levels of governance, and across different issue areas, shape and define how states and other actors can and do respond to forced displacement. The global governance of forced migration is nested within a broader institutional context, overlapping significantly with human rights, migration, humanitarian, development, and security regimes, in ways that can sometimes be complementary and sometimes contradictory to the overall scope and purpose of the refugee regime.

In particular, new layers of global governance have emerged in the twenty-first century that alter, challenge, and introduce new competitive dynamics to the refugee regime. First, global migration governance has created an array of means through which states now cooperate on migration management (Betts 2011; Koslowski 2012), some of which have significant effects on refugee protection, not least where they enable states to collectively restrict the movement of spontaneous-arrival asylum seekers. Second, humanitarian reform within the UN system, with the introduction of the so-called cluster approach has created a new logic of inter-agency competition in which all areas of humanitarian response—except for refugees—are now subject to inter-agency negotiation (Gottwald 2010; Weiss 2013).

Analytically, the refugee regime in particular has a number of features that make it apposite for exploring the dynamics of contemporary global governance. On a horizontal level, forced migration governance is closely intertwined with the politics and governance of a range of other policy fields and issue areas. It is impossible to understand the politics and governance of refugee protection, for instance, without engaging with its connections to migration, humanitarianism, human rights, development, and security (Betts 2009). On a vertical level, forced migration governance cannot be adequately understood without reflecting on the ways in which global norms are translated into practice at the national and local levels (Schmidt 2006; Betts 2013; Betts and Orchard 2014) or diffuse spatially from one region to another (Lambert, McAdam, and Fullerton 2013).

Non-state Actors

Far from being a 'statist' mode of governance, as it is often portrayed, the governance of forced migration now involves a range of non-state actors, including armed actors, NGOs, transnational civil society, and—increasingly—the private sector. A growing body of work in IR has recognized the emergence of private authority in policy fields relating to international political economy and security. However, this role has rarely been recognized or studied in relation to forced migration.

In migration more broadly, Gammeltoft-Hansen and Nyberg-Sørensen's (2013) work on the 'migration industry' points to the role of actors who, primarily motivated by profit, engage in activities relating to human mobility, including protection. Meanwhile Weiss's (2013) *Humanitarian Business*, although primarily focused on logics of competition between agencies, highlights the emergence of private actors in humanitarianism more broadly.

At the margins, private actors have always played a growing role in the refugee regime. In its early years, the UNHCR relied upon a grant from the Ford Foundation to provide assistance to refugees in Europe (Loescher 2001). Since the early 2000s, the role of the private sector has expanded massively (Betts, Bloom, and Omata 2012). The initial assumption was that firms would contribute to UNHCR largely on the basis of their corporate social responsibility (CSR) initiatives, wishing to be associated with a humanitarian brand, and sometimes working on particular projects. Over time, however, UNHCR has fostered links with firms and entrepreneurs whose role is not confined to philanthropy but extends to being active partners in offering expertise, networks, and policy guidance. Since 2012, UNHCR has a unit at headquarters known as 'UNHCR Innovation' which, based on an initial $110m grant from the IKEA Foundation, is working to pilot, prototype, and iterate scalable products and processes within refugee camps and urban areas (Betts, Bloom, and Omata 2012).

Transnational Political Mobilization

There has been growing recognition of the impact of refugee diasporas on the international political economy through remittance sending (Lindley 2010) and on international security as transnational armed actors (Salehyan 2009). These observations have led some authors to ask what diaspora and transnationalism do to our need to reframe core concepts of sovereignty and security (Adamson 2006). However, beyond these structural trends, there has been only limited work recognizing and theorizing the role of refugees and forced migrants themselves as political actors (Moulin and Nyers 2007).

Yet, historically, refugees and exiled populations have been significant actors in world politics. They have engaged in processes of transnational political mobilization, which are under-researched and under-theorized as either a dependent or an independent variable. During the Cold War and post-Cold War eras, exiled political groups have formed in ways that have contested the incumbent regime from outside.

In the context of illiberal regimes in Africa, such as Rwanda, Zimbabwe, Angola, and Eritrea, the national politics of contestation is transnational in nature, and depends crucially upon the role of exiled groups. In the absence of domestic political space, it is transnational political mobilization that allows the nation outside the state to challenge the incumbent regime. This emerging work on the 'transnational exile complex' not only allows refugees to be seen as political actors but also makes a contribution to reassess political authority sovereignty in the African context as inherently based on a form of networked sovereignty (Betts and Jones 2012).

CONCLUSION

The inherently political nature of forced migration means that concepts within IR should be of relevance to making sense of the interests, power relations, and ideas that shape the causes and consequences of, and responses to, displacement. Yet, forced migration has a number of distinguishing analytical features that should make it of interest to scholars of international relations. Its inherently complex relationship to sovereignty and the state system, its transnational dynamics, and position as intersecting with international political economy, security, and human rights make it an area from which a range of theoretical insights into world politics can be derived. The refugee regime in particular has a number of distinguishing features, lying between and relating to different policy fields, such as migration, development, and security, and working on the basis of a complex set of political relationships that connect global, national, and local dynamics.

International relations and forced migration therefore has immense potential not only to be an importer of concepts from IR but also to export ideas and to play a part in the development of a broader subdiscipline of IR that is today widely recognized to be 'up for grabs' in an increasingly transnational world. Many of the transnational themes that can be empirically explored through forced migration are those that IR needs to grapple with if it is to develop the conceptual tools to understand and engage with the challenges of the twenty-first century. Yet, so far, scholarship within international relations and forced migration has only scratched the surface of possible areas of inquiry. Beyond refugees, the international politics of other areas of forced migration remain mainly under-theorized, and there remain many empirical and conceptual puzzles that need to be explored in order to better understand—and so more effectively influence— the behaviour of states and other transnational actors in relation to forced migration.

REFERENCES

Adamson, F. B. (2006) 'Crossing Borders: International Migration and National Security'. *International Security* 31(1): 165–99.

Alter, K., and Meunier, S. (2009) 'The Politics of International Regime Complexity'. *Perspectives on Politics* 7(1): 13–24.

Barnett, M., and Finnemore, M. (2004) *Rules for the World: International Organizations in Global Politics*. New York: Cornell University Press.

Betts, A. (2009a) *Forced Migration and Global Politics*. Oxford: Wiley-Blackwell.

Betts, A. (2009b) *Protection by Persuasion: International Cooperation in the Refugee Regime*. Ithaca, NY: Cornell University Press.

Betts, A. (2010) 'The Refugee Regime Complex'. *Refugee Survey Quarterly*, 29(2): 12–37.

Betts, A. (ed.) (2011) *Global Migration Governance*. Oxford: Oxford University Press.

Betts, A. (2013) *Survival Migration: Failed Governance and the Crisis of Displacement*. Ithaca, NY: Cornell University Press.

Betts, A., Bloom, L., and Omata, N. (2012) 'Humanitarian Innovation and Refugee Protection'. Refugee Studies Centre Working Paper. Oxford: Refugee Studies Centre.

Betts, A., and Jones, W. (2012) 'The Transnational Exile Complex: How to Think about African Diaspora Politics'. Refugee Studies Centre Working Paper. Oxford: Refugee Studies Centre.

Betts, A., and Loescher, G. (2010) 'Refugees in International Relations'. Pp. 1–28 in A. Betts and G. Loescher (eds.), *Refugees in International Relations*. Oxford: Oxford University Press.

Betts, A., Loescher, G., and Milner, J. (2012) *UNHCR: The Politics and Practice of Refugee Protection*. London: Routledge.

Betts, A., and Orchard, P. (eds.) (2014) *Implementation and World Politics: How International Norms Change Practice*. Oxford: Oxford University Press.

Bull, H. (2010) 'Foreword'. In A. Betts and G. Loescher (eds.), *Refugees in International Relations*. Oxford: Oxford University Press.

Coles, G. (1989) 'Approaching the Refugee Problem Today'. Pp. 373–410 in G. Loescher and L. Monahan (eds.), *Refugees and International Relations*. Oxford: Oxford University Press.

Cronin, B. (2003) *Institutions for the Common Good: International Protection Regimes in International Society*. Cambridge: Cambridge University Press.

Cuenod, J. (1989) 'Refugees: Development or Relief'. Pp. 219–51 in G. Loescher and L. Monahan (eds.), *Refugees and International Relations*. Oxford: Oxford University Press.

Cuny, F., and Stein, B. (1989) 'Prospects for and Promotion of Spontaneous Repatriation'. Pp. 313–32 in G. Loescher and L. Monahan (eds.), *Refugees and International Relations*. Oxford: Oxford University Press.

Edwards, A., and Ferstman, C. (eds.) (2010) *Human Security and Non-Citizens: Law, Policy and International Affairs*. Cambridge: Cambridge University Press.

Gallagher, D. (1989) 'The Evolution of the International Refugee System'. Pp. 37–48 in G. Loescher and L. Monahan (eds.), *Refugees and International Relations*. Oxford: Oxford University Press.

Gammeltoft-Hansen, T., and Nyberg-Sørensen, N. (eds.) (2013) *The Commercialization of Migration and Markets for Migration*. Abingdon: Routledge.

Gibney, M. J. (2004) *The Ethics and Politics of Asylum: Liberal Democracy and the Response to Refugees*. Cambridge: Cambridge University Press.

Gordenker, L. (1987) *Refugees in International Politics*. New York: Columbia University Press.

Gottwald, M. (2010) 'Competing in the Humanitarian Marketplace: UNHCR's Organizational Culture and Decision-Making Process'. UNHCR Working Paper No. 190. Geneva: UNHCR.

Greenhill, K. (2010) *Weapons of Mass Migration: Forced Displacement, Coercion, and Foreign Policy*. Ithaca, NY: Cornell University Press.

Haddad, E. (2008) *The Refugee: The Individual between Sovereigns*. Cambridge: Cambridge University Press.

Hammerstad, A. (2010) 'UNHCR amd the Securitization of Forced Migration'. Pp. 237–60 in A. Betts and G. Loescher (eds.), *Refugees in International Relations*. Oxford: Oxford University Press.

Hurrell, A. (2010) 'Refugees, International Society and Global Order'. Pp. 85–104 in A. Betts and G. Loescher (eds.), *Refugees in International Relations*. Oxford: Oxford University Press.

Koslowski. R. (2011) *Global Mobility Regimes*. Basingstoke: Palgrave MacMillan.

Lambert, H., McAdam, J., and Fullerton, M. (eds.) (2013) *The Global Reach of European Refugee Law*. Cambridge: Cambridge University Press.

Lindley, A. (2010) *The Early Morning Phonecall: Remittances from a Refugee Diaspora*. New York: Berghahn.

Lischer, S. K. (2005) *Dangerous Sanctuaries: Refugee Camps, Civil War, and the Dilemmas of Humanitarian Aid*. Ithaca, NY: Cornell University Press.

Loescher, G. (1992) *Refugee Movements and International Security*. Adelphi Paper 268. London: Brasseys for The International Institute for Strategic Studies.

Loescher, G. (1993) *Beyond Charity: International Cooperation and the Global Refugee Crisis*. Oxford: Oxford University Press.

Loescher, G. (1996) *Beyond Charity: International Cooperation and the Global Refugee Crisis*. Oxford: Oxford University Press.

Loescher, G. (2001) *The UNHCR and World Politics: A Perilous Path*. Oxford: Oxford University Press.

Loescher, G., and Scanlan, J. (1987) *Calculated Kindness: Refugees and America's Half-Open Door*. New York: The Free Press.

Loescher, G., and Monahan, L. (eds.) (1989) *Refugees and International Relations*. Oxford: Clarendon Press.

Milner, J. (2009) *Refugees, the State and the Politics of Asylum in Africa*. Basingstoke: Palgrave Macmillan.

Moulin, C., and Nyers, P. (2007) 'We Live in a Country of UNHCR: Refugee Protests and Global Political Society'. *International Political Sociology* 1(4): 356–72.

Morris, E., and Stedman, S. J. (2008) 'Protracted Refugee Situations, Conflict and Security: The Need for Better Diagnosis and Prescription'. Pp. 189–213 in G. Loescher et al. (eds.), *Protracted*

Refugee Situations: Political, Human Rights and Security Implications. Tokyo: United Nations University Press and Brookings Institute Press.

Newman, E., and Van Selm, J. (eds.) (2003) *Refugees and Forced Displacement: International Security, Human Vulnerability, and the State*. Tokyo: United Nations University Press.

Owens, P. (2010) 'Beyond "Bare Life": Refugees and the "Right to Have Rights"'. Pp. 133–50 in A. Betts and G. Loescher (eds.), *Refugees in International Relations*. Oxford: Oxford University Press.

Roberts, A. (2010) 'Refugees and Military Intervention'. Pp. 213–36 in A. Betts and G. Loescher (eds.), *Refugees in International Relations*. Oxford: Oxford University Press.

Salehyan, I. (2009) *Rebels without Border: Transnational Insurgencies in World Politics*. Ithaca, NY: Cornell University Press.

Salehyan, I., and Gleditsch, K. S. (2006) 'Refugees and the Spread of Civil War'. *International Organization* 60(2): 335–66.

Schmidt, A. (2006) *From Global Prescription to Local Treatment—The International Refugee Regime in Tanzania and Uganda*. Department of Political Science, University of California, Berkeley.

Skran, C. (1995) *Refugees in Inter-War Europe: The Emergence of a Regime*. Oxford: Clarendon Press.

Snyder. J. (2010) 'Realism, Refugees, and Strategies of Humanitarianism'. Pp. 29–52 in A. Betts and G. Loescher (eds.), *Refugees in International Relations*. Oxford: Oxford University Press.

Stedman, S. J., and Tanner, F. (2003) *Refugee Manipulation: War, Politics, and the Abuse of Human Suffering*. Washington, DC: Brookings Institution Press.

Suhrke, A. (1998) 'Burden-Sharing during Refugee Emergencies: The Logic of Collective Action Versus National Action'. *Journal of Refugee Studies* 11(4): 396–415.

Thielemann, E. (2003) 'Between Interests and Norms: Burden-Sharing in the European Union'. *Journal of Refugee Studies* 16(3): 253–73.

Vertovec, S. (2004) 'Migrant Transnationalism and Modes of Transformation'. *International Migration Review* 38(3): 970–1001.

Weiner, M. (1993) *International Migration and Security*. Boulder, CO: Westview Press.

Weiner, M. (1995) *The Global Migration Crisis: Challenge to States and to Human Rights*. New York: Harper Collins.

Weiss, T. (2013) *Humanitarian Business*. Cambridge: Polity Press.

Zolberg, A. R. et al. (1989) *Escape from Violence: Conflict and the Refugee Crisis in the Developing World*. Oxford: Oxford University Press.

CHAPTER 6

....

ANTHROPOLOGY AND FORCED MIGRATION

....

DAWN CHATTY

INTRODUCTION

ANTHROPOLOGY, with its focus on people in groups, has had a pivotal role in the development of the modern interdisciplinary study of forced migration. Both before and after the birth of 'refugee' studies, anthropology's contribution to this new field has been and continues to be the prioritizing of the views of the uprooted, the displaced, and the dispossessed. Its emphasis on phenomenological and ethnographic field methods gives voice and agency to refugees, exiles, and other forced migrants. This chapter articulates anthropology's unique contribution to the field by setting out the conceptualizations and tools which have put the lived experience to the fore, documenting and further analysing what happens to people, their culture, and society when they are wrenched from their territorial moorings, be they refugees and exiles, development induced displaces, or mobile peoples evicted, restricted, and forced to remain in one place. In particular, it examines some of the important anthropological studies which pre-dated the 'fieldwork in a refugee camp' era of the early 1980s and after, and reflects on the significance of the 'view from below' centralized through anthropology's unique research tool and strategy: participant observation.

The chapter commences with an examination of anthropological studies of people who have been forced to move which pre-date the 1980s (Colson in the 1940s, Turnbull in the 1950s, Loizos in the 1960s, and Chatty in the 1970s). These contributions to the field clearly tied people to places from which they were dispossessed or evicted, a conceptualization in anthropology which was not challenged until the 1990s when Malkki's work gave rise to debates on deterritorialization, liminality, and belonging. The chapter then engages with the further elaboration in more recent anthropological studies which have come to question territorialization. As anthropology's foundation principles include the association of spaces with particular cultures and societies, the decoupling of territory and culture has been approached rather gingerly within the discipline. The emergence of transnationalism and diasporas as an area of anthropological scholarship area is a response to this reticence (Van Hear 2000; Monsutti 2005). Over time, the research agenda of anthropologists working in the field of forced migration has come to focus on certain other binaries: sedentism and mobility; those who remain and those who move; camp-based versus urban refugees; refugees in the global South and those in the global North; and more recently the circularity of forced migration including integration, return, and development.

THE HISTORY OF ANTHROPOLOGY AND THE ACADEMIC FIELD OF FORCED MIGRATION STUDIES

Anthropology developed as a discipline in the United States early in the twentieth century and was closely associated with protecting the rights and cultural memory of indigenous peoples, hence its early focus on phenomenological note taking and recording. In the United Kingdom and France, its growth and close association with European imperialism meant a disciplinary trajectory that focused on the theoretical and conceptual rather than the substantive, often in support of the colonial project. In whichever continent anthropology developed, the importance of the 'real' rather than the 'armchair' or desk study was prioritized. Thus participant observation, as a strategy and as a core method, became the hallmark of the discipline.

The academic interest in the study of migration as a specific field developed in the late nineteenth century with the work of the British demographer Ravenstein (Ravenstein 1889). This was followed by economists and sociologists in the USA mainly concerned with labour markets and immigration assimilation. Most of the migration research in the first half of the twentieth century in the USA was interested in immigrant absorption but not the immigrant experience. In Europe, pioneering work by the historian Ferdinand Braudel and others began to explore migrants' experiences; but this was also focused on national agendas and the priorities of the state. The experience or memory of migrants—forced or otherwise—were not on the research radar other than as elements which expanded or espoused ideas about national cultures (that is in terms of integration and assimilation). As Soguk saw the citizen as rooted in territorial space, the refugee was seen as uprooted, dislocated, and displaced from the community of citizens and thus the refugee lacked affinity with the national community. The refugee was a negative, an empty, or bare space in theory and in research (Soguk 1999). It took anthropologists with their fundamental interest in human experience and behaviour to turn the tide and bring the migration experience, the memory of dispossession and displacement, as well as the lived response to uprootedness into the core of a developing field of study (Sayigh 1979; Reynell 1989; Huseby-Darvas 1994; Malkki 1995; Das 1996; Hirschon 1998; Chatty 2010).

The twentieth century has been called the 'century of the refugee', so it is not surprising that the twenty-first century looks set to become known as the 'century of displacement and dispossession' (Colson 2003). Anthropologists have increasingly engaged in ethnographic studies of uprooting, displacement, migration, and resettlement. These interests reflect the current state of the world. For a field which sets out to understand the lived experience and which depends upon participant observation as its fundamental research tool, it is not surprising that forced migration has captured the attention of large numbers of anthropologists. This is so much so that the American Anthropological Association even contains a subgroup composed of those whose research interests focus on refugees, the internally displaced, and other involuntary migrants.

In the United States, anthropology developed through research on Native Americans, peoples who had been subjected to massive ethnic cleansings in the preceding two centuries. Much of that early work was with tribes who had been displaced, dispossessed, and involuntarily marched into resource-poor reservations. The anthropologists working with them thought they were engaging in a kind of salvage ethnography to record ways of life before they disappeared. These researchers largely ignored the impacts of displacement—the destroyed settlements, land occupation, non-viable reservations, inadequate welfare and hostile administrations, and lack of legal rights—and focused instead on trying to reconstruct memory culture of 'what life was like in the old days'. Nevertheless these studies gave us many of our basic concepts to describe the experience of uprootedness despite later embeddedness in gratuitously assumed stable modern societies. These fundamental anthropological concepts have become important in the discipline of forced migration studies. They include understandings of: role and identity, hierarchy, social networks, conflict mechanisms, reciprocity and trust, boundary creation, rites of passage, liminality, and the role of myths. Anthropological research in Africa also largely ignored the impacts of displacement on a continent which had seen much turmoil for the century before anthropologists had arrived. These largely British anthropologists also ignored the facts of displacement or dealt with partial systems of people living under colonial regimes.

Perhaps the earliest work with displaced populations was conducted by Elizabeth Colson between 1942 and 1943 at Poston War Relocation Camp in Arizona, where largely second-generation Japanese-Americans (Nisei) from California were interned during the Second World War. Here, the fact of displacement could not be ignored, and the thrust of the work was applied; to study the 'causes of resistance' to camp administration and to propose measures to ameliorate the effects of interment. Little work from that period has been published and is perhaps overshadowed by the long-term studies which Colson engaged in with the Plateau Tonga and the Gwembe Tonga from 1946 to the present. The latter represents the longest longitudinal study of forced migration—development induced displacement and resettlement—which we have. The work of Colin Turnbull whose two classic monographs were published in the 1960s but researched in the 1950s, *The Forest People* and *The Mountain People*, characterize the anthropological lens of the time perfectly. The first is a sympathetic study of a people—the pygmies of the Ituri forest—largely removed from much contact with the colonial regime. It is very much an ode to a harmonious way of life largely untouched by the twentieth century. The second, *The Mountain People*, largely ignored the displacement of these people from Uganda for the establishment of a National Game Reserve on their traditional grazing lands. It ignores their dispossession to the mountains of the Kenya/ Uganda border, their loss of livelihood, and their lack of legal rights. Instead it focuses on their social disintegration into a 'band' of hostile people whose only goal is individual survival. Published in the 1960s it was a study in societal breakdown which some saw as beginning to produce the same results in the West. This was classic anthropology: to study the other so as to better understand ourselves.

The 1970s saw a turn to greater introspection and holistic analysis. Peter Loizos was in many ways a pioneer in the study of the plight of refugees and in the emerging post-modernist lens. He was, to an extent, an accidental chronicler of displacement. His original Ph.D. study was intended to be on the 'dowry' in his father's Greek Cypriot village of Argaki, and yet processes of politicization in the early 1970s saw him shift emphasis to study politics in a Cypriot village. A few years later, in the aftermath of the Cypriot civil war, he found his village and his large extended family had become refugees and he returned to study how people had coped with dispossession and exile, what resources they had deployed, and how they had created new lives in difficult circumstances. Renee Hirschon also engaged in the determined study of a refugee group—some of the 1 million Orthodox Christians to be forcibly moved for 35,000 Muslim Turks after the 1922 Exchange of Populations. This international agreement resulted from the unsuccessful Greek attempt to retake Eastern Anatolia during the Turkish 'War for Independence' between 1918 and 1923. Hirschon set out to study the dispossessed and displaced Orthodox Christians from Asia Minor who were 'resettled' in the Greek port of Piraeus. She also sought to understand how people coped with exile and how they created new lives in difficult circumstances, and how second- and third-generation refugees identified themselves and structured the myths of origin. During this period a number of anthropological studies emerged looking at long-term dispossession among the Palestinian refugees in the Levant, as well as examining adaptation and innovation among dispossessed and stateless mobile groups (Chatty 1986; Peteet 1995). With regard to the latter, this involved anthropologists understanding competing concepts of sedentism and mobility and the way legal categories of territorial habitation were used to justify eviction such as *terra nullius* to justify the dispossession of 'the Other' in Australia, *vacuum domicilium* in the USA to justify the forced marches of Native Americans from their traditional territories, and *tabula rasa* in South West Africa to account for the genocide of the Herero by German colonialists.

Anthropology and the Formal Founding of the Discipline of Forced Migration Studies

The discipline was edging towards trying to understand the lives, the perceptions, and the aspirations of those who suffered forced migration whether caused by war or other forms of violence, or because the dominant view of the 'greater economic good' required removal. However, these ethnographies and the move towards defining a discipline rested on a problematic premiss. What right did social scientists have to study the suffering of others, unless it could be claimed—to use the old liberal assumption—that good research would contribute to better informed policy and practice and that such research would be for the betterment of both? That is not the same as saying that advocacy was an element in fieldwork, but rather that advocacy had a place in ameliorating desperate conditions. This positioning gave the new field a moral anchor significantly different from other disciplines grounded in traditional academic specializations such as sociology, politics, and geography where the traditions of knowledge were for knowledge's sake. The study of refugees and forced migrants had an ethical and individual moral imperative to give something back to the community studied, as a step to ameliorating suffering.

As early as the 1970s, studies were showing that the condition of involuntary movement and resettlement was not following the classical pattern established in the magisterial sociological study by Thomas and Znaniecki's work on Polish immigration to the USA (Thomas and Znaniecki 1996 (1918)). That study set out the way migrants used networks, established coherent ethnic communities, and reinforced links to the homeland, bypassing as much as possible contact with formal institutions provided by the host community where they felt powerless to control outcomes. What these new studies were showing was that voluntary migrants adjusted faster and their adjustment to their new physical and social environments was more stable and less conflict-ridden than those forced to move [or stay in one place] and officially relocated and under the control of a resettlement administration (Lieber 1977). Comparable findings for camp versus self-settled refugees in the Sudan emerged in Harrell-Bond's study (Harrell-Bond 1986) and those of Malkki for camp and self-settled refugees in Tanzania (Malkki 1995).

By the 1980s anthropologists were bringing together their findings from work on forced migration of various kinds, including refugees, internally displaced persons, those uprooted because others wanted their land or resources, and disaster victims. Many anthropologists had conducted this research thinking that it would have an impact on policy and make uprooting and readjustment less traumatic (Hansen and Oliver-Smith 1982; Oliver-Smith and Hansen 1982; Cernea 1985; Morgan and Colson 1987). Ethnographic studies of displacement for large development projects and biodiversity conservation protected areas had already aroused sufficient concern at the World Bank for guidelines to be drawn up evaluating social impacts on those at risk of involuntary displacement. However, these guidelines did not immediately provide any institutional means through which the displaced could appeal to an international constituency.

It was in this period that several institutions were established—largely by anthropologists—to find ways of taking their own research to the public and to policymakers and to give voice to the forced migrants, and other oppressed peoples. In 1971, a group of anthropologists framed the Barbados Declaration calling for the protection of the rights of indigenous people not to be dispossessed or assimilated by the nation states they found themselves in. The International Work Group for Indigenous Affairs (IWGIA) was set up at this time followed shortly thereafter by Cultural Survival in 1972 and its accompanying journal (*Cultural Survival*). The Refugee Studies Programme (RSP; now known as RSC) was established in the same tradition at the University of Oxford by Dr Barbara Harrell-Bond in 1982. It developed an academic focus emphasizing research and empirical findings and reached out to policymakers, practitioners, and refugees alike. It brought the broad critical study of humanitarianism squarely into anthropology and interrogated the motives, nature, and implications of humanitarian aid agencies'— and their staff's—interventions. By 1989, it had established both a journal (*Journal of Refuge Studies*) as well as a newsletter for practitioners (*Forced Migration Review*). In 2002, the RSC spearheaded a drive to protect the rights of mobile peoples—hunters and gatherers, pastoralists, and swidden agriculturalists—from eviction, dispossession, and forced settlement. That effort, the Dana Declaration on Mobile Peoples and Conservation was an advocacy effort based on research conducted at the RSC in the previous decade. Nonetheless, by and large, the RSC strengthened its academic credentials in teaching and research during this time. The IWGIA and Cultural Survival, on the other hand, emphasized service to the local communities, advocacy and activism bringing them and their plight to the attention of international public opinion.

The RSC, in the intervening decades, grew and became successfully integrated into the academic teaching and research programme of the University of Oxford. Barbara Harrell-Bond developed a broad-based teaching programme drawing on anthropological theories of the interconnectedness (holistic) of life that other disciplines generally dealt with separately. She recognized that people became (and remained refugees) because of largely national politics, and so she argued for research which examined the political contexts in which forced migration, dispossession, protection, and resettlement occurred. She also saw that vulnerable people who were abused or no longer protected by their own state needed to depend upon the international system to provide them with the basics of life (food, shelter, and water) and legal protection. Thus she included international law and international organizations into her teaching programme. Finally she put at the core of the teaching programme the immediate experience of displacement and dispossession and its aftermath. This she tied to a teaching module and practitioner training course on the psycho-social impacts of being a forced migrant. Overall, it took an anthropologist to see that what was needed was an interdisciplinary programme of teaching and research carried out by specialists in law, international relations, political science, anthropology, psychology, and other subjects including geography, sociology, and social policy. By incorporating representatives of other disciplines into the core programme at the RSP [RSC], Harrell-Bond followed a long-standing anthropological tradition. Anthropologists have always worked across interdisciplinary boundaries, which is why there is so much 'hyphenated anthropology': legal anthropology, medical anthropology, political anthropology, economic anthropology, cross-cultural psychology, etc. The programme she set up continues today and although there are now a handful of other 'refugee studies' programmes in the world—many founded by Harrell-Bond herself—the RSC remains uniquely holistic in its approach committed to the vision of its founder.

However, even with this strong interdisciplinary and holistic focus which shaped the field, there remains a tension between the phenomenological approach of anthropology and the 'refugee policy' concerns of law, politics, and international relations studies. The latter prioritized state-based agendas and state-based legal and political histories, while the former focused on people and their lived experience. This tension has seen sedentarist frameworks and liberal democratic statist orientations gain ascendancy in the field of forced migration studies. Notwithstanding this 'second place' positioning of anthropology among forced migration scholars, the concepts and concerns which anthropology have brought to the field have been ground-breaking.

CRITICAL ANTHROPOLOGICAL CONCEPTS IN THE DISCIPLINE OF FORCED MIGRATION STUDIES

The core anthropological concepts 'borrowed' at the founding of refugee and forced migration studies quickly matured and incorporated a 'postmodern' tint. As a reaction to the assumed certainty of scientific or objective efforts to explain reality, anthropology was quick to embrace and integrate social constructivism into its conceptual toolkit. Sceptical of explanations that claimed to be valid for all groups, cultures, and traditions, it promoted the position that reality was socially constructed and that there were no absolute truths. By the 1990s, mature social constructivist work by Malkki, Gupta and Ferguson, and Appadurai undertook a distancing from the 'roots' and territorial orientation of earlier studies (Gupta and Ferguson 1992; Malkki 1992; Malkki 1995; Appadurai 1995). Space and place, home and homeland came to be dramatically reconsidered as a result of this body of work and these concepts figured prominently in research with refugees, exiles, and other forced migrations. Their work challenged the inherent link between cultural difference and space or physical territory so prominent in earlier anthropological and political science structuralist/functionalist approaches. They criticized the partial incarceration of the native which saw the world as a colourful map where lines clearly delineated geographic territories (spaces) with distinctive cultures (places). Ideas and concepts regarding displacement assume a natural correspondence between people, geographic space, and place which anthropologists such as Malkki (1992) have now questioned for over two decades.

As Malkki shows, there is an abundance of 'botanical metaphors', largely derived from nineteenth-century nation-state ideologies, through which both anthropological and nationalist discourses have rooted people in the 'soil' of the nation or 'ethnic territory'. Yet despite this theoretical preoccupation with 'roots', historical research has consistently shown that migration is not the exception in human history, but rather more of a constant. Even more popular postmodern metaphors like 'grafting' transplanting and 'hybridization' continue this 'mother-earth' imagery. Contesting this popular conceptualization, Malkki makes clear in her work that people are chronically mobile and routinely displaced. They invent homes and homelands in the absence of territorial bases. It is through such memories that they can inhabit their imagined nation

(Malkki 1992). This undermining of the connections between peoples and places, which are imagined to be natural, has not led to cultural homogenization (Clifford 1988). Instead what has tended to happen with this blurring of places and localities is that ideas of cultural and ethnic distinctions are becoming more prevalent. Here, what we see is the 'imagined community' striving to become attached to imagined places (Anderson 1983). Dispossessed people everywhere remember their 'imagined' home-lands in a world that increasingly denies such firm identification of 'place' with 'geo-graphic space'. Remembered places have often served as symbolic anchors for forced migrants and other dispersed, diasporic, and transnational people. Thus 'homeland' is one of the most powerful unifying symbols for the dispossessed even though the way in which that place is constructed in the social imagination may be quite different among the far-flung members of the imagined community. Geographic space, as anthropol-ogy has long argued, is made meaningful by people. The experience of space is always socially constructed. Spatial meanings are thus established by those with the power to make places out of spaces.

Malkki, furthermore, argued that such territorialization is dominant in discourses of nationalism where biological or kinship metaphors are used to show the rootedness of nations to specific lands—the Fatherland or the Motherland. Thus the national order of things is considered to be normal while uprootedness and displacement are abnor-mal. According to Malkki, these 'sedentarist' approaches, based on the idealization of homeland, consider migration an anomaly and thus uprootedness and displacement are pathologized. These 'sedentarist' scholars viewed territorial displacement as a cause of identity loss and cultural stripping away (Rosaldo 1988). Thus, return to the homeland is regarded as the only durable solution.

Social constructivists such as Malkki, Appadurai, and Gupta and Ferguson argue that places and cultures are socially, politically, and historically constructed. They call for disengaging 'culture' and 'identity' from territorialized, nation-bounded concepts of place and space. For many of the dispossessed, the imagined 'homeland' acquires a mythical status and image. It is assumed to be unchanged by the departure and reloca-tion of its dispossessed. Yet the way in which the representation of the imagined com-munity is drawn and fixed rests largely with the people themselves. The past is smoothed out, pre-existing differences and ambiguities are often covered up or cleaned up, and the society and homeland is often assigned a primordial being by members of the dis-possessed group. This imagery is now being challenged by anthropologists and geog-raphers, among others, and is becoming the 'current orthodoxy' in the social sciences. Anthropology has had a special interest in this area as the practice of fieldwork, so cen-tral to the discipline, has long revolved around the idea that cultures are spatially located, which fits perfectly with the conception of the nation-state model that nations are 'natu-rally rooted' in the native soil of their people. It is perhaps because anthropology realizes it must abandon this idea of the natural, demarcated link between culture and nation, that there has been so much effort in the last decade or so to find ways of 'construct-ing' the field in 'unbounded' territory or multi-local and transnational milieus (Marcus 1998). As Malkki writes 'There has emerged a new awareness of the global social fact that now, more than perhaps ever before, people are chronically mobile and routinely displaced, and invent homes and homelands in the absence of territorial, national bases—not in situ, but through memories of, and claims on, places that they can, or will, no longer corporeally inhabit' (Malkki 1992: 24).

Yet, as David Turton and others point out, those who write on the subject of forced migration and displacement pay little attention to 'social and cultural constructions of the . . . places occupied by refugees and other forced migrants, preferring instead to concentrate on the physical and productive properties of these places' (Turton 2005: 276). It is ironic then that anthropological theorizing about 'place' and 'place-making' (emplacement) has not made more of a mark on those who study displacement (Allen 1996; Hammond 2004). It is as though the recognition of places as imagined and contested decouples or 'denaturalizes' the link between people and territorial space. This somehow is regarded as entering a minefield by those who seek to help or protect people such as refugees. Such conceptualizations, especially those which question and contest the 'natural' link between people, culture, and space, may be feared to play into the hands of governments and others who may wish to diminish or ignore the suffering of those who have been forced out of their homes. As we move ever more into a deterritorialized world we are coming to recognize that questions of space and place are very much more central to the concerns of both the dispossessed in their new resting places and those who remain.

With regard to return, the sedentarist positioning as the only durable solution, these social constructivists view this as problematic both because geographic spaces and cultural places change over time. The homeland existing in the imagination and memories of the uprooted may no longer correspond to realities on the ground. This historical and socially constructed notion of nations and national identity is well documented in the work of Benedict Anderson (1983). By decoupling nationalism from territory in his imagined communities he calls into question the discipline's heavy emphasis on the nation state, its sovereignty at the expense of the dispossessed, uprooted, and displaced.

Ethnicity is another broad concept important to forced migration studies which anthropologists have actively elucidated. For many anthropologists, ethnicity is generally defined as a sense of belonging to a group, based on shared ideas of group history, language, experience, and culture. Commonly in this sense, nationality and ethnicity are frequently interchanged with one another, while some anthropologists see nationalism as a variant of ethnicity (Eriksen 1993). There are several theoretical positions regarding the rise of ethnicity. Clifford Geertz, for example, regards ethnicity as being a 'primordial attachment', something pre-social, something one is born into (Geertz 1963). Fredrick Barth, on the other hand, sees ethnicity as socially constructed or created and emerging from the recognition of difference from neighbouring groups (1969). The differentiating markers are generally cultural characteristics such as language, shared history, religion, and customs. Other anthropologists see ethnicity as derived from instrumental need. These ideas have their roots in the work of Max Weber who identified organizational efforts by status groups to establish rules which exclude others (Weber 1968).

Whichever model is followed, ethnicity is often linked to political processes of boundary drawing between dominant groups and minorities. Becoming an ethnic minority rather than simply an ethnic community is a mechanism of marginalization which can have profound effects on how a community creates and maintains its social stability and cohesion. Being regarded as an ethnic community in a multicultural society is generally seen as a positive attribute. At the other extreme, however, is the ethnic minority in a dominant majority state whose presence is regarded as undesirable and divisive. The concept of ethnic minority generally implies some degree of marginalization or exclusion leading to situations of actual or potential conflict, dispossession, and displacement. These understandings support the 'holistic' turn of anthropology and confirm the importance of integrating the study of politics and international relations with that of the lived experience of dispossession and uprootedness in order to fully understand the processes of exclusion from the larger society and the state, the citizen and the non-citizen, the threats to state sovereignty and the international humanitarian regime.

CONCLUSION

Anthropology has given the growing field of forced migration studies its core conceptual binaries such as: place and space; home and homeland; territoriality and liminality; belonging and identity; social networks and capital; ethnicity and nationalism; displacement and emplacement; eviction and return; camp-based and self-settled; integration and assimilation. It has also given us sub-fields of investigation within this field such as the significance of gender and generation in camp ethnographies as well as humanitarian policies and practices; victimization and agency of the forced migrant, as well as refugee return and development in local hosting communities. Furthermore it has given the field two interrelated, fundamental research strategies and tools, participant observation and the ethnographic method, as well as permitting the development of critical approaches to concepts of agency, morality, and ethics in forced migration and humanitarianism studies. It is a body of work that has helped maintain a balance between state-centric work in politics, international relations, and law with a continuing interest in the refugees and forced migrants themselves. This above all else has been its most important contribution; the primacy of the vision of anthropology has been the perspective and voice of the forced migrant, the phenomenological encounter that permits the uprooted, the displaced, and the refugee to break out from the category of 'object of study' and to bring to life the individual experience of dispossession.

REFERENCES

Allen, T. (ed.) (1996) *In Search of Cool Ground: War, Flight and Homecoming in North East Africa*. London: James Currey.
Anderson, B. (1983) *Imagined Communities: Reflections on the Origin and Spread of Nationalism*. London: Verso.

Appadurai, A. (1995) 'The Production of Locality'. Pp. 204–25 in R. Fardon (ed.), *Counterworks: Managing the Diversity of Knowledge*. London: Routledge.

Barth, F. (ed.) (1969) *Ethnic Groups and Boundaries: The Social Organization of Culture Difference*. Oslo: Scandinavian University Press.

Cernea, M. (ed.) (1985) *Putting People First: Sociological Variables in Rural Development*. Oxford: Oxford University Press.

Chatty, D. (1977) 'Land Leaders, and Limousines: Emir Versus Sheikh'. *Ethnology* 16(4): 385–97.

Chatty, D. (1986) *From Camel to Truck: The Bedouin in the Modern World*. New York: Vantage Press.

Chatty, D. (2010) *Dispossession and Displacement in the Modern Middle East*. Cambridge: Cambridge University Press.

Clifford, J. (1988) *The Predicament of Culture: Twentieth-Century Ethnography, Literature, and Art*. Cambridge, MA: Harvard University Press.

Colson, E. (1945) 'The Makah: A Study of Assimilation'. PhD dissertation, Radcliffe College, Cambridge, MA.

Colson, E. (2003) 'Forced Migration and the Anthropological Response'. *Journal of Refugee Studies* 16(1): 1–16.

Das, V. (1996) 'Dislocation and Rehabilitation: Defining a Field'. *Economic and Political Weekly* 1(24): 1509–14.

Eriksen, T. H. (1993) *Ethnicity and Nationalism: Anthropological Perspectives*. London: Pluto.

Geertz, C. (1963) 'The Integrative Revolution: Primordial Sentiments and Civil Politics in the New States'. Pp. 105–57 in C. Geertz (ed.), *Old Societies and New States: The Quest for Modernity in Asia and Africa*. New York: Free Press of Glencoe.

Gupta, A., and Ferguson, J. (1992) 'Beyond "Culture": Space, Identity, and the Politics of Difference'. *Cultural Anthropology* 7: 6–23.

Hammond, L. (2004) *This Place Will Become Home: Refugee Repatriation to Ethiopia*. Ithaca, NY: Cornell University Press.

Hansen, A., and Oliver-Smith, A. (eds.) (1982) *Involuntary Migration and Resettlement: The Problems and Responses of Dislocated People*. Boulder, CO: Westview.

Harrell-Bond, B. E. (1986) *Imposing Aid*. Oxford: Oxford University Press.

Hirschon, R. (1998) *Heirs of the Greek Catastrophe: The Social Life of Asia Minor Refugees in Piraeus*. Oxford: Berghahn.

Lieber, M. (1977) *Exiles and Migrants in Oceania*. Honolulu: University Press of Hawaii.

Loizios, P. (1981) *The Heart Grown Bitter: A Chronicle of Cypriot War Refugees*. Cambridge: Cambridge University Press.

Malkki, L. H. (1992) 'National Geographic: The Rooting of Peoples and the Territorialization of National Identity among Scholars and Refugees'. *Cultural Anthropology* 7(1): 24–44.

Malkki, L. H. (1995) *Purity and Exile: Violence, Memory, and National Cosmology among Hutu Refugees in Tanzania*. Chicago: University of Chicago Press.

Marcus, G. (1998) *Ethnography through Thick and Thin*. Princeton: Princeton University Press.

Monsutti, A. (2005) *War and Migration: Social Networks and Economic Strategies of the Hazaras of Afghanistan*, trans. P. Camiller. New York: Routledge.

Morgan, S., and Colson, E. (eds.) (1987) *People in Upheaval*. New York: Center for Migration Studies.

Oliver-Smith, A., and Hansen, A. (1982) 'Introduction: Involuntary Migration and Resettlement: Causes and Contexts'. Pp. 1–9 in A. Hansen and A. Oliver-Smith, (eds.),

Involuntary Migration and Resettlement: The Problems and Responses of Dislocated People. Westview Special Studies. Boulder, CO: Westview.

Peteet, J. (1995) 'Transforming Trust: Dispossession and Empowerment among Palestinian Refugees'. Pp. 168–86 in E. V. Daniel and J. Knudsen (eds.), *Mistrusting Refugees.* Berkeley: University of California Press.

Ravenstein, E. (1889) 'The Laws of Migration'. *Journal of the Royal Statistical Society* 52(2): 241–305.

Reynell, J. (1989) *Political Pawns: Refugees on the Thai-Kampuchean Border.* Oxford: Oxfam.

Rosaldo, R. (1988) 'Ideology, Place and People without Culture'. *Cultural Anthropology* 3(1): 77–87.

Sayigh, R. (1979) *Palestinians: From Peasants to Revolutionaries.* London: Zed.

Soguk, N. (1999) *States and Strangers: Refugees and Displacements of Statecraft.* Minneapolis: University of Minnesota Press.

Thomas, W., and Znaniecki, F. (1996 [1918]) *The Polish Peasant in Europe and America: A Classic Work in Immigration History.* Urbana, IL: University of Illinois Press.

Turnbull, C. (1972) *The Mountian People.* New York: Touchstone Press.

Turton, D. (2005) 'The Meaning of Place in a World of Movement: Lessons from Long-Term Field Research in Southern Ethiopia'. *Journal of Refugee Studies* 18(3): 258–80.

Van Hear, N. (2000) 'People Abroad and People at Home in Societies under Strain'. *Forced Migration Review* 7: 33–6.

Weber, M., Roth, G., and Wittich, C. (eds.) (1968) *Economy and Society: An Outline of Interpretive Sociology.* New York: Bedminster Press.

CHAPTER 7

SOCIOLOGY AND FORCED MIGRATION

FINN STEPPUTAT AND NINNA NYBERG SØRENSEN

INTRODUCTION

WHEREAS migration historically has had an important role to play in sociology thanks to the Chicago School of urban sociology, it is only approximately 25 years ago that scholars began outlining a sociology of forced migration. Still in the context of the Cold War and without a clear sense of its transgression into a new epoch, *Current Sociology* published a special issue on 'The Sociology of Involuntary Migration'. The issue took stock of existing scholarly work and discussed future lines of inquiry, with the authors observing that the sociology of forced migration was at an 'embryonic stage' (Harrell-Bond 1988), empirical studies were largely uninformed by general sociological theory (Richmond 1988), and that they were of limited conceptual and theoretical sophistication (Mazur 1988). These flaws have routinely been repeated and lamented every now and then since 1988, and explained with reference to the inherently multidisciplinary nature of refugee and forced migration studies, the perception of refugee situations as ephemeral and temporary phenomena, and the lack of status associated with studies in this field.

The 1988 reference to a field of forced/involuntary migration is significant if we have in mind the critical discussion evolving in the 2000s (see Van Hear 2012) of whether and how policymakers and donors had influenced the transformation from the study of 'refugees' to the study of 'forced migration' that took place in the 1990s. It is clear from the 1988 issue that scholars considered refugees, exiles, and internally displaced populations—and to some extent also development induced displacement—as potentially forming part of their field due to the obvious commonalities in terms of the sociological questions these different processes raised. Furthermore, Richmond (1988: 13), leaning on Giddens's structuration theory, stated emphatically that 'from a sociological point of view' we cannot make clear distinctions between voluntary and involuntary migration, as little as we can distinguish clearly between economic and socio-political determinants of migration.

The authors also expressed the hope that sociologists in the future would contribute with their particular understanding of how factors and units of analysis at micro-, meso-, and macro levels could be jointly considered (individual, family, community, organizations, nation states, and world system), and how structure and agency play out in the field of forced migration. These studies would in turn contribute to sociology through the critical reflection of the concepts (such as 'refugee'), theories, methodologies, and praxis (Mazur 1988), and by breaking down the boundaries between the different disciplines that studies of forced migration draw upon (Harrell-Bond 1988).

In light of the above, in this chapter we address the most significant developments in forced migration studies when seen through the lens of sociology in terms of theory and concepts, themes and issues, and methodological questions. In conclusion we consider how, in retrospect, forced migration studies have contributed to sociology.

THEORIES AND CONCEPTS

As predicted in the 1988 issue of *Current Sociology*, sociological theory over the following 25 years contributed to studies of forced migration by way of providing general ideas of 'macro-level' or 'global' social transformation and to ideas of social dynamics at 'meso' and 'micro-' or 'local' level. This includes the linkages between the different levels and units of analysis, as well as the central sociological concern of how structure and agency are related. In fact, sociology has been suggested as a kind of meta-discipline which can 'help bring together all the varying [disciplinary] perspectives in an overall understanding of the social dynamics of forced migration' (Castles 2003: 22). In the wake of 9/11 and the preceding decade of globalization studies—including works by Bauman, Beck, and Castells—Castles gave one of the clearest, programmatic statements in this regard. In his overview article, 'Towards a Sociology of Forced Migration', he argued that sociologists should study forced migration because it has become an integral part of globalization, a system of selective inclusion and exclusion that exacerbates inequality and the North–South divide (in social rather than geographical terms). This system produces conflicts and forced migration and tends to blur distinctions between economic and forced migration. He furthermore stated that:

> It is clear that there can be no compartmentalized theory of forced migration. Theory, in this area, means analysing forced migration as a pivotal aspect of global social relations and linking it to an emerging new political economy in the context of US political and military domination, economic globalization, North-South inequality and transnationalism. (Castles 2003: 27)

The new conceptual lens of 'transnationalism', which entails a focus on transnational flows, networks, relations, different forms of capital, and social fields, represents the most significant break with the sociological tradition which otherwise has been insepa-rable from the nationalized 'container model' of society (Giddens 1995) and the perva-sive 'methodological nationalism' in social science (Wimmer and Glick-Schiller 2002). Despite being a field which to a large extent is defined by national or international leg-islation, forced migration studies have been much influenced by the transnationalist paradigm. This has been notable in the popularity of concepts such as 'diaspora' and in the imagination of a transnational alternative to the conventional durable solutions at international level (Sørensen, Van Hear, and Engberg-Pedersen 2002), but also as a model for solutions for IDPs who rather than having to return to their 'place of origin' might prefer to develop their 'mobile livelihoods' across rural-urban divides (Stepputat and Sørensen 2001a).

Despite its popularity, the theory of global social changes cannot explain the com-plexity of local responses to the conditions of selective exclusion/inclusion. Lindley (2010) provides a good example of a micro-sociological approach to understand-ing conflict-related mobility which gives a less homogenizing view of violent conflict and leaves more room for the agency of the people affected. As Turton (2003: 12) has remarked, the concept of 'forced migrant' tends to dehumanize people by denying them the role of being 'purposive actors' and thus ordinary people. Lindley shows that the way in which specific human capabilities and assets are affected and how socio-political protection changes in the trajectory of conflict inform peoples' decisions to flee or stay in an area of conflict. As the 'political economy of war' literature emphasized, war opens up opportunities for some people to thrive in such areas. In the same vein, Lubkeman (2005) suggests that violent conflicts affect patterns of migration in very different ways in different areas, giving the example of 'fragmented wars' (in areas of Mozambique) where local level dynamics are relatively more important factors of displacement than in the case of 'ethnic-nationalist' (Kosovo) or 'ethnic civil' wars (Rwanda).

In a conventional hierarchical definition of scales, the state occupies a middle posi-tion between the global and the local. Due to the legal or quasi-legal definitions of refu-gees and IDPs and the ambition of many scholars to influence a state-dominated policy field, forced migration has a 'symbiotic relationship' with the state (Betts 2009: 266). As the 1988 version of the sociology of forced migration indicates, this was not necessarily the way scholars saw it 25 years ago, since forced migration, in the 1970s and 1980s, was analysed as primarily an issue and responsibility of humanitarian agencies, that tended to bypass the host-state. However, since then, as Zetter (2007) also suggests, the state has taken centre stage in forced migration studies, if not explicitly then at least as the implied guarantor of human rights, the signatory of international conventions, and the ultimate arbiter in questions of territorial entry. In a sociological perspective, the rela-tionship to the state may be the primary distinguishing factor between forced and vol-untary movers (Hein 1993). The creation of refugees is part of the modern system of sovereign, territorial states, and indeed processes of state formation have been evoked as important drivers of forced migration (Zolberg 1983).

Rather than the process of decolonization that Zolberg used to build his hypoth-esis, policies in the 2000s associated the risk of forced migration with problems of governance and the legitimacy of 'fragile states'. Whereas state fragility could still be regarded as being related to a protracted process of state formation, we may also consider incorporating new trends in theoretical approaches to sovereignty, not least inspired by Agamben (1998). His work fitted so very well to the post 9/11 securitization of migration as part of the war on terror, but in particular to the mushrooming of camps and detention centres for asylum seekers and undocumented migrants who were kept at the 'threshold' of inclusion and exclusion and hence, in Agamben's theory, formed a ground for the performance and constitution of sovereignty. However, understanding sovereignty as being always tentative and precarious and hence contingent upon (threats of) violence visited with impunity upon the body, we may see the violence that is involved in displacement as linked to claims to sovereignty, not only of states but also of other political and moral communities: religious, national, or local communities, vigilante groups, drug cartels, warlords, etc. (Hansen and Stepputat 2005). This would account for many situations of forced migration which are not related to the state. In fact, if we look beyond the legal categorization, the degree of force involved in mobility, displacement, and emplacement may be what distinguishes particular forms of migration from others (Jansen and Löfving 2009).

THEMES AND ISSUES

As is the case with other disciplinary contributions, the gaze of those informed by sociology has tended to be defined by policy labels and categories, such as refugees, IDPs, flight/uprooting, local integration, resettlement, repatriation, or development induced displacement. Nonetheless, beyond this tendency, we discern classical sociological themes and issues which have made an impact in forced migration studies. These are questions of categorization and labelling, processes of integration and citizenship, and the analytical categories of gender, class, and ethnicity.

Labels and Categorization

Against the generally policy-defined nature of forced migration studies, a significant sociological contribution to the field has been pieces which, in the spirit of Foucault and Goffman (see Wood 1985), have analysed how policy labels and categorizations work in terms of power relations and with what effects (Zetter 2007; Bakewell 2008; Polzer 2008). Labelling is a particularly forceful attribute of bureaucracies and an important means of state performance. In Wood's words, labels tend to objectify people by 'de-linking' them from their 'story', turning them into standardized 'cases', and 're-linking' them to the institutions that administer the labelling and the actions—such as the issuing of documents—that depend on this process. The normalization of labels conceals the highly politicized role of labelling in structuring and mediating social relations (Zetter 2007: 188).

The linking of labels and resources tends to reinforce the identification with the label, but the literature has also amply shown how people move 'in' and 'out' of labels. This happens when people's life trajectories take them through different labels in slightly arbitrary ways, as in the case of pastoralists in the African Horn (Turton 1996), or because people have a very context-dependent and pragmatic relationship to 'their' label as in the case of IDPs in Peru, a case which also illustrates the relative weakness of the IDP label in terms of protection and entitlements (Stepputat and Sørensen 2001). Such cases also illustrate the point that there is little to show that traditional labels and categories of forced migration are 'sociologically significant in the sense of describing a set of characteristics that are innate or defining features of a theoretically distinct population group' (Black 2001: 64). This is also why people often do not live up to the expected characteristics that are 'bundled together' in the categories (Polzer 2008). This may lead institutional representatives and others to see people as being dysfunctional, cheating, or unauthentic as expressed in concepts such as 'illegal' or 'bogus' asylum seekers.

The political and bureaucratic dynamics of labelling constitute a constructive field of studies of itself, even as such studies tell us more about the agents, structures, and effects of labelling than about the people labelled. Labels have proliferated with the development and effects of the international migration regime (Zetter 2007), now including 'deportees' and 'trafficking victims', as well the definition of new challenges such as climate change and environmental degradation. One example is the politically significant notion of 'mixed flows', the 'complex' population movements of irregular migrants, refugees, and asylum seekers, stateless persons, unaccompanied minors, and other vulnerable persons travelling in an irregular manner along similar routes, using similar means of travel.

However, the focus on policy labels, and more broadly categorization, creates some analytical problems of categorical invisibility (Polzer 2008) as the relative invisibility of host populations, urban refugees, and self-settled displaced populations suggests.

(Re-)integration and Citizenship

Social integration has been a central theme in sociology, and in particular in its functionalist versions, as demonstrated by the Chicago School's dominant position in migration studies until the 1990s, when the focus on immigration and assimilation began giving way to transnational approaches. In regard to forced migration, functionalist approaches marked early developments, partly in studies of resettlement of South-East Asian refugees in developed countries in the 1970s–80s, and partly via studies of 'involuntary resettlement' in the South that theorized a phased, linear model of reintegration. They have since been criticized and superseded, but the notion of 'integration' continues to re-emerge, both in research and policy. However, more recent approaches explore integration as a more relational process, depending on the overall policy environment and acceptance; the livelihood opportunities of hosts and displaced people; and the mutual relationship between these groups (Jacobsen 2001).

One line of thinking developed around ideas of entitlements and socio-economic integration. Against the former studies, Cernea (1997) developed a non-linear, socio-economic model of 'impoverishment risks' in regard to development induced displacement. The model pinpointed the loss of job, land, and other assets, economic marginalization, and social disintegration that generally result from displacement, but it was also designed as an instrument to improve policies of restitution and reintegration. With a few additions (violence, the loss of education, and political participation), the model has been suggested as valid in relation to conflict induced displacement as well, but it has also been criticized for the limited space accorded to the agency and capabilities of displaced persons (Muggah 2000). Finally, 'involuntary immobility' is also associated with risks of impoverishment (Lubkeman 2008), resulting in 'displaced livelihoods' (Stepputat 2002) and implying a process of integration in reverse for those who stay in place.

Another line of thinking developed around the notion of citizenship. Against the normative assumption of equal citizenship within a state's territory, newer approaches have looked at how the practice of citizenship varies according to factors such as class, ethnicity, region, or religious identity. Whereas such factors often influence who becomes displaced in the first place, displacement makes it very visible how conditions of 'local citizenship' define processes of integration (Brun 2005).

When it comes to forced migrants who have crossed borders, the turn towards transnationalist approaches has also changed how integration is perceived. Against assimilationist approaches, more recent studies show that many refugees, maybe more so than other migrants, build intense political relations with their countries of origin and the wider 'diaspora'. However, the interesting point is that engagement in this kind of associational life does not seem to represent a hindrance for integration (Wahlbeck 1999).

Gender, Class, and Ethnicity

Influenced by the prevailing interpretation of the 1951 Convention as conferring individual status, forced migrants have generally been conceptualized as individuals, even when the right to family unity has been recognized. Within sociology, attempts to link micro-level occurrences to macro-level social transformation have received increasing attention (e.g. Castles 2003), as have the workings of the relationship between structure and agency (Bakewell 2010). At the micro-level, sociology understands migration as being influenced by and structured around social relations, in particular those relations pertaining to community, family, and gender (on the latter, see Fiddian-Qasmiyeh, this volume). Within each relational category, the main distinguishing or difference-producing factors have been analysed within the contexts of class, ethnicity, and generation, often 'embodied in hierarchies of power and social status, in positions in home and host communities, and in work and domestic relationships' (Van Hear 2010: 1531).

Sociologists interested in micro-level theory have pointed to family and gender relations as crucial to the refugee experience, in particular in regard to family separation during conflict, flight, or prolonged periods of family reunification arrangements (Jastram and Newland 2003). When conflicts break out, only few are able to flee as a family. Some family members may have died and remaining family members may be forced to take different routes. When societal institutions break down, the family may assume greater than usual importance. Family functions around physical care, protection, and emotional support are difficult to maintain during dispersal. From both a sociological and a feminist standpoint, the tendency to see women, men, or children in relation to idealized notions of 'family' has been criticized, as has the use of the family or household unit without regarding the gender and generational struggles taking place within it as well as the differentiated effects forced migration has on individual family members. In a special issue of *Forced Migration Review* in 1999, El-Bushra reiterated that forced migration impacts differently on women and men, that women's specific needs and aspirations have generally been ignored, but also that giving preference to women in assistance programmes may contribute to eroding men's traditional roles as protectors, providers, and decision makers. An example of conflicting 'traditional' versus 'changed' gender relations during flight among Guatemalan refugees in Mexico was highlighted by Pessar (2001). Here female Guatemalan refugees, under the tutelage of international NGOs, became exposed to human rights and women's rights discourses and through them came to see themselves and their citizenship claims beyond traditional gender norms. Upon return to Guatemala, however, their transnational rights discourses were thwarted by an entrenched and state-enforced patriarchy that sought to reinstall traditional gender hierarchy (Pessar 2001). Furthermore, Sørensen and Stepputat (2001) found that migration and refugee experiences impact differently on women and men of different generations precisely because local communities and states bestow authority on moving subjects according to gender.

Concerning class, Bauman (1998: 9), from a meso-sociological perspective, has argued that 'mobility has become the most powerful and coveted stratifying factor' in late modernity, connecting social hierarchies to movement and restriction on movement. Furthermore, as the costs of migration have multiplied with the increasingly restrictive international migration regime, migrants' and asylum seekers' socio-economic background has become ever more important in shaping the forms, patterns, and impacts of their movement. The better-off can reach more resourceful and secure destinations while the poorer become relegated to less secure forms of migration to less attractive destinations. While class to some extent explains the timing of exits in particular cases of forced migration—the better-off leaving first—it does not determine the outcome. Rather, class contributes explanations for the routes, forms, means, and destinations of particular movements.

Ethnicity, on the other hand, has remained somewhat of a 'hot potato' within sociology. Although one of the first to bring the term 'ethnic group' into social studies was the German sociologist Max Weber, generally sociologists have left the study of ethnicity to anthropologists. Weber (1978) defined ethnic groups as those who entertain a subjective belief in common descent because of similarities in phenotype, customs, historical memories of colonization or migration, or any combination of these. It is the effectiveness of social action and above all the political aspect of group action that inspires belief in common ethnicity and transforms group membership into a political culture (Malesevic 1988). Zolberg (1988) was among the first to point out how the spread of the nation state as a universal model for organizing political communities concomitantly produced refugees who did not fit national definitions of membership. The unprecedented scale of forced migration due to ethnicity during the twentieth century formation of nation states in former multi-ethic or colonial territories appears to confirm Zolberg's theory.

METHODOLOGIES

Castles defines the specific sociological focus as on the one hand 'connecting forced migration with social relations, ideas, institutions and structures at various levels (global, regional, national and local),' and on the other hand 'processes of loss of identity and of rebuilding community'. Whereas the field invites multidisciplinarity, 'the specific character of sociology lies in its theoretical and methodological approaches' (Castles 2003: 22–3). In general, research into forced migration has given more attention to those affected by it than to the processes causing the movements. However, one distinguishing factor of the sociology of forced migration is that it has developed in tandem with studies of voluntary/economic migration and focused attention on the social dynamics of the migratory process and processes of global social transformation in both areas of origin and destination. Thus attention to multi-locality is one distinguishing methodological aspect.

Over the years, forced migration research has been criticized for lacking sound methodological principles. Before 1988 data collection was often induced by the humanitarian, international agencies and their needs for improving logistics (Harrell-Bond 1988) and only few researchers applied participatory methods as a way of comprehending refugees' perspectives (Mazur 1988). Studies disproportionally emphasized camps and settlements over research into self-settled or spontaneously settled people (Bakewell 2008).

Reviewing the complete 2002 volume of *Journal of Refugee Studies*, Jacobsen and Landau (2003) found that the research published used a wide range of quantitative and (in particular) qualitative research designs and techniques. However, key methodological components often remained unrevealed, partly due to a tendency towards 'advocacy' with the explicit objective of alleviating the suffering of the people involved, partly due to security issues, both that of the people and communities involved ('do no harm') and that of the researchers (when risk does not justify adherence to principles). The review pointed to problems in data collection methods too often relying on snowballing or access through a particular NGO, church, or camp, and rarely on large-scale survey data sets. Furthermore, the lack of control groups made it 'difficult to assess the extent to which refugee-related variables cause the particular problem being discussed or whether other social, political or economic factors common to everyone living in the research area account for the variance' (Jacobsen and Landau 2003: 194). Finally, they found very little forced migration research to be replicable and comparable. Studies based on small samples or on stakeholder interviews, typically selected on the basis of accessibility, rarely yield a material that allows for testing of competing hypotheses and causal relationships, nor do they allow comparisons across different groups in a single location, or across time and space.

The inclination of forced migration research to have an impact on the problems of those affected and be able to influence policy has led to cooperation with related areas such as development and disaster studies. This relationship is also reflected in methodology, of which the livelihood approach probably has had the largest impact. Livelihood thinking dates back to the work of Robert Chambers in the mid-1980s, who developed the idea of 'sustainable livelihoods' with the intention to enhance the efficiency of development cooperation. The approach focuses on 'the capabilities and resources people possess (natural physical, human socio-political and financial assets) and how these are mobilized, and mediated by the wider structural environment (of policies, institutions and processes), to provide a means of living' (Lindley 2010: 28). In forced migration research, the approach has been adapted to account for changing distributions of power and wealth, societal change due to conflict, and people's capacity to adapt livelihood strategies for survival, coping in conflict-affected situations and locations. The sociological concept of 'mobile livelihoods' (Sørensen and Olwig 2002) furthermore emphasizes the ways in which making a living links up with wider patterns of mobility, the range and variation in mobility that population movements involve, the social institutions and networks facilitating, sustaining, or hindering mobile livelihoods, and the social and spatial practices of mobile populations.

Methodologically speaking, a mobile livelihood approach requires attention to mobility prior to, during, and after conflict. This resonates well with Lubkemann's suggestion to conduct empirical investigation of 'what may in fact be a much more complex, varied and ambiguous array of experiences that stem from wartime migration' (Lubkemann 2008: 456). While loss and disempowerment can be the effect of forced migration, displacement may equally produce an ambiguous mix of both loss and economic, social, and political empowerment. The relationship between migration and its social meaning or effects must therefore always be considered an empirical question, to be studied by including a baseline of the role that mobility already played in the life strategies and social organization of populations *prior to* displacement.

We end this short and partial review of methodological discussions in the sociology of forced migration by agreeing with Lubkemann (2008) and Castles' (2010) observations that ambiguity, complexity, diversity, context, and historical developments should be the building blocks in any middle range methodology. Sociologists would generally be well equipped to carry out such analysis from both a qualitative and quantitative angle.

Looking Back and Ahead

Looking back at the sociological contributions to the field of forced migration studies over the past quarter of a century, a number of continuities stand out. First, the problem of making clear distinctions between voluntary and forced migration has been a recurrent issue in sociological contributions which have pointed to new areas and processes, in which the distinction is hard to draw or where it makes little analytical sense to uphold. Second, it is striking that all of the considerable number of theoretical contributions have stated that the field lacks theoretical reflection and sophistication. Third, and also paradoxically, many have mentioned, yet challenged, the tendency of forced migration studies to be restricted by policy-defined labels and questions. Thus, in a way, these problems and paradoxes define the field and provide drivers of sociological analysis in terms of the continuous engagement with traditional themes such as structure/agency, integration as relation, and the political dynamics of labelling.

Yet there are also considerable changes which characterize the field, partly relating to the process of globalization and partly to the associated theoretical and methodological developments, such as transnationalism, the notion of diaspora, and multi-sited fieldwork. As Castles (2003) argued, forced migration may be seen as one of the defining characteristics of the current phase of globalization, and together with the more general issue of migration it has moved to the top of the political agenda, and increasingly so beyond the global North as well. The migration regime itself produces new forms of forced migration and indeed of 'involuntary immobility', including trafficking, encampment, and deportations which have disruptive effects on families, communities, and even nations. Furthermore, with the renewed scramble for resources, including for land, forced displacement is likely to take on even more importance, both in rural and urban areas. Indeed the sociology of evictions should be an expanding issue within studies of forced migration, moving on from the 'development induced' displacement paradigm.

As mentioned, the state has come to occupy an important position in the sociology of forced migration. However, there are several indications that studies should move beyond states and examine the role of private, non-state actors and the ways they relate to forced migration. The tendency towards outsourcing, privatization, and the concomitant creation of legal as well as illicit 'migration industries' (Sørensen and Gammeltoft-Hansen 2013) is one important field. Another is the role of non-state actors in displacing people from their homes (or restricting their mobility), be they corporations, communities, criminal organizations, or other entities that use force in the name of the community, development, security, or other forms of justification. Indeed, a central theoretical concern in future studies should be the use, legitimization, and effects of force that break the links between people and places or hinders the mobility necessary for upholding livelihoods.

In this regard, forced migration studies as a field where disciplines meet, overlap, and (ex)change has much to offer sociology. Good examples are ideas of 'mobile livelihoods' and other challenges to the 'sedentarist' thinking and 'container-images' of society that characterized forced migration studies some time before the emergence of the 'new' or 'critical mobilities' paradigm within sociology (Urry 2007).

REFERENCES

Agamben, G. (1998) *Homo Sacer: Sovereign Power and Bare Life*. Stanford, CA: Stanford University Press.

Bakewell, O. (2008) 'Research beyond the Categories: The Importance of Policy Irrelevant Research into Forced Migration'. *Journal of Refugee Studies* 21(4): 432–53.

Bakewell, O. (2010) 'Some Reflections on Structure and Agency in Migration Theory'. *Journal of Ethnic and Migration Studies* 36(10): 1689–708.

Bauman, Z. (1998) *Globalization: The Human Consequences*. Cambridge: Polity Press.

Betts, A. (2009) 'Forced Migration Studies: "Who are We and Where are We Going?"' Report on IASFM 12. *Journal of Refugee Studies* 23(2): 260–9.

Black, R. (2001) 'Fifty Years of Refugee Studies: From Theory to Policy'. *International Migration Review* 35(1): 57–78.

Brun, C. (2005). 'Women in the Local/Global Fields of War and Displacement in Sri Lanka'. *Gender, Technology and Development* 9(1): 57–80.

Castles, S. (2003) 'Towards a Sociology of Forced Migration and Social Transformation'. *Sociology* 37(13): 13–34.

Castles, S. (2010) 'Understanding Global Migration: A Social Transformation Perspective'. *Journal of Ethnic and Migration Studies* 36(10): 1565–86.

Cernea, M. (1997) 'The Risks and Reconstruction Model for Resettling Displaced Populations'. *World Development* 25(10): 1569–87.

El-Bushra, J. (1999) 'Gender and Forced Migration' (editorial) *Forced Migration Review* 9: 4–7.

Gammeltoft-Hansen, T., and Sørensen, N. N. (eds.) (2013) *The Migration Industry and the Commercialization of International Migration*. London: Routledge.

Giddens, A. (1995) *Nation-State and Violence*. Los Angeles: University of California Press.

Hansen, T., and Stepputat, F. (2005) *Sovereign Bodies*. Princeton: Princeton University Press.

Harrell-Bond, B. (1988) 'The Sociology of Involuntary Migration: An Introduction'. *Current Sociology* 36(2): 1–6.

Hein, J. (1993) 'Refugees, Immigrants and the State'. *Annual Review of Sociology* 19: 43–59.

Jacobsen, K. (2001) 'The Forgotten Solution: Local Integration for Refugees in Developing Countries'. Working Paper no. 45, New Issues in Refugee Research. Geneva: UNHCR.

Jacobsen, K., and Landau, L. B. (2003) 'The Dual Imperative in Refugee Research: Some Methodological and Ethical Considerations in Social Science Research on Forced Migration'. *Disasters* 27(3): 185–206.

Jansen, S., and Löfving, S. (2009) *Struggles for Home: Violence, Hope and the Movement of People*. Oxford: Berghahn Books.

Jastram, K., and Newland, K. (2003) 'Family Unity and Refugee Protection'. Pp. 555–603 in E. Feller, V. Türk, and F. Nicholson (eds.), *Refugee Protection in International Law: UNHCR's Global Consultations on International Protection*. Cambridge: Cambridge University Press.

Lindley, A. (2010) 'Leaving Mogadishu: Towards a Sociology of Conflict-Related Mobility'. *Journal of Refugee Studies* 23(1): 2–22.

Lubkemann, S. C. (2005) 'Migratory Coping in Wartime Mozambique: An Anthropology of Violence and Displacement in "Fragmented Wars"'. *Journal of Peace Research* 42(4): 493–508.

Lubkemann, S. C. (2008) 'Involuntary Immobility: On a Theoretical Invisibility in Forced Migration Studies'. *Journal of Refugee Studies* 21(4): 454–75.

Malesevic, S. (1988) *The Sociology of Ethnicity*. New York: Sage.

Mazur, R. E. (1988) 'Refugees in Africa: The Role of Sociological Analysis and Praxis'. *Current Sociology* 36(2): 43–60.

Muggah, R. (2000) 'Through the Developmentalist's Looking Glass: Conflict-Induced Displacement and Involuntary Resettlement in Colombia'. *Journal of Refugee Studies* 13(2): 133–64.

Pessar, P. (2001) 'Women's Political Consciousness and Empowerment in Local, National, and Transnational Contexts: Guatemalan Refugees and Returnees'. *Identities: Global Studies in Culture and Power* 7(4): 461–500.

Polzer, T. (2008) 'Invisible Integration: How Bureaucratic, Academic and Social Categories Obscure Integrated Refugees'. *Journal of Refugee Studies* 21(4): 476–97.

Richmond, A. H. (1988) 'Sociological Theories of International Migration: The Case of Refugees'. *Current Sociology* 36(2): 7–25.

Sørensen, N. N., and Stepputat, F. (2001). 'Narrations of Authority and Mobility'. *Identities: Global Studies in Culture and Power* 8(3): 313–42.

Sørensen, N. N., Van Hear, N., and Engberg-Pedersen, P. (2002) 'The Migration-Development Nexus: Evidence and Policy Options'. *International Migration* 40(5): 3–47.

Sørensen, N. N., and Olwig, K. F. (eds.) (2002) *Work and Migration: Life and Livelihoods in a Globalizing World*. London: Routledge.

Stepputat, F. (2002) 'The Final Move? Displaced Livelihoods and Collective Returns in Peru and Guatemala'. Pp. 202–24 in N. N. Sørensen and K. F. Olwig (eds.), *Work and Migration: Life and Livelihoods in a Globalizing World*. London: Routledge.

Stepputat, F., and Sørensen, N. N. (2001) 'The Rise and Fall of "Internally Displaced People" in the Central Peruvian Andes'. *Development and Change* 32: 769–91.

Turton, D. (1996) 'Migrants and Refugees: A Mursi Case Study'. Pp. 96–110 in T. Allen (ed.), *In Search of Cool Ground: War, Flight, and Homecoming in Northeast Africa*. London: James Currey.

Turton, D. (2003) 'Refugees, Forced Resettlers and Other "Forced Migrants": Towards a Unitary Study of Forced Migration'. Working paper no. 94, UNHCR, Evaluation and Policy Analysis Unit.

Urry, J. (2007). *Mobilities*. Cambridge: Polity Press.

Van Hear, N. (2010) 'Theories of Migration and Social Change'. *Journal of Ethnic and Migration Studies* 36(19): 1531–6.

Van Hear, N. (2012) 'Forcing the Issue: Migration Crisis and the Uneasy Dialogue between Refugee Research and Policy'. *Journal of Refugee Studies* 25(1): 2–24.

Wahlbeck, Ö. (1999) *Kurdish Diasporas: A Comparative Study of Kurdish Refugee Communities*. London: Macmillan.

Weber, M. (1978) *Economy and Society*. Berkeley: University of California Press.

Wimmer, A., and Glick-Schiller, N. (2002) 'Methodological Nationalism and beyond: Nation-State Building, Migration and the Social Sciences'. *Global Networks* 2(4): 301–34.

Wood, G. (1985) 'The Politics of Development Policy Labeling'. *Development and Change* 16: 347–73.

Zetter, R. (2007) 'More Labels, Fewer Refugees: Remaking the Refugee Label in an Era of Globalization'. *Journal of Refugee Studies* 20(2): 172–92.

Zolberg, A. R. (1983) 'The Formation of New States as a Refugee-Generating Process'. *Annals of the American Academy of Political and Social Science*, 467: 24–38.

CHAPTER 8

LIVELIHOODS AND FORCED MIGRATION

KAREN JACOBSEN

INTRODUCTION

MILLIONS of forcibly displaced people living in and outside camps seek to support themselves and their families often with minimal humanitarian assistance, and in the face of active resistance by governments and citizens of host countries. Yet it is important that displaced people be supported in their livelihood efforts so that they can provide for their families when humanitarian assistance is insufficient. Pursuing a livelihood can also help people recover aspects of their lives that have been disrupted by displacement, including psychosocial damage. Recognizing this, UNHCR and their implementing partners have sought to implement various forms of livelihood programming since the late 1990s.

This chapter contributes to a theory of 'displaced livelihoods'. I argue that such a theory is warranted because the pursuit of livelihoods by forced migrants is different from those of other migrants or those who are equally poor or discriminated against. There are three key differences, which create particular livelihood difficulties. First, all forced migrants begin from a position of loss, including the loss of assets, family and community, and often emotional and physical health. A second distinctive issue concerns the socio-political, legal, and policy factors in the host country. Forced migrants must try to re-establish their livelihoods in a policy context that is often weighted against them. One of the most obvious differences compared with other migrants is that refugees and internally displaced people (IDPs) are often required to live in camps. A third distinction is that refugees and IDPs, unlike other migrants, are often the recipients of humanitarian assistance, and increasingly, livelihoods programmes. While humanitarian assistance can support livelihoods, unexpected or indirect negative effects can arise, and sometimes such support can backfire.

As I will argue, these differences create specific disadvantages for forced migrants, and must be addressed if displaced livelihoods are to be supported. While the three issues are relevant for all forced migrants, I focus on refugees rather than IDPs, the most important difference being that IDPs are citizens rather than 'foreigners' and thus are not constrained by laws and policy pertaining to non-citizens. In any particular refugee setting, significant individual and group variation, even within the same host country, characterize each of these three distinctions. Not all refugees arrive at their places of asylum impoverished, and some nationalities do better than others. For example, in Cairo, many Iraqi refugees arrived with more assets, including education and financial assets, and are much less impoverished than other groups such as Ethiopians or Sudanese. A theory of displaced livelihoods must address these diverse outcomes.

The chapter begins with a brief discussion of the evolving theory of livelihoods and poverty, and social exclusion theory. I then explore the three distinctions in more detail and conclude with some proposals regarding future advocacy, programming, and research.

LIVELIHOODS THEORY AND FORCED MIGRATION

Most definitions of livelihoods stem from Chambers and Conway's 1992 definition: *the means of gaining a living*, including livelihood capabilities, tangible assets, such as stores and resources, and intangible assets, such as claims and access (cited in de Haan and Zoomers 2005: 27). The study of livelihoods of forced migrants straddles the poverty alleviation literature and the literature on undocumented migration, since many refugees live without formal status in host countries. During the 1990s, 'sustainable livelihoods' became an important theme in development policy, with sustainability defined in terms of 'long-term flexibility and ... ecological soundness' (de Haan and Zoomers 2005: 31). The sustainable livelihoods framework thus emerged, modelled as a system comprising the different capabilities, assets, and activities required to pursue a living. Livelihoods assets are more than simply material ones—such as land, livestock, or money—they include human capital such as health, education, skills and experience, and social capital. The latter is of particular importance to forced migrants, who draw on the social capital that comes from co-national networks already in place in their destinations. Such networks provide assistance when migrants first arrive and help them find housing and employment (Calhoun 2010).

However, households and individuals must be able to *access* their livelihoods assets. Refugees are often unable to utilize their human capital, such as skills and experience acquired in their home countries, because they are denied permission to work, lack the appropriate credentials, or are faced with discrimination at the workplace. A useful approach to understanding this denial of access is social exclusion theory, which portrays poverty as 'a failure caused by bottlenecks in access to capitals' (Bhalla and Lapeyre 1997; de Haan and Zoomers 2005: 33). The mechanisms of exclusion include monopolizing access to resources through property relations (laws, policies, and regulations) or by using 'certain social or physical characteristics such as race, gender, language, ethnicity, origin or religion to legitimize this fencing-in of opportunities.... This "social closure," a form of collective social action, results in exclusion and poverty and gives rise to social categories of eligibles and ineligibles' (de Haan and Zoomers 2005: 34). These power relations in the host context are crucial in understanding the livelihoods experience of forced migrants.

As scholarship on livelihoods has evolved, the importance of livelihood assets has come to be recognized beyond simply meeting basic needs. Rather, they are seen to give meaning to a person's world:

> Assets should not be understood only as things that allow survival, adaptation and poverty alleviation: they are also the basis of agents' power to act and to reproduce, challenge or change the rules that govern the control, use and transformation of resources. (Bebbington (1999), cited in de Haan and Zoomers 2005: 32)

If assets give people power to act, the loss of assets becomes doubly consequential. For refugees, losses incurred during the journey combined with lack of access to assets in the host country means they are deeply disempowered, constrained in their ability to act and to challenge rules and power structures. The strategies which refugees utilize to overcome such disempowerment are therefore of great interest, as they point the way to empowering other marginalized groups.

Lack of Data

Theory and related empirical work on refugee livelihoods is characterized by a notable lack of quantitative data from nationally representative probability samples that have refugees as the target population. Surveys of immigrants in the US and Spain have enabled cross-country comparisons (Connor and Massey 2010), but few studies have sought to focus on refugees in such data sets. Population-based studies focusing on the livelihoods of forced migrants in developing countries are almost completely absent, and there is a notable shortage of economic analysis of displaced livelihoods. There are a number of reasons for this paucity of data. In areas of conflict and displacement, reliable secondary data such as census data or household surveys are often unavailable because data collection is dangerous or logistically difficult. This lack of data means it has been difficult to quantify the impact of displacement on livelihoods (Amirthalingam and Lakshman 2009). Independent researchers not affiliated with aid agencies also find it difficult to work in such areas, their travel impaired by insecurity and high expense. Much of the research on livelihoods thus takes the form of qualitative studies, often by anthropologists, and evaluations or assessments by aid agencies. While these are valuable, there is a significant lack of comparative analysis or population-based studies.

Nonetheless, in recent years, a number of surveys and profiling studies have begun to fill the livelihoods data gap, including studies of Iraqi refugees in Syria (Doocy et al. 2012), of IDPs in Sri Lanka (Amirthalingam and Lakshman 2009), and of refugees and other international migrants in four African cities (Landau and Duponchel 2011). The author has also conducted a series of profiling surveys comparing forced migrants and their neighbours in a variety of urban settings (FIC 2012a). Many of these studies have sought to demonstrate how refugees differ from other populations, and our knowledge and understanding of refugee livelihoods and the contextual problems they face has increased. However, the extent of such data is still relatively small and unsynthesized, compared to other areas of refugee research, and there is much room for additional studies if we are to understand how best to address the livelihood problems of forced migrants.

How Displaced Livelihoods are Different

As suggested earlier, three distinguishing sets of factors influence the ability of refugees to regain their livelihoods.

Loss, Trauma, and Impoverishment

With displacement, whether elsewhere in the country or across borders, comes the loss of economic and non-economic assets. Compared with labour migrants who can better plan their journeys, refugees and other forcibly displaced people often have to move quickly and have to abandon assets in their home areas. A study of Colombian IDPs found that 83 per cent had their land taken from them or had to abandon it when they fled (Kirchhoff and Ibáñez 2001), and this experience is widespread globally. One of the first scholars to model displacement was Michael Cernea, whose impoverishment risk and livelihood reconstruction model identifies eight types of losses that increase the risk of impoverishment when people are displaced. These losses include the expropriation of land, the loss of wage employment, and of housing, cultural space, and common property assets. Each type of loss has an impact on economic power, but also has psychological or cultural impact, leading to reduced social status and 'a psychological downward slide of ... confidence in society and self ...' (Cernea 1997: 1572–3).

Another loss—in the form of a serious financial burden incurred by migrants and refugees—is debt arising from travel costs during the journey, including loans for smuggler fees. Migration-related debt is compounded when households borrow to smooth consumption needs, particularly upon arrival and before employment is secured. The following quote from a Colombian refugee in Ecuador is typical of many refugees' experience around the world:

> Before arriving here, we had a 'finca' (ranch) and we planted vegetables and fruit. We had a chicken farm too. We ate well and lived well. It was our land. Then the armed groups began telling us we were with them and not the other. They declared us 'objetivos militares' and we had to escape. But they controlled us and we had a curfew. They would only let us out from 9am–6pm. If we didn't follow their directions, they would kill us. Finally, we escaped by pretending my wife was sick. We left everything behind like engines and more than 700 chickens. When we left, we only had a motorbike, which we sold for very little to buy shoes and to escape to Ecuador. (FIC 2012b)

Many forced migrants also experience intense personal loss—both of family members and of their mental, physical, and emotional health—as a result of the homeland experience that forced them to flee and their harrowing journeys. The experience of violence, trauma, loss of family members, and community all take a toll on people's ability to restart their lives (Cernea 1997). Yet there is almost no research on how this psychosocial loss affects people's livelihoods. Existing psychosocial research focuses on what can be done to help people recover from trauma (Nickerson et al. 2011; Hardgrove 2009), but much less has explored how psychosocial issues affect the ability of forced migrants to restart or pursue livelihoods—or how livelihoods could help people recover. This is clearly a gap in the literature.

All these losses put forced migrants at an economic disadvantage upon arrival. Over time, unless they can recover their livelihoods, they are at risk of further impoverishment. However, recuperating asset losses after displacement can be extremely difficult, because of the social exclusion at work in the host country context.

Obstacles and Enablers in the Host Context

Livelihoods recovery for forced migrants is often less about accessing assets lost in the place of origin—because these are too difficult to regain[1]—and more about finding ways to access livelihood assets in the destination area. These can be assets refugees already possess, such as the education and skills they bring from their home country, or new assets available in the destination country. However, access to assets is often blocked by social and political exclusion processes that arise within both the host population and the various refugee communities, and at the level of the state and institutions. This section explores these processes by focusing on two components of livelihoods: access to employment and access to services, especially financial ones. For each, we explore how refugees have attempted to circumvent the exclusion mechanisms in order to pursue livelihoods.

STATE REFUGEE POLICY AND REGULATIONS

At the state level, exclusion mechanisms constraining livelihoods take the form of restrictive laws and policies, and the bureaucracies and authorities that implement these policies. International refugee conventions, such as the 1951 Convention, include several Articles pertaining to livelihoods. These include the rights not to be deported (*non-refoulement*), to freedom of movement, and to work and own businesses. Some of these rights pertain only to those who are legally defined as refugees; others, such as *non-refoulement*, pertain to all asylum seekers (Bailey 2004). However, it is host country policies, rather than international refugee law, that determine the extent to which refugees are able to exercise these rights. Most host governments, particularly those of neighbouring sending countries, view refugees as 'guests' and establish a policy environment that prevents or inhibits permanent settlement. One way to do this is to obstruct refugees' livelihoods and integration by limiting freedom of movement and their ability to work or own businesses or property. Policy mechanisms include encampment policy, while bureaucratic obstructions prevent access to business licences or work permits.

Encampment

Countries with large populations of refugees often require refugees to live in camps, where their basic needs are provided by UNHCR and other humanitarian agencies. In 2010, of the 71 host countries with more than 5,000 refugees, 19 had encampment policies, all of them in Africa or Asia (UNHCR 2011a). Livelihood activities outside camps are strongly discouraged, and governments try to restrict refugees to camp areas by limiting permission to work or travel beyond the immediate area. However, particularly in protracted situations, humanitarian agencies are not able to meet all basic needs in camps, including food requirements (either in terms of dietary diversity or quantity), and necessities such as firewood for cooking. To meet these and other needs, families seek livelihoods opportunities in and outside camps. Some family members remain in the camps where they can access food aid and other humanitarian assistance, and others move to urban areas to find work. In many host countries, large numbers of refugees live outside camps, often in informal settlements that lack facilities and livelihood prospects.

Refugees who seek work outside camps face significant travel and other transaction costs, often in the form of bribes. Authorities tolerate violations of restrictive policies by 'turning a blind eye', but such 'tolerance' can take the form of extortion by state officials. Reports of such extortion are widespread. An illustrative example is the case of Bangladesh, where Rohingya refugees from Burma have lived in Cox's Bazar district since 1978, some in camps but most outside the camps in informal settlements (UNHCR 2011b). The Rohingyas have been the primary workers at the port for fifty years. In 2011, the local MP decreed that Rohingyas were not to be hired at the docks since they did not have national ID cards. This rule was slackened immediately when the authorities found themselves facing a shortage of labour on the docks. However the Rohingyas do not receive fair wages, and are extorted by a variety of actors, including the local political leaders who dominate the port. In addition, Rohingyas who collect firewood in the jungles around the camps must bribe forestry officials to gain entry to the forests (WFP 2012).

The Bangladesh case is typical of host countries where governments refuse to allow refugees to become self-reliant, while nevertheless allowing state and civil society actors to exploit them economically. Economic desperation drives refugees in and outside camps to pursue highly risky livelihoods strategies (called 'negative coping mechanisms' in the literature) including entering the sex trade and being recruited by gangs and militias.

Legal Status and Documentation

While host country regulations differ, having formal legal status generally allows refugees to reside in the country outside camps, to work, and to access a range of services. In most developing countries, however, relatively few refugees have formal status; they are more likely to be asylum seekers or (especially those in camps) to have prima facie status, and lack the right to pursue livelihoods. In such contexts, documents proving legal status can be an important source of protection; even documents granting only prima facie status can reduce police abuses such as arbitrary arrest or extortion by having a paper to present when stopped. However, as Landau argues, documentation does not always prevent abuses. In South Africa, official documentation does not prevent corrupt police forces or civil servants from ill-treating refugees. Official documents are poorly designed—often handwritten and illegible, or flimsy and easily destroyed—and they do not look legitimate. Documentation must be recognizable by authorities, and authorities trained to act according to the rights conferred, in order to provide effective protection (Landau 2006).

The extent to which legal status enables livelihoods is not clear. Many refugees work in the informal sector, where law enforcement is lax and refugees can circumvent the need for paperwork (Prost 2006; Böhme and Thiele 2012). Although this could mean that legal status and supporting documentation is less important, lack of documentation nonetheless makes refugees vulnerable. For instance, employers can exploit undocumented refugees and migrants who are less likely to report abuses due to fear of arrest or deportation.

Legal status can thus be seen as a social exclusion mechanism, as are work permits and licences to own a business. Even if permitted to work, like all foreigners, refugees must usually obtain a work permit, and this process is often difficult and financially burdensome. Many refugees lack awareness of their rights, of what a work permit is and how to obtain it, and they often lack the financial resources required to navigate complex and expensive bureaucratic procedures. For example, Egypt hosts some 95,000 refugees, does not require them to live in camps, and allows refugees to work (according to Article 53 of the Egyptian constitution). However, Egyptian labour legislation requires all non-nationals with valid residence to obtain a work permit. Foreigners must find an employer sponsor and pay application fees. The cost for a yearly work permit varies by nationality: Sudanese and Palestinians pay only 200 Egyptian pounds (approximately US$40), but Somalis, Iraqis, Eritreans, and Ethiopians pay 4,530 Egyptian pounds (US$900). Applicants must also prove that they are uniquely qualified, and that their work cannot be performed by an Egyptian. This is particularly challenging as most refugees are low skilled—like poor Egyptians. Several other regulations make it difficult for refugees (and all non-nationals) to be hired or to open a business (Jacobsen, Ayoub, and Johnson 2012).

In sum, even when refugees are permitted to work or own businesses, social exclusion processes, including bureaucratic procedures, can make obtaining work documents so complicated and burdensome that most refugees forgo them. The host authorities then turn a blind eye—both to the work and the exploitation that goes with it—because refugees provide cheap labour, or labour that nationals are unwilling to do. By contrast, host governments can choose to promote refugees' self-reliance. For example, in Ecuador, the Constitution guarantees equal rights for refugees, and the Ministry of Labour provides all refugees with a free 'work permit' that helps clarify their status to potential employers and facilitates initial entry into the market (Asylum Access 2011).

Civil Society

At the level of civil society, social exclusion processes are played out through anti-migrant xenophobic attitudes and behaviours towards refugees. These take the form of discrimination (exclusion from jobs, services, and social spaces) and harassment, ranging from verbal and emotional abuse to physical harassment. Open extortion takes the form of forced payment of bribes and unwarranted detention. Such actions create a culture of fear and intimidation that affects refugees' ability to pursue livelihoods. One consequence is increased livelihood transaction costs in the form of bribes (often related to the lack of documentation[2]), higher rents (because of discrimination by landlords), and extra 'fees' charged by employers (who use refugees as cheap labour). A culture of harassment also means refugees face greater threats from criminals, who know they are less likely to seek recourse or protection from the authorities. In times of political crisis, such as the Arab Spring or national elections, xenophobia increases, as it does when economic competition is high (Jacobsen, Ayoub, and Johnson 2012). Under such conditions, refugees habitually choose to stay inside or keep their children out of school, and do not pursue self-employment initiatives where the risk of being jailed or extorted is higher than the amount earned.

Some refugee-hosting countries, such as South Africa and Israel, have active media and civil society organizations that publicize and criticize this phenomenon of anti-migrant violence. In other host countries, such as Bangladesh, Kenya, and Egypt, where xenophobia is equally widespread, there is much less civil society opposition.

INSTITUTIONS

The provision of financial, educational, and health services is another zone of social exclusion, in which organizations and institutions create rules of access for refugees. In some cases, legal status is required to use services, but more often access is limited by charging refugees higher fees, or requiring them to obtain special documentation. In Nairobi, harassment by the police and extortion are barriers for urban refugees in accessing services such as education, healthcare, legal aid, and livelihoods (Campbell, Crisp, and Kiragu 2011). When school fees and hospital bills exceed their monthly income, individuals must take out loans and become indebted to other community members, employers, or moneylenders.

One problem confronting refugees is lack of access to financial assets in the form of services from formal institutions such as banks and microfinance institutions (MFIs). Credit facilities are not available to refugees because banks and MFIs consider refugees to be poor credit risks. Refugees are also excluded from access to savings accounts or investment accounts, as well as most forms of insurance. To open a bank account one needs evidence of a residential address (such as a utility bill), and often a national identity card, and most refugees lack this kind of documentation. In some countries, advocacy organizations have worked with banks to expand their access. For example, in South Africa, some banks waive the required 13-digit identity number, allowing refugees and temporary residents to open accounts. However, this is uncommon, and lack of access to bank accounts means refugees have to carry their cash around with them, increasing the likelihood of being extorted by police and making refugees a target for criminals (Landau 2006).

The absence of formal credit facilities means refugees have to take out loans from other sources. A common coping strategy is to borrow from their community, but informal credit and loan practices can result in extortion and entrapment of refugees. For example, in Cox's Bazar, Bangladesh, Rohingya refugee fishermen become victims of entrapment by loan sharks. Many refugee fishermen are unable to afford fishing equipment, and they borrow from local rich fisheries owners. Market buyers refuse to buy the refugee fishermen's fish because they know the refugee fishermen must repay their loans to the powerful fishery owner first, by selling their fish to the owner. The fishery owners are therefore free to determine the price of the fish, which they set lower than the market. This exploitation persists because refugee fishermen rely on the loans—which are also used for bail when the police arrest them (WFP 2012).

Refugee livelihoods are therefore constrained by social exclusion mechanisms at all levels: by the state, in civil society, and through institutions. Refugees seek to work around these constraints by drawing on the resources of their own communities. Humanitarian agencies also seek to support them.

Humanitarian Assistance and Livelihoods

Since the 1990s, humanitarian agencies and UNHCR have recognized the need to support the livelihoods (or 'self-reliance') of the displaced, because over half of the world's displaced people live outside camps and cannot be fully supported by humanitarian aid. Most of the large international NGOs and UNHCR now have rural and urban livelihoods programmes. In the past few years, how-to manuals and strategic plans have been written, and donors have contributed large amounts of funding both to assess how livelihoods can be supported and to fund programmes. As the Women's Refugee Commission says, 'everyone, from local community-based organizations to international nongovernmental organizations to policy makers and donors, wants to support, fund and implement more effective programs to support the self-reliance of the displaced' (WRC 2009: iii). Livelihoods programmes for refugees generally seek to support self-employment and wage employment by building human capital through vocational training, and by supporting small businesses through, *inter alia*, the provision of microfinance and business development services, legal support, job placement, apprenticeships, and mentoring.

Several problems confront livelihoods programming, however, particularly for refugees. The most important problem is political. Host governments are generally opposed to livelihoods programs, first, because they are seen as an avenue to permanent settlement, and second because governments resist enabling refugees to compete on a more equal economic footing with citizens. Such competition often results in opposition by citizenry—an unappetizing prospect for governments. Government resistance means that advocacy for refugee livelihoods, including the right to work, must be undertaken very sensitively, recognizing that more harm than good can be accomplished if governments react adversely. In settings where the government tends to turn a blind eye to refugees working, overly enthusiastic promotion of 'the right of refugees to work' can backfire significantly. The government might cease to turn a blind eye and respond harshly, even changing its refugee policy for the worse. The author has been told (off the record) of situations where UNHCR's efforts to promote refugees' right to work have resulted in a souring of the government's attitude and threats of more vigorous enforcement of restrictive policies.

A second problem is the risk that livelihoods programming targeted at refugees can lead to resentment and hostility by the host population. Outside camps, refugees live amongst the host population, sometimes sharing their housing and land and often dependent on them for their good will. Targeting only refugees for livelihoods programming can jeopardize this good will and lead to problems long after the programme has come to an end or run out of funds. One way around this is to adopt an *inclusive* approach by designing programming that supports the livelihoods of both the host population and the refugees. There are several reasons why such targeting could improve the livelihoods context for refugees. First, the government is more likely to look favourably on such programmes since they provide benefits to their citizens. Second, bringing nationals and non-nationals together in a learning environment (such as vocational training or business services development) can benefit refugees in terms of networking, potential partnerships, and an increased understanding of the local context. Third, inclusive programming can build social capital with the host community and potentially reduce antagonism, both because refugees are seen to be bringing resources (in the form of programmes) and because working/learning together is good for social relations.

Conclusion

Forced migrants arrive in asylum contexts having experienced many losses, and then confront numerous challenges as they try to pursue livelihoods. Social exclusion mechanisms, ranging from encampment policies to xenophobia and harassment on the street, limit their rights and abilities to pursue economic activities. Refugees must find ways to generate income, whether for start-up funds to finance a business or to pay the necessary bribes to obtain documentation. However, their income-generating activities often create new risks and forms of exploitation. Aid agencies search for ways to support refugee livelihoods, but achieving effective and feasible livelihood programming has proven difficult. Government authorities and many in civil society see refugees' livelihood success in terms of the competition it poses, and as a pull factor for others in the sending country. These fears are expressed in xenophobic attitudes that create significant problems for refugees. Combating the resistance of host countries to refugee livelihoods is thus a key advocacy issue for UNHCR and other refugee agencies. It may be that, rather than bringing in new and expensive livelihood programmes, aid agencies can best serve as advocates and facilitators of livelihoods—by helping refugees make connections (both among other refugees and with the host population), supporting activities that promote integration, or providing business development services, mentoring, and training. Nonetheless, aid agencies can only do so much; in the end it is the communities in which the refugees live that will be the strongest source of support.

Notes

1. When people flee their homes and abandon their property, regaining ownership can be difficult, especially if others have claimed these assets and much time has passed. In Colombia, Ibáñez and Moya (2009) found that only one-quarter of IDP households were able to recover their original asset base.
2. The need for funds to pay bribes to obtain documents, work permits, and licences is widely reported. In South Africa, corruption plagues the process of obtaining asylum documents; applicants often have to offer fees in order to file their asylum claims, even though this process is free by South African law (Landau 2006: 317).

REFERENCES

Amirthalingam, K., and Lakshman, R. W. D. (2009) 'Displaced Livelihoods in Sri Lanka: An Economic Analysis'. *Journal of Refugee Studies* 22(4): 502–24.

Asylum Access Ecuador (2011) ' "To Have Work is to Have Life": Refugees' Experience with the Right to Work in Ecuador'. <http://rtwasylumaccess.files.wordpress.com/2011/03/asylum-access-right-to-work-in-ecuador.pdf> (accessed 28 October 2012).

Bailey, S. (2004) 'Is Legal Status Enough? Legal Status and Livelihood Obstacles for Urban Refugees'. Master of Arts in Law and Diplomacy Thesis, Fletcher School of Law & Diplomacy, Tufts University.

Bebbington, A. (1999) 'Capitals and Capabilities: A Framework for Analysing Peasant Viability, Rural Livelihoods and Poverty'. *World Development* 27(12): 2021–44.

Bhalla, A., and Lapeyre, F. (1997) 'Social Exclusion: Towards an Analytical and Operational Framework'. *Development and Change* 28: 413–33.

Böhme, M., and Thiele, R. (2012) 'Is the Informal Sector Constrained from the Demand Side? Evidence for Six West African Capitals'. *World Development* 40(7): 1369–81.

Calhoun, N. (2010) 'With a Little Help from our Friends: A Participatory Assessment of Social Capital among Refugees in Jordan'. New Issues in Refugee Research UNHCR Research Paper no. 189.

Campbell, E. Crisp, J., and Kiragu, E. (2011) 'Navigating Nairobi: A Review of the implementation of UNHCR's Urban Refugee Policy in Kenya's Capital City'. UNHCR Policy Development and Evaluation Service (PDES). <http://www.unhcr.org/4d5511209.html> (accessed 28 October 2012).

Cernea, M. (1997) 'The Risks and Reconstruction Model for Resettling Displaced Populations'. *World Development* 25(10): 1569–87.

Connor, P., and Massey, D. S. (2010) 'Economic Outcomes among Latino Migrants to Spain and the United States: Differences by Source Region and Legal Status'. *International Migration Review* 44(4): 802–29.

de Haan, L., and Zoomers, A. (2005) 'Exploring the Frontier of Livelihoods Research'. *Development and Change* 36(1): 27–47.

Doocy, S., Burnham, G., Biermann, E., and Tileva, M. (2012) 'Field Report: Household Economy and Livelihoods among Iraqi Refugees in Syria'. *Journal of Refugee Studies* 25(2): 282–300.

FIC (Feinstein International Center) (2012a) 'Summary of Urban Profiling Studies Conducted by the Feinstein International Center, 2005–2012' <fic.tufts.edu>.

FIC (2012b) 'Refugee Livelihoods in Urban Areas: Identifying Program Opportunities'. Case study: Quito, Ecuador. Feinstein International Center, Tufts University. Draft.

Hardgrove, A. (2009) 'Liberian Refugee Families in Ghana: The Implications of Family Demands and Capabilities for Return to Liberia'. *Journal of Refugee Studies* 22(4): 483–501.

Ibáñez, A. M., and Moya, A. (2009) 'Do Conflicts Create Poverty Traps? Asset Losses and Recovery for Displaced Households in Colombia'. Research Working Papers 10, MICROCON—A Micro Level Analysis of Violent Conflict. <http://www.microconflict.eu/publications/RWP10_AMI_AM.pdf>.

Ibáñez, A. M., and Vélez C. E. (2008) 'Civil Conflict and Forced Migration: The Micro Determinants and Welfare Losses of Displacement in Colombia'. *World Development* 36(4): 659–76.

Jacobsen, K., Ayoub, M., and Johnson, A. (2012) 'Remittances to Transit Countries: The Impact on Sudanese Refugee Livelihoods in Cairo'. Working Paper No. 2, Center for Migration and Refugee Studies, The American University in Cairo.

Jacobsen, K., and Furst Nichols, R. (2011) 'Developing a Profiling Methodology for Displaced People in Urban Areas. Final Report'. Feinstein International Center, Tufts University.

Kirchhoff, S., and Ibáñez, A. M. (2001) 'Displacement Due to Violence in Colombia: Determinants and Consequences at the Household Level'. Discussion Papers on Development Policy No. 41, p. 45, Center for Development Research, Bonn, October.

Landau, L. B. (2006) 'Protection and Dignity in Johannesburg: Shortcomings of South Africa's Urban Refugee Policy'. *Journal of Refugee Studies* 19(3): 308–27.

Landau, L. B., and Duponchel M. (2011) 'Laws, Policies, or Social Position? Capabilities and the Determinants of Effective Protection in Four African Cities'. *Journal of Refugee Studies* 24(1): 1–22.

Nickerson, A., Bryant, R. A., Silove, D., and Steel, Z. A. (2011) 'Critical Review of Psychological Treatments of Posttraumatic Stress Disorder in Refugees'. *Clinical Psychology Review* 31: 399–417.

Prost, A. (2006) 'The Problem with "Rich Refugees": Sponsorship, Capital, and the Informal Economy of Tibetan Refugees'. *Modern Asian Studies* 40(1): 233–53.

UNHCR (2011a) *Statistical Year Book 2010*, Annex, Table 17. <http://www.unhcr.org/4ef9c7269. html>.

UNHCR (2011b) 'States of Denial: A Review of UNHCR's Response to the Protracted Situation of Stateless Rohingya Refugees in Bangladesh'. PDES/2011/13 <http://www.unhcr.org/cgi-bin/texis/vtx/home/opendocPDFViewer.html?docid=4ee754c19&query=Bangladesh%20Rohingya>.

Women's Refugee Commission (WRC) (2009) 'Building Livelihoods: A Field Manual for Practitioners in Humanitarian Settings'. <http://www.womensrefugeecommission.org/>.

World Food Programme (WFP) (2012) 'The Contribution of Food Assistance to Durable Solutions in Protracted Refugee Situations: Its Impact and Role in Bangladesh. A Mixed Method Impact Evaluation'. Draft.

CHAPTER 9

GEOGRAPHIES OF FORCED MIGRATION

MICHAEL COLLYER

INTRODUCTION

UNLIKE other disciplines in the social sciences, geography is distinguished neither by a particular approach to methodology, nor by a set of perspectives established by a limited number of canonical texts. Rather, geography is defined by a range of characteristic themes such as the relationship between humanity and the environment or the nature of space. Interest in these themes is clearly not unique to geographers, though geographers typically claim a unique perspective on them. Geography was once considered a 'synthetic discipline' since it combines perspectives on these broad themes from a range of disciplines (Sidaway and Johnston 2007). It remains highly interdisciplinary, even at a time when cross-discipline research is common and has therefore produced a wide variety of perspectives on forced migration, many of them overlapping with cogent disciplines in the social sciences.

The broadest level of speciality within geography is between physical geography and human geography. Research into forced migration is dominated by subdisciplines of human geography, including political, economic, social, cultural, and development geographies, with much less engagement from physical geographers. There are two partial exceptions to this. First is the substantial research focus at the interface between physical and human geography examining the relationships between forced migration and the environment. This area has expanded considerably in recent years through examinations of the impact of environmental (particularly climate) change on migration. Second, developments in the range of remote sensing and Geographical Information Systems (GIS) applications, have often come from geographers, particularly those working on the more technical branches of the discipline or related areas of IT. Resulting tools have reached a level of sophistication that has led to their widespread use in emergency response planning.

In assessing the body of research across the subdisciplines of human geography, it is difficult to be more specific than Black (1993) in the collection *Geography and Refugees*, where he considers research simply in terms of the causes, consequences, and spatial patterns of refugee movement and (as Black says) interest in these topics is hardly specific to geography. In the introduction to that volume, Black is sceptical about both the possibility and desirability of a Geography *of* Refugees, though this is more or less the task I attempt in this section in relation to the broader category of forced migrants. I agree with Black that enumerating the physical locations of forced migrants is both a practically impossible and normatively questionable aim. Yet by the end of the 1990s, Hyndman identified an alternative understanding of a 'geography of forced migration' (Hyndman 1999, 2000). Drawing on feminist theory, and combining elements of cultural and political geography with post-structural understandings of space, it introduced a much more critical thread to geographical interpretations of forced migration which has remained popular and influential.

The notion that space is not fixed or easily measurable is an old one, most associated with philosophers like Liebniz, but the implications of this, in terms of the transformation of space to serve political or economic ends, have only been investigated in detail over the last few decades. Migration, particularly forced migration, has provided an important empirical support for some of this work. Abstract theoretical notions about the 'production' of space are illustrated clearly by objectives expressed at European Council meetings to create 'extra-territorial processing zones' to examine asylum applications to the European Union beyond EU territory or the brief insistence of the French government that the international zone of Charles de Gaulle airport was not part of France, allowing *refoulement* of transit passengers with impunity. Alison Mountz's (2010) analysis of the Canadian governments 'long tunnel thesis' also highlights the production of new disciplinary spaces. In response to large-scale arrivals by boat from the late 1990s onwards, certain detention sites were redefined as 'ports of entry' at which the rights of migrants who had officially arrived in Canada did not fully apply. The comparison to the tunnel through which passengers disembark an aircraft allowed this suspended status to be maintained during longer-term detention. Similarly, developing regimes of interdiction in the Mediterranean targeted at 'transit migrants' can only be understood through the changing levels of obligations that states owe to non-citizens once they reach that state's territory (Collyer 2012). The refugee camp itself has become emblematic of spaces of 'exception' in Giorgio Agamben's work that has inspired an entire strand of analysis of forced migration, though also considerable critical commentary (Ek 2006).

This chapter examines three interrelated aspects of the geography of forced migration. First, questions of data and categorization underpin most social scientific approaches but there is a geographical specificity in the attention paid to issues of space and scale. New geographic technologies of analysis (Geographical Positioning Systems (GPS), GIS, or remote sensing) promise more accurate data and provide invaluable support to emergency operations. Yet such technologies are not politically neutral and may also have negative consequences, justifying established critiques of the political context of data (Crisp 1999). Second, geographic research has dominated investigations of the relationship between the environment and forced migration, but here again, definitions and categories are important. Geographers have typically sounded a cautious note about the possibility of establishing a link between environmental change and migration and particular scepticism around the concept of the 'environmental refugee'. Finally, the fundamental geographical concern with location in relation to certain significant borders shapes definitions and approaches to forced migrants. These themes are overlapping and they highlight the ways in which central geographical themes of space, location, scale, and environment have generated a particular perspective on forced migration. The following three sections consider these aspects of the geography of forced migration in turn: data, environment, and location.

Data and Categorization

One thing common to the bulk of geographical research is a strong empirical grounding. Methodologically, geographical work on forced migration covers the whole range of social scientific approaches, from strongly positivist to firmly post-structural, and the importance placed on data varies. Nevertheless, any knowledge of where and who forced migrants are depends on methods of counting, systems of categorization, and the politics and practices of distribution of that information, so data and the means of categorization are important considerations. There are plenty of sources of statistical information about forced migrants, including international organizations (chiefly UNHCR), national governments, NGOs, and individual targeted pieces of research and a range of techniques for gathering such information, some more associated with geography than others. There is also a substantial literature critiquing the processes of identifying, categorizing, and counting forced migrants (Crisp 1999).

Given this range of sources, data itself has a geography. For example, where governments are responsible for examining individual claims for asylum quite detailed information is collected from individual asylum seekers, whereas in areas where refugee status is granted on a collective basis, precise data may be more difficult to come by. Even where data is accurate, access is not a given. A series of studies by geographers such as Koser (e.g. Koser and Pinkerton 2002) have drawn on classic geographical work on the diffusion of information to show that, despite what many Western European governments appear to believe, the information on which individual asylum seekers base migration decisions is lacking any level of detail on comparative policy regimes. Diffusing information on the danger of certain migration routes has become an important strategy to try to dissuade irregular migrants, but the effectiveness of such information campaigns is unproven. This highlights the geographically uneven nature of information but also a range of other problems with large-scale data collection.

The categories on which such data is typically collected do not correspond with the 'forced migration' focus of this volume; neither asylum seekers nor refugees correspond exactly with the broader category of forced migrants and data is collected in a huge variety of ways. Data on individual characteristics of forced migrants are equally hard to come by in most contexts, even basic data on sex or age are often lacking. This fuels arguments of systematic bias in the application of international protection, which go beyond critiques that men and women are treated differently to an argument that the entire system of international protection is structurally deficient in gendered ways (Crawley 2001).

The motivations for data collection may also be questionable. It goes without saying that institutions collect data for their own interests, which are not necessarily shared with those of forced migrants. This has important consequences for the ethics of any research that cooperates directly with such collection but also implications for the accuracy of such data. Where data manifestly serve interests of disciplining and controlling migrant populations, as is typically the case with state data, migrants may not cooperate or may even have an incentive to report inaccurate information. Even institutions focused more clearly on refugee and migrant welfare, such as UNHCR, may use data in ways that are contrary to the interests of individual migrants (Verdirame and Harrell-Bond 2005). Finally, even where data is collected and accurate it may not be easily available due to practical or political issues with distribution

Geographical techniques are now widely used in the collection and presentation of data about forced migrants, and are often considered to resolve problems of accuracy, quality, and presentation. One of the most widely discussed technologies is GIS, which describes any piece of software that links stores of information to geographical positions, allowing maps to be updated automatically as associated data changes. GIS software is now used routinely to coordinate emergency response planning in situations around the world, including monitoring and responding to related forced migration (Cutter 2003).

There are a number of significant technical hurdles to the widespread uptake of GIS (Emrich, Cutter, and Weschler 2011); three most significant are worth mentioning here, though all are gradually being overcome. First, GIS software is expensive and requires a degree of technical expertise to operate effectively; web-based GIS such as Google Earth are beginning to change this, since they are free and relatively easy to use and community monitoring of certain areas of high environmental sensitivity now occurs using GIS. Second, new data to be added must be geo-referenced, that is, its location must be known, and this usually requires the use of GPS, though this is also becoming easier as handheld GPS are becoming more affordable and frequently integrated into other devices, such as mobile phones. Finally, most software requires new data to be added to pre-existing maps, which may not be sufficiently accurate or up to date. This is likely to be a particular issue in responding to natural disasters, such as earthquakes, floods, or tsunami, which may themselves have altered the landscape through which people are forced to move.

Remote sensing provides a potential solution to the lack of up-to-date information on the ground. Given the development of ultra-high-resolution images, data from satellites, which includes measurement on non-visible spectrums allowing things like cooking sources to be identified, provides a useful means of estimating populations when on the ground censuses are not feasible. It is not likely that remote sensing data would be available sufficiently quickly to be of use in natural disaster management. Surveying new maps is often the only solution where road or river networks have been destroyed or substantially altered and urgent response is required. The high cost and expertise required for new surveys means that this is still concentrated in specialist UN agencies such as OCHA or specialist NGOs like MapAction (<http://www.mapaction.org>). When time frames are more extended, remote sensing can provide a worthwhile source of information. Recent research has highlighted the utility of remote sensing to obtain estimates of the total population of the Darfur camps in Kenya, for example, where computer calculations were shown to be as accurate, and much quicker, than analysis of satellite photos with the naked eye (Kemper et al. 2011). As satellite imagery and the software necessary to analyse it becomes more widely available this technique is likely to become more widespread in the monitoring and control of mobile populations.

New technology is obviously not apolitical. Although many of the uses of GIS, GPS, and remote sensing in monitoring and responding to situations of forced migration are justified as furthering support and solidarity towards those migrants, this is not necessarily always the case. In 2008, UNHCR teamed up with Google to develop a new layer for Google Earth that can be downloaded to show the location of refugee camps with the aim of further awareness and solidarity with refugees around the world. Palestinian activist groups quickly raised objections, since the 27 Palestinian refugee camps in the Occupied Territories, which have existed for more than 50 years but are not administered by UNHCR, were excluded from the refugees layer (Sabbah 2008). On a more theoretical level, Franke (2009) has associated the requirement to locate refugees with UNHCR's need to locate human rights within particular nation states, a tendency, he argues, which inevitably restricts human freedoms expressed in the ability to move in the first place. Such normative issues of spatial theory have become a more significant focus of critical geographical research and are explored in more detail in the final section. Before then, this chapter turns to the substantial body of geographical research on the impact of the environment on forced migration.

ENVIRONMENT AND FORCED MIGRATION

Interest in the potential impact of the environment on forced migration dates to the 1970s. Although it has continually been presented as 'new', Étienne Piguet and colleagues (2011) remind us that even Ravenstein, in one of the earliest attempts to theorize migration in 1889, suggested 'unfavourable environment' as a reason motivating migration. Climate change is already affecting the environment, but not in a uniform, predictable fashion. Extreme climatic events are becoming more common and environmental variability is increasing (IPCC 2007). Most of the research in this area has envisaged a direct relationship between environmental change and migration and a focus on the numbers of people likely to be forced to move has become common (e.g. Gemenne 2011).

Recent geographical work has challenged this orthodox approach in four significant ways: it has highlighted the vast differences in numerical estimates and questioned the logical possibility of reaching any kind of accurate estimate of the numbers of people who will be forced to move; it has emphasized the interconnections between different motivations to migrate and developed a much more critical position on the possibility of isolating the environment as a discrete cause of movement; it has investigated potential destinations of migration related to environmental factors; finally, it has questioned the basis for protecting those forced to move by environmental factors, particularly the desirability of the term 'environmental refugee'.

Mainstream work on the impact of climate change on society has typically sought to establish the significance of the issue in terms of the numbers of people who will be forced to move over the next few decades. Numerical estimates of resulting forced migration vary wildly, from the tens of millions to a billion (Gemenne 2011). The most basic approach to estimating numbers involved working out how many people live a certain distance above the mean water mark and assuming that they would all be forced to move by sea level rise of a similar magnitude. This is an oversimplified approach since environmental change is far more complex than a simple measure of sea level rise and includes much greater and still largely unpredictable forms of climate variability. It also assumes that migration is an impact of climate change whereas, for the entire history of human settlement, migration has been a form of adaptation to environmental stress. Indeed, migration is one of a number of proactive responses to environmental stress that should be built into development interventions (Boano, Zetter, and Morris 2008). Recognition of the complexity of environmental factors and the understanding of migration as an adaptive strategy have characterized much recent geographical work on this issue and led geographers to reject the possibilities of numerical estimates of migration as an impossible task (Gill 2010).

Once migration is understood as an adaptive strategy, rather than an impact of environmental change, the impossibility of isolating the environment as a discrete factor motivating migration becomes more obvious. Environmental change does not necessarily provoke new migration, but further complicates established migration systems in which people move for reasons which may be partly environmental but are also related to established economic, political, social, and cultural factors. Black and colleagues (2011) build on these insights to develop a new approach to environmentally induced migration. Rather than asking if climate change will cause migration their preferred approach is to investigate how climate change will affect existing drivers of migration. They select case studies in Ghana and Bangladesh to demonstrate that the evidence of migration responses to climate change is highly variable; in some cases increased flooding reduces the likelihood of migration, for example, whereas in others it results in new attempts to diversify livelihood strategies through migration. This approach to migration has been taken up by two large-scale research projects: the UK Government Office of Science (Foresight 2011) and the European Commission funded 'Environmental Change and Forced Migration Scenarios (EACH-FOR)' (Warner et al. 2009).

Relatively little attention has been paid to potential destinations of environmental related migration (Findlay 2011). Given the dominance of events at migrants' point of origin in any consideration of the topic, origin factors have generally been prioritized in this literature. Although numerical estimates of environmentally forced migration provide very limited details of intended destinations they are frequently interpreted as referring to south to north migration. This is inaccurate. It is now well established that most migration resulting from environmental stress will be over very short distances and often circular in nature, as individuals return once a crisis is over (Findlay 2011).

A final key question in this area concerns the resolution of incidents of environmentally related displacement. The term 'environmental refugee' is still widely popular, and highlights the responsibility of the international community to act. Yet this term is widely rejected by geographers since the analogy with refugees is questioned (Gill 2010). Refugees are people whose bond with their own state has broken down, whereas those forced to move by the environment are frequently assisted by their own state. Black (2001) argues that it is in the interests of states to insist on the 'environmental refugee' label since they are a group to whom states owe fewer obligations. Blitz (2011) shares this concern but suggests that in certain cases—notably small, low-lying, island states that will likely be wiped out completely by sea level rise—individuals will effectively become stateless and it may be possible to make use of the statelessness convention, which he argues, offers greater potential as the basis for some kind of international agreement.

The Place of Forced Migration: Location and Spatial Theory

Space, and the related notion of location, are key geographical concepts and though it also figures significantly in related social science disciplines geographers accord a particular attention to spatial issues and have developed a range of approaches to related concepts, such as scale and territory, that provide theoretical support to research into forced migration. As the first subsection of this chapter argued, location is a key determinant of the categorization of forced migrants and these concepts allow geographers to question binary distinctions that are central to the understandings and categorizations of forced migration. These include the nature of the nation state as a political entity and the key role played by the international border in definitions of refugees, the construction of global level spatial distinctions, such as North and South but also, relatedly, notions of migration, mobility, and immobility, which are typically distinguished by the crossing (or failure to cross) significant international borders. In developing theoretical approaches to these issues, geographers have drawn freely from other disciplines. This section examines these various trends in research into spatial theory and forced migration.

One of the most fundamental spatial categories, which is widely questioned by critical geographical research is that of the nation state itself. The international border is clearly fundamental to definitions of one particular group of forced migrants, refugees, but the issue of whether or not any forced migrant remains on the territory of their state of citizenship is determinant of the rights they can legitimately claim from the state and their access to international protection. Treating the results of such a historically contingent and dynamic process as the creation of international borders as fixed, given, or 'natural' ontological categories is widely questioned by geographers, especially in the field of migration. A seminal article by Agnew (1994), arguing that the nation state should be seen as a dynamic collection of institutions, has remained tremendously influential in geographical research. Research into forced migration has developed approaches to 'denaturalize' the nation state by focusing on the experience of individuals involved in implementing nation-state policies (Mountz 2010). Yet the 'essentialist' view of the nation state as linking territory and culture may inform the perspectives of forced migrants themselves (Brun 2001). Understandings of 'emplacement' or rootedness as identified with a single location have been widely criticized (e.g. Malkki 1995) but relationship to place is something that is potentially transferable as critical research into geographies of home has suggested (Blunt and Dowling 2006).

It is not just the nation state which can be seen as constructed or historically contingent. An influential strand of geographical work identifies scale as politically constructed (Delaney and Lietner 1997). As Marston summarizes, 'scale is not necessarily a preordained hierarchical framework for ordering the world—local, regional, national and global. It is instead a contingent outcome of the tensions that exist between structural forces and the practices of human agents' (2000: 220). In relation to research on forced migration this has typically been used in a political context to investigate the ways in which institutions of regional governance, such as the European Union, present themselves. Yet, as Marston argues, it can also inform research into social reproduction. These perspectives can help undermine the familiar view of 'nested' scales, through which local institutions defer to regional, to national, and to global in a constructed imagination of progressive importance. From the individual perspective, all action inevitably takes place at a local level so to attribute irresistible power to forces seen as 'global' may reflect on the impression of agency that individual migrants feel they possess.

Scale is therefore explicitly involved in the construction of boundaries, both those that are explicitly policed and those that are more broadly imagined, such as generalized distinctions between 'North' and 'South' at the global level. The distinction between mobility and migration depends on the crossing of these frequently ill-defined spatial and temporal boundaries. The mobilities paradigm has demonstrated that in many contexts 'mobility' is a more flexible term than 'migration', more suited to the realities faced by forced migrants. A special issue of the journal *Mobilities* has recently explored these links (Gill, Caletrio, and Mason 2011), highlighting the application of mobility studies to understand forced migration as more than an individual, linear movement. Discussion of mobility also leads more obviously to investigations of immobility, an increasingly common experience for forced migrants and one that requires a great deal more attention (Conlon 2011).

Space and location are central to refugee movement in terms of patterns of settlement or resettlement. Spatial patterns of movement and residence are increasingly incorporated into analysis of migration and social transformation (Castles 2003). Even in 1993 Black argued that geographers have analysed far more than the physical locations of refugee movement, including social and cultural elements of their engagement with those new locations. Nevertheless, spatial analysis was one of the consequences of migration that he felt geographers were particularly equipped to analyse. Both the construction of scale and the production of space are significant in analysing spatial practices such as the dispersal of asylum seekers or refugees (e.g. Robinson, Andersson, and Musterd 2003). In spatial terms, quantitative indexes for measuring segregation of particular populations were developed in classic geographical work in the 1970s (e.g. Peach 1975) and their use remains concentrated in particular schools of quantitative urban studies.

A final locational distinction worth investigating is between the camp and the city. The work of Giorgio Agamben has been particularly influential in geographical research on forced migration, though as in other areas, his challenging perspective is increasingly questioned (Ek 2006; Sigona 2015). For example, Darling (2009) working with destitute asylum seekers in the UK eventually turns away from Agamben's rigid rejection of any type of asylum determination, in favour of Derrida's more nuanced approach to hospitality. Similarly, Ramadan (2012) initially finds Agamben's approach useful in his analysis of Palestinian refugee camps but goes on to develop the 'beyond Agamen' perspective, finding Agamben too negative and offering too little space for refugee agency. This example demonstrates the willingness of geographers to borrow from other disciplines in the exploration of key geographical themes, but also the interest in using such theoretical approaches critically.

Conclusion

Geographical work on forced migration has come a long way since Black summarized it in terms of the 'causes and consequences' of migration—though of course much ongoing work would still fit that description. What is perhaps most interesting to note over the intervening period is how geography has developed a much more critical approach, so that a 'geography of forced migration', as Hyndman outlined, is no longer assumed to contain a catalogue of physical locations, but may explore the dynamic implications of space and location in terms of key social scientific questions on the distribution of power, the construction of social and political reality, and the place of individuals in society.

This chapter has highlighted the tremendous breadth of the geographical perspective on issues related to forced migration. As a geography of forced migration, it has not sought to enumerate the physical locations of forced migrants. As the first subsection sought to demonstrate, given the nature of data available, that is a near impossible task. Many also argue that it is normatively questionable, though geographical research, in the form of GIS and remote sensing has provided some of the tools to further that goal.

It has also reviewed new geographical approaches to the relationship between environmental change and forced migration and discussed further issues of categorization, particularly the label 'environmental refugees'. Finally, it has demonstrated the politically constructed nature of many understandings of location that are fundamental to key categorizations of forced migrants.

Categorization is one of the themes that has run through this chapter. Categorization of forced migrants is inevitable in both policy and academic contexts, though perhaps in different ways. An important ongoing division in geographical research in the area of forced migration exists between critical and applied policy research. Recent debate was fuelled by an article which claimed that critical research was inevitably distinct from applied policy research which served the interests of the state (Fuller and Kitchin 2004). Although this position has been disputed (e.g. Pain 2006) it does highlight an issue within geography where there is substantial suspicion of policy-related work. Geographical research in the area of forced migration, including much of the material discussed here, demonstrates that it is possible to develop a research agenda that is both critical and informed by policy.

References

Agnew, J. (1994) 'The Territorial Trap: The Geographical Assumptions of International Relations Theory'. *Review of International Political Economy* 1(1): 53–80.

Black, R. (1993) 'Geography and Refugees: Current Issues'. Pp. 3–13 in R. Black and V. Robinson (eds.), *Geography and Refugees: Patterns and Processes of Change*. London: Belhave Press.

Black, R. (2001) 'Environmental Refugees: Myth or Reality'. New Issues in Refugee Research Working Paper 34. Geneva: UNHCR.

Black, R., Kniveton, D., and Schmidt-Verkerk, K. (2011) 'Migration and Climate Change: Towards an Integrated Assessment of Sensitivity'. *Environment and Planning A* 43(2): 431–50.

Blitz, B. K. (2011) 'Statelessness and Environmental-Induced Displacement: Future Scenarios of Deterritorialisation, Rescue and Recovery Examined'. *Mobilities* 6(3): 433–50.

Blunt, A., and Dowling, R. (2006) *Home*. London: Routledge.

Boano, C., Zetter, R., and Morris, T. (2008) 'Environmentally Displaced People: Understanding the Linkages between Environmental Change, Livelihoods and Forced Migration'. Forced Migration Policy Briefing 1, Oxford: Refugees Studies Centre.

Brun, C. (2001) 'Reterritorialising the Relationship between People and Place in Refugee Studies'. *Geografisker Annaler* 83B: 15–25.

Castles, S. (2003) 'Towards a Sociology of Forced Migration and Social Transformation'. *Sociology* 37(1): 13–34.

Collyer, M. (2012) 'Migrants as Strategic Actors in the European Union's Global Approach to Migration and Mobility'. *Global Networks* 12(4): 505–24.

Conlon, D. (2011) 'Waiting: Feminist Perspectives on the Spacings/Timings of Migrant (Im)-mobility'. *Gender, Place, and Culture* 18(3): 353–60.

Crawley, H. (2001) *Refugees and Gender: Law and Process*. Bristol: Jordan Publishing.

Crisp, J. (1999) 'Who Has Counted the Refugees? UNHCR and the Politics of Numbers'. New Issues in Refugee Research Working Paper 12. Geneva: UNHCR.

Cutter, S. L. (2003) 'GIScience, Disasters and Emergency Management'. *Transactions in GIS* 7: 439–46.

Darling, J. (2009) 'Becoming Bare Life: Asylum, Hospitality and the Politics of Encampment'. *Environment and Planning D: Society and Space* 27: 649–55.

Delaney, D., and Lietner, H. (1997) 'The Political Construction of Scale'. *Political Geography* 16(2): 93–7.

Ek, R. (2006) 'Georgio Agamben and the Spatialities of the Camp: An Introduction' *Geografiska Annaler* 88 B(4): 363–86.

Emrich, C. T., Cutter, S. L., and Weschler, P. J. (2011) 'GIS and Emergency Management'. Pp. 321–43 in *The SAGE Handbook of GIS and Society*. London: Sage.

Findlay, A. M. (2011) 'Migrant Destinations in an Era of Environmental Change'. *Global Environmental Change* 21S: S50–S58.

Foresight: Migration and Global Environmental Change (2011) *Final Project Report*. London: The Government Office for Science.

Franke, M. F. N. (2009) 'Refugee Registration as Foreclosure of the Freedom to Move: The Virtualization of Refugees' Rights within Maps of International Protection'. *Environment and Planning D: Society and Space* 27: 352–69.

Fuller, D., and Kitchin, R. (2004) 'Radical Theory/Critical Praxis: Academic Geography beyond the Academy?' Pp. 1–20 in D. Fuller and R. Kitchin (eds.), *Radical Theory, Critical Praxis: Making a Difference beyond the Academy?* ACME e-bookseries.

Gemenne, F. (2011) 'Why the Numbers Don't Add up: A Review of Estimates and Predictions of People Displaced by Environmental Change'. *Global Environmental Change* 21S S41–S49.

Gill, N. (2010) ' "Environmental Refugees": Key Debates and the Contributions of Geographers'. *Geography Compass* 4(7): 861–71.

Gill, N., Caletrio, J., and Mason, V. (2011) 'Introduction: Mobilities and Forced Migration'. *Mobilities* 6(3): 301–16.

Hyndman, J. (1999) 'A Post Cold War Geography of Forced Migration in Kenya and Somalia'. *The Professional Geographer* 51(1): 104–14.

Hyndman, J. (2000) *Managing Displacement: Refugees and the Politics of Humanitarianism.* Minneapolis: University of Minnesota Press.

Kemper, T., Jenerowicz, M., Pesaresi, M., and Soille, P. (2011) 'Enumeration of Dwellings in Darfur Camps from GeoEye 1 Satellite Images Using Mathematical Morphology'. *IEEE Journal of Selected Topics in Applied Earth Observations and Remote Sensing* 4(1): 8–15.

Koser, K., and Pinkerton, C. (2002) 'The Social Networks of Asylum-Seekers and the Dissemination of Information about Countries of Asylum', Findings 165. London: Home Office.

McGregor, J. (1993). 'Refugees and the Environment'. Pp. 157–71 in R. Black and V. Robinson (eds.), *Geography and Refugees: Patterns and Processes of Change*. London: Belhaven.

Malkki, L. (1995) 'Refugees and Exile: From "Refugee Studies" to the National Order of Things'. *Annual Review of Anthropology* 24: 495–523.

Marston, S. A. (2000) 'The Social Construction of Scale'. *Progress in Human Geography* 24(2): 219–42.

Mountz, A. (2010) *Seeking Asylum: Human Smuggling and Bureaucracy at the Border.* Minneapolis: University of Minnesota Press.

Pain, R. (2006) 'Social Geography: Seven Deadly Myths of Policy Research'. *Progress in Human Geography* 30(2): 250–9.

Peach, C. (1975) *Urban Social Segregation*. London: Longman.

Piguet, E., Pecoud, A., and de Guchtenarire, P. (2011) 'Migration and Climate Change: An Overview'. *Refugee Survey Quarterly* 30(3): 1–23.

Ramadan, A. (2012) 'Spatialising the Refugee Camp'. *Transactions of the Institute of British Geographers*. doi: 10.1111/j.1475-5661.2012.00509.x

Robinson, V. Andersson, R., and Musterd, S. (2003) *Spreading the 'Burden'? A Review of Policies to Disperse Asylum Seekers and Refugees*. Bristol: Policy Press.

Sabbah, H. (2008) 'Lost Palestinian Refugee Camps on UN-Google Earth Map', 4 October. <http://www.sabbah.biz>.

Sidaway, J. D., and Johnston, R. J. (2007) 'Geography in Higher Education in the UK'. *Journal of Geography in Higher Education* 31(1): 57–80.

Sigona, N. (2015 forthcoming) 'Campzenship: Reimagining the Camp as a Social and Political Space', *Citizenship Studies* 19(1).

Verdirame, G., and Harrell-Bond, B. E. (2005) *Rights in Exile: Janus-Faced Humanitarianism*. Oxford: Berghahn Books.

Warner, K., Ehrhart, C., de Sherbinin, A., Adamo, S., and Chai-Onn, T. (2009) 'In Search of Shelter: Mapping the Effects of Climate Change on Human Migration and Displacement'. <http://ciesin.columbia.edu/documents/clim-migr-report-june09_media.pdf>.

PART II

SHIFTING
SPACES AND
SCENARIOS OF
DISPLACEMENT

CHAPTER 10

ENCAMPMENT AND SELF-SETTLEMENT

OLIVER BAKEWELL

INTRODUCTION

WHEN we think about where refugees live, the stereotypical view often takes us to the 'camp'. However, when we look at practices on the ground the idea of the camp becomes much more variegated, with different spatial, economic, and political configurations; we may be considering anything from areas enclosed by barbed wire, akin to prisons, to open villages. The range of possibilities becomes even wider if we turn to the alternative of self-settlement. This is hardly surprising given that refugees can be found in almost every country of the world, moving for a complex mix of reasons and living in vastly different conditions. Even if we restrict our focus to the developing world (as this chapter does), the historical, social, economic, and political contexts in which refugees are forced to claim—and states are obliged to offer—asylum vary enormously.

The academic debates about camps and settlements have ebbed and flowed over the years (Chambers 1979; Hansen and Oliver-Smith 1982; Van Damme 1995; Voutira and Harrell-Bond 1995; Black 1998; Crisp and Jacobsen 1998; Bakewell 2000; Hovil 2007) but there seems to be consensus about their general direction: the encampment of refugees is undesirable. Nonetheless, when it comes to policy, practice, and research, we very often end up back at the camp.

This chapter looks at some of the reasons for the rise of encampment and compares it with self-settlement, pointing to some of the main issues, raising critical questions and suggesting some avenues for further exploration. It argues that the rather narrow policy focus on camps as opposed to self-settlement obscures the much more flexible ways in which refugees live.

DIFFERENT SPACES OF PROTECTION

The emergence of the international refugee regime begged the question of how states could respond to the need for international protection in practice (see Goodwin-Gill, this volume). For those claiming asylum as persecuted individuals, the focus of the protection has tended to be on ensuring *non-refoulement* and also that refugees were granted economic and social rights in the country of asylum. The space in which this protection has been offered is hardly considered—individual refugees can settle as they please. In contrast, when it comes to the mass movement of refugees, this question of where protection should be available becomes extremely important for three basic reasons.

First, there is the concern about how large numbers of refugees can be incorporated within the society of the country of asylum. In particular, if the refugees come with very few possessions, and possibly in extremely poor physical and mental health, their arrival can herald a range of social challenges for the host society. They may be seen as adding to the existing problems, increasing the welfare burden on a state that is struggling to support its own population. The local population can react with suspicion, resentment, and even violence. In order to manage such problems arising from the presence of refugees, the response of states is generally focused on controlling where refugees should be allowed to stay. Perhaps not surprisingly, states focus on the control of the 'alien' in their midst rather than addressing the responses of their citizens.

A second concern is about the practicalities of providing for the immediate basic needs of the refugee population. How can food, water, shelter, and medical assistance be provided to a large group of refugees, whose numbers may overwhelm local services—especially if they arrive in remote border areas, as half a million Rwandans did when they crossed into north-western Tanzania in 1994? Faced with the daunting logistics of distributing aid to people, ensuring that they are located in known and accessible locations greatly eases the task.

A third concern, which is often the most pressing from the perspective of states, is that of security. If refugees stay close to the border they may attract hostile attention from military forces in their country of origin, especially if they are associated with one side of the conflict. There is a danger that refugees may be attacked from across the border as happened to Syrian refugees in Turkey in 2012. Some refugees may also engage in military activity if they can easily cross back into their country of origin ('warrior refugees' as described by Zolberg, Suhrke, et al. 1989). Hence moving refugees away from border areas is often a major priority for host states. If it is a large influx of refugees, especially if they are short of basic resources, states may also be concerned about the potential threat they may pose to the local population.

As a result, in the face of mass influxes of refugees, the most common—and in the humanitarian aid sector often the default—response has been the establishment of refugee camps. Today the poor refugee in the camp, sheltered under blue plastic sheeting in close proximity with others, provides one of the most prominent, stereotypical images associated with refugees. It is often forgotten that there are other possibilities, one of which provides the other theme of this chapter: self-settlement. Here the refugees make their own choices about where they reside and the state's role can vary enormously.

The extent to which these different approaches are adopted varies across the world. In Europe and North America, self-settlement is the norm: once a refugee's status has been determined, he or she is free to settle where they please (although refugee welfare provision may be limited to a particular location).[1] Since the closure of the European refugee camps in the aftermath of the Second World War, they have been used as a policy on the continent only once: during the influxes of refugees from the former Yugoslavia in the 1990s. In contrast, in the poorer regions of the world, encampment is used much more widely and self-settlement tends to be resisted by states. In such contexts, self-settlement—initiated by the refugees—often stands in opposition to encampment—initiated by the state. The focus of the encampment versus self-settlement debate has therefore been on Africa and Asia, where the largest numbers of refugees seek asylum and encampment is much more prevalent.

In this chapter, *encampment* refers to a policy which requires refugees to live in a designated area set aside for the exclusive use of refugees, unless they have gained specific permission to live elsewhere. The host state is obliged to ensure that the human rights of the refugees are upheld, including the rights to shelter, food, water, sanitation and healthcare, and education, but how these are delivered varies enormously.

When a camp is first established during the emergency phase of an aid operation, refugees are likely to be housed in very crude shelters, perhaps little more than a piece of plastic sheeting stretched over some sticks. In some cases, shelter is initially provided in dormitories made from large tents (or rub halls), in which each family is allocated a small section. If the refugees are likely to have to stay in the camp for any length of time, these very temporary shelters are likely to take a more permanent form, with grass roofs replacing plastic sheets and more permanent walls replacing cloth sheets dividing families in dormitories. Where refugees remain in camps for many years, the buildings may come to resemble the permanent structures of the local area. Buduburam refugee camp housing Liberian refugees on the edge of Accra, Ghana, has come to resemble a city suburb, and the older sections of Meheba refugee settlement in north-western Zambia resemble a collection of villages.

When it comes to the other basic rights, basic services of water and sanitation are provided and if the refugees are in place for some time, some provision is likely to be made for primary and sometimes secondary level education—in Dadaab camp in northern Kenya, there are even plans to open a campus of Nairobi University. Immediately after their arrival, refugees are likely to be supplied with food. This is usually in the form of a ration which they take home to cook for themselves. The refugee camps for Kosovo Albanians established in Macedonia in 1999 were exceptional as they provided individual ready meals for their residents: as many observers noted at the time, an extremely expensive approach that begs many questions about how rights are interpreted across the world.[2]

The question is what happens when the camp remains in place for any length of time. Providing food rations is very expensive and also tends to undermine the ability of refugees to provide for themselves and regain any sense of control over their lives. However, if rations are not provided, the refugees have to have some other means of securing food. This means that they need to gain access to either the labour market or land and agricultural inputs to cultivate their own food. Given that one of the rationales for establishing refugee camps in the first place has been to ensure that refugees do not overwhelm the capacity of the local area—whether flooding the labour market displacing local people from employment or creating potentially violent competition for resources such as land, pasture, water, or fuel—states have tended strictly to control the economic opportunities of refugees in camps.

One approach adopted during the 1970s and 1980s, primarily in Africa, was the creation of agricultural settlements for refugees (Rogge 1981). This policy was taken up most enthusiastically in Tanzania, Zambia, Sudan, and Uganda, which had large tracts of relatively fertile land in remote areas with low populations. In these settlements, each refugee household was allocated a plot of land for subsistence cultivation. Two alternative models were also adopted by Sudan: first rural wage-earning settlements established alongside mechanized agricultural projects—most famously at Qala en Nahal in Eastern Sudan; second, suburban settlements in larger towns where refugees were expected to make their living through petty commodity production. While some hailed such approaches as offering a longer-term solution of integration for African refugees, all these approaches were associated with the rejection of integration and self-settlement by states, as Kibreab argues (1989). The refugees were required to reside within the bounds of the settlements and, therefore, they remain a form of encampment.

The governance of the refugee camps and settlements also varies enormously with the security situation, the resources available, and government policy. Where refugees are seen as offering some sort of threat either as potential targets of attacks from the country of origin, or as 'warrior refugees' (Zolberg, Suhrke, et al. 1989), the camps are likely to be subject to control by either the security forces of the host state, or possibly international forces (see Kiljunen 1983 for examples from the Thai-Cambodia border). Here the movement of refugees in and out may be tightly circumscribed by the fences, guards, and checkpoints. In other cases, where security concerns are less prominent, the barrier to movement may be distance and the cost involved. In many cases, there are no physical constraints to movement but refugees caught out of place without the required papers will be subject to arrest.

This very brief overview of the many different forms of encampment shows that when we use the term refugee camp, we may be referring to anything from a small, militarized fenced centre housing refugees in dormitories guarded by soldiers, to a huge agricultural settlement (for example, Meheba refugees settlement in north-western Zambia extends over 20 kilometres) consisting of villages deeply embedded into the local economy (Jacobsen 2005). For the purposes of this chapter, I will refer to all these settlements as camps.

Of course, it would be futile to attempt to describe the different forms of self-settlement as they mirror the myriad forms of human settlement around the world. Even where policies of encampment are adopted, states often sanction self-settlement for those who gain the required permissions to live outside the camps. For example, this may be granted for those who need special medical attention in the capital city, for students winning scholarships, for those with sufficient resources to establish their own businesses, or for refugees with particular skills that are in short supply in the host country, such as qualified teachers and doctors. Hence, it is important not to equate self-settlement with illegal settlement. That said, in most countries, refugees who settle themselves outside the camps are for the most part in breach of the law. Many of them remain unregistered and largely out of view of the state. It is this form of self-settlement that is uncontrolled by the state, which is considered in this chapter.

THE SCALE OF ENCAMPMENT

Table 10.1 shows the latest data available on settlement forms from UNHCR's published statistics. The figures clearly show that the policy of encampment is one that is adopted almost exclusively in the poorer regions of the world. Second, they suggest that in all continents the number of refugees outside formal camps and settlements exceeds those within. Given that almost by definition self-settled refugees tend to remain outside the formal system, it is likely that official statistics overstate the proportion of refugees in camps.

In 1993, about 30 per cent of the persons of concern in Africa and 65 per cent in Asia remained outside camps. The percentage of refugees in camps fell dramatically in the

Table 10.1 Population of concern to UNHCR by type of accommodation (000s), end 2011

	Camps / centres	Individual accommodation (private)	Settlement	Undefined/ unknown	Total	% in camps / centres
Africa	3,990	1,610	4,346	3,107	13,054	31
Asia	1,330	7,106	332	5,475	14,243	9
Europe	15	483	—	2,806	3,303	0
Latin America	0	276	—	4,039	4,316	0
North America	—	—	—	483	483	0
Oceania	2	2	5	31	40	6
Total	5,338	9,478	4,683	15,942	35,440	15

Source: Adapted from UNHCR 2012 Global Refugee Trends Statistical Annex—Table 16.

late 2000s, when UNHCR started to report on the number of refugees whose whereabouts are unknown. This shift in the refugee calculus makes it difficult to identify clear numerical trends. However, it does indicate the slow recognition of the scale of self-settlement, which is now being acknowledged in the statistical records. It also demonstrates that only a minority of the world's refugees and persons of concern to UNHCR stay in formal camps and settlement. Nonetheless, in developing regions of the world, policy, practice, and research all tend to remain focused on them.

SELF-SETTLEMENT: THE REFUGEES' CHOICE?

Why do so many refugees in developing countries stay away from camps, regardless of the host government policy and the law, spurning the offer of humanitarian aid and services such as health and education? There seems little doubt that self-settlement can leave refugees in a more precarious formal legal position. Their refugee status may remain unrecognized by the state and even, in practice, by UNHCR, who may be unable to extend their effective protection to the self-settled. In particular, if refugees have settled themselves without making themselves known to the authorities—a strategy they may have to adopt if they are to avoid removal to a camp—they remain invisible to UNHCR and any protection it may offer. Despite such problems, self-settlement is often the option that people select if they have any choice. In any different context, many reasons can be put forward to explain the refugees' preference for self-settlement. These vary enormously but there are some that have been seen to recur in a range of settings; here just three are discussed, relating to their aspirations for return, access to livelihoods, and maintaining autonomy.

Research that has compared refugees in camps and the self-settled has noted that refugees may adopt very different strategies to achieve similar ends. Many refugees may share the asylum state's desire for their return. From the refugees' perspective, it may be much better to maintain as close a connection as possible to their homeland, sustaining regular contact and even being able to visit. Hence, they may prefer self-settlement close to the border in easy reach of their country of origin, as thousands of Afghan refugees have done in Pakistan, rather than being corralled into a distant camp.

Although states and aid agencies may suggest that the basic needs of refugees may be best met through encampment, the restrictions placed on refugees' movement, access to resources (in particular land), ownership of assets (such as livestock and vehicles), and limitations on business activities may act as a considerable brake on refugees' enterprise. Many refugees seem to weigh up the benefits of aid supplies and services in camps against these restrictions and find them wanting. Hence, they seek opportunities to settle in an area where they can make a better living for themselves.

Associated with such rationales that may be seen as political and socio-economic, there is a more psychological rationale: the desire of refugees to maintain their autonomy. One of the concerns about refugee camps is the extent to which the provision of humanitarian aid and free services to refugees in camps, especially over extended periods, instils a sense of 'dependency,' where refugees become reliant on the aid agencies. However, there is considerable evidence to suggest that refugees have always seized whatever options they can to improve their lives, incorporating aid where it is available (Kibreab 1993; Jacobsen 2005). By staying outside the camps, one may sacrifice the access to these resources but gain autonomy and other opportunities. For example, among self-settled Angolans in Zambia, staying outside the 'fence'—as they called the formal refugees settlement—opened up many more options for their livelihoods, repatriation, and integration into Zambia (Bakewell 2000). In practice things are rarely so clear cut and there may be strong social and economic links between self-settled refugees and those in camps.

Self-settlement is still sometimes referred to as 'spontaneous settlement', but this is a complete misnomer. Refugees cannot simply appear in another country and take over 'empty' space; they can only live in areas where they are able successfully to negotiate access with the local residents. In rural areas this may involve gaining the support of the village heads and traditional rulers. In urban areas, it is more likely to involve discussion with local community groups, gangs, or even local authorities. In practice, such negotiations require a good understanding of the language, the structure of the local society, and usually some pre-existing relationship. These conditions are most likely to be found when refugees flee across the border into the neighbouring country, especially when the border cuts across traditional lineages and chiefdoms— as they do across much of Africa. Such links facilitated the self-settlement of refugees from Liberia and Sierra Leone in the forest region of Guinea during the 1990s (Van Damme 1999).

The fact that refugees are able to negotiate their self-settlement also raises important questions about the extent to which staying outside the camps necessarily makes refugees' lives any more precarious in practice. While states may be very concerned about legal status, this may have very little impact on people's day-to-day lives. In poor countries where the reach of the state may be rather limited, those who live in remote rural areas may have very little contact with agents of the state. Moreover, in conditions where the local people are happy to receive refugees—perhaps because of shared language and culture or the expansion of local economy—they may collude with refugees to ensure they get access to basic services such as education and healthcare, or even citizenship papers for children. In this sense, those who are self-settled may gain a form of protection in practice that is stronger in everyday life than any protection in law that can be offered by the state.

Moreover, lives in camps may also be extremely precarious especially if the refugees are expected to be reliant on international aid for food, agricultural inputs, or other essential items. The aid pipeline is often vulnerable to problems with funding and logistics that mean goods are delivered in reduced volumes, late, or not at all. Refugees in camps may take every opportunity to supplement this international aid, but their initiatives may be very constrained by the rules of the camp, such as those that restrict mobility or prevent refugees keeping livestock.

The Encampment Turn

Such arguments drawing on the experience from many different settings suggest that self-settlement can and does play a very important role in the response to refugee crises. Where it is supported by the local population and it does not present a significant security threat, self-settlement has the potential to satisfy the concerns outlined at the beginning of this chapter. Moreover, the statistics suggests that many thousands of refugees are self-settled and it is only a minority that are housed in camps. Nonetheless, encampment remains fixed as the central pillar of refuge policy for states and aid agencies across Africa and Asia. This raises the question of why it has become so embedded in the mindsets of those involved in refugee aid policy. A common rationale for the use of camps is to refer to the concerns about finding the best of providing protection for refugees without undermining the rights to security and livelihoods of the host population. However, as I have shown, in some contexts self-settlement may address these as well as, or better than, encampment. This suggests that other factors must also be at work.

Where did the idea of putting refugees in camps come from? It may have become standard practice today, but refugee camps have a pedigree that is far removed from the humanitarian sphere. The response of encampment can be clearly identified with techniques of control and oppression used by various states throughout the twentieth century. The camp as a form of control has a much longer history in military use. The encampment of civilians was notoriously adopted as a tactic by the British in the Anglo-Boer War 1900–2 (Krebs 1992). The term 'concentration camp' was later adopted by the Nazi regime in Germany as part of its strategy of genocide in the Second World War. The idea of the *camp* as a controlled space housing people in wartime continues: whether for enemies (prisoner of war camps, internment camps, Guantanamo Bay, re-education camps in Vietnam and Cambodia) or civilians affected by war (refugee camps, 'protected villages').

For all these horrors associated with encampment, it has become established as part of the state's bureaucratic response to dealing with temporary crises where people are seen to be out of place, either in a place of danger or creating danger for others. The camp perhaps fills the imagination of the official faced with such problems. At the same time, this history also warns that the technology of the camp—the array of systems to manage and organize the space and those living within it—is fundamentally flawed with respect to human rights. It seems impossible to require people to live in such a space, withdraw their right to exit, and not create an environment for the abuse of rights; many have argued that this 'warehousing' of refugees is inimical to upholding their human rights (Smith 2004).

A second consideration that ensures encampment is favoured by states—in particular by host states—is the politics of aid. In many developing countries, and especially the least developed, the arrival of large numbers of refugees is accompanied by an international humanitarian response that sets out to provide for the basic needs of water, food, sanitation, shelter, and so forth. Such humanitarian aid for refugees involves a considerable transfer of resources. It also introduces a set of actors who have been immersed in the history of practice centred on camps. Refugee camps become a recognizable and familiar world for aid agencies and their creation enables a set of routines and systems to be established that facilitates smooth operations. For host governments who request international assistance in responding to refugees, the expectation that that there will be camps may be irresistible: Zetter (1995) recounts how international aid brought refugee camps to Malawi.

Moreover, aid that is focused on refugees will only flow as long as refugees are visible. Once refugees are in camps, for host states there are few incentives to allow them to move outside, where they may become integrated into the local host population. In due course the rationale for providing special refugee aid—rather than aid to the wider population—may disappear. In contrast, a refugee camp can be presented as a problem that requires ongoing funds for support that generates jobs, contracts, and overheads. For aid agencies that have received funds for helping refugees, working in a refugee camp makes it much easier for them to account for their work.

Donors, aid agencies, and host states have performed a long-standing dialogue about the problems of refugees caught in camps for long periods—so-called protracted refugee situations (see Milner, this volume). Much of this has been concerned with enhancing refugee rights in camps, enabling them more freedom to develop livelihoods and reducing their reliance on aid. In an initiative launched over 30 years ago, the 1981 International Conference on Assistance to Refugees in Africa (ICARA) and its successor ICARA II in 1984 debated self-reliance and introduced the idea of incorporating refugees in national development projects. Such ideas have resurfaced in the last decade with UNHCR's Convention Plus initiative, again with a strong focus on self-reliance. Throughout such discussions, there has been no suggestion that refugees should be allowed to leave camps and most host states, especially in Africa, have been adamantly against the integration of refugees.

This history of practice and the politics of aid contribute to make encampment as the default policy response. Above all, refugee camps segregate refugees from citizens, thereby upholding the primacy of the nation state as the arbiter of refugees' fate and ensuring that they are maintained as people amenable to management. 'The function of modern international organisations is to manage refugee populations in a manner that does not radically undermine the framework on which the nation-state rests' (Owens 2009: 571). The camp therefore plays a critical role, not only in upholding the symbolic power of the state[3] but also in constructing the idea of the 'refugee' that is reproduced by institutional practice and discourse.

This idea of the camp as a locus of power and abuse of power has been reinforced through academic discourse, where it constantly appears as a trope in literature drawing on the work of Foucault (1979), Arendt (1958), and Agamben (1998, 2005). Agamben has become particularly influential in making commonplace the idea of the camps as a 'place of exception', where refugees are reduced to 'bare life' to be subject to control as bodies without any regard for their humanity. Although such research has cast extremely valuable light on abuses and contradictions embedded in humanitarian aid, it has resulted in forced migration scholars working in poorer regions of the world focusing almost exclusively on camps. Hence, camps are deplored but the alternatives are little known or considered.

CONCLUSION

Academic arguments turn around the extent to which it is ever necessary to use refugee camps and who bears the main responsibility for their continued widespread adoption, whether it is host states, aid agencies, or donors. What is clear is that the responsibility for so many refugees remaining outside camps and settling themselves usually seems to lie with the refugees and the local society in which they settle. Given that the violations of people's rights observed in camps are so widespread, the fact that the majority manage to stay outside is something to be celebrated.

At the same time, it is important to remember that self-settlement is not readily available to all refugees. Even where self-settlement may be open to some, others may prefer to sacrifice some of their autonomy for the institutional support they can receive from aid agencies in camps. Many refugees arrive with very little having had to abandon their wealth as they fled. In addition, their social networks are likely to have been fractured as they fled and they may find themselves separated from family and friends who may have offered critical support at home. For example, elderly, disabled, or chronically sick people may struggle to re-establish new lives by themselves. Even if they do manage to stay together, their family may find it impossible to offer the required support in the face of the additional stresses caused by flight. For such people, some centralized aid provision, perhaps delivered in a refugee camp may provide an essential safety net.

One problem is that these discussions tend to revolve around these two approaches—encampment and self-settlement—as if they are mutually exclusive and represent the only conceivable possibilities. Where some refugees from a group settle themselves while others reside in camps, there is evidence (Van Damme 1999; Kaiser 2006) that critical interrelationships can develop between the two spaces with the continuous transfer of people and resources between them. The camp may offer a welfare safety net to some degree, while self-settlement opens up the door to much stronger livelihoods. Individual refugees may move between the camp and a settlement at different points in their lives. Hence, camp and settlement are not so separate, and perhaps there is plenty of room for new approaches that cover the space in between.

It is not difficult to envisage different models for delivering humanitarian assistance that enable refugees to live within the wider community. This may not entail delivering aid to individual refugees so much as ensuring that assistance is given that offsets any additional costs created by the added population. This may be particularly focused on expanding services such as education and healthcare and reduce the requirement for food aid. At the same time, where there is a need for refugees to be housed separately, it must be feasible to ensure their rights are upheld—and if it is impossible, there can be no justification for camps.

When it comes to developing a settlement policy for refugees, neither encampment nor self-settlement can be seen as good in themselves. The main concern is not about the settlement form so much as the freedom of refugees to choose how they live—exercising the same freedoms available to other citizens and immigrants. For now, the narrow focus on camps and limited work on self-settlement means that valuable lessons on how refugees are being received and settled to find temporary and perhaps even durable solutions—potentially outside any state interventions—are being lost.

NOTES

1. Here I am concerned with the treatment of refugees, whose claim to asylum is acknowledged by the state, rather than asylum seekers in wealthy states, who are often subject to severe constraints, including detention.
2. Miller and Simmons (1999).
3. This symbolic power—to demand that refugees stay in camps—may not directly relate to the actual power over refugees' actions, i.e. to make them stay in the camps.

REFERENCES

Agamben, G. (1998) *Homo Sacer: Sovereign Power and Bare Life*. Stanford, CA: Stanford University Press.

Agamben, G. (2005) *State of Exception*. Chicago: University of Chicago Press.

Arendt, H. (1958) *The Origins of Totalitarianism*. London: G. Allen & Unwin.

Bakewell, O. (2000) 'Repatriation and Self-settled Refugees in Zambia: Bringing Solutions to the Wrong Problems'. *Journal of Refugee Studies* 13(4): 356–73.

Black, R. (1998) 'Putting Refugees in Camps'. *Forced Migration Review* 2: 4–7.

Chambers, R. (1979) 'Rural Refugees in Africa: What the Eye Does not See'. *Disasters* 3(4): 381–92.

Crisp, J., and Jacobsen, K. (1998) 'Refugee Camps Reconsidered'. *Forced Migration Review* 3: 27–30.

Foucault, M. (1979) *Discipline and Punish: The Birth of the Prison*. Harmondsworth: Penguin Books.

Hansen, A., and Oliver-Smith, A. (eds.) (1982) *Involuntary Migration and Resettlement: The Problems and Responses of Dislocated People*. Boulder, CO: Westview Press.

Hovil, L. (2007) 'Self-settled Refugees in Uganda: An Alternative Approach to Displacement?' *Journal of Refugee Studies* 20(4): 599–620.

Jacobsen, K. (2005) *The Economic Life of Refugees*. Bloomfield, CT: Kumarian Press.

Kaiser, T. (2006) 'Between a Camp and a Hard Place: Rights, Livelihood and Experiences of the Local Settlement System for Long-Term Refugees in Uganda'. *The Journal of Modern African Studies* 44(4): 597–621.

Kibreab, G. (1989) 'Local Settlements in Africa: A Misconceived Option?' *Journal of Refugee Studies* 2(4): 468–90.

Kibreab, G. (1993) 'The Myth of Dependency among Camp Refugees in Somalia 1979–1989'. *Journal of Refugee Studies* 6(4): 321–49.

Kiljunen, K. (1983) 'The Tragedy of Kampuchea'. *Disasters* 7(2): 129–41.

Krebs, P. M. (1992). ' "The Last of the Gentlemen's Wars": Women in the Boer War Concentration Camp Controversy'. *History Workshop Journal* 33(1): 38–56.

Miller, T. C., and Simmons, A. M. (1999) 'Relief Camps for Africans and Kosovars: Worlds Apart'. *Los Angeles Times* 21 May. <http://www.essex.ac.uk/armedcon/story_id/000441.html>.

Owens, P. (2009) 'Reclaiming "Bare Life"? Against Agamben on Refugees'. *International Relations* 23(4): 567–82.

Rogge, J. R. (1981) 'Africa's Resettlement Strategies'. *International Migration Review* 15(1/2): 195–212.

Smith, M. (2004) 'Warehousing Refugees: A Denial of Rights, a Waste of Humanity'. Pp. 38–56 in M. Smith (ed.), *World Refugee Survey 2004—Warehousing Issue*. Washington, DC: United States Committee for Refugees.

Van Damme, W. (1995) 'Do Refugees Belong in Camps: Experiences from Goma and Guinea'. *Lancet* 346(8971): 360–2.

Van Damme, W. (1999) 'How Liberian and Sierra Leonean Refugees Settled in the Forest Region of Guinea (1990–1996)'. *Journal of Refugee Studies* 12(1): 36–53.

Voutira, E., and Harrell-Bond, B. E. (1995) 'In Search of the Locus of Trust: The Social World of the Refugee Camp'. Pp. 207–24 in E. V. Daniel and J. C. Knudsen (eds.), *Mistrusting Refugees*. Berkeley: University of California Press.

Zetter, R. (1995) 'Incorporation and Exclusion: The Life Cycle of Malawi's Refugee Assistance Programme'. *World Development* 23(10): 1653–67.

Zolberg, A. R., Suhrke, A., et al. (1989) *Escape from Violence: Conflict and the Refugee Crisis in the Developing World*. New York: Oxford University Press.

CHAPTER 11

··

URBAN REFUGEES AND IDPs

··

LOREN B. LANDAU

INTRODUCTION

PEOPLE displaced into urban areas due to war, persecution, or climatic crisis have claimed an increasingly prominent position in humanitarian operations and scholarship.[1] Those writing on 'urban refugees', a generic label, typically explain the urbanization of displacement and humanitarian action within broader global processes resulting in the rapid growth of cities and towns. This is sensible: if more than half the world's population is urbanized, it is unsurprising that the displaced follow suit. Given that the alternatives to urban settlement include decades in camps, administrative detention, or another 'protracted refugee situation' (see Bakewell, this volume), it is hardly surprising that the displaced increasingly find their ways to population centres. Although the urban displaced may not find golden paved streets, cities nonetheless offer at least faint promises of upward economic mobility and physical freedom.

In places like Kabul and Khartoum, cities surrounded by seemingly interminable conflicts, refugees and the internally displaced significantly contribute to cities' rapid population growth (Beall and Esser 2005: 6). Even where the displaced are proportionately less, their presence can rapidly reconfigure social and economic life. Elsewhere, the displaced move almost invisibly into cities, disappearing among longer-term residents who may share class, language, religious, or other commonalities.

The numbers alone make a compelling case for increased attention. According to the United Nations High Commissioner for Refugees (UNHCR 2009: 3), almost half of the world's refugees and displaced people (i.e. people of concern to the organization) are now found in urban areas. That translates to somewhat over 5 million people compared to the 3 million who live in purpose built camps and settlements (this, of course, excludes Palestinians). Of these, the vast majority are seeking profit, protection, and possibly passage elsewhere in the towns and cities of the 'global South'. Whereas camps disproportionately attract the most vulnerable among the displaced populations, those in urban areas typically reflect a population more representative of those in sending communities. If anything, they reflect population segments that may be more robust and resilient as the truly vulnerable are either immobile or find their way to sites where they can receive more focused, direct assistance.

It is important to note that while knowledge on urban refugees has expanded dramatically over the past decade, there are still significant gaps in our knowledge. Part of this is technical and logistical—characterizing social realities in rapidly transforming urban centres is difficult without the added challenge of hunting down new arrivals who may prefer to remain invisible (Jacobsen and Furst 2012). Many of the gaps are also due to particular forms of blindness in how we understand urban displacement. Although we know, for example, that small towns and peri-urban areas are the most rapidly growing in the developing world (UNDESA 2010), most studies focus on countries' primary cities.

Although it is unclear whether refugees' urban presence is as novel as many suggest—people have flagged their existence for decades (see Rogge and Akol 1989; Cooper 1992; Malkki 1995)—strong normative, political, and financial motivations have recently fixed the humanitarian gaze on what the eye had previously 'refused to see' (Kibreab 1996). Rather than crediting global socio-political processes with a growing attention to the displaced in urban settings, this chapter links the emergence of the 'urban refugee' as object of study to trends within the humanitarian and humanitarian studies field towards 'visibilization': to identifying and exposing the vulnerability of varied groups and defining them in terms that make them suitable objects of humanitarian action (see Polzer and Hammond 2008; Lubkemann 2010). That displaced persons who live in or pass through urban spaces—and the processes affecting them—ultimately fit so poorly in how scholars and practitioners typically understand and respond to humanitarian concerns means that many may ultimately lose interest. Given the close relationship between humanitarian action and the academic study of displacement (see Barnett, this volume), this will also undoubtedly diminish scholarly interest in displacement into urban areas.

A retreat from research on urban displacement will have important, negative implications for both humanitarianism and the scholarship thereof. If nothing else, this chapter suggests there are compelling normative and intellectual attention for sustained attention to both cities and the people seeking protection within them. However, such inquiries' potential will only be achieved through a substantial redefinition of the modes through which we 'see' and understand displacement and humanitarian intervention.

The remainder of this chapter proceeds through three sections offering a review of the stylized forms of knowledge that have been produced about 'urban refugees', a discussion of what this perspective overlooks, and a series of reflections on the practical and intellectual opportunities lost through such an approach. It concludes with tentative suggestions on how the 'urban refugee' may be redefined which recognize that doing so means challenging institutionalized structures within the academy and humanitarian field.

A few caveats before getting down to business. First, while critical of how urban refugees are framed in current debates, this chapter nonetheless follows current conventions in focusing almost exclusively on displaced persons and processes in 'Southern' cities. Although there are strong arguments for integrating stories of labour, social, and political integration in the global North with work elsewhere, this piece's scope is too limited to bridge that gap. It instead emphasizes issues of protection and assistance raised by displaced persons moving into/through the highly informalized environments that often characterize southern cities. Second, this entry by no means offers a comprehensive review of the ever more expansive work relevant to a discussion of displacement to and within urban areas.[2] More significant than missing references to specific studies or places is the exclusion of the broad, if imperfect, literature on urban poverty and mobility in the South. As such scholarship often includes stories of intra-city displacement due to housing 'upgrading', slum clearance, or other forms of development along with broader stories of marginalization, aid, and empowerment, it could and should contribute to our understanding of displaced people's urban experiences (see, for example, Watson 2006 and Simone 2009). This entry ends by advertising the benefits of future cross-fertilization.

Visibilizing the 'Urban Refugee'

Catalysed in large measure by the second Gulf War, which displaced hundreds of thousands of Iraqis through the politically sensitive Middle East, humanitarian and scholarly attention to urban refugees has grown remarkably over the past decade (see Sommers 2001; Jacobsen 2006; Bernstein and Okello 2007; Fábos and Kibreab 2007; Margesson, Sharp, and Bruno 2008; Lubkemann 2010). This attention not only bring us new stories and experiences, but also a further instance of the 'visibilization' imperative. This impulse to reveal hidden populations, processes, and patterns of marginalization not only informs, but to some extent still drives the study of displacement. From early inquiries into camp-based refugees, scholarship has expanded to include various categories of the displaced (especially those 'internally displaced'). More recently, scholars have added studies on people being involuntarily held in place, those left behind, returnees, and other groups. However, as Polzer and Hammond (2008: 421) note, this process of visibilization must be situated within a complex set of power relations: 'Invisibility is a relationship between those who have the power to see or to choose not to see, and on the other hand, those who lack the power to demand to be seen, or to protect themselves from the negative effects of imposed visibility.'

With this in mind there are reasons to interrogate how urban refugees moved from an academic side interest to the centre of considerable debate and attention. Until the 'noughties', UNCHR's own scepticism as to the veracity of refugee claims made in urban areas and fears over the spiralling costs of providing assistance in urban space contributed to their reluctance to engage in cities (Marfleet 2007; Kagan 2007; UNHCR 2009). However, after years of trepidation, the political imperative to respond to displaced Iraqis provided the institutional and financial incentives for change.

In response to new forms of massive and politically sensitive displacement in the Middle East coupled with long-standing frustration with its earlier approach, the UNHCR revised its 1997 policy on urban refugees, overtly recognizing, 'the need to address the issue of urban refugees in a more comprehensive manner' (UNHCR 2009: 2). Towards this end, the UNHCR has publicly moved away from its institutional scepticism towards the displaced in urban space and committed itself to maximizing, 'the protection space available to urban refugees and the humanitarian organizations that support them' (UNHCR 2009: 5). By its own admission, the UNHCR's policy document is aspirational, a kind of bill of rights that it hopes will be progressively realized. Critics will note that it remains vague, offering few concrete measures of success. Indeed, beyond their geographic demarcations, the recommendations for realizing such protection closely follow the principles accepted for refugee protection in dedicated settlements: promoting legal status, ensuring basic access to food and shelter, and prohibitions on *refoulement*. These principles provide neither the UNHCR nor its implementing partners with the empirical or ethical basis needed for work in the 'Southern' cities in which they are increasingly asked to operate.

As humanitarian analysts have peered into cities, they consistently relay a Malthusian vision, portraying both cities and those living therein as borderline catastrophes threatening descent into Hobbesian states of nature should rapid and firm intervention fail to arrive (see, for example Pavenello, Elhawary, and Pantuliano 2010; Women's Refugee Commission 2011). Within these accounts there remains a distinct tension. On one side are those who see refugees in urban areas as little different from those in camps: people needing to be indefinitely sustained by international and domestic humanitarianism. On the other, more sophisticated analyses suggest the need to revisit what humanitarianism means in urban environments. Yet even here the literature remains distinctly refugee-centric, both in its normative ambitions and its presumptions about those it aims to assist.

The refugee-centrism alluded to above reflects a general pattern within refugee studies and humanitarianism. Underlying the effort to highlight these forms of neediness is a humanitarian imperative, driven both by efforts to permanently remedy the unfortunate conditions of those in need and, perhaps more immediately, by the imperative to legitimize humanitarian assistance. As a result, there is a consistent effort to demonstrate how refugees—due to their displacement—have poorer access to social services, compete less effectively in the marketplace, and are regularly harassed, detained, and disadvantaged. Schoeller et al. (2012: 10) exemplify this position in their argument that: 'urbanization uproots individuals and households from these long-standing, kinship-based communities and drops them into informal settlements with a diverse population, forming a community of strangers.' The second generation of debates over urban refugees draws attention to the varied experiences of those who end up in urban centres and towns in ways that follow the predictable course of refugee-oriented scholarship: first focusing on women, then youth (and girls in particular), the aged, and the disabled.

What is notably absent from many of the accounts of vulnerability—which is undeniably real across many of the groups discussed—is a nuanced analysis of what results in vulnerability and varied forms of socio-economic marginalization. There is a largely untested faith that the observed challenges facing people are largely due to displacement. Consequently, the first impulse is to respond to this vulnerability with the same modalities evident in camp-based settings: direct assistance and documentation with a focus on 'classically' vulnerable groups, particularly women and children. In terms of modalities for assistance, here we see both continuity and adaptation without a fundamental reconsideration of what assistance may entail. While there are regular calls to engage local officials and service providers—rather than contracting implementing partners—the primary call to action is in the form of direct assistance. In South Africa—once considered the site for model urban refugee assistance—such direct assistance has proved both financially unsustainable and politically counter-productive as it has drawn negative attention to refugees from an equally deprived and under-serviced host population. Similarly, the kind of expensive direct assistance provided to Iraqi refugees in Jordan and elsewhere has proved problematic and is now recognized as a model that cannot be widely replicated.[3]

Through much of the discussion there remains an unchallenged premiss that assistance for refugees should come in the form of bespoke programmes exclusively targeting people of concern. Although many suggest the need to avoid building parallel programmes, they nonetheless demand initiatives aimed explicitly and, often exclusively, at the displaced. Indeed, humanitarian organizations fear that doing otherwise may decrease their aid effectiveness or undermine their ability to attract funding and act. The increased call from those supporting such operations—multi- and bilateral donors along with private foundations—for improved accountability, measurable output, and clearly defined beneficiaries has further encouraged the delineation of refugees from other groups while retaining an emphasis on direct service delivery. That there is so little longitudinal data or other information demonstrating dynamics within refugee communities—particularly the impact of interventions and policies on welfare and protection—further encourages organizations to rely on legitimized and immediately quantifiable programmes that conflate provision with protection.

Registration and legal status is perhaps the most notable assistance modality borrowed from camp-based assistance policies. Although there is evidence that national policy frameworks and refugees' individual legal status may have limited practical impact in the informalized environments in which they live, humanitarian organizations and the literature continue to emphasize the importance of formal documentation and legal frameworks (Kagan 2007; Landau and Duponchel 2011). In some instances such approaches undeniably open space for refugees and displaced people to pursue livelihoods and access services although there is little evidence within the literature to show that policies can affect such outcomes. Elsewhere such efforts may play important symbolic roles, signalling to refugees that their rights are protected and that governments are committed to protecting them.

In the attention to documentation we see the academic visibilization imperative realized in humanitarian practice. While there may well be potentially positive or benign consequences from legalization and registration, demands that refugees self-identify and organize access to services, livelihoods, or opportunities as refugees per se (rather than as urban residents, for example) all but ensures their continued segregation. In some instances, it may create a devils' bargain forcing individuals to choose between services accessible only to refugees and the precariousness stemming from publicly self-identifying to hostile governments and host populations. As Kibreab (2007: 31) argues, 'Though the economic crises facing African countries have nothing to do with the presence of refugees the latter are invariably blamed for being the causes of economic crisis and shortages of housing, transportation, water, electricity, employment, etc. Refugees are also blamed for theft, crimes, prostitution and other forms of anti-social behaviour.' Insisting on revelation to the state, to the United Nations, to humanitarian agencies, and to potentially hostile host populations may only encourage or facilitate such scapegoating.

What the Eye Won't See and the Hands Won't Do

Visibilization for the purpose of intervention relies heavily on concomitant processes of categorization and verification. The solidity of this trifecta is shaken by the sociological and political dynamics of displacement into urban areas in ways that fundamentally challenge the humanitarian imperative behind visibilization. This can be seen in three primary areas although others might also be included here. First and foremost is the inability to legally delineate who counts as a 'person of interest' to those humanitarians (and their donors) concentrating exclusively on the needs of the displaced. These tendencies are only exaggerated by a general suspicion among many within the UNHCR and elsewhere that those entering urban areas are substantively indistinguishable from other newly urbanized populations and should be treated as such. Indeed, there is considerable evidence that in many instances the two are more similar than different in terms of their urban experience if not the motivations for movement. The second factor frustrating conventional humanitarian thinking is the difficulty in distinguishing those needs that are inherently linked to displacement. Indeed, there may be traumas and disadvantage associated with forced movement, but the casual links are often rooted more in faith than in evidence. Third, and perhaps most fundamental, is the profound difficulty in verifying the effects of humanitarian interventions in urban areas.

As noted, much of the research and discussions on the displaced in urban areas focuses on the content of the policies itself and the presumed consequences for refugees and other people of concern. This work offers important critiques and draws attention to protection gaps, logical contradictions, and oversights. However, the tendency of existing scholarship to focus almost exclusively on the displaced and policies directly framed in terms of displacement unduly binds and limits the effects of our work. If we are to move beyond a focus on law as principle and ask how it translates into practice (see Kälin in this volume on the internally displaced), we would gain not only a more realistic understanding of the limits of formal policy in promoting protection, but a more comprehensive understanding of (a) the mechanisms through which positive and negative policies operate in loosely formalized and highly dynamic cities and (b) of processes by which progressive policy change might be promoted. By studying the policies and laws as outcomes alone, we often overlook the processes behind their production. Moreover, the policies most likely to help or hinder the displaced are rarely about refugees. Inasmuch as we ultimately hope to shift policies, laws, and their associated practices, we need to better understand their origins and the interests they serve.

Take for example the impressive work that has been accomplished around IDPs in and out of urban areas. As Lubkemann (2010) notes, there has been a tremendous amount of valuable work conducted on internally displaced people (IDPs) largely inspired and shaped by two seminal volumes by Cohen and Deng (1998). These texts collected case studies (heavily weighted towards Africa) while laying out the sociological predicament facing both the displaced and would-be humanitarians. Few would deny that this work has facilitated the adoption of the Guiding Principles of Internal Displacement, a document that has been widely hailed as the first international framework securing the protection of IDPs. However, there is little evidence that the guiding principles have translated into greater protection. In the words of the UNHCHR's special advisor of policy and evaluation, 'No comprehensive study has yet been undertaken to evaluate their actual impact' (Crisp n.d.: 16).

In terms of work on the displaced in urban areas, there is a similar disjuncture where we know little about how 'good' or 'bad' policies are actually formed, their impacts, and, perhaps most importantly, what constitutes a 'good' urban refugee policy. Even if dialogues on global, regional, and national refugee policy offer important opportunities for agenda setting, normative pronouncements, and symbolic action, there are good reasons to challenge the primacy of law and policy tools for achieving protection. The first comes from the observation that legal status and documentation have only limited practical protection effects in the informalized environments in which many refugees and the displaced reside. Work in South Africa, the most legalized state in sub-Saharan Africa and one that has been a pioneer in its progressive urban refugee policy, suggests that additional legislation is unlikely to be effective and may be counter-productive (Amit 2012). As indicated, such strategies have already provided incentives for continued self-segregation. Moreover, in the absence of a population that is sympathetic to refugees, specialized and highly visible programmes intended to promote refugee welfare have helped legitimize both popular and legislative backlash.

The second and more important blinder in the field relates to what is considered 'refugee' policy. Inasmuch as we retain faith in our ability to predictably translate policy into protection, there are a number of critical reasons why we should reconsider what substantive policies and whose polices we should be talking about. In this regard we need to step beyond the boundaries of humanitarianism if for no other reason that our continued emphasis on refugee and emergency policy makes it all the easier for governments to make commitments that they are unlikely to honour. By stepping into the space of policies where citizens or 'locals' have direct interests and working to ensure that these interests are aligned with humanitarians' 'people of concern' we can raise the odds that governments will dedicate the needed energies and resources.

Research on local government and urbanization—in the developing world and elsewhere—can provide considerable guidance into areas where we might dedicate our advocacy and scholarly activities. This work can provide an important complement to both the literature on international and regional policy instruments and debates regarding the connection between migration and development. We can take as our starting point Sandercock's (2004) demand that we rethink the role of planning and local authorities in an era of diversity and mobility. But this is not simply to demand that municipalities or local government authorities develop purpose built policies on refugees and the displaced, but that they—with assistance from scholars and advocates—understand the factors working against effective protection. While legal prohibitions on livelihoods and residence are clearly part of the picture, we need to consider more carefully the functional implications of decentralization; budgeting; vertical and horizontal cooperation; and popular participation. Many of these arrangements currently provide incentives for local authorities to ignore or exclude newcomers—citizens and foreign as well as voluntary and forced. Recognizing how these operate can also lead us to those areas where incentives might be realigned. While we should continue to work to maximize the impact that sound research and data play in decision making, we must also seek to understand the cognitive frames that lead to wilful ignorance or bias (Feldman and March 1981; Schmidt 2008). Where these frames can be reshaped, we should do so. Where they cannot, advocates must then learn to appeal to the interests and incentives with which they are confronted.

CONCLUSIONS

In summary, there are three analytical and practical divisions that need to be overcome in studying and intervening on behalf of the displaced in urban spaces. First, a definition of protection cannot accept the division of assistance and durable solutions into two discrete phases as such distinctions are often empirically and ethically indistinguishable—all the more so in urban areas. Second, protection interventions cannot focus exclusively on refugees. Any approach unduly enforcing distinctions between refugees and hosts not only requires (expensive) parallel assistance structures, but may also foster political resentments that will ultimately undermine its sustainability. Third, the nature of the increasingly informal urban economy means that we need a more nuanced vision of self-reliance and a model of assistance that shifts from incorporation into the formal labour market or gaining access to formal services. Instead, our metrics and efforts increasingly consider variegated income strategies and less formalized methods of service delivery. In this model, protection ceases to be solely about guaranteeing access to minimum levels of services—the welfarist ethos behind SPHERE and other such standards. It should instead be premissed on expanding people's effective choices about their livelihoods.

This means providing them with not only legal status to work, which is a first stage, but also the opportunity to organize politically to challenge discriminatory obstacles and, more importantly, to enhance the social networks that are so important in improving welfare and security. In this model, we no longer measure success solely in nutritive or legal status but by evaluating whether refugees are progressively able to expand the opportunities to achieve levels of welfare and security in line with local standards and their own heterogeneous objectives (Sen 1992: 5). This may make it difficult to evaluate the specific impacts of particular interventions and frustrate those seeking predictable, short-term quantifiable outcomes. Doing so will require that the UNHCR and its partners broaden the range of work they do, the skills they possess, and the ways they engage with local authority structures both formal and informal. Such efforts need not be more expensive than work in camps, but they will require considerable flexibility, adaptation, and learning. To some extent UNHCR has already begun to recognize these imperatives. However, there is still much organizational learning to do.

The normative and political engagement behind the visibilization project outlined above has resulted in a literature that exposes new forms of vulnerability. We have, as such, typically overlooked or expressly ignored work on urban refugees who are doing fine on their own or without humanitarian assistance. In my own work on urban refugees, fellow scholars and activists have encouraged me to suppress information demonstrating that self-settled refugees are often more economically successful than recent economic migrants from fear that it would result in funding cuts or a political backlash. This is a peril of the close relationship between scholarship and praxis which helps generate a 'miserabilist' bias. This is not to deny the horrendous consequences of displacement or the potential of humanitarianism to assist. Rather, it to recognize that we know little about the full array of effects that stem from displacement although what evidence we have suggests they are more complex, varied, and contradictory than the literature on urban refugees suggests. Cities vary in their ability to provide opportunities for new arrivals of all backgrounds. Sen's (1992) pioneering work on poverty also illustrates how, even among stable but 'marginalized' populations, entitlements and resilience differ according to an expansive matrix of variables including class, education, social networks, experience, and politics.

Do the points outlined above call, as do many of the other chapters in this collection, for us to approach refugee and forced migration studies as a distinct field of study? This chapter argues that by generating a self-delimited area of study focused on displacement and the displaced in urban areas, scholars and humanitarians have unnecessarily limited the scope of both their research and its potential positive impact. Rather than echoing tropes of marginalization or simply exposing/visibilizing urban refugees, there is a distinct and acute need for broader, more political engagement. This lesson applies across 'refugee studies', but needs foregrounding all the more in urban environments where substantive and empirical distinction map poorly with our analytical categories and impulses. Rather than continuing to treat urban refugees as a distinct population with economic and social identities shaped primarily or exclusively by their displacements, we—scholars and the urban displaced—would do better by integrating our studies with literature dedicated to understanding diasporization, urbanization, poverty, and public administration. This would not only advance our understanding of migrants' conditions and positions (and avoid having to start our work from scratch) but also expand our ability to engage in the policy and political processes that may better promote their rights and welfare. In the process, we will be able to add new dimensions to the study of other social phenomena, mainstreaming displacement through a dialogue that may ultimately help legitimize the study of forced migration beyond the bounds of refugee studies.

Notes

1. See, for example, *Forced Migration Review's* 2010 issue dedicated to Urban Refugees along with a range of other studies conducted in Africa, Asia, the Middle East, and Latin America by or on behalf of humanitarian organizations (Zetter and Deikun 2010) and a series of studies by such high-profile organizations as the Women's Refugee Commission (2011a and 2011b) and the associated International Rescue Committee (Lyytinen and Kullenberg 2013).
2. The UNHCR and others have completed more explicit literature reviews on 'urban refugees'.
3. The analysis of the Iraqi response stems from an interview with an official at the US State Department who spoke on the condition of anonymity.

References

Amit, R. (2012) *No Way In: Barriers to Access, Service and Administrative Justice at South Africa's Refugee Reception Offices.* Johannesburg: African Centre for Migration & Society.

Beal, J., and Esser, D. (2005) *Shaping Urban Futures: Challenges to Governing and Managing Afghan Cities.* Kabul: Afghanistan Research and Evaluation Unit.

Bernstein, J., and Okello, M. C. (2007) 'To Be or Not To Be: Urban Refugees in Kampala'. *Refuge* 24(1): 46–56.

Cohen, R., and Deng, F. M. (1998) *Masses in Flight: The Global Crisis of Internal Displacement.* Washington, DC: The Brookings Institution.

Cooper, D. (1992) *Urban Refugees: Ethiopians and Eritreans in Cairo.* Cairo: American University in Cairo Press.

Crisp. J. (n.d.) 'Forced Displacement in Africa: Dimensions, Difficulties and Policy Directions'. <http://www.cespi.it/CESPI-SID/Crisp-Forced_displacement_in_Africa.pdf> (accessed 12 September 2012).

Fábos, A., and Kibreab, G. (2007) 'Urban Refugees: Introduction'. *Refuge: Canada's Periodical on Refugees* 24(1): 1–19.

Feldman, M. S., and March, J. G. (1981) 'Information in Organizations as Signal and Symbol'. *Administrative Science Quarterly* 26(2): 171–86.

Jacobsen, K. (2006) 'Refugees and Asylum Seekers in Urban Areas: A Livelihoods Perspective'. *Journal of Refugee Studies* 19(3): 273–86.

Jacobsen, K., and Furst, R. (2012) *Developing a Profiling Methodology for Displaced People in Urban Settings*. Medford, MA: Tufts University.

Kagan, M. (2007) 'Legal Refugee Recognition in the Urban South: Formal v. *de Facto* Refugee Status'. *Refuge* 24(1): 11–26.

Kibreab, G. (1996) 'Eritrean and Ethiopian Urban Refugees in Khartoum: What the Eye Refuses to See'. *African Studies Review* 39(3): 131–78.

Landau, L. B., and Duponchel, M. (2011) 'Laws, Policies, or Social Position? Capabilities and the Determinants of Effective Protection in Four African Cities'. *Journal of Refugee Studies* 24(1): 1–22.

Lubkemann, S. (2010) 'Past Directions and Future Possibilities in the Study of African Displacement'. Unpublished scoping study for the Nordic Afrika Institute.

Lyytinen, E., and Kullenberg, J. (2013) 'Urban Refugee Research: An Analytical Report'. New York: International Rescue Committee.

Malkki, L. (1995) 'Refugees and Exile: From "Refugee Studies" to the National Order of Things'. *Annual Review of Anthropology* 24: 495–523.

Marfleet, P. (2007) 'Iraq's Refugees: "Exit" from the State'. *International Journal of Contemporary Iraqi Studies* 1(3): 397–419.

Margesson, R., Sharp, J. M., and Bruno, A. (2008) *CRS Report for Congress: Iraqi Refugees and Internally Displaced Persons: A Deepening Humanitarian Crisis?* Washington, DC: Congressional Research Service.

Pavenello, S., Elhawary, S., and Pantuliano, S. (2010) 'Hidden and Exposed: Urban Refugees in Nairobi, Kenya'. Humanitarian Policy Group Working Paper (March 2010).

Polzer, T., and Hammond, L. (2008) 'Invisible Displacement'. *Journal of Refugee Studies* 21(4): 417–31.

Rogge, J., and Akol, J. (1989) 'Repatriation: Its Role in Resolving Africa's Refugee Dilemma'. *International Migration Review* 23(2): 184–200.

Sandercock, L. (2004) 'Towards a Planning Imagination for the 21st Century'. *Journal of the American Planning Association* 70: 133–41.

Schoeller-Diaz, D. A., Lopez, V.-A., Kelly, J. J., and Patel, R. B. (2012) 'Hope in the Face of Displacement and Rapid Urbanization: A Study of the Factors that Contribute to Human Security and Resilience in Distrito de Aguablanca, Cali, Colombia'. Harvard Humanitarian Initiative Working Paper Series. September.

Schmidt, A. (2008) 'Negotiating Policy: Refugees and Security in Tanzania and Uganda'. Paper presented at the annual meeting of the ISA's 49th Annual Conventions, 'Bridging Multiple Divides', San Francisco, 26 March.

Sen, A. K. (1992) *Inequality Reexamined*. Oxford: Clarendon Press.

Simone, A. M. (2009) *City Life from Jakarta to Dakar: Movements at the Crossroads*. New York: Routledge.

Sommers, M. (2001) *Fear in Bongoland: Burundi Refugees in Urban Tanzania*. New York: Berghahn Books.

UN High Commissioner for Refugees (UNHCR) (2009) 'UNHCR Policy on Refugee Protection and Solutions in Urban Areas', September. <http://www.unhcr.org/refworld/docid/4ab8e7f72.html> (accessed 18 November 2012).

UNDESA, Population Division (2010) *World Urbanization Prospects: The 2009 Revision*. New York: United Nations.

Watson, V. (2006) 'Deep Difference: Diversity, Planning and Ethnics'. *Planning Theory* 12: 353–9.

Women's Refugee Commission (2011a) *Bright Lights, Big City: Urban Refugees Struggle to Make a Living in New Delhi*. New York: Women's Refugee Commission.

Women's Refugee Commission (2011b) *No Place to Go But Up: Urban Refugees in Johannesburg: South Africa*. New York: Women's Refugee Commission.

Zetter, R., and Deikun, G. (2010) 'Meeting Humanitarian Challenges in Urban Areas'. *Forced Migration Review* 34: 5–7.

CHAPTER 12

··

PROTRACTED REFUGEE SITUATIONS

··

JAMES MILNER

INTRODUCTION

THE search for 'permanent solutions for the problem of refugees' has been a core function of the Office of the United Nations High Commissioner for Refugees (UNHCR) since its creation in 1950 (UNGA 1950). Despite this long-standing recognition of the importance of 'durable solutions', the task of finding solutions for refugees has become increasingly difficult, and refugees have consequently spent longer periods in exile. In fact, UNHCR estimates that 'the average [duration] of major refugee situations...increased from nine years in 1993 to 17 years at the end of 2003' (UNHCR EXCOM 2004). This inability to ensure a timely solution for the plight of refugees has given rise to the phenomenon of 'protracted refugee situations', defined as a situation where refugees are in exile 'for five or more years after their initial displacement, without immediate prospects for implementation of durable solutions' (UNHCR EXCOM 2009).

A significant majority of the world's refugees are now to be found in protracted refugee situations. UNHCR estimates that 'some 6.4 million refugees were in a protracted situation by the end of 2012' (UNHCR 2013: 12). In addition, there are nearly 4.8 million Palestinian refugees registered with the United Nations Relief and Works Agency (UNRWA), which constitutes one of the world's largest protracted refugee situations. Recent concern for the rise of protracted refugee situations has been motivated not only by the scale of the problem, but also by the range of challenges associated with prolonged exile. Specifically, protracted refugee situations are frequently associated with poor protection environments and limitations on the rights of refugees, along with a range of challenges for states, UNHCR, and other actors.

The purpose of this chapter is to draw from recent research and policy discussions to provide an overview of the issue of protracted refugee situations. The chapter begins by considering the definition of protracted refugee situations and tracing the rise of the phenomenon. The chapter then discusses the causes and consequences of prolonged exile before turning to a more detailed discussion of how refugees, states, and UNHCR have responded to protracted refugee situations.

DEFINITIONS

In 2004, UNHCR characterized a protracted refugee situation as 'one in which refugees find themselves in a long-lasting and intractable state of limbo' (UNHCR 2004: 1) In identifying the major protracted refugee situations in the world at the time, UNHCR used the 'crude measure of refugee populations of 25,000 persons or more who have been in exile for five or more years in developing countries' (UNHCR 2004: 2). Over time, this characterization of *major* protracted refugee situations became the working definition of *all* protracted refugee situations. In a 2012 publication, for example, UNHCR defined a protracted refugee situation 'as one in which 25,000 or more refugees of the same nationality have been in exile for five years or longer in any given asylum country' (UNHCR 2004: 12). In this way, there has been a tendency to define a protracted refugee situation in both temporal (more than five years in exile) and quantitative (25,000 or more refugees) terms.

This definition is problematic as it excludes from our understanding of protracted refugee situations a number of populations that have been in exile for more than five years, but who number fewer than 25,000. For example, UNHCR reported in 2011 that there were some 11,500 Liberian refugees in Ghana, 14,000 Somali refugees in Djibouti, and 10,000 Sudanese refugees in Egypt (UNHCR 2011: 78–81). All of these populations have been in exile for more than a decade, but would be excluded from discussions of protracted refugee situations if the limit of 25,000 or more refugees remained in the definition. Likewise, quantitative limits on a definition are problematic given the difficulties frequently associated with refugee population statistics (Crisp 1999).

It is, therefore, significant that UNHCR's Executive Committee adopted a definition in 2009 that does not include a quantitative limit. Instead, it defined a protracted refugee situation as a situation where refugees have been in exile 'for five or more years after their initial displacement, without immediate prospects for implementation of durable solutions' (UNHCR 2009: preamble). This definition provides a more inclusive understanding of what constitutes a protracted refugee situation, and should therefore be used consistently as a basis for future discussions on the issue.

TRENDS

The significance of protracted refugee situations has grown over the past two decades with a shift in the balance between the number of refugees in emergency situations and those in prolonged exile. The early 1990s witnessed significant refugee movements in many regions of the world, including the Balkans, the Horn of Africa, Central Africa, West Africa, and South-West Asia. As a result, there was a dramatic increase in the global refugee population and the primary focus of the refugee regime was to deliver emergency life-saving assistance in many regions of the world, almost simultaneously. UNHCR reported that there were some 16.3 million refugees in the world at the end of 1993, the majority of which (52 per cent) were in emergency situations (UNHCR 2004: 2). Ten years later, many of these conflicts and associated refugee situations remained unresolved, with 64 per cent of the world's refugees no longer in an emergency situation, but a situation of prolonged exile. By the end of 2011, UNHCR estimated that almost 75 per cent of the refugee population under its mandate, some 7.1 million refugees, were in a protracted refugee situation (UNHCR 2012a). When the 4.8 million Palestinian refugees under the mandate of UNRWA are added to this total, it can be argued that 78 per cent of the world's refugees are now in a protracted refugee situation.

Some of the largest protracted refugee situations at the end of 2010 included: 1.9 million Afghans in Pakistan, 1.9 million Palestinians in Jordan, 1 million Afghans in Iran, 1 million Iraqis in Syria, 450,000 Iraqis in Jordan, and 350,000 Somalis in Kenya (UNHCR 2011: 78–81). In addition to these large situations, there are dozens of other protracted refugee situations around the world. Regardless of their size, all protracted refugee situations share an important feature: they are proving more difficult to resolve. UNHCR estimates that 'the average [duration] of major refugee situations...increased from nine years in 1993 to 17 years at the end of 2003' (UNHCR EXCOM 2004: 2). Ten years later, with many large situations of prolonged exile unresolved, it may be argued that the average duration of a refugee situation is now closer to 20 years. As a result, several generations of the same family can now be found in many refugee camps. For example, in the Dadaab camps in Kenya, there are some 10,000 third-generation Somali refugees, born to refugee parents who were themselves born in the camps (UNHCR 2012b).

CAUSES

While each situation has its own unique causes and dynamics, the growing prevalence of protracted refugee situations is generally understood to be the result of a similar set of causes. For its part, UNHCR has argued that:

> protracted refugee situations stem from political impasses. They are not inevitable, but are rather the result of political action and inaction, both in the country of origin (the persecution and violence that led to flight) and in the country of asylum. They endure because of ongoing problems in the country of origin, and stagnate and become protracted as a result of responses to refugee inflows, typically involving restrictions on refugee movement and employment possibilities, and confinement to camps. (UNHCR 2004: 2)

In fact, conditions in the country of origin and the responses of refugee-hosting countries are two important factors that help explain the rise of protracted refugee situations. Many situations of prolonged displacement originate from a number of so-called 'fragile states', such as Afghanistan, Iraq, and Somalia, where conflict and a lack of effective state institutions have been a primary driver of displacement. As noted by Long, however, not all protracted refugee situations are the result of the absence of government or state capacity, as in the case of Somalia, but may also be the result of particular types of government and the persecution of minority groups, as in the case of Myanmar or Bhutan (Long 2011: 6). Likewise, refugee situations remain protracted frequently in the midst of the policies of refugee-hosting states that deny refugees the opportunity to be self-reliant or to pursue a solution through local integration, as discussed below.

The prevailing situations in the country of origin and the policy responses of the country of asylum, however, provide only a partial explanation for the causes of protracted refugee situations, and it is consequently important to consider a broader set of causes that fall outside UNHCR's explanation. In particular, the challenge of solutions for refugees over the past 20 years has coincided with the introduction of more restrictive asylum policies by states in the global North. One consequence of these policies has been the 'containment' of refugee populations within their region of origin, thereby limiting solutions for refugees (Hyndman and Giles 2011). At the same time, there has been a marked decline in donor support for long-term refugee-assistance and repatriation programmes. The combination of restrictive asylum policies and declining donor engagement has resulted in concerns on the part of many refugee-hosting states that they are carrying a disproportionate share of the global responsibility for refugees, which, in turn, has reinforced restrictive asylum policies in countries of first asylum. For example, Crisp notes that by the late 1990s, 'donor states can be said to have exacerbated the decline in protection standards in Africa by making it increasingly clear that they [were] no longer prepared to support long-term refugee assistance efforts' (Crisp 2000: 6)

The response of UNHCR and the wider UN system has also contributed to the rise of protracted refugee situations. As noted by UNHCR, the typical response to large refugee movements in the 1980s and 1990s was the admission of refugees into countries of first asylum on a prima facie basis, the containment of these refugees in camps, and the long-term provision of food, shelter, and other needs by UNHCR and other humanitarian actors (UNHCR 2008). Over time, UNHCR 'assumed a progressively wider range of long-term refugee responsibilities' and functions within refugee camps, leading to concerns that UNHCR was acting as a 'surrogate state' and perpetuating refugee situations through long-term 'care and maintenance' programmes (Slaughter and Crisp 2008: 128). The past 20 years have also witnessed a marked decline in the engagement of other actors within the UN system to the causes and consequences of refugee movements. In particular, a lack of engagement on the part of various peace and security actors to address the conflict or human rights violations in the country of origin contributes to the prolongation of many refugee situations. Likewise, the limited engagement of development actors in countries of origin and asylum has weakened efforts to find solutions for refugees, especially through repatriation and local integration (Loescher et al. 2008).

CONSEQUENCES

The greatest consequence of prolonged displacement is for the human rights of refugees. As noted by Durieux, the significance of protracted refugee situations is not only in the 'duration of life in exile but also, and more significantly, about the quality of such life, which is seen to deteriorate over time as solutions remain elusive' (Durieux 2009: 60) Since the early 1990s, many states in the global South have required refugees to live in designated camps and have denied refugees a number of the rights enumerated in the 1951 Convention relating to the Status of Refugees, such as freedom of movement and the right to seek wage-earning employment (Smith 2004). Denial of these rights compounds refugees' vulnerability as they frequently become dependent on dwindling international assistance. Sexual and physical violence can also become prevalent in refugee camps, while refugee women, children, the elderly, and disabled all face particular protection challenges during prolonged encampment. Similarly, refugees in urban settings often find themselves in precarious situations, subject to harassment and exploitation. Without documentation, those in urban areas are left unprotected by either their home or host governments and suffer from discrimination, inadequate housing, and lack of employment and access to social services (UNHCR 2009).

In addition to these human rights and humanitarian concerns, protracted refugee situations can also lead to a number of political and security concerns for host states, the countries of origin, and the international community (Loescher and Milner 2005). The long-term presence of large refugee populations has been a source of tensions between states and regional instability, especially through the militarization of refugee camps. Armed groups have used refugee camps as a base to launch attacks against their country of origin. Other security concerns, such as arms trafficking, drug smuggling, human trafficking, and the recruitment of child soldiers, have also been documented in protracted refugee situations. In addition to these direct security concerns, protracted refugee situations also have indirect security implications. Tensions between refugees and the local population often arise as refugees are perceived to receive preferential access to social services such as health and education. Over time, competition between refugees and the host population over scarce resources can also become a source of insecurity.

These dynamics may lead host states to perceive the prolonged presence of refugees as a potential threat. This perception frequently reinforces the causes of protracted refugee situations, as states seek to 'contain' the refugee 'problem', typically in isolated refugee camps, while viewing pressures by the international donor community to encourage solutions for refugees through local integration as 'burden shifting' and an infringement of their sovereignty. Protracted refugee situations also have important consequences for the global refugee regime as they 'squander precious resources' (UNHCR 2004: 3) on long-term assistance programmes instead of activities to support durable solutions, serve as flashpoints for tensions between refugee-hosting states in the global South and donor states in the global North, and symbolize the inability of UNHCR to predictably fulfil one of its core functions. As noted by Long, 'the very fact of protracted displacement is evidence that existing approaches to "solving" displacement have failed' (Long 2011: 8).

RESPONSES

There are several important historical examples of the resolution of large and chronic refugee situations. In the late 1980s, for example, solutions were found for long-standing refugee populations from Indochina and Central America through Comprehensive Plans of Action (CPAs). As noted by Betts (2008), these past approaches shared a number of characteristics. They were *comprehensive* in the sense that they drew on all possible solutions: repatriation, resettlement, and local integration as well as expanding migratory opportunities. They were *cooperative* in that they were based on burden sharing between countries of refugee origin, host countries, and resettlement countries. And finally they were *collaborative*, meaning they involved a broad range of UN agencies, NGOs, and other actors. While it will be important to consider the limitations of these CPAs and the extent to which they may serve as models for resolving contemporary situations (Bradley 2011), these examples serve as important reminders that past responses to protracted refugee situations have resulted in solutions for millions of refugees.

Notwithstanding these past successes, the issue of protracted refugee situations received very limited international attention during the 1990s. As the decade's refugee emergencies subsided, however, and attention was drawn to the conditions of refugees in prolonged exile, greater attention was given to the need to develop more effective responses to protracted refugee situations. While researchers and advocacy groups have played an important role in raising the profile of this issue, UNHCR has provided the primary focus for global discussions on responses to protracted refugee situations. Beginning in 1999, UNHCR's Evaluation and Policy Analysis Unit commissioned a number of studies to better understand the dynamics and implications of prolonged displacement (Crisp 2003). The question of protracted refugee situations in Africa was subsequently discussed during UNHCR's Executive Committee in October 2001 (UNHCR 2001), and was the focus of a 2004 policy paper (UNHCR 2004). These initiatives helped highlight the significance of protracted refugee situations, while providing early analysis of their causes and consequences.

UNHCR's efforts to promote responses to protracted refugee situations, however, culminated in 2008 and 2009 around three events. The first event was the launch in June 2008 of the High Commissioner's Initiative on Protracted Refugee Situations, intended to 'reinvigorate possibilities for solutions to protracted refugee situations (PRS) and, in the interim, to improve the quality of life for populations that have lived in such exile for long periods of time' (UNHCR EXCOM 2008: 1). To launch the initiative, five priority situations were identified: Afghan refugees in Iran and Pakistan; Rohingya refugees in Bangladesh; Bosnian and Croatian refugees in Serbia; Burundian refugees in Tanzania; and Eritrean refugees in eastern Sudan.

The second event was the 2008 High Commissioner's Dialogue on Protection Challenges, which brought together representatives of governments, NGOs, UN agencies, and researchers to discuss responses to protracted refugee situations. In advance of the Dialogue, UNHCR released a discussion paper that outlined the importance of political action, international cooperation, coordination, and complimentarity in finding solutions for PRSs, in addition to discussing the challenges faced by the traditional durable solutions (UNHCR 2008). Arguably the most significant conclusion of the background document, however, was a call to move away from long-term 'care and maintenance' programmes to an approach focused more on self-reliance and local solutions for refugees. In the paper, UNHCR concluded that the care and maintenance model was 'flawed in several ways' and called for a new approach focused on livelihoods and self-reliance to prepare refugees for a durable solution, 'wherever that might be'.

The third significant event during this period was the negotiation of the 2009 EXCOM Conclusion on Protracted Refugee Situations. As is the tradition with EXCOM Conclusions, negotiations to draft a text acceptable to EXCOM's 70-plus member states produced multiple drafts and resulted in prolonged deliberations. In fact, when negotiations failed to produce a consensus text ahead of the normal meeting of the Executive Committee in October, many observers assumed that efforts to consolidate a decade of policy development and research into an EXCOM Conclusion had failed. The continuation of negotiations into November and the convening of a special EXCOM meeting in December to adopt the Conclusion is at least partially a reflection of the importance attached to the issues by UNHCR and a number of key EXCOM member states.

While it may be too soon to assess the impact of these three events on the resolution of individual protracted refugee situations, at least four important lessons emerged from these discussions. First, there are important differences within and between refugee populations, and there is consequently no 'one size fits all' approach to resolving protracted refugee situations. Second, UNHCR and humanitarian actors cannot resolve protracted refugee situations on their own. Instead, the sustained engagement of a broad range of stakeholders, especially peace and security and development actors within the UN system, is an important prerequisite for finding solutions for protracted refugee situations. Third, durable solutions need to be looked at in a comprehensive manner and approached in a complementary way, in addition to the reinforcement of the three traditional durable solutions of voluntary repatriation, local integration, and resettlement, as discussed elsewhere in this volume. Fourth, as noted, there is a pressing need to shift from a long-term 'care and maintenance' approach to protracted refugee situations to a 'solutions-oriented approach' based on increased self-reliance and livelihoods opportunities for refugees.

These four lessons, however, are indicative of long-standing weaknesses of the global refugee regime, and their implementation will involve overcoming a number of constraints within the regime itself. For example, the difficulties in negotiating the 2009 EXCOM Conclusion is not only a reflection of the complexity of the issues of protracted refugee situations and its close relation to core state interests, such as sovereignty and security, but also the wider challenge of cooperation within the global refugee regime. These tensions speak to the significant divide that remains between refugee-hosting states in the global South and the donor and resettlement countries in the global North. For their part, states in the global South tend to see discussions on solutions for protracted refugee situations as an effort by the global North to continue to contain the refugee issues in the South. In contrast, states in the global North see the policy choices of host states in the South as an impediment to solutions for refugees, especially through local integration.

Given these tensions, it may be significant that a number of governments have become more actively engaged in responses to protracted refugee situations. Among donor and resettlement countries, Canada assumed a leadership role by emphasizing the importance of the issues of protracted refugee situations within its multilateral relations, while domestically establishing an Interdepartmental Working Group on Protracted Refugee Situations in 2007 to help develop more comprehensive and integrated responses (Dion 2009: 28–9). More recently, the US Department of State has identified responses to protracted refugee situations as a US foreign policy priority.[1] While these initiatives have resulted in additional resettlement opportunities from some protracted refugee situations, such as those of Karen refugees in Thailand and Bhutanese refugees in Nepal, they have yet to have a demonstrated impact on the global response to protracted refugee situations.

In contrast, a limited number of states in the global South, including Sierra Leone, Liberia, and Tanzania, have started the process of resolving protracted refugee situations through the naturalization and local integration of refugees. While encouraging, it is important to note some of the limitations of these initiatives and the challenges that remain. For example, it was in 2007 that Tanzania first expressed its willingness to offer citizenship to some 220,000 Burundian refugees who had been in Tanzania since 1972. Through international support, the naturalization applications of nearly 163,000 individuals were approved by the government of Tanzania by mid-2010. Only a small number of these individuals, however, have received their citizenship papers due to domestic political constraints and concerns over diminishing support from the international donor community. As a result, the resolution of this protracted refugee situation has stalled (Milner 2013).

Given the limited impact of responses from UNHCR and states, it is especially important to consider how refugees themselves have responded to situations of prolonged exile. Although refugees in protracted refugee situations often live in restricted conditions and are officially denied many of the rights afforded to them by international refugee law, it would be wrong to assume that refugees have no agency and have not developed their own responses to protracted displacement. In fact, there is a growing recognition of the various means by which refugees have responded to prolonged exile and the failure of the refugee regime to identify a timely solution to their plight. For example, Lindley notes that in the case of Somali refugees who have been in Kenya for more than 20 years, refugees 'use a wide range of economic strategies to cope with life in exile', many of which are 'informal, refugee-driven, and occur beyond state regulation' (Lindley 2011: 39).

Indeed, many refugee camps have thriving informal economies, notwithstanding official prohibitions on such activities. Family members may also leave the camp to seek economic opportunities in surrounding communities or urban areas. Refugees from protracted refugee situations have increasingly sought their own solutions through onward migration outside their region of origin, regardless of the risks to their physical safety with such journeys. Refugee communities have also established elaborate transnational networks, linking camp-based refugees to those have been resettled or otherwise found access to the global North and establishing a flow of remittances to provide relief for those remaining in refugee camps.

This wide range of coping mechanisms speaks to the resourcefulness of refugees, the importance of recognizing their agency, and the benefits that would come from including refugees as central actors in the resolution of protracted refugee situations. It is, however, important to note that while these responses may enhance livelihood opportunities for refugees, even leading to de facto local integration (Long 2011: 22–6), such responses do not constitute a long-term solution. Moreover, these responses may also expose refugees to new vulnerabilities. For example, while camp-based refugees may respond to food shortages by borrowing from neighbours, finding informal work, or sending a family member out to beg, a smaller number of refugees may turn to so-called 'negative coping mechanisms', including prostitution. Likewise, refugees living in urban areas without official permission live with the daily risk of exploitation, detention, and possible deportation if caught.

Many of these vulnerabilities can be compounded when refugees respond to prolonged exile through 'irregular' migration. For example, Somali refugees have been found to resort to clandestine, costly, and frequently dangerous migration to Europe, South Africa, and elsewhere as a response to their prolonged exile in East Africa. In contrast, regional migration has been a more reliable coping strategy for Afghans in Pakistan and Iran and Sierra Leoneans and Liberians in West Africa, raising questions about the possibility of developing migration options as a possible 'fourth' solution for refugees (UNHCR 2008: 20–1). As noted by Long, however, the restrictive policies of states in the global North and South to the onward migration of refugees 'place clear limits on the extent to which refugee-directed mobility can offer a viable means of "unlocking" protracted refugee crises'. Moreover, Long notes that unless migration opportunities are linked to permanent legal status and full membership in a political community, 'migration cannot be considered a "fourth" solution' for refugees (Long 2011: 14–15 and this volume).

Conclusion

The past two decades have witnessed an important shift in the global refugee situation, with some three-quarters of the world's refugees now in a protracted refugee situation. As a result of the changing nature of conflict since the end of the Cold War, the introduction of restrictive policies by states in the global North and South, the legacy of responses by humanitarian actors, and the lack of engagement by other actors within the UN system, refugees now spend an average of some 20 years in exile. The consequences of such prolonged displacement include significant vulnerabilities for refugees, including the frequent violation of a number of their rights, in addition to concerns for host states, countries of origin, and the wider global refugee regime.

Despite the scale and importance of the issue, responses to protracted refugee situations have been limited in their impact. While UNHCR has sought to encourage a more meaningful international response through several initiatives in recent years, and while a number of states have developed responses, primarily to individual protracted refugee situations, the overall response to the global challenge of protracted refugee situations remains limited and ineffective. In contrast, refugees have demonstrated remarkable resilience and resourcefulness in finding their own responses to prolonged displacement. While demonstrating the importance of refugee agency, however, these responses have frequently compounded the vulnerability of refugees and underscore the central role that citizenship and the realization of rights need to play in the resolution of protracted refugee situations.

Although limited in their impact, efforts by the policy and research communities over the past decade to address protracted refugee situations have resulted in a clearer understanding of the significance of protracted displacement, its causes, and its various consequences. After more than a decade of discussions, however, it is important to focus on what practical steps can be taken to more systematically resolve protracted refugee situations. This may best be accomplished by focusing international attention on a prominent protracted refugee situation that is near resolution, such as the case of Burundian refugees in Tanzania, which could generate positive momentum and help unlock other situations. As outlined in this chapter, however, UNHCR and humanitarian actors cannot generate this momentum alone, but will require the meaningful engagement of a broader range of actors, especially those engaged in peace-building and development activities, along with sustained support from key political actors. More generally, however, key tensions within the global refugee regime, such as the impasse between states in the global North and South, will need to be addressed if responses to protracted refugee situations are to be more predictable.

There is an important role for future research in addressing these significant challenges. Specifically, future research could usefully work through case studies of historical and contemporary refugee situations to more systematically identify best practices of what has worked to address particular challenges and find solutions, and consider how these lessons may be applied elsewhere. Future research could also more systematically consider the links between prolonged displacement and other areas of international concern, such as peace-building, development, and regional politics, and how engaging with the interests of a broader set of actors can help unlock solutions for refugees. Likewise, additional research on the three 'traditional' durable solutions, other possible solutions, and the relationship between displacement, membership, and citizenship could identify new ways of understanding the meaning of solutions and how they may be pursued, while also considering the links with other forms of protracted displacement, especially statelessness. More fundamentally, however, the prevalence of protracted refugee situations highlights the shortcomings of the global refugee regime, the need for sustained and creative engagement, and the continuing need for international action to seek permanent solutions for the plight of refugees. This task remains as vital today as it was more than 60 years ago.

NOTE

1. See <http://www.state.gov/j/prm/policyissues/issues/protracted/index.htm> (accessed 31 July 2012).

REFERENCES

Adleman, H. (ed.) (2008) *Protracted Displacement in Asia: No Place to Call Home.* Aldershot: Ashgate.

Betts, A. (2008) 'Historical Lessons for Overcoming Protracted Refugee Situations'. Pp. 162–86 in G. Loescher, J. Milner, E. Newman, and G. Troeller (eds.), *Protracted Refugee Situations: Political, Human Rights and Security Implications.* Tokyo: United Nations University Press.

Bradley, M. (2011) 'Unlocking Protracted Displacement: Central America's "Success Story" Reconsidered'. *Refugee Survey Quarterly* 30(4): 84–121.

Brookings-Bern Project on Internal Displacement (2007) '*Summary Report: Expert Seminar on Protracted IDP Situations*'. Geneva, June.

Crisp, J. (1999) 'Who has Counted the Refugees? UNHCR and the Politics of Numbers'. New Issues in Refugee Research. Working paper No. 12. Geneva: UNHCR, June.

Crisp, J. (2000) 'Africa's Refugees: Patterns, Problems and Policy Challenges'. New Issues in Refugee Research. Working paper No. 28. Geneva: UNHCR, August.

Crisp, J. (2003) 'No Solutions in Sight: The Problem of Protracted Refugee Situations in Africa'. New Issues in Refugee Research. Working paper No. 75. Geneva: UNHCR, January.

Dion, A. (2009) 'Comprehensive Solutions: A "Whole-of-Government" Approach'. *Forced Migration Review* 33(September).

Durieux, J.-F. (2009) 'A Regime at a Loss?' *Forced Migration Review* 33(September).

Forced Migration Review (2009) 'Protracted Displacement'. 33(September). <http://www.fmreview.org/protracted.htm>.

Hyndman, J., and Giles, W. (2011) 'Waiting for What? The Feminization of Asylum in Protracted Situations'. *Gender, Place and Culture* 18(3)(June): 361–79.

Lindley, A. (2011) 'Between a Protracted and a Crisis Situation: Policy Responses to Somali Refugees in Kenya'. *Refugee Survey Quarterly* 30(4): 14–49.

Loescher, G., and Milner, J. (2005) *Protracted Refugee Situations: Domestic and International Security Implications*. Adelphi Paper no. 375. London: Routledge.

Loescher, G., Milner, J., Newman, E., and Troeller, G. (eds.) (2008) *Protracted Refugee Situations: Political, Human Rights and Security Implications*. Tokyo: United Nations University Press.

Long, K. (2011) 'Permanent Crises? Unlocking the Protracted Displacement of Refugees and Internally Displaced Persons: Policy Overview'. Oxford: Refugee Studies Centre, University of Oxford, October.

Milner, J. (2013) 'Two Steps Forward, One Step Back: Understanding the Shifting Politics of Refugee Policy in Tanzania'. New Issues in Refugee Research. Research paper No. 255. Geneva: UNHCR, July.

Slaughter, A., and Crisp, J. (2008) 'A Surrogate State? The Role of UNHCR in Protracted Refugee Situations'. Pp. 123–40. in G. Loescher, J. Milner, E. Newman, and G. Troeller (eds.), *Protracted Refugee Situations: Political, Human Rights and Security Implications*. Tokyo: United Nations University Press.

Smith, M. (2004) 'Warehousing Refugees: A Denial of Rights, a Waste of Humanity'. *World Refugee Survey 2004*. Washington, DC: US Committee for Refugees.

United Nations General Assembly (UNGA) (1950) 'Resolution 428(V): Annex: Statute of the Office of the United Nations High Commissioner for Refugees'. December.

United Nations High Commissioner for Refugees (UNHCR) (2001) 'Chairman's Summary: Informal Consultations on New Approaches and Partnerships for Protection and Solutions in Africa'. Geneva, December.

UNHCR (2008) 'Protracted Refugee Situations: A Discussion Paper Prepared for the High Commissioner's Dialogue on Protection Challenges'. UNHCR/DPC/2008/Doc. 2, 20 November.

UNHCR (2009) 'UNHCR Policy on Refugee Protection and Solutions in Urban Areas'. Geneva, September.

UNHCR (2011) *UNHCR: Statistical Yearbook 2010*. Geneva.

UNHCR (2012a) *UNHCR: Global Trends 2011*. Geneva, June.

UNHCR (2012b) 'News Story: Dadaab: World's Biggest Refugee Camp 20 Years Old'. 21 February, <http://www.unhcr.org/4f439dbb9.html> (accessed 31 July).

UNHCR (2013) *UNHCR: Global Trends 2012*. Geneva, June.

UNHCR, Executive Committee (EXCOM) (2004) 'Protracted Refugee Situations'. Standing Committee, 30th Meeting, EC/54/SC/CRP.14, 10 June.

UNHCR (EXCOM) (2008) 'Protracted Refugee Situations: Revisiting the Problem'. Standing Committee, 42nd Meeting, EC/59/SC/CRP.13, 2 June.

UNHCR (EXCOM) (2009) 'Conclusion on Protracted Refugee Situations'. No. 109 (LXI).

CHAPTER 13

....

INTERNAL DISPLACEMENT

....

WALTER KÄLIN

INTRODUCTION

THE 1998 Guiding Principles on Internal Displacement[1] describe internally displaced persons (IDPs) as

> persons or groups of persons who have been forced or obliged to flee or to leave their homes or places of habitual residence, in particular as a result of or in order to avoid the effects of armed conflict, situations of generalized violence, violations of human rights or natural or human-made disasters, and who have not crossed an internationally recognized state border.

This notion has become part of the legally binding 2009 African Convention on the Protection and Assistance for Internally Displaced Persons in Africa (hereinafter: Kampala Convention) as well as the Protocol on the Protection and Assistance to Internally Displaced Persons, adopted in 2006 by the Member States of the International Conference on the Great Lakes (hereinafter: Great Lakes IDP Protocol). The definition has also been incorporated into a series of national laws and policies, including in Uganda, Nepal, Iraq, and Sudan.

The coerced or otherwise involuntary character of movement and the fact that affected persons have not crossed 'an internationally recognized state border' are the two constitutive elements of this notion. The list of causes of displacement is only indicative, meaning that potentially a wide range of events that force people to leave their homes or places of habitual residence can count as a relevant cause.

It is important to stress that the notion of who is an IDP contained in the Guiding Principles is not a legal definition conferring a special legal status similar to refugee status. Rather, as citizens or habitual residents of an affected state who are in a situation of special vulnerability IDPs are entitled to the enjoyment of all relevant guarantees of human rights and humanitarian law applicable to the permanent population of the country concerned whether or not they are formally recognized as being displaced. This does not rule out the possibility of administrative measures such as registration by authorities or international organizations to identify those who are displaced and need special assistance and are entitled to special measures to address their specific vulnerabilities. However, lack of such registration would not deprive IDPs of their entitlements under applicable international human rights or humanitarian law.

INTERNAL DISPLACEMENT: CAUSES AND NUMBERS

With an estimated 28.8 million people displaced within their own countries by armed conflict and other forms of violence at the end of 2012, internally displaced persons outnumber the roughly 16–17 million refugees and asylum seekers by far. While the overall figure of IDPs has remained roughly the same for the past ten years situations are often very volatile: thus, in 2012 more than 6.5 million people were newly displaced while over 2.1 million IDPs were reported to have returned to their areas of origin (IDMC/NRC 2013a: 9–10). Typically, internal displacement caused by armed conflict lasts often very long and continues beyond actual hostilities. Protracted displacement where the process of finding durable solutions for IDPs is stalled and people remain in displacement for five, ten, or even 20 years and more exists in at least 40 countries (IDMC/NRC 2012: 14–15).

Very large numbers of people are displaced in the context of natural disasters with figures strongly fluctuating from year to year: while 14.9 million such IDPs were identified in 2011 the figure reached 42.3 million a year before and rose again in 2012 to 32.4 million (IDMC/NRC 2013b: 5). However, these estimates are incomplete particularly because smaller sudden-onset disasters are underreported and reliable figures of those displaced by slow-onset disasters such as drought are hardly available (IDMC/NRC 2012: 7). In many cases, people displaced by natural hazards are able to return after relatively short periods in displacement but there are also cases where, for instance due to a lack of sufficient support for rebuilding destroyed houses and infrastructure, people remain in protracted displacement.

Disaster induced displacement is likely to increase in the context of climate change (McAdam 2010). Five relevant scenarios have been identified in this context (Kälin 2010): (1) hydro-meteorological sudden-onset disasters such as flooding, hurricanes, or landslides; (2) slow-onset disasters such as drought or erosion of coastlines and salination of soil and groundwater due to rising sea levels; (3) low-lying small island states likely to become inhabitable due to sea-level rise, thus at risk of 'disappearing' as a whole; (4) designation of areas as high-risk zones too dangerous for human habitation or as areas set aside for mitigation (e.g. expansion of forest areas to create 'carbon sinks' binding greenhouse gases) or adaptation measures (e.g. creation of large water reservoirs built to address increasing drought); and (5) violent conflicts over diminishing resources such as water and pastures.

Finally, people may be forced to leave their homes because authorities or private actors implement development projects such as mines, dams, airports, and upgrading of urban areas or decide to protect forests and other natural habitats from human intrusion. Such decisions result in internal displacement where companies or authorities fail to relocate affected people and communities in accordance with international standards or do not properly compensate them. While information about the number of persons affected by projects funded by development banks are available, knowledge about development induced displacement outside this context remains scarce.

While the media often portray IDPs as people living in camps, the reality is different. In most countries affected by internal displacement, the majority of IDPs stay with host families, live in informal settlements, squat in public buildings, or manage to live on their own in rented houses or apartments. Many live in urban areas where it is often difficult to identify them, a challenge resulting in a certain degree of neglect by humanitarian actors (Fielden 2008; Beyani 2011: 7–18). Overall, more research on the dynamics of urban IDP flows is needed to develop appropriate approaches.

INTERNALLY DISPLACED PERSONS AND REFUGEES: A FUNDAMENTAL DIFFERENCE

Refugees and IDPs alike experience the perils of flight, find themselves in a new, often difficult environment, and hope to find a durable solution allowing them to rebuild their shattered lives. This is why some—in particular social scientists—regard both categories as essentially similar victims of forced migration (see Bakewell 2011: 15). Others, particularly legal scholars, insist that a sharp line must be drawn between the two (Hathaway 2007).

From a legal perspective, refugees are fundamentally different from IDPs: as they cannot turn to their own government for protection they are in need of protection abroad. The institution of asylum, the principle of *non-refoulement*, and the mandate of UNHCR[2] to provide protection and assistance to refugees are the cornerstones of such international protection. In contrast, IDPs have not left their own country and thus they remain under the jurisdiction of their government even in cases where governmental forces or authorities are responsible for their displacement. By virtue of state sovereignty, the international community is not entitled to substitute for national authorities but plays a subsidiary role of supporting or complementing governmental action. Thus, while refugee protection is essentially international protection, the protection of IDPs 'is primarily national protection' (UNHCR 2012: 120) even if in 'failed state' scenarios where a government has collapsed or withdrawn its presence from important parts of the country the international community may step into the vacuum.

To qualify IDPs as a kind of 'refugees' risks ultimately lowering the level of their rights: while refugees as foreigners regularly do not enjoy all the rights available to the citizens of a country, it is important to insist that IDPs do not lose *any* rights because they are displaced, even if in reality they may be discriminated against and treated as second class citizens.

INTERNALLY DISPLACED PERSONS: A DISTINCT CATEGORY OF CONCERN?

One of the current debates concerns the issue as to whether or not it is meaningful to look at IDPs as a distinct category of concern. The International Committee of the Red Cross, for instance, maintains that 'ICRC does not believe that someone displaced is automatically more vulnerable than someone who is not' (ICRC 2009: 20) and a study by the Overseas Development Institute stressed that identifying IDPs as a distinct category has not ameliorated their situation (Collinson, Darcy, and Waddell 2009: 53). Similarly, James Hathaway has asked: 'Why should they be treated as a category of concern distinguished from other internal human rights victims who have not been displaced?' (Hathaway 2007: 360).

Roberta Cohen, one of the key proponents of an IDP-specific approach, responded by asking whether Hathaway wanted to 'turn the clock back to an earlier time when only refugees, or individuals who flee across borders from persecution, could expect attention from the international community' (Cohen 2007: 370). Others too have insisted that there are good reasons to have a specific focus on IDPs in legal and operational terms (Kidane 2011).

This debate, however, is largely academic insofar as states clearly have accepted to look at IDPs as a specific category of concern and there are no indications that they want to depart from that approach: at the universal level, they regularly reaffirm their unanimous recognition of the Guiding Principles on Internal Displacement as an 'important international framework for the protection' of IDPs.[3] At the regional level, the adoption of the Kampala Convention is a strong reaffirmation of an IDP-specific approach; and at the domestic level the number of states adopting IDP specific laws, strategies, and policies is growing. Nevertheless, the question as to whether a deeper justification for a specific focus on IDPs exists is well founded and relevant.

That IDPs as citizens or permanent residents of the country they are displaced in are protected by human rights exactly as the rest of its population and are not necessarily more vulnerable than non-displaced people is often used as a key argument against looking at IDPs as a particular category of concern. While these observations are correct, they overlook the fact that IDPs have specific needs that non-displaced persons do not possess (Cohen and Deng 1998: 23–9; Mooney 2005; Kälin et al. 2010: in particular

19–22, 342–5, 377–82, 515–23). While their individual predicament may vastly differ—with some barely surviving and others quickly regaining normal lives in another part of the country—IDPs have in common that unlike non-displaced people they need to (1) be protected against being displaced; (2) be able to leave the danger zone and reach a safe location and not be forced to return to danger zones; (3) find a place to stay temporarily, whether in- or outside a camp; (4) be protected against discrimination on account of their being displaced, for instance regarding access to basic services or the labour market; (5) have lost personal documentation replaced and documents issued to children born during displacement even if, according to the law, documentation can only be obtained in the area of habitual residence; (6) be able to register as voters and participate in elections and referenda even if, according to the law, these political rights can only be exercised at the place of habitual residence; (7) have real estate and other property left behind protected against being taken over by others and, where this has happened, to have the appropriate assets restituted at a later stage; and (8) find a durable solution to their being displaced through sustainable return to the place of former habitual residence, or sustainable local integration where they had been displaced to, or in another part of the country. These eight displacement-specific needs of IDPs have been amply illustrated by the reports on country missions by the Representatives of the Secretary-General and the Special Rapporteur on (the Human Rights of) Internally Displaced Persons[4] but further empirical research would be useful.

Many IDPs face problems and vulnerabilities that are not limited to the displaced but become particularly relevant in the context of internal displacement: there is some evidence that without humanitarian assistance IDPs run a higher risk than those remaining at home to suffer malnutrition and be in need of food assistance; have their children recruited into armed forces or non-state armed groups; become victims of gender-based violence, particularly in camp situations; become separated from family members, particularly during flight; be excluded from education; suffer from more serious health problems than non-displaced people; or remain in extreme poverty without any access to adequate livelihood opportunities. In Afghanistan, for instance, the World Bank found that in urban settings 'IDP household heads have substantially lower literacy rates and formal levels of education', live 'in much more hazardous housing conditions' and earn substantially less than the urban poor (World Bank 2011: 7). Similarly, in Colombia IDPs belong to the poorest among poor urban populations and many became poorer after having been displaced from rural areas (Carrillo 2009: 534). However, in the Ivory Coast's largest city Abidjan IDPs were found to not be significantly more vulnerable than non-IDPs (Jacobsen 2008). While higher levels of vulnerability of IDPs have been observed in many situations, more research on the factors determining this outcome would be welcome.

Looking at IDPs as a specific category of concern should not be understood as a reason to provide them with humanitarian assistance to the detriment of other vulnerable people. Assistance should always be provided on the basis of assessed needs and vulnerabilities and not on grounds of categorization, but looking at IDPs as a specific category of concern helps to ensure that such assistance in fact meets their specific needs.

In this context, the notion of displacement-affected communities can be helpful to develop adequate responses. This notion acknowledges that host communities and communities expected to reintegrate IDPs once return becomes possible are also affected by the effects of internal displacement. To assist such displacement-affected communities, too, or to support them with area based development interventions (for instance by upgrading infrastructure such as water and sanitation or local health and education services) not only helps to reduce tensions between IDPs and local populations but also addresses the burden imposed on such communities by the arrival of displaced people.

PROTECTING INTERNALLY DISPLACED PERSONS: THE LEGAL FRAMEWORK

The Universal Level: The Guiding Principles on Internal Displacement

While internal displacement has been a reality since the advent of the nation state and the fixing of international borders, IDPs became the concern of the international community only as recently as the end of the Cold War, when it became possible to address an issue that hitherto had been widely regarded to belong to states' internal affairs. A particularly important step in this regard was the creation of the mandate of the Representative of the UN Secretary-General on Internally Displaced Persons (hereinafter: Representative) in 1992 by the then UN Human Rights Commission.[5]

The Representative early on stressed that as citizens or long-term residents of the country they are displaced in, IDPs are protected by international human rights law and in times of armed conflict also by international humanitarian law. His 'Compilation and Analysis of Legal Norms' submitted to the Human Rights Commission in 1995 found that present international law, despite several grey areas and a few gaps, sufficiently responds to most needs of IDPs; at the same time, the study highlighted that relevant human rights and humanitarian law guarantees, with only a very few exceptions, do not specifically address internal displacement and 'more specific right[s] ha[ve] not been articulated that would ensure implementation of the general norm in areas of particular need to internally displaced persons'.[6]

The Human Rights Commission agreed with this analysis and recognized 'that the protection of internally displaced persons would be strengthened by identifying, reaffirming and consolidating specific rights for their protection'. As a consequence, it called 'upon the Representative of the Secretary-General to continue, on the basis of his compilation and analysis of legal norms, to develop an appropriate framework in this regard for the protection of internally displaced persons'.[7] On the basis of this resolution, the Representative, supported by a team of experts, developed the 'Guiding Principles on

Internal Displacement' and submitted them to the Human Rights Commission in 1998 (Cohen 2004; Bagshaw 2005: 82–97; Weiss and Korn 2006).

This document sets out the rights of IDPs in 30 'Principles'. Covering all phases of displacement, they first present some General Principles. These include the important statement that 'the primary duty and responsibility to provide protection and humanitarian assistance to internally displaced persons' rests not with the international community but national authorities (Principle 3) (Brookings Institution 2005).

Principles relating to protection from displacement (Principles 5–9) contain, *inter alia*, the prohibition of arbitrary displacement which is violated, for instance, in cases of ethnic cleansing and similar practices; during 'armed conflict, unless the security of the civilians involved or imperative military reasons so demand'; or 'in case of disasters, unless the safety and health of those affected requires their evacuation' (Principle 6). The latter two examples indicate that not all instances of forced displacement are illegal. In this regard it is important to note that with few exceptions, the Guiding Principles apply to displacement regardless of whether it is arbitrary or not.

Principles relating to protection during displacement (Principles 10–23) enshrine a comprehensive list of guarantees addressing the specific needs and vulnerabilities of IDPs. They cover civil and political as well as economic, social, and cultural rights and usually start with highlighting the respective general guarantee as enshrined in international human rights and humanitarian law before going on to state the specific meaning of that guarantee for IDPs. Thus, for instance, Principle 20 first states the human right 'to recognition everywhere as a person before the law' as enshrined in Article 16 International Covenant on Civil and Political Rights and then provides, *inter alia*, that IDPs have a right to having personal documentation lost in the course of displacement restituted.

Principles relating to humanitarian assistance (Principles 24–6) contain the important statement that while international humanitarian actors only can work on behalf of IDPs once the state concerned has accepted their offer to provide services, such consent 'shall not be arbitrarily withheld, particularly when authorities concerned are unable or unwilling to provide the required humanitarian assistance' (Principle 25).

Finally, principles relating to return, resettlement, and reintegration (Principles 28–30) address the issue of durable solutions ending displacement. Particularly important is Principle 28 providing for, albeit in somewhat convoluted language, the right of IDPs to freely choose whether to return, integrate locally where they had been displaced to, or settle in another part of the country. Principle 28 also refers to the role of states to create conditions allowing for such solutions, but does not define when displacement ends. Return, for instance, does not automatically mean that IDPs can go back to their former life as they may not be able to recover property left behind, re-establish livelihoods, or avoid discrimination. There is agreement among humanitarian actors (IASC 2010) that displacement does not automatically end with return but can only be considered to be over when former IDPs no longer have displacement-specific needs, i.e. needs they would not have had they not been displaced.

Thus, according to the UN Framework on Durable Solutions (IASC 2010) finding durable solutions is a gradual process which is completed once IDPs enjoy, without discrimination, long-term safety and security; an adequate standard of living. This includes at a minimum access to adequate food, water, housing, healthcare, and basic education; access to employment and livelihoods; and restitution of their property or compensation for it. Depending on the context, they will also need access to and replacement of personal and other documentation; reunification with family members; the possibility to exercise their political rights; and access to effective remedies for displacement-related violations of their rights. While these criteria were derived from the practical experience of humanitarian and human rights actors, the issue of what makes solutions sustainable or causes them to fail is still not very well understood (see Long, this volume).

Legal Character

The Guiding Principles, while legally non-binding, derive their authority from the fact that, as their 'Introduction' stresses, they 'reflect and are consistent with international human rights law and international humanitarian law' and thus codify and progressively develop existing law rather than creating new rights and obligations. In fact, almost every Principle has a solid foundation in provisions enshrined in human rights instruments or international humanitarian law (Kälin 2008).

Despite this solid foundation, several governments objected to the Guiding Principles after Representative Deng had submitted them to the Human Rights Commission in 1998, criticizing not their content but rather the fact that they had been developed by a group of experts and not negotiated by states (Weiss and Korn 2006: 112–13). However, consensus slowly emerged, and in 2005, the UN World Summit of heads of state and government unanimously recognized the Guiding Principles as '[an] important international framework for the protection of internally displaced persons', language that since has been regularly reaffirmed by the General Assembly and the Human Rights Council.[8] They have also been invoked by regional human rights courts.[9] Thus, it is accurate to qualify them as international 'soft law' (Bagshaw 2005: 99–103; Orchard 2010) providing authoritative guidance to lawmakers as well as courts. The Constitutional Court of Colombia, for instance, recognized them as belonging to the body of international law that has to be considered when interpreting individual rights of the constitution in the context of internal displacement.[10]

In contrast, it would be premature to conclude that the Guiding Principles have already matured into international customary law (Schmidt 2004: 518–19), although they reflect to a considerable extent existing customary law (Goldman 2009: 68). This is particularly true for those Principles that are based on customary international humanitarian law. At the same time, they have also contributed to the formation of such customary law (Henckaerts and Doswald-Beck 2009: 195, 381, 424, 461, 465, 467–72), and at least two states have already clearly stated their conviction that the Guiding Principles have become part of international law.[11]

The Regional Level: Conventions

The Guiding Principles have also been recognized at regional and sub-regional levels. Several such organizations have welcomed the Guiding Principles and recommended to their member states to use them.[12]

Africa is the continent that has moved from soft to hard law. In 2006, the International Conference on the Great Lakes Region adopted the Great Lakes Protocol on the Protection and Assistance to Internally Displaced Persons. The Protocol obliges its presently 19 states parties to fully incorporate the Guiding Principles into their domestic legal order and thus provide them with the force of law.

With the 2009 Kampala Convention the African Union adopted the first treaty addressing internal displacement in a comprehensive and detailed manner (Abebe 2009; Maru 2011). It covers displacement caused by a wide range of causes—from conflict and human rights violations to natural or man-made disasters and development projects. While the Convention is based on the human rights of IDPs and reflects the Guiding Principles to a very large extent, it is formulated in terms not of rights of IDPs but of obligations of states and other relevant actors. It sets out standards for the protection of people from arbitrary displacement, the protection of IDPs while they are displaced, and durable solutions to their displacement. The Convention requires states parties to enact appropriate legislation, create an institutional framework for the coordination of IDP-related activities, and allocate the necessary funds to ensure implementation. On 6 December 2012, following the fifteenth ratification by a signatory state, the Kampala Convention entered into force.

The National Level: Laws and Policies

Without an adequate legal framework at the domestic level (Brookings-Bern Project on Internal Displacement 2008; IDMC/NRC/Brookings-LSE Project on Internal Displacement 2013) it is not possible for countries to live up to their responsibility to protect and assist IDPs. Experience shows that sectoral laws addressing issues such as security, health, education, housing, political rights, and other issues relevant for IDPs often fail to address the specific needs of IDPs. Many countries also lack the necessary institutional set-up to adequately respond to the challenges of internal displacement.

Today, more than 20 countries affected by internal displacement have enacted laws or strategies and policies specifically addressing IDPs.[13] These domestic instruments take rather different forms (Wyndham 2006: 8; Gouda 2009: 134), ranging from short declarations with a simple reference to the Guiding Principles and their domestic application (Burundi, Liberia), to rather detailed policies and strategies that, however, are limited to a specific cause or stage of displacement (Uganda, Georgia, Nepal, Sudan, Iraq), to IDP specific laws covering all phases of displacement (Kenya).

Regardless of the form and scope of domestic instruments it is important that they not only address the rights of IDPs but also the issue of institutional responsibilities and the allocation of resources. Protection of and assistance for IDPs is, as experience shows, seriously hampered if responsibilities are not clearly demarcated between different state institutions or if those responsible are not provided with the necessary powers and resources.

Assisting Internally Displaced Persons: The Operational Level

At the operational level, implementation of the rights of IDPs as codified in the Guiding Principles on Internal Displacement first and foremost happens with national or local authorities and humanitarian actors undertaking protection activities, that is 'activities aimed at obtaining full respect for the rights of the individual in accordance with the letter and the spirit of the relevant bodies of law'.[14]

While understanding of what this exactly means in practice, and how priorities should be determined, differs widely among agencies and other stakeholders (Ferris 2011: 270–85), protection activities are numerous and many different types can be observed in the field: they range from activities directly protecting people (such as evacuation from danger zones, lighting of water points and sanitation areas in camps and collective centres to prevent instances of gender-based violence, or the provision of legal aid to victims of human rights violations) to monitoring activities, advocacy with relevant stakeholders, and support for law-making or capacity building (Global Protection Cluster Working Group 2010).

Much of this work is undertaken by UN humanitarian agencies and their non-governmental partners. They join forces within the framework of what is called the 'Cluster Approach' (Bijleveld 2006), an arrangement set up by the UN to facilitate the coordination among organizations in humanitarian emergencies (see Russell and Tennant, this volume). Each cluster has a designated lead agency at the global and national levels. The lead agency is tasked with bringing relevant actors together in order to improve the overall humanitarian response through enhanced predictability, timeliness, and effectiveness. If no other organization is able to act it also has, subject to limits of access, security, and funding, to step in as a 'provider of last resort' to avoid gaps in the response (UNHCR 2012: 127). However, an evaluation in 2010 (Steets et al. 2010: 8–10) concluded that the Cluster Approach helped to better identify gaps in humanitarian assistance, reduce duplications, and thus improve coordination while cluster management and facilitation remained poor in many cases due to a lack of trained coordinators and coordination between clusters remained ineffective. The study criticized that 'clusters largely exclude national and local actors and often fail to link with, build on, or support existing coordination and response mechanisms' and thus have 'in several cases weakened national and local ownership and capacities'. Thus, despite several achievements, it is clear more efforts are needed to improve humanitarian action through improved coordination and ensure IDP protection can be delivered, not only as a legal framework but also in practice.

Notes

1. UN Doc. E/CN.4/1998/53/Add.2, 11 February 1998, Introduction, para. 2.
2. See Statute of the Office of the United Nations High Commissioner for Refugees, Annex to UNGA res. 428(V), 14 Dec. 1950.
3. 2005 World Summit Outcome, A/RES/60/1, 24 October 2005, para. 132; General Assembly resolutions: A/RES/62/153, para. 10; A/RES/64/162, para. 10; A/RES/66/165, para. 12. Human Rights Council resolutions: A/HRC/RES/6/32, para. 5; A/HRC/RES/14/6, para. 9; A/HRC/RES/20/9, para. 1; A/HRC/RES/23/8, para. 12.
4. These reports can be accessed at <http://www.ohchr.org/EN/Issues/IDPersons/Pages/Visits.aspx>.
5. Human Rights Commission resolution 1992/73.
6. E/CN.4/1996/52/Add.2, 5 December 1995, para. 411.
7. Human Rights Commission resolution 1996/52 of 19 April 1996, sixth preambular paragraph and paragraph 9.
8. See n. 3.
9. E.g. European Court of Human Rights, *Case of Doğan and Others v Turkey*, Applications nos. 8803–8811/02, 8813/02 and 8815–8819/02, Judgment of 29 June 2004, para. 154; Inter-American Court of Human Rights, *Case of the 'Mapiripán Massacre' v Colombia*, Judgment of 15 September 2005, para. 171.
10. Colombian Constitutional Court, Decision T-025 of 2004, in: Arango Rivadeneira 2009: 221.
11. Germany, Achter Bericht der Bundesregierung über ihre Menschenrechtspolitik in den auswärtigen Beziehungen und in anderen Politikbereichen, Deutscher Bundestag 16. Wahlperiode, Drucksache 16/10037, 16 July 2008, 76. Iraq National Policy on Displacement, July 2008, section 5, para. 3.
12. E.g. Council of Europe, Recommendation Rec(2006)6 of the Committee of Ministers to member states on internally displaced persons, 5 April 2006; Organization of American States, General Assembly resolution AG/RES. 2716 (XLII-O/12), 4 June 2012.
13. The text of national laws, policies, and strategies on internal displacement can be found at <http://www.brookings.edu/projects/idp/Laws-and-Policies/idp_policies_index.aspx> (accessed 2 August 2012).
14. IASC, IDP Protection Policy 1999. The definition was originally adopted by a 1999 Workshop of the International Committee of the Red Cross (ICRC) on Protection.

References

Abebe, A. M. (2009) 'Legal and Institutional Dimensions of Protecting and Assisting Internally Displaced Persons in Africa'. *Journal of Refugee Studies* 22(2): 155–76.
Arango Rivadeneira, R. (ed.) (2009) *Judicial Protection of Internally Displaced Persons: The Colombian Experience*. Washington, DC: Brookings-Bern Project on Internal Displacement.
Bagshaw, S. (2005) *Developing a Normative Framework for the Protection of Internally Displaced Persons*. Ardsley, NY: Transnational Publishers.
Bakewell, O. (2011) 'Conceptualizing Displacement and Migration: Processes, Conditions, and Categories'. Pp. 14–28 in K. Koser and S. Martin (eds.), *The Migration-Displacement Nexus: Patterns, Processes, and Policies*. New York: Berghahn Books.

Beyani, C., *Report of the Special Rapporteur on the Human Rights of Internally Displaced Persons, Chaloka Beyani*, UN Doc. A/HRC/19/54, 26 December 2011.

Bijleveld, A. W. (2006) 'Towards More Predictable Humanitarian Responses: Inter-Agency Cluster Approach to IDPs'. *Refugee Survey Quarterly* 25(4): 28–34.

Brookings–Bern Project on Internal Displacement (ed.) (2008) *Protecting Internally Displaced Persons: A Manual for Law and Policymakers*. Washington, DC: Brookings.

Brookings Institution (2005) *Addressing Internal Displacement: A Framework for National Responsibility*. Washington, DC: Brookings Institute.

Carrillo, A. C. (2009) 'Internal Displacement in Colombia: Humanitarian, Economic and Social Consequences in Urban Settings and Current Challenges'. *International Review of the Red Cross* 91(875): 527–46.

Christensen, A., and Harild, N. (2009) *Forced Displacement: The Development Challenge*. Washington, DC: The World Bank Group.

Cohen, R. (2004) 'The Guiding Principles on Internal Displacement: An Innovation in International Standard Setting'. *Global Governance* 10: 459–80.

Cohen, R. (2007) 'Response to Hathaway'. *Journal of Refugee Studies* 20(3): 370–6.

Cohen, R., and Deng, F. M. (1998) *Masses in Flight: The Global Crisis of Internal Displacement*. Washington, DC: Brookings Institution Press.

Collinson, S., Darcy, J., Waddell, N., et al. (2009) *Realising Protection: The Uncertain Benefits of Civilian, Refugee and IDP Status*. HPG Report 28. London: Overseas Development Institute.

Ferris E. (2011) *The Politics of Protection: The Limits of Humanitarian Action*. Washington, DC: Brookings Institution.

Fielden, A. (2008) *Ignored Displaced Persons: The Plights of IDPs in Urban Areas*. Geneva: UNHCR.

Global Protection Cluster Working Group (2010) *Handbook for the Protection of Internally Displaced Persons*. Geneva: UNHCR.

Goldman, R. K. (2009) 'Internal Displacement, the Guiding Principles on Internal Displacement, the Principles Normative Status, and the Need for their Effective Domestic Implementation in Colombia'. *Anuario Colombiano de derecho internacional* 2: 59–85.

Gouda, D. A. (2009). *Internal Displacement Law and Policy: Analysis of International Norms and Domestic Jurisprudence*. Lake Mary: Vandeplas Publishing.

Hathaway, J. (2007) 'Forced Migration Studies: Could We Agree Just to "Date"?' *Journal of Refugee Studies* 20(3): 349–69.

Henckaerts, J. M., and Doswald-Beck, L. (2009) *Customary International Law*, vol. i: *Rules* (3rd edn.). Cambridge: Cambridge University Press.

IASC (2010) 'Framework on Durable Solutions for Internally Displaced Persons'. Washington, DC: The Brookings–Bern Project on Internal Displacement.

ICRC (2009) *Internal Displacement in Armed Conflict: Facing up to the Challenges*. Geneva: ICRC.

IDMC/NRC (2012), *Internal Displacement Global: Overview of Trends and Developments in 2011*. Geneva: Internal Displacement Monitoring Centre.

IDMC/NRC (2013a), *Internal Displacement Global: Overview of Trends and Developments in 2012*. Geneva: Internal Displacement Monitoring Centre.

IDMC/NRC (2013b) *Global Estimates 2012: People Displaced by Natural Hazard-Induced Disasters*. Geneva: Internal Displacement Monitoring Centre.

IDMC/NRC/Brookings-LSE Project on Internal Displacement (2013), *National Instruments on Internal Displacement: A Guide to their Development*. Geneva: Internal Displacement Monitoring Centre.

Jacobsen, K. (2008) *Internal Displacement to Urban Areas: The Tufts-IDMC Profiling Study. Abidjan, Côte d'Ivoire: Case 2.* n.p.: Feinstein International Center/Tufts/NRC/IDMC.

Kälin, W. (2008) *Guiding Principles on Internal Displacement: Annotations* (2nd edn.). Washington, DC: The American Society of International Law.

Kälin, W. (2010) 'Conceptualizing Climate-Induced Displacement'. Pp. 81–103 in J. McAdam (ed.), *Climate Change & Displacement: Multidisciplinary Perspectives*. Oxford: Hart Publishing.

Kälin W. et al. (2010) *Incorporating the Guiding Principles on Internal Displacement into Domestic Law*. Washington, DC: American Society of International Law.

Kidane, W. (2011) 'Managing Forced Displacement by Law in Africa: The Role of the New African Union IDPs Convention'. *Vanderbilt Journal of Transnational Law* 44: 1–85.

McAdam, J. (ed.) (2010) *Climate Change & Displacement: Multidisciplinary Perspectives*. Oxford: Hart Publishing.

Maru, M. T. (2011) 'The Kampala Convention and its Contribution in Filling the Protection Gap in International Law'. *Journal of Internal Displacement* 1(1): 91–130.

Mooney, E. (2005) 'The Concept of Internal Displacement and the Case for Internally Displaced Persons as a Category of Concern'. *Refugee Survey Quarterly* 24(3): 9–26.

Orchard, P. (2010) 'Protection of Internally Displaced Persons: Soft Law as a Norm-Generating Mechanism'. *Review of International Studies* 36: 281–303.

Phuong, C. (2004) *The International Protection of Internally Displaced Persons*. Cambridge: Cambridge University Press.

Schmidt, P. (2004) 'The Process and Prospects for the U.N. Guiding Principles on Internal Displacement to Become International Customary Law: A Preliminary Assessment'. *Georgetown Journal of International Law* 35(3): 483–520.

Steets, J., Grünewald, F., Binder, A., de Geoffroy, V., Kauffmann, D., Krüger, S., Meier C., and Sokpoh, B. (2010) 'Cluster Approach Evaluation 2—Synthesis Report'. n.p.: u.r.d/GPPi.

UNHCR (2012) *The State of the World's Refugees: In Search of Solidarity*. Oxford: Oxford University Press.

Weiss, T. G., and Korn, D. A. (2006) *Internal Displacement: Conceptualization and its Consequences*. London: Routledge.

World Bank/UNHCR (2011) *Research Study on IDPs in Urban Settings: Afghanistan*. Kabul: The World Bank.

Wyndham, J. (2006) 'A Developing Trend: Laws and Policies on Internal Displacement'. *Human Rights Brief* (American University) 14/1: 7–12.

CHAPTER 14

REFUGEES, DIASPORAS, AND TRANSNATIONALISM

NICHOLAS VAN HEAR

INTRODUCTION

REFUGEES have figured strongly in the proliferation of diasporas over the last 25 years—broadly since the end of the Cold War and the subsequent reconfiguration of the global geopolitical order. These new or resurgent transnational social formations have consolidated, are enduring, have undertaken new or extended existing forms of transnational activity, and are becoming integrated into the global order, particularly in respect of relations between affluent countries and conflict-ridden societies. This chapter will explore the place of refugees in diaspora formation and transnational activities.

The chapter first tracks the emergence of diaspora and transnationalism as key concepts in the field of migration and refugee studies. It then explores the place of forced migration in the formation of diasporas, before turning to refugee engagement in transnational activities in conflict settings. Finally some thoughts about transnationalism and durable solutions for refugees are offered.

DIASPORA AND TRANSNATIONALISM AS KEY CONCEPTS IN REFUGEE STUDIES

The term diaspora broadly refers to the spread of migrant communities away from a real or imagined 'homeland'. Diasporas have three core features: dispersal from a homeland to two or more other territories; an enduring, although not necessarily permanent presence abroad; and some kind of flow or exchange—social, economic, political, or cultural—between or among the spatially separated populations comprising the diaspora (Cohen 1997/2008; Van Hear 1998). It is quite remarkable how this term has taken hold in migration studies and beyond, and it may make sense to distinguish between three understandings of the notion: a social science understanding of diaspora, a policy or governmental notion, and a vernacular understanding used by diasporas themselves and sometimes host populations in their discourse. The three understandings of diaspora shape and influence one another (Van Hear 2012). The rise in the importance of refugees in diaspora formation and transnational activities has unfolded in tandem with this growing conceptual hold of diaspora and transnationalism in migration and refugee studies from the mid-1990s and their subsequent take-up in the policy arena and the 'real world' in the 2000s, as the following account shows.

The emergence of diaspora and the associated notion of transnationalism as key concepts in migration and refugee studies may be tracked through a number of streams of scholarship that gathered pace from the 1990s and to some extent fed into one another. The current wave of interest in diaspora can perhaps be traced to a number of political scientists who from the 1980s saw the implications of increasing migration for politics and international relations. The political significance of diasporas was taken up in the contributions to a path-breaking volume edited by Sheffer (1986). For the most part, the political scientists were concerned with the political role of diasporas already in existence rather than their formation

A seminal article by Safran (1991), much drawn upon because of its helpful definition of diaspora, brought or reintroduced the concept to the anthropological and cultural studies milieu; at about the same time transnationalism was set out as 'a new analytical framework for understanding migration,' again starting from an anthropological perspective (Glick Schiller, Basch, and Blanc-Szanton 1992). The associated notions of diaspora and transnationalism were extensively interrogated subsequently. From the second half of the 1990s, the formation, consolidation, and unmaking of diasporas was taken up by those whose perspective on migration drew on political economy approaches, tempered by emphasis on human agency (Cohen 1997, 2008; Van Hear 1998). Since then the literature on diaspora and transnationalism has proliferated from different disciplinary perspectives, and the notions of diaspora and transnationalism have been subjected to meticulous and often well-founded critique, targeted mainly on the 'inflation' of the use of the terms—now ubiquitous in migration and refugee studies—and therefore their diminishing specificity and utility (Portes, Guarnizo, and Landholt 1999; Brubaker 2005).

Initially most of the scholarly attention was on migration, diaspora, and transnational engagement in relatively stable settings (Smith and Guarnizo 1998). To the extent that diaspora were considered in the context of conflict, it was largely as a negative force, fomenting or sustaining violence and insurgency. However in the 2000s there was a general shift in perception from ascribing diasporas a negative role in fomenting and supporting conflict as 'war mongers' or 'peace-wreckers' (Collier and Hoeffler 2004; Kapur 2007) to a more nuanced view that diasporas could assist with relief, peace-building, and post-conflict recovery as 'peace-makers' or 'peace-builders', or that their influence was ambivalent—sometimes negative and sometimes positive (Van Hear 2006a, 2006b; Smith and Stares 2007). Crucially, it was realized that while conflict undermined development by destroying assets and resources and by killing and displacing people, displacement itself contributed to the formation of diasporas which could themselves in time constitute a resource for conflict-ridden societies.

The notion of diaspora was rarely used in the policy world, nor in public discourse, until about 2000. Now it is ubiquitous in development and policy discourse, with agencies such as the World Bank, USAID, the European Commission, the IOM, the UK's Department for International Development, and German, Scandinavian, and other development agencies extolling the virtues of diaspora for development, looking to mobilize or galvanize the diaspora, and exploring the possibilities for diaspora engagement in development and in recovery in conflict settings (Van Hear and Sørensen 2003). The term is also increasingly used by states as they reach out to galvanize citizens abroad (Gamlen 2008). Moreover people in diasporas themselves increasingly use the label, partly because of its strong prevalence in the policy world, but also because of the realization of their growing influence on the world (Sökefeld 2006; Jeyaraj 2009).

THE MAKING OF REFUGEE DIASPORAS

The increased numbers of asylum seekers moving from the global South to the global North from the 1980s and the spate of major forced migration crises from the 1990s onwards increased attention on conflict as a source of diaspora formation. The crises included the break-up of the Soviet Union and the communist bloc after the fall of the Berlin wall in 1989; subsequent wars and 'un-mixing' of formerly ethnically diverse populations in parts of the former Soviet Union and the Balkans; the 'Gulf crisis' of 1990–1 and its associated mass exodus of refugees, of Asian and Arab migrant workers, and of Palestinians from Kuwait, Iraq, and elsewhere; the genocide, wars, and mass refugee movements in Central Africa from 1994; protracted conflict and massive displacement in Palestine, Afghanistan, the Horn of Africa, Sri Lanka, Colombia, and elsewhere; and the conflicts and refugee movements associated with the post-September 11 'war on terror' in Afghanistan (from 2001) and in Iraq (from 2003). Major new diasporas have formed from or been augmented by these and other conflict induced population movements over the last two decades (Van Hear 2012).

Common patterns of diaspora formation may be observed in these conflict settings over the last two decades or more (Van Hear 2006a, 2006b). Many people fleeing conflict make for safer parts of their country if they can, and are cast as internally displaced people. Others may look for refuge in a neighbouring country or countries if they are able to reach and cross a border. Together the internally displaced and those seeking asylum in neighbouring countries commonly account for most people seeking to escape conflict. Smaller numbers seek asylum in countries further afield, sometimes in other continents—usually those with which they have connections through previous migration of relatives or acquaintances. Some who initially seek refuge in neighbouring countries may later be resettled further afield, or migrate to new destinations as part of onward movements; they sometimes join those who have gone there directly. Dispersal that is enduring and consolidates in these different territories leads to the formation of what we may call refugee diasporas: those in neighbouring territories we might call the *near diaspora*, and those spread further afield we might term the *wider diaspora*. As time goes on, transnational connections often develop among these different locations: transnational social fields may be said to link those remaining at home, those in the near diaspora, and those in the wider diaspora.

Access to these different destinations is unequally distributed among those seeking safety. The increasingly stringent international migration and refugee 'regime' has limited access to more desirable affluent destinations—usually in the wider diaspora. Access to networks and money to pay smugglers or agents increasingly shape the capacity to migrate and determine the ability to reach such locations. Access to more prosperous and desirable destinations has therefore been increasingly limited to better resourced refugees: there tends to be a hierarchy of destinations that can be reached by those fleeing conflict, according to the resources—financial and network based—that they can call upon (Van Hear 2006b). Moreover diaspora formation also often features a number of waves or cohorts of migration over time—frequently professionals, elites, or political exiles, followed variously by students, labour migrants, refugees, and then those coming for family reunion or marriage to the 'primary' migrants. Furthermore, as time passes and diasporas consolidate, successive generations will unfold in the diaspora, each of which may have different orientations both to host- and homeland (Mannheim 1952; Loizos 2007). The net result of these processes is likely to be a variegated diasporic formation, with socio-economic position and politico-cultural outlooks shaped by age, gender, cohort of arrival, and generation.

Conflict induced movement in and from Afghanistan, Sri Lanka, and Somalia illustrate these patterns.

Afghans experienced large scale displacement from the late 1970s as the conflict in Afghanistan ebbed and flowed (Monsutti 2005). Large numbers of people were displaced within Afghanistan—around two million, depending on the state, phase, and nature of the conflict. Large numbers of refugees moved to Pakistan and Iran—three million and two million respectively at the peak of outflows. Sometimes the refugees followed former labour migration pathways: for example labour migration to Iran has been an important migration stream, and refugees followed these earlier labour migration and betterment pathways. At the same time substantial numbers of asylum seekers made for Europe, North America, and other affluent countries of the 'global North', these being usually better off than refugees in Pakistan and Iran. There have been return movements at various points, when conflict has abated, involving substantial movements of refugees and exiles back to Afghanistan (see Monsutti and Balci, this volume).

Tamils from Sri Lanka have been driven to flee by civil war since 1983, intensifying in the 1990s, resuming after an uneasy cease fire agreed in 2002 broke down in 2005, and culminating in a deadly military end-game in 2009 (Fuglerud 1999; Vimalarajah and Cheran 2010). Those displaced included poorer people and households moving to safety within Sri Lanka—between half a million and a million at any one time, according to the intensity of the conflict. Those who could muster some resources fled by boat to south

India—around 120,000 at peak in camps and cities of Tamil Nadu by the early 2000s. Some left conflict zones as labour migrants to the Middle East, both as a livelihood strategy and to escape the conflict. Others, with substantial resources to pay migrant smugglers and brokers, and often helped by earlier migrants, were able to make it as asylum seekers to affluent countries—notably the UK, Scandinavia, Switzerland, Canada, and Australia—contributing to the 800,000 or so Sri Lankan Tamils in wider diaspora. In addition to these movements, there has been movement back, between and among these various locations, varying over time with the conditions of conflict and with possibilities for migration (see Banerjee, this volume).

Somalis experienced state collapse and civil conflict from the late 1980s (Lindley 2009, 2010). Forms of forced migration have again included internal displacement for poorer households within what are known as the 'Somali regions', including southern Somalia, Somaliland, and Puntland in the north. Those who had some resources to move made for neighbouring countries Ethiopia, Kenya, Djibouti, and Yemen. There has also been migration to the Middle East as labour migrants and to set up small businesses both in pursuit of livelihoods and to escape the conflict and its consequences. As in the other cases there has been movement to western or other affluent countries, usually by those well endowed with resources and network connections, including onward movement of Somali refugees from Kenya to Europe (Kibreab, this volume).

As these cases show, people who move within and from conflict-ridden countries are spread among different kinds of location: some, typically the less endowed, are dispersed within their own countries as internally displaced people; some find their way to neighbouring countries; and still others, with the resources to do so, are able to move to countries further afield. The migrants include not just refugees, but people who move for a variety of reasons, and with varying degrees of force and choice. With their dispersal comes the establishment of transnational relations and networks among the dispersed groups and it is through these networks and relationships that diasporas can exert influence on their countries of origin.

REFUGEE DIASPORAS AND TRANSNATIONAL ENGAGEMENT

Diasporas formed as a result of conflict are of course shaped both by the society from which they have come and the new society in which they find themselves, as well as by their experience of conflict and flight: they carry with them some of the values of their homeland, while absorbing to a greater or lesser degree the values of their host society. These values, together with the socio-economic character of the diaspora—which is differentiated on class, ethnic, generational, and gender lines—help shape their disposition, their capacity, and inclination to influence the homeland.

One of the principal resources that diasporas contribute to relief during conflict and recovery afterwards are remittances and other transfers. It has been increasingly recognized that remittances often become key components of livelihood strategies in conflict settings—not for all, but at least for some people (Van Hear 2002, 2006a; Horst 2006; Lindley 2010). There are at least three settings in which diaspora transfers influence the living conditions of displaced and conflict-affected people. First, during the course of conflicts, such transfers provide a survival lifeline for those who cannot get out of conflict zones, or alternatively means of flight for those who can move out of such areas. Second, in neighbouring countries of first asylum, remittances might supplement other means of refugee survival and coping, such as humanitarian aid. Third, in post-conflict settings diaspora remittances and other transfers might enable households to get beyond survival to coping, and lay the basis for recovery. There has also been potential for diaspora contributions to broader economic and social recovery, beyond the immediate concerns of their kin in conflict areas. These kinds of interventions in conflict settings are considered further below.

The distinction should perhaps be drawn between the *capacity* and the *desire* to engage in conflict settings (Al-Ali, Black, and Koser 2001). *Capacity* to engage is shaped, among other things, by security of status, having an income above subsistence level, having the freedom to speak out, and developing social competence and political literacy—knowing how to lobby, campaign, speak in public, write leaflets, draw up funding proposals, and so on. The *desire* to engage is shaped by personal or private motivations, such as the imperative to protect one's family, kin, or friends; by wider humanitarian concerns for the community, society, or nation; and by harder political motivation, driven perhaps by ethno-nationalism.

The hope of humanitarian and development actors has been that, by virtue of gradual incorporation into Western societies, diasporas—or at least some of their members— would be drawn into nurturing 'liberal peace' in conflict-ridden societies (Duffield 2001). However, as in more stable environments, diaspora engagement in conflict settings tends to be privately oriented on family and community than concerned with broad societal renewal, as the next section indicates.

Spheres of Diaspora Engagement in Conflict Settings

Activities and engagement by diaspora groupings can be considered in three spheres, which feature different combinations of the private and public: the sphere of the household and the extended family, which is largely private and personal; the more public sphere of the 'known community', by which is meant collectivities of people that know each other or know of each other; and the largely public sphere of the 'imagined community', including ethnic, national, and other allegiances.

The household/extended family sphere. Engagement in the household and extended family is likely to be the most sustained of the three spheres. The most common, principal, and most tangible form of engagement is sending money—remittances—to assist extended family members to survive and cope in conflict settings. The money sent may be used for everyday needs, housing, schooling, healthcare, and sometimes to help people get out of zones of danger—this can involve paying an agent to organize migration abroad. Besides such transfers in cash and kind, diaspora members participate in life course events such as births, marriages, and funerals either 'virtually' or in person. Such engagement may involve visits, such as those by second generation Tamils who visited former conflict areas in northern Sri Lanka for the first time during the 2002–4 ceasefire and after the end of the war in 2009 (Vimalarajah and Cheran 2010). However, often of necessity in conflict settings, online connections and telephony replace face-to-face physical connection.

The 'known community' sphere. Engagement in the 'known community sphere' takes place in spaces where one lives or has lived, among people one knows or knows of. It is the realm of associational life: residentially and ethnically based associations and clubs, schools, religious bodies, mutual aid and welfare organizations, community-based and civil society organizations. Home town and home village associations and in particular old school associations have been important forms of organization and engagement, but their influence may decline in conflict contexts as time passes and connections grow weaker and cohorts of schoolmates are not reproduced. At the same time, engagement in these and other forms of associational life has expanded with the use of electronic media. Transfers to wider collectivities than households and extended families can be considered here: examples include donations made in temples, churches, or mosques for relief in the home country; the home town association or old school association that collects funds to rebuild a school, equip a hospital, or refurbish a library; collections by welfare organizations to provide relief for the victims of conflict; or, more darkly, the collections by supporters of insurgent groups for funds to buy weapons or otherwise support insurgency. These transfers, for more public or collective purposes, are somewhat different in nature from the more private remittances described above in the first, family sphere. In aggregate they are also probably smaller in scale than such private remittances. In conflict settings however the significance of such collective transfers goes beyond their immediate economic and material effects, since they can help repair the social fabric shredded by years of conflict, not least by helping to re-establish social linkages ruptured during war and rebuilding trust and confidence.

The 'imagined community'. In coining the notion 'the imagined community', Benedict Anderson referred to the nation to which one has an affinity without necessarily knowing its members personally (Anderson 1983/1991). The notion can be extended to other collectivities such as classes, co-religionists, and co-ethnics. Engagement here includes membership of or involvement in political parties and movements, and support for insurgent or oppositional groups. It might involve lobbying politicians or other influential people in the host country and/or at home, and engagement in political, social, or cultural debate in cyberspace or the blogosphere (Sökefeld 2006). This sphere is usually the most volatile of the three spheres and perhaps the least pervasive in terms of general and sustained participation: it requires greater degrees of social mobilization than do the more routine activities of the household and community spheres, considered further in the next section.

Diasporas, Lives, and Livelihoods in Conflict Settings

As already suggested, diaspora engagement can help individuals, households, families, and communities survive, cope, and perhaps even prosper under conflict conditions. Recent work on livelihoods in conflict is instructive here. Looking at conflict and other settings of severe strain, and taking Afghanistan as a case study, Bhatia et al. (2003: 74) suggest that, in the course of conflict, 'Broadly, households can be divided into those who profit (add to their asset base), those who cope or get along (non-erosion of assets) and those who survive (erosion of assets).'

Diaspora engagement in conflict settings can usefully be disaggregated along these lines:

Survival. During acute crisis, including intense violence, bombing, and shelling, resources from relatives may be sent to get people out of immediate danger of death or injury. Such transfers may also be necessary for poorer households simply to sustain life during times outside acute crisis when assets, resources, and means of livelihood are destroyed, looted, or have to be sold off.

Coping. Acute violence tends to be the exception rather than the rule in conflict settings. During the more usual condition of chronic instability and sporadic violence that characterizes such societies, resources from relatives and friends abroad may be sent to meet daily needs, so as to avoid having to dispose of assets to subsist. Money may again also be sent—often through informal channels—to assist people to leave when opportunities arise to escape from danger.

Accumulation. During ceasefires and while peace processes are under way, as well as after conflict abates, resources sent from those abroad may be used to reconstruct houses and perhaps to redevelop livelihoods or even start up businesses. Informal and formal systems of transfer may be used at this stage, since money and other markets may have been re-established. Some—among them conflict entrepreneurs who may profit from violence—may be able to accumulate not only during ceasefires and semi-peaceful interludes, but also during periods of conflict.

These outcomes and possibilities shift over time with the conditions and course of conflict in the homeland—outright war, acute and low-level violence, ceasefire, fragile or uneasy peace, reconstruction and recovery—and vary with the shape, composition, and position of the household in the conflict-ridden society. The three lines of engagement often coexist within a given conflict setting, since individuals, families, and communities will be affected differently by different conditions. Those conditions are also seldom clear-cut. Outcomes will vary with the capacity and inclination of diaspora members abroad to make transfers, as outlined above. As well as transfers to individuals and families, collective transfers may also be made for the same purposes—to enable a community to survive, cope, or rebuild and accumulate.

In conflict settings the 'accumulation' possibility is often the most challenging since conditions are often inimical to investment and helping kin to survive and cope takes precedence. Most forms of engagement—individual and collective—fall within the 'survival' and 'coping' rubric: together they form part of a safety net or a form of social security for people in conflict settings, a safety net that may also draw on humanitarian assistance and whatever other resources can be called upon to construct what has been called a 'livelihood portfolio' (Collinson 2003: 12). People, families, and communities in conflict areas need to balance different transnational and local resources in their livelihood portfolios.

Meanwhile, refugee households abroad in the diaspora have to balance the demands of their own livelihoods and futures (most importantly perhaps education of their children), those in other destination and transit countries, and those left at home, or in neighbouring countries of first refuge (Van Hear 2006a, 2006b; Lindley 2010). There is thus a countervailing 'portfolio of obligations' among those in the diaspora, as well as a portfolio of livelihood resources for those trying to manage in conflict settings. That portfolio of obligations may become unsustainable and debilitating, particularly if those in the diaspora have low, precarious incomes, as is often the case. Differences of wealth, resources, social capital, and class shape the capacity and level of support that can be offered and thus the circulation of resources among these different sites. This brings us back to the capacity and inclination—the disposition—of the diaspora to engage in conflict settings, which is in turn linked to the kind of recovery and development that might emerge as a result of diaspora engagement, and ultimately to the outcome of displacement.

Transnationalism as a Durable Solution?

As we have seen, the diasporas induced by conflict commonly comprise people spread among three main kinds of location—in the homeland, in neighbouring territories and in places further afield. Each of these domains corresponds to some extent to one of the locations or sites associated with the three 'durable solutions' that UNHCR is charged with pursuing for refugees: integration in the country of first asylum, resettlement in a third country, or return to the homeland (UNHCR 1995). Conventionally, these domains have been seen as distinct, but there are significant links across time and space among these places and statuses, as we have seen in this chapter. Indeed the literature on diasporas and transnationalism shows that this categorization is to some extent illusory: for example, it is conceivable that, either simultaneously or over time, a given household or family may have members at home, in a neighbouring country, in a country further afield, or moving between these locations. This has implications in relation to integration, resettlement, repatriation, and efforts to resolve conflicts at home (Van Hear 2006b).

As this chapter has suggested, in areas experiencing conflict or other severe strain, extended families often disperse to take advantage of different resources at different sites. Some stay at home, or become internally displaced, seeking refuge in other parts of their country. Of those who flee the country, the more vulnerable (perhaps the elderly, some women, and children) may stay in camps where they have access to health, education, and other services. Other members of the extended family may go to cities in search of employment or seek seasonal agricultural work; they may negotiate access to land or livestock in the host country, or find ways of maintaining control of their assets still in the homeland; or they may find trading niches between town and country or across international borders. Still other extended family members may go abroad as labour migrants, asylum seekers, undocumented workers, or through other migratory channels to find work and incomes for themselves and the family. Such 'strategies', if they may be called this, may well be in place before displacement, but the portfolio of strategies is likely to be broader after displacement, sometimes of necessity, sometimes by new opportunities opening up. Indeed access to social networks and mobility can be among refugees' most important resources. From this perspective, discouraging onward movements from 'first asylum' countries to more affluent states, which is one of the imperatives driving the migration policies of such states, may well be counter-productive, since they curtail what may be important elements of families' livelihood portfolios. Likewise concerns to prevent 'backflows' after repatriation may undermine cross-border networks that have been built up while in exile. Refugees may not want to go back permanently to their places of origin, but to re-establish access to their assets and to integrate them into their cross-border livelihood activities.

In these and other ways, transnationalism may in itself be a 'durable solution' for conditions of displacement—or at least an 'enduring' solution (Van Hear 2006b; Long 2010). As this chapter has shown, diaspora connections may be vital in sustaining societies in upheaval or conflict, and have the potential for reconstructing such societies once conflict lessens. Building on such potential involves understanding that the return of some members of a household or community to a 'post-conflict' society may be predicated on others staying abroad. The viability or durability of the return can be enhanced by this: by sending money home for example, those abroad may help to set up or sustain livelihoods established by returnees during start-up periods or during hard times. Sustainable livelihoods may then be established as the basis for subsequent returns of the displaced. The deployment of transnational connections in such ways is predicated on some elements of the diaspora having reasonably secure residence in the place of exile.

There are, of course, problems with such an approach. Not least of these is associated with differentiation within diasporas. As noted above their formation involves different waves, generations, and migratory forms (such as labour migrants, students, and marriage migrants as well as asylum seekers and refugees), and they may also be divided across lines of gender, class, and religion, among other social cleavages. This differentiation and diversity may lead to conflict within diasporas and, with respect to engagement in the homeland, may bring up questions of equity, for it tends to be those who are already better off who take prime positions in the transnational arena: encouragement of transnationalism may therefore reinforce inequalities.

Such problematic areas notwithstanding, diaspora connections and transnational practices can provide vital means for sustaining people caught up in conflict. Moreover, recovery after conflict will not only involve the homeland or the actual arena of conflict: transnational links and diaspora connections that develop to sustain societies in conflict are likely themselves to be irrevocably integral parts of the 'post-conflict' society. Taking advantage of transnational connections and practices requires taking account of the links among different domains of diaspora: this chapter has sought to offer a framework for considering the relations among these different domains.

REFERENCES

Al-Ali, N., Black, R., and Koser, K. (2001) 'The Limits to Transnationalism: Bosnian and Eritrean Refugees in Europe as Emerging Transnational Communities'. *Ethnic and Racial Studies* 24(4): 578–600.

Anderson, B. (1983/1991) *Imagined Communities: Reflections on the Origin and Spread of Nationalism*. London: Verso.

Bhatia, M., and Goodhand, J., with Atmar, H., Pain, A., and Suleman, M. (2003) 'Profits and Poverty: Aid Livelihoods and Conflict in Afghanistan'. Pp. 67–90 in S. Collinson (ed.), *Power, Livelihoods and Conflict: Case Studies in Political Economy Analysis for Humanitarian Action*. HPG Report 13. London: Humanitarian Policy Group, Overseas Development Institute.

Brubaker, R. (2005) 'The "Diaspora" Diaspora'. *Ethnic and Racial Studies* 28(1): 1–19.

Cohen, R. (1997/2008) *Global Diasporas: An Introduction*. London: Routledge.

Collier, P., and Hoeffler, A. (2004) 'Greed and Grievance in Civil War'. *Oxford Economic Papers* 56: 563–95.

Collinson, S. (2003), *Power, Livelihoods and Conflict: Case Studies in Political Economy Analysis for Humanitarian Action* HPG Report 13. London: Humanitarian Policy Group, Overseas Development Institute.

Duffield, M. (2001) *Global Governance and the New Wars: The Merging of Development and Security*. London: Zed Books.

Fuglerud, Ø. (1999) *Life on the Outside: The Tamil Diaspora and Long Distance Nationalism*. London: Pluto Press.

Gamlen, A. (2008) 'The Emigration State and the Modern Geopolitical Imagination'. *Political Geography* 27: 840–56.

Glick Schiller, N., Basch, L., and Blanc-Szanton, C. (1992) 'Transnationalism: A New Analytic Framework for Understanding Migration'. *Annals of the New York Academy of Sciences* 645: 1–24.

Horst, C. (2006) *Transnational Nomads: How Somalis Cope with Refugee Life in the Dadaab Camps of Kenya*. Oxford: Berghahn.

Jeyaraj, D. B. S. (2009). 'Deploying Diaspora'. *Frontline* 26(10). <http://www.flonnet.com/fl2610/stories/20090522261002600.htm> (accessed 1 June 2012).

Kapur, D. (2007) 'The Janus Face of Diasporas'. Pp. 89–118 in B. J. Merz, L. Chen, and P. Geithner (eds.), *Diaporas and Development*. Cambridge, MA: Harvard University Press.

Lindley, A. (2010) *The Early Morning Phone Call: Somali Refugees' Remittances*. Oxford: Berghahn.

Loizos, P. (2007) ' "Generations" in Forced Migration: Towards Greater Clarity'. *Journal of Refugee Studies* 20(2): 193–209.

Long, K. (2010) 'Home Alone? A Review of the Relationship between Repatriation, Mobility and Durable Solutions for Refugees'. PDES 2010/02. Geneva: UNHCR Policy and Evaluation Service.

Mannheim, K. (1952) 'The Problem of Generations'. In *Essays on the Sociology of Knowledge*. New York: OUP.

Monsutti, A. (2005) *War and Migration: Social Networks and Economic Strategies of the Hazaras of Afghanistan*. New York: Routledge.

Portes, A., Guarnizo, L., and Landholt, P. (1999) 'The Study of Transnationalism: Promises and Pitfalls of an Emergent Research Field'. *Ethnic and Racial Studies* 22(2): 217–37.

Safran, W. (1991) 'Diasporas in Modern Societies: Myths of Homeland and Return'. *Diaspora: A Journal of Transnational Studies* 1(1): 83–99.

Sheffer, G. (ed.) (1986) *Modern Diasporas in International Politics*. London: Croom Helm.

Smith, H., and Stares, P. B. (2007) *Diasporas in Conflict: Peace-Makers or Peace-Wreckers?* Tokyo: United Nations University.

Smith, M., and Guarnizo, L. (1998) *Transnationalism from Below*. New Brunswick, NJ: Transaction Publishers.

Sökefeld, M. (2006) 'Mobilising in Transnational Space: A Social Movement Approach to the Formation of Diaspora'. *Global Networks* 6(3): 265–84.

UNHCR (1995) *The State of the World's Refugees 1995: In Search of Solutions*. Oxford: Oxford University Press.

Van Hear, N. (1998) *New Diasporas: The Mass Exodus, Dispersal and Regrouping of Migrant Communities*. London: Routledge/University College London Press.

Van Hear, N. (2002) 'Sustaining Societies under Strain: Remittances as a Form of Transnational Exchange in Sri Lanka and Ghana'. Pp. 202–23 in K. Koser and N. Al-Ali (eds.), *New Approaches to Migration: Transnational Communities and the Transformation of Home*. London: Routledge.

Van Hear, N. (2006a) ' "I went as far as my money would take me": Conflict, Forced Migration and Class'. Pp. 125–58 in F. Crepeau, D. Nakache, and M. Collyer (eds.), *Forced Migration and Global Processes: A View from Forced Migration Studies*. Lanham, MD: Lexington/Rowman and Littlefield.

Van Hear, N. (2006b) 'Refugees in Diaspora: From Durable Solutions to Transnational Relations'. *Refuge* 23: 1.

Van Hear, N. (2012) 'Forcing the Issue: Migration Crises and the Uneasy Dialogue between Refugee Research and Policy'. *Journal of Refugee Studies* 25(1): 2–24.

Van Hear, N., and Sørensen, N. N. (eds.) (2003) *The Migration-Development Nexus*. Geneva: International Organization for Migration.

Vimalarajah, L., and Cheran, R. (2010) *Empowering Diasporas: The Dynamics of Post-War Transnational Tamil Politics*. Berghof Occasional Paper 31. Berlin: Berghof Conflict Research, Berghof Peace Support.

CHAPTER 15

FORCED MIGRANTS AS 'ILLEGAL' MIGRANTS

STEPHAN SCHEEL AND VICKI SQUIRE

INTRODUCTION

To describe forced migrants as illegal migrants is highly contentious, since it would appear to criminalize those who have no choice but to migrate (Schuster 2011; Hamlin 2012). To refer to 'forced migrants' is to highlight the extremity of conditions under which certain groups 'decide' to undertake the migratory journey. An emphasis on forced migration implies a series of factors such as political persecution, ethnic conflict, inequitable access to natural resources, declining living conditions, and chronic and pervasive human rights abuses marking a limited agency on the part of those migrating (Castles 2003). Based on this assumption of restricted agency, forced migrants are generally conceived of as legitimate if not strictly legal. Hence, Article 31 of the 1951 Geneva Convention stipulates that 'Contracting States shall not impose penalties [on refugees], on account of their illegal entry or presence' (as cited in Dauvergne 2008: 50).

By contrast, the term 'illegal migrant' implies a form of agential capacity that is less restricted than it is rendered suspect through its assumed (yet contestable) illegitimacy (Coutin 2005). The association of migration with criminality has occurred across wide-ranging regions, particularly since migrants increasingly resort to the services of smugglers under conditions marked by the closure of legal migratory options (Castles 2007; Khosravi 2007). In the UK and elsewhere, an emphasis on illegality has been more popularly adopted as a term of abuse, and widely conceived of as antithetical to the victimhood associated with forced migration (Squire 2009). 'Forced migrants' on this reading are not the same as 'illegal migrants': the former are victims of their circumstances, while the latter are deemed culpable for rendering the task of governing human mobility increasingly difficult.

This chapter provides an overview of research literatures in order to identify three interrelated readings of the heading 'forced migrants as illegal migrants'. These refer to the framing, the targeting, and the active production of 'forced migrants as illegal migrants'. The chapter shows that the labels of 'forced' and 'illegal' are integral to the governing of migration. Rather than using such labels as categories in themselves, it shows how different 'figures of migration' can be engaged as analytical lenses by which to trace shifting relations of migration. From this perspective, the currency of the rendering of 'forced migrants as illegal migrants' is less contentious than it is symptomatic of a particular conjuncture in the politics of mobility, in which 'illegality' has become the prevailing interpretative grid for the governing of migratory movements. While this argument is illustrated through the European context, similar observations have been made in regards to the politics of mobility in Australia (Inder 2010), North America (Mountz 2010), and beyond (Zetter 2007).

An analysis of different 'figures of migration' is not dissimilar to one based on the concept of labelling as developed by Roger Zetter in relation to the fractioning of the refugee label. The labelling approach explores 'how refugee status is distributed and how institutionalised practices seek to distinguish this status from other categories of migrants' (Zetter 2007: 174). Focusing on institutional practices and their consequences for the labelled, Zetter also seeks to provide a framework 'to examine the interaction between bureaucratic policy...and the reactions of the labelled' (1991: 41). It is this dynamic interplay between governmental interventions and particular forms and practices of migration which is underscored by the concept of 'figures of migration'. It emphasizes the historical emergence of different categories of migration and the contingency of the relations that these produce. Such an approach is helpful as a critical diagnostic of the heading 'forced migrants as illegal migrants', because it facilitates a tracing of the key figures of migration through which migrants have been problematized, targeted, and actively produced as both 'forced and illegal'.

The concept of 'figures of migration' is based on the argument that categorizations of people on the move such as the 'refugee' or the 'illegal migrant' do not represent distinct social groups sharing characteristic features. Rather, the currency of these historically contingent figures reflects particular relations of migration, which 'correlate to certain constellations of migration policy' (Karakayali and Rigo 2010: 129). Thereby, the focus on particular figures of migration enables the unearthing of several key dimensions of the politics of mobility. First, it allows for a consideration of the complex and dynamic interplay between different forms of migration and particular attempts to control or regulate these. Second, it moves beyond the prioritization of the 'refugee' in the labelling approach. Rather, the 'refugee' emerges as one among many figures of migration. Third, it shows how each of the figures of migration is related to particular framings of the agency of people on the move and how academic knowledge production has been implicated in their development. Thereby, academic knowledge production emerges, fourth, as both a battlefield and a stake in the politics of mobility.

The chapter proceeds in three parts. The first section shows how the framing of 'forced migrants as illegal migrants' involves problematic renderings of migrant agency and draws out the three different readings of this heading. The second section offers a diagnosis of how the framing of 'forced migrants as illegal migrants' has become intelligible, specifically by tracing the successive emergence of dominant figures of migration in Europe since the Second World War, including the 'guest worker', the '(bogus) asylum seeker' and the 'illegal migrant'. The third section concludes by highlighting ways that academic knowledge production might intervene in the contested politics of mobility in order to refuse, destabilize, or subvert the terms by which the rendering of 'forced migrants as illegal migrants' has become intelligible.

'Forced Migrants as Illegal Migrants': Critique and Three Readings

The rendering of 'forced migrants as illegal migrants' has been engaged across a range of sub-fields and disciplines. This includes the sub-fields of border studies (Tsianos and Karakayali 2010; Gerard and Pickering 2012), refugee and forced migration studies (Mortimer 1997; Bakewell 2008; Zimmermann 2009) and migration studies (Castles 2007). It is also one that fosters critical research across a range of disciplines, including anthropology (Khosravi 2007; Schuster 2011), law (Dauvergne 2008; Kneebone 2009; Inder 2010), politics and international studies (Betts 2010; Hamlin 2012), and geography (Black 2003; Mountz 2010). These literatures provide two important insights that allow for three different, but interrelated readings of the coupling of forced migration with illegal migration.

First, recent scholarship has underscored the impossibility of distinguishing voluntary from forced migration. The 1951 United Nations Geneva Convention is based on a clear-cut distinction between political and economic migrants, with the former qualifying as 'refugees' based on the fact of their 'well founded fear of persecution'. Numerous scholars have, however, argued that the underlying assumption, whereupon it is possible to distinguish between refugees and non-refugees in practice, is an illusion. Rather, 'forced' and 'voluntary' are conceived as poles of a continuum, with economic, political, environmental, and social factors shaping peoples' decisions to migrate being interdependent. The notion of the migration-asylum nexus seeks to underscore the blurring of forced and voluntary migratory movements at all stages of the migratory process. The motivations for movement are always mixed, while all migrants travel along the same routes, use the same means of transport and rely on social networks of compatriots upon arrival. Whereas the notion of migration-asylum-nexus was taken up in the migration policy discourse in the 1990s under the heading 'mixed migration', scholars have insisted that the nexus is by no means a new phenomenon (Castles 2007). From this perspective, the distinction between 'forced' (political) and 'voluntary' (economic) migrants enshrined in the 1951 Geneva Convention is conceived of as an artificial construct, albeit one with significant legal implications (Richmond 1988; Scalettaris 2007; Collyer 2010). Indeed, the refugee definition of the Convention is often regarded as too narrow and as excluding many types of forced migrants from profiting from protection (Castles 2003; Zetter 2007). For instance, the Geneva Convention has been criticized for not recognizing sexual violence and gender related prosecution as reasons for protection (Essed and Wesenbeek 2004).

Second, the divide between legal and illegal migration has been shown to be a complex and ambivalent one. Various authors have engaged critically with the concept of illegal migration, which is adopted here as a means to explore a juncture of the politics of mobility rather than as a term of analytical merit in itself (Black 2003; Karakayali 2008; Squire 2011). A growing body of literature shows how 'illegal migration' is a product of shifting policy and practice (Mountz 2010). This literature highlights restrictive migration legislation and the build-up of border controls as not controlling, but effectively *producing* 'illegal' migration (Samers 2004). Besides an emphasis on illegality as a produced and productive condition (De Genova 2002; Sigona 2012), there has also been a growing emphasis on illegality as a condition that is not fixed but which is complex and ambiguous in its functioning (Rigo 2011). This includes analyses that stress the blurred line between the illegal and illicit (Coutin 2005), as well as those unearthing the ways in which unauthorized migrants are incorporated in legal structures and practices (Sigona and Hughes 2012). Indeed, it has been demonstrated that migrants often lapse back and forth between statuses. In contrast to any clear-cut juridical definition, illegality has thus been shown to involve a plethora of forms and conditions (Sciortino 2004; Black et al. 2006; Chauvin and Garcés-Mascareñas 2012).

Together, the literatures on the migration-asylum nexus and on the production of illegality point to the problems of using labels such as 'forced' or 'illegal'. Of particular concern has been the search for a terminology that does not criminalize those to whom it refers. Many scholars have problematized the use of the prefix 'illegal', turning to alternatives such as 'undocumented migrant' or '*sans papiers*' (in the French context) that challenge assumptions regarding migrant criminality. Yet these alternatives are not always accurate, given that many migrants arrive and live with various forms of documentation (Khosravi 2007; Karakayali 2008; Chauvin and Garcés-Mascareñas 2012). This chapter directly mobilizes the term 'illegal migrant' in order to draw attention to the criminalization of migrants, not only by the law, but also through a plethora of practices (Black 2003; Dauvergne 2008). Instead of reifying such labels by using them as analytical categories, this chapter seeks to denaturalize them by engaging labels like 'refugee' or 'illegal migrant' as historically contingent figures. Engaging these 'figures of migration' as objects of inquiry in themselves reveals more about the conjunctures in the politics of mobility in which they flourish, than about the people they label. Thereby, the chapter underscores 'the extent to which bureaucratic interests and procedures are themselves crucial determinants in the definition of labels like refugee' (Zetter 1991: 41) 'forced migrant', or, indeed, 'illegal migrant'.

If we take seriously the insight that forced and voluntary are not a binary opposition, but ends of a continuum, and that legal and illegal are not clear-cut juridical statuses, but contested and ambiguous conditions, then the framing of 'forced migrants as illegal migrants' no longer simply appears as contentious. Rather, three different readings of this heading are made possible. 'Forced migrants as illegal migrants' can be read as a particular mode of *problematization*; as a particular form of *targeting* migrants; and/or as a process of actively *producing* forced migrants as illegal migrants. The first reading claims that many 'forced migrants' are in fact 'voluntary economic migrants' who abuse the asylum system and are therefore 'illegal'. This perspective has gained momentum in media coverage as well as among policymakers in the global North since the 1980s (Squire 2009), while some scholars have at times supported the validity of this claim (Chimni 1998). The second reading suggests that 'forced migrants' are increasingly regarded and treated as 'illegal migrants' through migration policies aimed at their deterrence and containment (Black 2003; Betts 2010). This creates critical distance from the assumption that 'forced migrants are illegal migrants'. Finally, the third reading indicates that many 'forced migrants', including those who would qualify for refugee status, are *actively produced* as illegal migrants (Schuster 2011; Hamlin 2012). The latter is supported by research that suggests some may prefer not to apply for asylum, since this can involve a denial of the right to work and/or detention (Bloch, Sigona, and Zetter 2011), or because restrictive asylum legislation and border control mechanisms prevent the application of asylum (e.g. Schuster 2011; Gerard and Pickering 2012).

It is important to note that these three readings of the heading of 'forced migrants as illegal migrants' are not mutually exclusive, but interrelated. While the first, acritical reading frames and problematizes forced migrants as illegal migrants, the second reading criticizes the policies and practices that are justified by this problematization of forced migrants as illegal migrants. The third reading builds on the previous two by proposing that it is through the problematization and targeting of forced migrants as illegal migrants that forced migrants are effectively produced as illegal migrants. This reading is important because it highlights the dynamic interplay between governmental categories and interventions and the practices and tactics of migration. As such, it draws attention to the struggles between migration and attempts to govern migration, which constitute the politics of mobility (Squire 2011). From this perspective, the heading of 'forced migrants as illegal migrants' is one that is less contentious than it is symptomatic of the contemporary conjuncture in the politics of mobility.

DIAGNOSING THE LABELLING OF 'FORCED MIGRANTS AS ILLEGAL MIGRANTS'

The problematization, targeting, and active production of 'forced migrants as illegal migrants' indicates a significant shift in the politics of mobility, which is characterized by the emergence of 'migration management' as a dominant paradigm in migration policy (Geiger and Pécoud 2010). 'Migration management' implicates a shift whereby the legal/illegal binary has eclipsed the forced/voluntary binary as the governmental grid and terrain for the politics of mobility. It revolves around a utilitarian economic logic, and entails the differentiation of migrants into various 'desirable' and 'undesirable' categories. Consequently, this new paradigm has not only effectively displaced the prominence of refugee protection, which constituted the dominant framework for the regulation of migration during the Cold War. It also implies a transformation of the post-war refugee protection regime itself (Betts 2010; Scheel and Ratfisch 2014).

Immediately after the Second World War, the forced/voluntary binary dominated the politics of mobility. A sharp distinction between 'forced' (political) and 'voluntary' (economic) migration was enshrined in the narrow definition of the 'refugee' in the Geneva Convention in 1951. The latter was heavily implicated in anti-communist politics at the onset of the Cold War as it afforded Western states a tool to claim moral superiority. At that time political agency was the defining feature of the 'refugee', who was imagined as 'white, male and anti-communist', fleeing political persecution for protection by Western states (Chimni 1998: 351). Consequently, the Geneva Convention effectively left many 'forced migrants' without access to protection. This included not only the thousands of people from the global South fleeing struggles over decolonization and state formation, but also those fleeing non-communist dictatorships in Southern European countries (Castles 2003). In this context, those who may otherwise be categorized as 'forced migrants' were faced with a choice of remaining where they were or migrating to Europe as 'voluntary economic migrants'. The latter is the case for the one million people who fled dictatorship and poverty in Portugal during the post-war period (Karakayali and Rigo 2010). Although clandestine, many of these migrants were able to regularize their status as 'guest workers' once they had found employment (Black 2003; Karakayali 2008).

Despite technically qualifying as 'illegal migrants' in the sense in which the term has been used in Europe over recent years, these groups were not problematized as such because they could integrate themselves within the matrix of migration policy under the figure of the 'guest worker' (Karakayali and Rigo 2010). 'Guest workers' were expected to stay and work only for a limited period in the Northern European countries before returning 'home'. Their right for residence was coupled to the duration of their labour contract. In this context, illegality was conceived as a transitional phase of 'guest workers' after arrival and channels of ex-post regularization were available in nearly all Western European countries until the mid-seventies (Sciortino 2004; Karakayali 2008). This example indicates that dominant figures of migration function as interpretative grids for all migration processes, thereby organizing the epistemological and political terrain of both migration and migration policy. It highlights, moreover, that all figures of migration entail certain representational barriers, which surface most prominently in particular renderings of migrants' agency (Karakayali and Rigo 2010). Whereas people fleeing dictatorships in Southern Europe did not comply with the figure of the 'refugee', who was imagined as imbued with political (anti-communist) agency in this period, they could, nevertheless, enter and remain in Northern Europe as 'guest workers', who were imagined as a *homo oeconomicus* with economic agency. This constellation in the politics of mobility is reflected in the discipline of migration studies, which was dominated by economic migration theories at that time (Massey et al. 1998).

Yet, significant shifts occurred in the politics of mobility from the mid-1970s onwards. First, moves toward the liberalization of mobility within the 'common market' of the European Economic Community was accompanied by a series of ad hoc measures that institutionalized migration as a security issue during the 1970s and 1980s (Huysmans 2006). The securitization of migration fed into a growing emphasis on the figure of the 'asylum seeker' during the 1980s and 1990s (Zetter 2007; Squire 2009). For those without family members in Northern Europe, the asylum system became the remaining legal channel of entry after the abolishment of guest-worker schemes (Mortimer 1997; Castles 2007; Karakayali 2008). In the absence of other legal migration channels, 'labour migrants in the 1970s and 1980s had to invent stories of 'political' persecution' (Karakayali and Rigo 2010: 129). Some who might previously have migrated as 'guest workers' or as 'Commonwealth migrants' (in the UK) were in this context better placed to claim asylum (Zetter 2007; Dauvergne 2008: 62). Migrants seeking to satisfy the requirements of governmental procedures often shaped their behaviour by appealing to the currency of the 'refugee' as a figure of migration (Karakayali and Rigo 2010: 130).

Second, there was an expansion of the 'refugee' definition to those fleeing war and communal violence in conjunction with the lifting of the geographical limitation of the Geneva Convention in 1967. This enabled people from the global South to seek protection in the global North. This shift was reflected in the expansion of refugee studies, which were subsequently dominated by a debate on these supposedly 'new asylum seekers' (Martin 1988). It implicated the construction of a 'myth of difference', according to which the features of forced migrants arriving from the global South were markedly different (Chimni 1998). The 'myth of difference' implied a reimagination of the figure of the 'refugee', who was now imagined as a poor and helpless person from the global South. A lack of political agency became the defining feature of the figure of the 'refugee' during this period (Malkki 1996; Nyers 2006). Most importantly, asylum seekers from the global South were also constructed as different with regard to their motivations for movement, precisely because they were imagined as deprived. They were suspected of not fleeing prosecution, but making an informed and beneficial migration choice. These developments heralded the emergence of the 'bogus asylum seeker' as the dominant figure of migration in the politics of mobility (Essed and Wesenbeek 2004; Karakayali and Rigo 2010).

It is the salience of the figure of the 'bogus asylum seeker' in media and policy discourses since the 1990s which signals the increasing *problematization* of 'forced migrants as illegal migrants' (Gabrielatos and Baker 2008). The figure of the 'bogus asylum seeker' rests on the assumption that asylum seekers falsely claim to be forced migrants in order to gain entry, but are in fact 'voluntary economic migrants' (Squire 2009). This suggests a shift from the forced/voluntary binary towards the legal/illegal binary as the dominant framework and terrain for the politics of mobility. In contrast to the figure of the 'refugee', whose defining feature is a lack of political agency, the 'bogus asylum seeker' is conceived as imbued with dangerous or excessive agency based on the suspected 'abuse' of the asylum system. The representational barriers of the figure of the 'refugee' implicated in the ascription of a lack of agency were played out in debates regarding the 'bogus asylum seeker'. Since migrating for economic reasons from the global South was politically unacceptable (particularly in times of recession in the global North), pro-migrant groups insisted on the humanitarian character of migratory movements (Karakayali and Rigo 2010). Ultimately, this debate led to the de-politicization of 'forced migration' by framing it either as a humanitarian or a law enforcement problem. Those claiming asylum in Europe were either criminalized as 'bogus asylum seekers' imbued with dangerous agency, or they were victimized as 'genuine refugees' in need of protection due to their lack of agency. That the application for asylum might entail a political dimension was precluded from this debate.

It was thus on the back of the figure of the 'bogus asylum seeker' that 'illegality' emerged as a dominant frame of migration during the 1990s (Karakayali and Rigo 2010). This is reflected in an explosion of publications on 'illegal migration', which had been previously treated as an appendix of labour and asylum migration (Black 2003). Many authors regard the end of the Cold War as a watershed in the global politics of mobility (Chimni 1998; Hamlin 2012). Refugee protection no longer held importance as an ideological tool proving the moral superiority of the West, and its rearticulation along the lines of a 'new humanitarianism' favoured the 'preventive protection' of forced migrants in the countries of origin. Various developments have been understood in light of these policies of containment: from Western wars in Bosnia and Iraq (Frelick 1992), through Australia's 'pacific solution' (Inder 2010), to the pursuit of interception policies against Haitian asylum seekers in the US (Hamlin 2012). This shift is highlighted, among others, by the problematization of 'internally displaced persons' (IDPs) in the 1990s, around which forced migration studies was established as a distinct academic field (Chimni 2009). Such developments ran alongside the *targeting* of 'forced migrants as illegal migrants', through policies of dissuasion and deterrence. These featured, among others, the introduction of visa restrictions for citizens from non-OECD countries, the invention of 'safe third country' rules and various temporary protection statuses as well as the detention of asylum seekers in isolated camps for prolonged periods.

Yet, these measures of targeting also conditioned a rise in 'illegal migration' (Samers 2004; Karakayali 2008: 180). On the one hand, the increasing rejection of asylum applications implicated the active 'manufacture of illegality' (Essed and Wesenbeek 2004). While some scholars have backed the claim by policymakers, whereupon falling recognition rates of asylum applications from 1985 onwards confirmed that most asylum claims were, in fact, unfounded, others have convincingly refuted this argument as circular, as it basically states: 'the system is fair because the applicants are bogus, and the applicants are bogus because the system says so' (Mortimer 1997: 202). Rather, declining recognition rates reflect the tightening of the criteria and procedures for recognizing asylum claims (Kneebone 2009; Mountz 2010; Hamlin 2012). As a result, asylum systems have become so inaccessible that many forced migrants now have to live as illegal migrants (Schuster 2011). On the other hand, asylum systems have become so repressive that some forced migrants now prefer to remain illegal in order to avoid detention and humiliating treatment (Black et al. 2006; Bloch, Sigona, and Zetter 2011). It is here that we can see how the targeting of 'forced migrants as illegal migrants' leads to the *active production* of 'forced migrants as illegal migrants'.

CRITICALLY INTERVENING THE POLITICS OF MOBILITY: INVENTING AND UNMAKING FIGURES OF MIGRATION

The problematization, targeting, and active production of 'forced migrants as illegal migrants' is indicative of the present conjuncture of the politics of mobility, in which 'illegality' has become the interpretative grid for all migratory movements, including those of 'forced migrants'. Though this shift is implicated by the emergence of 'migration management' as the dominant paradigm in the politics of mobility, a simple return to the refugee protection paradigm as a means to challenge the rendering of 'forced migrants as illegal migrants' appears as problematic. This is because the refugee protection regime of the Geneva Convention involves distinctions that are already inscribed within the legal/illegal binary, namely those regarding the legitimacy of forced (political) migration and the illegitimacy of voluntary (economic) migration (Scheel and Ratfisch 2014). Moreover, the dichotomous logic of the refugee protection regime implicates a depoliticization of migration. Through the interrelated processes of criminalization and victimization migrants' agency is either constructed as excessive or as impoverished. As such, migration is either reduced to a problem of law enforcement or to a problem affording humanitarian practices. Rather than seeking to recoup or rearticulate the agency of migrants in order to counter such depoliticizing manoeuvres, this chapter suggests that it is more appropriate to unearth and intervene in the struggles between migration and governmental attempts to regulate it.

To conclude, the chapter suggests two ways to develop such interventions. First, further work diagnosing how particular figures of migration emerge and become institutionalized as categorizations of migrant groups is required, specifically in order to guard against their uncritical use as analytical categories in academic research. Such analyses might examine how such categorizations not only shape forms of migration, but are also negotiated and appropriated by migrants for the realization of their migration projects. This involves an approach that pays attention to the *politics* of mobility and the subjectivities such politics involve and produce, without celebrating or denigrating migrants in this process. It also entails a refusal of the subdisciplinary boundaries of refugee or forced migration studies, whose agendas implicate such categorizations. Such (artificial) demarcations of knowledge fields constitute a veritable self-limitation, and overlook the impossibility of distinguishing univocally between people on the move in practice. Instead, a focus on the struggles between migration and attempts at migratory regulations allows for the consideration of various figures of migration as crucial *stakes* that are shaped by and mobilized in the politics of mobility (Squire 2011). Breaking down the barriers between different types of migration studies facilitates analysis of the ways in which migrants play into but also ultimately undermine the categories into which they are forced.

This leads to the second type of intervention that is important in guarding against the reproduction of governmental categories in academic research. Analyses that 'invent' or interrogate *ambivalent* figures of migration in order to disrupt or expose existing ones are of critical purchase here. For example, the analyses of Peter Nyers (2013) and Enrica Rigo (2011) highlight how 'illegal citizens' can contest and destabilize historically contingent ways of delimiting populations. Other examples include the relegitimization of 'irregular secondary movements' of recognized refugees as a form of 'self-resettlement' (Collyer 2010) and research on 'self-settled refugees' as a way to explore alternatives to the internment of forced migrants in camps in the course of interventions under the banner of humanitarianism (Bakewell 2008). These works neither simply adopt bureaucratic labels as analytical categories, nor fully distance themselves from them. They rather highlight how migratory regulations lie in constant tension with migratory practices. Thereby, they explore the politics of mobility in terms that open up key tensions to further question. To destabilize or contest dominant figures of migration in this regard moves beyond simply rejecting the heading of 'forced migrants as illegal migrants' due to the criminalization that this heading implies. Rather, it offers a possibility to critically intervene the politics of mobility through which such a heading becomes intelligible in the first place.

REFERENCES

Bakewell, O. (2008) 'Research beyond the Categories: The Importance of Policy Irrelevant Research into Forced Migration'. *Journal of Refugee Studies* 21(4): 432–53.

Betts, A. (2010) 'The Refugee Regime Complex'. *Refugee Survey Quarterly* 29(1): 12–37.

Black, R. (2003) 'Breaking the Convention: Researching the "Illegal" Migration of Refugees to Europe'. *Antipode* 35(1): 34–54.

Black, R., Collyer, M., Skeldon, R., and Waddington, C. (2006) 'Routes to Illegal Residence: A Case Study of Immigration Detainees in the United Kingdom'. *Geoforum* 37(4): 552–64.

Bloch, A., Sigona, N., and Zetter, R. (2011) *No Right to Dream: The Social and Economic Lives of Young Undocumented Migrants in Britain*. London: Paul Hamlyn Foundation.

Castles, S. (2003) 'Towards a Sociology of Forced Migration and Social Transformation'. *Sociology* 37(1): 13–24.

Castles, S. (2007) 'The Migration-Asylum Nexus and Regional Approaches'. Pp. 25–42 in S. Kneebone and F. Rawlings-Sanae (eds.), *New Regionalism and Asylum Seekers: Challenges Ahead*. London: Berghahn Books.

Chauvin, S., and Garcés-Mascareñas, B. (2012) 'Beyond Informal Citizenship: The New Moral Economy of Migrant Illegality'. *International Political Sociology* 6(3): 241–59.

Chimni, B. S. (1998) 'The Geopolitics of Refugee Studies: A View from the South'. *Journal of Refugee Studies* 11(4): 350–74.

Chimni, B. S. (2009) 'The Birth of a "Discipline": From Refugee to Forced Migration Studies'. *Journal of Refugee Studies* 22(1): 11–29.

Collyer, M. (2010) 'Stranded Migrants and the Fragmented Journey'. *Journal of Refugee Studies* 23(3): 273–93.

Coutin, S. B. (2005) 'Contesting Criminality: Illegal Immigration and the Spatialization of Legality'. *Theoretical Criminology* 9(1): 5–33.

Dauvergne, C. (2008) *Making People Illegal: What Globalization Means for Migration and Law.* New York: Cambridge University Press.

De Genova, N. (2002) 'Migrant "Illegality" and Deportability in Everyday Life'. *Annual Review of Anthropology* 31(3): 419–47.

Essed, P., and Wesenbeek, R. (2004) 'Contested Refugee Status: Human Rights, Ethics and Social Responsibilities'. Pp. 53–65 in P. Essed, G. Frerks, and J. Schrijvders (eds.), *Refugees and the Transformation of Societies: Agency, Policies, Ethics and Politics.* New York: Berghahn Books.

Frelick, B. (1992). '"Preventive Protection" and the Right to Seek Asylum: A Preliminary Look at Bosnia and Croatia'. *International Journal of Refugee Law* 4(4): 439–54.

Gabrielatos, C., and Baker, P. (2008) 'Fleeing, Sneaking, Flooding: A Corpus Analysis of Discursive Constructions of Refugees and Asylum Seekers in the UK Press, 1996–2005'. *Journal of English Linguistics* 36(1): 5–38.

Geiger, M., and Pécoud, A. (2010) 'The Politics of International Migration Management'. Pp. 1–20 in M. Geiger and A. Pécoud (eds.), *The Politics of International Migration Management.* Basingstoke: Palgrave.

Gerard, A., and Pickering, S. (2012) 'The Crime and Punishment of Somali Women's Extra-Legal Arrival in Malta'. *British Journal of Criminology* 53(3): 514–33.

Hamlin, R. (2012) 'Illegal Refugees: Competing Policy Ideas and the Rise of the Regime of Deterrence in American Asylum Policies'. *Refugee Survey Quarterly* 31(2): 33–53.

Huysmans, J. (2006) *The Politics of Insecurity: Fear, Migration and Asylum in the EU.* London: Routledge.

Inder, C. (2010) 'International Refugee Law, "Hyper-Legalism" and Migration Management: The Pacific Solution'. Pp. 220–51 in M. Geiger and A. Pécoud (eds.), *The Politics of International Migration Management.* Basingstoke: Palgrave.

Karakayali, S. (2008) *Gespenster der Migration: Zur Genealogie illegaler Einwanderung in der Bundesrepublik Deutschland.* Bielefeld: transcript.

Karakayali, S., and Rigo, E. (2010) 'Mapping the European Space of Circulation'. Pp. 123–44 in N. De Genova and N. Preutz (eds.), *The Deportation Regime: Sovereignty, Space, and the Freedom of Movement.* Durham, NC: Duke University Press.

Khosravi, S. (2007) 'The "Illegal" Traveller: An Auto-ethnography of Borders'. *Social Anthropology* 15(3): 321–34.

Kneebone, S. (2009) *Refugees, Asylum Seekers and the Rule of Law.* Cambridge: Cambridge University Press.

Malkki, L. (1996). 'Speechless Emissaries: Refugees, Humanitarianism, and Dehistoricization'. *Cultural Anthropology* 11(3): 377–404.

Martin, D. A. (1988) 'Introduction: The New Asylum Seekers'. Pp. 1–22 in D. A. Martin (ed.), *The New Asylum Seekers: Refugee Law in the 1980s.* Dordrecht: Martinus Nijhoff Publishers.

Massey, D., Arango, J., Hugo, G., Kouaouci, A., Pellegrino, A., and Edward Taylor, J. (1998) *Worlds in Motion: Understanding International Migration at the End of the Millenium.* New York: Oxford University Press.

Mortimer, E. (1997). 'The Treatment of Refugees and Asylum-seekers'. *Journal of Refugee Studies* 10(2): 199–207.

Mountz, A. (2010) *Seeking Asylum: Human Smuggling and Bureaucracy at the Border.* Minneapolis: University of Minnesota Press.

Nyers, P. (2006) *Rethinking Refugees: Beyond States of Emergency.* New York: Routledge.

Nyers, P. (2013) 'Liberating Irregularity: No Borders, Temporality, Citizenship'. Pp. 37–52 in X. Guillaume and J. Huysmans (eds.), *Citizenship and Security: The Constitution of Political Being.* London: Routledge.

Richmond, A. (1988). 'Sociological Theories of International Migration: The Case of Refugees'. *Current Sociology* 36(7): 7–25.

Rigo, E. (2011) 'Citizens despite Borders: Challenges to the Territorial Order of Europe'. Pp. 199–215 in V. Squire (ed.), *The Contested Politics of Mobility: Borderzones and Irregularity.* London: Routledge.

Samers, M. (2004) 'Emerging Geopolitics of Illegal Immigration in the European Union'. *European Journal of Migration and Law* 6(1): 27–45.

Scalettaris, G. (2007) 'Refugee Studies and the International Refugee Regime: A Reflection on a Desirable Separation'. *Refugee Survey Quarterly* 26(3): 36–50.

Scheel, S., and Ratfisch, P. (2014) 'Refugee Protection Meets "Migration Management": The UNHCR as a Global Police of Populations'. *Journal of Ethnic and Migration Studies*, special issue on 'International Organisations and the Politics of Migration', in press.

Schuster, L. (2011) 'Turning Refugees into "Illegal Migrants": Afghan Asylum Seekers in Europe'. *Ethnic and Racial Studies* 34(8): 1392–407.

Sciortino, G. (2004). 'Between Phantoms and Necessary Evils: Some Critical Points in the Study of Irregular Migrations to Western Europe'. *IMIS-Beiträge* 24: 17–43.

Sigona, N. (2012). ' "I have too much baggage": The Impacts of Legal Status on the Social Worlds of Irregular Migrants'. *Social Anthropology* 20(1): 50–65.

Sigona, N., and Hughes, V. (2012) 'No Way out, No Way in: Irregular Migrant Children and Families in the UK'. Oxford: ESRC Centre on Migration, Policy and Society.

Squire, V. (2009) *The Exclusionary Politics of Asylum.* Basingstoke: Palgrave MacMillan.

Squire, V. (2011) 'The Contested Politics of Mobility: Politicizing Mobility, Mobilizing Politics'. Pp. 1–30 in V. Squire (ed.), *The Contested Politics of Mobility: Borderzones and Irregularity.* London: Routledge.

Tsianos, V., and Karakayali, S. (2010) 'Transnational Migration and the Emergence of the European Border Regime: An Ethnographic Analysis'. *European Journal of Social Theory* 13(3): 373–87.

Zetter, R. (1991) 'Labelling Refugees: Forming and Transforming a Bureaucratic Identity'. *Journal of Refugee Studies* 4(1): 39–62.

Zetter, R. (2007) 'More Labels, Fewer Refugees: Remaking the Refugee Label in an Era of Globalization'. *Journal of Refugee Studies* 20(2): 172–92.

Zimmermann, S. E. (2009) 'Irregular Secondary Movements to Europe: Seeking Asylum beyond Refuge'. *Journal of Refugee Studies* 22(1): 74–96.

PART III

LEGAL AND INSTITUTIONAL RESPONSES TO FORCED MIGRATION

CHAPTER 16

HUMAN RIGHTS AND FORCED MIGRATION

JANE MCADAM

INTRODUCTION

As a matter of law, all people have human rights. They are safeguarded by a range of international, regional, and national legal instruments which articulate universal rights pertaining to all persons, as well as emphasizing particular rights for particular groups—such as women, children, and the disabled. It is widely accepted that human rights are indivisible, interdependent, and interrelated. Whether they are expressed as civil and political rights or as economic, cultural, and social rights, the fundamental notion underpinning human rights is that they are derived from the inherent dignity of every human being.

Forced migrants are entitled to enjoy the full range of civil, political, economic, social, and cultural rights set out in international and regional human rights treaties and customary international law. With very few exceptions (relating to the right to vote, the right to stand for public office, and the expulsion of aliens), the international human rights instruments make no distinction between the rights of citizens and (forced) migrants. Indeed, the principle of non-discrimination mandates that states respect and ensure human rights 'without discrimination of any kind as to race, colour, sex, language, religion, political or other opinion, national or social origin, property, birth or other status' (ICESCR, Art. 2(2); see also ICCPR, Art. 2(1)). That is not to say that all differential treatment amounts to discrimination, but rather that it will only be justified if the criteria for such differentiation are 'reasonable and objective' and the overall aim is 'to achieve a purpose which is legitimate' under human rights law (UN Human Rights Committee 1989: para. 13).

However, it is far too apparent that the rights of forced migrants are frequently violated. In some countries, asylum seekers are held in mandatory detention or even prison, live in destitution, are subject to whipping and other inhuman treatment, or live for decades in protracted situations with no durable solution in sight.

This chapter examines three ways in which human rights law can assist and protect such persons. To avoid overlap with other chapters, the focus here is on forced migrants who cross an *international* border but do not satisfy the legal definition of 'refugee' under the 1951 Refugee Convention (or its regional counterparts).

First, human rights law provides a basis on which an individual fleeing harm may be granted protection. This is because human rights law establishes minimum standards of treatment that states must afford to individuals within their territory or jurisdiction. If these rights are abused or denied, then people may flee their countries and seek protection elsewhere. Sometimes, such abuses are considered to be sufficiently severe (by their inherent nature or cumulative impact) to constitute 'persecution' under refugee law, and if the other elements of the refugee definition are also made out, then protection may be forthcoming on that basis. However, in other situations, a person may not meet the legal requirements of the refugee definition but still be at risk of harm if removed. This is where the expanded principle of *non-refoulement* in human rights law may provide protection. This is known by various terms but most commonly as 'complementary' or 'subsidiary' protection.

Second, human rights law is relevant to the legal status granted to forced migrants. It fleshes out the rights which forced migrants should receive when they are granted protection in another country. This is because of the minimum standards of treatment set out in the human rights treaties which states have agreed to guarantee to all persons within their territory or jurisdiction.

Finally, human rights treaties are 'living' instruments which evolve over time. This means that in the future, new groups of forced migrants may be able to secure protection as understandings of human rights develop.

FLEEING FROM HUMAN RIGHTS VIOLATIONS: COMPLEMENTARY PROTECTION

Settled Grounds of Human Rights-Based *Non-refoulement*

'Complementary protection' describes protection granted by states on the basis of an international protection need that falls outside the 1951 Refugee Convention framework. Such protection may be based on a human rights treaty, such as the International Covenant on Civil and Political Rights (ICCPR) or the Convention against Torture (CAT), or on more general humanitarian principles, such as assisting those fleeing generalized violence. It is premised on the expanded principle of *non-refoulement* (non-return) under human rights law, which at a minimum prohibits states from returning people to situations where they would face a real risk of being arbitrarily deprived of life or subjected to the death penalty; torture; cruel, inhuman, or degrading treatment or punishment; or enforced disappearance.[1] Complementary protection is typically granted where the treatment feared does not reach the level of severity of 'persecution', or where there is a risk of persecution but it is not linked to one of the Refugee Convention grounds.

Beginning with the case of *Soering v United Kingdom* in 1989, the European Court of Human Rights has led the way in articulating the grounds on which human rights law can offer protection to people at risk of harm elsewhere. These principles have since been adopted and extended by international treaty monitoring bodies, other regional courts (such as the Court of Justice of the EU), and domestic courts and legislatures.

As noted above, complementary protection protects people from return to circumstances where they are at risk of arbitrary deprivation of life, the death penalty, or being subjected to torture or cruel, inhuman, or degrading treatment or punishment. These rights are absolute: they have no exceptions, states cannot enter treaty reservations to them, and they cannot be derogated from during times of public emergency threatening the life of the nation. Their meaning has been the subject of considerable jurisprudence and scholarly analysis, and both the UN Human Rights Committee and the European Court of Human Rights have explained that they cannot be exhaustively defined since their meaning will evolve over time. For this reason, there is no definitive 'list' of proscribed treatment. Further, the individual circumstances of each case will have a bearing on whether the particular ill-treatment feared attains the minimum level of severity (which does not have to be as severe as 'persecution'). It is important to note that harm can result from positive acts (e.g. the actual infliction of harm) as well as from deprivation (e.g. resources being withheld) (Foster 2007).

Some other human rights are described as 'qualified' rights. This is because they are derogable in certain limited circumstances, they can be the subject of reservations, or they can be balanced against other competing considerations. For example, the right to freedom of expression can be restricted if this is necessary to protect national security, public order, public health, or morals, or to ensure respect for the rights or reputations of others (ICCPR, Art. 19). For this reason, in cases concerning qualified rights, applicants may try to show that the harm feared also constitutes 'inhuman or degrading treatment' (which is clearly recognized as a complementary protection ground). Most jurisprudence on human rights-based *non-refoulement* in fact focuses on this ground.

Additional Grounds

Despite the well-settled grounds for complementary protection, international and regional human rights bodies and courts have emphasized that this list is not closed and there may be other situations which preclude removal. The UN Committee on the Rights of the Child has made clear that the *non-refoulement* obligation is 'by no means limited to' provisions relating to threats to life or to torture or cruel, inhuman, or degrading treatment or punishment, and applies in *any* case where there are substantial grounds for believing that there is a real risk of 'irreparable harm' if the person is removed (2005: para. 27). The UN Human Rights Committee has accepted that the obligation may be triggered 'when considerations of non-discrimination . . . and respect for family life arise' (UN Human Rights Committee 1986, 1989, 2004).

The European Court of Human Rights has held that states must not return people to countries where they will face a 'flagrant denial of justice' (ECHR, Art. 6), such as when evidence obtained by torture is admitted in criminal proceedings (e.g. *Othman v UK*). It has also accepted, at least in principle, that a sufficiently flagrant breach of Article 5 (right to liberty and security) or Article 9 of the European Convention on Human Rights (ECHR) could give rise to a *non-refoulement* obligation (e.g. *Tomic v UK*; *Z and T v UK*).[2] In *Ullah*, the House of Lords (as it then was) acknowledged that a breach of *any* human right could potentially engage a *non-refoulement* obligation if the breach were so flagrant as to completely deny or nullify the right. However, both courts have pointed out that it would be difficult to envisage a case where a sufficiently flagrant violation would not already be encompassed by the prohibition on return to 'inhuman or degrading treatment' under Article 3 of the ECHR (*Z and T v UK*; *Ullah*).

Both courts also accept that Article 8 of the ECHR, which protects the right to respect for private and family life, may preclude return in certain circumstances (e.g. *Bensaid*; *Razgar*). The threshold is high and the interference must be balanced against considerations set out in Article 8(2)—whether the interference is 'necessary in a democratic society in the interests of national security, public safety or the economic well-being of the country, for the prevention of disorder or crime, for the protection of health or morals, or for the protection of the rights and freedoms of others'. This always involves striking 'a fair balance between the rights of the individual and the interests of the community', but '[d]ecisions taken pursuant to the lawful operation of immigration control will be proportionate in all save a small minority of exceptional cases, identifiable only on a case by case basis' (*Razgar*, para. 20; see also para. 59).

Finally, Article 3 of the Convention on the Rights of the Child mandates that in any decision involving a child, the child's best interests must be a primary consideration. This means that the child's interests should be considered first, and only outweighed if some other consideration (either individual or cumulative) is inherently more significant (*ZH*; *Wan*). While there is a general presumption in favour of family reunification, in some cases this will not be in the child's best interests. This might be because of the risk of harm in the place to which return is contemplated, or because of the risk represented by the parents themselves, such as if they have been involved in trafficking the child in the past, or are unable to protect the child from being trafficked in the future (UNICEF 2012: 42).

THE RELATIONSHIP BETWEEN REFUGEE LAW AND COMPLEMENTARY PROTECTION

Properly applied, complementary protection does not supplant or compete with the Refugee Convention. By its very nature, it is *complementary* to refugee status determination, which means it should only be considered following a comprehensive evaluation of a person's claim against the Refugee Convention definition and a finding that the applicant is not a refugee (UNHCR 2003: Goal 1, Objective 3; Executive Committee Conclusion No. 103, para. q). Thus, the legislative framework of the EU, Australia, and New Zealand, for instance, requires decision makers to assess refugee claims first, before turning to the complementary protection grounds.

This is intended to safeguard the 'primacy' of the Refugee Convention and ensure that decision makers remain mindful of the evolving meaning of 'persecution' in refugee law, thus developing refugee jurisprudence accordingly. Indeed, human rights law has been very influential on refugee law, helping to increase the latter's 'strength and relevance' (Fitzpatrick 2000). Superior courts around the world have recognized the Refugee Convention as a human rights treaty and have interpreted its provisions in light of other international law obligations arising under CAT, the ICCPR, the Universal Declaration of Human Rights, the Convention on the Elimination of All Forms of Discrimination against Women, and customary international law, thus enabling 'account to be taken of changes in society and of discriminatory circumstances which may not have been obvious to the delegates when the Convention was being framed' (*Islam*, 657). Human rights law has helped to inform key concepts such as the meaning of 'persecution' and 'particular social group'.

STANDARDS OF TREATMENT

Human rights treaties set out a comprehensive range of rights to which all people are entitled. Some of the most pertinent include:

ICCPR:
- the right to an effective remedy for breaches of human rights (Art. 2);
- the right to life (Art. 6);
- the right to freedom from torture or cruel, inhuman, or degrading treatment or punishment (Art. 7);
- the right to be treated with humanity and respect for the inherent dignity of the human person when deprived of liberty (Art. 10);
- the right to freedom from arbitrary detention (Art. 9);
- the right to freedom of movement (Art. 12);
- procedural rights against expulsion (Art. 13);
- the right to recognition before the law (Art. 16);
- the right to be free from arbitrary or unlawful interference with privacy or family (Art. 17);
- the right to protection of the family (Art. 23);
- the rights of children (Art. 24; see also the Convention on the Rights of the Child);
- the right to equal protection before the law and non-discrimination (Art. 26);

ICESCR:

- the right to work, as well as the right to just and favourable conditions of work (Arts. 6 and 7);
- the right to social security (Art. 9);
- the right of the family to the 'widest possible protection and assistance' (Art. 10);
- the right to an adequate standard of living (including food, clothing, and housing) (Art. 11);
- the right to the highest attainable standards of physical and mental health (Art. 12);
- the right to education (Art. 13).

In addition to being a ground on which removal to a country can be opposed, the prohibition on cruel, inhuman, or degrading treatment is central to safeguarding the proper treatment of asylum seekers and other forced migrants within the country in which they are seeking protection. At the very least, states must ensure that there are policies and structures in place so that no one is forced to live in inhuman or degrading conditions. In a series of cases concerning asylum seekers denied state support and the right to work, the UK courts said that treatment is inhuman or degrading 'if, to a seriously detrimental extent, it denies the most basic needs of any human being' (*Adam*, para. 7). While there is no general public duty to house the homeless or provide for the destitute, the House of Lords held that such a duty would arise if an asylum seeker 'with no means and no alternative sources of support, unable to support himself, is, by the deliberate action of the state, denied shelter, food or the most basic necessities of life' (*Adam*, para. 7). Relevant factors include the asylum seeker's 'age, gender, mental and physical health and condition, any facilities or sources of support available to the applicant, the weather and time of year and the period for which the applicant has already suffered or is likely to continue to suffer privation' (*Adam*, para. 8). The overall question is 'whether the treatment to which the asylum-seeker is being subjected *by the entire package of restrictions and deprivations* that surround him is so severe that it can properly be described as inhuman or degrading treatment' (*Adam*, para. 58). The highest appellate courts of France, Germany, Belgium, and South Africa have similarly acknowledged that even people without any formal immigration status are entitled to minimum health and other social services, as a matter of basic dignity (see cases cited in Bouteillet-Paquet 2002: 240; *Watchenuka*, para. 32).

Although it has not ruled directly on the matter of status in this context, the European Court of Human Rights has acknowledged that poor living conditions may violate Article 3 of the ECHR if they reach a minimum level of severity (e.g. *Pancenko*; *BB*; *HLR*; *Sisojeva*), which may include living without any social protection. The court's recent decision in *MSS v Belgium and Greece* suggests that asylum seekers must benefit from a minimum level of economic and social rights, irrespective of their formal recognition as refugees or beneficiaries of subsidiary protection. Elsewhere, the court has suggested that the longer a person remains in a country, the greater his or her personal, social, and economic ties, and the greater his or her claim on the state's resources (*Nasri*).

Refugees' rights are set out in the Refugee Convention and are supplemented by human rights law. When it comes to beneficiaries of complementary protection, state practice affirms that they should be accorded some form of domestic legal status. Whether this should be the same as that granted to Convention refugees has been the subject of some academic debate (Goodwin-Gill and McAdam 2007; McAdam 2007, 2009; cf. Hathaway 2010; Pobjoy 2010; Durieux 2013), but in the jurisdictions where domestic complementary protection exists, there is now a clear trend towards granting an identical status. Canada, New Zealand, and Australia provide the same status to refugees and beneficiaries of complementary protection, and a 2008 survey showed that most EU countries did so as well, even though the Qualification Directive did not require this at that time (ECRE 2008). The recast 2011 version of the Qualification Directive has significantly narrowed the gap between the status of Convention refugees and beneficiaries of subsidiary protection, although there are still differences in the length of residence permits granted (Art. 24), and social assistance can be limited to core benefits for beneficiaries of subsidiary protection (Art. 29) (although this is intended to be the exception rather than the rule). Furthermore, the regional African and Latin American refugee instruments envisage Convention refugee status extending to the broader categories of people they protect. UNHCR has argued that the rights and benefits granted to forced migrants should be based on need rather than the grounds on which a person has been granted protection, and that there is accordingly no valid reason to treat beneficiaries of complementary protection any differently from Convention refugees (UNHCR 2001, 2009).

However, some scholars are wary of this approach, arguing that it may undermine the refugee protection regime (Hathaway 2010; Durieux 2013). Implicit in their analysis is a concern that equal treatment might ultimately dilute the special protection provided to refugees by the Refugee Convention. While conceding that it may be 'good policy' to grant an identical legal status to both groups (Hathaway 2010: 506) and acknowledging the legal, political, and ethical dilemmas in trying to articulate a justification for a 'refugee privilege', they nevertheless place the international refugee regime on a pedestal, arguing that 'such an articulation [of a refugee privilege] is essential to the universal regime' (Durieux 2013: 253–4). Hathaway, in particular, has persistently argued that compared to other forced migrants, refugees are 'doubly deserving' of protection: 'not only is the risk they have fled profoundly serious, but their exposure to such risk is based on characteristics which are either unchangeable (like race or nationality) or so fundamental that they should not have to be renounced in order to be safe (like religion or political opinion)' (Hathaway 1997, 2007: 352).

Perhaps one's approach to this issue depends in part on whether refugee law is regarded as a subset of human rights law, or as a separate regime that needs to be quarantined to preserve the privileged status it extends to refugees. For human rights scholars, an insistence on the primacy of refugee status is counter-intuitive (if not inconsistent) with underlying premises of human rights law, such as the principle of non-discrimination. Relying on this principle, Pobjoy (2010) has argued that the protection granted to refugees and beneficiaries of complementary protection should be the same (see also Fitzpatrick 2000: 9–10; McAdam 2007: 220).

The Importance of Domestic Implementation

One of the main obstacles to the fulfilment of human rights in practice is translating them from international obligations into domestic law. In some countries, duties assumed under international treaties automatically become part of domestic law, but in others (such as the UK and Australia), they need to be formally adopted into national law before they are enforceable. Nevertheless, if a country fails to give effect to the human rights commitments that it has voluntarily undertaken by ratifying treaties, then it will be in breach of its obligations under international law (e.g. ICCPR, Art. 2).

Domestic human rights frameworks, such as bills of rights, provide a tool for measuring countries' compliance with their international obligations and for offering redress in circumstances where human rights are breached. They also facilitate the formulation of better laws and policies by requiring human rights issues to be taken into account at the beginning of the legislative process. The ECHR, Europe's regional human rights framework, has proved to be a very powerful mechanism for forced migrants—preventing removal through the expanded principle of *non-refoulement* and safeguarding rights in European host countries.

The absence of domestic human rights mechanisms on the rights of forced migrants is aptly illustrated by Australia's policy of mandatory detention. Introduced in 1992, it requires that all non-citizens who enter Australia without a valid visa be detained until they are either granted a visa or removed. Human rights law has an important role to play in establishing the limited circumstances in which a person may be detained and what constitutes acceptable standards of treatment during detention. Holding asylum seekers in immigration detention is not per se an impermissible breach of their rights, but the circumstances and length of detention may be such that the detention cannot be justified in the particular case. Deprivation of liberty strikes at the very heart of human rights protections, since without liberty a person is unable to enjoy other rights. In order for detention to be consistent with international human rights law, it must be shown to be necessary in the individual case (rather than the result of a mandatory, blanket policy); subject to periodic review by the judiciary or another authority, with the power to release detainees if detention cannot be objectively justified; be reasonably proportionate to the reason for the restriction (e.g. national security); and be for the shortest time possible. All the major UN human rights bodies have condemned Australia's system of mandatory detention as a violation of Article 9 of the ICCPR because it does not satisfy these conditions. However, without a domestic human rights instrument in place, there is no basis on which such detention, its length, or its conditions can be challenged in the Australian courts.

Finally, human rights provisions may also have procedural benefits for asylum seekers and refugees. For instance, in *Jabari v Turkey*, an asylum seeker successfully challenged a deportation order which had been issued because she had failed to lodge her asylum claim within five days (the time limit stipulated by Turkish law). The European Court of Human Rights held that, owing to the irreversible nature of the harm she feared if removed, Turkey had an obligation to conduct a meaningful assessment of her claim, notwithstanding the time limit in its domestic law. The court stated that the automatic and mechanical application of such a short time limit was at odds with the fundamental protection embodied in Article 3 of the ECHR. It also found that Turkey had violated the asylum seeker's right to an effective remedy.

CONCLUSION: THE EVOLUTION OF PROTECTION OVER TIME

The significant jurisprudential and legislative developments in human rights-based *non-refoulement* over the past 25 years, and the readiness of decision makers to reassess the classification of particular forms of harm over time, suggests that the kinds of ill-treatment from which forced migrants may be protected remains open, albeit not unlimited. Thus, much contemporary scholarship is concerned with the protection gaps and prospects for those displaced by the impacts of climate change and natural disasters (McAdam 2012; Kälin and Schrepfer 2012), development projects (Bennett and McDowell 2012), humanitarian crises (e.g. 'crisis migration'), and basic 'survival' needs (Betts 2010). The evolving nature of human rights law means that the protection needs of such groups will need to be perennially revisited against prevailing legal concepts. Irrespective of the potential scope of the principle of *non-refoulement*, however, states are already obliged to observe their voluntarily assumed responsibilities under human rights law with respect to all people within their territory and jurisdiction—including forced migrants. Even individuals who might ultimately be returnable have human rights that must be respected.

NOTES

1. Enforced disappearance does not form part of any state's complementary protection legislation. The obligation derives from the Disappearances Convention, Art. 16.
2. For a summary of cases other than Article 3 considered by the European Court of Human Rights, see *Ullah*, paras. 15–19, 24.

References

BB v France, App. No. 30930/96 (Commission, 9 March 1998).

Bennett, O., and McDowell, C. (2012) *Displaced: The Human Cost of Development and Resettlement*. New York: Palgrave Macmillan.

Bensaid v United Kingdom, App. No. 44599/98 (6 February 2001).

Betts, A. (2010) 'Survival Migration: A New Protection Framework'. *Global Governance* 16: 361.

Bouteillet-Paquet, D. (2002) 'Subsidiary Protection: Progress or Set-Back of Asylum Law in Europe? A Critical Analysis of the Legislation of the Member States of the European Union'. Pp. 211–64 in D. Bouteillet-Paquet (ed.), *Subsidiary Protection of Refugees in the European Union: Complementing the Geneva Convention?* Brussels: Bruylant.

Convention against Torture and Other Cruel, Inhuman or Degrading Treatment or Punishment (adopted 10 December 1984, entered into force 26 June 1987) 1465 UNTS 85.

Convention on the Elimination of All Forms of Discrimination against Women (adopted 18 December 1979, entered into force 3 September 1981) 1249 UNTS 13 (CEDAW).

Convention on the Rights of the Child (adopted 20 November 1989, entered into force 2 September 1990) 1577 UNTS 3.

Convention relating to the Status of Refugees (adopted 28 July 1951, entered into force 22 April 1954) 189 UNTS 137 (Refugee Convention).

Council Directive (EC) 2004/83 on Minimum Standards for the Qualification and Status of Third Country Nationals or Stateless Persons as Refugees or as Persons Who Otherwise Need International Protection and the Content of the Protection Granted [2004] OJ L304/12 (Qualification Directive).

Directive 2011/95/EU of the European Parliament and of the Council of 13 December 2011 on Standards for the Qualification of Third-Country Nationals or Stateless Persons as Beneficiaries of International Protection, for a Uniform Status for Refugees or for Persons Eligible for Subsidiary Protection, and for the Content of the Protection Granted (Recast), OJ 2011 No. L337/9.

Durieux, J.-F. (2013) 'The Vanishing Refugee: How EU Asylum Law Blurs the Specificity of Refugee Protection'. Pp. 225–57 in H. Lambert, J. McAdam, and M. Fullerton (eds.), *The Global Reach of European Refugee Law*. Cambridge: Cambridge University Press.

European Convention on Human Rights (Convention for the Protection of Human Rights and Fundamental Freedoms) (drafted 4 November 1950, entered into force 3 September 1953) ETS No. 5 (ECHR).

European Council on Refugees and Exiles (ECRE) and European Legal Network on Asylum (ELENA) (2008) *The Impact of the EU Qualification Directive on International Protection*.

Fitzpatrick, J. (2000) 'Human Rights and Forced Displacement: Converging Standards'. Pp. 3–25 in A. F. Bayefsky and J. Fitzpatrick (eds.), *Human Rights and Forced Displacement*. The Hague: Martinus Nijhoff Publishers.

Foster, M. (2007) *International Refugee Law and Socio-Economic Rights: Refuge from Deprivation*. Cambridge: Cambridge University Press.

Goodwin-Gill, G. S., and McAdam, J. (2007) *The Refugee in International Law* (3rd edn.). Oxford: Oxford University Press.

Hathaway, J. C. (1997) 'Is Refugee Status Really Elitist? An Answer to the Ethical Challenge'. Pp. 79–88 in J.-Y. Carlier and D. Vanheule (eds.), *Europe and Refugees: A Challenge?* The Hague: Kluwer Law International.

Hathaway, J. C. (2010) 'Leveraging Asylum'. *Texas International Law Journal* 45: 503.

HLR v France (1998) 26 EHRR 29.

International Convention for the Protection of All Persons from Enforced Disappearance (adopted 20 September 2006, entered into force 23 December 2010) UNGA res. 61/177, 14 IHRR 582 (Disappearances Convention).

International Covenant on Civil and Political Rights (adopted 16 December 1966, entered into force 23 March 1976) 999 UNTS 171 (ICCPR).

International Covenant on Economic, Social and Cultural Rights (adopted 16 December 1966, entered into force 3 January 1976) 993 UNTS 3 (ICESCR).

Islam v Secretary of State for the Home Department, R v Immigration Appeal Tribunal and another, ex parte Shah (Conjoined Appeals) [1999] 2 AC 629.

Jabari v Turkey, App. No. 40035/98 (11 July 2000).

Kälin, W., and Schrepfer, N. (2012) 'Protecting People Crossing Borders in the Context of Climate Change: Normative Gaps and Possible Approaches'. UNHCR Legal and Protection Policy Research Series, PPLA/2012/01.

McAdam, J. (2007) *Complementary Protection in International Refugee Law*. Oxford: Oxford University Press.

McAdam, J. (2009) 'Status Anxiety: The New Zealand Immigration Bill and the Rights of Non-Convention Refugees'. *New Zealand Law Review* 239–56.

McAdam, J. (2012) *Climate Change, Forced Migration, and International Law*. Oxford: Oxford University Press.

Minister of Home Affairs v Watchenuka (2004) 4 SA 326.

MSS v Belgium and Greece, App. No. 30696/09, 21 January 2011.

Nasri v France (1995) 21 EHRR 458.

Othman (Abu Qatada) v United Kingdom, App. No. 8139/09, 17 January 2012.

Pancenko v Latvia, App. No. 40772/98 (28 October 1999).

Pobjoy, J. (2010) 'Treating Like Alike: The Principle of Non-Discrimination as a Tool to Mandate the Equal Treatment of Refugees and Beneficiaries of Complementary Protection'. *Melbourne University Law Review* 34: 181.

Protocol relating to the Status of Refugees (adopted 31 January 1967, entered into force 4 October 1967) 606 UNTS 267.

R (Razgar) v Secretary of State for the Home Department [2004] 2 AC 368

R v Immigration Officer at Prague Airport; ex parte Roma Rights Centre [2005] 2 AC 1.

R v Secretary of State for the Home Department, ex parte Adam [2005] UKHL 66.

R v Special Adjudicator, ex parte Ullah [2004] UKHL 26.

Sisojeva v Latvia, App. No. 60654/00 (16 June 2005).

Soering v United Kingdom (1989) 11 EHRR 439.

Tomic v United Kingdom, App. No. 17837/03, 14 October 2003.

UNHCR (2001) UNHCR's Observations on the European Commission's Proposal for a Council Directive on Minimum Standards for the Qualification and Status of Third Country Nationals and Stateless Persons as Refugees or as Persons Who Otherwise Need International Protection 14109/01 ASILE 54.

UNHCR (2003) *Agenda for Protection* (3rd edn.) Geneva: UNHCR.

UNHCR (2009) 'UNHCR Comments on the European Commission's Proposal for a Directive of the European Parliament and of the Council on Minimum Standards for the Qualification and Status of Third Country Nationals or Stateless Persons as Beneficiaries of International Protection and the Content of the Protection Granted' (COM(2009)551, 21 October 2009).

UNHCR Executive Committee Conclusion No. 103 (2005).

UN Committee on the Rights of the Child (2005) 'General Comment No 6 (2005): Treatment of Unaccompanied and Separated Children Outside their Country of Origin'. UN Doc. CRC/GC/2005/6.

UN Human Rights Committee (1986) 'General Comment 15: The Position of Aliens under the Covenant'.

UN Human Rights Committee (1989) 'General Comment 18: Non-Discrimination'.

UN Human Rights Committee (1992) 'General Comment No 20: Replaces General Comment 7 concerning Prohibition of Torture and Cruel Treatment or Punishment (Art 7)'.

UN Human Rights Committee (2004) 'General Comment No 31: The Nature of the General Legal Obligation Imposed on States Parties to the Covenant'. UN Doc. CCPR/C/21/Rev.1/Add.13.

UNICEF and Office of the UN High Commissioner for Human Rights (Regional Office for Europe) (2012) *Judicial Implementation of Article 3 of the Convention on the Rights of the Child in Europe: The Case of Migrant Children including Unaccompanied Children.*

Universal Declaration of Human Rights (adopted 10 December 1948) UNGA res. 217A (III).

Wan v Minister for Immigration and Multicultural Affairs [2001] FCA 568.

Z and T v United Kingdom, App. No. 27034/05, 28 February 2006.

ZH (Tanzania) (FC) v Secretary of State for the Home Department [2011] UKSC 4.

CHAPTER 17

UNHCR AND FORCED MIGRATION

GIL LOESCHER

INTRODUCTION

THE Office of the United Nations High Commissioner for Refugees (UNHCR) was created by the UN General Assembly in December 1950 with a specific mandate to ensure the protection of refugees and to find a solution to their plight. Following a number of precedents during the interwar period, it was initially set up as a temporary organization with the sole responsibility of addressing the needs of refugees in Europe who had been displaced by the Second World War. Over time, however, its geographical focus was extended beyond Europe, and it has subsequently become a prominent international organization with global operations and policy concerns.

During the past six decades, the political and institutional contexts of UNHCR's work have constantly evolved resulting in a number of significant policy changes for the organization. This chapter will discuss UNHCR's normative agenda as well as the effectiveness of the Office's work for refugee protection within the context of a changing international political system, an expanding global mobility regime, and a growing and diverse group of displaced people in need of assistance and protection. Finally, the chapter will briefly address some of the key issues and problems UNHCR is likely to face in the future.

UNHCR AND THE GLOBAL REFUGEE REGIME

UNHCR is the UN's refugee agency and the UN High Commissioner for Refugees enjoys moral prestige as the spokesperson for the world's displaced. The Office's 1950 Statute sets out a clear mandate, defining the scope and role of the organization. The Statute defines UNHCR's core mandate as focusing on two principal areas. First, the Office was created to work with states to ensure refugees' access to protection from persecution and second, UNHCR works to ensure that refugees have access to durable solutions through reintegration within their country of origin or by permanent integration within a new country.[1]

UNHCR has also become the principal organization within the global refugee regime. The centrepiece of the regime is the 1951 Convention relating to the Status of Refugees which provides a definition of who qualifies for refugee status and sets out the rights to which all refugees are entitled. The 1951 Convention also explicitly identifies UNHCR as having supervisory responsibility for its implementation. The Office, therefore, has responsibility for monitoring and supporting states' compliance with the norms and rules that form the basis of the global refugee regime.

Despite these provisions in its Statute and the 1951 Convention, states ensured that the newly created UNHCR had a limited role. They initially restricted the Office's work to individuals who were refugees as a result of events occurring before 1951.[2] The refugee instruments also focused exclusively on refugees to the exclusion of other displaced persons. Furthermore, states originally required UNHCR to be a small, low-budget, and temporary organization that would play an exclusively legal advisory role rather than engaging in the provision of material assistance. Yet, from these inauspicious beginnings, the Office has over time expanded and adapted to become a permanent global organization with an annual budget of some $3.5 billion and over 7,000 staff in more than 125 countries, offering protection and assistance not only to refugees but also to IDPs, stateless persons, and other displaced people.

At key turning points in the past six decades, the Office has responded to changes in the political and institutional environment within which it works by reinterpreting and broadening its role and mandate.[3] From the 1960s on it expanded beyond its original focus on Europe to become a global organization. UNHCR shifted its focus from providing legal protection to refugees fleeing communist regimes in Eastern and Central Europe and became increasingly involved in refugee situations in the global South. During the 1960s, violent decolonization and post-independence strife generated vast numbers of refugees in Africa which required it to take on an ever greater role in providing material assistance. During the 1970s, mass exoduses from East Pakistan, Uganda, and Indochina, highly politicized refugee crises in Chile, Brazil, and Argentina, and the repatriation of refugees and internally displaced persons (IDPs) in southern Sudan expanded UNHCR's mission around the globe. The 1980s saw the Office shift away from its traditional focus on legal protection and assume a growing role in providing assistance to millions of refugees in camps and protracted situations in South-East Asia, Central America and Mexico, South Asia, the Horn of Africa, and Southern Africa. During the post-Cold War era, UNHCR assumed a wider role in providing massive humanitarian relief in intra-state conflicts and engaging in repatriation operations across the Balkans, Africa, Asia, and Central America. The late 1990s and early twenty-first century have seen UNHCR take on ever greater responsibility for the victims of some major natural disasters and to assume formal responsibility for the protection of IDPs. The expansion of the Office's work to include these new areas has often been controversial, and there have been concerns that UNHCR has sometimes acted in ways that contradicted or undermined its refugee protection mandate.

Within this process of adaptation and expansion, UNHCR has had limited political power. In the international refugee regime, states remain the predominant actors. But this does not mean that UNHCR is entirely without means either to uphold its normative agenda or exercise a degree of autonomy. UNHCR has at times assumed power beyond what states originally intended upon its creation.[4] In the past, most High Commissioners and their executive staff have realized that in order to shape state behaviour they had to exert their moral authority and leadership skills and use the power of their expertise, ideas, strategies, and legitimacy to alter the information and value contexts in which states made policy. The Office has tried to project refugee norms into an international system dominated by states that are, in turn, driven by concerns of national interest and security. Successful High Commissioners have convinced states that they can ensure domestic and inter-state stability and can reap the benefits of international cooperation by defining their national interests in ways compatible with protection norms and refugee needs. In promoting its normative agenda, UNHCR is further supported by non-governmental organizations (NGOs), which act as norm entrepreneurs through developing and disseminating new norms and through political advocacy and persuasion.[5]

UNHCR not only promotes the implementation of refugee norms; it also monitors compliance with international standards. Both the UNHCR Statute and the 1951 Convention authorize the organization to 'supervise' refugee conventions. This opens up the possibility for the UNHCR to make judgements or observations about state behaviour under refugee law and to challenge state policies when they endanger refugees. For example, in recent years, UNHCR has given legal opinions on matters such as access to protection and detention of asylum seekers before regional and international courts such as the EU Court of Justice and the European Court of Human Rights and elsewhere.

For most of its history, the Office has also acted as a 'teacher' of refugee norms. The majority of the UNHCR's tactics have mainly involved persuasion and socialization in order to hold states accountable to their previously stated policies or principles. For example, High Commissioners have frequently reminded Western states that as liberal democracies and open societies they are obliged to adhere to human rights norms in their asylum and refugee admissions policies. Because the UNHCR possesses specialized knowledge and expertise about refugee law, states at times have deferred to the Office on asylum matters. This was particularly the case before the 1980s when the UNHCR had a monopoly on information about refugee law and refugee movements. During the early decades of its existence, the Office enjoyed maximum legitimacy as it simultaneously tried to define the refugee issue for states, to convince governments that refugee problems were soluble, to prescribe solutions, and to monitor their implementation.

In recent decades, however, states have questioned UNHCR's moral authority or simply ignored UNHCR in the interest of pursuing more restrictive asylum and refugee policies. As the scope of the global refugee regime has increased, efforts to ensure international solidarity and burden sharing have been more problematic. For example, in recent years the global resettlement of refugees has declined and local integration in the global South remains exceedingly difficult. States have often sought means of pursuing their interests in the global refugee regime by attempting to shift responsibility to other actors and by avoiding additional responsibilities. Nevertheless, while its authority and legitimacy has consequently declined, the Office still tries to influence how states respond to refugees. During 2001–2, for example, UNHCR initiated the Global Consultations on International Protection which resulted in the adoption of an Agenda for Protection.[6] Moreover, since 2007 the High Commissioner's annual dialogues on Protection Challenges have provided a forum for states, NGOs, and experts to discuss action plans on issues such as mixed migration, burden sharing, protracted refugee situations, urban refugees, and environmental displacement. Finally, UNHCR provides training and promotes guidelines and standards for the international protection of refugees in a variety of forums involving not only states but also experts, NGOs, and regional and local actors around the world.

UNHCR has not only acted as a transmitter and monitor of refugee norms but also socialized new states to accept the promotion of refugee norms domestically as part of becoming a member of the international community. This socialization occurred first in the 1960s and 1970s in the newly independent countries of Africa and Asia and later in the 1990s in the republics of the former Soviet Union. The political leaders of most newly independent governments were concerned about their international image and reputation and sought international legitimacy through cooperation with the UNHCR. In addition, High Commissioners have repeatedly tried to link the refugee issue to states' material interests. Many new states, particularly in the global South, were willing to adapt their behaviour to UNHCR pressures for purely instrumental reasons. International humanitarian assistance has sometimes provided resource-strapped governments with the means to cope with influxes of refugees. In recent decades, especially in response to protracted refugee situations, the Office has even taken on the role of a surrogate state for both refugees and local host populations in remote areas of countries where government authorities have little reach.[7] Through a mixture of persuasion, socialization, and material incentives, UNHCR has communicated the importance of refugee norms and convinced many new states that the benefits of signing the refugee legal instruments and joining the UNHCR Executive Committee—either as a member or an observer—outweighed the costs of remaining outside the global refugee regime. Thus, while UNHCR is constrained by states, the notion that it is passive in the global refugee regime, with no independent agenda of its own or a mere instrument of states, is not borne out by the empirical evidence of the past 60 years.

CONSTRAINTS ON UNHCR: CHANGING STATE INTERESTS AND POLITICAL PROCESSES

While UNHCR has demonstrated its ability to act independently, its activities and evolution have been defined and, at times, constrained by global politics and the interests of states within the global refugee regime. The organization is dependent on voluntary contributions to carry out its work. This gives significant influence to a limited number of states in the global North who have traditionally funded the bulk of UNHCR's operational budget.[8] At the same time, UNHCR works at the invitation of states to undertake activities on their territories and must therefore negotiate with a range of refugee hosting states, especially in the global South. UNHCR is consequently placed in the difficult position of trying to facilitate cooperation between donor states in the global North and host states in the global South. At the same time, the Office works within changing global contexts, with changing dynamics of displacement, and with a range of partners, both within and outside the UN System. The humanitarian world is now characterized as a competitive marketplace which involves a vast range of actors each with their own mandate, institutional identity, and drive to protect their own interests. These political and institutional constraints affect the functioning of the global refugee regime and the ability of UNHCR to fulfil its mandate.

While UNHCR frequently finds itself caught between the norms that underpin the global refugee regime and the competing interests of states and other actors, these dynamics are further influenced by changes in world politics. For example, the end of the Cold War not only presented UNHCR with an unprecedented opportunity to resolve some of the world's longest-standing refugee situations through large-scale repatriation programmes but also presented new challenges to the organization.[9] In the early 1990s, the international community failed to effectively respond to a number of new intra-state conflicts and refugee crises, including the collapse of Somalia, the break-up of the former Yugoslavia, and genocide in Rwanda. Each of these crises witnessed significant and complex dynamics of forced displacement, and UNHCR was called upon to play a more prominent role. By engaging more directly in debates on new sources of national, regional, and international insecurity and by retooling itself to provide humanitarian assistance in intra-state conflicts, UNHCR sought to encourage sustained international action on behalf of refugees. Instead, governments often used humanitarian relief as a substitute for political action to address the root causes of mass displacement. This response placed a significant strain on UNHCR's operational ability to respond while upholding its mandate of ensuring protection.

Since the 1990s, it has become increasingly difficult for UNHCR to persuade states to host refugees and efforts to strengthen international cooperation have rarely been successful. In the North, the period since the end of the Cold War has been marked by a shift from asylum to containment where Western states have largely limited the asylum they offer to refugees and have focused on efforts to contain refugees in their region of origin. These measures included non-arrival policies, such as carrier sanctions and visa requirements, diversion policies, such as safe-third country agreements, an increasingly restrictive application of the 1951 Convention, and a range of deterrent policies, such as detention of asylum seekers and the denial of social assistance.

These developments have placed a significant strain on asylum countries in the South which continue to host the majority of the world's refugees. From the 1990s, states in the developing world also began to place restrictions on asylum. Some states closed their borders to prevent arrivals, pushed for the early and often unsustainable return of refugees to their country of origin, and, in exceptional cases, forcibly expelled entire refugee populations. More generally, states have been placing limits on the quality of asylum they offer to refugees, by denying them the social and economic rights contained in the 1951 Convention, such as freedom of movement and the right to seek employment. Many states in the South now require refugees to remain in isolated and insecure refugee camps for protracted periods, cut off from the local community, and fully dependent on international assistance. Millions of other refugees are stranded in sprawling urban areas with virtually no assistance and no livelihood.

The crisis of asylum in both the North and South has confronted UNHCR with a nearly impossible task. While mandated by the international community to ensure the protection of refugees and find solutions to their plight, UNHCR cannot fulfil this task without the cooperation of states. As the global crisis of asylum emerged, states largely excluded the Office and increasingly devised their own responses to insulate themselves from the growing number of refugees seeking access to their territories. The lack of cooperation by states, coupled with a global impasse over cooperation between Northern donor countries and Southern host states, has significantly frustrated UNHCR's activities in recent years.

Key Policy Challenges: UNHCR in the Broader World Community

UNHCR is unable to pursue its mandate independently of donor and host states. It is dependent on voluntary contributions from donors to carry out its work and it relies on host states for permission and cooperation to carry out its programmes. Thus the interest and priorities of donor and host states have consequently played a significant role in the work and evolution of the organization.

UNHCR's relationships with states have changed significantly over time. The most important of these relationships remains the Office's relationship with donors, who control the direction of UNHCR's work through the tight control of the organization's resources. At the same time, the Office has increasingly become a complex international organization with a truly global presence. In a wide range of operational contexts in host states, the Office must respond to local political realities, dynamics, and interests as it seeks to advance its mandate.

UNHCR's relationship with the wider UN system has also become increasingly important. In the past, the UN General Assembly played a crucial role in the expansion of UNHCR's mandate. For example, UNHCR turned repeatedly to the General Assembly throughout its early history to authorize the Office's involvement in emerging refugee situations in Africa and Asia. Notwithstanding this support, a critical problem today is the widespread perception within the UN system that refugees are UNHCR's 'problem'. This perception, likely a result of the territoriality and competition between

UN agencies, has resulted in the reluctance of other UN agencies to more fully engage in refugee issues and has frustrated recent efforts to articulate a more comprehensive and holistic engagement at the UN level in issues relating to refugees.

Another problem relates to the Executive Committee of the Program of the United Nations High Commissioner for Refugees (EXCOM) which currently has 87 states as members. EXCOM is responsible for approving the Office's budget and programme, for setting standards and reaching conclusions on international refugee protection policy issues, and for providing guidance on UNHCR's management, objectives, and priorities. It is the only specialized multilateral forum at the global level responsible for contributing to the development of international standards relating to refugee protection. In recent years, EXCOM has become too large and politicized and it is no longer an effective decision-making body. Not only are there too many participants, but the issues are complex, divisive, and numerous, and meetings are seldom a forum for organizational guidance. In addition, the increasing divide between industrialized states and developing countries makes international consensus of refugee matters exceedingly difficult to achieve. As a consequence of the breakdown in trust and cooperation, member states have failed for the first time since the creation of EXCOM in 1958 to adopt a Conclusion over the past few years.

Given the shortcomings of EXCOM as an authoritative decision-making body, individual donor governments and some key host states have come to establish the priorities that guide UNHCR's programme. In the early years of the Office, when its work was primarily focused on legal protection in Europe, UNHCR operated on a very modest budget. It was not until the global expansion of the Office in the 1970s and 1980s that UNHCR's budget began to increase dramatically. Contributions from the UN Regular Budget now account for less than 3 per cent of UNHCR's Annual Budget. As a result, UNHCR today is almost exclusively dependent on voluntary contributions from states to carry out its programmes.

This dependence is compounded by the fact that funding has tended to come from a relatively small number of so-called traditional donors in the industrialized world, with around three-quarters of its budget coming from its top ten donors. The unpredictability of funding and the concentration of donorship have placed UNHCR in a precarious political position. While the Office has attempted to safeguard the integrity of its mandate by being seen to be politically impartial, its ability to carry out its programmes depends upon its ability to respond to the interests of a relatively small number of donor states.

The influence of states is increased through their ability to specify how, where, and on what basis their contributions may be used by UNHCR. This practice, known as 'earmarking', remains commonplace. According to the 2011 UNHCR Global Report, 47 per cent of contributions to UNHCR that year were 'tightly earmarked' for specific countries and activities, while 26 per cent were 'broadly earmarked' for specific geographical regions and only 24 per cent came with no restrictions.[10] The practice of earmarking allows donors to exercise considerable influence over the work of UNHCR as programmes considered important by donors receive considerable support, while those deemed less important receive less support. For example, during the late 1990s, while the international community focused attention and resources on the crisis in Kosovo and East Timor, conflict and refugee crises in Africa were virtually ignored. This pattern continues over a decade and a half later as donor governments still give vastly disproportionate amounts of aid to a few well-known crises and trivial amounts of aid to dozens of other refugee programmes.

The fact that donors largely contribute to UNHCR on the basis of their own perceived interests makes the concentration of donors all the more problematic. In 2012, the top ten donors were the major industrialized states, with all other countries accounting for less than a quarter of contributions to UNHCR. As a result, the interests of a relatively small number of Northern states have been highly influential in determining UNHCR's activities.

The significant role played by a small number of donors and their interests places UNHCR in a challenging political position. Perhaps the most damaging effect of a concentration of donors is the perception by Southern states that UNHCR is beholden to a relatively small number of Northern donors and therefore is tied to their interests. These perceptions have further frustrated efforts at ensuring international cooperation within the global refugee regime. Reconciling the need to have an autonomous influence on states and supervising the refugee regime with being responsive to donor interests has sometimes been a difficult balancing act for the Office.

KEY POLICY CHALLENGES: THE REFUGEE REGIME COMPLEX

In recent decades the work of UNHCR has been further complicated by the dramatic increase in new forms of international cooperation at the bilateral, regional, and international levels in the areas of labour migration, international travel, human rights, humanitarianism, security, development, and peace building. In recent decades, a 'refugee regime complex'[11] has emerged in which these different institutions overlap, exist in parallel to each other, and influence states' policies towards refugees. These developments have had significant implications for refugee protection and for the work of UNHCR. The implications of the refugee regime complex has both positive and negative implications for UNHCR

Many of the new institutions offer states the opportunity to bypass UNHCR and the 1951 Convention when addressing their concerns with asylum. For example, new forms of inter-state cooperation on irregular migration enable many states to limit the access of asylum seekers and migrants to their territory. Regional forums have been established which enable states to develop bilateral agreements on issues such as visa control, readmission agreements, international zones at airports, and extra-territorial border management. The European Union border control agency FRONTEX has a mandate to intercept asylum seekers and migrants in the Mediterranean before they reach European shores to make asylum claims. Similarly, the Office must compete with other humanitarian actors for funds, visibility, and territory. Not surprisingly, UNHCR has spoken of an emerging 'humanitarian marketplace' within which the Office faces growing competition from other humanitarian service providers.[12]

While competition has clearly complicated UNHCR's work and effectiveness, the emergence of overlapping institutions has also enabled the Office to develop new partnerships that permit the Office to better fulfil its mandate. For example, a number of international human rights instruments provide sources of refugee protection for refugees fleeing persecution that come from outside international refugee law. At times, the Office has also collaborated with other institutions such as United Nations Development Programme or the International Organization for Migration in ways that have enabled it to engage with the development and migration implications of forced displacement. Much of the Office's recent work is also premised upon inter-agency collaboration through the UN's Inter-Agency Standing Committee. To date, however, the Office has resisted fully committing itself to the new focus within the UN on inter-agency integrated missions and to fully participating in unified responses to new humanitarian emergencies and crises. In the future, UNHCR will likely have to overcome its resistance to international coordination and will have to further expand its international links by establishing stronger complementary overlap with other institutions such as the Office of the High Commissioner for Human Rights, the World Bank, and the UN Peacebuilding Commission.

KEY POLICY CHALLENGES: CHANGING TRENDS IN FORCED MIGRATION

While the refugee problem remains as relevant as ever, the range of forced displacement challenges has become increasingly diverse. Today UNHCR faces the most rapid period of change in the nature of forced displacement in the six decades of its existence. Since 2005, UNHCR has assumed the lead in protecting IDPs in conflict situations. In addition, climate change, state fragility, food insecurity, and rapid urbanization all raise fundamental questions for new understandings of UNHCR's mandate and role in providing protection for populations displaced by these new developments.

International migration has increased rapidly in recent decades. UNHCR now works in a context in which asylum seekers and other groups of migrants are increasingly hard to distinguish. Both groups move for a variety of reasons including persecution, escape from violence, human rights violations, as well as in the search for employment and a better standard of living. Asylum seekers and migrants often use the same traffickers and migration routes and states often fail to differentiate between them. Thus, mixed migration poses a huge challenge for how UNHCR protects refugees. Moreover, as new drivers of cross-border displacement continue to emerge with the complex inter-action of state fragility, environmental change, and food insecurity, the Office faces the dilemma of how to respond to other categories of vulnerable migrants who have protection needs.

As new challenges emerge, UNHCR will face the question of how to adapt and how to define the boundaries of its 'population of concern'. It will need to judiciously decide when to and when not to take on new activities. And when new challenges are recognized as requiring an international response, it will need to carefully judge whether to take on such tasks or to encourage other actors to assume responsibility.

Towards a More Effective UNHCR

The expansion of UNHCR's programmes and population of concern has allowed the organization to grow and maintain its relevance both to the interests of key donor states and to some host states in the South. However, it has also led to a continuous expansion of UNHCR's activities, often in potentially contradictory ways. In fact, taking on an expanded role has sometimes had potentially negative consequences for protection and solutions. The Office has struggled to ensure that refugees have access to international protection and the range of rights contained in the 1951 Convention. States' unpredictable financial contributions and increasingly restrictive responses to refugees on their territories mean that protection needs are often inadequately met. In addition, UNHCR has not always been able to fulfil the solutions aspect of its mandate. For example, the average duration of a refugee situation has nearly doubled in the past decade to a staggering 18 years. In fact, some two-thirds of refugees in the world have been in exile for more than five years. These challenges further demonstrate the ongoing relevance of UNHCR's core mandate and the need to reinvigorate its focus on its central responsibilities. The prevalence of protracted refugee situations and the duration of their exile highlight the ongoing need to ensure refugees' timely access not only to durable solutions but also to encouraging states to adopt a more flexible approach to offering refugees migration opportunities and to long-term residency and citizenship. [13]

While the relevance of UNHCR's core mandate therefore remains as salient as ever, the nature of displacement is fundamentally changing in the twenty-first century. The Office has moved beyond its original focus on refugees to an involvement with other groups, including asylum seekers, returnees, stateless persons, and IDPs. UNHCR's work and policy concerns are interconnected in complex ways with broader issue areas such as migration, security, development, and peace building. In order to fulfil its core mandate of achieving protection and solutions for refugees, UNHCR cannot avoid engaging proactively with these areas. However, this is not an argument for UNHCR to infinitely expand its mandate and become a migration organization or a development organization. Rather, it is an argument for a UNHCR that plays a facilitative and catalytic role in mobilizing other actors to fulfil their responsibilities with respect to refugees. The Office will also need to become more focused and strategic in the advocacy, coordination, and facilitation role that it plays. To be able to play such a role, UNHCR will need to overcome some key challenges—its governance, transparency, and ability to secure funding—while developing ways of engaging more effectively with the UN system, regional organizations, and states.

UNHCR is a unique international organization, which has adapted and changed over time in order to balance its own institutional interests, the interests of states, the protection of refugees, and the need to uphold its normative agenda. The history of UNHCR highlights the significant role that an international organization can play as the guardian of an institutional framework over time in spite of changing configurations of interests and power relations. However, it also highlights how the tensions and contradictions implicit in this role can shape the trajectory of the organization itself and even affect its central role of the protection of refugees. It is only by confronting and responding effectively and creatively to these tensions and readjusting its structures and tactics that UNHCR will be able to fully realize its mandate of protecting refugees and finding solutions to their plight.

NOTES

1. Goodwin-Gill and McAdam (2007).
2. The temporal and geographic restrictions of the 1951 Convention were removed with the accession of the 1967 Protocol.
3. Betts, Loescher, and Milner (2012); Loescher (2001).
4. Barnett and Finnemore (1999, 2004); Loescher (2001).
5. Keck and Sinkink (1998).
6. Feller, Turk, and Nicholson (2003).
7. Crisp and Slaughter (2009).
8. Betts, Loescher, and Milner (2012).
9. Ogata (2005); Loescher (2001).
10. UNHCR (2011).
11. Betts (2009); Betts, Loescher, and Milner (2012).
12. Gottwald (2010).
13. Long (2011).

REFERENCES

Barnett, M., and Finnemore, M. (1999) 'The Politics, Power and Pathologies of International Organizations'. *International Organization* 53(4): 699–732.

Barnett, M., and Finnemore, M. (2004) *Rules for the World: International Organizations in Global Politics*. Ithaca, NY: Cornell University Press.

Betts, A. (2009) 'Institutional Proliferation and the Global Refugee Regime'. *Perspectives on Politics*: 53–8.

Betts, A., Loescher, G., and Milner, J. (2012) *The United Nations High Commissioner for Refugees: The Politics and Practice of Refugee Protection into the Twenty-First Century.* New York: Routledge.

Crisp, J., and Slaughter. A. (2009) 'A Surrogate State? The Role of UNHCR in Protracted Refugee Situations'. *New Issues in Refugee Research.* Working paper 168.

Feller, E., Türk, V., and Nicholson, F. (eds.) (2003) *Refugee Protection in International Law: UNHCR's Global Consultations on International Protection.* Cambridge: Cambridge University Press.

Goodwin-Gill, G., and McAdam, J. (2007) *The Refugee in International Law.* Oxford: Clarendon Press.

Gottwald, M. (2010) 'Competing within the Humanitarian Marketplace: UNHCR's Organizational Culture and Decision-Making Process'. *New Issues in Refugee Research.* Working paper No. 190.

Keck, M., and Sikkink, K. (1998) *Activists beyond Borders: Activist Networks in International Politics.* Ithaca, NY: Cornell University Press.

Loescher, G. (2001) *The UNHCR and World Politics: A Perilous Path.* Oxford: Oxford University Press.

Long, K. (2011) *Permanent Crises? Unlocking the Protracted Displacement of Refugees and IDPs.* Oxford: RSC.

Ogata, S. (2005) *The Turbulent Decade: The Refugee Crises of the 1990s.* New York. Norton.

UNHCR (2000) *The State of the World's Refugees: Fifty Years of Humanitarian Action.* Oxford: Oxford University Press.

UNHCR (2011) *UNHCR Global Report 2011.* Geneva.

CHAPTER 18

UNRWA AND PALESTINIAN REFUGEES

SUSAN AKRAM

INTRODUCTION

THIS chapter examines the legal situation of Palestinian refugees, assessing the main differences from other refugee situations, and the consequences of these differences.[1] The chapter explores the central role of the United Nations (UN) and its subsidiary agencies, particularly the United Nations Relief and Works Agency for Palestine Refugees (UNRWA) in the Palestinian refugee problem, especially on the right to durable solutions.

The unique character of the Palestinian refugee problem relates to the UN's ongoing involvement in Palestine. Since 1945, the UN's obligations towards resolution of the Palestinian refugee problem have rested on the Charter of the United Nations; its legal commitments to the majority population in Palestine prior to Partition;[2] and its partial responsibility for the flight or expulsion of hundreds of thousands of Palestinian refugees in the wake of the conflict following the Partition plan of UN General Assembly (UNGA) Resolution (Res.) 181(II) (29 November 1947) (see Akram and Lynk 2011: 502).

Resolution 181(II) recommended a division of Palestine into two states: a Jewish state with a 44 per cent Palestinian population and an Arab state with a 1 per cent Jewish population.[3] On 15 May 1948, the Mandate over Palestine expired and the British withdrew. Israel declared its state on 14 May, while war broke out, and the native Palestinians were forced out or fled as Israeli forces consolidated territory. In response to the expulsion and flight of approximately 800,000 refugees who became destitute and at the mercy of the international community, the UN took several important actions.

In 1948–9, the UN established a special regime comprising two agencies, the United Nations Conciliation Commission on Palestine (UNCCP) and UNRWA, with shared but distinct international obligations towards the displaced Palestinian population. Consequently, the UN decided to exclude Palestinians from the 'universal' refugee regime incorporated in the 1950 United Nations High Commissioner for Refugees

(UNHCR) Statute and the 1951 Refugee Convention. Over time, the key protection of durable solutions has been severed from the refugee definition, relegating Palestinians to weak and widely disparate rights protections around the world.

The consequences of ambiguous definitions, mandates, and benefits affect a huge global population. According to the most recent *Survey of Palestinian Refugees and Displaced Persons* (BADIL 2010–12), the worldwide Palestinian population is 11.2 million, 66 per cent of whom are displaced persons or refugees. Over half, or 5.8 million, are 1948 refugees and their descendants, 4.8 million of whom are registered with UNRWA. More than one million are 1967 displaced persons, and an additional 519,000 Palestinians are internally displaced on both sides of the Green Line.

Establishment of UN Agencies to Assist and Protect Palestine Refugees

The United Nations Conciliation Commission on Palestine (UNCCP)

On 1 December 1948, the UNGA passed Res. 194(III), which created the UNCCP, defined its durable solutions mandate towards the refugees, and established the framework for bringing about a final resolution to the conflict. The UNCCP was founded with a mandate of *refugee protection,* particularly to achieve a *specific durable solution* for the entire population of displaced Palestinians. UNCCP's mandate extended to all habitual residents or citizens of Palestine, who were either displaced by the 1947–8 conflict or were unable to return to territory under Israeli control.[4]

By the mid-1950s, it was evident to the UN and the parties involved that the UNCCP was unable to fulfil its dual mandate of mediator and international protection agency. Israel's opposition to repatriation made it impossible to solve the greater conflict while simultaneously implementing the required durable solution for the refugees. Although the UNCCP was never legally terminated, its operations shrank due to political impasse, lack of support, and de-funding by the UN. The UNCCP was never replaced by any international agency with an explicit mandate focusing on durable solutions for the entire Palestinian refugee population defined under Res. 194(III).

The United Nations Relief and Works Agency for Palestine Refugees (UNRWA)

On 8 December 1949, by Res. 302(IV), the UNGA created UNRWA. UNRWA was established at the outset as a short-term (three years, renewable) 'relief and works' agency. Its services initially extended to a subset of the population of UNCCP-defined 'Palestine refugees'—the subgroup that was 'in need'. By 1951, UNRWA had inherited a list of almost one million persons from the predecessor refugee agencies providing relief to the Palestinians. UNRWA's refugee definition as it has evolved today is not tied to specific eligibility for refugee protection, but covers groups and categories of vulnerable persons designated on the basis of need for services.

Resolution 302(IV) affirmed that para. 11 of Res. 194(III) was the frame of reference for the required durable solution, pending which UNRWA was to continue to provide relief to the refugees. In his *Note* of 9 April 1951, the UNCCP Legal Adviser clarified that para. 11's definition and its durable solutions formula related to *all those* who fled Palestine due to the conflict, not just those in the Arab states eligible for UNRWA's humanitarian assistance. However, unlike UNHCR, UNRWA has no enabling Statute or an Executive Committee. It rests its legal authority on three bases: its status as a subsidiary body of the UNGA; UNGA resolutions; and Commissioner-General statements and reports to the UN. The absence of clear statutory guidelines and its weak governing structure leave UNRWA without precise legal authority for many of its activities.[5]

UNRWA's initial focus on relief turned to 'works' after the Economic Survey Mission recommended instituting large-scale development projects to settle the refugees in the Arab host states. Political opposition towards host country integration blocked attempts to direct UNRWA's role away from humanitarian assistance. By the early 1960s, UNRWA had refocused its resources on education, and instituted an ambitious plan to build schools throughout the refugee camps. UNRWA services have continued to expand to broad health provision, social services, shelter and camp improvement, microfinance and microenterprise development programmes. In most of these areas, UNRWA has received approval by the UNGA and few challenges from states.

Following the 1967 war, UNRWA began responding to the increased need for human rights intervention and monitoring to protect individuals in ongoing conflict. UNGA resolutions increasingly used the language of 'protection' and 'legal rights' in conjunction with UNRWA's role and activities towards Palestinian refugees. These Resolutions fall into three categories: recommending the Secretary-General to take protection measures towards Palestinians in consultation with UNRWA; commending UNRWA for undertaking certain protection measures; and recognizing as fact that UNRWA's activities include 'assistance and protection'.[6]

In 1990, in the wake of the first *intifada,* the UN Security Council (UNSC) passed Res. 681, endorsing the establishment of the Refugee Affairs Officers (RAO) programme to monitor human rights violations of Palestinian refugees within the Occupied Territories. Despite pushback on the basis that RAO 'protection' activities went beyond UNRWA's mandate, they continued to operate through the early 1990s until the signing of the Oslo agreements. UNRWA has most recently instituted a 'Medium Term Strategy' (MTS) for 2010 to 2015 designed to mainstream protection throughout its operations as an internal matter, and expand protection activities as an external matter (UNRWA 2010). It has also engaged in ad hoc expansion of its fields of operations, for example collaborating with UNHCR to assist Palestinian refugees from Iraq following the two Gulf

Wars, and aiding Palestinians fleeing the current conflict in Syria to non-UNRWA fields such as Turkey (see LaGuardia and Van der Toorn 2011; UNRWA 2012).

UNRWA's mandate covers five geographic areas—Gaza, the West Bank, Jordan, Syria, and Lebanon—and not beyond. Within its five fields, UNRWA's mandate extends to groups or categories of vulnerable Palestinian refugees and displaced persons according to relief or protection criteria. Its designated categories and individuals can be dropped from the rolls or cease to be provided services based on changed priorities of need and vulnerabilities.

The United Nations High Commissioner for Refugees (UNHCR) and Palestinian Refugees

The UNHCR Statute adopted by UNGA Res. 428(V) in December 1950 incorporated an individualized 'universal' definition of refugee, which was later included in the Refugee Convention as Article 1A(2). Under Res. 428(V), the broad scope of UNHCR's mandate includes 'providing international protection' to refugees falling within its Statute, as well as to those displaced persons falling outside its statutory definition. UNHCR's core function, however, is to promote and secure *durable solutions for refugees*.

UNHCR's Statute limits its mandate vis-à-vis Palestinians. Chapter II, para. 7(c) states that the Agency's 'competence' shall not extend to a person 'Who continues to receive from other organs or agencies of the United Nations protection or assistance ...'. This 'exclusion clause' was incorporated into Article 1D of the Refugee Convention, and a second, 'inclusion' clause was added later in the Convention drafting process. Article 1D reads in full:

> This Convention shall not apply to persons who are at present receiving from organs or agencies of the United Nations other than the United Nations High Commissioner for Refugees protection or assistance.
>
> When such protection or assistance has ceased for any reason, without the position of such persons being definitively settled in accordance with the relevant resolutions adopted by the General Assembly of the United Nations, these persons shall *ipso facto* be entitled to the benefits of this Convention.

UNHCR's initial interpretation of Article 1D in its 1979 *Handbook* required that Palestinians claiming refugee status were to be assessed under the individualized criteria of Article 1A(2), rather than the group definition established under Res. 194—the protection definition operational for UNCCP. It required Palestinian refugees to demonstrate that they left the host countries owing to a 'well-founded fear of persecution' on the grounds cited in Article 1A(2). The *Handbook*'s oversight of the 'inclusion clause' encouraged a restrictive interpretation of Article 1D in a number of states.

UNHCR has amended its interpretation of Article 1D in two *Notes on the Applicability of Article 1D of the 1951 Convention Relating to the Status of Refugees to Palestinian Refugees* (2002 and 2009). The *Notes* define three categories of Palestinian refugees:

(a) 'Palestine refugees' in the sense of Res. 194(III), displaced from the part of Palestine that became Israel and unable to return there.

(b) 'Displaced Persons' within the sense of Res. 2252, who have been unable to return to the Occupied Territories due to Israeli policies since 1967.

(c) 'Palestinian refugees' neither 1948 nor 1967 displaced persons who are outside the Occupied Territories but are unable or unwilling to return there due to a well-founded fear of persecution under the meaning of Refugee Convention Article 1A(2).

Under UNHCR's current interpretation, Article 1D does not apply to category (c) refugees—who must instead satisfy the individualized persecution criteria of Article 1A(2)—but does apply to categories (a) and (b) since they are eligible to receive assistance from UNRWA. UNHCR recognizes that the second sentence of Article 1D is an 'inclusion clause', and states that categories (a) and (b) are Convention refugees simply because (*ipso facto*) they meet a group/category definition. They need not prove individualized persecution. UNHCR's Amended *Note* adds that categories (a) and (b) are entitled to the benefits of the Convention as long as they reside outside UNRWA areas. The *Note* clarifies that an individual refugee need not prove that s/he is outside UNRWA areas involuntarily due to circumstances outside his control. Finally, the *Note* states that descendants of 1948 and 1967 refugees are entitled to UNHCR and Convention protection even if they have never been in an UNRWA area.

Defining Palestine/Palestinian Refugees

The multiple refugee definitions that were drafted for different purposes, coupled with their widely divergent interpretations, have made the determination of who *is* a Palestinian refugee ambiguous and complex. The first discussion of a Palestinian refugee definition appears in a series of the UN Secretariat's 'working papers' related to the drafting of UNGA Res. 194(III). The Resolution does not define the 'refugees' covered under UNCCP's mandate, but UNCCP's 1950 *Analysis of Paragraph 11 of the General Assembly's Resolution of 11 December 1948* stated that 'the term "refugees" applies to all persons, Arabs, Jews, and others who have been displaced from their homes in Palestine'. The Legal Adviser *Note* to the UNCCP issued on 9 April 1951 defined the categories of Palestinian refugees covered by the terms of Res. 194 as:

1. 'persons of Arab origin who were Palestinian citizens and, after 29 November 1947, left territory at present under the control of the Israel authorities';

2. 'stateless persons of Arab origin who after 29 November 1947 left that territory where they had been settled up to that date';

3. 'Persons of Arab origin who were Palestinian citizens and left the said territory after 6 August 1924 and before 29 November 1947'; and

4. 'persons of Arab origin who had opted for Palestinian citizenship, left that territory before 6 August 1924, and retained their citizenship up to 29 November 1947'.

The second definition of 'Palestine refugee' is that found in UNRWA's Eligibility Regulations. After inheriting its caseload from the UN Relief for Palestine Refugees (UNRPR) and other relief organizations, UNRWA developed a working definition in order to reduce its relief records in response to donor pressure. UNRWA's initial working definition stated that a Palestine refugee 'is a needy person, who, as a result of the war in Palestine, has lost his home and his means of livelihood' (UNRWA 1950). This category incorporated 'Displaced Persons' (UNGA Res. 2252, 1967) who were forced from their homes in the 1967 conflict, but the category was discontinued when Jordan assumed responsibility for them. In 1993, UNRWA omitted both the requirement to establish 'need' and 'flight from Palestine as a result of the 1948 conflict' as criteria for registration; however, the need for assistance remains the determinant of eligibility for services (UNRWA 2009). UNRWA's current Consolidated Eligibility and Registration Instructions (CERI) define Palestine refugees—the largest group registered with UNRWA, but not the only category for UNRWA registration and services—as 'persons whose normal place of residence was Palestine during the period 1 June 1946 to 15 May 1948, and who lost both home and means of livelihood as a result of the 1948 conflict' (Part III.A.1).

The third definition applicable to Palestinians as refugees is the 'universal' definition incorporated into Article 1A(2) of the 1951 Refugee Convention. Article 1A(2) refers to refugees of any nationality or origin; it defines a refugee based on individualized assessment of fear of persecution due to one (or more) of five prescribed grounds—race, religion, nationality, political opinion, or particular social group. Article 1D, on the other hand, applies to Palestinians as an entire group or category, making these two definitions inconsistent in their application to Palestinians.

Adding to the complexity of Palestinian refugee status is the wide divergence in interpretations under state domestic policies and jurisprudence. BADIL's *Handbook on Protection of Palestinian Refugees* (BADIL 2005, 2011) is the most comprehensive study available, and reports that in 20 of the 23 states researched, 'Article 1D is either not incorporated or applied at all, or interpreted in a way that precludes recognition of Palestinian refugees as refugees under this provision' (BADIL 2005: 337). The Handbook concludes that 'due to the particular interpretation of Article 1D by national authorities and courts in these countries, Palestinian asylum-seekers have not derived any rights and benefits from Article 1D beyond the "right" to not be excluded from applying for refugee status under Article 1A(2) of the 1951 Refugee Convention' (BADIL 2005: 337–8).[7]

Recent European cases illustrate the inconsistent application of Article 1D. In *El-Ali v The Secretary of State for the Home Department* (26 July 2002) EWCA Civ. 1103. 1

WLR 95, an immigration court in the United Kingdom interpreted Article 1D's phrase 'at present receiving' as relating only to the date on which the Refugee Convention was signed. Thus, Article 1D applies only to those Palestinians who were born on or before 28 July 1951, and were in UNRWA areas on that date. The phrase 'protection or assistance has ceased for any reason' refers only to when UNRWA ceases to operate, and not to actual termination of services for any particular individual. In *Bolbol v Bevandorlasi es Allampolgarsagi Hivatal (BAH)* (June 2010) C-31/09, the European Court of Justice (ECJ) held the opposite, finding that the 'protection or assistance has ceased' language applied to individuals who have actually availed themselves of UNRWA's assistance, but which is no longer available. In 2012, the ECJ expanded this interpretation of 1D in *El Kott v BAH* (13 September 2012) C-364/11, finding that the phrase 'protection or assistance has ceased' refers to the protection or assistance to which individuals had actually availed themselves, and which is no longer provided to them for any reason beyond their control. The ECJ further found that the *ipso facto* clause of 1D means that if the prior conditions are satisfied, the individual Palestinian would be automatically entitled to refugee status in a member state.

Under either the *El-Ali* or the *Bolbol* decision, the vast majority of Palestinians who would be considered 'Palestine refugees' under the Res. 194(III) definition would not be considered 'Palestinian refugees' under Article 1D. Nor would they be recognized as refugees under the narrow definition of Article 1A(2). Following the *El-Ali* case, in the October 2012 decision of *Said v Sec'y of State for the Home Dept.* (26 October 2012) UKUT 00413 (IAC), the UK court stated that *Bolbol* overrules *El-Ali*; however, neither the UK nor any other jurisdiction has yet adapted domestic law to the broader ruling of *El Kott*, so its impact on Palestinian refugee claims remains to be seen.

The full meaning and scope of Article 1D are revealed in the Refugee Convention's *travaux préparatoires*. Although Article 1D is most commonly understood as an *exclusion* clause for Palestinian refugees, it may be most accurately described as a *contingent inclusion* clause: its first sentence operates to exclude Palestinians, but its second sentence re-includes them into the Refugee Convention upon the occurrence of certain contingencies. The Arab delegates who proposed the provision considered Palestinians to be different from all other refugees. First, they claimed that 'the existence of Palestine refugees...was the direct result of a decision taken by the United Nations itself, with full knowledge of the consequences. The Palestine refugees were therefore a direct responsibility on the part of the United Nations and could not be placed in the general category of refugees without betrayal of that responsibility' (UN GAOR 1950: para. 46).

Second, the Arab delegates viewed UNHCR and the new refugee treaty as essentially tasked with resettlement. The Palestinians, however, demanded and were entitled to repatriation: 'the obstacle to their repatriation was not dissatisfaction with their homeland [as required by Article 1], but the fact that a Member of the United Nations was preventing their return.' (UN GAOR 1950: para. 47). As the Saudi delegate stated, 'The Arab States desired that those refugees should be aided pending their repatriation, repatriation being the only real solution of their problem...Pending a proper settlement of the

Arab-Israeli Conflict, the Palestine refugees should continue to be granted a separate and special status' (UN GAOR 1950: paras. 52 and 62).

Third, the Arab delegates recognized the need to ensure that Palestinians would receive protection and assistance until the agreed durable solution could be realized. When the second sentence of 1D was later proposed, the Egyptian delegate stated: 'Once the United Nations assistance ceased, the Palestine refugees should automatically enjoy the benefits of the Convention' (UN Conference of Plenipotentiaries 1951). The amendment, however, left significant inconsistencies between the two sentences in the provision, and between Article 1D and the UNHCR Statute.

Some conclusions can be drawn from this brief overview of the drafting history concerning the key ambiguities in Article 1D. Article 1D does not include a definition of which refugees it covers (or excludes), but its reference to 'persons...at present receiving' can only be understood from the drafting history as incorporating the Res. 194(III) definition of 'Palestine refugee'. The 'organs or agencies' referred to are clearly UNCCP and UNRWA, both established before UNHCR. The loss of protection was the greater concern of the UN, as shown by the establishment of UNCCP, entrusted with a mandate to find a specific *durable solution* to the Palestinian refugee problem. As for the clause 'the position of such persons being definitively settled according to the relevant resolutions adopted by the General Assembly,' the drafting history also gives guidance. Since this clause does not appear in the UNHCR Statute, the relevant time period is the drafting of the second sentence of Article 1D. Between the fall of 1947 and July 1951, the UNGA had passed a series of Resolutions on Palestine/Israel related to the refugee issue, referring to the formula in Res. 194.[8] The UN's view of what the 'definitive settlement' of the refugee problem must entail was embodied in Res. 194(III), para. 11. This durable solutions formula was reaffirmed in all subsequent UNGA resolutions; thus, the clause referred to the formula of para. 11. Under the interpretation most consistent with the drafting history, every Palestinian refugee falling under any of the categories encompassed by the 194 definition is entitled to protection under the 1951 Convention.

Due to the complexity of the definitions, there is no uniform understanding of who is a Palestinian refugee; the benefits or durable solutions s/he is owed; which agency is to seek and implement the required durable solutions; which 'refugees' are represented in the peace negotiations between Israel and the Palestinians; and when refugee status terminates.

Implications for Durable Solutions

International protection and the search for a durable solution are distinct yet interrelated rights. UNHCR defines 'international protection of refugees' as an intervention 'on behalf of asylum-seekers and refugees to ensure that their rights, security and welfare are recognised and safeguarded in accordance with international standards' (Jastram and Achiron 2001: 129). UNHCR places primary importance on the key aspect of protection for refugees, 'the implementation of durable solutions' (Jastram and Achiron 2001: 129). UNRWA clarifies the distinction between the range of activities constituting international protection and the specific refugee protection right to durable solutions, noting that 'Neither humanitarian assistance nor international protection can substitute for, still less produce, a just and durable solution to the plight of Palestine refugees' (Morris 2008: 2). UNRWA also lists protection and durable solutions as separate components of its mandate towards Palestinian refugees (Morris 2008: 3).

International humanitarian assistance and international protection are also distinct but overlapping concepts; the former encompasses relief services undertaken by government and non-government agencies, while the latter relates to a broader range of human and civil rights normally provided by the state of nationality. In many ways the distinction between these concepts has become blurred as a general matter, and specifically in relation to UNRWA. At the general level, this is due to the evolution of humanitarian assistance work 'mainstreaming' human rights protection norms, and with regard to UNRWA, to the expansion of its activities into areas once considered international protection. For refugees and displaced persons, the core 'protection' right is to a durable solution, involving the right to return home or to a choice among available host country absorption or resettlement options; restitution of properties and compensation for losses; and increasingly, restorative and retributive justice (BADIL 2012: 90). Their recognition *as* refugees is tied directly to an international commitment that these durable solutions are to be realized for them. For the majority of the world's refugees, UNHCR is entrusted to carry out this commitment. Thus, refugee status recognition is the essential and necessary element that triggers international protection in the form of the right to durable solutions.

For Palestinians, three essential links are missing: (1) a clear, agreed-upon refugee definition that relates directly to access to *durable solutions*; (2) one or more agencies entrusted with realizing the durable solution rights for *all* those Palestinians qualifying under that definition; and (3) the recognition that all so-defined Palestinian refugees have been guaranteed the particular durable solutions formula embodied in Res. 194(III), and will be represented as such in a final resolution to their plight.

Eligibility for and Cessation of Refugee Status

On the first link, the most recognized 'refugee' definitions are mutually inconsistent: the category-based definition of Palestine refugee under Res. 194(III) as opposed to the individualized definition in the Refugee Convention that most states apply to Palestinians outside the UNRWA areas. The latter is particularly problematic. Since Palestinians usually arrive in non-UNRWA areas after residing for some time in an UNRWA area, states applying the Article 1A(2) persecution analysis relate it to one of the Arab host states, and usually find discrimination but not persecution. In contrast, if the Res. 194(III) category definition were applied, most Palestinians would automatically be recognized as refugees on the basis of the original persecution by Israel that dispossessed them of their homeland and denies the right to return to their homes and properties.

Another inconsistency between these two definitions is the application of the cessation clauses to refugee status. The status of a refugee defined under Article 1A(2) can terminate under the application of Article 1C of the Refugee Convention when s/he has taken steps to re-establish himself in his country of nationality or obtains nationality and protection in a new state; and under Article 1E when s/he has established residence in a second state that grants him rights equivalent to those of a national. For Palestinians, the application of these clauses is extremely problematic; long-term residence in an Arab host state would terminate any refugee status s/he may claim under the Convention. However, the Article 1C cessation clauses do not apply to Palestinians, as Article 1C states, 'This Convention shall cease to apply to any person *falling under the terms of section A*'. Article 1D refugees do not fall 'under the terms of Section A', hence 1C does not refer to Palestinians at all. The Article 1E cessation clause might apply to Palestinians, but that would be inconsistent with the termination clause under Article 1D. The termination of 1D refugee status for Palestinian refugees occurs when they are 'definitively settled in accordance with the relevant resolutions adopted by the General Assembly of the United Nations', that is, when the Res. 194(III), para. 11 formula has been fulfilled, and not by the application of other cessation or termination provisions.

Access to Durable Solutions

As for the second link, international agency mandates tied to refugee protection, UNRWA and/or UNHCR have not replaced UNCCP's broad mandate. UNCCP had a more expanded notion of protection in its obligations to resolve conflict issues, negotiate for restitution of the refugees' property, and secure return and compensation rights. At the same time, UNCCP did not have a clearly articulated mandate of day-to-day protection (UNCCP 1950). UNCCP's category definition relates to persecution by Israel and applies to Palestinians everywhere who fit that category, as well as their descendants. The UNGA has affirmed that Res. 194(III) also covers 1967 Displaced Persons and that 'just settlement', as it appears in later resolutions, refers to Res. 194(III)'s formula for durable solutions (i.e. UNSC 1967). Finally, UNCCP's mandate of international protection, including seeking durable solutions, terminates *as a legal matter* when the conditions of Res. 194(III) are satisfied for the entire category defined under that Resolution, and not otherwise (1951 Convention, Art. 1C & 1E).

UNRWA's Protection Role and Weaknesses in its Mandate

Addressing the third link, UNRWA's benefits or services are provided to individual 'registered' Palestinian refugees and categories of Palestinians on the basis of need for assistance or specified vulnerabilities. Following amendments made over time to accommodate subsequent groups of displaced Palestinians, UNRWA's registration and service eligibility have been bifurcated. After dropping the 'need' and 'flight' requirements, defined Palestine refugees and their descendants continue to be registered, but are not necessarily eligible for services. Later-displaced populations have also received services based on need for assistance, but are not registered on UNRWA's rolls. Such persons can be removed from UNRWA registration if they are no longer in need, or if the category itself is phased out.

Due to the lack of an authorizing statute or a governing body with clear legal authority by UN member states, UNRWA's mandate is on firmest ground as a legal matter regarding those activities clearly within its founding Resolution, or UNGA *authorizing* Resolutions (as opposed to after-the-fact commendatory Resolutions). It remains unproven whether UNRWA can effectively deliver the refugee protection activities described in its MTS, activities similar to those UNHCR undertakes to advance legal rights for its beneficiaries. UNRWA can, and routinely now does, collaborate with UNHCR to promote temporary absorption for Palestinians in and from UNRWA areas. However, UNRWA agrees that on the core refugee protection right, the search for and implementation of durable solutions, it has no mandate, other than to highlight the need for a just and comprehensive solution for the refugee problem.

Conclusions

Drawing conclusions from the various definitions and agency mandates, and the territories in which they operate as they affect Palestinian refugees, the protection gap is evident. As noted, the UNGA Res. 194(III) definition of 'Palestine refugee' applies today to a population of Palestinians, including a third generation, of approximately 6 million out of the 11.2 million Palestinians worldwide. The Agency that was to identify the beneficiaries of that definition and provide the full panoply of international protection functions, UNCCP, has become defunct as a practical, but not a legal, matter. UNHCR's interpretation of who is a 'Palestinian refugee' is inadequate to address the protection gap, because under its interpretation of Article 1D, a durable solution-related definition applies to only about half of the global Palestinian refugee or stateless population.

This anomaly is best illustrated by the lack of any intervention by UNHCR or UNRWA in negotiations between the parties to the Israel–Palestine conflict concerning durable solutions for Palestinian refugees. In contrast to dozens of conflicts in which UNHCR has protected the rights of refugees, this role is absent for Palestinian refugees. Despite promoting various durable solution plans in post-conflict agreements worldwide, UNHCR has never claimed a role to promote Palestinian refugee rights in any of the negotiations. UNRWA, on the other hand, has been excluded from even an 'observer' role in situations like the post-Madrid and the Oslo process. This reflects both political failure by states, and the limitations of UNRWA's mandate.

The full scope of the Palestinian protection gap includes the weak legal framework in the Arab world. None of the Arab host states is a party to the Refugee Convention or a regional convention with refugee protections (such as in Africa or the Americas). Hence, no treaty guarantees refugee rights in the territories where the majority of Palestinian refugees reside. The Arab states are not parties to the 1954 Convention on Stateless Persons, with its important rights-provisions for which UNHCR is the monitoring body. UNRWA would have no authority to monitor or implement the Refugee Convention or the Stateless Persons Convention in any case. The Arab states are parties to many individual human rights conventions, but UNRWA has limited capacity to monitor, intervene, file reports in the treaty bodies, or pressure for compliance concerning the Arab states' implementation of these treaties vis-à-vis Palestinians in their territories—a role even more constrained by its budget than perhaps the flexibility of its mandate. Although the Arab states are parties to the 1965 Casablanca Protocol, a region-wide treaty guaranteeing basic rights to Palestinians, they have widely disregarded their Protocol obligations (Akram and Rempel 2004: 164). UNHCR does not have treaty-based authority to intervene in the Arab states. UNHCR regularly engages with states and other agencies to pressure non-compliant actors through the UN human rights machinery. UNRWA claims competence to take on such monitoring, but has no treaty-based authority to do so, and is further limited by resource constraints. Thus, Palestinian refugees in the Arab region are outside a firm basis for agency intervention in this entire machinery for protection and promotion of their refugee rights, leaving them in indefinite protection limbo as a matter of refugee law.

Notes

1. The author thanks Danessa Watkins, Terry Rempel, Lex Takkenberg and Michael Lynk for input on this chapter.
2. Covenant of the League of Nations (28 April 1919) Article 22. UN Trusteeship Council, successor to the League Mandate System; UNGA Res. 106 (S-1) (15 May 1947) UN Doc. A/RES/106 (S-1) (establishing UNSCOP and UNSCOP Reports).
3. At the time, Jews were approximately one-third of the population of Mandate Palestine, and owned no more than 7 per cent of the land.
4. Para. 11 of Res. 194(III) states that the 'refugees wishing to return to their homes and live at peace with their neighbours should be permitted to do so at the earliest practicable date, and that compensation should be paid for the property of those choosing not to return.'
5. UNRWA is the sole UN programme without a governing body outside the UNGA, which devotes only about one day a year discussing its annual report and budget. (Thanks to Lex Takkenberg for this point.)
6. See UNGA Res. 37/120 (1982) Part (J), para. 1; UNGA Res. 49/35 (1994) Part E; UNGA Res. 61/114 (2006); Report Submitted to the Security Council by the Secretary-General in Accordance with SC Res. 605 (1987) para. 37.
7. The Handbook concludes that Article 1D is properly applied only in Finland, Hungary, and Norway.

8. See UNGA Res. 181(II) (the Partition Resolution); UNGA Res. 194(III) (establishing UNCCP); UNGA Res. 273(III) (11 May 1949) UN Doc. A/RES/273(III) (Israel's UN membership); UNGA Res. 302(IV) (establishing UNRWA); UNGA Res. 393(V) (2 December 1950) UN Doc. A/RES/393(V) (UNRWA assistance fund); UNGA Res. 394(V) (14 December 1950) UN Doc. A/RES/394(V) (protection measures of the refugees' rights, property and interests).

References

Akram, S. M., and Lynk, M. (2011) 'Arab–Israeli Conflict'. Pp. 499–525 in R. Wolfrum (ed.), *The Max Planck Encyclopedia of Public International Law*, vol. i. New York: Oxford University Press, Inc.

Akram, S. M., and Rempel, T. (2004) 'Temporary Protection as an Instrument for Implementing the Right of Return for Palestinian Refugees'. *Boston University International Law Journal* 22(1): 1–162.

BADIL (2012) *Survey of Palestinian Refugees and Displaced Persons: 2010–2012*, vol. vii. Bethlehem: BADIL Resource Center.

BADIL (2005) *Closing Protection Gaps: Handbook on Protection of Palestinian Refugees in States Signatories to the 1951 Refugee Convention*. Bethlehem: BADIL Resource Center.

Interim Report of the Director of the UNRWA, GOAR, 5th sess., suppl. 19. (6 October 1950). UN Doc. A/1451/Rev.1.

Jastram, K., and Achiron, M. (UNHCR) (2001) *Refugee Protection: A Guide to International Refugee Law* (1 December). <http://www.unhcr.org/3d4aba564.html>.

LaGuardia, D., and Van den Toorn, W. (2011) *Evaluation of UNRWA's Organizational Development (OD)*. Brussels: Transtec Project Management. <http://www.unrwa.org/userfiles/2012011541241.pdf>.

Morris, N. (2008) *Consultant's Report Dated 31 March 2008: What Protection Means for UNRWA in Concept and Practice*. <http://www.unrwa.org/userfiles/20100118155412.pdf>.

Report Submitted to the Security Council by the Secretary-General in Accordance with Security Council Resolution 605 (1987) (21 January 1988) UN Doc. S/19443.

UNCCP (1950) 'Analysis of Paragraph 11 of the General Assembly's Resolution of 11 December 1948' (15 May 1950) UN Doc. W/45.

UNCCP (1951) 'Definition of a "Refugee" under Paragraph 11 of the General Assembly Resolution of 11 December 1948' (9 April 1951) UN Doc. A/AC.25/W/61.

UNCCP (1962) Summary Record of the Three Hundred and Fifty-First Meeting (13 September 1962) UN Doc A/AC.25/SR.351.

UN Conference of Plenipotentiaries on the Status of Refugees and Stateless Persons: Summary Record of the Twenty-Ninth Meeting (28 November 1951) UN Doc. A/CONF.2/SR.29.

UN GAOR (1950) UN Doc. A/C.3/SR.328. 3d Comm., 5th Sess., 328th mtg (27 November).

UNHCR (1979) *Handbook on Procedures and Criteria for Determining Refugee Status under the 1951 Convention and the 1967 Protocol relating to the Status of Refugees*. HCR/IP/4/Eng/REV.1 (re-edited 1992).

UNHCR (2002) Note on the Applicability of Article 1D of the 1951 Convention relating to the Status of Refugees to Palestinian Refugees.

UNHCR (2009) Revised Note on the Applicability of Article 1D of the 1951 Convention relating to the Status of Refugees to Palestinian Refugees.

UNRWA (2009) *Consolidated Eligibility Registration Instructions (CERI).* <http://unispal.un.org/pdfs/UNRWA-CERI.pdf>.

UNRWA (2010). *UNRWA Medium Term Strategy. 2010–2015.* <http://www.unrwa.org/userfiles/201003317746.pdf>.

UNRWA (2012) *Outline of Protection Initiatives.* <http://www.unrwa.org/userfiles/file/publications/UNRWA-Protection.pdf>.

UN Secretariat (1950) *UNCCP Memorandum on Relations Between UNRWA and UNCCP* (30 March) UN Doc. A/AC.25/W/42.

CHAPTER 19

REFUGEES AND HUMANITARIANISM

MICHAEL BARNETT

INTRODUCTION

THIS chapter examines the intertwined history of the international refugee regime and the international humanitarian order. Both are responses to the inhumane consequences of a world organized around sovereignty. The major blood-soaked events of the last century are milestones for both: the First World War, Second World War, Biafra, Cambodia, Iraq, Bosnia, Somalia, and Rwanda. Those who wanted to protect refugees frequently sound the call of 'humanitarianism' to rally international sympathy, support, and action. The protection of refugees and displaced peoples, in turn, has been a defining element of the international humanitarian order. Over the last century humanitarianism has expanded to protect more kinds of peoples affected by forced migration, and the goal of finding permanent solutions to the plight of displaced peoples and refugees is a force behind the expansion of humanitarianism's scope and ambitions. Over the last decade the refugee regime has become more involved in natural disasters, far outside its original orbit of concern for peoples forcibly displaced because of persecution and war, and inching closer to more orthodox understandings of humanitarianism.

This chapter is organized in the following way. It begins by situating this discussion in the context of an international humanitarian order, and then proceeds to outline the nineteenth-century origins of the two major branches of humanitarianism that currently comprise this order. Following a distinction I introduced in *Empire of Humanity*, these two branches are: alchemical, wanting to eliminate all forms of suffering and its causes; and emergency, wanting to treat the symptoms of suffering caused by violence and natural disasters. Importantly, alchemists have historically been more inclined to address all kinds of suffering experienced by refugees and other displaced peoples, while emergency humanitarians have a more restricted vision.

The chapter then proceeds to discuss two distinct phases in the relationship of refugees and humanitarianism. The first phase begins in the late eighteenth century and ends with the First World War, and is defined by the *lack* of a relationship between refugees and humanitarianism. Specifically, modern humanitarianism dates to the initial attempt by those in the West to organize action on behalf of distant strangers, most dramatically on behalf of the slaves and aboriginal peoples in the global South; however, there was little interest in refugees, per se. The other nineteenth-century milestone in humanitarianism is the establishment of the Geneva Conventions and the International Committee of the Red Cross in 1864. Importantly, the ICRC's protection mandate included soldiers but not civilians or refugees. In short, neither camp paid much attention to refugees, per se. The simplest explanation for this neglect is that refugees were not an urgent 'problem' because states were not as fastidious about controlling their borders; it was possible for displaced peoples to reach safety in another country without slamming up against legal and political barriers.

The second phase begins with the First World War and continues through the present period, and at this moment the relationship between humanitarianism and refugees becomes much more intimate. I make three central points. First, humanitarianism helped to create a global concern for refugees, and refugees helped to create contemporary humanitarianism. Those who wanted to tend to refugees and other displaced people did so under the discursive sanctuary of humanitarianism, and modern humanitarianism includes a concern with refugees and other peoples that are forced to flee their homes because of violence. Second, the needs of refugees were not of equal concern to the alchemist and emergency camps. Specifically, alchemist agencies were much more responsive to the range of needs of refugees and other displaced peoples, while emergency agencies tended to limit their concern to moments of urgency and severe hardship. Third, because of the intimate relationship of humanitarianism and refugees, and because of the global forces that favoured alchemical humanitarianism, humanitarian organizations exhibited an impressive expansion in the kinds of populations of concern, particularly their attention to both the symptoms and causes of refugee flight. In order to illustrate this argument, I look at the humanitarianism of the UNHCR. Specifically, changes in the global environment and the international humanitarian order created the conditions for a UNHCR that was more open to an expansive definition of humanitarianism to go where few emergency agencies would.

Humanitarianism

For centuries there has existed an international humanitarian order dedicated to preserving and protecting human life. It includes: an interlocking set of norms, informal institutions, laws, and discourses that legitimate and compel various kinds of interventions to protect the world's most vulnerable populations; a surfeit of conventions and treaties that are designed to secure the fundamental right of all peoples—the right to life; a multitude of slogans and rallying cries—including 'never again' and the 'humanitarian imperative'—that accompany graphic and heart-wrenching photos of victims of vio-lence; a metropolis of states, international organizations, and non-governmental orga-nizations, some of which are dedicated to the goal of reducing suffering and others that will lend a hand under the right circumstances. These norms, laws, actors, and institu-tions are nestled in discourses of compassion, responsibility, and care, which, in turn, are attached to claims that the 'international community' has obligations to its weakest members. The international refugee regime, like the international humanitarian order, is comprised of various organizations, laws, and norms, including: the UNHCR and other international agencies like the Organization of International Migration, that are concerned with forced migration; non-governmental organizations such as Catholic Relief Services and Doctors Without Borders that provide relief; advocacy organiza-tions like Human Rights Watch; activists who help to develop international refugee law; and transnational campaigns like World Refugee Year.

Humanitarianism is the attempt to alleviate the suffering of distant strangers. Typically these strangers are not our neighbours or fellow citizens but rather live in other coun-tries. Because humanitarianism attempts to save lives at risk, action is typically urgent. Humanitarianism is also defined by several principles: humanity, the belief that all humans are equal and have inalienable rights; impartiality, the insistence that we help those who are most in need and that we do not play favourites; neutrality, the commitment to action that does not intentionally benefit or hurt one side or another; and independence, the attempt to ensure that the action is not connected to parties who have a stake in the political out-come of the emergency. We know who the humanitarians are because they act according to these principles and fulfil their duties to help distant strangers.

Although humanitarianism can be minimally understood as the attempt to relieve the suffering of distant strangers, in *The Empire of Humanity* I argue that two kinds have dominated the modern history of humanitarianism. The first, emergency humanitarian-ism, concerns the provision of relief to those in immediate peril, cleaves to the principles of neutrality, impartiality, and independence, and has a hands-off attitude toward poli-tics. Agencies that fall into this camp, including the ICRC and Médecins Sans Frontières (MSF), largely focus on keeping people alive. Their ability to do so, they argue, is depen-dent on following these aforementioned principles, which not only define their iden-tity but also provide the function of facilitating their access to populations at risk. If aid agencies are perceived by combatants or governments as partial, allied with a rival, or as having a vested interest in the outcome, then they will have difficulty reaching access to those in need, or worse, become enemy combatants. Best of all, these principles gener-ate a 'humanitarian space', a sanctuary for aid workers and victims. By adhering to the minimal goal of saving lives and doing so through these principles, humanitarianism ties itself to ethics and segregates itself from politics. Humanitarianism is and should remain apolitical. One of the implications is that it focuses on the symptoms and not the causes of suffering.

Alchemical humanitarianism, on the other hand, involves saving lives at risk *and* addressing the root causes of suffering. It operates with a less binding set of principles, and treats politics as a necessary and at times even a welcome feature of humanitarian action. Although Henry Dunant and the ICRC are often credited with starting modern humanitarianism in the 1860s, in fact it originated decades before, with various reform movements that wanted to stop unnecessary suffering and give people an opportunity for a fuller and healthier life. These moral visionaries can be credited for the launching the world's first international humanitarian movement—the abolitionists. Today some of the best-known aid organizations, including Oxfam, Catholic Relief Services, and CARE International, reside in the alchemical camp.

Alchemical humanitarians differ from emergency humanitarians in three significant ways. They are interested in reducing immediate suffering *and* tackling the root causes of suffering. What is the point of giving someone medical treatment if, when they leave the clinic, they will starve to death because of a lack of food, or be marked for death by a death squad, a warlord, or the state's internal security services? Alchemical humanitarians want to get at the root causes of suffering and make sure that the sick have access to medicines, that the malnourished have the ability to grow and buy food, that the poor can make a living, that people can leave their houses without fear of their rights being violated or experiencing violence. One consequence of this broader ambition is that alchemical humanitarians are less devoted to the principles of neutrality and independence. In certain circumstances, principles of independence and neutrality do not help the victims of genocide, ethnic cleansing, and crimes against humanity. If aid workers want to reduce the causes of suffering, then neutrality and independence can quickly become obstacles. Although alchemical agencies also value being perceived as apolitical, their interest in removing the causes of suffering invariably leads them to recommend interventions that redistribute power, wealth, and status, which often places them in opposition to local elites. Moreover, resource-starved agencies can and do appeal to states to intervene. Through lobbying, pleading, cajoling, and shaming, humanitarian organizations have, on occasion, persuaded states to respond to the tragedies around the world. Politics, far from being the enemy, can be a brother-in-alms. In general, while emergency and alchemical humanitarianism share a fundamental interest in eliminating unnecessary suffering, their different commitments and effects, generating dueling views of the purpose and principles of humanitarianism.

Emergency and alchemical humanitarianism also have differed in various ways over the years, including determining who, when, and how should they help. Emergency humanitarians tended to jump into action because of war, and slowly expanded their focus from soldiers to include civilians and other populations at risk. Alchemical humanitarians concluded that suffering was suffering, regardless of the cause, and that there was no principled reason to focus on soldiers before anyone else or to prefer humanly-made over natural disasters. Consequently, emergency and alchemical humanitarians have been differently disposed toward refugees. Although both are concerned with forced displacement caused by war, alchemists are more open to looking at the full range of needs required by refugees, both during and after the emergency, as well as the possible solutions to refugee flight. For various reasons global forces favoured a more expansive definition of humanitarianism, one that was closer to the characteristics of alchemical humanitarianism.

Humanitarianism without and with Refugees

For the first hundred years of modern humanitarianism, refugees were largely absent as a source of concern. Prior to the twentieth century states did not exert strict legal, political, and physical controls over their borders and hence for the most part people who were forced to flee their homeland had somewhere to go. Generally some form of sanctuary could be found elsewhere. In addition, because refugee flows were largely settled through ad hoc measures and did not require coordinated or permanent action, there were no international mechanisms for considering or handling refugees. Private voluntary agencies were sometimes organized to assist specific ethnic, national, or religious groups, and sometimes states cooperated with these groups, but there was no international mechanism for assistance. Consequently, while there were charitable societies that would help specific populations, humanitarian organizations spent most of their time focused on the suffering caused by deprivation and war. The closest humanitarianism got to helping 'displaced peoples' during the nineteenth century was slavery, slave-like conditions, and forced migration in the colonized global South. But no one imagined labelling slavery as an instance of forced displacement or calling slaves 'refugees'.

It was only with the rise of nationalism and the consolidation of national states in the late nineteenth and early twentieth centuries that governments began to introduce immigration laws, passports, and other legal and administrative barriers to entry. These changes made possible and necessary the legal category of refugee since it was only after these changes that individuals forced to flee their homes were unable to obtain citizenship or legal residence in another country.

Emerging state controls on entry set the stage for massive refugee crisis caused by the First World War. The war displaced hundreds of thousands of people, and then the Russian Revolution and the Russian famine of 1921 produced over a million Russian refugees. With millions of people unable to go home but unable to find sanctuary elsewhere, Europe faced a grave humanitarian emergency.

The First World War and its consequences produced several important developments that signalled the growing connection between humanitarianism and refugees. Refugees became a matter of international concern. At issue was not the compassionate desire to relieve the suffering of displaced peoples, but a fear that the mass movements of people was undermining peace and security. This demand to address the refugee flows was couched in terms of humanitarianism. Security-minded states and principled actors increasingly used this siren to demand action. There were various reasons to call such action humanitarian, but one of the immediate benefits was that it helped to depoliticize their assistance. In response to the demand for action and fearful of the destabilizing effects of refugees, states created their first multilateral organization to deal with the situation. The willingness by states to establish an organization dedicated to refugees was a remarkable innovation given the previous pattern of sustained indifference to refugees punctuated by isolated acts of charity.

Although the call to action was primed by the emergency situation of Russian refugees, many of the private voluntary agencies that got involved, and eventually the High Commissioner for Refugees (HCR), exhibited strong traces of alchemical sentiment. The relief organizations were concerned not only with the care of refugees during war but also in post-war reconstruction and providing solutions to the refugee crisis. The pull to do more was particularly evident in the case of the HCR. When states first created the HCR, it limited it to helping Russian refugees and insisted that it be a coordinating and not an operational body. Nevertheless, the first High Commissioner, the renowned Norwegian explorer Fridtjof Nansen, expanded his operations to assist refugees throughout the European region, articulating a set of refugee rights, and offering assistance that would allow refugees certain livelihoods and feel a degree of safety even though they were outside their homeland and were not granted citizenship by their host country. Nansen even went beyond helping refugees manage the long-term consequences of their displacement to try to address the root causes of specific refugee problems. In particular, he helped to oversee the permanent, compulsory, exchange of populations between Greece and Turkey which expelled and resettled nearly 500,000 people. The creation of both the HCR and the structure of the international refugee regime became a defining moment for the international humanitarian order.

THE EXPANDING ORBIT OF REFUGEES AND HUMANITARIANISM

Beginning with the Second World War, humanitarianism and refugees entered into an increasingly co-dependent relationship. Not only did the discourse of humanitarianism accompany all efforts to manage and mitigate the suffering of refugee flows but the scope and scale of humanitarianism expanded with every new major refugee flow. The growth of humanitarianism, in turn, made it much easier to demand new forms of ministration to more displaced peoples in more circumstances than ever before. This expansion of humanitarianism and concern with refugees and those in refugee-like circumstances was made possible by an alchemical-laced humanitarianism that became more interested in addressing the root causes of suffering.

In response to the refugee crises related to the Second World War, states established a refugee convention and international organization dedicated to the care of refugees. The major powers believed that a convention was necessary in order to provide legal protection and rights for refugees, an act not only of charity but also of survival, because of their anomalous status in international law and their invisibility in national law. Refugees also needed an agency to give a voice for these peoples existing in a transnational limbo.

States delivered a convention and agency, but these were limited by the amputated ethics of states, state sovereignty, and the desire to stay outside of politics and within humanitarianism. These limiting factors were evident in all the key dimensions of the refugee regime. Although there were millions of displaced peoples around the world, refugees would be protected only when they crossed borders and became legally entitled to be called a refugee. And not all those who crossed a border were eligible for refugee status, only those who were fleeing because of persecution. Accordingly, those who fled because of economic hardship, political events such as international and internal wars, famines, and authoritarianism did not count. States christened UNHCR a humanitarian organization, which meant that it was supposed to stay away from politics, and most importantly, the internal affairs of states. In this regard, the UNHCR was well advised to focus on the consequences—and not the causes—of refugee flight. Relatedly, 'protection' became legal protection; UNHCR was mandated to assist refugees by identifying who was eligible, giving them documents and papers, and pushing for greater protections. In other words, because of state sensitivities and sovereignty, UNHCR was supposed to wait on the other side of a border as refugees came to them—and stay out of the internal affairs of states. The limitations of sovereignty and humanitarianism also restricted the UNHCR to the solutions it proposed to refugee flight. UNHCR's statute outlined three solutions—integration into the asylum country, resettlement to a third country, and voluntary repatriation—and UNHCR was strongly encouraged to focus on the first two to the neglect of the third, which would steer it toward the internal affairs of states.

Over the next two decades UNHCR capitalized on world events and used its growing authority to significantly extend its activities, mandate, and working definition of a refugee. Its protection mission expanded from legal assistance to include other forms of assistance, and it began to provide assistance to non-statutory refugees. States sanctioned an organizational expansion that was in their (momentary) interests. But UNHCR was not a passive beneficiary of this process and strove to establish precedents at permissive moments, most famously when it invented new mechanisms such as the 'good offices'. The 'good offices' concept allowed UNHCR to extend protection and assistance to new groups and to transform what might have been a deeply politicized issue into a humanitarian and apolitical matter. This depoliticization benefited not only refugees but also UNHCR, for the concept alerted governments that the agency was apolitical. As a consequence, 'humanitarianism' was not only part of UNHCR's identity, it also proved to be instrumentally useful, a stealth weapon in the service of organizational expansion. States might have tagged UNHCR with a humanitarian mandate as a way of limiting its activities, but UNHCR used the label to insinuate itself into new areas. Refugees were finding a place in the international humanitarian order, and humanitarianism, in turn, was involved in the process of creating new categories of people to be administered and ministered.

While UNHCR was ready to break new ground when the occasion permitted, as far as it was concerned the occasion was never right if the displaced peoples still resided in their home country. Going global did not include walking into the spaces of sovereignty.

UNHCR remained an apolitical, emergency agency, honouring state sovereignty, waiting on the other side of the border to provide relief, and avoiding any consideration of the causes of refugee flight. For instance, when a delegation from Biafra went to Geneva in November 1967 to beg for UNHCR's assistance in helping the hundreds of thousands of displaced peoples caused by the civil war, High Commissioner Sadruddin Aga Khan unequivocally rejected any possible involvement on the grounds that Biafra was not a separate state. In a few decades, though, such an answer became nearly unthinkable.

Beginning in the late 1970s, and then accelerating with the end of the Cold War, several global developments led to a closer integration between humanitarianism and the refugee regime, and to UNHCR's more intimate association with alchemical humanitarianism and deeper involvement in the internal affairs of states. Beginning in the late 1970s both Western and Third World states began demonstrating 'refugee fatigue' and demanding that refugees go home as soon as possible. UNHCR had little choice but to play along, but it also believed that repatriation was, in principle, better and potentially more humane than the other options. The growing emphasis on repatriation led to considerable interest in the conditions in the refugee-producing country that represented an obstacle to repatriation and that caused refugee flight. Suddenly, UNHCR was moving into the internal affairs of states. UNHCR began slowly, simply escorting refugees back home to ensure that they had a 'safe and dignified' return. Then it introduced 'quick impact projects', which were designed to make it economically attractive to return and desirable to stay. After that UNHCR began to insinuate itself into the political situation of the refugees, becoming a more forceful spokesperson for the rights of minorities and peoples and keen to get at the 'root causes' of refugee flows.

A second global development was the creation of a more humanity-friendly definition of sovereignty and the rise of human rights. Although still respectful of the principle of non-interference, the emergence of human rights norms and popular sovereignty as a legitimating principle was shaping what states could not do vis-à-vis their populations and when the international community might have a right and duty to protect people at risk. States used to think of sovereignty as an absolute right and the principle of non-interference as sacrosanct. Increasingly, though, the international community was accepting the idea that sovereignty was conditional on how states treated their populations; if they mistreated their citizens, then their sovereignty could be suspended. The effect of this development was to give the international community both a right and a near duty to get involved; the curtain was now drawn back and the UN and states were increasingly commenting on how governments treated their populations and expecting governments to do better—or else.

Human rights and popular sovereignty were not only about principles, they also were about security, which led to the third global development: a change in the patterns of war and the concern that domestic security was related to international peace and security. By 1990 UNHCR began to legitimate its involvement in the circumstances of the refugee-producing country because of the apparent link between refugee flight and threats to international peace and security.[1] This was not mere conjecture. In an age where internal conflict was leading to massive refugee flows that caused regional instability, and where the displacement of populations was not simply a tragic by-product of war but rather was its intended effect, there were good reasons to see refugee flows as a cause and consequence of domestic and regional turmoil. Specifically, the end of the Cold War shifted the security agenda and the ideological fault lines, and there was growing acceptance of the claim that most wars are internal wars, that internal wars occur almost exclusively occur within illiberal states, and that these internal wars can represent 'threats to international peace and security'. As a result the international community had a reason to become deeply involved in the internal affairs of states. Because of the tight relationship between conflict and refugees, UNHCR became increasingly associated with international peace and security and the new human security agenda; and its interest in reducing the causes of refugee flows, which were frequently attributed to the breakdown of security, led to a growing interest in the internal conditions of states. In addition, UNHCR also became interested in helping refugees and other displaced peoples return to their homes, which, in turn, meant trying to create the conditions for peace and stability within states; UNHCR had become an important partner in the process of post-conflict reconstruction and building legitimate states.

There was one other development that represented a combination of the desire by states to retreat on their previous commitments to the refugee regime and the new patterns of conflict: the rise of the internally displaced people as a category of concern. The post-Cold War wars were causing millions of people to flee, but states were rolling up the welcome mat and refusing to let them cross the border. The consequence was that there were more and more people who were refugees in all but name—they would qualify for refugee status if states honoured their right to seek safety in another country. If states were not going to let UNHCR set up camps to receive these refugees, then it would have to go to them. Beginning with the 1991 Iraq War and then blossoming with Bosnia, UNHCR began to bring relief to displaced peoples instead of waiting for displaced peoples to cross an international border. This also meant that a UNHCR that was already taking care of refugees and those in refugee like circumstances was becoming more open to helping displaced peoples.

As UNHCR was expanding who it wanted to help, how it wanted to help, and where it wanted to help, it was becoming more involved in politics. Consequently, it began to debate whether it could maintain its 'humanitarian' and 'apolitical' standing given its growing involvement in the affairs of the refugee-producing country. UNHCR was long aware that measures might and should be taken to reduce the factors that caused refugee movements, but its 'humanitarian' and 'non-political' character prohibited it from becoming too intrusive. But now there seemed no turning back. According to the High Commissioner, Sadako Ogata, while some championed this activist role others feared that it would compromise its 'humanitarian' work and enmesh it in political disputes. The High Commissioner preferred to find a middle ground, one that defined as 'humanitarian' any action that increased the well-being of the individual while avoiding those controversies that were highly political and best handled by states. As a consequence, humanitarian assistance could include prevention, which was always preferable to the cure, and the attempt to foster respect for human rights, for this would help reduce refugee flows.

This response might have caused a political uproar during the Cold War, but not afterwards. UNHCR suddenly found itself carrying out new 'humanitarian' tasks in highly unstable domestic environments. In 1991 UNHCR's Working Group on International Protection considered whether it could maintain its apolitical credentials alongside its growing involvement in the refugee-producing country. It offered four observations and conclusions. First, 'the evolution of UNHCR's role over the last forty years has demonstrated that the mandate is resilient enough to allow, or indeed require, adaptation by UNHCR to new, unprecedented challenges through new approaches, including in the areas of prevention and in-country protection'. Refugee rights, the document noted, are part and parcel of human rights; thus, UNHCR's role as protector of refugee law legitimates its growing concern for the violations of human rights that lead to refugee flows. Second, UNHCR's humanitarian expertise and experience has, in fact, been recognized by the General Assembly as an 'appropriate basis for undertaking a range of activities not normally viewed as being within the Office's mandate.'[2] Third, 'the High Commissioner's non-political mandate requires neutrality'; but 'neutrality must be coupled with a thorough understanding of prevailing political and other realities.' Fourth, whereas once humanitarianism meant avoiding the 'political' circumstances within the home country and honouring the principle of non-interference, it soon began to include aspects of the state's internal affairs. UNHCR properly noted that it was not violating state sovereignty because it was operating with the consent of the state (except in those circumstances where there was no state to give consent), but there was little doubt that what was permissible under the 'humanitarian' label had significantly expanded.

CONCLUSION

When humanitarianism first came into existence in the early nineteenth century, humanitarian action was largely justified to discuss soldiers and others who needed to be saved because of extreme conditions, not refugees (in part because the legal and political category of refugees did not even exist). When refugees became a matter of international concern after the First World War, it was possible to find aid workers in areas without refugees, and refugees that did not trigger the attention of aid workers. After the Second World War states created the UNHCR as a 'humanitarian' organization to handle those populations that were forced to flee and crossed an international boundary, but refugees might be caused by various factors that had nothing to do with the kinds of circumstances that would trigger humanitarian action, i.e. individuals fleeing the Soviet Union for Europe, and there were situations of clear humanitarian urgency that did not grab the attention of officials from refugee agencies, i.e. Biafra in 1968.

Since the end of the Cold War, though, refugees and humanitarianism have become so closely associated that it is nearly impossible to imagine a situation in which one might exist without the other. One reason for this convergence is because of the patterns of conflict and other developments that have occurred since the end of the Cold War. But these 'objective' factors do not capture the crux of the matter: the world now thinks about humanitarianism and refugees in broader terms, and their mutual broadening is largely responsible for their meeting. Humanitarianism, at least according to the International Committee of the Red Cross, used to be limited to soldiers and to times of war; however, the international community now operates with a much broader definition of humanitarianism, including nearly all people who need to be lifted from conditions of immediate and long-term threats to their survival. Part of the reason why the international community decided to widen the definition of humanitarianism was because there were situations of mass displacement that needed attention but that did not quite meet the more narrow definition of humanitarianism. Likewise, the international community used to operate with a fairly narrow definition of refugees, but has since decided that nearly all displaced peoples, regardless of the reasons why they feel the need to leave their homes, should be a subject of international concern. And the international community has used the language of humanitarianism to justify its involvement, and to make it easier to protect these displaced peoples without becoming entangled in politics. Refugees have been good for humanitarianism, and humanitarianism has been good for refugees.

Refugees and humanitarianism are likely to continue to form a mutual aid society, at least if the agendas of the UNHCR and the UN's Office for the Coordination of Humanitarian Affairs (OCHA) are indicators. The UNHCR is increasingly interested in circumstances that cause mass movement for any reason, and it is nearly impossible to imagine a situation of mass movement that is not caused by events or developments that would not fit a contemporary definition of humanitarianism. UNHCR used to limit itself to those peoples who were forced to flee and cross an international border, but now it involves itself with internally displaced peoples of all kinds and 'people on the move'. UNHCR used to limit itself to situations of violence and persecution, but increasingly is becoming interested in conditions of flight triggered by climate change and natural disasters. UNHCR used to largely work in rural areas and working in large camps, but increasingly it is present in urban areas and working in more scattered surroundings. Although OCHA is just a child when compared to the relatively seasoned UNHCR, it has come a long way since its birth in 1998, and so, too, has a very broad understanding of what counts as a cause for humanitarian action. The UNHCR and OCHA work closely together, and it is increasingly difficult to imagine a situation that might arouse the concern of one but not the other.

NOTES

1. UNHCR 1990: 7.
2. UNHCR 1992: 4.

REFERENCES

Barnett, M. (2013) *Empire of Humanity: A History of Humaitarianism*. London: Cornell University Press.
UNHCR (1990) 'Note on International Protection'. Geneva: UNHCR, 27 August.
UNHCR (1992) 'Note on International Protection'. Geneva: UNHCR, 25 August.

CHAPTER 20

STATE CONTROLS: BORDERS, REFUGEES, AND CITIZENSHIP

RANDALL HANSEN

INTRODUCTION

THE study of forced migration and refugees, whether in a contemporary or historical context, cannot be understood without reference to the nation state and its borders. Historically, there is a strong contingent relationship between the emergence of the nation state and the (often violent) generation of large-scale refugee movements. Today, refugees are created through, and indeed are incomprehensible without, the interaction of migrants and borders.

The nation is, following Benedict Anderson, the imagined community of individuals who share some common sense of identity and who place their loyalty to each other above their loyalty to strangers (Anderson 2006). The state, made up of the legislature, executive, bureaucracy, courts, and army, is the final arbiter of disputes, holds a monopoly over violence, and is responsible for protecting, regulating, and redistributing property. Nations are roughly congruent with states, although there are many historical and contemporary exceptions: Germany in the interwar period (when a large German population lived in Poland), Hungary, Russia, and Québec today. The nation state is defined by its borders: externally, they constitute the limits of sovereignty; internally, residence and even mere presence within borders allow individuals to claim the protection of the nation state.

Despite tireless and somewhat tiresome efforts to find an alternate basis for citizenship, the status has no logic, power, or moral force outside a nation state (Hansen 2009). A citizen is one who enjoys the full panoply of rights—civil, social, economic, and political—accorded by a nation state; a citizen can call on his or her nation state, and only that nation state, to claim diplomatic protection; and the nation state can in turn demand the ultimate loyalty of its citizens, including the obligation to fight and die.

The international refugee system, as it has developed since the Second World War, has interacted with the state system in complex ways. On the one hand, the *non-refoulement* duty imposed by the 1951 UN Convention relating to the status of refugees and the Convention's 1967 Protocol is one of the few legal limitations on state sovereignty. States, in theory, cannot return or transfer refugees to countries where they face a 'well-founded fear of being persecuted for reasons of race, religion, nationality, membership of a particular social group, or political opinion'. On the other hand, the idea of refugees, in the sense understood by the 1951 Convention, is in theory and in practice incomprehensible without the international state system.

This chapter will outline the relationship between the nation state, borders, and refugees. The nation state has both the Weberian monopoly on violence *and* the sole capacity to protect human rights. Borders, in turn, define the limits, with a few exceptions, of nation-state sovereignty: they can fully protect only those within their borders. To be sure, citizenship does allow the state to extend its sovereignty to a degree: it is responsible for its citizens abroad. But outside its own borders, the state's capacity to protect those citizens is severely constrained, as imprisoned drug dealers around the world can attest. Asylum seekers become refugees by being recognized as such by the state. The state's obligations to asylum seekers—*non-refoulement* and the processing of the asylum claim—are triggered when the asylum seeker reaches the borders of that state and claims asylum (Loescher and Milner 2011: 194). And the end point in a successful asylum application is permanent residence and citizenship rights in the new state, ideally a liberal democratic one.

For the purposes of this chapter, 'refugees' are understood in both the popular and the legal sense. In the former, refugees are forced migrants; in the latter, following the 1951 UN refugee Convention, they are people with a 'well-founded fear of persecution' granted refugee status by a signatory state to the 1951 Convention. An asylum seeker, whether travelling alone or as part of a mass influx, is a person seeking that status.

Asylum Challenges to the Nation State

The contemporary asylum system challenges the very state system on which it depends. It does so for three reasons: first, because it is one of the few areas in which sovereignty is meaningfully restricted; second, because most Convention signatory states or their courts have articulated complex and lengthy legal procedures that make full asylum processing and subsequent appeals time consuming and expensive; and third, because deportation is extremely difficult. In the last, legal, moral, and financial limits mean that traditionally only a minority of those whose asylum cases were rejected were in fact deported. This fact led nation states to erect a wide variety of institutional and legal barriers designed to keep asylum seekers away from their borders: visa requirements, safe country of origin and safe third country rules, carrier sanctions, interdiction at sea, and the declaration of airports international zones (more on these below). These actions, in turn, threaten the institution of asylum itself. States and borders both sustain and undermine the asylum system.

BORDERS AND CITIZENSHIP

As a horizontal status, citizenship requires limits. It is, as Rogers Brubaker famously noted, 'internally inclusive' and 'externally exclusive' (Brubaker 1992: 21). For most people and in most cases, the limits of the borders are the limits of citizenship. Put another way, one can only be fully a citizen when resident in the state of one's citizenship. Even dual citizens, a naturally privileged category, enjoy no diplomatic protection when in the state of their other citizenship(s) and often find they have fewer social and political rights (to health care, to lower postsecondary education fees, or even to vote) when they do not reside in the state granting their citizenship.

BORDERS AND REFUGEES IN HISTORICAL CONTEXT

Borders are basic to the construction and creation of refugee movements in both historical and contemporary contexts. In the former, nation states have been built through mass flight and mass expulsions. In this sense, Europe's interwar period, in which there was a valiant and failed effort to match borders to people, was the exception. Both before and after the 1919–39 period, the norm was to match, through expulsion and murder, people to borders (Weinberg 2005: 895). Though often presented as an exceptional case, the expulsion of approximately 750,000 Palestinian Arabs from what is now Israel between November 1947 and September 1949 (Chatty and Farah 2005; Lentin 2005) is part of a broader pattern of displacement and dispossession that underpins the constitution of nation states. As discussed in more detail in Akram's chapter (this volume) on the establishment of the United Nations Relief and Works Agency for Palestinian refugees, the Zionist leadership from at least the 1890s privately floated the idea of transferring Arab populations out of Palestine (Morris 2004: 41–3). Liberal moral qualms, however, constrained the proposal until the 1930s (Morris 2004: 43). From then, partly in reaction to waves of Arab anti-Jewish violence in Palestine, these checks fell away (Morris 2004: 43–4). From the 1930s, onwards, a consensus, with some British support, emerged in favour of transferring Arabs from Palestine in order to make room for Jews and in order to prevent the emergence of a fifth column within the Jewish state (Morris 2004: 47–52). What the Zionists needed was the opportunity to implement that transfer; war provided it.

Rejecting UN General Assembly Resolution 181 of November 1947 on the Partition of Palestine, first Palestinians and, from May 1948, neighbouring Arab states attacked Israel, thereby providing the opportunity for the Jewish leadership to expel 400,000 Arabs from the new Jewish state (Morris 2008: chapter 3). As Arab attacks on Israeli positions intensified and as Jewish casualties mounted, attitudes hardened, and on 10

December 1947, Israeli tactics switched from one of attacks restricted to military targets. 'Aggressive defence', in which each attack would be followed by an aggressive counter-attack, reprisals, and the permanent seizure of Palestinian positions, became official policy (Morris 2004: 73; Chatty and Farah 2005: 468). By the end of the war, through a combination of flight and expulsion—the latter organized spontaneously by Israeli army units—750,000 Palestinians had fled their homes. Although there had been no overall plan and coordinated strategy for expulsion (hence 150,000 Arabs remained), preventing the return of those Arabs who had left became official Israeli policy, one '[g]enerally applied with resolution and, often, with brutality' (Morris 2004, 588–9).

It is often suggested that Israel was born with an original sin that blights, as original sin does, all that Israel has done since (Pappé 1992). What is less remarked on is that most moments of nation building occur against the background of ethnic cleansing.[1] A few examples illustrate this point. The creation of the American republic led to the subsequent mass transfer and murder of large numbers of Native Americans as well as to the flight or expulsion of some 60,000 Americans loyal to Britain (Jasanoff 2012: 357). By 1850, most Native Americans east of the Mississippi had been transferred west to 'Indian territory', and a massacre of California natives (aboriginals) living near goldfields occurred following the 1848 discovery of gold in the state (Grinde 2001: 374). Back in Europe, Turkey's emergence after the First World War from the ashes of the Ottoman Empire followed the expulsion of 1.5 million Armenians, of whom some 750,000 died (Pattie 2005: 15).

The 1941–51 period provided a particularly vivid illustration of the nation-building/refugee-production nexus. The creation of India and Pakistan led to the flight or expulsion of 8 million people. Poland and Czechoslovakia, among other East European countries, consolidated their post-1945 nations through the expulsion of their ethnic German populations (across Eastern Europe, 12 million Germans were expelled). Huge numbers of Poles had themselves been expelled as Stalin incorporated eastern Poland into the Soviet Union. More broadly, even after mass returns from war-torn Europe, there were after World War II 1.2 million displaced persons unwilling or unable to return to their homelands, including 400,000 Polish POWs and forced labourers; 150,000–200,000 Estonian, Lithuanian, and Latvian Wehrmacht and SS soldiers, slave labourers, and civilians fleeing the Soviets; 100,000–150,000 ethnic Ukrainians; and 250,000 Jewish refugees, including a small group who had survived the death camps and death marches (Cohen 2012: 5-6).

These nation-building exercises were accompanied, and perhaps made possible, by murder sprees of which the Israeli was numerically the smallest. At the end of the Second World War, some 700,000 Germans were killed through starvation, freezing, accidents, and murder; the rape and murder of women and the killing of children were common (Naimark 2002: 111; Snyder 2010: 332). Flight, expulsion, and deportation also resulted in 150,000 Polish, 250,000 Ukrainian, and 300,000 Soviet deaths during the same period (Snyder 2010: 332). In India and Pakistan, nationalist hardliners used ethnic and religious hatred to pursue, as nationalists often do, the creation of new states and the advancement of their careers. The partition of India and Pakistan occurred in and was made possible by a climate of intense religious hatred, by the systematic murder of civilians, by the decimation of whole villages, and by the mass expulsion and flight of millions of Hindus, Muslims, and Sikhs. It was carnage in which all religious groups were both perpetrators and victims. As Yasmin Khan concludes,

> Violence must sit at the core of any history of Partition... It affected women, children and the elderly as well as well-armed young men... Children watched as their parents were dismembered or burned alive, women were brutally raped and had their breasts and genitals mutilated[,] and entire populations of villages were summarily executed... Broken bodies lay along roadsides and on train platforms, while charred wood and rubble were all that remained of large quarters of Amritsar and Lahore.... Partition stories of Punjab in 1947 are marked by specific details and are layered in unique and entirely individual family memories. Yet these descriptions are also shot through with generic imagery and the haunting motifs that have entered the popular imagination of South Asia: the corpse-laden refugee train passing silently through the province, the penniless rows of refugees streaming across new international borders. (Khan 2007: 129–30)

The rape, mutilation, murder, and abduction of women and girls were a central part of India and Pakistan's nation-building process:

> Rape was used as a weapon, as a sport and as a punishment. Armed gangs had started to use rape as a tool of violence in Bengal and Bihar in 1946 but this now took on a new ubiquity and savagery in Punjab... [Many women] were snatched from their homes and villages by marauding gangs or literally carried away from the slow and under-protected *kafilas* that made their way on foot towards the border... Women's bodies were marked and branded with slogans of freedom, '*Pakistan Zindabad*' and '*Jai Hind*', inscribed on their faces and breasts. Those who survived were often humiliated and grossly scarred. They had become symbols of terror. (Khan 2007: 133–4)

There is no essential connection between nation building and the production of refugee movements any more than there is an essential connection between nation building and war, but there is a strong contingent one.

THREATENED BORDERS: CONTEMPORARY REFUGEE MOVEMENTS

If the drawing of borders was bound up with the production of refugee movements, so is the maintenance of those boundaries. This is true both legally and politically. Legally, both asylum seekers and refugees are created through the crossing of borders. The 1951 Convention creates a right not to asylum but, rather, a right to ask for it; the Convention imposes on states not a duty to recognize refugees but rather *not* to return them to countries where they face a well-founded fear of persecution (the *non-refoulement* requirement). In both cases, the process is initiated through crossing at least one border—when exiting the allegedly persecuting country—and reaching another—the country in which the applicant is seeking asylum (Long 2013: 1). As Article 1(A)2 of the 1951 Convention puts it, a refugee is one with a well-founded fear of persecution who is 'outside the country of his nationality and is unable or, owing to such fear, is unwilling to avail himself of protection of that country'. Subsequent international agreements, often with a more expansive definition of refugees than the 1951 Convention (the 1984 Cartagena Declaration on Refugees or the 1969 Organization of African Unity Convention Governing Specific Aspects of Refugee Problems), retain the emphasis on borders: they are activated when people flee their country (Loescher and Milner 2011: 191). Resettlement, in which individuals are selected from refugee camps, given asylum status under the Convention, and settled in the granting state, is the exception to this rule, but only 1 per cent of the world's refugees is considered for resettlement (UNHCR 2011). The corollary of these observations is that states wishing to prevent refugee movements obstruct border crossings. 'Border closures in the face of mass refugee influx,' observes Katy Long, 'are a visible demonstration of a state's refusal to accept the obligations of refugee protection as established under the existing refugee protection framework' (Long 2013: 464–7; see also Madokoro 2008).

During the Cold War, when metaphorical curtains and real bullets and barbed wire helped limit large-scale population movements from East to West, the refugee system worked rather well from the perspective of Western governments, which is to say that it caused few political problems (Loescher 2001: 54–7). Refugees were few in number, and, as they were often professional or artistic elites from the Soviet Union, their arrival was an economic or cultural boon, as well as evidence of the West's superiority over Communism. From the 1980s, however, as the costs of transportation declined, refugee migrations surged. After the end of the Cold War, they skyrocketed (see Bank, this volume).

Within scholarly circles, the combination of large numbers of asylum applications in Europe and large numbers of asylum seekers outside Europe encouraged the hypothesis, tested by several migration scholars, that governments had 'lost control' over their borders (Cornelius et al. 2004).

BORDERS AND REFUGEES

Governments soon reasserted that control over their borders. Across the West, states responded to these dynamics—the trigger of rights through the touching of domestic soil, and the limits on deportation—by efforts to block new asylum seekers' access to that soil and to expand efforts to return those they had rejected. States introduced a wide range of measures designed to keep asylum seekers from reaching national borders. They expanded visa requirements and introduced substantial fines for airlines that allowed asylum seekers to travel without correct documentation, thereby keeping asylum seekers off airplanes. They declared an often dubious list of countries 'safe' and therefore incapable of producing asylum seekers (thus allowing states to avoid processing the asylum claims of any nationals arriving from such countries). And they interdicted asylum seekers at sea, declared airports international zones outside the jurisdiction of courts, and expanded off-country detention (to prevent the lodging of asylum claims) (Hathaway 2005: 283–98; Goodwin-Gill and McAdam 2007).

The second and more recent response has involved expanded deportation. As a recent study concludes, there has been a prodigious rise in the use of deportation by liberal democratic states in the last two decades. In the USA and the UK, developments in infrastructural capacity and legal powers to deport, along with a new-found public and official enthusiasm for expulsion, have seen a tripling and doubling, respectively, of the number of non-citizens who leave these states under the threat of coercion. In the UK, deportations rose from 30,000 in 1997 to 67,000 in 2009 (the figure was 68,000 2008); in the US, they rose from 114,432 in 1997 to 400,000 in 2009 (Anderson, Gibney, and Paoletti 2011: 550). Many other countries, including Canada, France, Germany, and the Netherlands, have also become more serious about using deportation as a way of dealing with illegal migrants, failed asylum seekers, non-citizens convicted of criminal offences, and those suspected of involvement in terrorism. It is no exaggeration to talk of a deportation turn in the practices of Western states in their dealing with unwanted non-citizens (Anderson, Gibney, and Paoletti 2011: 547).

Scholars have argued that these efforts amounted to an attempt to bring refugee and asylum policy under the remit of military, security, and policing policy. Recent literature is replete with arguments that states have 'criminalized', 'securitized', and 'militarized' asylum and undocumented migration. As a recent review put it, 'prisons or immigration removal centres are singularly useful in the management of non-citizens because they enable society not only physically to exclude this population, but also, symbolically to mark these figures out as threatening and dangerous' (Bosworth 2008: 207–8).

These arguments display a flare for the metaphor, but they confuse ends with means. Governments have no a priori interest in criminalizing asylum seekers, not least because restrictions on migration and asylum attract so much criticism from *bien-pensant* commentators. Understanding such control measures requires taking them seriously as such: as measures designed to reduce asylum pressures. The question for students of public policy is why governments would adopt these measures rather than others, and this in turn requires reflecting on the aim common to all of them. What unites airline check-in employees flicking through passports and coast guards patrolling the seas is an effort to shift the border outwards. These and other measures aim to remove the burden of securing the border from those guarding the juridical line separating one country from another (Hansen and Papademetriou 2013). And states have been compelled to shift the border outwards because the traditional mechanism of border control has been undermined by the regular operation of the asylum system. States cannot simply line the physical border with guards who deny entry to undesirable migrants, because migrants acquire rights as soon as they reach the shores of a signatory state, and above all a liberal democratic signatory state.

For signatories of the UN Convention, an asylum application at the border triggers a complex, lengthy, and often expensive adjudication process. An asylum hearing must be arranged; lawyers must be appointed; a case and possibly an appeal must be heard; and, if unsuccessful, return procedures have to be initiated. Within the European Union, states are obligated to provide asylum seekers with minimum levels of housing and subsistence while their case is being determined (though the generosity and quality of that support varies in practice greatly across the Union). The average adjudication period in Europe in the late 1990s was six months (Hatton and Williamson 2004: 10). At the end of it all, only a minority of asylum seekers were successful: the 'dirty little secret' of asylum applications, as the late Arthur C. Helton put it, is that few asylum seekers are granted refugee status (Helton 2002: 169). By the most generous measures, less than 50 per cent of asylum seekers receive either refugee or non-Convention refugee status following the processing of their asylum applications. In most cases, the figure is under 30 per cent. The majority of asylum seekers were and are not refugees as understood either by the Convention itself or the principles underlying it (for instance, the idea that people persecuted by non-state actors, though not strictly speaking refugees, deserve protection).

Until recently, only a minority of those whose asylum applications were rejected were deported. Tracking down and deporting individuals was expensive; asylum seekers deliberately destroyed documentation in order to inhibit return; source countries were reluctant to take them without such documentation (and sometimes with it); and, as they could easily disappear in large cities, the state simply could not find the majority of illegal migrants (Gibney and Hansen 2003). And what this meant was that borders mattered both a great deal and very little. They mattered a great deal because the asylum adjudication process was initiated by crossing them. Whatever difficulties asylum seekers have in reaching a country that is a signatory to the 1951 UN Convention, dodging hostile boats and even bullets, once they arrive and claim asylum they enjoy rights: to the processing of the claim and, in Europe, to housing, social support, and legal advice. But borders also mattered very little because once asylum seekers crossed borders return became difficult, if not impossible.

THICKENING BORDERS

It was this dual dynamic—the initiation of the asylum process by touching the soil of a signatory country, and the generation by the liberal democratic polity of severe constraints on deportation—that led states to adopt measures designed to extend the border outwards and to remove through deportation failed asylum seekers residing within them. The former were so heavy handed in part because the rights enjoyed by asylum seekers who did reach liberal democratic soil were so robust. As Matthew Gibney noted in an important piece, there is a direct relationship between illiberalism outside the border and liberalism within it (Gibney 2003).

In the same vein, the American and British governments expanded deportation measures once it was clear that traditional mechanisms for border control—asylum processes in Europe distinguishing legitimate from illegitimate refugees, and the border itself in the United States— failed. Once the press politicized the issue by drawing attention to the gaps, literal and metaphorical, in British and American policy, both countries took measures that sharply increased deportation.

The last point takes us on to motivation. In much of the literature, scholars seeking to explain refugee policy adopt an implicit state autonomy model—a view of the state as an actor that governs the asylum process independently of wider political currents. On such views, governments, seemingly without reference to the publics that elect them, construct asylum as a problem. In doing so they generate public hostility to asylum seekers whom they would otherwise welcome or at least not notice, and then use this generated opposition as an excuse to implement restrictions (Hassan 2000; Abu-Laban and Garber 2005; Warner 2005–6; Nickels 2007). Such constructivist interpretations both give anti-migrant publics an undeserved pass and reflect a poor understanding of politics and the political process. It is only under the most ideal and unusual of conditions that politicians are masters of events; in almost all cases, they are reacting to them. They have no interest in stirring up political controversy. Indeed, the most desirable situation from a government's point of view is one in which the economy hums along, producing high employment and low inflation; there are no riots or demonstrations to disturb social peace; and international affairs are characterized by calm, cordial relations among affluent states producing no migrants. The first two conditions rarely obtain (and governments are almost guaranteed re-election when the first does); the last never does. It would be a foolish government that sought to generate an immigration crisis, replete as such crises are with negative public opinion, street demonstrations, activist and some degree of press hostility, and in the worst case anti-migrant violence. These crises, rather, are generated by those who profit from the government's discomfort. They can be opposition politicians, such as Anne Widdecombe, the British Shadow Home Secretary from 1999 to 2001 who savaged the Labour government over its supposed failure to control asylum, or Tom Tancredo, a Republican member of the US House of Representatives from Colorado who led a bitter campaign against illegal migration in the mid-2000s. These instigating actors can also be the press. In the UK, the *Daily Mail* whips up anti-asylum sentiment through lurid stories of asylum seekers abusing social benefits, enriching themselves through begging, or making shameless and unfounded appeals to sovereignty-destroying European courts; in the United States, CNN (under Lou Dobbs) and Fox News made 'broken borders' a consistent theme in US politics throughout the first decade of the millennium. But even these sparks require fuel: all these campaigns occurred against a backdrop of sharply rising migration: asylum applications in Britain and sharply rising undocumented migration to the United States.

Chronology bears these points out. In both Germany and the United Kingdom, efforts to reduce asylum applications through externalizing the border occurred after (a) a great upsurge in asylum seekers and (b) the politicization of asylum by extra-governmental actors. In the UK, the latter was provoked by the tabloid press; in Germany, it was federal states (which bear the costs of asylum seekers), far-right parties, and, most brutally and tragically, neo-Nazis who murdered first asylum seekers and then Turkish-Germans in the early 1990s. In the UK and the US, the 'turn to deportation' occurred after the British press and Conservative opposition got wind of the gap between asylum rejections and returns and after the CNN/Fox/Tancredo campaign against illegal (Latino) migrants (Anderson, Gibney, and Paoletti 2013).

Conclusion: Borders, Refugees, and Citizenship

This chapter has argued that borders are fundamental to the nation state; that borders are basic to the international system as they trigger the rights available under the UN Convention; that the nation state is the anchor of the international refugee system; and that, paradoxically, the asylum determination system threatens borders, the state, and the international refugee system itself. The account points to the importance of both structures and actors. Structurally, borders, rights-respecting states, and asylum seekers on the move interact in a manner that generates restrictive pressures that harm refugee protection internationally. Asylum seekers, both genuine refugees and those who use asylum when there are no other migratory entry points, activate robust rights when they cross borders and apply for asylum. These rights impose costs and obligations on states, and they militate against the deportation of failed asylum seekers in a manner that encourages states to determine and implement restrictions designed to keep asylum seekers from reaching the border and to deport those who have crossed. These restrictions, particularly those that 'thicken' the border, inevitably prevent genuine refugees from reaching the borders of 1951 Convention signatory states. And this means, equally inevitably, that states' defence of their borders risks undermining, and perhaps has in large measure already done so, the international refugee system.

Overly structuralist accounts should be viewed with suspicion, as they imply politics and policy without actors. This cannot be. None of the dynamics highlighted above can be initiated without actors who transform asylum into a political issue that threatens the government of the day. Such actors are diverse: opposition politicians, (often conservative) journalists, local officials, far-right parties, and, of course, avowed racist extremists. But this too only points to a further contradiction: liberal democracy, the values of which underpin the refugee system, generates through the normal operation of liberal democratic politics pressures that threaten that very system.

Note

1. In public debate, the expulsion of a roughly equal number of Jews from neighbouring Middle Eastern countries has also received little attention, although scholars have documented it. On the latter, for instance, see Shiblak (2005) on the expulsion of Iraqi Jews in the 1950s.

References

Abu-Laban, Y., and Garber, J. (2005) 'The Construction of the Geography of Immigration as a Policy Problem: The United States and Canada Compared'. *Urban Affairs Review* 40(4): 520–61.

Anderson, B. (2006) *Imagined Communities: Reflections on the Origins and Spread of Nationalism*. London: Verso.

Anderson, B., Gibney, M. J., and Paoletti, E. (2011) 'Citizenship, Deportation and the Boundaries of Belonging'. *Citizenship Studies* 15(5): 547–63.

Anderson, B., Gibney, M. J., and Paoletti, E. eds. (2013) *The Social, Political and Historical Contours of Deportation*. New York: Springer.

Betts, A., ed. (2011) *Global Governance Migration*. Oxford: Oxford University Press.

Bosworth, M. (2008) 'Border Control and the Limits of State Sovereignty'. *Social & Legal Studies* 2: 199–215.

Brubaker, R. (1992) *Citizenship and Nationhood in France and Germany*. Cambridge, MA: Harvard University Press.

Chatty, D., and Farah, R. (2005) 'Palestinian Refugees'. Pp. 465–471 in M. Gibney and R. Hansen (eds.), *Immigration and Asylum: From 1900 to the Present*, vol. 2. Santa Barbara, CA: ABC-Clio.

Cohen, G. D. (2012) *In War's Wake: Europe's Displaced Persons in the Postwar Order*. Oxford: Oxford University Press.

Cornelius, W. A., Tsuda, T., Martin, P. L., and Hollifield, J. F. (2004) *Controlling Immigration: A Global Perspective* (2nd edn.). Palo Alto, CA: Stanford University Press.

Eurostat (2012). *EU Member States Granted Protection to 84100 Asylum Seekers in 2011*. 19 June. <http://epp.eurostat.ec.europa.eu/cache/ITY_PUBLIC/3-19062012-BP/EN/3-19062012-BP-EN.PDF>.

Gibney, M. (2003) 'The State of Asylum: Democratization, Judicialization and the Evolution of Refugee Policy'. Pp. 19–46 in S. Kneebone (ed.), *The Refugee Convention 50 Years On: Globalization and International Law*. Croydon: Antony Rowe.

Gibney, M., and Hansen, R. (2003) *Deportation and the Liberal State: The Forcible Return of Asylum Seekers and Unlawful Migrants in Canada, Germany and the United Kingdom*. Geneva: United Nations High Commissioner for Refugees.

Goodwin-Gill, G., and McAdam, J. (2007) *The Refugee in International Law* (3rd edn.). Oxford: Oxford University Press.

Grinde, D. A. (2001) 'Indian History and Culture'. Pp. 369–79 in P. S. Boyer (ed.), *The Oxford Companion to United States History*. Oxford: Oxford University Press.

Hansen, R. (2009) 'The Poverty of Postnationalism: Citizenship, Immigration, and the New Europe'. *Theory and Society* 38(1): 1–24.

Hansen, R. and Papademetriou, D. (2013) 'Securing Borders: The Intended, Unintended, and Perverse Consequences'. Pp. 3–22 in R. Hansen and D. Papademetriou (eds.), *Managing Borders in an Increasingly Borderless World*. Washington, DC: Brookings Institution Press.

Hassan, L. (2000) 'Deterrence Measures and the Preservation of Asylum in the United Kingdom and the United States'. *Journal of Refugee Studies* 13(2): 184–204.

Hathaway, J. (2005) *The Rights of Refugees in International Law*. Cambridge: Cambridge University Press.

Hatton, T., and Williamson, J. (2004) *Refugees, Asylum Seekers and Policy in Europe*. Bonn: Institute for the Study of Labor.

Helton, A. C. (2002) *The Price of Indifference: Refugees and Humanitarian Action in the New Century*. Oxford: Oxford University Press.

Jasanoff, M. (2011) *Liberty's Exiles: America's Loyalists in the Revolutionary War*. New York: Alfred A. Knopf.

Khan, Y. (2007) *The Great Partition: The Making of India and Pakistan*. New Haven: Yale University Press.

Kneebone, S. (ed.) (2003) *The Refugee Convention 50 Years On: Globalization and International Law*. Aldershot: Ashgate.

Lentin, A. (2005) 'Israel'. Pp. 325–30 in M. Gibney and R. Hansen (eds.), *Immigration and Asylum: From 1900 to the Present*, vol. 1. Santa Barbara, CA: ABC-Clio.

Loescher, G. (2001) *The UNHCR and World Politics: A Perilous Path*. Oxford: Oxford University Press.

Loescher, G., and Milner, J. (2011) 'UNHCR and the Global Governance of Refugees'. Pp. 189–209 in A. Betts (ed.), *Global Governance Migration*. Oxford: Oxford University Press.

Long, K. (2013) 'In Search of Sanctuary: Border Closures, "Safe" Zones and Refugee Protection'. *Journal of Refugee Studies* 26(3): 458–76.

Madokoro, L. (2012) 'Borders Transformed: Sovereign Concerns, Population Movements and the Making of Territorial Frontiers in Hong Kong, 1949–1967'. *Journal of Refugee Studies* 25(3): 407–27.

Morris, B. (2004) *The Birth of the Palestinian Refugee Problem Revisited* (2nd edn.). Cambridge: Cambridge University Press.

Morris, B. (2008) *1948: A History of the First Arab–Israeli War*. New Haven: Yale University Press.

Naimark, N. M. (2002) *Fires of Hatred: Ethnic Cleansing in Twentieth Century Europe*. Cambridge, MA: Harvard University Press.

Nickels, H. C. (2007) 'Framing Asylum Discourses in Luxembourg'. *Journal of Refugee Studies* 20(1): 37–59.

Pappé, I. (1992) *The Making of the Arab–Israeli Conflict, 1947–1951*. London: I. B. Tauris.

Pattie, S. (2005) 'Armenian Diaspora'. Pp. 13–19 in M. Gibney and R. Hansen (eds.), *Immigration and Asylum: From 1900 to the Present*, vol. 1. Santa Barbara, CA: ABC-Clio.

Shiblak, A. (2005) *Iraqi Jews: A History of Mass Exodus*. London: Saqi.

Snyder, T. (2010) *Bloodlands: Europe between Hitler and Stalin*. New York: Basic Books.

UNHCR (2010) *UNHCR Projected Global Resettlement Needs 2011*. 30 June. <http://www.unhcr.org/5006ac509.html>.

Warner, J. A. (2005–6) 'The Social Construction of the Criminal Alien in Immigration Law, Enforcement Practice and Statistical Enumeration: Consequences for Immigrant Stereotyping'. *Journal of Social and Ecological Boundaries* 1(2): 56–80.

Weinberg, G. (2005). *A World at Arms: A Global History of World War II*. Cambridge: Cambridge University Press.

CHAPTER 21

....

THE SECURITIZATION OF
FORCED MIGRATION

....

ANNE HAMMERSTAD

INTRODUCTION

....

THE systematic inclusion of refugees, asylum seekers, and other categories of migrants on the research agendas of security scholars is a relatively recent phenomenon. Forced migrants were mostly ignored by Security Studies during the Cold War. The growth in interest in the security dimensions of forced migration has gone hand in hand with the widening of the security agenda taking place around the end of the Cold War. In this period, security came to be understood to include challenges beyond traditional preoccupations with weapons, war, and military invasion, both by analysts and policymakers. Refugee and migrant flows were among the earliest and most prominent new security issues proposed in the turbulent first years of the post-Cold War period (Wæver et al. 1993). Twenty years later there is a vast and diverse literature, covering a range of theoretical perspectives within Security Studies, on the relationship between forced migration and security.[1]

There are both empirical and theoretical reasons for this momentous growth in interest in the security dimensions of forced migration. Empirically, two developments in the early 1990s stand out as particularly significant. The break-up of the former Soviet Union led to exaggerated fears in Western Europe of mass immigration from the East. Tongue-in-cheek, but telling of the prevalent mood, *The Economist* magazine carried a front page in October 1990 ominously entitled 'The Russians are coming', illustrated by a picture of huddled refugees trudging through a winter landscape. The accompanying leader article on the consequences of the imminent collapse of the Soviet Union suggested that 'challenge number one for the world is how to respond to potential mass migration' (*Economist* 1990).

Concurrent with this rising fear of new mass migration, forced migrants also arrived on security agendas via another route. The first Iraq war in 1990 inaugurated an era of 'humanitarian intervention' wherein the UN Security Council determined with increasing regularity that it had a responsibility to tackle refugee situations as a matter of international peace and security, especially (but not only) if the displacement was caused by ethnic cleansing and atrocities against civilians (Loescher 1992; Roberts 1998). The many so-called 'New Wars' (Kaldor 2006) erupting in Bosnia, Rwanda, Burundi, Sierra Leone, Liberia, Kosovo, and elsewhere had at their heart the displacement of vast populations. Indeed in many of these wars ethnic cleansing was a primary war aim.

The inclusion of forced migration as a security issue was also part of the conceptual debate in the late 1980s and early 1990s between Realist scholars and their critics on the fundamental question of 'what is security'. For most of the Cold War period the broad consensus within Security Studies was that it should limit itself to '*the study of the threat, use, and control of military force*' (Walt 1991: 212). In the post-Cold War era, economic, environmental, and identity security concerns were posited as of similar importance to the defence of state sovereignty and territorial integrity. Refugees and asylum seekers were proposed as potential threats to all these 'new' types of insecurity.

The Constructivist Turn

This conceptual debate soon took a constructivist turn. After all, the passionate debate over 'what is security' revealed that the answer is not an objectively given fact. Security and insecurity are social constructions: friend/enemy distinctions are intersubjectively constituted, built on a community's sense of history, identity, and values. Security threats are not objectively given, either. Even the threat of nuclear weapons depends at least to some extent on the horizon of the beholder: whether one state views another state's nuclear arsenal as threatening or unthreatening depends on past relations, present perceptions of amity/enmity, and assumptions of behaviour.

Foremost among the constructivist approaches to security is the *securitization* approach, developed by the Copenhagen School in the 1990s (see Buzan, Wæver, and de Wilde 1998). Over time, the securitization approach has developed into an influential, mainstream school of Security Studies. This school has displayed a strong preoccupation with the construction of refugees and asylum seekers as security threats—or in other words: the securitization of forced migration.

Applying the insights of the securitization approach, the remainder of this chapter will discuss the questions of how, why, in what context, and with what consequences, refugees and asylum seekers (as well as other migrants) can be constructed as security issues. Different versions of the securitization approach are used to shed light on different securitization processes. The three versions are the speech act approach of the Copenhagen School, the sociological approach inspired by Foucault, and the 'inclusive security' approach focused on human or common security. All three have been influential in shaping security scholars' attempts to understand the security dimensions of forced migration.

The idea of positive securitizations offered by the 'inclusive security' approach stands in stark contrast to the combative, controlling, and communitarian understanding of security discourses and practice presented by Copenhagen School and Foucauldian analysts. Because these latter two securitization schools complement each other in many ways, as recognized by the emergence of a 'second generation' of securitization theorists (Stritzel 2011: 2492), I will combine their insights in my discussions of the securitization of immigrants, asylum seekers, and refugees as threats to communal cohesion and identity. I then turn to the 'inclusive security' approach to discuss the use of security language as a means with which to achieve a heightened sense of urgency and greater cooperation to resolve the 'root causes' of displacement and conflict. The discussion of these three versions of the securitization approach is by necessity brief and simplified. The empirical examples should be treated as such, not as case-studies. The aim is to give an overview of the direction of the changing debate on the securitization of forced migration.

The Development of Securitization Theory

Starting with the premiss that there is no objectively true answer to the question 'what is security', the securitization approach focuses instead on the question, 'what are the processes through which security threats are constructed?' The Copenhagen School's first formulations of securitization theory focused on the discursive level of 'speaking security'. Securitization is understood as a *speech act*: by declaring an issue a matter of security, its urgency and priority becomes established. The issue is taken out of ordinary politics and into the sphere of emergency politics, where existential threats must be countered by urgent response and where exceptional measures (including violence) are justified due the existential nature of the threat (Buzan, Wæver, and de Wilde 1998: 26).

The Copenhagen School has been criticized for relying too heavily on speech acts. Inspired by Foucault's concept of biopolitics, a more sociological understanding of securitization has been promoted, which focuses on the role of power relations, bureaucratic politics, and institutional interests in determining who or what becomes securitized, and what sort of security practices are promoted to deal with 'threats'. In this view, securitization processes are less about dramatic speech acts, and more about controlling populations through bureaucratic procedures, surveillance, and risk management—techniques of government (Huysmans 2006: 38). This approach tends to posit migration as a pre-eminent example of how certain 'risk populations' are securitized (Bigo 2005; Huysmans 2006).

The Foucauldian approach to securitization shares with the Copenhagen School an understanding of security language and security practices as ultimately pernicious, since they create or reinforce divisions between 'us' and 'them', using the enemy 'other' on the outside as a tool for strengthening the community bonds between insiders. The Copenhagen School and the Foucauldian approaches also share an understanding of the political potency of security: a successful securitization ensures that considerable resources and energy are spent on countering the depicted threat. Obstacles to draconian and extreme measures can be swept aside in the name of security. Building on this, the Foucauldian approach also emphasizes that securitization processes serve to increase the reach of state control over the population and to strengthen and consolidate power in the hands of established elites. Security discourses of fear and unease, positing particular groups or phenomena as threats to the in-group's cohesion, identity and 'way of life', are employed to justify ever more intrusive and draconian government control measures.

These insights are not new. Long before the international relations term 'securitization' was coined, students of Nationalism such as Benedict Anderson (1991) discussed how (imagined) communities were constructed and maintained by consciously setting community members apart from, and contrasting them with, those whom they are not. Unyielding boundaries between group members and outsiders were erected through new practices such as passport regimes and border control. Nationalism studies often focus on the close relationship between nation building and state building, observing how the authority and legitimacy of state institutions were bolstered by the claim that they embody the national community. The primary task of the state became to defend and protect the national community (no longer only the sovereign). Simultaneously a communal duty fell on citizens to display patriotic loyalty towards the state. In this view, to defend the state is to defend the community, and vice versa.

Thus, identity/societal security, defined by Buzan (1991: 19) as 'the sustainability, within acceptable conditions for evolution, of traditional patterns of language, culture and religious and national identity and custom', became a central aspect of nation building. Nation building in turn became vital for state building. From this reasoning, the securitization of identity ends up casting migrants and refugees as security threats. Migrants are by definition outsiders aiming to come in and settle among the insiders. Depending on how insular and traditionalist the communal identity of the host population is (notice Buzan's caveat of 'acceptable conditions for evolution'), how culturally different migrants are to their hosts, the nature of the historical relationship between host community and migrant sending community, and the sheer magnitude of the migrant influx, migration can become securitized as an existential threat to the identity, cohesion, and way of life of the host community.

Real-Life Securitizations

Anxiety over immigration and asylum has become a potent political force. In Europe, the growth in asylum applications, combined with growing international migration numbers, led to what Huysmans (2006) has described as a politics of *unease*, where migrants and asylum seekers were not directly and individually described as threats and enemies. Instead they were lumped together with other more traditionally 'scary' trends such as international crime (people smuggling and trafficking). At the same time immigration figures were presented as unsustainably high, overburdening schools, healthcare, employment, and social services.

The securitization of migration intensified in the aftermath of the 11 September 2001 terror attacks on New York and Washington. The amorphous but potent discourse of unease about 'floods' of migrants evolving in the 1990s, now became accompanied by alarmist speech acts depicting (some) asylum seekers and migrants as threats to national security (Newland et al. 2002: 4). A direct link was made between lax immigration control and international terrorism. Governments across the world announced major immigration reform and tightening of border control in the name of 'homeland security'. Although almost all of the 9/11 hijackers had arrived in the US on six-month tourism visas, and none as asylum seekers, asylum procedures were highlighted as particularly open to abuse by terrorist networks. As a result, there was a marked rise in the use of the exclusion clauses of the Refugee Convention in the aftermath of 9/11 (Blake 2003: 445–7). In many countries, asylum seekers were routinely incarcerated in detention centres, and even in prisons. Thus, the post 9/11 securitization of (particularly Muslim) asylum seekers as a high-risk group eroded asylum seekers' rights in the name of security, allowing exceptional measures such as long-term detention without trial.

Since 2008, the economic downturn has hit migrant-receiving countries severely. As a result, migration-terrorism-related anxieties have been compounded by fears related to the economic well-being of the host populace. As unemployment has risen, the immigrant as job-stealer has perhaps overtaken the image of the immigrant as terror risk. Policy practices in security mode have become commonplace, as currently seen in the Southern European response to Mediterranean boat migrants.

Mediterranean Boat Migrants: Securitizing the Vulnerable

In Europe, irregular migrants from sub-Saharan Africa who arrive in overloaded boats on Southern European shores, are commonly treated as a hostile invasion force. Greece is building vast prison-like detention and deportation centres for irregular migrants (Smith 2012), while Italy pursues an aggressive anti-immigration rhetoric and a policy practice of returning migrant boats to North Africa (HRW 2012). When civil war broke out in Libya in 2011, the Italian Foreign Minister, Franco Frattini, warned of a 'wave of 200,000 to 300,000 immigrants', adding that '[i]t is a Biblical exodus' (quoted in *Der Spiegel* 2011). The foreign minister stated that the 'collapse of Colonel Gaddafi's regime could result in a tidal wave of refugees and illegal immigrants pouring into Europe' (*Telegraph* 2011). Meanwhile, at least 1,500 migrants and refugees died in the attempt to cross the Mediterranean in 2011, and both merchant ships and NATO vessels failed to pick up boat migrants in distress (Council of Europe 2012). The perilous journeys are not abating. On 3 October 2013, a fishing boat carrying more than 500 Eritreans caught fire and sank off the coast of the tiny Italian island of Lampedusa, killing at least

364 people. A week later another boat sank in the same area, this time with around 250 Syrian refugees, of which at least 38 drowned (Davies 2013).

The lack of responsiveness to the fate of migrants and refugees perishing in the Mediterranean is symptomatic of a securitized phenomenon. The concept of national security has aggressive as well as defensive aspects. The threatening discourse to describe migrants takes away their humanity and depicts migration as a natural disaster rather than a normal (and perennial) human activity—mobility. Such dehumanization is commonplace in the construction of enemy images and makes it is easier to detain, deport, and ignore the distress signals of boat migrants.

This hardening of attitudes against irregular migrants is a stark example of the consequences for human rights and humanitarian values of the securitization of migrants. It is also a vivid example of what happens to *forced migrants* once the general category of migration becomes securitized. The UN Refugee Convention relies on the ability and willingness of state officials to distinguish between refugees and asylum seekers (individuals claiming refugee status), on the one hand, and 'ordinary' economic migrants, on the other, based on the *motivations* for their migration. While economic migrants are thought to relocate due to a mix of economic push and pull factors (e.g. unemployment at home and better job opportunities abroad), forced migrants migrate because they believe they have no choice. Furthermore, to fit the definition of 'refugee', the reason for fleeing must be political and man-made, such as war and persecution, not economic or environmental, such as poverty or drought (although the distinction between political and non-political motivations is often difficult to uphold, as when persecution of a minority takes the form of economic repression, making it difficult for the group to survive, or if warfare makes harvest impossible and causes famine).

The crucial distinction, from the point of view of the international refugee protection regime, between the economic 'pull' motives of voluntary migrants and political 'push' motives of forced migrants tends to vanish once the overall phenomenon of migration becomes securitized. It is indeed true that refugees may use the same migration channels as undocumented migrants, since very few legal channels to the North are available through which an asylum seeker can lodge their application. The UN High Commissioner for Refugees (UNHCR) has used the term 'mixed flows' in recognition of this phenomenon, in an attempt to distinguish between refugees' motives for migration (protection from fear) and the way in which they may travel (mixed with 'ordinary' migrants and using irregular routes). The right to seek asylum, the UNHCR admonishes, should not be affected by the legality (or not) of how the asylum seeker travelled to safety (Lubbers 2004).

Despite this intention, the term 'mixed flow' suits a securitizing discourse well. It allows the audience to focus more on the worrying term 'flow' than the ambiguous term 'mixed'. Whether forced or voluntary, or somewhere in between, the Mediterranean boat migrants become conflated in the securitizing discourse into one group whose main characteristic is that it is threatening to the host community. Refugees taking this route are judged by, first, the manner in which they travel (clandestinely and illegally, thus making their journey a criminal act); and, second, by their impact on the host community (which is considered threatening, since they are seen as a part, or the vanguard, of a flood). Thus the refugee is criminalized and securitized through the act of attempting to seek asylum.

AUTOCHTHONY, DISPLACEMENT, AND INSECURITY IN THE KIVUS

The securitization of forced migration is also noticeable in the global South, including in sub-Saharan Africa. The Great Lakes region of Africa, in particular, vividly exemplifies how historical cycles of displacement, counter-displacement, and securitized identity politics lead to intractable conflict between rebel and self-defence groups claiming to represent particular ethnic communities, and who are invariably supported by a selection of local, national, and foreign government backers. As Perera (2012) describes, conflict in the Great Lakes is fuelled by autochthonous tropes, wherein a range of competing ethnic groups assert their claim of being the 'original' inhabitants of the same geographical space and demand control and domination of that space. Myths of migrations of alien 'Nilotic' tribes such as the Tutsi to the Great Lakes region in some distant (and unrecorded) past have cast the Tutsi as foreign invaders pitched against the original 'Bantu' sons of the soil such as the Hutu.

The North and South Kivu provinces of eastern Democratic Republic of Congo (DRC) is a distilled and intensified microcosmos of the inter-communal security dilemmas created by the vicious cycle of autochthonous claims, conflict, and displacement in the Great Lakes. The Kivus have for decades served as a territory where losers of the Hutu-Tutsi conflict could flee and regroup (Mamdani 2001: 234). Placed at the eastern periphery of the vast, dysfunctional DRC (formerly Zaïre), the Kivus host numerous ethnic groups, including the Banyamulenge, Congolese Tutsis who arrived in the Kivus from Rwanda in several refugee waves from the late nineteenth century. Since the aftermath of the Rwandan genocide in 1994, the Kivus have also hosted Rwandan Hutu Power rebel groups, who are embroiled in the local Congolese conflict dynamics while also harbouring dreams of retaking Rwanda from the Tutsi-minority regime of President Paul Kagame and his Rwandan Patriotic Front.

Decades of persecution and marginalization of the Tutsi Banyamulenge in Zaïre/DRC, combined with the more recent influx of Hutu groups, have provided constant fuel for conflict and rebellion in the Kivus. Members of both ethnic groups have been securitized as threats to local stability and national security. The Banyamulenge, stripped during the Mobutu regime of their Congolese citizenship, and viewed as outsiders by other Kivutian ethnic groups, have responded to threats to their existence and belonging by joining numerous rebel movements over the years, including the Rwandan backed rebellion by Laurent Kabila that led to Mobutu's downfall in 1996.

The arrival in the Kivus in 1994 of Hutu Power groups added to the Banyamulenge's sense of existential insecurity, due to their hateful anti-Tutsi ideology and their attacks on Tutsi civilians. Conversely, the Hutu Power groups such as the FDLR (Forces Démocratiques de Libération du Rwanda), have their own sense of existential insecurity, being pursued by Rwandan government, international peacekeeping and, in recent years, Congolese government forces. Fearing for their lives if they return to Rwanda, members of the FDLR perceive their struggle as a matter of survival—as individuals and as a community.

By aiming the spotlight at securitized and exclusionary identities, it becomes easier to understand the protracted and desperate nature of conflict in the Kivus. It also becomes easier to understand the region's chronic displacement cycles. The displacement of populations in the Kivus is sometimes a side-effect of fighting and looting. But it is often, and arguably at heart, the result of various ethnic-based militias claiming exclusive control over the same territory, and with that the monopoly on political power and economic gain that comes with 'ownership' of that territory. Until a way can be found to accommodate the identity security needs of the Kivus' many ethnic communities, including Tutsis and Hutus, the region's cycle of conflict and displacement, where each feeds into the other, will continue. Such a process would have to include the development of a less territorial and exclusionary understanding of ethnic identities.

Inclusive Securitization: Human Security and Protecting the Vulnerable

So far the securitization of migration and displacement has been presented as an unmitigated disaster from the perspective of migrants (and often also for their hosts). Such downwards spiralling insecurity is by no means an inevitable result, but is in line with the analytical assumptions of the Copenhagen School and, particularly, the Foucauldian approach to securitization. Both warn about the exclusive, divisive, and conflict-prone nature of security discourse and practices.

Not all securitization scholars agree with this gloomy view of security politics as a confrontational zero-sum game between us and them, friend and enemy. Instead, they argue, the urgency intrinsic to the concept of security can be utilized to forge strong coalitions of actors to *defuse* security threats in proactive, inclusive, and collaborative ways. Such ideas are inspired by Critical Security Theory (Booth 1991), a normative-theoretical approach that seeks to undermine and eventually overthrow the traditional state-centric and competitive understanding of security. In Booth's words, 'Security is emancipation', or at least it can become so if analysts and activists lay bare the power political and self-serving basis of elites' use of security language.

Critical Security Theory is not so much an empirical research programme as a normative agenda for change (Wyn Jones 1999). As such it has not achieved the mainstream presence within academia that the securitization approach has done. It has nevertheless inspired some securitization scholars and activists to attempt the transformation of security into a more 'people-friendly' and cooperative concept. These theorists agree with the Copenhagen school that securitization is a potent political tool. But they suggest that an issue can be securitized in a positive 'win-win' manner by concentrating minds and bringing people together to find solutions to pressing common problems. Most of this research has focused on environmental politics, for instance on how the presentation of climate change as an existential threat could add urgency to intergovernmental climate negotiations (Beck 1999; Trombetta 2008). But others have attempted, particularly in the 1990s and early 2000s, to present forced migration as *human security* or *common security* problems, in order to convince governments to deal proactively with the root causes of flight and find permanent solutions to refugee problems.

It is this securitization of forced migration as human insecurity that will be discussed here. The concept of human security has been criticized as an all-inclusive vessel containing problems ranging from poverty, unemployment, lack of access to education and healthcare, to war and genocide (Paris 2001). But influential scholars have argued that the concept has more analytical and political value if it is reserved for what Suhrke (1999: 272) describes as 'extremely vulnerable' people: those finding themselves balanced on the edge of calamity and death, whether due to natural or human made threats. Suhrke includes refugees among the extremely vulnerable, as do most human security advocates. Kaldor (2007: 183) describes displacement as a 'typical feature of contemporary crises' and argues that '[p]erhaps the indicator that comes closest to a measure of human security is displaced persons.'

The aim of securitizing forced migration as a human security or common security issue was popular throughout the 1990s, but less an academic endeavour than an activist one. Most empirical studies of the securitization of forced migration have concluded that there is faint possibility of achieving a positive, pro-active, and inclusive securitization of forced migration. At the same time, this literature highlighted the agenda-setting power of successful securitizations. Many activist NGOs, and indeed the UNHCR itself, took interest in the political power of the concept of security in the belief, in accordance with Critical Security Theory, that the status quo can be challenged and the concept of security redefined in a more people-friendly and inclusive manner. The end of the Cold War, the peaceful dismantling of the Berlin Wall, and what looked like a more cooperative spirit among the veto powers of the UN Security Council, raised hopes that the forging of a common international security agenda was a realistic possibility for the post-Cold War period.

For the UNHCR in the early 1990s, hopes were high of convincing states to find permanent solutions to refugee problems and deal with the 'root causes of flight' by elevating displacement to a security matter requiring urgent priority. The UNHCR dramatically reinterpreted its mandate, and began to frame displacement as a security problem which states left to fester at their own and the international community's peril.

The refugee agency attempted to convince donor and refugee host governments that their security interests and those of displaced populations could be aligned (e.g. Ogata 1995, 1997).

The UNHCR had some notable successes with its security discourse (Hammerstad 2011). It transformed into a major humanitarian organization, obtained a frequent voice in Security Council debates, and became a central and visible actor aiding the victims of the many conflicts erupting in the 1990s. Its security discourse, which promoted a combination of human security language and the argument that promoting the security of refugees was in the security self-interest of states, contributed to the trend of securitizing forced migration and thus to placing refugees higher on the political agendas of states.

Despite this, the UNHCR abandoned its security language by the early 2000s, disillusioned by the stubborn quality of the concept of security of reverting to its traditional national security tropes when push comes to shove. The aftermath of the Rwandan genocide was a turning point. The UNHCR argued strongly, in the media, in donor meetings and in the Security Council, that unless the Hutu refugee camps in eastern DRC (then Zaire) were demilitarized and protected, their presence would destabilize the African Great Lakes Region. The UNHCR was correct. The existence of the camps, controlled by Hutu genocidaires, became a rallying point for Congolese rebels and a justification for Rwandan invasion. In 1996 a rebel coalition led by Laurent Kabila, supported by the Rwandan army, overran the refugee camps and went on to take Kinshasa. This sparked what has been called Africa's first world war, embroiling all of Congo's neighbours. The UNHCR drew the lesson that security interests remain selfish: the Security Council powers, whose national security concerns were unaffected by the situation in the Great Lakes, were contented with funding a civilian humanitarian aid operation in the camps. The Rwandan RPF government, on the other hand, viewed the camps as an existential threat, and eventually attacked them, leading to a great loss of refugee lives (Hammerstad 2014: 213–28).

As sentiments turned against asylum seekers in the aftermath of 9/11, the UNHCR distanced itself from any further security discourse. After 9/11, the UNHCR's aim became instead to *desecuritize* forced migration: to take it out of the realm of security politics and practices and return it to the realm of humanitarian and human rights politics. Erika Feller, head of the UNHCR's protection work, urged states 'to de-dramatise and de-politicise the essentially humanitarian challenge of protecting refugees and to promote better understanding of refugees and their right to seek asylum' (UNHCR 2001).

CONCLUSION

Whether focused on the backlash against asylum seekers in the North or violent conflict in ethnically diverse and politically weak states in the South, securitization studies have in common the wish to understand better when, why, and how forced migration can lead to unease, fear, hostility, and even enmity among communities. Most securitization analysts have focused on identity security, and the potential pernicious effects this has on the treatment of 'outsiders' and on inter-group relations. 'The politics of insecurity is…always also a politics of belonging' (Huysmans 2006: 63). The securitization of migration is at heart about the defence of existing communities and their entitlements, against outsiders whose numbers and differentness are seen as an existential threat to communal identity, rights, and privileges.

In contrast to this understanding of the quest for security as almost by necessity leading to the insecurity of others, some scholars have explored the possibility of a 'positive' securitization of forced migration as human security or common security, which reinforces a sense of solidarity with forced migrants and encourages finding solutions to the root causes of displacement. The aim has been to harness the power of the concept of security to forge coalitions and action plans to 'really do something' about the refugee problem. Research conducted so far suggests that the transformation of the concept of security is yet to happen, at least in the case of refugees and asylum seekers. Over the same period that migrants and refugees have become securitized at an unprecedented scale, we have also seen a withering of the international refugee protection regime based on the 1951 UN Refugee Convention. Indeed, the securitization of population movement has contributed to making the plight of forced migrants less visible. Asylum and refugee protection have instead become only one aspect of a range of migration management—and migration reduction—practices. In the case of forced migration, Huysmans (2006: xii) seems right to assert that security knowledge has 'a specific capacity for fabricating and sustaining antagonistic relations between groups of people'. This said, not all securitizations consist of an amorphous sense of 'unease', as when refugee camps become rebel recruitment grounds or mass influxes of refugees lead to cholera epidemics in the host area. The task ahead is not to repress security concerns as illegitimate but to base responses to forced migration on considered analysis rather than alarmist notions of fear and unease.

NOTE

1. See the References for some prominent contributions to this literature.

REFERENCES

Anderson, B. (1991) *Imagined Communities: Reflections on the Origin and Spread of Nationalism*. London: Verso.

Beck, U. (1999) *World Risk Society*. Cambridge: Polity Press.

Bigo, D. (2005) 'From Foreigners to "Abnormal Aliens": How the Faces of the Enemy Have Changed Following September the 11th'. In E. Guild and J. van Selm (eds.), *International Migration and Security: Opportunities and Challenges*. Abingdon: Routledge.

Blake, N. (2003) 'Exclusion from Refugee Protection: Serious Non-political Crimes after 9/11'. *European Journal of Migration and Law* 4(4): 425–47.

Booth, K. (1991) 'Security and Emancipation'. *Review of International Studies* 17(4): 313–26.

Buzan, B. (1991) *People, States and Fear: An Agenda for International Security Studies in the Post-Cold War Era* (2nd edn.). Hemel Hempstead, Hertfordshire: Harvester Wheatsheaf.

Buzan, B., Wæver, O., and de Wilde, J. (1998) *Security: A New Framework for Analysis*. London: Lynne Rienner.

Davies, L. (2013) 'Why Lampedusa Remains an Island of Hope for Migrants'. *The Guardian*, 16 October. <http://www.theguardian.com/world/2013/oct/16/lampedusa-island-of-hope> (accessed 10 December 2013).

Economist (1990) 'The Russians Are Coming'. *The Economist*, 20–6 October.

Hammerstad, A. (2011) 'UNHCR and the Securitization of Forced Migration'. In A. Betts and G. Loescher (eds.), *Refugees in International Relations*. Oxford: Oxford University Press.

Hammerstad, A. (2014) *The Rise and Decline of a Global Security Actor: UNHCR, Refugee Protection and Security*. Oxford: Oxford University Press.

Huysmans, J. (2006) *The Politics of Insecurity: Fear, Migration and Asylum in the EU*. Abingdon: Routledge.

Kaldor, M. (2006) *New and Old Wars: Organized Violence in a Global Era* (2nd edn.). Cambridge: Polity Press.

Kaldor, M. (2007) *Human Security: Reflections on Globalization and Intervention*. Cambridge: Polity Press.

Loescher, G. (1992) *Refugee Movements and International Security*. Adelphi Paper No. 268. London: IISS.

Lubbers, R. (2004) 'Closing Statement by Mr. Ruud Lubbers, United Nations High Commissioner for Refugees, at the Fifty-fifth Session of the Executive Committee of the High Commissioner's Programme (ExCom)'. Geneva, 8 October.

Mamdani, M. (2001) *When Victims Become Killers: Colonialism, Nativism and the Genocide in Rwanda*. Oxford: James Currey.

Newland, K., Patrick, E., Van Selm, J., and Zard, M. (2002) 'Introduction'. *Forced Migration Review*, special issue 13, June.

Ogata, S. (1995) 'Assuring the Security of People: The Humanitarian Challenge of the 21st Century'. Stockholm, 14 June.

Ogata, S. (1997) 'Peace, Security and Humanitarian Action'. London: IISS, 3 April.

Paris, R. (2001) 'Human Security: Paradigm Shift or Hot Air?' *International Security* 26(2): 87–102.

Perera, S. (2012) 'Displacement, Identity and Conflict in the African Great Lakes'. Unpublished Ph.D. thesis, University of Kent, September.

Roberts, A. (1998) 'More Refugees, Less Asylum: A Regime in Transformation'. *Journal of Refugee Studies* 11(4): 375–95.

Smith, H. (2012) 'Greek Crackdown on Illegal Immigrants Leads to Mass Arrests'. *The Guardian*. <http://www.guardian.co.uk/world/2012/aug/07/greece-crackdown-illegal-immigrants-arrest?INTCMP=SRCH> (accessed 7 August 2012).

Spiegel Online International (2011) 'Libyan Crisis: Italy Warns of a New Wave of Immigrants to Europe'. 24 February. <http://www.spiegel.de/international/europe/libyan-crisis-italy-warns-of-a-new-wave-of-immigrants-to-europe-a-747459.html> (accessed 7 November 2012).

Stritzel, H. (2007) 'Towards a Theory of Securitization: Copenhagen and Beyond'. *European Journal of International Relations* 13(3): 357–83.

Stritzel H. (2011) 'Security as Translation: Threats, Discourse, and the Politics of Localization'. *Review of International Studies* 37(5): 2491–517.

Suhrke, A. (1999) 'Human Security and the Interests of States'. *Security Dialogue* 30(3): 265–76.

Telegraph (2011) 'Libya: Up to a Million Refugees Could Pour into Europe'. London, 21 February. <http://www.telegraph.co.uk/news/worldnews/africaandindianocean/libya/8339225/Libya-up-to-a-million-refugees-could-pour-into-Europe.html> (accessed 7 November 2012).

Trombetta, M. J. (2008) 'Environmental Security and Climate Change: Analysing the Discourse'. *Cambridge Review of International Affairs* 21(4): 585–602.

UNHCR (2001) 'Care Urged in Balancing Security and Refugee Protection Needs'. Press release Geneva: UNHCR, 1 October.

Walt, S. (1991) 'The Renaissance of Security Studies'. *International Studies Quarterly* 35: 211–39.

Wyn Jones, R. (1999) *Security, Strategy, and Critical Theory*. London: Lynne Rienner.

Wæver, O., Buzan, B., Kelstrup, M., and Lemaitre, P. (1993) *Identity, Migration and the New Security Agenda in Europe*. London: Pinter.

CHAPTER 22

....

PROTECTION GAPS

....

VOLKER TÜRK AND REBECCA DOWD

INTRODUCTION

FOR it to be effective, the international protection of refugees and other forcibly displaced people requires a solid legal and institutional underpinning, which is reflected primarily in international and regional legal instruments for the protection of refugees, notably the 1951 Convention and 1967 Protocol relating to the Status of Refugees. Effective protection also greatly depends on the genuine commitment of states to implement these instruments, both individually and through international cooperation. At the institutional level, the United Nations High Commissioner for Refugees (UNHCR) was established as the main global refugee institution in the wake of the Second World War. Given the particular character of refugees as people who lack the protection of their own countries, UNHCR was created as the legal entity able to intercede on their behalf, as best illustrated by its supervisory responsibilities in respect of international refugee and statelessness instruments. The effective exercise of UNHCR's mandate both presupposes and is underpinned by the commitment from states to cooperate with it. From the outset, one of the main challenges has been addressing gaps in protection both as regards the legal regime and how it operates in practice.

PROTECTION GAPS AND RESPONSES

Against this background, 'protection gaps' is a term that has generally been used to describe inadequacies in the protection afforded to refugees and other forcibly displaced persons[1] where existing provisions of international law, notably international refugee law, are either not applicable, non-existent, or inadequate in scope, or are not interpreted and/or applied in an appropriate manner. In 1994, UNHCR observed that '[s]ignificant numbers of people who are in need of international protection are outside the effective scope of the principal international instruments for the protection of refugees.'[2] Almost 20 years later, and 60 years after the 1951 Convention was adopted, there are still critical gaps in the 'effective scope' of the international refugee protection regime. The following analysis groups these into three areas: application gaps, implementation gaps and normative gaps, and includes examples of steps taken by the international community to fill them.

APPLICATION GAPS

As noted in UNHCR's 2012 State of the World's Refugees, '[t]he refugee protection system is weakened by its less than universal application.'[3] The most significant application gap early on in refugee law concerned the geographic and temporal limitations contained in the refugee definition of the 1951 Convention. This was filled with the adoption of the 1967 Protocol which removed both limitations. The most apparent gap today lies in the non-applicability of international refugee instruments where a country has either not acceded to them, or maintains reservations to its provisions. One hundred and forty-eight states are currently party to the 1951 Convention and/or its 1967 Protocol. There is significant regional variation in their applicability, with the majority of non-states parties situated in the developing world. Yet this is not necessarily mirrored in the actual provision of protection: in 2011, more than 40 per cent of refugees under UNHCR's mandate were hosted by states that had not acceded to either instrument, notably in Asia and the Middle East.[4]

For decades, UNHCR has periodically encouraged countries to accede to the international and regional refugee instruments and to remove reservations. States have made similar appeals through the United Nations General Assembly,[5] UNHCR's Executive Committee,[6] and in the outcome documents of ministerial-level events organized by UNHCR.[7] Over time, the number of states parties has steadily increased. International and regional human rights law,[8] regional refugee law instruments,[9] and the recognition of the principle of *non-refoulement* as a norm of customary international law by the international community at large have, to some extent at least, helped fill gaps linked to the non-applicability of the international refugee instruments. However, accession to the international refugee instruments or withdrawal of reservations would ensure that these gaps are filled in a comprehensive and predictable manner.

IMPLEMENTATION GAPS

In 1989, UNHCR's Executive Committee adopted a Conclusion specifically on implementation of the 1951 Convention and its 1967 Protocol, which underlined 'again' the need for full and effective implementation and called on states to take 'a positive and humanitarian approach' in a manner fully compatible with their object and purposes.[10] Yet in 2014, significant discrepancies remain in the ways in which states interpret and implement their obligations under the 1951 Convention and 1967 Protocol, both in terms of determining who comes within their scope and the rights and entitlements of recognized refugees. Serious differences can lead to lower standards of protection for fewer people, which can in turn affect asylum flows and cause secondary movements of refugees.

Consistent with the Vienna Convention on the Law of Treaties, the 1951 Convention needs to be interpreted in good faith in accordance with the ordinary meaning of its terms in their context and in light of its object and purpose.[11] The Preamble to the 1951 Convention makes clear its purpose—to ensure that refugees enjoy the widest possible exercise of their fundamental rights and freedoms without discrimination. As is the case with international human rights treaties, the 1951 Convention is a living instrument which 'must be interpreted in light of present-day conditions'.[12] The UK House of Lords, for example, has explained that 'while its meaning does not change over time its application will',[13] noting that '[i]t is clear that the signatory states intended that the Convention should afford continuing protection for refugees in the changing circumstances of the present and future world'.[14] The Supreme Court of Canada has similarly recognized that '[i]nternational conventions must be interpreted in the light of current conditions'.[15] In construing the term 'particular social group', an Australian High Court judge explained that '[i]t would be an error to construe the [refugee] definition so as to ignore the changing circumstances of the world in which the Convention now operates'.[16] A recent New Zealand case also emphasized that the 1951 Convention 'should not be applied in an improperly or overly restrictive manner', noting that it should be given 'a purposive and dynamic interpretation'.[17]

Indeed, over the past 60 years, the 1951 Convention and its 1967 Protocol have afforded refugee protection to people fleeing a wide range of risks and threats in their countries of origin. Examples include draft evaders and deserters, persons who fear persecution by non-state actors,[18] women as members of a particular social group, persons who fear persecution on the grounds of sexual orientation or gender identity,[19] victims of trafficking, and victims of organized gangs. Yet a number of decision makers continue to exploit the ambiguities in the Convention definition, meticulously dissecting its terms and interpreting them narrowly so as to minimize the scope of their protection obligations. Some states, for example, do not accept obligations on grounds not explicitly listed in Article 1A(2) of the Convention, such as gender. A recent study on the 'particular social group' ground concludes that analysis 'has largely become more stringent and presents a greater hurdle for applicants wishing to rely on [this] ground alone'.[20] Another example of divergent and at times restrictive interpretations relates to refugees fleeing armed conflict and the indiscriminate effects of generalized violence. Approaches vary markedly between states that have accepted a wider refugee definition in regional instruments, states parties to the 1951 Convention that interpret its definition broadly to encompass some in this group, states that offer complementary/subsidiary forms of protection to persons fleeing generalized violence, and states that deny any entitlement to international protection to such persons.

Discordant views on different elements of the refugee definition give rise to varying rates of refugee recognition among states, with asylum seekers subjecting their futures to what has been described as an 'asylum lottery'.[21] In relation to Afghan asylum seekers, for example, refugee recognition rates in 2011 among eight European countries ranged from 3 per cent in the Netherlands to 33 per cent in Austria. When other forms of protection such as complementary protection, subsidiary protection, and humanitarian status are included in this equation, the gap is even more drastic, ranging from 11 per cent in Greece to 73 per cent in Sweden.[22] This is despite the ongoing development of a Common European Asylum System, which was set in place to ensure that any person seeking protection in Europe would be treated in the same way irrespective of where they apply. Despite some positive progress towards this goal, a 2010 evaluation of the implementation of the European Qualification Directive found that 'the objective of creating a level playing field with respect to the qualification and status of beneficiaries of international protection and to the content of the protection granted has not been fully achieved during the first phase of harmonization.'[23]

UNHCR strives, pursuant to its supervisory responsibility, to fill implementation gaps relating *inter alia* to interpretation and implementation of the refugee definition. This supervisory responsibility is laid down explicitly in paragraph 8(a) of the UNHCR Statute and is mirrored in Articles 35 and 36 of the 1951 Convention and Article II of the 1967 Protocol. UNHCR is therefore competent *qua* its Statute and international treaty law to supervise all conventions relevant to refugee protection. Moreover, most regional refugee instruments also explicitly establish a link to UNHCR's supervisory function as regards the application of their provisions.[24] In essence, states parties to regional and international refugee instruments undertake to cooperate with UNHCR in the exercise of its functions, and in particular to facilitate its duty of supervising these instruments. In some country operations UNHCR has been directly involved in national status determination procedures and national decision making: at present, UNHCR itself conducts more than 1 in 11 of the world's individual refugee status determinations. UNHCR has also worked closely with the judiciary by providing *amicus curiae* briefs on leading cases, and has set out the Office's legal and protection position through the issuance of Guidelines on International Protection on various aspects of Article 1A(2), or Eligibility Guidelines in respect of particular country situations. In addition, soft law conclusions adopted by UNHCR's Executive Committee serve an important role in providing clarity and building consensus on key aspects of the 1951 Convention, including its definition.

In relation to the implementation of states' obligations towards recognized 1951 Convention refugees, the gaps are manifold, and the quality of protection offered in different parts of the world varies considerably. A number of states parties to the 1951 Convention have not fully incorporated their obligations into domestic law or, where they have, do not always comply with them. A particular gap has arisen in situations where asylum seekers and refugees are deterred from reaching a territory, including when travelling by sea. Measures to deter or prevent the arrival of asylum seekers include tightened entry controls, border closures, restrictive visa requirements, offshore border controls, interception at sea, mandatory detention on immigration grounds with few protection safeguards, and even in some instances push-backs and *refoulement*. Where asylum seekers are able to access the territories of states, they often lack meaningful access to asylum systems due to practical issues such as cost, language barriers, or huge case backlogs, or where decision makers are not sufficiently sensitive to the situation they have fled and/or their particular needs.

Many refugees are unable to enjoy basic rights to documentation, education, and protection against sexual and gender-based violence, particularly in urban settings. There is also often a gap in meeting fundamental needs in areas such as nutrition, access to clean water, and primary healthcare. In addition, the particular protection needs of women, children, older persons, LGBTI individuals, and persons with disabilities are not always adequately responded to. These issues can be linked to the legal framework in place in a given state, which may perpetuate or fail to address certain types of discrimination, to a lack of resources or capacity, and/or to political unwillingness to provide protection and assistance to certain groups. In response, UNHCR and other humanitarian actors often step in operationally, even de facto replacing state structures, both in convention and non-convention states. Activities range from setting up camps, to providing assistance and protection interventions in urban areas, to working on solutions. UNHCR's supervisory role in relation to states' compliance with their international obligations towards refugees and asylum seekers (as well as stateless persons) is an integral part of its core mandate and directly linked to ensuring a principled application of the international protection regime. A direct emanation of this responsibility is, *inter alia*, that UNHCR has prompt and unhindered access to asylum seekers and refugees, wherever they are,[25] and is allowed to supervise their well-being.[26]

Normative Gaps

The extent to which the existing international refugee law framework is capable of responding to the needs of persons forcibly displaced outside a more classic refugee context, is the subject of ongoing debate. As early as 1996, UNHCR's Executive Committee observed that 'the underlying causes of large-scale involuntary population displacements are complex and interrelated and encompass gross violations of human rights, including in armed conflict, poverty and economic disruption, political conflicts, ethnic and inter-communal tensions and environmental degradation, and that there is a need for the international community to address these causes in a concerted and holistic manner.'[27] Forced displacement today is being further impacted by the global economic crisis, the effects of climate change, and large-scale complex emergencies and natural disasters. An increasing number of people are forced to move—more frequently within, but also across, state borders—for a complex mix of reasons. Among them will often be economic migrants in search of a better life, but also persons for whom leaving their country was not a choice, but a necessity. Often, they also travel alongside refugees.

Where persecution is one reason for their displacement, irrespective of others, such persons are entitled to protection under the 1951 Convention. There may also be circumstances in which some persons displaced in the context of climate change, natural disaster, severe deprivation or a combination of these—in the absence of more 'traditional' forms of persecution—may fall within the scope of the 1951 Convention.[28] However, it is well known that even the most flexible and principled application of the Convention will exclude some forcibly displaced persons who may have a legitimate need for protection. The main obstacle to obtaining 1951 Convention protection is the requirement that a claim be linked to one of five grounds, which more often than not precludes its application to claims based on generalized, indiscriminate suffering, or threats that are not human made.

Normative gaps may also emerge in the case of persons whose need for protection arises when they are already outside their country of origin. Stranded migrants, for example, can be vulnerable to abuse, exploitation, and human rights violations/deprivations during their journey and following arrival.[29] They are often left in a situation of 'legal limbo' and have been described as 'fall[ing] into a protection and human rights gap'.[30] The plight of displaced migrant workers has also come into the spotlight following the displacement of hundreds of thousands from Libya to Egypt and Tunisia in 2011. They, too, fall into a 'legal grey zone'.[31]

Various initiatives at the national, regional, and international levels have served to fill a number of normative gaps. In the context of environmental or natural disaster, for example, some national legislation provides for the grant of temporary protected status,[32] stays of removal,[33] subsidiary protection,[34] temporary protection,[35] special temporary residence status,[36] or residence permits.[37] At the regional level, some normative gaps—notably for persons fleeing situations of generalized violence—were filled through the adoption of region-specific instruments, such as the 1969 OAU Refugee Convention in Africa and the 1984 Cartagena Declaration in Latin America. As mentioned, over the last ten years the European Union has also codified a legal framework covering asylum, reception conditions, asylum procedures, and temporary protection applicable to the member states. Existing protections against *refoulement* in regional and international human rights law instruments can protect some persons against return, but do not provide for a right of stay or a legal status, even if only on a temporary basis. Further, the scope of *non-refoulement* in such circumstances is not clearly defined. Specifically in relation to climate change, states have reached agreements[38] and made pledges[39] to *inter alia* improve understanding with regard to climate change and displacement, enhance coordination and cooperation, identify best practices, and work towards a more coherent and consistent approach on how best to assist and protect affected people.

There are also substantive gaps in the 1951 Convention that go beyond its refugee definition. Critically, the Convention is not explicit on admission to territory or access to asylum procedures. In fact, asylum seekers are not explicitly covered by the 1951 Convention, even though some of its most fundamental protections equally apply to them. Further, the 1951 Convention does not include a framework for addressing some of the key protection challenges that have confronted the international community for decades, such as protracted situations, large-scale influxes, maritime protection, or secondary movements of refugees. While the Convention is predicated on international solidarity, there are no agreed parameters for predictable burden and responsibility sharing. This is compounded by the fact that the majority of refugees are situated in countries without the resources to adequately meet their needs. The Convention also does not provide standards for the timely realization of durable solutions. Besides the OAU Convention, there is currently no hard law on voluntary repatriation, local integration, or resettlement.

Such normative gaps have often been addressed in Executive Committee Conclusions[40] and General Assembly resolutions,[41] and also through the adoption of signed documents of a contractual nature or non-signed documents of a declaratory nature. Agreements that are not legally binding per se may still reflect important political commitments of states to act in a predictable manner. Traditionally, special agreements have been used in the context of promoting voluntary repatriation[42] and agreeing on the implementation of its operational modalities. Arrangements have, however, gone beyond this aspect. By way of examples, the final document of the Comprehensive Plan of Action for Indo-Chinese Refugees was agreed upon at an international conference in 1989. While the agreed plan did not contain normative or interpretative guidelines, it established roles and responsibilities on how to address a particular refugee situation. Another example is the CIREFCA process. A 1989 conference agreed on measures to resolve the mass displacements caused by the long-running conflicts in Central America. Following the outbreak of the crisis in the former Yugoslavia, UNHCR convened an international conference in 1992 and presented a comprehensive plan of action that was endorsed by the international community. The document was a policy framework dealing with elements, such as temporary protection and solutions, and proved instrumental in steering the humanitarian response for years. Similarly, a CIS Conference, held in Geneva in May 1996, adopted a Programme of Action covering a broad range of migration and displacement issues resulting from the demise of the Soviet Union.[43]

UNHCR has undertaken a number of high-level initiatives over the years to analyse gaps—application, implementation, and normative—and explore ways to respond. A particularly important process was the Global Consultations on International Protection in 2001–2, which focused on the tools available to the international community and those in need of development, and resulted in the adoption of an Agenda for Protection.[44] In the wake of the Global Consultations, UNHCR launched the Convention Plus initiative in 2003 to promote the development of multilateral agreements to complement the 1951 Convention, which led to the adoption of a Multilateral Framework of Understandings on Resettlement in 2004. Since 2007, the High Commissioner's annual Dialogues on Protection Challenges have provided a forum to discuss both normative and operational gaps, leading mostly to action plans at various levels. In 2011, UNHCR organized a series of expert events[45] in the context of the 60th anniversary of the 1951 Convention, culminating in a Ministerial Meeting at which states made a number of concrete pledges to fill protection gaps.[46]

Way Forward

The 1951 Convention and 1967 Protocol remain the foundation of the international refugee protection regime, as reaffirmed by states on both the 50th and 60th anniversaries of the Convention.[47] However, while these instruments remain an essential governance framework, they do not alone suffice. This, too, has long been recognized. Twenty years ago, UNHCR acknowledged in relation to normative gaps that 'the present system of ad hoc international responses and domestic national arrangements to protect persons in need, but outside any existing international regime, needs to be strengthened.'[48] In 2001, states similarly recognized that the international refugee protection regime should be developed further, as appropriate, and in this connection called on UNHCR to explore areas that would benefit from further standard setting, such as Executive Committee Conclusions or other instruments to be identified at a later stage.[49] In 2011, states again acknowledged the need to deepen their understanding of 'evolving patterns of displacement' and agree upon ways to respond to the challenges they present.[50]

Considerable work has been done in recent years to identify the most pertinent normative and implementation gaps in the international refugee protection regime. The international community now needs to build strong consensus around these gaps, and make a concerted effort to fill them. The identification of good practices at national and regional levels has proven useful, and should continue to inform the way forward. There is also a need to clarify the role of UNHCR and other actors in addressing forms of cross-border displacement that fall outside the scope of the existing international refugee protection framework. Numerous recommendations have been made to address protection gaps, such as the development of a global guiding framework on normative gaps, guiding principles on displacement in the context of natural disasters, a tool to introduce greater predictability and foreseeability to burden and responsibility sharing, temporary or interim protection arrangements, or the strengthening of human rights protection in the context of *non-refoulement* and other refugee rights.

Ultimately, the feasibility of suggestions to fill protection gaps will depend on the commitment of states. However, it is clear that the effectiveness of measures to address protection gaps would be limited if conceived in only abstract, conceptual, and theoretical terms. If such measures are not tied to specific, concrete problems or situations, which elicit a measure of political interest and a willingness to cooperate, their feasibility would be doubtful. It is likely that states would be reluctant to commit themselves to models or mechanisms in the abstract. If at all, these would then remain vague, and thus add little as a tool or to increase predictability of responses.

NOTES

1. Whilst protection gaps do exist in relation to internally displaced persons and stateless people, this chapter focuses on cross-border displacement.
2. UNHCR (1994: para. 68).
3. UNHCR (2012b: 9).
4. UNHCR (2012b: 9).
5. See, for example, General Assembly Resolution 66/133, 19 March 2012.
6. See, for example, UNHCR Executive Committee General Conclusion on International Protection No. 108/2008. In 1986, the Executive Committee adopted Conclusion No. 42 (XXXVI) specifically on accession.
7. Ministerial Communiqué, 8 December 2011, HCR/MINCOMMS/2011/6; Declaration of States Parties, 16 January 2002, HCR/MMSP/2001/09.
8. See, for example, Article 22 of the 1989 UN Convention on the Rights of the Child. See also the 1969 American Convention on Human Rights 'Pact of San José, Costa Rica', 1144 UNTS 123, Article 22(8). Explicit or implicit protections against *refoulement* are included in a number of human rights instruments, including the 1984 Convention Against Torture and Other Cruel, Inhuman or Degrading Treatment or Punishment, the 1966 International Covenant on Civil and Political Rights, and the 1950 European Convention for the Protection of Human Rights and Fundamental Freedoms.
9. See, for example, the OAU Convention Governing Specific Aspects of Refugee Problems in Africa, 1969, 1001 UNTS 45 and the Cartagena Declaration on Refugees, 22 November 1984, Annual Report of the Inter-American Commission on Human Rights, OAS Doc. OEA/Ser.L/V/II.66/doc.10.
10. See UNHCR Executive Committee, Conclusion No. 57 (XL) on Implementation of the 1951 Convention and the 1967 Protocol Relating to the Status of Refugees, 1989.
11. Article 31(1).
12. *Hirsi Jamaa and Others v Italy*, Application no. 27765/09, Council of Europe: European Court of Human Rights, 23 February 2012, para. 175. See also *Tyrer v United Kingdom* (1979–80) 2 EHRR 1, para. 31.
13. *Sepet (FC) and Another (FC) (Appellants) v Secretary of State for the Home Department (Respondent)* [2003] UKHL 15.
14. *R v Secretary of State for the Home Department, Ex p Adan* [2001] 2 AC 477, 500, per Laws LJ. [NB: This is a classic error of citation. The quotation in the text is rightly attributed to Lord Justice Laws (Laws LJ). Laws LJ is not now and was not then a member of the House of Lords; he is a judge in the Court of Appeal. The error arises from the fact that the judgment of the Court of Appeal in the cited case is reproduced in [2001] 2 AC 477 at 481–504; the judgment of the House of Lords itself begins at 507].
15. *Suresh v Canada (Minister of Citizenship and Immigration)* [2002] 1 SCR 3 (Canada), para. 87.
16. *A v Minister for Immigration & Ethnic Affairs* (1997) 190 CLR 225, para. 227.
17. *AC (Syria)*, [2011] NZIPT 800035, New Zealand: Immigration and Protection Tribunal, 27 May 2011, para. 62. See also *Refugee Appeal No 74665* [2005] NZAR 60; [2005] INLR 68 at [56] (RSAA) per Haines QC.
18. Türk 2002.
19. UNHCR, 'The Protection of Lesbian, Gay, Bisexual, Transgender and Intersex Asylum-Seekers and Refugees: Discussion Paper prepared for a UNHCR Roundtable on

Asylum-Seekers and Refugees Seeking Protection on Account of Their Sexual Orientation and Gender Identity', Geneva, Switzerland, 22 September 2010.

20. Foster 2012.

21. See the website of the European Council on Refugees and Exiles <http://www.ecre.org/topics/areas-of-work/protection-in-europe.html>.

22. UNHCR, *Global Trends 2011*, 18 June 2012.

23. European Commission, Report from the Commission to the European Parliament and the Council on the Application of Directive 2004/83/EC of 29 April 2004 on minimum standards for the qualification and status of third country nationals or stateless persons as refugees or as persons who otherwise need international protection and the content of the protection, 16 June 2010.

24. See, for instance, Article VIII of the OAU Convention (n. 9). A reflection of UNHCR's supervisory responsibility can also be found in recommendation (e) of the *1984 Cartagena Declaration* and the *Preamble* to the *1957 Agreement Relating to Refugee Seamen*. Furthermore, European Union law also demonstrates the commitment of its member states to cooperate with UNHCR in the implementation of the international refugee instruments, which extends to UNHCR's supervisory role. For example, Article 78(1) of the Treaty on the Functionings of the European Union stipulates that a common policy on asylum, subsidiary protection, and temporary protection must be in accordance with the 1951 Convention. Further, Declaration 17 to the Final Act of the *1997 Treaty of Amsterdam*, which foresees consultations with UNHCR in the area of harmonization of refugee law and policies, can be seen as a concrete implementation by European Union member states of their responsibility to cooperate with UNHCR. UNHCR is also specifically mentioned in the EU Qualification Directive and the EU Procedures Directive.

25. See also UNHCR Executive Committee Conclusions No. 22(III), 33(h), 72(b), 73(b)(iii), 77(q), 79(p).

26. See UNHCR Executive Committee Conclusions No. 22(III), 48(4)(d).

27. UNHCR Executive Committee Conclusion No. 80 (XLVII) 1996, 'Comprehensive and Regional Approaches within a Protection Framework', Preamble. See also UNHCR, Note on International Protection, 9 September 1991, A/AC.96/777, para. 5, which observes that 'population movements are compelled by persecution, other forms of human rights violation and conflict, but are also caused by natural or ecological disaster, extreme poverty, or by a mix of these reasons'.

28. In relation to climate change, see, for example, UNHCR 2009: 9–10. In relation to economic deprivation, see the UNHCR *Handbook and Guidelines on Procedures and Criteria for Determining Refugee Status under the 1951 Convention and the 1967 Protocol Relating to the Status of Refugees*, as reissued in 2011(<http://www.refworld.org/docid/4f33c8d92.html>), para. 63, and Foster 2007: 13.

29. See Dowd 2008.

30. Global Migration Group, 'Building Partnerships for Identifying, protecting, Assisting and Resolving the Situation of Stranded and Vulnerable Migrants', Background Paper, Session 2, Parallel Working Group B, Practitioners Symposium, Geneva, 27–8 May 2010.

31. K. Koser, 'Migration, Displacement and the Arab Spring: Lessons to Learn', Brookings, 22 March 2012.

32. *Immigration and Nationality Act*, United States of America (last amended March 2010), s. 244(b)(1)(B)(i).

33. *Immigration and Refugee Protection Regulations* (SOR/2002-227), Canada (last amended 10 April 2012), s. 230(1)(b).
34. *Aliens Act*, 2005, Chapter 5, Section 1(2).
35. *Act No. 221/2003 Coll. on Temporary Protection of Aliens of 26 June 2003*, Czech Republic, Articles 2 and 3.
36. *Decree 616/2010—Regulation of Migration Law No. 25.871 and amendments*, Argentina, 6 May 2010, Title II, Chapter I, Article 24(3)(h).
37. *Aliens Act 301/2004*, Finland, s. 88a (323/2009), para. (1).
38. Nansen Conference on Climate Change and Displacement in the 21st Century, Oslo, 6–7 June 2011, Nansen Principles, Principle IX; Outcome of the Ad-Hoc Working Group on Long-Term Cooperative Action under the Convention, Cancún, December 2009.
39. See the pledge made by Norway and Switzerland, and joined by Germany and Mexico. UNHCR, 'Pledges 2011: Ministerial Intergovernmental Event on Refugees and Stateless Persons', Geneva, May 2012.
40. A recent example is UNHCR Executive Committee Conclusion on Protracted Refugee Situations, No. 109 (LXI), 2009.
41. See, for example, UN General Assembly, Declaration on Territorial Asylum, 14 December 1967, A/RES/2312(XXII).
42. A quick review of UNHCR's organizational practice reveals that there have been some 24 special agreements dealing with voluntary repatriation.
43. 'Regional Conference to Address the Problems of Refugees, Displaced Persons, Other Forms of Involuntary Displacement and Returnees in the Countries of the Commonwealth of Independent States and Relevant Neighbouring States', 11 June 1996, CISCONF/1996/5.
44. UNHCR, 'Agenda for Protection' (3rd edn.), October 2003.
45. Documentation from a series of expert events in 2011, on topics such as climate change and displacement and international cooperation, is available at <http://www.unhcr.org/pages/4d22f95f6.html>.
46. See UNHCR, 'Pledges 2011' (n. 39).
47. See n. 7.
48. UNHCR, 'Protection of persons of concern to UNHCR who fall outside the 1951 Convention: a discussion note', EC/1992/SCP/CRP.5, 2 April 1992.
49. Declaration of States Parties (n. 7).
50. Ministerial Communiqué (n. 7).

References

Chairperson's Summary (2011) *The Nansen Conference on Climate Change and Displacement in the 21st Century*. Oslo, 6–7 June.

Dowd, R. (2008) 'Trapped in Transit: The Plight and Human Rights of Stranded Migrants'. *UNHCR New Issues in Refugee Research*. Research paper No. 156, June.

European Commission (2010) *Report from the Commission to the European Parliament and the Council on the Application of Directive 2004/83/EC of 29 April 2004 on minimum standards for the qualification and status of third country nationals or stateless persons as refugees or as persons who otherwise need international protection and the content of the protection.*

European Council on Refugees and Exile (2008) *The Impact of the EU Qualification Directive on International Protection*.

Foster, M. (2007) *International Refugee Law and Socio-Economic Right*. Cambridge: Cambridge University Press.

Foster, M. (2012) *The 'Ground with the Least Clarity': A Comparative Study of Jurisprudential Developments Relating to 'Membership of a Particular Social Group*. Geneva: UNHCR Legal and Protection Policy Research Series.

Global Migration Group (2010) 'Building Partnerships for Identifying, Protecting, Assisting and Resolving the Situation of Stranded and Vulnerable Migrants'. *Practitioners Symposium*, Geneva, 27–8 May 2010.

Türk, V. (2002) 'Non-State Agents of Persecution'. Pp. 95–109 in V. Chetail and V. Gowlland-Debbas (eds.), *Switzerland and the International Protection of Refugees*. The Hague: Kluwer Law International.

UNFCC (2010) 'Report of the Ad Hoc Working Group on Long-term Cooperative Action under the Convention'. *Cancun Climate Change Conference*. Cancún, Mexico, December 2009.

UNHCR (1992a) *Persons covered by the OAU Convention Governing the Specific Aspects of Refugee Problems in Africa and by the Cartagena Declaration on Refugees* (Submitted by the African Group and the Latin American Group), EC/1992/SCP/CRP.6, 6 April.

UNHCR (1992b) *Protection of Persons of Concern to UNHCR who Fall Outside the 1951 Convention: A Discussion Note*. EC/1992/SCP/CRP.5, 2 April.

UNHCR (1994) Note on International Protection, A/AC.96/830, *Executive Committee of the High Commissioner's Programme*, 45th Session, 7 September.

UNHCR (2002) *Declaration of States Parties to the 1951 Convention and or its 1967 Protocol Relating to the Status of Refugees*, HCR/MMSP/2001/09, 16 January, Geneva.

UNHCR (2007) *Asylum in the European Union: A Study of the Implementation of the EC Qualification Directive*.

UNHCR (2009) Forced Displacement in the Context of Climate Change: Challenges for States under International Law, Submission to the 6th Session of the Ad Hoc Working Group on Long-Term Cooperative Action under the Convention, *Cancun Climate Change Conference*, Cancún, Mexico, 20 May.

UNHCR (2010) High Commissioner's Closing Remarks, *Dialogue on Protection Challenges: Protection Gaps and Responses*. Geneva: Palais des Nations, 9 December.

UNHCR (2011) Ministerial Communiqué, HCR/MINCOMMS/2011/6, 8 December, Geneva.

UNHCR (2012a) *Pledges 2011: Ministerial Intergovernmental Event on Refugees and Stateless Persons*. Geneva.

UNHCR (2012b) *The State of the World's Refugees: In Search of Solidarity*. Geneva.

UNHCR (2012c) *Pledges 2012: Ministerial Intergovernmental Event on Refugees and Stateless Persons*. Geneva.

United Nations (2012) *General Assembly Resolution 66/133: Office of the United Nations High Commissioner for Refugees*, 19 March.

CHAPTER 23

··

STATELESSNESS

··

ALICE EDWARDS AND LAURA VAN WAAS[1]

INTRODUCTION

THREE years after the adoption of the 1951 Convention relating to the Status of Refugees (1951 Refugee Convention), the 1954 Convention relating to the Status of Stateless Persons (1954 Stateless Convention) was agreed by a similar Conference of Plenipotentiaries. Initially designed as a protocol to the 1951 Convention, the later Convention became a stand-alone instrument, heralding a parting of the ways for refugees and stateless persons who had previously been seen as two sides of the same problem: an absence of international protection. While less significant for the fate of refugees, who succeeded in retaining the attention of the international community in the decades that followed, this parting was a pivotal moment in the history of the international response to statelessness. For the following four decades, statelessness as an international protection problem was largely neglected, although international legislative efforts in this area continued, including the entry into force of the 1961 Convention on the Reduction of Statelessness (1961 Convention). Several important human rights instruments also incorporated statelessness into relevant provisions on nationality.

Almost 60 years after the adoption of the 1954 Stateless Convention and 50 years after the 1961 Convention, there remain up to 12 million stateless persons worldwide, although the figure could be even higher. Statelessness continues to affect people in all regions, both on an individual basis as the by-product of the regular operation of states' nationality laws and on a large scale as a product of exclusive or discriminatory citizenship policies. Among the larger and more protracted situations of statelessness are the Bidoon in Kuwait, the Rohingya in Myanmar, and people of Haitian descent in the Dominican Republic. Although individual circumstances vary from one state or from one stateless person to another, statelessness generally has a deeply detrimental impact on people's lives. It can obstruct the enjoyment of a wide range of rights, as well as contributing to human insecurity, forced displacement, or conflict. As such, the issue has long been of concern to the international community.

This chapter explores the historical development of the international legal regime for the protection of stateless persons, and the prevention and reduction of statelessness. It looks at the relationship with the closely related international refugee regime, outlines some of the contemporary challenges in the area of statelessness, and comments on a number of promising developments that may pave the way for further progress in this field.

THE 1954 CONVENTION ON THE STATUS OF STATELESS PERSONS

The Ad Hoc Committee on Statelessness and Related Problems, appointed by the UN's Economic and Social Council (ECOSOC) in 1949, was tasked with considering (a) the desirability of a revised and consolidated convention relating to the international status of refugees and stateless persons, and drafting a text if appropriate; and (b) how to eliminate the problem of statelessness.[2] Although refugees and stateless persons were discussed hand in hand during the early debates on a possible treaty, it soon became evident that the problem of refugees was seen as 'acute' and the need for a convention urgently required, whereas the elimination of statelessness was considered a longer-term problem. While there was some concern raised about the separation of the two issues, the Ad Hoc Committee's report to ECOSOC offered the text of a draft refugee convention, while proposing an additional protocol on stateless persons to be drafted subsequently. Such an additional protocol, it was suggested, might extend the application of the Refugee Convention, *mutatis mutandis*, to stateless persons to whom it did not otherwise apply.[3] Measures to eliminate statelessness received even less attention, being dealt with in a Danish proposal of 10 articles to be used as a basis for drafting a convention on the issue (see section below). [4]

In December 1950, the General Assembly decided to convene a Conference of Plenipotentiaries to complete the draft convention relating to the status of refugees *and* the draft protocol on stateless persons,[5] but discussion on the draft protocol was postponed and referred back to the appropriate organs of the UN for further study.[6] Nearly four years later, on 26 April 1954, ECOSOC adopted a Resolution to convene a second Conference of Plenipotentiaries to 'regulate and improve the status of stateless persons by an international agreement'.[7]

The Conference adopted the 1954 Stateless Convention as an independent treaty, rather than as a protocol to the 1951 Refugee Convention. Like the 1951 Refugee Convention, the 1954 Stateless Convention sets out a definition of a stateless person and specifies the rights and duties of such persons. In respect of the definition, Article 1 provides that a stateless person is 'a person who is not considered a national by any State under the operation of its law'. Despite the preceding work of the ILC to deal with the distinctions between de jure and de facto statelessness, and the passionate appeal by the Special Rapporteur Mr Roberto Cordova to include both categories in any instrument (he argued that '*de facto* statelessness is much worse than *de jure* statelessness not only quantitatively but also qualitatively'),[8] the Conference decided only to cover 'de jure' stateless persons. As discussed further herein, this definition requires establishing a negative condition, which can make it particularly complex to apply in practice. Nevertheless, the non-binding Final Act of the Conference called on states parties to accord to persons who have renounced the protection of their nationality for valid reasons (de facto stateless persons) the benefits of the Convention.

It is critical to note that, in the absence of any obligations to grant nationality under international law to stateless persons, the status that they receive under the Convention is to be recognized as 'stateless persons': in other words, their status as a person without a nationality is merely confirmed. Article 32 of the Convention, like Article 34 of the Refugee Convention, does however urge states parties to consider granting nationality to stateless persons.

In other areas, the two treaties also share many like provisions. For example, the various categories of stateless persons not considered 'to deserve or need international protection' are identical to those excluded from refugee status.[9] In terms of rights entitlements, the rights envisaged for stateless persons are nearly identical to those provided to refugees, but lower than had been proposed by the ILC. Two important distinctions are worth highlighting. First, there is no protection from *refoulement* to a threat to life or freedom in the 1954 Convention, and second, there is no protection against penalization for illegal entry or stay. Presumably these rights were omitted as the 'stateless person' in which the Convention was interested was not necessarily outside their country of habitual residence, but rather was seen as requiring the legal remedy of nationality rather than protection. Where a stateless person is also a refugee, he or she will enjoy protection from *refoulement* under the terms of the refugee instrument. A final notable difference is that UNHCR was not assigned supervisory responsibility over stateless persons, although a role for UNHCR has since emerged thanks to the 1961 Convention and subsequent General Assembly resolutions.

One downside to the stateless convention, which stems from its joint history with the refugee convention, is that the overarching principle as regards treatment is that 'Contracting States shall accord to stateless persons the same treatment as is accorded to aliens generally' (Article 7). With regard to a number of rights, such as education and access to courts, a higher standard of treatment is prescribed, but this is the overall bottom line. This does not seem entirely appropriate in all situations, not least where stateless persons may have been arbitrarily deprived of their nationality by their countries of origin, including because of ethnic or gender discrimination. In other words, persons deprived of the nationality by their country of origin or habitual residence would be entitled only to treatment equivalent to aliens in many areas, whether they remain in that country or have moved abroad.

THE 1961 CONVENTION ON THE REDUCTION OF STATELESSNESS

Satisfied that a framework was now in place to meet the protection needs of those who had been left stateless by the Second World War, the international community turned its attention to a second objective: to ensure that, in future, no new cases of statelessness would arise.[10] The idea was to turn the aspiration of Article 15 of the Universal Declaration of Human Rights 1948 into concrete standards for states to incorporate in their nationality laws. In particular, the notion that 'everyone has the right to a nationality' would be further codified in an international convention, through a set of safeguards that indicate which nationality a person is entitled to when he or she would otherwise be stateless.

The necessity of such a convention—and ultimately the underlying cause of statelessness—lay in the fact that 'at the core of sovereignty was the unfettered discretion to set the terms of membership'.[11] In other words, states have traditionally been free to establish their own rules for the acquisition and loss of nationality, in accordance with their own interests and ideology.[12] Where such rules are exclusionary or there is a conflict between the rules of different states, statelessness may result.[13] The function then, of what would become the 1961 Convention on the Reduction of Statelessness, was to agree some restrictions on states' freedom in nationality matters.

It was not the first time that international norms on the regulation of nationality were pursued. Earlier instruments included the Hague Convention on Certain Questions Relating to the Conflict of Nationality Laws and the Protocol Relating to a Certain Case of Statelessness (both adopted in 1930), as well as the Convention on the Nationality of Married Women (1957). Each of these contained some standards that would help to limit the incidence of statelessness, but none provided a rigorous or comprehensive framework for this purpose.

In fact, two draft texts were submitted by the ILC to the General Assembly for its consideration: one focusing on the elimination of future statelessness, the other on reduction. Both provided for the avoidance of statelessness in a variety of conflicts of laws scenarios, but the former proposal elaborated safeguards in rigid, absolute terms, while the latter granted a margin of discretion to states.[14] Governments favoured a more flexible approach and proceeded to discuss the latter text.

The 1961 Convention seeks to prevent statelessness in three basic contexts: acquisition of nationality at birth (Articles 1 to 4); loss, deprivation, or renunciation of nationality in later life (Articles 5 to 9); and regulation of nationality following state succession (Article 10). In each case, the Convention outlines the responsibility of the state(s) concerned by dictating when it must allow the individual to either acquire or retain nationality. The common thread throughout—and what makes it a convention on the reduction of statelessness rather than an instrument for the harmonization of nationality laws—is that the obligations only go into effect where statelessness would otherwise result. For instance, in Article 1, the convention does not compel states to adhere to the *jus soli* doctrine, but it does require them to grant nationality to a child born on their territory *if he or she would otherwise be stateless.*

A drawback of this approach is that the Convention does not comment on the legality of nationality laws. For example, as a general principle the Convention provides that if, as a consequence of any change in the personal status of a person (i.e. marriage, divorce), the law of the contracting state leads to loss of nationality, such loss must be conditional upon the possession or acquisition of another nationality. Likewise, children deprived of nationality owing to discriminatory nationality laws should not be rendered stateless. Yet it does not otherwise make comment on the legality or otherwise of discriminatory nationality laws. In other words, as long as statelessness is avoided in individual cases, it is irrelevant if the national system maintains and perpetuates not only patrilineal nationality laws, but also laws contrary to other areas of international law. The only exception to this general rule about the scope of the 1961 Convention is its Article 9 which does provide for a blanket prohibition of deprivation of nationality on racial, ethnic, religious, or political grounds—a policy that is considered untenable even if statelessness does not result.

Another decision taken in the drafting process that left an even greater mark on the Convention's effectiveness relates to its enforcement machinery. The reference in the ILC draft text to the establishment of a 'tribunal' that would be empowered to rule on the application of the convention's standards was dropped during the deliberations. In the Convention, only a weaker supervisory mechanism remained: an agency that can assist a person claiming the benefit of the convention in presenting his or her claim to the appropriate authority (Article 11). Since the adoption of the instrument, the designated agency has been UNHCR.

Regardless of these, and other, shortcomings, the 1961 Convention, along with the 1954 Convention, remains a key tool for states in their efforts to prevent new cases of statelessness from emerging.

The Main Challenges Confronting Statelessness Today

While international 'statelessness law' shares its origins with international refugee law, there is a sharp contrast in the way the two fields have developed since their inception. The 1951 Convention was quick to gain states' support, accruing the necessary ratifications to enter into force in under three years and it now has close to 150 state parties. Its sister instrument, the 1954 Stateless Convention took double the time to gather enough parties to enter into force and the level of ratification is still only half that of the refugee instrument. The 1961 Convention, meanwhile, took a full twelve years to secure the six ratifications needed for entry into force and to date has less than 55 state parties. Moreover, refugee law has been the subject of research, teaching, and debate, as well as achieving progressive development thanks to expansive jurisprudence. 'Statelessness law', on the other hand, is not even a term in use.

Indeed, the relative dearth of interest that the statelessness instruments—and even the phenomenon itself—suffered has left some serious challenges relating to their interpretation and implementation unmet. The international community's understanding of the problem of statelessness and states' experiences of tackling it lag far behind as compared to refugee issues. With interest in statelessness now on the rise, there are numerous hurdles to be examined and overcome. The following paragraphs briefly present three of these fundamental challenges.

Defining a Stateless Person: The Great 'De Facto'–'De Jure' Debate

Central to the application of any legal standards is agreement about what or who they apply to. Where statelessness is concerned, this most basic of questions has been a matter of ongoing debate. The major sticking point is what obligations exist towards so-called de facto stateless people and when, in fact, a person can be deemed to be de facto stateless. As explained above, those who meet the definition of a stateless person provided by the 1954 convention have commonly been described as de jure stateless. The premiss is that these people are stateless, i.e. hold no nationality, as a matter of law. At the same time, there are others about whom this cannot be concluded, yet who are similarly situated. A widely held view was that 'persons with no effective nationality are, for all practical purposes, stateless, and should be labelled and treated as such'.[15] These individuals have therefore frequently been labelled as de facto stateless.

In spite of the arguments in favour of extending the protection offered to stateless people (de jure) to those whose nationality is ineffective in some way, there is no international legal regime for the de facto stateless. International law does not define the term, nor has there been consistency in the use of the concept by scholars or (international) organizations in their work. The early view was that de facto statelessness referred to persons outside their country of nationality who had been refused diplomatic and consular protection by their state of nationality.[16] The Secretary-General's 1949 *Study of Statelessness* added to the de facto statelessness notion those who have themselves renounced the assistance and protection of their country(ies) of nationality.[17] Later the question of the effectiveness of nationality emerged, partly linked to the two aforementioned formulations, but also taking on broader dimensions. Indeed, it is no easy task to agree on how to measure the effectiveness of nationality and at what point difficulties in effectuating the rights usually associated with nationality tips the balance such as to render a person de facto stateless. In some cases, the meaning of the term has been stretched significantly, even beyond the already problematic notion of an ineffective nationality.

Despite the aforementioned difficulties surrounding the concept, in the scarce literature on statelessness, de facto statelessness has received a disproportionate amount of attention. In contrast, there has been little discussion of the application of the definition of a stateless person that *is* provided by international law and to which rights are attached. Because of the lack of clarity around the notion of de jure statelessness, many commentators and advocates have opted to use de facto statelessness as something of a catch-all category. This has had the unintended consequence of leaving the international legal concept of statelessness (de jure) to be interpreted very narrowly. UNHCR has cautioned that those who qualify as 'stateless persons' under Article 1(1) of the 1954 Convention need to be recognized as such and not mistakenly referred to as de facto stateless persons, otherwise they may fail to receive the protection guaranteed under the 1954 Convention.[18]

Lack of Procedures for the Determination of Statelessness

A closely related challenge is the lack of procedures for the identification of statelessness in most national jurisdictions. This gap is particularly remarkable in those states which have acceded to the 1954 Convention, given that the instrument is virtually identical in aim, style, and content to the 1951 refugee convention. In fact, only a handful of states have developed *statelessness* status determination (SSD) procedures. This presents a serious obstacle for stateless people to access protection and the rights specifically accorded to them under the 1954 Convention. For instance, where stateless people turn up in a migration context, without a dedicated determination procedure, they may be reliant solely on state discretion to grant the right to remain, without necessarily even having their status as a stateless person established. At the same time, gaps in the statistical reporting on statelessness show that, more generally, efforts to identify statelessness are still woefully inadequate. Another problem is that studies or platforms on statelessness tend to adopt their own definition of 'statelessness', and the information is not therefore easy to disaggregate.

There has been little research, to date, into the treatment of stateless people around the globe. For instance, a comprehensive assessment of the implementation of the 1954 convention by state parties remains outstanding, although biennial updates on statelessness are produced by UNHCR. Where studies have been conducted, a causal link has nonetheless been traced between the inadequate provision for the SSD and some serious protection concerns. For instance, mapping projects completed by UNHCR in 2011 conclude that the absence of dedicated SSD procedures has left many stateless people trapped in a hopeless cycle of detention and destitution.[19]

Furthermore, inadequate means for identifying relevant cases can also be highly problematic in the context of the prevention and reduction of statelessness. For instance, in order to guarantee that all children receive a nationality at birth, there must be an opportunity to identify those children whose circumstances—country of birth and nationality or statelessness of parents—would leave them stateless. Similarly, failing to identify a person as stateless will mean that he or she is unable to benefit from facilitated access to naturalization, where a state has established a more favourable naturalization regime for the stateless, in line with Article 32 of the 1954 Convention.

Persistent Gaps and Discrimination in Nationality Laws

Another impediment to the prevention and reduction of statelessness is the persistence of a variety of provisions in states' nationality laws which are known to cause or dramatically heighten the risk of statelessness, or obstruct its resolution. Men and women, for example, have historically enjoyed different treatment in the field of nationality, thanks to a patriarchal view of nationality and the principle of unity of nationality within the family. Policies which exclude particular religious or ethnic communities from accessing nationality were once also commonplace, as states sought to construct or maintain a homogeneous national identity. Some such policies remain in place today, despite international standards relating to non-discrimination, and are contributing to the creation of new cases of statelessness.

In March 2012, UNHCR identified 26 countries where there is still significant gender discrimination in place.[20] It is widely documented that women are particularly disadvantaged in their right to transmit nationality to their children and to a non-national spouse, and likewise may be stripped of their nationality upon marriage or divorce. This can lead to statelessness where children are unable to acquire a nationality from their father—for instance because they are born out of wedlock, in which case it is often difficult or impossible to acquire the father's nationality. It can also prolong statelessness because a stateless man does not enjoy facilitated access to nationality through marriage to a citizen—whereas a stateless woman often does in the reverse scenario. Likewise, women marrying men in another country can have their nationality automatically removed without acquiring the nationality of their husband, as their husband's country may require additional conditions to nationality acquisition, such as a certain period of residence in the country. Statelessness has similarly arisen or become firmly entrenched where racial or religious discrimination has not been addressed in a state's nationality laws, or where nationality laws are applied in a discriminatory way to deprive or prevent persons from obtaining nationality. Minority groups are especially vulnerable to exclusionary policies of denial or deprivation of nationality, which can be exacerbated in the context of conflict or state succession.

Besides these troubling forms of discrimination, nationality laws can exhibit other flaws that contribute to statelessness. Indeed, few countries have watertight guarantees in place to prevent statelessness from arising within their jurisdiction. Many states have yet to adopt the safeguards designed under international law to ensure that all children acquire a nationality at birth or that no one becomes stateless in later life due to loss, deprivation, or renunciation of their only nationality. Moreover, as mentioned, even

the 1961 Convention, in which the most important such safeguards have been codified, admits that these are not absolute and the number of new cases of statelessness
will therefore be reduced rather than eradicated completely. Today, with fresh concern
about the protection of national security, some states are making it easier to withdraw
nationality or rediscovering long-forgotten powers to do so, with the risk of an increase
in statelessness cases. Naturalization policies in many states are also tightening, including through the introduction of more complex integration requirements and related
tests, meaning that the resolution of existing cases of statelessness is becoming more of
a challenge.

Future Opportunities?

The foregoing paragraphs paint a somewhat bleak picture and there is clearly some way
to go if statelessness is to achieve a fully effective response. Yet, the past decades—and
the last several years in particular—have seen numerous developments which are cause
for optimism. Most significant among these is the emerging role of human rights law in
both protecting the rights of stateless people and promoting the avoidance of statelessness. Both the 1954 and 1961 statelessness conventions, which are themselves steadily
attracting accessions, now sit within a broader framework of international legal standards relevant to statelessness. This means that both interest in and obligations towards
the problem of statelessness extend far beyond the borders of the state parties to the two
dedicated conventions. Statelessness has become a truly global concern and the human
rights system provides an invaluable complementary regime for tackling the issue.

To begin with, there has been significant effort to settle the de jure–de facto debate.
UNHCR has drafted guidelines on the definitional and other questions, a first step
towards the creation of a much needed handbook for understanding international
'statelessness law'. This new guidance should therefore help to facilitate implementation
of the relevant standards, reduce possible protection gaps, and lay the great de jure–de
facto debate to rest.

A second set of UNHCR statelessness guidelines aim to assist states in applying the
definition in practice, in particular on SSD procedures.

Finally, with regards to the aforementioned incidences of discrimination or gaps
in nationality laws that can cause or prolong statelessness, there are some especially
encouraging developments. First, although it was noted that the 1961 Convention has
attracted only a limited number of state parties to date, the solutions it prescribes enjoy
wider acceptance. They have been adopted by many more countries as a simple and pragmatic answer to certain conflicts of laws situations that would otherwise lead to statelessness. Second, thanks to the recognition of the right to a nationality as a human right,
the issue can and has been pursued before various human rights bodies. Furthermore,
such discrimination in nationality law is also becoming increasingly uncommon as key
reforms are passed in a number of countries. Last, over the same period, a number of

states made a dramatic effort to resolve previously large-scale and protracted situations of statelessness within their jurisdiction, demonstrating that it is possible to act decisively to restore the enjoyment of a nationality and stop statelessness in its tracks.

NOTES

1. The views expressed in this chapter are those of the authors and do not necessarily reflect those of the UN or the UNHCR. The authors would like to thank Mairead de Faoite for her help with final editing.
2. Economic and Social Council (ECOSOC), Resolution 248 (IX) B, 8 August 1949.
3. Report of the Ad Hoc Committee on Refugees and Stateless Persons, 16 January to 16 February 1950, E/AC.32/8; E/1850, annex III, available at: <http://www.unhcr.org/refworld/publisher,AHCRSP,,,3ae68c248,0.html>.
4. Report of the Ad Hoc Committee on Refugees and Stateless Persons, annex V. For more on the historical background, see Goodwin-Gill (2010).
5. General Assembly, Resolution 429(V), 14 December 1950 (The draft protocol on stateless persons appears in the report of the Ad Hoc Committee on Refugees and Stateless Persons, 14 to 25 August 1950, E/AC.32/8/;E/1850/, annex II; the Committee had been renamed in the interim).
6. See the resolution in para. III of the Final Act of the Conference of Plenipotentiaries on the Status of Refugees and Stateless Persons, 25 July 1951, A/CONF.2/108/Rev.1, available at: <http://www.unhcr.org/refworld/docid/40a8a7394.html>.
7. ECOSOC, Resolution 526 A (XVII), 26 April 1964.
8. International Law Commission (1954a) at 37.
9. Articles 1D, 1E, and 1F of the 1951 Refugee Convention and Article 1 of the 1954 Stateless Convention exclude from their protection those persons presently receiving protection or assistance from United Nations agencies other than the UNHCR, those enjoying in fact the rights and obligations of citizenship in their country of residence, and war criminals, serious non-political criminals, and similar cases.
10. See UN General Assembly, Resolution 319 (IV): Provisions for the functioning of the High Commissioner's Office for Refugees, 3 December 1949, available at: <http://www.unhcr.org/3ae69ef54.html>.
11. Spiro (2011).
12. See, for instance, Permanent Court of International Justice, *Advisory Opinion No. 4: Nationality Decrees Issued in Tunis and Morocco*, 7 February 1923, 24.
13. A commonly cited example of a conflict of nationality laws is where *jus soli* and *jus sanguinis* legal regimes collide. Thus, if a child is born to parents whose country of nationality grants citizenship to all children born on state territory (*jus soli*), but the child is born abroad in the territory of a state that grants nationality based on parental lineage (*jus sanguinis*), there is a negative conflict of laws that leaves the child stateless. In the opposite scenario, there is a positive conflict of laws that can result in dual nationality.
14. The full text of the two drafts can be found in International Law Commission 1954b.
15. Weissbrodt and Collins (2006).
16. Intergovernmental Committee on Refugees, 'Statelessness and its Causes: An Outline', March 1946, at 2, cited in Massey (2010).
17. United Nations Department of Social Affairs (1949).

18. UNHCR (2012a: para. 8).
19. UNHCR (2011a); UNHCR (2011b).
20. UNHCR (2012d).

References

Bauböck, R., and Wallace Goodman, S. (2010) *Naturalisation*. EUDO Citizenship Policy Brief No. 2.

Edwards, A. (2009) *Displacement, Statelessness and Questions of Gender Discrimination under the Convention on the Elimination of All Forms of Discrimination Against Women*. UNHCR Legal and Protection Policy Research Series.

Edwards, A., and van Waas, L. (eds.) (forthcoming) *Nationality and Statelessness under International Law*. Cambridge: Cambridge University Press.

De Groot, G., Vink, V., and Honohan, I. (2010) *Loss of Citizenship*. EUDO Citizenship Policy Brief No. 3.

Goodwin-Gill, G. S. (2010) *Convention Relating to the Status of Stateless Persons*. United Nations Audiovisual Library of International Law. <http://untreaty.un.org/cod/avl/pdf/ha/cssp/cssp_e.pdf>.

International Law Commission (1954a) 'Nationality, including Statelessness: Third Report on the Elimination or Reduction of Statelessness'. Report by Roberto Cordova, Special Rapporteur. A/CN.4/81. <http://untreaty.un.org/ilc/documentation/english/a_cn4_81_corr1.pdf>.

International Law Commission (1954b) *Report of the International Law Commission Covering the Work of its Sixth Session*. A/2693. <http://untreaty.un.org/ilc/reports/english/a_cn4_88.pdf>.

Massey, J. (2010) 'UNHCR and De Facto Statelessness'. UNHCR Legal and Protection Policy Series. <http://www.unhcr.org/refworld/pdfid/4bbf387d2.pdf>.

Spiro, P. (2011) 'A New International Law of Citizenship?' *American Journal of International Law* 105: 694–746.

UNHCR (2010/2011) 'Expert Meeting Conclusions on Statelessness (Prato, Geneva, Dakar): Statelessness Special Features in Refworld' <http://www.unhcr.org/refworld/statelessness.html>.

UNHCR (2011a) *Mapping Statelessness in the United Kingdom*. 22 November. <http://www.unhcr.org/refworld/docid/4ecb6a192.html>.

UNHCR (2011b) *Mapping Statelessness in the Netherlands*. November. <http://www.unhcr.org/refworld/docid/4eef65da2.html>.

UNHCR (2012a) 'Guidelines on Statelessness No. 1: The Definition of "Stateless Person" in Article 1(1) of the 1954 Convention Relating to the Status of Stateless Persons'. 20 February, HCR/GS/12/01.

UNHCR (2012b) 'Guidelines on Statelessness No. 2: Procedures for Determining whether an Individual is a Stateless Person'. 5 April, HCR/GS/12/02.

UNHCR (2012c) 'Guidelines on Statelessness No. 3: The Status of Stateless Persons at the National Level'. 17 July, HRC/GS/12/03.

UNHCR (2012d) 'Background Note on Gender Equality, Nationality Laws and Statelessness'. 8 March.

United Nations Department of Social Affairs (1949) *A Study of Statelessness*. Lake Success, NY. August, E/1112; E/1112/Add.1.

Van Waas, L. (2008) *Nationality Matters: Statelessness under International Law*. Antwerp: Intersentia.

Weis, P. (1962) 'The United Nations Convention on the Reduction of Statelessness, 1961'. *International and Comparative Law Quarterly* 11: 1073–96.

Weissbrodt, D., and Collins, C. (2006) 'The Human Rights of Stateless Persons'. *Human Rights Quarterly* 28: 245–76.

CHAPTER 24

HUMANITARIAN REFORM: FROM COORDINATION TO CLUSTERS

SIMON RUSSELL AND VICKY TENNANT

INTRODUCTION

THE emergence of internal displacement as a focus of international concern in the 1990s was accompanied by a debate on the most appropriate institutional arrangements for addressing the needs of internally displaced persons. A decade later, the Humanitarian Response Review identified several persistent shortcomings in the preparedness and response capacity of humanitarian agencies. The most significant was in protection of IDPs, particularly in situations like Darfur where the government itself was responsible for grave abuses.

This chapter analyses the changes in the architecture for addressing internal displacement brought about by the Humanitarian Reform process initiated in 2005, and its subsequent evolution. It reviews ongoing debates about institutional mandates and responsibilities and examines its implementation in practice, drawing on field experience and recent evaluations of operations where elements of the reform have been applied.

BACKGROUND

In the decade following the creation of a Representative of the Secretary-General (RSG) on IDPs in 1992, several measures were undertaken to address the need for a more effective and coordinated humanitarian response to internal displacement, including the designation of the Emergency Relief Coordinator as the UN 'reference point' for IDPs, and the establishment in 2002 of an Internal Displacement Unit (later the Inter-Agency Internal Displacement Division) within UNOCHA (Turton 2011).

Despite these measures significant gaps persisted, and in 2005 a multi-donor review concluded that the humanitarian system had failed to adequately address a 'continuing and substantial deficit' in the protection of IDPs (Borton et al. 2005). A key question was where in the UN system responsibility for addressing the humanitarian consequences of internal displacement should be placed. Should this take the form of a framework for collaboration, shaped at country level by the presence and capacity of agencies on the ground, or was a more predictable model needed, with defined responsibilities at global level? Should the primary responsibility be assigned to a single agency, either by transforming UNHCR into a 'UN High Commissioner for Forced Migrants' (Martin et al. 2005), or by establishing a new organization specifically for this purpose (Crisp 2009)?

Views on the appropriate parameters of UNHCR's role with IDPs were, and continue to be, divergent. Beginning in 1972, the Office increasingly became involved with IDPs, particularly alongside its role supporting the voluntary repatriation of refugees. In the 1990s its presence in the Balkans and elsewhere expanded in tandem with an increasing focus on in-country protection and assistance (Lanz 2008). At the same time, the rapid increase in the number of IDPs after the Cold War led to the view that events taking place inside a country were a legitimate matter of international concern and put pressure on UNHCR to assume greater responsibility for IDPs.

The suggestion that UNHCR should assume global responsibility for IDPs not only elicited strong opposition from other UN agencies but also a range of both practical and principled concerns from UNHCR. These included the fear that such added responsibility would overwhelm UNHCR's operational capacity; the potential to undermine the right to asylum by engagement in IDP situations; the challenge to state sovereignty implied by granting a formal IDP mandate to one agency; and the potential impact on UNHCR's refugee operations by engagement in politically sensitive IDP situations (Merheb et al. 2006; Lanz 2008; Betts 2009; Crisp 2009). As a result, UNHCR's role with IDPs remained 'inconsistent and unpredictable' (Mattar 2005).

Consequently, the 'collaborative approach' was developed under the auspices of the ERC and OCHA, under which a broad range of actors would work together to respond to the needs of IDPs based on their mandates and experience. It, however, proved unable to generate the level of leadership, predictability, and accountability required to ensure a systematic and effective humanitarian response.

Humanitarian Reform

The failure of the collaborative approach led to a decision by the ERC to commission a comprehensive review of the response system. The Humanitarian Response Review of August 2005 found major shortcomings in humanitarian preparedness and response, finding that 'as a sector, protection requires special and urgent attention'. Its recommendations focused on three key areas: humanitarian leadership, funding, and coordination. These became the three initial pillars of the Humanitarian Reform process, later joined by partnership, linked to the development of the Global Humanitarian Platform Principles of Partnership.

A key component of the reform was the adoption of the 'cluster approach', adopted by the Inter-Agency Standing Committee in September 2005, as a means of bringing together relevant humanitarian actors (including the UN, Red Cross/Red Crescent movement, NGOs and governments) at global and (where needed) at country levels to address gaps in seven key areas: nutrition, health, water/sanitation, emergency shelter, camp coordination and camp management, protection, and early recovery, each with a designated 'cluster lead'. Two additional 'service' clusters were established, for logistics and emergency telecommunications (IASC 2006). Clusters were also subsequently created for food security and education, bringing the total to eleven.

The stated aim of the cluster approach was to strengthen humanitarian preparedness and response by ensuring predictable leadership, accountability, and partnership in sectors in which these had hitherto been lacking, under the overall leadership of the ERC at global level and the Humanitarian Coordinator at country level. The cluster approach was introduced in parallel with measures to strengthen the Humanitarian Coordinator system and to improve the timeliness and adequacy of humanitarian funding, including through the Central Emergency Relief Fund (CERF).

UNHCR was designated as global cluster lead for protection, and co-lead of the emergency shelter and camp coordination/camp management clusters. At country level, the agency was designated as cluster lead in situations involving conflict induced internal displacement, but not (as a general rule) in natural disasters. Country-level leadership of the protection cluster in natural disasters and in complex emergencies without significant displacement was to be agreed case-by-case through consultation between UNICEF, the Office of the High Commissioner for Human Rights (OHCHR) and UNHCR (IASC 2006). A central element of the cluster approach is the concept of 'provider of last resort' by which cluster leads are committed to do their utmost to ensure an adequate response, stepping in to fill gaps if necessary.

Two important stakeholders opted to remain outside the cluster system. Médecins Sans Frontières (MSF) in a policy paper in April 2007 challenged what it termed 'political' strategies of coordination and integration of humanitarian actors in a global framework in which humanitarian action was structurally subordinated to political strategies (MSF 2007).

ICRC also determined that it would not become a cluster lead or a cluster member, as this would entail accountability to the UN system, and would therefore be inconsistent with its mandate. It nevertheless affirmed its commitment to coordinating 'with' (as opposed to being coordinated 'by') a range of UN and non-UN actors, including global and country level cluster leads, with the aim of ensuring effective operational complementarity and an improved response (ICRC 2006).

Whilst the gaps identified in relation to the humanitarian response to internal displacement were a key driving force behind the establishment of the cluster approach, the 2006 Guidance Note was clear that the new model was not designed for internal displacement crises only. It nonetheless aimed at achieving a 'significant improvement in the quality, level and predictability' of the response to IDP crises and was conceived as representing a 'substantial strengthening of the collaborative response' (IASC 2006).

Overall Impact of the Cluster Approach

An early series of evaluations and reviews sought to capture some initial lessons from the rollout of the cluster approach. In 2007, UNHCR undertook a series of real-time evaluations of the impact of the cluster approach in its own operations, and the first report of a two-phase evaluation commissioned by the IASC (Cluster Evaluation I) was published in late 2007. Despite concerns about the rapid roll-out of the cluster approach, which was viewed by some as having been imposed with little consultation beyond the UN system, and a degree of confusion around the concept and its objectives, early assessments were cautiously positive (Stoddard et al. 2007).

The Cluster Evaluation I concluded that the cluster approach provided more pre-dictability, professionalism, and automaticity in a system 'long characterised by volunteerism and best effort'. It stated that 'short of more radical reform and consolidation of the UN agency structure to create a single line of management and accountability through the Humanitarian Coordinator, a strengthened and fully realised cluster approach would seem to be the most promising avenue'.

UNHCR's own evaluations also found that the cluster approach had resulted in a number of positive outcomes, including fostering a common strategic vision at country level, clarifying roles and responsibilities, strengthening resource mobilization, and improvements in coordination (UNHCR 2007b).

A review of NGO engagement with the humanitarian reform process, completed in 2010, highlighted significant gaps in humanitarian leadership, which (it argued) undermined the other components of the reform. Overall, it found that progress had been 'patchy', and that despite some improvements (for example, NGOs acting as cluster co-leads in some operations), NGOs were still not regarded as equal partners, and did not view the system as sufficiently accountable to crisis-affected communities. National and local NGO engagement was particularly weak, and the clusters were assessed as having failed to ensure appropriate linkages with national authorities, whilst preserving the neutrality, impartiality, and independence of humanitarian action (Street et al. 2009).

The Cluster Evaluation II, also concluded in 2010, found that with additional efforts the approach had significant potential for further improving humanitarian response, with a direct impact on affected populations. Conversely, the cluster approach was found largely to exclude local and national actors, on occasion to threaten humanitarian principles, and to be susceptible to becoming process rather than action oriented (Steets et al. 2010).

Subsequent analysis, such as the *State of the Humanitarian System* (SOHS) report, published in July 2012, has tended to confirm that the cluster approach has contributed to some tangible progress towards more systematic, better coordinated, and more predictable humanitarian engagement in new and protracted emergencies, but that significant problems persist as a result of insufficient funding and political and security-related access challenges (Taylor et al. 2012). Several commentators have noted that in an increasingly competitive humanitarian environment there is an inherent tension between coordination based on essentially voluntary arrangements and the drive to retain autonomy by individual agencies.

IMPACT ON THE PROTECTION OF IDPs

UNHCR's Role

A significant consequence of the cluster approach was the systematization of UNHCR's leadership role on protection, reflected in a new strategy developed through consultations with UNHCR's Executive Committee and formally presented in June 2007. Entitled '*UNHCR's role in support of an enhanced humanitarian response to situations of internal displacement*', it committed UNHCR to becoming a 'predictable and reliable partner in efforts to address and resolve the plight of [IDPs]' (UNHCR 2007a).

Consequently, the scope of UNHCR's engagement with IDPs significantly increased. The number of IDPs 'of concern' to UNHCR had hovered between 4 and 6 million between 1995 and 2004. By the end of 2005, when the cluster approach was introduced, it was 6.6 million. By 2007 that number had jumped to 13.7 million, and in 2011 it was 15.5 million—just over half the number of those internally displaced by conflict and violence that year (UNHCR 2005, 2007c, 2011c; IDMC 2012). By 2011, of the 28 protection clusters activated globally, 20 were led by UNHCR, and the agency was engaged with IDPs in 31 countries (UNHCR 2011).

The expansion of UNHCR's engagement was also visible in operations where it had previously not had significant or systematic IDP programmes, such as in Somalia, northern Uganda, and the DRC. In Uganda the activation of the cluster approach significantly changed the way humanitarian business was conducted and protection operationalized. The protection cluster's focus on freedom of movement of the IDPs rather than long-term assistance in camps eventually led to a situation where the vast majority returned to their homes (Crisp et al. 2007).

Criticisms of the agency's role have nonetheless continued. One view is that the agency has not only expanded too far in a bid to avoid irrelevance, but has done so at the expense of its 'core' mandate (Betts 2009). Others—in particular NGOs—have argued that UNHCR's commitment to IDPs is still insufficiently embedded within the organization, and that refugees are still seen as the priority.

Role of the Protection Cluster

The Cluster Evaluation I identified a number of areas in which tangible progress in protection had been made, and noted the increased presence and leadership of UNHCR in several IDP operations. It nonetheless highlighted that the cluster faced significant challenges in securing a common vision of the concept of protection and achieving a cohesive approach. While agencies with specific expertise had undertaken to act as focal points for thematic areas: child protection (UNICEF), gender-based violence (UNFPA/UNICEF), land, housing, and property (UN-Habitat), and mine action (UNMAS), the evaluation noted the need to avoid an atomized response, in which the protection cluster becomes fragmented into 'silos', and noted that more needed to be done to articulate expectations of the focal point roles.

Despite the work of the Global Protection Cluster Working Group to secure a common understanding of the concept of protection, based on the definition adopted by the IASC in 1999, disagreements about how this should be operationalized, and how priorities should be determined, have often resulted in field-level strategies shaped by the mandates and work plans of participating partners rather than on the basis of context-driven needs assessments.

The operational impact of a fragmented protection response can be significant. As an example, in Nepal, the protection cluster's contingency plans for a mega-disaster in 2002 consisted of four documents, running to over 140 pages. There is also often a lack of general agreement among protection actors that the focus should always be on acute protection concerns rather than chronic human rights/development problems.

Despite these challenges, considerable efforts have been made to raise standards and there is now a multiplicity of guidance on various aspects of protection. As far back as 2007 the UNHCR Director of International Protection noted that 'the challenge for the cluster now is to link these tools and knowledge to actual field operations. The "predicament" of the cluster is that it is still seen as something distant and separated from field operations.'[1] There is a risk that the production of tools and guidance materials becomes a headquarters-based 'cottage industry' and that these are not effectively disseminated to the field.

At field level, the work of the protection clusters has focused on three elements: first, the delivery of goods and services which have a specific and measurable protection outcome, e.g. mine action, legal aid to restore property, the removal of children from armed groups and their reintegration; and second, protection 'mainstreaming', ensuring that interventions in other sectors take into account vulnerability and the different needs of beneficiaries taking into account their age, gender, and diversity. A third aspect is the gathering and analysis of information, through IDP profiling, conflict analysis, protection monitoring, and vulnerability mapping, on which evidence-based programming and advocacy can then be based.

Funding shortfalls are also a serious constraint. The SOHS report noted with concern the persistent underfunding of protection as compared with other sectors (only 43 per cent of stated needs were covered in 2009–10). Even the Central Emergency Response Fund, intended to cover gaps in funding, allocated no funds to protection in its $128 million allocation to the Horn of Africa in 2011 (UNOCHA 2011).

Relevance of the 'IDP' Category

The evolution of the cluster approach has been accompanied by a debate on the validity of the IDP 'category' as an adequate and useful approach. A number of NGOs and analysts have argued that whilst displacement may be an indicator of increased vulnerability, and may often entail specific protection risks, the 'status-based' approach entailed by an operational focus on IDPs amounts to privileging them at the expense of others whose needs may be less visible, but even more acute (Turton 2011; Ferris 2011). The ICRC also approaches internal displacement as part of a broader approach to the civilian population as a whole, and has raised concerns that segmenting the humanitarian response and splitting beneficiaries into categories risks overlooking the needs of those most at risk (ICRC 2006).

There has consequently been a shift from a primary focus on IDPs to broader protection issues affecting populations in conflict and natural disasters, in which displacement is one among a range of problems. This has also been linked to an increased focus on the concept of 'protection of civilians' at a global level (United Nations 2009; Stensland and Sending 2011). Indeed, the protection of civilians has become the main priority of the majority of clusters in the field, with some notable successes. For example, in Afghanistan the protection cluster adopted protection of civilians as its sole objective and, with the monitoring, analysis, and reporting of UNAMA, advocated successfully for changes in ISAF tactical directives[2] to prioritize the protection of civilians in ISAF operations, leading to a decrease in the number of deaths attributable to pro-government forces (UNAMA 2008).

REMAINING CHALLENGES

Engagement with National Actors and Non-traditional Partners

Reviews of the cluster approach have consistently found that engagement with national and local actors is insufficient. The Cluster Evaluation II was particularly critical, noting that the cluster approach risked taking away a sense of responsibility from the government and undermining existing local capacity. The challenges in interfacing with pre-existing capacity were demonstrated in practice in the activation of the cluster approach in Kenya in 2008 after disputed presidential elections triggered a wave of violence concentrated in the Rift Valley, which displaced some 600,000 people. The protection and camp management responsibilities assigned to UNHCR were quickly challenged by the highly capable Kenya Red Cross, which felt no need to coordinate its actions with newly arrived international agencies.

There are nonetheless also some positive examples of progress in engaging national actors. For example, whilst the clusters established in Myanmar after Cyclone Nargis were initially run in an 'isolationist manner', a year into the response, significant improvements had been noted with regard to engagement with both the government and other local actors. Language is highly relevant: in the Haiti earthquake response, meetings were held in English or French, but not in Haitian Creole. Conversely, in Myanmar, the protection cluster provided translation into Burmese, and in Yemen, the protection cluster includes more local NGOs than international ones, and works in Arabic.

A key consequence of the lack of inclusion of national and other actors is that situation analysis is often poor and the role and impact of international agencies overemphasized. As one recent study shows, in practice it is communities who ensure their own protection, and from their perspective, the contribution of international actors to their protection is rarely the most significant (South 2012).

The engagement of international humanitarian actors other than traditional partners is also limited. For example, the Emirati and Turkish Red Crescent Societies regularly provide relief to populations in conflict settings but are rarely included in cluster priority-setting exercises and often work to different standards, with consequences for the entire humanitarian operation.[3]

Engagement with Integrated UN Missions and non-UN Military Actors

The humanitarian reform process evolved in the context of a broader drive towards 'coherence' within the UN system, rooted in the 1997 report of the Secretary-General—*Renewing the United Nations—A Programme for Reform*. This was built upon by the Brahimi Report (2000), which laid the basis of the 'integrated approach' now applied in conflict and post-conflict settings where a multidimensional UN peacekeeping or political mission is deployed; the Humanitarian Response Review (2005) in relation to UN (and non-UN) humanitarian agencies, and the High-Level Panel on System-Wide Coherence 2006, which laid the basis for the 'Delivering As One' approach.

At the same time, governments have increasingly embraced 'stabilization' approaches to their engagement in fragile states and complex emergencies, combining military, humanitarian, political, and economic instruments with the aim of bringing 'stability' to such areas (Collinson et al. 2010). In certain countries, such as Afghanistan, there may be close links between an integrated UN mission (there, UNAMA) and an international military engagement (NATO) shaped by stabilization doctrine. The protection of civilians is an increasingly important component both of the mandates of UN missions, and stabilization objectives, and as such, some degree of coordination between humanitarian actors and these entities becomes critical.

Nonetheless, there is a pervasive uneasiness amongst humanitarians about such engagement. A study completed in 2011 found that in 'high-risk environments' much greater caution is called for in establishing integrated arrangements which structurally subsume and/or very visibly link humanitarian actors to a political or peacekeeping mission (Metcalfe et al. 2011).

In some operations, UN missions have played a direct role in the cluster approach. In Afghanistan and the DRC, missions have played a direct role as protection cluster co-lead. Conversely, in South Sudan, UNMIS was rarely engaged with the protection cluster. The involvement of peacekeeping and political missions in the work of the clusters remains controversial, but arguably, this tension between the political and military and the humanitarian needs to be overcome if action to promote protection of civilians is to advance.

Protection Cluster Leadership in Natural Disasters

As noted above, no systematic arrangement was reached in relation to country-level protection cluster leadership in natural disaster situations. Instead, it was agreed that this would be determined on a case-by-case basis in consultation between UNICEF, OHCHR, and UNHCR, under the leadership of the Humanitarian Coordinator. A review commissioned by UNHCR in 2010 found that of 58 natural disasters in the preceding five-year period, UNHCR had an operational involvement in 13 and supported another five (Deschamp 2010). The lack of predictability inherent in these arrangements has attracted significant criticism (Cohen 2008) particularly if, as expected, the size and frequency of sudden-onset natural disasters increases as a consequence of climate change (Ferris 2011).

In 2009, the High Commissioner told UNHCR's Executive Committee he wanted to see UNHCR take on a more systematic engagement in leading protection clusters in natural disasters, viewing this as a 'logical extension' of the agency's current responsibilities (UNHCR 2009). This suggestion received a mixed response and in his 2011 EXCOM opening statement, the High Commissioner noted that as agreement had not yet been reached on more predictable arrangements, the existing approach would be maintained (UNHCR 2011b).

REFUGEES AND HUMANITARIAN REFORM

From the outset, it had been clear that the cluster approach, which had been designed to address accountability and leadership gaps, would not apply to refugee operations, in which UNHCR's responsibilities were clear (IASC 2006). Nonetheless, as the cluster approach began to move beyond its initial gap-filling role, in effect becoming the standard operating mechanism for humanitarian coordination, questions began to be raised as to whether refugees should not also be brought within the cluster framework. The Cluster Evaluation I recommended that in 'mixed' situations—where refugee crises unfolded in the context of broader humanitarian emergencies, or where refugees were living alongside IDP populations and/or in host communities also affected by crisis, where the cluster approach had been activated—UNHCR should consider working through a single coordination framework (Stoddard et al. 2007).

This recommendation was formally rejected by the UNHCR on the basis that the lines of accountability established under the cluster approach (to the Humanitarian Coordinator at country level and the Emergency Relief Coordinator at global level) were not compatible with the High Commissioner's mandate under international law for refugee protection and solutions, for which he is accountable to the General Assembly. UNHCR's mandate encompasses a leadership role, along with host governments, in the provision of assistance—viewed as an integral part of protection—to refugees, and requires it to maintain the capacity to act as 'provider of last resort' where necessary.[4]

The five years following the humanitarian reform saw major emergencies characterized by large-scale internal displacement in which the cluster approach was applied. In 2011 and 2012, there was a shift in this pattern, as a series of crises in Côte d'Ivoire, Libya, Somalia, Sudan, Mali, and Syria triggered major refugee emergencies.

The Liberia refugee crisis highlighted that humanitarian reform had brought about changed expectations of those exercising leadership and coordination responsibilities, whether or not the cluster approach is applied (Balde et al. 2011). As a result, UNHCR has recently taken steps to strengthen key functions such as information management and resource mobilization, as part of an overall strategy to strengthen its leadership and coordination functions in refugee operations and to reinforce its engagement with both implementing and operational partners.

Conclusion

The humanitarian reform process, despite criticism, has now come of age and is widely regarded as having brought about tangible improvements in the international humanitarian response to crises.

Nonetheless, significant flaws persist, as demonstrated by the weak coordination of the response to the 2011 Haiti earthquake and Pakistan floods. The Emergency Relief Coordinator has now launched a 'Transformative Agenda', with a particular focus on strengthening and accelerating response in the critical early phase of a 'Level 3' (i.e. large-scale) emergency, and introduced specific measures to reinforce the three pillars of leadership, coordination, and accountability (IASC 2011).

But central problems of international coordination persist. Can this new phase of the humanitarian reform bring about meaningful change in a competitive humanitarian 'marketplace' characterized by a multiplicity and proliferation of actors, each with their own mandate, institutional identity, and drive to protect their own interests?[5] According to a view expressed by a number of analysts, agencies benefit from the current system, in which the 'drive to articulate and to preserve agencies' mandates and turf, and to do so quickly, is more important than collaboration to maximise collective impact' (Hoffman and Weiss 2006; Ramalingham and Barnett 2010). In an increasingly competitive environment a system, which depends on voluntary agreement, with no real mechanisms for accountability or sanctions for underperformance, may only have limited effectiveness.

Experience suggests that agencies are willing to 'coordinate' only insofar as this does not result in a loss of autonomy and decision-making capacity. Their operating environment has also been progressively occupied by private sector contractors, military, and civilian advisers in peacekeeping or stabilization missions. Despite these challenges allied with persistent problems of leadership and funding, progress has undoubtedly been made. As a new wave of major emergencies unfolds, it is more critical than ever that the collective capacity of the humanitarian system is effectively harnessed.

NOTES

1. Report of the Protection Cluster Working Group Retreat, Geneva, 15–16 November 2007.
2. COMISAF Tactical Directive, 2 September 2008.
3. In northern Yemen, the Emirati Red Crescent ran an IDP camp at an annual cost of $16m, more than the entire UNHCR programme, where IDPs received three cooked meals a day but could not keep their livestock at the camp.
4. Guy Goodwin-Gill has nonetheless challenged the extent to which the provision of assistance to refugees should or needs to remain a particular operational responsibility for UNHCR, arguing that a more effective collaborative response under the cluster approach would enable UNHCR to divest itself of many of its assistance activities and refocus on 'core' protection functions (Goodwin-Gill 2006).
5. The SOHS report notes that there are now more than 4,400 NGOs worldwide engaged in humanitarian action.

REFERENCES

Balde, M. D., et al. (2011) 'Shelter from the Storm: A Real-Time Evaluation of UNHCR's Response to the Emergency in Côte d'Ivoire and Liberia'. UNHCR.

Betts, A. (2009) 'Institutional Proliferation and the Global Refugee Regime'. *Perspectives on Politics* 7(1): 53–8.

Borton, J., et al. (2005) 'Support to Internally Displaced Persons: Learning from Evaluation'. Swedish International Development Cooperation Agency (Sida).

Brahimi Report (2000) Report of the Panel on United Nations Peace Operations (Brahimi Report) 2000, A/55/305-S/2000/809.

Cohen, R. (2008) 'For Disaster IDPs: An Institutional Gap'. The Brookings Institution, 8 August.

Collinson, S., et al. (2009) 'Realising Protection: The Uncertain Benefits of Civilian, Refugee and IDP Status'. Humanitarian Policy Group Report 28, Overseas Development Institute, September.

Collinson, S., et al. (2010) 'States of Fragility: Stabilisation and its Implications for Humanitarian Action'. Humanitarian Policy Group Working Paper, Overseas Development Institute, August.

Crisp, J., et al. (2007) 'Real-Time Evaluation of UNHCR's IDP Operation in Uganda'. UNHCR.

Crisp, J. (2009) 'Refugees, Persons of Concern, and People on the Move: The Broadening Boundaries of UNHCR'. *Refuge* 26(1): 73–6.

Deschamp, B. (2010) 'Earth, Wind and Fire: A Review of UNHCR's Role in Recent Natural Disasters'. UNHCR.

Ferris, E. (2011) 'Megatrends and the Future of Humanitarian Action'. *International Review of the Red Cross* 93: 915–38.

Global Protection Cluster Child Protection Working Group (2011) 'Too Little, Too Late: Child Protection Funding in Emergencies'. Geneva.

Goodwin-Gill, G. (2006) 'International Protection and Assistance for Refugees and the Displaced: Institutional Challenges and United Nations Reform'. Paper Presented at the Refugee Studies Centre Workshop, 'Refugee Protection in International Law: Contemporary Challenges'. Oxford, 24 April.

Hoffman, P. J., and Weiss, T. G. (2006) *Sword & Salve: Confronting New Wars and Humanitarian Crises*. London: Rowman and Littlefield Publishers, Inc.

ICRC (2006) 'ICRC Position on Internally Displaced Persons (IDPs)', ICRC, May.

Inter-Agency Standing Committee (IASC) (2006) 'Guidance Note on Using the Cluster Approach to Strengthen Humanitarian Response'. Inter-Agency Standing Committee (IASC), 24 November.

Inter-Agency Standing Committee (2011) 'IASC Transformative Agenda—2012: Chapeau and Compendium of Actions'. Inter-Agency Standing Committee (IASC), December.

Internal Displacement Monitoring Centre (IDMC) (2012) 'Global Overview 2011: People Internally Displaced by Conflict and Violence'. Norwegian Refugee Council.

Lanz, D. (2008) 'Subversion or Reinvention? Dilemmas and Debates in the Context of UNHCR's Increasing Involvement with IDPs'. *Journal of Refugee Studies* 21(2): 192–209.

Martin, S., et al. (2005) *The Uprooted*. Lanham, MD: Lexington Books.

Mattar, V., and White, P. (2005) 'Consistent and Predictable Responses to IDPs: A Review of UNHCR's Decision-Making Processes'. UNHCR.

Médecins Sans Frontières (2007) 'MSF: What Relation to the Aid System?' Médecins Sans Frontières, April.

Merheb, N., et al. (2006) 'The State of the World's Refugees: Human Displacement in the New Millennium'. UNHCR.

Metcalfe, V., et al. (2011) 'Integration and Humanitarian Space: An Independent Study Commissioned by the UN Integration Steering Group'. Humanitarian Policy Group/ Overseas Development Institute and the Stimson Centre, December.

Ramalingham, B., and Barnett, M. (2010) 'The Humanitarian's Dilemma: Collective Action or Inaction in International Relief?' Background Note, Overseas Development Institute, August.

Steets, J., et al. (2010) 'Cluster Approach Evaluation 2: Synthesis Report'. Groupe Urgence, Réhabilitation, Développement/Global Policy Institute.

Stensland, A. O., and Sending, O. J. (2011) 'Unpacking the Culture of Protection: A Political Economy Analysis of OCHA and the Protection of Civilians'. Norwegian Institute of International Affairs.

Stoddard, A., et al. (2007) 'Cluster Approach Evaluation: Final'. Center on International Cooperation/Humanitarian Policy Group, Overseas Development Institute, November.

Street, A., et al. (2009) 'Review of the Engagement of NGOs with the Humanitarian Reform Process: Synthesis Report'. NGOs and Humanitarian Reform Project/International Council of Voluntary Agencies, October.

Taylor, G., et al. (2012) 'The State of the Humanitarian System'. ALNAP/Overseas Development Institute. London.

Turton, D. (2011) 'The Politics of Internal Displacement and Options for Institutional Reform'. Pp. 2–24 in *Deportate, estuli, profughe. Rivista telematica di studi sulla memoria femminile* 17(November).

United Nations Assistance Mission in Afghanistan (UNAMA) (2008) Afghanistan: Annual Report on Protection of Civilians in Armed Conflict.

United Nations Assistance Mission in Afghanistan (UNAMA) (2009) Afghanistan: Annual Report on Protection of Civilians in Armed Conflict.

UNHCR (2005) 'Global Report 2005'. UNHCR.

UNHCR (2007a) 'UNHCR's Role in Support of an Enhanced Humanitarian Response to Situations of Internal Displacement: Policy Framework and Implementation Strategy'. Executive Committee of the High Commissioner's Programme, UNHCR, 4 June.

UNHCR (2007b) 'Real-Time Evaluations of UNHCR's Involvement in Operations for Internally Displaced Persons and the Cluster Approach: Analysis of Findings'. Executive Committee of the High Commissioner's Programme, UNHCR, 29 August.

UNHCR (2007c) 'Global Report 2007'. UNHCR.

UNHCR (2010) 'High Commissioner's Opening Statement to the 62nd Session of ExCom'. 4 October.

UNHCR (2011a) 'UNHCR's Role in Support of an Enhanced Humanitarian Response for the Protection of Persons Affected by Natural Disasters'. Executive Committee of the High Commissioner's Programme, UNHCR, 6 June.

UNHCR (2011b) 'High Commissioner's Opening Statement to the 62nd Session of ExCom'. 3 October.

UNHCR (2011c) 'Global Report 2011: Reaffirming our Responsibilities'. UNHCR.

United Nations (2009) *Protecting Civilians in the Context of UN Peacekeeping Operations: Successes, Setbacks and Remaining Challenges*. New York: United Nations, November.

UNOCHA (2011) 'Central Emergency Response Fund 2011 Annual Report'. United Nations.

PART IV

ROOT CAUSES OF DISPLACEMENT

....

CHAPTER 25

CONFLICT AND CRISIS INDUCED DISPLACEMENT

....

SARAH KENYON LISCHER

Introduction

....

When faced with political violence, or threats of violence, a person has the choice to fight, to attempt escape, or to give up and likely suffer terrible consequences. Considering that in most situations of conflict and crisis the person being threatened is unarmed and usually in one or more categories of vulnerability or particular risk (female, child, elderly, sick), a common response is the attempt to escape. However, the seemingly simple equation of conflict and escape is, like all political phenomena, complex and constantly shifting. Addressing the topic of conflict and crisis induced displacement requires an examination of three dimensions: theoretical, methodological, and practical. Deriving from an analysis of the literature on conflict and crisis induced displacement, this chapter briefly examines each of these three dimensions, and stresses the need for increased integration among the different theoretical and methodological approaches. In light of the breadth of the topic, it is necessary to begin by specifying how the concepts of conflict and crisis are used in this context. Subsequently, there is a discussion of theories and methods, including an assessment of their contributions to the field and a discussion of the practical requirement for developing and testing explanations. The conclusion in turn addresses current gaps and areas for future research.

In this chapter, the terms 'conflict' and 'crisis' refer to political violence occurring in the country of origin.[1] The term crisis often indicates the necessity for decision making in the face of impending danger. A crisis can affect an individual or family when weighing the risks of staying or fleeing. In politics, the term crisis describes an unsustainable situation which will rapidly degenerate without countervailing action. Using the terms crisis and conflict in this broad conceptualization takes into account the many types of political violence that cause displacement, as well as the varying levels of intensity in violence. These can range from violent political oppression to full-scale civil war.[2] Such violence causes displacement when people flee their homes in response to the conflict. They may flee across international borders or remain within the borders of their own state as internally displaced people (IDPs). In addition to the broad definition of conflict, this chapter adopts a broad definition of displaced people since the legal definitions provided in the 1951 Geneva Convention, its 1967 Protocol, and the OAU Convention exclude many of the displaced, particularly those who do not cross state borders or those who are denied official refugee status. The Guiding Principles on Internal Displacement are perhaps most useful for states which are amenable to helping IDPs, but the Principles arguably have little influence with states hostile to the IDPs.

Theories of conflict and crisis induced displacement can be disaggregated into numerous avenues of research. Some of the most important questions, as demonstrated by the level of scholarly attention and practical importance, focus on the types of conflict and crises which induce forced migration. Related analyses seek to understand the location and timing of displacement, and the determinants of individual and family decision-making processes. Researchers aim to establish how the affected people interpret their own situations, as well as the larger political and historical context of the displacement. Finally, two overarching questions are how regional and international factors affect conflict induced displacement and how displacement, in turn, affects political processes.

The increasing recognition of the political and security implications of displacement has broadened the theoretical lens through which scholars view the issue (also see Hammerstad, this volume). An international relations analysis, for example, focuses more on the relationship between traditional security threats and forced migration (Zolberg, Suhrke, and Aguayo 1989; Loescher 1992; Terry 2002; Stedman and Tanner 2003; Lischer 2005; Loescher and Milner 2005; Muggah 2006; Greenhill 2008). This has had a mixed effect: the issue of displacement receives more attention outside the humanitarian realm, but that attention may lead policymakers to securitize the response to the crisis in a way that undermines refugee protection. One response to this trend is an increasing emphasis on 'human security' (Newman and Van Selm 2003). The Human Security Report Project explains that the 'term *human security* is now widely used to describe the complex of interrelated threats associated with international war, civil war, genocide, and the displacement of populations. Human security means, at minimum, freedom from violence, and from the fear of violence' (Human Security Report 2008).

The methodologies employed are as rich and diverse as the theoretical. Scholars have examined the causal factors of displacement using methods such as intensive field research, comparative case studies, and large-n statistical studies. The different methods adapt themselves to different levels of analysis ranging from macro-historical and global trends to micro-level analysis of why individuals decide to flee. The following sections examine both the theoretical and methodological approaches used in analyses of conflict induced displacement.

THEORIES OF CONFLICT INDUCED DISPLACEMENT

The initial motivating question for most scholars of migration is 'why do people flee?' (Thorburn 1996; Weiner 1996; Schmeidl 1997; Davenport, Moore, and Poe 2003; Neumayer 2005; Melander and Öberg 2006; Adhikari 2013). Within the parameters of this chapter, the guiding question is 'given the presence (or threat of) political violence, why do people flee?' The significance of this research question is demonstrated by the extensive political, security, and humanitarian impacts of displacement. In addition, the importance of this inquiry often derives from the normative desire to reduce violence in general or to reduce the suffering caused by displacement crises. Overall, the importance of conflict induced displacement within academia is evidenced by the growth of the sub-field of refugee and forced migration studies and the integration of displacement issues in many social sciences and humanities disciplines. From the perspective of critical theory, Hyndman reminds us that the issue of forced migration has broad and interdisciplinary importance, far beyond the field of Refugee Studies. She observes that 'Combined with the increased mobility of space-time compression, questions of travel, identity formation, and displacement represent a major tour de force in the social sciences and humanities' (Hyndman 2000: 36).

Theories of conflict induced displacement focus on both root causes and proximate causes. Analysing root causes of displacement, such as persistent oppression and inequality, provides background data and predictive possibilities.[3] However, such conditions generally combine with a proximate cause, such as ethnic cleansing, riots, and war, before forced displacement occurs. Indeed, many states are characterized by conditions and processes that are described as root causes of displacement, such as political oppression, inequality, or historical enmity; furthermore, such conditions can persist for years without any significant forced displacement taking place.

With the above in mind, this chapter examines political violence as a proximate cause of forced displacement. One common finding in the literature in this regard is that, while there are many types of political violence, it is a few types of violence which cause most large-scale forced displacement around the world. As discussed herein, these are genocide, politicide,[4] and civil war. Schmeidl's regression analysis confirms the widely held hypothesis that political violence is the most significant cause of refugee movements: 'The relative strength and consistency of genocides/politicides in predicting change in refugee stock supports Fein's (1993) and Jonassohn's (1993) claims that the majority of all refugee migrations are caused by genocides' (Schmeidl 1997: 302). Much of the research on conflict induced displacement thus focuses on the characteristics of the conflict in the country of origin and the conditions under which they lead to forced migration, with hypotheses subsequently seeking to explain a wide range of phenomena, from broad determinants of refugee flows in general to individuals' decisions within specific conflicts.

In research that investigates broad patterns, as well as specific phenomena, Hyndman offers a theoretical approach which provides a macro-level analysis of global patterns of power and resource allocation, making the claim that 'the politics of mobility is a useful tool for analyzing migration, specifically because it recognizes the variable movement of refugees and other disenfranchised groups' (Hyndman 2000: 32). Such a transnational geopolitics of mobility compares the movement of people and resources, particularly money, across borders. This analysis gains strength from its firm empirical grounding in the Horn of Africa. In the case of the Kenya/Somalia border, Hyndman finds that 'humanitarian capital crosses borders much more easily than refugees can traverse the same frontiers' (Hyndman 2000: 59).

Similar reliance on comparative frameworks of analysis has led to a greater level of detail and variation in research on conflict and migration. Drawing from the literature on civil war, researchers have identified the need to disaggregate concepts such as conflict and violence (Kalyvas 2006). The reasoning is that the type of political violence that spurred flight will help determine the nature of the displacement crisis and the potential solutions to both the original conflict and the resulting forced migration. In examining the causes of displacement through the lens of Kalyvas's model, Lischer focuses on civil conflict and international conflict. She divides the former into four categories: civil war, genocide, failed state, and persecution; the category of international conflict in turn includes border wars, third party intervention, and invasion. The benefit of disaggregation is that it 'allows the researcher to examine how conflict affects displacement and also how aspects of the displacement crisis may in turn affect the conflict' (Lischer 2007: 145).

Such disaggregated analyses demonstrate that forced displacement often functions as a central strategy in civil wars and, as such, can be considered in the political as well as humanitarian realm. An example of the central strategic role of forced migration is the conflict in Darfur which rapidly prompted a massive refugee and IDP crisis: Kofi Annan labelled Darfur as the 'world's worst humanitarian crisis' of the time (Reuters, 29 December 2005). The statistics in Darfur may have given the impression that massive displacement and destruction were the tragic by-product of war. In reality, however, forced migration was a strategic tool used by the Sudanese government to permanently alter landownership and population patterns in Darfur: 'the massive displacement is not merely a consequence of the attacks, but rather a central war aim of the attackers, who are clearing entire areas of their original inhabitants' (Tubiana 2007: 69). The terrifying abuses that accompanied this displacement, such as mass rapes and widespread torture, ensured the future reluctance of internally and internationally displaced persons to return home. Considering the political motives underpinning displacement, the almost exclusively humanitarian response unsurprisingly did not lead to a solution.

In light of such experiences of abuse and the strategic political motivations underpinning conflict induced displacement, scholars are also increasingly asking why people stay. Indeed, insight into why people flee is gained by asking why they do not flee. This requires the researcher to analyse the causes of displacement by comparing different populations and not just the displaced groups. Steele, for instance, argues that the question of why people leave is not universally applicable, indicating that, based on her fieldwork in Colombia, 'many people stay in spite of violence' (2009: 420), while Melander and Öberg focus on the population which stays behind, noting that over time, that group becomes 'increasingly unwilling or unable to relocate' (2006: 129). Thus, it becomes important to identify and analyse the conditions that influence decisions to stay in order to advance our understanding of why other people decide to leave.

In addition to domestic factors, a greater understanding of the complex relationship between refugee crises and regional politics has emerged over time, starting with the seminal work by Zolberg, Suhrke, and Aguayo, *Escape from Violence*, published in 1989. In effect, although much literature focused on the ways in which refugees affected politics in the host state, the ways in which host state politics caused refugee flows remained under-theorized until the 1990s. Weiner, in his seminal article 'Bad Neighbors, Bad Neighborhoods' (1996), identifies the causal relationship between regional conflicts and refugee crises. First, he categorizes types of conflicts which produce refugees: inter-state wars, anti-colonial wars, ethnic conflicts, non-ethnic conflicts, and flights from authoritarian and revolutionary regimes. From his analysis of global refugee trends between 1969 and 1992, he finds that regional effects play an important role in forced migration, arguing, effectively, that refugees come from 'bad neighborhoods' (Weiner 1996: 9). He elaborates on the empirical observation that civil wars tend to occur in regional clusters as follows:

> Conflicts within countries often spill across borders, sometimes because the conflicts themselves are rooted in the division of ethnic communities by international boundaries, sometimes because the weaker party in a conflict successfully finds allies in a neighboring country, and sometimes because the refugees themselves become the source of conflict within or between countries. (Weiner 1996: 28)

In addition to his finding vis-à-vis the creation of refugee flows, Weiner notes that refugees can also be causes of conflict. He gives the example that 'The flow of some ten million refugees from East Pakistan was not the result of the war between India and Pakistan in 1972, but took place during the civil war in 1971. The refugee flow was one of the causes of the war, not its consequence' (Weiner 1996: 19).

The empirical observation regarding the clustering of civil wars is further examined by Saleyhan and Gleditch, who focus more on the effects rather than the causes of displacement. Their research is guided by the question: 'what are the exact causal mechanisms behind the international diffusion of civil war' (2006: 2)? From this general question, they narrow the focus on refugees, hypothesizing that '*the presence of refugees from neighboring countries increases the probability that a country will experience civil war*' (2006: 15, emphasis in the original). Their statistical study finds that states hosting refugees are more likely to experience civil war than those without. Saleyhan and Gleditch are interested in a similar question to Weiner, although they do not attempt to replicate that research. Instead, their quantitative work sheds further light on the earlier findings. The following section will explore such different methodological approaches in greater detail.

METHODOLOGICAL DIVERSITY

Scholars have used a welcome diversity of methodological approaches and research methods to study the causes of conflict induced displacement, in part due to the interdisciplinary nature of the field of refugee and forced migration studies. Indeed, researchers from different disciplines, such as anthropology, sociology, and political science, bring their own disciplinary practices to bear on similar questions. Scholars engage in both theory building and empirical research that test existing hypotheses. Within qualitative approaches, there are numerous ways to study the causes of conflict induced displacement. These include anthropological thick description, controlled case studies, elite interviewing, and others (George and Bennett 2005). In turn, the most common quantitative method is large-n statistical analysis, with quantitative scholars often relying on existing datasets or developing their own; more recently, some work has moved into computer modelling and other technical tools (Edwards 2008). The following section provides some examples of these methods and analyses the general advantages and disadvantages of each.

Qualitative

A traditional anthropological method is ethnographic in nature and may include long-term participant observation and the collection of detailed oral histories and life stories; by telling their own stories to the researcher, refugees themselves and the ethnographer her or himself are able to develop a narrative analysis to interpret the reasons for their displacement. Eastmond (2007) finds that narratives can help researchers uncover the causes of displacement by listening to the voices of the displaced:

> With the more interpretive approach, narratives have become interesting also for what they can tell us about how people themselves, as 'experiencing subjects', make sense of violence and turbulent change. From personal accounts we may also glean the diversity behind over-generalized notions of 'the refugee experience'.

However, Eastmond continues with the caveat that 'narratives are vital in the research process, but also offer considerable challenges as a methodology' (2007: 249). In particular, scholars undertaking such intensive anthropological work are confronted with the difficulty of interpreting the stories they collect: 'Representing stories in ways that do narrators justice is not only a general problem of researchers' authority, but one which needs particular attention in relation to vulnerable categories of people' (Eastmond 2007: 261).

In the field of political science a common qualitative approach is controlled case studies and elite interviewing. This may be less intrusive and time consuming than the above-mentioned narrative analysis and lends itself to comparative research questions, with qualitative research designs developed to compare a wide variety of variables including types of violence, ethnic affiliation, host state characteristics, and historical context. The ideal design is able to control for many explanatory variables while observing variation in the factors of interest (George and Bennett 2005).

On the one hand, qualitative and micro-level research offers rich and deep data, allowing accurate analysis of the cases being studied. On the other hand, however, there are limits on the generalizability of such data. Indeed, qualitative scholars face a high barrier (although not an impossible one) to demonstrating generalizability, as the standards of evidence must be rigorous, particularly since much of the research is not perfectly replicable. Citing research which finds a consistent and direct relationship between violence and displacement, Steele calls for 'a more rigorous conceptualization of risk perception and threat' as a way to 'illuminate existing findings and direct attention to areas for further research' (2009: 421). Case studies which are well selected for the purposes of controlled comparison will offer the greatest potential for generalizability and theory building and testing (see King, Keohane, and Verba 1994).

Quantitative

A strength of quantitative work is its ability to provide a stronger base to claim the generalizability of existing hypotheses, most notably that political violence is a major cause of forced displacement. As Moore and Shellman comment, most of the existing work 'assumes that the connection between state behavior and forced migration is obvious, yet explicit causal arguments are rare' (2004: 727). Sociologist Schmeidl developed a benchmark study of the causes of forced migration using quantitative methods, considering the existing causal explanations of refugee flows which include a variety of causal factors such as human rights abuses, political oppression, economic factors, and civil wars. Qualitative methods provided in-depth data for a variety of cases while quantitative methods allowed a more generalizable analysis of these explanations. The result is broader knowledge of which causes—civil wars with international intervention and generalized violence—have the most predictive power for large-scale forced migration (Schmeidl 1997). While Schmeidl recognizes potential pitfalls in large-n statistical analysis, warning that 'quantitative analysis can be only as good as its indicators' (Schmeidl 1997: 305), this mixed-methods research demonstrates a rigorous and theoretically rich use of regression analysis and highlights its value in building on existing research and testing hypotheses.

Later work has also examined hypotheses which have taken on the status of conventional wisdom and yet remain under-examined. An example of such quantitative research is that of Davenport, Moore, and Poe, who test the hypothesis that people flee due to perceived threats to their physical security, most often manifested during civil war, genocide, and violent rebellions. As they state: 'This is our basic argument: all other things constant, people leave their homes when they feel that their physical security is threatened' (Davenport et. al. 2003: 31). They further specify that countries which are experiencing civil war or 'organized violent rebellions' are more likely to produce refugees (Davenport, Moore, and Poe 2003: 34). Their findings in support of those hypotheses are based on a statistical analysis of 129 countries over the years 1964–89.

Importantly, statistical research and dataset analysis does not necessitate a macro-level perspective. For instance, Moore and Shellman examine individual decision making and hypothesize that 'one will leave one's home when the probability of being a victim of persecution becomes sufficiently high that the expected utility of leaving exceeds the expected utility of staying' (2004: 727–8). Within a rationalist framework and based on a global sample covering the years 1952–95, they find that 'the violent behavior of governments and dissidents (and their interaction) are the primary determinants of forced migration flows' (2004: 742). In their conclusion, however, the authors caution that 'these results—like those of all large-N statistical analyses—are average effects: they tell us precious little about the specific impact of covariates in any given forced migration event' (2004: 742). They subsequently recommend analysis of time series case studies to provide more specific information. As a way to test these existing theories of behaviour, Adhikari examines individual decision making through quantitative analysis, using a public opinion survey undertaken in Nepal, and provides confirmation of existing hypotheses (2013: 82–9).

In addition to the value of testing existing hypotheses and generating theory, a significant contribution of quantitative research is the collection and aggregation of data. New datasets, particularly when in the public domain, enrich the wider literature as subsequent research uses or further develops the datasets. The paucity of data on many variables of interest hinders scholars, and the compilation of reliable data is therefore essential. Writing from the qualitative perspective, Weiner warns 'All aggregate statistics on refugee flows should thus be interpreted with care' (1996). For example, UNHCR data on refugee demographics varies widely by country, creating challenges for researchers who want to use age or gender as variables in a global dataset (UNHCR Global Trends 2011).

Two concerns are often mentioned regarding large-n studies in general. These are the risk of reductionism and of reliance on poor data. Both of those will weaken or invalidate findings. This critique is the inverse of the risk of qualitative data in which too much detail impedes comparison across cases. The more general the perspective, the harder it is to capture the wide diversity of displacement crises. In every dataset, variation is sacrificed. This can result in incorrectly coded or missed cases. One example is the case of the Rwandan refugee flows in 1994, commonly coded as a flight due to genocide. As one large-n study explains:

> In instances of genocide and politicide, governments seek to exterminate an entire people and to force any who remain out of their sovereign territory. Obviously this leads members of that group to quite rightly fear for their security and to flee. Collectively these personal decisions result in acute refugee/displacement situations like that which occurred during the exodus from Rwanda, in 1994, when nearly a third of the country's 7.5 million people abandoned their homes. (Davenport et al. 2003: 33; see also Schmeidl 1997 for similar coding)

The implicit assumption in this coding is that the two million refugees were fleeing genocide. Yet in actuality, this massive refugee flow in the context of genocide was *not* primarily composed of the group identified as the target of the genocide (the Tutsi), but of group identified as the perpetrator group (the Hutu). This may be an unusual situation, but considering that the Rwandan outflow was one of the largest and most violent of the 1990s, it is important since its miscoding could skew the findings.

Other methodological considerations pertain to the level of analysis. Micro-level studies often focus on individual choice, whereas in many situations the decision to flee is a communal or family choice. Many of the rationalist frameworks take into account only an individual's fear for his or her own safety, rather than the more likely decision factor of family safety. Threats to one's children or other vulnerable relations are likely to prompt flight, even if one is not as concerned about one's own safety. For example, the threats of abduction facing children in northern Uganda were calculated to terrorize adults, not about their own safety, but about that of their children (Gates and Reich 2010). Rationalist studies could fruitfully use the family or household as the unit of analysis in addition to or rather than the individual.

PRACTICAL APPROACHES TO CRISIS AND CONFLICT INDUCED DISPLACEMENT

The study of causes of forced migration is intrinsically related to the search for solutions, both to migration crises and the larger contexts of violence. However, focusing myopically on either causes or solutions narrows the usefulness of a research agenda, since, in order to identify meaningful solutions it is first necessary to learn about the causes of the crisis. Indeed, understanding the characteristics of conflict can help predict, and hopefully prevent, displacement as policymakers note warning signs. For example, wars in Iraq and Syria created large outflows of refugees and IDPs which could have been predicted, and even prevented, had more attention been paid to the causes of conflict induced displacement. This effort requires political attention and resources to ensure the validity of research and the application of findings, rather than merely adopting an apolitical lens and promoting a palliative humanitarian response.

At a practical level, the validity of the theoretical and methodological approaches used to understand displacement rests on the quality of the data used to formulate and test explanations. Asking good questions about the causes of conflict- and crisis induced displacement is the first step. As discussed earlier, major areas of inquiry include individual decision making, macro-level historical trends, and the relationships between cases of displacement crises and their solutions. Answering these questions requires a rigorous methodological framework, which, in turn, rests on reliable, accurate data. This is true for large-n data sets, as well as for detailed field interviews.

In many instances, better information on specific social groups, processes, and dynamics would remedy problems created by research based on faulty or incomplete data. For example, while necessary to understand conflict induced displacement, numerous information gaps remain vis-à-vis family decision-making processes in contexts of conflict and crisis induced displacement. Filling these gaps, however, is problematic for numerous reasons. At the statistical level, the limitations of available demographic data pertaining to the periods before, during, and after displacement impede research on social and economic trends affecting forced migration. A further challenge is related to the sharp increase in and attention to the internally displaced, as research on IDPs and the causes of their flight is dependent on researchers' ability to operate in dangerous areas. Indeed, UNHCR expresses concern that the causes of displacement are increasingly related to internal conflict and, thus, humanitarians work more in actual conflict zones that in the past; the agency notes that 'contemporary forms of violence force people to flee their homes to destinations that are less predictable, less circumscribed, and often themselves also insecure' (UNHCR 2012: 12, quote p. 18). Finally, as many NGOs point out, numerous conflict zones, such as the civil war in Mali which flared in 2012, receive little attention from policymakers, the public, or researchers. This leads to the question of how knowledge about those crises can be generalizable to more high-profile situations.

In effect, humanitarian organizations sometimes have a privileged position to observe micro-level phenomena, seeing trends before they reach the attention of scholars and policymakers. However, despite their potential for complementarity, research, humanitarian action, and public policy do not always fit together, as evidenced by the tension that exists between scholarly endeavours and policy relevance. Indeed, Bakewell warns that a strict pursuit of policy relevance can constrain research in a way that excludes important populations and categories of explanations (Bakewell 2008). A different tension afflicts humanitarians, as they are often hard pressed to concentrate on the causes of the crisis when they are in an emergency situation, trying desperately to protect the rights of the displaced, and find a solution to the crisis. These frictions cannot be easily resolved, even though there is a general consensus about the ultimate desired outcome: the prevention or resolution of refugee crises within the context of peace and security.

Conclusion

This chapter has explored diverse approaches to understanding the causes of conflict- and crisis induced displacement, arguing that the existing academic literature on conflict induced displacement would benefit from increased integration, rather than a continual reinvention of typologies, datasets, and conceptualizations. Current scholarship often takes place within narrow boundaries of discipline, geographic focus, and methodological approach, and yet, ideally, qualitative and quantitative researchers alike would learn from the positive contributions of each type of scholarship, recognizing the benefits of complementarity—one remedy is collaboration between scholars conducting intensive field research and those collecting data for large-n analysis.

Importantly, conflict and crisis induced displacement cannot be viewed in isolation from other causes. Resource scarcity, for example, can lead to political violence as different groups struggle to control the government, and thereby control diverse resources. Acknowledging the interaction among various root causes can help explain the crisis. For example, Newland notes that 'a number of the ethnic conflicts that have erupted into violence and generated refugees in the developing world can be characterized as resource wars, in which battle lines reflect ethnic or tribal affiliations' (Newland 1993: 90). Indeed, UNHCR recognizes that 'in contemporary contexts, the distinction between armed conflict and violence used as a means of securing or reinforcing social or economic power is often blurred' (2012: 15). When scholars and policymakers remain narrowly focused on their area of expertise, they may miss an important factor which could help solve the crisis—since displacement crises have so many interwoven causes, a holistic approach is necessary for creating rigorous, generalizable explanations for forced migration.

NOTES

1. Other types of crises, such as environmental and development issues which can cause forced migration are addressed in Zetter and Morrissey's and McDowell's chapters respectively (in this volume).
2. In this chapter, references to conflict induced displacement include the concept of crisis.
3. Observing global trends, Schmeidl distinguishes among root causes, proximate conditions, and intervening factors, giving an overview of each type (Schmeidl 1997: 286). At the regional level, Thorburn (1996) and Neumayer (2005) focus on root causes analysis in the context of forced migration in Europe.
4. Schmeidl defines politicide as the attempt by a government to eliminate a target group based on political orientation (1997: 294).

REFERENCES

Adhikari, P. (2013) 'Conflict-Induced Displacement: Understanding the Causes of Flight'. *American Journal of Political Science* 57: 82–9.

Bakewell, O. (2008) 'Research beyond the Categories: The Importance of Policy Irrelevant Research in Forced Migration'. *Journal of Refugee Studies* 21(4): 423–53.

Davenport, C. A., Moore, W. H., and Poe, S. C. (2003) 'Sometimes You Just Have to Leave: Domestic Threats and Forced Migration, 1964–1989'. *International Interactions* 29: 27–55.

Eastmond, M. (2007) 'Stories as Lived Experience: Narratives in Forced Migration Research'. *Journal of Refugee Studies* 20(2): 248–64.

Edwards, S. (2008) 'Computational Tools in Predicting and Assessing Forced Migration'. *Journal of Refugee Studies* 21(3): 347–59.

Fein, H. (1993) 'Accounting for Genocide after 1945: Theories and Some Findings'. *International Journal on Group Rights* 1: 79–106.

Gates, S., and Reich, S. (eds.) (2010) *Child Soldiers in the Age of Fractured States.* Pittsburgh: University of Pittsburgh Press.

George, A., and Bennett, A. (2005) *Case Studies and Theory Development in the Social Sciences.* Cambridge, MA: MIT Press.

Greenhill, K. M. (2008) 'Strategic Engineered Migration as a Weapon of War'. *Civil Wars* 10(1): 6–21.

Human Security Report Project (2008) 'miniAtlas of Human Security'. May. <http://www.miniatlasofhumansecurity.info/en/access.html>.

Hyndman, J. (2000) *Managing Displacement: Refugees and the Politics of Humanitarianism.* Minneapolis: University of Minnesota Press.

Jonassohn, K. (1993) 'Prevention without Prediction'. *Holocaust and Genocide Studies* 7: 1–13.

Kalyvas, S. (2006) *The Logic of Violence in Civil War.* Cambridge: Cambridge University Press.

King, G., Keohane, R. O., and Verba, S. (1994) *Designing Social Inquiry: Scientific Inference in Qualitative Research.* Princeton: Princeton University Press.

Lischer, S. K. (2005) *Dangerous Sanctuaries: Refugee Camps, Civil War, and the Dilemmas of Humanitarian Aid.* Ithaca, NY: Cornell University Press.

Lischer, S. K. (2007) 'Causes and Consequences of Conflict-Induced Displacement'. *Civil Wars* 9(2) (June): 142–55.

Loescher, G. (1992) *Refugee Movements and International Security.* London: Brassey's for IISS.

Loescher, G., and Milner, J. (2005) *Protracted Refugee Situations: Domestic and International Security Implications.* Adelphi Paper 375. New York: Routledge.

Melander, E., and Öberg, M. (2006) 'Time to Go? Duration Dependence in Forced Migration'. *International Interactions* 32: 129–52.

Melander, E., and Öberg, M. (2007) 'The Threat of Violence and Forced Migration: Geographical Scope Trumps Intensity of Fighting'. *Civil Wars* 9(2) (June): 156–73.

Muggah, R. (ed.) (2006) *No Refuge: The Crisis of Refugee Militarization in Africa.* London: Zed Books.

Neumayer, E. (2005) 'Bogus Refugees? The Determinants of Asylum Migration to Western Europe'. *International Studies Quarterly* 49: 389–409.

Newland, K. (1993) 'Ethnic Conflict and Refugees'. *Survival* 35(1) (Spring): 81–101.

Newman, E., and Van Selm, J. (2003) *Refugees and Forced Displacement: International Security, Human Vulnerability, and the State.* Tokyo: United Nations University Press.

Reuters (2005) 'Fear, Terror Still Stalk Sudan's Darfur: Annan'. *New York Times* 29 December.

Salehyan, I., and Gleditch, K. S. (2006) 'Refugees and the Spread of Civil War'. *International Organization* 60(2) (April): 335–62.

Schmeidl, S. (1997) 'Exploring the Causes of Forced Migration: A Pooled Time-Series Analysis, 1971–1990'. *Social Science Quarterly* 78(2) (June): 284–308.

Stedman, S. J., and Tanner, F. (eds.) (2003) *Refugee Manipulation: War, Politics, and the Abuse of Human Suffering.* Washington, DC: Brookings Institution Press.

Steele, A. (2009) 'Seeking Safety: Avoiding Displacement and Choosing Destinations in Civil Wars'. *Journal of Peace Research* 46(3): 419–30.

Terry, F. (2002) *Condemned to Repeat: The Paradox of Humanitarian Action.* Ithaca, NY: Cornell University Press.

Thorburn, J. (1996) 'Root Cause Approaches to Forced Migration: Part of a Comprehensive Strategy? A European Strategy'. *Journal of Refugee Studies* 9(2) (1996): 119–35.

Tubiana, J. (2007) 'Darfur: A Conflict for Land?' Pp. 68–91 in A. de Waal (ed.), *War in Darfur and the Search for Peace*. Cambridge, MA: Global Equity Initiative, Harvard University.

UNHCR (2012) *The State of the World's Refugees*. Oxford: Oxford University Press.

Weiner, M. (1996) 'Bad Neighbors, Bad Neighborhoods: An Inquiry into the Causes of Refugee Flows'. *International Security* 21(1) (Summer): 5–42.

Zolberg, A. R., Suhrke, A., and Aguayo, S. (1989) *Escape from Violence*. Oxford: Oxford University Press.

CHAPTER 26

DEVELOPMENT CREATED POPULATION DISPLACEMENT

CHRISTOPHER MCDOWELL

INTRODUCTION

THROUGHOUT modern history, state-directed population displacement and involuntary resettlement have been at the centre of nation building, modernization, and development. It was not until the 1950s, however, and the adoption by the International Labour Organization (ILO) of the Indigenous and Tribal Populations Convention, that the inherent conflict in the development process involving the state, developers, and populations 'in the way of progress', was officially recognized. Earlier in the twentieth century, as we shall see in the example of Soviet collectivization, states, and in particular colonizing states, moved people around their territories using powers of eminent domain, or simply illegally and by force, to achieve national development objectives. It will also be shown that involuntary resettlement, rather than merely a by-product of a development project, is frequently an objective in itself aimed at accelerating the modernization process. This chapter explores the evolution of the governance of development created displacement that has shifted involuntary resettlement from a purely sovereign matter to one that, partially at least, is in the domain of international humanitarian and human rights law. The recognition of development created displacement as a global political and humanitarian problem, and the calls for greater protection and understanding of its negative socio-cultural and economic impacts, particularly on minority populations, has come about as a result of actions taken by multilateral institutions from the 1990s, civil society engagement including resistance to displacement among affected populations, and increased academic interest.

Displacement and the Achievement of Modernization

Stalin's 'total collectivization' of the early 1930s across the republics of the Soviet Union is one of the earliest and most ambitious programmes of population displacement, deportation, and involuntary resettlement undertaken to achieve political, social, and economic transformation. Collectivization depended upon, and helped to create, a centralized administrative-command system, that was able to sequester millions of mainly rural people onto newly created collective and state farms, and into factories (Scott 1998: 193–221). The model of agrarian and demographic change was subsequently employed by Russian-backed socialist states in Asia and Africa from the 1960s to the 1980s, leading to forcible rural resettlement in large-scale villagization programmes (Hyden 1980; Scott 1998: 223–61).

Relocations in pursuit of collectivization in the former Soviet Union were both local and international, with millions resettled from distant republics. The Central Asia republic of Kirghizia, for example, received 'settlers' and deportees from Russia, Belarus, and the Ukraine from the 1920s, and from the Caucuses from the 1930s and 1940s, in such large numbers that the relocated rapidly outnumbered the indigenous populations. The presence and labour of those relocated consolidated the collective farm system and created what today is termed 'super-diversity' (Vertovec 2006). The motivations behind collectivization while being primarily developmental (to mechanize and modernize agriculture) were also directly political, in that collectivization was fundamental to achieving the socialist transformation of the new republics, and guaranteeing the concentration of power in the hands of the Communist Party and Soviet institutions.

The displacement, resettlement, and relocation of populations as a result of state-defined development processes is, therefore, not only a matter of happenstance where people are moved because they are 'in the way' of new infrastructure. Rather the displacement of people and communities is frequently an essential element of economic and political modernization, and a means of social and political change.

The displacement and resettlement of more than 1.3 million people in China between 1997 and 2007 as a result of the construction of the Three Gorges Dam on the Yangtse River is a case in point. The Chinese government was praised for making substantial investments in the Three Gorges Project (TGP) resettlement programme through the construction of new relocation villages and towns and developing new suburbs of existing cities, for their policy of reserving jobs for resettlers in the new locations, and also for providing training opportunities and subsidized housing. This so-called Resettlement with Development (RwD) approach is generally regarded as an improvement on past resettlement practice in China (McDonald and Webber 2002), not least for allowing affected populations to choose between rural relocation and a continuation of farming, or urban relocation and a change in livelihoods. Nonetheless, concerns remain about the quality of construction in the relocation sites, the viability of the new livelihood opportunities in both rural and urban areas, the short-term nature of post-resettlement support, and the voluntariness and degree of real choice underpinning these processes (Jackson and Sleigh 2000).

It is clear, however, that for the state authorities resettlement contributed to wider social objectives and the resettlers themselves were key drivers of the modernization they embodied. Resettlers originated mainly from rural areas, pursued a largely subsistence form of farming producing crops of low value and high cost, or were employed in state-owned enterprises that were failing to compete in China's rapidly mechanizing and centralizing production and export-oriented economy. Either way, those targeted for resettlement represented the 'old China', largely dependent on the state for housing, employment, and state subsidies, often living in remote areas, and far less productive than China's fast growing urban population in regional economic hubs such as Chongqing. The transformation brought about by the resettlement proved to the Chinese and the wider world that the government was firmly in control of the country's development, and was able to undertake large-scale and 'coercive' social projects, despite the ever present threat of rural unrest linked to local corruption, and the frequent heavy-handed implementation of relocation.

The lives of hundreds of thousands of rural Chinese, rehoused in high-rise blocks fringing major towns and cities, and overlooking the new industrial zones in which they were expected to be employed, were transformed from a horizontal to a vertical existence. The former reliance on the state was rapidly replaced by a requirement for self-reliance as people adjusted to the realities of the new socialist market economy, taking out mortgages on their apartments, and receiving bills for healthcare and education. For those who remained in the countryside, the relocation villages shunned the spatial arrangements of their former village farms, with clustered two-storey housing separating the people from their animals, and setting aside space for commercial enterprises, to encourage diversified economic activity. While the expected benefits of relocation in the new villages have been held back by a rural economy which has not shared the rates of growth seen nationally, and which has struggled to absorb a new population of workers, the social transformations achieved were nonetheless significant.

The historical example of Soviet collectivization and the TGP in China reveal the ways in which the displacement and resettlement of populations can be both a means to achieve political and development objectives, and a consequence of political decisions about development that require managing. The following section considers the evolution of the management of land acquisition and involuntary resettlement by examining shifts in national and global governance that have seen the survival of colonial era eminent domains laws into the modern era, but at the same time, have supported attempts at strengthening the legal protection of development-affected people through international humanitarian and human rights legislation.

Governance of Development Created Involuntary Resettlement

It is estimated that 280–300 million[1] people over the past 20 years (15 million people annually) were displaced and involuntarily resettled as a result of the construction of both public and private sector infrastructure development projects (Cernea 2008: 20). The majority of such displacement and resettlement occurring as a result of state-defined development processes is taking place in the fast industrializing countries of China and India. Whilst principally as a result of infrastructure projects in the hydropower and transport sector, significant numbers of people are also resettled due to industrial development (including the creation of Special Economic Zones in Asia), urban upgrading, and tourism. It has been estimated that 60 million people in India were displaced between 1947 and 2004 (Fernandes 2008: 91), while in China the construction of hydro-power projects led to the involuntary resettlement of 12 million people between 1950 and 1985. Between 1993 and 2003, the conversion of farmland to industrial or housing displaced a further 36.4 million people in China, and from 2003 to 2010 the Chinese authorities oversaw the resettlement of approximately 3.3 million people each year as a result of state-land acquisitions (Fuggle et al. 2000: 12; ADB 2007: 1). In Latin America there is also considerable further displacement and resettlement related to new dam construction, and as a result of shifts in agriculture away from small-scale farms and towards large-scale, often foreign-owned and -operated mechanized cash crop production across the developing world. Globally, the construction of climate change mitigation and adaptation infrastructure projects, such as coastal defences, as well as afforestation and other land preservation programmes, will require further land acquisition with the likelihood of future large-scale involuntary resettlement (McDowell 2013).

In recent decades the financing of infrastructure development has become more international and commercial; while the World Bank and other international financing institutions (IFIs) remain significant lenders to governments for large schemes, countries such as India, China, and Brazil are able to raise the necessary capital through their domestic economies, or to secure loans on the international money markets. As we shall see, such shifts in the pattern of infrastructure financing have affected the national and global governance of involuntary resettlement.

The governance of development created involuntary resettlement has undergone important changes over the past two decades. Beginning in the late nineteenth century, governments gained considerable legal powers in the acquisition of land for public purpose, where the intended use was for projects that were in the 'national interest'. Colonial era laws of eminent domain defined the rights of the state in land acquisition, but failed to define the rights of people against unjust resettlement and losses, in the form of either guarantees for compensation for lost assets, or relocation. Governments have long recognized the benefits of eminent domain as a legal principle, and pressures from civil society to refine such laws, and to redress the imbalance between the state and the citizen in land acquisition, meet with continued resistance. Conflicts inherent in development activities, including over land acquisition for development purposes, were recognized in the 1950s when the ILO oversaw an early attempt at reducing such conflicts through the Convention on Indigenous and Tribal Populations (ILO 1957), and in the 1970s the UN's Food and Agriculture Organization published what Butcher (1971) described as the earliest manual for resettlement. However, according to Scudder (2005: 45), the beneficial impacts of these early voluntary instruments were rarely felt beyond the immediate project of which they were a part.

In the 1970s, with concern growing about delays and disruptions to projects it sought to fund in the developing world, the World Bank built up its social and environmental division in an attempt to understand, anticipate, and manage those social risks. It adopted its first resettlement policy in 1980, and in the 1990s, building on the voluntary OECD DAC guidelines on Involuntary Resettlement (1992), the Bank led a number of important initiatives which opened up discussion between governments and civil society on the issue of land acquisition and involuntary resettlement in the development process. Responding to high-profile resettlement controversies, the Bank strengthened its social safeguard policies on involuntary resettlement requiring borrowers to anticipate the resettlement risks involved in any infrastructure project for which a loan was sought, and demanding from borrowers credible and fully funded plans to mitigate and address risks, including, where appropriate, the identification and purchase of alternative replacement land, and a livelihood restoration plan. An important contribution to the Bank's reassessment of involuntary resettlement was an internal review of the outcomes of resettlement operations in Bank-funded projects which found that in the majority of cases the resettlement component of projects had failed, and that the policy declarations and principles available at the time were insufficient to ensure adequate protection (World Bank 1996). Borrowers' lack of expertise in planning properly for resettlement was recognized as a weakness and, furthermore, the costs of resettlement were externalized resulting in insufficient money being available for compensation or land replacement: what money was available was either paid late, in an inappropriate manner, or not at all. A crucial anti-development outcome of Bank-funded projects was found to be the impoverishment of resettled people. The findings were far reaching, informing the enquiry into the future environmental and economic viability, and public acceptability of large dams undertaken by the World Commission on Dams (WCD 2000), and stimulating new academic research on the socio-economic (McDowell 1996) and cultural impacts (Downing 1996) of involuntary resettlement. The latter included the generation of analytical models for better understanding resettlement-related impoverishment (Cernea 2000), as well as the refinement of earlier models. The World Bank findings, in addition, encouraged research into the conceptualization of forced migration, including the similarities and dissimilarities of the refugee and development displacee experience (Cernea and McDowell 2000), and importantly, into the ethics of development and displacement (Penz, Drydyk, and Bose 2011).

The World Bank's safeguard policies on involuntary resettlement had the positive further effect of obliging borrower governments to develop resettlement expertise within their ministries, and coinciding with the Bank's growing engagement with civil society, local and international NGOs monitored more closely states' and lenders' activities in resettlement operations. An increasing number of requests for the inspection of resettlement matters received by the independent Inspection Panel of the World Bank attested to a growing interest in the 1990s in projects that created involuntary resettlement in the developing world, as well as the potential for policy failure. The Asian Development Bank (ADB) (later followed by the other regional development banks) adopted its own involuntary resettlement safeguards that were very similar to those of the World Bank. The ADB, in addition, used the growing body of academic knowledge in the late 1990s and 2000s, and its own influence on important Asian lenders, to deploy technical assistance funds to support governments in developing and adopting their own national resettlement policies with the aim of extending the safeguards principle beyond only externally IFI-funded projects.

The development banks' influence also extended, although with less penetration, into the private sector. A number of large companies engaged in construction, the oil and gas industry, and power, adopted human rights, social and environmental 'statements' that drew mainly on the International Finance Corporation's (IFC) Performance Standards on involuntary resettlement. These Standards are less comprehensive and less stringent than the development banks' safeguard policies, and in the absence of proper accountability or comprehensive external and independent scrutiny, the effectiveness of such voluntary codes, and their compliance with international standards set down in the UN Global Compact or the Equator Principles III, is limited. However, the private sector's increasing role in involuntary resettlement, which has seen companies rather than governments managing the resettlement process, has increased public and academic scrutiny of such activities.

Despite the gains made, the World Bank's leadership in setting global standards on involuntary resettlement in the development process receded from 2000, in part due to the eastward shift in economic power and a view increasingly held by the rapidly industrializing countries of Asia and Latin America, that the Bank's conditionalities, including on resettlement, functioned as obstacles to national development. With China and India less reliant on IFI money, commercial loans at higher rates of interest, but with fewer strings attached, became increasingly appealing. As the influence of the development banks on global standard setting declined, however, important parallel developments in the governance of development created involuntary resettlement, took place among a different constituency elsewhere in Washington DC and Geneva.

The Guiding Principles on Internal Displacement (1998), built around the norm that sovereign states must earn their sovereignty, and failure to do so may result in them forgoing some of that sovereignty, posit that a central responsibility of the state is to protect its citizens against displacement, to assist those who are unavoidably displaced enabling them to build a new a life in a new location (see Kälin, this volume). By including development created displacement as a potential cause of human rights violations arising out of state complicity or neglect, the architects of the Guiding Principles sought to shift development created displacement into the legal humanitarian and human rights domain, and away from the governance-weak domain of development-related voluntary standards, commercial statements, and project-dependent safeguards. The Principles, combining elements of international refugee, human rights, and humanitarian law, address widely observed weaknesses in humanitarian operations and legal frameworks, by identifying those people displaced within the borders of their own countries for whom protection was severely lacking and against whom human rights violations were widespread. Principle 5, 2 (c) recognized that displacement resulting from 'large-scale development projects' which cannot be 'justified by compelling and overriding public interests' should be considered 'arbitrary', and where shown to be so, the Principles would offer a basis for protection and assistance during displacement, and define guarantees for safe return, resettlement, and reintegration.

As Robinson (2003) noted, the Guiding Principles place the responsibility on governments to justify any planned resettlement as compellingly in the national interest, and to show that displacement has been avoided or minimized in project planning wherever possible. Where displacement could not be avoided, the process had to be legal, involve consultation leading to consent, full compensation had to paid, and any harmful consequences, particularly in the case of minority populations, had to be addressed (2003: 53). The application of the Principles to land acquisition and involuntary resettlement, however, was not straightforward. The question of what constitutes 'compelling public interest', which is not defined in the Principles, remains contentious (Petterson 2002), with governments, business and citizens sharing diverse opinions about what should be the correct development path for a country, how its resources should be exploited, and how decisions about development should be taken. The emphasis on 'large-scale projects' is misguided because it is the larger projects for which international financing is sought that are more likely to be subject to development bank safeguards, or the voluntary codes outlined above; furthermore, external and independent scrutiny tends to follow large projects more closely than it does the thousands of smaller projects which together displace many more people each year. Concurrently, the meaning of 'compensation' is always problematic in resettlement operations, from the micro-problems of asset valuation, to the challenge of compensating for individual and community owned assets for which no monetary value can easily be attached (such as shrines or graves). Finally, the requirement for 'consent' in compulsory acquisition and involuntary resettlement is anomalous because compulsory and legal land acquisition in the public interest will always by definition, and in practice, be involuntary; the requirement of land acquisition and resettlement by consent would have major implications for the future of infrastructure development in the developed and developing world.

Weak and Fractured Governance

While the Guiding Principles are not binding on states, and are unlikely to become so, the backing of the UN Security Council and the creation of a Special Representative on the Human Rights of IDPs, has ensured that the Principles inform discussions between states, the UN system and civil society about the rights and needs of development displaced people, and the responsibilities of governments towards them. However, there is little evidence that the Principles have brought about significant changes in the policies or operations of governments in any high-profile development project involving involuntary resettlement. Nonetheless, the educative contribution of the Principles have been successful in assisting governments in preparing IDP laws that incorporate the protection principles, although the implementation of such laws, and the extension of victim status to those displaced by what are described as development projects, remains inconsistent. Part of the problem in drafting legislation to protect people displaced by development, is that such displacement frequently occurs in conditions of conflict where control of land and its productive capacity is achieved by driving people off land, and involves acts that may or may not have state involvement. The neatness of the causations of displacement outlined in the Principles therefore break down in the everyday realities of competition over resources, as does the identification of responsibility. The Principles also played a further role in influencing the adoption of the African Union Convention on the Protection and Assistance of Internally Displaced People in Africa (Kampala Convention) in October 2009. However, the obligation placed on states by the Convention (which was not yet legally enforceable in Summer 2013) to prevent 'as much as possible' displacement due to development projects carried out by public and private actors (Article 10.1) is far from onerous. There is no mention of consent, and nor are the issue of land tenure rights, or livelihood re-establishment, addressed.

While the Guiding Principles gave impetus to improving the policy and legal frameworks within which development created displacement take place, the actual protection afforded remains weak, in large part because the land tenure rights of individuals and communities are themselves far weaker than eminent domain laws. Important efforts have been made at the international level, led by the UN Declaration on the Rights of Indigenous Peoples to respect and strengthen land tenure systems, and these have been further endorsed by the UNDP Initiative on Legal Empowerment of the Poor (LEAP), and further recognized in successive World Development Reports. In addition, the World Bank has increased its investments in land-tenure related projects, and NGOs have published numerous policy statements urging the strengthening of land tenure. However, as pressure on land grows, the rules, norms, and institutions that govern access to and control over traditional lands are being placed under immense strain, not least when eminent domain rights are employed to expropriate land. Beyond state expropriation, however, land increasingly is being acquired for development purposes through the market, and protection for the weaker parties involved in so-called 'willing-seller-willing-buyer' transactions (which are commonplace in development-related land acquisitions, and indeed are recommended by lenders such as the EBRD and the IFC), involving complex contracts and asset valuation techniques, are generally not set down in law.

As outlined above, most eminent domain laws reflect the values and needs of nineteenth-century colonial powers who viewed the land they occupied as unowned, and compensation for its taking required only recompense for the temporary labour that its 'users' invested. Such eminent domain powers did not recognize the far-reaching social, psychological, and economic harm that displacement and dislocation brought to individuals and communities. While many governments have modified their colonial laws,[2] the Nehruvian idea that certain citizens should make sacrifices for the good of the nation,[3] are engrained in many countries' political culture. Enhanced protections offered to affected populations in more recently adopted resettlement instruments are readily set aside, for example, on the declaration of an emergency, or are found wanting when the source of funding and management of a project is international rather than local; and the failure to enforce resettlement laws and policies has been widely noted (WCD 2000: 10). The lack of political will is often very difficult to challenge by displaced people who are likely to originate from a marginalized community and often a minority population, who speak a different language to the majority, perhaps of a different faith, living in remote areas of the country and at a distance from the centre of power. Such affected communities exist on the edges of the formal economy and lack meaningful representation. While civil society organizations are giving 'voice' to displaced communities, and there are examples of effective and organized resistance from within those communities, the challenge of defending rights in unstable countries with an ineffective judiciary and limited freedom of expression and protest, are immense.

Weaknesses in the governance of land and resource acquisition, involuntary resettlement, compensation, and population relocation at the national and international level, by states, IFIs, corporations, and international organizations including the UN, have had wide-ranging negative impacts on the individuals and communities which are most disempowered in the development process. Governance is far from global, and cooperation between states, the private sector, and civil society, which is arguably necessary to tackle the globalized aspects of contemporary development processes, is not yet in evidence. Voluntary codes are not adhered to and the lack of transparent and independent scrutiny undermines accountability. The IFIs' policies, including those such as the IFC and EBRD that lend to the private sector, are narrowly project specific and fail to address the much wider political, social, and environmental consequences of what are regarded as one-off investments.

There is ample research evidence showing that the experience of displacement and resettlement as a result of land acquisition in pursuit of economic development is one of increased impoverishment and social and political marginalization, as a consequence of such fractured governance and the weak protection offered to the majority of displaced and resettled people. The multidimensionality of the impoverishment process is better understood (McDowell 1996), and studies have demonstrated that resettlement created impoverishment is persistent even over two or more generations (Bennett and McDowell 2012). Furthermore, Downing (2002) has argued that involuntary resettlement may create new forms of impoverishment that are not fully recognized in traditional poverty studies, and which involve the rapid unravelling of key social institutions, the undermining of social capital, and the loss of cultural rooting that is essential both for coping with the stresses and practical challenges of displacement and for livelihood

re-establishment. In particular, anthropological analysis helps us understand the significance of loss of place and home, and the detachment from what is familiar (Appardurai
1990; Gupta and Ferguson 1992).

Conclusion

Development investments in infrastructure are an increasingly globalized and transboundary phenomenon, and yet, as explored in this chapter, infrastructure development is an activity in which states have largely failed to adopt binding international
agreements overseen by fully accountable international institutions. States retain considerable autonomy in how they conduct infrastructure development and also in determining their land acquisition and resettlement policies. This means that governments,
even more so where they tend to authoritarianism, are able to pursue economic and
industrial policies where land acquisition is no serious impediment to the rapid achievement of growth objectives. The fragmentation of involuntary resettlement governance
reinforces the power of states and private companies in the development process. This
raises the question, following Betts's (2009) discussion of the governance of international migration, of what might be a normatively desirable and politically feasible
framework for land acquisition and involuntary resettlement governance in the development process, and, indeed, what the prospects are of such governance being achieved.

The past decade has seen 'bottom-up' attempts at formulating such governance. It has
been suggested that development induced population displacement is a form of forced
migration and as such could arguably fall under the remit of a new UN agency (such
as the proposed High Commission for Forced Migration) charged with enforcing a
new binding convention on the rights of displaced persons to include development displacees. Although the UN Guiding Principles on IDPs had the potential to become such
a binding convention, all indications are that it will remain as a form of embedded soft
law. Nonetheless, it was significant that the Principles, as a soft law framework, were the
product not of traditional policymaking based on the interests of states, but rather were
the product of the tenacity of multiply situated international lawyers whose affiliations
were essentially non-governmental and think tank in nature whilst allied in creative
ways with powerful UN institutions and backed financially by some European governments (Weiss and Korn 2006).

Elsewhere through the UN's humanitarian reform process, designed to identify and fill
gaps in humanitarian protection, there have been serious discussions among UN agencies and NGOs about the status of development displaced persons as 'people in need'
of humanitarian protection and warranting a humanitarian response (see Tennant
and Russell, this volume). While the UNHCR has expanded its mandate to include the
responsibility to protect not only refugees but also those who have not crossed a border and yet are in a refugee like situation, the agency has repeatedly rejected an expansion of the definition of displacement to include those people who lose their homes and

their assets in the development process. To date it would appear that land acquisition and involuntary resettlement will not be considered as warranting humanitarian protection, unless displaced people find themselves fleeing alongside refugees escaping from conflict and whose rights are clearly being violated. This position is understandable given that the humanitarian world faces a significant challenge dealing with conflict- and disaster induced displacement, often struggling to finance their operations and facing an ever-present concern that states in both the developed and developing world are questioning the relevance of the 1951 Refugee Convention and may seek revisions which would reduce their legal obligations to protection and asylum. There is a danger that the sheer number of development displacees (some 15 million annually) would eclipse the number of refugees and IDPs in conflict situations and divert resources accordingly. There is the further concern that including development displacees in statistics pertaining to the globally displaced would broaden the definition of displacement, confuse public understanding and ultimately reduce public sympathy for refugees fleeing from armed conflict. For these reasons, the future protection of development created displacement and involuntary resettlement will remain, principally, the responsibility of states.

NOTES

1. Due to under-reporting and hidden displacement, this number is likely to be a significant underestimation.
2. Most notably the adoption by the Indian Government of the Land Acquisition, Resettlement and Rehabilitation Act (LARR) on 26 September 2013.
3. In 1948, Jawaharlal Nehru famously told villagers protesting against their displacement from the Hirakud Dam, 'If you are to suffer, you should suffer in the interests of the country'.

REFERENCES

Appardurai, A. (1990) 'Disjuncture and Difference in the Global Cultural Economy'. *Public Culture* 2(2): 1–24.

Asian Development Bank (2007) *Capacity Building for Resettlement Risk Management: People's Republic of China Country Report*. Manila: Asian Development Bank.

Bennett, O., and McDowell, C. (2012) *Displaced: The Human Cost of Development and Resettlement*. New York: Palgrave Macmillan.

Betts, A. (2009) *Forced Migration and Global Politics*. London: Blackwell.

Butcher, D. (1971) *An Organisational Manual for Resettlement*. Rome: FAO.

Cernea, M. (2000) 'Risks, Safeguards and Reconstruction: A Model for Population Displacement and Resettlement'. Pp. 11–55 in M. Cernea and C. McDowell (eds.), *Risks and Reconstruction: The Experiences of Refugees and Resettlers*. Washington, DC: The World Bank.

Cernea, M. (2008) 'Compensation and Investment in Resettlement: Theory, Practice, Pitfalls, and Needed Policy'. In M. Cernea and H. M. Mathur (eds.), *Can Compensation Prevent Impoverishment?* Delhi: Oxford University Press.

Cernea, M., and McDowell, C. (eds.) (2000) *Risks and Reconstruction: The Experiences of Refugees and Resettlers.* Washington, DC: The World Bank.

Downing, T. E. (1996) 'Mitigating Social Impoverishment when People Are Involuntarily Displaced'. Pp. 33–48 in C. McDowell (ed.), *Understanding Impoverishment: The Consequences of Development-Induced Displacement.* Oxford: Berghahn.

Downing, T. E. (2002) *Avoiding New Poverty: Mining-Induced Displacement and Resettlement.* Mining, Minerals and Sustainable Development Working Paper No. 58. London: International Institute for Environment and Development.

Fernandes, W. (2008) 'India's Forced Displacement Policy and Practice: Is Compensation up to its Function'. In M. Cernea and H. M. Mathur (eds.), *Can Compensation Prevent Impoverishment?* Delhi: Oxford University Press.

Fuggle, R., Smith, W. T., Hydrosult Canada Inc., and Androdev Canada Inc. (2000) *Experience with Dams in Water and Energy Resource Development in The People's Republic of China.* Cape Town: World Commission on Dams.

Gupta, A., and Ferguson, J. (1992) 'Beyond "Culture": Space, Identity, and the Politics of Difference'. *Cultural Anthropology* 7(1): 6–23.

Hyden, G. (1980) *Beyond Ujamaa in Tanzania: Underdevelopment and an Uncaptured Peasantry.* London: Heinemann.

Jackson, S., and Sleigh, A. (2000) 'Resettlement for China's Three Gorges Project: Socio-economic Impact and Institutional Tensions'. *Communist and Post-Communist Studies* 33: 223–41.

McDonald, B., and Webber, M. (2002) 'Involuntary Resettlement in China: A Model of Good Practice'. *Forced Migration Review*, 14: 38–9.

McDowell, C. (ed.) (1996) *Understanding Impoverishment: The Consequences of Development-Induced Displacement* Oxford: Berghahn.

McDowell, C. (2002) 'Involuntary Resettlement, Impoverishment Risks and Sustainable Livelihoods'. *Australasian Journal of Disaster and Trauma Studies*, 6(2).

McDowell, C. (2013) 'Climate Change Adaptation and Mitigation: Implications for Land Acquisition and Population Relocation' *Development Policy Review*, 31: 677–95

McDowell, C., and Morrell, G. (2010) *Displacement beyond Conflict: Challenges for the 21st Century.* Oxford: Berghahn.

Penz, P., Drydyk, J., and Bose, P. (2011) *Displacement and Development: Ethics, Rights and Responsibility.* Cambridge: Cambridge University Press.

Petterson, B. (2002) 'Development-Induced Displacement: Internal Affair or International Human Rights Issue?' *Forced Migration Review* 12: 16–20.

Robinson, C. (2003) *Risks and Rights: The Causes, Consequences and Challenges of Development-Induced Displacement.* Washington, DC: The Brookings Institution.

Scott, J. C. (1988) *Seeing Like a State: How Certain Schemes to Improve the Human Condition Have Failed.* New Haven: Yale University Press.

Scudder, T. (2005) *The Future of Large Dams: Dealing with Social, Environmental, Institutional and Political Costs.* London: Earthscan.

Vertovec, S. (2006) 'The Emergence of Super-Diversity in Britain'. Working Paper No. 25. Oxford: COMPAS.

Weiss, T., and Korn, D. (2006) *Internal Displacement and its Consequences.* London: Routledge.

World Bank (1996) 'Resettlement and Development: The Bankwide Review of Projects Involving Involuntary Resettlement 1986–1993'. Departmental Working Paper No.1. Washington, DC.

CHAPTER 27

THE ENVIRONMENT-MOBILITY NEXUS: RECONCEPTUALIZING THE LINKS BETWEEN ENVIRONMENTAL STRESS, (IM)MOBILITY, AND POWER

ROGER ZETTER AND JAMES MORRISSEY[1]

INTRODUCTION

AN extensive academic and policymaking discourse exists on the links between climate change and population displacement. As a whole, the mainstream approach regarding this nexus is apolitical and neo-liberal in nature (Felli and Castree 2012), with a largely managerialist frame claiming that environmental variables shape mobility decisions in contexts of environmental stress. After introducing the reasoning which dominates current research and policy analysis on this relationship, this chapter challenges this discourse by using a 'local' lens and empirical data drawn from four case-study countries (Bangladesh, Ethiopia, Kenya, and Ghana[2]), to explain (im)mobility decisions in terms of structures of political and social power and disempowerment that condition the livelihoods of vulnerable households. The chapter argues for the saliency of recognizing the dominant 'hinge points' of power which explains the relationships between actors and institutions that shape access to resources and, in turn, mediate mobility decisions in contexts of environmental stress.

CLIMATE CHANGE AND POPULATION DISPLACEMENT

From the mid-1980s the assumption has grown that deteriorating environmental conditions associated with anthropogenically driven climate change will become a major cause of population displacement in the twenty-first century, especially in the developing world (El-Hinnawi 1985). Livelihoods rendered more vulnerable by the increasing incidence of both rapid-onset events such as extreme weather events, and the slow-onset impacts of desiccation, rising sea levels, salination, and river bank erosion, have underpinned the contention that a new form of 'forced migration' has been emerging with climate change the driver and the newly labelled 'climate' and 'environmental' 'refugees' the consequence (Myers 1993; Bates 2002; Christian Aid 2007). Concerns about the potential scale of this displacement process are highlighted, *inter alia*, by reports by the Intergovernmental Panel on Climate Change (2007); awareness of protection gaps for the 'environmentally displaced' (Zetter 2009, 2010a; McAdam 2010; UNHCR 2011); concerns at security threats caused by competition for depleting resources (Barnett and Adger 2007); new programmes such as the Nansen Initiative (2013); and rights advocacy to fill these protection gaps (Kälin 2010). Other initiatives include attempts to establish a new category of migrant (Laczko and Aghazarm 2009), and even proposals for a new Geneva Convention mirroring the 1951 'Refugee Convention' but for environmental refugees (CRIDEAU 2008; Docherty and Giannini 2009).

Debates on the displacement impacts of increasingly threatening scenarios of climate change gathered momentum (Morrissey 2012), with so-called 'maximalists' (Suhrke 1994), such as Myers and Kent (1995) and Myers (2002), assessing that there might be up to 200 million people forced to move by the middle of the century. Despite a general presumption that migration and displacement can be linked to deteriorating environmental conditions and slow-onset climate change, the 'minimalists' conversely pointed to the conceptual fallacy of a cause-effect, 'deterministic' relationship and argued that empirical evidence on these links was both limited and often highly contested (Black 2001; Piguet 2011; Morrissey 2012). For example, maximalists ignored that adaptation and resilience strategies might reduce threatened communities' susceptibility to displacement. Moreover, climate scientists are now less certain about the time scale and the intensity of climate change, rendering the 'who', 'how many', 'when', and 'where to' questions similarly uncertain.

Conceptually, it is therefore difficult to disaggregate environmental factors from the nexus of socio-political and economic processes and contexts which condition mobility decisions (Zetter 2010a). Empirical evidence similarly points towards complex and non-linear processes and interactions. This is not to deny the significance of environmental change and stressed environments in people's decisions to migrate, nor, in extreme circumstances, the directly instrumental effects, such as rising sea levels, which will compel people to leave their habitual environments. Rather, the impacts of changing environmental conditions must be set within a wider context of social, economic, and political factors that induce or constrain people's decisions to migrate.

Environmental Stress, Mobility, Power, and Disempowerment

If we are to understand the relationship between environmental stress and human (im-)mobility, we need to explore the nexus of socio-political processes and the distribution of social and political power that shape and mediate household access to resources, and thus their propensity/capacity to migrate in the context of environmental stress. The presence and the combination of these structural factors conditioning mobility patterns and processes vary between countries and localities. Consideration of the contingency of structures of 'power' is an established message in the vulnerability, political ecology, and environment-society literature (Adger and Kelly 1999; Wisner et al. 2004), but one which has been largely absent in the discourse on the nexus between environmental change and human mobility, and ignored entirely by policymakers.

An overarching question is thus what structural features cause some people to respond to environmental stress by migrating while others do not, or cannot?

Research data from Bangladesh, Ethiopia, Kenya, and Ghana, invoking a novel focus on structural conditions at the local level, shows that vulnerable, or potentially vulnerable, communities are distinguishable by their exclusion from the structures of power which might normally allow either access to the material means necessary to secure their livelihoods and minimize exposure to hazards (e.g. through adaptation and resilience strategies or facilitating mobility), or the decision-making processes required to ensure relevant interventions (e.g. through participatory approaches to resettlement).[3]

POWER STRUCTURES AND THEIR EFFECTS IN CONTEXTS OF ENVIRONMENTAL STRESS

In the remainder of this chapter, we take a wide perspective when elaborating the nature and effect of 'power' in this context. This includes political power, for example the power of elected representatives or informal power brokers in local communities; economic power, which may include the role of landowners, money lenders, traders, and others who control access to livelihood resources; and hegemonic socio-cultural norms including practices of collective decision making, resistance to migration and deference to traditional/customary norms such as those governing access to land, burial practices, and sharing and mutual support in times of livelihood adversity.

Three examples illustrate the relevance and application of these concepts.

Bangladesh

In Bangladesh, rural livelihoods are compromised by multiple environmental stresses, and yet it is how the extant power structures mediate the impacts of such stress that dominates explanations of livelihood (in)security and subsequent human (im)mobility.

In a country where the majority of Bangladesh's population is landless and absolute landlessness is steadily increasing, our research shows that under conditions of a centralized but weak state with limited accountability, power is, in effect, ceded to local elites, comprising bigger landowners or small businessmen, often linked to the local clergy and with political, social, and business relations based on patronage. These actors exploit a corrupt and inefficient land registration system to acquire land from usually illiterate groups or to forcefully expel people from their land with impunity. It is these processes that, combined with environmental stress (rather than the stress itself), increase household vulnerability and thus the propensity for (im)mobility. The consequences play out in two ways.

First, marginalized social groups typically move to marginal lands leaving them with poorer crops and more vulnerable to environmental stresses and disasters (flooding, river bank erosion, salinity). Concomitantly the impact of these stresses further entrenches power inequalities: while the impacts of erosion are theoretically ameliorable—erosion in one place results in deposition and accretion in another—accreted land is considered too unstable for housing and is given to established landholders who have land for their household elsewhere and who can thus turn this land over to production (usually through hired labour constituted by landless groups). Similarly, while there is an established procedure for providing government (*Khas*) land as compensation for households whose livelihoods are undermined by erosion, such land is insufficient to provide for all those who are entitled to it, and much of what is available is appropriated by local elites. Thus power inequalities act to render certain groups more vulnerable to environmental stresses and disasters, while the redistribution of resources in the aftermath of such events frequently acts to further entrench those self-same inequalities.

A second outcome of these processes is that marginalized groups become increasingly reliant on larger landowners for their livelihoods, whether as tenants and/or as daily labourers. In addition to richer landowners having the best lands, new environmental stresses have also endangered productivity, sometimes leading to shifts in agricultural patterns. In Moralganj for instance, increasing salinity has forced most landlords to shift from rice cultivation, with two crops a year a few decades ago, to shrimp farming, which only produces one harvest a year, and thus requires less labour. For landowners, shrimp farming remains a profitable enterprise and the switch in livelihoods effectively insulates them from the impacts of environmental stress. For those without land, however, the shift to shrimp farming, and resultant reduction in work opportunities, has significant impacts on livelihoods, effectively halving an already meagre income base. These economic dynamics reinforce the power of rural elites and traditional hierarchies whilst further accentuating disempowerment of the landless labourers.[4]

Ethiopia

Similarly, in Ethiopia, localized power is the dominant structural feature manifest under conditions of extensive state power, but limited bureaucratic reach. Here, however, the main brokers are not landed elites but local officials, appointed as party loyalists who are given powers to make decisions regarding access to the most basic means of production and forms of income (land, jobs, credit, and food aid). They can act with relative autonomy, given the state's limited capacity to monitor their administrative actions, and no effective channels for citizens to challenge their accountability. This creates space for highly localized politics with large discrepancies in, and often highly personal interpretations of, what is believed to be formal state policy and/or law.

In a context where rural and urban livelihoods are similarly precarious—the former being reliant on a fickle and degraded biophysical environment and the latter being characterized by saturated labour markets—rural–urban migration does not offer a panacea to the problems of livelihood insecurity generated by environmental stress. As such, once major demographic features (in this case age) have been accounted for, it is the local officials—acting as gatekeepers for the goods required to secure livelihoods—who become central in explaining who migrates and who does not in a context of environmental stress.

The expansion of local officials' power lies in central government's desire to coerce votes. This has been achieved by expanding the number of local political administrative units, which has in turn allowed the state to better observe individual behaviour and thereby identify voices of dissent. The control of resources vital for survival, particularly in the rural areas, is then used as a means to punish opposition and reward compliance.

As such, while it is environmental stress that shapes much of the livelihood insecurity in Ethiopia and which, in turn, motivates the desire to move, it is the context of political *coercion*, and the resultant devolution of power over vital resources to local actors, which shapes (im)mobility decisions and the subsequent conditions of human (in)security.

In a context similar to that in Bangladesh, pressure on landholding also shapes mobility dynamics in Ethiopia. Ironically, however, in Ethiopia such pressures are the outcome of revolutionary, rather than customary, practices. In Ethiopia all the country's land is held by the state, with a prohibition on any transfer of land by private sale. Such conditions have been in place since the socialist *Derg* government replaced the imperial regime of Haile Selassie, and have been maintained by the current government since it came to power in the early 1990s. The outcome is that it requires the state to administer periodic, centralized redistributions of land to allow new households to acquire properties large enough to support themselves. Under conditions of population growth, however, such redistributions have resulted in increasingly fractionalized landholdings. Consequently, landholdings in the north of the country are now too small to allow many households to sustain themselves for an entire year, even under perfect agricultural conditions, let alone with the added impact of social and environmental stress. Thus, the state has declared that there will be no further redistribution of land, while at the same time refusing to change its position on the potential for private transfer by sale.

Such conditions exacerbate the impacts of environmental stress. Where larger land-holdings might have allowed households to produce a sufficient harvest, under worsening rainfall conditions, the small landholdings to which people currently have access make this impossible. Similarly, the impacts of reduced landholdings could be ameliorated by better bio-physical conditions, thereby lessening the imperative to move. In addition, among people who were too young to receive land in the last major redistribution, there is the problem of intractable landlessness. These individuals currently have no land and no means of attaining land outside inheritance, which is inadequate given the extent to which fertility rates outstrip mortality rates in the country, particularly in rural areas. In such a context, environmental stress interacts with a lack of land to increase the imperative to move, by reducing the opportunity cost of not doing so.

Again, understanding such conditions requires an appreciation of the macro-scale politics informing the current government's decision to maintain state ownership of the country's land and its refusal to allow any form of private transfer by sale.

In Bangladesh and Ethiopia, decentralized and highly disaggregated power structures mediate the nature and impact of environmental stress for poor people, and the migratory consequences. Kenya offers a contrasting account of the local power structures that affect the impacts of environmental stress and mobility. Here, our evidence shows how a configuration of collective socio-political alliances comprising family, customary, and collective community power structures mediate environmental stress creating constraints and resistance to migration.

Kenya

In Kenya, customary cultural norms dominate a hierarchy of power structures primarily in the form of patrilineal and extended family dynamics. Thus, in the arid and drought-prone Kalkalcha village, for instance, the decision to move rests at the family level. Wealthy pastoralists secure their access to pasture by moving to more fertile areas in the Tana basin and delta, while intermediate and poor households, supported by relatives who have already migrated, also opt for migration. In both Budalangi and Kalkalcha villages, the network of relatives is an important factor in the decision process for (im)mobility. The justification of immobility is often the absence of a support network. Conversely, the family network opens potential for migration and intervenes in the choice of the destination. Most of the migrants in our fieldwork, in the slums of Eldoret and Nairobi, acknowledge that they have not specifically chosen either the place or the kind of job they wanted to undertake: their destinations and employment reflect the fact that they have relatives able to assist them through providing short-term and/or permanent accommodation as well as a job and financial assistance.

Customary power and collective community (often superimposed by ethnicity) in Kenya embodies another kind of power structure, above the family level. It is manifest through political and judicial power which is codified and regulated by pre- and post-colonial customary institutions, comprising councils of elders, and by socio-economical power. Politico-judicial power is wide-ranging but relevant, for example, in regulating access to resources such as land, pasture, and water and cattle-rustling, all of which are critical elements in local livelihoods where the traditional, customary power of the elders not only plays a critical role in mediating environmental stress but also in orchestrating adaptation to environmental change. In this regard, decisions might be made to set aside areas for pasture recovery, organizing the migration of animals, and the search for pasture during periods of drought. In the particular case of a pastoralist system, the mobility decision rests upon the community.

Recently, however, customary power has tended to be eroded. Although among Pokots, organization is still partly based on the customs and elders' power system, for the Ormas, it seems to be more degraded, and even more so for the Luhya farmers of Budalangi. The decline in customary power structures can be explained, in the main, by the degree of penetration by exogenous agencies, ranging from formal intervention by state administrative infrastructure to religious groups and NGOs who play an increasingly important role in food security, as in Ethiopia. At the same time, attitudes are changing to the exercise of traditional power within these and other communities. In particular, this diminution of power may also be explained by the fact that young people are more inclined to break away from traditional norms.

Alongside these customary, politico-judicial manifestations of power is the informal socio-economic collective power of the community which links community members through collective access to, and management of, key livelihood resources. How this form of power is exercised has great relevance to the way in which environmental stress and shocks are absorbed by the community and how they configure mobility decisions in that context. For example, in most of the rural locations of our study, people pay for the water they collect from wells; the funds are then reinvested for the maintenance and future exploitation of water sources, which in turn conditions the extent to which livelihoods can be sustained, and out-migration resisted.

Nevertheless, collective resource management goes much further, illustrated by the way in which other scarce resources or environmental shocks are mediated. Amongst the Pokot community, solidarity is an essential mechanism to alleviate the impacts of environmental shocks. When families face economic difficulties because they have lost animals and have no other means of livelihood support, they are fed or hosted by another family. A traditional loan and insurance system, often extending inter-generationally, also enables households whose cattle have been stricken by disease and drought to restock. Furthermore, trade and marriage interactions between contiguous villages provide the basis of mutual support. When one village is flooded, wives return to their parents' village for support and new seeds, for instance. This spontaneous mechanism facilitates recovery for those affected by floods. Likewise, during the dry season, when pasture is particularly scarce, pastoral communities convene a dry season truce and agree on shared access to resources.

Although we cannot be conclusive at this stage, our evidence suggests, albeit to differing extents among different groups, that these collective configurations of socio-political alliances as well as the collective way in which environmental shocks may be faced in Kenya, have typically constrained out-migration as a response to environmental stress. This conclusion is reinforced by evidence of strong cultural resistance to migration. Environmental shocks are traditionally dealt with by cultural communal solidarity, rather than by 'running away': the communities encourage resistance to migration by fuelling fears of the exterior, exclusion, and insecurity once outside the community's boundaries, fears which are underpinned by the endemic violence of Kenya's border areas. Elders' discourse and stories sustain collective resistance and the counter-incentive to migration.

However, it is clear that environmental stress, with extending periods of drought affecting all households, is increasingly placing these norms under pressure: collective mechanisms are decreasingly able to cope with the vulnerability or impoverishment of community members. Thus, as with the declining reach of politico-judicial power, so too does the declining capacity of collective socio-economic power structures (under conditions of environmental stress as well as social change) open space for more formal, exogenous agencies to intervene. These dynamics alter the locus and exercise of power, with potentially far-reaching consequences for: who migrates, who does not, where they go and what the prospects for livelihood security look like post-migration, in both the sending and receiving areas.

How Does the Exercise of Power Differ across Different Social Groups?

Just as the characteristics and effects of power structures differ between and within countries, we must similarly appreciate how institutional and other relationships structure power across different social groups—how women, men, children, the elderly, and different communities and ethnic groups might be differentially predisposed to conditions of human insecurity and vulnerability resulting from environmental stress, and how this manifests in (im)mobility.

For example, in Bangladesh the nexus of environmental stress, vulnerability and disempowerment generates out-migration by young women. More detailed analysis of data from Kenya illustrates why such disaggregation is important to understand the differential impacts of power structures in the context of environmental stress and the propensity to migrate. Amongst the Budalangi, spiritual attachment to the land impedes migration from their locality, as some members of the community are reluctant to leave the home that offers a physical tie to the spirits. The family's gods are attached to that place, and the deceased are buried in the familial courtyard. Nonetheless, whilst this attachment to place is evident amongst the older generation, the younger generation are less influenced by these traditional beliefs, manifest in their greater willingness to pursue the social and economic opportunities that migration potentially offers. By extension, we might argue that under conditions of environmental stress, younger people are more likely to challenge prevailing cultural norms and opt to migrate as a way of averting increasing vulnerability. Our data show that if they do not migrate, it is more because of the lack of economic opportunities or social networks elsewhere, than because of cultural constraints.

Other traditional norms are confronted by contemporary pressures. Many ethnic groups in Kenya (other than some nomadic groups) have a patrilineal system of land inheritance and subdivision. Polygamy and population growth have progressively reduced the size of the plots, threatening the scope for all the male children to sustain their traditional livelihoods on inheritance. In this context, environmental stress, declining agricultural productivity, and thus increasing vulnerability, concomitantly act as strong incentives for migration. Some migrants in Nairobi testified that they preferred to go to the city and radically change their lifestyle because of this complex and seemingly irreversible nexus of constraints in the rural areas.

Understanding how structural determinants mediate the impacts of environmental stress (and in some instances generate and perpetuate environmental stress) is core to our analysis. And yet this begs supplementary questions of how such power structures are able to exist, how they are legitimized, how they sustain their influence, and their differential impacts.

The Legitimization, Maintenance, and Contestation of Power Structures

The dynamics of these power structures are similarly diverse. In Ghana, for example, the legitimacy of the power structures stems from hegemonic deference to traditional authority structures such as village elders and earth priests. In relation to the mid-country destinations for migrants from the north of Ghana, by conferring burial rights for migrants' relatives, the earth priests provide migrants with a rite of passage from sojourners to settlers. Also important to note here is the relationship between competing power structures and the fact that the government allows traditional authority to persist alongside the formal institutions of the state.

In contrast, as we have seen in the case of Bangladesh, the existence of local informal power brokers (and corruption) arises because of the inherent weakness of the state, whereas in Kenya it arises from the balancing of complex and diverse ethnic interests in land as well as the competing balance between customary and government/state institutions and power structures. In Kenya mistrust of the state, and especially its role in resettlement schemes, creates resistance to the presence of the state, instead perhaps reinforcing local power and decision-making structures. By contrast again, we suggest that evidence as to the coercive power of the state, often represented by local administrators as in Ethiopia, has critical importance in demonstrating how policies aiming to manage environmental stress (and related migratory impacts) are enacted and implemented.

Alongside the existence and legitimacy of the power structures is their maintenance and contestation; indeed, the three dynamics are intertwined.

On the one hand we have identified processes through which unequal access is maintained and enforced. For example, the legitimacy of the power held by the local officials to distribute land in Ethiopia lies, to a large extent, in the coercive power of the state which also maintains the power structures in the context of a wilfully blind international community. In Bangladesh, the power of local landowners is maintained by patronage and through provision of employment to landless peasants; however, here their legitimacy arises because of the power vacuum which exists between a weak state and powerless local authorities. The threat of exclusion from basic income grants, social welfare support, and food aid in Ethiopia, or through eviction in Bangladesh and social exclusion in Kenya, reinforce the maintenance of powerlessness.

These examples of the ways power structures reproduce themselves indicate how local communities, and especially individual households, can become increasingly marginalized and thus increasingly vulnerable in conditions of environmental stress. In turn, it is these conditions that translate into decisions to migrate or not in order to reduce vulnerability and defend livelihoods at a minimal level.

On the other hand, although the above examples have tended to cast power in a negative light, institutional power can be used to ensure rights and better-informed decision making on migration. This is evident in acts of charity among citizens in Ethiopia, acts of community solidarity in Kenya, the role of Muslim philanthropy in Bangladesh, as well as the vital role played in all countries by social networks (a representation of collective power) in mitigating some of the negative impacts of disasters and droughts and facilitating mobility by easing access to urban shelter and labour markets. Such features are central to the processes of securing rights and livelihoods and thus cannot be excluded from our explanations of how power mediates the impacts of environmental stress in the case-study countries.

Moreover, other informal strategies enable individuals and communities to contest such power relations and assert their claims to resources. For example, in Bangladesh, certain communities experience greater levels of land tenure security, having organized themselves, at times with the advocacy of local NGOs. In Kenya, local communities' embedded suspicion of government policies on land issues—notably to planned resettlement projects and the practice of forced evictions—tends to reinforce their recourse to customary cultural precepts and beliefs as the factors conditioning their responses to environmental stress. Furthermore, in Kenya, as in Bangladesh and Ethiopia, many rural households in the country's more vulnerable regions rely on substantial and sustained emergency food aid distributed by the government, the Kenyan Red Cross, and other NGOs. This may act as a safety valve in relation to decisions to migrate, by protecting customary coping mechanisms and underpinning livelihoods. Indeed, it is remarkable how much this assistance appears to be fully, and almost automatically, integrated as a coping mechanism in household livelihood strategies in Kalkalcha and North Pokot, for example. Whether the combined effect of customary practices and food aid are sustainable in the longer term is highly questionable.

These examples demonstrate how local communities find ways of successfully challenging overbearing or repressive power structures and develop strategies to increase livelihood security (Scott 1997). Cases such as these suggest that in some situations these groups have been able to make or organize these claims, whilst others have been unable to do so; the cases also suggest that there are limits to these actions of contestation (Scott 1997). With this security comes the potential to reduce or limit vulnerability to environmental stress and other shocks and thus also to reduce the extent to which migration may be the necessary or only means of accommodating these stresses and shocks.

Nonetheless, a further important aspect of this research is that the exercise of power is not static. New dynamics come into play, for example, when community and customary power structures become less capable of coping with increasing vulnerability and conditions of environmental stress, and space is consequently opened up for exogenous agencies to reconfigure the locus and form of power. This has potentially far-reaching consequences for the ways in which local communities can respond to continuing environmental stress, with the likely effect of further decreasing their autonomy over crucial decision-making areas such as migration.

Conclusion

This chapter has presented a fundamental challenge to the apolitical framing of the environmental stress-mobility nexus. As such it challenges the managerial focus on disaster risk, adaptation, and resilience policies for those susceptible to the displacement impacts of environmental stress. In addition, it challenges calls, principally by external advocacy groups and agencies, for rights protection norms and frameworks for what some claim to be a newly emerging category of forced migrants. Although these policies and instruments are necessary, in allowing for 'solutions' they ultimately ignore the core issue of the distribution of power and, in so doing, potentially maintain, or even exacerbate such inequality.

Thus, the silence of a rights-based discourse on environmental stress and displacement in the affected countries speaks to the appropriation of power either by the state through coercive practices (e.g. in Ethiopia), or by political and landed elites (e.g. in Bangladesh and Kenya, and to a lesser extent in Ghana). In the context of fragile governance structures, vulnerable people, almost by definition, have neither access nor power to invoke rights to protect their interests, or to reduce their vulnerability to environmental stress. As such, this high degree of disempowerment raises profound questions about the apolitical framing of the environmental stress-mobility nexus.

These findings therefore lay the foundations for continuing research in two main areas: first, on questioning the viability of adaptation—currently promoted as the primary response to environmental stress—in situations where power is so unequally available; and second, on the greater significance of understanding the socio-economic and cultural determinants of livelihoods at the household level which shape mobility decisions in the context of environmental stress, with less attention paid to the role of so-called 'environmental drivers' per se.

Reframing challenges in terms of power and politics is therefore to suggest that these challenges need to be addressed in structural rather than instrumental terms.

NOTES

1. This chapter is based on research funded by the John D and Catherine D MacArthur Foundation entitled 'Environmentally displaced people: rights, policies and labels', Grant No 10-94408-000-INP. The authors are grateful for the support of the Foundation. Thanks are also due to the research team, Jane Chun, Marie Pecoud, Malika Peyraut, and Augustine Yelfaanibe. An earlier version of this chapter entitled 'Migration, Rights and Power: Understanding the Links between Environmental Stress and (Im-)mobility' was presented at the 'Crisis Migration Roundtable' held by the John D. and Catherine D. MacArthur Foundation, in Chicago in February 2013.

2. Although our research also includes Vietnam, space limitations constrain reference only to Bangladesh, Ethiopia, Kenya, and Ghana.

3. Our work on the conjuncture of environmental stress and mobility is contextualized by wider questions about the political and historical framing of migration policies and the national level migration discourse in each of the countries. These 'macro' level structural conditions—notably episodic and often traumatic migration histories and thus the complex political milieu and sensitivities within which internal migration sits make this a highly sensitive phenomenon in all five countries—are explored in a complementary paper (Zetter and Morrissey 2014).

4. Although not part of the present discussion, mobility is acknowledged as an important option. In our study areas, most poor rural families have now at least one member engaged in a migratory process to an urban area, whether on a temporary basis or a permanent relocation. Ironically, they may reside with urban area living standards that may be worse than in the rural areas of origin. Moreover, while landownership confers prestige and power in Bangladesh, landlessness is largely stigmatized and of itself a factor in out-migration.

REFERENCES

Adger, N. W., and Kelly, P. M. (1999) 'Social Vulnerability to Climate Change and the Architecture of Entitlements'. *Mitigation and Adaptation Strategies for Global Change* 4(3): 253–66.

Barnett, J., and Adger, W. N. (2007) 'Climate Change, Human Security and Violent Conflict'. *Political Geography*: 1–17.

Bates, D. C. (2002) 'Environmental Refugees? Classifying Human Migrations Caused by Environmental Change'. *Population and Environment* 23(5): 465–77.

Black, R. (2001) 'Environmental Refugees: Myth or Reality?' Working Paper No. 34. Geneva: UNHCR.

Christian Aid (2007) *Human Tide: The Real Migration Crisis*. <http://www.christianaid.org.uk/Images/human_tide3__tcm15-23335.pdf>.

CRIDEAU, CRDP, and Faculty of Law and Economic Science at the University of Limoges (2008) *Draft Convention on the International Status of Environmentally-Displaced Persons*. <http://www.cidce.org/pdf/Draft%20Convention%20on%20the%20International%20Status%20on%20environmentally%20displaced%20persons.pdf>.

Docherty, B., and Giannini, T. (2009) 'Confronting a Rising Tide: A Proposal for a Convention on Climate Change Refugees'. *Harvard Environmental Law Review* 33: 349–403.

El-Hinnawi, E. (1985) *Environmental Refugees*. Nairobi: United Nations Environmental Programme.

Felli, R., and Castree, N. (2012) 'Commentary'. *Environment and Planning A* 44: 1–4.

Intergovernmental Panel on Climate Change (2007) *Contribution of Working Group II to the Fourth Assessment Report of the Intergovernmental Panel on Climate Change*. Cambridge: Cambridge University Press.

Kälin, W. (2010) 'Conceptualizing Climate-Induced Displacement'. Pp. 81–104 in J. McAdam (ed.), *Climate Change and Displacement in the Pacific: Multidisciplinary Perspectives*. Oxford: Hart Publishing.

Laczko, F., and Aghazarm, C. (eds.) (2009) *Migration, Environment and Climate Change: Assessing the Evidence*. Geneva: IOM.

McAdam, J. (ed.) (2010) *Climate Change and Displacement in the Pacific: Multidisciplinary Perspectives*. Oxford: Hart Publishing.

Morrissey, J. (2012) 'Rethinking the "Debate on Environmental Refugees": From "Maximilists and Minimalists" to "Proponents and Critics"'. *Journal of Political Ecology* 19: 36–49.

Myers, N. (1993) 'Environmental Refugees in a Globally Warmed World'. *BioScience* 43(11): 752–61.

Myers, N. (2002) 'Environmental Refugees: A Growing Phenomenon of the 21st Century'. *Philosophical Transactions of the Royal Society* 357: 609–13.

Myers, N., and Kent, J. (1995) *Environmental Exodus: An Emergent Crisis in the Global Arena*. Washingdon, DC: The Climate Institute.

Nansen Initiative (2013) <http://www.nanseninitiative.org>.

Piguet, E., Pecoud, A., and de Guchteneir, P. (2011) *Migration and Climate Change*. Cambridge and Paris: Cambridge University Press and UNESCO.

Scott, J. (1997) *Seeing Like a State: How Certain Schemes to Improve the Human Condition Have Failed*. New Haven: Yale University Press.

Suhrke, A. (1994) 'Environmental Degradation and Population Flows'. *Journal of International Affair* 47(2): 473–96.

UNHCR (2011) *Summary of Deliberations on Climate Change and Displacement*. Geneva: UNHCR. April. <http://www.unhcr.org/cgi-bin/texis/vtx/home/opendocPD-FViewer.html?docid=4da2b5e19&query=Summary%20of%20Deliberations%20on%20Climate%20Change%20and%20Displacement%20April%202011>.

Wisner, B., Blaikie, P., Cannon, T., and Davis, I. (2004) *At Risk: Natural Hazards, People's Vulnerability and Disasters* (2nd edn.). London: Routledge.

Zetter, R. (2009) 'Protection and the Role of Legal and Normative Frameworks'. Pp. 285–441 in F. Laczko and C. Aghazarm (eds.), *Migration Environment and Climate Change: Assessing the Evidence*. Geneva: IOM.

Zetter, R. (2010a) *Protecting Environmentally Displaced People: Developing the Capacity of Legal and Normative Frameworks*. University of Oxford, Refugee Studies Centre, report commissioned by UNHCR and Governments of Switzerland and Norway.

Zetter, R. (2010b) 'Protecting People Displaced by Climate Change: Some Conceptual Challenges'. Pp. 131–50 in J. McAdam (ed.), *Climate Change and Displacement in the Pacific: Multidisciplinary Perspectives*. Oxford: Hart Publishing.

Zetter, R., and Morrissey, J. (2014) 'Environmental Displacement and the Challenge of Rights Protection'. Forthcoming in S. Martin, S. Weerasinghe, and A. Taylor (eds.), *Crisis Migration, Causes, Consequences and Responses*. London: Routledge.

CHAPTER 28

TRAFFICKING

BRIDGET ANDERSON

INTRODUCTION

THERE is an extensive but relatively recent literature on trafficking spanning academia, policy, and non-governmental organizations. 'Trafficking' is applied to highly heterogeneous phenomena from child labour in Bangladesh to tobacco farming in Kazakhstan to underage prostitution in the European Union. The states of origin and of destination for people identified as victims of trafficking (VoT) are multiple: victims from Burma have been identified in Thailand, VoT from Thailand identified in the UK, victims from Benin have been identified in Nigeria, and victims from Nigeria have been identified in Italy and so on. Anti-trafficking activity is not restricted to a single state and trafficking is treated as a crime requiring international cooperation, although it is also recognized as occurring within states. It is a field where there is considerable engagement between policymakers, academics, and activists, often incorporating surprising alliances between, for example, radical feminists and evangelical Christians (Weitzer 2007).

While there is considerable interest in trafficking it is also bedevilled by conflicting agendas and analyses. This chapter will first consider the history of trafficking legislation policies with a particular focus on the landmark Trafficking Protocol of 2000. It goes on to consider how force and coercion have been understood and debated depending on whether trafficking is regarded as a problem of prostitution, or of forced labour. It will then examine how the focus on migration raises difficult questions for activists and for states, both with reference to trafficking and labour migrants and trafficking and asylum. It will end with a brief consideration of the politics of trafficking.

ANTI-TRAFFICKING: A BRIEF HISTORY

Between 1904 and 1933 there were four international instruments suppressing 'the White Slave Traffic', the procurement by force or deceit of a white girl or woman for 'immoral purposes'. The initial trigger for this response was growing female migration from Europe and Russia to the Americas and parts of the British Empire (Doezema 2010). At that time there was also anxiety in the USA about the trafficking of white women because of their perceived vulnerability to the depredations of free black men. In 1949, the newly created United Nations adopted the Convention for the Suppression of the Traffic in Persons and of the Exploitation of the Prostitution of Others, a legally binding instrument that punished persons who 'to gratify the passions of another procures or exploits the prostitution of a person . . . even with the consent of that person' (United Nations 1949: Art. 1). This was not ratified by many states, and for over four decades following 1950 trafficking was not a focus of international interest.

State concerns about trafficking resurfaced in the late 1990s, and in 2000 the UN General Assembly adopted the Convention Against Transnational Organized Crime. This was supplemented by three additional protocols dealing with Trafficking in Firearms, Smuggling of Migrants, and the Protocol to Prevent, Suppress and Punish Trafficking in Persons Especially Women and Children. The latter is known as the Trafficking Protocol, or the Palermo Protocol. There were several factors that contributed to states' readiness to re-engage with trafficking as a policy problem at this time. Some were nationally specific: Argentina was proposing a new convention against trafficking in minors (Gallagher 2010) and the United States had issued a memorandum on measures to be taken to combat violence against women and trafficking (Chuang 2010). However, there were also global pressures at work. Europe was witnessing an increase in intra-European migration following the fall of the Berlin Wall. Emigrants from former Communist states had previously been limited to relatively small numbers of political refugees recognized by the 1951 UNHCR Refugee Convention. But by the 1990s there was significant out-migration, particularly of women, from these same states. This movement was now classed as a movement of economic migrants rather than of political refugees and European states and institutions were beginning to develop punitive responses. More generally, improved and lower cost international transport, proliferation of conflicts, and increasing global integration were resulting in an increase in movements of people across borders, and women were becoming increasingly visible as migrants (the so-called 'feminization of migration').

Definitions and the Trafficking and Smuggling Protocols

The Protocol drafting occurred within a context of intense preoccupations with immigration, prostitution, and the vulnerabilities of children. Given these very different preoccupations, one of its achievements is often held to be agreement reached on the first internationally recognized definition of trafficking:

> 'Trafficking in persons' shall mean the recruitment, transportation, transfer, harbouring or receipt of persons, by means of the threat or use of force or other forms of coercion, of abduction, of fraud, of deception, of the abuse of power or of a position of vulnerability or of the giving or receiving of payments or benefits to achieve the consent of a person having control over another person, for the purpose of exploitation. Exploitation shall include, at a minimum, the exploitation of the prostitution of others or other forms of sexual exploitation, forced labour or services, slavery or practices similar to slavery, servitude or the removal of organs. (United Nations 2000: Art. 3(a))

This defines trafficking as a matter of process. The end point of slavery, sexual exploitation, removal of organs, etc. is *not* what is identified as trafficking. To count as trafficking an act must have three elements: 'transportation...by means of...for the purpose of exploitation'. In this sense it is akin to the criminalization of the slave trade rather than the criminalization of slavery. The Trafficking Protocol is not a human rights instrument, it is an instrument designed to facilitate cooperation between states to combat organized crime. The emphasis is on intercepting traffickers and on punishing and prosecuting them. Border control, not human rights protection, lie at its heart.

Although the protocol is a supplement to the Convention on Transnational Organized Crime, the transportation element of trafficking does not have to occur across national boundaries and neither is entry into a state necessarily illegal. Thus anti-trafficking policies can illegalize mobility that is otherwise, *qua* mobility, legal. Movement by EU nationals within the EU for example, or mobility of under-18s for the purposes of work within and between states of the global South, can under certain circumstances and if it is for the purpose of labour/prostitution be criminalized as trafficking. 'Internal' trafficking has received more research and policy attention in the global South. Its associated policies are typically focused on the prevention of child movement and child labour, and the sensitization and education of families perceived as ignorant and poverty stricken (see e.g. Howard 2012). In the global North anti-trafficking is associated with the expansion of criminal networks and mafia-type organizations. Whether an internal or an international migrant, the victim of trafficking is often depicted as hailing from a 'traditional' background, oppressed by both 'culture' and poverty.

The Smuggling Protocol has received far less academic and activist attention but in practice the differentiation between trafficked and smuggled persons is crucial to the management of anti-trafficking regimes. Both protocols seek to criminalize the facilitation of certain types of mobility, but in contrast to trafficking, smuggling is concerned with the illegal crossing of international borders. The Smuggling Protocol sets a transnational duty to criminalize irregular border crossing. States of origin are required for instance, not only to readmit smuggled nationals, but also to actively facilitate the travel and re-entry of both nationals and permanent residents. Thus it effectively 'converts an issue traditionally conceived as purely a matter of domestic law (the right of states to sanction persons who aid or assist persons unlawfully to enter their territory) into a transnational legal obligation' (Hathaway 2008: 27). Through the Trafficking and Smuggling protocols, countries of origin and transit are conscripted into a global project of mobility control.

Both smuggling and trafficking protocols have received considerable international support, with 112 states having signed the Smuggling Protocol and 117 signed the Trafficking Protocol by January 2013. In contrast, only 34 states have signed the UN Convention on the Protection of the Rights of All Migrant Workers and their Families, approved by the UN ten years earlier in 1990. Following the Trafficking Protocol there were a number of regional instruments developed including the Council of Europe Convention on Action Against Trafficking in Human Beings (CoE Convention), which entered into force in 2008, and the Council Directive on the Short-Term Residence Permit Issued to Victims of Action to Facilitate Illegal Immigration or Trafficking in Human Beings Who Co-operate with the Competent Authorities. These have greater emphasis on victim protection but nevertheless this is generally only extended to those who cooperate with authorities. Other regional legal instruments include the SAARC Convention on Preventing and Combating Trafficking in Women and Children for Prostitution (signed by Bhutan, Nepal, Sri Lanka, India, Pakistan, Maldives, Bangladesh), and the ASEAN Declaration Against Trafficking in Persons (signed by Brunei, Cambodia, Indonesia, Lao, Malaysia, Myanmar, Philippines, Singapore, Thailand, and Vietnam). The United Nations Global Initiative to Fight Human Trafficking (UN GIFT) launched by the International Labour Organization, the Office of the United Nations High Commissioner for Human Rights, the United Nations Office on Drugs and Crime, the International Organization for Migration (IOM), and the Organization for Security and Cooperation in Europe (OSCE) has also played a prominent part in anti-trafficking coordination and capacity building.

In addition to international and regional anti-trafficking instruments, national governments have developed their own legislation and as of 2009, 177 states had anti-trafficking policies (Cho, Dreher, and Neumayer 2011). The USA has played a key role both in monitoring the scope of trafficking and in encouraging the global roll-out of anti-trafficking policy and practice, particularly in those states that are recipients of US aid. The United States' Victims of Trafficking and Violence Protection Act (VTVPA) was signed into law in 2000 shortly before the Palermo Protocol. It established the State Department Office to Monitor and Combat Trafficking in Persons and required any country receiving economic or security assistance from the USA to report annually on trafficking and anti-trafficking measures. The Trafficking in Persons (TiP) Report is published annually by the US State Department, assessing and ranking countries according to their anti-trafficking efficacy and commitment. Countries that do not meet minimum standards can have US non-humanitarian aid withdrawn and the US will oppose similar assistance from the IMF and multilateral development banks.

The Palermo Protocol saw a massive expansion in political initiatives, research, and publications about trafficking, and the number of organizations active on the issue multiplied (Kempadoo 2005). However, despite the significant injection of funds into anti-trafficking work there continues to be confusion over the extent of trafficking, with estimates differing ranging from 2.5 to 27 million (see the UNESCO trafficking statistics project for data comparisons <http://www.unescobkk.org/index.php?id=1022>). There seems to be general agreement that numbers are 'increasing', yet when scientifically interrogated trafficking estimates tend to reduce significantly (Feingold 2010). The US Government Accountability Office's (GAO) analysis of State Department spending on trafficking contrasts the large numbers of claimed victims, with the considerably smaller number of people offered official assistance (United States' Government Accountability Office 2006: 51).

Trafficking and 'Force'

The problem with estimating numbers points to continuing confusion about what precisely trafficking is despite the Palermo Protocol, and, relatedly, *why* trafficking is a problem (Bacchi 2001). For lawmakers and service providers, this is manifest in the difficulty of differentiating between trafficking and smuggling, between voluntary and involuntary movement. It is in the matter of force versus consensuality, victimhood versus agency, compulsion versus choice that 'trafficking' both is distinguished from smuggling, and overlaps with forced migration. However, to use the definitional terms given by the protocol, what is meant by 'force' and 'coercion' is very contested. How it is so contested depends on whether trafficking is perceived as principally a problem of prostitution, forced labour, or migration, and each poses different but related challenges.

Trafficking, Force, and Prostitution/Sex Work

The victim of trafficking is first and foremost imagined as a migrant woman or girl forced into prostitution, and the degrading nature and stigmatization of prostitution/ sex work is rarely interrogated. 'Sexual exploitation' was highlighted by the VTVPA and subsequent US funded activities, and under the Bush administration anti-trafficking funds were only available to groups prepared to declare their opposition to prostitution (Weitzer 2007). Taking prostitution as the starting point emphasizes relations of gender domination and there has been a persistent focus on female victims and male perpetrators. The Trafficking Protocol is particularly concerned with female and child labour. It is the Protocol to Prevent, Suppress and Punish Trafficking in Persons *Especially Women and Children*.

Academic and political debates about trafficking need to be contextualized within the highly polarized and often bitter feminist controversy about sex work/prostitution (Anderson and O'Connell Davidson 2003). On the one side are those who might be termed 'radical feminists' (who use the terminology of prostitution and prostituted women) and on the other those who argued for 'sex workers' rights'. Radical feminists such as MacKinnon, Dworkin, and Barry have argued and continue to argue that prostitution is a symptom of and compounds patriarchal domination, affecting all women negatively by consolidating men's rights of access to women's bodies. They hold that no woman can voluntarily consent to her own exploitation and consequently recognize no distinction between 'forced' and 'free' prostitution. In tolerating, regulating, or legalizing prostitution, they consider states permit the repeated violation of women's rights to dignity and sexual autonomy. For this group, trafficking is a manifestation of the global problem of prostitution. The Coalition against Trafficking in Women (CATW) has been extremely influential in promoting this position as has the European Women's Lobby, an umbrella organization of women's associations that is highly actively at the EU level. The radical feminist analysis of trafficking as prostitution was strongly supported by the Bush administration in the US and by the Swedish government. The 'Swedish model' of criminalizing the client has been adopted by Norway and is currently being considered by a number of other states.

In contrast, feminists such as Doezma, Kempadoo, and James adopt what might be termed a 'sex workers' rights' perspective and reject the idea that all sex work is intrinsically degrading. They view sex work as a service sector job and argue that it is the lack of protection for workers in the sex industry, rather than the existence of a market for commercial sex in itself, that gives rise to disproportionate exploitation in the sector. Opposing the radical feminists, they maintain that sex work is a form of low waged labour and distinguish between forced prostitution and consensual sex work, holding that 'trafficking' is a problem associated with forced labour and servitude which can include certain situations of prostitution but is not restricted to prostitution and does not apply to all sex work (Andrijasevic 2010). They argue that the solution to abuse lies in bringing the sex sector above ground, and regulating it in the same way that other employment sectors are regulated and robustly oppose claims that measures to eradicate the market for prostitution are necessarily anti-trafficking measures, and vice versa. Broadly speaking their views are reflected at an activist level by the Global Alliance Against Traffic in Women (GAATW) and national and international groups and networks of sex workers.

The debates around the drafting of the Protocol reflected these deeply opposing feminist positions, and although the final wording is ambivalent there is particular and special reference made in the protocol to sexual exploitation and exploitation of the prostitution of others.

Trafficking, Force, and Labour

Although the Trafficking Protocol explicitly mentions forced labour, trafficking initially tended not to be analysed as a labour issue. If trafficking begins as being a problem of prostitution, then suggesting labour rights as a solution is highly contentious for those who hold that it is commodification of certain types of human (sexual) relations that is the source of the problem. This parallels a common response to child labour, where the problem is typically located in the engagement of children in contractual commodified relations. Thus for child labour activists, as for radical feminists, the problem cannot be ameliorated through improvement in conditions, and the relation itself must be abolished. Concern about child trafficking had initially focused on child pornography and prostitution with impetus from first world congress against commercial sexual exploitation of children in 1996. Child labour became strongly associated with child trafficking, and the International Labour Organization's (ILO) International Programme on the Elimination of Child Labour (IPEC) has taken anti-trafficking work as a key priority. 'Trafficking' comprises one of the 'worst forms of child labour', though the relation between 'trafficking' which is a process, and 'form of labour' is not clear.

The ILO has not confined itself to the issues raised by child labour and has played an important part in broadening the debate on trafficking to include questions of labour relations and labour rights (including for sex workers). In 2005 the ILO published a Global Report on Forced Labour, finding that sectors such as agriculture, mining, and domestic labour were prone to forced labour, and presenting the forced labour extracted from migrants, both internal and international, as 'trafficking':

> The global movement against trafficking has certainly given an impetus to the understanding of, and action against, forced labour; and . . . it may potentially present law- and policy-makers with an option. (GAAFL 2005: ch. 1 para. 21)

Trades unions, sex workers groups, and NGOs such as the Anti-Slavery Society and Free the Slaves have all been galvanized by taking a forced labour perspective on trafficking. This has required attempts to differentiate, *inter alia*, between 'forced labour', 'slavery', and 'debt bondage' but these are often contradictory (O'Connell Davidson 2010). Workers cannot be divided into two entirely separate and distinct groups—those who are working involuntarily in the misery of slavery-like conditions in an illegal or unregulated economic sector, and those who work in a well-regulated job they choose to do for pleasure. This dichotomy means labour activists and sex workers' rights feminists are faced with distinguishing between coerced and consensual labour, raising the difficult question not only what is 'forced labour' but what is 'free labour'? (This is not a problem when it comes to child labour because children (defined as anyone under 18) are not held capable of 'consenting'.) While arguably this can be helped by thinking of a continuum between forced and free rather than a dichotomy (Anderson and O'Connell Davidson 2003), but the problem remains that the fewer one's alternatives, the more likely one is to consent to a situation which can be labelled 'unfree'. That is, the matter cannot be reduced purely to one of consent. Attempts to distinguish between free and forced labour in practice reveal 'a moral/political judgment about the kinds of pressures to enter and remain at work that are considered legitimate and those that are not' (Steinfeld 2008).

Furthermore trafficking is not only about force, freedom, and consent, but also 'exploitation'. This too is a very difficult term to define and to instrumentalize. When is exploitation simply a legitimate recovery of investment or profit making, and when is it unacceptable? Often 'exploitative' is used as a short hand to indicate poor conditions and low wages, but when are these so poor and so low that they constitute 'trafficking'? One of the rhetorical devices drawn on by both anti-prostitution and anti-forced labour activists for distinguishing between trafficking and exploitative conditions is the language of 'modern day slavery' (Bales 2005). Free labour is *not slavery*. But certainty about the immorality of slavery (very few people today would argue that 'slavery' is morally acceptable) does not mean certainty about what precisely is meant by the term. 'Modern slavery' can indicate ownership, domination, or unfreedom. Rather than clarify what forced labour is, this terminology serves to situate the fight against trafficking firmly within the context of the transatlantic slave trade. Anti-trafficking campaigners are described as modern day abolitionists (see for example the 2012 TiP report <http://www.state.gov/documents/organization/192587.pdf>)—indeed radical feminists are often referred to as 'feminist abolitionists' thereby conflating aspirations for the abolition of prostitution with past campaigners for the abolition of slavery. This arguably contradicts the radical feminist and child labour activist positions as it identifies freedom with the ability to sell one's labour in the marketplace, the opportunity offered by capitalism, while they are explicitly against the extension of contract to certain types of relations. Moreover, what tends to be forgotten in the comparison it invites with the transatlantic slave trade is that 'modern slavery' (unlike contemporary governance of labour migration) is not a mode of organizing labour in any contemporary state. The language of 'modern day slavery' lends itself to a strong association with transcontinental forced mobility for the purpose of labour but also overlooks a critical difference for contemporary labour migrants: we cannot assume that migrants, even those working illegally in highly exploitative conditions, have been wrenched from lives where they wanted to remain.

Trafficking, Force, and Migration

Trafficking seems to indicate a rare site of consensus in immigration politics, where migrants' organizations can find common cause with states. However, analysing trafficking as principally a problem for migrants raises challenging questions for activists, who typically locate the *problem* of trafficking in the end point (prostitution, forced labour) rather than the process. If the problem is one of prostitution or forced labour, why is migration at issue? Why is it worse to be forced to prostitute oneself abroad rather than in one's home town?

At first sight this seems less problematic for states, which are concerned with criminalizing a process, but in fact using a migration lens to interrogate anti-trafficking can also reveal difficult policy tensions, both with reference to labour migration and with reference to asylum.

The Trafficked Migrant as Worker

As discussed, what constitutes 'force' and 'exploitation' raises serious challenges for those implementing and promoting anti-trafficking policies. These problems are exacerbated when migration issues are introduced. Migrants, whether internal or international, have different frames of reference, and potentially different forces acting to determine the legitimacy or otherwise of their consent to enter and to remain in particular employment conditions. While economic migrants are often depicted as rational choice actors, weighing costs and benefits and making trade-offs, victims of trafficking are usually presented as embedded in social relations of gender, religion, ethnicity, and 'culture'. In situations which are framed as those of 'poverty,...lack of access to education, chronic unemployment, discrimination, and the lack of economic opportunities' (VTVPA section 102 paragraph 4) how are 'consent' and 'exploitation' to be understood? The extent of inequalities mean that it can be difficult in practice to differentiate between issues of voluntariness (no one could voluntary choose to work in such a situation) and issues of fairness (it is not fair that anyone should have to choose to work in such a situation). While those who support migrant workers' rights, and some migrants themselves, may find that appealing to trafficking protections may gain access to resources and state support that is not otherwise available, particularly in the case of undocumented migrants, there are also political costs. The 'trafficked' must be distinguished from the mundanely exploited, creating a hierarchy of oppression that can be very divisive between migrants. This also risks setting acceptable labour standards for migrants below those acceptable for citizens, i.e. if a migrant is 'only' below the minimum wage and not beaten they are compared to the imagined situation of the VoT rather than the acceptable minimum for the citizen worker.

For non-citizens the employment contract dramatically affects the legal and political status of the worker, and can have consequences, most obviously for the right to reside, that are way beyond the employment relationship. While the right to leave an employer and to work for whom one wishes is regarded as a defining element of what constitutes 'free' labour (Steinfeld 2001), this is not a right that non-citizens necessarily have. Miles (1987) famously argued that the limitations on migrants' entitlement to commodify their labour power that result from state imposed restrictions (as with sponsorship) generate a form of unfree labour. In this way immigration restrictions are an important mechanism of domination. Concern with trafficking focuses on borders and immigration controls while missing the crucial point that immigration controls produce relations of domination and subordination. It can be very difficult for migrants, whatever their legal status, to object to poor working conditions and abuses because of their dependence on their employer for their immigration status. It could be argued then that migrants' susceptibility to trafficking as 'forced labour' then lies not so much in organized crime's control over the (illegal) migratory process as in immigration controls themselves. This is in contrast to state' usual presentation of immigration controls and enforcement as an important means of *protecting* migrants from traffickers and as points of intervention where individual abusers and criminal gangs can be identified and brought to justice.

The Trafficked Migrant and Asylum

In Europe the figure of the victim of trafficking as a rights claimant emerges in the early 2000s at the same time as the rights claims of refugees become contested, and the non-citizen subject of human rights morphs from the asylum seeker to the victim of trafficking (Anderson 2013). The rise to prominence of anti-trafficking policy, law, and activism and support offered to VoT has run alongside growing concern about abuse of refugee processes and the reluctance of states in the global North to accept asylum seekers. Both the genuine refugee and the VoT are recognized as subject to human rights abuse (increasingly VoT are described as subject to 'torture', further aligning them with the refugee), both seek protection from a non-liberal Other. In the case of refugees this Other may be a state, but in the case of VoT, this is organized crime. However, the relation between trafficking and asylum is more complex than simple replacement. The Victim of Trafficking may also have a valid claim for refugee status. They may fear being persecuted because of their membership of a particular social group and reprisals and ostracism on the basis of having been trafficked may constitute persecution in this sense (UNHCR 2006). There is an acknowledged overlap, and the refugee or displaced person is often regarded as especially vulnerable to trafficking, particularly if they are a child (UNHCR 2009).

Both VoT and genuine refugee must be distinguished from smuggled people, and they should not be penalized for illegal entry. However, while refugees may, theoretically at least, be protected by flight, migrant workers as potential victims of trafficking are it seems protected by not being able to move in the first place. For VoT, mobility per se is treated as problematic (both consequence and reason for the use of slavery terminology), but for refugees, mobility is recognized as a solution. Thus VoT protections can be accommodated within mainstream immigration controls and enforcement, but asylum must be kept distinct. When it comes to return, what for a refugee would constitute *refoulement*, for a VoT is voluntary return and reintegration. Very few states will permit VoT permanent residence and most allow temporary residence only for those who are cooperating with authorities.

THE POLITICS OF TRAFFICKING

Much of the literature on trafficking emphasizes the extremes of suffering and victimization experienced by those forced to work in the sex sector. In contrast to the 'economic migrant', the VoT regularly speaks (or 'testifies') at an international level (Cheng 2010). Her account is heard, selected, and promulgated by a range of anti-trafficking activists. But although heard, the VoT is heard only under very specific conditions and the only option for her is to be rescued, as any suggestion of agency undermines victim status (Enns 2012). This has been criticized by some who protest that this leaves VoT, and by extension, migrant women, sex workers, and children, as non-autonomous subjects (Stenvoll and Jacobsen 2002; Sharma 2003). 'Trafficking' turns 'us' into moral actors, but, as Enns and others have argued, the politics of this kind of movement are incredibly limited: 'What status quo are we buttressing when we reduce the lives and aspirations of the disenfranchised into uncomplicated stories of poverty and abuse by traffickers?' (Cheng 2010: 216). Furthermore, by emphasizing the criminal and moral nature of the traffickers, the role of the state in the production of vulnerability goes unexamined. Too often the same body that is charged with protecting vulnerable migrants from harm is also charged with creating and policing the boundaries between citizens and non-citizens, and with deporting them if they are found to be in breach of the law.

REFERENCES

Anderson, B. (2013) *Us and Them? The Dangerous Politics of Immigration Control*. Oxford: Oxford University Press.

Anderson, B., and O'Connell Davidson, J. (2003) *Is Trafficking in Human Beings Demand Driven? A Multi-Country Pilot Study*. Geneva: International Organization for Migration.

Andrijasevic, R. (2010) *Migration, Agency and Citizenship in Sex Trafficking*. London: Palgrave Macmillan.

Bacchi, C. (2001) *Women, Policy and Politics: The Construction of Policy Problems*. London: Sage.

Bales, K. (2005) *Understanding Global Slavery*. Berkeley and Los Angeles: University of California Press.

Brace, L. (2010) 'The Opposites of Slavery? Contract, Freedom and Labour, Human Rights, Victimhood and Consent'. *Social, Legal and Political Dilemmas of Victimhood*, Bergen 10–12 June.

Cheng, S. (2010) *On the Move for Love: Migrant Entertainers and the U.S. Military in South Korea*. Philadelphia: University of Pennsylvania Press.

Cho, S., Dreher, A., and Neumayer, E. (2011) 'The Spread of Anti-Trafficking Policies: Evidence from a New Index'. CESifo Working Paper No. 3376. <http://www.cesifo.org/wp>.

Chuang, J. (2010) 'Rescuing Trafficking from Ideological Capture: Prostitution Reform and Anti-Trafficking Law and Policy'. *University of Pennsylvania Law Review* 158: 1655–728.

Doezma, J. (2010) *Sex Slaves and Discourse Masters: The Construction of Trafficking*. London: Zed Books.

Enns, D. (2012) *The Violence of Victimhood*. Pennsylvania: Pennsylvania University Press.

Feingold, D. (2010) 'Trafficking in Numbers: The Social Construction of Human Trafficking Data'. Pp. 46–74 in P. Andreas and K. Greenhill (eds.), *Sex, Drugs and Body Counts: The Politics of Numbers in Global Crime and Conflict*. New York: Cornell University Press.

Gallagher, A. (2010) *The International Law of Human Trafficking*. Cambridge: Cambridge University Press.

Global Alliance Against Forced Labour (GAAFL) (2005) *Global Report under the Follow-up to the ILO Declaration on Fundamental Principles and Rights at Work*. International Labour Conference 93rd Session, report 1B. Geneva: International Labour Office.

Hathaway, J. (2008) 'The Human Rights Quagmire of "Human Trafficking" '. *Virginia Journal of International Law* 49(1): 1–59.

Howard, N. (2012) 'Accountable to Whom? Accountable for What? Understanding Anti-Child Trafficking Discourse and Policy in Southern Benin'. *Anti-Trafficking Review* 1: 43–59.

Hua, J. (2011) *Trafficking Women's Human Rights*. Minneapolis: University of Minnesota Press.

International Labour Office (2008) 'Fighting Human Trafficking: The Forced Labour Dimensions (Background Paper)'. Geneva: ILO.

Jacobsen, C., and Stenvoll, D. (2010) 'Muslim Women and Foreign Prostitutes: Victim Discourse, Subjectivity and Governance'. Social Politics International Studies in Gender, State and Society 17(3): 270–94.

Kempadoo, K., Sanghera, J., and Pattanaik, B. (eds.) (2005) *Trafficking and Prostitution Reconsidered: New Perspectives on Migration, Sex Work and Human Rights*. Boulder, CO: Paradigm Publishers.

Miles, R. (1987) *Capitalism and Unfree Labour: Anomaly or Necessity?* London: Tavistock Publications Ltd.

O'Connell-Davidson, J. (2010) 'New Slavery, Old Binaries: Human Trafficking and the Borders of "Freedom" '. *Global Networks* 10(2): 244–61.

O'Connell Davidson, J. (2011) 'Outside Liberal Fictions of Disembodiment: Dilemmas of Intimate Labour'. Rethinking Intimate Labor through Inter-Asian Migrations Workshop. Bellagio, 6–10 June.

Sharma, N. (2003) 'Travel Agency: A Critique of Anti-Trafficking Campaigns'. *Refuge* 21: 53–65.

Steinfeld, R. J. (2008) 'Coercion/Consent in Labour'. COMPAS Annual Conference: Theorizing Key Migration Debates. St Anne's College, University of Oxford.

UNHCR (2006) 'Guidelines on International Protection: the Application of Article 1(A)2 of the 1951 Convention and/or 1967 Protocol Relating to the Status of Refugees to Victims of Trafficking and Persons at Risk of being Trafficked'. <http://www.justice.gov/eoir/vll/benchbook/resources/UNHCR_Guidelines_Trafficking.pdf>.

UNHCR (2009) 'Human Trafficking and Refugee Protection: UNHCR's Perspective'. Ministerial Conference: Towards Global EU Action Against Trafficking in Human Beings. Brussels, 19–20 October.

United States' Government Accountability Office (2006) *Human Trafficking: Better Data, Strategy and Reporting Needed to Enhance U.S. Anti-Trafficking Efforts Abroad*. Washington, DC: US GAO.

Weitzer, R. (2007) 'The Social Construction of Sex Trafficking: Ideology and Institutionalization of a Moral Crusade'. *Politics and Society* 35(3): 447–75.

PART V

LIVED
EXPERIENCES AND
REPRESENTATIONS
OF FORCED
MIGRATION

....

CHAPTER 29

THE POLITICS OF REFUGEE VOICES: REPRESENTATIONS, NARRATIVES, AND MEMORIES

....

NANDO SIGONA[1]

INTRODUCTION

....

THIS chapter reflects on existing debates surrounding the politics of 'refugee voices' by examining the relationship between representations, narratives, and memories of refugees' experiences. Drawing on literature framed by post-structuralist and critical theories, the chapter problematizes assumptions regarding the existence of 'a refugee voice' on the one hand, and the extent to which academic and policy discourses often fail to listen to or to hear such voices on the other. It does so by identifying different configurations of the production and consumption of emic narratives of forced migration and displacement (that is, produced by forced migrants themselves), exploring the factors shaping these narratives and the embedded power relations that permeate them. In particular, the chapter explores the practices and spaces which refugees enact and embody to contest the processes which lead to the silencing and marginalization of their narratives and experiences. To do so, the chapter is divided in three main sections which in turn address different yet interlinked manifestations of the 'refugee voice'.

SITUATING NARRATIVES

....

A number of personal, domestic, and international factors contribute to shape both the production of such narratives and the ways they are received, interpreted, and acted upon. The 'refugee voice' is far from singular, as is the case of the plurality of 'refugee experiences' (Turton 2003). As Soguk argues (1999: 4):

> There are a thousand multifarious refugee experiences and a thousand refugee fig-
> ures whose meanings and identities are negotiated in the process of displacement in
> time and place.

Recounting these experiences is also not a straightforward process, since narratives
'are produced in relation to socially available and hegemonic discourses and practices'
(Anthias 2002: 511), and also in relation to the immediate and broader contexts to which
they are a dialectic response.

Indeed, storytelling is part of people's everyday life, a cultural and intersubjective
experience to the core (Eastmond 2007) in which a person draws on the cultural reper-
toires at his/her disposal to make sense of, imagine, and negotiate with others the world
around them; such an exercise, this chapter argues, is simultaneously individual and
collective, positional and situated, rooted in the past as well as in the present and future.
For Jackson (2002: 18), 'by constructing, relating and sharing stories, [forced migrants]
contrive to restore viability to their relationship with others, redressing a bias towards
autonomy when it has been lost, and affirming collective ideals in the face of disparate
experiences'.

As the chapters in this part of the Handbook well document, gender and sexual
orientation (Fiddian-Qasmiyeh, this volume), age (Hart, this volume; Bolzman, this
volume), different abilities (Mirza, this volume), 'race', ethnicity, and social class all
contribute to make refugees' experiences plural and diverse. However, this plurality
does not necessarily translate into humanitarian, academic, and media discourses, as
these tend to privilege a one-dimensional representation of the refugee which relies
heavily on feminized and infantilized images of 'pure' victimhood and vulnerability
(Malkki 1995; see also Wright, this volume). By abstracting displaced people's predicaments from specific political, historical, and cultural milieus, these representations
ultimately lead to the silencing of refugees (Malkki 1997).

In line with the above, the chapter's first section focuses on the relationship between
humanitarian actors' (etic) representations of refugees on the one hand, and forced
migrants' claims for rights and political subjectivity on the other. A case-study of
Sudanese refugees' three-month-long sit-in in front of the UNHCR headquarters in
Cairo in 2005 offers the opportunity to explore the tension between dominant representations of the refugee as an agency-less object of humanitarian intervention, and
refugees' quest for recognition as political subjects. It shows the disruptive potential
of refugees appropriating the vocabulary of humanitarian organizations and directing
their claims for rights towards them.

The second section examines places such as national asylum tribunals and immigration offices where the 'refugee voice', while heard, is also probed, scrutinized, and
dissected. It briefly discusses issues of truth and credibility in the asylum process and
brings to the forefront the impact which the culture of disbelief that pervades the asylum system in Western liberal democracies has on forced migrants and their voices.

Moving away from the workings of the international humanitarian regime and
national asylum systems, the third section in turn addresses the politics of memory and

memorialization of experiences of mass persecution and displacement and the extent to which the refugee voice does or does not become part of diasporic identities and state-building projects in post-conflict settings, long after the events have taken place.

Finally, the chapter concludes by outlining some of the epistemological and methodological challenges for researchers engaging with the scholarly endeavour of 'prioritizing the views of the uprooted, the displaced and the dispossessed' (Chatty, this volume).

POLITICS OF COMPASSION AND REFUGEE'S AGENCY

Drawing on debates in social sciences on agency and subjectivation rooted in Foucaldian tradition, this section looks at the 'refugee voice' as a vehicle for expressing refugees' political subjectivity. It argues that to understand what it means to be political as a refugee (in a broader sense), entails engaging not only with the causes and consequences of forced displacement but also with discourses and practices of the 'humanitarian government' (Agier 2008) and the politics of compassion that underpins it (Fassin 2011).

In Foucault's work (1979) subjects are produced in and by power relations and they embody and experience the social relations of which they are products. The Foucauldian subject, Butler (1997: 94) argues, 'is never fully constituted in subjection. It is repeatedly constituted in subjection, and it is in the possibility of a repetition that repeats against its origin that subjection might be understood to draw its inadvertently enabling power'. Nonetheless, the performative effort of naming can only attempt to bring its addressee into being since the interpellated subject's recognition of the name is a necessary prerequisite for this to happen. In this regard, refugees' narratives of displacement and asylum are produced within a set of pre-given discourses and power relations, and yet by acting upon them and being political (Isin 2002), refugees can open up transformative opportunities and unsettle given truths on the colonial footings of the humanitarian regime and its moral order (see Spivak 1988).

Following a brief introduction on etic representations of forced displacement by agencies variously involved in supporting displaced people, both internationally and at the national level, this section explores more closely the tension between, on the one hand, dominant representations of the refugee as speechless and traumatized and, on the other, refugees' quest for political recognition.

Victimhood and Agency

While negative representations of refugees in media and political discourse tend to generate significant academic interest, much less critical attention has been devoted to date to investigate the ways in which pro-asylum organizations and advocates represent forced migration and refugees, and to what effect (Rajaram 2002; Pupavac 2008; Fiddian-Qasmiyeh 2014). Research shows how Western humanitarian organizations frequently resort to a vocabulary of trauma and vulnerability to describe the condition of refugees and others who have survived conflict and persecution. This discursive frame operates in conjunction with other forms of interventions within what Malkki terms 'the international order of things' to produce refugees as a universal and dehistoricized category of humanity (Malkki 1995). The depoliticization of refugees happens in two ways: at the micro-level, by neglecting and/or denying the importance of the political in their experience of exile (Essed, Frerks, and Schrijvers 2004); and at the macro-level, by concealing behind the discourse of the West's humanitarianism present and past involvement in producing the causes of conflict and forced migration.

The kind of sympathy mobilized by the trauma-centred discourse, Pupavac (2008: 280) points out, 'unlike political solidarity, is not based on a relationship between equals, but one of dependency, in which those with impaired capacity are released from normal responsibilities' and their capacity for self-determination and political subjectivity is called into question (cf. Fiddian-Qasmiyeh 2014). They are consigned to a 'mute and faceless physical mass' (Rajaram 2002: 247) and denied the right to present narratives that may disturb the dominant *truth* on asylum.

The trauma discourse and the pathologization of refugees, while disabling for the objects of humanitarian intervention, makes Western 'experts' and support organizations the only trustworthy voice to speak for refugees and about the experience of forced displacement, turning refugee lives into 'a site where Western ways of knowing are reproduced'[2] (Rajaram 2002: 247). In the following section, a discussion of the 2005 sit-in of Sudanese refugees in front of the UNHCR office in Egypt will be used to explore some of the challenges that refugees' voices can pose to the humanitarian government and the international order of things.

Claiming Rights: The 2005 Sit-in of Sudanese Refugees in Cairo

In September 2005, dozens of Sudanese asylum seekers and refugees commenced a sit-in near the UNHCR headquarters in Cairo. 'Trapped in an untenable state—unwilling to repatriate, unable to integrate locally, and without the option of moving on' (Lewis 2011: 81), protesters complained for their living conditions in Egypt and the UNHCR's suspension of individual refugee status determination procedures following the signing of the Comprehensive Peace Agreement between the Government of Sudan and the Sudanese People's Liberation Movement at the beginning of 2004 (Fiddian 2006). The sit-in was the result of long-standing grievances that Sudanese refugees had about the way the UNHCR office handled their cases: an 'opaque, defensive, all-powerful, and above all inaccessible' office to those it was meant to serve, in the words of an observer (Danielson 2008: 19).

Protesters set up a permanent camp at Mustafa Mahmoud Park, the area that served as screening grounds for nearby UNHCR, and their number rapidly grew to an average of 1,800 to 2,500 residents including single individuals and families, children and elders, and remained at those levels throughout the following three months. Meetings and negotiations among the sit-in leadership, UNHCR, and other parties failed to meet the demonstrators' requests. On 30 December 2005, Egyptian security forces violently removed the protesters; 28 were killed (Azzam 2006).

When the sit-in started, protesters delivered a 'list of requests' to UNHCR. They articulated their demands employing the vocabulary of the 'humanitarian government'—the requests directed to UNHCR abound in terms such as 'human rights', 'resettlement', 'protection', 'refugee'. However their very appropriation and use of these terms, as well as the institutional target of their grievances, broke the unwritten rules of the international (moral) order of things (to paraphrase Malkki), producing an 'interruption of the UNHCR's monopoly over the language of protection, care, and resettlement' (Moulin and Nyers 2007: 363, Danielson 2008). Inversely, UNHCR's initial refusal and successive denial of refuges' requests and, particularly, its attempt to undermine the protestors' legitimacy to make political claims to the Agency by refusing, at least initially, to call them 'refugees' and therefore not of their concern, demonstrates a sense of discomfort with a political initiative by a group of *self-proclaimed* refugees that challenges the UNHCR's position in the humanitarian government as the sole authority entitled to make *true* claims, in the Foucaldian sense, 'over the care of abject populations' (Moulin and Nyers 2007: 369).

The next section discusses issues of truth and credibility in refugee status determination processes and the culture of disbelief that pervades the asylum system in Western liberal democracies.

TRUTH AND CREDIBILITY

A growing body of literature has investigated the encounter between asylum claimants, mainly in Western liberal democracies, and the bureaucratic apparatus governing the refugee status determination (RSD). Such studies have explored, *inter alia*, the underpinning cultural beliefs that inform asylum case workers (Jubany 2011) and the ways that immigration judges, barristers, and community lawyers conduct the examination and cross-examination of a claimant's narrative (Coutin 2000; Good 2007; Morris 2010). Other academics have documented and assessed the structural factors shaping the assessment and judicial processes and how the legal truth is ascertained (Feldman 2011), and those that shape the claimant's narrative and that may lead in some circumstances and for some claimants to their voices being silenced (Berg and Millbank 2009; Chase 2010; Johnson 2011).

This section focuses on places such as asylum tribunals where refugees are expected to narrate their experience as part of the process of assessing the genuineness and truthfulness of their asylum claims. In the first part, it discusses how the refugee voice is dismembered and reassembled as a legal narrative during the assessment process. In the second part, it argues that the emergence of some voices and the disappearance of others may have more to do with emerging global sensitivity to specific identities and issues than with an individual claimant and his/her story.

Refugee Truth and Refugee Status Determination

A widespread and pervasive culture of disbelief underpins the asylum process, with public attitudes to asylum seekers in many Western countries being overwhelmingly negative, tending to see 'them' as liars or 'bogus' claimants.

Decisions on asylum claims, in the paucity of objective evidential proof, rely heavily on the claimant's personal account and the way she or he recollects and pieces together the events that led to their forced departure. Such is the disbelief in asylum seekers that their voices, in order to be heard, increasingly need to be corroborated by more trustworthy voices such as those of country and medical experts; this has developed to such a degree that, according to Fassin and d'Halluin (2005: 606), the medical certificate (i.e. confirming torture or sexual violence) becomes 'the tenuous thread on which hangs the entire existence—both physical and political—of the asylum seeker'.

During the asylum assessment, the *subjective* voice of the claimant is dissected and scrutinized in search for *objective* legal truths. This is achieved primarily via a twofold assessment of the claimant's credibility and of the coherence and plausibility of their account vis-à-vis the general known facts (UNHCR 1992). Internal coherence and external consistency guide the decision-making process on the claimant's credibility and the genuineness of their claim to the point that credibility is often conflated with 'truth' (Sweeney 2009), and incongruences and inconsistencies in one aspect of an applicant's account, even if not directly pertinent to the case or of secondary importance, may exercise a significant weight on the decision of the claim for protection (Coffey 2003; Griffiths 2012).

Given the presumption that all asylum applicants are 'bogus' until proved otherwise that seems to inform government-led RSD in Western states (Sales 2002), it is unsurprising that developing a capacity to unearth incongruences is a central feature of the training of new recruits who, according to Jubany (2011), are socialized in their role not so much by being taught about refugees in terms of their rights and options, but through techniques to unmask lies and inconsistencies in asylum seekers' narratives.

Adopting internal coherence and external plausibility as the main criteria informing asylum decisions, however, can be problematic. Evidence in medical and anthropological research, for example, shows that torture victims may find it unbearably hard to tell their story of persecution in court as the physical pain of torture 'does not simply resist language but actively destroys it' (Scarry 1985: 4). It also demonstrates that there are multiple factors that may affect the capacity of victims of violence, rape, and traumatic events to recount their past experiences in court in a linear, accurate, consistent, detail-rich, rule-oriented, and emotionally vibrant way, all features appreciated by adjudicators (Shuman and Bohmer 2004).

Whose Voice?

Despite the 1951 Convention Relating to the Status of Refugees constructing the definition of the refugee in relation to an individualized well-founded fear of persecution, in RSD processes, the refugee often loses her or his individual identity. This is a by-product of the *formalism* and *formulism* of asylum courts. The former is used to denote the protocol that provides the script that actors must follow in the asylum court, and the latter the way in which, through the mediation of a claimant's legal representative,[3] asylum narratives must be structured and verbalized in order to address the grounds of the Refugee Convention.

The way adjudicators make decisions vis-à-vis asylum cases also reflects and reproduces this process of standardization of the 'refugee experience', denying that an asylum applicant, of all people, is a 'candidate for the unusual' (Lord Justice Schiemann in *Adam v Secretary of State* [2002]). Drawing on ethnographic fieldwork with immigration authorities in Spain and the UK, Jubany (2011) argues that immigration officers in deciding upon actual asylum cases refer to what they consider a 'normal case'. 'Officers categorize individuals into different types, according to certain "patterns", used as indicators to determine how deserving of asylum status applicants are' (Jubany 2011: 82).[4]

The key question is: what makes previously unheard narratives loud and visible in asylum courts? Especially given the strictly scripted set of rules, protocol, and discursive practice governing the working of asylum courts, the emergence of previously unheard voices is possible insofar as the 'normal' patterns mentioned earlier are redefined. This process of redefinition begins outside the court and informs the work of adjudicators as much as asylum advocates.[5] However, it is never fully complete, as Morris's analysis of British case law on access to welfare for asylum seekers shows; rather, judgments become an argumentative terrain of negotiation and contestation where different ideas of rights, entitlements, and personhood are played out (2010).

The recent emergence of LGBTI narratives in the asylum process (Fiddian-Qasmiyeh, this volume), for example, can be interpreted as the result of a societal transformation and a global movement which has also reached the asylum courts and plays into existing ideological divides. As such, although LGBTI narratives are not new in and of themselves, asylum applicants' voices are now heard by the actors inside the court, including adjudicators (Millbank 2002). Similarly, one can detect a growing attention to and audibility of the voices of disabled asylum claimants (Mirza, this volume).

Conversely, the accounts of persecution and forced displacement experienced by unaccompanied and separated children seeking asylum are less visible, as their stories are hidden and systematically denied by a protection regime that grants them protection as long and insofar as they are 'children', imposing a special type of 'pure humanity' while deeming them unworthy of protection as individuals claimants as soon as they reach the adult age (Sigona and Hughes 2012; Schuster and Majidi 2013; Hart, this volume). Furthermore, information gathered while in care as deserving children is used to judge their credibility as adult claimants, reducing even further their chances for recognition of status (Crawley 2007).

SHARED MEMORIES AND CONTEMPORARY POLITICS OF BELONGING

Narratives of exile, violence, and persecution are produced and circulate in multiple public and private spheres, even long after the actual events had happened. After having briefly discussed the 'refugee voice' in relation to the international humanitarian regime and its discursive order, and to the ways nation states assess and decide upon asylum claims, this section turns to how refugees' narratives of persecution, violence, and exile play or not a role, first, in the creation and reproduction of diasporic identities across generations, and, secondly, as part of nation-building projects in post-conflict settings, as in the case of post-genocide Rwanda. Overall, it highlights the role that politics and practices of memorialization and commemoration play in enabling some refugee narratives and disabling others.

Refugee Narratives and Diasporic Identities

Remembering the traumatic events that led to displacement and loss of home and/or homeland is a central feature of diasporic communities (on diasporas and displacement, see Van Hear, this volume). Memories are socially constructed and culturally specific, always mediated 'but also censured, publicly and privately, officially and unofficially' (Chamberlain and Leydesdorff 2004: 229). The *yizker bikher*, or memorial books—a Jewish memorial tradition developed among diasporic communities—are exemplar of the agential and strategic nature of memory making and transmission to future generations. They were prepared in exile by survivors of the Nazi pogroms and contain historical accounts of community life before and after the destruction that annihilated their individual communities. For Hirsch (1996), these memorial books are 'acts of witness and sites of memory' around which diasporic Jewish communities construct a shared sense of belonging and where 'subsequent generations can find a lost origin, where they can learn about the time and place they will never see' (Hirsh 1996: 665). Memorial books and similar remembrance practices in which the individual voices and testimonies of refugees are collected to create a collective *memory of community* serve an important role in defining and reproducing the boundaries of the diasporic community as a living *community of memory* where new imaginings and politics of community can be produced and 'critical alternatives (both traditional and emergent) can be expressed' (Clifford 1994: 315). These shared memories bridge the more private and intimate space of the family (Tschuggnall and Welzer 2002) with the wider imagined community (Anderson 1981) and provide the raw material on which new generations can construct their post-memory (Hirsch 1996) of exile and displacement as well as renegotiate and reinforce notions of who does and does not belong to a polity (Glynn and Kleist 2012; Lacroix and Fiddian-Qasmiyeh 2013).

Official Memories and Dissonant Voices

> Historical events are worth remembering only when the contemporary society is motivated to define them as such. (Schwartz, Zerubavel, and Barnett 1986: 149)

Commemorations, anniversaries, memorials, and other remembrance practices are often contentious affairs, as they constitute occasions when selective memories are produced, mobilized, and activated, and ideas of inclusion and exclusion can be created, reproduced, challenged, as well as thought anew. They become the arena where social actors compete to decide 'who has what rights to determine what should be remembered and how' (Jelin 1998: 24–5), inevitably producing politics of exclusion and spaces of 'non-existence' (Coutin 2003).[6] This is particularly relevant in conflict and post-conflict settings, where alternative narratives of the recent and past events compete for dominance and where a large part of those who are or were affected by such events may no longer live as a result of the conflict.

In the 1990s, South Africa's Truth and Reconciliation Commission arguably provided one of the most ambitious attempts in recent history to bridge, on the one hand, the individual dimension—i.e storytelling as therapeutic for the victim, based on an unproblematic link between 'voice' and 'dignity' and between 'voice' and 'being heard' (Ross 2003)—and, on the other hand, the collective dimension—i.e. a wider nation-building project in which individual memories of violence and suffering are placed at the centre of the imaginative work of forging a new public imaginary and sociality.[7]

Post-genocide Rwanda provides another example of a nation-building project basing its political capital and legitimacy, internally and internationally, on the remembrance of mass violence and persecution. However, in this case the voices of those affected by the genocide, including those forcibly displaced as a result of mass violence, are forced in various ways to conform with the government-led official narrative or to stay hidden. The Rwandan government's official version of history has been that the genocide of the Tutsi was motivated by racial hierarchies that were colonial in origin. In this context, Hintjens argues (2008: 32), 'progress and modernity, RPF style, seem to be about protecting Rwandans from themselves, since their attitudes are irrevocably tainted with colonialism and race ideologies'. In the process, the memory of genocide is also mobilized in everyday political interactions to police dissent—i.e. policing *through* the collective memory of genocide. Through the accusation of divisionism and harbouring a 'genocide mentality', the state exercises tight control over the public expression of political identities and produce a narrowing of the political space, generating uncertainty amongst civil society activists and political opposition 'as to what issues they can raise with the government and how critical they can be before incurring legal sanction or other form of intimidation' (Beswick 2010: 247), but also among *ordinary* Rwandans both in the country and to a lesser extent in the diaspora.

CONCLUSION

This chapter has identified and explored different contexts of production and reception of refugee narratives of exile, violence, and suffering to argue for a more critically engaged and theoretically informed understanding of the 'refugee voice' in refugee and forced migration studies that considers refugees' emic narratives as situated, positional, and relational. It locates refugee narratives within more powerful discursive fields such as those produced by the international humanitarian regime, national asylum courts, and diaspora and nation-building projects and examines the extent to which those narratives can be heard, and what strategies refugees have adopted to address the specific narrative and power configurations of these fields. Unsettling the 'voice' vs. 'silence' binary, this approach opens situated and contingent spaces for refugee agential intervention. It shows, for example, the extent to which claims for rights and recognition towards the UNHCR can disrupt (even if only temporarily) the totalizing narratives of humanitarianism; the power of silence as an expression of refugee agency in highly scripted asylum hearings and in the context of a widespread culture of disbelief towards asylum seekers; and the ways emic narratives of violence and suffering can be used to reproduce diasporic identities across generations.

Refugee voices have multiple footings that inescapably also permeate the encounter with the researcher that sets to collect and communicate (with) them. Interviews are 'saturated by images of the social dynamics of the interview itself, projections of the social context in which it takes place, the roles and power dynamics of interviewer and respondent, and their respective agendas, [. .. and by] the imagined texts that will be created through the use of interview data' (Briggs 2003: 246). This is particularly true for refugees who may have experienced mistrust and disbelief during the RSD process (Hynes 2003). It is crucial to bear in mind these elements in order to avoid what Bourdieu termed 'the biographical illusion' (Bourdieu 1994) and the risk of 'naturalising' interview data as a 'stable set of social facts that have an objective existence independent of the linguistic and contextual settings in which they are expressed' (Briggs 2003: 247). The interview (with the researcher as much as with the media—see Wright, this volume) is a situated and mediated (often via translators and interpreters) encounter and a performance in which the meanings of questions and responses are contextually grounded and jointly constructed.

However, there are also other power relations that shape the encounter between researched and researcher, namely that between the researcher and those who have the power to shape the agenda of refugee research and access to refugees (Harrell Bond and Voutira 2007; Eastmond 2007; Bakewell 2008; Marlowe 2010).

Reflecting on and incorporating the analysis of the 'refugee voice' within these multiple footings may also contribute to shedding light on what Bourdieu terms *doxa*, 'that which is taken for granted' (Bourdieu 1977: 165) and that which defines 'the space of the conceivable and utterable' (Hoffman 2011: 1) in refugee and forced migration scholarship.

NOTES

1. I wish to thank Nora Danielson, Alexandra Délano, and Jenny Allsopp for their bibliographic suggestions, and Elena Fiddian-Qasmiyeh for her thorough feedback on the draft.
2. For Rainbird (2012), such an exclusive position of expertise vis-à-vis asylum seekers' and refugees' predicaments enable organizations supporting asylum seekers and refugees to maintain a degree of influence in government policy, and to ensure a competitive edge in the privatized arena of service provision.
3. Research with legal advisory services for Salvadorian refugees in the USA shows that legal advisers select clients for legal support judging their likelihood of success on how much their story fits with the dominant narrative of deservingness (Coutin 2003).
4. However, scholars have also shown that asylum narratives with recurring storylines are approached with suspicion by immigration officers (Barsky 2000). Similarly Ticktin (2005) shows that French adjudicators feel compassion (and grant status) through notions of the applicants being 'exceptional'—and these assessments are intrinsically gendered in nature.
5. The extent to which religious persecution is prioritized by lawyers in order to fit into Orientalist and Islamophobic discourses, even if their clients do not identify with the terms and frames of the claim, is discussed in Akram (2000).
6. Embracing Butler's proposal (2010) to investigate the politics of recognition in remembrance practices and shed light on the conditions under which we mourn some lives while leave others unrecognized and silent, Délano and Nienass's work on the 9/11 memorial reveals the absence of Mexican undocumented migrants from the list of those 'deserving' remembrance and shows how the condition of 'non-existence' (Coutin 2003) in which undocumented migrant workers had been confined before the event projects long shadows also on their afterlife (Délano and Nienass 2012).
7. However, it also highlights the challenge for those who testified (Ross 2003: 325) of witnessing their testimonies developing a social 'life' outside their control.

REFERENCES

Adam, N. M. v Secretary of State for the Home Department [SSHD] [2002] EWCACiv265, 4 March 2003.

Agier, M. (2008) *On the Margins of the World*. Cambridge: Polity.

Akram, S. M. (2000) 'Orientalism Revisited in Asylum and Refugee Claims'. *International Journal of Refugee Law* 12(1): 7–40.

Anderson, B. (1981) *Imagined Communities: Reflections on the Origin and Spread of Nationalism*. London: Verso.

Anthias, F. (2002) 'Where do I Belong?' *Ethnicities* 2(4): 491–514.

Azzam, F. (ed.) (2006) *A Tragedy of Failures and False Expectations: Report on the Events Surrounding the Three-Month Sit-in and Forced Removal of Sudanese Refugees in Cairo, September–December 2005*. Cairo: Forced Migration and Refugee Studies Programme, American University in Cairo.

Bakewell, O. (2008) 'Research beyond the Categories: The Importance of Policy Irrelevant Research into Forced Migration'. *Journal of Refugee Studies* 21(4): 432–53.

Barsky, R. (2000) *Arguing and Justifying: Assessing the Convention Refugees' Choice of Moment, Motive and Host Country*. Aldershot: Ashgate.

Berg, L., and Millbank, J. (2009) 'Constructing the Personal Narratives of Lesbian, Gay and Bisexual Asylum Claimants'. *Journal of Refugee Studies* 22(2): 195–223.

Beswick, D. (2010) 'Managing Dissent in a Post-Genocide Environment: The Challenge of Political Space in Rwanda'. *Development and Change* 41(2): 225–51.

Bourdieu, P. (1977) *Outline of a Theory of Practice*. Cambridge: Cambridge University Press.

Briggs, C. (2003) 'Interviewing, Power /Knowledge and Social Inequality'. Pp. 911–22 in J. Holstein and J. F. Gubrium (eds.), *Inside Interviewing: New Lenses, New Concerns*. Thousand Oaks, CA: Sage.

Butler, J. (1997) *The Psychic Life of Power: Theories in Subjection*. Stanford, CA: Stanford University Press.

Butler, J. (2010) *Frames of War: When is Life Grievable?* New York: Verso.

Chamberlain, M., and Leydesdorff, S. (2004) 'Transnational Families: Memories and Narratives'. *Global Networks* 4(3): 227–41.

Chase, E. (2010) 'Agency and Silence: Young People Seeking Asylum Alone in the UK'. *British Journal of Social Work* 40(7): 2050–68.

Clifford, J. (1994) 'Diasporas'. *Cultural Anthropology* 9(3): 302–38.

Coffey, G. (2003) 'The Credibility of Credibility Evidence at the Refugee Review Tribunal'. *International Journal of Refugee Law* 15: 377–417.

Coutin, B. S. (2000) *Legalizing Moves: Salvadoran Immigrants' Struggle for U.S. Residency*. Ann Arbor: University of Michigan Press.

Coutin, S. B. (2003) 'Borderlands, Illegality and the Spaces of Non-existence'. Pp. 171–202 in R. Perry and B. Maurer (eds.), *Globalization and Governmentalities*. Minneapolis: University of Minnesota Press.

Crawley, H. (2007) *When is a Child Not a Child? Asylum, Age Disputes and the Process of Age Assessment*. London: ILPA.

Danielson, N. (2008) 'A Contested Demonstration: Resistance, Negotiation and Transformation in the Cairo Sudanese Refugee Protest of 2005'. M.Phil. thesis (unpublished), University of Oxford.

Délano, A., and Nienass, B. (2012) 'Between Absence and Invisibility: Undocumented Migration and the September 11 Memorial'. Presented at the conference *From the Art of Memory to Memory and Art: A One Day Conference Honoring Professor Vera L. Zolberg's Career*. The New School, New York, 28 April.

Eastmond, M. (2007) 'Stories as Lived Experience: Narratives in Forced Migration Research'. *Journal of Refugee Studies* 20(2): 248–64.

Essed, P., Frerks, G., and Schrijvers, J. (2004) *Refugees and the Transformation of Societies: Agency, Policies, Ethics and Politics*. Oxford: Berghahn Books.

Fassin, D. (2011) *Humanitarian Reason: A Moral History of the Present*. Berkeley and Los Angeles: University of California Press.

Fassin, D., and d'Halluin, E. (2005) 'The Truth from the Body: Medical Certificates as Ultimate Evidence for Asylum Seekers'. *American Anthropologist* 107(4): 597–608.

Feldman, G. (2011) *The Migration Apparatus*. Stanford, CA: Stanford University Press.

Fiddian, E. (2006) 'Relocating: The Asylum Experience in Cairo'. *Interventions: International Journal of Postcolonial Studies* 8(2): 295–318.

Fiddian-Qasmiyeh, E. (2014) *The Ideal Refugees: Gender, Islam and the Sahrawi Politics of Survival*. Syracuse, NY: Syracuse University Press.

Foucault, M. (1979) *The History of Sexuality, i: The Will to Knowledge*. London: Allen Lane.

Glynn, I., and Kleist, O. (2012) *History, Memory and Migration: Perceptions of the Past and the Politics of Incorporation*. London: Palgrave Macmillan.

Good, A. (2007) *Anthropology and Expertise in the Asylum Courts*. Abingdon: Routledge.

Griffiths, M. (2012) ' "Vile Liars and Truth Distorters": Truth, Trust and the Asylum System'. *Anthropology Today* 28(5): 8–12.

Harrell-Bond, B., and Voutira, E. (2007) 'In Search of "Invisible" Actors: Barriers to Access in Refugee Research'. *Journal of Refugee Studies* 20(2): 281–98.

Hintjens, H. (2008) 'Post-Genocide Identity Politics in Rwanda'. *Ethnicities* 8(1): 5–41.

Hirsch, M. (1996) 'Postmemory in Exile'. *Poetics Today* 17(4): 659–86.

Hoffman, S.-L. (2011) 'Introduction: Genealogies of Human Rights'. Pp. 1–26 in S.-L. Hoffman (ed.), *Human Rights in the Twentieth Century*. Cambridge: Cambridge University Press.

Hynes, T. (2003) 'The Issue of "Trust" or "Mistrust" in Research with Refugees: Choices, Caveats and Considerations for Researchers'. *New Issues in Refugee Research* (Working Paper No. 98). Geneva: UNHCR.

Isin, E. (2002) *Being Political: Genealogies of Citizenship*. Minneapolis: University of Minnesota Press.

Jackson, M. (2002) *The Politics of Storytelling*. Copenhagen: Museum Tusculanum Press.

Jelin, E. (1998) 'The Minefields of Memory'. *NACLA Report on the Americas* 32(2): 23–30.

Johnson, T. A. M. (2011) 'On Silence, Sexuality and Skeletons: Reconceptualising Narrative in Asylum Hearings'. *Social & Legal Studies* 20(1): 57–71.

Jubany, O. (2011) 'Constructing Truths in a Culture of Disbelief: Understanding Asylum Screening from Within'. *International Sociology* 26(1): 74–94.

Lacroix, T., and Fiddian-Qasmiyeh, E. (eds.) (2013) 'Refugee and Diaspora Memories: The Politics of Remembering and Forgetting'. *Journal of Intercultural Studies*, special issue 34(6) (December).

Lewis, T. (2011) 'Come, we kill what is called "persecution life": Sudanese Refugee Youth Gangs in Cairo'. *Oxford Monitor of Forced Migration* 1(1): 78–92.

Malkki, L. H. (1995) 'Refugees and Exile: From "Refugee Studies" to the National Order of Things'. *Annual Review of Anthropology* 24(1): 495–523.

Malkki, L. (1997). 'Speechless Emissaries: Refugees, Humanitarianism, and Dehistoricization'. Pp. 223–54 in K. F. Olwig and K. Hastrup (eds.), *Siting Culture. The Shifting Anthropological Object*. London: Routledge.

Marlowe, J. M. (2010) 'Beyond the Discourse of Trauma: Shifting the Focus on Sudanese Refugees'. *Journal of Refugee Studies* 23(2): 183–98.

Millbank, J. (2002) 'Imagining Otherness: Refugee Claims on the Basis of Sexuality in Canada and Australia'. *Melbourne University Law Review* 26: 144–77.

Morris, L. (2010) *Asylum, Welfare and the Cosmopolitan Ideal: A Sociology of Rights*. Abingdon: Routledge.

Moulin, C., and Nyers, P. (2007). ' "We Live in a Country of UNHCR": Refugee Protests and Global Political Society'. *International Political Sociology* 1: 356–72.

Pupavac, V. (2008) 'Refugee Advocacy, Traumatic Representations and Political Disenchantment'. *Government and Opposition* 43(2): 270–92.

Rainbird, S. (2011) 'Asylum Seeker "Vulnerability": The Official Explanation of Service Providers and the Emotive Responses of Asylum Seekers'. *Community Development Journal* 47(3): 405–22.

Rajaram, P. (2002) 'Humanitarianism and Representations of the Refugee'. *Journal of Refugee Studies* 15(3): 247–64.

Ross, F. C. (2003) 'On Having Voice and Being Heard'. *Anthropological Theory* 3(3): 325–41.

Sales, R. (2002) 'The Deserving and the Undeserving'. *Critical Social Policy* 22(3): 456–78.

Scarry, E. (1985) *The Body in Pain*. Oxford: Oxford University Press.

Schuster, L., and Majidi, N. (2013) 'What Happens Post-Deportation? The Experience of Deported Afghans'. *Migration Studies* 1(2): 221–40.

Schwartz, B., Zerubavel, Y., and Barnett, B. M. (1986) 'The Recovery of Masada: A Study of Collective Memory'. *Sociological Quarterly* 27(2): 147–64.

Shuman, A., and Bohmer, C. (2004) 'Representing Trauma: Political Asylum Narrative'. *Journal of American Folklore* 117(466): 394–414.

Sigona, N., and Hughes, V. (2012) *No Way Out, No Way In: Irregular Migrant Children and Families in the UK*. Oxford: COMPAS.

Soguk, N. (1999) *States and Strangers: Refugees and Displacements of Statecraft*. Minneapolis: University of Minnesota Press.

Spivak, G. C. (1998) 'Can the Subaltern Speak?' In C. Nelson and L. Grossberg (eds.), *Marxism and the Interpretation of Culture*. Urbana, IL: University of Illinois Press.

Sweeney, J. (2009) 'Credibility, Proof and Refugee Law'. *International Journal of Refugee Law* 21(4): 700–26.

Ticktin, M. (2005) 'Policing and Humanitarianism in France: Immigration and the Turn to Law as State of Exception'. *Interventions* 7(3): 346–68.

Tschuggnall, K., and Welzer, H. (2002) 'Rewriting Memories: Family Recollections of the National Socialist Past in Germany'. *Culture & Psychology* 8(1): 130–45.

Turton, D. (2003) 'Conceptualising Forced Migration'. RSC Working Paper No. 12. Oxford: RSC.

UNHCR (1992) *Handbook on Procedures and Criteria for Determining the Refugee Status*. Geneva: UNHCR.

CHAPTER 30

CHILDREN AND FORCED MIGRATION

JASON HART

INTRODUCTION

SITTING in neat rows in makeshift classrooms under canvas, or waiting in line for food or medical treatment, children have dominated the imagery of humanitarian response to situations of forced migration. Popular imagination has been fired by photographs of the young having their basic needs met by relief agencies. In consequence such imagery has helped to mobilize financial and political support for interventions. Over many years, the common assumptions about children as the most vulnerable section of a displaced population whose experience is dominated by trauma and whose needs are self-evident discouraged serious enquiry from most parts of academia apart from psychology and social work. More recently, however, studies from a broader array of scholars have emerged, providing a more complex picture and challenging practitioners to consider their interventions afresh. In this chapter I seek to explore how the understanding of the situation of children in settings of forced migration is evolving as a result of research that brings a more socially engaged aspect to a field of study conventionally the provenance of researchers whose focus has been largely on the individual. Such enquiry will entail consideration of diverse ideas about the needs and competencies of the young and their interaction with the social environment.

BRIEF OVERVIEW OF THE CURRENT STATE OF PLAY

The United Nations High Commission for Refugees (UNHCR) suggests that of the 33.9 million 'people of concern' to that organization around half are under 18 and thus classified as 'children'.[1] This figure includes refugees, those seeking asylum, the internally displaced, as well as recent returnees. Not included in the UNHCR statistics are the roughly 3 million young Palestinians a large proportion of whom, but not all, are registered with the United Nations Relief and Works Agency (UNRWA). In addition there are surely innumerable young forced migrants who slip under the radar of institutional registration and data collection. While the total number of displaced children cannot be ascertained with great accuracy, we are clearly speaking of a phenomenon of immense proportions.

Not all of those children who may be considered as 'forced migrants' within one of the categories suggested above have experienced displacement during their own lifetimes. There are numerous populations that have remained displaced over decades. Amongst those now referred to by the institutional label 'Protracted Refugee Situation' are the Sahrawi in Algeria, the Bhutanese in Nepal, the Karen in Thailand, and the Palestinians in Lebanon, Syria, and Jordan. In each of these cases it is not the youngest generation but their parents, grandparents, or even great-grandparents who were forced to flee. Yet, the lives of the children are shaped in diverse and significant ways by this experience of displacement. They must contend, as a part of daily life, with the constraints of existence in a country where citizenship is at best hedged with ambiguity and more typically withheld entirely. Even in cases when asylum is offered and full citizenship attained, children are often faced with challenges of a personal or familial nature arising from their own or their parents' experience of violent displacement (Almqvist and Brandell-Forsberg 1997; Miller et al. 2008).

Displacement, in whichever form it takes, can entail upheaval on many levels—societal, familial, and institutional—with specific consequences for those in the early years of life. For example, formal education for some children may be curtailed either due to lack of provision in the new location or through denial of access. Conversely, displacement can sometimes open up the possibility of schooling that had been unavailable previously. Beyond assistance in the so-called 'four primary life-saving areas'[2]—water and sanitation, nutrition, healthcare, and shelter—education has become an increasingly prominent element of humanitarian intervention. As a result children housed in displacement camps or other settings supported by aid agencies may be able to enter a classroom—however rudimentary—for the first time.

From a legal perspective forced migration can place the young in a highly ambiguous position. Throughout most of the world the state bears responsibility as the ultimate guarantor of the basic rights and well-being of children, intervening when parents fail. This role has been strengthened by the near universal ratification of the United Nations Convention on the Rights of the Child (1989). Yet forced migrant children are often distanced from state bodies and denied the rights enjoyed by citizens, including those pertaining to freedom of movement and assembly, access to basic services, and family reunification. For internally displaced or refugee children living 'under the radar' the state represents nothing so much as a threat with which it is vital to minimize interaction for fear of imprisonment, violence, or expulsion.

To summarize briefly, while the number of forced migrant children at any moment is impossible to calculate with accuracy it seems reasonable to suppose that the total is well in excess of 20 million globally. Any estimate must take account of children known to the major UN organizations supporting refugees as well as those who are 'self-settled' or who have never sought formal registration. Forced migrant children may be found throughout much, if not all, of the globe: from refugee camps in remote areas of various African countries to the asylum processing/detention centres in certain European states. Displacement may impact upon children's lives directly and in a diverse range of ways that are both individual and communal. Moreover, the effects can be immediate and direct or may be more diffuse and long-term: as in situations of protracted exile spanning generations or within families engaged in resettlement.

Principal Lines of Enquiry

With this brief overview in mind I shall now consider the main trends of study in relation to the subject of children and forced migration. At the risk of being overly schematic I have organized the discussion in accordance with three broad approaches: 'mental health and social work', 'legal', and 'ethnographic'. Each of these is shorthand for a number of different academic disciplines and fields of study and none is incompatible with either of the other two. However these three can be differentiated in methodological and epistemological terms as well as in the manner that each construes their object of study. I do not intend to suggest that these three approaches between them cover all possibilities: there is a growing interest amongst scholars in the field of international relations, for example, that indicates alternatives. Nevertheless, I would argue that between them these three represent the most significant approaches in shaping a field of study around the subject of children and forced migration. They have also, to differing but important degrees, influenced policy and practice.

The Mental Health and Social Work Approach

Although displaced children have been considered within numerous studies over many years, scholars working within the various branches of mental health and social work have played the greatest part in bringing into being a distinct field of enquiry focused on the young. Indeed, it may be said that the 'refugee child' as a distinct object of research has been constructed most especially by psychologists and colleagues in cognate disciplines (e.g. Eisenbruch 1988; Athey and Ahearn 1991; Rousseau 1995). Of particular concern to researchers in this tradition have been the effects of displacement upon the mental and emotional state of children. In order to assist those still living in situations of danger the broad aim of research has been to understand how best to promote coping. The emphasis of work in settings of refuge is more likely to be upon the means of healing and bringing closure (e.g. Westermeyer and Wamenholm 1996).

Over the more than a quarter-century that mental health scholars have been focusing upon displaced children and those living in conflict-affected zones there have been notable changes in the ideas and interests that inform research. In the 1990s the majority of work was explicitly focused on 'trauma' with particular attention given to diagnosis using criteria devised in the West, such as those specified in the Diagnostic and Statistical Manual of Mental Disorders (DSM) created by the American Psychiatric Association. These criteria have been utilized as the basis for various questionnaires and other tools intended specifically to capture instances of trauma expressed in the form of 'Post-Traumatic Stress Disorder' (PTSD). Examples of such questionnaires developed with and applied to war-affected and displaced children include the 'Harvard Trauma Questionnaire'[3] (Ahmad, von Knorring, and Sundelin-Wahlsten 2008), and the 'Childhood War Traumas Questionnaire' (Macksoud 1992). Research has been concerned not only with the development of diagnostic tools but with techniques for the resolution of trauma: often piloting and evaluating new projects with a view to informing large-scale programming across diverse settings within an approach that may be broadly described as 'curative' (Kalksma-Van Lith 2007).

The trauma-focused model is concerned particularly with children's exposure to specific kinds of events deemed damaging, often with the view that exposure will necessarily entail negative consequences, or sequelae, for the young. In this there is a presupposition that children are inherently and universally vulnerable by virtue of their age or stage in the developmental process. The intervention of experts, generally outsiders, is necessary to alleviate suffering. This model has met with growing dissatisfaction amongst mental health scholars for many of whom it is overly mechanistic. In consequence recent years have witnessed the development of an approach that differs in at least two important respects. First, it suspends assumption of an inevitable cause and effect relation between exposure to certain events and children's reaction, suggesting instead that how the young are affected by such events will be strongly mediated by a host of environmental factors. Second, this approach asserts that the child is potentially able to withstand negative experiences as a result of the interaction between the intra-personal and environmental.

The approach which has emerged in recent years replaces the central focus on 'trauma' with a concern for 'resilience'.[4] Numerous studies have been undertaken that explore the means by which displaced children and those still living in zones of armed conflict may be supported to withstand the challenges to their mental and emotional well-being arising from exposure to potentially traumatising events (e.g. Daud, Klinteberg, and Rydelius 2008; APA 2010; Stermac, Clarke, and Brown 2013). The assumption of resilience resonates with a perception of children as agentive beings negotiating the conditions of their existence that has grown in popularity within the academy and amongst practitioners. Such perception has been prompted particularly by the emergence of a sociological field of childhood studies in the early 1990s and the rise of the rights-based approach within the field of international development. In practice this perception has served to encourage the pursuit of more participatory, and less objectifying, humanitarian efforts including the delivery of mental health projects to the young. Thus we may discern both in mental health scholarship and in practice something of a shift in the construction of the 'displaced child' over the past quarter-century. A once dominant view of the young as inevitably traumatized objects of concern requiring expert assistance now contends with the assertion that even in the midst of dire and dangerous conditions children are potentially resilient social actors who may act in meaningful ways upon their situation.

Social work shares the aim of mental health disciplines to inform intervention that ameliorates the situation of displaced children. The ways in which this may be achieved are various and while social work scholars have often engaged with traumatic experience, the focus is also upon the challenges of resettlement and integration. These are explored at both a practical level and in non-material terms: such as in relation to children's sense of identity (Fantino and Colak 2001; Kohli 2007; Kohli and Mitchell 2007). A considerable body of work is focused explicitly on social work practice with displaced children, particularly those who are unaccompanied/separated (Christie 2002; Wade, Mitchell, and Graeme 2006). While mental health research has been undertaken in locations across the globe, including in settings where children first experience displacement or are encamped, social work scholars have predominantly worked in Western nations. Here refuge and resettlement are managed on an individual or (nuclear) familial basis rather than in respect of larger collectives such as clans or villages. Given the general lack of interest of social work in the collective dimensions of people's lives, it is unsurprising that research with displaced children tends also towards the individualistic, paying little attention to their allegiances and political concerns.

The Legal Approach

The legal landscape that forcibly displaced children traverse is complex and multifaceted. In their various elements International Humanitarian Law and International Human Rights Law speak both directly and by implication about the protection and rights of young displacees.[5] Moreover children—both individually and in family or other groupings—are subject to national and regional laws in host countries that govern many aspects of everyday life and that may, in certain respects, stand at odds with international law.

A body of research has been amassed that considers the laws and legal systems as they relate to children. Thus, for example, studies have been conducted that look at the rules on asylum within specific jurisdictions, examining the consequences for unaccompanied/separated minors (e.g. Ruxton 2003; Bhabha and Finch 2006). A particular emphasis of much of this work has been upon the actual workings of a particular legal system and how those involved—officials as well as children and their families—negotiate the rules and procedures (Bhabha and Young 1999; Lidén and Rusten 2007). Scholars conducting such research come from a range of disciplinary backgrounds, in addition to legal studies, and often employ methods of a sociological kind. Their work is commonly undertaken with a direct view to addressing policy and often in collaboration with think tanks and lobby groups (e.g. Rutter 2003; Crawley/ILPA 2006).

In contrast to the field of mental health, which has constructed a clear vision of the 'refugee child' as 'passive victim' and (more latterly) as resilient actor, legal scholarship lacks a singular understanding. Rather, the young are considered according to various categories of experience—such as 'trafficked', 'unaccompanied/separated', 'internally displaced', etc.—or in relation to specific violations deemed common as a cause or as part of the process of flight: sexual violence, forcible recruitment, detention, denial of access to basic services, and so on. Research is often conducted in accordance with these categories of experience and violations. A large proportion of such work is commissioned by the major child-focused agencies, such as UNICEF and Save the Children, sometimes with explicit reference to elements of International Law, especially the United Nations Convention on the Rights of the Child (UNCRC). Human/child rights organizations such as Human Rights Watch and Defence for Children International have also been active in compiling studies around specific forms of violation. An important impetus was given to such work by the publication of the United Nations study on the *Impact of Armed Conflict on Children* compiled by Graça Machel (1996). The primary emphasis in this report is upon the various forms of risk to the young as indicated by the following excerpt:

> During flight from the dangers of conflict, families and children continue to be exposed to multiple physical dangers. They are threatened by sudden attacks, shelling, snipers and landmines, and must often walk for days with only limited quantities of water and food. Under such circumstances, children become acutely undernourished and prone to illness, and they are the first to die. Girls in flight are even more vulnerable than usual to sexual abuse. Children forced to flee on their own to ensure their survival are also at heightened risk. Many abandon home to avoid forced recruitment, only to find that being in flight still places them at risk of recruitment, especially if they have no documentation and travel without their families. (Machel/ UN 1996: 23)

The legal/human rights research conducted in settings of displacement has paid particular attention to the issue of child recruitment since the early years of this century, prompted by various initiatives at the United Nations including promulgation of the Optional Protocol to the UNCRC on the Involvement of Children in Armed Conflict in February 2002 and the adoption of several resolutions by the Security Council beginning with Resolution 1261 in August 1999. Child recruitment has been the subject of numerous studies of academic, practitioner, and popular orientation (e.g. Goodwin-Gil and Cohn 1994; UNICEF 2002; Brett and Specht 2004; Rosen 2005; Singer 2005; Beah 2007). Much of this work speaks about child recruitment in general terms. Consideration of the particular connection between forced migration and involvement with military groups is discussed in passing—for example when fear of abduction causes children to flee. There is, however, a small body of research that has examined the ways in which displacement may render the young vulnerable to recruitment, whether through some form of coercion or by their own volition (e.g. Alfredson 2002; Reich and Achvarina 2006; Hart 2008). The issue of military participation has also been a focus of study in relation to the treatment of children in the asylum system of Western countries. Studies have focused on whether or not former child soldiers may be considered ineligible for asylum under Article 1F the 1951 Refugee Convention which stipulates that an application may be refused on the grounds that the individual has committed a war crime. This brings up obvious questions of volition. On the other hand, fear of recruitment might be considered grounds for a child to claim asylum (Happold 2002; Cepernich 2010).

The Ethnographic Approach

Studies undertaken by scholars from diverse disciplines have utilized elements of an ethnographic approach in order to obtain data. For example, participant-observation with the young in the settings of their daily lives has been undertaken by mental health scholars keen to develop a more grounded understandings of children's psycho-emotional state than that afforded by employment of questionnaires and checklists organized around 'trauma' (e.g. Eyber and Ager 2004). However, in speaking of an 'ethnographic approach' I seek to draw attention to a research paradigm that constructs its object of study in a manner distinct from those of mental health and social work, and legal/human rights studies. Within these latter approaches displacement and its ill-effects constitute the *raison d'être* of research: study seeks to understand how children are negatively impacted and/or how such impact may be mitigated. Research according to these approaches invariably has at least one eye towards practice or policy.

By contrast the ethnographic approach, which has been principally but not exclusively pursued by anthropologists, sociologists, and human geographers, focuses on displacement not primarily as cause but as context for children's experience. Forced migration is not assumed to have a necessarily negative impact but to inform a set of circumstances in which everyday life and aspirations continue to be pursued by the young. Indeed, the possibility is held open that forced migration may present opportunities, for example for the renegotiation of conventional hierarchies built around age, gender, or socio-economic class. As with those mental health scholars interested in resilience, ethnographers consider children as social actors who may mediate the negative experience of forced migration for themselves and others (e.g. Hinton 2000). Moreover, some studies have sought also to explore the experiences that children themselves find distressing rather than assuming that certain events and stressors conventionally associated with displacement will inevitably have the greatest negative effect (e.g. de Berry et al. 2003; Nelems 2008).

Researchers undertaking ethnographic study of children in settings of forced migration have not always taken great account of the immediate agendas of practitioners and policymakers. However, their work can have considerable implications for the ways in which displaced children and their needs are conceptualized by those seeking to assist them. A notable example of this are studies that examine how the young may be rendered vulnerable by specific circumstances and processes (e.g. de Berry 2004). These studies call attention to the importance of agencies engaging with, for example, discriminatory attitudes and practices, lack of or inappropriate services, and poor governance in order to reduce the risk to displaced children, rather than assuming that vulnerability to harm is an inherent and inevitable property of the young.

Themes explored by ethnographers in settings of displacement have included children's political engagement (e.g. Evans 2008; Fiddian-Qasmiyeh 2012), their education (e.g. Bash and Zezlina-Phillips 2006), and their friendships and networks of support (e.g. Mann 2008). Each of these has an important bearing upon aspects of humanitarian assistance calling into question assumptions that commonly inform policy and programming at a global level. For example, the research exploring the political mobilization of displaced children challenges the narrow manner in which young people's agency and their role as social actors is conventionally conceived by humanitarian organizations, often revealing their willing engagement in confrontational politics in pursuit of social and political change. Applying these insights to practice suggests the need for a broader and more politically savvy approach to participatory programming.

Some scholars have applied an ethnographic approach to exploration of children's experience of humanitarian organizations' assistance, often revealing questionable assumptions that inform such work (e.g. Tefferi 2007; Evans and Mayer 2012). Similarly, shortcomings in the asylum system have been brought to light by researchers working closely with unaccompanied children negotiating their way around the demands and assumptions of immigration officials (e.g. Crawley 2009).

A particular feature of the ethnographic approach is the tendency to locate study of forced migration in historical terms, which includes documenting the process of displacement and resettlement/encampment to contextualize data emerging from participant-observation and other methods. Study may also entail exploring children's experience as members of a generational cohort situated differently from parents or grandparents in a setting of long-term encampment. Or it may involve documentation of the life history of displaced children, locating this within larger historical processes. How children articulate ideas around 'homeland' or 'return' at certain moments in time has been of particular interest (e.g. Hart 2004; Hoodfar 2008).

The ethnographic approach which, via a range of methods, engages with children over an extended period is inevitably challenging to pursue in many settings of displacement. In some cases researchers may need to be prepared and have permission to move together with the subjects of their study if they wish to continue their work. In many of the world's displacement camps access for a researcher is hard to obtain or may be limited: preventing participant-observation during certain times of the day, most typically during evening and at night. These are obstacles faced to an inevitably lesser extent by researchers pursuing the approaches typical to mental health, social work, and legal/rights studies whose methods typically entail a far shorter period 'in the field' and for whom observation of everyday life has limited importance.

CONCLUSION

In this chapter I have sought to provide a necessarily brief overview of some of the key features of the study of children and forced migration as this has been pursued over approximately the last quarter-century. This has been structured in terms of three broad scholarly approaches that I have labelled as 'mental health and social work', 'legal', and 'ethnographic'. These are neither exhaustive nor are they mutually exclusive. Thus, for example, elements of an ethnographic approach may be employed in the study of how legal systems operate or in order to gain a more localized understanding of the terms in which the impact of displacement upon children is construed.

With regards to the impact of these three approaches upon policy and practice, I would suggest that mental health and social work scholarship has had an especially influential role. This may be partly accounted for by the fact that researchers pursuing this approach are especially oriented towards ameliorating the situation of displaced boys and girls through targeted interventions. However, it is arguably also the case that the mental health and social work approach is encouraged by policymakers and practitioners for reasons that are extrinsic to the academic disciplines involved. In a multipolar world when the geopolitical issues surrounding displacement are complex and potentially comprising for states, it is unsurprising that many governmental donors seek to address the frustrations, anxieties, and aspirations within a psychosocial framework: a move suggestive of the term 'therapeutic governance' (Pupavac 2005). For their part, UN agencies and major international NGOs are often caught in the tension between the need to be seen to deliver for displaced children, on one hand, while not challenging the agendas of donor governments and powerful interests, on the other. Conceptualizing the needs of young forced migrants in primarily psycho-emotional terms can help to resolve this dilemma by providing a domain in which to appear efficacious while sidestepping those priorities articulated by young people themselves that might be politically sensitive to address. A stronger involvement by scholars undertaking ethnographic and legal research in debates surrounding policy and practice could help to challenge the current status quo, confronting donors and major agencies with their obligations to act in ways that are accountable to displaced populations and to international law. However, there is also an important role for the fields of politics and international relations in questioning the current agenda of policymakers and practitioners. There are signs that some scholars working in these disciplines are becoming aware of the profoundly political questions surrounding the ways that young forced migrants are managed within the current global humanitarian architecture.

NOTES

1. <http://www.unhcr.org/pages/49c3646c1e8.html> (accessed 9 December 2012).
2. <http://www.sphereproject.org/handbook/> (accessed 2 December 2012).
3. <http://hprt-cambridge.org/?page_id=42> (accessed 12 December 2012).
4. For a helpful explanation of the focus of research into resilience, see <http://resilienceproject. org/> (accessed 19 December 2012).
5. See Ressler, Boothby, and Steinbock (1988: s. III, pp. 209–80) for a useful summary of international law as it relates to displaced children.

REFERENCES

Achvarina, V., and Reich, S. (2006) 'No Place to Hide: Refugees, Displaced Persons, and the Recruitment of Child Soldiers'. *International Security* 31(1): 127–64.

Ahmad, A., von Knorring, A. L., and Sundelin-Wahlsten, V. (2008) 'Traumatic Experiences and Post-Traumatic Stress Disorder in Kurdistanian Children and their Parents in Homeland and Exile: An Epidemiological Approach'. *Nordic Journal of Psychiatry* 62(6): 457–63.

Alfredson, L. (2002) 'Child Soldiers, Displacement and Human Security'. *Disarmament Forum* 3: 17–27.

Almqvist, K., and Brandell-Forsberg, M. (1997) 'Refugee Children in Sweden: Post-Traumatic Stress Disorder in Iranian Preschool Children Exposed to Organized Violence'. *Child Abuse & Neglect* 21: 351–66.

APA (2010) *Resilience and Recovery after War: Refugee Children and Families in the United States*. Washington, DC: American Psychological Association.

Athey, J. L., and Ahearn, F. L. (1991) 'The Mental Health of Refugee Children: An Overview'. Pp 3–19 in F. L. Ahearn and J. L. Athey (eds.), *Refugee Children: Theory, Research, and Services*. The Johns Hopkins series in contemporary medicine and public health. Baltimore: Johns Hopkins University Press.

Bash, L., and Zezlina-Phillips, E. (2006) 'Identity, Boundary and Schooling: Perspectives on the Experiences and Perceptions of Refugee Children'. *Intercultural Education* 17(1): 113–28.

Beah, I. (2007) *A Long Way Gone: Memoirs of a Boy Soldier*. London: Harper Perennial.

Bhabha, J., and Finch, N. (2006) *Seeking Asylum Alone: Unaccompanied and Separated Children and Refugee Protection in the UK*. <http://idcoalition.org/wp-content/uploads/2009/06/seeking-asylum-alone.pdf> (accessed 20 December 2012).

Bhabha, J., and Young, W. (1999) 'Not Adults in Miniature: Unaccompanied Child Asylum Seekers and the New US Guidelines'. *International Journal of Refugee Law* 11(1): 84–125.

Brett, R., and Specht, I. (2003) *Young Soldiers: Why they Choose to Fight*. Boulder, CO: Lynne Reiner Publishing Inc.

Cepernich, D. (2010) 'Fighting for Asylum: A Statutory Exception to Relevant Bars for Former Child Soldiers'. *Southern California Law Review* 83(5): 1099–134.

Christie, A. (2002) 'Responses of the Social Work Profession to Unaccompanied Children Seeking Asylum in the Republic of Ireland'. *European Journal of Social Work* 5(2): 187–98.

Crawley, H./ILPA (2006) *Child First, Migrant Second: Ensuring that Every Child Matters*. London: Immigration Lawyers Practitioner Association. <http://www.ilpa.org.uk/data/resources/13270/ilpa_child_first.pdf> (accessed 20 December 2012).

Crawley, H. (2009) 'Between a Rock and a Hard Place: Negotiating Age and Identity in the UK Asylum System'. In N. Thomas (ed.), *Children, Politics and Communication: Participation at the Margins*. Bristol: Policy Press.

Daud, A., Klinteberg, B., and Rydelius, P.-A. (2008) 'Resilience and Vulnerability among Refugee Children of Traumatized and Non-Traumatized Parents'. *Child and Adolescent Psychiatry and Mental Health* 2(7)(March): 1–11.

de Berry, J. (2004) 'The Sexual Vulnerability of Adolescent Girls during Civil War in Teso, Uganda'. In J. Boyden and J. de Berry (eds.), *Children and Youth on the Front Line: Ethnography, Armed Conflict and Displacement*. Oxford: Berghahn Books.

de Berry, J., Fazili, A., Farhad, S., Nasiry, F., Hashemi, S., and Hakimi, M. (2003) *The Children of Kabul: Discussions with Afghan Families*. Kabul: Save the Children USA/UNICEF.

Eisenbruch, M. (1988) 'The Mental Health of Refugee Children and their Cultural Development'. *International Migration Review* 22: 282–300.

Evans, R. (2008) 'The Two Faces of Empowerment in Conflict'. *Research in International and Comparative Education* 3(1): 50–64.

Evans, R., and Mayer, R. (2012) 'Global Priorities against Local Context: Protecting Bhutanese Refugee Children in Nepal'. *Development in Practice* 22(4): 523–35.

Eyber, C., and Ager, A. (2004) 'Researching Young People's Experiences of War: Participatory Methods and the Trauma Discourse in Angola'. In J. Boyden and J. de Berry (eds.), *Children and Youth on the Front Line: Ethnography, Armed Conflict and Displacement.* Oxford: Berghahn Books.

Fantino, A. M., and Colak, A. (2001) 'Refugee Children in Canada: Searching for Identity'. *Child Welfare* 80(5): 587–96.

Fiddian-Qasmiyeh, E. (2012) 'Transnational Childhood and Adolescence: Mobilising Sahrawi Identity and Politics across Time and Space'. *Journal of Ethnic and Racial Studies* 35: 875–95.

Goodwin-Gill, G. S., and Cohn, I. (1994) *Child Soldiers: The Role of Children in Armed Conflict.* Oxford: Clarendon.

Happold, M. (2002) 'Excluding Children from Refugee Status: Child Soldiers and Article 1F of the Refugee Convention'. *American University International Law Review* 17(6): 1131–76.

Hart, J. (2004) 'Beyond Struggle and Aid: Children's Identities in a Palestinian Refugee Camp in Jordan'. In J. Boyden and J. de Berry (eds.), *Children and Youth on the Front Line: Ethnography, Armed Conflict and Displacement.* Oxford: Berghahn Books.

Hart, J. (2008) 'Displaced Children's Participation in Political Violence: Towards Greater Understanding of Mobilisation'. *Conflict, Security & Development* (8)3: 277–93.

Hinton, R. (2000) 'Seen but not Heard: Refugee Children and Models for Intervention'. Pp. 199–212 in C. Panter-Brick and M. T. Smith (eds.), *Abandoned Children.* Cambridge: Cambridge University Press.

Hoodfar, H. (2008) 'The Long Road Home: Adolescent Afghan Refugee Children in Iran Contemplate "Return"'. In J. Hart (ed.), *Years of Conflict: Adolescence, Political Violence and Displacement.* Oxford: Berghahn Books.

Kalksma-Van Lith, B. (2007) 'Psychosocial Interventions for Children in War-Affected Areas: The State of the Art'. *Intervention* 5(1): 3–17.

Kohli, R. S. (2007) *Social Work with Unaccompanied Asylum Seeking Children.* London: Palgrave Macmillan.

Kohli, R. S., and Mitchell, F. (eds.) (2007) *Unaccompanied Asylum Seeking Children: Issues for Policy and Practice.* London: Palgrave Macmillan.

Lidén, H., and Rusten, H. (2007) 'Asylum, Participation and the Best Interests of the Child: New Lessons from Norway'. *Children & Society* 21(4): 273–83.

Machel, G./United Nations (1996) *Impact of Armed Conflict on Children.* <http://www.unicef.org/graca/a51-306_en.pdf> (accessed 21 December 2012).

Macksoud, M. (1992) 'Assessing War Trauma in Children: A Case Study of Lebanese Children'. *Journal of Refugee Studies* 5(1): 1–15.

Mann, G. (2008) 'Doing Nothing and Being Good: Social Relationships and Networks of Support among Adolescent Congolese Refugees in Dar es Salaam'. In J. Hart (ed.), *Years of Conflict: Adolescence, Political Violence and Displacement.* Oxford: Berghahn Books.

Miller, K. E., Kulkarni, M. S., and Kushner, H. (2006) 'Beyond Trauma-Focused Psychiatric Epidemiology: Bridging Research and Practice With War-Affected Populations'. *American Journal of Orthopsychiatry* 76(4): 409–22.

Miller, K. E., Kushner, H., McCall, J., Martell, Z., and Kulkarni, M. S. (2008) 'Growing Up in Exile: Psychosocial Challenges Facing Refugee Youth in the United States'. In J. Hart (ed.), *Years of Conflict: Adolescence, Political Violence and Displacement*. Oxford: Berghahn Books.

Nelems, M. (2008) *The Unity Circle Project: Experiences of Iraqi Children and Parents Living in Amman, Jordan*. Amman: Save the Children, IICRD, UNICEF, Relief International.

Pupavac, V. (2005) 'Human Security and the Rise of Global Therapeutic Governance'. *Conflict, Security and Development* 5(2): 161–81.

Ressler, E., Boothby, N., and Steinbock, D. (1988) *Unaccompanied Children: Care and Protection in Wars, Natural Disasters and Refugee Movements*. Oxford: Oxford University Press.

Rosen, D. (2005) *Armies of the Young: Child Soldiers in War and Terrorism*. Camden, NJ: Rutgers University Press.

Rousseau, C. (1995) 'The Mental Health of Refugee Children'. *Transcultural Psychiatric Research Review* 32: 299–331.

Rutter, J. (2003) *Working with Refugee Children*. London: Joseph Rowntree Foundation. <http://www.jrf.org.uk/sites/files/jrf/1859351395.pdf> (accessed 20 December 2012).

Ruxton, S. (2003) *Separated Children and EU Asylum and Immigration Policy*. Save the Children. <http://www.separated-children-europe-programme.org/publications/reports/report_separated_child_eu_policy.pdf> (accessed 20 December 2012).

Singer, P. W. (2005) *Children at War*. New York: Pantheon.

Stermac, L., Clarke, A. K., and Brown, J. (2013) 'Pathways to Resilience: The Role of Education in War-Zone Immigrant and Refugee Student Success'. In C. Fernando and M. Ferrari (eds.), *Handbook of Resilience in Children of War*. New York: Springer.

Tefferi, H. (2007) 'Reconstructing Adolescence after Displacement: Experience from Eastern Africa'. *Children & Society* 21(4): 297–308.

UNICEF (2002) *Adult Wars, Child Soldiers*. New York: UNICEF. <http://www.unicef.org/eapro/AdultWarsChildSoldiers.pdf> (accessed 21 December 2012).

Wade, J., Mitchell, F., and Graeme, B. (2006) *Unaccompanied Asylum Seeking Children: The Response of Social Work Services*. London: British Association for Adoption and Fostering.

Westermeyer, J., and Wahmanholm, K. (1996) 'Refugee Children'. Pp 75–103 in R. J. Apfel and B. Simon (eds.), *Minefields in their Hearts: The Mental Health of Children in War and Communal Violence*. New Haven: Yale University Press.

CHAPTER 31

....

GENDER AND FORCED MIGRATION

....

ELENA FIDDIAN-QASMIYEH

INTRODUCTION

THIS chapter analyses the development of academic and policy attention to 'women' and 'gender' in forced migration contexts,[1] highlighting the transition from documenting the particularities of female experiences, to a re-evaluation of the multiple ways in which processes of and responses to forced migration influence gender identities, roles, and relations. The chapter is divided into three main sections. First, it offers a brief historical overview of feminist contributions to analyses of forced migration. The second section then addresses gendered causes and experiences of forced migration by engaging with two sets of debates: gendered evaluations of individualized persecution on the one hand, and gendered experiences of conflict induced mass displacement on the other. The first subsection explores the gendered nature of refugee status determination processes, highlighting the biases underpinning 'neutral' legal definitions and policies, and documenting emerging sensitivity to the intersections between sexual orientation, gender identity, and asylum. The second subsection in turn traces developments in responses to sexual and gender-based violence in mass displacement contexts, and argues in favour of the continued incorporation of displaced men and boys into gender analysis and programming. In the third section, the chapter subsequently examines responses to displacement, again focusing on two sets of debates: the first regarding the paradoxical implications of policies designed to promote gender equality and empowerment in camp contexts, and the second on the nexus between gender and the three traditional durable solutions.

A Brief History of Feminist and Gendered Analyses of Forced Migration

From the 1970s, feminists challenged the processes which rendered women invisible across the social sciences. Even when women were recognized as members of the socio-political systems being analysed, a range of theoretical, conceptual, and methodological barriers to their meaningful inclusion in such studies were identified. For instance, feminist anthropologists argued that

> a great deal of information on women exists, but it frequently comes from questions asked of men about their wives, daughters, and sisters, rather than from the women themselves. Men's information is too often presented as a group's reality, rather than only part of a cultural whole. Too often women and their roles are glossed over, under-analyzed, or absent from all but the edges of the description. (Reiter 1975: 12)

Feminists thus advocated 'placing women at the center, as subjects of inquiry and as active agents in the gathering of knowledge', in order to make 'women's experiences visible' and thereby reveal 'the sexist biases and tacitly male assumptions of traditional knowledge' (Stacey and Thorne 1985: 303).

Such approaches deeply influenced shifts within Development Studies, which have in turn been paralleled by gendered analyses of displacement from the 1980s to the present. The remainder of this section briefly illustrates the main feminist and gendered paradigms within Development Studies (known as WID, WAD, and GAD), and emphasizes their relevance to forced migration scholarship.

From WID, WAD, and GAD to WIFM and GAFM[2]

The first paradigm, known as Women In Development (WID), aimed to 'add women and stir' into the existing development framework. Largely associated with American liberal feminism, proponents of WID argued that 'women's experience of development and of societal change differed from that of men', making it 'legitimate for research to focus specifically on women's experiences and perceptions' (Rathgeber 1990: 491). This approach thus aimed to 'find' women in order to redress historical lacunae, and also to integrate them into socio-economic systems as a means of maximizing their productivity in future; these practical aims were prioritized rather than interrogating why women had been excluded from these systems, and to what effect.

The Women And Development (WAD) approach subsequently emerged in the 1970s, drawing on neo-Marxist feminism to argue that class structures, global inequalities, and exploitation were pivotal in the development system. Stressing the relationship *between* women and development, those espousing the WAD framework argued that women had always played central roles in economic development, and yet were excluded and exploited through different means. While ultimately underdeveloped in WAD, the significance of the *intersections* of identity markers such as gender, class, and race, and of power structures including patriarchy, classism, and racism emerged. For instance, WAD noted that non-elite 'Third World' men were exploited alongside 'Third World' women, and that Western middle-class women often exploited Other women, rather than assuming universal sisterhood across time and space.

In turn, Gender And Development (GAD) developed in the late 1980s, informed by socialist feminism and post-colonial theory. While WAD recognized the experiences of non-elite men within the development industry, both WID and WAD explicitly placed 'women at the centre'. In contrast, the GAD paradigm critiqued the social construction of gender—understood as being intrinsically *relational*, context specific, and changeable—and the processes by which gender roles, identities, and responsibilities come to be naturalized by socio-economic and political systems. GAD therefore laid the foundations to critique the invisibility of women and girls in earlier studies, programmes, and institutions, but also to interrogate the spaces and roles available for different groups of men and boys.

Since a gender analysis recognizes that the social attributes, expectations, and opportunities related to 'being' female or male can change over time and space, it is clear that these can be influenced by processes of accelerated social change, including conflict and displacement. Equally, by recognizing both females and males as active agents of social change, GAD demanded a commitment to structural change and the disruption of unequal social and institutional power relations to achieve gender equality and female empowerment.

Despite the centrality of *relational* dynamics in conceptualizations of gender and the recognition that gendered experiences must be analysed as '*part of the broader socio-cultural context... [as] other important criteria for socio-cultural analysis include class, race, poverty level, ethnic group and age*',[3] the tendency to equate 'gender' with 'women' often remains in practice. Indeed, while 'rapidly be[coming] outmoded in development discourse', the WID model has 'had great staying power in actual programming' (Indra 1999: 11). Tellingly, the newly established UN Entity for Gender Equality and Empowerment of Women is officially named *UN Women*, and not UN Gender.

Evolving approaches to women and gender within development studies have broadly been paralleled by shifts in the study of forced migration, leading to the Women *In* Forced Migration (WIFM) and the Gender *And* Forced Migration (GAFM) paradigms (respectively analogous to WID and GAD; Indra 1999: 17). With the interdisciplinary field of refugee and forced migration studies emerging in the early 1980s, many forced migration scholars and practitioners were aware of over a decade of extensive feminist critiques of the social sciences and development programming. Nonetheless, Camus-Jacques argued in 1989 that refugee women remained ' "the forgotten majority" on the international agenda' (cited in Hajdukowski-Ahmed, Khanlou, and Moussa 2008: 2). In contrast, Indra argues that Women In Forced Migration gained relative prominence from the mid-1980s and 1990s, 'becoming a fully legitimate, institutionalised element of forced migration discourse' (1999: 17). This institutionalization is reflected, *inter alia*, by the United Nations High Commissioner for Refugees' (UNHCR) 1990 *Position Paper on Gender-Related Persecution,* and its adoption of the *Guidelines on the Protection of Refugee Women* in 1991.

Nevertheless, forced migration academics and practitioners largely identified, depicted, and responded to 'refugee women' as apolitical and non-agentic victims, either as *madonnalike* figures (Malkki 1992: 33, 1996: 389), or as weakened, dependent, and vulnerable 'womenandchildren' (Enloe 1991). While increasingly recognizing that women's experiences of displacement differed from men's, these accounts often reduced such experiences to women's vulnerability to sexual violence, rather than exploring how and why women were victim*ized* and persecuted, or recognizing that displaced women could simultaneously be victim*ized* and yet remain active agents deserving of respect, and not simply pity (Hajdukowski-Ahmed, Khanlou, and Moussa 2008: 6).

GENDERED CAUSES AND EXPERIENCES OF FORCED MIGRATION

With this development of feminist and gendered analyses of forced migration in mind two bodies of literature are particularly pertinent when considering the gendered causes and experiences of forced migration: one pertaining to gender and refugee status determination, and the other with reference to mass conflict induced displacement.

Gender and Refugee Status Determination

Since the 1980s, feminist critiques of the 1951 Geneva Convention refugee definition have included denunciations that 'By portraying as universal that which is in fact a male paradigm...women refugees face rejection of their claims because their experiences of persecution go unrecognized' (Greatbatch 1989: 518). Pittaway and Bartolomei (1991: 26) refer to 'a classic case, cited by international human rights lawyers in their fight to change the legal recognition of the experience of refugee women', which is summarized as follows:

> A man was tied to a chair and forced at gunpoint to watch his common-law wife being raped by soldiers. In determining the case for refugee status, he was deemed to have been tortured. His partner was not.

Critics have therefore argued that the Convention itself is both androcentric and heteronormative, demanding, for instance, that the refugee definition be rewritten to include gender as a basis (of fear) of persecution, and that 'persecution' itself be redefined in order to recognize the political nature of female resistance to systems of oppression and violence within both the public and private spheres (Indra 1987).

UNHCR currently recognizes that 'historically, the refugee definition has been interpreted through a framework of male experiences, which has meant that many claims of women and of homosexuals have gone unrecognised' (UNHCR 2002: n. 1).[4] However, rather than advocating to include gender as an enumerated ground of persecution to redress a historical absence, the mainstream policy position maintains that gender bias in RSD can be adequately addressed through gender-sensitive *interpretations* of the existing framework. This has led to the development of numerous international and national guidelines, the first of which were UNHCR's 1991 *Guidelines on the Protection of Refugee Women*, closely followed by the first state-produced guidelines: the Canadian Immigration and Refugee Board's 1993 *Guidelines on Women Refugee Claimants Fearing Gender-Related Persecution* and the United States Immigration and Naturalization Service's 1995 *Considerations for Asylum Officers Adjudicating Asylum Claims from Women.*

Subsequent state and international advice on gender-sensitive interpretations has often drawn on ground-breaking legal cases: for instance, *Attorney-General of Canada and Ward* (1993) established that persecutory actors did not have to be state actors, granting the precedent of offering asylum to women who have experienced persecution at the hands of non-state actors (including family members); *Kasinga, 211 and N. Dec 357* (BIA 1996) was the first US decision to recognize female genital mutilation as a form of gender-based persecution; and the UK's *Islam v Secretary of State for the Home Department* offered asylum to two Pakistani women who had suffered domestic violence and were at risk of being accused of adultery if returned to Pakistan.

Whilst highlighting the limitations of earlier interpretations of the 1951 Convention by focusing on women, these and other documents have reproduced a prevailing view that 'refugee women and girls have *special* protection needs that reflect their gender' and '*special* efforts may be needed to resolve problems faced specifically by refugee women' (UNHCR 1991). While women were 'added to' existing frameworks, they were effectively included on the implicit understanding that they were exceptions to the norm: they required 'special' guidelines precisely because they were conceptualized as a 'particularly vulnerable social group' which was distinctly unlike the 'normal' refugee.

Women, and subsequently 'other social groups' for whom similar guidelines have been developed—such as children (UNHCR 1994) and lesbian, gay, bisexual, transsexual and intersex (LGBTI) asylum seekers (UNHCR 2012)—have thus been identified as fleeing 'different', 'extraordinary', and 'unconventional' forms of persecution requiring 'special efforts' to offer them protection. This thereby suggests that the so-called 'gender neutral' Convention was developed with adult male, heterosexual asylum applicants in mind, raising questions as to whether 'adding and stirring' women, children, and LBGTI applicants via 'exceptional' guidelines adequately addresses the conceptual biases and protection gaps emerging when assessing the causes of forced migration. The tendency to situate these 'exceptional' cases in the scope of the 1951 Convention through the grounds of 'membership of a particular social group' rather than recognizing these forms of persecution through the nexus of political opinion, nationality, or religious identity has received scrutiny for over a decade (Crawley 2000).

Sexual Orientation and Gender Identity

Indeed, although feminist critiques laid the foundations for more nuanced assessments of asylum applications submitted by LGBTI individuals on the basis of sexual orientation and/or gender identity, this issue remains a relatively new area of academic inquiry and policy implementation (see Jansen and Spijkerboer 2011; Forced Migration Review's 2013 special issue). The *Yogyakarta Principles on the Application of International Human Rights Law in Relation to Sexual Orientation and Gender Identity* were only drafted in 2007, and Jansen and Spijkerboer note that 'In light of the recent nature of these developments, it can scarcely be surprising that LGBTI asylum issues have only recently begun to receive attention' (2011: 14). Such attention has started to highlight the challenges experienced by LGBTI asylum seekers and refugees in their countries of origin, asylum, and resettlement: these include homophobia, transphobia, and the criminalization of same-sex relationships, and gender-specific forms of persecution such as the 'corrective rape' of lesbian asylum seekers, forced sterilization and forced marriage of LGBTI individuals, and 'corrective surgery' of intersex individuals.

UNHCR published its *Guidance Note on Refugee Claims Relating to Sexual Orientation and Gender Identity* in 2008, followed by its 2011 *Need to Know Guidance* on working with LGBTI persons and the aforementioned revised 2012 Guidelines. In the European Union, Article 10(1)(d) of the Qualification Directive was amended in 2011 to explicitly recognize that sexual orientation *and* gender identity may fall under the ground 'membership of a particular social group'. The EU Directive is limited not only because only a small number of EU member states offer protection on this basis either through offering asylum, subsidiary protection, or another form of protection (Jansen and Spijkerboer 2011: 7), but also because it continues to associate LGBTI cases with membership of a particular social group. In effect, UNHCR's 2012 Guidelines clearly stress that 'other grounds may...also be relevant depending on the political, religious and cultural context of the claim; for example advocacy by LGBTI activists may be seen as going against prevailing political or religious views and/or practices' (Gray and McDowall 2013: 22). Transcending the equation between women and gender on the one hand, and between women's and LGBTI asylum applications and membership of a particular social group on the other, remains a major challenge within academia and policy alike.

Gender and Conflict Induced Displacement

In addition to feminist and gendered contributions to understandings of individual persecution, studies of gender and armed conflict have, *inter alia*, examined how conflict is itself founded upon gendered aims and institutions and how conflict is implemented through gendered tactics and protection narratives (i.e. Abu-Lughod 2002). Initially, feminist investigations aimed to render women and girls *visible* as social groups affected by war, and to document female-specific experiences of conflict. In particular, female experiences of sexual violence were recognized as prompting and accompanying processes of forced migration.

Such research influenced ground-breaking changes in international responses to sexual violence against women in the 'new wars' of the early 1990s, especially following the widespread rape of women in former Yugoslavia, and subsequently in Rwanda: rape and sexual slavery in conflict were recognized for the first time as crimes against humanity by the International Criminal Tribunal for the Former Yugoslavia (1993)[5] and the International Criminal Tribunal for Rwanda (1994). Article 7(1g) of the Rome Statute of the International Criminal Court, in force since 2002, includes 'Rape, sexual slavery, enforced prostitution, forced pregnancy, enforced sterilization, or any other form of sexual violence of comparable gravity' as crimes against humanity when they are committed in a widespread or systematic way.

By identifying women's roles as human rights and peace advocates, this literature also implicitly recognized that women might be persecuted due to their political activism. More explicitly, this work influenced the international community's commitment to women's increased participation in the 'prevention and resolution of conflicts' and in the 'maintenance and promotion of peace and security' as asserted in UN Security Council Resolution 1325 on Women, Peace, and Security (2000).

Whilst enhancing understandings of women's multiple positions within conflict and displacement situations, and recognizing female agency rather than depicting women as non-agentic victims, these studies often reproduced representations of women's 'natural' propensity to 'care for' populations affected by violence. Extensive critiques have now deconstructed the naturalization of women's roles as 'victims', 'carers', or inherent 'peacemakers', and the corresponding depiction of men's 'innate' violence within a broader oppressive patriarchal system. In particular, investigations have explored not only the experiences of women, but how women *and* men, girls *and* boys, are differentially involved in, and affected by, conflict situations which lead to mass displacement.

For instance, it has been acknowledged that women may themselves directly participate in or incite acts of violence, transcending long-standing binary depictions of women as victims and men as perpetrators (Moser and Clarke 2001). With reference to the latter, studies are increasingly documenting certain men and boys' vulnerabilities to gender-specific violence and persecution, including boys and men being targeted for forced recruitment, summary execution, and sex-specific massacres (as was the case, for instance, of Muslim boys and men killed en masse in Srebrenica). More broadly, male experiences of sexual violence in displacement situations are increasingly being documented, with the rape and sexual mutilation of men and boys being committed by both male and female perpetrators around the world (Dolan 2003; Carpenter 2006).

Such studies challenge mainstream understandings of sexual and gender-based violence as "Any act or threat *by men or male-dominated* institutions that inflicts physical, sexual, or psychological harm *on a woman or girl because of their gender* (Reeves and Baden 2000: 2, emphasis added). It also pushes international organizations to transcend their policies of focusing on men and boys 'as agents of change for gender equality and bringing an end to violence [against women]' (UNHCR EXCOM 2012: 5), in order to recognize men and boys as potentially *subjected to* sexual and gender-based violence (SGBV), rather than as either *perpetrators of* SGBV against, or *protectors of*, women. Recognizing male experiences of gender-based violence has been welcomed by many gender analysts, whilst others argue that addressing this issue detracts academic and policy attention from, and limited financial resources for, women and girls.

Gender and Responses to Forced Migration

A third major set of debates pertains to responses to different stages of forced migration, including with reference to gender and camps on the one hand, and gender and durable solutions on the other.

Gender and Encampment

Numerous studies have highlighted the vulnerability of 'womenandchildren' in refugee and IDP camps, often based upon the premiss that camps are criminalized spaces where political and power structures reinforce and strengthen patriarchal tendencies of the displaced community (see Callamard 1999: 198; Fiddian-Qasmiyeh 2014). Indeed, camps and host cities alike often do not provide a 'sanctuary' for displaced persons; instead, they may be subjected to a repetition or re-initiation of cycles of violence and abuse experienced in their countries of origin, or may experience physical and sexual abuse for the first time in exile (Fiddian 2006). The dangers encountered in such spaces often arise due to the disruption of social systems and safety nets such as family protection and socio-religious authority mechanisms, although, as noted, it is now simultaneously recognized that the domestic sphere may itself have been a space of persecution rather than safety in the context of origin.

Importantly, however, UNHCR's *Age, Gender and Diversity Mainstreaming* (AGDM, now AGD) strategy has prompted a shift away from UNHCR's earlier reliance on essentialist categorizations of 'pre-identified groups of "vulnerable" or "extremely vulnerable persons"', towards 'the broader concepts of age, gender and diversity' (UNHCR EXCOM 2010). Rather than 'simply label[ling] individuals as "vulnerable"', UNHCR staff and partners are now encouraged 'to analyse the protection context of persons of concern and identify the different vulnerabilities and capacities of all age and gender groups' (UNHCR EXCOM 2010). This has resulted in the development and implementation of diverse policies to identify *risk* factors which can be addressed to maximize the *prevention of* SGBV in camp situations (UNHCR 2004, 2008), rather than merely *responding* to SGBV *post facto*.

Furthermore, displacement has also been identified as potentially providing a space for 'positive' change and gender empowerment precisely because of the disruption of traditional social systems and the reconfiguration of the gendered division of labour arising from displacement. Indeed, UNHCR has the *responsibility* to promote gender equality as part of its protection mandate (UNHCR 2008: 23), and its aims include facilitating 'Empowerment and enhancement of productive capacities and self-reliance of refugees, particularly of women, pending durable solutions' (UNHCR EXCOM 2003: D/33).

Paradoxical Impacts of Gender Equality and Empowerment Policies in Camps

Despite the rationale underpinning UNHCR's gender equality and empowerment policies (where 'gender' generally continues to be synonymous with 'women'), studies have increasingly examined their paradoxical impacts. For instance, Turner's research with Burundian refugees in camps in Tanzania (2010) argues that UNHCR's gender equality policy led to refugees' common perceptions that 'UNHCR is a better husband,' which 'illustrates very aptly this feeling that masculinity was being taken away from the male refugees and appropriated by the UNHCR' (Turner 2012: 72). Rather than reconfiguring relations between women and men, Turner's research reveals both a continuation of male authority over female refugees, and the ways in which the gender equality policy unexpectedly provided opportunities for young men to outmanoeuvre the old patriarchal order by replacing the older generation of men as the new 'big men' in the camp.

While Turner's interviewees rejected gender equality as undesirable, and male refugees struggled to 'rehabilitate' their masculinity and their positions within their families and broader camp community, the international discourse regarding gender equality and female empowerment has officially been embraced by refugees in other contexts, often with equally paradoxical effects. With reference to the protracted Sahrawi refugee situation, for instance, UNHCR's Refugee Women and Gender Equality Unit has declared that Sahrawi refugee women's empowerment in the Algeria-based Sahrawi refugee camps is 'unique', identifying the camp-based National Union of Sahrawi Women (NUSW) as an 'ideal partner', and explicitly presenting the camps as an example of 'good practice on gender mainstreaming' (Fiddian-Qasmiyeh 2010, 2014). Without dismissing the significance of women's contributions throughout social, political, and administrative sectors and spaces within the camps, Fiddian-Qasmiyeh (2014) argues that Sahrawi refugees' political representatives have formally adopted international donors' rhetoric vis-à-vis gender equality and female empowerment to ensure a continuation of political and humanitarian support. Her research reveals that official affirmations (by Sahrawi refugees and UNHCR alike) that the camps are characterized by gender equality and that Sahrawi women have an 'ideal' and 'unique' position within the camps, have reinforced the marginalization not only of 'non-ideal' women, but also of girls, boys, and young men (Fiddian-Qasmiyeh 2014).

As such, although Turner's study argues that young men became the new 'big men' in the Tanzanian camps, the Sahrawi case illustrates that the position of the older generation of elite Sahrawi women over both younger females *and* males in the camps has been reinforced through a range of policies and programmes ostensibly designed to maximize 'gender equality' and 'female empowerment'. In the Sahrawi context, the older generation of elite Sahrawi women *and* men have ultimately monopolized the camps' political, economic, and social spheres, despite the younger generation having been educated to higher levels in numerous locations around the world (Fiddian-Qasmiyeh 2009, 2014). The significance of gender, age, and political status in these studies therefore reinforces the value of intersectionalist analyses of displacement situations; it also illustrates the diverse ways in which displaced populations respond to international policies and discourses, and the multifaceted impacts of policies on relations between men and women, and also between different groups of men, and different groups of women. Indeed, Fiddian-Qasmiyeh's research also confirms the importance of transcending mainstream Western feminist definitions of patriarchy 'as the power of men over women' to recognize a plurality of patriarchal systems, including Joseph's conceptualization of 'patriarchy in the Arab context as the prioritising of the rights of males and elders (*including elder women*)' (1996: 14, emphasis added). Further research remains to be conducted regarding LGBTI experiences of encampment and different structures of oppression and control including patriarchy, homophobia, and transphobia, and the impacts of recent policies designed or amended to uphold the rights of LGBTI displaced persons in such contexts.

Engendering Durable Solutions

Although they are presented as gender neutral, the three durable solutions available to the international community—local integration, repatriation, and resettlement—are also gendered in terms of access, experiences, and implications. One key question is whether a given durable solution can ever be appropriate for all members of a displaced community. With reference to local integration, for example, certain individuals and social groups may be able to access the legal, political, social, and economic rights necessary for both de facto and de jure integration to take place; however, an individual's gender, sexual orientation, and gender identity, age, personal status, religion, and health/ disability status may influence their ability to safely 'integrate' in their host environment. Amongst other experiences, the continuation or instigation of violence and persecution against particular individuals and groups in host cities indicates that third-country resettlement might be the only *viable* source of meaningful protection, even if it might not be *available* for the vast majority of refugees.

Importantly, although women and girls have historically been perceived to be particularly 'vulnerable' to different forms of abuse and violence throughout all phases and spaces of displacement, both access to and decisions in the asylum process, and submissions for resettlement have largely remained androcentric (Boyd 1999). Since being recognized as a refugee is a main requirement for inclusion on resettlement states' 'guest lists',[6] the former has major implications for the latter (Fiddian 2006).

The gender bias in global resettlement processes was officially recognized in 2006 by UNHCR EXCOM Conclusion 105, since only 5.7 per cent of all resettlement cases submitted to UNHCR in 2005 were women-at-risk. EXCOM Conclusion 105 declared that at least 10 per cent of all cases submitted to UNHCR for resettlement should correspond to 'women-and-girls-at-risk'.[7] The UNHCR's Heightened Risk Identification Tool (HRIT) was developed in 2008 as a means of recognizing that 'While many persons in a displaced community may find themselves at risk, the challenge is to identify those individuals who are at heightened risk, requiring early intervention' (2010: 3). Although the HRIT is used in conjunction with the Age, Gender, and Diversity strategy to identify high-risk cases in camp contexts, its main use is not to assess who may need particular support in a *host* environment, but more specifically to identify priority cases for resettlement.

A more recent policy development is the expansion of the 'at-risk' category to include LGBTI individuals, as reflected for the first time in the latest version of the HRIT published by UNHCR in 2010 (Turk 2013: 8). As in the case of 'women-at-risk', however, LGBTI individuals' access to resettlement is typically contingent upon being recognized as a refugee, which is itself a major challenge in countries of first asylum due to limited understandings of the nature of LGBTI experiences of persecution in private and public spheres (as indicated earlier). A further difficulty emerges when policy (and political) decisions to promote repatriation as the preferred durable solution for a given refugee community has the potential to place LGBTI survivors of persecution at particular risk in their countries of origin. For instance, in 2004 the peace-deal being brokered in Sudan meant that UNHCR ceased interviewing (non-Darfuri) Sudanese asylum applicants in Cairo, thereby preventing 'exceptional' LGBTI asylum seekers from informing refugee status decision makers that they had been persecuted in Sudan, and in Egypt, due to their sexual orientation and gender identity, and that the nature of their claim therefore remained unchanged by the peace-deal (see Fiddian 2006).

Indeed, while Gruber notes that repatriation 'cannot presuppose a return to the *status quo ante*' and that 'negotiation of what may be profoundly altered ways of life and familial and communal structures should be recognised as intrinsic to any repatriation initiative' (1999: 9), certain elements of the *status quo ante* may indeed remain or be strengthened in the country of origin. These include patriarchal, xenophobic, and homophobic structures and attitudes which may have underpinned the causes of persecution before seeking asylum, and may continue doing so upon 'return'.

While rendering ongoing experiences of violence and persecution visible, the development of gender-sensitive protection tools like the original and revised Heightened Risk Identification Tool continue to focus on 'exceptional' refugees, rather than interrogating the foundations of mainstream assumptions which led to women, children, and LGBTI refugees and asylum-seekers being excluded to begin with. By typically highlighting a particular form of risk (primarily sexual and gender-based violence) refugee status determination systems and such protection tools embody a form of institutional violence which 'privileges forms of life or humanity not constituted as right-bearing individuals, but as corporeal victims of sexual violence, innocent, non-agentive, and apolitical' (Ticktin 2005: 367).

As suggested above, all three 'solutions' are characterized by ongoing processes of social integration which are both intrinsically gendered and potentially violent. On the one hand, multiple individual, familial, and collective challenges exist when negotiating gendered experiences and expectations for the present and future. On the other hand, integrating into a host state, resettlement state, or country of origin may equally lead to new or repeated forms of exclusion and marginalization. For instance, given the prevalence of homophobia and transphobia across the global North and global South, LGBTI refugees will likely continue to encounter stigmatization and perhaps even criminalization if same-sex relationships are considered to be illegal in their resettlement state. In turn, Muslim refugee women, whose religious identity may be particularly visible if they are veiled, may experience new forms of discrimination such as Islamophobia and racism, in addition to a continuation of patriarchal structures of oppression in countries of asylum or resettlement alike (Fiddian-Qasmiyeh and Qasmiyeh 2010).

Conclusion

Refugees' and asylum seekers' experiences of seeking a secure and dignified life through asylum and any one of the three durable solutions (and, indeed, protracted encampment), are framed by overlapping identity markers such as gender, age, religion, and sexual orientation, and structures such as patriarchy, xenophobia, and homophobia. Major conceptual, theoretical, and practical challenges remain to recognize and uphold the agency of displaced individuals and groups, whilst simultaneously ensuring that all individuals' experiences of persecution are 'legible' to decision makers, and that policies to offer meaningful protection are neither paternalistic nor patriarchal in and of themselves (Pittaway and Bartolomei 1991). Indeed, this chapter has suggested the extent to which power imbalances and systems of control are potentially reproduced, rather than being challenged, through programmes designed to promote 'gender equality' and 'female empowerment'. Future research must therefore continue to critique the assumption that 'gender' has been successfully 'mainstreamed' into academia, policy, and practice by recognizing both who and what has been rendered visible, but also who and what has been rendered invisible throughout feminist and gender studies of forced migration to date. That sensitivity to the intersections between masculinity and forced migration on the one hand, and sexual orientation, gender identity, and asylum on the other should be so recent, and contested, demonstrates precisely how urgent this ongoing research agenda is.

NOTES

1. This chapter can usefully be read alongside Anderson's discussion of gendered discourses of trafficking and smuggling; Edwards and Van Waas's analysis of gender and statelessness; and Stepputat and Sørensen on micro-level sociological studies of familial and individual experiences of forced migration (all in this volume).
2. This section draws in particular on Rathgeber (1990) and Indra (1999).
3. <http://www.un.org/womenwatch/osagi/conceptsanddefinitions.html>, emphasis added.
4. As noted by Chloe Lewis, by failing to specify 'heterosexual male experiences' in this context, UNHCR 'seems to reify the emasculation of gay men' (personal communication, 22 June 2013).
5. Pittaway and Bartolomei (1991) argue that the development of this legal framework as a response to the mass rape of *Caucasian* women in the former Yugoslavia must be examined through an intersectional lens of race and gender.
6. On Australian and Canadian humanitarian resettlement programmes for women-at-risk who may not have been recognized as refugees per se, see Manderson et al. (1998) and Boyd (1999), respectively.
7. Importantly, this category in turn risks perpetuating patriarchal systems by assuming that 'a woman without a man is a woman at risk'—see Manderson et al. (1998).

REFERENCES

Abu-Lughod, L. (2002) 'Do Muslim Women Really Need Saving? Anthropological Reflections on Cultural Relativism and its Others'. *American Anthropologist* 104: 783–90.

Boyd, M. (1999) 'Gender, Refugee Status and Permanent Settlement'. *Gender Issues* 17(1): 5–25.

Callamard, A. (1999) 'Refugee Women: A Gendered and Political Analysis of the Refugee Experience'. Pp. 194–214 in A. Ager (ed.), *Refugees: Perspectives on the Experience of Forced Migration*. London: Continuum.

Camus-Jacques, G. (1989) 'Refugee Women: The Forgotten Majority'. Pp. 141–7 in G. Loescher and L. Monaham (eds.), *Refugees and International Relations*. Oxford: Oxford University Press.

Carpenter, C. (2006) 'Recognizing Gender-Based Violence against Civilian Men and Boys in Conflict Situations'. *Security Dialogue* 37: 83–103.

Crawley, H. (2000) 'Gender, Persecution and the Concept of Politics in the Asylum Determination Process'. *Forced Migration Review* 9: 17–20.

Dolan, C. (2003) 'Collapsing Masculinities and Weak States: A Case Study of Northern Uganda'. Pp. 57–83 in F. Cleaver (ed.), *Masculinity Matters: Men, Masculinities and Gender Relations in Development*. London: Zed Books.

Enloe, C. H. (1991) '"Womenandchildren": Propaganda Tools of Patriarchy'. Pp. 89ff. in G. Bates (ed.), *Mobilising Democracy: Changing the US Role in the Middle East*. Monroe, ME: Common Courage Press.

Fiddian, E. (2006) 'Relocating: The Asylum Experience in Cairo'. *Interventions: International Journal of Postcolonial Studies* 8(2): 295–318.

Fiddian-Qasmiyeh, E. (2010) '"Ideal" Refugee Women and Gender Equality Mainstreaming: "Good Practice" for Whom?' *Refugee Survey Quarterly* 29(2): 64–84.

Fiddian-Qasmiyeh, E. (2014) *The Ideal Refugees: Gender, Islam and the Sahrawi Politics of Survival*. Syracuse, NY: Syracuse University Press.

Fiddian-Qasmiyeh, E., and Qasmiyeh, Y. (2010) 'Muslim Asylum-Seekers and Refugees: Negotiating Politics, Religion and Identity in the UK'. *Journal of Refugee Studies* 23(3): 294–314.

Gray, A., and McDowall, A. (2013) 'LGBT Refugee Protection in the UK: From Discretion to Belief?' *Forced Migration Review* 42: 22–5.

Greatbatch, J. (1989) 'The Gendered Difference: Feminist Critiques of Refugee Discourse'. *International Journal of Refugee Law* 1(4): 518–27.

Hajdukowski-Ahmed, M., Khanlou, N., and Moussa, H. (2008) 'Introduction'. Pp. 1–24 in M. Hajdukowski-Ahmed, N. Khanlou, and H. Moussa (eds.), *Not Born a Refugee Woman: Contesting Identities, Rethinking Practices*. Oxford: Berghahn Books.

Indra, D. M. (1999) 'Not a "Room of One's Own": Engendering Forced Migration and Practice'. Pp. 1–22 in D. M. Indra (ed.), *Engendering Forced Migration: Theory and Practice*. Oxford: Berghahn Books.

Jansen, S., and Spijkerboer, T. (2011) *Fleeing Homophobia: Asylum Claims Related to Sexual Orientation and Gender Identity in Europe*. Amsterdam: COC Nederland, Vrije Universitei.

Joseph, S. (1996) 'Patriarchy and Development in the Arab World'. *Gender and Development* 4(2): 14–19.

Malkki, L. (1992) 'National Geographic: The Rooting of Peoples and the Territorialization of National Identity among Scholars and Refugees'. *Cultural Anthropology* 7(1): 24–44.

Manderson, L., Kelaher, M., Markovic, M., and McManus, K. (1998) 'A Woman without a Man is a Woman at Risk: Women at Risk in Australian Humanitarian Programs'. *Journal of Refugee Studies* 11(3): 267–83.

Moser, C., and Clarke, F. (eds.) (2001) *Victims, Perpetrators or Actors? Gender, Armed Conflict and Political Violence*. London: Zed Books.

Pittaway, E., and Bartolomei, L. (1991) 'Refugees, Race, and Gender: The Multiple Discrimination against Refugee Women'. *Refuge* 19(6): 21–32.

Rathgeber, E. M. (1990) 'WID, WAD, GAD: Trends in Research and Practice'. *Journal of Developing Areas* 24: 489–502.

Reeves, H., and Baden, S. (2000) *Gender and Development: Concepts and Definitions*. BRIDGE Report No. 55.

Reiter, R. (1975) 'Introduction'. Pp. 10–19 in R. Reiter (ed.), *Toward an Anthropology of Women*. New York: Monthly Review Press.

Stacey, J., and Thorne, B. (1985) 'The Missing Feminist Revolution in Sociology'. *Social Problems* 32(4): 301–16.

Turner, S. (2012) *Politics of Innocence: Hutu Identity, Conflict and Camp Life*. Oxford: Berghahn Books.

UNHCR (2012) 'Guidelines on International Protection No. 9: Claims to Refugee Status based on Sexual Orientation and/or Gender Identity within the context of Article 1A(2) of the 1951 Convention and/or its 1967 Protocol relating to the Status of Refugees'. Geneva: UNHCR.

UNHCR EXCOM (2012) 'Age, Gender and Diversity Approach', EC/61/SC/CRP.14.

CHAPTER 32

....

OLDER REFUGEES

....

CLAUDIO BOLZMAN[1]

INTRODUCTION

FROM UNHCR figures, it is estimated that, at the end of 2011, no more than 3 per cent of all refugees, i.e. some 315,000 for a population of 10,400,000, were aged 60 years or more (UNHCR 2012).[2] The same figures can be extrapolated for the internally displaced and for other persons in refugee-like situations. At the outset, it appears to be a very low proportion; moreover, one should bear in mind that the proportion of older refugees is a dynamic phenomenon. It should not be reduced to a matter of statistical data, whether accurate or inaccurate, but rather should be tackled as a qualitative reflection of a series of factors—such as when, for example, exile took place, at what age the person was exiled, and for how long.

Equally, it is important to differentiate those persons who grew old while they were refugees and those who were already considered to be old when they became refugees or internally displaced. There is more research about those who have grown old after they became refugees than about those who were already old when forced to migrate (Scott and Bolzman 1999). In spite of the disequilibrium of data, I will try to give an overview of both categories of refugee within this chapter.

After a brief outline of the general context, the chapter draws on interviews with older refugees collected in studies I carried out previously, mainly in Switzerland[3] (Bolzman 1996; Scott and Bolzman 1999; Bolzman et al. 2008), and on secondary literature on refugees in Europe and, to a lesser extent, in North America. The chapter aims to address, in the first part of the chapter, the main disruptions and challenges met by refugees from a life course perspective. Special attention will be paid in the second section to intergenerational relationships and to coping strategies of families in a context of stress and resource reduction. The third section will deal with the health situation of older refugees. Similarities and differences with older people from minority ethnic groups shall be examined. The main risks of specific health troubles and mental illness will also be dealt with.

The last section will present the main forms of community support for older refugees in host countries, and will address the question of durable solutions for older refugees. The conclusion will address the need for more research in order to gain a better understanding of the phenomenon of older refugees.

EXILE AND THE LIFE COURSE PERSPECTIVE

In most cases exile represents a radical severance with a person's home country or region of origin resulting in the loss of the primary social and economic resources that structured everyday life. For every migrant, but more specifically for refugees, arriving in a new country or region represents significant changes and dilemmas related to the acquaintance of a new social context whereby many issues that were formerly routine go on to become a problem (Bolzman 1994).

These conditions are felt particularly by older people who are, in general, less flexible than younger people in the process of adaptation to new social situations. Even affluent older migrants that moved voluntarily from Northern to Southern European countries try to reproduce their former way of life in the new environment (Casado-Diaz, Kaiser, and Warnes 2004; Huber and O'Reilly 2004). Cultural shock overwhelms those without much prior experience or knowledge of urban life in industrialized societies, as was experienced by the many older Vietnamese boat people who sought refuge in Europe and North America during the 1970s and 1980s (Ahmed, Tims, and Kolker 1981; Allard 1987). Mental distress tends to increase when refugees are subsequently separated from their larger social networks in the country of asylum, as was the case for refugees from South-East Asia in Europe and North America (Montero 1979; Simon-Barouh 1984). Here again, older people have been seen to feel the effects of separation more intensely than younger people, as in the case of those moving to join their adult children (Bolzman et al. 2008).

These feelings of loss are particularly intense when refugees perceive their situation in the country of exile to be permanent—knowing that they may never see their country or region of origin again. The Latin American refugees from the 1970s as well as Central and East Europeans from the 1940s and 1950s are a good illustration. Exile, for them, was at the beginning a transitory situation—they had hoped that the political situation within their own countries would be changed and that they would be able to return within a few years. This perception was voiced by Francisco, a Chilean refugee who, as former trade union leader, was imprisoned and then expelled by the military junta. He arrived in Switzerland in 1976 when he was 52 years old. He said:

> My wife and children were not feeling good at the beginning. The fight for our country, for our people, was very important and met with strong conviction. It allowed us to feel at ease with ourselves, to be always together, to build up a more organized life in exile, to think always about our country, about the return.[4]

However, forced migration is a dynamic situation. Perceptions of this situation are modified not only with time but also by the socio-historical context. For instance, when older Latin American refugees realized that exile would be a permanent reality and that they could never return to their country of origin, they were overwhelmed with profound feelings of emptiness. Like Ismael, a now retired Chilean:

> If I were conservative, passive, I would be very happy in Switzerland. But if you like to do things, to participate, in this country there is nothing to do. (Quoted from Bolzman 1996: 192)

They felt that there was no place for them in the country of asylum other than within their ethnic community, that there was no place for older people with strong political convictions.

Scott (1998), in her study of Polish exiles in Scotland, considered the implications of long-term exile mainly from the perspectives of displacement lost youth, and a lifetime struggle to reach a sense of personal reconciliation to the realities of exile. For those who left the country as young people in 1945, with the expectation of a temporary departure, in time discovered that it had become a permanent state of exile. For these generations of men and women who represent a whole generation of Central and East Europeans displaced in their youth by the ravages of war, the celebration of the end of war each year in May has been a silent commemoration of their lost families, friends, comrades, and their homeland.

Kalemkaryan and Ohanian (1996), in a survey on some 500 older Armenian people living in the London Borough of Hounslow, the majority of whom had been born in Turkey or in the Middle East, believe that the experience of persecution leaves an indelible mark. They argue that this damage becomes further engrained when the greater part of the person's life has been lived under colonial or dictatorial regimes, such as those in Syria, Iran, or Lebanon. They suggest that older people, in particular, have not only had the greater experience of one or other form of persecution, but that their survival presents an additional set of concerns. For Armenian older refugees, the experience of surviving the systematic destruction of their own nation in Ottoman Turkey and then living as refugees in societies where freedom of expression had been denied for many years, continues to haunt and influence the way they perceive the world and society, even now, in the more liberal/multicultural Britain (1996: 2).

What seems clear is that for the first generation of refugees and displaced, the feeling of identification with their country or region of origin remains strong, even after a long residence in the country or region of asylum. This is supported by Leser and Seeberg (1992) who, in their study of Hungarian refugees settled in Switzerland after 1956, noted that there was a rebirth of identification with the country of origin and with the idea of return, but only after the end of the Cold War. The shattering of the Iron Curtain opened up the Eastern part of Europe and triggered more intense relations with the home country. Scott (1997) also reports that some older Polish people living in Scotland, did return to Poland, but some found the transition after more than a half-century too difficult to cope with. They returned with deeper disappointment and a sense of utter failure. We will focus again on this point in the last section of this chapter.

OLDER REFUGEES AND FAMILY LIFE

Forced migration does not impact on individuals alone but affects their whole family. Significant and critical changes occur in the social context which often deeply alters the interactions amongst family members. Transformations within family life can be more or less significant according to the possibility for each family member to participate in the decision—in this case, to leave the country and decide on the conditions of departure. Another significant factor is the possibility for each member of the family as well as the family as a whole to adopt, at least to some extent, their previous ways of life in the asylum society.

Forced migration is an arduous challenge for families, disrupting everyday life for each individual, but also causing physical separation of family members. Indeed, in many cases, some family members stay in the home country, others find refuge in the first country of asylum, and others still need to leave for another country. Usually, older people stay behind because their mobility opportunities are more reduced. Indeed, we have seen that they constitute a minor proportion of refugees. During this period of separation, family life needs to be reframed. Hence family members develop transnational ties. Despite the distance, they try to communicate through various media (telephone, email, Skype, tape/CD recordings, letters, etc.). Expressions of 'long distance closeness' (Coenen-Hutter, Kellerhals, and Von Allmen 1994), which may be more or less close and regular, persist between the generations across borders. Women from both the older and the younger generation play a central role in maintaining these ties (Bryceson and Vuorela 2007).

For those who migrate to a single country of asylum, the redefinition and reconstitution of families becomes a major challenge. As showed by the study conducted by Vatz Laaroussi (2009) about migrant and refugees families in Canada, social and professional conditions can affect the ability of refugee families to stay together. Moreover, it may be that the concept of family is not the same for particular refugees as for those resident in the asylum country. Ways of living and practices within and outside the family can also be different. Therefore, the family, as a close network of relatives, can take on new meaning; and the need to reaffirm their identity as the core of the family unit becomes a central task for those in exile. Scott (1997) has analysed how non-blood kinship has developed amongst older Poles, many of whom arrived as single individuals, comparing those who married within their ethnic groups with the small number who married outside it. In this context, she argues, extended 'family networks' have been created through affiliations amongst exiles and have been tied through a series of symbolic adoptions, such as the allocation of godfathers in the Catholic rite. This specific affiliation, like blood kinship, such as consanguinity, created expectations regarding intergenerational support and provided stability to the reconstituted family.

Bolzman, Fibbi, and Vial (2001) see the family network as a 'reservoir' in which resources—material, symbolic, social—are gathered and mobilized whenever the need arises. In an ideal situation, continuous intergenerational support takes place 'spontaneously' and without prior conditions having to be established. However, within exiled groups, forced migration has been found to disrupt established inter-generational support mechanisms and to force families to negotiate new ways of coping. For many older people in exile, the cultural value linked to age decreases, because, for example, the elderly in urban and industrialized societies are usually seen as non-economically viable and therefore dependent. The higher status assigned to an older person in their home country/region—in recognition of their life experi-ence, knowledge, and wisdom—is not matched in the new place of residence. Instead, respect and honour given to a person based on his or her age is often shifted in favour of the younger generation.

Older people therefore face these cultural differences, especially within the redefined and reconstructed family, and their expectations to occupy a central place in this unit meet with disappointment. For example, many Chilean refugees fear being alone at the time of retirement. They dream of being able to return to Chile, where they imagine that the support of family and their wider social network will be much better. Although some older Chileans at the time of the study were enjoying good health, had family ties in Switzerland, and participated actively in voluntary associations and within the com-munity, there was a significant number of older people who experienced the loss of their specific roles and/or commitment; this had led to low self-esteem and increased depen-dency on their families (Bolzman 1996). Loneliness was a reality for these older people, and even when the family was trying to be supportive, life in exile is often associated with social and economic difficulties, which burdens the younger members of the fam-ily. Older people, often trapped in the cycle of poverty become dependent upon their children for their livelihood in everyday life. This was, for example, the case with Silvia, an older Chilean woman, who needed her children to live with her, so that they could help her to pay the rent of the apartment:

> The problem is that the children want to leave the house... They are already too old as one of them is married and want to live alone with her husband. That is my dilemma. I feel somehow guilty to try to keep them here because of my low income. I am used to living with my family. To live without family here is like to be sent to die in an older person's home: that is the way they do it here. (Quoted from Bolzman 1996: 221–2)

Family plays a central role in the life of older refugees. The economic dimension of care, as shown above, is relevant. The central question, however, is whether they can feel reassured about the future. Older refugees hope that as they grow older and become more dependent their children will continue to play an active role in provid-ing support for them. The way societies offer care for older people varies greatly, and for older refugees the idea of living the rest of their lives in nursing homes is particu-larly stressful, and contrary to their expectations. They hope that the younger mem-bers of their family will play an important role in their care, particularly in the areas of health and material assistance.

HEALTH OF OLDER REFUGEES

Older refugees, like other older immigrants, often experience a lower quality of life accompanied by poor physical and mental health compared to the majority of the elderly population. Bollini and Siem (1995) defined this phenomenon as the 'exhausted migrant effect'. The health problems of former migrant workers are related to precarious living and work conditions, both in the home country as well as in their new country of residence. For refugees, the situation is even more difficult, as persecution and collective violence have deeply marked their lives and had a strong impact on their physical and mental health, contributing to greater deterioration in the later years of their life (also see Ager, this volume). While professional dequalification and lasting unemployment can have an influence on low self-esteem and depression, these feelings are also strongly linked to the psycho-social conditions imposed through forced migration. For the majority, the reality is that forced migration remains dominant in their memories, and continues to be as complex in its political content as it is in terms of that person's response to it (Bowling 1990; Scott 1997). In later life, trauma and its many concomitants can re-emerge and take the form of various mental conditions, such as depression, anxiety, neurosis, and paranoia (Baker 1983; Bram 1983). They can also take the form of physical health problems, as can be observed in the case of refugees and asylum seekers from the Balkans in Switzerland (Bolzman 2012).

In a research study carried out in the early 2000s, Bolzman, Poncioni, and Vial (2012) compared the situation of older migrants and refugees from former Yugoslavia to that of older migrants from Italy and Spain. About 30 per cent of former Yugoslavians in the sample, especially Bosnians and Albanians from Kosovo, came to Switzerland to escape from violence and war in their home country during the 1990s. Most of the indicators relative to the health conditions of the former Yugoslavians were particularly alarming: a high proportion of them were suffering from bad health according to self-assessment indicators, a high level were registered disabled, physically and/or mentally. Those fleeing the violence in Bosnia and Kosovo and who had subsequently been living for many years with a precarious legal status (especially as asylum seekers, or as individuals with temporary admission) and in precarious social conditions in Switzerland were particularly affected. Though younger than other elderly immigrants (most of former Yugoslavian immigrants were aged 55 to 64, while most Spanish and Italian immigrants were aged 65 or older), their health was poorer (Bolzman, Poncioni, and Vial 2012). At the same time, their access to the various health services, as asylum seekers or temporarily admitted, was more limited due to financial or legal restrictions (Subilia 2002).

For the majority, the reality of forced migration perseveres within their memories and remains greatly complex both in its content and in terms of their political personal response to it (Braito 1988; Bowling 1990). In old age, injuries and their side-effects may resurface and also take the form of various mental health conditions such as depression, anxiety, neurosis, or paranoia (dubbed the 'Polish disease') (Bram 1983). As noted by Braito with reference to refugees from Eastern and Central Europe after the war:

> The paranoia of refugees is also a problem. Certain groups like the Poles or Ukrainians were separated from their homeland by the war, locked in concentration camps and used as a labour force. This experience in itself can create health problems. Moreover, behaviours designed to cope with these experiences may have contributed to the survival but constitute a problem in a new and different environment. (1988: 10)

For older refugees, forced migration was in itself traumatic and life threatening, but this constituted only one aspect of the damage caused to them as it also went on to negatively influence their future lives. Other phenomena are added. For example, the transition from rural areas to highly industrialized and urbanized environments leads to many challenges in adaptation to a new society. Faced with the reality that the return home may not be possible in the short term, if at all, the initial optimism of escape from danger can later give way to despair and nostalgia. Equally, having to face up to and live in the knowledge of being the only survivor while others perished continues to cause feelings of guilt, making it very difficult to find reconciliation with the survivor. Whilst time is generally considered to be a healer and a means of distancing a person from personal tragedy, it seems that for refugees it is not the case. Refugees' previous traumatic experiences seem to become accentuated, more real, and to affect them more as time passes. This is what Davidson (1980) observed from the study of Jewish survivors of the Nazi genocide, and Scott (1997) in the case of older Polish who were prisoners in labour camps during the Second World War: traumatic memories of concentration camps still affected them. It is therefore not surprising that mental illness is one of the health problems most frequently detected among older refugees. Forced migration often exposes individuals and groups to inhumane conditions and experiences, and these require professional intervention, clinical awareness, sensitivity to the uniqueness of each person's experience, and the appropriate skills and competences to treat them.

For today's older refugees, this understanding of their traumatic experiences may have come too late to be of any long-term benefit. Nonetheless, there is an urgent need to consider how mental health conditions are diagnosed and treated amongst older refugees. Dementia, as one condition affecting mainly an older population, needs to be particularly taken into account in the personal biographies and life experiences of the patients and when considering how therapeutic resources might be best mobilized. The need for mental health support for refugees has now been somewhat recognized, particularly in the case of torture victims whose physical injuries are quite visible, but mental welfare still remains a decidedly challenging area. Too often older refugees are misunderstood in terms of the nature of their condition and their response to externally provided services. Labelling, as a social phenomenon, becomes a common practice amongst professionals in mental health especially when there is a failure on their part to correlate today's behaviour with yesterday's experience. For example symptoms of paranoia and persecution may perhaps not be so unusual if they are understood in the context of a person's own life course and how, for example, he or she endured forced migration.

Social Support and Enduring
Solutions for Refugees

There is a general consensus in the literature that ethnic minority communities provide an essential support network to refugees, particularly in the early stages of exile when contact with the local population can be difficult. This also provides a means of creating a bridge between past and present, which will also affect the future. The ethnic minority communities in the host country create, according to different identity criteria (ideological resemblances, shared religion, same geographical origin, etc.), informal groups or associations that allow the newcomers a chance to meet other refugees and to share experiences in the new environment, which is often very different to that of their homeland (Griffiths, Sigona, and Zetter 2005). Refugees can also themselves trigger the stimulus for self-help and support, whether it is material, social, psychological, or cultural: what remains important is how the community responds to their requests for support. As Oerster (1986) pointed out in the case of Switzerland, self-help initiatives were facilitated when refugees were settled in close proximity to each other. These spaces facilitate the necessary transition from one society to another and allow refugees to regain some control over their own lives after many disrupting events. It is also in these groups and associations that they are able to develop forms of ethnic minority support. This can be useful particularly to older refugees initially, but also later on, in meeting their long-term care needs as they become older.

However, in many cases, the institutions of the host society consider that integration will take place faster if refugees are dispersed throughout an area, including being individually placed in small towns, as is the case for instance in Canada (Labman 2009). However, research shows that these efforts to integrate the newcomers in this way are unsuccessful as refugees tend to move as soon as possible and to resettle in places, mainly urban areas, where they can join other members of their social or ethnic networks (Vatz Laaroussi 2009). In fact, while institutional social support is important for them, the role of informal social support within their close network is far more crucial for regaining a sense of well-being in their host society. However, the quality of social support given by the ethnic minority community does depend on its collective resources, i.e. its capacity for self-organization and self-help.

These two qualities do not necessarily go hand-in-hand. For instance, in Switzerland, Chilean refugees did organize themselves in the very early stages of their exile, but they only became concerned with self-help when they realized that exile was not a transitory phenomenon. From that point on, they began to create various associations in order to respond to the different perceived needs of community members, including those of the more isolated older members (Bolzman 1996).

Social support from the ethnic minority community is very important for local integration in the long run but also in the short run. Older migrants and refugees need spaces where they can communicate in their mother tongue and share with other people who have gone through similar life experiences.

However, for some older refugees the best solution is to return to their home country. Generally this solution is preferred by those who have kept strong symbolic and cultural ties with their home society (Bolzman, Fibbi, and Vial 2006) during the years of exile. If political conditions allow it, they will try to go back and rebuild their life as it was before their forced migration. They will probably experience a situation of 'des-exile' (Benedetti 1984), that is to learn to live again in what has become a new reality.

FINAL REMARKS

This chapter has mainly focused on issues related to older refugees living in Western societies. It would also be helpful to explore specific problems of older refugees living in camps and cities in less developed countries. Life and health conditions in such camps and host cities are much more precarious compared to the living accommodations for refugees in Western Europe. In fact, refugee camps in developing countries provide only minimum survival standards. They are set up as provisional solutions to cope with emergency situations. However, these transitional spaces often become long-term places of residence for refugee populations, which has a strong, negative impacts on the most fragile of them, especially those who are older. There is therefore a clear need to document these situations.

More broadly speaking, while research on older migrants, generally, has greatly increased, providing valuable information, there has not been a similar increase in the research on older refugees specifically. The problems faced by these forced migrants remain relatively unexplored and there is a growing need to better understand their experiences and to provide them with support in managing their memories. This task is not only needed in improving the quality of life and well-being of older exiles, but also in order to better help the host societies to respond appropriately to the needs of these victims of forced migration.

NOTES

1. This chapter is a revised and updated version of a previous paper by Scott and Bolzman (1999). The author wishes to acknowledge the contribution of Helena Scott. Finally, many thanks are due to Joy Mellor for her detailed editorial assistance with this chapter.
2. Generally speaking, the sourcing of reliable statistics on refugees and internally displaced persons is problematic, as is data collection. The collection of these data may be flawed in methodology, and/or influenced by the ways and means individual states decide on the particular and general details they shall focus on during data collection (Minority Rights Group 1990). We must not forget that etymologically the word 'statistics' has its roots in the word *stato* (state); statistics offer an account of what states perceive to be important and

how this should be quantified (Bolzman and Golebiowska 2012). The means by which data are scaled and gathered, i.e. the range and type of variables used, can also greatly influence the outcome. For instance, some countries may record only the head of the refugee family, while others make a record of every member.

3. Some quotations from the study by Bolzman (1996) about Chilean refugees in Switzerland will be used in this chapter to illustrate the meaning of exile for older refugees.

4. Quoted from Bolzman (1996: 143). All the individual quotations that follow are from this study about Chilean refugees in Switzerland.

References

Ahmed, P. I., Tims, F., and Kolker, A. (1981) 'After the Fall: Indochinese Refugees in the United States'. Pp. 61–74 in G. V. Coelho and P. I. Ahmed (eds.), *Uprooting and Development: Dilemmas of Coping with Modernisation*. New York: Plenum Press.

Allard, D. (1987) *L'Insertion socioculturelle des réfugiés vietnamiens*. Geneva: Mémoire de licence, Département de Sociologie, University of Geneva.

Baker, R. (ed.) (1983) *The Psychosocial Problems of Refugees*. London: British Refugee Council.

Benedetti, M. (1984) *El desexilio y otras conjeturas*. Madrid: El País.

Bollini, P., and Siem, H. (1995) 'No Real Progress Towards Equity: Health of Migrants and Ethnic Minorities on the Eve of the Year 2000'. *Social Science and Medicine* 41: 819–28.

Bolzman, C. (1994) 'Stages and Modes of Incorporation of Exiles in Switzerland: The Example of Chilean Refugees'. *Innovation* 7(3): 321–33.

Bolzman, C. (1996) *Sociologie de l'exil. Une approche dynamique. L'exemple des réfugiés chiliens en Suisse*. Zurich: Seismo.

Bolzman, C. (2012), 'Democratization of Ageing: Also a Reality for Elderly Immigrants?' *European Journal of Social Work* 15(1): 97–113.

Bolzman, C., Fibbi, R., and Vial, M. (2001) 'La Famille. Lne source de légitimité pour les immigrés après la retraite? Le cas des Espagnols et des Italiens en Suisse'. *Revue européenne des migrations internationales* 17(1): 55–78.

Bolzman, C., Fibbi, R., and Vial, M. (2006) 'What to do after Retirement? Elderly Migrants and the Question of Return'. *Journal of Ethnic and Migrations Studies*, 32(8): 1359–75.

Bolzman, C., and Golebiowska, K. (2012) 'Modes de catégorisation, statuts administratifs, assignations sociales et géographiques'. Pp. 123–37 in C. Belkhodja and M. Vatz Laaroussi (eds.), *Immigration hors de grands centres: enjeux, politiques et pratiques dans cinq états fédéraux*. Paris: L'Harmattan.

Bolzman, C., Hirsch-Durret, E., Anderfuhren, S., and Vuille, M. (2008) 'Migration of Parents under Family Reunification Policies: A National Approach to a Transnational Problem. The Case of Switzerland'. *Retraite et société*, 93–121.

Bolzman C., Poncioni, R., and Vial, M. (2012) 'Elderly Immigrants in Switzerland: Exploring their Social and Health Situation'. *Analele Ştiintifice* 5(1): 175–90.

Bowling, B. (1990) *The Development, Co-ordination and Provision of Services to Elderly People from the Ethnic Minorities: A Report on Four Innovatory Projects*. London: Age Concern Institute of Gerontology, King's College.

Braito, R. (1988) 'The Polish Immigrant Experience and its Relevance of Quality of Life Issues Among the Elderly'. Paper presented at the Annual Meeting of the British Sociological Association. Edinburgh, 28–31 March.

Bram, G. (1983) 'Breakdown in Elderly Polish Refugees'. Pp. 39–42 in R. Baker (ed.), *The Psychosocial Problems of Refugees.* London: British Refugee Council.

Bryceson, D., and Vuorela, U. (2007) *The Transnational Family: New European Frontiers and Global Networks.* Oxford: Berg.

Casado-Diaz, M. A., Kaiser, C., and Warnes, A. W. (2004) 'Northern European Retired Residents in Nine Southern European Areas: Characteristics, Motivations and Adjustment'. *Ageing & Society* 24: 353–81.

Coenen-Hutter, J., Kellerhals, J., and Von Allmen, M. (1994) *Les Réseaux de solidarité dans la famille.* Lausanne: Réalités sociales.

Davidson, S. (1980) 'The Clinical Effects of Massive Psychic Trauma in Families of Holocaust Survivors'. *Journal of Marital and Family Therapy* 6: 9–21.

Griffiths, D., Sigona, N., and Zetter, R. (2005) *Refugee Community Organisations and Dispersal: Networks, Resources and Social Capital.* Bristol: Policy Press.

Huber, A., and O'Reilly, K. (2004) 'The Construction of Heimat under Conditions of Individual Modernity: Swiss and British Elderly Migrants in Spain'. *Ageing & Society* 24: 327–51.

Kalemkaryan, E., and Ohanian, M. (1996) *Survey Report of Armenian Older People Living in Houston.* London: Portee for Armenian Information and Advice.

Labman, S. (2009) *Refocus Concern for Refugees.* Winnipeg: Winnipeg Free Press.

Lesser, M., and Seeberg, B. (1992) *Alter und Migration. Eine empirische Untersuchung an ungarischen Migranten in Basel.* Basel: Bad Kissingen.

Minority Rights Group (1990) *Refugees in Europe: A Minority Rights Group Report.* London: Minority Rights Group.

Montero, D. (1979) 'The Vietnamese Refugees in America: Toward a Theory of Spontaneous International Migration'. *International Migration Review* 13: 624–48.

Oerster, K. (1986) *Les Réfugiés en Suisse. Aspects de l'intégration.* Lucerne: Caritas.

Scott, H. (1997) 'Ageing in Multicultural Europe: Making the Challenge—Setting the Agenda'. Paper presented for the Age Concern Scotland Scottish European Symposium for the European Year of Older People & Solidarity between Generations, 15–16 December.

Scott, H. (1998) 'Invisible and Involuntary Exiles: A Generation of the Polish Community in Scotland'. Draft M.Phil thesis. University of Edinburgh.

Scott, H., and Bolzman, C. (1999) 'Age in Exile: Europe's Older Refugees and Exiles'. Pp. 168–86 in A. Bloch and C. Levy (eds.), *Refugees, Citizenship and Social Policy in Europe.* Houndmills: Macmillan Press.

Simon-Barouh, I. (1984) 'L'Accueil des réfugiés d'Asie du Sud-Est à Rennes'. *Pluriel* 28: 23–55.

Subilia, L. (2002) 'Impact du durcissement de la politique d'asile sur la santé physique et mentale des requérants d'asile'. *Cultures & sociétés* 16–17: 173–81.

UNHCR (2012) *Statistical Yearbook 2011.* Geneva: UNHCR.

Vatz Laaroussi, M. (2009) *Mobilités, réseaux et resilience. Le cas des familles immigrantes et réfugiées au Québec.* Quebec: Presses de l'Université du Québec.

CHAPTER 33

DISABILITY AND FORCED MIGRATION

MANSHA MIRZA

INTRODUCTION

THE World Health Organization estimates that people with disabilities comprise about 15 per cent of the world's population (World Health Organization 2011). When this global disability estimate is applied to displaced populations we get nearly 6.4 million persons with disabilities among the world's 42.5 million people believed to be forcibly displaced. The actual numbers could be higher since displacement is often characterized by conditions that increase risk of acquiring disability, such as violence, malnutrition, and poor healthcare (Rockhold and McDonald 2009). People with disabilities thus represent a substantial subgroup among displaced populations. Yet disability issues have been mostly neglected within displacement-focused humanitarian programmes. This historical neglect has had far-reaching consequences including serious unmet needs and human rights violations among displaced persons with disabilities (Kett and van Ommeren 2009).

However there have been promising developments in the humanitarian field over the past five years. The plight of displaced persons with disabilities has recently occupied centre stage in scholarly publications and practice bulletins, and has also captured the attention of the United Nations Commissioner for Human Rights (Mirza 2011a). Furthermore, the United Nations Convention on the Rights of Persons with Disabilities (Article 11) has also played a role in highlighting the dire situation of disabled persons affected by humanitarian emergencies (United Nations Commission on Human Rights 2007).

This chapter contributes to this growing momentum and summarizes disability issues within the context of forced displacement. The chapter begins with a description of conceptual models of disability followed by an exposition of disability experiences in displacement settings. Next, the chapter explores how disability affects access to durable solutions. The chapter concludes with propositions for future research and practice in this area.

CONCEPTUAL MODELS OF DISABILITY

Conceptualizations of disability have evolved over time. Prior to the 1980s, disability was predominantly viewed as a medical problem located within the individual (Craddock 1996). To counter this 'medical model' of disability, British disability rights activists proposed an alternative conceptualization known as the 'social model' of disability. The social model considers disability the result of physical, social, economic, political, and cultural barriers that limit opportunities for people with biological impairments. This radically different view of disability calls for a shift in approach from individual remediation and cure to addressing environmental barriers (Oliver 1996). A third conceptual framework proposed by the World Health Organization attempts to merge biomedical and social/environmental conceptualizations of disability. This framework, titled the 'International Classification of Functioning, Disability, and Health' identifies disability as an umbrella term encompassing changes in an individual's functioning and participation as the result of dynamic interplay between person-level and environmental factors. Thus the framework incorporates multipurpose goals of addressing environmental access and societal discrimination as well as individual treatment and rehabilitation, where desired (WHO 2001).

It is important to carefully weigh the applicability of the models described above in relation to the cultural and geographical context of displacement. The UNHCR stipulates that four-fifths of forcibly displaced persons live in impoverished developing countries (United Nations High Commissioner for Refugees 2012). Much of the debate on conceptual models of disability has emerged from the global North, and is being increasingly called out for ignoring important issues affecting people with disabilities living in resource-poor conditions of the global South (Meekosha 2008; Miles 2011). Therefore, when drawing on the above models to guide interventions for displaced persons with disabilities, it is important to recognize that responses will need to be multifaceted and will vary by context, type of disability, and individual choice. These responses might range from medical care, rehabilitation, and psychosocial interventions, to addressing environmental and attitudinal barriers affecting various life domains (Officer and Groce 2009).

DISABILITY EXPERIENCES IN DISPLACEMENT SETTINGS

There is now a growing body of literature that documents the situation of displaced persons with disabilities living in displacement camps and urban settlements. This literature comprises information from desk research and field research conducted in various post-conflict and post-disaster settings dispersed throughout the world. Despite the multiplicity of displacement settings, findings across existing research are remarkably consistent with regard to disabled people's access (or lack thereof) to humanitarian programmes and facilities.

An important factor that detrimentally affects disabled persons' access to humanitarian programmes and facilities is the layout and infrastructure of camps and urban settlements. Within displacement camps, common facilities such as food distribution centres, water collection points, sanitation facilities, schools, health clinics, and administrative offices are often inaccessible, particularly for people with physical and visual impairments. Uneven terrain and long distances between living shelters and various offices and facilities further exacerbate their physical inaccessibility (Reilly 2010; Shivji 2010).

The problem of physical inaccessibility is direr for disabled persons in urban settings. First, urban settlements where displaced populations seek refuge are frequently located in impoverished regions of the world, which lack legal regulations and mandates promoting accessibility for people with disabilities. Second, opportunities to adapt physical infrastructure are fewer and more difficult to implement in urban settings than in camps (Women's Refugee Commission 2008).

Problems with physical access have broad ramifications for people with disabilities and impede their ability to avail of services in other areas such as food rations, healthcare, education, and vocational opportunities. A closer look at each of these areas reveals additional barriers for displaced persons with disabilities.

For example, food distribution in camp settings is characterized by long queues and jostling crowds. Such scenarios significantly disadvantage persons with disabilities. Barring few exceptions, there is little evidence of disabled people being prioritized during food distribution or being given special food rations when needed (WRC 2008). In some settings humanitarian agencies offer extra food rations to 'extremely vulnerable individuals' (Kett and Trani 2010). However, such measures tend to be fugacious given their dependence on budget surpluses.

Budget constraints also limit availability of other services for persons with disabilities, most importantly healthcare services. Research shows that disabled people experience serious barriers in accessing mainstream health services owing to physical inaccessibility of clinics and misperceptions among humanitarian health actors who view disabled people's needs as outside their area of expertise (Shivji 2010; Mirza 2011a). This situation is true of camps as well as urban settings. In camps specialized services such as rehabilitation, surgical and pharmacological interventions, and psychosocial supports are also severely limited. Rehabilitation services, where available, tend to focus on prosthetic rehabilitation for amputees and land mine survivors (Shivji 2010; Mirza 2011a). It is also rare for individuals who need specialized services to be referred to outside clinics or hospitals (WRC 2008). Lack of trained professionals and poverty of local infrastructure further exacerbate this situation (Mirza 2011a).

Specialized medical services might be more readily available in urban settings. However, urban settled refugees often lack legal living permits, and therefore might be reluctant to avail of services for fear of being apprehended. Furthermore, humanitarian actors in urban settings tend to be limited in their knowledge of locally available services for persons with disabilities. Thus disabled persons in these settings might be disconnected from specialized services even when their legal status is not a concern (WRC 2008).

Aside from healthcare, access to livelihood opportunities is another area where displaced people with disabilities experience significant barriers. Livelihood opportunities are in general severely constricted for displaced populations, be they camp-dwelling or urban settled. For camp-dwelling refugees, few opportunities exist to live and work outside camps. Such opportunities, where they exist, favour young, educated, and able-bodied males while disadvantaging women, elderly people, and people with disabilities (Hyndman 2000). Those without educational and financial resources seek surreptitious alternatives to live and work illegally in surrounding towns and cities. The associated risks and uncertainty again preclude women and people with disabilities from taking advantage of these alternatives.

Vocational skills training and adult literacy courses are frequently available in displacement camps. People with disabilities are either actively excluded from these opportunities and when included, the trainings are poorly designed to meet their needs. There is growing evidence of vocational trainings targeted exclusively at disabled camp inhabitants. However, these trainings mostly benefit those with less severe disabilities. Additionally, while these opportunities give a semblance of occupational activity, they seldom translate into economically viable livelihood opportunities (WRC 2008). Nevertheless, the situation is still better for camp-dwellers versus urban settlers. Although scarce, economic avenues for camp-dwelling persons with disabilities exist in the form of small business loans and affirmative hiring policies of certain humanitarian agencies. On the other hand, those living in urban settlements have to compete for livelihood opportunities against non-disabled workers in the open market (WRC 2008).

Access to education comprises the one area where most advances have been made for displaced persons with disabilities, particularly those living in camps (Pinnock and Hodgkin 2010). Positive examples have been reported from camps in Nepal, Thailand, and Kenya. These examples include early intervention for children with developmental disabilities, full inclusion of disabled children in mainstream schools, special schools for deaf and blind children, and life skills training, special learning centres, and educational home visits for children with more severe disabilities. However, in some camps barriers to educational access persist such as physically inaccessible classrooms, lack of teaching aids, and dearth of trained teachers. Disabled children among urban settled populations face similar barriers along with the additional barrier of restricted access to public schools (WRC 2008).

Disabled people also experience special protection concerns. Across displacement settings, disabled persons report harassment, physical and emotional abuse, stigmatization, and discrimination from their own communities as well as from members of the host community (WRC 2008). This is especially true for persons with intellectual disabilities and mental health conditions. Evidence of sexual and gender-based violence in this population is more mixed. While persons with mental disabilities might be more vulnerable to abuse, those with physical disabilities, particularly women, might be more protected since they are less likely to venture out for activities such as collecting fuel for cooking (WRC 2008; Bombi 2010). What is evident, however, is that disability is generally not considered in planning of sexual and domestic abuse interventions (Bombi 2010).

Durable Solutions and Persons with Disabilities

Little is known about the experiences of persons with disabilities as they undergo return, repatriation, or resettlement. There is also a lack of information on official policies for including disabled people in planning durable solutions, each of which is considered in detail in this section.

Voluntary Repatriation and Local Integration

People with disabilities face several challenges during voluntary repatriation. For example, information on repatriation schedules and supports might be inaccessible to persons with hearing, vision, or intellectual disabilities. Return transportation sponsored by humanitarian agencies might be inaccessible for people using mobility aids such as crutches or wheelchairs (Bombi 2010; Shivji 2010). Availability of repatriation supports might also be contingent on conditions such as ability to rebuild one's house. Such conditions, together with discriminatory rules related to land and property ownership, might work against some people with disabilities (Kett and Trani 2010).

People with disabilities might also face long-term challenges after repatriation to environments that are fragile and emerging from a crisis situation. Such environments are frequently devoid of sustainable livelihood opportunities and comprehensive human care infrastructure. While this situation affects all individuals, it could be particularly challenging for individuals with disabilities. Ironically, as disability awareness grows within the humanitarian arena, displaced people with disabilities are likely to encounter appropriate services for the first time in displacement camps. Limited availability of such services post-repatriation might be a major deterrent to their return (Gulu Disabled Persons Union 2010; Shivji 2010).

Integration in the country of first asylum might also be fraught with challenges for people with disabilities. Asylum countries often lack adequate infrastructure to support the needs of persons with disabilities, be they native citizens or forced migrants (Mirza 2011a). In addition, forced migrants with disabilities might face active discrimination in access to the meagre resources that are available in first asylum countries (Kett and Trani

2010). Disabled migrants might also find it difficult to compete for labour-intensive work opportunities in asylum countries. Those without alternative sources of financial and social support such as family members and friends are likely to be worst off in such situations.

Disability in Resettlement

Resettlement remains an elusive option for all forced migrants. Resettlement opportunities are even more limited for persons with disabilities mostly due to unclear and contradictory resettlement policies implemented by UNHCR and resettlement countries.

Over the years, UNHCR's official position on resettlement for disabled refugees appears to have evolved, but inconsistencies persist. The agency's 1996 guidelines on assisting disabled refugees favour 'integration of the disabled in their own communities' over resettlement (UNHCR 1996). In contrast, the 2011 edition of UNHCR's *Resettlement Handbook* acknowledges disabled refugees' eligibility for resettlement like all other refugees. The handbook recognizes disabled refugees as an important subgroup with specific protection needs while also acknowledging disability as an important cross-cutting issue across all populations of concern.

Yet, perplexingly, the 2011 *Resettlement Handbook*, like the UNHCR's 1996 guidelines, maintains that 'well-adjusted' disabled refugees are 'generally not to be considered for resettlement' (UNHCR 2011: 198). Furthermore, resettlement for persons with disabilities is discussed predominantly under the medical needs category rather than the legal/physical protection needs category. Guidelines for resettlement submissions in the former category are based on strict diagnostic and prognostic criteria rather than protection needs. For example, the applicant's underlying condition should be likely to worsen without treatment, treatment should be unavailable locally or under UNHCR's medical referral scheme, and there should be a favourable prognosis following treatment or resettlement (UNHCR 2011).

The available guidelines thus betray UNHCR's contradictory and possibly discriminatory position on the issue of disabled refugees' resettlement. Contradictions on paper can translate into confusion on the ground. Field reports indicate confusion about resettlement prospects for disabled refugees among applicants as well as resettlement officers (WRC, 2008).

Similar contradictions and undercurrents of discrimination are mirrored in the resettlement policies of receiving countries. For example, Australia categorically restricts the admission of refugees with disabilities, citing undue costs and encumbrance on the country's healthcare and social service systems (UNHCR 2011: Australia chapter). Countries like Portugal and the UK appear to have discontinued their resettlement quotas for persons with disabilities and medical needs. Even countries generally open to resettling persons with disabilities (e.g. Brazil, Canada, Finland, Iceland, Ireland), and those that reserve a percentage of their resettlement quotas for persons with disabilities and medical needs (e.g. Denmark, Netherlands, New Zealand, Norway), employ additional criteria such as integration potential, prospects of recovery, and availability of treatment options. A notable exception to this trend is the USA, which offers priority resettlement to people with disabilities along with other groups deemed to have specific protection risks (UNHCR 2011).

Sporadic positive examples notwithstanding, the preceding discussion indicates that resettlement policies are generally dominated by the medical model of disability, which could be detrimental for disabled refugees. Resettlement policies based on medical need call for medical professionals to act as resettlement gatekeepers rather than recognizing disabled people's right to resettlement like all other refugees. Second, resettlement priorities based on need for medical treatment might preclude opportunities for people with disabilities whose condition might not be treatable. There are a large number of physical and cognitive impairments for which no known cure or treatment exists even in the most developed countries. Resettlement opportunities contingent on medical need and treatment availability thus allow receiving countries a backhanded excuse to limit the resettlement of persons with untreatable, and therefore more severe, disabilities, while professing ostensibly equitable and progressive resettlement policies (Mirza 2014).

Disability and Asylum Procedures

Applying for asylum constitutes another avenue for forced migrants to settle in a third country. The asylum application process presents several barriers for persons with disabilities. Neither the UN Refugee Convention nor UNHCR provide guidelines on accommodating the needs of disabled asylum applicants. Similarly, a review of the Common European Asylum System indicates minimal guidance in this area. The directives that do address this issue do not acknowledge disabled people as a particular social group nor do they recognize the diversity of disability experiences (Straimer 2010). The absence of appropriate guidelines has triggered concerns that disabled asylum seekers may face impediments to presenting their asylum claims due to lack of needed supports such as sign language interpreters and allowances for people with cognitive and psychiatric disabilities who might be unable to establish credibility of their claims in a coherent and consistent manner (Amas and Lagnado 2010; Crock, McCallum, and Ernst 2011).

Another concern is related to unsuitability of reception and detention conditions for persons with disabilities. For example, the European Union Commission does not prohibit the detention of asylum seekers with disabilities, but emphasizes that detention be used only as a last resort. European Union Directive 2003/9 requires that asylum legislation of member states consider the situation of people with disabilities when planning material reception conditions, including administrative detention centres (Beduschi-Ortiz 2010). However, owing to the extensive discretionary power granted to national authorities, implementation of the above obligations remains weak among member states. It is common practice for asylum seekers, including those with disabilities, to be held in detention centres, which are often not adapted to meet the needs of disabled people (Beduschi-Ortiz 2010). Furthermore, disabled asylum seekers continue to live in detention for long periods of time without adequate access to healthcare (Refugee Council 2005), and in conditions that are likely to worsen the physical and mental health of persons with disabilities (Cutler 2005).

Disability also intersects with asylum detention in indirect ways. The idea and image of disability is being increasingly deployed by human rights advocates to question asylum detention practices. Several reports highlight the negative impact of detention on the mental and physical health of asylum seekers, thus suggesting that detention practices can produce disability among those otherwise healthy and non-disabled (e.g. Laban et al. 2008; Amaral 2010). Rights-based organizations and legal advocates also support the idea that disability can be an important ground for mounting legal challenges against detention (Burnham 2003; Cutler 2005).

The above trends are problematic because they signify disability as a strictly medical issue by heightening the role of medical professionals in diagnosing acquired disabilities among detainees. This practice also results in unnecessary labelling of people as 'vulnerable' or as having medical conditions that might not align with their own understanding of their situation (Mirza 2014). Additionally, constant association of disability with the notion of 'vulnerability' suggests that people with disabilities are essentially weak and needy. Given cost-burden arguments used by states against accepting disabled refugees and asylum seekers, portraying them as vulnerable defeats the purpose of contesting their detention (Straimer 2010).

A final issue at the nexus of disability and asylum pertains to asylum claims based on disability-related persecution. A nascent argument is emerging in favour of disability-sensitive interpretations of the Convention definition of a refugee. Preliminary data indicate that disability-related asylum claims fail to meet the 'fear of persecution' criterion (Crock, McCallum, and Ernst 2011). Pejorative treatment of persons with disabilities in their country of origin tends to be construed as discrimination rather than persecution. However, legal advocates argue that discrimination in multiple realms (e.g. freedom of mobility, employment, reproductive rights) amounts to persecution and a failure of states to protect disabled persons' rights, especially if these states are signatories to the UN Convention on the Rights of Persons with Disabilities (Parekh 2009; Crock, McCallum, and Ernst 2011). Even if this explanation holds, there remains the challenge of establishing that persecutory conduct arises from disabled persons' membership in a particular social group by virtue of possessing innate and unchangeable characteristics. Such a position would be at odds with the social model of disability, which does not view disability as innate and unchangeable but rather as the result of potentially mutable environmental barriers (Crock, McCallum, and Ernst 2011).

Post-resettlement and Post-asylum Supports

There is a growing body of research documenting the experiences of forced migrants with disabilities after being resettled or being granted asylum in a third country. Research findings are strikingly consistent across varied settings.

Research in the UK and the USA has highlighted disabled refugees' struggles with inaccessible living quarters and inaccessible English language and job training courses (Roberts and Harris 2002; Mirza and Heinemann 2012). Resettlement policies in the USA emphasize early self-sufficiency for refugees, yet disabled refugees are provided with few employment supports and opportunities (Mirza 2012). In Canada, research with disabled refugee women has demonstrated added struggles for this group in terms of finding stable housing and meaningful employment, resulting in their characterization as unworthy welfare recipients (Dossa 2009).

Research in the UK and USA has also revealed that disabled refugees have minimal contact with local disability service organizations and experience difficulties with accessing disability-related social services owing to language or literacy barriers and cultural incongruence between mainstream disability providers and refugee communities. Refugee service providers have also been found to lack knowledge about disability rights, services, and entitlements while mainstream disability organizations have been found to lack awareness about the needs and social service eligibility of refugees (Ward, Amas, and Lagnado 2008; Mirza and Heinemann 2012). As a result, cross-referrals between these service systems are minimal and efforts toward outreach and collaboration are limited by resource constraints. Similar paucity of cross-referrals, dialogue, and interactive learning between mainstream disability service agencies and ethnic community organizations has been documented in research with refugee communities in Canada (Pegg 2004).

These service gaps detrimentally affect disabled refugees' access to services, their long-term well-being, and quality of life. It does not help that UNHCR's handbook on reception and integration of resettled refugees provides no information on planning services for refugees with disabilities. One positive example comes from New Zealand where a mainstream disability organization has partnered with the country's main reception centre for newly arrived refugees. The partnership is intended to conduct comprehensive needs assessments and to educate disabled refugees and their families about available resources in their destination communities (Brandon and Smith 2010).

Research shows that disabled asylum seekers face similar challenges as those experienced by disabled refugees following resettlement. However, the situation of asylum seekers is more precarious because their undecided refugee status further hinders their access to support services. For example, disabled asylum seekers in Belgium face difficulties in accessing medical and social care due to their contested legal status and lack of acceptable proof of disability (Albrecht, Devlieger, and Van Hove 2009). Similarly, in the UK, while statutory support exists for disabled asylum seekers, access is hindered by confusion around eligibility, fragmented and inconsistent services, and supports being cut off without fair assessment of needs. Additional barriers include discontinuity of care due to dispersal policies, and contested responsibility between local and federal authorities for disabled asylum seekers (Harris and Roberts 2004; Amas and Lagnado 2010).

Conclusions and Future Directions

Clearly a lot needs to be done to ensure that the rights of persons with disabilities are protected and that their needs are adequately addressed in contexts of forced displacement. In the recent past there have been some promising developments in this regard both at the official level and at the grassroots level.

Official developments include the 2010 Executive Committee Conclusion for Refugees with Disabilities and Other Persons with Disabilities Protected and Assisted by UNHCR, UNHCR's 2007 guidelines for The Protection of Older Persons and Persons with Disabilities, and UNHCR's 2011 guidelines on Working with Persons with Disabilities in Forced Displacement. Even the Sphere Handbook, a key text for responding to large-scale human displacement, recognizes disability as a cross-cutting issue and endorses the implementation of minimum standards for disability access across all facets of service provision.

Grassroots developments include examples of forced migrants with disabilities and their allies coming together to mobilize resources and pursue disability rights. For example, the Karen Handicapped Welfare Association, a Disabled Persons' Organization in Mae La refugee camp in Thailand, set up a residential care facility that offers emotional support, rehabilitation care, and vocational training for landmine survivors in the camp who lack family support (WRC 2008). Similarly in Dzaleka camp in Malawi, disabled refugees of various nationalities have come together to form an association called Umoja, the Swahili word for unity. Members of the association work with humanitarian staff for better access to camp resources and for the development of respite care and community awareness programmes (Mirza 2011b). Efforts toward disability inclusion in refugee camps have also emerged from allied constituencies, such as indigenous women's groups in the Karen refugee camps in Thailand and the Bhutanese camps in Nepal (Mirza 2011b).

Similar examples of disability advocacy and organizing can also be found among urban settled refugees and internally displaced persons. The Association of Refugees with Disabilities and the Disabled Refugees' Project are examples of grassroots organizations of disabled refugees in Kampala and Johannesburg respectively. Likewise, the Gulu Disabled Person's Union (GDPU), a network of five advocacy groups, promotes the inclusion of internally displaced persons with disabilities in Uganda's post-conflict reconstruction and peace-building efforts (GDPU 2010). These examples are testament to a proliferating disability consciousness in situations of forced displacement and a reminder that displaced persons with disabilities are not passive aid recipients, but rather people with skills, ideas, and a growing awareness of their rights.

It is vital that the humanitarian community make concerted efforts to build upon the developments described here. Experts in the field recommend a twin-tracking approach, which combines inclusion of disabled people in mainstream programmes while developing special programmes targeted at this group (Kett and van Ommeren 2009). Engaging grassroots coalitions of persons with disabilities is vital for achieving both goals not only in displacement camps and urban settlements, but also in post-resettlement contexts. Grassroots coalitions can serve as a conduit between the professional humanitarian sector and the local disability community, and can aid in soliciting local input and planning initiatives (Stein et al. 2009). Grassroots actors can also play an important role in monitoring the inclusion of people with disabilities and the impact of disability inclusion on various outcomes such as disabled persons' quality of life in displacement camps or after resettlement, and their access to resettlement and asylum opportunities.

There is an urgent need, however, to develop appropriate indicators, which are currently lacking, for the purpose of monitoring and evaluation (Kett and van Ommeren 2009). It is also important to address the current information gap with regard to the numbers of persons with disabilities in various displacement contexts, their needs, and the resources available to them (Simmons 2010). Without accurate numbers, disabled persons will continue to be a hidden group among displaced populations. The UNHCR's 'proGres' registration system (WRC 2008) offers a good source for gathering population-level data on numbers of persons with disabilities and their needs. It is important to ensure that such data collection tools are comprehensive enough to capture information on the range of disability experiences, including physical, intellectual, and psychiatric disabilities.

Finally, there is need for a broad research agenda that goes beyond gathering numbers. Such a research agenda would need to include multiple methodological strategies incorporating survey-based research, narrative research, policy analysis, discourse analysis, and operations-based logistical research to illuminate the complex phenomena associated with disability and forced migration and to inform effective interventions.

REFERENCES

Albrecht, G. L., Devlieger, P. J., and Van Hove, G. (2009) 'Living on the Margin: Disabled Iranians in Belgian Society'. *Disability & Society* 24(3): 259–71.

Amaral, P. (2010) *Becoming Vulnerable in Detention: Civil Society Report on the Detention of Vulnerable Asylum Seekers and Irregular Migrants in the European Union (The Devas Project)*. Brussels: Jesuit Refugee Service—European Regional Office.

Amas, N., and Lagnado, J. (2010) 'Failing London's Disabled Refugees'. *Forced Migration Review—Theme Issue on Disability and Displacement* 35: 27–8.

Beduschi-Ortiz, A. (2010) 'Reception of Asylum Seekers with Disabilities in Europe'. *Forced Migration Review—Theme Issue on Disability and Displacement* 35: 29–30.

Bombi, F. (2010) 'Perception and Protection in Sri Lanka'. *Forced Migration Review—Theme Issue on Disability and Displacement* 35: 14–15.

Brandon, C, and Smith, C. (2010) 'Early Engagement'. *Forced Migration Review—Theme Issue on Disability and Displacement* 35: 26–7.

Burnham, E. (2003) *Challenging Immigrant Detention: A Best Practice Guide*. London: Immigration Law Practitioners' Association and Bail for Immigration Detainees.

Craddock, J. (1996) 'Responses of the Occupational Therapy Profession to the Perspective of the Disability Movement, Part I'. *British Journal of Occupational Therapy* 59(1): 17–22.

Crock, M., McCallum, R., and Ernst, C. (2011) 'Where Disability and Displacement Intersect: Asylum Seekers with Disabilities'. Discussion paper prepared for the Vulnerable Persons Working Group International Association of Refugee Law Judges World Conference. Bled, Slovenia, 7–9 September.

Cutler, S. (2005) *Fit to Be Detained? Challenging the Detention of Asylum Seekers and Migrants with Health Needs*. London: Bail for Immigration Detainees.

Dossa, P. (2009) *Racialized Bodies, Disabling Worlds: Storied Lives of Immigrant Muslim Women*. Toronto: University of Toronto Press.

Gulu Disabled Persons Union (2010) 'More than a Ramp'. *Forced Migration Review—Theme issue on Disability and Displacement* 35: 16–18.

Harris, J., and Roberts, K. (2004) ' "Not our Problem": The Provision of Services to Disabled Refugees and Asylum Seekers'. Pp. 151–61 in D. Hayes and B. Humphries (eds.), *Social Work, Immigration and Asylum*. London: Jessica Kingsley Publishers.

Hyndman, J. (2000) *Managing Displacement: Refugees and the Politics of Humanitarianism*. Minneapolis: University of Minnesota Press.

Kett, M., and Trani, J.-F. (2010) 'Vulnerability and Disability in Darfur'. *Forced Migration Review* 35: 12–13.

Kett, M., and van Ommeren, M. (2009) 'Disability, Conflict, and Emergencies'. *Lancet* 374(9704): 1801–3.

Laban, C. J., Komproe, I. H., Gernaat, H. B., and de Jong, J. T. (2008) 'The Impact of a Long Asylum Procedure on Quality of Life, Disability and Physical Health in Iraqi Asylum Seekers in the Netherlands'. *Social Psychiatry and Psychiatric Epidemiology* 43(7): 507–15.

Meekosha, H. (2008) 'Contextualizing Disability: Developing Southern/Global Theory'. Keynote paper given at the 4th Biennial Disability Studies Conference, Lancaster University, 2–4 September.

Miles, M. (2011) 'The "Social Model of Disability" Met a Narrative of (In) Credulity: A Review'. *Disability, CBR and Inclusive Development* 22(1): 5–15.

Mirza, M. (2011a) 'Unmet Needs and Diminished Opportunities: Disability, Displacement and Humanitarian Healthcare'. New Issues in Refugee Research Working Paper Series. Research paper number: 212. Geneva: UNHCR, Policy Development and Evaluation Service.

Mirza, M. (2011b) 'Disability and Humanitarianism in Refugee Camps: The Case for a Traveling Supranational Disability Praxis'. *Third World Quarterly* 32(8): 1527–36.

Mirza, M. (2012) 'Occupational Upheaval during Resettlement and Migration: Findings of Global Ethnography with Refugees with Disabilities'. *OTJR: Occupation, Participation and Health* 32(1): 6–14.

Mirza, M. (2014) 'Refugee Camps, Asylum Detention, and the Geopolitics of Transnational Migration: Disability and its Intersects with Humanitarian Confinement'. Forthcoming in L. Ben-Moshe, C. Chapman, and A. Carey (eds.), *Disability Incarcerated: Imprisonment and Disability in North America*. New York: Palgrave Macmillan.

Mirza, M., and Heinemann, A. W. (2012) 'Service Needs and Service Gaps among Refugees with Disabilities Resettled in the United States'. *Disability & Rehabilitation* 34(7): 542–52. doi: 10.3109/09638288.2011.611211

Officer, A., and Groce, N. (2009) 'Key Concepts in Disability'. *Lancet* 374(9704): 1795–6.

Oliver, M. (1996) *Understanding Disability: From Theory to Practice.* Basingstoke, Macmillan.

Parekh, G. (2009) 'Is there Refuge for People with Disabilities within the 1951 Convention Relating to the Status of Refugees?' *Critical Disability Studies* 1. <http://pi.library.yorku.ca/ojs/index.php/cdd/issue/view/1440> (accessed 19 February 2013).

Pegg, S. (2004) *Disability, Culture and Service Engagement among Chinese, Somali and Tamil Communities in Toronto.* Toronto: The Roeher Institute.

Pinnock, H., and Hodgkin, M. (2010) 'Education Access for All'. *Forced Migration Review— Theme issue on Disability and Displacement* 35: 34–5.

Refugee Council (2005) *A Study of Asylum Seekers with Special Needs.* London: Refugee Council.

Reilly, R. (2010) 'Disability among Refugees and Conflict-Affected Populations'. *Forced Migration Review—Theme Issue on Disability and Displacement* 35: 8–10.

Roberts, K., and Harris, J. (2002) *Disabled People in Refugee and Asylum-Seeking Communities in Britain.* Bristol: The Policy Press.

Rockhold, P., and McDonald, L. (2009) 'The Hidden Issue in International Development Aid: Health and Disability in Conflict-Affected Settings in Sub-Saharan Africa'. *Journal for Disability and International Development* 1: 4–11.

Shivji, A. (2010) 'Disability in Displacement'. *Forced Migration Review—Theme Issue on Disability and Displacement* 35: 4–7.

Simmons, K. (2010) 'Addressing the Data Challenge'. *Forced Migration Review—Theme Issue on Disability and Displacement* 35: 10–12.

Stein, M. A., Stein, P. J., Weiss, D., and Lang, R. (2009) 'Health Care and the UN Disability Rights Convention'. *Lancet* 374: 1796–8.

Straimer, C. (2010) *Vulnerable or Invisible? Asylum Seekers with Disabilities in Europe.* Research paper No. 194. Geneva: United Nations High Commissioner for Refugees.

United Nations Commission on Human Rights (2007) A/RES/61/106, Annex I. *Convention on the Rights of Persons with Disabilities.* New York: United Nations.

United Nations High Commissioner for Refugees (1996) *Community Service Guidelines on Assisting Disabled Refugees: A Community Based Approach* (2nd ed.). Geneva: UNHCR. <http://www.unhcr.org/refworld/docid/49997ae41f.html> (accessed 19 February 2013).

United Nations High Commissioner for Refugees (2011) *UNHCR Resettlement Handbook.* Geneva: UNHCR. <http://www.unhcr.org/4a2ccf4c6.html> (accessed 19 February 2013).

United Nations High Commissioner for Refugees (2012) *UNHCR Global Trends 2011: A Year of Crises.* Geneva: UNHCR. <http://www.unhcr.org/4fd6f87f9.html> (accessed 6 March 2013).

Ward, K., Amas, N., and Lagnado, J. (2008) *Supporting Disabled Refugees and Asylum Seekers: Opportunities for New Approaches.* London: Refugee Support/Metropolitan Support Trust.

Women's Refugee Commission (2008) *Disabilities among Refugees and Conflict-Affected Populations.* New York: Women's Refugee Commission.

World Health Organization (2001) *International Classification of Functioning, Disability and Health (ICF).* Geneva: WHO.

World Health Organization (2011) *World Report on Disability.* Geneva: WHO.

CHAPTER 34

HEALTH AND FORCED MIGRATION

ALASTAIR AGER

Introduction

THE last century has seen a major improvement in health indicators worldwide. While improvements in life expectancy were led by progress in higher-income countries, middle- and lower-income settings have also seen steady progress. Life expectancy in Latin America increased from 68.2 to 73.6 between 1990 and 2010, and in South Asia from 57.8 to 64.6 in the same period. Even in sub-Saharan Africa, where progress has been slowest, life expectancy at birth increased from 49.9 to 54.2 in this 20-year period (World Bank 2013).

This global progress is relevant to an analysis of the health of forced migrants because of the factors that are generally acknowledged to have driven such trends. In general, improvements in health status have been the result not of major advances in medicine but rather those in the field of public health. In particular, two streams of activity have been crucial: first, a broad range of environmental improvements regarding water, sanitation, housing, working conditions, and other means of reducing health risks; second, the development of preventive health systems addressing, in particular, maternal, neonatal, and child through such measures as immunization, growth monitoring, and antenatal care.

These streams of activity share a common commitment to *public* health, that is understanding and responding to health as a population, rather than individual, issue. While the role of civil society and the private sector in public health response is increasingly acknowledged, the foundation for such activity remains state and civic provision. What has driven the remarkable progress in health over the century has thus been the development of laws, environmental measures, and health systems to protect the health of the populations for whom states and civic authorities are responsible.

State and civic commitment to health makes sense in terms of social and economic development. The growing awareness that the majority of deaths before old age are from causes preventable by effective, often low-cost interventions, has created a subtle but significant change in thinking about the global burden of disease. It now makes some sense to conceptualize premature death and disability as an avoidable burden upon social and economic development. Increasingly, thinking on health is informed by a global, normative standard of healthy years of life lived (Murray et al. 2012). Investing in health is seen as a sound economic policy supporting national interests.

Understanding state responsibility, capacity, and interest in population health is foundational to considering health in forced migrant populations who, either as internally displaced persons (IDPs) or as refugees, are owed state protection. The analysis above suggests that access to the protection, provision, and systems of the state is fundamental to the health of populations. With this perspective, we should therefore view the health of displaced populations not principally in terms of the specific health risks associated with their migration experience (although these may be considerable), but more in terms of the health vulnerabilities associated with weak protection, provision, and systems access resulting from their status as forced migrants.

The forces shaping weak protection, provision, and systems access are recurrent themes within this volume: a complex interplay of state, institutional, and community interests. In relation to access of forced migrants to health services in South Africa, for example, while both the Constitution and Refugee Act of 1998 guarantees that no one—regardless of nationality, documentation, or residency status—may be refused emergency medical treatment, a national study of refugees and asylum seekers found that 17 per cent of all respondents had been denied emergency medical care (Belvedere 2003). Landau and Monson note how:

> in these practices—and accompanying forms of social exclusion—we see the citizenry enforcing a kind of closure that at times reflects the state's strong anti-immigration legislation but often contradicts state commitments to providing asylum, the rule of law and universal human rights. (2008: 323)

While we have established that analyses of health must address the wider forces shaping the vulnerability of refugee and displaced populations to lack of state and community protection we should not ignore health as an issue of significance in its own right. With health being a prerequisite for active engagement in re-establishing individual and household well-being post-flight, it is often highlighted by the displaced themselves as a key priority. Such perspectives typically reinforce a holistic view of health. While it is still common to view health as the 'absence of disease' (Boorse 1977) or 'a state of physical well-being' (Callahan 1973), a broader perspective has been promoted since the adoption by the World Health Organization in 1948 of a definition that sees health as 'a state of complete physical, mental and social well-being and not merely the absence of disease or infirmity' (WHO 1948). It is this broader perspective that will be adopted as the appropriate framing of the health of refugees and other displaced persons in this chapter.

HEALTH NEEDS AND PROVISION IN THE CONTEXT OF COMPLEX HUMANITARIAN EMERGENCIES

Priority Health Issues

In the last 20 years there has been significant accumulation of knowledge and expertise vis-à-vis addressing health needs in contexts of acute humanitarian crisis. The professionalization of rapid medical response by agencies such as Médecins Sans Frontières (MSF), alongside growing emergency preparedness and response capacity of national governments within middle- and higher-income contexts, means that key actions to control disease outbreaks can prevent the escalation of mortality seen in previous mass population displacements. With the increased adoption of consensus professional standards such as Sphere (Sphere Project 2011) to guide response, the greatest barrier to the provision of emergency response is now typically the lack of 'humanitarian space' allowing deployment of such assistance in a timely manner (Karunakara 2011).

Formally, a health emergency is defined by a mortality rate of more than 1 death per 10,000 people per day. This corresponds to 3 deaths per 1,000 people per month. This was a rate that, during the course of the 1990s, was exceeded more than threefold amongst displaced populations in a range of contexts including Iraq, Sudan, Bhutan, Mozambique, Bosnia, Burundi, Rwanda, Angola, and Somalia. Improvements in the management of health in emergencies have contributed to a reduction in such excess mortality amongst displaced populations over the last decade, but the health emergency threshold has continued to be exceeded in a number of situations (e.g. Afghanistan, Bartlett et al. 2002; Darfur, Guha-Sapir, and Degomme 2005; and Democratic Republic of Congo, HNTS 2011).

Elevated mortality rates reflect increased risk for all members of a population, but the most vulnerable to premature death are typically children, with women also facing increased risks. As noted by Al Gaseer, the origins of such differential vulnerability are a combination of biological and social factors:

> Biology is responsible for women's higher risk of reproductive tract infections and infants' unique dietary needs. Sociocultural norms may dictate that women have little control over financial resources and transport. (Al Gaseer et al. 2004: 9)

Karunakara and Stevenson (2012) have also signalled the relative neglect of attention in humanitarian contexts to older persons, whose vulnerabilities may be exacerbated not only by physical frailty, but the disruption of support networks (see Bolzman, in this volume).

In the immediate aftermath of a disaster or conflict causing major population movement, the most pressing health issues typically concern infectious disease and poor nutrition, reflecting disruption of access to adequate water and sanitation facilities and food supply respectively. These risks may be strongly associated with the conditions of flight and emergency settlement, but often will predate such circumstances. In the case of both slow onset environmental disasters and gradually escalating insecurity, households will typically have experienced deteriorating health and nutritional status for many months, indeed years, before displacement. Such increased physical vulnerability, which may itself be a factor determining a household's ultimate decision to flee from home, livelihood, and assets, clearly places individuals at elevated risk of mortality.

The conditions of refugee and IDP camps—while facilitating access of health programmes to displaced populations—present health challenges of their own, with crowded conditions creating additional risks for rapid transmission of disease. Significant risk for transmission of water-borne diseases such as cholera and hepatitis E has been documented in camp settings.

Camps also typically present conditions that lead to the disruption of cultural norms, social conventions, and community governance. Conflict and disaster in general contribute to an erosion of structures and practices regarding sexual behaviour (e.g. Muhwezi et al. 2011). However, there are particular risks regarding unsafe sexual practices and transactional sex in such environments. With the power that military personnel and camp staff potentially have over displaced persons in camps, their sexual behaviour is an important factor that can further exacerbate risk. The humanitarian 'efficiency' of camps thus creates population density and anonymity that strains accountability and exposes populations resident there to increased risk of exploitation and abuse (Ager 2012).

A broader framing of health—inclusive of mental and social as well as physical well-being—puts such issues as gender-based violence (GBV) firmly within the analysis of the public health needs of displaced populations. Despite challenges of measurement and reporting (Stark and Ager 2011) and uncertainty of the attribution of such violence to the circumstances of displacement, pre-existing gender dynamics, or a complex interaction of the two (Stark et al. 2010), GBV is a prominent feature of the daily experience of displaced women (and, it is increasingly recognized, men)[1] in numerous contexts. While much attention has been focused on the notion of rape as a 'weapon of war', with concomitant focus on the behaviour of military personnel and fighting forces, women are commonly at greatest risk of sexual assault from within their own community. Stark et al. (2010) found women in IDP camps in northern Uganda to be at eight to ten times greater risk of violent assault by their husband than by a stranger. 52 per cent of women reported physical abuse and 41 per cent forced sex by husbands in the preceding year, compared with 5 per cent reporting rape by a stranger. As noted, displacement frequently erodes social norms and—with disruption of traditional mechanisms of community order and accountability—creates conditions of impunity for perpetrators of violence. Along with the loss of sources of male self-esteem and autonomy through lack of work and restrictions on employment, this may result in significant vulnerability for women:

The men have become mad…they go drinking, watching videos and come back home late, beat and chase us out of our houses. (Woman interviewed in context of protracted IDP crisis in Northern Uganda, Lira 2006, fieldnote.)

Strategies of Response

Whether internally displaced—and thus with rights to protection as citizens—or refugees—owed protection by countries of asylum under international convention obligations—the state is a key duty bearer with respect to the health needs of forced migrants. However, the sudden onset of population displacement (following natural disaster or rapid escalation of conflict) and/or the volume of such migration commonly overwhelm state capacities. Facilitating response to the health needs of displaced populations is thus one of the core foci of international humanitarian response.

The coordination of such response is usually through the activation of the 'cluster' mechanism, with UNICEF generally taking the cluster lead and convening planning meetings with all UN and international NGO partners with operational capacity in the situation (O'Keefe and Rose 2010). The Red Cross and MSF are commonly leading providers of emergency health assistance, although the cluster mechanism provides for engagement with a wide range of actors, including national NGOs. The cluster approach anticipates joint convening of sectoral clusters by the relevant government ministry, such as the Ministry of Health in the case of the health sector. However, government engagement in such mechanisms has typically been weak, whether due to capacity constraints, lack of political commitment, or a combination of the two (Binder and Grünewald 2010). In contexts of extremely weak states or states in active conflict, health provision by military medical teams has emerged as a significant trend. Such developments have, however, raised major concerns within the NGO community given the risk of militarization of humanitarian response threatening neutrality and reducing the humanitarian space available to agencies in settings of ongoing political conflict.

The lack of engagement with government providers is a serious weakness given that disruption of, or dislocation from, the routine services of a basic health system is a major driver of disease burden once the acute 'spike' of emergency health issues has been addressed. The continuity of care provided by even a weak health system—through such services as provision of family planning, antenatal care, post-natal care, growth monitoring, and immunization—is crucial to the protection of population health. In Dadaab in Kenya a group of five non-governmental agencies manage a de facto health system (comprising three hospitals and a network of 22 health posts) on a continuing basis (UNHCR 2012). In general, however, the strengthening of government health provision in areas impacted by significant forced migration represents a more coherent and sustainable option. The challenges of such a strategy share many of the features of integrating services for refugees in countries of asylum and resettlement discussed in the next section.

Health in Countries of Asylum and Resettlement

It is important to approach understanding of the forces shaping the health of refugees in countries of asylum and resettlement with an appreciation of the evidence regarding the so-called 'healthy migrant' effect (Fennelly 2007). Essentially, this describes the general trajectory of the health status of migrants to be one from having better health than is typical for the 'host' population to one where, over a period of years, health status declines towards—and often then below—that of the 'host' population. Migrants' typical initial health advantage is generally seen as related to factors associated with mobility, including economic standing and educational attainment. Subsequent declines in health status can be attributed to a number of causes. Diet has been implicated as a major factor, with the high fat, low vegetable diet of the urban underclass into which many migrants are assimilated driving increased risks of coronary heart disease, stroke, diabetes, and a range of other chronic diseases. Restricted access to health services—whether as a result of legal, economic, or cultural barriers—is another major cause, and there is also increasing evidence to suggest that it is the 'embodiment' of the experience of exclusion and marginalization that also significantly drives decrements in the health status of migrant populations (Spitzer 2011).

To what extent is this general pattern echoed in the specific experience of forced migrants? Evidence regarding initial health status is somewhat contradictory. Refugees who secure resettlement to third countries will typically have demonstrated significant resourcefulness in negotiating not only initial flight but also subsequent processes of seeking asylum, paralleling the self-selection bias seen to underpin the initial positive health status of general migrants. Further, the US Refugee Resettlement Act, for example, requires prospective refugees to undergo a medical examination prior travelling to the USA, with identification of 'Class A' conditions (such as tuberculosis, HIV, and syphilis) leading to denial of permission to travel unless granted an explicit waiver by authorities (RHTAC 2013). Such processes are clearly likely to result in those refugees securing resettlement in third countries having better health status than those not successful in securing resettlement.

However, there is much evidence that the health challenges associated with pre-flight circumstances will frequently outweigh the benefits of such selection bias. Burnett and Peel (2001: 544) summarize numerous studies of the burden of disease evident in resettling refugees:

> ...in the United States...15% of Cambodians were found to be positive for hepatitis B surface antigen...in Spain, 21% of migrants from sub-Saharan Africa were chronic carriers of hepatitis B...3.4% of refugees arriving in the United States had tuberculosis...Gastrointestinal symptoms were reported by 25% of a group of asylum seekers in Australia.

Tiong et al. (2006) found the most common health problems identified amongst newly arrived African refugees in Melbourne, Australia, to be inadequate vaccinations, nutritional deficiencies (vitamin D and iron), infectious diseases (gastrointestinal infections, schistosomiasis, and latent tuberculosis), and dental disease. In the same location Paxton et al. (2012) reported Karen resettling refugees presenting high rates of nutritional deficiencies (again including vitamin D and iron) and infectious diseases (including hepatitis, schistosomiasis, and faecal parasites). The addition of criteria of vulnerability—including mental and physical disability—to prioritization of resettlement cases has increased the likelihood of individuals with major health needs successfully securing resettlement in a third country (Mirza 2010). The UN Declaration of Commitment on HIV/AIDS in 2001 recognized that refugees were at increased risk of exposure to HIV infection (UNAIDS 2007).

In consequence, refugees are often considered at risk of being relatively 'unhealthy migrants' compared to those immigrating on the basis of principally economic motives. Such an assumption underpins a number of domestic health screening programmes that are instituted in countries of resettlement (Paxton et al. 2012; CDC 2013). Importantly, however, while refugees may not reflect the positive initial health profile associated with the 'healthy migrant' effect they are clearly at risk to the drivers of *declining* health associated with settlement.

Structural Barriers to Accessing Health Services

Addressing the health needs of refugees in countries of resettlement needs to be predicated on the assumption that, in addition to risks and vulnerabilities associated with pre-migratory experience and flight, refugees (as part of the broader class of migrants) face a range of forces predictive of poorer health outcomes. Principal amongst these are structural factors that restrict access to health services. Legal and economic barriers to access reflect national policies and resettlement conditions. In the UK, for instance, where a significant number of forced migrants are asylum seekers seeking protection as refugees under the 1951 Geneva Convention, there have been fierce debates over the entitlement to access to health services before adjudication of an asylum claim or, following an unsuccessful claim, during the period of an appeal (Taylor 2009). Government policy is motivated to restrict access to National Health Service facilities until formal claims to state protection have been adjudicated; physicians and refugee advocates have generally argued for facilitating access on the basis of the World Medical Association's 1948 commitment 'to provid[e] competent medical service in full professional and moral independence, with compassion and respect for human dignity'. In Canada, Caulford and Vali (2006) report that, despite formal 'waiting periods' for eligibility being much shorter, refugee patients took on average over two years to establish public health insurance coverage.

Such delays appear to reflect not only restrictive national policies but also weak local implementation of that provision that is potentially protective of refugees. Miedema,

Hamilton, and Easley (2008) note, for example, how the provisions of the Interim Federal Health (IFH) programme in Canada frequently do not translate into health access for refugee households. Family physicians were found to be either unfamiliar with the programme or reported the reimbursement requirements too cumbersome. One resettlement worker noted how:

> The [after-hours] clinics will not accept the IFH papers anymore because IFH is so difficult to work with that the accounting staff of all these doctors hate doing IFH. Because it's time-consuming to fill out the forms and it's months and months before they get their payment. (Miedema, Hamilton, and Easley 2008: 335)

Other local contextual factors, such as the provision of translation services, can also have a marked influence on access. The provision of effective translation services was noted as a key contribution to supporting access to primary healthcare provision in a study of local integration amongst refugees in the UK:

> I did not find any difficulty accessing services because when I go to my GP I am ask if I need interpreter or not. So if I need one, they find one...telephone connection...telephone service. It is not difficult. (Ager and Strang 2004: 6)

Trust in health providers has also been indicated as a key factor influencing service access. Asgary and Segar (2011: 510), studying asylum seekers in New York, found that although research participants did not report arrests or deportations due to inter-actions with the healthcare system 'they had a pervasive preoccupation with their health-care-related bills, fearing that lack of documentation or inability to pay would lead to subsequent arrest, detention, and deportation'.

Social and Cultural Influences on Health

Although access to the health system is an important prerequisite to support health out-comes, the broader social determinants of health are increasingly recognized as a key contributor to health inequalities. Such determinants include a wide range of influences on diet and lifestyle. Rondinelli et al. (2011), for example, report on factors shaping both under- and over-nutrition among refugees in San Diego County, California. A number of studies have also documented the role of culture in exacerbating health inequalities through shaping expectations of clinical encounters or presentation of health needs

However, there is increasing recognition of the role of social processes of margin-alization and discrimination in influencing health outcomes for refugees. Social dis-connection, downward employment mobility and the experience of racial harassment all induce significant social stress that not only contributes to mental ill-health, but also physical suffering (Asgary and Segar 2011; Spitzer 2011). The latter represents an embodiment of social conditions that is increasingly acknowledged as a major factor shaping public health outcomes. Recent analyses of the social determinants of health, for example, strongly support the relationship between income inequality and mortality at the population level (Marmot 2005). Anthropological analyses of the 'othering' of refugees—defining and treating them as separate, distant, and disconnected from host communities in receiving countries (Grove and Zwi 2006)—are very pertinent in this regard. As noted by Grove and Zwi, such processes of othering risk the creation of 'vulnerable, marginalised under classes with very real consequences for population health' (2006: 1939). Spitzer's (2011) collection of studies of migrant experience in Canada vividly illustrates the complex mechanisms by which the social positioning of forced migrants can have a major impact on their embodiment of social stresses and their impact on health and well-being.

MENTAL HEALTH NEEDS

A 1993 review for the Harvard Project on International Mental and Behavioral Health (Ager 1993) provides insight into conceptualization and policy regarding mental health in refugee populations in the 1990s. Extensive literature documented the potential risk factors for mental ill-health associated with various elements of the 'refugee experience', from pre-flight conditions through to resettlement or return. However, other than a few ground-breaking evaluations of psychiatric service provision for resettled refugees, there was little in the way of systematic analysis of programmatic intervention targeting improved adjustment. There was also significant concern at the potential for the use of a psychiatric lens to distort the experience of refugees by focusing inappropriately on issues of acute trauma at the time of flight (rather than broader, subsequent acculturative stressors) and insufficiently addressing refugees' agency and their adaptive capacities.

Twenty years on, perspectives have significantly evolved. Debate has resulted in an increased emphasis on the provision of culturally appropriate social and community supports as a means to secure psychosocial well-being. In emergency settings, interventions have been shaped by evolving consensus from field studies and reflection on practice (Mollica et al. 2004; IASC 2007) to a point where it is widely acknowledged that:

> a community-development approach is most appropriate to the needs of the whole population because it aims to restore the capacity of communities...[through] strengthening family and kinship ties, promoting indigenous healing methods, facilitating community participation in decision-making, fostering leadership structures, and reestablishing spiritual, religious, social, and cultural institutions and practices that restore a framework of cohesion and purpose for the whole community. (JH/IFRC 2008: 216)

In resettlement contexts, studies have similarly increasingly reflected broader ecological understandings of the multiple influences on refugee adjustment and well-being. The work of Miller and colleagues exemplified this trend towards elucidating the stresses and losses of displacement, documenting how Bosnian refugees in the USA:

contrasted their current experience of isolation with the rich social networks to which they belonged before going into exile; the lack of social support in their present lives was seen against a prewar backdrop of close friends, family members, and neighbors to whom one could turn for assistance in times of need. (Miller et al. 2002: 344)

Such analyses have informed a more preventive approach to work with resettling refugee communities. Reflecting on advances in understanding the complex dynamics shaping refugee identity and well-being, Weine (2011) has recently proposed a number of characteristics that should mark such work. These include working at multiple systemic levels given that refugees are typically

exposed to multilevel stressors (traumatic, economic, familial, community, work, and school) [and]...are interacting with multiple systems (resettlement agency, schools, clinics, neighborhoods, other families, workplace, state welfare system) that do not necessarily communicate or collaborate effectively with one another. (Weine 2011: 415)

CONCLUSIONS

The lens of health, arguably a comparatively neglected area of study within the field of forced migration, provides significant insight into multiple dimensions of the lived experience of refugee populations. Health status is a consistent marker of the political subjugation and marginalization within societies that may promote population displacement. The disintegration of health services and the social stress associated with civil conflict—with predictable impacts on population morbidity and mortality—is a common precursor or accompaniment to internal displacement within war-affected nations. The provision of access to health services is a reliable indicator of state commitment to legal obligations to asylum seekers and refugees within countries of temporary refuge or resettlement.

Throughout this chapter, analysis of health and health systems has sought to locate such concepts within both the priorities and agendas of marginalized populations and the obligations and capacities of states with responsibility to address these. Such principles are played out somewhat differently in the two contexts focused upon in the chapter—complex humanitarian emergencies and countries of resettlement—but remain crucial in orienting appropriate practice and policy. In all settings, health and well-being are shown to reflect not just physical and material circumstances but also the dynamics of social place, engagement, and identity. While marginalization, discrimination, and downward social mobility have clear implications for the mental health of refugees, such stresses are also embodied in a manner that has significant and enduring impact on physical health.

Building upon the above, key areas for further investigation in the field of health and forced migration reflect the changing global dimensions of such displacement: protracted displacement, the increasing urbanization of refugee settlement and the increasing linkage of criminality and enforced migration (through trafficking and related activity). With respect to each of these trends, the dynamics of health risk—and the service mechanisms to address them—are being flexed in new ways. Protracted displacement, for example, is resulting in the ageing of refugee populations in a manner that leads to chronic diseases emerging as a key service focus. New models of service delivery, emphasizing continuity of care rather than 'episodic' provision (such as the Family Health Team approach being piloted in UNRWA health clinics serving Palestinian refugees, UNRWA 2011), will be required to address such challenges.

The increasing urban settlement of refugees creates health risks—and required service delivery systems—very different from those of the classic setting of the refugee camp. Spiegel (2010) describes how the UNHCR Public Health and HIV Section is exploring models of response in urban settings through:

> a three-pronged strategy—focusing on advocacy, support of existing capacities and monitoring of delivery—to work with its partners to increase access to affordable and good quality health services for urban refugees.

Such analysis recognizes that in urban settings effective, quality health services will often be available, but that legal, political, social, and economic barriers will frequently restrict displaced persons' access to them.

A recent WHO (2012) review has acknowledged that there has been little systematic research on the health needs of survivors of trafficking. However, work conducted to date on the physical, sexual, and mental health of women trafficked for sexual exploitation suggests high prevalence of general fatigue, chronic pain, sexual and reproductive health problems, and significant weight loss, as well as enduring mental health symptoms. The insecure legal and economic position of such forced migrants clearly renders sustained health provision to address these needs challenging, although such support may be seen as crucial to the long-term adjustment and settlement of such individuals.

NOTE

1. There is increasing recognition of the vulnerability of men to sexual violence in contexts of displacement (e.g. Nagai et al. 2008)

REFERENCES

Ager, A (1993) *Mental Health Issues in Refugee Populations: A Review*. Boston: Harvard Centre for the Study of Culture and Medicine.

Ager, A. (2012) 'Health on the Move: The Impact of Forced Migration on Health'. *World Disasters Report*. Geneva: International Federation of the Red Cross and Crescent.

Ager, A., Boothby, N., and Bremer, M. (2009) 'Using the Framework of the "Protective Environment" to Analyze the Protection Needs of Children in Darfur'. *Disasters* 33(4): 548–73.

Ager, A., and Strang, A. (2004) 'The Experience of Integration: A Qualitative Study of Refugee Integration in the Local Communities of Pollokshaws and Islington'. Home Office Online Report 55/04.

Al Gaseer, N., Dresden, E., Keeney, G. B., and Warren, N. (2004) 'Status of Women and Infants in Complex Humanitarian Emergencies'. *Journal of Midwifery & Women's Health* 49(S1): 7–13.

Asgary, R., and Segar, N. (2011) 'Barriers to Health Care Access among Refugee Asylum Seekers'. *Journal of Health Care for the Poor and Underserved* 22(2): 506–22.

Bartlett, L. A. et al. (2002) 'Maternal Mortality in Afghan Refugees in Pakistan, 1999–2000'. *Lancet* 359(9307): 643–9.

Belvedere, F. (2003) *National Refugee Baseline Survey: Final Report*. Johannesburg: Community Agency for Social Enquiry.

Binder, A., and Grünewald, F. (2010) IASC Cluster Approach Evaluation, 2nd Phase Country Study, April. Haiti: Global Public Policy Institute and Groupe URD, 1–74.

Boorse, C. (1977) 'Health as a Theoretical Concept'. *Philosophy of Science* 44(4): 542–73.

Burnett, A., and Peel, M. (2001) 'Health Needs of Asylum Seekers and Refugees'. *British Medical Journal* 322(7285): 544–7.

Callahan, D. (1973) 'The WHO Definition of "Health"'. *Hastings Center Report* 1(3): 77–87.

Caulford, P., and Vali, Y. (2006) 'Providing Health Care to Medically Uninsured Immigrants and Refugees'. *Canadian Medical Association Journal* 174(9): 1253–4.

Center for Disease Control and Prevention (CDC) (2013) 'Guidelines for the U.S. Domestic Medical Examination for Newly Arriving Refugees'. <http://www.cdc.gov>.

Fennelly, K. (2007) 'The "Healthy Migrant" Effect'. *Minnesota Medicine* 90(3): 51–3.

Grove, N. J., and Zwi, A. B. (2006) 'Our Health and Theirs: Forced Migration, Othering, and Public Health'. *Social Science & Medicine* 62: 1931–42.

Guha-Sapir, D., and Degomme, O. (2005) 'Mortality Estimates from Multiple Survey Data'. *Louvain: Centre for Research on the Epidemiology of Disasters*. <http://www.cred.be>.

HNTS (2011) 'Democratic Republic of Congo Analysis: March 2011'. <http://www.thehnts.org/useruploads/files/drc_analysis_03_03_2011.pdf>.

IASC (2007) 'IASC Guidelines on Mental Health and Psychosocial Support in Emergency Settings'. Geneva: Inter-Agency Standing Committee.

JH/IFRC (2008) *Public Health Guide in Emergencies* (2nd edn.). Geneva: Johns Hopkins and Red Cross and Red Crescent.

Karunakara, U. (2011) 'Keynote Address: Articulating an Agenda for Humanitarian Education and Training'. <http://www.cerahgeneve.ch/conferences/colloques/Finalreport.pdf>.

Karunakara, U., and Stevenson, F. (2012) 'Ending Neglect of Older People in the Response to Humanitarian Emergencies'. *PLoS Med* 9(12): e1001357.

Landau, L. B., and Monson, T. (2008) 'Displacement, Estrangement and Sovereignty: Reconfiguring State Power in Urban South Africa'. *Government and Opposition* 43(2): 315–36.

Marmot, M. (2005) 'The Social Determinants of Health Inequalities'. *The Lancet* 365: 1099–104.

Miedema, B., Hamilton, R., and Easley, J. (2008) 'Climbing the Walls: Structural Barriers to Accessing Primary Care for Refugee Newcomers in Canada'. *Canadian Family Physician* 54(3): 335–6.

Miller, K., Worthington, G. J., Muzurovic, J., Tipping, S., and Goldman A. (2002) 'Bosnian Refugees and the Stressors of Exile: A Narrative Study'. *American Journal of Orthopsychiatry* 72(3): 341–54.

Mirza, M. (2010) 'Resettlement for Disabled Refugees'. *Forced Migration Review* 35: 30–1.

Mollica, R. F., Cardozo, B. L., Osofsky, H. J., Raphael, B., Ager, A., and Salama, P. (2004) 'Mental Health in Complex Emergencies'. *The Lancet* 364(9450): 2058–67.

Muhwezi, W. W., Kinyanda, E., Mungherera, M., Onyango, P., Ngabirano, E., Muron, J., Kagugube, J., and Kajungu, R. (2011) 'Vulnerability to High Risk Sexual Behavior (HRSB) Following Exposure to War Trauma as Seen in Post-Conflict Communities in Eastern Uganda: A Qualitative Study'. *Conflict and Health* 5(1): 22.

Murray, C. J. L., et al. (2012) 'Disability-Adjusted Life Years (DALYs) for 291 Diseases and Injuries in 21 Regions, 1990–2010: A Systematic Analysis for the Global Burden of Disease Study 2010'. *The Lancet* 380(9859): 2197–223.

Nagai, M., et al. (2008) 'Violence against Refugees, Non-Refugees and Host Populations in Southern Sudan and Northern Uganda'. *Global Public Health* 3(3): 249–70.

O'Keefe, P., and Rose, J. (2008) 'Relief Operations'. Pp. 506–13 in K. Heggenhougen (ed.), *International Encyclopedia of Public Health*. Amsterdam: Elsevier.

Paxton, G. A., Sangster, K. J., Maxwell, E. L., McBride, C. R. J., and Drewe, R. H. (2012) 'Post-Arrival Health Screening in Karen Refugees in Australia'. *PLoS ONE* 7(5): e38194.

Refugee Health Technical Assistance Center (RHTAC) (2013) 'Health Assessments'. <http://www.refugeehealthta.org/physical-mental-health/health-assessments/>.

Rondinelli, A. J., Morris M. D., Rodwell, T. C., Moser, K. S., Paida, P., Popper, S. T., and Brouwer, K. C. (2011) 'Under- and Over-Nutrition among Refugees in San Diego County, California'. *Journal of Immigrant and Minority Health* 13(1): 161–8.

Sphere Project (2011). *Humanitarian Charter and Minimum Standards in Humanitarian Response: The Sphere Project*. London: Practical Action Publishing.

Spiegel, P. (2010). 'Urban Refugee Health: Meeting the Challenges'. *Forced Migration Review* 34: 21–2. <http://www.fmreview.org/sites/fmr/files/FMRdownloads/en/urban-displacement/FMR34.pdf>.

Spitzer, D. (ed.) (2011) *Engendering Migrant Health: Canadian Perspectives*. Toronto: University of Toronto Press.

Stark, L., and Ager, A. (2011) 'A Systematic Review of Prevalence Studies of Gender Based Violence in Complex Emergencies'. *Trauma, Violence, & Abuse* 12(3): 127–34.

Stark, L., Roberts, L, Wheaton, W., Acham, A., Boothby, N., and Ager, A. (2010) 'Measuring Violence against Women amidst War and Displacement in Northern Uganda Using the "Neighborhood Method"'. *Journal of Epidemiology & Community Health* 64(12): 1056–61.

Taylor, K. (2009) 'Asylum Seekers, Refugees, and the Politics of Access to Health Care: A UK Perspective'. *British Journal of General Practice* 59(567): 765–72.

Tiong, A. C., Patel, M. S., Gardiner, J., Ryan, R., Linton, K. S., Walker, K. A., Scopel, J., and Biggs, B. A. (2006) 'Health Issues in Newly Arrived African Refugees Attending General Practice Clinics in Melbourne'. *Medical Journal of Australia* 185(11–12): 602–6.

UNAIDS (2007) 'HIV and Refugees Policy Brief'. Geneva: UNAIDS and UNHCR. <http://www.unaids.org/en/media/unaids/contentassets/dataimport/pub/briefingnote/2007/policy_brief_refugees.pdf>.

UNHCR (2012) 'Health and Nutrition Sector Update: Dadaab Refugee Camps 14th–20th April, 2012'. Nairobi: UNHCR.

UNRWA (2011) 'Modern and Efficient UNRWA Health Services: Family Health Team Approach. Update No. 40'. UNRWA: Jordan.

Weine, S. M. (2011) 'Developing Preventive Mental Health Interventions for Refugee Families in Resettlement'. *Family Process* 50(3): 410–30.

WHO (1948) 'WHO Definition of Health'. <httbp://www.who.int/about/definition/en/print. html>.

WHO (2012) 'Understanding and Addressing Violence against Women: Human Trafficking'. <http://apps.who.int/iris/bitstream/10665/77394/1/WHO_RHR_12.42_eng.pdf>.

World Bank (2013) 'Data: Life Expectancy at Birth'. <http://data.worldbank.org/indicator/ SP.DYN.LE00.IN>.

CHAPTER 35

RELIGION AND FORCED MIGRATION

DAVID HOLLENBACH, SJ

INTRODUCTION

THE nexus between religion and forced migration is highly complex, in part because religious communities have diverse self-understandings and act in different ways. Analysis of religion's multifaceted influences on conflict, humanitarian crises, and forced migration can shed useful light on the important role played by religious communities in assisting people driven from their homes and how religious faith helps sustain the displaced in the face of their losses. Such study can also lead to a better understanding of how religion sometimes contributes to conflicts that lead to forced migration. This chapter examines the religion-forced migration nexus, discussing the normative traditions of several monotheistic and Asian religious communities on the needs and rights of forced migrants. While such normative traditions are not always adopted in practice by these communities or their individual members, the analysis shows how different faiths understand their responsibilities to aid displaced populations. The chapter also explores several of the distinctive strengths and special challenges faced by faith-based agencies in their efforts to aid the displaced today.

THE HISTORICAL TRAJECTORY

Throughout most of pre-modern history, religious traditions were the principal fonts of the charity and compassion that led people to assist those forced from their homes by war, natural disaster, or extreme poverty. Well into the nineteenth and early twentieth centuries the humanitarian movement had strongly religious roots, particularly the anti-slavery movement, the founding of the International Committee of the Red Cross, and the expansion of Christian missionary engagement with poverty (Barnett 2011: 57–94). In contrast, after the Second World War humanitarian action appeared to undergo a notable secular-ization and the engagement of religious agencies seemed to decline. However, over the past decade much of the expansion in responses to humanitarian crises and displacement has been faith-based, leading to an increasing interest in faith-based humanitarianism by academics and practitioners alike (see Fiddian-Qasmiyeh 2011).

Particularly notable has been the establishment of new Christian NGOs with an evan-gelical orientation and of several Islamic humanitarian agencies. Indeed, religiously inspired responses to forced migration continue to be strong today. Although estimates of the revenues of some religious organizations cannot be very precise, the revenue expended in international assistance work by the major United States-based religiously affiliated groups in 2004 was approximately equal to the expenditures by secular agen-cies (McCleary and Barro 2008). The operating budgets of some major secular and religious humanitarian NGOs, drawn from their 2012 annual reports, are presented in Tables 35.1 and 35.2.

Thus, as Barnett comments, 'It is impossible to study humanitarianism without being impressed by the importance of religion' (2011: 17).

This continuing importance of faith-based organizations runs counter to the secu-larization hypothesis held until recently by many sociologists (see Luckmann 1967; for reassessment, see Berger 1999). Secularization can refer either to a *decline* of religion, with fewer believers than in earlier days, or to the *privatization* of religion, with less influence in public domains such as the state or economy. Neither of these phenomena

Table 35.1 Secular humanitarian organizations

Secular NGO	Annual Budget 2012
Oxfam Confederation	€990 million
Save the Children	$596 million
Care USA	$585 million
International Rescue Committee	$396 million
Norwegian Refugee Council	NOK 1,415 million (approx. $232 million)

Data compiled by the author from annual reports.

Table 35.2 Religious humanitarian organizations

Religious NGO	Annual Budget 2012
World Vision	$2,128 million
Catholic Relief Services	$732 million
Samaritan's Purse	$382 million
Islamic Relief Worldwide	£96 million
Islamic Relief USA	$51 million
Hebrew Immigrant Aid Society (2011)	$27 million

Data compiled by the author from annual reports.

has been occurring in most parts of the world in recent decades. Indeed, Casanova argues that 'religious traditions throughout the world are refusing to accept the marginal and privatized role which theories of modernity as well as theories of secularization had reserved for them' (1994: 5). The continuing public influence of religion seems particularly notable in international politics (Toft, Philpott, and Shah 2011).

Faith communities' international activity can, of course, have both positive and negative effects on forced migrants. Religion's negative face is evident in the politicized assertions of religious identity and self-defensive fundamentalisms involved in several of the world's conflicts today. On the other hand, religious communities and religious leaders such as Mohandas Karamchand Gandhi, Martin Luther King, the Dalai Lama, Pope John Paul II, and Archbishop Desmond Tutu have played significant roles in the pursuit of human rights, peace, and reconciliation. Appleby (2000) has thus argued that religion plays an 'ambivalent' role in international politics.

A key question, therefore, is what *kind* of faith and faith-based tenets motivate activities influencing forced migration. If faith leads to respect for the dignity and rights of all persons, including people of other faiths, and sees the state as a secular guarantor of the rights of all, the believing community can make positive contributions to peace and to the protection of those forced from home. Appleby (2000) and Toft, Philpott, and Shah (2011) have shown that many religious communities today possess these characteristics. On the other hand, they have also shown that if a religious community holds that only its own members possess full dignity and rights, or that the state should protect only those holding 'the true faith', conflict will likely result, making the creation of refugees likely. Thus the way a religious community understands the values within its own tradition and how these values shape the community's relations with other communities will have very important effects for forced migration. The following section will therefore provide an overview of several major religious traditions' key normative ideas relevant to displacement.

NORMATIVE STANCES OF RELIGIOUS COMMUNITIES

Migration and exile play central roles in the founding narratives of many world religions. Followers of three major monotheistic faiths—Judaism, Christianity, and Islam—all see themselves as descendants of the Patriarch Abraham, whose experience of God's call led him to migrate from his home in present-day Iraq to the land of Canaan, in present-day Israel. This section presents an overview of the normative perspectives shaping the response of these monotheistic faiths to forced migrants, followed by a brief discussion of the normative stances underpinning Asian religious traditions. It is important to note that the ways faith communities' normative values promote protection of displaced people are dynamic realities and are sometimes violated in notable ways, just as normative political ideas, such as democracy or the rule of law, are evolving and sometimes violated by their adherents. Despite this caveat, the way a faith community interprets its normative traditions helps shape the community's role in relation to forced migration.

Judaism

The story of the Exodus—a migration from slavery in Egypt to freedom in the land of God's promise—forms the identity of Judaism. In this narrative, the Israelites had been forced to migrate to Egypt by famine in their homeland. After a period in which they had been welcomed in Egypt, the Egyptians came to fear them and laid on them 'the whole cruel fate of slaves' (Exodus 1: 11–14). God saw their misery, liberated them through Moses' leadership, formed them into a people through bonds of a covenant, and led them into the land that became their home (Exodus 3: 7–8). Because of the way God freed the Jewish people from oppression and exile, a special duty to respect the strangers and migrants they encountered in the land of Israel itself came to form a core tenet of Judaism: 'You shall not oppress an alien; you well know how it feels to be an alien, since you were once aliens yourselves in the land of Egypt' (Exodus 23: 9). Thus this normative identity, as presented in the law and prophets of the Hebrew Bible, calls the Jewish people to exercise special responsibilities towards displaced persons. Judaism, like other religious communities, may not always live up to these normative standards, for example in some members' stance toward displaced Palestinians. Nonetheless, the foundational texts show why Judaism ought to support a vigorous humanitarian response to the needs of forced migrants (Wechsler 2003).

In a biblical perspective, God's covenant with the Jewish people is also seen as the basis of a special relation to the land of Israel. Importantly, this perceived special relation to the land of Zion is an underlying source of unresolved conflict today between Israel and the Palestinians. In much Jewish self-understanding, however, the place of the land of Israel in God's covenant does not justify the denial of the fundamental rights of non-Jews, including Palestinians. Indeed, the former Chief Rabbi of the United Hebrew Congregations of the Commonwealth, Jonathan Sacks, has argued that Jewish particularism should give Jews a special sensitivity to the duty to protect the distinctive identities of peoples different from themselves (2003: 45–66). Further, the narrative of the particularistic covenant with Israel is accompanied by the book of Genesis's story of the universal creation of every human being in the image and likeness of God (Genesis 1: 27). This universalist orientation is reinforced by the covenant with Noah (Genesis 9: 1–17), which sees God's care extending to all persons and to the entire earth, giving the Jewish people strict duties to respect the common humanity of all people.

Judaism, therefore, is a blend of particularist values that require special support for members of the Jewish community, and universalist values that call for respect for all people. These values, in different ways, point toward strong obligations toward forced migrants, both Jews and non-Jews. They energize vigorous efforts by members of the Jewish community to work on behalf of refugees, and can challenge some of the practices of the Israeli state and its citizens today.

Christianity

The New Testament portrays Jesus as a second Moses who is the leader of a new Israel. Therefore most of the perspectives that shape Jewish response to forced migrants are also normative within Christianity. There are also several distinctive themes that are important for the Christian stance.

The Gospel of Matthew explicates how just after his birth in Bethlehem, Jesus' 'flight into Egypt' with Mary and Joseph was due to King Herod's effort to destroy the infant Jesus as a threat to his regime. This can be seen as a form of persecution, and since it involved flight across a border, anachronistically we could say that Jesus met the contemporary international Convention's definition of a refugee. Therefore, as followers of Jesus, when Christians adhere to central tenets of their religion they should have special sensitivity to the needs of forced migrants. Also, in Matthew's Gospel Jesus teaches that on the Day of Judgement one of the criteria that will determine an individual's salvation or damnation will be whether one has welcomed the stranger. As Jesus puts it in Matthew's account, 'just as you did it to one of the least of these...you did it to me' (Matt. 25: 40). In following this teaching, Christians will see aiding the 'stranger' as offering assistance to Jesus himself. Thus response to the forced migrant is closely linked with the way Christians understand their relation with Jesus and with God.

In Luke's Gospel, Jesus' parable of the Good Samaritan is used to illustrate the meaning of love of neighbour. When a man on the road from Jerusalem to Jericho falls among thieves and is left half-dead by the roadside, it is neither the priest nor the Levite who comes to his aid, but rather a Samaritan—someone whom the Jews of Jesus' time regarded as a religious outsider. However, it is just this outsider that Jesus holds up as an example of the love of neighbour that is one of the two great commandments. When the parable ends with the words 'go and do likewise,' it challenges Christians to see in-group/out-group boundaries of religion, ethnicity, or nationality as irrelevant to their response to humanitarian crises and forced migrants (Christiansen 1996; Dulles 2003).

Jesus' radically inclusive understanding of neighbour-love reflects the Book of Genesis's affirmation that all persons have been created in the image of God and are brothers and sisters in a single human family no matter what their nationality or ethnicity. As St Paul declared, 'From one single stock [God]...created the whole human race so that they could occupy the entire earth' (Acts 17: 26). This challenges any understanding of the moral significance of borders that leads to denying refugees the kind of respect and care that are required by the commandment to love them as oneself. *Sub specie aeternitatis* there are no foreigners; all humans are equally brothers and sisters to one another. Extending care only to those who are 'like us' is thus religiously unacceptable in a Christian normative perspective. This does not mean, of course, that Christian communities and Christian-influenced societies always live up to these standards. There have been clear examples of Christian violation of such standards in the past, such as the Crusades and missionaries' support for colonialism, and they continue to occur today, for example in the former Yugoslavia. Nonetheless, the normative Christian approach helps explain the Christian inspiration and affiliation of many NGOs working with forced migrants today.

Islam

Within Islam, the Prophet Muhammad's *hijra* or migration from Mecca to Medina (622 CE) is considered the founding event of the Muslim religious community. The Prophet was fleeing persecution by the Quraysh, the dominant clan in Mecca. Once again anachronistically, we could say that the Prophet Muhammad met the contemporary definition of a refugee. The Prophet fled so he could preserve the integrity of the message of monotheism he had begun setting forth in the early suras (chapters) of the Qur'an. The Quraysh's continuing adherence to their culture's many gods led to a conflict with the Prophet Muhammad's central message of the oneness of God. The conflict was also rooted in the Quraysh's desire to retain their economic power and their control over the *ka'bah* as a central pilgrimage site of pre-Islamic traditions. Thus the Prophet Muhammad's migration was motivated both by the commitment to belief in the oneness of God in the face of religious persecution, and by threats he and his followers faced from those holding political and commercial power (Casewit 1998). The origins of Islam, therefore, are closely intertwined with an event of forced migration.

In continuity with this founding experience, the tenets of Islam include a core commitment to offer assistance and protection to 'needy travellers'. Being a traveller has been part of the Muslim experience from its beginning; one of the five pillars of Islam is each Muslim's duty, if possible, to make the *hajj* (pilgrimage) to Mecca. Both the founding *hijra* and the requirement of *hajj* call Muslims to appreciate the needs of people on the move, including refugees and other forced migrants. Thus the Qur'an sees emigrants (*muhajirin*) such as Abraham, the Jewish people, and, above all, the Prophet Muhammad and his companions in the *hijra* as falling under the special care of Allah (Qur'an 9: 100). Those who welcomed the Prophet Muhammad and his fellow migrants to Medina are known as the *ansar* (the helpers) and they are held to be especially blessed. The Qur'an notes that forced migrants, in their flight from oppression, continue to face special vulnerabilities, and that Muslims have special responsibilities toward them (Qur'an 28: 4). These responsibilities include the duty to provide asylum, including for non-Muslims. Surah 9: 6 notes: 'If anyone of the disbelievers seeks your protection, then grant him protection so he may hear the word of Allah and then escort him to where he will be secure' (Qur'an 9: 6). These and other Islamic teachings have led the Organization of the Islamic Conference, working with UNHCR, to conclude that 'Respect for migrants and those seeking refuge has been a permanent feature of the Islamic faith' (UNHCR and OIC 2005; Guterres 2012).

A full picture of the Islamic tradition's response to forced migration also requires noting some less admirable components. The Prophet's flight from Mecca to Medina is seen as a form of struggle (*jihad*) against the adversaries of his monotheistic faith in the oneness of Allah. *Jihad*, of course, does not necessarily mean armed struggle; *jihad* on behalf of Islam can be undertaken through persuasive words and the witness of an exemplary life. Nonetheless, there are strands of Islamic tradition that have led some extremist groups to endorse armed *jihad* as appropriate in the struggle against Western colonialism and continuing Western influence in the Muslim world. This stance, however, is in only partial continuity with the broad Islamic tradition (Masud 1990). In the larger tradition, struggle through word and example remains central, including through care for refugees and 'needy travellers'. This has led to Muslim efforts to respond to the displaced throughout the history of Islam and to the foundation of Muslim agencies that respond to forced migrants with notable effectiveness today, such as Islamic Relief.

Hinduism and Buddhism

A relative paucity of literature published in European languages exists regarding the normative stances of Asian religious traditions towards forced migrants. Nonetheless, this section reflects on some of the core concepts underpinning responses to forced migrants in the religions of Asia, specifically in Hinduism and Buddhism.

The Hindu concept of *dharma* ('duty' or 'justice') requires that 'One should never do that to another which one regards as injurious to oneself' (*Mahabharata* XX: 113, 8, cited in Sharma 2003: 5). *Dharma,* however, also refers to duties based on caste and to citizens of one's own group (Mehta 2011). *Dharma,* therefore, can prompt and require positive responses to the needs of forced migrants, such as India's welcome of millions from Pakistan at the time of the India/Pakistan partition and of many from Tibet more recently. It can also threaten to lead to conflict with India's non-Hindu neighbours and thus threaten to cause displacement. Thus like the monotheistic religions, Hinduism has an ambivalent impact on forced migration.

Buddhism is often regarded as a spirituality of meditation and withdrawal from engagement with the struggles of social and political life. While Buddhists have often followed this path, there are significant resources within the Buddhist tradition that are increasingly being tapped to energize engaged efforts to alleviate the suffering of the victims of humanitarian crises (Queen and King 1996). The first of the 'four noble truths' taught by the Buddha after his enlightenment was the pervasiveness of suffering. Followers of the Buddha who are on the path to enlightenment should respond to this suffering with compassion, even delaying their own enlightenment in order to help others become free of suffering. Those on such a path of active compassion are called *bodhisattvas.*

What the Vietnamese Buddhist monk Thích Nhất Hạnh (1987) has called 'engaged Buddhism' has led to several new forms of Buddhist engagement with forced migrants and the causes that have driven them from home. Among such engaged Buddhists are Maha Ghosananda, the Buddhist patriarch of Cambodia. Ghosananda began his leadership of a series of 'pilgrimages for truth' in the refugee camps on the Thai border to which many Cambodians had fled from the atrocities of the Khmer Rouge. Other Buddhists, such as Sulak Sivaraksa of Thailand and the Dalai Lama of Tibet have also led non-violent campaigns that seek to address some of the deep causes of forced migration (Queen and King 1996; Appleby 2000: 121–43). The Taiwanese Buddhist nun Cheng Yen founded Tzu Chi, a Buddhist NGO with several million members in many countries engaged in international relief work, including work with the displaced. Cheng Yen teaches this work is a way of 'following and applying the teachings of Buddha in our daily lives and transforming ourselves into living Bodhisattvas' (Tzu Chi n.d.).

Buddhism, of course, like the other religions explored here, does not have an entirely positive record in relation to forced migration. It has been intertwined with the violent Sinhalese nationalism that contributed to the Sri Lankan civil war that displaced hundreds of thousands (Norwegian Refugee Council 2012). Nonetheless, also within Sri Lanka the Buddhist movement Sarvodaya Shramadana has sought a non-violent resolution of the conflict (King 2009: 83–90). Thus the key factor affecting the impact of Buddhism on forced migration in Sri Lanka as elsewhere is how its adherents understand and enact the normative principles of their tradition.

Contributions and Challenges

The contributions made by faith-based agencies responding to situations of displacement also raise challenges that need to be addressed with care.

Meaning in the Face of Suffering

Humanitarian emergencies fracture the taken-for-granted worlds of the displaced, shattering and reshaping the relationships that give meaning to the routines of ordinary life. Such crises also affect those seeking to help, who have to face the suffering of those they assist in a way that can lead to secondary trauma and burn-out. Thus humanitarian crises and forced migration often raise questions about ultimate meaning that are, in essence, religious. Is continuing to struggle pointless in the face of loss, or can one trust, however tentatively, that there is a deeper source of hope? Such trust is a form of faith that can enable the victims of crisis to carry on and to struggle actively for a better future.

Following a review of existing empirical literature, Walker et al. (2012) conclude that religion and spirituality help people cope with trauma in four ways: providing meaning in the face of grave loss, helping reduce anxiety, connecting victims to social support, and, in a more explicitly religious way, enabling them to attain communion with the sacred. Although the data on the ways in which these religious forms of support function in the midst of humanitarian crises are chiefly anecdotal, Walker and his co-authors believe that 'there is a strong case to be made for the critical role supporting faith can have in improving survival and recovery from the trauma of major humanitarian crisis' (2012: 132; also see Fiddian-Qasmiyeh and Ager 2013). Indeed, Goździak notes how Islam helped Kosovar Albanians cope with the trauma of their displacement (2002), and Parsitau's ethnographic research with internally displaced populations in Kenya (2011) concludes that the displaced have actively drawn on their own faith in grappling with the challenges of forced migration.

Further, Barnett and Stein note that secular humanitarianism itself possesses an orientation to meaning that transcends what is feasible politically, giving humanitarian work itself a kind of faith dimension (2012b). In their view, this blurs the lines between religious and secular humanitarianism, pointing to the fact that forced migrants' struggles call for a kind of meaning and hope that is either religious or analogous to that provided by religion as more traditionally understood. At the same time, faith-based organizations are convinced of the importance of their distinctive traditions for their effectiveness and such claims should not be overlooked.

Inclusiveness, Accountability, and Accompaniment

Faith-based organizations vary considerably in the way their faith influences the style of their work. Some evangelical Christian agencies stress their explicitly religious mission, such as Samaritan's Purse, which states that it responds to the needs of victims of war and natural disasters in the name Jesus Christ: 'Our ministry is all about Jesus—first, last, and always' (Samaritan's Purse n.d.). In contrast, Catholic Relief Services is motivated by the gospel but also by seeing the gospel as supporting values such as human dignity and justice. CRS, like many other faith-based organizations, explicitly states that it works inclusively 'to assist people on the basis of need, not creed, race or nationality' (n.d., online). In a similar way, Islamic Relief 'provides support regardless of religion, ethnicity or gender and without expecting anything in return' (n.d., online). Such faith-based organizations thus share many of the commitments of secular humanitarian organizations, including their criticism of proselytization by evangelical groups in disaster situations (Ferris 2005).

In stressing that their approaches overlap with those based on humanistic, reason-based values, faith-based organizations like CRS and Islamic Relief indicate that they are ready to be held accountable to the professional standards of effectiveness increasingly operative in the humanitarian world. Accountability to these standards is a precondition today for obtaining necessary financial support, including support from governments. One can ask, however, whether, such standards may threaten the religious identity of faith-based organizations and perhaps even the secular humanitarian goal of providing care without calculating the cost (Stein 2008; Barnett 2012). For example, the Jesuit Refugee Service identifies 'accompaniment' of the displaced as one of its three objectives, along with service to and advocacy on behalf of the displaced. It describes accompaniment as a 'direct and personal approach of individual interaction and cooperation with refugees which mutually empowers refugees and JRS personnel alike' (n.d., online). Whether such a personalized approach can continue when organizations must administer the complex bureaucratic systems needed to assure they can be held accountable to donors is a serious question for the entire humanitarian enterprise, religious and secular alike. Religious NGOs may in effect be better situated to combine personalized care with the requirements of accountability because of their frequently well-organized efforts to retain their identity by training their staff in the practical implications of that identity (Paras and Stein 2011–12).

Tensions between Advocacy and Service

Similar questions about identity emerge when humanitarian organizations become involved in advocacy that addresses the political and social causes of the crises affecting those they serve. Even in natural disasters, destructive effects are often due to governmental failure to take preventive steps to reduce the risk. Thus advocacy can call into question an agency's commitment to the political neutrality often seen as a defining characteristic of humanitarianism. Addressing root causes and advocating long-term solutions can run the risk of entangling the humanitarian organization in politics. The commitment to justice that some faith-based groups see as an essential aspect of their identity has been moving an increasing number of them in this direction.

For example, Catholic Relief Services failed to take steps to help prevent the 1994 Rwanda genocide despite its presence in Rwanda for many years. This experience led CRS to examine its operating philosophy and to adopt a 'justice lens' that tries to identify and respond to deeper causes of crisis (1998). CRS now seeks to contribute to the prevention of crises through systemic, long-term action for both justice and peace. However, acting on this commitment could lead to CRS being denied access, for political reasons, to people who are suffering, and thus being unable to serve their urgent needs. Action that might be perceived as political could also risk having negative impact on the funding that makes CRS's work possible, especially the funding it receives from the US government.

It can be argued that avoiding these risks will be more likely if the faith-based organization retains a strong rootedness in the values that shape its identity. Clarity about an organization's identity will help it stay alert to when its values call for a categorical stand and when compromise is appropriate. Catholic and ecumenical Protestant organizations have dealt with how to link their explicit work for social justice with their Christian identity throughout much of the twentieth century. It is possible, therefore, that Christian agencies could share what they have learned from experience to help clarify ways of negotiating the relationship between neutrality and advocacy both with other faith-based bodies and with secular humanitarian organizations who serve forced migrants (Ferris 2011).

CONCLUSION

The role of religion in addressing the causes and experiences of forced migration and the responses to it, both by the displaced themselves and by organizations seeking to help them, is clearly a complex matter. While faith-based agencies continue to play important public roles in the humanitarian sector, religious contributions to the needs of the displaced vary both across and within religious traditions. These contributions have notable strengths and yet raise continuing challenges: faith often helps displaced themselves to carry on in the face of their losses and may energize the response of the agencies that come to their assistance, and yet it can sometimes itself be a factor in causing displacement. This chapter shows that while much is known about these matters, further investigation and research is needed, for this area has received less academic and practitioner reflection that its importance warrants. Additional reflection could surely help both faith-based and secular agencies alike respond more effectively to the needs of displaced people, a goal shared by all in the humanitarian community.

REFERENCES

Appleby, R. (2000) *The Ambivalence of the Sacred: Religion, Violence, and Reconciliation.* Lanham, MD: Rowman and Littlefield.

Barnett, M. (2011) *Empire of Humanity: A History of Humanitarianism.* Ithaca, NY: Cornell University Press.

Barnett, M. (2012) 'Faith in the Machine: Humanitarianism in an Age of Bureaucratization'. Pp. 188–210 in M. Barnett and J. Stein (eds.), *Sacred Aid: Faith and Humanitarianism.* Oxford: Oxford University Press .

Barnett, M., and Stein, J. (eds.) (2012a) *Sacred Aid: Faith and Humanitarianism.* Oxford: Oxford University Press.

Barnett, M., and Stein, J. (2012b) 'Introduction: The Secularization and Sanctification of Humanitarianism', in M. Barnett and J. Stein (eds.), *Sacred Aid: Faith and Humanitarianism.* Oxford: Oxford University Press, 1–36.

Barnett, M., and Weiss, T. (eds.) (2008) *Humanitarianism in Question: Politics, Power, Ethics.* Ithaca, NY: Cornell University Press.

Berger, P. (1999) *The Desecularization of the World: Resurgent Religion and World Politics.* Grand Rapids, MI: Eerdmans.

Casanova, J. (1994) *Public Religions in the Modern World.* Chicago: University of Chicago Press.

Casewit, D. (1998) 'Hijra as History and Metaphor: A Survey of Qur'anic and Hadith Sources'. *Muslim World* 88(2): 105–28.

Catholic Relief Services (n.d.) 'Mission Statement'. <http://crs.org/about/mission-statement/>.

Catholic Relief Services (1998) *Applying the Justice Lens to Programming: Ideas, Examples, and Initial Lessons.* Baltimore: Catholic Relief Services.

Christiansen, D. (1996) 'Movement, Asylum, Borders: Christian Perspectives'. *International Migration Review* 30(1): 7–11.

Dulles, A. (2003) 'Christianity and Humanitarian Action'. Pp. 5–20 in K. Cahill (ed.), *Traditions, Values, and Humanitarian Action.* New York: Fordham University Press and Center for International Health and Cooperation.

Eikelman, D., and Piscatori, J. (eds.) (1990) *Muslim Travellers: Pilgrimage, Migration, and the Religious Imagination.* Berkeley and Los Angeles: University of California Press.

Ferris, E. (2005) 'Faith-based and Secular Humanitarian Organizations'. *International Review of the Red Cross* 87(858): 311–25.

Ferris, E. (2011) 'Faith and Humanitarianism: It's Complicated'. *Journal of Refugee Studies* 24(3): 606–25.

Fiddian-Qasmiyeh, E. (2011) 'Special Issue on Faith-Based Humanitarianism in Contexts of Forced Displacement'. *Journal of Refugee Studies* 24(3).

Fiddian-Qasmiyeh, E., and Ager, A. (eds.) (2013) *Local Faith Communities and the Promotion of Resilience in Humanitarian Situations*. Refugee Studies Centre & Joint Learning Initiative Working Paper 90. Oxford: Refugee Studies Centre.

Goździak, E. (2002) 'Spiritual Emergency Room: The Role of Spirituality and Religion in the Resettlement of Kosovar Albanians'. *Journal of Refugee Studies* 15(2): 136–52.

Islamic Relief (n.d.) 'Who We Are/About Us'. <http://www.islamic-relief.com/Whoweare/Default.aspx?depID=2>.

Guterres, A. (2012) Opening Remarks of the United Nations High Commissioner for Refugees, at Organization of Islamic Cooperation Ministerial Conference on Refugees in the Muslim World, Ashgabat, 11 May. <http://www.unhcr.org/4fb270979.html>.

Jesuit Refugee Service (n.d.) 'Accompaniment'. <http://www.jrs.net/accompaniment>.

King, S. (2009) *Socially Engaged Buddhism*. Honolulu: University of Hawai'i Press.

Luckmann, T. (1967) *The Invisible Religion: The Problem of Religion in Modern Society*, trans. from the German. New York: Macmillan.

McCleary, R., and Barro, R. (2008) 'Private Voluntary Organizations Engaged in International Assistance, 1939–2004'. *Nonprofit and Voluntary Sector Quarterly* 37(3): 512–36.

Masud, M. (1990) 'The Obligation to Migrate: The Doctrine of Hijra in Islamic Law'. Pp. 29–49 in D. Eikelman and J. Piscatori (eds.), *Muslim Travellers: Pilgrimage, Migration, and the Religious Imagination*. Berkeley and Los Angeles: University of California Press.

Mehta, P. B. (2011) 'Hinduism and the Politics of Rights in India'. Pp. 193–212 in T. Banchoff and R. Wuthnow (eds.), *Religion and the Global Politics of Human Rights*. Oxford: Oxford University Press.

Nhất Hạnh, T. (1987) *Interbeing: Fourteen Guidelines for Engaged Buddhism* (3rd edn.). Berkeley and Los Angeles: Parallax Press.

Norwegian Refugee Council (2011) *Global Overview 2011: People Internally Displaced by Conflict and Violence*. Châtelaine: Internal Displacement Monitoring Centre.

Paras, A., and Stein, J. (2012) 'Bridging the Sacred and Profane in Humanitarian Life'. In M. Barnett and J. Stein (eds.), *Sacred Aid: Faith and Humanitarianism*. Oxford: Oxford University Press, 211–39.

Parsitau, D. (2011) 'The Role of Faith and Faith-Based Organizations among Internally Displaced Persons in Kenya'. *Journal of Refugee Studies* 24(3): 493–512.

Queen, C., and King, S. (eds.) (1996) *Engaged Buddhism: Buddhist Liberation Movements in Asia*. Albany, NY: State University of New York Press.

Sacks, J. (2003) *The Dignity of Difference: How to Avoid a Clash of Civilizations* (rev. edn.). London: Continuum.

Samaritan's Purse (n.d.) 'About Us'. <http://www.samaritanspurse.org/our-ministry/about-us/>.

Sharma, A. (2003) *Hinduism and Human Rights: A Conceptual Approach*. New Delhi: Oxford University Press.

Stein, J. (2008) 'Humanitarian Organizations: Accountable—Why, to Whom, for What, and How?' In M. Barnett and T. Weiss (eds.), *Humanitarianism in Question: Politics, Power, Ethics*. Ithaca, NY: Cornell University Press, 124–42.

Toft, M., Philpott, D., and Shah, T. (2011) *God's Century: Resurgent Religion and Global Politics*. New York: W. W. Norton.

Tzu Chi (n.d.) 'Master's Teachings'. <http://www.tw.tzuchi.org/en/>, at 'Our Founder'.

United Nations High Commissioner for Refugees (UNHCR), in collaboration with the Secretariat of the Organization of the Islamic Conference (OIC) (2005) 'Enhancing Refugee Protection in the Muslim World'. Working Document, 18 March. <http://unispal.un.org/UNISPAL.NSF/0/A761F9F2A351670E852570060053D50D>.

Walker, P., Mazurana, D., Warren, A., Scarlett, G., and Lewis, H. (2012) 'The Role of Spirituality in Humanitarian Crisis Survival and Recovery'. In M. Barnett and J. Stein (eds.), *Sacred Aid: Faith and Humanitarianism*. Oxford: Oxford University Press, 115–39.

Wechsler, H. (2003) 'For the Sake of my Kin and Friends: Traditions, Values, and Humanitarian Action in Judaism'. Pp. 21–40 in K. Cahill (ed.), *Traditions, Values, and Humanitarian Action*. New York: Fordham University Press and Center for International Health and Cooperation.

Zaat, K. (2007) 'The Protection of Forced Migrants in Islamic Law'. UNHCR, Policy Development and Evaluation Service, December. Research Paper No. 146.

....

CHAPTER 36

THE MEDIA AND REPRESENTATIONS OF REFUGEES AND OTHER FORCED MIGRANTS

....

TERENCE WRIGHT[1]

The only Europeans who were there were aid workers, and you weren't, you were just a journalist, and at that particular moment I couldn't think of a more useless occupation.

Michael Buerk 2008

INTRODUCTION

....

THIS chapter examines the changing patterns in representation of forced migration in the media between 2000 and 2012. During this period, dramatic social and cultural changes have taken place that have had a profound influence on the media portrayal of refugee crises and forced migration. Not only have there been significant historical events (e.g. the 'Arab Spring') that have changed the patterns of forced migration across the globe, but also a number of campaigns have been launched, with the aim of heightening public awareness and drawing attention to media representations of refugees. For some (e.g. Sulaiman-Hill et al. 2011), media reporting on forced migration has been subject to changing political agendas, particularly in the post-2001 world. For others (Robinson 1999), it can be the media that play a major role in influencing the political agenda. Awareness campaigns, such as those initiated by the Institute for Public Policy Research (IPPR) (see Greenslade 2005) and Oxfam (2007) have aimed to raise public consciousness regarding the reporting of forced migration. And, partly influenced by the World Trade Center attacks (see Wright 2004), other initiatives have campaigned to improve media coverage of the Developing World. Indeed the list of grievances about mainstream media reporting of the subject appears to be universal. For instance, concerns over the behaviour of western media is echoed in Kaur's (2007: 10) study of Malaysian media reports on refugees which 'highlight accusations and fear of their spreading infectious diseases, gansterism, theft, violence among the different groups, and involvement in other criminal activities leading to a rise in crime in areas where these people reside'.

The growing ease of cross-border travel and increase of global migrations has high-lighted refugees as a group, and yet refugees are very diverse and often defy the usual media stereotypes employed to represent them. Few refugee news stories make the con-nection between 'there' and 'here': sympathetic coverage of those in far-off lands affected by disaster and war appears in stark contrast to the media treatment of those seeking asylum in the West. At the same time, European news media organizations have become subject to budget cuts in overseas reporting and an increasing dependence upon the 'mobile phone images' produced by 'citizen journalists' and 'refugee journalists' (as in journalists who become refugees, and in the case of refugees who are journalists in camps and urban settings etc., especially in protracted refugee situations). This has put a new range of dramatic, yet questionable, images into circulation with a new kind of immediacy (Danziger 2005).

Meanwhile the very definition of 'The Media' itself has undergone some radical transformations. With the introduction of digital communication technologies, such concepts as 'publication' and 'broadcasting' have changed substantially. In the pre-9/11 era, Robinson found that the 'new technologies appeared to reduce the scope for calm deliberation over policy, forcing policy-makers to respond to whatever issue journal-ists focused on' (1999: 301). But since then, the dominance of international news and broadcasting networks has been eroded by the increasingly democratic medium of the Internet—though widening access and production has led to an uncertainty about accuracy in a new era of information. Consequently it has become increasingly difficult to adhere to 'traditional' media categorizations: mass media/local media; professional/amateur. This more diffuse climate presents problems for researchers in attempting to define the ways and means by which people obtain information about the world. Newspapers, radio, and television no longer provide the authorial voices that become the major determinants of public opinion. The Internet, Twitter, cellular phone texting combine with traditional media forms (television, documentary film, newspapers, and journals) all contributing to our world outlook. At the same time, the terms 'multime-dia' or 'media-mix' prove inadequate to account for this phenomenon. They have either taken on new connotations or appear inappropriate to account for the multiple infor-mation flows of the digital media era. This state of affairs has led Madianou and Miller (2012) to coin the term 'polymedia', as an acknowledgement 'that most people use a con-stellation of different media as an integrated environment in which each medium finds its niche in relation to others' (Madianou and Miller 2012: 3). In this context, families that have become separated (whether 'forced' or 'economic' migrants) can maintain their relationships and family ties through a network of systems: email, instant mes-saging, social networking sites, webcam, and texting. All made available through the accessibility and usability of new digital technologies. However this global and cultural complexity of media systems is further compounded by unequal distribution. While the technology has bypassed some refugees and forced migrants, others have had the opportunity to embrace it. Or, as we shall see later in this chapter, some groups of forced migrants range from those who are non-literate to those who are running their own global communications networks.

First, the chapter considers some of the central issues concerning the 'mainstream' media's portrayal of refugees and pinpoints some of the factors that lead to media misrepresentation. It then reviews some of the studies and campaigns that have aimed for a climate of more balanced reporting of refugee crises. It is proposed that the proliferation of new technologies has the potential to undermine 'traditional' news media hierarchies, bringing about the possibility of refugees controlling their own media images. However, this state of affairs is highly dependent upon access to technology and training in journalistic skills.

THE REFUGEE IMAGE

Since the 1890s when technological advances made it possible to reproduce photographs in newspapers, pictures have become an essential part of news reporting. Not only could readers get an idea of the 'look' of the news, but also the telegraph gave them increased speed of access. With the arrival of television and more recently the Internet, the visual image and the immediacy of news (together with an increase in 'democratization' of news channels) has given the viewing public unprecedented levels of access. However, regardless of such developments, many of the media representations of refugees appear to have been left in a time-warp, often visually represented in a manner reminiscent of biblical iconography: the much repeated 'Madonna and Child' image, for example (Wright 2002). Despite the scale of a refugee crisis or humanitarian disaster, one of the problems in reporting is that much of the visual imagery promulgated by the mainstream media remains the largely same. Following Hurricane Andrew's devastation of the south-eastern USA in 1992, ABC reporter Dave Marash referred to the numbing effect on audience compassion due to repetition of imagery which he called 'TV Codes': 'Palm trees bending to the gale, surf splashing over the humbled shore, missing roofs, homeless people showing up in local gyms. You see it once or twice most years' (Marash 1995: 9). In an African refugee context, anthropologist Liisa Malkki found another range of stereotypes employed in a news photograph of a 'grouping of people—women clothed in colorful wraps, children in ragged T-shirts and shorts, walking barefoot out of Burundi— [who] had just become generic refugees and generic Africans in whose societies tribal violence periodically flares up' (Malkki 1996: 389). Malkki notes that the image that appeared in the *New York Times* was not accompanied by a story. This (and other examples) lead her to conclude that 'The visual conventions for representing refugees...have the effect of constructing refugees as a bare humanity—even as a merely biological or demographic presence' (1996: 390). However, this regard for refugees can be relative to cultural distance or racial difference. For example, if the refugee crisis is European,

Western audiences find it easier to relate to their plight. 'What made the Kosovans popular refugees was the ability of Westerners to see themselves—and their families, friends and neighbours—in the Kosovans' suffering' (Gibney 1999: 5).

In addition to our own prejudices and perspectives, the *institutional discourses* of television reporting have not been kind to refugees. Rather than being allowed to speak for themselves, they are more commonly spoken about by NGO reps, translators, television reporters, TV studio anchorpersons, and politicians. In addition, the news bifurcation of 'foreign' news and 'home' news divide refugees (i.e. those 'over there') from asylum seekers ('over here') and rarely acknowledges that war and disaster victims, who generally have the sympathy of the public, are the self-same people seeking shelter in Western states. This is compounded by the fact that the very state of displacement automatically places refugees at a social disadvantage. This increases the likelihood of the media treating them as anonymous passive victims. For example, they do not always have the language skills or security to express themselves in media interviews—let alone the ability to lobby the media in a bid to improve their situation. In this context, it is important to keep in mind that the television news institution does not provide viewers with a 'transparent' view of the world, but it operates more as a television *genre* whereby world events are represented to standard formulae and inserted into specific time-slots.

CHANGING THE PICTURE

Over the last 12 years, various pressure groups have launched initiatives that have aimed to raise public and press awareness in order to amend the media coverage of refugees and forced migrants. While there has been a general improvement from some media outlets, overall the cultural mindset of the media remains unchanged. Nonetheless a report from The Hague Process on Refugees and Migration draws little success from these efforts. 'The policy and public mood towards migration is often more negative than it was ten years ago' (2012: 15) and much of this stems from 'inconsistent media coverage' (p. 16). Indeed an initiative established by the Institute for Public Policy Research (Greenslade 2005) reviews a little-changing picture of asylum-seeker reporting in British newspapers since the 1940s. More recently in 2012, an ICAR report (Information Centre about Asylum and Refugees) provides an update on this state of affairs, but in both instances (along with many other media analyses of refugee reporting) studies are mostly limited to print journalism and do little to address broadcast media and even less to account for the rapidly expanding Internet/'New Media' culture. At this point, it is worth noting that UK television, unlike the newspapers, has a statutory requirement to provide balanced and fair reports. For instance, 'impartiality' is written into the BBC's charter:

> The Agreement accompanying the BBC Charter requires us to do all we can to ensure controversial subjects are treated with due impartiality in our news and other output dealing with matters of public policy or political or industrial controversy.[2]

Consequently, the newspapers have become easy targets for research as discriminatory standpoints are relatively unrestricted and are often quite transparent. For example, Bradimore and Bauder (2011: 657) identify negative reporting in the Canadian press with 'concerns about fleeing terrorists, economic migrants, abuses of Canada's generosity, and "highly infectious diseases such as tuberculosis"'. They maintain that such reports have a direct impact on the national political agenda. Pickering (2001: 169) shows how the Australian 'quality' newspapers construct refugees as a 'deviant' problem 'both implicitly and explicitly'. Nonetheless, despite requirements for impartiality, the television refugee image is subtler, rarely 'explicit' in this regard, but can carry subconscious, 'implicit' negative messages of which the television editors themselves may not be aware. For example, it is often the case that video footage to illustrate asylum seekers in the UK is of men, while with 'overseas' migrants from disaster, women and children are usually shown. The underlying message suggests a sense of potential aggression and threat from men hanging around 'our' streets in contrast to helpless passive victims of circumstances beyond their control (for more on the gendered nature of refugee representations see Seu 2003). While television's 'balanced approach' (and this is evident in editorial policy in showing two sides of the story) does not always pay due care and attention to the implied messages of its news stories. Reporters can unconsciously adopt the common currency of newspaper rhetoric and, automatically resort to newspaper-style metaphors and refer to 'the tide of immigration'; 'floods of refugees'; 'at first a trickle, then a stream'; etc. From the perspective of the television production side, the urgency and buzz of the news gallery allows little time to check news content to the same precise level of detail as the study of a media analyst. This is becoming an increasingly controversial topic with new technologies having widened and accelerated the news gathering process.

Another dimension to newsworthiness is that stories from the *Developing World* seldom make the Western news agendas unless either the disaster is on such a scale that it is impossible to ignore, or it has a strong Western connections (e.g. British tourists among the victims). Though since the World Trade Center attacks of 2001 and the Arab Spring of 2010, journalists have been a little less reluctant to let 'marginal' countries lie idle, particularly if it is possible that terrorism or insurrection is brewing behind closed doors. Nonetheless, the chances of broadcast for any news story will be increased if dramatic video footage is available—this can be measured by public donations to the disaster. For example, when cyclone 05B hit Orissa in 1999 it was estimated that around 10,000 people died and 15 million people were affected. A year later the Mozambique floods caused 700 deaths and affected some 2 million people. However, despite suffering more than ten times the number of deaths to Mozambique, the Orissa disaster only raised £7 million in aid in comparison to Mozambique's £31 million (Eaton 2001). This disparity can be ascribed to the lack of dramatic imagery of the Orissa disaster. In contrast, Mozambique received unprecedented levels of media attention and dramatic scenes of helicopter rescues etc. More rarely, if the journalistic approach is more innovative or unusual it can generate viewers' interest. This might depend upon individual journalists choosing to champion a particular cause that they feel should be of public concern (see Wright 2011).

WINDS OF CHANGE

The first decade of the twenty-first century wrought havoc with the systems that supported and nurtured the journalism industry, challenging
many of the sacred cows that underpinned the modern practice of reporting news. Old ways of working...became increasingly obsolete while new
supply models remained nascent and untested.

Jones and Salter 2012: 73

On 26 December 2004 the 9.3 magnitude Sumatra–Andaman earthquake created a
massive tsunami wave (as high as 25m) that killed about 300,000 people around the
Indian Ocean the area covering a wide arc from Indonesia to South Africa. The disaster
displaced about 1.7 million persons (Rofi, Doocy, and Robinson 2006: 340). However
the scale, locations, and duration of the disaster had a profound effect on the media
coverage. First, no one could immediately determine the exact location of the disaster to focus the media reporting. Second, 'amateur' coverage of the disaster reached
unprecedented levels, particularly in those areas populated by tourists, because of the
recent and rapid proliferation of video recording capabilities of mobile phones that
increasingly characterize modern communications. However, this phenomenon had
negative result in creating a distorted picture—giving the false impression that these
were the worst-hit areas. As a consequence, news organizations first concentrated their
efforts on the areas from where the pictures emerged; meanwhile the worse affected
'non-tourist' areas remained invisible so were largely ignored until weeks after the
initial impact of the tsunami. This compounded the Western news media's tendency
to focus on disasters that involve westerners, such as tourists who get caught up in
events—revealing hierarchies of inequality in media attention (see also Gibney 1999;
Joye 2011).

Third, the disaster demanded coverage of a vast geographical area for such a long
duration (to sustain media attention) that about ten days into the disaster, journalists
had run-out of stock headlines, metaphors, computer simulations, and picture clichés.
There was danger that the constant repetition of the same old images, would result in
severe 'compassion fatigue' for viewers. Ironically, some newspapers were forced to take
a much more adventurous line and, to maintain readership interest and attention, began
to produce reports and imagery that would not look out of place in a contemporary art
gallery (see Wright 2008: 133–5). Indeed the 2004 Sumatran tsunami was so large in
scale that the news media could hardly cope and had been tested to the limits. However,
the most obvious change in disaster coverage was the mainstream media's high reliance
on amateur footage, which provided key images functioning in a headline capacity for
news broadcasts worldwide. The substantial increase and wide (albeit uneven) distribution of this form of technology (Zickuhr and Smith 2012), accompanied by considerable improvements in broadcastable quality images established the 'citizen journalist'
as an essential component in the chain of news gathering, as well as instigating a new

'eye-witness' aesthetic of the shaky amateurish hand-held camera style of the mobile phone often accompanied by ad hoc spontaneous and panicky commentary.

CITIZEN JOURNALISTS AND REFUGEE JOURNALISTS

> The reality is that if you have an iPhone with a 3G service you can pretty much be a broadcaster.
>
> Jon Williams, BBC World News editor

The changes in media technology mean that both journalists and 'ordinary' citizens, possessing such equipment as smartphones and iPads, have the ability to capture and broadcast images of events as they happen. While the kind of footage recorded by tourists or User Generated Content (UGC) during the Sumatran Tsunami was opportunist and unsystematic, achieved more by luck than judgement, some of the material was undoubtedly unique and provided 'breaking news', but did not necessarily reflect journalistic research, strategy, or contextualization. Furthermore, video material produced by these means is not always trustworthy or representative of the overall state of affairs.

The citizen journalist is one who is engaged in 'participatory journalism'. Bowman and Willis define this as:

> The act of a citizen, or group of citizens, playing an active role in the process of collecting, reporting, analyzing and disseminating news and information. The intent of this participation is to provide independent, reliable, accurate, wide-ranging and relevant information that a democracy requires. (Bowman and Willis 2003: 9)

However, in reality, the very concept of the 'citizen journalist' is quite imprecise. As we find a middle-ground, between 'journalists' and 'citizen journalists', occupied by the *freelancers* who range from experienced seasoned reporters to anyone who happens to buy a camera, a plane ticket and turns up with his/her backpack at the scene of a war or humanitarian disaster. This was the case with the recent Libyan revolution with some 400 such reporters based in Benghazi. According to Hannah Storm of the International News Safety Institute, 'there has been this blurring of what it means to be a journalist, with the rise of citizen journalism and journalist-activists...coming at the same time that journalists are increasingly being targeted around the world' (quoted in Beaumont 2011). Indeed Jon Williams (BBC) will reject material, no matter how good, if he suspects the 'journalist' has taken unnecessary risks in order to acquire the story or footage (Williams 2012). While Western media organizations are cutting back on foreign reporting, gaps are most likely to be filled by untrained citizen/freelance opportunists and the problems associated with riskily acquired material are likely to escalate. So while UGC does not operate in a journalistic context, unable to provide broader contextualization, it is not required to fit into journalistic ethical guidelines. Most news organizations take the opinion that UGC should only be used if nothing better is available 'you should only run them if you've got nothing else' (Witschge 2012: 124). And among journalists a general view exists that UGC is of limited value just to supply pictures to give a competitive advantage and to 'aid to authenticity' (Witschge 2012: 126). This type of visual imagery is likely to be far from the considered investigative fact-finding use of the camera in the tradition of documentary film, for example, more a type of moving-image snap-shot that can provide wallpaper imagery to accompany journalistic comment.

For the representation of refugees, the likely outcomes for the use of UGC are that the citizen journalists will operate on a simple point-and-shoot policy, believing the camera will provide a transparent record of events, or they will consciously attempt to emulate mainstream news reports gained through their familiarity with watching news—not through a broader understanding of the story gained through research. However, as in the tsunami example, UGC divides the 'haves' from the 'have nots' with regard to mobile phone ownership and while some relatively well-to-do refugees may be able to provide UGC of their own state of forced migration, others will remain invisible. However, refugees and internally displaced persons (IDPs) attempting to report on their own conditions may be facing increased dangers of their own. While 'conventional' journalists have an increased ability to be 'on the spot' with mobile phones, satellite links, laptops, etc., they are facing increased hostility—another factor affecting the reporting of refugee crises. According to the International News Safety Institute 'One thousand journalists and support staff have died trying to report the news around the world in the past 10 years: an average of two a week' (INSI 2007: 7) and a recent update suggests that the situation has not improved (Storm 2013).

The large international agencies are able to enlist their reporters into hostile environment training schemes, which include role-play on how to cope with dangerous locations, they are also able to provide more accurate assessments of the situation: the likely presence of unexploded ordnance; refusal of visas; illegal entry; 'escape plans'; for example. In addition they have the expertise at hand to assess the 'balanced risk' of the situation. Freelancers (who are prepared to go to less secure environments than staff journalists) and journalists working in their own countries are less likely to be able to obtain such support mechanisms. While much has been made of the harsh treatment that refugees have been given by the media, both 'sides' of the argument have tended to adopt an 'us' and 'them' dichotomy. However it might be a worthwhile reminder that not all refugee crises occur in war zones. And ironically, it is not war zones that have the highest journalist casualties. These occur among journalists working in their own countries and in peacetime. For example the Agence France-Presse (AFP) news agency provides a chilling account of the dangers experienced by newspaper journalists working in the Mexican border town Ciudad Juarez (AFP 2011). Not only do local journalists who might be exposing criminality, corruption, drugs, or human trafficking become targets, but also the authorities are unlikely to investigate the murder of journalists. Such is the extent of this worldwide problem that in 2002 La Maison des Journalistes (The House of Journalists) was set up in Paris to provide a temporary sanctuary for journalists who have become refugees themselves fleeing persecution in their home countries (Thisse 2008).

THE REFUGEE MEDIA EXPERIENCE

The 'flip-side' of this unstable state of affairs where journalists fleeing repression have been forced to become refugees, is where refugees themselves take up journalism to promote their cause. In this context, the 'new technologies' have created another kind of opportunity for 'citizen journalism' with refugee communities actively using the media to assist members of their own community as well as heighten awareness of their situation to a wider public. This opens up the possibilities that citizen journalists can redress the balance of inaccurate reporting whereby refugees generate their own positive news reporting.

For example, the Karenni migrant community in Houston has been proactive in its own use of the media through engagement with local 'traditional' media as well the use of the Internet. In 2012 the Business section of the local newspaper *The Houston Chronicle* included a review of a visual arts exhibition of textiles produced by Karenni immigrants (Luks 2012). The exhibition 'Weaving Home: Textile Traditions from Houston's Karenni Community'[3] provided a valuable example of how unique cultural characteristics of an immigrant group could be used to create a positive refugee story within the host community. The exhibition functioned as an expression of identity and drew upon the cultural resources of the refugees. It had created an inroad into the local business economy based on the Karenni's skills and cultural traditions. Furthermore, the Houston press coverage did not limit itself to discussing arts and crafts. It gave a fair and factual (if brief) report of the Burmese political situation that included interviews with Karenni speaking freely about the repression they had escaped. In general, it constituted a refreshing break from usual patterns of local news media coverage of refugees: using a 'human interest' media opportunity to 'hook' readers, and via a local business concern, to move on the story to address a wider international social and political issue.

However, in view of the wide distribution of Karenni resettled across the state of Texas, the community itself has used the Internet to maintain contact through the *Karenni Connection BlogSpot*[4] and the online *Shadaw Journal*[5]. The websites feature 'the hardships, opportunities, and daily lifestyles our Karenni people are facing in America' not only for those who have resettled, but also for Karenni in refugee camps and those still living in Myanmar.[6] The *Shadaw Journal* website also features aspects of Karenni popular culture: cartoons, fashion, job adverts, music and video downloads. Furthermore, the idea of the Karenni taking charge of their own media representations is not limited to those resettled in the West. Linked to the BlogSpot initiative is the *Kantarawaddy Times* (*KT*) started in 2004 by a group of exiled Karenni based in Thailand:

> we believe in providing accurate, fair and balanced news...KT is also dedicated to the impartial documentation of the current situation in Burma, and its members are

driven by the desire to promote democracy in all Burma while giving a voice to all Karenni people. In addition to this website, KT publishes a monthly newspaper in Burmese and Karenni, broadcasts radio news in Karenni each week, runs a training program for budding Karenni journalists, and sends out news releases over email.[7]

The hard-copy newspaper and website provide information, discussion space, links to other sites of potential interest, and a sense of social cohesion for the entire Karenni diaspora whether still living in Myanmar, in Thai refugee camps, or those resettled in Finland, New Zealand, and the USA. Indeed it forms a central hub for the kind of 'poly-media' referred to by Medianou and Miller at the beginning of this chapter.[8]

The editorial offices of the *Kantarawaddy Times* can be found in a remote village in the Shan Hills, close to the Burmese border and some 26 km from the town of Mae Hong Son. Though lacking running water and modern sanitation, a small wooden house is equipped with an Internet connection and half a dozen laptop computers. From there the newspaper is assembled and transmitted to the printers. Later, hard copies arrive to be distributed among the Karenni in the Thai refugee camps. In con-trast to media communications of the pre-digital era, stories are not only dissemi-nated amongst the Karenni diaspora, but also along the entire refugee trail from those still living in the villages in the remote mountains of the Burmese/Thai border to those starting a new way of life in the Western urban metropolis. Within a generation the Karenni working on the website and publication have leap-frogged twentieth-century technologies based on the Industrial Revolution and embraced digital media in a global network.

With a recent relaxation of the Burmese regime's grip on the country the *KT* is now freely distributed in the Karenni regions of Myanmar/Burma, though this is on the condition that the Rangoon authorities can keep an eye on its contents. So the *KT* is not fully independent and for its funding the journal and website have relied on Internews: 'an international non-profit organization whose mission is to empower local media worldwide to give people the news and information they need, the ability to connect and the means to make their voices heard.'[9] Internews provided the initial training in journalism that encouraged the small group of Karenni to launch the paper and supported its production and distribution in formative years. Internews continues to provide follow-up training in journalism making an important contribution, given the rapid changes in communications technology. Notwithstanding, the *KT* staff are finding that grant applications and fundraising to keep the network alive account for more of their time.

One key motivation for groups creating their own media stems from dissatisfac-tion with the existing 'official' media channels and the Karenni use of the media is by no means unique. Madianou and Miller's study of the Filipino diaspora suggests an increasing global dependency on new forms of communication among migrant groups. Furthermore, 'home grown' digital media can have the added benefit of increasing agency and boosting self-esteem (Couldry 2012).

Conclusions

Worldwide, the present political landscape is in a state of flux and unrest. This has led to changing patterns of human migration. At the same time, technological innovation moving from the analogue to the digital has resulted in dramatic changing patterns in the 'media landscape'. Overall the picture remains discriminatory in that it depends on refugees' access to technology. Yet it also depends upon journalistic training if this brand of citizen journalism is to produce balanced, accurate, informative, and meaningful reports and does not follow the prejudicial patterns of some of the mainstream media outlets. So while some refugees remain passive victims to Western media reporting, others possess substantial opportunities in gaining control of a more democratized media. At the same time, it is essential to remain alert to the negative accounts of Western media reporting and maintain pressure on media institutions to be responsible in their coverage of migration issues. Media reports, which do not always reflect the reality of the situation, have a strong effect on public opinions, but people's perceptions can determine the reality. From an optimistic perspective, it may be that the new 'social media' could provide a platform to bring together mainstream public opinion and refugee voices (Sigona, this volume). In the future it may prove to be a key factor in developing a positive media attitude to refugees and forced migrants.

Notes

1. The author wishes to thank Say Reh Soe of the *Kantarawaddy Times* and Oo Reh Sor of the Karenni Community of Texas for their help and valuable cooperation in the preparation of this chapter.
2. <http://www.bbc.co.uk/editorialguidelines/page/guidelines-impartiality-introduction>.
3. <http://www.youtube.com/watch?v=bMg9ofCSxos>.
4. <http://www.karenniconnection.blogspot.com>.
5. <http://journal.shadaw.net>.
6. For a detailed a count of the Karenni media experience see Gawthrop 2009. In contrast, an interesting autobiographical account from the Kayan (Padaung) perspective can be found in Pascal Khoo Thwe's *From the Land of Green Ghosts* (2002). It provides a first-hand view of the hill tribe experience of the Myanmar regime.
7. <http://www.ktimes.org>.
8. Not only does Horst (2006) describe the use of new media by Somali refugees, but also she finds the internet provides the kind of interaction that facilitates research into refugee diasporas.
9. <http://www.internews.org>.

REFERENCES

Agence France-Presse (AFP) News agency (2011) 'A Life of Danger for Mexico's Journalists'. Online report 22 June. <http://www.youtube.com/watch?v=e6Vsxgf4eQg&feature=rel mfu> (accessed 6 June 2012).

Beaumont, P. (2011) 'Reporting Libya: Freelance Coverage, Full-Time Dangers'. *The Guardian* Sunday 13 November. <http://www.guardian.co.uk/media/2011/nov/13/reporting-li bya-freelance-dangers> (accessed 6 June 2012).

Bowman, S., and Willis, C. (2003) *We Media: How Audiences are Shaping the Future of News and Information.* Reston, VA: The Media Center at the American Press Institute.

Bradimore, A., and Bauder, H. (2011) 'Mystery Ships and Risky Boat People: Tamil Refugee Migration in the Newsprint Media'. *Canadian Journal of Communication* 36: 637–61.

Buerk, M. (2008) On this Day 1950–2005 Correspondents. <http://news.bbc.co.uk/onthisday/ hi/correspondents/newsid_2626000/2626349.stm> (accessed 6 June 2012).

Couldry, N. (2012) *Media, Society, World: Social Theory and Digital Media Practice.* Cambrdge: Polity.

Danziger, N. (2005) 'History in the Raw'. *The Times* 3 September: 12–13.

Eaton, I. (2001). *A Choice of Disasters: BBC Television News Coverage of Earthquakes, Storms and Floods.* Oxford: Reuters Institute for the Study of Journalism.

Gawthrop, D. (2009) 'Circumventing the Junta:How Burmese Exiles Use Independent Media to Foster Civic Culture and Promote Democracy'. MA dissertation. Royal Roads UniversityVictoria, Canada.

Gibney, M. J. (1999) 'Kosovo and Beyond: Popular and Unpopular Refugees'. *Forced Migration Review* 5 August: 28–9.

Greenslade, R. (2005) *Seeking Scapegoats: The Coverage of Asylum in the UK Press.* London: Institute for Public Policy Research.

The Hague Process on Refugees and Migration (2012) *GLOBAL HEARING on Refugees and Migration.* Report on meeting 4–5 June 2012. The Hague. <http://www.un.org/esa/ population/meetings/eleventhcoord2013/THP-Global_Hearing_Report_2012.pdf>.

Horst, C. (2006). 'In "Virtual Dialogue" with the Somali Community: The Value of Electronic Media for Research amongst Refugee Diasporas'. *Refuge* 23(1): 51–7.

ICAR (Information Centre about Asylum and Refugees) (2012) 'Asylum Seekers, Refugees and Media'. <http://www.icar.org.uk/Asylum_Seekers_and_Media_Briefing_ICAR.pdf> (accessed 22 January 2013).

INSI (2007) *Killing the Messenger: The Deadly Cost of News.* Brussels: International News Safety Institute.

Jones, J., and Salter, L. (2012) *Digital Journalism.* Los Angeles: Sage Publications.

Joye, S. (2011) 'The Hierarchy of Global Suffering'. *Journal of International Communication* 15(2): 45–61.

Kaur, K. (2007) 'Media Reporting on Refugees in Malaysia'. *UNEAC Asia Papers* 13: 8–12.

Luks, J. (2012) 'The Art of Survival: *Weaving Home* Reveals the Courage of Houston's Karenni Refugees in Cloth'. *Houston Chronicle* 23 May.

Madianou, M., and Miller, D. (2012) *Migration and New Media: Transnational Families and Polymedia.* London: Routledge.

Malkki, L. H. (1996) 'Speechless Emissaries: Refugees, Humanitarianism, and Dehistoricization'. *Current Anthropology* 11(3): 377–404.

Marash, D. (1995) 'Big Story, Small Screen'. *Columbia Journalism Review* July/August: 9.9–10.

Oxfam (2007) *Forward Together: Ideas for Working with Asylum Seekers, Refugees, the Media and Communities*. Oxford.

Pickering, S. (2001) 'Common Sense and Original Deviancy: News Discourses and Asylum Seekers in Australia'. *Journal of Refugee Studies* 14(2): 169–86.

Robinson, P. (1999) 'The CNN Effect: Can the News Media Drive Foreign Policy?' *Review of International Studies* 25: 301–9.

Rofi, A., Doocy, S., and Robinson, C. (2006) 'Tsunami Mortality and Displacement in Aceh Province, Indonesia'. *Disasters* 30(3): 340–50.

Seu, B. I. (2003) 'The Woman with the Baby: Exploring Narratives of Female Refugees'. *Feminist Review* 72: 158–65.

Storm, H. (2013) 'Journalist Safety: Killing the Messenger'. 4 March. <http://www.fairobserver.com/article/journalist-safety-killing-messenger> (accessed 20 March 2013).

Sulaiman-Hill, C. M. R., Thomson, S. C., Afsar, R., and Hodliffe, T. L. (2011) 'Changing Images of Refugees: A Comparative Analysis of Australian and New Zealand Print Media 1998–2008'. *Journal of Immigration and Refugee Studies*: 345–66.

Thisse, T. (2008) 'A Refuge for Refugee Journalists in the Heart of France'. *UNHCR News Stories* 6 May. <http://www.unhcr.org/481b4b304.html> (accessed 6 June 2012).

Thwe, P. K. (2002) *From the Land of Green Ghosts: A Burmese Odyssey*. London: Harper Collins.

Williams, J. (2012) Interviewed in radio broadcast *Life and Death on the Frontline*. A Perfectly Normal Production for BBC Radio 4, London. Producer: Richard Clemmow. 20:00 Tuesday 1 May. 38 minutes.

Witschge, T. (2012) 'Changing Audiences, Changing Journalism'. Pp 117–34 in P. Lee-Wright, A. Phillips, and T. Witschge (eds.), *Changing Journalism*. London: Taylor & Francis.

Wright, T. (2002) 'Moving Images: The Media Representation of Refugees'. *Visual Studies* 17(1): 53–66.

Wright, T. (2004) 'Collateral Coverage: Media Images of Afghan Refugees, 2001'. *Visual Studies* 19(1): 97–111.

Wright, T. (2008) *Visual Impact: Culture and the Meaning of Images*. Oxford: Berg.

Wright, T. (2011) 'Press Photography and Visual Rhetoric'. Pp. 317–36 in E. Margolis and L. Pauwels (eds.), *The SAGE Handbook of Visual Research Methods*. London: Sage.

Zickuhr, K., and Smith, A. (2012) *Digital Differences*. Pew Research Center's Internet & American Life Project. <http://pewinternet.org/Reports/2012/Digital-differences.aspx>.

PART VI

RETHINKING DURABLE SOLUTIONS

CHAPTER 37

....

RETHINKING 'DURABLE' SOLUTIONS

....

KATY LONG

INTRODUCTION

....

THE international refugee regime was designed not just to protect refugees, but to *solve* refugee crises. However, in recent years researchers, policymakers and practitioners have become increasingly concerned about the failures of traditional 'durable solutions'. This has prompted a new drive to develop innovative approaches to solving refugee crises. In particular, there has been a surge of interest in the role that migration and mobility might play in improving life in exile and resolving displacement (UNHCR 2008a; Long 2009, 2010, 2013a).

This chapter examines why conventional solutions to refugee and IDP crises can be said to have failed, and asks whether migration might offer a 'fourth solution' to complement the conventional trinity of repatriation, local integration, and resettlement. Can refugees become migrants—and does this offer a novel solution for those otherwise trapped in protracted displacement?

This chapter argues that to escape the trap of protracted displacement, we must first rethink the problem, recognizing the inherent 'sedentary bias' that shapes state-centred responses to migration during conflict and crisis (see Bakewell 2008). The failure to 'solve' forced migration reflects in part the deliberate construction of the 'refuge problem' in terms of physical dislocation, rather than focusing on the denial or refugee and IDPs' political rights as citizens. Yet in fact, freedom of movement may offer important opportunities for the displaced (and other poor citizens in underdeveloped states) to obtain access to the full set of rights, goods, and services (especially social and economic) that are needed to live a good life. Far from being 'the problem', migration may actually be part of the solution.

The chapter is divided into five parts. It first considers how conventional solutions—repatriation, local integration, and resettlement—have failed to unlock protracted crises. It then argues that to rethink solutions, we must first understand how the international community has chosen to frame the 'refugee problem'. Third, the chapter considers recent developments in both research and policy that have argued for an incorporation migration and mobility into the international community's framing of 'solutions'. The fourth part of the chapter considers how a migration-centred approach to durable solutions might help to reframe long-term displacement as a development, and not just a humanitarian challenge. The fifth section of the chapter then explores attempts to implement official mobility-centred solutions strategies in West Africa and Afghanistan. The chapter concludes by considering the prospects for successful implementation of such a mobility-focused strategy given contemporary political hostility towards general migration flows.

THE FAILURE OF CONVENTIONAL SOLUTIONS

Resolving refugee crises—restoring the 'normal' order of things after the disruption of sudden, traumatic displacement—is in the obvious interests of both refugees and states. When appointed High Commissioner for Russian refugees in 1921, Fridtjof Nansen's primary task was (alongside determining their legal status) to facilitate the resolution of the refugee crisis by securing the refugees' 'emigration or repatriation' (League of Nations 1921). UNHCR's statute mandates the agency to seek 'permanent solutions for the problems of refugees' (UNGA 1950).

Conventional accounts repeat the mantra that there are three 'durable solutions' that can bring refugees' exile to an end. These are repatriation (return to the country of origin), local integration (permanent residency or naturalization in the first country of asylum) and resettlement (ordered migration to a third country). However, as the following chapters by Hammond (repatriation), Hovil (local integration), and Van Selm (resettlement) make clear, all three solutions face serious challenges.

Repatriation—which remains the 'ideal solution' for many policymakers, is often neither possible—due to continuing conflict and instability—nor desirable—especially for younger and second generation refugees who may often not know the 'home' to which they are returning (see Long 2013a). States' continued support for repatriation as the *best* solution arguably reflects their own political interests in retaining a 'national order of things', rather than a concern with refugees' welfare (Malkki 1995). As Hovil argues, local integration is not so much the 'forgotten solution' as the forbidden solution: a reality which occurs between and beneath laws which are deliberately intended to prevent refugees mixing with host communities and restrict access to citizenship. Van Selm underlines that resettlement numbers are tiny—UNHCR estimates only 1 per cent of refugees will benefit from a resettlement place.

The result, as Milner's chapter in this Handbook underlines, is that today some seven million refugees—over two-thirds of all registered refugees—are trapped in a 'long-lasting and intractable state of limbo' (UNHCR 2004). These protracted refugees' lives are not necessarily at risk: but their access to more than 'bare life' beyond a humanitarian space of exception is strictly curtailed. Quite clearly, the traditional 'solutions' are not enough.

In addition, any new twenty-first-century approach to 'solutions' needs to consider the particular challenges involved in solving internal displacement. A durable solution for IDPs is usually described as 'when internally displaced persons no longer have any specific assistance and protection needs that are linked to their displacement and can enjoy their human rights without discrimination on account of their displacement' (UNGA 2009). This can involve return and reintegration in their place of origin, sustainable integration in a host community, or resettlement to a new location (within the state). As with refugees, however, the numbers of IDPs trapped in prolonged displacement are indicative of many IDPs' inability to access these solutions and states' interests in prioritizing return over integration. The non-discrimination benchmark focuses attention on the need to secure equal citizenship, but also raises new questions about the role of the international community and in particular the interface between humanitarian and development actors in brokering sustainable solutions for displaced populations. Can the international community talk of durable solutions if these only return IDPs to an level of suffering in extreme poverty and insecurity endured equally by all citizens?

Rethinking the Problem

It seems clear that conventional solutions are failing to free the majority of refugees and IDPs from protracted displacement. The question that must be asked is: why? At least three potential obstacles can be identified: an excessive focus on repatriation as the *only* viable solution; a failure to engage with broader development issues in refugee-producing and refugee-hosting regions, and a tendency to focus on the physical symptoms of displacement rather than the political causes.

The claim that the existing durable solutions framework is in urgent need of revision is not new. In the late 1980s and 1990s, the shift to prioritize refugee repatriation over resettlement provoked a set of critiques from experts (see e.g. Chimni 2004). These commentators warned that the new push for 'durable solutions' was in fact intended to open up the space for the practice of early repatriation and even containment, in order to reduce Western states' physical burden-sharing responsibilities. Most researchers, however, have tended to critique the specific dynamics of repatriation, local integration, or resettlement separately, rather than focus upon the concept of 'durable solutions' as an integrated whole (for an account of these critiques, see Van Selm, Hovil, and Hammond, this volume).

In recent years, however, academics have returned to question once again the structures of the durable solutions framework, in particular arguing that the continued fixation on three separate solutions by today's policymakers fails to recognize a fundamental need to move away from understanding all solutions simply in terms of 'fixing' people in places. As early as 2003, Van Hear argued for a shift in policymaking to encompass transnational diaspora, and a new language of 'enduring solutions' to better capture the continued fluidity of displacement and migration:

> If transnational activities across locations at home and in exile are [this] pervasive... does the continued use of the categories home, country of first asylum, and resettlement country, which accompany the notion of 'durable solutions', make sense? (Van Hear 2003)

More recently, Long has also argued that 'host and donor states have remained excessively fixed on permanent physical returns of the displaced as "the" solution to exile' (Long 2011). She argues that this imbalance must be redressed: first by recognizing the possible roles migration and mobility can play in securing rights for the displaced, and then by considering how the international community can work to ensure the protection of freedom of movement. For Long and Van Hear, as well as a growing number of other researchers, addressing the failure of the traditional durable solutions framework therefore requires not just a rethinking of the solution, but also a rethinking of the 'refugee problem'.

Policy instruments frequently refer to the need to solve 'the refugee problem' (e.g. ECOSOC 1958). Yet in fact, this turn of phrase is misleading, because it implies that displacement can be viewed as a single, structural problem. In fact, we should ask more questions: *which* structures, and *whose* problem? Refugee and state perspectives on the problems displacement creates are often very different: it follows they are likely to demand very different solutions.

For host states, refugees are beyond all else *foreigners* on their *territory*, threatening to disrupt political and social order by competing with existing citizens for (limited) resources. Host states therefore understand their 'refugee problem' as a *physical* problem, requiring the removal of refugees—and ideally, their return to their state of origin, restoring the 'normal' order of nation states. Yet as the seminal work of Arendt (1967) reminds us, to focus on the physical symptom of displacement distracts us from recognizing that the refugee's or IDP's problem is fundamentally one of political exclusion. Physical dislocation may result in very real suffering, but it is only a reflection a broader inability to access the rights of citizenship. Refugees' views of their 'problem' underline that, for the vast majority of the displaced, any 'solution' is best understood in terms of realizable rights, providing the possibility of leading a dignified and autonomous life: physical security, a livelihood, opportunities for education and development. The solution to refugees' problems, then, is political inclusion, rather than physical removal.

Any successful reimagining of durable solutions—assuming success is to be measured in the number of refugees able to escape protracted exile—must therefore wrestle with these two very different understandings of the 'refugee problem', one physical and one political. Yet these approaches are perhaps less far apart than might initially be considered the case. Both suggest a need to reframe 'durable solutions' not just as the end of humanitarian action, but an integral part of a continuing long-term and imperfect development and peace-building process. How, then, might this be achieved? One possible answer—which has been the focus on increasing interest from both policymakers and researchers in recent years—is to consider the roles that migration and mobility might play in allowing refugees to move *between* places, building their own solutions.

Refugees and Migration: A New Policy Arena?

Recent Developments: A New Approach?

Policymakers' interest in the contribution migration and mobility-centred approaches could make in the search for durable solutions has grown significantly since 2007, in part because of increasing concern with what are termed mixed migration flows (see Squire and Scheel, this volume). These shifts can be traced in part through a study of UNHCR policy documents. In 2008, a discussion paper prepared for that year's High Commissioner's Dialogue on protracted refugee situations noted that:

> Refugees…could perhaps be admitted to the migrant worker and immigration programmes maintained by states that are unable to meet their own labour market needs. Many of these programmes, it should be noted, also offer opportunities for long-term residence and naturalisation, and thus offer the prospect of a durable solution as well as an interim one. (UNHCR 2008a)

Earlier that year, UNHCR's new *Return and Reintegration Policy* had also stressed that post-return migration—often from a rural to an urban setting—should not be viewed in itself as proof of the failure of return (UNHCR 2008b). A year later, UNHCR's Resettlement Service, with Sweden as co-chair, presented a paper at the Annual Tripartite Consultations on Resettlement in Geneva, suggesting that resettlement states should consider opening up parallel migration channels for suitably qualified refugees. In September 2012, UNHCR and ILO held a joint two-day workshop to further consider the possible engagement of refugees as labour migrants. Moving from migration-friendly policy words to mobility-centred active practice, however, has proved far more difficult.

These policy developments have been mirrored by growing evidence from researchers regarding the normative, empirical, and political value of reconsidering the relationship between refugees and migration (e.g. Monsutti 2008; Chatelard 2010). In particular, ethnographic studies of the ways in which refugees and IDPs already use migration to secure income (particularly through trade), attend schools, and lay the foundations for a gradual and sustainable repatriation from Afghanistan to Somalia to Sudan have helped to reinforce these policy shifts, and underlined the extent to which distinctions between refugee and migrant are policy constructions rather than observed realities.

However, just as critiques of durable solutions are not new, this recent interest in rethinking durable solutions by adopting a migration-centred approach is not as new or radical as is sometimes claimed. In fact, early international efforts to solve Europe's interwar refugee crises were centred on facilitating refugees' migration. Arguably the greatest achievement of the pre-1950 refugee protection regime, the Nansen passport system was devised to furnish otherwise stateless refugees with a legal identity, in order to allow refugees to move across borders in search of employment. At the outbreak of the Second World War, Nansen passports were recognized by 52 states and had been issued to some 450,000 refugees. It was in fact only in the 1960s that 'refugee' and 'migrant' identities were definitively separated, in part to ensure refugees' humanitarian protection (see Long 2013b).

There is today general agreement that the Convention Travel Document system that succeeded the Nansen passport is now both out-dated and 'dysfunctional' (Author's interviews, 2012 and 2013). Yet the inability of the modern refugee to protect rather than constrain real prospects for refugee mobility should be seen as a serious failing of the modern refugee protection regime and a political choice, rather than an inevitable side-effect of offering humanitarian assistance.

Mobility and Migration: Towards Development-Centred Durable Solutions?

Defending freedom of movement in the abstract is one thing: considering how freedom of movement can contribute in concrete terms to mobility and migration-centred solutions to displacement crises is another. Why might these sorts of mobility and migration-centred approaches offer a viable alternative? Recognizing that displacement is a political and not a physical problem, and that conventional approaches to solving displacement have failed because of this is one thing. It does not immediately follow that *continued* movement is the solution.

Clearly, as the following chapters in this Handbook demonstrate, in the right circumstances, repatriation, local integration, and resettlement can provide a durable solution.

Arguably the crucial difference with a mobility-centred approach is that instead of equating a solution to a displacement crisis with the end of movement (as is the case with traditional approaches to repatriation, local integration, and resettlement), advocates of a mobility-centred approach explicitly couple the undertaking to end forced movement with a different parallel commitment: that individuals should be *free* to move. If we consider repatriation, local integration, and resettlement in turn, we can begin to see that mobility and migration could help to address some of the difficulties faced today in trying to solve protracted displacement.

First, let us take repatriation. As Hammond shows, the most serious obstacle preventing the use of refugee repatriation as a means of ensuring political inclusion is the chronic weakness of many states of origin. These states—even when early peace has been brokered—are often insecure, with poor infrastructure and limited socio-economic absorptive capacity. Even when persecution has ended, poverty may prevent a sustainable return. In other words, repatriation is above all a development (and usually a peace-building) challenge.

This helps to provide some insight into why a migration-centred approach to solving displacement might unlock some protracted crises. The potential for migration to play a role in fostering development is well recognized (Nyberg-Sørensen, Van Hear, and Engberg-Pedersen 2002). The fruits of migration, then, could actually help to strengthen peace-building initiatives and make return more sustainable by providing capital and skills to be transferred back to a country of origin, and by allowing refugees to *choose* when to return (see Hovil 2010; Kaiser 2010).

Turning to local integration, part of the reluctance of developing states to accept refugees' local integration as a formal solution is their conviction that recognizing even long-term refugees as citizens would allow them to make new claims on limited state resources, potentially leading to new conflicts with existing citizen groups. Underlying hostility towards official local integration, then, is partly a response to a humanitarian economy that characterizes and pays for refugees as 'burdens' in settings where local communities are also often neglected or marginalized by underdeveloped or poorly governed states. Again, this suggests that local integration must be viewed as a development issue (see Long 2011; Lindley 2011).

Solving refugee crises by turning refugees into citizens is therefore highly problematic. But if refugees cannot become citizens, could those who have already built businesses or family links integrate as migrants? This approach could build on regional citizenship initiatives (such as common citizenship of the Economic Community of West African States, ECOWAS, or the East African Community, EAC) to allow self-supporting refugees to move outside humanitarian space and work as migrants, circumventing national politics, and laying foundations for development that would benefit both the displaced and their host communities.

The third durable solution, resettlement, is intended to function above all as a form of protection, offering a solution to a limited numbers of refugees selected on the basis of humanitarian need. Yet in essence, resettlement *solves* displacement by offering migration to a limited number of refugees. The value attached to resettlement by refugee communities themselves is expressed not just in terms of safety and protection, but often viewed above all as an opportunity to earn money, access education, and migrate legally to the West (Author's fieldwork, 2012). This is an option which increasing contemporary restrictions in Europe, Australia, and North America on low and medium-skilled extra-regional migration have otherwise removed. Yet opening up new *migration* pathways to the West (to complement existing humanitarian resettlement programmes) could establish new channels for economic and social development, helping to build transnational networks (see Van Hear, this volume).

A migration and mobility-centred approach may therefore offer one means to unlock traditional durable solutions by circumventing political obstacles and directly contributing to development needs. Yet arguably the most important contribution such an approach can make is to challenge the very structure of 'durable solutions', imagined as three separate and distinct options. Migration and mobility may not only enhance existing solutions: they offer a means of connecting them, allowing refugees to build their own composite solutions that reflect complex identities, particularly for those refugees who have spent considerable time in exile and may have family or other social ties to their host community, speak the language, own a business, or attend school there.

Furthermore, not only do migration and mobility break down the distinctions between different solutions, such an approach may help to blur the lines between 'exile' and 'solution', focusing attention of the international community on the need to make displacement itself less traumatic. Accepting mobile, complex identities as an expected result of protracted displacement, and viewing these as an opportunity rather than a threat allows 'solutions' to displacement to better reflect the coping strategies that displaced communities establish during exile. These frequently rely upon mobility between a place of economic production (usually the place of origin) and a place of protection. Congolese in Uganda, Iraqi refugees in Jordan, and Afghans in Pakistan all often practise 'commuter' displacement, returning frequently to check on family or landholdings (Monsutti 2008; Chatelard 2010; Author's fieldwork, 2012). IDPs may travel frequently between towns (sites of protection) and rural villages (sites of economic production). Across nearly all displacement crises, evidence from practitioners and anthropologists is clear: movement is a normal, rational coping strategy for populations with scarce resources and migration patterns often pre-date current conflicts, drawing on traditional seasonal and temporary routes as well as existing transnational diaspora. This suggests that it is international interventions in refugee and IDP crises, and international approaches that frame durable solutions as an *end* to migration, that need to adapt if such solutions are to better meet the needs of the displaced.

Mobility and Migration as Solutions to Displacement in Practice

In the past decade, there has been greater recognition of refugees' and IDPs' existing use of mobility and migration—often through informal channels—to carve out some form of 'enduring solution'. However, it is far more difficult to identify formal programmes that have incorporated mobility and migration. This in part reflects the fact that while humanitarian actors have been prepared to recognize the *potential* value of migration in solving protracted displacement, states have been far more cautious. Many states are reluctant to move away from repatriation-focused strategies because of the political costs that are seen to be associated with allowing refugees to become migrants in a host state (widespread popular hostility and xenophobia can be observed from the UK to Kenya to Pakistan) or because the return of refugees is closely associated with the return of peace and stability and the end of conflict.

Nevertheless, a few limited initiatives suggest that a mobility-centred approach to resolving refugee and IDP crises can play an important role in addressing residual casel-oads, in acknowledging long-term development challenges in countries of origin, and in recognizing the particular needs of long-term (including second- and third-generation) displaced, who may often wish to restore or maintain links with their country of origin and a long-term host community.[1]

Regional citizenship structures have offered one means of putting mobility-centred solutions into practice. Regional citizenship is most developed in the European Union, but West and East African communities also grant the citizens of member states freedom to move, reside, and work throughout a region. In particular, pre-existing ECOWAS freedom of movement protocols were used between 2007 and 2010 to broker a solution for residual caseloads of Sierra Leonean and Liberian refugees in Nigeria and the Gambia.

Following the end of the brutal Liberian and Sierra Leonean civil wars in the early 2000s, the majority of refugees repatriated from neighbouring West African states. However a sizeable group—some 117,000 Liberians and 18,000 Sierra Leoneans—did not wish to return, either because they were sceptical about their potential to reinte-grate, or because they had established significant economic and social ties during decades of exile. None of the three traditional durable solutions met these refugees' needs. However, existing ECOWAS citizenship law entitled these refugees to remain in the host communities, as Liberian and Sierra Leonean *migrants*.

In June 2007, a quadripartite agreement was signed for the integration of Liberian and Sierra Leonean refugees in Nigeria. Under the terms of this agreement, the Liberian and Sierra Leonean governments issue passports to those refugees still residing in Nigeria, who are then issued with a three-year renewable ECOWAS residence permit by the Nigerians. A similar programme was later adopted in the Gambia. In taking up these offers, par-ticipating refugees were asked to explicitly confirm that they were voluntarily re-availing themselves of the protection of their country of origin (Multipartite Agreement 2007). This initiative thus used existing legislation designed to further economic development to provide refugees with a composite solution combining local integration with formal repa-triation (but not physical return). As Adepoju, Boulton, and Levin concluded in 2007, this initiative suggests a need to rethink the shape of 'durable solutions':

> Integration is a notion ordinarily associated with permanence. It is thus somewhat counter-intuitive to suppose that integration can be achieved through greater mobil-ity. Yet it is precisely this possibility that the ECOWAS protocols present for refugees who are citizens of one Community country residing in another community coun-try. (Adepoju, Boulton, and Levin 2007: 20)

The other major international initiative intended to help support refugees in securing a durable solution by protecting their mobility has arguably proved less successful. It was quickly recognized by researchers and UNHCR that the sustainability of the massive Afghan repatriation that followed the fall of the Taliban in 2002 would depend on meeting three distinct challenges. First, the majority of Afghan refugees who remained in Pakistan and Iran had been born there, and had a limited desire to return 'home'. Second, the Afghan state was extremely fragile and had limited absorptive capacity. Third, transnational and seasonal migration networks from Afghanistan to Iran and Pakistan had long pre-dated conflict in the region and were a normal part of economic livelihood strategies in the region. A successful solution to the Afghan refugee crisis therefore depended upon accepting significant continued Afghan migration in the region, and in 2003, UNHCR urged that the post-2005 Afghan refugee situation should be addressed not simply as a repatriation exercise, but as a 'migration and development challenge' (UNHCR 2003).

In the ensuing decade, various initiatives have attempted to build a platform for Afghan migration as part of a sustainable peace in the region. This has in part rested upon evidence that facilitating labour migration, particularly of breadwinners, may help to lay the foundations for eventual repatriation by providing access to a sustainable livelihood. In 2007, 2.14 million Afghans in Pakistan were registered not as Afghan refugees, but 'Afghans living in Pakistan' (Tennant 2008). This was seen as a significant step forward.

The impact of such policies, however, has been limited; at least in part because the growing fragility of the Pakistani state and the increasing isolation of Iran mean that both states have continued to insist for political reasons that return is the only option. Since 2010 there has been a renewed insistence on return, with UNHCR facilitating a repatriation 'surge' despite evidence that prospects for sustainable integration are weak, while the Pakistani government has announced plans to revoke Afghans' status in July 2013 with the aim of accelerating repatriation. In Iran, Afghans have been offered a series of limited work-permits (conditional upon surrendering refugee cards and returning non-working family members to Afghanistan). Yet some observers have concluded that this initiative has in fact contributed only to a narrowing of protection space within Iran and turned many refugees into illegal migrants, vulnerable to deportation. This is the direct opposite of what migration and mobility-centred strategies were intended to achieve.

CONCLUSION: NO PANACEA, BUT MANY POSSIBILITIES

The ECOWAS and Afghan cases illustrate both the potential opportunities and pitfalls that mobility-centred strategies offer. Critics have certainly warned of the need to recognize the limits of migration as a 'fourth solution'. Migrant status is not equivalent to citizenship, and the difficult lives faced by many migrant labourers—including potential exploitation by employers and police—mean that migration is no panacea. Some researchers have warned that advocating for refugees to 'become migrants' risks diminishing much-needed protection space in host countries, allowing states to evade their responsibilities under Refugee Law to provide access to work, education, and freedom of movement. Others voice concerns that if migration is seen as an acceptable alternative to sustainable return, such strategies risk substituting one type of forced migration (political) for another (economic).

These are real risks. Yet acknowledging these risks does not mean that we should stop considering how freedom of movement can help provide durable solutions for the displaced. What it does suggest is that we need to not only rethink *solutions*, but also rethink *protection*. Such strategies can make displacement itself better, by allowing the displaced—when they are able—to move beyond humanitarian space and engage in development, exercising choice and autonomy, even if this does not amount to an ideal 'durable solution'.

The restrictions that existing approaches to refugee protection often place on refugees' and IDPs' capacity to move may in fact place those in need of protection at risk of harm. There is little doubt that many forced migrants, faced with economic needs and aspirations that cannot be met through humanitarian care and maintenance, chose to 'solve' their displacement through illegal migration, increasing vulnerability to trafficking and other exploitation. There is also clear evidence that those with financial capital often chose to move as migrants rather than as refugees, avoiding the constraints associated with formal asylum protections and instead living as exiles. In attempting to address prolonged displacement, the first step may thus be to stop talking about solutions, and concentrate instead on making displacement better, making mobility not an end point for displacement, but an integral component of international efforts to maximize refugees' choices.

The real difficulty, however, lies in persuading states that the costs of protracted displacement—of failing to solve refugee crises for generations—are not an acceptable price to pay for the illusion of migration control. States—and their voters—remain firmly committed to a system in which it is the citizen who has the 'right to have rights'. Given the global rise in hostility towards migrant flows since the economic crisis, it is likely that the insistence that refugees should return 'home' will continue, and prospects for a broad embrace of mobility as a key component of development in post-conflict settings look bleak. This is why the best chance for encouraging states to adopt mobility-centred refugee policy is to continue to link migration with repatriation, and to carry out further research to map the ways in which facilitating the mobility of displaced people can contribute to broader development and peace-building aims. For it is clear that the real challenge is not to make a normative case for freedom of movement, but to make it politically possible to implement such a solution in practice.

Note

1. The following case studies are drawn from Long (2009).

References

Adepoju, A., Boulton, A., and Levin, M. (2007) 'Promoting Integration through Mobility: Free Movement and the ECOWAS Protocol'. New Issues in Refugee Research. UNHCR Working Papers. December.

Arendt, H. (1967) *The Origins of Totalitarianism* (2nd edn.). New York: Harvest.

Bakewell, O. (2008) 'Keeping Them in their Place: The Ambivalent Relationship between Development and Migration in Africa'. *Third World Quarterly* 29(7): 1341–58.

Chatelard, G. (2010) 'Cross-Border Mobility of Iraqi Refugees'. *Forced Migration Review* 34: 60–1.

Chimni, B. (2004) 'From Resettlement to Involuntary Repatriation: Towards a Critical History of Durable Solutions to Refugee Problems'. *Refugee Survey Quarterly* 23(3): 55–73.

Hovil, L. (2010) 'Hoping for Peace, Afraid of War: The Dilemmas of Repatriation and Belonging on the Borders of Uganda and South Sudan'. New Issues in Refugee Research. UNHCR Working Paper Series No. 196.

Kaiser, T. (2010) 'Dispersal, Division and Diversification: Durable Solutions and Sudanese Refugees in Uganda'. *Journal of Eastern African Studies* 4(1): 44–60.

League of Nations (1921) *Russian Refugees: Summary of the Documents Received by the Secretariat on this Subject since the 12th Session of the Council*. 16 June. C.126.M.72.1921.VII; LN, Les Réfugiés Russes. Adopted by Council 27 June 1921, C.133l.M.131ust 1921, C.292a.1921.VI.

Lindley, A., and Haslie, A. (2011) 'Unlocking Protracted Displacement: Somali Case Study'. RSC Working Paper No. 79. August.

Long, K. (2009) 'Extending Protection? Labour Migration and Durable Solutions for Refugees'. New Issues in Refugee Research. UNHCR Working Paper Series No. 176. October.

Long, K. (2010) 'Home Alone? A Review of the Relationship between Repatriation, Mobility and Durable Solutions for Refugees'. UNHCR Evaluation. January.

Long, K. (2011) 'Permanent Crises? Unlocking the Protracted Displacement of Refugees and Internally Displaced Persons'. Oxford: RSC. October.

Long, K. (2013a) *The Point of No Return: Refugees, Rights and Repatriation*. Oxford: Oxford University Press.

Long, K. (2013b) 'When Refugees Stopped Being Migrants'. *Journal of Migration Studies* 1(1) (March): 4–26.

Malkki, L. (1995) 'Refugees and Exile: From "Refugee Studies" to the National Order of Things'. *Annual Review of Anthropology* 24: 495–523.

Monsutti, A. (2008) 'Afghan Migratory Strategies and the Three Solutions to the Refugee Problem'. *Refugee Survey Quarterly* 27(1): 558–73.

Multipartite Agreement (2007) Multipartite Agreement for the Integration of Liberian and Sierra Leonean Refugees in Nigeria between the Governments of Liberia, Sierra Leone and Nigeria. ECOWAS.

Nyberg-Sørensen, N., Van Hear, N., and Engberg-Pedersen, P. (2002) *The Migration-Development Nexus: Evidence and Policy Options*. Geneva: IOM.

Tennant, V. (2008) 'Afghan Situation Regional Policy Review'. UNHCR Internal Document. PDES/2008/02. April.

UN Economic and Social Council (ECOSOC) (1958) 'UN Economic and Social Council Resolution 672 (XXV): Establishment of the Executive Committee of the Programme of the United Nations High Commissioner for Refugees'. E/RES/672 (XXV). 30 April.

UN General Assembly (1950) 'Statute of the Office of the United Nations High Commissioner for Refugees'. A/RES/428(V). 14 December. <http://www.unhcr.org/refworld/docid/3ae6b3628.html>.

UN General Assembly (2009) 'Report of the Representative of the Secretary-General on the human rights of internally displaced persons'. Walter Kälin. Addendum: Framework on Durable Solutions for Internally Displaced Persons'. A/HRC/13/21/Add.4, 29 December.

UNHCR (2003). 'Towards a Comprehensive Solution for Displacement from Afghanistan'. July. <http://www.unhcr.org/refworld/docid/3f1be2224.html>.

UNHCR (2004) 'Protracted Refugee Situations'. Executive Committee of the High Commissioner's Programme, Standing Committee, 30th Meeting, UN Doc.EC/54/SC/CRP.14. 10 June: 2.

UNHCR (2008a) 'Protracted Refugee Situations: A Discussion Paper Prepared for the High Commissioner's Dialogue on Protection Challenges'. Geneva. December. <http://www.unhcr.org/492ad3782.html>.

UNHCR (2008b) 'UNHCR's Role in Support of the Return and Reintegration of Displaced Populations: Policy Framework and Implementation Strategy'. February. <http://www.unhcr.org/refworld/docid/47d6a6db2.html>. EC/59/SC/CRP.5.

Van Hear, N. (2003) 'From Durable Solutions to Transnational Relations: Home and Exile among Refugee Diasporas'. UNHCR New Issues in Refugee Research. Working Paper Series No. 83. <http://www.unhcr.org/3e71f8984.html>.

CHAPTER 38

LOCAL INTEGRATION

LUCY HOVIL

INTRODUCTION

As one of the three 'durable solutions' along with repatriation and resettlement, local integration—whereby refugees become full members of their host community in their first country of asylum—has been described as the 'forgotten solution' (Jacobsen 2001). Yet this notion is misleading. At a national and international policy level, local integration is not so much forgotten as evaded. And among refugees, it is very much remembered and acted upon: it is an area in which refugees show their ability to claim for themselves forms of belonging that the wider policy structure often seeks to withhold from them. Therefore, despite official neglect of local integration as a means to ending exile, in situations where repatriation seems unlikely, and where resettlement numbers are highly restricted, it is often the most viable of the three 'solutions'.

In official policy terms, local integration as a *durable solution* is about receiving the citizenship of the country of exile (as opposed to those who are resettled, and for whom obtaining citizenship is something of an assumed outcome of the process). This principle is clearly established in international refugee law through the 1951 UN Refugee Convention, which focuses on the importance of citizenship in achieving durable solutions. According to Article 34 of the Convention, 'the contracting states shall as far as possible facilitate the assimilation and naturalisation of refugees. They shall in particular make every effort to expedite naturalisation proceedings.'[1]

Yet in practice, local integration is about far more—and far less—than the acquisition of citizenship. When refugees, members of the host population, governments, policy-makers, or academics talk about local integration, they are often referring to fundamentally different processes and outcomes. Thus, while governments go to great lengths to ensure that refugees are *not* able to obtain citizenship—and, therefore, do not meet the legal criteria of local integration as an officially sanctioned durable solution—refugees constantly vote with their feet and generate varying levels of locally based integration.

As a result, local integration as broadly understood is hard to define, hard to quantify, hard to categorize, and hard to evaluate.

In order to frame the discussion, this chapter uses two recognized categories of local integration (albeit categories that are neither neat nor exclusive), namely de facto and de jure local integration, as a point of departure. It focuses primarily on refugee situations in Africa, where local integration—both as an idea and a reality—has been particularly salient, and provides valuable lessons for situations in other parts of the world where local integration is being, or should be, pursued.

DE FACTO AND DE JURE INTEGRATION

De facto integration is an informal process that takes place primarily at a local level whereby refugee individuals or groups negotiate belonging in the locality in which they are living. Integration takes place on a spectrum and can function on multiple levels—whether economic, social, cultural, and, at times, political—and is strongly context specific. The relationship between refugees and the host population (often including local government officials) is key to their ability to integrate locally: for instance, their legitimacy to live in the area might be built on localized understandings of belonging that transcend national identities, or through recognition of refugees as a potential asset. However, local integration is characterized by its informality and is often illegal and temporary—although not necessarily so. Therefore, it must not be over-romanticized: while it demonstrates the extraordinary resourcefulness of those who find themselves in exile, it can also leave them vulnerable and lacking in formal mechanisms of protection.

De jure local integration, on the other hand, is primarily about national belonging (despite the misleading notion of 'local'). It is represented by the formal process of obtaining a new citizenship and is an overtly political process. This acquisition of a new national identity represents, at least in theory, the gateway to rights as citizens of that state in as much as citizenship is 'the right to have rights' (Arendt 1986). Legally, therefore, it can be called a durable solution. However, as stated above, this particular option is continually evaded by governments that prefer an approach to citizenship that is both exclusive and protectionist, and instances of naturalization as a means to ending exile are the exception rather than the rule.

Most importantly, however, formal citizenship does not necessarily translate into inclusion for former refugees: the legitimacy to belong is a far more complex process. On the one hand, local belonging is unstable without national recognition: localized forms of integration have the potential to be undermined should external circumstances change. On the other, national citizenship holds little promise if individuals and groups fail to be accepted within a particular locality.

This chapter therefore argues that in order to deliver on its promise as a genuinely *durable* solution whereby former refugees have access to the full ambit of rights due any citizen of the country (the right to have rights is not synonymous with citizenship, but the former is strongly contingent upon the latter), local integration *in practice* needs to take place at both a local and national level.

LOCAL INTEGRATION IN THE LITERATURE

Literature on local integration is characterized broadly by its neglect. As Fielden states, 'local integration is actually not a forgotten solution, but an undocumented one' (2008: 1). In many respects this is not surprising given the nature of local integration which, for the most part, has been de facto (and therefore off the official policy radar and hard to quantify), rather than de jure (legally achieved and therefore quantifiable).

In the case of de facto integration—which generally takes place outside of, and in defiance of, the settlement structure—relatively little is known about the millions of refugees who have opted out of the system and chosen to self-settle within the host population, in direct contrast to the ample documentation that exists on the problems associated with the encampment of refugees (Hovil 2007). This lack of information reflects a global trend in which self-settled and urban refugees have remained relatively under-researched, despite the fact that the majority of refugees in Africa have opted out of the settlement system (Bakewell 2005).

More recently, however, there has been growing interest in the potential for local integration as a durable solution, particularly in the context of so-called 'protracted' refugee contexts (Crisp 2004). A growing body of literature has emerged that focuses on self-settled refugees and their strategies towards local integration, documenting the economic, social, and cultural processes of unofficial integration that have been taking place (Refugee Law Project working paper series; Jacobsen and Landau 2003; Briant and Kennedy 2004).

Much of this literature—which also talks about the closely related notion of 'self-reliance'—emphasizes the extent to which local integration, particularly economic and social integration (but not exclusively so), takes place *despite* government and international refugee policy, not because of it, and points to the ways in which refugees seek out their own forms of protection that official structures fail to meet. For instance Sommers (2001) talks of the unrecognized and unrealized potential of refugee youth living in Dar es Salaam, alienated by their lack of official recognition and the fact that the policy environment forces them to hide, while Sperl (2001) critiques UNHCR's reluctance to provide assistance to urban refugees, particularly where they are unable to reach self-reliance.

From the perspective of de jure integration, examples that might be documented are few and far between. Documented cases of formally sanctioned local integration processes taking place include a situation in which a residual group of Mozambicans remained in Malawi post-repatriation (Ferris 1996), and the situation of Liberians in Côte d'Ivoire where the government opposed the settlements policy and allowed refugees to settle freely among the population (Harrell-Bond 2002). Indeed, there

are indications that governments in West Africa are showing a readiness to provide long-term residence rights to refugees and former refugees, underpinned by
the ECOWAS Protocol on the Free Movement of People (Crisp 2012). Most recently,
Tanzania's offer of naturalization to approximately 200,000 Burundian refugees, as discussed below, is perhaps the clearest example of a situation in which a government has
taken a decision to offer citizenship to a group of refugees within a broader international
refugee policy context.

LOCAL INTEGRATION IN ITS HISTORICAL CONTEXT

In the past, local integration has played a more central role in international efforts to
'solve' refugee crises than it does in current thinking. In the 1950s, it was seen as the
principle means of resolving refugee situations (Meyer 2008). Certainly from the 1960s
until the 1980s, with the break-up of colonialism in Africa and the conflicts that were
spawned as a result, many African countries admitted large numbers of refugees and
allowed for de facto local integration. However, the acceptance of refugees soon became
eroded by the exclusive policies on which the post-colonial state was built. Notions of
belonging had changed irrevocably with the advent of colonialism: the movement of
people within specific areas was now labelled 'cross-border' and became increasingly
regulated.

As a result, from the 1980s governments grew progressively more protectionist in
their approach to refugees and, therefore, increasingly hostile to the notion of free integration. This exclusive notion of belonging formed the basis for the encampment policy,
which continues to be the default policy for 'managing' refugees. Governments have
repeatedly used the rhetoric of xenophobia to support their policies, emphasizing the
extent to which refugees are a security threat and an economic drain on resources. In the
case of the former, this argument was reinforced by the exodus following the 1994 genocide in Rwanda, in which militias fled with genuine asylum seekers (Lawyers Committee
for Human Rights 2002). Refugees, therefore, needed to be kept in camps where they
could be monitored from a security point of view, and where they could provide a visible humanitarian category that forced a humanitarian, rather than developmental and
political, response to their plight.

There has also been an assumption that refugees who are allowed to integrate are less
likely to eventually return to the country they fled from. These assumptions underpinning the encampment of refugees have been challenged, but with limited impact. (See,
for example, Hovil 2002.)

Even Tanzania, which held onto pan-African notions of inclusion and belonging longer than most governments in Africa, eventually caved in to this exclusivist logic and
stopped giving refugees sufficient land in settlement areas and a number of villages. As

a result, refugees who arrived in the 1970s were given adequate land that enabled them to become net contributors of food within the country, while those who fled in the 1990s were put into 'camps' where they were dependent on humanitarian relief.

Meanwhile at a policy level, since the 1970s there has been a growing awareness of the need for refugee issues to be addressed within the wider context of development, and for the need for 'burden-sharing' (see Gottwald, this volume). The main attempts by UNHCR to generate international cooperation to address regional refugee situations within Africa have been the International Conferences on Assistance to Refugees in Africa of 1981 and 1984 (ICARA I and II). The ICARA conferences were then followed by the International Conference on Refugees in Central America (1987–94), the Indo-Chinese Comprehensive Plan of Action (1988–96), and the Convention Plus Initiative (2003–5).

On the ground, however, this approach led to a number of initiatives that tried to create a tightly controlled and managed form of temporary 'local integration'. In Uganda in the early 2000s, for instance, the Self-Reliance Strategy (SRS) for refugees was implemented throughout the country as part of UNHCR's wider global strategy of Development Assistance to Refugees (DAR), a component of the Convention Plus Initiative. The SRS was introduced in 1999 as a developmental response to refugee management that was intended to integrate assistance to both refugees and their hosts. Its main objective was to allow refugees to become self-sufficient by giving them a small plot of land to farm and gradually reducing their rations, the expectation being that refugees would reach a point of self-reliance. Yet the SRS fundamentally failed: the idea of refugees becoming self-reliant within the restrictions of a settlement structure—whereby refugees have no freedom of movement and no freedom of choice—somewhat predictably proved to be a contradiction in terms.

Despite the intention behind such initiatives, therefore, the opportunities for local integration have remained sorely neglected. There was something of a change in 2005 when UNHCR's Executive Committee reached conclusion No. 104 (LVI) on local integration, which highlighted its importance as a burden sharing. Yet in reality, this official recognition of the potential of local integration has been somewhat akin to old wine in new bottles, inasmuch as the restrictive encampment policy has continued to trump efforts at local integration.

Obstacles to Local Integration

The settlement policy, therefore, has been one of the primary obstacles to allowing for de facto integration. It is effectively a holding exercise—a way of managing refugees until such time as they can be repatriated or, for a minority, resettled. Yet the protracted nature of many refugee situations, and the ongoing insistence that refugees must remain in camps (being driven by political and donor agendas) has meant that temporary solutions have evolved into quasi-permanent solutions, and refugees have been left heavily reliant on aid that is 'completely undependable, erratic and inadequate' (Harrell-Bond 2000: 4; see also Verdirame and Harrell-Bond 2005).

Local integration—and, therefore, a degree of self-reliance—can only take place if people have freedom of movement and freedom to make their own choices of where to live, how to support themselves, how to best utilize the limited resources that they have, and which markets to access. It is not surprising, therefore, that thousands of refugees have opted out of the settlement structure and have 'self-settled' amongst the national population, where many have reached a strong level of economic, social, and cultural integration.

In the case of de jure local integration, the main barrier has been a lack of political will to offer refugees new citizenship in order to end their exile. As outlined above, the protectionist and exclusivist approach adopted by governments throughout the world has meant that local integration as a durable solution has been deeply unpopular. The offer of citizenship, which renders an official end to exile, has been seen as taking hospitality a step too far. Instead, governments have preferred to hold out for repatriation to take place, relying on erratic donor funding to maintain expensive camps in the meantime.

The current situation facing Rwandan refugees is a case in point. Rwandan refugees have been living in a number of states across the region for decades. Many have reached a significant level of de facto local integration, although few are likely to have acquired new citizenship. Yet since UNHCR recommended cessation of refugee status for Rwandan refugees who fled between 1959 and 1998, these refugees have suddenly become visible as governments seek to return them to Rwanda: UNHCR's 'Comprehensive Strategy for the Rwandan Refugee Situation', which set in motion the ending of refugee status for Rwandans, emphasizes voluntary return as one of its main components. While the strategy does also refer to local integration, to date only Zambia has indicated that it is considering other legal status as an alternative to repatriation. There has also been some discussion in the media in Uganda about the possibility of naturalization for Rwandan refugees (IRIN 2012), but whether or not this will translate into citizenship remains to be seen. Overall, therefore, the lack of government will to seriously consider allowing for naturalization, along with heavy-handed pressure from the Rwandan government that is determined to ensure all its citizens return home as evidence of the country's stability, means that an opportunity for local integration as a durable solution to exile is being passed over.

'Invisible' Integration

Despite these obstacles, refugees repeatedly demonstrate the ability to be far more innovative than government policies, and many people have reached a point of economic and social integration *despite* the national and international policy climate. In order to do this, they have deployed coping strategies that allow them to live, work, farm, marry, trade, pay local taxes, and even vote in local elections. But in order to do this, they have to hide their identity as refugees and forgo official protection—such as it is.

As Kibreab states, 'Invisibility is a powerful weapon deployed by transmigrants and certain sections of forced migrants... to access certain bundles of citizenship rights and privileges they are not formally entitled to, by diminishing the ability of the state on the one hand to exercise sovereignty over its borders and, on the other, diminishing its ability to accord differentiated bundles of rights of citizenship to diverse categories of people...' (Kibreab 2012). Becoming 'invisible', therefore, is a highly creative and, in many cases, effective coping strategy that challenges humanitarian and political categorizations of peoples.

But it also has serious limitations. For the main part, this strategy is technically illegal, and when those who are invisible become visible to the state (as in the case with Rwandan refugees, for example) or when the host population feels threatened by their presence for one reason or another, the vulnerability of their situation is suddenly exposed. They lose their legitimacy to belong, and can quickly become excluded as outsiders. Therefore it can be both a source of 'empowerment and freedom', but also of 'vulnerability and marginalisation' (Kibreab 2012). Being locally integrated but effectively stateless is not a position of safety, not least in a geopolitical context in which states invest considerable resources and energy in security apparatus and invisibility is something of an illusion.

At the end of the day, therefore, governments are likely to turn a blind eye to economic and social/cultural integration, not least as this often benefits them directly or indirectly (through paying local taxes, for instance), but the *legal* dimension to integration is a political concern that has to be led and endorsed by governments themselves.

The Tanzania Case Study: Lessons to be Learnt

The 'local integration' process for Burundian refugees living in Tanzania is the only recent example of an attempt to provide solutions for a mass caseload through naturalization, and provides a telling case study of the potentials and pitfalls inherent in a document-focused approach to integration.

In 2008, the Tanzanian government, with considerable encouragement from UNHCR, took the decision to offer citizenship to approximately 200,000 Burundian refugees who had fled their country in 1972 and had since been living as refugees in Tanzania. While some of this group of refugees opted to repatriate to Burundi, 162,000 took up the offer of applying for naturalization. Obtaining citizenship was, for many, a logical step: many of this group were born in Tanzania (and, technically, were already entitled to Tanzanian citizenship) and had reached a significant level of 'local' integration. They were heavily integrated into the local economy, were exporting food across the country, and many had married Tanzanians.

Yet still, there was always a ceiling to their integration. Most remained within the confines of the settlement structure where, technically, they were supposed to obtain travel permits to leave the camp, and they were still identified as 'refugees' by the surrounding population (Hovil and Kweka 2008). Therefore, despite living in the area for almost four decades and having reached significant levels of integration, in the absence of national belonging in the form of citizenship their situation always remained temporary and unstable. The offer of naturalization presented the possibility to remove this ceiling and legitimize their belonging at both a local and national level. However, there was a catch: once they had made their choice to apply for naturalization, they were informed that, despite having been accepted for naturalization (in as much as their identification numbers had been listed on a board indicating that they had been accepted), they were told that they would not receive their citizenship certificates until they relocate elsewhere in Tanzania.

This has created an impasse. On the one hand, the former refugees believe that relocating to other parts of a country has the potential to unravel much of the informal and local-specific integration that has taken place over the past four decades. Therefore, they are concerned that if they relocate their citizenship will become meaningless: if they are not accepted in the specific locality in which they are living, their ability to support themselves will be jeopardized (Hovil 2013).

At the same time, however, the way in which citizenship has been constructed in Tanzania for decades has been premissed precisely on such ruptures in location taking place: on precipitating a break with localized expressions of 'tradition' that ensures that citizenship is built on 'new' (i.e. non-ethnic) forms of social affiliation. Recent research shows that the need to break with the past was recognized not only by Tanzanians and local government officials living and working in the settlement areas, but also by a few of the former refugees themselves (Hovil 2013).

Therefore, the process has become ensnarled in *realpolitik* and practicalities, none of which are insurmountable, but that are going to demand a fair amount of compromise from every side—a compromise that encourages relocation but that does not make citizenship contingent upon it.

It is likely that, with time, many former refugees will relocate themselves around the country, and incentives for doing so can and should be offered to those who are willing and able to move, just as Tanzanians are likely to move into the former settlement areas vacated by those who have moved. Indeed, unofficially this has already started to take place. At the same time, those who are unable or unwilling to move should be allowed to remain where they are—but still receive their citizenship certificates. Most importantly, any action that is taken needs to be cognizant of the fact that tying people to specific geographical locations is a recipe for exclusion. Inclusive citizenship, on the other hand, is based on integration and flexibility (Hovil 2013).

The issue of relocation has also become something of a smokescreen for the government, which has not been unified in the decision to offer mass-naturalization: the decision to offer naturalization was inadequately debated within government, and is only now being tabled before Parliament. As a result, the current process is currently in jeopardy and there are very real concerns that the entire group, having renounced their Burundi citizenship and without completing the process of becoming Tanzanian, could become stateless.

Furthermore, the proof of the success of this exercise will not only lie in the declaration that these former refugees are now Tanzanian citizens, but also in ensuring the realization of the rights attached to that citizenship. In order for that to happen, these former refugees need both the legitimacy of *national* belonging, and the opportunity to forge and reinforce *local* forms of belonging. The two are intimately connected and need to be mutually reinforced (Hovil 2013).

By the same token, it would be a tragedy if this process ultimately fails, not only for this specific group of former refugees, but for others who are living in protracted situations of exile around the world. Tanzania has the opportunity to demonstrate a radically different approach to belonging that offers an alternative to the exclusive approaches that are being witnessed across the region in the form of premature cessation, forced returns, and expulsions, which violate both international and national law and undermine refugee protection. Genuine local integration that is built on local and national forms of legitimacy offers a powerful antidote to this current trend.

Local Integration Moving Forward

Local integration, as both a temporary and long-term solution to the exclusion of exile, holds out enormous possibilities. There is something liberating in its emphasis on the agency of refugees, as opposed to the humanitarian premiss of refugees as victims. Those who have managed to obtain a degree of local integration have mostly done so against the odds, and often as a result of asserting and claiming rights, such as freedom of choice and freedom of movement, that would otherwise be denied them. However, as a form of empowerment it should not be over-romanticized: local integration is often a strategy that creates incredible hardship and vulnerability and remains out of reach for those who have no choice but to live in a settlement.

Over the past decades, local integration as a durable solution has, in effect, been everywhere except on the political agenda. Yet this resistance at an official level is possibly beginning to change. With growing emphasis on regional mechanisms and belonging, as well as greater awareness of the need for increased freedom of movement, there appears to be increasing opportunity for there to be a shift. This change has already taken place to some extent in West Africa, where movement between ECOWAS states has already shifted the displacement landscape. Yet, of course, far more needs to be done, and the protectionist approach to citizenship remains a significant stumbling block (see Long, this volume).

Furthermore, policy changes are not the only factor: for local integration to function as a genuinely durable solution, it has been argued that both de facto and de jure integration need to be promoted alongside each other. Informal local integration, while thriving in many contexts—not least due to the fact that governments often choose to turn a blind eye—needs to be encouraged and supported. But it needs to be supported with great care: de facto local integration takes place as a result of a complex and finely tuned process of negotiation between refugees and the host population, and represents a process that would likely be undermined if external actors sought to interfere in inappropriate ways.

The most important way of reinforcing localized forms of belonging is to give refugees the legitimacy to belong at a national level, as represented by the offer of citizenship. Local and national forms of belonging need to reinforce rather than oppose each other. Therefore, for local integration to function as a genuinely durable solution—by which refugees end their exile through obtaining a new citizenship, encompassing the 'right to have rights'—both local *and* national integration need to take place. It needs to be driven by governments inasmuch as it needs to have political sanction (in the form of citizenship), but it also needs to chime with localized forms of belonging and therefore function as a grassroots-driven process.

NOTE

1. Article 34 of the 1951 Convention Relating to the Status of Refugees, Adopted on 28 July 1951 by the United Nations Conference of Plenipotentiaries on the Status of Refugees and Stateless Persons convened under General Assembly Resolution 429 (V) of 14 December 1950; entry into force 22 April 1954, in accordance with Article 43.

REFERENCES

Arendt, H. (1986) *The Origins of Totalitarianism*. New York: Andre Deutsch.

Bakewell, O. (2005) 'Refugee Aid and Protection in Rural Africa: Working in Parallel or Cross-Purposes?' New Issues in Refugee Research. UNHCR Working Paper No. 35.

Briant, N., and Kennedy, A. (2004) 'An Investigation of the Perceived Needs and Priorities Held by African Refugees in an Urban Setting in a First Country of Asylum'. *Journal of Refugee Studies* 17(4).

Crisp, J. (2004) 'The Local Integration and Local Settlement of Refugees: A Conceptual and Historical Analysis'. New Issues in Refugee Research. UNHCR Working Paper No. 102.

Crisp, J. (2012). 'Twenty-Five Years of Forced Migration'. *Forced Migration Review*—25th Anniversary Collection. November.

Ferris, E. (1996) 'Refugees: New Approaches to Traditional Solutions'. <http://www.forcedmigration.org>.

Fielden, A. (2008) 'Local Integration: An Under-Reported Solution to Protracted Refugee Situations'. New Issues in Refugee Research. UNHCR Working Paper No. 158.

Harrell-Bond, B. (2002). 'Towards the Economic and Social "Integration" of Refugee Populations in Host Countries in Africa'. <http://www.stanleyfoundation.org/reports/hrp/HRP02B.pdf>.

Hovil, L. (2007) 'Self-Settled Refugees in Uganda: An Alternative Approach to Displacement?' *Journal of Refugee Studies* 20(4): 599–620.

Hovil, L. (2013) ' "I can't be a citizen if I am still a refugee': Former Burundian Refugees Struggle to Assert their New Tanzanian Citizenship'. International Refugee Rights Initiative (IRRI). Citizenship and Displacement in the Great Lakes Region. Working Paper No. 9. February.

Hovil, L. and Kweka, O. (2008) 'Going Home or Staying Home? Ending Displacement for Burundian Refugees in Tanzania'. International Refugee Rights Initiative (IRRI), Centre for the Study of Forced Migration and Social Science Research Council. Citizenship and Displacement in the Great Lakes Region. Working Paper No. 1. November.

IRIN (2012) 'Uganda: Government Plans Naturalisation of Refugees'. <http://www.irinnews.org/report/95701/UGANDA-Government-plans-naturalization-of-refugees>.

Jacobsen, K. (2001) 'The Forgotten Solution: Local Integration for Refugees in Developing Countries'. New Issues in Refugee Research. UNHCR Working Paper No. 45.

Jacobsen, K., and Landau, L. B. (2003) 'The Dual Imperative in Refugee Research: Some Methodological and Ethical Considerations in Social Science Research on Forced Migration'. New Issues in Refugee Research. UNHCR Working Paper No. 19.

Kibreab, G. (2012) 'Invisible Integration in the Greater Horn Region of Africa'. Pp. 69–110 in K. Mengisteab and R. Bereketeab (eds.), *Regional Integration in the Greater Horn Region*. Oxford: James Currey Publishers.

Lawyers Committee for Human Rights (2002) *Refugees, Rebels and the Quest for Justice*. New York.

Meyer, S. (2008) Forced Migration Online Research Guide on Local Integration. <http://www.forcedmigration.org/guides/fm0045/>.

Refugee Law Project working paper series. <http://www.refugeelawproject.org>.

Sommers, M. (2001) 'Young, Male and Pentecostal: Urban Refugees in Dar es Salaam, Tanzania'. *Journal of Refugee Studies* 14(4): 347–70.

Sperl, S. (2001) *Evaluation of UNHCR's Policy on Refugees in Urban Areas: A Case Study Review of Cairo*. UNHCR EPAU. June. Geneva: UNHCR.

CHAPTER 39

'VOLUNTARY' REPATRIATION AND REINTEGRATION

LAURA HAMMOND

INTRODUCTION

FOR people involuntarily displaced from their homes, return might seem like an ideal solution. Yet deciding whether or not to return, when and how to do so, and facing the prospect of rebuilding a life in the country of origin can be fraught with challenges. This chapter examines these challenges of repatriation and return. It considers several bodies of literature concerned with different aspects of return and the experiences of forced migrants at different stages of the return process.

Repatriation research has centred on three major areas. The first considers the decision to return and the conditions that determine whether that decision is made freely and in a context of safety. The second concerns the experience of the actual move to the country or area of origin (keeping in mind that not all return movements are to the displaced person's precise area of origin); this includes the preparation, physical relocation, and immediate experience of repatriation or return. The third probes experiences after return, as returnees seek to establish themselves and their livelihoods; this process is usually referred to as reintegration, even though it may be more of a creative process of innovation and developing of new strategies than a return to a pre-existing way of life (see Hammond 1999).

The chapter considers repatriation in its various forms—from the most voluntary to more coerced forms of deportation and return—as well as the post-return experience of (re)integration and homecoming/homemaking. A critical perspective on repatriation and return is offered, based on the need to develop identifiable benchmarks and goals for successful return. I argue that clearer benchmarks are needed for identifying what constitutes viable and sustainable reintegration, and that these must be based on a firm understanding of the conditions in the areas of return, the needs and expectations of returnees, and the prospects for peace and development in the area of return.

RETURN IN HISTORICAL CONTEXT

When the 1951 Geneva Convention Relating to the Status of Refugees was first drafted, it was meant as a response to forced migration caused in the aftermath of the Second World War. Given the redrawing of national borders and political alliances in Europe during that period, displacement was largely expected to be a permanent move. Most of the language of the 1951 Convention therefore focuses on the need to define and protect a category of persons fleeing persecution without much concern for an eventual resolution of their condition of being displaced. Preston notes that 'with notable exceptions, from 1947 until the 1970s, repatriation was unlikely to be perceived as the long-term plan for refuge-seeking groups'. Citing Larkin (1992) she refers to a 'post-Second World War reticence to recommend repatriation as the conclusion to exile, since it was feared that legitimate repatriation would quickly facilitate *refoulement*' (1999: 20).

By the time further elaboration of the conditions and means by which return should be facilitated was given in the 1980s, refugee law and UNHCR's mandate had expanded both geographically to include refugees worldwide and those displaced as a result of events that had occurred after the Second World War. Large refugee populations were being generated in Central America and Africa as a result of post-colonial and Cold War proxy wars. The decade of conflict in Central America that began in the late 1970s generated more than 2 million refugees, IDPs, and undocumented 'externally displaced' persons (Betts 2006). As of 1981, it was estimated that there were 5 million refugees living in Africa, more than half of the world's total refugee population. The resolution of some of the wars that had generated these refugees, coupled with the international community's interests in relieving the 'burden' suffered by poor host countries, saw the initiation of two separate processes involving UNHCR and other UN agencies as well as host and donor states which were designed to encourage repatriation.

First, in Africa in 1981, an International Conference on Assistance to Refugees in Africa (ICARA) focused primarily on trying to raise funds for provision of relief assistance to refugees. This was followed in 1984 by a second conference aimed at finding solutions to the problems of protracted displacement on the continent. ICARA II brought the idea of durable solutions—return, local integration, and resettlement—to the fore; here repatriation was identified as the 'best option' to resolve long-standing problems of displacement (Stein 1994). Shortly thereafter a second process was launched in Central America—known as the International Conference on Central American Refugees, or CIREFCA, and involving a series of meetings held between 1987 and 1994—to establish a blueprint for simultaneously facilitating repatriation, promoting post-conflict rehabilitation, and consolidating the fragile peace that was taking hold in the region. In both of these processes, the need to overcome developmental obstacles to facilitating return led to the adoption of 'cross-mandate' approaches to enhance cooperation between UNHCR, UNDP, and other UN agencies and NGOs. These initiatives formed the precursors to more recent trends in facilitation of repatriation and return through engagement with development processes in areas of return, and a de facto widening of UNHCR's mandate to consider not only protection of refugees but promotion of durable solutions. Despite the geographic distance between them, the two processes in part informed each other, as was evident in the repatriation of Eritrean refugees from Sudan in the early 1990s, which explicitly borrowed lessons from the CIREFCA process (see McSpadden 1999).

The 1990s saw the declaration of a 'decade of repatriation' in which hundreds of thousands of refugees were returned, some of the largest moves being to Afghanistan, Mozambique, Cambodia, Eritrea, and Ethiopia. These moves were made possible largely by the realignment of global power and the end of the Cold War. UNHCR experienced a major expansion in its operational capacity and an increasing acceptance of its vital role in repatriation. Yet much of the euphoria over the prospect of return occasioned by these changing geopolitical relations was tempered by the realization that facilitation of return was an extremely complex process that went beyond a single agency's ability to implement. For the formerly displaced, return was recognized as marking not so much the end of the migration experience as the beginning of a new chapter of adjustment and adaptation, sometimes involving further mobility and migration.

The Decision to Return

Literature that considers the decision to return and whether it is freely made under conditions of safety and dignity has been largely dominated by legal scholars (see for example Chetail 2004; Zieck 2004; Krever 2011), although some anthropologists and sociologists have also conducted research into the conditions surrounding repatriation choices (see contributions to Black and Koser 1999; Bakewell 2002). The decision to repatriate is a far from straightforward choice for a number of reasons. First, there is the legal requirement that return must not amount to *refoulement*; assessing likely threats to returnees may be difficult and fraught with political considerations. Concerns that genocidaires were living among the refugee populations in Zaire/Democratic Republic of Congo (DRC) and Tanzania led to the forced return of approximately half a million refugees to Rwanda in 1996, including many civilians (see Stein 1997; Whitaker 2002). In addition, when displacement has been prolonged, many refugees have become established in their new place of settlement and their desire or willingness to return may diminish. Gale (2008) describes how Liberian refugees living in Guinea decided to stay in the refugee camps even after UNHCR had withdrawn its assistance in order to continue to exploit the opportunities of living along the border and taking advantage of the economy and social networks of both Guinea and Liberia; Byrne (2013) documents a similar trend amongst Liberians in Ghana. Second-generation refugees may have no desire to 'return' to a country that they left when they were so young that they do not remember it or else were born in exile (Abbasi-Shivazi et al. 2008). Moreover the socio-economic challenges of returning to a country that is emerging from conflict, as in Eritrea, or the discomfort they may encounter upon returning to live with people whose grievances against them persist after the cessation of formal hostilities, as in the case of Bosnia, may dissuade many people who were displaced from opting to return, even if in principle they may express a desire to return one day.

Here the question of *who* in a household makes the decision to return is crucial. If men have sole decision-making power, women may be obliged to return regardless of their feelings on the matter.[1] Martin points out that 'along the Thai-Cambodian border in the 1980s, in eastern Zaire/DRC in the mid-1990s and in West Timor in the late 1990s, many women and children were in effect captives of the resistance groups that controlled the camps and were prohibited from repatriating' (2004: 107). Elderly relatives also often have little or no say about whether they will return. Pressure may be placed by political leaders or others in positions of authority to oblige people to return who might not volunteer on their own.

Often people 'choose' to return because they have no other option. The refugee camp may be closing and there may be no option for people to legally remain in the country of exile. The 'choice' then is to remain in the country illegally or to return to an uncertain fate. Refugees who have fled conflict are often pressured by political parties and factions to return in order to demonstrate their political support for one group or another once the conflict has ended; they may be used as political pawns and the 'free' nature of their decision to return may be suspect. Often the determination of whether the conditions that gave rise to the refugee outflux have been ameliorated, and whether it is safe to invoke the cessation of refugee status (and thus protection) are made by governments or other parties rather than by the refugees themselves (Chimni 1999); such determinations can overlook the real threats that persist for sections of the refugee population.

Those who are resettled in third countries, often in the global North, face different kinds of challenges in thinking about return. Like those weighing the possibilities and risks of returning from neighbouring countries, these potential repatriants must consider the security conditions in the areas to which they would likely return. But often factors such as the likely sacrifices in living standards they would have to make—including access to healthcare, education in the language that their children are accustomed to, as well as the conveniences of Western living—may be significant barriers to their return (see Muggeridge and Doná 2006). The issue of whether their skills can be transferred back to a local job market may also be significant. Changes in gender roles acquired while in exile may also complicate decisions about return (see McSpadden 2003 on Eritrean refugees; Grabska 2010 on South Sudanese; Stefansson 2003 on Bosnians).

PROCESS AND EXPERIENCE OF RETURN

Research concerning UNHCR-assisted repatriation often focuses on a particular aspect of the return process. In preparation for return, UNHCR works together with the countries of origin and return to organize an information campaign aimed at letting potential returnees know what conditions, services, and challenges they can expect to find upon return. They may also arrange escorted trips for community leaders so that they can see the return areas for themselves and discuss with locals with whom they will be living (see Koser 1997 on Mozambicans returning from Malawi). This may convince many people to return; others may be more reluctant to consider return under the conditions being proposed if they fear that their own circumstances and identity might make them vulnerable to persecution when they return, or if they fear being unable to support themselves economically upon return (Hardgrove 2011: 496).

Research on tripartite agreements between UNHCR, the country of origin, and the refugee-hosting country centres around the politics of such negotiations (see McSpadden 1999 on Eritrean repatriation). Other researchers have examined the politics and ethics of repatriation. Long (2012) considers repatriation as a 'statebuilding tool', a 'process of political rapprochement between citizen, community and state' (see Gibney, this volume, for further details).

In cases where governments decide that safe return is possible and that a cessation of refugee status is warranted, those who decide not to return may find themselves stateless. No longer welcome in the country of exile and either unable or unwilling to return to their country of origin, they remain in the insterstices of legality, and experience a new kind of vulnerability related to their lack of legal documentation and permission to live, work, study, or travel in the area that they have been residing in, often for a generation or more (Refugees International 2009).

Unassisted Return

As important as it is to protect the right to return voluntarily in safety and dignity, it is also true that every year thousands of refugees return to places where conflict continues to rage, where landmines pose significant threats of injury and loss of life, and where no assistance has been prepositioned (see Cuny and Stein 1994). People engage in such unassisted or 'spontaneous repatriation' when they are willing to incur considerable risks in order to preserve or reclaim their property, restart their agricultural activities, or be reunited with family members who have remained behind. Hendrie (1990) documents the return of Tigrayan refugees to northern Ethiopia in 1985–7, just months after they had fled war and famine. Approximately 200,000 people returned to their homes in Ethiopia despite the continuation of the civil war. (Many more refugees remained in the camps in Sudan until the war ended in 1991 and assisted repatriation was started in 1993; see Hammond 2004.) In another example, half a million refugees returned from Zaire/DRC to Rwanda in 1996 following the genocide. Pottier argues that while some refugees may have freely chosen to return, many were effectively forced to return by local militias and the Kigali government. Despite this, an estimated 700,000 remained in Zaire/DRC, 'disappearing' into local towns and refugee settlements that international organizations had limited or no access to (Pottier: 1999).

Of great concern are the cases in which refugees are forced against their will to return to dangerous environments. This has occurred in Kenya, Burundi, Iran, and Thailand, to name but a few countries. This often happens when refugees overstay their welcome in host countries—their numbers become so large and their perceived or actual drain on resources is so great that there is little public will to continue hosting them. It may also happen if refugees are perceived as constituting a security threat to the host country. Thailand has been accused of deporting Rohingya to Burma in 2012–13; UNHCR and human rights groups have repeatedly called on the Thai government to suspend the deportations, which the latter defends on the grounds that the migrants are not refugees; international observers and the Rohingya themselves claim that they do have a valid claim to refugee status (Human Rights Watch 2013). Infringements of the right of *non-refoulement* are difficult to hold to account: no international court has ever ruled against a country for forcibly returning refugees.

The Return Process

Once a tripartite agreement has been signed, people willing to repatriate have been identified and authorities are satisfied that their decision to return has been made freely, the voluntary repatriation programme must also prepare for and carry out the physical transportation of refugees to their country of origin. This can be an extraordinarily complex logistical challenge. In the host country it requires conducting further information campaigns about what to expect during the transport phase—what people can bring with them, what they should leave behind, what facilities and services to expect, etc. It also involves providing health screening of the population to ensure that vulnerable and disabled people are adequately provided for during and after the operation. It will involve providing basic supplies that the returnees will need while en route to their destinations; if the distances are very large this may also involve setting up transit centres for people to spend the night at along the journey, or reception centres where people can be dispersed in smaller numbers to their final destination once they have arrived in-country (such work may require coordination between assistance staff in both host and return countries).

In the country of return, reception areas and final settlements need to be prepared prior to the arrival of any returnees. This includes setting up distribution sites for reintegration assistance, identification of land for agriculture and/or pastoralism, demarcation of house sites, procurement of housing materials, construction of water points, and building and equipping health and education facilities. Although ideally these should all be in place before any returnees arrive, in practice, assistance is often provided late, not all provided at once, or provided at an inconvenient time of year (for example, uncleared land being distributed right before planting season, housing materials only being provided for construction after people have already arrived so that they must live in the open air for several days, plough oxen or tractor ploughing not made available on time, etc.). Hammond's research

(2004) with a community of Ethiopian Tigrayan returnees who returned from Sudan in the early 1990s describes the challenges encountered by returnees in the early days following their return and the processes through which assistance was provided.

REINTEGRATION

Reintegration of returnees is a highly problematic concept. To what standard are people being reintegrated? Is the goal to help returnees achieve the same standard of living as the local communities with whom they will be living? Is it to make sure they meet certain international standards of well-being, such as the Sphere Project's Minimum Standards in Humanitarian Response (2011) or other benchmarks? Is it to ensure that they do not suffer a drop in the standard of living that they were accustomed to while living as refugees? Each of these criteria may have something attractive about it, but each is also problematic. If the goal is to reach parity with local communities, but the local community has suffered from deprivation as a result of conflict, famine, or other calamity, then the entire population will continue to be extremely vulnerable. In practice, repatriation often occurs before states have been able to establish effective systems of rule of law or adequate socio-economic systems to support large numbers of returnees (see Long 2013). If the goal is to keep standards from the refugee hosting environment, but these are much better than (or much worse than) those of the local community, then tensions could mount between the two groups and conflict could result.

UNHCR's Handbook for Repatriation and Reintegration Activities (2004) does not include criteria for measuring the success of reintegration activities. Historically repatriation assistance has been offered for periods of between a few months and one full year of assistance, but this is often based on rather arbitrary ideas about the costs of establishing oneself post-repatriation. Multiple studies suggest that it can take two years or more to establish self-sufficiency following return (see Hammond 2004; Dolan and Large 2004). In the longer term, there are important questions to be asked about how long returnees should be considered to comprise a group distinct from refugee, internally displaced, or local populations living with or near them. Although UNHCR has increasingly come to see returnees as 'people of concern' where they live near refugees and sometimes internally displaced persons, there may still be a danger of impeding their integration and causing tension between different groups if they are treated as special cases when they do not have vulnerabilities which would justify such an approach.

HOME-MAKING AND EMPLACEMENT

Return does not and should not necessarily mean a return to a prior way of life. Such nostalgic notions of what it means to repatriate are commonly held by external actors as well as by refugees themselves; however, they are largely unrealistic and impractical. Returnees may have to settle in areas other than those they originated from—in urban areas rather than on their farms, for instance, or on new land because the property they once held has been taken over by someone else. Former refugees may have adopted new livelihood activities while in exile that they want to continue upon return, making post-return life more like a new beginning than a return to a former one (see Hammond 1999). In this way we may say that repatriation and integration are forward-looking processes which are about creating new ties to places, people, and markets so that (ideally) life can become sustainable.

Several studies of post-return adjustments have problematized the idea of 'home-coming', given that people return to their country of origin but not necessarily to the communities they were displaced from. Hammond (2004)'s study of Tigrayan return considers the process of emplacement—of creating new bonds to an environment, and indeed forging a new sense of community, where people had no pre-existing attachment. She found that emplacement was a process that was more likely to take generations than to fit into government's and UNHCR's frameworks of thinking about repatriation as a one or two-year process. Grabska's (2010) work on repatriation to South Sudan and Stefansson's (2003) analysis of return to Bosnia from Denmark also deal with these themes.

Repatriation and return may involve a process of negotiating one's political identity as well—(re)establishing one's citizenship rights and place within a particular political community (see Long forthcoming). Returnees may face hostility from those who remained behind as they compete with these 'stayees' for jobs, resources, and political voice.

OTHER LESS VOLUNTARY FORMS OF RETURN

In addition to organized voluntary repatriation, a range of returns may also be relevant to a consideration of refugee return. Assisted Voluntary Return (AVR) programmes sometimes involve people who freely choose to return to their country of origin, but may also be extended to failed asylum seekers. Such programmes have become an important aspect of migration management systems since the late 1990s, particularly in Europe (Bradley 2006). In some cases, return migrants taking part in such programmes are clearly volunteers who want to return; they may want to play a part in the post-war reconstruction process. Participants in the Qualified Expatriate Somali Technical Support—Migration for Development in Africa (QUESTS-MIDA) programme, for instance, are given job placements inside the government administration for periods of up to three years. They use the return as a chance to reconnect with family and to explore the possibility of longer-term residence in their country of origin, as well as to contribute to the development of their homeland. Participants in this kind of programme are skilled professionals who have usually succeeded in obtaining durable residence rights in the country of exile. For them, the ability to go back into exile if return does not live up to their needs or expectations is an important insurance policy.

Forcible return of failed asylum seekers and illegal migrants is often carried out without providing any support (save transportation to the country of origin). Some deportees are seen as having 'internal flight alternatives'. The country which has denied asylum or settlement to a migrant may determine that while returning a person to the locality of origin might constitute *refoulement*, it may be possible to return them to another part of the country where security conditions are substantially different so that it is expected that they will not face persecution of the sort referred to as grounds for granting refugee status. Many human rights groups have expressed concern about the lack of follow-up in such cases to determine what happens to deportees and whether they may be returned to dangerous settings; the risks that a deportee faces may be enhanced by virtue of the fact that they are known to have attempted to claim asylum from their home country.

The Right (but not the Intention?) to Return

In some instances, there may be a distinction between the *right* to return and the *intention* to return. Having one's right to return recognized may be seen as acknowledgement that they have been displaced from a place that they had a right to reside in, that they have lost property which they are entitled to be compensated for. This recognition may be tied to a central claim to identity. Bosnians who had fled their homes and resettled in Western Europe, for instance, sought compensation for the houses that had been taken over after they were displaced; when their property rights were restored, many people sold their houses in Bosnia and remained in their adopted homes outside the country. Similarly for Palestinians the right of return is a central political mobilizing platform; many Palestinian refugees have been displaced for so long that the homes they originally were displaced from are no longer standing. The right of return is tied to their need to have their displacement recognized both by Israel and the international community and not having this right recognized is seen as a major obstacle to reconciliation (see Dumper 2006).

Transnational Mobility: An Alternative to Return?

Increasingly, many long-term refugees are opting not to return to their country of origin permanently but rather to establish themselves in multiple locations at the same time.

A single family may have some members living in their country of asylum while others return to the country of origin for some or all of the year (Long, this volume; Van Hear, this volume). These 'revolving returnees' (Hansen 2007) or 'part-time returnees' (Hammond et al. 2011) often pursue economic and political projects in multiple places. Their engagement in multiple places helps them to also manage the risks of return; if conditions turn out not to be as safe and secure as they had hoped, they can relocate to join their relatives in other countries. Yet at the same time they can contribute to economic and political development and manage family affairs in their country of origin. This option may be particularly attractive for people from developing countries who have come to more developed countries to settle. Security conditions, education and health services, employment, and investment possibilities may not be conducive to bringing the whole family back, but part-time return may work very well. Thus far, such transnational practices have been pursued largely without any assistance (although some part-time returnees do take advantage of assisted voluntary return support, for instance by being employed temporarily by one of these schemes upon return). Yet even without assistance millions of returnees are opting for this kind of return. Helping to support people who opt for this partial return strategy may have important positive development implications (Long, this volume).

Conclusion: Towards Improved Repatriation and Reintegration Assistance

Repatriation and return will likely continue to be the most favoured durable solution, not only for those hosting refugees but for many refugees themselves. For hosting countries, when refugees return they are relieved of the financial, security, social, and political costs of providing safe haven for refugees. Donor countries prefer repatriation to expensive care and maintenance programmes for refugees as well as to accepting them for resettlement. Countries of origin see refugees as highly politicized symbols; their return sends a strong public message that the fear of persecution that kept people outside their country is no longer present; repatriation can be a major vote of confidence for a new government in particular.

For refugees themselves, return is often an ideal that they hold dear even when the realistic prospects for return are negligible. The dream of return can help bind together refugee communities living in exile, including even people who know that they are unlikely to return. For those who do repatriate, the challenges of re-establishing their economic livelihoods, political capital, and social networks can be extremely difficult. Many may address this difficulty by engaging in continued mobility at least for some time as they spread risk and maximize opportunities in both the country of asylum and that of origin.

For those who want to and are able to return safely, much more can be done to help ensure that the process of post-return integration goes smoothly. Refugees and locals in return areas could be included more in the preparations for return. Better monitoring and evaluation could help to ensure that reintegration assistance provided is adequate, appropriate, and lasts long enough for people to achieve some degree of stability in their lives post-return. Moreover allowing people to maintain highly mobile livelihood strategies can help to minimize their vulnerabilities and also help them to contribute to social integration in the areas of return.

NOTE

1. Zimmermann (2011) discusses Somali women's lack of agency in deciding when or where to leave their homes during the civil war; their limited role in repatriation decisions is also evident.

REFERENCES

Abbasi-Shivazi, M. J., Glazebrook, D., Jamshidiha, G., Mahmoudian, H., and Sadeghi, R. (2008) 'Second Generation Afghans in Iran: Integration, Identity and Return'. Kabul: Afghanistan Research and Evaluation Unit (AREU). <http://www.refworld.org/cgi-bin/texis/vtx/rwmain?docid=4846b2062>.

Adelman, H., and Barkan, E. (2011) *No Return, No Refuge: Rites and Rights in Minority Repatriation*. New York: Columbia University Press.

Bakewell, O. (1999) 'Returning Refugees or Migrating Villagers? Voluntary Repatriation Programmes in Africa Reconsidered'. New Issues in Refugee Research. UNHCR Working Paper No. 15.

Betts, A. (2006) 'Comprehensive Plans of Action: Insights from CIREFCA and the Indochinese CPA'. New Issues in Refugee Research. Working Paper No. 120. <http://www.unhcr.org/43eb6a152.html>.

Black, R., and Koser, K. (eds.) (1999) *The End of the Refugee Cycle? Refugee Repatriation and Reconstruction*. Oxford: Berghahn Books.

Bradley, M. (2006). 'Return of Forced Migrants'. Expert Guide for Forced Migration Online. <http://www.forcedmigration.org/research-resources/expert-guides/return-of-forced-migrants/managing-return>.

Byrne, J. (2013) 'Should I Stay or Should I Go? National Identity and Attitudes towards Local Integration among Liberian Refugees in Ghana'. *Refugee Survey Quarterly* 32(1): 50–73.

Chetail, V. (2004) 'Voluntary Repatriation in Public International Law: Concepts and Contents'. *Refugee Survey Quarterly* 23(3): 1–32.

Chimni, B. S. (1999) '*States, Banks and Crisis: Emerging Finance Capitalism in Mexico and Turkey*'. New Issues in Refugee Research. UNHCR Working Paper No. 2. May.

Cuny, F., and Stein, B. (1994) 'Refugee Repatriation during Conflict: Protection and Post-Return Assistance'. *Development in Practice* 4(3): 173–87.

Dolan, C., and Large, J. (2004) 'Evaluation of UNHCR's repatriation and reintegration programme in East Timor, 1999–2003'. Geneva: UNHCR. <http://www.unhcr.org/cgi-bin/texis/vtx/research/opendoc.pdf?tbl=RESEARCH&id=403f62e17>.

Dumper, M. (ed.) (2006) *Palestinian Refugee Repatriation: Global Perspectives*. London: Routledge.

Gale, L. A. (2008) 'The Invisible Refugee Camp: Durable Solutions for Boreah "Residuals" in Guinea,' *Journal of Refugee Studies* 21(4): 537–52.

Grabska, K. (2010) 'In-Flux: (Re)negotiations of Gender, Identity and "Home" in Post-War Southern Sudan'. Ph.D. dissertation. Brighton: University of Sussex.

Hammond, L. (1999) 'Examining the Discourse of Repatriation: Towards a More Proactive Theory of Return Migration'. Pp. 227–44 in R. Black and K. Koser (eds.), *The End of the Refugee Cycle? Refugee Repatriation and Reconstruction*. Oxford: Berghahn Books.

Hammond, L. (2004) *This Place Will Become Home: Refugee Repatriation to Ethiopia*. Ithaca, NY: Cornell University Press.

Hammond, L. (2006) 'What Does "Adequate Assistance" Mean in the Context of Promoting Viable Return and Appropriate Compensation? Lessons from the Horn of Africa'. Pp. 132–53 in M. Dumper (ed.), *Palestinian Refugee Repatriation: Global Perspectives*. London: Routledge.

Hammond, L., Awad, M., Dagane, A. I., Hansen, P., Horst, C., Menkhaus, K., and Obare, L. (2011) *Cash and Compassion: The Role of the Somali Diaspora in Relief, Development and Peacebuilding*. Nairobi: UNDP.

Hansen, P. (2007) 'Revolving Returnees: Meanings and Practices of Transnational Return Among Somalilanders'. Copenhagen: University of Copenhagen.

Hardgrove, A. (2011) 'Liberian Refugee Families in Ghana: The Implications of Family Demands and Capabilities for Return to Liberia'. *Journal of Refugee Studies* 22(4): 483–501.

Hendrie, B. (1990) 'The Politics of Repatriation: The Tigrayan Refugee Repatriation 1985–87'.

Human Rights Watch (2013) 'Thailand: Don't Deport Rohingya "Boat People"'. <http://www.hrw.org/news/2013/01/02/thailand-don-t-deport-rohingya-boat-people>.

Koser, K. (1997) 'Information and Repatriation: The Case of Mozambican Refugees in Malawi'. *Journal of Refugee Studies* 10(1): 1–18.

Krever, T. (2011) 'Mopping Up: UNHCR, Neutrality and *Non-Refoulement* since the Cold War'. *Chinese Journal of International Law* 10(3): 587–608.

Larkin, M. A. (1992) 'Preface'. Pp. vii–xii in M. A. Larkin, F. C. Cuny, and B. N. Stein (eds.), *Repatriation under Conflict in Central America*. Washington, DC: Hemispheric Migration Project, Georgetown University.

Long, K. (2012) 'Statebuilding through Refugee Repatriation'. *Journal of Intervention and Statebuilding* 6(4): 369–86.

Long, K. (2013) *The Point of No Return: Refugees, Rights and Repatriation*. Oxford: Oxford University Press.

Long, L., and Oxfeld, E. (eds.) (2004) *Coming Home? Refugees, Migrants and Those who Stayed Behind*. Philadelphia: University of Pennsylvania Press.

Markowitz, F., and Stefansson, A. (2004) *Homecomings: Unsettling Paths of Return*. Lanham, MD. Lexington Books.

Martin, S. F. (2004) *Refugee Women* (2nd edn.). Lanham, MD: Lexington Books.

McSpadden, L. A. (1999) 'Contradictions and Control in Repatriation: Negotiations for the Return of 500,000 Eritrean Refugees'. Pp. 69–84 in R. Black and K. Koser (eds.), *The End of the Refugee Cycle? Refugee Repatriation and Reconstruction*. Oxford: Berghahn Books.

Muggeridge, H., and Doná, G. (2006) 'Back Home? Refugees' Experiences of their First Visit back to their Country of Origin'. *Journal of Refugee Studies* 19(4): 415–32.

Pottier, J. (1999) 'The "Self" in Self-Repatriation: Closing Down Mugunga Camp, Eastern Zaire'. Pp. 142–70 in R. Black and K. Koser (eds.), *The End of the Refugee Cycle? Refugee Repatriation and Reconstruction*. Oxford: Berghahn Books.

Preston, R. (1999) 'Researching Repatriation and Reconstruction: Who is Researching What and Why?' Pp 18–38 in R. Black and K. Koser (eds.), *The End of the Refugee Cycle? Refugee Repatriation and Reconstruction*. Oxford: Berghahn Books.

Refugees International (2009) *Nationality Rights for All: A Progress Report and Global Survey on Statelessness*. Washington, DC: Refugees International. <http://www.refugeesinternational. org/sites/default/files/RI%20Stateless%20Report_FINAL_031109.pdf>.

Sphere Project (2011) *The Sphere Handbook: Humanitarian Charter and Minimum Standards in Humanitarian Response*. <http://www.spherehandbook.org>.

Stefansson, A. (2003) 'Sarajevo Suffering: Homecoming and the Hierarchy of Homeland Hardship'. Pp. 54–75 in F. Markowitz and A. H. Stefansson (eds.), *Homecomings: Unsettling Paths of Return*. Lanham, MD: Lexington Books.

Stein, B. (1994) 'Returnees and Development'. <http://www.unhcr.org/cgi-bin/texis/vtx/search ?page=search&docid=3bd40fb24&query=barry%20stein%20icara>.

Stein, B. (1997) 'Refugee Repatriation, Return and Refoulement During Conflict'. Paper presented to USAID Conference, Promoting Democracy, Human Rights, and Reintegration in Post-Conflict Societies, Washington, DC. <http://pdf.usaid.gov/pdf_docs/PNACD092. pdf>.

UNHCR (2004) Handbook for Repatriation and Reintegration Activities. <http://www.unhcr. org/411786694.pdf>.

Webber, F. (2011) 'How Voluntary are Voluntary Returns?' *Race and Class* 52(4): 98–107.

Whitaker, B. E. (2002) 'Changing Priorities in Refugee Protection: The Rwandan Repatriation from Tanzania'. *Refugee Survey Quarterly* 21(1/2): 328–44.

Zieck, M. (1997) *UNHCR and Voluntary Repatriation of Refugees: A Legal Analysis*. Dordrecht: Martinus Nijhoff Publishers.

Zieck, M. (2004) 'Voluntary Repatriation: Paradigms, Pitfalls, Progress'. *Refugee Survey Quarterly* 23(3): 33–54.

Zimmermann, S. E. (2011) 'Danger, Loss and Disruption in Somalia after 1991: Practicalities and Needs behind Refugee Decision-Making'. *Refugee Survey Quarterly* 30(2): 45–66.

CHAPTER 40

REFUGEE RESETTLEMENT

JOANNE VAN SELM

INTRODUCTION

RESETTLEMENT is one of the three durable solutions to refugeehood, alongside local integration and return and involves the organized movement of pre-selected refugees to a destination country in which their settlement is expected to be permanent. This chapter will focus on three issues that are central to understanding and thinking about refugee resettlement: the question of how, who, and why to resettle; the challenges of the 'good refugee/bad asylum seeker' binary; and the integration of resettled refugees.

BACKGROUND INFORMATION

Some 28 countries worldwide currently offer resettlement opportunities, including nine traditional resettlement states with larger, longer-established programmes. The United States has the largest resettlement programme by far, and one that is much more nationally driven than those of most other resettlement countries, which rely heavily on UNHCR's direction. The USA, Canada, and Australia collectively provide 90 per cent of global refugee capacity. A further 8 per cent is offered by 16 European states, including Norway, Sweden, Finland, Denmark, the Netherlands, and the UK, which have established, annual resettlement programmes exceeding 200 refugees per year, and eight other EU member states which have smaller programmes.[1] Belgium and Germany offer at need places, such as for the 2011 Global Resettlement Solidarity Initiative for non-Libyan refugees fleeing Libya for Tunisia.

Much of the global discussion on resettlement focuses on capacity and numbers, and the resettlement countries' perspective. As a solution for the few, the refugees' hopes and wishes for resettlement have a relatively low profile in the literature. UNHCR has recently established an internet community exclusively for resettled refugees, where they can share experiences and offer advice to newly resettling people (UNHCR 2012a). Global resettlement needs, according to UNHCR, could be as high as 800,000 refugees; however, only some 85,000 places are available on an annual basis (UNHCR 2012b).

Historically, resettlement was significant in the Cold War context, and reached a high-point as an instrument in refugee protection in the 1970s and 1980s, being used to relieve countries of first asylum for the Indo-Chinese, and offer protection to 'boat people' (Robinson 1998). By the end of this programme the movement had essentially become a migration, rather than protection, flow. The reputation of refugee resettlement was sullied, and some countries, particularly in Europe, closed their programmes completely or only offered a few emergency or medical cases resettlement each year.

Since the Cold War there have been fluctuations in the use of resettlement. The USA, Canada, Australia, New Zealand, and the Nordic countries maintain 'traditional' programmes, that is they accept refugees for resettlement annually, offering a consistent number of places, selection criteria, and an established integration path. Australia has, since the mid-1990s, linked the number of resettlement places to the number of onshore arrivals—but also made a multi-year commitment unlike other countries, which have annual programmes. Its programme has also increased in total size from 12,000 to 13,500 annually over that period. The US programme, however, faced post-9/11 concerns about refugee-candidates for resettlement's potential links to terrorist groups ('material support'), and has adapted its approach to refugee admissions both through new rules and a shift in emphasis in terms of regions of origin (see e.g. Fullerton 2010). Asian refugees, for example the Bhutanese and Burmese, have benefited from proportionally more resettlement opportunities since the mid-2000s, whereas the programme focus in the late 1990s was more on Africa.

In the past decade, some European resettlement programmes have been revived, and more EU member states are becoming resettlement countries, with encouragement and support from the European Commission. In March 2012 the EU announced funding to stimulate increased resettlement, from priority situations.

Resettlement clearly cannot be the solution for all refugees as the number of places available is simply too low. However, it is the only viable solution for some refugees who cannot be protected in their region of origin. In the past decade, UNHCR and resettlement countries have promoted the 'Strategic Use of Resettlement', arguing that resettlement can occasionally be used to achieve other goals. Examples of these goals could be opening the way for other refugees to achieve greater local integration through changes in government policies, or as a form of solidarity with host governments which allows them to maintain open borders and access to asylum. As such, a 'strategic use of resettlement' should benefit other refugees as well as offering a path to a new life for particular refugee families. However, assessment of Strategic Use's impact to date is mixed, with positive opinions being based more on hope and belief than actual evidence.

Much of the academic literature on refugee resettlement focuses on aspects of integration for resettled refugees, in particular health, employment, education, and housing, frequently from the point of view of communities and states, or in comparison with asylum seekers or other migrants (see e.g. Bevelander, Hagström, and Rönnqvis 2009; Brolan 2010; Connor 2010; Valtonen 2008). There has been some interest in policy literature in the question of whether (more) states should practise resettlement in the last decade, including some attention to the links between resettlement and asylum as elements in a comprehensive refugee policy; selection; processing; 'strategic use of resettlement'; and the role of resettlement in a more managed approach to refugee protection as a migration category (ECRE 2006; Van Selm 2007). There has been relatively little written about resettlement from the refugee perspective (UNHCR 2012c): how individuals decide to apply and accept resettlement; how they adapt to often completely different circumstances, particularly if moving from decades in a camp to a bustling North American city; how they motivate themselves to make the best of their new situation, particularly once the assistances and services of the most immediate post-arrival period are phased out and they must sink or swim.

How, Who, and Why to Resettle?

Having decided that resettlement will be both useful for them and offer international protection, governments determine the criteria according to which they will select refugees (given the imbalance of supply of places to demand for solutions). They then establish the range of actors that will be involved in different aspects of their resettlement programmes. Programmes vary from country to country but most frequently include: identifying resettlement candidates (often carried out by UNHCR); preparing cases for status determination and resettlement eligibility processing (often UNHCR or NGOs); selection missions (immigration services); preparing refugees for movement and settlement (often IOM); transportation (usually IOM) and assistance with settlement and integration after arrival (often NGOs and some government departments and services).

The traditional resettlement countries' programmes all differ in the way they are crafted and implemented. They have nationally driven characteristics, and also differ simply on the basis of objective factors such as the numbers offered places and the distance from the countries or regions of origin of refugees being resettled, as well as in their relationship to both broader immigration traditions and patterns and asylum systems.

Given the limited number of resettlement places available—less than 1 per cent of the total refugee population—resettlement countries have to set eligibility criteria to make programmes manageable. Beyond the confirmation of refugee status and indication of objective need, they can essentially pick and choose. There are often suggestions that certain resettlement countries (particularly those with strong immigration traditions) 'cream off' the more economically resourceful refugees. This should not be the case, although it will often happen that refugees with skills have a strong role in a camp or refugee community in a first country of asylum, and will either hear sooner about a resettlement programme, be more efficient in ensuring they submit an application, and/or have connections that get them onto referral lists. There have been discussions, particularly in Europe, about using 'integration criteria' in identifying the few refugees who will be resettled. However, other than 'community building' criteria in selecting the broad group characteristics and, one could argue, family resettlement categories, there are to date no such explicit integration-oriented criteria in use. No resettlement country actively pursues only refugees from places where there are 'employable' candidates, or purposefully and explicitly seeks only those candidates.

The history of modern refugee resettlement in the USA dates back to the Second World War and the resettlement of some 250,000 Europeans, which was followed in 1948 by legislation and the resettlement of a further 400,000 displaced persons (see Martin, this volume). The current US Refugee Admissions Program (USRAP) was established under the 1980 Refugee Act, prompted by the resettlement of hundreds of thousands from Indo-China. Since 1975 some 3 million refugees have been resettled to the United States. The programme is divided into three 'priority' categories, formally designated by Congress on an annual basis. The priority designations and all changing political and practical information on the USRAP are set out in an annual report to Congress (See e.g. USDoS 2012).

Priority 1 (P1) are individually referred refugees, put forward by UNHCR, US embassies, or designated NGOs, who can be identified in any country (although for practical purposes of selection mission travel there have to be substantial numbers involved). In the 1980s and 1990s this was a relatively small channel for resettlement arrivals in the USA, but it has been growing since the early 2000s, particularly for UNHCR referrals from situations in which there is little chance of agreement being reached on a Priority 2 (P2) designation.

P2 is for group referrals of specified ethnic, national, or religious groups in specific locations. The characteristics assigned need to be objectively assessable: Bhutanese in Nepal, for example, or Iraqis associated with the USA, where employment contracts can be verified. The State Department decides to assign P2 referral status to a group in consultation with UNHCR embassies, and NGOs. P2s can be 'open access' (any individual can apply to be considered part of the group) or 'pre-defined group access' (an existing group e.g. in a camp situation).

P3 was not used for four years after significant fraud was discovered in 2008: it is a category for family sponsorship, open to specified nationalities. The category was being reopened in 2012/13 with enhanced measures for verifying relationships.

Involving up to 70,000 refugees annually, the USRAP can be used relatively flexibly by the USA itself to align refugee admissions with foreign and domestic policy interests, as well as to make international humanitarian statements. It is the resettlement programme which can definitively impact a refugee crisis, single-handedly, or with fellow resettlement countries assisting by offering places for the same groups. At the same time, it is the resettlement programme which is least open to external influence in spite of the widespread consultations. Having a programme that numerically is greater than the resettlement programmes of all other countries combined simply means that the USA is dominant in refugee resettlement.

Like the USA, Australia's modern history of refugee resettlement dates to arrangements following the Second World War, and was punctuated by Cold War movements, including Hungarians in 1956, as well as Indo-Chinese resettlement and legislative changes in the late 1970s and early 1980s.

The Australian Refugee and Humanitarian Programme includes an onshore and an offshore component. The offshore part is broken down into two categories: refugees and Special Humanitarian Visas (SHVs) for people in need of protection, but who do not meet the refugee definition. The Australian programme is unique in combining the two components—onshore asylum and offshore resettlement—into one statistical target. Since 2006 the numerical range has been between 13,000 and 13,800 total acceptances, with around 6,000 refugees being resettled each year, while the number of SHVs has fluctuated relating to the number of asylum cases onshore that have been accepted. In 2006/7, for example, there were 5,183 SHVs and 1,793 onshore acceptances, while in 2010/11 there were 2,973 SHVs and 4,828 onshore acceptances.

The Australian programme's recent focus has been on refugees from the Middle East and Asia, although African refugees did make up a majority of the resettlement intake in the early 2000s. The Australian discourse around asylum and resettlement, in terms of 'waiting in line' is a constant policy and public debate factor, both in terms of its role and impact in Australian politics and in terms of its export value to discussions on asylum (and resettlement) policies in Europe in particular.

Canada's programme has both Government Assisted Refugees and Privately Sponsored Refugees. Those who receive government assistance for their first year in the country must be referred by UNHCR or another recognized agency. Private sponsors, approved groups including churches, or five or more citizens can refer a refugee whom they will commit to support during their first year in Canada. In special cases resettled refugees can be jointly assisted by the government and private groups. The Government Assisted part of the programme can be used by UNHCR and the Canadian government to address particular situations, whereas the private sponsorship element reflects individual's and families' interests and networks.

In Europe programmes vary widely. The Nordic countries (Sweden, Finland, Denmark, and non-EU Norway) each have their own selection missions to locations in which they, in consultation with UNHCR, have determined that they will focus for a given year. However, Finland, for example, looks particularly at groups and nationalities that could be expected to integrate well in a relatively isolated society, so they will return for multiple years to a given country of first asylum to build communities among the refugees who are resettled. Sweden and Norway accept more UNHCR proposals for new locations. All of these countries have some places for people with urgent medical needs and/or other particular vulnerabilities.

The UK started its 'Gateway' programme in 2004, and now offers 750 places annually: previously the UK had run a 'twenty or more' programme for medical evacuees. The Netherlands had also reduced its resettlement numbers to medical needs during the late 1990s and early 2000s, but has reinvigorated its programme to have a broader focus for 500 cases annually: 100 each for four UNHCR priority situations and 100 for emergency needs.

There are several reasons for renewed interest in resettlement in Europe in recent years. One is the sense that resettlement arrivals can be managed and limited in number, compared to the fundamental inability to manage asylum flows. This brings public relations benefits with regard to national populations. Governments are also better able to manage the image of certain asylum arrivals if they can show that there are obviously refugees from those locations, since they are also resettling some, although this has two sides. The flip side is the potential for allegations of 'queue jumping'—that those seeking asylum 'should' have waited their turn to be resettled. Another perceived PR benefit that has encouraged European governments to engage in resettlement is that resettlement appears to offer a visible demonstration of humanitarian commitment despite rising levels of xenophobia among European populations leading to anti-asylum seeker sentiment.

Resettlement offers permanent status. On departure towards the country to which they are being resettled, a refugee will already have been granted that status (unlike an asylum seeker), and have visa, entry, and residence documentation in hand. They will be permitted to work. They will also have been through some kind of orientation course giving them information on what to expect in their new home country: those courses try to explain all manner of things from language and broad culture to how to get around. They will be met on arrival by those organizations (governmental, NGO, family, and/or sponsors according to the system in the resettlement country) who will assist them in their first weeks or months. There should be housing ready for them, although in some countries they will first go to a dedicated shelter for more assistance. For some time they will be classed as immigrants or permanent residents, and they will have access to naturalization as part of their choices in how they integrate. Nothing stops resettled refugees later choosing to return to their country of origin, especially if peace is brokered there. However, they are likely to return with an additional passport, or at least to maintain residency rights in their resettlement country.

THE CHALLENGES OF THE 'GOOD REFUGEES/ BAD ASYLUM SEEKERS' AND 'EASY TO RESETTLE/DIFFICULT' SYNDROMES

Political discourse on resettlement sometimes simplifies: if refugees want a new life, with protection and a solution, in developed countries then rhetoric suggests they should wait their turn to be resettled. Resettlement offers states far greater control over deciding who to admit. A resettling country selects people who fit the refugee definition and eligibility criteria like country of origin, country of first asylum, thereby region of the world and potentially race, ethnicity, and religion. Yet, that same resettling country when faced with asylum seekers cannot select where they come from or anything about them, but only assess their refugee status, and if they prove to be in need of protection grant them their right to stay.

As a result, a binary discourse implies that the refugees who 'wait' for resettlement are 'good' and that those who seek their own path to safety and travel, arriving in a developed country to seek asylum, are somehow 'bad'. Those who take the asylum path are sometimes also labelled 'bad' because they are automatically grouped with irregular migrants broadly. One challenge in explaining resettlement in policy and real-life terms is to try and move beyond this simplification. With so few resettlement spaces and so many refugees, it is clear that not all refugees can be resettled. Many refugees do not want to resettle: fleeing for safety from a homeland where a person previously had a 'normal' life does not make that person suddenly want to move halfway around the world. Some resettle happily, seeing the opportunities a new life can bring for them or their children. Others are reluctant, but see it as the only way to move forward. International law is clear that all persons have a right to seek and enjoy asylum, and the travel and communication means of the twenty-first century permit them to exercise that right around the world—even if the vast majority of refugees never seek asylum in the developed world.

The suggestion arises from time to time that if resettlement were offered in larger numbers, asylum seeking would decrease—and the 'difficulties' associated with 'unmanaged' migration would reduce commensurately. However, the relationship is not so clear cut: those refugees who would be resettled if more places were available are not necessarily the same refugees who would otherwise undertake hazardous journeys to seek asylum. It is also possible that offering more resettlement could pose a 'pull factor' making a particular destination country seem more welcoming, thus if one did not gain entry to the resettlement programme one might be inspired to seek asylum. Resettlement countries could not possibly offer enough resettlement places to ensure that all refugees who need a solution or might seek one through asylum would, in a short period of time, be safe.

Australia's approach as described above is an attempt at balancing international commitments with a sense that a large part of the voting public does not welcome asylum seekers. The numerical balance goes together with measures to process asylum seekers arriving by boat in offshore locations, particularly the Pacific Islands of Nauru and Papua New Guinea. That approach is beyond the remit of this chapter (see McNevin, this volume), but it also goes some way towards illustrating this challenge.

A further part of the 'good refugee, bad asylum seeker' challenge is the goals for which resettlement is used. Beyond fitting those to be resettled to the refugee definition and eligibility criteria there are different purposes for which resettlement is used: emergency, protection purposes, and solution purposes.

Emergencies can be personal, such as major illness or injuries that cannot be treated in a country of first asylum, or more widespread: a sudden major event that exposes significant protection needs that cannot be met in the region. In the latter cases removal for resettlement would for protection needs not due to the lack of any other solution: such a crisis could be resolved and repatriation opportunities arise. Evacuation for protection purposes might also be needed if, for example, neighbouring countries are small, have limited resources and/or their own tensions. Then evacuation demonstrates burden sharing and solidarity by the international community.

Should such evacuations for protection purposes—rather than as solutions per se—be considered resettlement, or should alternatives be used, such as temporary protection? One relatively recent example is the humanitarian evacuation programme (HEP) for Kosovars displaced during the NATO campaign in response to Serbian aggression in 1999. The HEP was intended to show solidarity: relieve Macedonia of some of the 200,000 Kosovars who had entered the country, challenging its own ethnic balance. The evacuating countries diverged in the status granted to Kosovars. The USA offered resettlement places; Canada granted rights to the Kosovars immediately, and allowed them to apply for asylum in the country (Amnesty International 1999; Van Selm 2000). However, the Europeans offered temporary protection and Australia created new safe haven visas, with no permanent residence rights. Both expected return might be possible. Return did become possible for many, but not all. However, not all those who could return wanted to, leading to deportations as well as voluntary repatriations. Some could claim additional protection or humanitarian reasons for staying in the country to which they had been evacuated. Those who were resettled to the USA, or gained asylum in Canada, did not need to return to Kosovo, as their status in those countries was linked to longer-term residence rights, and cessation was not applied. Yet many Kosovar Albanians did return from North America.

The sense that something needed to be done for Kosovars was again one of the 'good' and the 'bad': the refugees seemed 'just like us' (Gibney 1999). The outpouring of positive sentiment across Europe in particular meant that from a public relations perspective governments had to step in to protect (Van Selm 2001). But, with few resettlement programmes in place at the time, a permanent status might have been a step too far. Soon after the end of the HEP and the conflict, Kosovars heading to the EU were quickly branded 'illegal immigrants', not even asylum seekers.

In the more recent case of the Arab Spring, while Tunisia and Egypt, having just faced their own revolutions and associated displacement, received hundreds of thousands of Libyans and third country nationals fleeing the conflict in Libya, EU governments appeared to panic in the face of some 40,000 asylum seekers. They did offer some resettlement for third country nationals whom UNHCR could demonstrate had been determined to have refugee status in Libya, but the overall approach was labelled 'shameful' by Amnesty International, as the status quo approach to boat arrivals being, as is the case in Australia too, labelled almost 'invasion forces' and by definition 'irregular' was maintained (Amnesty International 2011). The resettlement that was undertaken was sought by UNHCR as a 'strategic use', although some European ministers clearly questioned this, suggesting that this emergency/protection resettlement should not be prioritized, rather existing strategic uses for durable solutions elsewhere in the world should be the focus (Garlick and Van Selm 2012).

An example of the benefits of resettlement coming to those who have waited might be the Bhutanese in Nepal. They form the largest post-Cold War group of refugees whose situation has been addressed by the international community through mass resettlement. With neither return to Bhutan nor integration in Nepal being practically or politically possible after 25 years of exile, the international community embarked on resettlement in 2007 in the hope of opening the path to other solutions (Banki 2008). By 2012 some 70,000 out of the 100,000 refugees had been resettled, or places made available for them—60,000 would be resettled to the USA. Resettlement in this case might offer a long-term solution (although neither return nor integration had happened for the remaining population by early 2013) and relieve the burden on Nepal, but some would also suggest that the Bhutanese population is a relatively 'easy' population for countries to resettle.

Refugee resettlement is also seen by some as juxtaposed to 'bad' ways of seeking protection in the developed world. This suggests that resettlement and new opportunities are a reward for many years, if not decades, in a difficult situation of limited protection in a neighbouring state, awaiting a return (see Hovil, this volume), or chance to just get on with life in the fullest sense, that never comes. If so, resettled refugees could be expected to have limited personal resources of any kind left to actually make use of those opportunities, yet as a lasting solution to their need for protection in a world of states, resettlement is a permanent situation, and one which will only succeed if the refugees successfully integrate into their new countries and communities.

The Integration of Resettled Refugees

The success of refugee resettlement depends very much on the integration of those refugees who are resettled with their host country and community. The establishment and maintenance of effective integration programmes can be challenging (see Ager and Strang 2008). Key elements in effective integration programmes include pre-departure orientation; language and other skills training with an emphasis on self-reliance and employment potential; recognition of and support for vulnerable groups, including the provision of appropriate services; support from and engagement of host communities; coordination across government at the national and local levels in policy, practice, service provision, etc.; and coordination between government and non-governmental partners (UNHCR 2002).

One of the reasons behind the relatively small number of places offered for resettlement is the challenge, and costs, of integration. Different resettlement countries handle integration in different ways, reflecting cultural and sociological norms and standards that prevail in their domestic settings.

The new focus on resettlement in the EU has given rise to initiatives led by UNHCR, IOM, and ICMC drawing attention to integration for resettled refugees reflecting the European culture of entitlements in the welfare state context (ICMC 2011). The 'Linking-In EU' resettlement initiative brings together resettlement actors in a network and virtual community, using web-based tools for the sharing of experiences and best practices (2012). The network focuses particularly on the integration of resettled refugees. UNHCR is also promoting the development of benchmarks to measure integration outcomes for resettled refugees. The European Parliament, which has played a significant role in highlighting the potential of a joint EU resettlement programme, has emphasized the integration of resettled refugees as key in demonstrating the quality, sustainability, and effectiveness of resettlement.

The literature on integration of resettled refugees in Europe reflects on the relatively small programmes in numerical terms, and high quality of assistance and care targeted at these newcomers. The way in which integration is handled differs between European countries—but much of the practical approach is centred on housing, education, and healthcare (see e.g. Valenta 2010). Employment opportunities are lower down the list of issues to be addressed.

This is quite different in North America. In the USA, the focus of orientation and integration is generally on employment, as both the government and voluntary agencies involved are very aware that funding for resettled refugees lasts only a few months. After that, they must, unless they fall under limited other assistance programmes, make their own way. For some this means accepting work well below their past experience and expectations; for some it means taking on multiple jobs and working long hours to make ends meet. For many it means adapting to the 'American way of life', and seeking success on the economic ladder and using their social network, if they have one: some manage, some do not, and there is little by way of a safety net (Beaman 2012). Thus the orientation materials refer to work, whether the nominal core subject is housing, transportation, education, or cultural life (CAL 2013).

Resettled refugees could be said to have the advantage over asylum seekers and other low-skilled immigrants of knowing that they will remain, and not having to fight for their legal status. This means that they can focus on establishing the substance of their new lives, rather than having to fight the system for the chance to get started. In addition, in all resettlement countries there are organizations and systems to offer assistance, at least in the beginning, from finding initial housing, to locating a healthcare provider, to finding schools, and in some cases finding jobs too. In Canada there is even assistance in the provision of winter clothing.

Where that assistance can run out, however, be it after weeks (as in the USA), months, or a year (as in Canada) the refugees may or may not have found their feet by the time they have to really stand on them. They may have status, but whether they can make use of the opportunities presented to them or not is very much down to individual skills and opportunities. Whereas some assume that those refugees who 'make it' were selected on that basis, it is often not the case. The 'Lost Boys of Sudan' can hardly be said to have been chosen for resettlement to the USA on the basis of their great career prospects, yet many have succeeded in their education and employment paths to date (Bixler 2005). The strong motivation to succeed can come from an understanding of being, in some sense, 'the chosen ones', although it is not easy to achieve education and employment goals in a 'sink or swim' system (see e.g. PBS 2004, 2007).

Conclusions

The research on resettlement to date broadly covers government policies, UNHCR's interests and approaches, offers some thinking on why societies will accept (or reject) certain refugee groups and managed arrivals, and elements of the integration of resettled refugees, in their own right, and in contrast with the integration of asylum seekers and of immigrants more broadly.

There has been, however, little focus on the point of view of the refugees themselves: how do they decide whether to apply for resettlement? Is resettlement something that simply 'happens' in the process of their displacement, or are active choices involved? How do resettled refugees react to the cumulative changes in their lives of displacement, a period (perhaps extended) with no solution, followed by a solution to their status and safety but new challenges of adjustment?

If resettlement is to be useful in addressing the challenges of protracted displacement and the continuing protection needs of the twenty-first century's refugees information and insights from the refugee perspective would be useful in adapting government and international policymaking to reflect lived reality, so that individual experiences, or data coming from a range of individual experiences, help inform debates about not only enhancing resettlement for those who are selected, but also about the role of resettlement as a refugee solution, as a protection tool, and as an approach to an international problem that impacts both individuals and states.

Note

1. Bulgaria, the Czech Republic, France, Hungary, Ireland, Portugal, Romania, and Spain.

References

Ager, A., and Strang, A. (2008) 'Understanding Integration: A Conceptual Framework'. *Journal of Refugee Studies* 21(2): 166–91.

Amnesty International (1999) *The Protection of Kosovo Albanian Refugees*. 19 May. EUR 65/03/99. <http://www.unhcr.org/refworld/docid/3ae6a9c914.html> (accessed 19 October 2012).

Amnesty International (2011) 'Letter to Mr Herman Rompuy: The European Union's response to the Refugee and Migrant Crisis in North Africa'. Ref B1089. Brussels. 20 June.

Banki, S. (2008) 'Resettlement of the Bhhutanese from Nepal: The Durable Solution Discourse'. Pp. 29–58 in H. Adelman (ed.), *Protracted Displacement in Asia: No Place to Call Home*. London: Ashgate.

Beaman, L. A. (2012) 'Social Networks and the Dynamics of Labour Market Outcomes: Evidence from Refugees Resettled in the U.S.' *Review of Economic Studies* 79(1): 128–61.

Bevelander, P., Hagström, M., and Rönnqvist, S. (2009) 'Resettled and Included? The Employment Integration of Resettled Refugees in Sweden.' Malmö: Institute for Studies of Migration, Diversity and Welfare (MIM), Malmö University.

Bixler, M. (2005) *The Lost Boys of Sudan: An American Story of the Refugee Experience*. Athens, GA: University of Georgia Press.

Brolan, C. E. (2010) 'Joint EU Resettlement Programme: The Health of Refugee and Humanitarian Arrivals'. *Eur J Public Health* 20(3): 248–9.

Connor, P. (2010) 'Explaining the Refugee Gap: Economic Outcomes of Refugees versus Other Immigrants'. *Journal of Refugee Studies* 23/3: 377–97.

CAL (2013) Cultural Orientation Resource Center. <http://www.culturalorientation.net/>.

ECRE (2006) 'The Way Forward: "Towards a European Resettlement Programme"'. <http://ecre.org/topics/areas-of-work/resettlement/103-the-way-forward-towards-a-european-resettlement-programme.html>.

Fullerton, M. (2010) 'Terrorism, Torture, and Refugee Protection in the United States'. *Refugee Survey Quarterly* 29/4: 4–30.

Garlick, M., and Van Selm, J. (2012) 'From Commitment to Practice: The EU Response'. *Forced Migration Review* 39. <http://www.fmreview.org/en/north-africa/garlick-vanselm.pdf>.

Gibney, M. (1999) 'Kosovo and Beyond: Popular and Unpopular Refugees'. *Forced Migration Review* 5. <http://www.fmreview.org/FMRpdfs/FMR05/fmr5full.pdf>.

ICMC (2011) *Paving the Way: A Handbook on the Reception and Integration of Resettled Refugees*. <http://www.icmc.net/pubs/paving-way-a-handbook-reception-and-integration-resettled-refugees>.

Linking-In (2012) <http://www.resettlement.eu/>.

PBS (2004, 2007) 'Interviews: In Search of a Durable Solution with Sasha Chanoff, Mapendo International'. <http://www.pbs.org/pov/lostboysofsudan/special_interviews_sc_new.php>.

Robinson, W. C. (1998) *Terms of Refuge: The Indochinese Exodus & the International Response*. London: Zed Books.

UNHCR (2002) *Refugee Resettlement: An International Handbook to Guide Reception and Integration*. UNHCR and the Victoria Foundation for Survivors of Torture.

UNHCR (2012a) 'The World Wide Community of Resettled Refugees'. <http://www.unhcr.org/5077e5d96.html> (accessed 7 March 2013).

UNHCR (2012b) 'UNHCR Projected Global Resettlement Needs 2013'. <http://www.unhcr.org/5006aff49.html> (accessed 8 March 2013).

UNHCR (2012c) 'Durable Solutions: Breaking the Stalemate'. Pp. 65–89 in *State of the World's Refugees: In Search of Solidarity*. Geneva: UNHCR.

USDoS (United States Department of State), United States Department of Homeland Security, United States Department of Health and Human Services (2012) 'Proposed Refugee Admissions for Fiscal Year 2012'. Report to the Congress. <http://www.state.gov/documents/organization/181378.pdf>.

Valenta, M., and Bunar, N. (2010) 'State Assisted Integration: Refugee Integration Policies in Scandinavian Welfare States: The Swedish and Norwegian Experience'. *Journal of Refugee Studies* 23(4): 463–83.

Valtonen, K. (2008) *Social Work and Migration: Immigrant and Refugee Settlement and Integration*. Aldershot: Ashgate.

Van Selm, J. (ed.) (2000) *Kosovo's Refugees in the European Union*. London: Continuum.

Van Selm, J. (2001) 'Perceptions of Kosovo's Refugees'. Pp. 251–65 in M. Buckley and S. Cummings (eds.), *Perceptions of the Crisis in Kosovo*. London: Pinter-Continuum.

Van Selm, J. (2007) 'The Europeanization of Refugee Policy'. Pp. 79–110 in S. Kneebone and F. Rawlings-Sanaei (eds.), *New Regionalism and Asylum Seekers: Challenges Ahead*. New York: Berghahn Books .

CHAPTER 41

BURDEN SHARING AND REFUGEE PROTECTION

MARTIN GOTTWALD

INTRODUCTION

THE origins of the concept of international burden and responsibility sharing in relation to refugees are found in Paragraph 4 of the Preamble of the 1951 Convention Relating to the Status of Refugees, which expressly acknowledges that 'the grant of asylum may place unduly heavy burdens on certain countries, and that a satisfactory solution of a problem of which the United Nations has recognized the international scope and nature cannot therefore be achieved without international cooperation'.

States, notably developing countries hosting larger numbers of refugees, often use the term 'burden-sharing' to emphasize the perceived and real inequalities in the distribution of direct and indirect costs that accrue when dealing with refugees both in situations of mass influx and in long-standing refugee situations. In such situations, receiving states often have to tackle serious political, security, social, environmental, developmental, economic, and infrastructural problems which arise from the influx and the protracted presence of refugees.

Conversely, humanitarian organizations stress a more positive image of refugees and a stronger framework for international cooperation, and thus prefer the term 'responsibility sharing'. Such cooperation to share the burdens and responsibilities can take different forms ranging from prompt material and in-kind assistance during refugee emergencies, financial assistance at all stages of displacement, resettlement of refugees from first asylum countries in the global South to industrialized countries, and efforts to resolve conflicts and prepare the ground for durable solutions.

States' definition of the burden and their approach to address it has significantly evolved over the past six decades. The drafters of the 1951 Convention Relating to the Status of Refugees approached refugee issues in a state-centric, sedentary, and linear manner. First, they focused on the 'refugee problem' rather than the 'problem of refugees'. They treated this as a 'tame' problem that is well defined and with a definite stopping point, i.e. the end or reversal of movement. Second, they viewed refugees as passive individual actors in the displacement cycle that need to be protected by states. Third, they treated displacement and onward mobility as sources of instability that need to be reversed. Hence their use of the term 'burden' that implies that refugees are a drain on receiving states and a security problem for the international community. Fourth, framing refugee displacement in a linear cause-effect manner, they delinked forced population movements and responses to these flows from other issues, overlooking root causes of displacement and the potentially destabilizing impact of their own interventions.

Since 1951, state interests in refugee protection have evolved considerably. In the 1980s, the massive rise in refugee movements coupled with economic recession and the election of conservative governments in many Western states resulted in increasingly restrictive asylum policies (Loescher 2008). Norms of humanitarian intervention started superseding the norm of non-intervention which prepared the ground for an increasingly 'proactive, home-land oriented and holistic' approach in countries of origin (UNHCR 1995). At the same time, the political interest of industrialized and developing countries in comprehensive regional and international burden- and responsibility-sharing regimes as part of comprehensive solutions has further increased. Intergovernmental meetings such as those held at the Global Consultations in 2001 and on the occasion of the 60th anniversary of the 1951 Convention in 2011 reflect states' growing awareness of the substantive relationship between burden sharing and refugee protection in the South, and immigration, security, and trade. Yet the failure of initiatives such as the Convention Plus Initiative (2003–5) show that Western states are not yet prepared to translate their verbal commitment to responsibility sharing into normative frameworks on international burden sharing.

This chapter examines to what extent Western states' evolving interests have led to a paradigm shift away from atomistic and mono-dimensional (Cartesian) interventions in countries of asylum to holistic and multi-dimensions approaches in refugee source regions, and the implications this has for 'burden sharing'.

Paradigms

The term 'paradigm' refers to a set of shared worldviews that emerge from scientific theories and frame the way we see the world and solve problems (Kuhn 1970). In the international relations context, a paradigm can be defined as 'a mixture of beliefs, theory, preconceptions and prejudices that shapes ideas of how the international systems works, generates expectations and prescribes appropriate behavior' (MccGwire 2001).

A paradigm provides model problems and solutions to a community of practitioners and thus binds a culture together. At the same time, it acts like a filter that not only gives incoming data a particular interpretation, but also determines which kinds of data enter. As a result, it may blind practitioners to things that would not make sense within the paradigm's interpretative framework (Kuhn 1970).

Paradigms may 'shift' thanks to developments in science, which usually triggers a period of pervasive change. These shifts occur when anomalies between existing theory and observation arise, when an alternative paradigm is available, and when a critical mass of people have changed their beliefs (Kuhn 1970). Using two different paradigms in the analysis of forced migration helps approaching forced migration issues from different frames and define patterns of change.

The Cartesian paradigm is associated with the views of classical scientists such as Newton and Descartes (Capra 1997). Cartesians propose that the world is composed of independent elements and that the behaviour of complex systems can best be analysed in terms of the properties of the part. The sum total of the behaviour of these parts then constitutes the behaviour of the complex entity which in the first place was broken up.

Systems thinking, in turn, draws on discoveries made in the fields of physics and biology in the twentieth century. Systems thinkers understand the world as an interconnected system, that is, an integrated whole whose properties cannot be reduced to smaller parts, because they arise from the interaction of the parts. It is only by understanding the whole that one understands the parts constituting the whole and their symbiotic relationships with the whole and each other (Capra 1997).

What is the 'Burden'?

Practitioners and academics refer almost ritualistically to 'burden' and 'burden sharing' as accepted terms of art in the approach to refugee protection as if it were an objectively given fact that refugees are a 'burden'. And yet the applicability and scope of these terms vary significantly depending on whether one views refugee movements from a Cartesian or a systems perspective.

Cartesians believe that static equilibrium is the natural, ideal state. Hence for them disequilibrium generated by man-made or natural disasters and resulting population movements is in itself a 'burden'. To regain the perception of control they seek to restabilize the situation into a static equilibrium. They do so by breaking down the multitude of interconnected problems associated with the disequilibrium into lower level 'tame problems', allocate costs to them and address them in isolation from one another using conventional methods. In terms of refugee protection, Cartesians tend to reduce a complex phenomenon such as armed conflict to its immediate consequences for asylum countries, thus ignoring root causes and dissociating the humanitarian response from other issues areas.

Conversely, for complexity theorists it is static equilibrium that puts complex adaptive systems at risk. Bounded instability, i.e. a state between stability and instability, is for them more conducive to evolution than either stable equilibrium or explosive instability. As the 'edge of chaos' provides opportunities for collective evolution, there is no use in applying prejudicial terms such as 'burden' to it (Pascale 2001). Rather problems and solutions should be formulated in terms of the whole system instead of individual components.

In forced migration, systems thinkers view refugee movements in the broader context of global political, economic, and social interdependencies and the resulting disturbances. They do so based on the belief that most social planning problems are 'wicked problems' (Rittel 1973), i.e. problems where the dynamic and behavioural complexities are high, where stakeholders hold different assumptions, values, and beliefs, and where component problems cannot be solved in isolation from one another.

Systems theory also allows for burdens to turn into benefits. Short-term costs associated with specific components may translate into long-term gains for the entire system. For example, while refugees' regular or irregular arrival in industrialized countries may 'overburden' asylum systems in the short term, over time positive feedback effects may emerge that can benefit both the origin state and the destination state. Remittances and return movements with additional skills, contacts, and know-how may positively contribute to the national economy of the source country. Equally, the arrival of refugees may benefit destination states in that it responds to relative scarcity and/or productivity gains, increasing the general productivity of the economy. For example, when Andras Grof fled in 1956 from Austria to Hungary with a bundle of belongings, he may have been a drain on the resources of Austria, which temporarily admitted him to safety, and of the USA, to which he was eventually resettled. When in 1968, as Andrew Grove, he became CEO of the newly founded Intel company, which quickly became very profitable, the receiving state certainly no longer considered him a 'burden' (UNHCR 2006).

The drafters of the 1951 Convention approached the problem of refugees primarily from a Cartesian perspective. First, the use of the term 'burden' in the Preamble reflects states' negative association with population movements. Second, they focused in a reactive manner on the immediate emergency phase of refugee mass influxes, thus overlooking the pre-emergency and post-emergency phases and hence the root causes of displacement. And third, while refraining from explicitly defining the 'burden', discussions at the plenipotentiary conference suggest that states had a rather narrow definition of 'burden' in mind. They thought primarily of the direct costs of protecting and assisting refugees in emergency situations, thus neglecting possible indirect effects on the political, economic, security, and social fabric of both receiving and non-receiving countries.

Since then, the problem definition and thus the scope of the perceived 'burden' have gradually expanded. In countries of first asylum, states' initial focus on the direct costs associated with protection and assistance of refugees during emergencies gradually widened to other issues areas, including refugees' impact on economic, social, environmental, and security issues (EXCOM 1999, 2004; UNHCR 2000). These include the cost involved in maintaining asylum adjudication processes, care for and maintain asylum seekers, refugees' distorting effects on labour markets, and economic, social, cultural, and community relations, as well as refugees' impact on foreign relations and national security as part of the 'burden' (Brown 1999).

The scope of the 'burden' also expanded in terms of the time frame associated with the 'burden'. While up to the 1960s, 'burden' was primarily linked with the immediate emergency phase, the UN General Assembly implicitly widened in its 1967 Declaration on Territorial Asylum the time frame by referring to the continuation of asylum and thus the post-emergency phase. Equally, EXCOM gradually expanded the concept from a narrow association of burden with the immediate emergency phase (EXCOM 1979) to a wider definition that explicitly links the concept of 'burden' with the post-emergency phase and the three traditional durable solutions (EXCOM 1981; UNHCR 2010).

The geographic scope of the burden expanded when Western states started addressing root causes of displacement in refugee source countries. The UN's 1992 Agenda for Peace specifies that these preventive efforts may take various forms, including preventive diplomacy prior and during conflict, peacemaking, and peacekeeping. The new homeland approach reflected a growing recognition that root causes of refugee crises must be addressed so as to prevent refugee movements in the first place and successfully reverse displacement. States engaging with preventive efforts were thus seen as carrying a part of the overall 'burden' through their 'proactive contributions' (EU 1995; Thieleman 2006).

In sum, over the past 60 years, the scope of 'burden' has widened in two ways. First, the focus shifted from direct emergency reception costs in asylum countries to a more systemic consideration of refugees' longer-term impact on host states' socio-economic and political fabric. Second, practitioners gradually acknowledged that the concept of 'burden' needs to be associated not only with the emergency phase but holistically with all stages of the refugee displacement cycle including prevention of and solutions to displacement in territories other than countries of asylum. The growing recognition that these stages are interdependent also meant that the 'burden' was no longer associated solely with the humanitarian sector but now also entered the realm of development, political, and economic actors.

While this evolution reflects a clear departure from Cartesian thinking, it still falls short of whole systems thinking. First, affluent asylum countries maintain a short-term frame of costs resulting from refugee movements and thus view these as inherently burdensome. This in turn reflects Cartesians' view that static equilibrium is favourable over dynamic disequilibrium. Second, from a systems point of view, refugee practitioners and academics still overlook many of the indirect costs that non-refugee hosting countries in and outside the region face as a result of conflict and forced displacement. Third, the root causes debate focuses exclusively on factors in refugee source countries, thus ignoring structural causes at the global level which contribute to creating conflict and displacement.

Who is Affected by the 'Burden'?

The Cartesian paradigm explains the world in terms of direct, linear causality, that is, a force moves in one direction only and affects objects in its path. Causes and effects have thereby a proportional relationship, in that small changes in original conditions can induce consistent changes in their effects. This can be visualized as a row of dominoes falling one after the other. In other words, the effects of refugee displacement are primarily borne by countries of first asylum while indirect effects on non-receiving countries are overlooked.

In contrast, complexity science proposes circular causality, that is, the emphasis is on forces moving in many directions simultaneously, not simply a single event caused by a previous one. Conflict and refugee displacement in one part of the world may trigger consequences for the entire world (Sköns 2005). In a globalized economy, non-receiving countries—in or outside the region—may in some cases bear even higher costs than those borne by refugee source and receiving countries. For example, the Libya crisis in 2011 heavily affected Bangladesh both in terms of the sudden return of some 40,000 unemployed migrant workers and lost remittances which have a significant macro- and micro-economic role for the country. Nonetheless, Bangladesh was the second-largest donor of in-kind contributions, as a result of providing the services of its national air carrier to transport returning migrants (IOM 2011; Kelly 2012).

The drafters of the 1951 Convention clearly approached the consequences of conflict and refugee displacement in a linear-causal manner in that they associated the 'burden' exclusively with asylum countries affected by mass influx and thus ignored the effects on non-receiving countries. Since then, their view of countries affected by the consequences of conflict and displacement has widened. From an initial focus on countries of first asylum (EXCOM 1979), states came to acknowledge that refugee movements can also impose significant intra-regional burdens (EXCOM 1996), for then eventually concluding that countries other than those hosting refugees permanently, including transition countries (EXCOM 1997) as well as countries receiving secondary movers as well as smuggled and trafficked people (UNHCR 2010) may face a 'burden'. The next logical step was the realization that mass influx situations pose 'challenges' not only for receiving states but also for other states in the region and for the international community as such (EXCOM 2004).

In sum, refugee practitioners and scholars increasingly acknowledge that conflict and forced displacement entail regional and global costs, thus endorsing systems theorists' view of an interdependent world. This view reflects scholars' proposition that refugee protection—and more generally conflict prevention and resolution—should be seen as international public goods that benefit the entire world (Suhrke 1999).

WHO SHOULD ADDRESS THE 'BURDEN'?

International Realist theorists draw on Cartesians' hierarchical and atomistic assumptions in two ways. First, in the absence of a supreme coordination instance, they consider nation states as the primary actors in international relations. Second, in analogy from Newtonian physics, Realists see states as isolated atoms which rationally and autonomously pursue their self-interest. Doing so, they regularly collide with each other. In terms of the refugee 'burden'-sharing debate, this implies that it is national self-interest that drives states' contribution to the prevention and resolution of conflicts, protection, and solutions (Betts 2009).

Against that background, the state-centric and fragmented manner in which the 1951 Convention assigns responsibilities for refugee protection clearly reflects the Cartesian paradigm. First, the drafters of the Convention did not consider that 'protection' may be provided by actors other than states. Accordingly, refugees are seen as 'individual' actors requiring protection rather than as an interconnected collective with self-managing capacities. Second, while the responsibilities of refugee-receiving countries are clearly established, there are no binding rules concerning the role of other countries, including countries of origin. In particular, the rather vague reference to international solidarity enshrined in the Preamble cannot be seen as the basis for a legally binding refugee distribution mechanism.

Throughout the Cold War period, powerful Western states assumed a hegemonic role in terms of the physical distribution of refugees. They agreed, based on foreign policy interests, to admit refugees to their territories. In response, first countries of asylum—increasingly located in the global South—committed themselves to temporarily admitting refugees to their territories, until they were resettled to the global North. When Western states shifted in the 1980s to increasingly restrictive asylum policies and thus abandoned their hegemonic distribution role, developing countries of asylum responded to the perceived defection by adopting non-admission policies too. This triggered in terms of the Prisoners' Dilemma a downward spiral of mutual defection, which can also be described as 'chicken games', that is, states signalling each other that no one has the intention of providing for refugees, through restricting entry and refraining from supplying provisions (Kritzman-Amir 2008).

The perceived mutual defection was reframed following the end of the Cold War and Western states' increasing intervention in refugee source countries. Practitioners and scholars started arguing that preventive diplomacy, peacemaking, and peacekeeping are intrinsically linked to the displacement solutions phases and thus should be considered as contributions to 'burden' and responsibility sharing (EU 1995; Thieleman 2006). In short, this view suggests that the implicit regime had widened, with different states, based on their comparative advantage, making contributions in regard to the global public goods of international peace and security.

The shift from a culture of 'reaction' to 'prevention' also meant a redefinition of state sovereignty that was no longer seen as centred on the prerogatives of the state but on its primary responsibility to protect its citizens. The concept of Responsibility to Protect (R2P) reflects the idea that if a state cannot provide protection it forfeits its sovereignty (ICISS 2001), and the international community steps in not only to protect, but to prevent and rebuild. The emphasis that R2P lies first and foremost with the state concerned implied that responsibilities relating to conflict prevention, emergency response, and refugee solutions were formally shifted from Western states to states and regional organizations in the South. The 'New Deal' for Western states' engagement in fragile states includes their commitment to support country-led and country-owned transitions out of fragility. This implies a new role for Western states that increasingly define their responsibilities in terms of building institutional capacities in Southern states to prevent conflict and displacement, and cope with their consequences.

These new approaches to 'responsibility' sharing had one important aspect in common: protection action remained the prerogative of the sovereign nation state, and, by default, the international humanitarian community (South 2012). Yet the growing awareness that the increasing number and complexity of trans-sovereign problems exceeds the problem-solving and regulatory capacities of the traditional humanitarian actors, encouraged Western states and humanitarian organizations to also reconceive the role of refugees and other non-governmental actors. First, while throughout the Cold War, affected populations were viewed as passive victims, the new humanitarianism of the post-Cold War period meant that refugees were increasingly seen as active rights-holders who should be involved in agencies' key decisions and processes that influence their lives (South 2012). Second, international organizations started outsourcing an increasing number of prevention, protection, and solutions-related activities to NGOs. Third, Western states are now also engaging with for-profit organizations and other private sector actors to leverage innovation and strategic knowledge so as to ensure more effective humanitarian action.

While refugees' new status as 'stakeholders' allowed them to influence decision making, protection continued to be seen as an activity undertaken primarily by outsiders, on behalf of vulnerable communities, for several reasons. First, states in the global South have proven reluctant to articulate their own protection obligations to fulfil their obligations under R2P. This impacted Western states' capacity-building programmes which, in the absence of Southern states' political will to assume protection responsibilities, were not seen as sustainable. Second, the global financial crisis has forced Western states to reduce their financial commitments in the global South. Increasingly aware of communities' local self-protection capacities, traditional donor countries have thus started emphasizing self-protection capacities of affected populations, based on the concept of 'resilience'.

This concept draws on ideas from multiple disciplines such as systems theory and can be defined as 'the ability of a system, community or society exposed to a crisis to resist, absorb, accommodate to and recover from the effects of a crisis in timely and efficient manner, including through the preservation and restoration of its essential basic structures and functions' (UNISDR 2009). In short, Western states have started viewing societies in the global South as complex adaptive systems that have the capacity to shoulder and self-manage the burden at all stages of emergencies. In a similar vein, confronted with the recurrent lack of funds for financing the achievements of the Millennium Development Goals, Western states and international organizations have become increasingly interested in private transfers by refugees and migrants as an alternative source of finance. Indeed, estimates suggest that the annual value of remittances is about twice as much as the value of official development assistance and close to equalizing the total amount of foreign direct investment in poor countries (World Bank 2012).

In sum, responsibilities to address the 'burden' associated with conflict and displacement have gradually shifted from countries in the global North to different state and civil actors in conflict-affected and refugee-receiving countries in the region. For systems theorists, states' growing recognition of the self-managing capacities of affected populations at the society and community level is a healthy development as they see these as better placed to regulate systems disturbances than outsiders. Yet while affluent states increasingly practise systems thinking in regard to the factors internal to the countries and regions of origin as causes of refugee movements, they continue to overlook the international dimension of the causes. That is, affluent states' self-interested pursuit of foreign policy and security objectives is seen as fuelling conflict and displacement (Chimni 2000). Furthermore, affluent states' continued interest in unilaterally controlling migration to their territories means that transnational mobility as an important coping mechanism of affected populations is curtailed. Indeed, the growing literature on transnational social networks suggests that displaced families and communities frequently disperse to different locations both internally and across international borders, as part of increasingly complex collective coping strategies that aim at mutual support (Van Hear 2003).

Burden Sharing, Burden Shifting?

Cartesians address complex phenomena such as armed conflict and its causes and consequences by splitting them into smaller pieces and addressing them in isolation. The atomistic approach reflects the assumption that the whole is nothing more than the sum of its parts and that fixing components of a system contributes to stabilizing the whole. This results in the adoption of specific international legal frameworks for each of the components, the establishment of different categories of conflict-affected people, and the creation of specialized agencies with tall bureaucratic hierarchies, specialized functions, and mandates for specific situations and people. It also translates into humanitarian principles that emphasize the independence from action relating to other components.

The 1951 Convention reflects the atomistic assumptions of the Cartesian paradigm in that it adopts a reactive, exile-oriented, and refugee-centric approach to forced migration. The atomistic way in which Western states conceived refugee protection translated into operational and institutional ineffectiveness and thus threatened affluent states' interest in containing forced population movements in regions of origin. First, by overlooking root causes to displacement and disconnecting refugee protection from other issues areas, humanitarian actors ended up with protracted care and maintenance refugee situations in countries of the global South when Western states shifted to restrictive asylum policies. Second, the neglect of other population groups often implied that gains made in regard to the protection of refugees translated into a further deterioration of IDPs and resident populations. Third, international agencies' narrow focus on specific issue areas and categories of people meant that uncoordinated agency programmes frequently undermined each other's impact. In short, the Cartesian approach to refugee protection often increased rather than decreased the overall burden.

The shift to a proactive, home-land oriented, and holistic approach with the end of the Cold War signalled a growing awareness among affluent states that root causes and issues areas are interconnected and thus need to be addressed in a holistic manner. This new approach had important operational, geographic, and institutional consequences. Operationally, states increasingly acknowledged that the interdependence of forced migration with other issues areas requires integrated and context-sensitive interventions. For example, relief and development were no longer viewed as self-contained and mutually exclusive. Equally, concepts such as 'conflict sensitivity' and 'sustainable development' signalled States' increasing preparedness for longer-term systems thinking. Second, forced migration-related issues were increasingly seen as trans-sovereign and multidimensional, thus requiring regional multi-sector approaches. Third, actors came to conclude that comprehensive protection approaches must encompass all population groups affected by armed conflict.

Building on successful comprehensive approaches in Central America and South-East Asia, states launched at the Global Consultations the concept of 'comprehensive solutions' without specifying its meaning. Scholars suggest that the term 'comprehensive' reflects not only the increasingly holistic thinking characterizing the post-Cold War period. It is also the entry point for systems theory, in that it refers to the ability to obtain a full understanding of interwoven issues in the field of forced migration and deal with them in an inclusive manner (Gottwald 2012).

Institutionally, actors involved realized that a systems approach to 'burden' sharing required concerted action among humanitarian, development, political, and security actors which contrasted with agencies' traditional silo cultures. This led to the adoption of the Humanitarian Reform and its humanitarian coordination architecture and UN initiatives such as Integrated Missions and Delivering as One. Agencies and Western donor countries seek to mirror these interagency network arrangements with whole-of-organization and whole-of-government approaches.

While these developments reflect a clear shift from Cartesian thinking to systems thinking, doubts arise as to whether in practice these approaches have translated into systemic action. Despite institutional reform efforts, governments and international organizations remain in essence hierarchical bureaucracies operating on unilateral control values and assumptions. It is thus the Cartesian paradigm that continues to govern their actions. Conversely, affected populations in conjunction with other civil actors are—when comprised of diverse, independent, decentralized individuals and groups— much more effective in collectively embracing the complexity of their environment and adapting to changing circumstances. For example, local communities in Somalia and Somali refugees in the Dadaab refugee camps in Kenya have set up strong networks with the Somali diaspora in the USA, including an informal system of communication and banking operated by Somalis around the world (Horst 2008). These networks enable Somalis to stay in Somalia despite the food crisis, and Somali refugees to survive in the camps notwithstanding insufficient international aid.

Yet in pursuit of their self-interest to contain populations in regions of origin, states and international organizations have tended to implement systems approaches on a regional basis rather than globally. This closed system approach reflects the structural inequality that characterizes North–South relations (Chimni 2000), contradicts refugees' transnational strategies, and contributes to irregular population movements to the global North.

Conclusions

The systems approaches that have emerged in the past decade have translated into four changes in the 'burden'-sharing debate. First, practitioners and scholars increasingly recognize that conflict and displacement result from a multitude of interconnected causes and entail multidimensional costs not only for refugee source and host countries but also for non-receiving countries at the regional and global level. This has encouraged them to broaden the definition of 'burden' and include interventions such as prevention, protection, and solutions, as these are contributing to international peace and security. It has also prompted them to promote the concerted action of humanitarian, development, political, and security actors in both countries of asylum and origin, and at all stages of conflict. Second, Western states have come to acknowledge that the trans-sovereign nature and complexity of root causes and their negative cross-sector externalities exceed not only their own problem-solving and redistribution capacities, but also those of international organizations such as UNHCR. Hence their shift from exclusive executive multilateralism to inclusive multipartite forms of global governance that draw on the responsibilities and capacities of states in the South and an expanding range of non-state actors such as refugees' transnational networks, NGOs, and private-sector organizations.

Yet the Western states continue to act in ways which reflect their ambiguity regarding the emergent heterarchical world order. While Western states have emphasized systems thinking in regard to the factors internal to refugee countries and regions in the global South, they continue to ignore the international causes of conflict, including their self-interested pursuit of foreign and security interests. Second, Western states' restrictive attitude towards immigration from the South has meant that they seek to contain population movements in regions of origins through a closed systems approach which interferes with affected populations' collective transnational coping mechanisms.

This leads to the final question. Can the global North continue dictating the terms of 'burden' and responsibility sharing? Multipartite collaboration between Northern and Southern states, intergovernmental, international, and private actors aimed at collectively managing trans-sovereign problems could strengthen global governance such as defined by the West and thus confirm Western states' primary authority. But equally, given the failure of this burden-sharing system, the increasing diversification of actors in the 'burden'-sharing domain could mean that the traditional 'burden'-sharing system will be overtaken by non-traditional systems that are much more adaptive to environmental turmoil than the formal networks established by Western states and the UN. For if states' refugee problem—and refugees' problems—are to be comprehensively addressed in the twenty-first century, it seems clear the West will need to continue to reimagine 'burden sharing' to encompass multiple actors, continuing movements, and the principles of systems theory.

References

Anderson, M. (1999) *Do No Harm: How Aid Can Support Peace—or War*. Boulder, CO: Lynne Rienner Publishers.

Betts, A. (2009) *Forced Migration and Global Politics*. New York: Wiley-Blackwell.

Brown, M., and Rosecrance, R. (1999) *The Costs of Conflict: Prevention and Cure in the Global Arena*. Lanham, MD: Rowman & Littlefield.

Capra, F. (1997) *The Web of Life: A New Scientific Understanding of Living Systems*. New York: Anchor Books.

Chimni, B. S. (2000) *International Refugee Law*. New Delhi: Sage Publications.

Chimni, B. S. (2003) 'Aid, Relief, and Containment: The First Asylum Country and Beyond'. *International Migration* 40: 5.

EU Council (1995) 'Resolution on Burden-Sharing with Regard to the Admission and Residence of Displaced Persons'.

EXCOM Conclusions, No. 15 (1979), 22 (1981), 79 (1996), 81 (1997) 87 (1999), 100 (2004).

Gottwald, M. (2012) 'Back to the Future: The Concept of Comprehensive Solutions'. *Refugee Survey Quarterly* 31: 3.

Hommon, R. J. (1996) 'Social Complex Adaptive Systems: Some Hawaiian Examples'. Working paper. <http://www.santafe.edu/media/workingpapers/95-07-066.pdf>.

Horst, C. (2008) *Transnational Nomads: How Somalis Cope with Refugee Life in the Dadaab Camps of Kenya*. New York: Berghahn Books.

International Commission on Intervention and State Sovereignty/ICISS (2001) *The Responsibility to Protect*. Ottawa: International Development Research Centre.

IOM (2011) *Migrants Caught in Crisis: The IOM Experience in Libya*. <http://publications.iom. int/bookstore/free/MigrationCaughtinCrisis_forweb.pdf>.

Kelly, B., and Wadud, A. J. (2012) 'Asian Labour Migrants and Humanitarian Crises: Lessons from Libya'. IOM, Issue in Brief No. 3.

Krasner, S. (1983) *International Regimes*. Cambridge: Cornell University Press.

Kritzman-Amir, T. (2008) 'Not in my Backyard: On the Morality of Responsibility-Sharing in Refugee Law'. <http://works.bepress.com/tally_kritzman_amir/1>.

Kuhn, T. (1970). *The Structure of Scientific Revolutions*. Chicago: University of Chicago Press.

Loescher, G., Betts, A., and Milner, J. (2008) *The United Nations High Commissioner for Refugees (UNHCR)*. New York: Routledge.

Luttwak, E. (1999) 'Give War a Chance'. *Foreign Affairs* (July/August).

MccGwire, M. (2001) 'The Paradigm that Lost its Way'. *International Affairs* 77(4): 777–803.

South, A., and Harragin, S. (2012) 'Local to Global Protection in Myanmar (Burma), Sudan, South Sudan and Zimbabwe'. Network Paper No. 72.

Suhrke, A. (1999) 'Burden-Sharing during Refugee Emergencies: The Logic of Collective versus National Action'. *Journal of Refugee Studies* 11(4): 396–415.

Pascale, R., Milleman, M., and Goja, L. (2001) *Surfing the Edge of Chaos*. New York: Three Rivers Press.

Rittel, H., and Webber, M. (1973) 'Dilemmas in a General Theory of Planning'. *Policy Sciences* 4: 155–69.

Sköns, E. (2005) 'The Costs of Armed Conflict'. Pp. 169–90 in International Task Force on Global Public Goods (ed.), *Peace and Security*. Stockholm: International Task Force on Global Public Goods.

Surowiecki, J. (2005) *The Wisdom of Crowds*. New York: Anchor Books.

Thielemann, E., and Dewan, T. (2006) 'Why States Don't Defect: Refugee Protection and Implicit Burden-Sharing'. *West European Politics* 29(1).

UNHCR (1995) *The State of the World's Refugees: In Search of Solutions*. Oxford: UNHCR.

UNHCR (2000) 'Burden-Sharing'. Discussion paper submitted by UNHCR Fifth Annual Plenary Meeting of the APC.

UNHCR (2006) 'Where Are They Now? The Hungarian Refugees, 50 Years On'. *Refugees Magazine* 144(3).

UNHCR (2010) 'International Cooperation, Burden Sharing and Comprehensive Regional Approaches'. Breakout Session 2, High Commissioner's Dialogue on Protection Challenges.

UNISDR (2009) UNISDR terminology on disaster risk reduction. <http://www.unisdr.org/eng/terminology/terminology-2009-eng.html>.

Van Hear, N. (2003) 'From Durable Solutions to Transnational Relations: Home and Exile among Refugee Diasporas'. New Issues in Refugee Research. Working Paper No. 83.

World Bank (2012) *Migration and Remittances during the Global Financial Crisis and Beyond*. Washington, DC: The World Bank.

PART VII

REGIONAL STUDIES: CURRENT REALITIES AND FUTURE CHALLENGES

CHAPTER 42

FORCED MIGRATION IN WEST AFRICA

MARION FRESIA[1]

INTRODUCTION

SINCE the 1960s, West Africa has long had a reputation of stability and economic growth driven by Senegal, Ghana, and Côte d'Ivoire, and yet political and economic crises leading to mass displacements across the region have multiplied over the last 20 years. Since the 2000s, West Africa has also been identified as a major hub for human trafficking, and portrayed as a departure point for thousands of desperate 'illegal' migrants trying to reach Europe when 80 per cent of migratory movements actually take place within the region (Gnisci 2008). This chapter discusses these recent evolutions by situating regional dynamics of different types of forced displacement in historical perspective. It highlights some of the unintended effects which the development of a West African 'protection' regime have had in terms of labelling processes, the development of increasingly rigid categories of belonging, and, at times, the accentuation of certain conflicts. It also outlines regional specificities such as the role of the Economic Community of West African States (ECOWAS) vis-à-vis displaced populations, and the influence of the European Union (EU) immigration agenda in framing regional discourses and initiatives in relation to forced migration.

'West Africa' in this context refers to ECOWAS member states (Benin, Burkina Faso, Cap Verde, Côte d'Ivoire, Gambia, Ghana, Guinea, Guinea-Bissau, Mali, Niger, Nigeria, Liberia, Senegal, Sierra Leone, and Togo) and Mauritania, which withdrew from ECOWAS in 2000. This chapter does not comprehensively cover the situation of all these countries, but rather highlights significant trends vis-à-vis dynamics of displacement identified broadly across the region through an extensive review of the literature. However, while West Africa shares a common heritage of slavery, colonization, and migratory patterns as well as a common framework with ECOWAS, not all dynamics identified necessarily have an intrinsically regional character: the politics and practices of asylum, for instance, remain strongly dependent on national contexts while labelling processes are closely articulated to wider, global, dynamics. Nevertheless, the regional scale facilitates an analysis of the intra-regional dimension of a majority of displacements in West Africa, and a reflection on the potential for ECOWAS to address cross-border challenges whilst simultaneously recognizing the importance of mobility in the everyday lives of displaced populations.

'Refugees' of Pre-colonial and Colonial Times

Forced displacement is not a recent phenomenon in West Africa and its causes have always been multiple. During pre-colonial times, constant micro-displacements took place as small groups of people fled lineage disputes over power, chiefdom leadership, and land. These micro-displacements played a key role in West African population dynamics and in the construction of pre-colonial political organizations, as migrants sought to reproduce the political structures of their society of origin in new areas of settlement (Kopytoff 1987). Larger population movements throughout this period were also induced by *razzias* (raids) of goods and animals and by political and religious conquests, including *jihad* movements across the Sahel undertaken by the Almovarides in the Middle Ages and subsequently by Muslim Fulani in the nineteenth century (Amselle and M'Bokolo 1989).

Concurrently, the most documented and most extensive form of forced migration in West Africa remains the external slave trade. While slavery had always existed in the region, it took a new dimension with the trans-Saharan (8th–18th centuries) and the trans-atlantic trades (16th–19th centuries), when local slave systems started to supply captives for slave markets outside the region. Slaves were first captured at the periphery of medieval West African empires and sent to North Africa and the Middle East. With the transatlantic trade, an estimated 12 million people were then captured across the coastal regions, including 6 million deported to the Americas. The most affected regions were Benin, Guinea, and Senegambia, and yet they were also the most developed ones (Manning 1996). After its abolition in the early eighteenth century, slavery also brought about so-called 'return movements' of emancipated slaves from the Unites States to Liberia and Sierra Leone, organized by a philanthropic American movement. These 'returns' created a structural division in Liberia and Sierra Leone between 'Afro-Americans' and those asserting their 'autochthony', a divide which was subsequently manipulated by both countries' elites, contributing to the devastating conflicts of the 1990s.

Colonization equally caused important forced displacements. Within French West Africa, it induced new kinds of micro-displacements as inhabitants fled the census, head taxes, the requisition of forced labour, and military recruitment. People attempted to escape by moving from one circumscription to the other or fleeing to inaccessible rural areas. Until the 1950s, both the inner Sahel bush and tropical forests of West Africa became 'refuge zones' (Marchal 1999). Many were also forcibly requisitioned to work on plantations, mines, or for construction. This was the case of the Mossi resettled from Upper Volta to work on plantations in Côte d'Ivoire. As for Diola and Malinke, the Mossi migration was afterwards promoted under the Houpouet Boigny presidency to provide planters with a steady labour supply and, years later, the politicization of the presence of these migrants was one of the factors which led Côte d'Ivoire to civil war. In the Upper Volta alone, Marchal (1999) estimates that 1.8 million people were forcibly displaced between 1900 and 1950.

Forced displacements prior to 1960, which continue to this date, were eventually caused by harsh climate conditions combined with socio-economic, demographic, and political factors (Morrissey 2014). Major events in this regard have included the famines of 1900–3 and 1913 in the Niger delta and the dramatic droughts of the 1970s, which provoked the displacement, and sometimes forced sedentarization of thousands of Moorish, Tuareg, and Fulani nomads leading to a dramatic increase in pressure on land in the Sahel.

Overall, forced displacements in the past have either intensified existing migration patterns towards existing towns or contributed to the development of new communities, whose relationships with established communities have varied between absorption or domination (Skinner 1963). Social scientists have outlined the key role played by local intermediaries such as the figure of the *jatigui* in facilitating the social integration of strangers in new areas and contributing to fluid politics of belonging (Chauveau Jacob, and Le Meur 2004). Yet they also show that colonial practices solidified boundary-making processes between existing populations and newcomers by encapsulating them into reified ethnic categories, and nourishing tensions over access to resources which were to reappear years after independence (Amselle and M'Bokolo 1989).

Contemporary Forced Displacements

Since the 1960s, processes of displacement across West Africa have often been induced by multiple and overlapping factors as in the past and have sometimes resulted from conflicts over resources provoked by previous displacements. However, contemporary types of displacement are distinct since they now occur in the context of nation states and are framed according to bureaucratic categories such as 'refugees', 'internally displaced persons' (IDPs), or 'trafficked persons'. The following section explores regional trends vis-à-vis three key types of displacements—conflict induced displacement, forced expulsions induced by economic crisis, and 'child trafficking'—which may, however, have interrelated causes in practice. Importantly, it must be noted that mass displacements such as those related to the Mano River wars and more recently 'mixed migration' towards Europe have been much more extensively documented than other types of movements which are either more recent or have received less media coverage.

Conflict Induced Displacements

Conflicts have been a major cause of contemporary forced migration in West Africa (Kotoudi 2004). Apart from the liberation struggle of Guinea-Bissau, most conflicts have been intrastate, related to nation-state-building processes and struggles over the control of power and resources, and often articulated around the language of ethnicity or religion. Political tensions have at times also arisen from the militarization of the political sphere or from post-election crises.

Until the late 1980s, such conflicts remained localized in a region reputed to be stable. They took the form of secessionist movements like the Biafra war in Nigeria (1967–70) and the Casamance independence movement in Southern Senegal (1980–present), and generated more internal displacement than refugee flows. If the Biafra war was relatively short and provoked large-scale internal displacement, the Casamance conflict was much longer, and induced fewer displacements. Despite several ceasefires, the conflict continued into the 1990s and took a wider dimension as Zighinchor, the capital, was no longer spared from violence. Approximately 17,000 (Robin 2006) displaced people started crossing to Guinea-Bissau and Gambia. Yet, rebels amongst the refugees not only perpetrated sporadic violent attacks in Casamance but also took part in the 1998–9 Guinean civil war, generating another 400,000 IDPs (Robin 2006). A system of conflict thus slowly emerged in the Senegambia area, fostered by cross-border solidarities and arms trafficking, creating chronic instability.

The development of the Casamance conflict reflects the way in which regional displacement dynamics have evolved since the mid-1990s: a growing circulation of actors and factors of conflicts, massive cross-border refugee movements which have sometimes nourished new tensions and new displacements following the militarization of refugee camps. This evolution has been fuelled by historical links between cross-border populations, and by the increasing involvement in intrastate conflicts of various actors, including humanitarian organizations, ECOWAS, the UN, or other states. Its most significant illustration is the well-known imbrication of the civil wars in Sierra Leone and Liberia, which induced, at the pick of the war in 1996, the displacement of around 755,000 Liberians and 355,000 Sierra Leoneans to neighbouring countries (Gnisci, Tremoliers, and Hussein 2003: 20–3).

Although the consequences of these refugee movements in Guinea has been well documented (Van Damme 1999; Milner 2009), their impact in Côte d'Ivoire is less known. The concentration of Liberian and Sierra Leonean refugees in the west of the country, where many Ivoirians of Burkinabe and Malian origin had been established since the colonial times, significantly increased an already important demographic pressure on land, at a time when Côte d'Ivoire was experiencing a major economic crisis and the redistribution of power among its elites (Gnisci, Tremoliers, and Hussein 2003). Their presence contributed to an exacerbation of the ongoing politicization of autochtony, and facilitated the circulation of arms and mercenaries (Ero and Marshall 2003). The subsequent civil war in Côte d'Ivoire (2002–7, 2010–11) further displaced Liberian and Sierra

Leonean refugees but also led to the massive expulsions of Ivoirians of Burkinabe origin, the internal displacement of thousands of Ivoirians, and the flight of 250,000 others abroad (UNHCR 2011: 110), about whose situation there is a salient lack of research. The current situation in and around Côte d'Ivoire remains volatile, especially as return movements have created new tensions over access to land, as in Burkina-Faso (Zongo 2008), and as war itself increasingly becomes a survival mode attracting unemployed youth (Ero and Marshall 2005).

A final illustration of such systems of conflict is the situation in northern Mali as of October 2012. Throughout the 1960s and 1990s, Mali faced Tuareg separatist insurgencies accompanied by sporadic population displacement to Algeria and Libya. And yet the Tuareg Mouvement National de Libération de l'Azawad has recently received further support following the return of Malian Tuareg from Libya well armed with weapons circulating since Qaddafi's demise, prompting the displacement of hundreds of thousands of Malians to border countries in areas severely affected by droughts. Several armed Islamist movements have also joined and sometimes supplanted the Tuareg uprising. The progressive establishment of so-called 'radical Islam' in the Sahel, which rearticulates local political agendas in a new manner, illustrates the importance of extra-regional dynamics on conflict and displacement in West Africa.

Current trends therefore suggest that conflict induced displacement in the coming years may be increasingly related to the apparition of 'nomadic' war economies, which fuel local conflicts related to nation-state-building processes, and become an attractive activity for marginalized youth. The politicization of refugee camps and humanitarian aid may also be part of the problem as they simultaneously reinforce cross-border alliances and foster politics of autochthony in hosting areas. Such an evolution risks spreading chronic instability around Côte d'Ivoire, the Mano River countries, and the Sahel, leading refugees to find asylum not only in bordering countries but also increasingly in other countries of the region.

Forced Expulsions and 'Mixed Migration'

If war has been a major cause of forced displacement, other processes have predominantly resulted from economic crises leading to violence targeted against foreigners. At times of economic recession, West African states have sometimes taken radical measures, such as the mass expulsion of 200,000 Nigerians and other foreigners from Ghana in 1969 (Bump 2006). In 1983 and 1985, Nigeria followed Ghana's example, with its military government expelling over 1.2 million Ghanaians, accusing them of taking jobs from Nigerians (Bump 2006). Yet, these expulsions did not bring fundamental changes to migration dynamics, as migrants quickly returned to Nigeria and Ghana. In a different context, Mauritania and Senegal also organized the forced repatriation of thousands of their citizens in 1989, after a border incident provoked an outburst of violence against Moorish traders in Senegal and against Senegalese citizens in Nouakchott. However, in Mauritania the authorities also used the forced returns of Senegalese as a pretext to expel 120,000 Mauritanian citizens belonging to the same ethnic groups, and who had historically controlled the country's only fertile lands, which became increasingly strategic after the sedentarization of 70 per cent of Moorish nomads during the 1970s droughts (Fresia 2009).

Since the early 2000s, forced expulsions of West Africans have, however, mainly happened at the periphery of the region, from North African and European countries, as a result of restrictive European immigration policies and strengthened surveillance of North African borders and maritime routes. Within the international policy arena, this context has raised attention to the increased risk of *refoulement* faced by West African asylum seekers using the same routes as other migrants (the 'mixed migration' problematic). In parallel, a rich literature documenting the migratory experiences of West Africans attempting to reach Europe outlines the difficulty of drawing a clear line between forced and voluntary migration. Scholars have also focused on the situation of those expelled from North Africa or Europe, demonstrating that the majority are not in a position to return home due to lack of funds and fear of experiencing shame, thereby tending to either remain in so-called 'transit' countries that turn out to be dead ends or attempting to migrate again (Schmitz 2008). Poutignat and Streiff-Fénart (2008) outline how the European immigration agenda has contributed to the stigmatization of certain migrant communities established for decades in Senegal, Mauritania, or Mali as 'illegal' migrants, generating xenophobia against them. Restrictive European policies have ultimately been described as the cause of the growing sophistication of human smuggling networks in West Africa, which has in turn produced a discourse criminalizing intermediaries such as the *jatigui* despite their role often also being positive in facilitating migrants' journey and integration in foreign countries (Pian 2010).

Child Trafficking or Youth Migration?

Since the United Nations adopted the Palermo Protocol on trafficking on persons in 2000, West Africa has also been increasingly framed as a major human trafficking region. Child trafficking has particularly been denounced as a key regional challenge, generating considerable grey literature. Three main exploitation routes have repeatedly been identified: adolescent boys from Mali and Burkina Faso transported to work in the cocoa agricultural industry in Côte d'Ivoire and Ghana; young girls from Benin and Togo taken to Gabon and Nigeria to be employed as domestic servants or street beggars; and young women taken from Nigeria and Ghana mainly to Europe and the Middle East to work as sex workers. Liberia, Sierra Leone, Guinea, and Côte d'Ivoire are also associated with the forced enrolment of children in armed forces and child labour in mines (Sawadogo 2012).

Research remains scarce on the topic and academics are more cautious than NGOs to qualify certain practices as human trafficking. Castles and Diarra (2003) highlight the need to adopt a more nuanced perspective given the history of child migration in the region, where the *confiage*[2] of children to a relative for educational purposes has always been widespread, and adolescents' working experience abroad has often been perceived as a necessary rite of passage or an emancipatory adventure. Some researchers underline the socio-economic transformations that may explain why such historical practices have sometimes become abusive, such as the globalization of criminal networks, surging food prices or women's accession to monetary economy which creates greater needs for domestic labour (Abega, Abé, and Mimche 2007). They also note the region's demographic explosion, which redefines young people's roles as becoming increasingly responsible for financially supporting their parents. In this context, youth mobility becomes the best if not the only option to secure their family's life. Scholars insist on the need to restore parents' and youth's agency within the human trafficking discourse, highlighting the unintended effects of an approach which criminalizes and homogenizes such practices (Huijsmans and Baker 2012).

THE WEST AFRICAN 'PROTECTION' APPARATUS

In parallel with and as a response to contemporary displacements, West African states have developed national and regional legal and political frameworks to ensure the management of displaced populations. This contemporary 'protection' apparatus has been shaped by international and regional norms on refugee rights, but has never fully replaced former mechanisms of migration regulation such as kinship solidarity or the *jatigui* institution. This section provides a brief overview of the history of this apparatus, how it has been mobilized by governments, and the role ECOWAS, the EU, and UNHCR have played in shaping it.

The Politics and Practices of Asylum

West Africa has a well-developed legal framework vis-à-vis refugee protection. During the 1960s and 1970s, all ECOWAS member states acceded to the Geneva Convention relating to the Status of Refugees (1951) and its additional Protocol (1967), as well as the OAU Convention Governing the Specific Aspects of Refugee Problems in Africa (1969). Throughout the 1990s and 2000s, all ECOWAS countries except Cape Verde adopted national laws on asylum, responding to these decades' massive refugee movements and UNHCR's advocacy work. Furthermore, since 2009, all ECOWAS countries save Niger and Cape Verde have either signed or ratified the Kampala Convention on IDPs and by 2012 half of them had acceded to the UN Conventions relating to the Status of Stateless Persons of 1954 or 1961. Since the early 2000s, a majority of ECOWAS countries as well as Mauritania have eventually established their own national commissions for refugee status determination (RSD).

There is a lack of systematic research regarding the actual practices of asylum in the region, and yet investigations conducted in Guinea (Milner 2009) and Senegal (Fresia 2009), in addition to World Refugee Surveys, can give us insights into how West African states have mobilized this framework in practice. First, it appears that they may not have followed the same path as other sub-Saharan African states depicted as having had a 'golden age' of asylum up to the 1980s followed by a crisis in hospitality since the 1990s (Crisp 2006). Rather, they have always upheld broadly open asylum policies combined at certain times with restrictive practices. Since the 1960s, they have continuously hosted massive refugee influxes on their territories granting them prima facie refugee status. Hosting policies have also been characterized as laissez-faire, taking place through a combination of kinship solidarities, *jatigui* hosting mechanisms, and spontaneous refugee settlements; these processes have been paralleled by the establishment of more standardized refugee camps since the mid-1990s along with the Mano River conflicts (Van Damne 1999). Camps in West Africa however have rarely reached the size of those in Eastern Africa and West African states have not formulated encampment policies nor formally restricted refugees' freedom of movement or right to work. Far from being embedded in so-called African 'hospitality', this can be explained by diverse factors including long-lasting economic and kinship links across border populations, the ECOWAS framework, political interests in hosting a given refugee population, the perceived advantage of receiving international assistance and the extent and length of the demographic pressure exerted by refugee populations (Milner 2009: 171–88). West Africa may not have yet reached 'refugee fatigue' as massive and continuous cross-border movements have only occurred since the 1990s.

Nonetheless, West African states have, at different times, adopted restrictive policies towards refugees, often because of geopolitical interests or in response to the militarization of refugees. In Guinea, Milner (2009: 144–5) has documented President Conté's harsh reaction to the 2000–1 cross-border incursions, which provoked the detention of thousands of refugees. The Senegalese authorities also decided not to issue Mauritanian refugees with adequate ID cards in the late 1990s, as their political activism became a subject of diplomatic tensions with Mauritania (Fresia 2009). The failure to issue ID cards or to recognize existing ones is actually a widespread limit to refugee protection across the region, which hampers refugees' formal freedom of movements.

Another significant component of restrictive policies relates to individual RSD. West African states with national eligibility committees still lack a fair procedure and, apart from Guinea, the main hosting countries in the region have extremely low recognition rates.[3] Recent research conducted in Ghana and Senegal shows, for instance, that both states tend to suspect that all applicants who have moved beyond their first country of asylum are preparing an 'illegal' trip to Europe and are abusing their asylum system (Charrière and Fresia 2008). This has direct consequences on refugees originating from non-ECOWAS countries but also on Sierra Leoneans, Liberians, and Ivoirians who move throughout the region and are in need of protection. In both countries, RSD therefore appears to have been mobilized more as an instrument of exclusion, asserting national sovereignty, than as an instrument of protection.

As for durable solutions, West African state practices have varied between repatriation and local integration, often combining the two for the same population. After the independence of Guinea-Bissau, thousands of Guinean refugees were repatriated, while many remained in Senegal. Since the early 2000s, the official return of refugees became the 'favourite' durable solution, as it is perceived as a strong political signal symbolizing the return to peace in previously unstable countries. Sierra Leoneans, Liberians, Togolese, and Mauritanians were officially repatriated when many of them had either already returned spontaneously or found a solution through transnational coping strategies. Yet, the early 2000s can concurrently be characterized as an era of 'local integration' (Milner 2009: 34). UNHCR has indeed actively promoted the latter to address protracted refugee situations and several governments have so far responded positively to the idea of officially integrating refugees who cannot repatriate, either through naturalization or via the regularization of their often de facto integration as migrant workers through the ECOWAS framework.

The ECOWAS Framework

ECOWAS was created in 1975 to promote economic integration across the region through its 1979 Protocol Relating to Free Movement of Persons, Right of Residence and Establishment for all ECOWAS citizens, and its supplementary protocols. This framework has the potential to further protect refugees who are ECOWAS citizens by facilitating their economic integration in member states and recognizing the importance of mobility in their lives. In practice, however, the ECOWAS Protocols have been scarcely implemented (Gnisci 2008). ECOWAS citizens still encounter difficulties with moving freely in the region as they are subject to informal taxes or arbitrary detention. At borders, legal distinctions between ECOWAS and non-ECOWAS citizens, migrants, and refugees are of little relevance. Rather, discrimination appears to function between nationals of bordering countries and the 'others'. Likewise, ECOWAS citizens coming from countries other than bordering ones face greater difficulties in accessing employment and resident permits. In Senegal, for instance, there are discriminatory administrative practices between 'Sahel people' and people from the 'tropical forests', which particularly affect Anglophone refugees (Charrière and Fresia 2008).

While its role in terms of economic integration has remained limited, ECOWAS has nevertheless developed a new function in the area of peace-building during the 1990s. An additional protocol was signed in 1999 establishing the ECOWAS Mechanism for Conflict Prevention and Peace Keeping. It institutionalized the ECOMOG West African intervention force—an ad hoc ceasefire monitoring group which intervened in the Mano River countries and Guinea-Bissau—and led to the creation of an ECOWAS department of Humanitarian Affairs. For Levitt (2001), ECOWAS is the African regional organization with the most advanced experience in terms of refugee protection via peacekeeping. However, its actions have also contributed to prolong the Liberian civil war, and its lack of resources and internal divisions remain major weaknesses.

ECOWAS's role vis-à-vis displaced persons has nevertheless received increased interest through several initiatives. First, UNHCR has closely worked with several ECOWAS member states to encourage them to recognize that the Protocols on free movements should apply to Liberians and Sierra Leoneans, whose refugee status has ceased (Adepoju, Boulton, and Levin 2007). This strategy led to the adoption, in 2007, of a 'Memorandum on equality of treatment for refugees and other ECOWAS nationals' which constitutes an innovative first step towards considering not only local integration but also legal mobility as a fourth durable solution for ECOWAS refugees. If this solution is de facto the one already adopted by a majority of refugees for whom mobility is at the heart of coping strategies, its implementation could allow legal recognition of the latter and secure their rights.

Second, the ECOWAS framework has gained interest with regard to combating human trafficking with the adoption of the 2006 Ouagadougou Action Plan against the trafficking of women and children. Parallel to these initiatives, 12 countries out of 15 have signed the Palermo Protocol on Trafficking between 2009 and 2012 including Benin, Togo, and Burkina-Faso and 12 of the 15 states have passed national laws on human trafficking. IOM has also developed a regional programme of assistance for the return and reintegration of trafficked children (IOM/UNHCR 2011). Nonetheless, the impact of these counter-trafficking initiatives remains to be evaluated, especially when they tend to homogenize practices that may be of different natures. Besides, their focus on women and children tends to overshadow the situation of men who may be equally exposed to labour exploitation.

The Weight of the EU Immigration Agenda

A third aspect of the West African protection 'apparatus' is its articulation with the EU immigration agenda. The multiplication, since the early 2000s, of bilateral agreements between EU countries and West African states vis-à-vis migration management have contributed to shape regional priorities (Gnisci 2008). First, it has legitimized the need to reinforce national capacities with regard to border management, which may contradict ECOWAS Protocols. Second, it has framed West Africa as a region of departure of 'illegal migrants', entailing a shift of attention away from refugee movements. Third, while it may signal West African states' will to gain ownership on asylum, the recent establishment of RSD systems in the region can also be interpreted as a consequence of European pressure to have them better control their migration flows.

These evolutions have, however, been partially counter-balanced in 2008 by the 'ECOWAS Common Approach of Member States to Migration' in which the will is reaffirmed to speed up the implementation of the Protocols while asserting the need to protect refugees and trafficked persons, and the right of residence in member countries for ECOWAS refugees. UNHCR has also initiated trainings on 'protection sensitive' border management and convened several inter-agency conferences with IOM and ECOWAS on the 'protection of refugees and other people on the move within mixed migration contexts' (IOM/UNHCR 2011). Overall, these initiatives have contributed to a discursive shift within the region from 'refugee protection' to 'mixed migration', recognizing both that the boundary between forced and voluntary migration is not always clear, and yet that the 'specific' protection needs of different categories of people on the move should be addressed.

Conclusion

While forced displacements have always existed in West Africa, the past 50 years have witnessed dramatic changes in the way they have been framed and addressed.

First, the development of a 'protection' apparatus in the region has contributed to the production of 'refugeehood' by constructing a boundary between refugees and migrants, which have been juxtaposed to former, and yet still existing, mechanisms of migration regulation which were based on more fluid categories of belonging. Since the early 2000s, under the influence of EU, UNHCR, and IOM, this apparatus has entered a new phase with a shift of focus from 'refugee protection' alone to the protection of different categories of 'people on the move'. This shift reflects a wider, global, evolution towards a multiplication of labels of displaced persons paradoxically combined with the recognition that refugees and other migrants may have similar experiences of migration. If these labelling processes have the potential to offer more protection to displaced persons in West Africa, they may also have unintended consequences such as the stigmatization of the figure of the stranger ; the criminalization of intermediaries such as the *jatigui*; the production of victimhood ; and the homogenization of practices related to youth migration. Yet, research work has also shown that these labelling processes have enhanced new forms of political mobilization and citizenship among displaced persons, and new migratory and labour opportunities for certain social actors (Fresia 2009). Further research is therefore necessary to fully understand how this West African protection apparatus contributes to alter regional and local political and historical dynamics.

A second regional evolution is the growing role played by individual recognition of refugee status. There is currently almost no research on the politics and practices of national eligibility committees. It only appears that West African states seem more generous to provide prima facie protection to refugees coming from neighbouring countries, than to provide individual recognition to asylum seekers coming from farther countries. The mobilization of RSD to exclude more than to protect could therefore become a challenge to be closely followed.

A third recent trend is the growing political will to use ECOWAS not only as an instrument of regional economic integration but also as a tool to enhance protection and innovative durable solutions. This positive evolution yet raises several challenges including ECOWAS's capacity to implement such ambitious goals; the concern that ECOWAS's increased role is too closely articulated to the EU migration agenda and may be a way for European countries to shift a number of burdens on West African states; and the risk of accentuating an already existing discrimination between ECOWAS and non-ECOWAS citizens in terms of access to asylum, durable solutions, or labour migration.

Last, this chapter has outlined the increasing imbrications between system of conflicts and displaced populations. This is probably the most important challenge the region will continue to face in coming years, despite being recently overshadowed by the 'mixed migration' discourse, whether on policy or research agendas. Further research on the circulation of actors and factors of conflicts is therefore needed, including by following the implications of recent major repatriation operations that, far from being the end of refugee cycles in the region, may be characterized by a range of new challenges.

NOTES

1. The author is grateful to Laura Rezzonico who conducted the literature review for this chapter, Elena Fiddian-Qasmiyeh for her detailed comments as well as Étienne Piguet.
2. Literally referring to 'entrusting' the child to a relative or friend, *confiage* can be understood as a form of fostering.
3. Recognition rates in 2007: Benin 3.6%; Côte d'Ivoire 8%; Senegal 5%; Ghana 3.6%; Guinea 63.1% (Charrière and Fresia 2008).

REFERENCES

Abega, S. C., Abé, C., and Mimche, H. (2007) 'Le Trafic des enfants. Étude d'une forme d'abus à l'égard des cadets sociaux'. *Sociétés et jeunesses en difficulté* 3. < http://sejed.revues.org/353> (accessed 17 December 2013).

Adepoju, A., Boulton, A., and Levin, M. (2007) 'Promoting Integration through Mobility: Free Movement and the ECOWAS Protocol'. New Issues in Refugee Research. UNHCR Working Paper No. 150.

Amselle, J.-L., and M'Bokolo, E. (1989) *Au cœur de l'ethnie: ethnies, tribalisme et État en Afrique*. Paris: La Découverte.

Bump, M. (2006) 'Ghana country profile, Migration information source'. <http://www.migrationinformation.org/USFocus/display.cfm?ID=38>. (accessed 20 December 2012).

Castle, S., and Diarra, A. (2003) *The International Migration of Young Malians: Tradition, Necessity or Rites of Passage?* London: London School of Hygiene and Tropical Medicine.

Charrière, F., and Fresia, M. (2008) *West Africa as a Space of Migration and Protection*. Geneva: UNHCR.

Chauveau, J. P., Jacob, J. P., and Le Meur, P. Y (2004) 'L'Organisation de la mobilité dans les sociétés rurales du Sud'. *Autrepart* 30: 3–25.

Crisp, J. (2006) 'Forced Displacement in Africa: Dimensions, Difficulties and Policy Directions'. New Issues in Refugee Research. UNHCR Working Paper No. 126.

Ero, C., and Marshall, A. (2003) 'L'Ouest de la Côte d'Ivoire. Un conflit libérien?' *Politique africaine* 89: 88–101.

Fresia, M. (2009) *Les Mauritaniens réfugiés au Sénégal. Une anthropologie de l'asile et de l'aide humanitaire*. Paris: L'Harmattan.

Gnisci, D. (2008) *West African Mobility and Migration Policies of OECD Countries.* Issy-les-Moulineaux: West African Studies/OECD.

Gnisci, D., Tremoliers, M., and Hussein, K. (2003) 'Interactions entre conflits et migrations involontaires en Afrique de l'Ouest. Pour une approche régionale intégrée et concertée'. Club du Sahel et de l'Afrique de l'Ouest, Scoping Study.

Huijsmans, R., and Baker, S. (2012) 'Child Trafficking: Worst Form of Child Labour, or Worst Approach to Young Migrants?' *Development & Change* 43(4): 919–46.

Kotoudi, I. (2004) *Les Migrations forcées en Afrique de l'Ouest.* Dakar: The Panos Institute West Africa.

Kopytoff, I. (1987) *The African Frontier: The Reproduction of Traditional African Societies.* Bloomington-Indianapolis: Indianapolis University Press.

Levitt, J. (2001) 'Conflict Prevention, Management, and Resolution: Africa—Regional Strategies for the Prevention of Displacement and Protection of Displaced Persons'. *Duke Journal of Comparative and International Law* 11: 39–79.

Manning, P. (ed.) (1996) *Slave Trades, 1500–1800: Globalization of Forced Labour.* Aldershot: Ashgate Variorium.

Marchal, J.-Y. (1999) 'Frontières et réfugiés en Afrique Occidentale Française: 1900–1950'. Pp. 209–26 in V. Lassailly-Jacob, J.-Y. Marchal, and A. Quesnel (eds.), *Déplacés et réfugiés. La mobilité sous contrainte.* Paris: IRD editions.

Milner, J. (2009) *Refugees, the State and the Politics of Asylum in Africa.* Basingstoke: Palgrave Macmillan.

Morrissey, J. (2014) 'Environmental Change and Human Migration in Sub-Saharan Africa'. Pp. 81–109 in E. Piguet and F. Laczko (eds.), *People on the Move in a Changing Climate.* Global Migration Issues, vol 2. Dordrecht: Springer.

Pian, A. (2010) 'Variations autour de la figure du passeur'. *Plein droit* 85(1): 21–5.

Poutignat, P., and Streiff-Fénart, J. (2008) 'Nouadhibou "ville de transit"?' *Revue européenne des migrations internationales* 24(2): 193–217.

Robin, N. (2006) 'Le Déracinement des populations en Casamance. Un défi pour l'état de droit'. *Revue européenne des migrations internationales* 22(1): 153–81.

Sawadogo, W. S (2012) 'The Challenges of Transnational Human Trafficking in West Africa'. *African Studies Quarterly* 13(1–2): 95–115.

Schmitz, J. (2008) 'Migrants ouest-africains: miséreux, aventuriers ou notables?' *Politique Africaine* 109: 2–15

Skinner, E. P (1963) 'Strangers in West African Societies'. *Africa: Journal of the International African Institute* 33(4): 307–20.

UNHCR Global Reports (West Africa) (2011).

UNHCR/IOM (2011). *Protecting Refugees and Other Persons on the Move in the ECOWAS Space.* Dakar.

Van Damme, W. (1999) 'Les Réfugiés du Libéria et de Sierra Leone en Guinée forestière (1990–1996)'. Pp. 343–82 in V. Lassailly-Jacob, J.-Y. Marchal, and A. Quesnel, *Déplacés et réfugiés. La mobilité sous contrainte.* Paris: IRD editions.

World Refugee Survey USCRI (country updates) (2007 to 2011).

Zongo, M. (2008) 'Accueil et réinsertion des "rapatriés" en zone rurale au Burkina Faso'. Pp. 139–63 in L. Cambrézy, S. Laacher, V. Lassailly-Jacob, and L. Legoux, *L'Asile au sud.* Paris: La Dispute.

CHAPTER 43

....

FORCED MIGRATION IN SOUTHERN AFRICA

....

JONATHAN CRUSH AND ABEL CHIKANDA

INTRODUCTION

....

OVER the last 50 years, Southern Africa (here viewed as coterminous with the 15 member states of the Southern African Development Community) has experienced successive waves of forced migration primarily as a result of armed conflict and civil war. Some states, such as Angola and Mozambique, have generated significant refugee outflows and internal displacement; others, such as Botswana, Malawi, Swaziland, Tanzania, and Zambia have been states of refuge; still others, such as Namibia, South Africa, and Zimbabwe have sent and received refugees. Other forms of forced migration include trafficking, which is not a significant issue in this region, and deportations, which are.

Saul (1993) depicts the independence struggles against colonial and white settler rule in Southern Africa as the 'thirty years war'. However, forced migration within the region did not begin with the struggle for independence nor end when it was attained. To understand both the volume and longevity of forced migration in Southern Africa, it is necessary to revisit the history of involuntary population movement in the pre-colonial and colonial periods. Colonialism itself set the stage for what we refer to here as Southern Africa's 'fifty years war' of struggle for independence and post-independence strife which has disrupted lives, destroyed livelihoods, and displaced millions of people internally and across borders. At the regional scale, the total number of refugees in Southern Africa rose steadily between 1960 and the late 1970s, fell in the early 1980s, and then rapidly escalated to a peak of 1.8 million in 1992 (Figure 43.1). Since then, the numbers have declined, risen and then fallen again. However, at no point between 1967 and 2011 has the number of refugees outside their home countries ever dropped below 400,000. No comparable time-series data exists for Internally Displaced Persons (IDPs) whose numbers peaked in different countries at different times. According

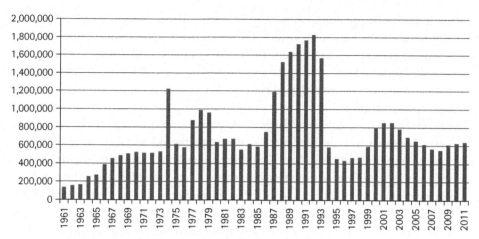

FIGURE 43.1 Refugee flows within Southern Africa, 1961–2011

Source: UNHCR Statistical Online Population Database (<http://www.unhcr.org/statistics/populationdatabase>, accessed 20 June 2012).

to the UNHCR, the highest number of IDPs was 4 million in Mozambique (in 1992), 2.1 million in the DRC (2009), and 300,000 in Angola (in 1994).

This chapter begins with a brief overview of pre-colonial and colonial forced migration. It then periodizes the fifty years war from 1960 to the present. The first phase accompanied the wars of independence of the 1960s, 1970s, and 1980s. The second began when anti-colonial forces turned on each other, often with outside backing. The third phase, primarily in the 1990s, saw the voluntary return and reintegration of many refugees, especially to Mozambique. The fourth phase, which began in the early 1990s, has seen increasing numbers of forced migrants from other African countries entering Southern Africa. The final, and current, phase has witnessed a mass exodus of people from Zimbabwe and mass deportations of migrants, asylum seekers, and refugees to other states. Against this backdrop, the chapter surveys the divergent policy responses towards forced migrants, paying particular attention to the differences between control-oriented and protection-oriented approaches.

PRE-COLONIAL AND COLONIAL FORCED MIGRATION

Forced migration in Southern Africa has deep historical roots. In pre-colonial times, forced migration was a product of factors such as territorial invasions by outside groups or dwindling resources due to population pressure, drought, disease, and pestilence, and inter-ethnic conflict. Pre-colonial forced migrations were never entirely endogenous, however, as they often occurred at the interface between local and outside political and economic forces. Many disruptions were exacerbated and even instigated by contact with the expansionist European powers. The transatlantic slave trade, for example, forcibly removed millions of people from the region and consolidated slave raiding kingdoms in the modern states of Angola and the Democratic Republic of Congo (DRC). These kingdoms not only raided weaker states for slaves for export but caused massive population displacement.

In the early nineteenth century, large-scale population movements occurred within Southern Africa during the *Mfecane* ('scattering') period as clans were expelled or took refuge from the militarist Zulu Kingdom under Shaka. The modern-day Basotho nation (Lesotho) was formed from refugee groups fleeing the *Mfecane* to the north-east. A defining characteristic of pre-colonial forced movements was their geographically unrestricted character because of the absence of international boundaries. In colonial mythology, the expansionist Zulu state and associated forced migration were a product of 'tribal' warfare. Later historical scholarship demonstrated that the pressures of expansion of white settlement and trade played a major catalytic role in the *Mfecane* (Hamilton 1995).

Colonialism fundamentally changed the nature of forced migration in Southern Africa. Conquest was sometimes relatively peaceful (as in Botswana, Lesotho, and Swaziland) and sometimes extremely bloody (as in the Anglo-Zulu wars of the nineteenth century and the genocidal policies pursued by the Germans in Namibia in the early twentieth) (Olusoga and Erichsen 2010). The partition of the region grouped pre-colonial enemies under the same European flag, while ethnic groups with shared cultures and histories were separated and forced to serve different masters. Several inter-ethnic conflicts in Africa can be traced to this arbitrary process. Furthermore, colonialism led to the massive internal displacement of peasant communities as fertile land was forcibly expropriated for white settlement in many colonies. In South Africa, over 85 per cent of the entire land surface was expropriated. Many people continued to live on expropriated land, until the apartheid state began forced removals in the 1960s.

THE COLONIAL RETREAT

The collapse of Belgian, British, French and Portuguese colonialism and white minority rule in Southern Africa in the late twentieth century brought the promise of a new era of economic opportunity and political rights. Across the region, the struggle for independence was often protracted and bloody. Although the colonial retreat from some countries was relatively peaceful, even these former British colonies of Botswana, Lesotho, Malawi, Swaziland, Tanzania, and Zambia were caught up in the regional maelstrom, becoming destinations for forced migrants fleeing wars of liberation in neighbouring countries.

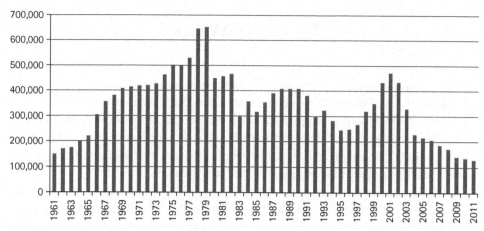

FIGURE 43.2   Refugee flows from Angola, 1961–2011

The independence wars against Portugal (in Angola and Mozambique) and white settler rule (in Namibia, South Africa, and Zimbabwe) were the most violent. The independence war in Angola lasted from 1961 to 1974 and led to hundreds of thousands fleeing to neighbouring countries such as Zambia and Zaire (now the Democratic Republic of Congo (DRC)). By the early 1970s, over 400,000 had left the country (Figure 43.2). The independence war ended after a military coup in Lisbon in 1974, paving the way for Angolan independence in 1975.

Portugal's refusal to voluntarily leave Angola was mirrored in Mozambique which experienced a decade-long war of liberation between 1964 and 1974. As the nationalist Frente de Libertação de Moçambique (FRELIMO) made territorial gains, Portuguese repression intensified, including the massacre of civilians who were supporting FRELIMO. Whole communities fled to neighbouring countries from northern Mozambique. In 1967, 67,000 Mozambican refugees were living in Tanzanian camps. As in Angola, the war in Mozambique ended abruptly in 1974.

The wars of independence also produced significant internal displacement and cross-border refugee migration. By the late 1970s, over 200,000 people had fled Zimbabwe for countries such as Mozambique and Zambia. Namibia, too, experienced a liberation war from 1966 to 1988 between the South-West Africa People's Organization (SWAPO) and the occupying South African army (Leys and Saul 1995). Many SWAPO members went into exile in Angola and joined the guerilla war. In the late 1970s and 1980s, the number of refugees leaving Namibia exceeded 70,000.

In South Africa, the apartheid government's repression of its black population led to the internal displacement of an estimated 3.5 million people. By comparison, the numbers who left the country were relatively small. Refugees were mainly anti-apartheid activists who pursued the struggle against white rule from other countries. By the late 1980s, nearly 40,000 South Africans were in political exile.

Uncivil Wars

Forced migration, both internally and across borders, escalated after the end of colonial rule in three of the most populous states: the DRC, Angola, and Mozambique. In a fourth, Zimbabwe, the Mugabe government sent the North Korean trained Fifth Brigade into southern Zimbabwe in the early 1980s to suppress dissent in Operation Gukurahundi (CCJP 2007). At least 3,000 people died and nearly 10,000 fled to neighbouring Botswana where they were accommodated in camps.

The DRC, formerly the Belgian Congo and then Zaire, became an independent state in 1960, following a series of violent altercations between the Belgian and Congolese armies in the late 1950s. Secession attempts in Katanga province shortly after independence led to the death of thousands including Prime Minister Patrice Lumumba. In the late 1970s, further disturbances in Katanga were only suppressed with Moroccan and French intervention. At the height of the conflict, more than 260,000 refugees left the country while many more were displaced internally. Ethnic tensions in neighbouring Great Lakes countries spilled into the DRC, leading to the First Congo War of 1996–7. In 1997, more than 170,000 people fled as refugees as the Kabila-led Tutsi army swept Mobutu from power.

A second war began soon after Kabila took power and withstood attacks by Rwandan and Ugandan-backed rebels with support from Angola, Namibia, and Zimbabwe. Kabila was assassinated and replaced by his son in 2001, but violent conflict continued to generate forced movements. The number of DRC refugees in neighbouring countries remained above 350,000 after 2000 and was estimated at close to 500,000 in 2011. IDPs were estimated to be close to 1 million in 2007 but fell to about 800,000 in 2011.

In Angola and Mozambique, bitter civil wars began almost immediately after the Portuguese had departed. Neither would have been as traumatic and lengthy without outside interference (Minter 1994). In Angola, the two main anti-colonial movements, the Popular Movement for the Liberation of Angola (MPLA) and the National Union for the Total Liberation of Angola (UNITA), took up arms against each other. The United States and South Africa sided with UNITA while Cuba and the Soviet Union backed the MPLA. By the late 1980s, Angola had 800,000 IDPs and 400,000 refugees in Zaire and Zambia. After nearly 30 years, the war ended in 2002 when Jonas Savimbi, the UNITA leader, was killed.

Independence in Mozambique led to heightened civil conflict as white-ruled Rhodesia and South Africa set out to destroy the new socialist FRELIMO government (Minter 1994). The civil war in Mozambique was fought between FRELIMO and the Mozambican Resistance Movement (RENAMO). With support from South Africa, RENAMO launched a terror campaign which resulted in destruction of infrastructure, an increasingly traumatized society, and widespread displacement (Table 43.1). An estimated 200,000 people died and millions were displaced internally and across borders to Tanzania, Malawi, Zimbabwe, Swaziland, and South Africa. Unlike in Angola, the

Table 43.1 Flow of Mozambican refugees and IDPs

Year	No. of Refugees*	Estimated No. of Internally Displaced People**	Total of Refugees & IDPs (Estimate)
1984	51,200	400,000	450,000
1985	72,250	700,000-1.8 million	770,000-1.9 million
1986	193,550	900,000-1.8 million	1.1-2.0 million
1987	635,000	2.0 million	2.6 million
1988	921,238	1.5-2.0 million	2.4-2.9 million
1989	1,120,758	1.7 million	2.8 million
1990	1,247,992	2.0 million	3.2 million
1991	1,316,636	2.0 million	3.3 million
1992-3	1,445,474	4.0 million	5.4 million

Sources: *UNHCR Statistical Online Population Database; **Azevedo (2002: 4).

war in Mozambique ended quickly with the collapse of apartheid and the end of South African support for RENAMO.

THE RETURN OF THE REFUGEE

The end of apartheid brought major shifts in patterns of forced migration in Southern Africa. First, South Africa's proxy wars in Angola, Namibia, and Mozambique, and its suppression of internal dissent, came to an end. During the 1990s, South Africa, Namibia, and Mozambique ceased to be major refugee-generating states. Second, forced migrants began to return home in large numbers to Mozambique and Angola. SWAPO and ANC political exiles also returned to Namibia and South Africa (Simon and Preston 1993). The orderly nature of refugee repatriation to Namibia and South Africa contrasted with the disorganized manner in which refugees returned to Mozambique. The majority of refugees self-repatriated because of the failure of the official repatriation programmes (Englund 2002). By the time the official programme was launched in Malawi, most of the refugees had already returned. Third, most Mozambican refugees in South Africa were not interested in return (Azevedo 2002). The UNHCR instituted a voluntary return programme which included financial assistance with resettlement to Mozambique. The programme was not a great success, the vast majority of refugees electing to stay in South Africa where they were living and working.

After the 1994 elections, the post-apartheid government ratified the OAU and UN Refugee Conventions and passed the Refugees Act of 1998. This did not resolve one policy dilemma since most Mozambican refugees in South Africa no longer qualified for Convention protection. The South African Cabinet eventually approved an amnesty for ex-refugees from Mozambique. Although this was plagued by procedural delays, an estimated 130,000 Mozambicans acquired identity documents and permanent residence in South Africa.

When the civil war in Angola ended in 2002, more than 457,000 Angolans were living as refugees in neighbouring countries. Zambia had more than 225,000 refugees, some of whom had integrated into Zambian society. In four years of repatriation between 2003 and 2006, UNHCR organized the return of 140,000 refugees and assisted another 117,000. A further 154,000 refugees returned without UNHCR assistance.

New Forced Migrants

Since the late 1980s, Southern Africa has become a new destination for asylum seekers from the rest of Africa, particularly from the Horn and Great Lakes region (Long and Crisp 2011). The most dramatic increase in the volume of inward forced migration was experienced by the DRC and Tanzania. In the DRC, the number of refugees increased from just over 100,000 in 1990 to a peak of nearly 1.6 million in 1994 as hundreds of thousands of people fled the genocide in Rwanda. By 2011, the number of refugees in DRC had fallen again to 74,000. In Tanzania, the refugee population grew from 177,000 to 832,307 by 1994 at the height of the Rwandan genocide. By 2011, the number of refugees still in Tanzania had dwindled to less than 70,000.

Rwandan refugees also moved in much smaller numbers to other Southern African countries in the 1990s. However, the most notable feature of the last 20 years has been the steady increase in the number of African asylum seekers from more distant countries in East, West, and North Africa. In 1990 (excluding the DRC and Tanzania as destinations), there were only 3,400 refugees registered by the UNHCR from outside the region in Southern Africa. This number rose to 21,000 in 2000 and to nearly 60,000 in 2011 (Figure 43.3). The main destination countries are South Africa and Zambia, which combined hosted 83 per cent of the total in 2010. The actual numbers of forced migrants in Southern Africa may well be much larger since some countries are notoriously resistant to providing protection to asylum seekers from countries that are not deemed by governments to be 'refugee generating'.

The idea has gained currency that refugee protection systems are collapsing under the weight of bogus claims by economic migrants. In the UNHCR lexicon 'mixed migration' streams combine genuine refugees and voluntary economic migrants seeking to legitimize their irregular status through making applications for asylum (van der Klaauw 2009). In 2010, the Government of Tanzania, the UNHCR, and the International Organization for Migration (IOM) convened a regional conference on mixed movements and irregular migration to Southern Africa. The conference developed an Action Plan which, amongst other things, offered technical support to governments to distinguish genuine refugees from 'irregular migrants'. Migration from Zimbabwe to its neighbours is seen as a good example of the phenomenon of 'mixed migration' and the challenges it poses.

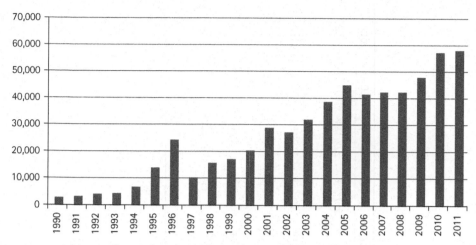

FIGURE 43.3   African refugees from outside Southern Africa

Source: UNHCR Statistical Online Population Database.

The South African government has shown great interest in the notion of 'mixed migration' for it perfectly buttresses its argument that the country's refugee system is being abused by non-refugees. However, when it comes to Zimbabwe, South Africa has been extremely reluctant to acknowledge that there is any forced migration at all (Crush and Tevera 2011). The number of asylum applications lodged by Zimbabweans in South Africa rose dramatically after 2003 and reached nearly 150,000 in 2009 and 2010 (Table 43.2). In total, Zimbabweans have lodged nearly half a million asylum applications in South Africa since 2000 (over 50 per cent of the total number received). In 2010 alone, over 80 per cent of total asylum applications were made by Zimbabweans.

The dramatic increase in the number of applications for asylum by Zimbabweans partly reflects the fact that continuing human rights violations and political persecution in Zimbabwe are forcing people out of the country to seek protection. It also reflects a different kind of forced migration driven by sheer economic desperation. Between 2003 and 2010 (excluding 2008 for which data is not available), bureaucratic ineptitude and reluctance to process claimants meant that only 53,144 Zimbabwean asylum applications (or 15 per cent) had been adjudicated. Of these, 98 per cent were rejected. In other words, 348,819 applications for refugee protection yielded a mere 1,119 successful claims, an extraordinarily low rate of 2.1 per cent. As the number of applications increased, so the success rate declined. To reduce the pressure on the refugee protection system by Zimbabweans, the South African government ran an amnesty programme in 2010–11. Approximately 250,000 applications for four-year work and residence permits were received, many from individuals holding asylum-seeker permits.

Although there is no reason why Zimbabwean migrants cannot continue to apply for asylum, after December 2011 the South African Department of Home Affairs refused to issue asylum permits to Zimbabweans unless they had previously acquired an 'asylum transit permit' at the border when they entered the country. Not only was this a violation

Table 43.2 Zimbabweans claiming asylum in South Africa, 2001–2010

	2000	2001	2002	2003	2004	2005	2006	2007	2008	2009	2010	Total
Asylum Applications by all Nationalities in South Africa	3,132	4,294	55,426	35,920	32,565	28,522	53,361	45,637	207,206	222,324	180,637	869,024
No. of Zimbabwean Applicants	0	4	115	2,588	5,789	7,783	18,973	17,667	111,968	149,453	146,566	460,906
% Applications by Zimbabweans	0.0	0.1	0.2	7.2	17.8	27.3	35.6	38.7	54.0	67.2	81.1	53.0
Zimbabwean Claims Adjudicated				25	93	271	1,981	1,894	n/a	15,701	33,179	53,144
Granted Refugee Status				9	24	83	103	271	n/a	200	429	1,119
% Accepted				36.0	25.8	30.6	5.2	14.3	n/a	1.3	1.3	2.1

Source: UNHCR Statistical Online Population Database; UNHCR Statistical Yearbooks (Various Reports).

of South Africa's international and regional Convention obligations, it transpired that it was virtually impossible to obtain a transit permit on entry. Recognizing Zimbabweans as legitimate refugees would amount to criticizing a government and leader which the South African government has been extremely reluctant to antagonize. There was a moratorium on deportations during the amnesty but they resumed in 2012 when 43,000 Zimbabweans were forcibly deported.

The end of apartheid brought major increases of intra-regional cross-border migration in Southern Africa. Most of this movement was economically motivated and of a temporary and circular nature focused on those countries with stronger economies such as Botswana, Namibia, and South Africa. However, economic migration from other countries in the region was widely viewed as a threat by citizens and governments in destination countries, despite their common membership of the Southern African Development Community. Efforts to craft a regional Protocol on freer movement continuously foundered on the rocks of territorial sovereignty and opposition from individual governments. Levels of xenophobia and hostility towards all migrants are extraordinarily high and often culminate in physical violence. In 2008, for example, over 100,000 migrants were internally displaced from urban communities in South Africa following xenophobic attacks throughout the country which killed over 70 people.

Legal avenues for migrants from one country to go and work in another are extremely restricted leading to considerable undocumented migration and irregular employment. The response of most states has been to try and control the influx with border fortification (for example between South Africa and Zimbabwe and Botswana and Zimbabwe), army patrols, and 'homeland' policing. In South Africa, the policy of rounding up migrants at work and on the streets and summarily deporting them to neighbouring countries began in the apartheid period (Figure 43.4). This form of forced migration intensified after 1994. Since 1990, over 3 million people have been forcibly removed from

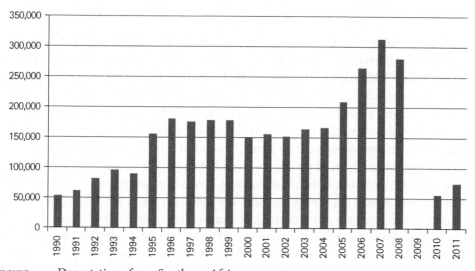

FIGURE 43.4   Deportations from Southern Africa, 1990–2011

South Africa through deportation. The passage of the Immigration Act of 2002 provided even more draconian enforcement provisions and deportations exceeded 300,000 in 2006 alone (LHR 2008).

These policies enjoy widespread popular support. If anything, governments are regarded as too lenient by their citizens. A survey conducted by SAMP in 2010 sought to establish the attitudes of South Africans on refugee rights. Forty two per cent of the respondents felt that refugees should never enjoy freedom of speech, a quarter felt that they should never enjoy legal protection, such as access to lawyers and the courts, and a similar number that they should never enjoy police protection. Attitudinally, South Africans tend to group refugees together with other foreign citizens and subject them to the same kinds of intolerance and abuse. Somali refugees have become particular targets in violent attacks in the country.

Refugees and asylum seekers are regularly caught up in the dragnet which the police use to catch, identify, and deport irregular migrants. A vast corruption industry has grown up around enforcement and often it is easier for refugees to simply pay the bribes demanded by the police rather than risk having their documents destroyed and being arrested and deported with a minimum of due process (Klaaren and Ramji 2001). The refugee protection system is not protecting and the immigration enforcement machinery is engaged in a ruthless form of forced migration which clearly violates Convention principles of *non-refoulement*. South Africa is simply the most prominent example of a regional phenomenon. Forced migrants in other countries in the region face similar kinds of treatment and abuse of their rights. At the heart of the issue is a clash between rights-based and control-oriented approaches and policy perspectives on forced migration.

CONTROL VERSUS PROTECTION

All of the countries in the Southern African region are signatories to the 1951 UN International Convention governing the recognition and protection of refugees. With the exception of Mauritius, Madagascar, and Namibia, all have also ratified the 1969 Organization of African Unity Convention Governing the Specific Aspects of Refugee Problems in Africa (OAU Convention) with its broader definition of the meaning of 'refugee'. In addition, all countries have their own legislation defining who qualifies as a refugee, how refugee status is defined, and the conditions of sojourn in the host country (Table 43.3). However, the actual rights given to refugees in individual countries vary considerably in terms of freedom of movement, access to employment, and eligibility for naturalization. Part of the reason for variations in the approach to refugee protection is based on how refugee laws have evolved. The earliest laws were control oriented in their approach, aimed at controlling the entry of refugees into the respective countries. The first laws were enacted in the 1960s and include Tanzania's Refugee Control Act of 1966, Botswana's Refugee (Control and Recognition) Act of 1968, Zambia's Refugee (Control)

Table 43.3 Refugee legislation in Southern Africa

| | UN Convention (Year Signed)[a] | OAU Convention (Date of Ratification)[b] | Refugee Legislation[c] | Rights Given to Refugees in Practice[d] | | | | | Refugee determination process | |
				Freedom of movement	Confinement to camps	Naturalisation	Access to employment		Prima Facie determination	Individual status determination
Angola	23 Jun 1981	30 April 1981	Law No. 8/1990 of 26 May 1990, Law on Refugee Status	✓	5	–	✓		5	✓
Botswana	06 Jan 1969	4 May 1995	Refugees (Recognition and Control) Act, Cap. 25:03 (1968)	✓	✓	5	5		5	✓
Lesotho	14 May 1981	18 Nov 1988	Refugee Act 1983	✓	5	✓	–		✓	✓
Malawi	10 Dec 1987	4 Nov 1987	Refugee Act (1989)	5	✓	5	5		5	✓
Mozambique	16 Dec 1983	22 Feb 1989	Act No. 21/1991 of 31 December 1991 (Refugee Act)	✓	5	✓	✓		5	✓

(Continued)

Table 43.3 (Continued)

| | UN Convention (Year Signed)[a] | OAU Convention (Date of Ratification)[b] | Refugee Legislation[c] | Rights Given to Refugees in Practice[d] | | | | | |
| | | | | Freedom of movement | Confinement to camps | Naturalisation | Access to employment | Refugee determination process | |
								Prima Facie	Individual status determination
Namibia	17 Feb 1995	11 Nov 2009	Namibia Refugees (Recognition and Control) Act, 1999	5	✓	-	-	5	✓
South Africa	12 Jan 1996	15 Dec 1995	Refugees Act (No. 130, 1998)	✓	5	✓	✓	✓	✓
Swaziland	14 Feb 2000	16 Jan 1989	The Refugees Control Order, 1978	5	✓	-	-	✓	5
Tanzania	12 May 1964	10 Jan 1989	Refugees Act, 1998	5	✓	5	5	✓	✓
Zambia	24 Sep 1969	30 July 1973	Refugee (Control) Act, 1970	5	✓	5	5	✓	✓
Zimbabwe	25 Aug 1981	28 Sept 1985	Refugee Act, 1983	5	✓	5	5	✓	✓

[a] UNHCR website <http://www.unhcr.org/3b73b0d63.html>; Makhema (2009).
[b] Africa Union website <http://www.au.int/en/treaties>.
[c] UNHCR Refworld <http://www.unhcr.org/cgi-bin/texis/vtx/refworld/rwmain>.
[d] Klaaren and Rutinwa (2004).

Act of 1970, and Swaziland's Refugee Control Order of 1978. More importantly, the laws of all four countries permitted the restriction of movement of refugees.

The refugee laws that emerged in the region after 1980 were more concerned about the protection of refugees and were more consistent with the extended definitions and parameters of the OAU Convention. They include Zimbabwe's Refugees Act of 1983 and Lesotho's Refugee Act of 1983, which made provisions for individual refugee status determination including appeals. Other countries which adopted protection-oriented refugee laws in this period include Angola's Law on Refugee Status of 1990, Mozambique's Refugee Act of 1991, South Africa's Refugee Act of 1998, and Namibia's Refugees (Recognition and Control) Act of 1999. Tanzania repealed the Refugees Control Act of 1966 and replaced it with a protection-oriented Refugee Act of 1998.

In terms of refugee status determination, two main procedures are used: prima facie status and individual status determination. Prima facie procedures give the minister responsible for refugee affairs the power to declare any class of persons to be refugees under any acceptable definition. Countries whose legislation has such provisions include Lesotho, South Africa, Swaziland, Tanzania, Zambia, and Zimbabwe. On the other hand, individual status determination of asylum applications is allowed under the laws of Angola, Botswana, Namibia, Lesotho, Malawi, Mozambique, South Africa, Tanzania, and Zimbabwe. Furthermore, countries such as Malawi, Tanzania, Zambia, Namibia, Swaziland, and Zimbabwe require refugees to reside in specific settlements while Angola, South Africa, and Mozambique allow them to engage in gainful employment activities. Finally, Lesotho, Mozambique, and South Africa have provisions in their legislation which make it possible for refugees to naturalize.

New hope for the protection of IDPs in Africa is provided by the African Union Convention for the Protection and Assistance of Internally Displaced Persons in Africa (the 'Kampala Convention') which entered into force on 6 December 2012. The Convention binds governments to provide legal protection for the rights and well-being of those forced to flee inside their home countries due to conflict, violence, natural disasters, or development projects. By January 2013, a total of 37 states had signed the Convention and 16 had ratified it. In Southern Africa, eight of the 15 states had signed the Convention (Angola, DRC, Lesotho, Mozambique, Namibia, Tanzania, Zambia, and Zimbabwe). However, only three (Lesotho, Swaziland, and Zambia) had ratified it, none of which have significant numbers of IDPs. The major IDP-generating countries of the region, past and present (including Angola, the DRC, Mozambique, and South Africa) had not ratified the Convention by early 2013, presumably because they are reluctant to accept responsibility for the state obligations towards IDPs that the Convention requires.

CONCLUSION

For five decades, Southern Africa has been one of the world's major forced migration-generating regions. The vast majority of forced migration movements have been between countries within the region. Although the drivers of forced migration and the affected parts of the region have varied over time, there is sufficient continuity to permit several generalizations to be made. First, forced migration in Southern Africa did not begin with the anti-colonial struggles of the late twentieth century nor did it end with political independence from colonial rule. Forced migration has a very long history in the region, dating deep into the pre-colonial period. Pre-colonial forced migration was not, however, a purely endogenous phenomenon and was partly stimulated by European encroachment on the continent. The colonial period saw the first major example of internal forced displacement in the region as land was expropriated for white settlers and the residents were relocated into reserves.

In recent decades, armed struggle against colonial rule and the assault by states on their own populations have been the most important causes of forced migration in the region. Whether instigated by repressive colonial and white settler regimes, the apartheid government's assault on its own black population and newly independent states, or civil conflict between competing political groups, many countries have undergone periods of extreme disruption and insecurity. In almost every case, outside influence and interference played an important role. Some colonial powers, especially the Portuguese, only decolonized with great reluctance. White settler regimes, emboldened by outside support, fought to retain power for far too long at incalculable human cost. The apartheid regime destabilized many independent states for the best part of a decade. Cold War protagonists also had their proxy wars in the region, especially in Angola.

Forced migration across borders and internal displacement have generally involved large-scale mass flight, calling for massive humanitarian emergency assistance from the UNHCR. The essentially temporary nature of many of these movements has meant that once the flight conditions have resolved, large-scale repatriation has generally followed. The major exception to this was the case of Mozambicans in South Africa in the 1990s who preferred to remain where they were, despite the difficulties of remaining in a country where they were not wanted by the state or the citizenry.

Southern Africa's 'fifty years war' shows encouraging signs of finally winding down. South Africa is no longer the region's rogue state. Angola and Mozambique are amongst Africa's fastest-growing economies. All, with the exception of Zimbabwe and Swaziland, are now relatively robust democracies. The numbers of refugees and internally displaced within Southern Africa are lower than they have been for decades. Poverty, inequality, and unemployment are certainly endemic but, with the exception of Zimbabwe, are not prompting displacement and flight by communities in fear of their lives. The biggest challenge currently facing Southern Africa is not protecting forced migrants but repatriating and integrating returnees and IDPs.

At the same time, there remain four emerging policy challenges with regard to forced migration. First, there is substantial evidence of growing intolerance and xenophobia directed against refugees by citizens. Governments are reluctant to acknowledge this reality, much less take steps to mitigate its pernicious effects. Second, the influx of asylum seekers from other areas of Africa (and the use of the region as a 'transit point' for asylum seekers attempting to reach other regions) is a growing policy challenge that governments are not responding to particularly well, opting for control- rather than protection-oriented solutions. Third, by defining deportations as a form of forced migration, this chapter draws attention to a phenomenon that achieves very little except the disruption of livelihoods, the abuse of migrant and refugee rights, and the enrichment of corrupt enforcers. Finally, while each state has its own refugee legislation, there is little harmony in approach or perspective amongst states. A strong case has been made by the Migration Dialogue for Southern Africa (MIDSA) for the harmonization of laws and practices across the SADC (Klaaren and Rutinwa 2004). However, this call has yet to be acted on by governments.

References

Azevedo, M. (2002) *Tragedy and Triumph: Mozambique Refugees in Southern Africa, 1977–2001.* Portsmouth, NH: Heinemann.

CCJP (Catholic Commission for Justice and Peace in Zimbabwe) (2007) *Gukurahundi in Zimbabwe: A Report on the Disturbances in the Matabeleland and the Midlands.* London: Hurst and Company.

Crush, J., and Tevera, D. (eds.) (2011) *Zimbabwe's Exodus: Crisis, Migration, Survival.* Cape Town and Ottawa: SAMP and IDRC.

Englund, H. (2002) *From War to Peace on the Mozambique–Malawi Borderland.* Edinburgh: Edinburgh University Press.

Hamilton, C. (ed.) (1995) *The Mfecane Aftermath: Reconstructive Debates in Southern African History.* Johannesburg: Witwatersrand University Press.

Klaaren, J., and Ramji, J. (2001) 'Inside Illegality: Migration Policing in South Africa after Apartheid'. *Africa Today* 48: 35–47.

Klaaren, J., and Rutinwa, B. (2004) *Towards the Harmonization of Immigration and Refugee Law in SADC.* Cape Town: SAMP/MIDSA.

Leys, C., and Saul, C. (1995) *Namibia's Liberation Struggle: The Two-Edged Sword.* London: James Currey.

LHR (2008) 'Monitoring Immigration Detention in South Africa'. Report for Lawyers for Human Rights. Pretoria.

Long, K., and Crisp, J. (2011) 'In Harm's Way: The Irregular Movement of Migrants to Southern Africa from the Horn and Great Lakes Regions'. Research Paper No. 200 Geneva: UNHCR.

Makhema, M. (2009) 'Social Protection for Refugees and Asylum Seekers in the Southern Africa Development Community (SADC)'. World Bank Social Protection Discussion Papers 49168. Washington, DC.

Minter, W. (1994) *Apartheid's Contras: An Inquiry into the Roots of War in Angola and Mozambique.* London: Zed Books.

Olusoga, D., and Erichsen, C. (2010) *The Kaiser's Holocaust: Germany's Forgotten Genocide and the Colonial Roots of Nazism.* London: Faber and Faber.

Saul, J. (1993) *Recolonization and Resistance in Southern Africa in the 1990s.* Toronto: Between the Lines Press.

Simon, D., and Preston, R. (1993) 'Return to the Promised Land: Repatriation and Resettlement of Namibian Refugees, 1989–1990'. Pp. 47–63 in R. Black and V. Robinson (eds.), *Geography and Refugees: Patterns and Processes of Change*. London: Belhaven Press.

van der Klaauw, J. (2009) 'Refugee Rights in Times of Mixed Migration: Evolving Status and Protection Issues'. *Refugee Survey Quarterly* 28: 59–86.

CHAPTER 44

··

FORCED MIGRATION IN THE GREAT LAKES AND HORN OF AFRICA

··

GAIM KIBREAB[1]

INTRODUCTION

AFTER briefly discussing the nexus between the violence that accompanied the twin processes of decolonization and state building, this chapter examines the causes and types of forced migration in the Great Lakes region (GLR) and the Horn of Africa (HoA), and presents evidence to show that the institution of asylum in the two regions is under pressure.

The GLR (comprising Burundi, Democratic Republic of Congo (DRC), Kenya, Rwanda, Tanzania, and Uganda) and the HoA (composed of Djibouti, Eritrea, Ethiopia, Somalia, South Sudan, and Sudan) broadly comprise the Greater Horn of Africa, with the exception of DRC and Tanzania. All but Tanzania have over time produced refugees and IDPs, although neither Tanzania nor Rwanda currently have IDPs. The histories of the two regions are inextricably linked with protracted crises of conflict and displacement, with all of the countries having hosted large numbers of refugees. The data in Figures 44.1 and 44.2 do not include IDPs and the hundreds of thousands, if not millions, who are invisibly integrated because they share common culture, language, and way of life with their hosts and therefore are indistinguishable from nationals (Kibreab 2012).

All the countries in the GLR and HoA, save Eritrea, are parties to the 1951 UN Convention on the Status of Refugees, its 1967 Protocol and the Organization of African Unity (OAU) 1969 Convention Governing the Specific Aspects of Refugee Problems in Africa. The countries in the GLR except Kenya, Sudan, and South Sudan are also signatories to the 2006 Kampala Convention on Assistance and Protection of IDPs which came into force on 6 December 2012. All the countries in the GLR are also signatories to the Pact on Stability, Security, and Development signed in December 2006 which includes 10 Protocols, two of which are on refugees and IDPs. Although the adoption of

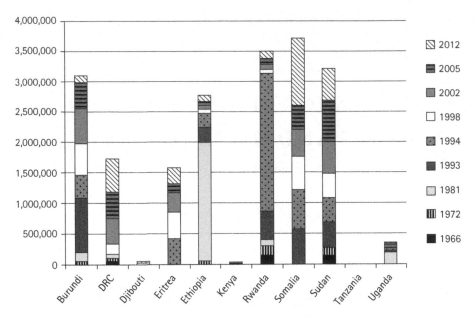

FIGURE **44.1** Total number of refugees from countries in the Great Lakes and Horn of Africa, by country of origin

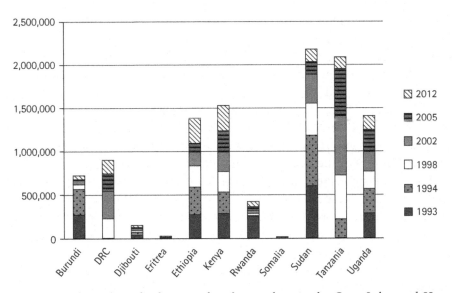

FIGURE **44.2** Total number of refugees and asylum seekers in the Great Lakes and Horn of Africa, by country of asylum

such frameworks is a step in the right direction, there is no evidence to show that these frameworks have led to better treatment of forced migrants.

CAUSES AND TYPES OF DISPLACEMENT

Historically, the refugee and IDP problem in the GLR and HoA has been inextricably linked with the anti-colonial struggles for independence and the post-colonial process of nation building. Decolonization unleashed new political forces that were suppressed during the colonial period, as in Rwanda, Burundi, and Sudan. The reasons for this are many. First, the colonial and post-colonial political boundaries brought together disparate cultural groups, and the dearth of carefully crafted power-sharing arrangements engendered violent conflicts. Second, the colonial powers pursued a systematic policy of 'divide and rule' which eroded the prospect of building united post-colonial states, as was the case in Burundi, Rwanda, Sudan, and even Uganda. In Sudan, northerners were even prohibited from visiting Southern Sudan between 1922 and 1946 because of the Condominium's policy of separate development. The violent conflict that ensued in 1955 on the eve of independence was therefore unsurprising. Third, the colonial powers did not effect structural transformation of the economies of the GLR and the HoA because they did not invest in manufacturing, education, and infrastructure which could have, *inter alia*, created urbanized population and working classes separated from the means of production—land—and particular places. This would have contributed to the development of shared values which would have facilitated the project of nation building based on unity.

In the following section, the causes of displacement in the particular countries that have generated large numbers of refugees and IDPs will be discussed briefly in historical perspective.

THE GREAT LAKES REGION

Rwanda

Rwanda was afflicted by violent conflict on the eve of its independence. Historically, the Hutu and the Tutsi shared common culture, religion, and language and lived side by side in peace benefiting from a mutually beneficial economic relationship. All this changed during the German and Belgian rules which favoured the Tutsi, and yet on the eve of independence, the Belgian rulers changed sides favouring the Hutu majority. In an attempt to rectify the injustice they suffered, the Hutu tried to seize power and in the turmoil that ensued, many Tutsis were killed. Rwanda became a republic under a Hutu president for the first time in its history and a vicious civil war broke out which forced over 100,000 Tutsis to flee the country to seek asylum in Burundi, Uganda, Tanzania, and Zaire. Soon after, some of the refugees formed secret cells known as *Inyenzi* to over-throw the Hutu-led government. In 1963, the *Inyenzi* launched a major attack which was easily repelled but resulted in the massacre of between 10,000 and 13,000 Tutsi civilians and tens of thousands fled to the neighbouring countries.

The Tutsi refugees who were unable to return home in safety or integrate into the host societies after three decades maintained hope of retuning as liberators. In 1980, some of those in Uganda joined Museveni's National Resistance Army and occupied short-lived, but prominent positions. In response to public resentment, especially amongst the Buganda, Museveni abandoned the Tutsi refugees. The latter realized that they had no future outside Rwanda and in 1987 they formed the Rwandan Patriotic Front, attack-ing Rwanda in 1990. An attempt at power-sharing resulting from the Arusha agreement of August 1993 produced no results. The situation imploded in the immediate after-math of the death of President Juvenal Habyarimana of Rwanda and President Cyprien Ntaryamira of Burundi in a plane crash on 6 April 1994. Hutu militants used this as a pretext to seize power and attack Tutsi civilians and moderate Hutus: about 800,000 people were killed in five months. Approximately one million Hutus fled to Zaire and Tanzania whilst 1.5 million were internally displaced (USCR 1995: 7).

Burundi

Burundi's social and political history is the mirror image of the preceding account. In 1972, a Hutu-led coup attempt resulted in the death of thousands of Tutsis and in retaliation, the Tutsi army massacred thousands of Hutus, over 300,000 of whom fled to Tanzania. During the first half of the 1990s, the situation became increasingly tense. In October 1993, the democratically elected Hutu president, Melchior Ndadaye, was murdered by Tutsis, triggering an outbreak of violence which resulted in the killing of thousands of Tutsis and Hutus. To escape the violence, about 700,000 Hutus fled to Rwanda. The hostility between the Tutsi and Hutu continued unabated and a series of coups and assassinations left the country's population traumatized. Another coup took place in 1996 which triggered another civil war forcing tens of thousands of Hutus to flee to Tanzania.

Zaire/Democratic Republic of the Congo

The tragic history of Zaire is inextricably linked with its enormous resource endow-ment which goes back to the pillage and destruction presided over by King Leopold II of Belgium. The latter destroyed the social fabric of Congolese society, engendering mas-sive suffering and internal displacement. Independence unleashed new and powerful national and international political forces, and the country was ripped apart by conflict which resulted in the mysterious death of the first Prime Minister, Patrice Lumumba in 1960. The country was plagued by unrest and rebellion between 1960 and 1965, forcing tens of thousands into internal displacement. Many also fled to Congo Brazaville, Central African Republic, Uganda, Rwanda, Sudan, Burundi, Tanzania, Angola, and Zambia. Approximately 100,000 people were killed. Mobutu ruled the country between 1965 and 1997 with an iron fist which resulted in the death and displacement of millions. After the end of the Cold War, Mobutu lost his Western allies and the country sank into internecine civil war. The situation was exacerbated by the genocide in Rwanda and interventions by governments from within and outside the region. Reyntjens (2009) has labelled the theatre of war that engulfed the country in the aftermath of the genocide in Rwanda as 'The Great African War'.

A variety of interlocking factors lay at the heart of the violence that afflicted Eastern Zaire. These included competition over land; fiercely contested identities in the context of a sham process of democratization; and regional and international intervention driven by greed for precious minerals. In the process of so-called democratization, the national identity of the Banyarwanda (Hutu and Tutsi) comprising several groups—the 'natives' established since pre-colonial days, the 'immigrants' and the 'transplanted' of the colonial period, the 'infiltrators' and the 'clandestines' before and after independence and the Tutsi and Hutu 'refugees'—was fiercely contested (Reyntjens 2009: 13). In 1993, the so-called 'indigenous' inhabitants of north Kivu, such as the Hunde, Nande, and Nyanga, together with their respective militias, attacked the Banyarwanda.

The arrival of nearly one million Hutu refugees, amongst whom were the Intrahamwe, mixed with peaceful civilian refugees accentuated existing tensions. The Intrahamwe not only intended to return to Rwanda and held the refugees hostage with Mobutu's acquiescence, but they also victimized the Banyamulenge in Eastern Zaire. The Alliance of Democratic Forces for the Liberation of Congo–Zaire (ADFL), under the leadership of Lauren Kabila in alliance with the Rwandan army, launched an offensive in the east of the country prompting tens of thousands of Bemba who sided with Mobutu during the ADFL offensive to flee to Tanzania. Soon after, Mobutu's government collapsed, and rebel groups, neighbouring governments, and diverse state and non-state actors tried to access and control a share of the country's resources. Between 1998 and 2003, c.3.3 million people died and tens of thousands fled the country. As of December 2010, there were 1.68 million IDPs in DRC, primarily in DRC's eastern provinces. Between May 2012 and early 2013, the ongoing fighting between the M23 militia and government forces has also displaced about 800,000 people (BBC 2013).

The Horn of Africa

The HoA region is located in arid and semi-arid climatic zone and hence suffers from frequent seasonal droughts and famines. The region is also conflict prone, including due to competition over scarce resources; weak and corrupt regulatory institutions; the proliferation of small weapons; and weak or heavy-handed governments that are either unable to enforce their own laws or maintain law and order, or breach the fundamental human rights of their citizens. During the Cold War, the HoA was a theatre of super-power rivalry. In the last six decades, millions of people have fled their places of origin to become refugees or IDPs due to the interplay between political, economic, social, and environmental factors.

Sudan

The problem of refugees and IDPs in Southern Sudan emerged in 1955, a few months before independence, when the southern units of the Sudanese army mutinied, result-ing in bloodshed, destruction, and displacement. The people in Southern Sudan dif-fer from northerners in terms of culture, language, and way of life. These differences were exacerbated by the colonial policy of separate development, and at independence Arabic was imposed as a national language which was rejected by politicians from the south. A guerrilla movement known as Anyanya was born and the conflict escalated between 1962 and 1965, generating mass internal displacement and large numbers of refugees who fled to CAR, Zaire, Uganda, and later to Ethiopia. When the Addis Ababa Peace Agreement was signed in 1972, there were 166,000 refugees in the neighbouring countries and an unknown but large number of IDPs. The majority returned home after the Agreement through large-scale repatriation operations.

In September 1983, Nimeiri's government introduced a new penal code which included the five canonical Islamic punishments and promised to work towards full Islamization of the country, its laws, institutions, and political system. The war lasted 21 years and resulted in the death and external displacement of hundreds of thousands, and forced millions into internal displacement. At the end of 2010, there were 5.2 mil-lion IDPs from **South** Sudan. Between 2003 and 2011, there were 2,666,115 IDPs from Northern and Southern Darfur (IDMC 2012). Although the Comprehensive Peace Agreement was signed in 2005 and South Sudan achieved its independence in July 2011, independence has not stemmed the flow of IDPs, especially in light of the conflict in Abyei.

Eritrea

In accordance with a 1950 UN resolution, the Italian colony of Eritrea was federated with Ethiopia in 1952 under the sovereign rule of the Ethiopian Emperor against the expressed wish of nationalist Eritreans. After the Ethiopian government began disman-tling the symbols of Eritrean autonomy, the Eritrean Liberation Front was established to fight for independence in September 1961, and in 1962, Ethiopia annexed Eritrea. The Eritreans fought a bloody 30 years war of liberation. In February–March 1967, about 30,000 Eritreans fled to Sudan after their villages were razed to the ground. From that year onwards, a wave of violence prompted tens of thousands to flee the country. During the Thirty Years War, nearly 600,000 people fled to Sudan. A substantial proportion emigrated to the Gulf States, North America, Europe, and Australia, using Sudan as a point of transit. Eritrea achieved its independence de facto in May 1991 and de jure in May 1993, after 99.8 per cent of the population voted in favour of independence in a UN supervised referendum.

It was expected that those who were in exile would return in response to independence and that Eritrea would cease being a major producer of refugees. However, independence has not stemmed the flow of large numbers of refugees. Between May 1998 and June 2000, a vicious inter-state war broke out between Eritrea and Ethiopia, killing over 100,000 people and displacing about 1.35 million IDPs in both countries (*circa* one million in Eritrea and 350,000 in Ethiopia). Although a state of no-war-no-peace exists between the two governments, all IDPs have returned to their villages. The border dispute was referred to an international arbitration—the Eritrea–Ethiopia Border Commission (EEBC)—whose decision the two governments agreed would be final and binding. The EEBC delivered its award in April 2002, and yet Ethiopia refused to accept the decision and the Eritrean government, using the threat of war as a pretext, has turned the obligatory 18 months' national service for all Eritrean men and women between 18 and 40 years into an open-ended obligation. The national service has therefore degenerated into forced labour and has since then been the major cause of forced migration. Tens of thousands have been fleeing to Sudan and Ethiopia and from there to the rest of the world to escape from what many refer to as a modern form of slavery (Kibreab 2009, 2013).

Ethiopia

Emperor Haile Selassie's autocratic regime was overthrown in 1974 and was replaced by a brutal military dictatorship which tore apart Ethiopian society, resulting in the death of thousands of students, peasants, workers, members of the old regime, members and sympathizers of opposition groups, such the Ethiopian People's Revolutionary Party (EPRP), Tigray People's Liberation Front (TPLF), Oromo Liberation Front (OLF), Ogaden National Liberation Front (ONLF), and many other liberation movements; simultaneously, hundreds of thousands fled to neighbouring countries, such as Djibouti, Sudan, and Kenya. In 1977–8, Ethiopia and Somalia went to war over the Ogaden, a war in which the USA and the USSR were embroiled. Over half a million ethnic Somalis fled to Somalia, while Siad Barre's government invaded the Ogaden in pursuit of its goal of creating 'Greater Somalia'. However, this project was thwarted due to the massive supply of weapons from the Soviet Union and the direct involvement of Cuban soldiers on the side of Ethiopia.

The war in Tigray also caused the displacement of tens of thousands to Sudan and many others were displaced internally. The Derg suffered a humiliating defeat at the hands of the combined forces of the Eritrean People's Liberation Front (EPLF) and Ethiopian Peoples' Revolutionary Democratic Front (EPRDF) in May 1991. Whilst some 'voted with their feet' homewards, many Derg members and sympathizers, and their families, in addition to members of the different ethnic groups that feared 'reprisals' from the Tigrean-dominated EPRDF, fled to Kenya, Sudan, and Djibouti.

Somalia

In 1960, the former British and Italian colonies merged and formed the United Republic of Somalia. Until Siad Barre seized power in a coup in 1969, the country was ruled by democratically elected governments. In 1977, as mentioned above, the Somali army invaded the Ogaden, the home of ethnic Somalis. After a spectacular initial success, Somalia's army was defeated and driven out from the Ogaden in 1978 as a result of a sudden shift of superpower alliances. In 1977, a leftist demagogue, Mengistu, had seized power in Ethiopia, and in response the USSR and the US governments swapped sides. Soviet military advisers and Cuban soldiers, as well as massive shipments of Soviet weapons, led to the defeat of the Somali army in 1978. Barre's government never recovered from the humiliating defeat his army suffered in the Ogaden, sounding the gradual 'death knell' not only of Barre's government, but also of the Somali State in 1991.

Soon after, clan-based armed groups, such as the Somali Salvation Democratic Front (SSDF) and the Somali National Movement (SNM) emerged and mobilized their clan groups against the central government. In response, the government deployed counter-insurgency operations leading to the death and internal and external displacement of thousands and the destruction of Hargeisa town. Gradually, the legitimacy of Barre's government was eroded and he fled the country in 1991 when Mogadishu was captured by rival clan militias. In this failed state, a state of lawlessness and chaos which caused the death of hundreds of thousands, and the displacement of two million refugees and IDPs was caused by brutal war lords who competed for resources with impunity; intra-clan internecine civil wars; the proliferation of small weapons; drought; famine; and Ethiopian military intervention. As of November 2012, there were 1.36 million IDPs and 1,003,513 Somali refugees in Yemen, Djibouti, Ethiopia, Kenya, Uganda, Eritrea, and Tanzania (UNHCR 2012).

HUMAN TRAFFICKING

The countries in the GLR and the HoA are also major sources, transit, and destinations of an unknown number (estimated to be tens of thousands) of victims of human trafficking. The causes of trafficking in the regions include conflict, poverty, and lack of employment, corruption, and limited policing capability. In the GLR, the majority of victims of trafficking are reported to be women and children and to a lesser extent men. Women and girls are trafficked for domestic labour and forced prostitution whilst men are trafficked for forced labour in agriculture, construction, and crime (UN Office on Drugs and Crime 2007). In turn, in the HoA, men, women, and children are kidnapped and trafficked and held hostage mainly in eastern Sudan and the Sinai. The hostage tak-ers demand tens of thousands of dollars for their lives. Failure to pay the ransom leads to torture and death. The victims are also subjected to vicious sexual violence and organ harvesting, with hundreds of Eritrean hostages currently languishing in the Sinai and eastern Sudan in the hands of Bedouin and Rashaida traffickers and hostage takers (van Reisen et al. 2012). In turn, in Eritrea, as mentioned above, the open-ended national ser-vice lies at the heart of the problem of trafficking of both men and women.

THE DEMISE OF ASYLUM?

Although all governments in the GLR and HoA were hostile to the self-settlement of refugees from the outset, between the 1960s and the first half of the 1980s, most of these states pursued open-door policies, receiving refugees as temporary guests. However, from the mid-1980s onwards, these governments' policies changed dra-matically, reflected, *inter alia*, in the increased intensity with which the policy against self-settlement is enforced. In the aftermath of the Rwandan genocide, Kenya, Uganda, and Tanzania have declared an open war on self-settlement. In the following some of the indicators of major policy shifts are discussed.

Phasing out of Self-sufficiency Programmes in Favour of Camps

With few exceptions, during the 1960s, 1970s, and the first half of the 1980s, refugee camps housed asylum seekers and prima facie refugees in the interim period until UNHCR with its partners and host governments identified suitable sites for land-based self-sufficiency projects. At that time, it was common for UNHCR to field expert mis-sions to undertake reconnaissance surveys and feasibility studies to determine the suitability of proposed sites for agricultural production. The only exceptions were the 35 camps in Somalia and Wad Sherife Camp in eastern Sudan. As of 1982, there were 86 self-sufficiency projects in the GLR and in the HoA where, in the majority of cases, refugees were allocated cultivable land by host governments. UNHCR built settlement infrastructure, NGOs provided services, and the World Food Programme provided food aid until the first two or three harvests. By then, the refugees were expected to become self-sufficient. Between 1982 and 1985, Kagera in Tanzania, Kayaka II in Uganda, Mufaza in Eastern Sudan, and 19 settlements for Ugandan refugees in Southern Sudan were established. The latter were closed down following to their repatriation.

The last refugee settlement was established in 1985, and yet camps have proliferated since then. Not only have host governments ceased establishing self-sufficiency projects, but some countries, such as Uganda, Tanzania, and Sudan have closed down successful refugee settlements either to transfer their inhabitants to camps or to induce them to return to their countries of origin even when the conditions that prompted them to flee have not been eliminated. Even the Tanzanian government's highly celebrated decision to naturalize Burundian refugees has been dependent on the refugees' willingness to relocate from the settlements where they lived since 1972 (Oakland Institute 2011). The Sudanese government also closed down the relatively successful six settlements in Qala en Nahal and transferred the refugees to the overcrowded and bleak refugee camp of Um Gargour in 2004.

In Sudan many of the refugee camps, such as Wad Sherife, the three camps in Shagarab, Kilo 26, Kashm el Girba, and the three camps in Es Suki have become institutionalized. Burundian refugees who arrived in Tanzania in the 1990s were also warehoused in camps rather than being settled in self-sufficiency projects as was the case in the 1970s. They were only given land for housing and small gardens, receiving no land for cultivation. Indeed, even the so-called local settlements were designed to perpetuate refugee status rather than to promote integration.

Local Settlements

Contrary to UNHCR's, analysts', and practitioners' mistaken assumptions, I argue that the aim of 'local settlement' is to prevent the integration of refugees into host societies. Indeed, the aim of local settlements is to keep refugees in spatially segregated sites until the factors that prompted them to flee are perceived to be eliminated. Local settlements are therefore designed to perpetuate, rather than to bring to an end, refugee status. There are a number of reasons why host governments in the two regions place refugees in spatially segregated sites and round up, harass, detain, mistreat, and deport self-settled refugees to countries of origin even when the conditions that promoted them to flee persist.

Maintenance of Separate Refugee Identity

One of the major objectives of local settlement in the two regions is to prevent integration contrary to the spirit and letter of the Statute and the 1951 UN Convention. Integration is a function of social and economic interactions between refugees and host populations, and yet camp- and settlement-based refugees and asylum seekers lack freedom of movement and residence and therefore cannot interact with host populations. In effect, freedom of movement is a *sine qua non* for the enjoyment of other rights, such as education, employment, self-employment and choice of residence.

Keeping refugees in spatially segregated sites enables governments to isolate refugees from host populations indefinitely. In the GLR and HoA, the segregated sites are designed to prevent integration. For example, Ahmed Karadawi, Sudan's former Assistant Commissioner for Refugees, stated: 'how realistic is the approach that aims at helping the refugees to settle permanently in the Sudan and become Sudanese? *The strategy of what is called 'integration' by the aid agencies is a European import oblivious to the local processes that have brought refugees into the Sudan'* (in Kibreab 1996: 140, emphasis added). Equally, Hassan Attiya, who was Commissioner for Refugees in Sudan during the second half of the 1980s, also told UNHCR's *Refugee* Magazine:

> *If you talk of integration as a sort of naturalization, this is completely rejected in Sudan... Being a refugee in a country for 20, 30 or 100 years, I don't think will deprive you of your own nationality, your own origin... That is why in Sudan you hear... this policy of local settlement, rather than local integration...* (Kibreab 1996: 142, emphasis added)

As such, the aim of 'local settlement' is to provide refugees with a confined geographical space where they can maintain and perpetuate their 'Otherness' without being able to intermingle with nationals. In Attiya's own words,

> *Refugees should be given a certain place to live in, to continue their own sort of relations with their own people [not of course with Sudanese], not to forget their country, because we are not interested that they will forget their countries; they have to go back. We don't want more population in this country: it is enough.* (Kibreab 1996: 142, emphasis added)

This is true throughout the GLR and HoA. The Tanzanian Minister for Foreign Affairs went much further by asserting:

> Experience has proved that such measures as granting of permanent refugee status, permanent settlement are not a formula for a permanent solution to the refugee crisis. The solution indeed lies in the countries of origin rather than in the countries of asylum which are burdened with obligations on the refugees. (In Rutinwa 1999.)

Securitization

In the aftermath of the Rwandan genocide, all states in the region have placed refugees on the security agenda, this being the main reason why governments keep refugees in specially segregated sites where their movements and political activities can be controlled. For example, in the 1990s Tanzania restricted the movement of refugees in settlements to a four-kilometre radius from the centre (IRRI 2008). The head of the Sudanese State Security accused the self-settled refugees of representing a threat to national security (quoted in Kibreab 1996). The Vice-President also declared that 'The government has... decided to phase out spontaneous settlement' (Kibreab 1996: 142). Securitization often results in unrelenting rounding up, extortion, arbitrary detention, harassment, and eviction of self-settled refugees and, in the worst case scenario, *refoulement* to countries of origin (Karadawi 1984; Kibreab 1996; HRW 2007). The measures emanate from the assumption that refugees represent a socio-economic burden and danger to national and societal security. The best way to avert the burden and the risks is said to be by placing all asylum seekers and refugees in spatially segregated sites where their political activities can be controlled, their freedom of movement blocked, and their possibility to make ends meet by competing with nationals thwarted.

There is well-thought-out reasoning underlying the notion of securitization in the two regions (also see Hammerstad, this volume). Once an issue is framed in security terms, it justifies any measure taken to ward off the actual or the imagined threat. In the absence of such a threat, the measures host governments take would be regarded as a violation of international human rights standards. Once an issue is securitized, however, it is presented as a question of life and death which 'justifies any means': 'Something is presented as existentially threatened, and on this basis it is argued that "we" must use extraordinary means to handle the threat' (Waever in Kibreab 2000: 271). Mandel argues that 'Portraying concerns as security issues can elevate them into crisis requiring extreme emergency measures that may be unwarranted' (1994: 16), and Buzan underscores the same view noting that 'The appeal to national security as a justification for actions and policies which would otherwise have to be explained is a political tool of immense convenience for a large variety of sectional interests in all types of state' (1991: 11). It was under the pretext of the protection of national security that Tanzania and Uganda expelled Rwandan and Burundian refugees, and other states restricted refugees' movement in their territories.

Undue Pressure

Governments in the GLR and the HoA have been putting self-settled refugees under much pressure to induce them to return home. For example, in Tanzania, asylum seekers and refugees are required to remain in spatially designated sites with no freedom of movement and choice of residence (section 17 [5]), and non-compliance is a criminal offence (section 17 [6]). This requirement is systematically enforced by the authorities, including by the armed forces (see HRW 2007). For example, on 5 December 1996 a joint government–UNHCR statement declared that 'all Rwandese refugees in Tanzania are expected to return home by 31 December 1996' (in Whitaker 2002). The Foreign Minister in a similar vein as the Sudanese Commissioner for Refugees declared: 'We are saying enough is enough. Let us tell the refugees that the time has come for them to return home and no more should come' (in Rutinwa 1999).

In Uganda, residence outside refugee camps and settlements is also considered a criminal offence. In the 1990s, asylum seekers and refugees found residing outside government designated camps and settlements were charged with treason. Researchers identified 30 such refugees in Luzira Upper Prison detained together with persons accused of capital offences (Lomo 1995: 5). Lomo states that these refugees committed no crimes, but were 'apprehended because they had been found to be out of their settlements. Some had been arrested in markets where they were trading their rations for basic necessities or simply moving along a road between their settlement and the market' (Lomo 1995: 5) This shows that the severity of limitation imposed on refugees' freedom of movement is as harsh in Uganda as in Sudan and Tanzania. Since 2009, Rwandan refugees in Nakivale and elsewhere in Uganda live under imminent threat of deportation (IRRI and RLP 2010).

In Kenya, the majority of refugees and asylum seekers are confined in spatially segregated camps and the prospects for integration of those who reside outside camps without being able to render themselves invisible is bleak. This is also true for those urban refugees residing in Nairobi (see Campbell 2006; Pavanello et al. 2010). In Kakuma and Dadaab refugee camps where most refugees reside, there is no freedom of movement or residence. In 2006, the government of Kenya passed a Refugee Act, but its provisions fall far below the standards enshrined in the 1951 Convention. Consistent with its 'encampment' policy, the government expects all refugees to reside in camps. The government's 'encampment' requirement is not accompanied with the designation of specific places for such a purpose, and this therefore creates confusion and renders many refugees vulnerable to arbitrary detention, harassment, extortion, and gross violation of their rights at the hands of the police (Pavanello et al. 2010): 'There is a widespread belief within the police that refugees should be restricted to camps... Police officers also typically assume that refugees are criminally minded, while Somalis in particular may be suspected of links with terrorist organisations'. Even those with a recognized status are not receiving meaningful protection (Pavanello et al. 2010: 17).

Concluding Remarks

Although many of the states in the GLR and the HoA pursued repressive policies that prompted tens of thousands of their citizens to flee in search of protection, prior to the demise of the bipolar division of the world, these states nonetheless pursued relatively 'open door' policies towards those who fled their countries in search of sanctuary. It appears that the end of the Cold War has sounded the 'death knell' of such a generous refugee policy. Most governments in the two regions have been gradually, but surely, rejecting the once touted 'local integration' (read local settlement) as the 'second most durable solution'. Most governments in the region have also declared war on self-settlement of refugees which has hitherto been working by enabling hundreds of thousands, if not millions, of asylum seekers, refugees, and mixed migrants to be integrated into host societies informally.

Note

1. A debt of gratitude is due to Elena Fiddian-Qasmiyeh for her detailed constructive suggestions and editorial comments.

References

BBC News (2013) 'DR Congo: M23's Makenga and Rniga factions "Clash"'. 25 February. <http://www.bbc.co.uk/news/world-africa-21578357>.

Buzan, B. (1991) *People, States & Fear: An Agenda for International Security Studies in the Post-Cold War Era* (2nd edn.). London: Harvester Wheatsheaf.

Campbell, E. (2006) 'Urban Refugees in Nairobi: Problems of Protection, Mechanisms of Survival, and Possibilities for Integration'. *Journal of Refugee Studies* 19(3): 305–27.

Human Rights Watch (2002) 'Hidden in Plain View: Refugees Living without Protection in Nairobi and Kampala'. 21 November.

Human Rights Watch (2007) Human Rights Watch letter to President J. M. Kikwete. 8 May.

IRRI (2011) 'Resisting Repatriation: Burundian Refugees Struggling to Stay in Tanzania'.

IRRI and RLP (2010) 'A Dangerous Impasse: Rwandan Refugees in Uganda'. Citizenship and Forced Migration in the Great Lakes Region. Working Paper No. 4.

Kibreab, G. (1996) 'Eritrean and Ethiopian Refugees in Khartoum: What the Eye Refuses to See'. *African Studies Review* 39(3): 131–78.

Kibreab, G. (2000) 'Resistance, Displacement and Identity: The Case of Eritrean Refugees in Sudan'. *Canadian Journal of African Studies* 34(2): 249–96.

Kibreab, G. (2009) 'Forced Labour in Eritrea'. *Journal of Modern African Studies* 47(1): 41–72.

Kibreab, G. (2012) 'Invisible Integration in the Greater Horn Region of Africa'. Pp. 69–110 in K. Mengisteab and R. Bereketeab (eds.), *Regional Integration in the Greater Horn Region*. Oxford: James Currey Publishers.

Kibreab, G. (2013) 'The National Service/Warsai-Yikealo Development Campaign and Forced Migration in Post-independence Eritrea'. *Journal of Eastern African Studies* 7(4): 630–49.

Lomo, Z. (1999) 'The Role of Legislation in Promoting "Recovery": A Critical Analysis of Refugee Law and Policy in Uganda'. Unpublished paper.

Mandel, R. (1994) *The Changing Face of National Security: A Conceptual Analysis*. London: Greenwood Press.

Oakland Institute (2011) 'Understanding Land Deals in Africa: AgriSol Energy and Pharos Global Agriculture Fund's Land Deals in Tanzania'. June.

Pavanello, S., et al. (2010) 'Hidden and Exposed: Urban Refugees in Nairobi, Kenya'. HPG.

Rutinwa, B. (1999) 'The End of Asylum? The Changing Nature of Refugee Policies in Africa'. Issues in Refugee Research. Working Paper No. 5.

UN Office on Drugs and Crime (2007) 'Vulnerabilities of Conflict and Post-Conflict Countries'. Regional UN.GIFT Meeting. Kampala. 19–22 June.

van Reisen, M., et al. (2012) *Human Trafficking in the Sinai: Refugees between Life and Death*. Brussels: Tilburg University and Europe External Policy Advisors.

Whitaker, B. (2002) 'Changing Priorities in Refugee Protection: The Rwandan Repatriation from Tanzania'. New Issues in Refugee Research. Working Paper No. 53.

CHAPTER 45

··

FORCED MIGRATION IN THE MIDDLE EAST AND NORTH AFRICA

··

SARI HANAFI[1]

INTRODUCTION

THERE is a long history of forced displacement to, from, and within the Middle East and North Africa (MENA), understood here to refer to the countries of North Africa (also referred to as the Maghreb: Morocco, Western Sahara/Sahrawi Arab Democratic Republic, Algeria, Tunisia, Libya, and Egypt), the Levant (also known as the Mashreq: Lebanon, Syria, Jordan, Iraq, Palestine/the Occupied Palestinian Territories, and Israel) and the Gulf (Saudi Arabia, Yemen, Oman, Bahrain, Qatar, UAE, and Kuwait).[2] The causes of forced displacement in the twentieth and twenty-first centuries have included colonial experiences (as in the case of Palestinians expelled from the territory which became Israel), post-colonial contexts (such as Sahrawi and Kurdish refugees), civil war (Lebanese refugees), and conflict and post-conflict situations (Iraqi refugees). Alongside experiences of internal displacement, the region has also witnessed intersecting processes of forced displacement and forced sedentarization of mobile and nomadic populations for whom movement and mobility are central parts of their lives and livelihoods.

Since the establishment of nation states in the region, the borders between Middle Eastern countries have remained porous, enabling refugees to move relatively easily throughout the sub-region over the past century, to reach states which have broadly tolerated their presence on an official level: these include c.800,000 Palestinians hosted across the region since the 1940s; an estimated two to four million Sudanese who have fled to Egypt since the 1980s; and one million Iraqis displaced in the 1990s and 2.4 million Iraqis since 2003. In spite of this high degree of movement on the one hand, and official tolerance on the other, Middle Eastern and North African nation states have nonetheless marginalized numerous populations, excluding them from 'the right to have a right', to paraphrase Arendt. Indeed, the sub-region's nation states have developed policies which define who is inside or outside the nation, thereby producing a mass of non-citizens and stateless groups, such as c.150,000 Kurds in Syria and thousands of children born to Lebanese mothers and foreign fathers who are stateless due to Lebanon's nationality laws. In the Gulf area more specifically, the modern petro-monarchs defined nationality in a very narrow fashion, resulting in the exclusion of 'undesirable' tribes and undermining the long history of these tribes' habitual mobility across and beyond the Arabian Peninsula. This has generated a phenomenon of stateless Bedouins, referred to as the *bidoon*, in all the countries of this region but especially in Kuwait, where an estimated 100,000 *bidoon* are based.

Due to the wide range of displacement situations in the MENA region, this chapter uses a small selection of case studies to highlight the diversity of the causes, experiences, and responses to forced migration from different perspectives. A range of major refugee and IDP crises are introduced, including Iraqis who fled their country because of the civil war; the protracted Palestinian refugee camp crisis in Lebanon; and, most recently, the displacement of Syrian refugees and IDPs due to authoritarian repression during the Arab Spring. Other forms of displacement are also briefly discussed with reference to climate induced displacement, trafficking, and statelessness, all of which have had significant impacts on individual, collective, and national experiences in the region. Thematically, the chapter focuses on the host-displacee relationships, and the major challenges of using refugee camps as a residential solution for refugees in the region.

Regional Political and Legal Frameworks

The vast majority of refugees in the MENA region are Palestinians, constituting about 4.3 million refugees out of the total of 5.1 million refugees currently residing in the region (56 per cent of all forced migrants). In light of the protracted Palestinian displacement, a special relationship between MENA states and the 'international' refugee regime has been established. While the history and present of the UN Relief and Works Agency for Palestine Refugees (UNRWA) and its relationship with the UN High Commissioner for Refugees (UNHCR) is the focus of Akram's chapter earlier in this volume, a brief overview of the regional regime in place to assist Palestinian refugees is necessary at this stage.

Between 1948 and 1949 the United Nations (UN) General Assembly accorded mandates to two separate UN agencies to provide relief and protection to Palestinian refugees: the UN Conciliation Commission for Palestine (UNCCP), and the UN Relief and Works Agency for Palestine Refugees (UNRWA) (Remple 2002). The UNCCP mandate included the provision of protection for all refugees and displaced persons in Palestine and the facilitation of durable solutions as delineated in paragraph 11 of the resolution (i.e. return, restitution, and compensation based on individual refugee choice). The singularity of the UN agency for Palestinians makes Middle Eastern states' relationship with UNHCR very complex: Middle Eastern states, with the exception of Yemen, were reluctant to ratify the 1951 Convention and its Protocol as they were afraid that UNHCR would promote the durable solutions of local integration or resettlement for Palestinians at the expense of Palestinians' right of return. In contrast, North African states (apart from Libya and Egypt) are all signatories of the 1951 Convention and its 1967 Protocol, although none has to date developed national asylum systems.

Despite UNHCR being established to provide international *protection* and seek permanent solutions for refugees worldwide, UNRWA was conceived as a *service provider* organization for Palestinian refugees upon its creation in 1950, and was given a specific mandate by the UN which did not encompass protection or return. Despite this strict mandate, however, there have been some transgressions during the past 15 years, including the provision of 'passive protection' for Palestinian refugees during the first Intifada. Indeed, since its 2004 Geneva donor meeting, UNRWA has linked service provision to advocacy, and a rights-based approach to their humanitarian mandate is emerging. Relatively strong language is notably used in UNRWA publications to attract the attention of the international community about the continuous plight of Palestinian refugees. However, focusing on housing, children's and women's rights and other rights does not mean that the right of return has become part of UNRWA's advocacy strategy. In effect, the USA and a number of UNRWA's European donors consider that if UNRWA seeks a durable solution such as return, a dangerous politicization will have taken place; nonetheless, UNHCR's case has effectively shown that being involved in the search for durable solutions does not conflict with an essentially humanitarian mandate (Takkenberg 2007).

While UNRWA has played a very important role in empowering Palestinian refugees by providing education, health, and sometimes work, this has not been sufficient to enable Palestinians to integrate into their host societies. UNRWA has at times accepted host states' policies of keeping Palestinian refugee camps as temporary spaces. The advantages, disadvantages, opportunities, and risks of self-settlement, policies of encampment,and local integration of refugees have been extensively debated (see Bakewell, this volume), and yet further research is necessary to critically examine MENA states' preference for particular types of refugee camps in the region. Many refugee groups (including Palestinians across the Levant and Sahrawis in Algeria) have been spatially segregated in urban and desert-based camps with minimum opportunities for social and cultural integration over the course of numerous decades, and yet in the 2000s Syria received the largest group of urban refugees in the Arab world, integrating them very quickly in different cities. In effect, a refugee camp that was created in July 2003 to host Iraqis in Hassakeh had been closed by June 2004 (Dorai 2007: 9). Why certain states have placed specific refugee populations in camps while other refugee groups have been encouraged to locally integrate in urban settings remains to be investigated in detail, especially in light of MENA states' responses to displacement following the Arab Spring.

In addition to the UN legal framework for Palestinian refugees, MENA states have developed resolutions through the Arab League to facilitate Palestinians' living and livelihood conditions in Arab host countries. Some MENA countries ratified the 1965 Protocol for the Treatment of Palestinians in Arab States (known as the 'Casablanca Protocol'), giving Palestinian refugees the right to work and to own property in signatory states. Seven states (Jordan, Algeria, Sudan, Iraq, Syria, Egypt, and Yemen) ratified the Protocol with no reservations; Lebanon, Kuwait, and Libya ratified the Casablanca Protocol with reservations (for instance excluding Palestinians from the right to work in certain sectors); while by 2013 Saudi Arabia, Morocco, and Tunisia had not yet ratified the Protocol.

Beyond the Arab League, two other bodies are pertinent in this context. First, the Organization of the Islamic Conference and its Islamic Committee for the International Crescent, established in 1977, is mandated to '[help] alleviate the sufferings causes by natural disaster and war'. Second, a number of North African states are members of the African Union and have signed the 1969 Organisation of African Unity Convention Governing the Specific Aspects of Refugee Problems in Africa. The OAU Convention is applicable in Algeria, Egypt, Libya, and Tunisia, offering the possibility for asylum seekers' cases to be assessed in relation to the broader regional refugee definition in addition to the 1951 Geneva Convention definition.

With reference to internally displaced persons, by Spring 2013 five states (Algeria, Libya, Egypt, Tunisia, and the Sahrawi Arab Democratic Republic[3]) had signed the African Union Convention for the Protection and Assistance of Internally Displaced Persons in Africa, although the impact which this regional IDP Convention will have in signatory states remains to be assessed (also see Kalin, this volume).

REGIONAL TRENDS REGARDING CAUSES AND TYPES OF DISPLACEMENT

Refugees and IDPs

Major refugee populations in the region in the 2000s have included Iraqis in Syria and Jordan; Somali, Ethiopian, and Sudanese refugees in Egypt; Somalis and Eritreans in Egypt and Yemen; and finally Syrian refugees displaced to Jordan, Lebanon, and Turkey in 2012–13. Statistics from 2011 clearly show that in addition to receiving 6,680,635 refugees from the above-mentioned populations, the MENA region was also the region of origin for 7,512,968 refugees and asylum seekers, of whom 4,319,991 are Palestinian (see Tables 45.1 and 45.2). The Palestinian territory, Jordan, and Lebanon are the most important refugee receivers as a percentage of their population, while Iraq, Libya, and Yemen have the largest IDP populations registered by the UNHCR (1,773,242).

Table 45.1 MENA forced migrants by country of asylum

	Asylum seekers	IDPs	Refugees	Total displaced population of concern
Algeria	816		94,148	94,964
Bahrain	160		199	359
Egypt	18,938		95,087	114,025
Iraq	4,196	1,332,382	35,189	1,371,767
Jordan	4,975		451,009	455,984
Kuwait	1,118		335	1,453
Lebanon	1,736		8,845	10,581
Libya	2,894	93,565	7,540	103,999
Morocco	615		736	1,351
Oman	43		83	126
Palestine			5,100,000[a]	5,100,000
Qatar	49		80	129
Saudi Arabia	80		572	652
Syria	1,830		755,445	757,275
Tunisia	555		3,048	3,603
UAE	45		677	722
Yemen	5,878	347,295	214,740	567,913
Total	43,928	1,773,242	6,767,733	8,584,903

Source: UNHCR (2011).
[a] Estimated Number of Palestinians in the Arab World, End Year 2012 (PCBS 2012).

Protracted Refugee Situations

Over two-thirds of the world's refugees are trapped in protracted refugee situations, with key cases characterizing the MENA region: Palestinians displaced since the 1940s; Kurds originating from Iraq, Syria, Turkey, and Iran; and the Sahrawi, who are identified by UNHCR as 'one of the most protracted refugee situations worldwide' and correspond to the organization's second oldest refugee caseload (Fiddian-Qasmiyeh 2011). These cases demonstrate the major difficulties in achieving durable solutions, and the challenges faced by individuals, families, and collectives in these contexts. Protracted refugee situations are caused by the combined effect of inaction or unsustained international action both in the country of origin and the country of asylum, with protracted refugees often subsisting without socio-economic or civil rights such as rights to work, practise professions, run businesses, and own property (also see Milner, this volume).

Protracted refugees are often confined to camps or segregated settlements where they are virtually dependent on humanitarian assistance. While the Sahrawi refugee camps in South-West Algeria have been identified as 'ideal' self-sufficient camps by Western observers who celebrate their democratic, secular, and female-friendly socio-political structures (Fiddian-Qasmiyeh 2014), refugee camps elsewhere in the region have been seen as 'insecurity islands' (a term used by Lebanese right-wing politicians), being treated

Table 45.2 MENA forced migrants by country of origin

	Asylum seekers	IDPs	Refugees	Refugees Under UNRWA jurisdiction[a]	Total
Algeria	1,991		6,120		8,111
Bahrain	46		215		261
Egypt	2,477		7,934		10,411
Iraq	23,981	1,332,382	1,428,308		2,784,671
Jordan	519		2,248	1,858,362	1,861,129
Kuwait	121		1,120		1,241
Lebanon	1,354		15,013	270,000[b]	286,367
Libya	1,505	93,565	3,335		98,405
Morocco	1,104		2,312		3,416
Oman	2		60		62
Palestinian territories	1,635		94,121	1,739,266	1,835,022
Qatar	7		95		102
Saudi Arabia	98		745		843
Syrian Arab Republic	14,117		19,900	442,363	476,380
Tunisia	1,599		1,951		3,550
United Arab Emirates	12		486		498
Western Sahara	289		116,476[c]		
Yemen	1,114	347,295	2,322		350,731
Total	51,682	1,773,242	1,586,285	4,309,991	7,721,200

Source: UNHCR (2011).
[a] *Source*: United Nations Relief and Works Agency for Palestine Refugees in the Near East (UNRWA).
[b] Although at present there are in excess of 400,000 Palestinian refugees registered with UNRWA, only approximately 270,000 refugees are currently residing in Lebanon, according to an AUB–UNRWA survey (Hanafi, Chaaban, and Seyfert 2012).
[c] *Source*: UNHCR 2014, data for mid-2013.

as a space of exception and an experimental laboratory for control and surveillance. In such contexts, the host country and humanitarian organizations alike have dealt with protracted refugees as objects to be administered, rather than as potential subjects of historical or social action. Nonetheless, this does not mean that protracted refugee subjects cannot emerge and resist this control, but rather that state sovereignty and humanitarian governmentality attempt to reduce the subjective trajectories of these individuals.

The case of Palestinian refugees' presence in Lebanon is particularly pertinent as it is characterized by deep ethno-national divisions, political confrontation, and, in the post-civil war years, ideological controversy. Of the 260,000–270,000 refugees residing in Lebanon, up to two-thirds live in refugee camps served by UNRWA, or in small communities (known as 'gatherings') adjacent to the camps where people have access to UNRWA services and those offered by Palestinian and other NGOs.

Distrust between refugees and citizens in Lebanon is well documented, with many Lebanese citizens (especially Christian Maronites) holding Palestinian refugees responsible for the civil war. The majority of Lebanese citizens vehemently oppose the permanent integration of Palestinians in the country. Importantly, *tawteen* (the Arabic for 'implantation' or settlement), is also strongly rejected by Palestinians who insist on the right of return to Palestine. References to *tawteen* often accentuate public phobia against Palestinians' basic rights. Debates in Lebanon about Palestinians' civil and economic rights typically start by affirming that the objective should not be *tawteen*, and Palestinians' rights have systematically been substituted by humanitarian or security solutions. Indeed, in a deeply divided political and sectarian context, the only common ground between the various Lebanese political parties is that *tawteen* is a taboo. The Lebanese position on the local integration of Palestinians also translates to discriminatory policies as, after 60 years' living in Lebanon, Palestinian refugees' legal status remains like that of a foreigner, with the Lebanese state having implemented restrictive policies with regard to Palestinians' social, economic, and civil rights (Hanafi and Tiltnes 2008).

Policies of protracted encampment are very problematic on numerous levels. In the case of the Palestinian refugees in the Palestinian territory and in Lebanon, one can witness that camp dwellers have developed a specific identity which is related to the very nature of the camp. The camp as a closed space forms the very conditions for facilitating the use of specific types of politics by the host countries and UNRWA, as refugees are gathered in a centralized and controlled place where they can be under constant surveillance. In the pretext of facilitating service provisions, the camp is conceived as the only possible space, and yet this 'care, cure and control' system has transformed refugee camps into disciplinary spaces.

The case of the Algerian-based Sahrawi camps studied by Fiddian-Qasmiyeh (2011, 2014) also suggests a problematic mode of governance. Established by the Polisario Front in 1975–6 with Algerian support, the Sahrawi refugee camps are estimated to house between 90,000 and 125,000 refugees, and they have been administered by the Polisario with substantial support from the UN, humanitarian agencies, and civil society networks. Fiddian-Qasmiyeh (2011: 1) critically assesses the status of the camps as follows:

> while the camps are consistently represented [by the Polisario] to humanitarian observers as 'ideal' self-sufficient refugee camps which meet donors' priorities regarding 'good governance,' [there is an] urgent need to question mainstream assumptions regarding conditions and dynamics within the Sahrawi refugee camps, and to develop policy and programming responses accordingly. This is particularly significant given that idealized depictions of life in the Sahrawi refugee camps potentially risk normalising the status quo, thereby hiding the anomalous nature of the Sahrawi's protracted displacement and failing to engage with the political causes, impacts and potential solutions to the conflict.

In addition to the significance of host–refugee relations highlighted in the case of Palestinians in Lebanon, the Sahrawi case demonstrates the ways in which international actors, including UNHCR but also European and North American civil society networks and NGOs, influence refugees' experiences and representations of protracted encampment in the region. The implications of these national and international interventions, ranging from discourses of 'good governance', conditionalities of aid, and/or policies which promote or impede self-sufficiency, will be particularly important areas to be examined and addressed with reference to recent and ongoing processes of displacement resulting from the Arab Spring.

Recent Conflicts in 1990s and 2000s

Tables 45.1 and 45.2 do not show the dynamics of the displacement which has taken place in the region over time, or how individuals and families have responded to the conflict situations which have prompted displacement both inside their respective countries and into the neighbouring MENA countries. Iraqis, for example, constituted the largest group of newly displaced people in the second half of the 2010s. As of September 2007, there were estimated to be over 4.4 million displaced Iraqis around the world, including some 2.2 million internally displaced in Iraq and a similar number in neighbouring countries: Jordan and Syria received the largest numbers, an estimated 450,000–500,000 and 800,000 respectively (Fafo 2007), while some 200,000 are hosted further afield (UNHCR 2007).

A Fafo survey identified a range of key aspects characterizing the Iraqi households and individuals present in Jordan in May 2007: the migration of Iraqis to Jordan has predominantly been family based, with the highest volume of population movement taking place in 2004 and 2005, according to the Jordanian border authorities. The majority of Iraqis have lived on savings or remittances, with 42 per cent receiving such transfers from Iraq. This has made a large segment of Iraqis in Jordan at risk of becoming vulnerable as their savings have been depleted, and one in every five Iraqis in 2007 had concrete plans to emigrate to a third country. A wish to go to a third country is found in all parts of the Iraqi population, but it is particularly true for the poorer cohorts and those belonging to non-Muslim religions. With the widespread destruction and displacement arising from the recent Arab Spring, Iraqi refugees in conflict-affected counties such as Syria have increasingly faced the dilemma of staying in their unsafe host context or returning to the persistent insecurity of Iraq.

Indeed, the recent uprisings across the Middle East and North Africa have triggered mass displacement and mixed-migration flows within and from Egypt, Libya, Tunisia, and Syria. The case of Syrian refugees is particularly critical, with the UNHCR estimating in April 2013 that three million are internally displaced, and two million Syrian refugees had fled to Turkey, Jordan, and Lebanon. Xenophobia and inhuman living conditions characterize the Jordanian refugee camps for Syrians, and urban hosting contexts in Lebanon. In this regard it is also notable that while Jordan promptly established the Zaatari camp for Syrian refugees, the Lebanese government has refused to erect refugee camps for those Syrians (and indeed Palestinians formerly hosted in Syria) who have crossed into the country, fearing, *inter alia*, the possibility of another protracted refugee situation becoming entrenched on its territory.

CHALLENGES AND ONGOING POLICY DEVELOPMENTS

The Environment and Displacement Nexus

Three particularities of the MENA region make people affected by environmental pressures particularly prone to displacement: the dearth of water, the transboundary nature of this water, and creeping urbanization. Based on the OFDA/CRED International Disaster Database of the Université Catholique de Louvain, Table 45.3 compiles data related to MENA countries and key neighbouring states. The database encompasses 342 disasters[4] over the last 20 years (1991–2010), affecting more than 33 million people, mainly by being uprooted and displaced from the place where the disasters occurred. While Sudan, Somalia, and Mauritania are not covered directly in this chapter, they are categorized as Arab countries by the OFDA/CRED database, and are particularly pertinent given that populations displaced from these countries often find themselves crossing into neighbouring MENA states. According to the Database, Sudan is considered to be the most affected Arab country, with 18 million displaced by natural disasters (half the total number of the whole Arab world), followed by Somalia (8 million), Mauritania (2 million), and Syria (1.6 millions) (see Table 45.3). Floods constitute the most common type of disaster having occurred 3,820 times in North Africa and the Horn of Africa, and 1,093 times in the Arab East (the Levant) during 1991–2010.

Figures of affected populations are, however, limited since they do not indicate whether mobility and migration is permanent or temporary. Indeed, the prevalence of short-distance, circular migration in the context of land degradation and desertification, especially in areas relying primarily on rain-fed agriculture, can effectively be seen to be a form of income diversification that may involve the same activity—farming—in different locations, or temporarily engaging in non-farm activities, especially when less labour is required in the fields. Household members may also move to urban centres, especially when there is demand for migrant labour, and send remittances home on a regular basis. There is little research that directly explores the impact of environmental factors on income diversification and mobility in the region. However, there is much evidence showing that these interrelated strategies are substantial elements of the livelihoods of both rural and urban dwellers (Tacoli 2009). As such, it can be expected that, building on existing patterns and trends, such income diversification will become an increasingly important element of adaptation to slow-onset climate change in the region (also see Zetter and Morrissey, this volume).

Table 45.3 The impact of natural disasters in the Arab countries (1991–2010)

Country	No of Disasters	Killed	Total Affected	Damage US$
Sudan	60	7,594	18,272,810	526,200
Somalia	56	6,396	8,486,022	100,020
Mauritania	23	157	1,938,202	–
Syria	6	118	1,629,375	–
Djibouti	14	288	977,572	2,119
Algeria	50	4,012	480,136	5,762,846
Morocco	23	1,740	444,352	1,567,059
Yemen	30	943	390,658	1,611,500
Jordan	9	41	348,237	401,000
Comoros	11	86	294,112	–
Egypt	20	1,451	262,813	1,342,000
Lebanon	4	26	121,590	155,000
Iraq	12	83	77,783	1,300
Tunisia	5	45	33,708	–
Saudi Arabia	10	428	24,118	900,000
Oman	4	129	20,083	3,951,000
Palestine	2	–	500	–
Kuwait	2	2	201	–
Bahrain	–	–	–	–
Libya	1	–	–	42,200
Qatar	–	–	–	–
United Arab Emirates	–	–	–	–
Total	342	23,539	33,802,272	16,362,244

Source: EM-DAT: The OFDA/CRED International Disaster Database. <http://www.em-dat.net>–
Université Catholique de Louvain–Brussels–Belgium.

Trafficking

Human trafficking in the MENA region is particularly notable with regards to the exploitation of workers in the Gulf area, including domestic workers and migrant workers from South-East and East Asia. However, although 13 MENA states had signed the United Nations Anti-Trafficking Protocol (known as the Palermo Protocol) by the end of 2013, there have been few indications of a decrease in human trafficking in the region and MENA authorities' responses have been particularly limited in tackling the different forms of trafficking in the region. Indeed, despite increasing attention to forced labour, the discourse on trafficking has typically reduced trafficking to a single category of female and children sex workers (Mahdavi and Questioning 2011; see Anderson, this volume, for a critique of trafficking discourse and policy). With reference to the latter, for instance, the trafficking and sexual exploitation of women has long been identified in Iraq, as have forced marriage and domestic servitude. However, since the US-led invasion of Iraq, the number of trafficked women has reportedly increased significantly to Jordan and Syria, but also to Saudi Arabia and the United Arab Emirates (UAE) (Sarhan

2011). Indeed, UAE has been seen as a major locus for such practices. According to the US Department of State 2008 *Trafficking in Persons Report*,

> UAE is a destination country for men and women trafficked for the purposes of labor and commercial sexual exploitation… [We recommend that the UAE] continue to increase law enforcement efforts to identify, prosecute and punish acts of sex trafficking… In practice, government authorities continue to interpret the anti-trafficking law to exclude some who have been forced into commercial sexual exploitation of labor.

In addition to challenging MENA states to develop and interpret anti-trafficking legislation in line with the Palermo Protocol, international and non-governmental campaigns have attempted to encourage states in the region to curb trafficking. Furthermore, academic research critiques the Palermo Protocol's focus on trans-border trafficking by highlighting the existence and implications of internal trafficking within MENA states, as examined, for instance, by Jureidini through the case of exploited domestic workers in Egypt who originate from rural areas and are recruited through local agencies (Jureidini 2010).

Statelessness

In addition to stateless Palestinians, statelessness is a phenomenon found primarily in the Gulf area. As noted, there are approximately 100,000 *bidoons*, or stateless people in Kuwait, representing 10 per cent of the national population. Originating in the tribes of Northern Arabia, they are undistinguishable from Kuwaiti citizens and yet have been prevented from obtaining nationality. Despite their role in the construction of the modern state, the *bidoons* were classified as 'illegal migrants' in 1986, and the non-national, grey situation of the *bidoons* has continued to be an invisible domestic matter (Beaugrand 2010).

Recently, some state policies in the Gulf have started to deal with the acute problem of statelessness. For instance, Oman's nationality law was designed to integrate populations repatriated from Zanzibar, and in Bahrain, the issue was addressed in 2001 by the then Sheikh Hamad Bin 'Isa al-Khalifa, who granted Bahraini nationality as a sign of 'royal generosity' (*makruma*), to c.10,000 to 20,000 *bidoons* of mostly Iranian ('*ajam*) origin in an attempt to diffuse social and sectarian tensions. In turn, in the UAE, the issue came to the fore in October 2006 when President Sheikh Khalifa Bin Zayd Al-Nahyan pledged to solve the issue, leading, two years later, to the registration of nationality applications. In Saudi Arabia and Qatar, statelessness has not yet come to be a prominent issue, although it is certain that it affects the kingdom significantly; whether or not it affects Qatar to the same extent remains unclear.

CONCLUSION

Refugees, IDPs, and other groups of forced migrants will continue to represent a major issue worldwide but perhaps particularly in the MENA region due to the problematic setting of refugee camps in the region, but also given ongoing processes of national identity formation and the challenges protracted refugees in the region continue to face.

First, although the construction of national identity in the Arab region began during the British and French mandates, the crystallization of this national identity is a relatively recent phenomenon, and one which is effectively still underway in many contexts. Due to the relative tenuousness of this process of crystallization, the state in the MENA region became a nationalizing state; that is to say, that after making Syria, Lebanon, Tunisia, and Jordan, it faced the challenge of constituting the Syrians, the Lebanese, the Tunisians, and the Jordanians. The process of state formation has a major impact on identity formation, as do, of course, the processes of revolutions and post-conflict reconstruction which both affect and create citizens and refugees alike. The state–citizen relationship becomes an exclusionary force that embodies the techniques and processes by which states secure their legitimacy in the eyes of the people they govern, and this relationship can equally be decoupled when that legitimacy and the very integrity of the nation state are destabilized, as in the case of the Arab Spring. The processes underpinning the constitution and solidification of citizenship are not only related to democratization (or indeed authoritarianism), but also to struggles that are at the very heart of state legitimization strategies, including the formation and transformation of political identities and communities; the distribution and redistribution of rights, responsibilities, and resources; and negotiations over representation and participation. As MENA states continue to struggle to affirm their legitimacy, and are challenged by citizens, refugees, and stateless populations alike, the region will equally continue to be characterized by diverse processes of displacement and dispossession.

In addition to recent, ongoing, and likely future cases of displacement, protracted refugees continue to be in an exceptionally vulnerable situation across the region. The exodus of Palestinian refugee workers expelled from Kuwait to Jordan, Syria, and Lebanon in the 1990s following the Iraqi invasion of this country, as well as the recent case of the Sahrawi and Palestinian refugee workers and students displaced by the 2011 Libyan uprising suggest the urgency, as Fiddian-Qasmiyeh (2012) has argued, for a 'critical assessment of the protection mechanisms in place to support refugees who "voluntarily" migrate for economic and educational purposes. Such an evaluation is particularly important given policy-makers' increasing interest in presenting mobility as a "fourth durable solution". For her, protracted refugees who engage in 'voluntary migration' to find employment in neighbouring countries must not be conceptualized as having lost their claims to the refugee label and the protection which it entails. Rather, she argues in favour of a new conceptual framework of 'overlapping' and 'multiple' refugeehoods (2012), which is particularly apt in the context of the MENA region where protracted refugees have so frequently experienced secondary and tertiary displacements from their host countries, and will most likely continue to do so in the foreseeable future.

NOTES

1. The author would like to thank Elena Fiddian-Qasmiyeh for her extensive work reviewing this chapter.

2. There are many definitions of the 'MENA' region, ranging from a minimalist one that consists of countries whose official language is Arabic (as adopted by the Arab league and UNDP), to a maximalist definition which also includes Turkey and Iran (as used by the World Bank).

3. The Sahrawi Arab Democratic Republic is a full member of the African Union and is therefore a state signatory to the Convention despite not being recognized as a state by the United Nations (see Fiddian-Qasmiyeh 2011).

4. Disasters are included in the database if they fulfil at least one of the following criteria: 10 or more people reported killed; 100 or more people reported affected; declaration of a state of emergency; call for international assistance.

REFERENCES

Assal, M. (2007) 'Refugees from, and to Sudan'. Paper presented at Conference on Migration and Refugee Movements in the Middle East and North-Eastern Africa. Cairo: The Forced Migration and Refugee Studies (FMRS) at the American University in Cairo (AUC). 23–5 October.

Beaugrand, C. (2010) 'Statelessness and Transnationalism in Northern Arabia: Biduns and State Building in Kuwait, 1959–2009'. Ph.D. thesis, London School of Economics and Political Science.

Dorai, M. K. (2007) 'Iraqi Refugees in Syria'. Paper presented at Conference on Migration and Refugee Movements in the Middle East and North-Eastern Africa. Cairo: The Forced Migration and Refugee Studies (FMRS) at the American University in Cairo (AUC). 23–5 October.

Fafo (2007) *Iraqis in Jordan: Their Number and Characteristics*. Oslo: Fafo.

Fiddian-Qasmiyeh, E. (2011) 'Protracted Sahrawi Displacement: Challenges and Opportunities beyond Encampment'. Policy Briefing 7. Oxford: Refugee Studies Centre. May.

Fiddian-Qasmiyeh, E. (2012) 'Invisible Refugees and/or Overlapping Refugeedom? Protecting Sahrawis and Palestinians Displaced by the 2011 Libyan Uprising'. *International Journal of Refugee Law* 24(2)(May): 263–93.

Fiddian-Qasmiyeh, E. (2014) *The Ideal Refugees: Gender, Islam and the Sahrawi Politics of Survival*. Syracuse, NY: Syracuse University Press.

Hanafi, S., Chaaban, J., and Seyfert, K. (2012) 'Social Exclusion of Palestinian Refugees in Lebanon: Reflections on the Mechanisms that Cement their Persistent Poverty'. *Refugee Survey Quarterly* 31(1): 34–53.

Hanafi, S., and Tiltnes, Å. A. (2008) 'The Employability of Palestinian Professionals in Lebanon'. *Knowledge, Work and Society*, 5(1): 127–50.

Jureidini, R. (2010) 'Are Contract Migrant Domestic Workers Trafficked?' <http://www.iom.int/jahia/webdav/shared/shared/mainsite/microsites/IDM/workshops/ensuring_protection_070909/human_trafficking_new_directions_for_research.pdf>.

Mahdavi, P., and Sargent, C. (2011) 'Questioning the Discursive Construction of Trafficking and Forced Labor in the United Arab Emirates'. *Journal of Middle East Women's Studies* 7: 6–35.

PCBS (2013) 'Palestinians at the End of 2012'. <http://www.pcbs.gov.ps/portals/_pcbs/PressRelease/Press_En_PalestiniansEOY2012E.pdf>.

Rempel, T. (2002) 'UNHCR, Palestinian Refugees, and Durable Solutions'. BADIL—Information & Discussion Brief. Issue No. 7.

Sarhan, J. (2011) 'Arab Spring Doesn't Curb Trafficking of Women'. <http://www.policymic.com/articles/arab-spring-doesn-t-curb-trafficking-of-women>.

Tacoli, C. (2009) 'Crisis or Adaptation? Migration and Climate Change in a Context of High Mobility'. Paper prepared for Expert Group Meeting on Population Dynamics and Climate Change. UNFPA and IIED in Collaboration with UN-HABITAT and the Population Division. UN/DESA. 24–5 June.

Takkenberg, L. (2006) 'The Search for Durable Solutions for Palestinian Refugees: A Role for UNRWA?' Pp. 231–50 in S. Hanafi, E. Benvenisti, and C. Gans (eds.), *Palestinian Refugees and Israel*. Heidelberg: Max Planck Institute for Comparative Public and International Law.

UNHCR (2007) 'Statistics on Displaced Iraqis around the World. September 2007. Global Overview'. <http://www.unhcr.org/cgi-bin/texis/vtx/home/opendoc.pdf?tbl=SUBSITES&id=470387fc2>.

UNHCR (2011) Statistics on Displaced Iraqis around the World. September 2011. Global Overview.

UNHCR (2014) '2014 UNHCR Regional Operations Plan—North Africa (Western Sahara Territory)'. <http://www.unhcr.org/pages/49e4861f6.html>.

CHAPTER 46

FORCED MIGRATION IN BROADER CENTRAL ASIA

ALESSANDRO MONSUTTI AND BAYRAM BALCI

INTRODUCTION

CENTRAL Asia—as understood here—covers the former Soviet republics of Kazakhstan, Kyrgyzstan, Tajikistan, Uzbekistan, Turkmenistan, alongside Afghanistan, with a total population of almost 100 million. In the latter period of the Cold War and following the collapse of the USSR, these countries underwent political and social upheavals that have caused voluntary and forced migrations on internal and international levels. However, a high level of population mobility in its various forms—as related to pastoralism, trade, pilgrimage, conquest, but also administrative impositions or planning schemes such as collectivization—has marked the region's socio-political landscape throughout its history. This chapter offers an overview of past, current, and future challenges in this highly volatile region characterized by both the ethnicization of public life and the proliferation of Islamist groups. The first part examines the case of Afghanistan, one of the most massive and protracted refugee crises in the last 60 years, which has played a crucial role in the final period of the Cold War and debates on the manipulation of humanitarian action. The second part addresses the former Soviet Republics, which have been affected since their independence by significant population displacements caused by a series of conflicts and environmental disasters. The case of Central Asia, including Afghanistan, demonstrates both that migration is a constitutive feature of social life and that massive displacements of people have been caused by conflict and process of nation—and state building.

A Long History of Conflicts and Displacements

For over 2,000 years, a succession of nomadic confederacies have dominated the Eurasian steppes and repeatedly intervened in the affairs of the settled states of East Asia, South Asia, the Middle East, and Eastern Europe (Barfield 1989). The balance of power changed only recently, when European colonial expansion redrew the region's political map during the nineteenth century. The Central Asian *khanates* lost their independence, while Afghanistan was maintained as a buffer state between the Russian and British Empires, engaged in the strategic rivalry known as the 'Great Game'. Subsequently, the authorities of the newly created Soviet Union implemented forced collectivization in the 1920s and 1930s, provoking a cycle of uprisings and repressions that caused the displacement of large segments of the population (also see McDowell, this volume). In Afghanistan the state-building process also reshaped society, with the central government relocating thousands of people to weaken centrifugal forces and increase its grip on distant provinces.

The Russian quest for warm water ports resumed during the Cold War and brought further turmoil. In Afghanistan, the 1978 Communist coup d'état and the Soviet intervention the following year provoked the flight of millions of people. In the 1980s, many social scientists worked with and about Afghan refugees in Pakistan. Afghans who went to Iran were comparatively understudied due to access barriers. In the 1990s, research progressively included Iran and returnees, or examined the vast transnational networks set up by Afghans. Policy and academic debates critically assessed the three solutions to the problem of the refugees promoted by the United Nations High Commissioner for Refugees (UNHCR), in particular return, and were influenced by concerns over global security.

In Central Asia, the dissolution of the old political order in 1991 led to the independence of the various republics, while the spread of international and non-governmental organizations and Islamic militant groups unsettled the new states' fragile sovereignty. The new countries experienced the political transition in contrasted ways. In Uzbekistan and Turkmenistan, former elites maintained strong control over state and society. Kyrgyzstan opened its borders to international trade and external assistance but underwent social strife. In the Fergana Valley, riots between Kyrgyz and Uzbeks in 1990 and 2010 caused the flight of tens of thousands of people. In Tajikistan, the civil war that raged between 1992 and 1997 caused an important displacement of population within and outside the national territory.

AFGHANISTAN: A MASSIVE CRISIS WITH GEOSTRATEGIC DIMENSIONS

The territory that today constitutes Afghanistan emerged as a modern nation during the eighteenth and nineteenth centuries. Supported by British subsidies, the emir Abdur Rahman (1880–1901) extended his authority on the whole country by overcoming resistance. In this process, entire tribal sections were massacred or forcibly relocated to other regions. Although Afghanistan's political unity was forged during his reign, his harsh tactics created long-lasting enmities within the population.

The 1978 Communist coup d'état and the Red Army's intervention in 1979 resulted in an unprecedented level of violence that triggered the social, political, and economic tensions accumulated since the late nineteenth century. In its scale and duration, the conflict that has been tearing Afghanistan apart caused one of the gravest humanitarian crises since the creation of the United Nations. Using ancient migratory routes, millions of Afghans sought refuge in neighbouring countries, and in 1990 Afghans formed the largest group of displaced persons in the world, accounting for 40 per cent of the people of concern falling under UNHCR's mandate. In 1990 there were 6.22 million Afghan refugees, in their huge majority between Pakistan and Iran, and up to an estimated 1.5 million internally displaced people (Colville 1998).

Large numbers repatriated after the Soviet withdrawal (1989) and the capture of Kabul by resistance forces (1992), but over the following years this trend reversed as more outward flows accompanied the new outbreaks of fighting. Again, the fall of the Taliban regime in late 2001 and the establishment of a government in Kabul backed by the international community have caused an unprecedented wave of returns. It is considered by the UNHCR to be the largest repatriation campaign in its history, with some 3.5 million refugees returning to Afghanistan between 2002 and 2005.

Afghan Refugees in Pakistan

During the 1980s, Afghans were presented in the West as the victims of Communist expansionism. The United States saw UNHCR as an efficient partner in anti-Soviet propaganda and contributed significantly to its budget. Pakistan, a key American ally during the Cold War era, served as a training ground for the *mujahedeen*. Directly involved in this new Great Game and supported financially and militarily, the country hosted the most numerous refugee population of the time while it was party neither to the 1951 Refugee Convention nor the 1967 Protocol.

Many Afghans taking refuge in Pakistan were installed in so-called Afghan Refugee Villages (ARVs), most of which were situated near the border, in the North-West Frontier Province and Baluchistan. They were not fenced and little distinguished them from neighbouring Pakistani villages. Most refugees were Pashtuns from East and South

Afghanistan and they lived in Pakistan among a population sharing their language, cultural references, and value system (Ahmed 1986; Edwards 1986).

Afghans in Pakistan defined themselves in different ways in the 1980s (Centlivres 1988). First, through the 1951 Convention the international figure of the refugee conveys the image of a person in need of legal protection and socio-economic assistance from the international community. To receive food rations and benefit from health services and education facilities, Afghans quickly learned to display signs of distress when meeting organizations participating in the international refugee regime. The second identity pole was related to Islam, with Afghans envisaged as having repeated the migration of the Prophet Muhammad and his followers from Mecca to Medina (*hejrat*) when they left a country ruled by an impious government to go to Muslim lands. They were therefore entitled to be called *mohâjerin*, the 'emigrants'. This terminology does not designate victims in need of international compassion but proactive people ready to brave all dangers for their faith. The third model is the Pashtun tribal code. Here Afghans represent themselves as armed people struggling against a more powerful enemy and taking temporary refuge among fellow tribesmen on the other side of an international border that is not perceived as a cultural and social boundary. Afghans in Pakistan had the ability to take benefit of the various facets of their situation, alternatively putting forward one or another figure according to the context. The status of refugee thereby coexisted with other labels, which often valued proactive characteristics.

After the heydays of humanitarian aid in the 1980s, rations decreased in the following decade due to donor fatigue and the declining geo-strategic relevance of the region (Marsden 1992). Many Afghans went to urban centres to find menial jobs, joining the ranks of so-called self-settled refugees. After 2001, the pressure on Afghan refugees increased further due to the international military intervention in Afghanistan, the American-launched global war on terrorism, and the increasing fractures of Pakistani society. Tensions between Kabul, Islamabad, and UNHCR culminated with the crisis of summer 2007, when the Pakistani authorities officially closed several camps, including Jalozai and Gacha Gari (respectively with some 100,000 and 65,000 residents), in spite of vehement protests by the UN refugee agency. Even if these camps were not totally emptied of their population, Pakistan clearly no longer offers a safe haven for Afghans fleeing violence.

Afghans in Iran

Alienated from the Western bloc, post-revolutionary Iran did not have a massive presence of UN agencies and international NGOs, despite the country having ratified the Refugee Convention and its Protocol as early as 1976. In sharp contrast to the situation in Pakistan, it is assumed that only *circa* 3 per cent of Afghans lived in refugee camps (Colville 1998; Abbasi-Shavazi and Glazebrook 2006). The majority of these were Persian-speaking with an overrepresentation of Shiites (especially Hazaras). In the 1980s, they were welcomed as Muslim brothers fleeing their country where they were unable to practise Islam, and most of them were integrated into the labour market—occupying a series of menial jobs in sectors such as construction, industrial mills, quarry, or agriculture—at a time when Iranian youth were involved in the war against Iraq.

After the Soviet withdrawal from Afghanistan in 1989 and the fall of the Najibullah regime in 1992, the Iranian authorities' attitude towards the Afghan presence became progressively tougher. In August 1998, the Taliban captured the northern Afghan city of Mazar-e Sharif and murdered several Iranian diplomats and journalists. Tehran reacted by deploying troops along the border with Afghanistan. This military response and the public outcry contributed to further worsen the situation of Afghans in Iran. This trend was not reversed by the intervention in Afghanistan of an international coalition led by American forces, which caused the fall of the Taliban in late 2001 but is widely conceived as a threat in Iran.

The authorities have increasingly implemented a policy to limit the number of Afghans and to push them back across the border, arguing that their home country is now peaceful. Labour market regulation became stricter, with police controlling building sites and factories, and employers hiring illegal Afghan workers being severely fined. Welfare facilities in education and health sectors have been progressively withdrawn. Under pressure, several hundred thousand Afghan refugees and migrants decided to repatriate.

Nonetheless, in 2005, over one million documented Afghans remained in Iran. There were also c.500,000 undocumented labour migrants (Abbasi-Shavazi and Glazebrook 2006) who have left their families behind in Afghanistan and regularly move back and forth. Iran has needed Afghan manpower (especially during the Iran–Iraq war and the ensuing reconstruction), but the government also wanted to avoid a Pakistani-style situation—where Afghans have monopolized several sectors of the economy—and it has therefore taken various steps to discourage integration and long-term residence.

Return to Afghanistan and Solutions to the Refugee Problem

The massive wave of returns to Afghanistan following the fall of the Taliban in late 2001 was widely considered to be a success by the major stakeholders. In 2002 alone, UNHCR estimated that over 1.5 million Afghan refugees from Pakistan and some 250,000 from Iran had returned to their country of origin, with as many as 4,678,094 Afghans returning between 2002 and 2012 (UNHCR 2012). In the period of optimism that followed the fall of the Taliban, such large-scale and rapid assisted repatriation represented a vote of popular support for the interim government of Afghanistan. It also represented a reduction in the burden of hosting and supporting a large refugee population for Pakistan and Iran as well as for UNHCR and the donor community.

However, these official figures must be viewed with caution. Turton and Marsden (2002) very early questioned the veracity and sustainability of such a large return movement, which primarily served the interests of the international community. They showed that many registered returnees might be 'recyclers'—repatriating to Afghanistan, receiving assistance packages, and then going back to Pakistan or Iran. Some others might be seasonal migrants with no intention of staying in Afghanistan on a long-term basis. Concurrently, repatriation has been a tool for Pakistan and Iran to put donors or the Afghan government under pressure. In a changing political environment, Afghan refugees were again pawns in the international arena.

Over the years, many returnees have amassed in the cities, especially Kabul, often with vulnerable livelihoods that have prompted secondary displacements (Majidi 2011). Indeed, return to Afghanistan does not necessarily mean the end of mobility. Many Afghans have been shifting from one place to the next for years—some never returning to their place of origin, others only on a temporary basis before deciding to return into Iran, Pakistan, or further afield. Migration to Afghanistan's neighbouring countries, and the very significant sum of remittances sent home, can be seen as a response to war and insecurity, but also as an efficient economic strategy for households and a crucial contribution to the country's economy as a whole. Blurring any clear-cut distinction between voluntary and involuntary migration, a certain level of ongoing individual mobility and family dispersion lie at the core of the strategies developed by many Afghans, who have over time established transnational networks linking distant places (Monsutti 2005).

Based on its long presence in the region and its analysis of the political situation, UNHCR itself became aware of the limitations of its action. Soon after 2002, the year with the highest level of returns, internal documents (UNHCR 2003, 2004) acknowledged the necessity of defining a new approach. UNHCR established the Afghanistan Comprehensive Solution Unit, a policy bureau aiming to consider the refugee problem in its wider context and to identify durable solutions for those Afghans remaining in exile. This innovative initiative stemmed from several observations. First, the absorption capacity inside Afghanistan was limited due to economic and demographic factors. Second, the national economy benefited from the inflow of cash and commodities financed by migrants, and full repatriation was therefore neither feasible nor desirable. Indeed, implemented at all costs, it could destabilize the fragile equilibrium of the renascent Afghan state and have negative effects on the neighbouring countries. Policy-wise, a more comprehensive solution needed to take into account the full range of strategies and responses developed by the Afghan population, including the transnational networks and back-and-forth movements between Afghanistan, Pakistan, Iran, and beyond (Stigter and Monsutti 2005).

Through the Afghan case, UNHCR became progressively aware of the necessity to develop a new paradigm supplementing the three classical solutions to the refugee problem (voluntary repatriation, local integration, and resettlement) (Crisp 2008), which are based on the idea that movement must stop (Monsutti 2008). Such an evolution reflected both a changing political context (with the Soviet withdrawal and the end of the Cold War, the subsequent conflict between factions, the rise and fall of the Taliban, and the establishment of a government backed by the international community in Kabul) and a progressive learning from social realities (mobility as an asset and not only as a problem).

The Unmaking of the Soviet Union and the Making of Nation States

Throughout its relatively short history, the Soviet Union witnessed various forced displacements of peasants opposed to collectivization or minorities resisting state intervention. During the Second World War, many peoples and sometimes whole ethnic groups were deported far from the front where it was feared they may collaborate with the Nazi troops. Crimean Tatars, Meskhetian Turks, Karachays, and Chechens were among the main victims of this policy. When Mikhail Gorbachev took over in 1985 and started glasnost and perestroika, voices called for the right to return. In such a rapidly changing political environment, local authorities were reluctant to answer positively to the demands of deported populations. After the various republics were granted independence in 1991, they proved even less willing to listen to such claims, in the fear it could jeopardize the nation-building process in a context of fierce competition over the control of natural resources and power.

The Soviet republics had all intentionally been made multi-ethnic entities under the close eye of Moscow. In 1991, for example, Kazakhstan was a 16 million nation composed of only 53 per cent Kazakhs and an important proportion of Russians. Uzbekistan was more homogeneous, and yet the 70 per cent ethnic Uzbeks lived alongside several minorities. In turn, Kyrgyzstan's population in 1999 consisted of 65 per cent ethnic Kyrgyz, 13 per cent Uzbeks, and Russians. Similar characteristics were observed in Tajikistan. By contrast, post-Soviet republics underwent a process of ethnicization after their independence. Power was exercised in the name of the eponymous nation and minority groups were marginalized.

THE *DRANG NACH WESTEN* OF RUSSIANS AND GERMANS

The last Soviet census released in 1989 showed 9 million Russians in the Central Asian republics, about 20 per cent of the whole population: 37 per cent in Kazakhstan, 21 per cent in Kyrgyzstan, 9 per cent in Turkmenistan, and 8 per cent in Uzbekistan. Less than a decade later, millions of Russians had migrated to Russia, considered as their homeland although they had been established in Central Asia for several generations. In the newly independent states, nationalism became the administration's ideology and Russians turned from a privileged to a marginalized minority. The indigenization of political elites encouraged by Moscow had started in the 1970s and accelerated after independence with the replacement of the Russian language by the vernacular language in the administration, educational system, and public scene (Peyrouse 2008). Russians were suddenly downgraded to a second-class status.

As for the Volga Germans, they did not return to the Volga basin where they came from, with most of them choosing to settle in reunified Germany. Like many, they had been deported to Central Asia during the Second World War. The German embassy in Kazakhstan stated that 900,000 Volga Germans officially immigrated to Germany between 1989 and 2005. In Kyrgyzstan, in the same period, their population shrank from some 100,000 individuals to about 26,000.

Were these migration flows forced or not? Although these populations were not forced out by overt violence, the creeping ethno-nationalistic political context combined with harsh socio-economic difficulties put heavy pressure on these groups and pushed them to leave the places where they had been born.

NATION BUILDING AND CONFLICT

Other population movements in Central Asia leave no doubt on their forced nature. These may result from localized conflict, civil war, or state repression. The Fergana Valley, which is divided between Uzbekistan, Kyrgyzstan, and Tajikistan, was the location of several tragic events that triggered the displacement of hundreds of thousands of people.

During the summer of 1989, Meskhetian Turks were the victims of brutal riots. Ethnically and linguistically close to the Anatolian Turks, they originate from south-western Georgia and were deported in 1944 to Central Asia. The quickly deteriorating living conditions in the period immediately preceding the collapse of the Soviet Union led to unspeakable acts of violence against this educated but politically isolated minority. The violence lasted only a few days but left hundreds of casualties. Since then, the exodus of Meskhetian Turks has been uninterrupted. If some chose Azerbaijan and even Turkey, where they were granted citizenship, a group of 13,000 remain stateless and live in highly precarious conditions in the Krasnodar region of Southern Russia. Not a single family was ever reported to have returned to the homeland, despite all the promises received from the Georgian government to facilitate return (Nahajlo 2006).

The civil war that raged in post-Soviet Tajikistan also forced important masses to migrate. From the early days of its independence, the country was the scene of fierce competition over power. Tensions turned to open violence after the contested presidential elections in 1991: parties took arms, and after only a few months the civil war had left 50,000 victims, 800,000 IDPs, and 80,000 refugees in neighbouring countries. The warring factions were not organized along ethnic lines but on regional solidarity and clan ties. The government was controlled by people from Kulab and Leninabad, the original stronghold of Tajik communists, while the so-called Islamic and democratic alliance was rooted in Gharm, Penjikent, and the Pamir.

To prevent the conflict from spreading across Central Asia, the United Nations and regional powers pushed for national reconciliation and the war ended in 1997.

UNHCR took responsibility for the uneasy task of facilitating refugees' return. A solution was found for the ethnic Tajiks but not for other displaced people. All 12,000 Turkmens who lived in Tajikistan before the civil war settled in Turkmenistan, where they are still waiting for the authorities to recognize them as citizens (UNHCR 2011).

In May 2005, in the Fergana Valley again, the Uzbek city of Andijan saw a popular anti-government uprising. People stormed the town jailhouse, ransacked official buildings, and demonstrated in the city centre. The subsequent military repression is estimated to have left between 187 people (according to official figures) and up to 1,000 people dead. Over 2,000 people crossed the border to Kyrgyzstan. Tashkent put pressure on Bishkek and immediately and repeatedly demanded the return of all refugees. Although 400 individuals were granted UNHCR's protection and resettlement in Europe, Kyrgyzstan expelled 86 persons to Uzbekistan in breach to the principle of *non-refoulement* (Colville 2006). The crisis led UNHCR to end all operations in Uzbekistan, the only country in Central Asia that is party neither to the 1951 Convention nor the 1967 Protocol.

Another major crisis took place not far from Andijan, in the Kyrgyz city of Osh. The urban population is composed of a large majority of ethnic Uzbeks. Tensions between communities already arose in 1990, and in June 2010 political instability following the dismissal of President Bakiev two months earlier, combined with persistent economic difficulties, triggered a violent conflict. Uzbek neighbourhoods were attacked by groups of Kyrgyz men from the surrounding mountain villages with the possible involvement of the police. Thousands of homes were destroyed and for four days the city slipped out of governmental control. While Kyrgyz authorities acknowledge only 400 casualties, Uzbek sources state that 2,000 people were killed. A hundred thousand people crossed the border to Uzbekistan and yet Tashkent, fearing the spread of political Islam, was reluctant to welcome those fleeing violence, even if they were in majority ethnic Uzbeks. Most of them were sent back to Kyrgyzstan just a few weeks after the pogroms.

This outburst of violence was soon described as resulting from old animosities and hatred between two ethnic groups. However, the causes are deeply intertwined, including political and economic competition and rivalry; frustration and animosity against the successful minority of city dwelling Uzbeks while rural or recently urbanized Kyrgyz feel marginalized in their own country; control of the drug trafficking routes that cross the region; and increased competition for resources brought by international and non-governmental organizations. The ethno-nationalist ideology developed by successive governments in Bishkek since independence reinforced these fault lines (Balci 2011). Two years after the events, Uzbeks are still the prey of local Kyrgyz authorities, indicating that conflict may erupt at any time; and yet they are not welcomed in Uzbekistan. As such, Uzbeks in Kyrgyzstan occupy a political interstice between two nation states without being fully accepted by either one (Liu 2012).

BEYOND CONFLICT INDUCED
DISPLACEMENT

Statelessness

In addition to conflict induced displacement, significant populations became stateless after the collapse of the USSR without moving from their place of residence. With the independence of the Central Asia republics, many people continued to use their Soviet passports, which had become invalid, because they did not bear any identity documents established by the new states. More than twenty years later, statelessness has not completely disappeared in Central Asia (Farquharson 2011). According to UNHCR, there are 9,000 stateless individuals in Kyrgyzstan alone. Some of them are ethnic Kyrgyz who fled the civil war in Tajikistan and could not obtain Kyrgyz citizenship in spite of promises made by the authorities. In Kazakhstan in 2007, more than 7,500 persons were living on the national territory without any citizenship. Some of them were Kazakhs from Mongolia, China, and other countries whose settlement was encouraged by the government in order to reinforce the Kazakh element in the population. In Uzbekistan, the issue of statelessness is even more pronounced and problematic: over 500,000 people are in an inextricable situation, possessing no passport and therefore unable to cross an international border even if they have the internal document allowing them to work and travel inside the country.

Human Trafficking

In addition to the emergence of statelessness following independence, human trafficking in Central Asia increased dramatically since 1991 despite having been insignificant under the Soviets. The deepening poverty and the establishment of labour relations not only with Russia but also Western Europe and the Middle East contributed to the development of criminal activities linked to human trafficking. The most important component remains prostitution. In Kyrgyzstan, for instance, the south region of Osh, afflicted by conflict and extreme poverty, is a major point of recruitment both for sexual and labour exploitation (Tashybaeva 2011). Every year thousands of women and girls are involved in sexual trafficking between Central Asia and countries like UAE, Turkey, and Israel (Kelly 2005).

Environmental Questions and Forced Migrations

Finally, environmental issues and ecological catastrophes resulting from industrial or agricultural activities have also forced people from their homeland (Gemenne and

Reuchlin 2008). Environmental disasters are always combined with other causes and reasons for leaving, whether forced or voluntary. The ecological argument may trigger or emphasize the migration process, but it does not explain it fully.

In Semipalatinsk (Kazakhstan), for instance, the Soviet regime established one of its most important nuclear test sites. From 1949 to 1989, 456 weapons tests were conducted underground, on the surface, and in the atmosphere. The impact on public health was kept a state secret for decades. Epidemiological studies were not undertaken, and little is therefore known on the health consequences of high levels of radioactive gases in the atmosphere. Kazakh nationalist groups and activists were the first to denounce the nuclear tests at the end of the 1980s. According to different sources, between 1980 and 1990 over 161,000 people had to leave the test area due to life-threatening pollution levels (Sulaimanova 2004).

Further south, the Aral Sea, lying on the border between Uzbekistan and Kazakhstan, used to be the fourth largest intercontinental locked body of salt water on the planet. In the 1960s, the Soviet regime intensified cotton monoculture by digging draining canals from both the Syr Darya and the Amu Darya. The Aral Sea paid the high price for this development policy that disregarded the region's ecological conditions to grow a water-greedy plant like cotton. The rivers' waters no longer reached the Sea, and the abuse of pesticides and defoliant chemicals polluted the rivers and groundwater, endangering numerous animal and plant species. Desertification accelerated, as did the salinization of soils that soon became unusable for any kind of agriculture.

Without water, food, or health services, the population was forced to leave. It has been estimated that 100,000 people were displaced during the 1980s and 1990s for ecological reasons in the Aral Sea Basin, 50,000 people having left Karakalpakstan alone (Médecins Sans Frontières 2003). The migration process is ongoing, although its scope is difficult to measure as the Uzbek authorities are reluctant to provide data on this sensitive issue.

CONCLUSION

As demonstrated in this chapter, forced migration in Central Asia is not a new phenomenon and can be caused by a multiplicity of often overlapping reasons. The current volatile situation linked to the withdrawal of international forces from Afghanistan and a range of major challenges in the former Soviet republics raise the prospects of ongoing and new forms of displacement in the whole region.

In Afghanistan, the Soviet military occupation in the 1980s provoked one of the world's largest forced displacements of population since the Second World War. Millions of Afghan refugees have been welcomed in Pakistan, a country that has not ratified the 1951 Convention or the 1967 Protocol. The political conditions of the time, more than humanitarian concern, made this situation acceptable for the UNHCR, the host country and the Western bloc, which was the major source of financial support. By contrast Iran has been snubbed by donors, while it harboured almost as many Afghan refugees and was an early party to the international texts relating to the status of refugees. Twenty years later, another intervention—this time by the United States—has produced further turmoil. Despite hundreds of millions of dollars of foreign aid money, Afghanistan still ranks at or near the bottom of many human development indicators, including infant mortality, life expectancy, and indices of societal violence. The urban population continues to swell, while rural areas are unable to integrate more people due to demographic pressures and limited agricultural potential. More attention has been paid to security issues than to structural social and demographic trends, which may induce further displacement. Unfortunately for the Afghan population, their options may seem significantly more limited today than they were during the anti-Soviet *jihad*. The strategic context has changed and neither Pakistan nor Iran seem possible host countries for Afghan refugees anymore, an extremely worrying situation considering the US and NATO pullout of 2014 and a possible new deterioration of the situation in the following years.

Besides violence and conflict, the very process of state building has also prompted displacement, as shown by events surrounding the independence of the Central Asian republics. After the collapse of the Soviet Union, nationalism has been gaining ground and is jeopardizing the social and ethnic status quo. This trend is illustrated by the anticipatory movement of European minorities, who have left the region en masse without having been targeted by violence but in response to a loss of status and the ethnicization of political life. Many people remain stateless, while large minority groups, trapped and marginalized, have grown resentful and frustrated in the newly established nation states. Environmental mismanagement is another factor to be considered, as sadly illustrated by the demise of the Aral Sea. Despite international efforts, the sea continues to shrink and is predicted to soon disappear, thus threatening the survival of 5 million people living in its basin. The pressure on water and conflicts over resources add further constraints to the regional context; the risk for new tragic developments is high. Over two decades after their independence, the Central Asian republics are still struggling to reinvent themselves under the threat of many potential social conflicts as well as destructive natural disasters.

The various cases of displacements discussed above show the weight of political and strategic considerations when compared with humanitarian law. The experience of the Afghanistan Comprehensive Solution Unit, whose scope goes beyond the specific case, shows that UNHCR has progressively acknowledged the need to imagine a fourth solution to the refugee problem, taking into account ongoing mobility. Indeed, in the absence of legal solutions to their plight, people labelled as refugees strive to utilize the interstices between the various interests of states and humanitarian organizations. They are increasingly exploring their own alternative strategies to maximize opportunities and spread risks, frequently involving transnationalism and irregularity. Even if they meet constant obstacles, these strategies show the inventiveness and agency of refugees. They should be included, in one way or another, into the international system of protection.

References

Abbasi-Shavazi, M. J., and Glazebrook, D. (2006) *Continued Protection, Sustainable Reintegration: Afghan Refugees and Migrants in Iran*. Kabul: Afghanistan Research and Evaluation Unit.

Ahmed, A. S. (1986) 'The Afghan Refugees'. Pp. 165–85 in *Pakistan Society: Islam, Ethnicity and Leadership in South Asia*. Karachi: Oxford University Press.

Balci, B. (2011) 'Identité nationale et gestion du fait minoritaire en Asie centrale. Analyse des affrontements interethniques d'Och en juin 2010'. *Cahiers d'Asie centrale* 19–20: 470–84.

Barfield, T. J. (1989) *The Perilous Frontier: Nomadic Empires and China, 221 BC to AD 1757*. Oxford: Blackwell.

Centlivres, P. (1988) 'Les Trois Pôles de l'identité afghane au Pakistan'. *L'Homme* 28(4): 134–46.

Colville, R. (1998) 'Afghan Refugees: Is International Support Draining away after Two Decades in Exile?' *Refuge* 17(4): 6–11.

Colville, R. (2006) 'How the World Rallied round the Refugees from Andijan'. *Refugees* 143(2): 14–19.

Crisp, J. (2008) *Beyond the Nexus: UNHCR's Evolving Perspective on Refugee Protection and International Migration*. Geneva: UNHCR Policy Development and Evaluation Service.

Edwards, D. B. (1986) 'Marginality and Migration: Cultural Dimensions of the Afghan Refugee Problem'. *International Migration Review* 20(2): 313–25.

Farquharson, M. (2011) *Statelessness in Central Asia*. Geneva: UNHCR. <http://www.unhcr.org/4dfb592e9.html>.

Gemenne, F., and Reuchlin, P. (2008) 'Climate Change and Displacement in Central Asia'. *Forced Migration Review* 31: 14–15.

Kelly, L. (2005) *Fertile Fields: Trafficking in Persons in Central Asia*. Geneva: International Organization for Migration. <http://publications.iom.int/bookstore/index.php?main_page=product_info&products_id=184>.

Liu, M. Y. (2012) *Under Solomon's Throne: Uzbek Visions of Renewal in Osh*. Pittsburgh: University of Pittsburgh Press.

Majidi, N. (2011) *Urban Returnees and Internally Displaced Persons in Afghanistan*. Washington, DC: Middle East Institute; Paris: Fondation pour la recherche stratégique.

Marsden, P. (1992) 'Afghan in Pakistan: Why Rations Decline'. *Journal of Refugee Studies* 5(3–4): 289–99.

Médecins Sans Frontières (2003) *Karakalpakstan: A Population in Danger. The Impact of the Aral Sea Disaster and a Worsening Economic Climate on the Health and Wellbeing of the People of Karakalpakstan*. Tashkent: Médecins Sans Frontières.

Monsutti, A. (2005) *War and Migration: Social Networks and Economic Strategies of the Hazaras of Afghanistan*. New York: Routledge.

Monsutti, A. (2008) 'Afghan Migratory Strategies and the Three Solutions to the Refugee Problem'. *Refugee Survey Quarterly* 27(1): 58–73.

Nahajlo, B. (2006) 'Grappling with Stalin's Legacy'. *Refugees* 143(2): 23–5.

Peyrouse, S. (2008) 'Les Russes d'Asie centrale, une minorité en déclin face à de multiples défis'. *Revue d'études comparatives est-ouest* 39(1): 149–77.

Stigter, E., and Monsutti, A. (2005) *Transnational Networks: Recognising a Regional Reality*. Kabul: Afghanistan Research and Evaluation Unit.

Sulaimanova, S. (2004) 'Migration Trends in Central Asia and the Case of Trafficking of Women'. Pp. 377–400 in D. Burghart and T. Sabonis-Helf (eds.), *In the Tracks of Tamerlane: Central Asia's Path to the 21st Century*. Washington, DC: National Defense University Press.

Tashybaeva, A. (2011) *Human Trafficking in the Southern Kyrgyz Republic*. Oslo: Norwegian Institute of International Affairs.

Turton, D., and Marsden, P. (2002) *Taking Refugees for a Ride? The Politics of Refugee Return to Afghanistan*. Kabul: Afghanistan Research and Evaluation Unit.

UNHCR (2003) 'Towards a Comprehensive Solution for Displacement from Afghanistan'. Discussion Paper. Geneva: UNHCR.

UNHCR (2004) *Afghanistan: Challenges to Return*. Geneva: UNHCR.

UNHCR (2011) *Statelessness: More than 3,000 Stateless People Given Turkmen Nationality*. Geneva: UNHCR. <http://www.unhcr.org/4edf81ce6.html>.

UNHCR (2012) *Afghanistan Update on VolRep and Border Monitoring October 2012*. Geneva: UNHCR. <http://www.unhcr.org/50ab463b6.pdf>.

CHAPTER 47

FORCED MIGRATION IN SOUTH ASIA

PAULA BANERJEE

INTRODUCTION

IN colonial times massive displacements took place across South Asia due to conflict, contest over resources, exploitation by colonial masters, and subsequent protests. Although partition was intended to end all possible hostilities, conflicts, and displacements, extreme violence and subsequent displacements followed. Indeed, South Asia emerged from a violent partition that displaced over 15 million people (Bose 2010), killing 100,000 and leading to the abduction of more than 50,000 women from both sides of the border, many of whom were forcefully repatriated, thereby suffering double displacements. It has thus been argued that 'Partition lives on in post-colonial time to such an extent that we should truly prefer the phrase "partitioned times" to the more common "post-colonial times"' (Samaddar 2003: 21). This chapter addresses both the root causes of displacement and the experiences of forced migrants in South Asia. In particular, it focuses on conflict induced displacement, internal displacement resulting from development projects, and statelessness in the region. In addition to highlighting the gendered nature of displacement, the chapter places the region's contemporary displacement situations in historical context, and concludes by reflecting on South Asia's future challenges.

LEGAL FRAMEWORKS AND REFUGEES IN SOUTH ASIA

Although no South Asian states (here understood to include India, Sri Lanka, Pakistan, Bangladesh, Nepal, Maldives, and Bhutan) have signed either the 1951 Refugee

Convention or the 1967 Protocol, these countries have nonetheless ratified many other human rights instruments in the recent past: all seven have ratified the 1969 International Convention on the Elimination of All Forms of Racial Discrimination, the 1989 Convention on the Rights of the Child, and the 1981 Convention on the Elimination of All Forms of Discrimination Against Women, in addition to the four Geneva Conventions.[1] While South Asian states have been reluctant to accept the 1951 Refugee Convention, states have offered no official reasons for such a decision, and certain states, including India, have offered refugee status to specific groups of non-citizens, including partition refugees and others both before and after partition.

Key South Asian Refugee Populations in India

In India, like all other migrants, refugees fall under the jurisdiction of the Foreigners Act (1946) and the Passport Act (1955). These Acts are relevant to all non-citizens and they make entering India without valid papers an offence. However, India has given refugee status to specific groups: apart from the partition refugees, these include Tibetan refugees, followed by Bangladeshis, Sri Lankans, and Bhutanese.

The Tibetan problem emerged in 1959, when the Dalai Lama and 13,000 of his followers fled Tibet fearing persecution by the Chinese and arrived in upper Assam, with Prime Minister Jawaharlal Nehru responding positively to the Dalai Lama's request for asylum. Tibetans in India initially numbered about 80,000, with up to 150,000 currently living in the country (HRLN 2007). These refugees were accommodated in 37 settlements and 70 scattered communities which broadly reflected three sectors: agriculture, agro-based, and carpet weaving and handicrafts. Whilst provided with free rations, clothing, cooking utensils, and medical facilities, they faced initial problems. Those settled in either Missamari camp in Assam or Buxa camp in West Bengal could not survive the hot, humid, and moist climate, and many monks contracted tuberculosis. The Dalai Lama requested that the government of India (GOI) move them to a more clement climate, and the refugees were subsequently sent to cooler areas such as Kashmir, Kalimpong, and Darjeeling. The government tried to make the refugees economically independent, and many of them were given jobs in road construction. Registration cards were also given to the children of the refugees who were born in India. However, as Tibetans continued to arrive, the GOI did not stop them from entering India but neither was the government so forthcoming with registration cards and other benefits; nonetheless, the Tibetans have lived in comparative peace in India.

Ten years after Tibetans refugees fled to India, East Pakistani refugees started entering the east and north-east of India fleeing Pakistani persecution. Ayub Khan stepped down from his position of power and handed over the reins of Pakistani government to Yahya Khan who promised to hold on to power until he could hand over the government to an elected representative. Rather, in his effort to hold on to power he persecuted the East Pakistanis whose leader Mujibur Rahman had won the elections. The violence began in March 1971 and after two days it was feared that 100,000 people had been killed. The Parliament of India adopted a resolution expressing their solidarity with the 'freedom fighters of Bangladesh',[2] and as a result of atrocities committed by the Pakistani army refugees started fleeing to India en masse. By late 1971 there were refugees in West Bengal, Tripura, Assam, and Meghalaya. Initially the refugees were given residence permits for three months and some relief assistance, the cost of which were borne by the GOI. It is estimated that over the course of a few months about 10 million people came to India as refugees from East Pakistan (Saha 2003: 213).

On 17 December 1971 Bangladesh became an independent nation and by then most refugees were becoming impatient to return to their villages. When they arrived many of these refugees were suffering from acute health problems as a result of which 800 refugees reportedly died in local hospitals. It is said that while the refugees remained in India they were treated fairly, and when they desired repatriation the Indian government rendered considerable assistance, with the GOI working in collaboration with international aid agencies in the rehabilitation of refugees; UNHCR worked as the focal point of these agencies. The estimated cost for providing aid for ten months was US$1,100 million, with foreign assistance amounting to US$234 million: c.21 per cent. It was fortunate, as one practitioner comments, that the 'country's political policies and humanitarian policies had converged' (Saha 2003: 242).

The Tamils were the next group of refugees to come to India. When Sri Lanka became independent in 1948 it soon passed an Act that denied citizenship to one of the two distinct groups of Tamils in the country: the Indian Tamils. This was the beginning of the attacks on the Tamil community as a whole. Shortly after the Sri Lankan Freedom Party (hereafter SLFP) came to power in 1956, there were talks of a new legislation that would make Sinhala the only official language. The Sinhala Only Act and other repressive Acts enraged the Tamils, and by 1975 the Tamils prepared to combat this repression. Tamil nationalism took the form of armed struggle and in 1976 the Liberation Tigers of Tamil Eelam (LTTE) was created.

In July 1983, the LTTE launched a deadly ambush on a Sri Lanka Army patrol team killing an officer and 12 soldiers. Ethnic tensions between the Tamils and Sinhalese heightened and Sri Lanka experienced major anti-Tamil riots in July 1983 (where thousands of Tamils were killed) as a result of which more than 150,000 Tamil civilians fled the island, seeking asylum in other countries. This is considered the beginning of the civil war in Sri Lanka. The first refugees, numbering about 30,000, fled to India immediately after the anti-Tamil riots of July 1983. By May 1985 the number of Sri Lankan refugees grew to 100,000 and two years later to 134,053. In 1989 25,585 refugees were repatriated to Sri Lanka, and yet after 1989 Sri Lankans started fleeing to India once more. By 1990, the number of refugees had grown to 125,000, and by 1997, to 164,000. While almost half of them lived in refugee camps, the remaining half lived outside of these, often with relatives. Between 20 January 1992, after the assassination of Rajiv Gandhi, and March 1995, 54,188 refugees voluntarily repatriated to Sri Lanka (*The Hindu* 2002). In 2009 Mahinda

Rajapakse's army defeated and annihilated the top leadership of LTTE, and from that time onwards the number of Sri Lankan refugees decreased. According to UNHCR, by July 2011 some 1,200 refugees had repatriated from India to Sri Lanka (UNCHR 2012). Those who opted to stay in camps were given free shelter, subsidized food, free medical care, and free medication (Manivannan 2001: 54–6), and were allowed to take up jobs outside the camps. Initially, those Sri Lankan refugees whose children were born in India were entitled to acquire Indian citizenship; however, after 1 July 1987 only those children with one parent who was Indian could obtain Indian citizenship.

While massive displacement was underway in Sri Lanka thousands of people belonging to ethnic minorities in Myanmar were about to be displaced as a result of the oppressive military rule (on Myanmar's displaced, see McConnachie, this volume). Since 1991, the UN General Assembly has adopted annual resolutions concerning the violation of human rights across Burma, and in June 1999, the International Labour Organization announced that the Burmese authorities had not desisted from carrying out or from condoning practices such as forced labour, arbitrary detention, torture, and rape. There are recent indications that the international community is relaxing its pressure on the Burmese regime due to its apparent move towards political transition and discussions with various ethnic groups; and yet it must be remembered that the widespread repression has led to many ethnic minorities being forcefully displaced within Burma. According to one observer, 'because of the diversity among Burma's 135 officially recognized ethnic groups generalizing about them is risky. However, there clearly exists a country-wide pattern to the abuses suffered by Karen, Karenni, Mon, Shan, Kachin, Chin, Arakanese, Rohingya, and other ethnic women.' Due to continuing lack of access and information, the enormity of the situation is difficult to verify. Although UNHCR has granted 2,000 Burmese official refugee status, unofficial estimates suggest that there are approximately 40,000 displaced Burmese in India. Most Burmese enter India from the north-east and very few asylum seekers who travel to Delhi are recognized as refugees by the UNHCR. The UNHCR in Delhi assists some Burmese refugees, the majority of whom originate from Chin state. The organization provides the more vulnerable individuals with a small monthly stipend, which is often insufficient to cover basic necessities (HRLN 2007).

Other displaced populations in India include some 9,000 Afghan refugees, about 200 Somali refugee families, over a million forced migrants from Bangladesh, and an indeterminate number of Lhotshampas (see next section). Among the most recent refugee groups are the 160 Palestinians who arrived in India after the fall of Saddam Hussein.

OTHER SOUTH ASIAN REFUGEE SITUATIONS

Bhutanese refugees are another significant population of forced migrants in South Asia, living both in Nepal and India. Like all South Asian states, Bhutan is multi-ethnic in nature, including a major population of Lhotshampas of Nepali origin who began settling in Bhutan in the nineteenth century. In the 1980s the Lhotshampas began to be perceived as a security threat by the Bhutanese government. When a string of measures were passed that discriminated against their group, the Lhotshampas organized a series of public demonstrations for which they were branded as anti-nationals. Several thousand Southern Bhutanese were imprisoned, and more than 2,000 tortured, according to *Amnesty International*. Very few of them were formally charged. Thousands fled to India and Nepal. Since the ethnic conflict between the ruling Drukpas of Bhutan and the ethnic Bhutanese of Nepali origin started in 1990, around 15,000 Bhutanese refugees of ethnic Nepali origin took shelter in Shiliguri and Jalpaiguri districts of West Bengal and Kokhrajhar district of Assam. The government of India does not recognize them as refugees and hence, provides no assistance. However, under the 1949 Indo-Bhutan Friendship Treaty, they are allowed to stay in India and can engage in employment activities. Nepal and Bhutan continue with bilateral discussions as an attempt to find an amicable solution to the problems.

In 1958, when the first Citizenship Act was passed in Bhutan, the Lhotshampas were granted full citizenship. However, in the 1980s the situation changed drastically and the Citizenship Act of 1985 clearly stated that those who could not give evidence that they had been living in Bhutan in 1958 were to be deprived of their citizenship. It became unlawful to venture outdoors unless one wore the ethnic costume worn by the northern Bhutanese, and the Nepali language was removed from schools. The southern Bhutanese who protested were expelled, and slowly many people were deprived of their citizenship for a variety of reasons, becoming stateless as a result. The number of southern Bhutanese in UNHCR camps in Nepal grew to 100,000 with those outside camps growing to about 35,000. Given the protracted nature of this situation, UNHCR has successfully brokered an agreement for third-country resettlement: currently over half of the Bhutanese refugees from UNHCR-run camps have been resettled in third countries such as the United States of America, with growing hope that most of the camp refugees will be resettled in the coming years.

Pakistan is also a major hosting country for protracted refugees, with UNHCR estimating a population of 1.7 million refugees in the early 2010s, the majority of whom are Afghans who started entering Pakistan during the Soviet occupation of Afghanistan and whose situation is addressed in more detail in Monsutti and Balci (this volume). Since March 2002, UNHCR has facilitated the return of approximately 3.7 million registered Afghans from Pakistan, and in the first eight months of 2011 nearly 34,000 Afghans returned to their country of origin (UNHCR 2012a). In addition to the approximately 1.7 million refugees in the country, there are currently approximately 420,500 people who have been internally displaced due to conflict in Khyber Pakhtunkhwa (KPK) and the Federally Administered Tribal Areas (FATA). UNHCR, in collaboration with other humanitarian partners, is supporting Pakistan's efforts to address the protection and other basic needs of this group and their return to their own communities.

Bangladesh hosts another significant protracted refugee population in the region: the Rohingya, who are a stateless ethnic and religious minority group originally displaced from Rakhine State in Myanmar. UNHCR estimates that approximately 200,000 undocumented individuals from Myanmar are in a refugee-like situation in Bangladesh, 30,000 registered Rohingya refugees currently live in two official camps (Nayapara and

Kutupalong in the district of Cox's Bazar), and an estimated 36,000 are based in unregistered camps such as the Leda Site and Kutupalong Makeshift Site (Kiragu, Rosi, and Morris 2011: 1). Bangladesh, like all other South Asian countries, has not signed either the refugee or statelessness conventions; although the Bangladesh Constitution grants some basic rights to refugees, and the Ministry of Food and Disaster Management is responsible for refugee-related issues and coordinating activities in relation to camp-based refugees (Vijayakumar 2001: 9), in practice, both registered and unregistered refugees do not enjoy access to basic rights such as freedom of movement or the right to work. In June 2012, the government of Bangladesh closed its border with Myanmar, preventing the entry of, and pushing back, Rohingya attempting to escape violence and persecution in Rakhine State; furthermore, the resettlement process was stopped at the government's request in November 2010, while conditions for Rohingya within the country continued to deteriorate. Rohingya refugees' main protection risks in official camps include sexual and gender-based violence (*inter alia*, domestic violence, rape, early or non-consensual marriage, child labour and trafficking), detention for illegal presence, extortion, and exploitation (Kiragu, Rosi, and Morris 2011: 13). Between May and December 2011, 76 cases of sexual and gender-based violence including two rape cases, three kidnappings, and three sexual assaults were reported.

As outlined above, since there are no legal mechanisms in place for the protection of South Asian refugees, refugee protection is usually tendered in an ad hoc manner; overall, most groups seeking refuge have at least initially been offered sanctuary within the region. However, refugees are neither the only nor the largest group of forced migrants in South Asia, with internally displaced populations being equally important in understanding the construction, determination, and delineation of the region's history, present, and future.

INTERNALLY DISPLACED PEOPLE IN SOUTH ASIA

Since the 1990s, South Asia has seen a dramatic escalation in the number of internally displaced people (IDPs), and yet to date not a single state in this region has formulated any legal mechanism in line with the Guiding Principles on Internal Displacement (Banerjee, Raychowdhury, and Das 2005). The reasons behind these displacements are numerous including conflict, controversial development projects, ecological problems, climate related hazards, and change in laws such as forest laws.

Development Induced IDPs

The largest numbers of displacements occur due to development projects such as the construction of dams building projects, mining, shrimping, urban beautification projects (such as the beautification of Dhaka during the South Asian Federation games which displaced thousands from the city's slums and brothels), and most recently the formation of Special Economic Zones.

The development paradigm favoured by much of the post-colonial world, including countries in South Asia, has inevitably resulted in massive displacements of the vulnerable sections of the population. This is because the cost of development is not borne equally by all sections of the society: the poor largely bear the cost while the rich benefit (also see McDowell, this volume). It is estimated that the construction of over 4,300 dams in India alone has resulted in the displacement of between 21 and 40 million people (Taneja and Thakkar 2000). Most of these are indigenous people, who have historically inhabited areas which are rich in coal and other minerals throughout South Asia. Very often, indigenous people affected by such programmes are considered as having been 'evicted' rather than 'displaced' once they are moved from their land, since, if they are denominated as IDPs they automatically accrue certain rights within the legal system (also see Kälin, this volume). The total number of those displaced due to development projects is calculated to be as many as 50 million.[3] The effects of displacement often lead to loss of traditional means of employment, loss of resources, disrupted community life, change of environment, marginalization, and profound psychological trauma. Yet even though development induced displacement disrupts lives in so many ways and increases morbidity and mortality, it continues in the name of national interest.

Any mapping of development induced displacement in India must begin with the oustees of the Sardar Sarovar Dam Project, which is the second largest project in the Narmada Valley in terms of both the total area submerged and the numbers of people displaced (Baviskar 1995). Proponents have promoted the project as the lifeline of Gujarat, stating that the project will make it possible to irrigate large tracts of the land, and to generate electricity and provide drinking water to thousands. According to Berger and Morse's independent review conducted for the World Bank, once completed the Sardar Sarovar Dam Project was to submerge approximately 37,000 hectares of land for the reservoir, and approximately 80,000 hectares for the extensive canal works. It was to displace at least 100,000 people who resided in approximately 245 villages. Approximately 140,000 additional farmers were to be affected by the canal and irrigation system (Berger and Morse 1992: xii–xiii). Much later, however, a project by Tata Institute for Social Sciences calculated that an unknown number of people, ranging somewhere in the neighbourhood of 300,000 would be affected by the project (TIISS 2008). One recent report stated that the project's irrigation system has never been completed, and the Narmada waters do not reach the intended beneficiaries. If the dam is completed, its reservoir will submerge 376 square kilometres of land and displace approximately 240,000 people. The canal network will displace even more people. The Indian Supreme Court ruled that the dam oustees need to receive cultivable replacement land and housing plots, and yet the TIISS report finds that this binding order has never been complied with, and that the replacement land for the oustees is not available (TIISS 2008).

The north-east of India, known as the powerhouse of India, has also been gravely affected by development-related displacement The region's development projects have directly affected the poor and powerless tribes both in the hills and plains, with an absence of adequate resettlement and rehabilitation policies for the displaced leading to further pauperization, marginalization, and helplessness among the oustees.

As in the case of the Sardar Sarovar dam project outlined above, Assam has faced mass displacements as a result of mega dams, including the Pagladiya Dam Project which is being constructed in Nalbari District of Lower Assam, the 2000 MW Lower Subansiri project to be constructed on the border areas of Assam and Arunachal, and the Dumbar Dam of the Gumti Hydel Project in South Tripura district. The Pagladiya dam will displace almost 105,000 mostly tribal people, while the Lower Subansiri project (which is opposed by civil society and the governments of both Assam and Arunachal) will adversely affect 100,000 tribal people of Arunachal Pradesh and physically displace approximately 15,000. To date, the Gumti Hydel project has displaced a total of 5,845 tribal families (between 35,000 to 40,000 individuals), who primarily belong to the Reang community. As the affected Reang communities are mostly Jumma tribal peoples, they have no land records even of their homestead land and it is therefore virtually impossible for them to obtain compensation without legal documentation. The rich biodiversity found in these regions will be gravely affected: the Gumti Hydel project will submerge 3,436 hectares of land, including 42 hectares of land in the Tulley Valley reserve forest which is home to innumerable rare animal species.

In addition to mega dams, other development projects related to oil, paper mills, urbanization and mining are displacing hundreds of thousands across north-east India. New oil townships have been established across Upper and Lower Assam displacing the inhabitants of those areas, the Tuli paper mill of Nagaland has displaced hundreds of tribal families and affected the rich biodiversity and environment of the region, and the Jagiroad and Cachar mills in Assam have respectively displaced people belonging to the Tiwa tribes and badly affected the bamboo forest in area neighbouring the Barak Valley. More generally, urbanization processes are displacing tribal people across this region of India, with the urban expansion of Guwahati city displacing peoples mostly belonging to the Karbis and Bodos tribes, pushing them out of the city to the periphery.

Large-scale displacement is also occurring due to mining, although this is a slow and gradual process. Despite complex procedures to acquire land in order to obtain mining leases for exploration, prospecting, and extraction, in reality and as reflected in the New Mineral Policy of 1993, mining projects are sanctioned as a means of encouraging and catering to the interests of the mining industries rather than to protect the interests of the local communities and the other natural resources in the mining areas.

Impacts on Women

Like many development projects, mining has had an insidious effect on women. When mining projects are established, both rural and tribal women are completely alienated from their access to natural resources and rights. The testimonies of women from the coal mining areas of Orissa (Talcher) demonstrate that displacement and the loss of land were the most serious problems affecting their lives, as their livelihoods, economic and social status, health, and security all depended on land and forests (Bhanumathi et al. 2004). Whenever villages and their inhabitants have been displaced or affected, women have been pushed into menial, marginalized, and socially humiliating forms of labour, for instance as maids and servants, as construction labourers, or into prostitution.

The detrimental effect of development induced displacement on women is also extensively documented in studies conducted among displaced persons. For instance, although tribal sex ratios are usually high because the social status of tribal women is higher than the status of her caste counterparts, studies of populations displaced by the National Aluminium Company in Orissa revealed a surprisingly low sex ratio of 739 among teenaged tribal girls. As noted by Menon, as long as land and other resources continue to be communally controlled, tribal women have a say in their management and they are an economic asset unlike in the settled agriculture-based dowry-paying groups that consider tribal women an economic liability (Menon 1995: 101). Equally, findings regarding the health status of girls following their alienation from their land and the other resources that sustained them, indicate that there is greater incidence of diseases among children, particularly girls, than among adults: in Arunachal Pradesh, for example, the incidence of most diseases was 50 per cent higher among girls. Burra's study confirms broader findings that 60 per cent of all child labourers are girls (Burra 1995), and among the project-displaced families of West Bengal, boys constituted a third, and girls two-thirds of the children who were prematurely withdrawn from school to work for an income (Fernandes et al. 2006).

Resistance

Protests against development induced displacement are becoming increasingly visible and frequent across India. A notable example is that of the Tatas' protest against the acquisition of 403 hectares of land for the Nano factory in Singur, for the production of the cheapest car in Asia. This was further compounded by the protest against a Special Economic Zone and a chemical hub in Nandigram. These protests led to 14 deaths in West Bengal in 2008. This is not unique as such deaths had become commonplace in other parts of the country such as Orissa. Nonetheless, West Bengal was exceptional as it was administered by a pro-labour left-wing state government and the anti-state people's movement resulted in the 33-year-old left-front state government being toppled in West Bengal in 2011.

Conflict Induced IDPs

Other than development-related displacement, conflict is a major cause of internal displacement. On the India–Pakistan border, for instance, it is estimated that 265,000 people are still displaced. In 2008, the violence between Bodos and Muslims in Assam caused the displacement of 128,000 individuals. The number increased manifold in the ongoing conflict in 2012: according to one estimate 'there were altogether 4,85,921 [sic] refugees in 340 relief camps during the height of the violence which began on July

19 [2012] claiming 96 lives' (*The Hindu* 2012). These reportedly currently include over 31,000 displaced Brus (Reangs) in Mizoram and Tripura. On the Pakistani side of the border there are reports that more than 45,000 people had been displaced as of June 2012. Many of these are unable to return to their homes even temporarily because their villages have been mined in anticipation of an Indian ground attack.

Since 1996, Nepal has experienced an internal armed conflict between the Communist Party of Nepal and the government of Nepal. The Informal Sector Service Centre (INSEC) reports that 10,985 people had lost their lives by 2005 (INSEC 2005), and at its height there were approximately 500,000 displaced people in Nepal (NRC 2004). Despite the end of the conflict and the closure of the only official IDP camp, thousands of IDPs are still unable to return because their land has been taken.

In the context of internal displacement in Sri Lanka, there were already 300,000 'old' IDPs when a further 200,000 people were displaced in the final stages of the conflict between the state and the LTTE. From 2009, the Sri Lankan state has attempted to return IDPs to their areas of origin with the help of UNHCR, which has provided transportation and cash grants as a key feature of its operational support to the 2009–10 return process (Eintwisle 2010). Thousands of individuals in Sri Lanka remain in a state of displacement in 2013.

Disaster Induced IDPs

In addition to internal displacement arising from development induced displacement and conflict, South Asia periodically experiences cyclones, earthquakes, and floods that displace thousands and at times millions of people (as was the case following the 2004 Indian Ocean Tsunami). Every year severe floods in the Bengal-Bangladesh border displace an indeterminate number of people. As in other contexts around the world, those displaced internally by disasters in South Asia cannot be neatly categorized: it is often the case that those who have been displaced once can face multiple displacements, sometimes due to conflict, then for ecological disasters, and later after settling in a place that is marked for a developmental project. It is therefore sometimes impossible to establish whether displacement has arisen as a result of conflict, development, or ecological conditions. What remains clear is the increasing vulnerability of numerous populations, which leads to protracted situations of displacement (also see Zetter and Morrissey, this volume).

STATELESSNESS IN SOUTH ASIA

Stateless peoples in South Asia (individuals and groups holding no effective nationality or the protection that nationality should offer), include the Chakmas in Arunachal Pradesh; the Chhitmahals in the Indian enclaves in Bangladesh; the above-mentioned Llotshampa Bhutanese of Nepali origin presently living in the eastern and north-eastern parts of India; displaced Hindus from Pakistan living in the Jammu valley and in the districts of Bikaner, Barmer, Jaisalmer and Ganganagar of Rajasthan; the Tamils of Indian origin who migrated from Sri Lanka and took shelter in different settlements in the southern part of India; Bihari Muslims from Bangladesh living mainly in West Bengal and Rajasthan; Nepali Madheshis in the north-eastern states of Insia; and the Chinese of Kolkata.

The situation of the Chakma and Hajong peoples exemplifies the challenges and discrimination experienced by stateless groups across the region. According to the government of India estimates, by the middle of 1964, at least 140,000 persons (over 2,900 families) including Chakmas and Hajongs had migrated to Assam. The then-government of Assam expressed their inability to settle such a large number of migrants in the state and consequently requested that they be relocated elsewhere. A suggestion was also made that a substantial number of families could be accommodated in the then-North East Frontier Agency (NEFA) as 'some surplus land was available there' and 'NEFA agreed to accommodate some new migrants including the Chakmas and Hajongs under the already approved scheme' (CCRCAP, Committee for Citizenship Rights of the Chakmas of Arunachal Pradesh, n.d.: 2). During 1964–8, 2,902 Chakma/Hajong families were settled in the NEFA in three districts of Lohit, Tirap, and Subansiri.

The Chakma issue evolved through three interrelated stages: although the issue has its origins in the larger decolonization process in South Asia, it was born with the commissioning of the Kaptai hydroelectric project in what was then East Pakistan, and the consequent displacement of the Chakmas and other indigenous communities in the Chittagong Hill Tracts in 1964. When NEFA became the separate state of Arunachal Pradesh in 1986, the indigenous tribes challenged their social and political exclusion: a landmark court judgment in 1996 gave the verdict in favour of the right to life and protection of the Chakma, falling short of conferring citizenship on them. Notwithstanding the landmark verdict, Chakmas continue to face discrimination and both de jure and de facto statelessness.

FUTURE CHALLENGES

The contemporary situation of refugees, IDPs, and the stateless in South Asia is highly problematic as there are few if any national or regional mechanisms that can help them to redress their claims. The case of the Chakmas demonstrates that even if a state is willing and legal judgments are made in support of the rights of minority groups, local communities can undermine the ethical and just treatment of such marginalized populations. Equally, although the resettlement and rehabilitation policies of different countries lay the necessary foundations to help those displaced by development projects, such laws cannot be enforced. Furthermore, in those cases where state policies themselves result in displacement, obtaining redress clearly becomes even more problematic.

Although the partition of South Asia was meant to solve all divisive identity issues, the establishment of newly independent states failed to solve these problems. Rather, fissures created during the partition often became fault-lines on which battles were fought, and new minorities emerged who were even more vulnerable to ongoing and new forms of displacement. Indeed, forced migration as a phenomenon in South Asia largely affects vulnerable populations including religious and ethnic minorities, and oppressed castes and classes; women and children in these minority groups are often doubly and triply victimized by virtue of their religious, ethnic, caste, and class identities in addition to their gender and age (see Fiddian-Qasmiyeh, this volume).

In spite of these processes of victimization, policies for forced migrants are developed and implemented by powerful elites who have little concern for those displaced and dispossessed by conflict, development, or disasters. Any help, relief, and rehabilitation offered to forced migrants is seen, not as an inalienable human right, but as humanitarian aid which should be gratefully received. Thus the root causes of forced migration are rarely addressed by the states in question, and those policies which are developed are typically merely cosmetic changes which often reinforce rather than challenge the status quo. Since forced migrants are often disempowered by a multiplicity of structures, including xenophobia, caste hierarchies, and patriarchy, those state and non-state actors who victimize forced migrants or allow their persecution continue to go unchallenged. Nonetheless, South Asia is also home to many successful civil society movements advocating for the rights and justice of vulnerable sections of the population. The ongoing challenge for South Asian human rights communities is therefore to rise above the divisions created by the partition and centralize the protection of forced migrants within their advocacy agendas.

NOTES

1. This chapter can usefully be read alongside McConnachie's overview of forced migration in South-East and East Asia (this volume).
2. Government of People's Republic of Bangladesh (1984: 663).
3. Shibaji Pratim Basu, 'The "Other" in the "Self": IDPs in India (A Status Report)', a seminar paper. <http://www.southasianrights.org/wp-content/uploads/2012/03/IDP-Report-India.pdf>.

REFERENCES

Banerjee, P. (2005) 'Resisting Erasure'. In Banerjee, Raychowdhury, and Das (2005).

Banerjee, P., Raychowdhury, S. B., and Das, S. (eds.) (2005) *Internal Displacement in South Asia*. New Delhi: Sage.

Baviskar, A. (1995) *In the Belly of the River*. Oxford: New Delhi.

Berger, B., and Morse, T. (1992) *Sardar Sarovar: The Report of the Independent Review*. Ottawa: Resource Futures International.

Bhanumathi, K., Kalpa, N. N., Shankar, G. V. S. R., Vanka, S., and Gunavathi, B. (2004) Conferencia Internacional Mujeres y Mineria. Visakhapatnam, India. 1–9 October.

Bose, S. (2010) *Contested Lands: Israel-Palestine, Kashmir, Bosnia, Cyprus and Sri Lanka*. Cambridge, MA: Harvard University Press.

Burra, N. (1995) *Born to Work: Child Labour in India*. New York: Oxford University Press.

Eintwisle, H. (2010) 'The End of the Road? A Review of UNHCR's Role in Return and Reintegration of Internally Displaced Populations'. PDES/2010/09. July.

Fernandes, W. (2007) 'Development-Induced Displacement: The Class and Gender Perspective'. Paper presented at the International Conference on The Emerging Woman in the Indian Economy. Christ College, Bangalore. 26–7 November.

Fernandes, W., Chhetri, S., Joseph, S., and Lama, S. (2006) *Development-Induced Displacement and Deprivation in West Bengal 1947–2000: A Quantitative and Qualitative Database on its Extent and Impact*. Guwahati: North Eastern Social Research Centre (mimeo).

Government of People's Republic of Bangladesh (1984) *Bangladesh War of Independence Documents*, vol. xiv, Dhaka: Government of People's Republic of Bangladesh.

The Hindu (2002) 'Repatriating Refugees'. <http://hindu.com/2002/07/06/stories/2002070600381000.htm>. 6 July [accessed 13 March 2014].

The Hindu (2012) 'New Refugees Arrive in Kokrajhar Barpeta'. 4 September. <http://www.thehindu.com/news/national/other-states/new-refugees-arrive-in-kokrajhar-barpeta/article3855744.ece> [accessed 13 March 2014].

HRLN (2007) 'Report of Refugee Populations in India'. November. <http://www.hrln.org/admin/issue/subpdf/Refugee_populations_in_India.pdf> [accessed 15 January 2012].

INSEC (2005) <www.insec.org.np> [accessed 13 January 2005].

Kiragu, E., Li Rosi, A., and Morris, T. (2011) *States of Denial: A Review of UNHCR's Response to the Protracted Situation of Stateless Rohingya Refugees in Bangladesh*. Geneva: PDES UNHCR.

Manivannan, I. V. (2001) 'Rehabilitation of Refugees'. Pp. 54–6 in UNHCR, *Marking Fifty Years of Refugee Protection*. New Delhi: UNHCR.

Menon, G. (1995) 'The Impact of Migration on the Work and Tribal Women's Status'. Pp. 79–154 in L. Schenken-Sandbergen (ed.), *Women and Seasonal Labour Migration*. New Delhi: Sage.

Norwegian Refugee Council (NRC)/Global IDP Project (2004) *Profile of Internal Displacement: Nepal*. Geneva. September. <http://www.idpproject.org> [accessed 13 March 2014].

Saha, K. C. (2003) 'The Genocide of 1971 and the Refugee Influx in the East'. P. 213 in R. G. G. Deschaumes and R. Ivekovic (eds.), *Directed Countries, Separated Cities: The Modern Legacy of Partition*. New Delhi: Oxford University Press.

Samaddar, R. (2003) 'The Last Hurrah that Continues'. P. 21 in G. G. Deschaumes and R. Ivekovic (eds.), *Directed Countries, Separated Cities: The Modern Legacy of Partition*. New Delhi: Oxford University Press.

Taneja, B., and Thakkar, H. (2000) 'Large Dams and Displacement in India'. Submission no. SOC166 to the World Commission on Dams, Cape Town.

TIISS (2008) 'Performance and Development: Effectiveness of Sardar Sarovar Project'. <http://www.indiaenvironmentportal.org.in/content/performance-and-development-effectiveness-sardar-sarovar-project> (accessed 13 March 2014).

UNHCR (2012a) 'Pakistan—2012 UNHCR Country Operations Profile'. New Delhi: UNHCR.

UNHCR (2012b) '2012 Regional Operations Profile—South Asia'. New Delhi: UNHCR.

Vijayakumar, V. (2001) 'A Critical Analysis of Refugee Protection in South Asia'. *Refuge* 19(2) (January): 6–16.

CHAPTER 48

FORCED MIGRATION IN SOUTH-EAST ASIA AND EAST ASIA

KIRSTEN MCCONNACHIE

INTRODUCTION

THIS chapter considers forced migration in South-East Asia and East Asia, a vast region that includes Brunei Darussalam, Cambodia, China, Hong Kong, Indonesia, Japan, Lao People's Democratic Republic, Macau, Malaysia, Myanmar, the Republic of Korea, the Democratic People's Republic of Korea, the Philippines, Singapore, Thailand, Timor-Leste, and Vietnam.[1] The chapter opens with a broad overview of regional dimensions of forced migration. The second section provides more detail about selected individual country contexts. The third section examines two protracted refugee situations that have dominated this regional context: refugees from Indochina and refugees from Myanmar.

A REGIONAL OVERVIEW

'South-East and East Asia' is a region of tremendous economic, political, and social diversity. To the extent that a shared regional experience of forced migration can be identified, it is one of large mixed migration flows but very limited formal legal protection. Few nations in the region have ratified the 1951 Refugee Convention (with the exception of China, Cambodia, Japan, the Republic of Korea, Timor-Leste, and the Philippines) while none has acceded to the 1961 Convention on the Reduction of Statelessness and only one (the Philippines) has acceded to the 1954 Convention on the Status of Stateless Persons. There is much wider acceptance of general human rights instruments with all states in the region as signatories to the Convention on the Rights of the Child and the Convention on the Elimination of All Forms of Discrimination Against Women; including, perhaps surprisingly, such 'pariah states' as Myanmar and the Democratic People's Republic of Korea.[2]

Remaining outside the global refugee regime does not mean that states in the region have refused to grant asylum, Thailand, in particular, has absorbed large-scale refugee flows continually for the past four decades. It does mean, however, that approaches to asylum have not been mediated by formal legal obligations. As in much of the rest of the world, South-East and East Asian nations' primary concern has been with controlling irregular migration rather than with humanitarian objectives of asylum. Furthermore, with no binding document equivalent to the 1951 Refugee Convention or the Organization of African Unity's regional Convention, the 'Asian approach' to forced migration has been founded on respect for sovereignty and the pursuit of economic development rather than on international human rights or refugee law (Davies 2008; Hedman 2009).

In 2013, the total 'population of concern' to UNHCR in South-East Asia, East Asia, and the Pacific was slightly more than 2.75 million people. Of this population approximately 1.4 million are stateless persons, 750,000 are refugees, and 500,000 are IDPs assisted by UNHCR (UNHCR 2013: 116). Primary refugee-generating countries in the region include Myanmar and Vietnam and, to a much lesser extent, Indonesia, Cambodia, Laos, and the Philippines. Primary refugee-hosting nations include Thailand, Malaysia, and again to a much lesser extent, Indonesia. There are large IDP populations in Indonesia, Myanmar, and the Philippines.[3] Statelessness exists throughout the region and is the consequence of both indirect denial of citizenship (i.e. children born to refugee parents) and the direct exclusion of particular ethnic groups. The latter includes the Rohingya, who were denied nationality by the Burmese Citizenship Law of 1982 and have endured extreme persecution and discrimination in Myanmar and throughout the region (Human Rights Watch 2013).

Political conflict and repression have been at the root of the largest refugee outflows in recent decades, from Vietnam, Cambodia, Laos, North Korea, and Myanmar. Forced migration has also been catalysed by ethnic conflict, religious persecution, state-sponsored 'development' projects,[4] famine (in North Korea), and natural disaster (including Cyclone Nargis in Myanmar and the 2011 Tōhoku earthquake in Japan). Of course, it is not always possible to identify a single cause of displacement as multiple causes often exist simultaneously. Likewise, the line between 'forced' and 'voluntary' migration is often hard to determine (Turton 2003). This widely recognized problem is particularly acute in Asia, where uneven economic development across the region has generated massive labour migration. Migrant worker transit routes intersect with smuggling and trafficking pathways, creating extremely complex contexts of mixed migration which typify the 'asylum-migration nexus' (Castles and Van Hear 2005—for a critique of trafficking discourse and policy, see Anderson, this volume).

Regional agendas have primarily focused on irregular migration rather than asylum, with the recent adoption of the Bali Process on People Smuggling, Trafficking in Persons and Related Transnational Crime and a number of other initiatives establishing a common framework.[5] In contrast, there is no comprehensive regional strategy for refugee protection but rather 'weakly institutionalized regional cooperation and a patchwork of intra-regional protocols and bilateral agreements' (Hedman 2010: 34). One example of such regional cooperation is the Bangkok Principles on the Status and Treatment of Refugees (1966). Drafted under the auspices of the intergovernmental Asian African Legal Consultative Committee, the Bangkok Principles have been widely adopted and serve as a guideline framework for refugee protection. However, they are merely declaratory, non-binding, and unenforceable and as such 'have had little discernible effect on Asian state practice in relation to refugees' (Davies 2008: 3).[6]

The most significant regional initiative with implications for forced migration policy is the Association of South-East Asian Nations (ASEAN), established by the 1967 Bangkok Declaration between Malaysia, Indonesia, the Philippines, Singapore, and Thailand and later expanded to its current membership of ten nations (with Brunei Darussalam, Cambodia, Lao PDR, Myanmar, and Vietnam). ASEAN was established to 'reassert individual sovereignty, mutual protection from foreign influence and ensure that each member was equally protected from another member's influence' (Cook 2010: 440). A core policy principle was that of non-interference in the affairs of other states. The ideal of the 'ASEAN way' is that solidarity between ASEAN nations in public keeps a door open for private dialogue and negotiation (Acharya 2008). This approach has had important successes in individual cases (as, for example, in the ASEAN intervention to secure international aid access to Myanmar in the aftermath of Cyclone Nargis (Marr 2010; Cook 2010)) but it has fundamentally restricted ASEAN's capacity to shape a regional agenda on forced migration—at least, one that is not solely based on security objectives. While the creation of an ASEAN Intergovernmental Commission on Human Rights (AICHR) in 2009 hinted that ASEAN may take a more active role in developing a harmonized regional approach that reflects human rights goals, as a consensus-based institution the AICHR is likely to be restricted by the same political relationships that inhibit ASEAN overall.

The limited institutional framework for refugee protection lends particular importance to the role of civil society. At the regional level, the Asia Pacific Refugee Rights Network was established in 2008 to conduct advocacy, information sharing, and capacity building on refugee rights. By 2013, it had 160 organizational members. Key agendas include lobbying states to adopt the 1951 Refugee Convention and 1967 Protocol, and to enact domestic legislation to protect refugees' rights. The APRRN has also engaged with ASEAN to raise the profile of refugee and statelessness issues within the organization and its member nations. These agendas have been pursued at the national level by APRRN members such as the Thai Committee for Refugees and the Japan Association for Refugees. In addition, local community-based organizations are often crucial in providing basic resources and assistance to forced migrants, including education, healthcare, and legal aid. Such organizations and informal networks play a central role in protection activities in areas where international agencies have had no or limited access (including much of Myanmar (South 2012)) as well as in the management of refugee camps in Thailand (McConnachie 2014), and in the urban environments of Bangkok and Kuala Lumpur (Smith 2012: 15; Palmgren 2013).

RECEIVING REFUGEES: SELECTED NATIONAL CONTEXTS

The lack of formal refugee protection continues at the domestic level as most countries do not have codified national legislation or procedures for asylum claims (with one recent exception including the Republic of Korea, where a national Refugee Act came into force in 2013). During the Indochinese refugee crisis, camps were established throughout the region, including in Thailand, Hong Kong, Malaysia, Indonesia, and the Philippines. Today, in contrast to responses to refugee flows in much of Africa, relatively few refugees in South-East Asia are confined to camps (with the notable exception of approximately 130,000 refugees from Myanmar in Thailand).

While this is broadly positive, the absence of mechanisms for verifying asylum means that refugees are not distinguished from economic migrants and instead all are lumped together as undocumented 'illegal' migrants, vulnerable to arrest, detention, and deportation. This creates acute protection challenges. Immigration detention is widely used throughout the region but detention conditions in many countries in the region fall far short of international standards; as, for example, in Malaysia, where punishments for immigration offences include whipping and caning (APRRN 2013: 9).

At one end of the spectrum, Japan cooperates with the international refugee regime as both a donor country and as a resettlement country but it also has a domestic political climate that broadly opposes immigration and a legal system that imposes harsh penalties for illegal migration. The launch of Japan's resettlement programme was heralded as 'historic' (UNHCR 2008) but only 55 refugees were resettled in its first three years of operation (APRRN 2013).

Other countries receive much larger populations of forced migrants but 'border control' is all but indistinguishable from 'refoulement'. China is one of the few regional state parties to the 1951 Convention and during the Indochinese refugee crisis accepted more than 300,000 Vietnamese refugees (mostly ethnic Chinese) for resettlement. In recent refugee situations, however, its response has been rather less generous. Tens of thousands of North Koreans have crossed illegally to China to escape famine and political and religious discrimination. Most, if not all of those leaving would likely meet the criteria for refugee status under the 1951 Convention (Cohen 2012). Nonetheless, if found in China they are considered irregular economic or 'food' migrants and returned to North Korea where they face interrogation and detention in prison, forced labour camps, or re-education camps (Human Rights Watch 2013; Haggard and Noland 2011). In 2012, mass repatriations were conducted to return thousands of ethnic Kachin who fled to China after the collapse of a ceasefire between the Kachin Independence Army and the Myanmar government. Both North Korean and Kachin women have become primary targets for trafficking in China (Haggard and Noland 2011; KWAT 2013).

There are many more examples of rejections, push-backs, and *refoulement* across South-East and East Asia. Khmer Krom asylum seekers who fled persecution in Vietnam have been forcibly returned from both Cambodia and Thailand. In 2009, more than 4,000 Hmong who fled from Laos to Thailand were detained in camps and detention centres, before being forcibly repatriated as illegal migrants (Mydans 2009). Rohingya boat arrivals to Thailand have been pushed back or, under the euphemistically named 'help on' policy, provided with some food, water, and other resources before being moved on to Malaysia or Indonesia.

Thailand and Malaysia receive the largest number of asylum seekers, though neither country has enacted domestic legislation for the recognition and protection of refugees. Instead, huge populations of undocumented migrants are 'managed' through a combination of border control, regularization campaigns, and criminal sanctions (Hall 2012: 6).[7] These efforts to control irregular migration sit uneasily with an economic dependence on unskilled migrant labour. As Grundy-Warr (2004: 252) writes, 'The fact is that the Kingdom of Thailand, like so many other political economies, continues to officially restrict but unofficially (or less officially) encourage, or at least tolerate, very large numbers of undocumented migrants on her soil.' Undocumented migrants—a population including potentially hundreds of thousands of people who would qualify for refugee status— thus exist in a precarious space of tolerated illegality. They also represent a dual source of revenue to their host states: as a source of cheap labour and as an income stream through migrant worker registration and regularization programmes (Grundy-Warr 2004: 252).

The protection environment for refugees and migrants is often bleak but there is some (albeit limited) cause for optimism. In Malaysia, 'illegal' migrants live under an ever-present fear of arrest and detention, in a context where police corruption is widespread (Smith 2012: 59–60). Nevertheless, there have been some improvements in the treatment of refugees and asylum seekers in recent years. Refugees recognized by UNHCR and in possession of a 'UNHCR card' are less likely to be detained and since 2009, UNHCR has been able to negotiate the release of more than 9,000 people from immigration detention (Crisp, Obi, and Umlas 2012: 13–14). However, thousands more remain in detention, in a network of more than 40 camps and centres throughout the nation (Chin Refugee Committee 2012: 25).

In 2012, the Indonesian Ministry of Foreign Affairs consulted with civil society in drafting 'Standard Operating Procedures' which recognized the right to temporary asylum and right to *non-refoulement* and established refugees' entitlements to local integration, freedom of movement, right to education, right to work, and freedom of religion. More than a year later they had still not been formally adopted by the Indonesian Government (APRRN 2013: 15).

REGIONAL REFUGEE CRISES

The brief introduction above gives some sense of the complexity of forced migration at the country level. In terms of refugee situations with regional impact, the recent history of forced migration in South-East and East Asia has been dominated by two situations: refugees from Indochina (1975–95) and refugees from Myanmar (late 1970s–present). These situations have obvious differences but also some important similarities, including rejection of the international refugee regime, regional cohesion around shared political objectives, and the potential for international cooperation in the search for durable solutions.

The Indochina Refugee Crisis

The Indochinese refugee crisis has been described as one of the 'great population shifts in history' (Robinson 1998: 50). Between 1975 and 1995, more than 3 million people from Vietnam, Laos, and Cambodia sought asylum in surrounding countries. From the outset, the response of South-East Asian nations was that this massive exodus was not their responsibility and that granting asylum would only lead to a larger influx. Instead, they consented to provide temporary asylum only if resettlement places were secured in other nations; a position sealed when Malaysia and Thailand began pushing back boatloads of arrivals (Loescher 1993: 87).

Initially, the majority of resettlement places were provided by the United States, a situation that echoed regional and international perceptions of responsibility for the refugee flows and which, while hardly the preference of the US government, also afforded significant political capital as a symbol of both the undesirability of communist regimes and American generosity and tolerance. However, as the number of asylum seekers outpaced the number of available resettlement places, South-East Asian nations became 'increasingly determined, in the face of regional instability, to maintain their domestic stability by stemming the flow of asylum seekers and guarantee international assistance' (Davies 2006: 14). ASEAN foreign ministers issued a joint statement that their countries had 'reached the limit of their endurance and would not accept any new arrivals' unless international resettlement places were guaranteed (Robinson 1998: 50). Tens of thousands of people who had travelled long distances in flimsy, overcrowded boats were turned back or towed away from the Philippines, Indonesia, Singapore, and Thailand. Most international attention was focused on the Vietnamese boat people, but even larger numbers of people were trying to cross overland from Cambodia to Thailand. These people too were pushed back—into minefields and Khmer Rouge controlled areas—in a process of mass *refoulement* as a result of which unknown numbers died (Robinson 1998).

By July 1979, the situation had become desperate and the United Nations convened an international conference in Geneva with the goals of preserving temporary first asylum, securing resettlement places, and reducing clandestine departures from Vietnam. The conference was a success, as participating nations pledged 260,000 resettlement places and US$160 million in donations, and the government of Vietnam agreed to establish an Orderly Departures Programme to permit legitimate departures (for family reunion and humanitarian cases) and prevent clandestine departures. The situation was temporarily resolved, though the dynamics of its resolution had troubling implications: violating international law had provided South-East Asian nations with the outcome that they desired, where granting asylum had threatened to burden them with the sole responsibility for the refugee crisis. The lesson for all concerned was that 'hard hearts could drive hard bargains' (Robinson 1998: 31).

For much of the next decade, resettlement places exceeded arrivals and the agreement held. As population outflows continued into the 1980s, however, both Asian and Western nations began to view the automatic grant of resettlement places as a 'pull factor' for economic migrants as well as genuine refugees. A second international conference was convened, leading to the adoption of the Comprehensive Plan of Action (CPA) for Indochina (1989), which maintained the same objectives as the previous agreement (to preserve temporary asylum, reduce clandestine departures, and provide resettlement places) but added two new elements in a requirement of status determination and the incorporation of repatriation as well as resettlement. The process would be that those already based in camps would be resettled but all new arrivals thereafter would be screened to separate genuine refugees from economic migrants. The former would be resettled while the latter would be repatriated.

Between 1975 and 1995, the CPA and its predecessor agreement processed the asylum claims of 1,436,556 people and resettled 1,311,183 (UNHCR 2000: 98). More than 3 million people left Indochina during these years, and in preserving the grant of first asylum agreement this process provided some measure of protection and security for many of them. As such it must surely be considered a successful international response to a desperate humanitarian emergency. As a collaborative multinational response to a regional refugee situation it also established a powerful paradigm for north–south burden sharing (UNHCR 2006: 147; Betts 2006). Yet its impact on regional and international refugee policy was arguably less positive. Regionally, the success of the 'asylum for resettlement' bargaining strategy arguably consolidated South-East Asia as a region outside the global refugee regime and entrenched the belief among those nations that the global refugee regime was not in their regional interests (Davies 2006), while the scale of arrivals engendered suspicion of resettlement that would continue for decades to come (Robinson 1998: 324).

UNHCR played a central role in securing international cooperation and the CPA process was a crucial period in the agency's history (Loescher 2001: 203–14). Yet here too, the lasting consequences of the operation are complex: did UNHCR's pragmatic approach preserve asylum and uphold the principle of *non-refoulement* for Indochinese refugees, or was the agency tainted by complicity in forced repatriations and political bargaining with the right to seek asylum (Robinson 1998; Loescher 2001: 211)? Finally, while the CPA established the potential for burden sharing, its precedential value is questionable. Humanitarianism may have had something to do with Western nations' support for and participation in the CPA, but Cold War politics also played a significant role: just how significant is perhaps most apparent when the Indochinese experience is compared with a more recent refugee situation, that of refugees from Myanmar.

Myanmar's Displaced

Where the plight of Indochinese refugees is frequently described as a crisis, forced migration from Myanmar is more accurately described as chronic: persistent displacement over decades in a population exodus that has been somewhat less dramatic than that of Indochinese refugees but which in numerical terms is likely comparable. This context also differs from the Indochinese situation in that there is not one primary catalyst for forced migration but a conjunction of causes including political violence, statelessness, religious and ethnic discrimination, economic insecurity, and environmental disaster. The result has been a complex and continually evolving field of forced migration, populated with multiple generations of forced migrants with very different experiences in and of displacement (South 2007).

Myanmar was ruled by a series of military regimes from 1962 to 2011, when political leadership was nominally transferred to a civilian government (though one in which military and former military members continue to play a leading role). Over its half-century of military rule Myanmar became synonymous with political oppression and the brutal suppression of dissent. Thousands of pro-democracy activists were forced into exile, particularly in the aftermath of public protests in 1988 and in 2007. Many more people were displaced in and from ethnic border regions, consequent to armed conflict, discrimination and persecution, state-sponsored 'development' projects, and general livelihoods insecurity (South 2007).[8] In 2012, it was estimated that there were at least 400,000 IDPs in south-east Myanmar alone (TBBC 2012: 2). These are predominantly members of Kayin (Karen), Kayah (Karenni), and Mon ethnic groups in contexts of long-term displacement, in conditions which range from intense insecurity in short-term hiding-sites, to established camps and settlements, to strictly controlled government relocation sites. International access to these populations has been very limited but strong community protection structures have developed, often linked to ethnic insurgency organizations or to faith-based organizations (South 2012).

Recent political liberalization in Myanmar appears to have altered patterns of displacement but has not stopped it occurring. Displacement in eastern Myanmar was much reduced in 2012 (almost certainly related to a provisional ceasefire between the Karen National Union and the Myanmar government) (TBBC 2012). However, during the same period around 85,000 people were displaced in Kachin State and Shan States, and up to 140,000 Rohingya and Burmese Muslims were displaced by sectarian violence and ethnic cleansing (UN OCHA 2013; Human Rights Watch 2013). Stateless and persecuted in Myanmar, unwanted in Bangladesh, and often turned away from Thailand and Malaysia, the Rohingya are one of the most vulnerable refugee populations in the world today. However, while anti-Rohingya violence has a long heritage in Myanmar, recent attacks have also been directed at the Kaman (a Muslim minority group who, unlike the Rohingya, are formally recognized as Burmese citizens) and against Muslims more widely.

In addition to the large populations of internally displaced, more than 3 million people from Myanmar are estimated to have crossed international borders illegally in the past two decades (Hall 2012). Only a small fraction of these have been formally granted asylum. At the end of 2013, in Thailand, around 130,000 refugees from Myanmar were living in nine camps in the border region, but even among this population only 82,539 were registered with UNHCR.[9] In Malaysia, 94,670 people from Myanmar were registered with UNHCR, but tens of thousands more were unregistered.[10] In late 2013, UNHCR in Malaysia undertook a 'mobile registration' to conduct initial registration of asylum seekers from Myanmar. It was anticipated that up to 20,000 people would be registered through this programme. Millions more throughout the region subsist in shadow zones as illegal migrant workers, with all the vulnerabilities and risks that entails. In contrast to the coordinated response for refugees from Indochina, the plight of Myanmar's refugees has generated limited international concern. At the regional level, Myanmar was accepted into ASEAN in 1997, and other ASEAN members have maintained a policy of 'constructive engagement' based on the belief that continuing dialogue with the Myanmar regime offered the best avenue for regional influence. The principle of non-interference largely prevailed, although ASEAN foreign ministers have made public statements after particularly egregious actions by the Myanmar regime, expressing 'revulsion' after the suppression of the 'Saffron Revolution' in 2007 and intervening to ensure access for international relief agencies in the aftermath of Cyclone Nargis (Loescher and Milner 2008; Marr 2010). Given Myanmar's position as ASEAN Chair in 2014, the centrality of ASEAN to Myanmar's political rehabilitation is likely to grow over the coming years.

The absence of regional and international cooperation has been particularly damaging for prospects of durable solution. As in most recent protracted refugee situations in the post-Cold War era (see Milner, this volume), the primary challenge has been a lack of available durable solutions: repatriation was impossible while conflict and political repression continued in Myanmar, and both local integration and large-scale resettlement were rejected by host nations. Initially wary of repeating the mass influx that had occurred during the Indochinese crisis, the Royal Thai government eventually conceded to a resettlement programme for camp-based refugees, and between 2005 and 2013 more than 100,000 refugees were resettled to third countries. However, the total population in camps barely decreased as new arrivals came to replace those who had left. Refugees in camps in Thailand have repeatedly claimed that their preferred durable solution is to return safely to Myanmar (Banki and Lang 2008: 78) and for the first time in decades this is beginning to seem a credible possibility.

However, it is essential that the conditions in Myanmar permit safe return and that repatriation is truly voluntary. This is a particularly pertinent concern in the Myanmar context, where in 1994–5, UNHCR cooperated in the forced repatriation of 230,000 Rohingya from Bangladesh to Myanmar, returning these people to statelessness, insecurity, and continued persecution (Loescher and Milner 2008: 313). This process serves as a tragic reminder that caution must prevail in assessing security in Myanmar.

As noted above, there is a high level of community organization within many of Myanmar's displaced populations. To ensure voluntary repatriation, it is essential that these representatives are part of any and all discussions about return. The Karen Refugee Committee (2013) issued a statement identifying ten preconditions that must be met for repatriation to be feasible; these points include the existence of a nationwide ceasefire; sustainable peace; respect for human rights; the removal of landmines from relocation areas; the availability of land for those returning; monitoring and oversight of repatriation conditions; and agreement between all concerned organizations (including refugee community organizations) that there is a genuine peace in Myanmar. This statement highlights many important issues that are relevant for other displaced populations from Myanmar, and indicates the scale of the challenges that lie ahead.

The need for a 'comprehensive' approach to Myanmar's displaced has been widely recognized both in terms of the need for regional cooperation (Loescher and Milner 2008) and for the inclusion of all forced migrants (Banki and Lang 2008). Certainly, responding to displacement is an essential task before any genuine political transition can take place in Myanmar. However, it remains to be seen whether the expertise, resources, and political will exist to design and sustain an appropriately wide-ranging response. In particular, it remains to be seen whether there is a genuine political will from the Myanmar government and military, which, as yet, has singularly failed to acknowledge its responsibility in creating one of the world's largest and most complex displacement situations.

CONCLUSION

The experiences of refugees from Indochina and Myanmar highlight important dimensions of refugee protection in the region of South-East and East Asia, notably the difficulty of protecting refugees in the absence of binding legal obligations. Davies (2008) has argued that Asian 'rejection' of the 1951 Refugee Convention and 1967 Protocol is rooted in the perception of these documents as Eurocentric and unsuited to refugee contexts in Asia. Other commentators (Abrar 2000) have suggested that it is also due to Asian nations' unwillingness to bind themselves to the humanitarian obligations underwriting that system; a position bolstered by comments such as those made by the Malaysian Foreign Minister in 2012 that accession to the Refugee Convention would create obligations 'to treat these people better than our own people' (Naidu 2012).

The failure of many South-East and East Asian nations to distinguish 'real' refugees from 'voluntary' migrants has deeply problematic consequences for forced migrants, including vulnerability to arrest and detention, to labour exploitation and trafficking, and to *refoulement*. Contradictory responses to migrant labour—on the one hand, national economic dependence, on the other, a desire to control illegal movement—place millions of vulnerable people in a limbo-state of insecurity. However, while there is much to criticize in these national policy approaches, in their fundamental objectives and strategies they conform to the approach taken throughout Europe and America: securitization objectives, the criminalization of migration, and a culture of disbelief with regard to asylum seekers.

This raises the question of whether adoption of the 1951 Convention regime is really the 'solution' to refugee protection in South-East and East Asia. Asian nations may indeed be more likely to support the 1951 Convention regime if it is perceived as a truly global system that pursues parity of responsibility through genuine cooperation and burden sharing. However, enhancing the protection environment for forced migrants will also require a transformation in perceptions of forced migration, particularly in rejecting the notion that forced migrants are always and inevitably a threat to security. Taking into account the clear strengths of regional cohesion and a sense of shared interests, and bearing in mind the vast numbers of forced migrants within the region, the most effective avenue for strengthening protection may be to focus on mechanisms and strategies that work within that context and which operate to counterbalance (if not entirely to overcome) the security priorities that have prevailed thus far. Such strategies might include strengthening regional and domestic civil society in advocating for domestic legislation and supporting those organizations in enabling forced migrants to enforce their rights under such legislation.

Notes

1. UNHCR regional categories consider 'East Asia and the Pacific' as the geographical scope, which includes all of the states listed above and Australia, New Zealand, Papua New Guinea, and the Pacific Island Countries. The latter group of states are covered in McNevin's chapter in this volume.
2. For ratification of human rights treaties see: <http://treaties.un.org/pages/ParticipationStatus.aspx>. Regional non-recognition of the 1951 Convention is reflected in the UNHCR Executive Committee with only China, Japan, and the Philippines as current EXCOM members.
3. Timor-Leste experienced massive internal and cross-border displacement between 1999 and 2010. In 2010, it was announced that there were no more IDPs in the country, though the true sustainability of returns remains unclear (IDMC 2011: 93).
4. See McDowell (this volume) regarding development induced displacement in the context of China.
5. Including the Regional Roundtable on Irregular Movements by Sea in the Asia-Pacific region and ASEAN Declarations on Trafficking in Persons (2004) and the Protection and Promotion of Rights of Migrant Workers (2007).
6. The Bangkok Principles were revised in the late 1990s and formally readopted by the Asian-African Legal Consultative Organization on 24 June 2001.
7. Thailand's National Security Council distinguishes four target groups for a new strategy on irregular migration: stateless people (approximately 700,000 people); illegal migrant workers (approximately 2 million people of Myanmar, Laos, and Cambodian nationality); migrants who are 'threats to national security' (from Myanmar and North Korea)

and illegal immigrants who have overstayed their visa (IOM Migrant Information Note October 2012).

8. Myanmar has eight recognized 'ethnic nationalities' (Bamar, Shan, Mon, Kayah [Karenni], Kayin [Karen], Chin, Kachin, and Rakhine) and many more ethnic subgroups.

9. In an earlier 'era' of forced migration from Myanmar to Thailand, UNHCR was permitted to register Burmese 'students' who fled after the suppression of election results in 1990 (Loescher and Milner 2008: 306–7).

10. Of 103,010 refugees and asylum seekers in total. See *UNHCR Malaysia: Figures at a Glance*: <http://www.unhcr.org.my/About_Us-@-Figures_At_A_Glance.aspx>.

REFERENCES

Abrar, C. (2000) 'Legal Protection of Refugees in South Asia'. *Forced Migration Review* 10: 21–3.

Acharya, A. (2008) *ASEAN: Constructing a Security Community in Southeast Asia*. London: Routledge.

APRRN (2013) *Asia-Pacific Refugee Rights Network Annual Report 2012*. Bangkok: APPRN.

Banki, S., and Lang, H. (2008) 'Protracted Displacement on the Thai–Burmese Border: The Interrelated Search for Durable Solutions'. Pp. 59–81 in H. Adelman (ed.), *Protracted Displacement in Asia: No Place to Call Home*. Aldershot: Ashgate Publishing.

Betts, A. (2006) 'Comprehensive Plans of Action: Insights from CIREFCA and the Indochinese CPA'. New Issues in Refugee Research. UNHCR Working Paper No. 120.

Castles, S., and Van Hear, N. (2005) *Developing DFID's Policy Approach to Refugees and Internally Displaced Persons*. Oxford: Refugee Studies Centre.

Chin Refugee Committee Malaysia (2012). *Annual Report 2012*. <http://malaysiacrc.org/reports/2013-03-06-10-28-50>.

Cohen, R. (2012) 'China's Repatriation of North Korean Refugees'. Testimony submitted to the Congressional-Executive Committee on China. <http://www.brookings.edu/research/testimony/2012/03/05-china-repatriation-cohen>.

Cook, A. D. B. (2010) *Operationalising Regimes and Recognising Actors: Responding to Crises in Southeast Asia*. Asia Security Initiative Policy Series.

Crisp, J., Obi, N., and Umlas, L. (2012) *But When Will our Time Come? A Review of the Implementation of UNHCR's Urban Refugee Policy in Malaysia*. Geneva: UNHCR Policy Development and Evaluation Service.

Davies, S. (2006) 'Saving Refugees or Saving Borders? Southeast Asian States and the Indochinese Refugee Crisis'. *Global Change, Peace & Security* 18(1): 3–24.

Davies, S. (2008) *Legitimising Rejection: International Refugee Law in Southeast Asia*. Leiden: Martinus Nijhoff Publishers.

Grundy-Warr, C. (2004) 'The Silence and Violence of Forced Migration: The Myanmar–Thailand Border'. Pp. 228–72 in A. Ananta and E. N. Arifin (eds.), *International Migration in South East Asia*. Singapore: Institute of Southeast Asian Studies.

Haggard, S., and Noland, M. (2011) *Witness to Transformation: Refugee Insights into North Korea*. Washington, DC: Peterson Institute for International Economics.

Hall, A. (2012) *Myanmar and Migrant Workers: Briefing and Recommendations*. Mahidol Migration Centre.

Human Rights Watch (2012) 'Ad Hoc and Inadequate: Thailand's Treatment of Refugees and Asylum Seekers'. <http://www.hrw.org/sites/default/files/reports/thailand0912.pdf>.

Human Rights Watch (2013). 'All You Can Do is Pray'. <http://www.hrw.org/reports/2013/04/22/all-you-can-do-pray-0>.

IDMC (2011) 'Internal Displacement in South and South-East Asia'. At <http://www.internal-displacement.org>.

KWAT (2013) *Pushed to the Brink: Conflict and Human Trafficking on the Kachin–China Border*. New York: KWAT.

Loescher, G. (2001) *The UNHCR and World Politics*. Oxford: Oxford University Press.

Loescher, G., and Milner, J. (2008) 'Burmese Refugees in South and Southeast Asia: A Comparative Regional Analysis'. Pp. 303–32 in G. Loescher, J. Milner, E. Newman, and G. Troeller (eds.), *Protracted Refugee Situations: Political, Human Rights and Security Implications*. New York: United Nations University Press.

McConnachie, K. (2014) *Governing Refugees: Justice, Order and Legal Pluralism*. Abingdon and New York: Routledge.

Marr, S. (2010) 'Compassion in Action: The Story of the Asean-Led Coordination in Myanmar'. ASEAN. Jakarta.

Mydans, S. (2009) 'Thailand Begins Repatriation of Hmong to Laos'. *New York Times* 27 December.

Nah, A. (2010) 'Refugees and Space in Urban Areas in Malaysia'. *Forced Migration Review* 34: 29–31.

Naidu, S. (2012) 'Malaysia Finds "Conflict" in UN Refugee Convention'. Australia Network News. 13 November.

Palmgren, P. A. (2013) 'Irregular Networks: Bangkok Refugees in the City and Region'. *Journal of Refugee Studies*. doi: 10.1093/jrs/fet004

Robinson, W. C. (1998) *Terms of Refuge: The Indo-Chinese Exodus and the International Response*. London: Zed Books.

Robinson, W. C. (2000). 'Flight from Indochina'. In UNHCR, *State of the World's Refugees*. Geneva: UNHCR.

Smith, A. (2012). *In Search of Survival and Sanctuary in the City: Refugees from Myanmar/Burma in Kuala Lumpur, Malaysia*. London: International Rescue Committee.

South, A. (2007) 'Burma: The Changing Nature of Displacement Crises'. Refugee Studies Centre Working Paper.

South, A. (2012) 'The Politics of Protection in Burma: Beyond the Humanitarian Mainstream'. *Critical Asian Studies* 44(2): 175–204.

TBBC (2012) 'Changing Realities: Poverty and Displacement in South East Burma/Myanmar'. New York: TBBC.

Turton, D. (2003) 'Conceptualising Forced Migration'. Refugee Studies Centre Working Paper.

UNHCR (2000) *State of the World's Refugees*. Geneva: UNHCR.

UNHCR (2008) 'Japan to Start a Pilot Resettlement Programme'. Briefing Notes. 19 December. <http://www.unhcr.org/494b7e3011.html>.

UNHCR (2013) *Global Appeal 2013 Update*.<http://www.unhcr.org/ga13/index.xml>.

UN OCHA (2013) *Humanitarian Bulletin*. Myanmar, 18 April–31 May.

Vungsiriphisal, P., Bennett, G., Poomkacha, C., Jitpong, W., and Reungsamran, K. (2011) *Analysis of Royal Thai Government Policy Towards Displaced Persons from Myanmar*. Chulalongkorn: Asian Research Center for Migration, Institute of Asian Studies, Chulalongkorn University.

Zolberg, A. R., Suhrke. A., and Aguayo, S. (1989) *Escape from Violence: Conflict and the Refugee Crisis in the Developing World*. Oxford: Oxford University Press.

CHAPTER 49

FORCED MIGRATION IN AUSTRALIA, NEW ZEALAND, AND THE PACIFIC

ANNE MCNEVIN

INTRODUCTION

THIS chapter provides an overview of forced migration in relation to Australia, New Zealand, and the Pacific. Its focus is upon Australia and New Zealand as destinations for asylum seekers and refugees, and Pacific Island states as source countries for climate induced and other forms of forced migration. It begins with a historical introduction to forced migration within the region, as well as twentieth-century histories of refugee reception. It then outlines the legal architecture and policy frameworks that currently shape responses to forced migrants and humanitarian resettlement. The chapter then addresses the political context shaping these responses before concluding with a discussion of the challenges confronting a region that is likely to face significant forced migration flows in the decades to come.

HISTORICAL BACKGROUND

The histories of Australia, New Zealand, and the Pacific contain many examples of what we might today call forced migration, including the transportation from Britain of approximately 162,000 convicts between 1788 and 1868 who were forced to serve their sentences in the early Australian colonies. The British colonies of Australia and New Zealand and European colonies in the Pacific were, in addition, founded on the displacement and dispossession of indigenous people from their ancestral lands—a process that extended well into the twentieth century with the practice of removing Aboriginal and Maori people into institutional care, for example (Nethery 2009: 73–5).

The mid- to late nineteenth century also saw the transit of several thousand Melanesians from the Solomon Islands and present-day Vanuatu to work in the cotton and cane fields of Queensland in northern Australia. Labour migration of this kind was based on a mixture of coercion and economic necessity. The practice was associated with highly exploitative working conditions and was only legally regulated from 1872. In 1901, one of the new Australian Commonwealth parliament's first acts was to authorize the deportation of over 4,000 such Islanders, despite their protests and despite the fact that many had by then made their long-term homes in Australia (Nicholls 2009; Connell 2010). The same year saw the introduction of Australia's infamous dictation test (a test administered in any language chosen by officials for any aspiring migrant to Australia) as the cornerstone of a 'white Australia policy' that would shape the racist nature of the country's twentieth-century immigration regime, which in turn, profoundly impacted the selective basis upon which displaced persons were subsequently chosen for resettlement.

In the second half of the twentieth century, Australia and New Zealand came to be known as destination states for many forced migrants. However, until the 1930s the region remained isolated from most of the world's major refugee movements. By 1945, Australia and New Zealand had together accepted several thousand Jews fleeing Nazi persecution but not without a degree of reluctance on the part of parliamentarians concerned about the transfer of European 'racial' problems to the antipodes (Neumann 2004: 15–26; Beaglehole 2009: 108). Between 1947 and 1972, some 260,000 displaced persons and refugees were resettled in Australia, first from central European camps and later in the wake of uprisings in Communist-controlled Hungary and Czechoslovakia. The schemes were highly selective, based on criteria for age, occupation, and financial resources in line with Australia's post-war drive to 'populate or perish' and to bolster shortfalls in its workforce. Those considered economically unproductive or socially undesirable—the elderly, disabled, chronically ill, or single mothers—were vetted from the schemes. There was also administrative discretion to restrict on the basis of race, resulting in the early post-war years in a preference for fairer East Europeans rather than southerners. Non-European refugees were generally not accepted for resettlement (Neumann 2004).

One of the lesser known episodes in Australia's engagement with forced migration concerns several thousand West Papuans in the 1960s and 1970s who claimed to be resistance fighters and crossed into Papua New Guinea (PNG) which operated under Australian administration until 1973. During the transfer of West Papua from Dutch to Indonesian control, Australian authorities in PNG tended to grant asylum only to those West Papuans who were sponsored by the Dutch and feared being targeted as collaborators. Many others who attempted to cross into PNG were refused at the border in an ad hoc process from which the UNHCR was excluded. The Australian government preferred to handle the border crossings with discretion in order to preserve diplomatic relations with Indonesia (Neumann 2004; Palmer 2006). Tensions between Australia and Indonesia on the matter of West Papuan asylum seekers resurfaced in the twenty-first century, when asylum seekers fled directly to Australian territory.

The decision by immigration officials in 2006 to grant 43 West Papuans refugee status prompted the Howard government to attempt to remove the entire Australian mainland from the national migration zone (limiting access to asylum) and to reassure Indonesia that every effort was being made to avoid the possibility of similar events in the future.

New Zealand resettled fewer people than Australia in the post-war years—just under 7,000 UN or otherwise sponsored refugees between 1945 and 1966. However, its immigration schemes were less driven by racial and other instrumental criteria. Notably, for example, New Zealand accepted Asians fleeing persecution in Idi Amin's Uganda where Australia did not. In 1959, New Zealand became the first country to accept for resettlement families with one or more person with a disability, though the numbers remained relatively small, and in the 1980s and 1990s, New Zealand accepted 'hard to resettle' cases as a matter of policy priority, including refugees with HIV/AIDS. Approximately 30,000 refugees have been resettled in New Zealand since 1944 when they were first distinguished as an administrative category (Verbitsky 2006).

In the late 1970s and in response to the Indo-Chinese conflict, Australia and New Zealand developed distinct policies on refugee reception which would later extend to annual quotas for resettlement. While most refugees resettled on account of conflict in Indo-China (some 60,000 in Australia and over 10,000 in New Zealand) were accepted directly from camps in Malaysia, c.2,000 mostly Vietnamese 'boat people' arrived spontaneously on Australian territory. At this time, Vietnamese 'boat people' were received relatively uncontroversially and public debate surrounding their plight bore little of the suspicion that infuses its present-day equivalent. In the 1980s both New Zealand and Australia also resettled significant numbers of Cambodians, Lebanese, and Chileans. A second 'wave' of Cambodian 'boat people' and asylum applications from Chinese students in Australia coincided with events in Tiananmen Square and the end of the Cold War. The latter would profoundly change the political context in which asylum seekers were received. In the 1990s and 2000s source countries for refugees accepted into both Australia and New Zealand reflected civil disorders in the former Yugoslavia, Sri Lanka, and African states including Ethiopia, Somalia, Sudan, and Eritrea, and ongoing conflicts and persecution in Iran, Iraq, and Afghanistan. The latter group was prominent amongst asylum seekers arriving by boat in the late 1990s and early 2000s.

In 2012 Australia increased its yearly intake of migrants under humanitarian streams from approximately 13,500 to 20,000 while New Zealand resettles approximately 750 persons annually. Because few countries commit to resettlement quotas in this way, Australia and New Zealand claim that their resettlement schemes are comparatively generous and accord with a long tradition of humanitarian reception for those displaced by conflict and persecution. Such claims are perplexing on at least three fronts. First, as Neumann (2004) has demonstrated in the case of Australia, the historical narrative relies on a highly selective reading of Australia's past humanitarian record which has been far more instrumental than is generally acknowledged. Second, and less controversially, Australia and New Zealand's combined annual humanitarian intake is equivalent to only a tiny fraction of the world's refugees (less than 0.1 per cent of 15.4 million in 2012) and even fewer of those considered by the UN to be in refugee-like situations. On a per capita basis, in 2012 Australia and New Zealand respectively ranked 58th and 88th on the list of refugee hosting countries and compared even less favourably (77th and 94th) when relative wealth (GDP per capita) was taken into consideration.[1] That the numbers hosted are so comparatively low belies the extent, third, to which the issue of asylum seekers has become so politically charged.

LEGAL AND POLICY FRAMEWORKS

Within the region, signatories to the 1951 Refugee Convention and the 1967 Protocol include Australia, Fiji, Nauru, New Zealand, PNG, Samoa, Solomon Islands, and Tuvalu. While PNG continues to host several thousand West Papuan refugees, Australia and New Zealand are the only states to have well-established refugee status determination systems and resettlement programmes. Refugees selected for resettlement via offshore schemes are provided with a comprehensive package of assistance which enjoys general public support. By contrast, asylum seekers who arrive spontaneously provoke much public anxiety. The Australian response to 'irregular' arrivals (asylum seekers without passports or relevant visas) is by far the most controversial aspect of forced migration governance in the region and therefore provides the starting point for this section.

From the 1990s, Australia's legal and policy framework with respect to asylum seekers has been characterized by two key aspects: (1) deterrence and (2) an increasingly narrow interpretation of the Refugee Convention in determining the status of and protection obligations owed to asylum seekers. Deterrents to asylum seekers have, since 1992, included mandatory and remote detention for irregular arrivals, in locations removed from adequate legal and community support services for periods of up to seven years in extreme cases. Temporary protection visas (TPVs) were introduced in 1999 as a punitive deterrent. The visas required those found to be refugees to re-establish their refugee status after a three-year period, during which time they were not entitled to resettle their families in Australia.

Between 1999 and 2000, the numbers of irregular boat arrivals increased fourfold. While absolute numbers (4,175 in the year to June 2000) remained relatively low by global comparison, the rate of increase prompted policymakers to harden the deterrence framework. The resulting suite of laws—collectively dubbed 'The Pacific Solution'—was introduced in the wake of the *Tampa* affair in August 2001. The *Tampa*, a Norwegian container ship that had rescued 433 mainly Afghan asylum seekers from their distressed vessel north-west of Australia's Christmas Island, was refused entry into Australian waters and redirected under guard by Special Air Services troops to Indonesia. Following the incident, Australian authorities were given expanded powers to pursue, board, and deter vessels suspected of carrying asylum seekers and effectively to prohibit access to territory in which Australian obligations to provide protection applied. Second, Australian island territories were excised from Australia's migration zone with the implication that asylum seekers arriving in those territories would have no automatic access to asylum-seeking processes, statutory oversight, or judicial review as they operated on the mainland and could be removed to third countries. Third, Australia negotiated with neighbouring Pacific countries to host asylum seekers intercepted en route to Australia: Australia financed detention centres in Nauru and Papua New Guinea to which asylum seekers were transferred and held while their claims were processed under the auspices of the UNHCR.

The Pacific Solution attracted widespread international attention. For other countries also keen to prevent asylum seekers from entering their territories, the Australian initiative proved to be an influential model, inspiring proposals in the European context for offshore transit processing centres for asylum seekers and others seeking entry to Europe (see Bank, this volume). Australia's increasing emphasis on border control *against* asylum seekers is in line with cooperative European efforts to increase surveillance and interdiction on the European frontier. Likewise, Australia's experiments in offshore processing resonate with the externalization of the European border for the purposes of asylum—a process that includes dubious bilateral arrangements for interdiction, detention, and deportation of irregular migrants en route to Europe with states from North Africa to the Caucuses (Schuster 2005; Afeef 2006).

From other perspectives, the Pacific Solution was strongly criticized for its cruel and detrimental effects on individual asylum seekers and for breaches of the spirit if not the letter of international law (for a summary, see Crock et al. 2006). While a new Labor government in 2007 abandoned both the TPV system and offshore processing, promising a more humane approach, the changes did not challenge the overall deterrence framework. In 2012, under pressure from rising numbers of irregular boat arrivals (approximately 17,000) the Gillard Labor government reinstated offshore processing on Nauru and PNG. Work rights and family reunion were denied to boat arrivals found to be refugees for up to five years after their status determination under a scheme that claimed to give 'no advantage' to asylum seekers over refugees applying for resettlement from camps in Asia and Africa. In 2013 the same Labor government passed the legislation that the former Howard government had failed to achieve, effectively excising the Australian mainland from the national migration zone and ending any mainstream party opposition to the deterrence policy framework.

Australia's Pacific Solution in its first and second phases is portrayed by policy advocates as part of a regional border protection strategy (see for example Bowen 2012). Regional governments are increasingly embedded in governance networks and collaborative processes relating to forced migration and border control, as members of the IOM and a number of security initiatives relevant to irregular migration and as part of the International Governmental Consultations on Migration, Asylum, and Refugees. Along with a number of Pacific states, Australia and New Zealand are also participants in the Bali Process—an important Asia Pacific intergovernmental dialogue on People Smuggling, Trafficking in Persons and Related Transnational Crime as well as the Pacific Immigration Directors' Conference, a similar collaborative framework for Pacific states. Much of the collaborative activity emanating from these processes falls within the context of law enforcement and consists of initiatives to upgrade and integrate border management systems, criminal legislation relating to smuggling and trafficking, and information and intelligence sharing. This emphasis on border control has serious implications for asylum seekers who may not have timely access to consular services but will find it increasingly difficult to cross borders without appropriate documentation. The 2011 Ministerial Conference of the Bali Process endorsed the advancement of a non-binding regional cooperation framework (RCF) that paves the way for a regional approach to refugee protection. Current schemes promoted under the RCF appear, however, to be consistent with a framework of deterrence rather than with the design of effective protection and resettlement options for refugees and others in need of protection in the Asia-Pacific region.

Australia's recent bilateral initiatives demonstrate this point well. From 2001, Australia entered into a tripartite agreement with Indonesia and the IOM. Indonesia agreed to the return of asylum seekers intercepted en route to Australia and to increased efforts to prevent their departure from Indonesia. Towards these ends, Australia provides equipment and training for relevant Indonesian authorities tasked with border control. Australia also funds IOM operations in Indonesia where they relate to material assistance for asylum seekers awaiting UNHCR status determination, an expanded detention infrastructure across the archipelago, and public communications strategies designed to encourage villagers, fishermen, and port authorities to report on human smuggling activities. Similar arrangements have existed between Australia and PNG since 2005 (Taylor 2010). Such schemes operate against the backdrop of the UNHCR's limited resources in Indonesia and PNG and the difficulties faced by asylum seekers attempting to access a timely status determination procedure there (Taylor and Rafferty-Brown 2010). As Taylor (2010) indicates, there is mixed opinion as to the extent of Australia's legal responsibilities towards asylum seekers administered by partner countries and the IOM under these arrangements. There is little doubt, however, that such schemes are designed to prevent asylum seekers from claiming asylum on Australian territory and under Australian law.

POLITICAL CONTEXT

The numbers of asylum seekers likely to reach Australia, New Zealand, and the Pacific are inevitably limited by island geography, isolation, and in the case of Pacific states by poor access to status determination procedures. Hosting only very small numbers of refugees and asylum seekers, Pacific states remain preoccupied with the ever increasing prospect of displacement induced by climate change. In Australia, however, considerable financial resources are devoted to controlling asylum seekers via onshore and offshore detention networks, coastal surveillance, and proxy funding for regional containment systems.[2] Asylum seekers attract persistent media attention and are the focus of significant public anxiety. What can account for the hardline response to border control directed against asylum seekers? Why has the public discourse related to the issue been far less vitriolic in New Zealand than in Australia and what explains the two countries' different policy approaches in recent years?

Australia and New Zealand are not alone amongst the world's wealthier countries in increasingly restrictive approaches to border control. The trend is often represented as a realist policy response to changed external conditions following the end of the Cold War, including the relaxation of exit controls in former Soviet states, the dislocating effects of global economic restructuring, and new types of wars that systematically target and displace civilian populations. Together, these conditions have been identified as 'push factors' for irregular migration, raising concerns about ensuing threats to the labour markets, welfare capacities, and cultural cohesion of migrant receiving states (for a summary see Zolberg 2001). Yet the trend towards restrictive border control is also a result of the problematization of migration in general and forced migration in particular as a security issue, over and above a humanitarian one (Watson 2009). In the post-Cold War era, politicians and policymakers increasingly represented the arrival of asylum seekers as a direct assault on state sovereignty and, in the post 9/11 context, as a potential avenue for terrorism. In Australia, this type of discourse has been central to public anxiety vis-à-vis asylum seekers, particularly in the wake of the *Tampa* affair, which, in the immediate aftermath of the New York terrorist attacks, was debated in terms of sovereign and existential threats. Elsewhere I have argued that this type of framing has been deployed in Australia as part of a political strategy to deflect anxiety about increasing exposure to global markets (McNevin 2011). Scapegoating asylum seekers for the uncertain trajectory of globalization accounts at least in part for the disproportionality between the numbers of asylum seekers reaching Australia directly and the extraordinary lengths to which successive governments have gone to prevent their access to Australian territory and law.

Other factors more specific to Australia's history and political culture also play a part in explaining the resonance of border control in the popular imagination. Since the founding of the first colony in New South Wales, Australia's national identity has been shaped by a sense of cultural and geopolitical vulnerability as a white European outpost in an alien Asian region. An 'invasion anxiety' (Burke 2001) played into racially restrictive immigration policies implemented by pre- and post-federation governments as well as a persistent expectation that government should exercise strong control over all forms of immigration as part of a highly orchestrated nation-building project (Jupp 2007). This emphasis on the necessity of an orderly and selective immigration system has survived the demise of the system's overtly racist dimensions (the White Australia policy was abandoned in 1972). The post-*Tampa* reforms, for example, were justified in part on the basis of system integrity and attendant policy rhetoric pursued this theme relentlessly. Politicians distinguished between 'real' refugees waiting patiently in UNHCR administered camps for selection for resettlement and 'queue jumpers' (the targets of the post-*Tampa* reforms) who attempted to subvert the system by arriving uninvited. The sincerity of the latter's refugee status was implicitly questioned in such comparisons, despite a high recognition rate in subsequent status determinations.[3] Historic fears and targeted discourse coalesced around the symbolic arrival of boats that were taken to signal a potential 'flood' of 'unruly' migrants of morally dubious character. A sustained push to remove the bulk of border policing against such people to offshore locations and to represent people smugglers as the new target of criminal sanctions has perpetuated border control as a keystone of what Australian governments consider an electable platform.

New Zealand has not been immune from broader global trends to securitize humanitarian migration. Some conservative commentators and politicians have attempted to generate moral panic about refugees and immigrants as cultural and economic threats (Devere et al. 2006). The far right party, New Zealand First, ran an anti-immigrant platform in the 1990s similar in content to that of Australia's One Nation and the far-right parties that emerged throughout Europe at the same time. However, in contrast to Australia, the conservative social agenda of New Zealand First was not adopted by the governing mainstream party, and the rhetoric on border control gained far less traction. The events of 9/11 likewise had an impact in New Zealand: unauthorized arrivals were subsequently detained (although for limited periods) and in a highly controversial case, Ahmed Zaoui, an Algerian asylum seeker and subsequent refugee, was detained without charge for two years on account of appearing on a watch list for terrorist suspects. Notwithstanding this significant exception, New Zealanders have been less inclined than Australians to see themselves as a target for terrorists, and therefore less susceptible to generalized associations between asylum seekers and security threats. Rather, New Zealand has adopted a broader human security agenda within the scope of its foreign and defence policies with less emphasis on the traditional security concerns and alliances that preoccupy Australia (Devetak and True 2006). Consequently, New Zealand's political culture has been less susceptible to scape-goating and fear-mongering in relation to forced migration and the reception of refugees.

Indeed, New Zealand's offer to resettle 150 refugees who had been aboard the *Tampa* was, for some commentators, indicative of the 'chasm between... [Australia and New Zealand] in terms of reaction to a refugee crisis' (Devere et al. 2006: 362). New Zealand's geographic remoteness may be an important factor in its different approach. The country has not been a target destination for asylum seekers in transit from Indonesia and has seen reduced numbers of asylum applications in recent years, largely due to pre-flight screening of passengers. In 2012, however, the conservative government responded swiftly to ten Chinese nationals en route to New Zealand by boat who ultimately claimed asylum in Australia. Official rhetoric echoed the deterrence tactics of the Australian government (Guy 2012). Later in the year, Immigration Minister Nathan Guy proposed legislation for six months' mandatory and renewable detention for irregular boat arrivals as well as forms of temporary protection and limits to family reunion. Prime Minister John Key's support for a regional refugee processing centre suggests, in addition, that a more hardline response may be taken should geography fail to provide a natural defence.

FUTURE CHALLENGES

Australia's administrative system and policy approach with respect to asylum seekers has been at a point of crisis for a sustained period of time. The offshore and onshore detention network, in particular, has been the focus of numerous inquiries and government-commissioned reports that have questioned the extent to which the system upholds domestic and international law, identified repeated failures in privatized service provision, documented cases of wrongful detention and damaging effects on detainees (including exacerbation of acute mental illness), as well as deaths in custody (see for example Joint Select Committee on Australia's Immigration Detention Network 2012). In 2011, the Secretary of the Immigration Department, in statements to a Parliamentary Inquiry, questioned the rationale of the detention system in terms of its intended deterrence function. Detainees have consistently protested against their conditions—most importantly against the uncertainty attached to prolonged periods of detention and suspensions on the processing of applications for protection from citizens of states deemed 'safe' for return (in 2010, Afghanistan and Sri Lanka were temporarily characterized in this way). That such protests have frequently taken the form of hunger strikes and other acts of self-harm is an indication of the levels of frustration and injustice felt by detainees. Asylum seekers continue to drown at sea en route to Australia or to die in circumstances related to the asylum-seeking process: estimates account for 1487 such deaths between 2000 and 2013.[4]

The integrity of Australia's refugee status determination system remains controversial. The numbers of negative assessments of the refugee status of irregular maritime arrivals overturned on appeal (over 82 per cent in 2011–12) raises questions about the legitimacy of the process, at least at its elementary levels, and about discrepancies between the process applying to plane versus boat arrivals (Department of Immigration and Citizenship 2013: 12; Joint Select Committee on Australia's Immigration Detention Network 2012: 152). More broadly, a significant distinction remains in Australian policy practice between a generally effective resettlement scheme for offshore refugees and a punitive response to spontaneous asylum applicants. Successive governments have deferred any efforts to engage the public with informed debate about the ongoing reality of forced migration in the region and the need to address in a sustainable way the serious protection and resettlement gaps that generate the need for spontaneous arrivals per se.

Australia, New Zealand, and Pacific states will doubtless be confronted with significant challenges on account of forced migration in the South-East Asian and Pacific region in the medium- to long-term future. Predicted trends and plausible scenarios in forced migration in these regions are, moreover, unlikely to fall within the scope of refugee status as defined by the Refugee Convention. There is, for example, significant potential for both episodic and entrenched civil conflict in Melanesian societies such as Solomon Islands, PNG, Fiji, and Vanuatu, and in East Timor. In 1999, 80 per cent of East Timorese fled violence that erupted following the aspiring state's independence referendum and an additional 150,000 were displaced from Dili in 2006 when their homes were seized or destroyed. By the early 2000s, civil war in the Solomon Islands had resulted in 30,000 internally displaced people or 10 per cent of the population. While displaced populations in these two cases have since been returned or resettled, ongoing tensions remain on account of post-independence development and state-building processes, along with high unemployment and lack of basic services (IDMC 2012). Should such tensions escalate, they may prompt the need for provisional protection measures for vulnerable groups, and possibly permanent forms of complementary protection in alternative resettlement countries (Leach and Nethery 2008).

Asia and the Pacific are also the regions most likely to be severely affected by climate change and climate-related natural disasters with large populations living in high-risk zones with limited capacity to reduce their vulnerability (see Zetter and Morrissey, this volume). Indonesia, the Phillipines, Burma, Malaysia, and Thailand are amongst the top 20 countries whose populations are at risk from increased sea level by 2050; PNG faces the risk of landslides in the highlands and coastal flooding while Pacific island states such as Kiribati, Marshall Islands, and Tuvalu face more immediate pressures on freshwater sources and uninhabitablity (Asian Development Bank, 2012). While most climate induced migration may be internal, the next 30 to 50 years are likely to see significant rises in cross-border migration both as a last resort and as a planned adaptation strategy. Yet global and regional policy on climate induced migration remains underdeveloped, highlighting an obvious protection gap in existing legal architecture applying to forced migrants.

Some commentators have suggested that temporary guestworker schemes may alleviate some of the migration pressures facing the Pacific region (Leach and Nethery 2008). In 2005, New Zealand established a guestworker scheme both to address seasonal labour shortages in the horticulture and viticulture industries, and to open formal avenues for migration from targeted Pacific states. The scheme's success prompted Australia to run a similar pilot scheme from 2008 and to expand the programme in 2012, incorporating migrant workers from Kiribati, PNG, Tonga, Vanuatu, Nauru, Samoa, Solomon Islands, Tuvalu, and East Timor. While there may be benefits from expanded schemes of this kind for both sending and receiving states—particularly those facing environmental pressures—they represent only part of the effort required to address forced migration in the longer term.

The need for a genuinely regional approach to refugee and complimentary protection is acknowledged overwhelmingly by intergovernmental organizations like the UNHCR, by a range of domestic and regional refugee advocacy networks, and by government-appointed expert panels.[5] However, current initiatives justified within the scope of such an arrangement resemble Australia's original 'Pacific Solution' much more than genuinely innovative collaborations. Proposals for regional processing centres have so far failed to demonstrate how refugee status determination could be completed in countries (including Pacific island states) that lack the legal, financial, and administrative resources to ensure the integrity of the process. Proposals have also failed to establish realistic resettlement options for those claimants found to be in need of protection. Neither Australia nor New Zealand has seriously raised the prospect of helping to alleviate the significant numbers of refugees hosted by South-East Asian neighbours (over 86,000 in Malaysia and over 89,000 in Thailand).

In Australia, New Zealand, and the Pacific, political support for a policy direction that addresses such issues comprehensively requires a commitment to reorient the nature of debate on forced migration. While the practical necessity is clear, it remains to be seen whether the political will exists to challenge the securitization of humanitarian migration with a policy framework less beholden to an either/or choice between sovereign and migrant rights. Without such a shift, the deterrence policy framework is likely to persist in domestic contexts and to limit the terms of reference for collaborative Asia-Pacific responses to forced migration.

Notes

1. All population figures are calculated from UNHCR (2013).
2. For details of *c.*$1.05 billion allocated to 'Offshore Asylum Seeker Management' in 2011–12, see Spinks et al. (2011: 6–7)
3. Between 70 and 97 per cent of asylum seekers arriving by boat at different times between 1998 and 2011 have been determined to be refugees (Phillips 2011: 7–8).
4. Australian Border Deaths Database <http://artsonline.monash.edu.au/thebordercrossing observatory/publications/australian-border-deaths-database/>.
5. See for example Houston et al. (2012) and a statement in support of the RCF by the Asia Pacific Refugee Rights Network: <http://refugeerightsasiapacific.org/2011/09/16/apprn-statement-on-a-new-approach-to-regional-cooperation-on-refugee-protection/>.

References

Afeef, K. F. (2006) 'The Politics of Extraterritorial Processing: Offshore Asylum Policies in Europe and the Pacific'. Refugee Studies Centre Working Paper No. 36.

Asian Development Bank (2012) *Addressing Climate Change and Migration in Asia and the Pacific*. Manila: Asian Development Bank.

Beaglehole, A. (2009) 'Looking Back and Glancing Sideways: Refugee Policy and Multicultural Nation Building in New Zealand'. Pp. 105–23 in K. Neumann and G. Tavan (eds.), *Does History Matter? Making and Debating Citizenship, Immigration and Refugee Policy in Australia and New Zealand*. Canberra: ANU e-press.

Bowen, C. (2012) Interview: Malaysia Arrangement, Indonesia, turning back the boats, Autralian Labor Party, Budget, Defence reviews. *Meet the Press*: Channel Ten Broadcast. 11 March.

Burke, A. (2001) *In Fear of Security: Australia's Invasion Anxiety*. Sydney, Pluto Press.

Connell, J. (2010) 'From Blackbirds to Guestworkers in the South Pacific: Plus ça change?' *Economic and Labour Relations Review* 20: 111–22.

Crock, M., et al. (2006) *Future Seekers II: Refugees and Irregular Migration in Australia*. Sydney: The Federation Press.

Department of Immigration and Citizenship (2013) *Asylum Statistics—Australia. Quarterly Tables—March Quarter 2013*. Canberra: Commonwealth of Australia.

Devere, H., et al. (2006) '"Just a Refugee": Rights and Status of Refugees in New Zealand'. Pp. 343–67 in F. Crépeau et al. (eds.), *Forced Migration and Global Processes*. Lanham, MD: Rowman & Littlefield.

Devetak, R., and True, J. (2006) 'Diplomatic Divergence in the Antipodes: Globalisation, Foreign Policy and State Identity in Australia and New Zealand'. *Australian Journal of Political Science* 41: 241–56.

Guy, N. (2012) 'New Measures to Deter People-Smugglers Announced'. Media Release, New Zealand National Party. 30 April.

Houston, A., et al. (2012) *Report of the Expert Panel on Asylum Seekers*. Canberra: Commonwealth of Australia.

IDMC (Internal Displacement Monitoring Centre) (2012) *Country Pages for Solomon Islands and East Timor*. Geneva. <http://www.internal-displacement.org>.

Joint Select Committee on Australia's Immigration Detention Network (2012) *Final Report*. Canberra: Commonwealth of Australia.

Jupp, J. (2007) *From White Australia to Woomera*. Cambridge: Cambridge University Press.

Leach, M., and Nethery, A. (2008) 'Forced Migration in the Asia-Pacific: Prospects and Implications for Australia'. Pp. 102–19 in S. Totman and S. Burchill (eds.), *Global Crises and Risks*. South Melbourne: Oxford University Press.

McNevin, A. (2011) *Contesting Citizenship: Irregular Migrants and New Frontiers of the Political*. New York: Columbia University Press.

Nethery, A. (2009) '"A Modern-Day Concentration Camp": Using History to Make Sense of Australian Immigration Detention Centres'. Pp. 65–80 in K. Neumann and G. Tavan (eds.), *Does History Matter? Making and Debating Citizenship, Immigration and Refugee Policy in Australia and New Zealand*. Canberra: ANU e-press.

Neumann, K. (2004) *Refuge Australia: Australia's Humanitarian Record*. Sydney: University of New South Wales Press.

Nicholls, G. (2009) 'Gone with Hardly a Trace: Deportees in Immigration Policy'. Pp. 9–23 in K. Neumann and G. Tavan (eds.), *Does History Matter? Making and Debating Citizenship, Immigration and Refugee Policy in Australia and New Zealand*. Canberra: ANU e-press.

Palmer, D. (2006) 'Between a Rock and a Hard Place: The Case of Papuan Asylum-Seekers'. *Australian Journal of Politics and History* 52: 576–603.

Phillips, J. (2011) *Asylum Seekers and Refugees: What are the Facts?* Canberra: Parliamentary Library, Commonwealth of Australia.

Schuster, L. (2005) '*The Realities of a New Asylum Paradigm*'. COMPAS Working Paper No. 20.

Spinks, H., et al. (2011) *Australian Government Spending on Irregular Maritime Arrivals and Counter-People Smuggling Activity*. Canberra: Parliamentary Library, Commonwealth of Australia.

Taylor, S. (2010) 'Australian Funded Care and Maintenance of Asylum Seekers in Indonesia and Papual New Guinea: All Care But No Responsibility?' *UNSW Law Journal* 33: 337–59.

Taylor, S., and Rafferty-Brown, B. (2010) 'Difficult Journeys: Accessing Refugee Protection in Indonesia'. *Monash Law Review* 36: 138–61.

UNHCR (2013) *Global Trends 2012: Statistical Annexe*. Geneva: UNHCR. <http://www.unhcr.org/51c071816.html>.

Verbitsky, J. (2006) 'Refugee Policy'. Pp. 651–61 in R. Miller (ed.), *New Zealand Government and Politics*. Melbourne: Oxford University Press.

Watson, S. D. (2009) *The Securitization of Humanitarian Migration: Digging Moats and Sinking Boats*. Abingdon: Routledge.

Zolberg, A. R. (2001). 'Introduction: Beyond the Crisis'. Pp. 1–25 in A. R. Zolberg and P. M. Benda (eds.), *Global Migrants, Global Refugees: Problems and Solutions*. New York: Berghahn Books.

CHAPTER 50

FORCED MIGRATION IN SOUTH AMERICA

JOSÉ H. FISCHEL DE ANDRADE[1]

INTRODUCTION

WHILE the international protection of refugees at the global level dates back to the 1920s, the protection regime in Latin America in general and in South America in particular is partially the result of a tradition developed over the past 200 years. The Latin American protection regime codified the subcontinent's tradition, practice, and values which preceded the 1951 Refugee Convention and the 1920s League of Nations' first instruments for the protection of Russian and Armenian refugees (Fischel de Andrade 1996). In fact 'exile has been a key institution of international society in...South America since independence,...performing a crucial function during the period of state-formation, and constituting, well into the twentieth century, one of the features that distinguished international society in the sub-continent from the progressively globalizing European model' (Jones 2011). Asylum practices were adopted during the revolutionary era so that the diplomatic recognition of newly established governments by major foreign states would not be jeopardized, and exile simultaneously acted as a regulatory mechanism, given that Latin American countries were unable to create pluralistic and inclusive models of participation, developing from an elite, in the nineteenthth century, to a mass phenomenon in the twentiethth century (Sznajder and Roniger 2009).

Against this backdrop, this chapter introduces the regional legal framework and organizations aimed at the protection of forced migrants in South America, and subsequently examines the region's main forced migration trends. Importantly, in so doing, it is impossible to dissociate forced migration in South America from the context of Latin America and the Americas more broadly, and the chapter therefore recognizes the significance of cross-fertilization with the other sub-regions of the American continent.

REGIONAL LEGAL FRAMEWORKS AND PROTECTION ORGANIZATIONS

Since independence in the early nineteenth century most Latin American countries have developed a sophisticated and advanced system of regional international law and institutions that are the basis of their society.

This section maps the legal framework for the protection of forced migrants in South America, giving special attention to the different legal statuses of 'asylees' and 'refugees'. It then introduces the Organization of American States' organs and human rights machinery to which recourse can be made in order to ensure the protection of the rights of forced migrants.

Legal Frameworks for the Protection of Forced Migrants

The Legal Institution of Asylum: Refugee Status and Asylee Status

The Americas, Latin America, and South America have a regional and also a subcontinental legal framework for the protection of forced migrants which complete the international, global legal framework, whose cornerstone is the 1951 Refugee Convention and its 1967 Protocol.

Latin American academic literature has during the second half of the twentieth century dwelt extensively with the difference between the so-called 'legal institutions' of *Asilo* (Asylum) and *Refugio* (Refuge), the latter meaning the UN protection regime and the former meaning the Latin American protection regime. This dualism is, however, anachronistic and should nowadays be avoided. As defined in 1950 by the Institute of International Law during its Bath session, '[a]sylum is the protection which a State grants on its territory or in some other place under the control of its organs to a person who comes to seek it'. Therefore asylum can be territorial or diplomatic,[2] the latter being granted in the diplomatic premises of the asylum seeker's receiving state. However, there is only one *legal institution* as such: that of Asylum.

Those persons in need of international protection who are not outside their country of nationality may enjoy Territorial Asylum under different *legal statuses*. The most common one is 'refugee status', which normally derives from the refugee-receiving state's obligations resulting from the 1951 Refugee Convention and national legislation which may also have—and this has been the case in several South American countries—widened the 1951 Refugee Convention definition. These refugees enjoy 'Convention' refugee status. 'Refugee status' may also ensue from UNHCR's refugee status determination procedures conducted in line with its 1950 Statute and subsequent General Assembly resolutions and international customary law. These refugees, in turn, enjoy 'Mandate' refugee status. Both 'Convention' and 'Mandate' refugees enjoy refugee status.

In Latin America, in addition to refugee status, there exists 'asylee status' (*asilado*), which derives from the regional or sub-regional asylum treaties and corresponding implementing national legislation.

Finally, as in any other continent, Latin and South American countries may accord another migratory legal status to a person in need of international protection, i.e. a complementary form of protection, the choice for not granting refugee or asylee status being grounded either on the asylum seekers' unsuitability vis-à-vis the 'refugee' or 'asylee' definitions, or on a political decision privileging another migratory status.

Ultimately, instead of having a dichotomy between *Asilo* and *Refugio* as converging but also competing legal institutions, one should place Asylum as a genus from which the two most relevant protective legal statuses granted in Latin and South America to persons in need of international protection derive, namely 'refugee status' and 'asylee status'.[3] The ensuing questions are: what is the legal basis, at the regional and sub-regional level, from which asylee status derives? What are the most relevant differences and similarities between refugee status and asylee status?

The Legal Basis for Asylee Status

Although the origins of the Inter-American System of Human Rights date back to the 1826 Panama Congress (Gil-Bazo and Nogueira 2013), a first and failed attempt at regulating and defining the concept of asylum in South America took place during a congress in 1867 (Yundt 1988). The codification of the practice that progressively developed of granting territorial and diplomatic asylum to those politically persecuted came to fruition only during the 1889 First South American Congress on Private International Law. The 1889 Montevideo Treaty deals with both territorial and diplomatic asylum and captured already at that early stage of codification, in its Article 15, a rudimentary provision on the principle of non-refoulement.

The following treaty to be adopted was the 1928 Convention on Asylum, which regulates matters pertaining to both political and diplomatic asylum. Subsequently, in 1933 the Convention on Political Asylum was adopted; this made some advancements regarding asylum procedures—in particular as to which state is to decide on the non-political nature of crimes that may have been committed prior to the asylum request—and also stating the humanitarian character of political asylum. In 1939, during the Second South American Congress on Private International Law, a Treaty on Asylum and Political Refuge was adopted which deals with both territorial and diplomatic asylum.

Following the 1950 Colombian-Peruvian Asylum case where the International Court of Justice found that there is so much uncertainty and contradiction, fluctuation, and discrepancy in the exercise of diplomatic asylum by Latin American states that an international custom respecting asylum could not be implied, both the Convention on Diplomatic Asylum and the Convention on Territorial Asylum were adopted in 1954.

The legal basis from which asylee status derives, at the international regional level, is the various regional and sub-regional instruments mentioned above but also the practices or methods in applying asylum which are followed for more than a century by most Latin and South American States. At the national level, the legal basis includes domestic regulations, implementing decrees enacted for the internalization of international instruments (in case they are not regarded as self-executing), provisions of general migration legislation,[4] or specific legislation on asylee status.[5]

Differences and Similarities between Refugee Status and Asylee Status

Asylee status and refugee status—species which derive from the same genus, the institution of Asylum—share relevant differences and similarities. While the rights and duties which construe these two legal statuses may in most cases be the same, this is not always the case. In this regard, with a slight change of approach, what this writer stated in the late 1990s (Fischel de Andrade 1998) may still be held as valid:

- Refugee status derives in most cases from the country of asylum's legal obligations captured in the 1951 Convention, which is an international global legal instrument. Regional developments complete the 1951 Convention refugee definition; this is the case in Africa, as a result of the 1969 Convention Governing the Specific Aspects of Refugee Problems in Africa, and also in the many countries of Latin America which have incorporated the extended definition of a refugee captured in the non-binding 1984 Cartagena Declaration. Refugee status may also be granted by the UNHCR on the basis of the refugee definition of paragraphs 6 and 7 of its 1950 Statute as well as by the Organization's subsequent practice. Asylee status, in its turn, is a legal regime regulated only by Latin or South American regional legal instruments, *none* of which refer to the 1951 Convention;
- Refugee status can only be enjoyed by persons who find themselves outside the territory of their country of nationality, or of former habitual residence, in the case of stateless persons. This is not the case of asylee status, since diplomatic asylum may be enjoyed in the diplomatic premises of the asylee-receiving state located in the territory of his or her country of nationality;
- To be granted refugee status, the person concerned needs to show a well-founded fear of persecution. This persecution may not necessarily have materialized by the time the refugee claim is lodged. Asylee status, on the other hand, is premissed upon an actual persecution and thus a sense of 'urgency';
- Refugee status, according to the 1951 Convention, is granted on the basis of five grounds: race, religion, nationality, membership to a particular social group or political opinion, and yet UNHCR practice and regional developments in Africa and Latin America have extended these grounds. The grounds for granting asylee status, however, are limited to political offences, political reasons, or political crimes;
- The enjoyment of refugee status may be supervised by UNHCR, which is the main component of the institutional pillar of the contemporary international global refugee protection regime. The enjoyment of asylee status, on the other hand, does not benefit from the supervision of an international institutional, the role of the Inter-American Commission and Court of Human Rights being rather limited;

- The determination of refugee status is a procedure whereby it is declared whether or not an asylum-seeker is a refugee. It is hence about a declaratory act that recognizes—or not—'refugeehood', a de facto situation that exists prior to the determination and granting of refugee status. The determination of asylee status, in turn, is a procedure that has a constitutive nature, the person becoming an asylee only *after* this legal status is conferred upon him or her.

Notwithstanding the differences between refugee status and asylee status, these statuses are nonetheless complementary and share the same premiss, namely the protection of persecuted individuals. After comparing and contrasting asylee and refugee status, and when identifying the best regime to protect persecuted persons, the global refugee regime is generally recognized as being much more precise, modern, progressive, and up to date, and as granting the best and widest international protection—i.e. refugee status—to those in need of it. The regional asylum regime—and its asylee status—is considered narrower and inferior in scope and inadequate to respond to the challenges of contemporary forced migration flows.

The Organization of American States' Organs and Human Rights Machinery and Forced Migrants

The legal framework for the protection of forced migrants in South America is also based on the organs and human rights machinery established regionally by the Organization of American States (OAS). On 2 May 1948—thus preceding the Universal Declaration of Human Rights—the first ever international (though not global) general human rights instrument, the American Declaration on the Rights and Duties of Man, was adopted, stating in its Article XXVII that '[e]very person has the right, in case of pursuit not resulting from ordinary crimes, to seek and receive asylum in foreign territory, in accordance with the laws of each country and with international agreements'.

In turn, the Washington-based Inter-American Commission of Human Rights (the Commission) was created in 1959. It first inspected the human rights situation in an OAS member state in 1961, and in 1965 its seven commissioners were expressly authorized to examine specific cases of human rights violations. In 1969, the guiding principles behind the American Declaration were taken, reshaped, and restated in the American Convention on Human Rights (the American Convention, also known as 'Pact of San José'). The American Convention ordered the establishment of the Inter-American Court of Human Rights (the court) and is currently binding on 22 of the OAS's 34 member states.

The two provisions of the American Convention which are most relevant to asylum issues are paragraphs 7 and 8 of Article 22 (Freedom of Movement and Residence), respectively stating that 'Every person has the right to seek and be granted asylum in a foreign territory...in the event he is being pursued for political offences or related common crimes', and enshrining the principle of *non-refoulement*. So far there has been only one case submitted to the court[6] which addresses violations of these two provisions: Case No. 12,474, Pacheco Tineo Family, Bolivia. The case concerns violations that occurred in the context of refugee status determination (RSD) procedures, and as a result of the fact that the Peruvian asylum-seeking family was returned from Bolivia to their country of origin without a serious determination of their fear of persecution. In 2013 the court gave judgment for the first time in a contentious case both on the issue of a state's obligation to give proper consideration to asylum requests and the principle of non-refoulement. In the judgment, the court establishes a series of minimum guarantees for asylum and expulsion proceedings derived from the American Convention.

There have been, however, a few cases heard by the court which are relevant to the broader issue of forced migration issues. In a 1998 case against Peru (Case of *Castillo-Páez v Peru*), the court established that the applicant was entitled to compensation for moral damages as a result of the psychological distress suffered because of her brother's disappearance, unknown whereabouts, and death, which forced her to live in the Netherlands as a refugee.

In a 2006 case (Case of the *Ituango Massacres v Colombia*) the court found that Colombia was responsible for the violation of the protected rights of 702 persons who were forcibly displaced. The court went further to say that when the former inhabitants decided to return, their security should be guaranteed and monitored by the state, and that if return was not possible the authorities should provide the necessary and sufficient resources to enable resettlement to a place chosen freely and voluntarily by the displaced persons affected.

In another, similar case against Colombia in 2005 (*Case of the Mapiripán Massacre v Colombia*), the court dwelt upon the phenomenon of internal displacement and the broad range of human rights affected or endangered by it, in particular the circumstances of special weakness, vulnerability, and defencelessness in which the displaced population generally finds itself, and the social dimension and cultural prejudices that hinder the integration of the displaced population in society and that can lead to impunity regarding the human rights violations against them. In a very pragmatic manner, the court examined the state guarantees of safety of the displaced persons who decided to return and determined that actions to ensure their safety should be designed in consultation with the beneficiaries of the measures. The court made a remarkable and innovative move by involving the victims in the solution of their situation, what goes *pari passu* with the idea that victims are not objects but rather subjects of rights.

In some cases the court has also used provisional measures to ensure that the immediate needs of forcibly displaced persons are met, that no further displacement occurs and that displaced persons may return to their villages of origin. In some cases the court has called upon states to establish a continuous monitoring and permanent communication mechanism in the so-called 'humanitarian refuge zones'.[7]

In the exercise of the court's advisory function, the advisory opinion that is most relevant to forced migration issues is that of 2003 on *Juridical Condition and Rights of the Undocumented Migrants* (OC-18). The court established that the right to due process must be recognized as one of the minimum guarantees that should be offered to any migrant, irrespective of their migratory status. The broad scope of the preservation of due process should encompass all matters and all persons, without any discrimination. Most importantly, the migratory status of a person cannot constitute a justification to deprive them of the enjoyment and exercise of human rights. This rationale has also been used with regard to RSD procedures.

REGIONAL FORCED MIGRATION TRENDS

This section stresses the importance of the Cartagena Declaration in South America and lays out considerations on recent initiatives regarding resettlement, the IDP phenomenon in Colombia, and statelessness.

The Heritage of the Cartagena Declaration in South America

Although the Cartagena Declaration was conceived as a result of and to address the forced displacement that occurred in the 1980s in Central America, since the 1990s it has influenced quite significantly the refugee acts and legislation enacted in South American countries.

Conclusion No. 3 of the 1984 Cartagena Declaration stated that

> the definition or concept of a refugee to be recommended for use in the region is one which, in addition to containing the elements of the 1951 Convention and the 1967 Protocol, includes among refugees persons who have fled their country because their lives, safety or freedom have been threatened by generalized violence, foreign aggression, internal conflicts, massive violation of human rights or other circumstances which have seriously disturbed public order.

This definition implies that those to be protected fulfil two characteristics: on the one hand, that a threat to life, security, or freedom exists and, on the other hand, that this threat results from one of the five grounds listed in the text (Gros Espiell et al. 1990). It is thus a humanitarian and pragmatic approach, which rules out the concept of individual persecution in order to emphasize objective criteria.

Although the 1984 Cartagena Declaration was not intended to be a legally binding instrument, but rather aspirational in character, throughout the years and because of its acceptance and application by several states, it has achieved significant persuasive force. It has been argued by a renowned scholar and former President of the Inter-American Court of Human Rights that the 1984 Cartagena Declaration is part of the origin of the creation of a Latin American and Caribbean regional custom and that its persuasive force derives from the fact that there was generalized *opinio juris* (i.e. the belief that an action was carried out because it was a legal obligation) when it was formed (Gros Espiell 1995). In addition, there has been a constant practice premised upon this binding quality in its concrete application. Being considered an atypical, spontaneous, and crystallized source of law, the 1984 Cartagena Declaration may have a binding effect vis-à-vis states which have unilaterally recognized it, or acted in such a way as to imply recognition of its normative nature. Consequently, states which have not embodied the refugee definition outlined in the 1984 Cartagena Declaration in their domestic legislation but apply it in practice would be bound by it owing to its standing as a rule of customary international law. The progressive rationale offered by Gros Espiell is sound, although it may be subject to criticism; Grahl-Madsen for instance has argued that in 'customary (unwritten) international law there is no such thing as a generally accepted definition of "refugee". It follows that it has no meaning to speak of "refugees in the juridical sense" or "der Begriff des Flüchtlings" except in the context of a particular legal instrument' (Grahl-Madsen 1966: 73).

Furthermore, although originally intended to be applied within the specific context of Central America, the 1984 Cartagena Declaration received the active support of several South American countries such as Colombia, Venezuela, and Uruguay. Indeed, the principles embodied in, and the practice resulting from the 1984 Cartagena Declaration achieved a regional reach, influencing refugee protection in several South American countries.

The 1984 Cartagena Declaration's refugee definition is embodied—word for word or by way of inspiration—in the Refugee Acts of Argentina (2006), Bolivia (2012), Brazil (1997), Chile (2010), Colombia (2009), Paraguay (2002), Peru (2002), and Uruguay (2006). Despite the inexistence of a domestic legislation capturing the Cartagena expanded refugee definition, Venezuela applies it in practice—although not uniformly—for asylum seekers fleeing generalized violence. Finally, in an unfortunate development, in 2012 Ecuador derogated the previous legislation (1992) that captured the recommended Cartagena refugee definition.

Durable Solutions and the Solidarity Resettlement Programme

The Mexico Plan of Action (MPA) was adopted by 20 Latin American countries in 2004. The MPA is an innovative protection initiative for the region, addressing both refugee and IDP movements, focusing on urban settings and marginalized border areas. Apart from areas related to protection and doctrine, the MPA comprises three strands relating to durable solutions: Solidarity Resettlement, Cities of Solidarity, and Borders of Solidarity (Piovesan and Jubilut 2011).

Solidarity Resettlement was born out of a Brazilian initiative to establish a regional resettlement programme based on responsibility sharing with a view to supporting Latin American countries that host large refugee populations (Jubilut and Carneiro 2011). That initiative was preceded by Brazil's resettlement experience during the post-war resettlement efforts of the International Refugee Organization (Fischel de Andrade 2011), by the resettlement in mid-1980s to Brazil of about 50 families (200 persons) of Iranian Bahais (Fischel de Andrade and Marcolini 2002a), by Brazil's 1997 Refugee Act, and on a pilot-project initiated in 2002 (Fischel de Andrade and Marcolini 2002b). Argentina, Brazil, and Chile, in addition to Uruguay and Paraguay have subscribed to the Solidarity Resettlement Programme by signing framework agreements with UNHCR. From 2004 to December 2011, almost 1,000 persons were resettled to the Southern cone.

Over the past years, the Solidarity Resettlement Programme has also importantly contributed to the extension and consolidation of the protection networks in the concerned countries, greatly due to the decentralization policy. As a result of this policy the Programme is now being implemented in more than 20 cities in Brazil, and in Chile and Argentina more provinces have joined the Programme, like Iquique (Chile) and Rosario and Mendoza (Argentina). Another significant development is that the Latin American resettlement countries have opened towards receiving cases from extra-regional asylum countries, as is the case with Palestinian refugees from Jordan and Syria who have been accepted by Brazil and Argentina.

The south-south resettlement programme is also an effective contribution to the regional response to the Colombian crisis. The emerging resettlement countries do not impose quotas, and yet their reception capacity depends entirely on the availability of financial resources and technical capacity.

A recent evaluation of the Solidarity Resettlement Programme in Argentina, Brazil, and Chile (White 2012) concluded that in order for this initiative to continue and have a future, barriers to the integration of refugees should be identified and alternative and creative ways to address them with the collaboration of all partners involved—NGOs, governments, and UNHCR—should be designed. The diversification of resources and partnerships was also highlighted as important, as well as the need to strengthen good practices and the chances of sustainability.

Internal Displacement in Colombia

At the end of 2013 there were 5,087,092 IDPs and people in IDP-like situations protected and/or assisted by UNHCR in Colombia. The recent increase of more than one million IDPs is due to the national registry having been updated on the one hand, and a 2013 Constitutional Court decision to include those displaced by post-demobilization armed groups and criminal gangs as IDPs on the other. If the current peace process is not successful, the numbers tend to increase. Although the overall figure encompasses only those people who have been displaced since 1996, the IDP problem in Colombia dates back to 1948 when 'The Violence' (*La Violencia*) started. The IDPs are the outcome of internal armed conflict and human rights violations resulting from drug trafficking, disputes over the control of land, and the actions of state forces and illegal armed groups, such as guerrillas and paramilitary groups.

Most Colombian IDPs are Afro-Colombian and indigenous communities, particularly in areas such as the Pacific Coast and borders with Ecuador and Venezuela. Half of the IDP population is living in urban centres, partly for the reason that 70,000 landmines affect 22 per cent of the Colombian territory. The IDP concentration in urban centres renders them—and particularly female IDPs—more vulnerable: according to the UN Entity for Gender Equality and the Empowerment of Women 50 per cent of displaced women are victims of sexual and other forms of gender-based violence.

The Colombian authorities have been pro-active and civil society has been very vocal in protecting and assisting IDPs. In 1997 a Law on internal displacement was enacted, adopting measures for the prevention of forced displacement and for the assistance, protection, socio-economic consolidation, and stabilization of persons internally displaced by violence. Its implementation, however, was rather limited due to the lack of a comprehensive strategy to address internal displacement, which should include, *inter alia*, the integration of the issue of displacement into the peace process.

Most recently, the legislature adopted in 2011 a Victims and Land Restitution Law, whose purpose is to guarantee the enjoyment of the rights to truth, justice, and reparation for victims. This law is an instrument of transitional justice which aims at the reconciliation of Colombians. Despite making a breakthrough in some areas, the new law is also a source of concern regarding e.g. its definition of 'victim', which is narrower than that of IDPs that one finds in the 1997 IDP Law; the return model to be adopted has not been defined; and the difficulty in addressing the vulnerabilities of the Afro-Colombian and indigenous communities which result from the fact that they come from strategic areas under the control of armed groups.

Efforts to Address Statelessness in South America

The main reasons for the 12 million stateless persons worldwide are gaps in nationality laws, arbitrary deprivation of nationality, and restrictive administrative practices. Situations of statelessness are considered rare in South America given both the conferment of nationality through parentage (*jus sanguinis*) as well as on the basis of birth within its borders (*jus soli*), and the very few existing legal gaps, an example of which is the difficulty of women to transfer their nationality to their children in Suriname.

Only Bolivia, Brazil, Ecuador, and Uruguay are state parties to both the 1954 Convention on the Status of Stateless Persons and the 1961 Convention on the Reduction of Statelessness. Argentina is only bound by the 1954 Convention and Paraguay has recently acceded to the 1961 Convention.

During and following the December 2011 Intergovernmental Ministerial Event organized in Geneva by UNHCR, Argentina, Bolivia, Brazil, Colombia, Ecuador, and Uruguay made pledges either on the accession to the 1954 or 1961 Conventions, the adoption of national mechanisms for the determination of the status of stateless persons, or the revision of national legislation on nationality. As a result, the Colombian Congress recently passed legislation on the accession to both international instruments on statelessness, accession discussions are underway in Argentina and Peru, and draft legal norms based on a draft model law developed by UNHCR to set up national determination procedures of the status of statelessness persons are currently being discussed in Bolivia, Brazil, Ecuador, and Uruguay.

A recent indication of a South American country's resolve to address statelessness was Brazil's amendment in 2007 of its Constitution to repeal a requirement that children born to Brazilians abroad must return and reside in Brazil to acquire Brazilian nationality. Applied retroactively, this amendment resolved the stateless status of approximately 200,000 children born to Brazilians abroad and prevents future statelessness from arising.

CONCLUSIONS

The phenomenon of forced migration has marked Latin America in general and the South American sub-region in particular, for the last 200 years. At present, however, the number of refugees in South America is comparatively small (337,354 persons, 96.5 per cent of whom are in Ecuador (123,436) and in Venezuela (202,022); UNHCR 2012) and the instances where asylee status is granted is very limited and yet highly topical. Two recent cases are the diplomatic asylum granted at the Brazilian Embassy in Tegucigalpa in 2009 to former Honduran president, Manuel Zelaya, who since 2010 enjoys territorial asylum as an asylee (*asilado*) in the Dominican Republic, and the diplomatic asylum granted at the Ecuadorian Embassy in London to Wikileaks spokesperson Julian Assange in 2012. Of more relevance in South America today is the internal forced displacement taking place in Colombia (see Kälin, this volume).

South American countries have faced forced migration by developing a protective legal framework at the regional level that completes the international protection regime. Legally binding and non-binding instruments abound and have been key in inspiring domestic legislation. Although there has been a concern regarding the adoption of specific laws on refugee protection and the harmonization of national asylum procedures, as remembered by the 2000 Rio de Janeiro Declaration on the Protection of Refugees, recent initiatives have focused mostly on a regional approach aiming at resettlement, migratory regularization alternatives, and cooperation mechanisms between institutions that deal with refugee issues, as called for by the 2010 Brasília Declaration on the Protection of Refugees and Stateless Persons in the Americas (Costa 2011) and the 2012 Mercosul Declaration of Principles on the International Protection of Refugees, which was concluded in Fortaleza, Brazil, during a meeting of the ministers of Interior and Justice of Mercosul members Argentina, Brazil, Uruguay, and Venezuela, and two associated countries, Bolivia and Chile.

If one witnesses an indication of political will expressed by innumerable non-binding initiatives such as declarations, plans of actions, recommendations, and conclusions, there are nevertheless accelerated procedures which do not comply with internationally established due process guarantees, some RSD procedures are not regulated through domestic laws (USCRI and AAE 2013), and most of the existing refugee status determination bodies still lack the training, efficiency, independence, and expertise that are to be found in other parts of the world. Worse still: Ecuador's June 2012 decision to withdraw the extended, Cartagena-inspired definition from its legislation and Venezuela's decision in September 2012 to denounce the American Convention on Human Rights are indicative of the unstable and fragile political framework in which the protection of human rights in general and that of forced migrants in particular is implemented in South America.

Nonetheless, despite recent setbacks, the overall assessment cannot be but promising: all South American countries (with the exception of the non-Latin American Guyana) are state parties to the 1951 Convention and/or the 1967 Protocol; all ten Latin/ South American countries have refugee status determination bodies, of which eight apply refugee legislation which has—in different degrees—incorporated the expanded, Cartagena-inspired refugee definition, bridging a protection gap by according refugee status instead of complementary or other forms of protection, such as subsidiary or humanitarian protection. Furthermore, this sub-region is becoming a destination of resettled refugees, with its potential yet to be fulfilled, and is also indicating a willingness to address statelessness through commitment to international instruments, enactment or revision of domestic legislation, and the establishment of national determination procedures.

Notes

1. The views expressed in this chapter are those of the author and do not necessarily reflect those of the French National Court of Asylum (CNDA) or the UNHCR.
2. Only in the American continent is it now possible to find operative multilateral conventions intended to recognize the institution of asylum in its two forms—territorial and diplomatic—and to define the legal regime that governs it.
3. In Europe other protective legal statuses coexist with that of refugee status, the most relevant ones being 'subsidiary protection' and 'humanitarian protection' statuses.
4. For instance, Articles 28 and 29 of Brazil's 1980 Foreigners Act partially defines the legal status of asylees (*asilados*).
5. Such is the case of Peru's Asylum Law 27,840 of 12 Oct. 2002, which refers only to asylee status.
6. For the case law of the Inter-American Commission on Human Rights on asylum-related issues, see Cantor and Barichello 2013.
7. These include the I/A Court H.R. *Cases of: The Communities of Jiguamiandó and Curbaradó v Colombia; The Peace Community of San José de Apartadó v Colombia; Pueblo Indígena de Kankuamo v Colombia*; and *Pueblo Indígena de Sarayaku v Ecuador*.

References

Cantor, D. J., and Barichello, S. (2013) 'Protection of Asylum-Seekers under the Inter-American Human Rights System'. In A. Abass and F. Ippolito (eds.), *Regional Organizations and the Protection of Asylum-Seekers*. London: Ashgate.

Costa, D. (2011) 'Introductory Note to the Brasília Declaration on the Protection of Refugees and Stateless Persons in the Americas'. *International Legal Materials* 50(3): 357.

Fischel de Andrade, J. H. (1996) *Direito internacional dos refugiados. Evolução histórica (1921–1952)*. Rio de Janeiro: Renovar.

Fischel de Andrade, J. H. (1998) 'Regional Policy Approaches and Harmonization: A Latin American Perspective'. *International Journal of Refugee Law* 10(3): 389–409.

Fischel de Andrade, J. H. (2011). 'Brazil and the International Refugee Organization (1946–1952)'. *Refugee Survey Quarterly* 30(1):65–88.

Fischel de Andrade, J. H., and Marcolini, A. (2002a) 'Brazil's Refugee Act: Model Refugee Law for Latin America?' *Forced Migration Review* 12: 37–9.

Fischel de Andrade, J. H., and Marcolini, A. (2002b) 'A política Brasileira de proteção e de reassentamento de refugiados. Breves comentários sobre suas principais características'. *Revista Brasileira de Política Internacional* 45(1).

Gil-Bazo, M. T., and Nogueira, M. B. B. (2013) 'Asylum in the Practice of Latin American and African States'. Research Paper No. 249. Geneva: UNHCR.

Grahl-Madsen, A. (1966) *The Status of Refugees in International Law*, vol. i. Leiden: Sijthoff.

Gros Espiell, H. (1995) 'La Declaración de Cartagena como fuente del derecho internacional de los refugiados en América Latina'. In *Memoria del Coloquio International. 10 Años de la Declaración de Cartagena sobre Refugiados*. Colloquium of San José de Costa Rica, 5–7 December 1994. San José: ACNUR/IIDH.

Gros Espiell, H., et al. (1990) 'Principles and Criteria for the Protection of and Assistance to Central American Refugees, Returnees and Displaced Persons in Latin America'. *International Journal of Refugee Law* 2: 83–117.

Jones, C. A. (2011) 'Exile as an Institution of South American International Society, 1808–1881'. Paper presented at the III World International Studies Committee (WISC) conference, August. Porto (unpublished).

Jubilut, L. L., and Carneiro, W. P. (2011) 'Resettlement in Solidarity: A New Approach towards a More Humane Durable Solution'. *Refugee Survey Quarterly* 30(3): 63–86.

Piovesan, F., and Jubilut, L. L. (2011) 'Regional Developments: Americas'. In A. Zimermann (ed.), *The 1951 Convention Relating to the Status of Refugees and its 1967 Protocol: A Commentary*. Oxford: Oxford University Press.

Sznaider, M., and Roniger, L. (2009) *The Politics of Exile in Latin America*. Cambridge: Cambridge University Press.

UNHCR (2012) *UNHCR Global Trends 2011*. Geneva: UNHCR.

USCRI and AAE (2013) *Refugee Status Determination in Latin America: Regional, Challenges & Opportunities*. <http://www.refworld.org/docid/51704a564.html>.

White, A. G. (2012) *A Pillar of Protection: Solidarity Resettlement for Refugees in Latin America*. Research Paper No. 239. Geneva: UNHCR.

Yundt, K. W. (1988) *Latin American States and Political Refugees*. New York: Praeger.

CHAPTER 51

FORCED MIGRATION IN CENTRAL AMERICA AND THE CARIBBEAN: COOPERATION AND CHALLENGES

MEGAN BRADLEY

INTRODUCTION

DISPLACEMENT runs deep in the history of Central America and the Caribbean.[1] Myriad labels have been applied to the region's forced migrants, from refugees, internally displaced persons (IDPs), and exiles; to evacuees, 'illegals', returnees, and deportees. In earlier eras, the majority of the region's forced migrants were indigenous communities ousted by European colonialists and slaves forced across the Atlantic from Africa. In the twentieth century, the poverty, inequality, rights violations, and armed conflicts engendered by the region's history of colonialism, corruption, and economic exploitation gave way to multiple displacement crises, the largest of which unfolded over the course of the 1980s and early 1990s, as more than 3 million Nicaraguans, Salvadorans, and Guatemalans were uprooted by interlinked civil wars (García 2006: 2). In addition to forced migration attributed primarily to conflict and human rights violations, over the past century millions of people across the region have been displaced by natural disasters including earthquakes, hurricanes, and volcanic eruptions.

This chapter explores the dynamics of displacement in Central America and the Caribbean. The first section examines past and present trends in the causes and types of displacement, while the subsequent sections address the diversity of responses to forced migration from and within the region, including the role of legal frameworks, regional organizations and initiatives, solidarity movements, and grassroots mobilization. The chapter highlights emerging challenges that are likely to shape the future regional dynamics of forced migration, including displacement connected to increasingly severe natural disasters, as well as the complex relationship between undocumented migration and the sustainable resolution of displacement. In particular, the chapter emphasizes the striking ways in which cooperation at the regional, national, and grassroots levels has shaped responses to displacement in Central America and the Caribbean. In the third section, an examination of efforts to resolve displacement emerging from Central America's civil wars is used to bring these multi-level cooperation dynamics into focus. While this case is often hailed as an all-too-rare success story, this re-examination suggests that it was far from a clear-cut victory: this case demonstrates innovative cooperative approaches to responding to forced migration, but also the negative effects of inequitable access to assistance and the persistent difficulties the region faces in successfully supporting the resolution of displacement.

CAUSES AND CONSEQUENCES OF DISPLACEMENT

In recent years, 'newer' causes of displacement have attracted increased attention, such as organized crime and disasters associated with the effects of climate change. However, these drivers of displacement are clearly linked to the region's longer history of forced migration, underdevelopment, socio-economic inequalities, and conflict.

In the colonial era, Central America and the Caribbean witnessed mass forced migration through the slave trade to the Caribbean and the seizure of indigenous peoples' traditional lands by *conquistadores*. Particularly in Guatemala, many of the millions of indigenous citizens uprooted during the country's civil war (1960–96) trace their dispossession to a much earlier crisis, the arrival of Spanish colonizers in the sixteenth century. In some cases, independence struggles resulted in renewed displacement, as did the dictatorships that ruled several Central American and Caribbean countries in the post-colonial era. For example, Rafael Trujillo's rule of the Dominican Republic from 1930 to 1961 saw the exodus of Dominicans fleeing repression and executions by death squads, and the culmination of his *Antihaitianismo* ('anti-Haitianism') policy in *El Corte* ('the cutting')—the 1937 murder by government agents of an estimated 20,000–30,000 Haitians and Dominicans of Haitian origin. Intended to rid the borderlands of Haitians, despite the long-standing practice of Haitian labour migration to work in Dominican sugar cane fields, many people—most of them Dominican citizens—were killed while attempting to escape to Haiti. In spite of this atrocity, by 1939 Haitians resumed labour migration to the Dominican Republic—a testament to the depth of economic deprivation in Haiti and the blurred lines between 'voluntary' and 'forced' migration in the region (Jadotte 2009). While less bloody, the 1959 Cuban Revolution prompted a significant outflow of Cubans, 'many of them ardent supporters of the revolution initially', to seek shelter abroad, mostly in the United States but also in countries including Canada, Mexico, Spain, Italy, and Sweden (Pedraza 2007: 1). Between 1959 and 2004, more than 1.3 million citizens, totalling

12–15 per cent of the population, left Cuba by various means, and with varying degrees of force (Pedraza 2007: 1–3). Under the Duvalier regime in the 1960s, Haiti also saw large, politically motivated movements, predominantly to North America.

Displacement in the region reached its apex in the 1980s and early 1990s as millions of Central Americans fled civil wars in Nicaragua, Guatemala, and El Salvador.[2] While shaped by Cold War rivalries, on a deeper level these wars were rooted in the same, drastically inequitable distributions of political power, land, and economic resources that fuelled displacement across the region in the colonial and early post-colonial eras. These dynamics prompted the development of left-wing insurgencies, which were brutally opposed in El Salvador and Guatemala through scorched earth campaigns in the early 1980s. In Guatemala, the war became a genocide as the majority of the 200,000 who died or disappeared and the 2.3–3 million displaced were indigenous Maya. In El Salvador, 500,000 were internally displaced between 1979 and 1982, and over a million fled to the United States, Mexico, and camps in Honduras (Bradley 2011: 88, 90).

Although UNHCR argued that Guatemalans and Salvadorans who fled their states after the start of the scorched earth campaigns should be granted prima facie refugee status, the recognition of asylum claims, particularly in Mexico and the United States, became grossly politicized. Wary of antagonizing its northern and southern neighbours, Mexico granted refugee status to only 45,000 of the estimated 200,000 Guatemalans who fled to Mexico. The United States, unwilling to acknowledge the consequences of the lethal policies embraced by Washington-backed governments, accepted only 1.8 per cent of Guatemalan asylum applications filed between 1983 and 1990, and 2.6 per cent of those filed by Salvadorans (Montes 1988; Bradley 2011: 89–90). Recognizing that they were highly unlikely to be granted formal refugee status, the vast majority of those fleeing Guatemala and El Salvador simply went underground. While displacement from Nicaragua had a similarly regional character, with most forced migrants seeking shelter internally, in neighbouring states, or in the United States, the conflict took a different track, with the leftist Frente Sandinista de Liberación seizing power from the ruling Somoza family in 1979. Alongside the return of left-wing exiles, middle-class and wealthy Nicaraguans left en masse; a handful formed the Contras, which fought to topple the Sandinistas. Amongst Nicaragua's 350,000 IDPs and 72,000 refugees were many unaligned indigenous Miskitos who fled the conflict with the Contras and government efforts to forcibly resettle them.

In Central America and the Caribbean, large-scale displacement due to armed conflict has waned, with only 2 per cent of the world's refugees located in Latin America and the Caribbean, and no reliable data available on how many remain internally displaced in Guatemala (UNHCR 2012: 46; IDMC 2013: 34). Asylum-seeking patterns remain highly regional, with applicants seeking shelter in neighbouring countries or, more commonly, in North America. Although the numbers are modest compared to earlier periods, in 2011 and 2012, El Salvador, Guatemala, Haiti, and Honduras ranked in the top ten source countries for asylum applications in Canada and the United States, with a total of 11,785 applications filed in 2011 and 13,660 in 2012. The United States, which receives the majority of asylum applications from the region, has been reluctant to recognize those fleeing new drivers of displacement in Central America, including gang violence: between 2007 and 2013, 74,449 Guatemalans, Salvadorans, and Hondurans sought refuge in the United States, but only 2,250 (3 per cent) were accepted (Kennedy 2013).

Natural disasters remain a major cause of displacement in Central America and the Caribbean, with more than 78,000 people displaced by disasters in Central America in 2012, and over 483,000 uprooted in the Caribbean (IDMC 2012a: 46). Much of this displacement is associated with increasingly severe storms linked to the effects of climate change, compounded by persistent poverty and lack of state capacity in countries such as Haiti. This renders citizens more vulnerable to repeated and protracted displacement, as they are likely to lack effective early warning and preparedness systems, well-constructed homes located in safe areas, and the finances and tenure security required to rebuild them if necessary. Preparedness and response capacities vary dramatically across the region and, in a sad irony, repeated exposure to disasters often undercuts the ability of states and communities to weather major disasters.

For example, in 2012, Hurricane Sandy displaced 343,000 in Cuba and 32,000 in Haiti, and yet the Cuban government was exponentially better prepared to respond to the disaster, preventing it from becoming a crisis (IDMC 2012a: 17). In contrast, in Haiti the arrival of storms such as Sandy is almost invariably a crisis. One of the poorest countries in the world, Haiti has the highest relative level of displacement due to natural disasters: between 2008 and 2012, 1.9 million Haitians were displaced due to disasters, totalling 19 per cent of the population (IDMC 2012a: 7). Many of the 2 million left homeless by the massive 2010 earthquake had previously been displaced due to natural disasters, and the 147,000 who remained in IDP camps in early 2014 continue to face high risk of repeated displacement due to hurricanes, floods, and mudslides (IDMC 2012a: 35). Weak governance, environmental degradation, and, in particular, the difficulty of resolving displacement in urban environments with complex social problems that long pre-date and intersect with the IDP crisis have undermined the hope that the billions flowing into reconstruction would enable Haiti to 'build back better'. Instead, most urban Haitians live in informal settlements, inadequate rental housing, or IDP camps. Although new building codes have been adopted, the government is unable to enforce them, particularly as Haitian families themselves undertake the construction and repair of an estimated 40,000 homes each year. Many unplanned settlements have emerged in areas susceptible to landslides and flooding, setting the stage for further displacement (IDMC 2012a; Ferris and Ferro-Ribeiro 2012).

As in other regions, displacement that is primarily attributable to conflict, human rights violations, and natural disasters in Central America and the Caribbean occurs alongside movements that states often label 'voluntary', but which occupy a grey zone between compulsion and choice, and raise a host of concerns for forced migration scholars and practitioners, including deportation and statelessness. For example, for generations Haitians have migrated to the Dominican Republic to seek work. Whether such movement is meaningfully voluntary is a matter of debate given the impoverished conditions in Haiti, but it is incontrovertible that constitutional amendments adopted in 2010 (formalizing a policy in place since 2007) have rendered as many as 200,000 individuals of Haitian descent in the Dominican Republic de facto if not de jure state-less, as they cannot prove their citizenship, or legally attend school or work. These amendments—adopted the same year as the Haiti earthquake, when migration to the Dominican Republic surged—restrict *jus solis* laws that formerly accorded citizenship to the vast majority of those born in the country. Under the amendments, backstopped by an October 2013 Dominican Constitutional Court decision, only those whose parents were legally resident—which most cannot prove—are entitled to citizenship, leaving scores in limbo. Further, the Constitutional Court decision, decried by many observers as racist, instructs Dominican officials to audit birth records to identify who is ineligible for citizenship, exacerbating the precarious status of scores of long-time residents of the Dominican Republic (*Economist* 2011; Abiu Lopez 2013; Archibold 2013). The 2010 constitutional amendments follow a longer history of efforts to restrict the presence of Haitians in the Dominican Republic, including not only *El Corte* in 1937 but also large-scale, collective expulsions in 1991, 1996–7, and 1999 (Fletcher and Miller 2004).

Deportation is also an increasingly important dynamic in the forced movement of people between Central America and the United States, with the United States establishing hundreds of new detention centres and spending millions to remove an estimated 22,000 to 41,000 individuals from Honduras, El Salvador, and Guatemala in 2012 alone (Kennedy 2013). Officials justify these removals on the grounds that the deportees are economic migrants without legal rights to remain in the United States, and yet some suggest that many have legitimate, if unacknowledged, asylum claims as they are fleeing increasingly powerful transnational criminal organizations (TCOs) in El Salvador, Honduras, and Guatemala. These TCOs 'wield considerably more arms, money and power than each nation's military,' have an estimated 40–70 per cent of government officials on the take, and control entire municipalities and sections of national governments (Kennedy 2013: 50). These groups' efforts to instil fear, persecute their opponents, and expand their power are becoming a significant source of displacement in the region, particularly of children and young people, who make up the majority of recruits (willing or otherwise) into gangs. Although the number of immigrants caught unlawfully attempting to enter the United States is at a '40-year low, the number of children coming illegally and alone is surging, largely as a result of increasing drug-fuelled violence in Central America... One in 13 people caught by the Border Patrol last fiscal year were under 18' (Nazario 2013). US officials estimate that in the 2013–14 fiscal year, the number of unaccompanied minors unlawfully entering the United States will rise by approximately 70 per cent; however, rather than acknowledging and systematically responding to this increasingly important source of forced migration in the region, the United States is poised to continue its policy of intensified deportation efforts, despite the tendency of such removals to fuel the development of TCOs. Indeed, it was the forced return of individuals who 'illegally' fled the civil wars in Central America and subsequently joined gangs in the United States that led to the transnational spread of these organizations, laying the foundations for continued undocumented forced migration today (Kennedy 2013).[3]

COOPERATION TO ADDRESS DISPLACEMENT

Responses to forced migration in Central America and the Caribbean are character-ized by strikingly high levels of cooperation from the international to the grassroots levels. Important legal frameworks structuring regional governments' responses to dis-placement include the 1951 Refugee Convention[4] and the 1984 Cartagena Declaration on Refugees. Adopted by government officials at the Colloquium on the International Protection of Refugees in Central America, Mexico and Panama, the Cartagena Declaration expands the refugee definition applicable in the region to include not only those fleeing persecution, but also those 'who have fled their country because their lives, safety, or freedom have been threatened by generalized violence, foreign aggression, internal conflicts, massive violations of human rights or other circumstances which have seriously disturbed public order' (Part III, Conclusion 3). The Declaration, which has been integrated into several national asylum laws, emphasizes the search for durable solutions to displacement, and recommends cooperation between the Organization of American States (OAS) and UNHCR.[5]

The OAS and in particular the Inter-American Commission on Human Rights (IACHR) and the Inter-American Court of Human Rights, stand out as critical ele-ments of the region's cooperation system related to forced migration, grounded in regional standards including the OAS Charter, the 1948 American Declaration on the Rights and Duties of Man,[6] and the 1969 American Convention on Human Rights.[7] The Inter-American Court has a long history of addressing cases related to displace-ment and awarding reparations to the victims of massacres leading to massive forced migration. For example, in 2004 the court determined that the Guatemalan state was responsible for the notorious 1982 Plan de Sánchez massacre, and ordered the govern-ment to extend almost US$8 million in financial redress to the survivors, the court's highest award on record. The IACHR has also investigated the predicament of various displaced groups across the region, from refugees fleeing the 1959 Cuban Revolution and Guatemalan IDPs mobilized as 'Communities of Peoples in Resistance' (IACHR 1994) to, more recently, those displaced in connection with the activities of non-state actors including paramilitaries and *maras* (gangs). In 2011, the IACHR moved towards more concertedly addressing the rights and well-being of the displaced by expanding the mandate of the IACHR Rapporteur on the Rights of Migrants to include 'asylum seekers, refugees, complementary protection seekers and beneficiaries, stateless per-sons, victims of human trafficking, internally displaced persons and other vulnerable groups within the context of human mobility' (IACHR n.d.). While the IACHR cannot compel governments to change their policies, by drawing attention to the plight of dis-placed communities in an intergovernmental setting, it can encourage and incentivize improved responses.

In addition to the Inter-American human rights system, Central America and the Caribbean host several regional organizations concerned with displacement in the context of disaster risk management, including, most prominently, Central America's Coordination Center for Natural Disaster Prevention (CEPREDENAC) and the Caribbean Disaster Emergency Management Agency (CDEMA), as well as the Panama-based Regional Inter-Agency Coordination Task Force for Risk, Emergency and Disasters (REDLAC), which serves as a catalyst for enhanced regional-level coordination and cooperation. As Fagen (2008: 5–6) remarks,

> To a greater extent than in other regions, Latin American and Caribbean governments have established regional entities to help them define needs, share information and training opportunities and elaborate projects… What is truly exceptional in the Latin America/Caribbean region is the commitment of virtually every regional organization to incorporate disaster management and disaster risk reduction in their institutional mandates and to support national institutions in these areas.

This cooperation is perhaps unsurprising, as Latin America and the Caribbean is one of the most disaster-prone areas in the world. However, just as the region's governments have dramatically different response capacities, the efficacy of these organizations varies considerably. They remain largely dependent on international donors; effective, cooperative responses to disasters are also hindered by 'over-reliance on military sector leadership' and 'lack of political will to devote national resources to disaster management and particularly to disaster prevention,' in addition to a tendency for international actors to bypass the complex process of regional-level capacity building (Fagen 2008: 5; Ferris and Petz 2013).

Looking back on Central America's 'Success Story'

Just as mutual challenges and interests prompted significant regional cooperation related to disasters, they served as the impetus for unprecedented cooperation, from the grassroots to the international level, in response to the displacement crisis sparked by Central America's civil wars. Popular mobilization to support solutions for displaced Central Americans has been celebrated as a grassroots victory, while the International Conference on Central American Refugees (CIREFCA) process has been lauded as 'the most successful example of North–South cooperation in the history of the global refugee regime,' and a remarkable instance of regional cooperation (Betts 2009: 109). It is questionable, however, whether this cooperation translated into a recognizable 'success' for the majority of forced migrants: under these processes, the bulk of support was channelled towards the fraction of those displaced who managed to obtain formal refugee status. As UNHCR itself acknowledges, projects supported through international cooperation efforts touched only the 'tip of the iceberg' (Betts 2006: 12). In the absence of safe, dignified, and socio-economically sustainable solutions for the legions displaced across the region, 'peace' remained reminiscent of war in its uncertainty and often unrelenting violence.

International and Regional Cooperation through CIREFCA

Central America's regional and national peace processes gained traction in the late 1980s and during the 1990s. Regional efforts included the 1987 Esquipulas II agreement, which acknowledged displacement as a critical element in the region's conflicts. Building on Esquipulas II, CIREFCA was not just an event or a declaration but a process to support solutions to displacement that played out between 1989 and 1995, drawing together regional governments, donors, and NGOs, under the leadership of UNHCR and UNDP. Motivated by an 'integrated development approach', the CIREFCA process aimed to be comprehensive, cooperative, and collaborative: that is, it advanced a range of solutions to displacement, promoted burden sharing, and engaged a diversity of actors (Betts 2009: 91, 2006). CIREFCA's proponents underscored the links between the resolution of forced migration and the consolidation of peace, security, and development, and leveraged governments' interests in these issues to gain support for durable solutions. CIREFCA's primary tangible contributions include $422.3 million to support projects intended to backstop the local integration or return of 45,000 Guatemalans, 62,000 Nicaraguans, and 27,000 Salvadorans. The Development Program for Displaced Persons, Refugees and Returnees in Central America (PRODERE) channelled $115 million to the region to support reintegration activities. In addition, CIREFCA protagonists promoted political dialogues that resulted in Tripartite Agreements on Repatriation to Guatemala and Nicaragua. Although governments generally encouraged return as the 'preferred' solution to displacement, support for local integration gradually increased, such that many were able to select a solution most appropriate to their needs (Betts 2009: 87–9).

Grassroots Cooperation in Support of Solutions

Alongside regional and international cooperation efforts, remarkable grassroots campaigns for safe, dignified, and ultimately just solutions for Central America's displaced populations unfolded, largely at the initiative of refugees and IDPs themselves. The emergence of solidarity networks connecting uprooted *campesinos* (peasants) with supporters worldwide, and the mobilization of displaced Salvadorans and Guatemalans to negotiate their own durable solutions have been applauded as grassroots triumphs. Rooted in long histories of resistance and belief systems including liberation theology, this 'self-help' approach was premised on the recognition that international assistance would be inevitably limited; the region's governments had not fundamentally reformed; and the search for solutions—and peace—would be a long-term process in which the displaced could play a leading role, promoting 'state-making from the margins' (Stølen

2007: 203). Salvadoran refugees in Honduras served as catalysts in this mobilization effort. Beginning in 1985, the refugees began organizing themselves to achieve a collective return to El Salvador. This 'repopulation' movement encountered opposition from the Salvadoran government, which attempted to prevent them from returning to areas under Frente Farabuno Martí para la Liberación Nacional (FMLN) control; from UNHCR, which feared it could not guarantee returnees' safety; and from the FMLN, which had strategic interests in maintaining the camps and controlling the refugees' movements. However, the refugees showed 'new and enormous capacity for negotiation, insisting on the right to return to communities irrespective of locale, and develop them without harassment' (Sollis 1992: 55–6; Silber 2011: 65). The organized repopulation of communities such as El Barillo and Tenancingo 'opened up the way for subsequent groups,' including IDPs, 'to move back more spontaneously in a way that consolidate[d] the reborn settlements and surrounding areas' (Sollis 1992: 54–5; Todd 2004). Refugees and IDPs engaged in the repopulation process were represented by a wide range of organizations with a common commitment to holding the government accountable to its citizens and promoting sustainable development. Cooperation between these groups helped to diminish competition over resources in repopulated communities.

Inspired by the Salvadoran returnees, Guatemalan refugees in Mexico organized a network of Permanent Commissions of Guatemala Refugees (CCPP) dedicated to negotiating their organized, collective return. (A similar mobilization process was undertaken by some 32,000 Guatemalan IDPs organized into 'Communities of Populations in Resistance'.) The Commissions negotiated the 1992 October Accord, the first agreement on return concluded between exiled citizens and their government, which declared that the 'return of the refugees must be a voluntary decision, individually expressed, undertaken in a collective and organized fashion, under secure conditions, and with dignity'. The agreement recognized returnees' rights to security, free movement, and freedom of association, and established processes through which the returnees could reclaim their lost lands, or access new lands. While a remarkable accomplishment, implementation efforts floundered, and, at any rate the agreement's relatively progressive provisions directly benefited only 5 per cent of uprooted Guatemalans, leading to resentment amongst the non-displaced and IDPs covered only by the less ambitious 1994 Accord on the Resettlement of the Population Groups Uprooted by the Armed Conflict (Stølen 2007: 1–2; Bradley 2013: 99–120).

These efforts were complemented by international sanctuary and accompaniment campaigns. The latter were, in the eyes of many displaced Central Americans, essential to enabling returns: 'without international accompaniment,' one returnee reflected, 'the people are like worms the army can step on' (García 2006: 82). In North America, sanctuary movement activists numbered more than 70,000 by the late 1980s. Committed to preventing deportations and supporting local integration, the movement was also instrumental in working with the Central American diaspora community to secure 'legalization' opportunities for undocumented migrants, and pushing for an end to the scorched earth warfare that fuelled the displacement crisis (Coutin 2000; Bradley 2011: 99–100, 118–19).

A Success in Retrospect?

In light of these innovative, cooperative approaches to resolving displacement, the Central American case is often held up as a success story or even a 'best case scenario' (Worby 2000: 17). Certainly, this case demonstrates the value of synergies between 'bottom-up' and 'top-down' approaches; the significance of addressing the development and justice dimensions of durable solutions; and the importance of equitable access to assistance and choice between solutions. However, closer examination highlights that this case was far from a straightforward success. International resettlement opportunities were seriously limited, while internal resettlement or relocation processes were highly militarized. Local integration opportunities were contingent on large numbers of refugees having already returned. Countless returnees were exposed to violence, threats, and intimidation; while the promised land redistribution and development programmes often never got off the ground, or simply lined the pockets of those responsible for displacement in the first place. As such, access to

> protection and support was highly uneven: UNHCR estimates that only ten percent of forced migrants benefitted from international assistance. Those least likely to be able to secure support included IDPs . . . asylum seekers who were denied refugee status through grossly politicized determination procedures; and the hundreds of thousands of Central American forced migrants who understood that they were unlikely to be recognized as refugees, and therefore moved 'under the radar' to Mexico and the US. (Bradley 2011: 85)

Indeed, the role of undocumented migration in this case is highly significant if underexamined by forced migration scholars. Undocumented migration undoubtedly relieved the pressure on the humanitarian system, but Salvadorans' experiences highlight the tensions inherent in this 'quasi-solution' to displacement. Before the war, Salvadorans had no history of mass migration, yet by 1988 1 million had escaped to the United States, and began sending remittances in the order of $4 million a day. Although most eventually 'became legal', the long-standing risk of deportation exacerbated the marginalization of the community: Salvadorans who had 'graduated from the school of clandestine and illegal survival' were obliged to use 'mechanisms of concealment, self-defense, and solidarity' to survive (Montes 1988: 124). This created an environment conducive to the development of gangs and, in combination with families' growing dependence on remittances, left many effectively trapped: although many Salvadorans in the United States wanted the option to return, whether permanently or temporarily, this was often untenable given the risk of travelling without documentation and the need to continue sending money home. The longer-term implications of this strategy for the durability of 'traditional' solutions such as return and local integration are uncertain. Undoubtedly, '[m]igration that began in the context of war provided [a degree of] personal security for those who got away', but the effects of this and subsequent migration may in fact be exacerbating on-going problems of political destabilization' and underdevelopment in El Salvador. As a result of this migration, communities—disproportionately, those most stricken by the war—lose their human capital and experience rising property prices and diminished agricultural production as comparatively affluent diaspora members buy up land they do not cultivate (Garni 2010: 326). This in turn exacerbates unemployment and dependence on remittances in repopulated communities: as of 2009, remittances accounted for 16 per cent of El Salvador's GDP, with 77 per cent of remitted money being spent on food. Returnees to Chalatenango who subsequently joined the flow of illicit migrants to the United States depict their homeland as 'una tierra expulsadora' (a land that expels), suggesting that in some cases such movements may represent a continuation of displacement (Garni 2010: 324–5; Bradley 2011: 108–10; Silber 2011: 19).

Conclusion: 'Onwards, for the struggle continues'

Central American refugees' mantras 'Onwards, for the struggle continues' and 'Struggle to return! Return to struggle!' reflect that those uprooted in the region's largest displacement crisis never expected their story to be an unfettered success, but a long fight for justice, equality, and development. Cooperation between various actors on multiple levels was undoubtedly critical to the achievements that were made in responding to this crisis, however qualified they may be in retrospect. Moving forward, multi-level cooperation is likely to continue to play a key role in responding to the diverse challenges facing the region, including increased displacement linked to organized crime, natural disasters, and development projects from dams to urban 'renewal' efforts that tend to advance the interests of the region's elite to the detriment of its marginalized citizens. While this volume underscores the value of forced migration as a distinctive field of study, experiences in this region also attest to the need for scholars and practitioners alike to better understand the past and present ways in which purportedly voluntary, undocumented movements intersect with displacement, and affect efforts to resolve it.

Notes

1. Thank you to Ana Vucetic for her assistance with this chapter.
2. For a comprehensive discussion of the Central American displacement crisis, see García (2006).
3. In the 1980s and 1990s, gangs grew in Central American diaspora communities partly because undocumented migrants could not rely on the police or other state services for protection and assistance.

4. All UN member states in the region have signed the 1951 Convention and its 1967 Protocol, with the exception of Barbados, the Cayman Islands, Cuba, Grenada, Guyana, and Saint Lucia. St Kitts and Nevis has only signed the 1951 Convention, and Venezuela has only signed the 1967 Protocol.

5. For further discussion of the Cartagena Declaration, see Fischel De Andrade's chapter in this volume.

6. See Article XXVII on the right to asylum and Article VIII on rights relating to choice of residence and freedom of movement.

7. Article 22 sets out detailed rights on freedom of movement and residence, including the right to seek and be granted asylum, and the right to leave and enter one's country.

REFERENCES

Abiu Lopez, E. (2013) ' "Stateless" Haitians Gain Legal Foothold in the Dominican Republic'. *Huffington Post*. Last updated 16 January. <http://www.huffingtonpost.com/2013/01/17/stateless-haitians-dominican-republic_n_2497033.html> (accessed 11 June 2013).

Archibold, R. (2013) 'Dominicans of Haitian Descent Cast into Legal Limbo by Court'. *New York Times*, 24 October: A1.

Betts, A. (2006) 'Comprehensive Plans of Action: Insights from CIREFCA and the Indochinese CPA. New Issues in Refugee Research'. Research Paper No. 120. Geneva: UNHCR.

Betts, A. (2009) *Protection by Persuasion*. Ithaca, NY: Cornell University Press.

Bradley, M. (2011) 'Unlocking Protracted Displacement: Central America's "Success Story" Reconsidered'. *Refugee Survey Quarterly* 30(4): 84–121.

Bradley, M. (2013) *Refugee Repatriation: Justice, Responsibility and Redress*. Cambridge: Cambridge University Press.

Coutin, S. B. (2000) *Legalizing Moves: Salvadoran Immigrants' Struggle for US Residency*. Ann Arbor: University of Michigan Press.

Economist (2011) 'Stateless: When is a Dominican Not One?' <http://www.economist.com/node/21542182> (accessed 11 June 2013).

Evans, J. (2009) 'International Migrations, Remittances and Labour Supply: The Case of the Republic of Haiti'. UNU-WIDER Working Papers No. 2009/28. Helsinki.

Fagen, P. W. (2008) 'Natural Disasters in Latin America and the Caribbean: National, Regional and International Interactions'. Humanitarian Policy Group Working Paper. October. London. <http://www.odi.org.uk/sites/odi.org.uk/files/odi-assets/publications-opinion-files/3415.pdf> (accessed 11 June 2013).

Ferris, E., and Ferro-Ribeiro, S. (2012) 'Protecting People in Cities: The Disturbing Case of Haiti'. *Disasters* 36(S1): 43–63.

Ferris, E., and Petz, D. (2013) *In the Neighborhood: The Growing Role of Regional Organizations in Disaster Risk Management*. Washington, DC: Brookings-LSE Project on Internal Displacement.

Fletcher, L., and Miller, T. (2004) 'New Perspectives on Old Patterns: Forced Migration of Haitians in the Dominican Republic'. *Journal of Ethnic and Migration Studies* 30(4): 659–79.

García, M. C. (2006) *Seeking Refuge: Central American Migration to Mexico, the United States and Canada*. Berkeley and Los Angeles: University of California Press.

Garni, A. (2010). 'Mechanisms of Migration: Poverty and Social Instability in the Postwar Expansion of Central American Migration to the United States'. *Journal of Immigrant and Refugee Studies* 8: 329–30.

IACHR (1994) *Special Report on the Human Rights Situation in the So-Called 'Communities of Peoples in Resistance' in Guatemala.* Washington, DC: Inter-American Commission on Human Rights.

IACHR (n.d.) *Rapporteurship on the Rights of Migrants.* <http://www.cidh.oas.org/migrants.background.htm> (accessed 11 June 2013).

IDMC (2013a) *Global Estimates 2012: People Displaced by Disasters.* Geneva: IDMC.

IDMC (2013b) *Global Overview 2012: People Displaced by Conflict and Violence.* Geneva: IDMC.

Kennedy, E. (2013) 'Refugees from Central American Gangs Denied'. *Forced Migration Review* 43: 50–2.

Montes, S. (1988) 'Migration to the United States as an Index of the Intensifying Social and Political Crises in El Salvador'. *Journal of Refugee Studies* 1(2): 107–26.

Nazario, S. (2013) 'Child Migrants, Alone in Court'. *New York Times.* 11 April: A23.

Pedraza, S. (2007) *Political Disaffection in Cuba's Revolution and Exodus.* Cambridge: Cambridge University Press.

Silber, I. C. (2011) *Everyday Revolutionaries: Gender, Violence, and Disillusionment in Postwar El Salvador.* New Brunswick, NJ: Rutgers University Press.

Sollis, P. (1992) 'Displaced Persons and Human Rights: The Crisis in El Salvador'. *Bulletin of Latin American Research* 11(1): 49–67.

Stølen, K. A. (2007) *Guatemalans in the Aftermath of Violence: The Refugees' Return.* Philadelphia: University of Pennsylvania Press.

Todd, M. (2004) *Beyond Displacement: Campesinos, Refugees, and Collective Action in the Salvadoran Civil War.* Madison: University of Wisconsin Press.

UNHCR (2012) *UNHCR Global Trends 2011.* Geneva: UNHCR.

Worby, P. (2000) 'Security and Dignity: Land Access and Guatemala's Returned Refugees'. *Refuge* 19(3): 17–24.

CHAPTER 52

....

FORCED MIGRATION IN
NORTH AMERICA

....

SUSAN F. MARTIN

INTRODUCTION

....

THIS chapter examines North American responses to forced migration with reference to the United States and Canada's position vis-à-vis the international refugee regime. These countries have ratified the principal instruments that provide protection to refugees and have helped promulgate the Guiding Principles for protection of displaced persons; offer substantial financial support to the UN High Commissioner for Refugees (UNHCR) and other international humanitarian organizations; accept tens of thousands of refugees each year for permanent resettlement; provide asylum and temporary protection to still further persons arriving spontaneously on their territory; have systems in place to offer protection to victims of trafficking; and have pledged to help reduce statelessness. While the USA and Canada are often identified as key proponents of an effective international system for assistance and protection of refugees and forced migrants in light of the above, their policies regarding refugees and other forced migrants are not without a basis for criticism (Adelman 1991).

Indeed, both countries are nations of immigrants, founded largely by people seeking safety from persecution and religious intolerance, albeit often in turn displacing indigenous populations living in settlement areas. The USA and Canada shifted their immigration policies in the 1920s, however, towards more restrictive standards that provided few exceptions for refugees (Kelley and Trebilcock 2010; Martin 2011). These policies and other efforts to restrict refugee admissions proved tragic as millions lost their lives in the Holocaust. The saga of the *St Louis*, which sailed from Hamburg to Cuba on 13 May 1939, was emblematic. When no Western Hemisphere government allowed the ship to land, the *St Louis* headed back to Hamburg. Only about half survived the Holocaust (Martin 2011).

However, with concerns growing about Soviet dominance of Eastern Europe and the large number of refugees in still unstable Western Europe, the USA and Canada initiated programmes to admit displaced persons for permanent resettlement, with Canada admitting approximately 165,000 displaced persons between 1946 and 1953, and the USA enacting legislation in 1948 for the admission of 220,000 displaced persons (the number later increased to 415,000). Significantly, neither country initially ratified the 1951 Convention on the Status of Refugees, preferring to operate under its own domestic refugee legislation rather than international standards. Canada ratified the Convention in June 1969 when it also acceded to the 1967 Protocol, while the USA ratified only the Protocol in November 1968.

The Cold War served as the backdrop for Canadian and American refugee policy throughout the next half-century. Until the Refugee Act of 1980 was adopted, the USA explicitly defined refugees as persons fleeing persecution in Communist countries, reflecting the importance of Cold War policy in determining admissions. Both countries admitted Hungarians and Czechs in 1956 and 1968, respectively; Vietnamese, Cambodians, Laotians, Soviet Jews and other religious dissidents, Afghans and refugees displaced by surrogate Cold War conflicts in Africa and Latin America in the 1970s and 1980s. Furthermore, the USA admitted particularly large numbers of refugees from Cuba in the years after the revolution in that country. Overall, although Canada, in particular, also admitted refugees from Chile and other countries in which left-leaning governments were overthrown by rightist ones, these numbers paled in comparison to the numbers admitted from Communist countries.

In the post-Cold War period, US and Canadian policies related to refugees and displaced persons have evolved. The two countries remain major contributors to international protection and assistance programmes for refugees whilst also providing significant resources to internally displaced persons (IDPs), through support for UNHCR, the UN Relief and Works Administration for Palestinian Refugees (UNRWA), International Organization for Migration (IOM), and other UN agencies.[1]

The refugee resettlement programmes remain at the heart of their admissions programmes but increasing attention has been paid to spontaneous arrival of asylum seekers. Equally, as concepts of forced migration have broadened to include those affected by natural disasters, trafficking, and statelessness, Canada and the USA have also responded to these forms of displacement in different ways. The remainder of this chapter describes and assesses policies these areas.

RESETTLEMENT PROGRAMMES

Canada and the United States have long resettled refugees, granting them permanent admissions[2] and a pathway towards citizenship. Of the 79,800 refugees that UNHCR reports were admitted to 22 resettlement countries in 2011, the United States resettled

51,500 and Canada resettled 12,900. Together, they therefore account for 80 per cent of all refugee resettlement.

The two countries differ somewhat in the mechanisms used for resettlement.[3] In Canada, principal responsibility for refugee resettlement rests with Citizenship and Immigration Canada, which handles both the processing of applications and settlement assistance. Responsibility is more diffuse in the USA, with the Bureau of Population, Refugees and Migration in State Department and US Citizenship and Immigration Services in the Department of Homeland Security sharing admissions responsibility and PRM and the Office of Refugee Resettlement in the Department of Health and Human Services sharing responsibility for assistance to refugees.

Of the two, Canada has a broader definition of persons eligible for admission through the resettlement programme, with two classes of eligible applicants: (1) Convention Refugee Abroad Class covers persons who meet the definition in the 1951 UN Convention Relating to the Status of Refugees; and (2) Country of Asylum Class covers those who are outside their home country or the country where they normally live and have been, and continue to be, seriously and personally affected by civil war or armed conflict, or have suffered massive violations of human rights. In both cases, applicants must be referred by the UNHCR or another referral organization. Only the Convention class is eligible for government funded resettlement, while others must be privately sponsored (sponsorship class) or demonstrate they have the funds needed to support themselves and any dependents after arrival in Canada (Bloemraad 2006).

In turn, the US resettlement programme is open only to those who meet the definition of a refugee in the Refugee Act of 1980, which is similar to the UN Refugee Convention definition. The USA does not have a provision for admitting victims of civil war or armed conflict or of massive violations of human rights that do not fall under the Convention refugee definition. However, legislation does permit the designation as refugees of persons still inside their countries of origin if they otherwise meet the eligibility requirements (Legomsky 2009), which allows processing of refugees in countries of origin as occurred in the former Soviet Union, Vietnam, Haiti, and Cuba. US law also recognizes that persons who have suffered particularly serious forms of past persecution are eligible for admission, even if they are no longer at risk of future persecution.

Both countries put certain restrictions on admissions. Refugees must demonstrate they have not established residence in a country of first asylum and they are subject to security and criminal checks. US legislation specifies that refugees who provided material support to a terrorist organization are ineligible for admission. Terrorist organizations are broadly defined to include most insurgent groups, whether or not they use terrorist means towards their goals and there is no exception for coercion, so refugees who have been forced to provide material support or paid ransoms to free themselves or their relatives are inadmissible for entry into the United States unless a waiver is granted. Thousands of persons recognized as refugees are awaiting resettlement in countries such as Jordan, Syria, Ecuador, and Thailand, often in very difficult circumstances, because security checks have not been completed (Schoenholtz and Hojaiban

2008; Martin 2010). Often, the problem is a lack of information to confirm that someone is not a security risk, rather than credible documentation that he or she is a risk.[4]

The Canadian government passed legislative changes in June 2012 that will increase the number of refugees to be resettled. In 2013, as many as 14,500 refugees were to be resettled (CIC 2013). Funding for resettlement assistance was set at CAN$54 million in 2013. The decision to increase resettlement has been part of an overall effort to reduce perceived abuse in the asylum system. While the overall target is set by legislation, decisions on which groups of refugees should be resettled are made through annual planning processes that involve consultations with UNHCR and private sponsors. In the early 2010s, groups given priority for resettlement included Bhutanese, Karen, and Iraqi refugees.

Under the Refugee Act of 1980, there is no targeted number of refugees to be resettled in the USA. Instead, the President determines how many refugees will be admitted each year and how that number will be allocated by region. In September 2012, President Obama determined that 'the admission of up to 70,000 refugees to the United States during Fiscal Year (FY) 2013 is justified by humanitarian concerns or is otherwise in the national interest' (White House 2012). Priorities for resettlement within regional allocations are: (1) cases involving persons facing compelling security concerns; (2) cases involving persons from specific groups of special humanitarian concern to the United States; and (3) family reunification cases involving close relatives of persons admitted as refugees or granted asylum (Bruno 2102). The Lautenberg Amendment, after its principal sponsor, establishes a presumption of eligibility for refugee status to certain religious minorities from Iran and the former Soviet Union (e.g. Jews, Christians, and Baha'is) (Bruno 2012).

In Canada, government-assisted refugees are eligible for up to one year of support, or until they are able to support themselves, whichever happens first. Private sponsors are responsible for providing aid for the same duration (CIC 2013). All refugees are also eligible for the programmes that CIC offers to immigrant newcomers, including free language instruction in English or French. The US refugees are eligible for cash and medical coverage during their first eight months in the country and language training and other social services. The programmes are funded through a mix of public and private funds.

Asylum Policy

In recent years, the number of asylum seekers in Canada and the United States has exceeded the number of resettled refugees. According to UNHCR's data, Canada received approximately 23,000 asylum seekers in 2010 and 25,000 in 2011. The five main countries of origin in 2011 were Hungary, China, Colombia, Namibia, and Pakistan (UNHCR 2011; Showler 2013). The USA in turn had an estimated 56,000 and 74,000 asylum seekers in 2010 and 2011, respectively.[5] The largest number of applications came from China, Mexico, El Salvador, Guatemala, and India (UNHCR 2011). In

2010, UNHCR reports, Canada granted Convention refugee status to 47 per cent of the cases in which the claim to asylum was adjudicated (12,305 approved/13,642 rejected). Sixty-four per cent of those adjudicated for asylum claims were approved in the USA (19,043 approved/10,524 rejected), and yet the number of cases closed for other reasons (40,457) exceeded the number actually adjudicated in the country.[6]

Sharing a long common border, Canada and the USA entered into an agreement in 2004 defining allocation of responsibilities to decide asylum claims. Under the US-Canada Safe Third Country Agreement, the country into which the asylum applicant first arrives has the responsibility for adjudicating the case. If the asylum seeker is found entering the other country, he or she will be returned to the country of first arrival. Exceptions are made for asylum seekers with family in the country they are attempting to reach. The agreement was made at the behest of the Canadian government which received far more asylum seekers transiting the USA than vice versa.

The asylum processes differ in the two countries. Canada has a two-tiered system for its asylum programme, designating applicants as Convention refugees or persons in need of protection because removal to their home country would subject them to the danger of torture, a risk to their life, or a risk of cruel and unusual treatment or punishment (Bechard and Elbersma 2011; CIC 2013). In the USA, asylum is granted only on the basis of the 1951 Refugee Convention or the 1948 Convention against Torture, as adopted in US legislation.

The process for determining eligibility for refugee status within Canada is in transition as a result of legislation adopted in June 2012. The changes were promoted by the government to make the procedures faster and fairer. Prior to the 2012 legislation, decisions in asylum cases were made by members of the Immigration and Refugee Board (IRB). The IRB appointment process was criticized by supporters and opponents of the asylum system as one encouraging patronage over merit (Macklin 2009). Under the new legislation, civil servants decide on initial refugee claims, which are, in some cases, appealable to a new Refugee Appeals Division (RAD), which consists of GIC appointments. The new appeals process was welcomed by UNHCR as an improvement in Canada's process but other aspects of the new law have been more controversial (UNHCR 2012).

The legislation granted the Minister of Citizenship and Immigration Canada the authority to establish a list of Designated Countries of Origin (DCO) that are deemed safe enough to raise serious questions about the credibility of an asylum claim from nationals of those countries. The DCO cases will be heard on an expedited basis (within 45 days if the claim is made at a port of entry and within 30 days if made inland) and cannot be appealed to the RAD if the case is rejected. Also by legislation, 'irregular arrivals'—defined as persons whose identity or admissibility cannot be verified in a timely manner or who appear to have been smuggled into the country by a criminal organization or terrorist group—face mandatory detention, with their incarceration reviewed after 14 days and six months. During the period in which the claim is being adjudicated, asylum seekers are no longer eligible for work permits or for many forms of social assistance, including non-emergency healthcare. These changes were argued as cost-saving measures that would also have deterrent effects.

According to Canadian Border Services Agency (CBSA), 'one of the key principles of Canada's new asylum system will be the timely removal of individuals whose refugee claims have been refused' (CBSA 2013). To aid this process, CBSA is implementing an Assisted Voluntary Return and Reintegration (AVRR) pilot programme in the Greater Toronto Area, through which it will refer unsuccessful asylum seekers to the International Organization for Migration for education, counselling, and departure assistance in Canada and services in their home country (CBSA 2013).

The USA had adopted a number of similar changes as early as 1995, including streamlined adjudications, limitations on work authorization, and bars on access to social benefits. The USA has two separate procedures—one affirmative and the other defensive. The affirmative asylum process is for those who voluntarily apply for status with US Citizenship and Immigration Services (USCIS) in the Department of Homeland Security (DHS). They must apply for asylum within one year of entry into the USA, unless there are compelling reasons for the delay (for example, due to changed circumstances in the country of origin). The claim is heard by an Asylum Officer in a non-adversarial setting against the refugee definition. The Asylum Officer has the authority to grant asylum but, in the majority of cases, must refer questionable cases to an Immigration Judge in the Executive Office of Immigration Review (EOIR) in the Justice Department. The Immigration Judges hear referred cases *de novo* although they do receive the information that was submitted to the Asylum Officer. The Immigration Judges also hear defensive cases—that is, those involving applicants who seek asylum after they are arrested by immigration authorities.

At the court stage, the process is adversarial. The government is represented by an attorney; the asylum seeker has the right to counsel but not at government expense. Studies have shown asylum seekers who are represented are six times more likely to succeed in their claim (Schoenholtz and Jacobs 2002). The decision of the Immigration Judge can be appealed by either the government or the asylum seeker to the administrative Board of Immigration Appeals, whose decisions can be appealed to the federal Judiciary.

An expedited process is in place for those who are apprehended at ports of entry attempting to use fraudulent documents or have no documents at all. Inspections officers in the Customs and Border Protection (CBP) agency within DHS have the authority to administratively remove all persons attempting to enter the country without legitimate documentation. If, on questioning, the apprehended person expresses fears about return to their home country, he or she is referred to an Asylum Officer in USCIS to determine if the expressed fear is credible. If the decision is affirmative, the individual is then referred to an Immigration Judge for a full hearing of the asylum claim.

Interdiction of migrants attempting to enter illegally by sea has been a persistent aspect of US policy since 1981. The Supreme Court determined in 1993 that the *non-refoulement* obligation did not apply outside the United States, giving the Executive Branch considerable discretion in decisions on return of those interdicted on the high seas. Affecting more asylum seekers has been the one-year time limit on asylum applications. Schrag et al. (2010) estimated that the Department of Homeland Security 'rejected more than 15,000 asylum applications (involving more than 21,000 refugees) that would otherwise have been granted' had the case been fully adjudicated. Those rejected on this basis can apply for cancellation of removal (the US provision for *non-refoulement*[7]) or protection under the Convention against Torture. Although beneficiaries may not be at risk of deportation, they are not eligible for family reunification, permanent residence, or citizenship (Legomsky 2009).

The securitization of asylum is of concern in both countries, which preceded the terrorist attacks on 11 September in both countries but hardened thereafter (Bourbeau 2011; Martin 2011). It applies to both terrorism and organized crime. As examples, the material support bars on admission through the US resettlement programme also affect asylum seekers (Schoenholtz and Hojaiban 2008). In implementing the new provisions regarding irregular arrivals, the Canadian Minister of Public Safety stated: 'Human smuggling is a dangerous and despicable crime—it puts lives at risk and threatens the integrity of Canada's immigration system as well as the security and safety of Canadians' (Public Safety Canada 2012).

The quality of asylum decisions has been an area of concern in both countries. The US system has been described as 'Refugee Roulette' because outcomes for applicants from countries vary significantly depending on the individual adjudicator and office (Ramji-Nogales, Schoenholtz, and Schrag 2011). A Canadian Broadcasting Company analysis of Canadian asylum decisions found similar fluctuations in the approval and denial rates depending on the adjudicator.[8]

At the same time, Canada and the United States can be credited with taking leadership regarding other aspects of asylum adjudications. For example, they have been leaders in establishing that fear of persecution by non-state actors can be a basis for asylum if the government of the country of origin is unwilling or unable to protect the applicant. Canada and the United States were also the first countries to provide guidance to asylum adjudicators regarding gender-based persecution, issuing guidelines in 1993 and 1995 respectively (Martin 2004). These guidelines focused on two aspects of gender and asylum—(1) that persecution can be gendered, as in the case of rape and sexual abuse; and (2) persecution can be on account of gender, particularly in cases involving sexual orientation, domestic violence, and female genital mutilation (Martin 2004).

Temporary Protection

The United States enacted legislation in 1990 to provide temporary protected status (TPS) to persons 'in the United States who are temporarily unable to safely return to their home country because of ongoing armed conflict, an environmental disaster, or other extraordinary and temporary conditions' (USA Immigration Act 1990). Environmental disasters may include 'an earthquake, flood, drought, epidemic, or other environmental disaster in the state resulting in a substantial, but temporary, disruption of living conditions in the area affected' (Wasem and Ester 2011). In the case of environmental disasters, as compared to conflict, the country of origin must request designation of TPS for its nationals.

Those granted TPS are eligible to work in the United States. They are not considered to be residing in legal status, however, for purposes of receiving social benefits and they are not able to bring family members into the country to join them. Importantly, TPS only applies to persons already in the United States at the time of the designation. The designation is discretionary, to be made by the Secretary of Homeland Security in consultation with the Secretary of State. If it were determined that as a group TPS recipients cannot return home, special legislation, which would require a super-majority (three-fifths) of Senators for passage, is needed to allow them to remain permanently. At the same time, lifting temporary protected status has equally proven to be very difficult. Currently, the designation is still in effect for citizens of Honduras and Nicaragua (since 1998), El Salvador (2001), Somalia (2001), Sudan (2004), and Haiti (2010).[9] This leaves more than 300,000 TPS recipients in limbo (Wasem and Ester 2011).

Canada may declare a temporary suspension of removals when a country's general conditions (e.g. war or natural disaster) put the safety of the general population at risk. According to regulation, 'the guiding principle of generalized risk is that the impact of the catastrophic event is so pervasive and widespread that it would be inconceivable to conduct general returns to that country until some degree of safety is restored' (CIC 2010: 33). The suspension ends when country conditions improve and the public is no longer in danger. For example, in a controversial move, the suspension of removal was lifted in 2009 for nationals of Burundi, Rwanda, and Liberia. Recognizing that some had been in Canada for an extended period, these nationals were given the opportunity to apply for humanitarian and compassionate consideration for permanent residence in Canada. Such considerations as the best interests of any child directly involved, establishment in Canada, integration into Canadian society, and other factors put forward by the applicant are taken into account in determining if an applicant will be permitted to remain in Canada. Canada also undertakes a Pre-Removal Risk Assessment in determining if persons denied asylum would be at risk of other serious harm if removed to their country of origin.

Trafficking

Canada and the United States ratified the Protocol to Prevent, Suppress and Punish Trafficking in Persons, especially Women and Children, of the UN Convention on Organized Transnational Crime in 2002 and 2005, respectively. Domestic policies in both countries provide some level of protection to those who have been coerced or deceived into entering the countries for the purpose of exploitation, typically for sexual exploitation or forced labour. Both countries also organize their policies around the international standard that emphasizes the 4Ps: prevention of trafficking; protection of trafficking victims; prosecution of traffickers; and partnerships for more effective action against trafficking (on trafficking, see Anderson, this volume).

Both countries have mechanisms that enable trafficking survivors to remain at least temporarily. In Canada, CIC can issue a Temporary Resident Permit (TRP) to foreign nationals who have been trafficked into Canada. The TRP is valid for 180 days and is renewable. In some cases, a TRP may be issued for up to three years. Those granted the status have access to health care and counselling. They may apply for a fee-exempt work permit which gives them the legal right to work in Canada. Victims of trafficking are not required to assist in any criminal investigation or testify against their trafficker. The TRP is seen as a mechanism to help trafficking survivors recover and reflect upon their next steps—whether to return home or attempt to remain in Canada.

In the USA, the Victims of Trafficking and Violence Protection Act (VTVPA) of 2000 established a separate visa category (T-visa) for victims of trafficking. Unlike the Canadian programme, to qualify, applicants must comply with a law enforcement agency in the investigation or prosecution of human trafficking.[10] They must also demonstrate that they would suffer extreme hardship involving unusual and severe harm if removed from the United States. After three years of continuing residence, T-visa holders are eligible to become permanent residents of the United States. They may also sponsor family members who may be endangered by traffickers in their home country. T-visa holders have access to the same benefits that are available to refugees in the USA. Principal countries of origin for foreign victims have been Thailand, India, Mexico, Philippines, Haiti, Honduras, El Salvador, and the Dominican Republic, the majority of whom are trafficked for forced labour (US State Department 2011).

Identification of trafficking victims is the largest hurdle to protecting them (Brennan 2009–10; Okech Morreau, and Benson 2012). A Congressional Research Service (CRS) report points out that there were only 2,500 applications for the T-visa between 2002 and 2009, during a period in which the government estimated that at least 14,500 persons were trafficked into the USA each year, although the number of grants has increased in recent years (Wyler, Siskin, and Seelke 2009/2012).

STATELESSNESS

There are no statistics on the number of stateless persons in Canada and the United States. Canada and the USA recognize all children born on their territory as citizens regardless of the legal status of the parent or the duration of the parent's stay in the country,[11] and as a result, statelessness does not arise for the children of foreigners born on their territory. Statelessness is a problem, however, for foreigners who are not recognized as citizens by their country of birth or previous residence and who are unable to naturalize because they do not meet the requirements of the USA and Canada. For instance, they may be illegally present, on temporary visas, or be permanent residents who do not meet naturalization requirements such as duration of stay and their knowledge of English.

Neither Canada nor the USA has explicit policies to offer permanent residence and citizenship to stateless persons except in very specific situations. In Canada, for example, special consideration may be given to providing permanent resident status (and eventual access to naturalization) to the children of Canadians born abroad who would otherwise be stateless. This situation arose when legislation was adopted in 2009 that limits citizenship by descent to the first generation born or adopted outside Canada with certain exceptions for government employees.

In both countries, depending on the reasons for statelessness, persons may be eligible for asylum. For example, those stripped of their nationality because of race, religion, nationality, political opinion, or membership in a particular social group may fit the refugee definition. However, other reasons for statelessness are not considered grounds for asylum.

CONCLUSIONS

Canada and the USA have come a long way since the highly restrictive policies that closed the doors on refugees from Nazi Germany. Certainly, in respect to the priority given to refugee resettlement, their policies constitute a North American approach, resettling together more than 80 per cent of refugees brought to third countries for permanent residence. They are also among the most important donors to the UNHCR. Since the 1990s, they have put in place asylum adjudication processes that provide access to long-term protection for a significant proportion of those whose hearings are completed. Furthermore, they have together been leaders in ensuring protection for those fearing persecution on account of their gender and sexual orientation.

Nevertheless, there are reasons to be cautious about both countries' policies. The numbers who are resettled today are significantly lower than those of the early 1980s and well below the need for global resettlement. The multiple security checks imposed on applicants for resettlement leave applicants neither approved nor denied but instead awaiting clearance. And, most troubling, the asylum systems still have significant gaps, particularly in provisions such as interdiction, detention, arbitrary deadlines, and security checks that make them inaccessible for too many asylum seekers with credible claims for protection.

NOTES

1. In 2011, Canada's contributions to UNHCR were US$58,543,383 and the USA's were US$698,168,056. In absolute terms, Canada ranked 8th among donors, and on per capita and GDP bases, it ranked 16th and 17th, respectively. The United States was the largest

donor in absolute terms and ranked 13th on both a per capita and GDP basis. Both governments provide general support as well as earmarked funds for specific programmes. In 2011 Canada and the United States also provided US$35 million and US$375 million to IOM for its operational programmes. The majority of these funds were earmarked to programmes for displaced persons and refugee resettlement activities. Initiatives, such as the evacuation of migrants from Libya, received special attention in 2011, with Canada and the United States contributing US$3.7 and US$27.1 million respectively. Canada and the USA contributed $15 and $239 million, respectively, to UNRWA.

2. In the United States, refugees have a one-year conditional admission and apply for permanent resident status after that period.
3. The Quebec government selects the refugees who settle in Quebec under policy guidance from the national government. For the purposes of this chapter, only the federal policies are discussed.
4. During a field visit to Amman Jordan in January 2012, the author interviewed Iraqi refugees in this situation. They had met all requirements for admission to the United States but no decision had been made on their security clearance.
5. US data come from two separate agencies using different measures. The Department of Homeland Security provides statistics on cases. The statistics assumes 1.4 members per case. The Justice Department reports on individuals.
6. Cases may be closed because of the failure of applicants to pursue their claims or because they are eligible for other relief from deportation. Alternatively, they may be closed because the applications were made after the one-year filing deadline discussed herein.
7. The standard for cancellation is a clear probability of persecution whereas the standard for asylum is well-founded fear. If there is a clear probability, the decision to cancel removal is mandatory. On the other hand, the grant of asylum is discretionary.
8. <http://www.cbc.ca/news/politics/story/2009/12/17/f-refugee-claims.html>.
9. In 2007, TPS ended for Liberians but the Administration decided to grant Deferred Enforced Departure (DED) for those who had had Temporary Protected Status. As of this writing (February 2013), it is still in force. DED also provides work authorization and protection against removal.
10. There are exceptions in policy, though not always in practice, for minors and those who have suffered psychological harm <http://www.uscis.gov/portal/site/uscis/menuitem. eb1d4c2a3e5b9ac89243c6a7543f6d1a/?vgnextoid=02ed3e4d77d73210VgnVCM10000008 2ca60aRCRD&vgnextchannel=02ed3e4d77d73210VgnVCM100000082ca60aRCRD>.
11. The only exceptions apply to the children of diplomats.

REFERENCES

Adelman, H. (ed.) (1991) *Refugee Policy: Canada and the United States*. New York: Center for Migration Studies.

Bechard, J., and Elbersma, S. (2011) *Refugee Protection in Canada*. Ottawa: Library of Parliament.

Bloemraad, I. (2006) *Becoming a Citizen: Incorporating Immigrants and Refugees in the United States and Canada*. Berkeley and Los Angeles: University of California Press.

Bourbeau, P. (2011) *The Securitization of Migration: A Study of Movement and Order*. New York: Routledge.

Bruno, A. (2012) *Refugee Admissions and Resettlement Policy*. Washington, DC: Congressional Research Service.

Brennan, D. (2009–10) 'Key Issues in the Resettlement of Formerly Trafficked Persons in the United States'. *University of Pennsylvania Law Review* 158: 1581–608.

Canadian Border Security Agency (CBSA) (2013) *Refugee Reform Initiative: Improving Canada's Asylum System*. <http://www.cbsa-asfc.gc.ca/agency-agence/refugee-refugie/menu-eng.html>.

Citizenship and Immigration Canada (CIC) (2010) *Removals*. <http://www.cic.gc.ca/english/resources/manuals/enf/enf10-eng.pdf>.

Citizenship and Immigration Canada (CIC) (2013) *Refugees*. <http://www.cic.gc.ca/english/refugees/index.asp>.

Kelley, N., and Trebilcock, M. (2010) *The Making of the Mosaic: A History of Canadian Immigration Policy* (2nd edn.). Toronto: University of Toronto Press.

Legomsky, S. (2009) 'Refugees, Asylum and the Rule of Law in the USA'. Pp. 122–70 in S. Kneebone (ed.), *Refugees, Asylum Seekers and the Rule of Law: Comparative Perspectives*. Cambridge: Cambridge University Press.

Macklin, A. (2009) 'Asylum and the Rule of Law in Canada'. Pp. 78–121 in S. Kneebone, *Refugees, Asylum Seekers and the Rule of Law: Comparative Perspectives*. Cambridge: Cambridge University Press.

Martin, S. (2004) *Refugee Women* (2nd edn.). Lanham, MD: Lexington Books.

Martin, S. (2011) *A Nation of Immigrants*. New York: Cambridge University Press.

Okech, D., Morreau, W., and Benson, K. (2012) 'Human Trafficking: Improving Victim Identification and Service Provision'. *International Social Work* 55/4: 488–503.

Price, P. J. (2012) 'Stateless in the United States: Current Reality and a Future Prediction'. Emory Legal Studies Research Paper No. 12-229.

Public Safety Canada (2012) 'Harper Government Takes Action against Human Smuggling'. <http://www.publicsafety.gc.ca/media/nr/2012/nr20121205-1-eng.aspx>.

Ramji-Nogales, J., Schoenholtz, A., and Schrag, P. (2011) *Refugee Roulette: Disparities in Asylum Adjudication and Proposals for Reform*. New York: New York University Press.

Schoenholtz, A. I., and Hojaiban, J. (2008) 'International Migration and Anti-Terrorism Laws and Policies: Balancing Security and Refugee Protection'. Institute for the Study of International Migration, Transatlantic Perspectives on Migration, Policy Brief No. 4.

Schoenholtz, A. I., and Jacobs, J. (2002) 'The State of Asylum Representation: Ideas for Change'. *Georgetown Immigration Law Journal* 16/4: 739–72.

Schrag, P. G., Schoenholtz, A., Ramji-Nogales, J., and Dombach, J. P. (2010) 'Rejecting Refugees: Homeland Security's Administration of the One-Year Bar to Asylum'. *William & Mary Law Review* 52: 651–804.

Showler, P. (2013). *By the Numbers: Refugee Statistics*. Research and Education Centre, University of Ottawa. <http://www.cdp-hrc.uottawa.ca/projects/refugee-forum/projects/Statistics.php>.

UNHCR (2011) *Asylum Levels and Trends in Industrialized Countries*. Geneva: UNHCR. <http://www.unhcr.org/4e9beaa19.html>.

UNHCR (2012) Submission on Bill C-31 Protecting Canada's Immigration System Act, Ottawa. UNHCR. May. <http://www.unhcr.ca/resources/documents/RPT-2012-05-08-billc31-submission-e.pdf>.

US State Department (2011) *Trafficking in Persons Report*. Washington, DC: US State Department.

Wasem, R. E., and Ester, K. (2011) *Temporary Protected Status: Current Immigration Policy and Issues*. Washington, DC: Congressional Research Service.

White House (2012) Presidential Memorandum: Annual Refugee Admissions Numbers. <http://www.whitehouse.gov/the-press-office/2012/09/28/presidential-memorandum-annual-refugee-admissions-numbers>.

Wyler, L. S., Siskin, A., and Seelke, C. R. (2009/updated 2012) *Trafficking in Persons: U.S. Policy and Issues for Congress*. Washington, DC: Congressional Research Service.

CHAPTER 53

FORCED MIGRATION IN EUROPE

ROLAND BANK

INTRODUCTION

EUROPE has a long history of producing forced migration flows, in particular in the context of the atrocities committed before and during the Second World War, as well as a more recent record of providing a safe haven for those fleeing persecution, war or other human rights violations. Standards and law on dealing with such forced migration flows in Europe have been developed both under the auspices of the Council of Europe (CoE) and by the European Union (EU). The CoE, with its broad membership and mechanisms governed by the principles of intergovernmental cooperation and international law, provides the framework for binding norms of international human rights law as well as a forum for standard setting through soft-law instruments. The EU has created norms which are binding under European law and have the full force flowing from the supranational framework.

After a short historical overview of forced migration in the context of Europe, the frameworks and achievements for the protection of forced migrants shall be explored. The EU's endeavours in the field of the harmonization of asylum policies shall be examined in particular detail given their importance for the shaping of international refugee law and standards. As groups posing particular challenges, the situation of victims of trafficking and stateless persons will also be discussed.

HISTORICAL BACKGROUND

Before the last decades of the twentieth century, Europe was a continent of emigration. Most European states attracted little voluntary immigration from other continents and from other European states (Bade 2003). Within Europe, significant flows of forced migrants took place in the context of the Second World War. In the last decades of the twentieth century, Western European states became countries of destination for voluntary migration and for persons in need of international protection from all over the world.

Europe was at the heart of the creation of international regimes for refugee protection when refugee situations arrived at the international agenda as a result of immigration restrictions introduced during and after the First World War. The 1922 'Nansen passport' system, the first institutional approach to refugee problems on the international level, was designed to address the situation of refugees from the Russian revolution and subsequently applied in similar terms to certain groups of refugees from the Ottoman Empire. The first refugee convention of 1933 covering these arrangements in addition to the 1938 Convention focusing on refugees from Nazi Germany concerned refugee flows from European states. The atrocities committed before and during the Second World War and the resulting refugee flows inspired the adoption of the 1951 Convention Relating to the Status of Refugees (1951 Convention). It also prompted the recognition and codification of human rights which in Europe led to the foundation of the CoE and the adoption of the 1950 European Convention on Human Rights (ECHR).

For the first decades, the post-war history of forced migration was determined by the effects of the Cold War and by persons fleeing communism to Western European states. Those refugees were welcome for political reasons and did not usually arrive in big numbers, with the exception of refugee movements following the crises in Hungary in 1956 and in Czechoslovakia in 1968. Since the 1970s, asylum seekers from all over the world have arrived in Western Europe. Within Europe, the refugee crises in the context of the wars and ethnic persecution in the Former Yugoslavia—in the early 1990s in Bosnia and in the late 1990s in Kosovo—led to significant flows of persons in need of protection.

In the 2010s, Europe has continued to receive a significant proportion of the asylum seekers arriving in the *industrialized* world, amounting to approximately 75 per cent of asylum claims submitted in industrialized countries in 2011 (UNHCR 2012a: 8); however, according to UNHCR numbers those arriving in Europe are fewer than 15 per cent of the world refugee population (UNHCR 2012b: 13). Main countries of origin among asylum seekers in European states in 2010 and 2011 were Afghanistan, Iraq, Serbia and Kosovo, Russian Federation, and Pakistan (UNHCR 2012a: 23). In 2011, the Arab Spring prompted significant migration movements to Europe; in many cases however, those persons did not ask for international protection (for instance, in Italy more than 25,000 Tunisians arrived in the first three and a half months of 2011 and yet in the entire year, only some 4,500 applied for asylum (*New York Times* 2011; Eurostat 2012). An exception has been the crisis in Syria which has not only forced masses to leave the country for neighbouring states but also increased the number of Syrian asylum seekers in Europe (UNHCR 2012d: Table 3).

Legal and Policy Framework and Political Context

The European legal and policy landscape is characterized by a basic divide between those countries which are part of the EU and therefore take part in the shaping of the

Common European Asylum System (CEAS) under the EU's supranational framework, and those which are not, even though they may participate in the intergovernmental cooperation endeavours at the CoE.

There is an important reciprocal influence between the systems of the EU and CoE. Whereas CoE member states outside the EU look at the EU with a view to the interpretation of international refugee law and standard setting, the EU sphere of asylum policies is also heavily influenced by the CoE, in particular regarding the interpretation of the obligations flowing from the ECHR as per the European Court of Human Rights (ECtHR) and the Court of Justice of the European Union (CJEU), in particular when applying the EU Charter of Fundamental Rights (Costello 2012). This not only affects the interpretation of ECHR-relevant aspects but has also influenced EU legislation on questions of international protection.[1]

EU Asylum Policies

EU asylum policies are determined by a supranational framework providing a significant level of guarantees for asylum seekers and refugees who have reached the EU. Concurrently, restrictive visa policies and a panoply of border control measures including through the EU border agency Frontex have been established. As a consequence, access to Europe and thereby to protection in Europe has become a matter of financial investment—through the payment of 'fees' to smugglers and document forgers—and of risking one's life in a perilous journey. Moreover, in the context of extraterritorial border control measures, in particular at the high seas, obligations under international refugee law and human rights law have not always been respected (Bank 2011).

Institutional Setting

The current situation has been preceded by a long period of pure intergovernmental cooperation. Until 1993, cooperation in the field of asylum and refugees had taken place outside the European institutional framework. The Treaty of Maastricht then established the so-called Third Pillar of the European Union providing for intergovernmental cooperation within the EU, and it was only in 1999 that the Treaty of Amsterdam brought about the transfer of the policy area into European Community Law aiming at harmonization of all of the most important areas of refugee protection, in particular reception conditions, procedures, criteria for eligibility, and rights to be granted. Simultaneously, the 1951 Convention was established as the yardstick for all refugee law instruments to be adopted in the EU framework. However, elements of intergovernmental cooperation were maintained for a transitional period of five years, in particular by requiring unanimity in the Council and excluding the European Parliament from co-decision in legislation. In this way, member states maintained full control of the contents of legal instruments adopted during this first harmonization phase. On the other hand, regulations and, under certain additional conditions, directives adopted in the area could apply directly in the member states.[2] The Commission's competence to oversee the transposition and implementation of these, including the power to initiate procedures for treaty infringement, also provided a strong supranational tool which, however, was hardly used at all in practice by the Commission.

Since the Treaty of Lisbon entered into force in 2009, EU asylum policies have been governed by a fully-fledged supranational institutional framework (Peers 2011: 303–7). The second harmonization phase—supposed to foster further harmonization and to provide the basis for the CEAS by revising the instruments adopted—has been taking place under the usual system of qualified majority voting in the Council and with full co-decision powers of the European Parliament.

Instruments in all areas governing asylum systems were adopted in the first harmonization phase thereby establishing the EU asylum-*acquis*. The Temporary Protection Directive was designed for situations of mass-influx of persons in need of protection, but remained unused in practice. The so-called Dublin-II-Regulation establishes criteria to determine which member state is responsible for processing an asylum application. In addition to all EU member states, Iceland, Liechtenstein, Norway, and Switzerland participate in the Dublin system. In turn, the Reception Conditions Directive (RCD) guarantees a certain minimum level of reception conditions for asylum seekers, including far-reaching provisions on the treatment to be accorded to persons with special needs, for instance, unaccompanied minors, single parents with minor children, or victims of violence. The Asylum Procedures Directive (APD) contains provisions on all aspects of the procedure including fundamental guarantees for the applicants. Finally, the Qualification Directive (QD) defines the criteria for eligibility for refugee status under the 1951 Convention in more detail than provided in the Convention itself (Storey 2008). Moreover, the QD established criteria for subsidiary protection in order to close protection gaps arising under the 1951 Convention for persons in need of protection for human rights-related reasons or because of extreme violence in the context of an armed conflict (McAdam 2007: 53–110). Furthermore, this directive defines a minimum standard of rights to be granted to refugees and subsidiary protection beneficiaries. All of these acts of secondary legislation have been revised in the second harmonization phase with a view to improving the legal basis for harmonization.

The State of Harmonization after the First Phase

Despite the above-mentioned adoption of legal instruments, harmonization in practice still remains *in statu nascendi*: laws, standards, and protection rates vary widely. Studies carried out by UNHCR (UNHCR 2007, 2010, 2011a) have revealed important discrepancies in the transposition but most relevantly in the application of secondary EU legislation, partly due to piecemeal approaches in EU law: some of the Directives, in particular the APD, partly leave huge discretion to member states through numerous optional clauses. For instance, out of 12 countries examined in a UNHCR study, only three had adopted a list of safe countries of origin. There was only one country—Ghana—which was on all of the lists; in the UK, however, safety was presumed only for male Ghanaians (UNHCR 2010: 336). The QD has been met with some reasonably accurate transposition legislation, but in practice questions of interpretation remain and different answers are given on the domestic level (UNHCR 2007, 2011a). Furthermore, it seems, country of origin information is interpreted differently by the national authorities (UNHCR 2011), and protection rates for asylum seekers from specific countries vary dramatically. For instance, in 2010, according to UNHCR figures protection rates for Afghan applicants after first instance decisions stood at 9.7 per cent in the UK and 62.4 per cent in Belgium; for Iraqi applicants at 10.9 per cent in the UK and 78.5 per cent in Belgium; and for Somali applicants at 34.3 per cent in the Netherlands and 89.4 per cent in Germany (UNHCR 2011: 7).

Moreover, certain compulsory concepts may have also remained irrelevant in practice at least in some states. The prime example for this is the provision on subsidiary protection in the context of armed conflict (Article 15c QD). According to a UNHCR study in six EU member states in 2010, Article 15c was applied only in Belgium and Sweden to a significant extent (UNHCR 2011: 24–8). This was partly due to the lack of congruence in identifying situations with a level of generalized violence so high as to trigger the protection of Article 15c (UNHCR 2011: 33–5).

As a consequence, chances of obtaining protection largely depend on which state is responsible for processing the claim under the Dublin-II-Regulation. Most frequently, responsibility is determined by the point of first illegal entry into EU territory, turning the travel route of asylum seekers into a lottery for their chances of a positive decision. This puts into doubt whether the Dublin system can be justified, and such doubts are reinforced by fragmentation of the legal situation: non-EU member states participating in the Dublin system are not even part of the harmonization process and are not bound by EU minimum standards. Moreover, certain EU member states have also preferred not to be bound by those standards: the UK, Ireland, and Denmark have chosen not to apply some of the instruments adopted while still taking part in the Dublin system.

Drastically substandard practices in some of the EU member states have not only put the Dublin system under strain but may have also turned the CEAS into a remote, perhaps even unrealistic aim. The most prominent example has been Greece, which failed to establish a functioning asylum system to the extent that European courts explicitly ruled out the transfer of asylum seekers to Greece.[3] Another example is Hungary, with UNHCR documenting serious shortcomings because of the sweeping use of detention under extremely problematic conditions as well as lack of a substantive review of asylum claims if applicants are returned under the Dublin system (UNHCR 2012e: paras. 20 and 50).

The Start into the Second Phase: Limited Impulses for Harmonization

In the second phase, all first-phase instruments of the asylum-*acquis*, with the exception of the Temporary Protection Directive, were revised in order to establish a solid basis for the CEAS. However, many provisions still lack a decisive push for increased harmonization. In particular, optional concepts have remained in some central areas, certain concepts lacking harmonized interpretation in practice were not clarified any further, and in some instances, diversity rather than harmonization is promoted.[4]

One of the reasons for the limited impulse for harmonization may be found in the prevalence of national over European thinking in the EU Council negotiations. National delegations appear to have aimed predominantly to maintain the national status quo. Rather than addressing the gaps which became evident in the course of applying the first-phase instruments, some member states raised fundamental objections to starting the second harmonization phase. It was claimed that aiming to establish new standards was inappropriate since certain EU states were still incapable of fulfilling the standards adopted in the first phase (UNHCR 2011b: 6, 7). The frequent point of reference for this argument was the dysfunctional asylum system in Greece. However, the failure of one member state in running an asylum system is ill-placed to provide an argument against amendments in the details of the asylum-*acquis* applying to all participating EU member states: the complete failure of one system cannot provide an argument against refining and further harmonizing the standards for other functioning systems. Moreover, unclear or optional provisions in the directives had failed to guarantee clear minimum standards and therefore indeed did require revision.

Another aspect potentially limiting states' aims to establish higher and more harmonized standards of refugee protection may be rooted in the particular challenges faced by some states which have a high share of new arrivals. For instance, Malta as a small island of only some 400,000 inhabitants struggled with between 1,300 and 2,600 asylum seekers per year in 2007–11 (with the exception of 140 in 2010), placing Malta at the top of industrialized countries regarding the rate of asylum applications per capita (UNHCR 2011: 13, 20). The government reacted by detaining asylum seekers, often under deplorable conditions, and called for other states to act in solidarity by accepting some of the persons determined to be in need of international protection. In addition, Greece, situated on one of the main migration routes to EU-Europe, has faced particularly high numbers of arrivals which are routinely detained under appalling conditions. After release from detention, Greece does not provide access to an asylum procedure nor any kind of reception arrangements for the vast majority of would-be asylum seekers. The situation of homeless migrants living in the streets of Athens in turn may have supported negative prejudices and fuelled xenophobia.

EU endeavours to establish the CEAS are accompanied by a policy of strict border controls. In the Stockholm Programme, a five-year programme for policies on justice, home affairs and migration, and border control measures are outlined as a priority—before addressing asylum questions—with the aim of curbing illegal migration and trans-border crime (EU 2010). While various measures are envisaged in this regard in the programme, including a reinforcement of the mandate of the EU's border agency (Frontex), it is claimed that the access of persons in need of international protection must continue to be guaranteed. The programme, however, fails to explain how these conflicting aims may be reconciled, and, in particular, how it can be assured that persons in need of international protection would not be impeded in their access to safety in EU-Europe by the establishment of increased border controls.

The External Dimension of EU Asylum Policies

In contrast to internal asylum policies, cooperation with other states outside the EU, the so-called external dimension of EU asylum policies (Baldaccini 2007), is of rather limited scope. 'Regional Protection Programmes' have been devised with the aim of reinforcing protection capacities on the part of governments and NGOs in countries in a region of transit (Eastern Europe: Belarus, Moldova, and Ukraine) or of asylum (African Great Lakes: Tanzania). New programmes have been initiated since 2010 in the Horn of Africa (Kenya, Yemen, and Djibouti) and Eastern North Africa (Egypt, Libya, Tunisia). Aiming at creating conditions conducive to durable solutions (repatriation, local integration, resettlement), projects are carried out, for instance, with the aim of improving the general protection situation, reception conditions, the situation of the local population, or establishing refugee status determination procedures. The rationale behind this may have been to increase the reliability of protection systems in regions of origin and transit and potentially reduce refugee flows to the EU. Whether this has worked is impossible to determine without detailed research of the functioning and effects of the programmes in the respective host countries, and yet a significant impact does not appear likely. The programmes were intended to be combined with measures of solidarity by accepting a number of persons in need of protection into Europe by way of resettlement. Commitment of EU member states in this respect, however, remains largely lacking.

Performance of the EU member states in the field of resettlement has generally been rather mediocre on quantitative terms in the last years. For instance, in 2008 and 2009, EU member states failed to meet the mark of 10,000 persons they had set themselves by a EU Council conclusion (27/28 November 2008) for the resettlement of Iraqi refugees from Syria and Jordan based on a German initiative to this end. By the end of 2009 and also taking into account Iraqi refugees resettled from 2007 to 2009 under existing quotas, a total of 8,444 Iraqi refugees were resettled (ICMC/ICR 2010: 16). Moreover, in 2012, EU member states contributed less than 8 per cent of resettlement places offered around the world (UNHCR 2012c). In March 2012, however, the EU adopted a joint resettlement programme.[5] While participation in the programme is voluntary, it aims to increase the contribution of resettlement places by EU countries by way of increased cooperation and through financial incentives usually amounting to 4,000 euros to be paid out of the European Refugee Fund for any refugee resettled under the criteria of the programme. These criteria include, in particular, resettlement from a country or region designated for a regional protection programme or of a particularly vulnerable person as established in the Decision, or a person resettled in accordance with the EU's resettlement priorities.

The CoE: *Non-refoulement* and Standards for Asylum Systems

In the CoE, a binding international law framework has been established on some aspects of high relevance for forced migration issues. Moreover, governed by the principles of intergovernmental cooperation, some non-binding standards have also been adopted under its auspices.

The European Convention on Human Rights in its interpretation by the European Court of Human Rights has become a stronghold in the human rights of forced migrants. It has substantially limited state parties' discretion in adopting migration policies, in particular through the court's jurisprudence on *non-refoulement* under ECHR Articles 2 and 3, including rulings on the relevance of Article 3 in the EU's Dublin system and reception conditions provided to asylum seekers. Other central areas of the court's jurisprudence on forced migrants relate to the review of detention of asylum seekers under Article 5, and the rights to family unity and social links to the host society under Article 8. Not least, the court has refused to balance the absolute protection against torture and inhuman and degrading treatment against state security considerations.[6]

Moreover, factual reports of human rights institutions of the Council of Europe, in particular the Committee for the Prevention of Torture and the Commissioner for Human Rights, have become a highly relevant source of information on asylum-relevant questions, in particular regarding the detention and reception conditions for asylum seekers.

Finally, the Committee of Ministers and the Parliamentary Assembly have engaged in some standard-setting exercises by adopting soft-law instruments on issues such as the harmonization of asylum procedures, detention of asylum seekers, or training matters. Furthermore, the CoE has adopted two international law agreements binding upon ratifying states: the European Agreement on the Abolition of Visas for Refugees and the European Agreement on Transfer of Responsibility for Refugees, the latter complementing provisions of the 1951 Convention on this question.

PARTICULAR GROUPS OF FORCED MIGRANTS

Victims of Human Trafficking

Particular attention has been devoted in the shaping of EU asylum policies to the special needs of particularly vulnerable asylum seekers and persons granted protection, as indicated by a significant number of provisions to this end in EU asylum instruments. The needs and rights of trafficked persons have increasingly come to the forefront in recent years, as evidenced not least through explicit references added in the recast versions of the asylum directives. The particularity of this group in comparison to other vulnerable groups, however, is that they are in need of some additional specific protection against dangers prevailing *in the host country.*

The scope of this phenomenon and thereby the number of persons in need of such additional measures of protection is difficult to assess. It is estimated that only one in 20 trafficked persons is detected; on the basis of this estimate, UN organizations extrapolate a number of 140,000 trafficked persons in West and Central Europe in 2006.[7] Both the CoE and the EU have devoted particular attention to anti-trafficking initiatives. The CoE adopted the Convention on Action against Trafficking in Human Beings in 2005, which entered into force in February 2008 and had been ratified by 37 member states of the CoE by the end of 2012. The Convention aims to prevent trafficking, protect the rights of victims, and prosecute traffickers, and an expert body has been established as a monitoring mechanism. In turn, the EU has adopted the Directive on Preventing and Combating Trafficking in Human Beings and Protecting its Victims in 2011 which repealed an earlier Council Framework Decision. It recognizes trafficking in human beings as a crime and a human rights violation, and maintains that the protection of victims of trafficking shall be enhanced by provisions on non-prosecution, assistance and support, protection in criminal proceedings, particular measures applying to child victims, and compensation. Moreover, EU member states are obliged to take measures for the prevention of trafficking such as training, education, and awareness raising. Finally, national reporting mechanisms shall be established under the Directive.

These endeavours notwithstanding, the core question for trafficked persons regarding their effective protection will often be their access to legal residence in their host country. While victims of trafficking and potential victims alike will often qualify as refugees if there is a danger of a human rights violation upon return to the country of origin (see UNHCR 2006), their position may be precarious in the host state if refugee protection is denied. Unless the host country provides for a durable stay on the basis of residence permits granted on humanitarian reasons, the legal stay of victims of trafficking is habitually dependent upon criminal procedures against the perpetrators of the trafficking crimes and conditional on the victim's cooperation with the judicial authorities. The EU Directive on residence permits for victims of trafficking (Council Directive 2004/81/EC) provides for a minimum duration of six months and a prolongation according to the needs of the investigation or judicial proceedings. Such permits of limited duration, however, do not provide any perspective in the host country and thereby makes it more difficult for victims of trafficking to overcome the long-term effects of their suffering.

Stateless Persons

The 1954 Convention Relating to the Status of Stateless Persons conveys the message that this group of persons is in need of almost the same rights as refugees. European states, however, often do not guarantee these rights to stateless persons if they do not simultaneously qualify as refugees. Given that many European countries do not properly determine, register, and count stateless persons, it is not only difficult to assess the number of stateless persons but it is also clear that European states are not always willing to devote much attention to the situation of stateless persons in their countries. A significant number of European states have also abstained from ratifying any of the statelessness conventions (including four EU member states), and even more countries have limited their commitment to the 1954 Convention Relating to the Status of Stateless Persons while not ratifying the 1961 Convention on the Reduction of Statelessness (including another eight EU member states). While the EU lacks a specific competence for dealing with stateless persons, the CoE has addressed the problem on various occasions and adopted two treaties of particular relevance to the subject: the 1997 European Convention on Nationality containing some general provisions on the avoidance of statelessness (20 ratifications at the end of 2012) and the more specific 2006 Convention on the Avoidance of Statelessness in Relation to State Succession (only six ratifications at the end of 2012).

The roots of the problems faced by stateless persons present in European states are often due to the lack of transposition of the 1954 Convention into national law and the granting of legal residence on the basis of the determination as a stateless person. For instance, the UK Immigration Rules do not contain a reference to the 1954 Convention and thereby do not provide for a possibility of stateless persons to claim the protection of that Convention, in particular regarding protection against expulsion under its Article 31. In addition, and in contrast to the legal position of refugees, there is no provision in the Immigration Rules granting leave to enter or remain to persons based on their statelessness (UNHCR/Asylum Aid 2011: 68). Similarly, German immigration law does not provide for a residence permit explicitly based on statelessness, but rather allows status to be granted on the basis of the impossibility of return to another country (Section 25 (5) Residence Act) which, however, does not provide for the full scope of rights guaranteed under the 1954 Convention to stateless persons legally staying in a host country. These approaches are representative of many European states where access to protection as a stateless person is very limited.

CONCLUSION: FUTURE CHALLENGES

Overall, in light of Europe's record regarding forced migration, it is not possible to identify Europe as a stronghold of human rights or a region taking a liberal approach to guaranteeing the protection to forced migrants and assuming a strong role in contributing to the solutions to problems of forced migration worldwide. The record is rather mixed: on the one hand, almost all European states are members of the Council of Europe and most of its human rights instruments. Some European states—despite certain shortcomings—may be said to provide a protection system on a quantitatively and qualitatively high level. Furthermore, within the EU, a significant level of guarantees has been established in the context of creating the Common European Asylum System. On the other hand, some European states continue to use persecution as a political tool and thereby can themselves be identified as inducing refugee flows. In the reality of the EU's Common European Asylum System, practice often falls seriously short of complying with the standards thus established and of producing harmonized results. As a consequence, even if the main obstacle in accessing protection—access to EU territory despite all heightened measures for controlling borders—has been overcome, presence on the EU territory does not necessarily correspond with access to a fair and efficient review of protection needs and the granting of protection if necessary. Moreover, regarding its contribution to resolving problems of forced migration worldwide, the record on resettlement could be much improved.

In those asylum systems within Europe which function reasonably well, prospects for success may very much depend on the country responsible for processing a claim. The denial of protection status based on restrictive approaches which are not in line with international law puts those affected into a very vulnerable situation. Moreover, with regard to certain groups of forced migrants, protection needs are frequently ignored: in many countries, stateless persons are neither offered a statelessness determination procedure nor a status regulating their residence. Similarly, even though attention to the phenomenon of human trafficking has increased significantly, such attention has not led to a focus on facilitating access to protection and stability of residence in order for victims to be able to restore their lives. Addressing these shortcomings will remain a challenge for all policies on forced migrants throughout Europe.

Specifically regarding the EU's asylum policies, the development of legislation on asylum matters and its interpretation in the EU send strong signals to the interpretation of international refugee law all over the world. However, the EU faces the fundamental challenge of improving its record on harmonization, unless it wants to risk losing the credibility and legitimacy of its endeavours to establish a Common European Asylum System. The record over the past years has been limited if judged by the high degree of variance in the design and outcome of the asylum procedures across the different EU member states. However, a full set of norms was established binding member states to a significant extent, in an area which until recently was regarded as a stronghold of national sovereignty. Rooting such rules into the national systems takes time and must overcome the barriers of national customs. The CJEU has played an increasingly important role and will probably continue to be confronted with questions on ambiguous clauses and concepts contained in the EU asylum-*acquis*. The European Asylum Support Office (EASO), endowed with the task, in particular, of supporting harmonization through practical cooperation was only established in 2010. Its role may include a certain amount of monitoring which—in contrast to the practically non-existent monitoring by the EU Commission—could provide important impulses for increased harmonization. However, it remains to be established how far the EASO will take over monitoring functions at all. Effectively, the long and tedious process of harmonization of asylum policies has only just begun.

Notes

1. For instance, the new provision on an internal protection alternative in Article 8 (1) QD (2011/95/EU) transposed into EU law the requirements on accessibility as set out by the ECtHR in *Salah Sheek v The Netherlands*, 11 January 2007, para. 141.

2. A 'regulation' is a legislative act of the EU which is legally binding and directly applies in the EU member states participating in the application of the act. A 'directive' is a legislative act of the EU which is binding upon participating EU member states but which is not directly applicable in EU member states. Rather, it sets out certain end results or minimum standards to be achieved by adopting national legislation. If a directive or a specific provision of it is not transposed at all or not accurately by a member state within the deadline set in the directive, and this provision is specific enough to be applied directly, it applies with direct effect to the benefit of individuals.

3. ECtHR, *M.S.S. v. Belgium and Greece*, 21 January 2011; CJEU, N.S. (C-411/10) and M.E. (C-493/10), 21 December 2011.

4. For instance, the concept of European lists of safe countries of origin and of safe third countries is given up in the revised recast proposal of the EU Commission for the APD (Com (2011) 319 final, <http://ec.europa.eu/home-affairs/news/intro/docs/110601/319/1_EN_ACT_part1_v12[1].pdf>), where it is foreseen that the member states can individually designate third countries as safe (Articles 37–9 amended recast APD).

5. Decision No. 281/2012/EU of the European Parliament and of the Council of 29 March 2012, OJ L 92/1.

6. See for instance, ECtHR, *Saadi v Italy*, 28 February 2008.

7. UNHCHR et al., Prevent, Combat, Protect—Human Trafficking—Joint UN Commentary on the EU Directive, 2011, p. 16.

References

Bade, K. J. (2003) *Migration in European History*. Oxford: Wiley-Blackwell.

Baldaccini, A. (2007) 'The External Dimension of the EU's Asylum and Immigration Policies: Old Concerns and New Approaches'. Pp. 277–298 in A. Baldaccini et al. (eds.), *Whose Freedom, Security and Justice?* Oxford: Hart.

Bank, R. (2011), 'Refugees at Sea'. Pp. 815–52 in A. Zimmermann (ed.), *The 1951 Convention Relating to the Status of Refugees and its 1967 Protocol: A Commentary*. Oxford: Oxford University Press.

Costello, C. (2012) 'Courting Access to Asylum in Europe: Recent Supranational Jurisprudence Explored'. *Human Rights Law Review* 12(2): 287–339.

EU (2010) 'The Stockholm Programme: An Open and Secure Europe Serving and Protecting Citizens'. Official Journal C 115 of 4 May.

Eurostat (2012) Press Release 46/2012.

ICMC/ICR (2010) '10 000 Refugees from Iraq: A Report on Joint Resettlement in the European Union'.

McAdam, J. (2007). *Complementary Protection in International Refugee Law*. Oxford: Oxford University Press.

New York Times (2011) 'On Journey, Young Tunisians Need Only a Final Destination'. 19 April. <http://www.nytimes.com/2011/04/20/world/europe/20france.html?pagewanted=all>.

Peers, S. (2011) *EU Justice and Home Affairs Law*. Oxford: Oxford University Press.

Storey, H. (2008) 'The EU Qualification Directive: A Brave New World?' *IJRL* 20(1): 1–49.

UNHCR (2006) 'Guidelines on International Protection No. 7: The application of Article 1A(2) of the 1951 Convention and/or 1967 Protocol Relating to the Status of Refugees to Victims of Trafficking and Persons at Risk of Being Trafficked.'

UNHCR (2007) 'Asylum in the European Union: A Study on the Implementation of the Qualification Directive.'

UNHCR (2010) 'Improving Asylum Procedures: Comparative Analysis and Recommendations for Law and Practice.'

UNHCR (2011a) 'Safe at Last? Law and Practice in Selected EU Member States with Respect to Asylum-Seekers Fleeing Indiscriminate Violence.'

UNHCR (2011b) '60 Jahre Genfer Flüchtlingskonvention. Herausforderungen für die deutsche Flüchtlingspolitik.' <http://www.unhcr.de/fileadmin/user_upload/dokumente/07_presse/60_Jahre_GFK_-_Herausforderungen_fuer_die_deutsche_Fluechtlingspolitik.pdf>.

UNHCR (2012a) 'Asylum Levels and Trends in Industrialized Countries'. Geneva: UNHCR.

UNHCR (2012b) 'Global Trends 2011'. Geneva: UNHCR.

UNHCR (2012c) 'Statement by UNHCR spokesperson Melissa Fleming on 30 March'. <http://www.unhcr.org/4f7589ef9.html>.

UNHCR (2012d) 'Asylum Levels and Trends in Industrialised Countries, First Half 2012'. <http://www.unhcr.org/507c000c9.html>.

UNHCR (2012e) 'Hungary as a Country of Asylum: Observations on the Situation of Asylum-Seekers and Refugees in Hungary'. Geneva: UNHCR.

UNHCR/Asylum Aid (2011) 'Mapping Statelessness in the United Kingdom'. Geneva: UNHCR/Asylum Aid.

Name Index

Subject Index

Note: all law cases are indexed together under 'legal cases'. Bold entries refer to tables.

United States (*Cont.*)
  Central American refugees 666–7, 668,
    673–4
  Cold War influences on policy 678
  deportation 259, 260, 668
  detention 668
  ethnic cleansing 256
  protracted refugee situations 158
  Refugee Act (1980) 678, 680
  resettlement programme 512, 513, 678–80
    disabled refugees 426
    eligibility 679–80
    health of refugees 438
    Indochinese refugee crisis 631
    integration 521
    numbers resettled 678–9, 680
    Refugee Admissions Program 515
    responsibility for 679
    support 680
  statelessness 685–6
  temporary protection status 683–4
United States-Canada Safe Third Country
    Agreement (2004) 681
United States Committee for Refugees 3
United States Immigration and Naturalization
    Service 399
Universal Declaration of Human Rights 39,
    42, 293
  asylum 42
urban refugees 8
  assistance ensures continued
    segregation 144
  challenges for humanitarian assistance 144
  characteristics of 139–40
  direct assistance to 143
  disabled migrants 422
    access to healthcare 422–3
  focus on legal status and documentation in
    assistance to 143–4
    counter-productive 145
  gaps in knowledge about 140
  health risks 443
  increased attention to 13, 139, 141
  limitations of scholarship on 144–5
  local government 146
  modalities of assistance 143
  new approaches to 146–7, 148

  numbers of 139
  reconsideration of policies 145–6
  refugee-oriented analysis of 142–3
  as scapegoats 144
  successes among 147
  United Nations High Commissioner for
    Refugees 141–2
  urbanization 139
  visibilization 144
    within humanitarian field 140, 141
urbanization, and urban refugees 139
Uruguay 658, 659, 660
User Generated Content (USG), and
    media representation of forced
    migration 466–7
Uzbekistan 599, 600, 606, 607, 608

vacuum domicilium 77
Vanuatu 647, 648
Venezuela 658, 661
Victims of Trafficking and Violence Protection
    Act (VTVPA, USA) 358, 359, 685
Vienna Convention on the Law of Treaties
    (1969) 44, 47n23, 280
Vietnam 626, 627, 628
  Indochinese refugee crisis 631
  refugees from 629
Vietnamese boat people 410, 513, 631, 641
visibilization:
  power relations 141
  reliance on categorization and
    verification 144
  urban refugees 140, 141
vocational training, and disabled
    migrants 423
voice, *see* refugee voice
Volga Germans 606
voluntary repatriation 42–3

West Africa 11–12, 541–2
  anti-trafficking initiatives 550
  asylum practices 548
  child trafficking 546–7
  child/youth migration 546–7
  colonial period 542–3
  conflict-induced displacement 544–5
  durable solutions 549

Lightning Source UK Ltd.
Milton Keynes UK
UKOW04f0609250517

301982UK00002B/5/P